The SAGE Handbook of
Mentoring

The SAGE Handbook of Mentoring

Edited by
David A. Clutterbuck,
Frances Kochan,
Laura Gail Lunsford,
Nora Dominguez and
Julie Haddock-Millar

Los Angeles | London | New Delhi
Singapore | Washington DC | Melbourne

SAGE Publications Ltd
1 Oliver's Yard
55 City Road
London EC1Y 1SP

SAGE Publications Inc.
2455 Teller Road
Thousand Oaks, California 91320

SAGE Publications India Pvt Ltd
B 1/I 1 Mohan Cooperative Industrial Area
Mathura Road
New Delhi 110 044

SAGE Publications Asia-Pacific Pte Ltd
3 Church Street
#10-04 Samsung Hub
Singapore 049483

Editor: Susannah Trefgarne
Editorial Assistant: Matthew Oldfield
Production Editor: Rudrani Mukherjee
Copyeditor: Sunrise Setting Ltd.
Proofreader: Derek Markham
Indexer: Martin Hergeaves
Marketing Manager: Emma Turner
Cover Design: Wendy Scott
Typeset by Cenveo Publisher Services
Printed and bound by
CPI Group (UK) Ltd, Croydon, CR0 4YY.

Editorial arrangement © David A. Clutterbuck, Frances Kochan, Laura Gail Lunsford, Nora Dominguez and Julie Haddock-Millar 2017

Chapter 1 © David A. Clutterbuck, Frances Kochan, Laura Gail Lunsford, Nora Dominguez and Julie Haddock-Millar 2017
Part 1 © Frances Kochan 2017
Chapter 2 © Bob Garvey 2017
Chapter 3 © Carol A. Mullen 2017
Chapter 4 © Julie Haddock-Millar 2017
Chapter 5 © Nora Dominguez 2017
Chapter 6 © Jeffrey Yip and Kathy E. Kram 2017
Chapter 7 © W. Brad Johnson 2017
Chapter 8 © Beverly J. Irby, Jennifer Boswell, Nahed Abdelrahman, Rafael Lara-Alecio and Fuhui Tong 2017
Part 2 © Julie Haddock-Millar 2017
Chapter 9 © Chandana Sanyal 2017
Chapter 10 © Julie Haddock-Millar 2017
Chapter 11 © David A. Clutterbuck and David Megginson 2017
Chapter 12 © Lis Merrick 2017
Chapter 13 © Sadhana Bhide 2017
Chapter 14 © Vicki L. Baker 2017
Chapter 15 © Eileen Murphy and Jane Lewes 2017
Chapter 16 © Terezia Koczka 2017
Chapter 17 © Rodney K. Goodyear, Tony Rousmaniere and Jeff Zimmerman 2017
Chapter 18 © Rose Opengart and Laura Bierema 2017
Part 3 © Laura Gail Lunsford 2017
Chapter 19 © Stella S. Kanchewa, Sarah E.O. Schwartz and Jean E. Rhodes 2017
Chapter 20 © Laura Gail Lunsford, Gloria Crisp, Erin L. Dolan and Brad Wuetherick 2017
Chapter 21 © Andrew J. Hobson 2017
Chapter 22 © Roxanne B. Reeves 2017
Chapter 23 © Deirdre Cobb-Roberts, Talia Esnard, Ann Unterreiner, Vonzell Agosto, Zorka Karanxha, Makini Beck and Ke Wu 2017
Chapter 24 © Nora Dominguez and Faith Sears 2017
Chapter 25 © Kirsten M. Poulsen 2017
Chapter 26 © Vicki L. Baker and Aimee LaPointe Terosky 2017
Chapter 27 © Gary M. Crow and Margaret Grogan 2017
Chapter 28 © Diane M. Ryan and Jeffrey D. Peterson 2017
Chapter 29 © Donnel Nunes and Leslie Dashew 2017
Chapter 30 © Laura Bierema 2017
Part 4 © David A. Clutterbuck 2017
Chapter 31 © Hilary Geber and Moyra Keane 2017
Chapter 32 © Melissa Richardson 2017
Chapter 33 © Aline Maria de Medeiros Rodrigues Reali, Maria da Graça Nicoletti Mizukami and Regina Maria Simões Puccinelli Tancredi 2017
Chapter 34 © Kathleen Bury and Amanda Edwards 2017
Chapter 35 © Mikaela Nyström and Eeva-Liisa Heinaro 2017
Chapter 36 © Matteo Perchiazzi 2017
Chapter 37 © Vasudha B and Farah Palmer 2017
Chapter 38 © Jennybeth Ekeland and Åse Velure 2017
Chapter 39 © Wendy Baker and Warrant Officer Viti Flanagan 2017
Chapter 40 © Mariola Czechowska-Fraczak, Anna Jarzębska and Malgorzata Jastrzebska 2017
Chapter 41 © Ana Oliveira Pinto 2017
Chapter 42 © Hoang Anh Thi Le and Laura Rana 2017
Chapter 43 © Esther Cavett 2017
Chapter 44 © Paula King 2017
Chapter 45 © Mariano Ulanovsky and Patricia Pérez 2017
Chapter 46 © Tim Bright and David Megginson 2017
Chapter 47 © Joanne Leck and Catherine Mossop 2017
Chapter 48 © Rebecca Viney and Denise Harris 2017
Chapter 49 © Emily Cosgrove and Petra Lockhart 2017
Chapter 50 © Vanessa Fudge and Akram Sabbagh 2017
Chapter 51 © Anna Blackman 2017
Chapter 52 © Ridwanah Gurjee 2017
Chapter 53 © Judie Gannon 2017
Chapter 54 © Sally Lawson 2017
Chapter 55 © Fiona McInnes-Craig 2017
Chapter 56 © Tim Bright 2017

Apart from any fair dealing for the purposes of research or private study, or criticism or review, as permitted under the Copyright, Designs and Patents Act, 1988, this publication may be reproduced, stored or transmitted in any form, or by any means, only with the prior permission in writing of the publishers, or in the case of reprographic reproduction, in accordance with the terms of licences issued by the Copyright Licensing Agency. Enquiries concerning reproduction outside those terms should be sent to the publishers.

Library of Congress Control Number: 2017930948

British Library Cataloguing in Publication data

A catalogue record for this book is available from the British Library

ISBN 978-1-4129-6253-7

Contents

List of Figures	xi
List of Tables	xii
Notes on the Editors and Contributors	xiii
Acknowledgements	xxxv

1 Introduction 1
   David A. Clutterbuck, Frances Kochan, Laura Gail Lunsford,
   Nora Dominguez and Julie Haddock-Millar

**PART I THE LANDSCAPE OF MENTORING:
         PAST, PRESENT, AND FUTURE   11
         FRANCES KOCHAN**

2 Philosophical Origins of Mentoring: The Critical Narrative Analysis 15
   Bob Garvey

3 Critical Issues on Democracy and Mentoring in Education:
   A Debate in the Literature 34
   Carol A. Mullen

4 Critical Issues in Mentoring Research 52
   Julie Haddock-Millar

5 A Research Analysis of the Underpinnings, Practice, and Quality of
   Mentoring Programs and Relationships 67
   Nora Dominguez

6 Developmental Networks: Enhancing the Science and Practice
   of Mentoring 88
   Jeffrey Yip and Kathy E. Kram

7 Ethical Considerations for Mentors: Toward a Mentoring Code of Ethics 105
   W. Brad Johnson

8 New Horizons for Mentoring Research: Exploring the Present and Past to
   Frame the Future 119
   Beverly J. Irby, Jennifer Boswell, Nahed Abdelrahman,
   Rafael Lara-Alecio and Fuhui Tong

PART II	THE PRACTICE OF MENTORING *JULIE HADDOCK-MILLAR*	139
9	The Effective Mentor, Mentee and Mentoring Relationship *Chandana Sanyal*	143
10	The Mentoring Cycle *Julie Haddock-Millar*	156
11	Working with Goals in Mentoring *David A. Clutterbuck and David Megginson*	169
12	Design of Effective Mentoring Programmes *Lis Merrick*	185
13	A Case Study of the Operations and Perceived Attributes of Successful Multi-Country Mentoring Programmes *Sadhana Bhide*	202
14	Organizational Contexts: Aligning Individual and Organizational Outcomes *Vicki L. Baker*	212
15	Measuring the Effectiveness of Mentoring Programmes *Eileen Murphy and Jane Lewes*	227
16	The Role of the Mentoring Programme Co-ordinator *Terezia Koczka*	246
17	Supervision of Mentoring *Rodney K. Goodyear, Tony Rousmaniere and Jeff Zimmerman*	261
18	Keeping Emotions IN It: Emotionally Intelligent Mentoring *Rose Opengart and Laura Bierema*	274
PART III	THE CONTEXTS OF MENTORING *LAURA GAIL LUNSFORD*	291
19	Mentoring Disadvantaged Youth *Stella S. Kanchewa, Sarah E.O. Schwartz and Jean E. Rhodes*	295
20	Mentoring in Higher Education *Laura Gail Lunsford, Gloria Crisp, Erin L. Dolan and Brad Wuetherick*	316
21	The Terrors of Judgementoring and the Case for ONSIDE Mentoring for Early Career Teachers *Andrew J. Hobson*	335

22	Mentoring Newcomer Immigrants: Tactics of and Recommendations for Successful Mentors *Roxanne B. Reeves*	358
23	Race, Gender and Mentoring in Higher Education *Deirdre Cobb-Roberts, Talia Esnard, Ann Unterreiner, Vonzell Agosto, Zorka Karanxha, Makini Beck and Ke Wu*	374
24	Mentoring Diverse Populations *Nora Dominguez and Faith Sears*	389
25	Mentoring Executives at the Workplace: A View of Practice and Research *Kirsten M. Poulsen*	406
26	Early Career Faculty Mentoring: Career Cycles, Learning and Support *Vicki L. Baker and Aimee LaPointe Terosky*	421
27	Mentoring in Educational Leadership for Organizational Transformation *Gary M. Crow and Margaret Grogan*	436
28	Mentoring in the Military *Diane M. Ryan and Jeffrey D. Peterson*	451
29	An Historical Exploration of the Research and Practice of Familial Mentoring *Donnel Nunes and Leslie Dashew*	466
30	eMentoring: Computer Mediated Career Development for the Future *Laura Bierema*	482
PART IV	**CASE STUDIES OF MENTORING AROUND THE GLOBE** *DAVID A. CLUTTERBUCK*	**499**
31	*Ubuntu* and Transformational Mentoring in South Africa: 7 Principles of a Culturally Integrated Mentoring Response *Hilary Geber and Moyra Keane*	501
32	E-mentoring Women in Resources: Lessons Learned from an Australian Programme *Melissa Richardson*	508
33	Mentoring Novice Teachers: An Online Experience in Brazil *Aline Maria de Medeiros Rodrigues Reali, Maria da Graça Nicoletti Mizukami and Regina Maria Simões Puccinelli Tancredi*	513

34	Mowgli Foundation – Mentoring to Empower Entrepreneurial and Economic Development *Kathleen Bury and Amanda Edwards*	520
35	Rhea Challenge Mentoring Learning Alliance Program for Female Entrepreneurs in Finland *Mikaela Nyström and Eeva-Liisa Heinaro*	527
36	Intercultural Relationships and Mentoring: The Italian Air Force on an Afghanistan NATO Training Mission, Shindand *Matteo Perchiazzi*	531
37	The Virtual Māori Mentoring Programme, Massey Business School, New Zealand *Vasudha B and Farah Palmer*	539
38	Statoil Mentoring Program for Leaders in Projects *Jennybeth Ekeland and Åse Velure*	545
39	A Case Study of Mentoring in a Military Context *Wendy Baker and Warrant Officer Viti Flanagan*	549
40	Sanofi Aventis Case Study, Poland *Mariola Czechowska-Fraczak, Anna Jarzębska and Malgorzata Jastrzebska*	554
41	The WomenWinWin Mentoring Programme (WWWMP), Portugal *Ana Oliveira Pinto*	560
42	Youth Business International *Hoang Anh Thi Le and Laura Rana*	565
43	Mentoring in Music and the City: A Comparison of Schemes for City Businesswomen and High-Performing Early-Career Professional Musicians *Esther Cavett*	570
44	Mentoring Irish Rugby Players For Life After Rugby *Paula King*	575
45	Peer Mentoring: A Powerful Tool to Accelerate the Learning Experience *Mariano Ulanovsky and Patricia Pérez*	582
46	A Multi-country Mentoring Programme across Eurasia with Anadolu Efes *Tim Bright and David Megginson*	587

47	Mentoring Women in Canada's Financial Sector *Joanne Leck and Catherine Mossop*	590
48	Coaching and Mentoring Doctors and Dentists – A Case Study *Rebecca Viney and Denise Harris*	595
49	Swarovski Case Study *Emily Cosgrove and Petra Lockhart*	600
50	Mentoring across an Industry – the Recruitment Industry in Australia and New Zealand *Vanessa Fudge and Akram Sabbagh*	604
51	Commonwealth of Australia Statutory Authority *Anna Blackman*	610
52	UCLan, Centre for Volunteering and Community Leadership: Mentoring Practice *Ridwanah Gurjee*	614
53	The Bacchus Mentoring Scheme: Enhancing the Alumni and Student Experience *Judie Gannon*	618
54	How Might Mentoring Work? Starting to Lift the Lid on the Black Box *Sally Lawson*	623
55	Crossing Thresholds Career-Mentoring Programme for Women in the UK Civil Service *Fiona McInnes-Craig*	629
56	A Self-managed Mentee-Led Mentoring Programme for Vodafone Turkey *Tim Bright*	633
Index		636

List of Figures

I.1	The developmental conversation	6
6.1	Differences in network density	94
6.2	Levels of analysis in mentoring research	99
12.1	Differences between sponsorship and developmental mentoring	186
12.2	The Talent Mentoring Wheel	188
12.3	Characteristic approaches to executive mentoring by country	189
12.4	Comparison of stepped approaches to designing a mentoring programme	189
12.5	A schema for mentor development and supervision	193
15.1	Stakeholders' group	229
15.2	Logic Model	233
15.3	Evaluation Model	235
15.4	The new world Kirkpatrick Model	235
15.5	Investors in people framework	242
16.1	Phase 1 Striving for mentoring	249
16.2	Phases 2 and 3 Preparation and design of the proposal	250
16.3	Phases 4 and 5 Implementation and evaluation of the mentoring programme	252
17.1	Supervision's proximal and distal effects	262
19.1	Model of Change	304
22.1	Proposed model for describing multiple meanings conferred on the term inter-cultural mentoring	360
25.1	Career transition points	408
25.2	Evolution/foci of mentoring definitions	409
25.3	Situational mentoring – the mentor's many roles	417
33.1	CTLE themes developed by Novice Teachers I and A assisted by Mentor MI	515
34.1	The three critical stages of an entrepreneur's journey when they need a mentor	522
35.1	A kick-off with all mentors and mentees was held in March and a mid-review in October. A workshop related to time and stress management was held in December; and a closing evaluation and feedback session was held in April 2016, when the one-year program came to an end	528
35.2	Different roles of the mentor	529
36.1	Afghan Army mentee by ethnicity	533
36.2	Constraints of mentoring relationship	534
36.3	Strengths of mentoring relationship	534
36.4	Details of military ethics and values in mentoring relationships	535
36.5	Details of values shown in mentoring relationships in the categories 'military ethics' and 'culture'	536
36.6	Details of values shown in mentoring relationships in the categories 'religion' and 'relationship'	537
40.1	First edition of the Mentoring Program – the project flow	556
40.2	Testimonials of the mentee – after closing the first edition of the Mentoring Program	558
40.3	Testimonials of the mentors – after closing the first edition of the Mentoring Program	559

List of Tables

2.1	Underpinning philosophies	30
3.1	Primary mentoring tensions in the scholarly literature	37
6.1	Example of a name generator	90
6.2	Example of name interpreter questions	91
6.3	Example of a matrix	92
8.1	Methods employed	121
13.1	Industry grouping (survey options)	204
15.1	Evaluation plan: output indicators	238
15.2	Evaluation plan: outcome indicators	239
15.3	EMCC competence framework	242
18.1	Three streams of definitions of Emotional Intelligence	276
18.2	Four-point perspective of Emotional Intelligence (EI)	277
18.3	Low and high EIM and their impact on the mentoring relationship	283
18.4	Emotional intelligence and mentoring relational skills matrix	284
20.1	Purpose, types, and outcomes of mentoring for undergraduates, graduate students, and faculty members	327
21.1	The five empirical research projects examined	337
21.2	ONSIDE Mentoring	349
23.1	Articles reviewed for meta-synthesis	383
29.1	Representation of categories in literature search	472
30.1	Comparing tMentoring and eMentoring	488
30.2	Virtual mentoring process models	492
31.1	Contrasting worldview perspectives	504
33.1	TLE themes developed by Novice Teachers I and A assisted by Mentor MI	515
33.2	Phases/steps of the Teaching and Learning Experiences (TLE) conducted by the novice with the mentors' supervision	518
40.1	Data gathered at the end of the mentoring programme	557
50.1	PEARL mentoring-programme participants	607
50.2	PEARL Programme 2015 – mentee feedback on programme impact	608
50.3	PEARL Programme 2015 – mentor feedback on programme impact	609
51.1	Implementation process	612
51.2	Coachee expectations	613

Notes on the Editors and Contributors

THE EDITORS

David A. Clutterbuck is visiting professor at four UK universities and co-founder of the European Mentoring and Coaching Council, for which he is now special ambassador. Author, co-author or editor of 65 books, he leads a global community of trainer-consultants in mentoring and in team coaching, Coaching and Mentoring International. His book *Coaching the Team at Work* (2007) was the first to offer an evidence-based exploration of the subject, and he continues an active programme of research into both theory and good practice in this area.

Frances Kochan is a Wayne T. Smith Distinguished Professor, Emerita, at Auburn University, Al. She is series editor for *Perspectives in Mentoring* published by Information Age Press. She has written, edited or co-edited over 75 publications on the topic. Her research focuses on establishing and assessing mentoring relationships and programs, and on the cultural aspects that must be considered in the mentoring process. She served on the Board of the International Mentoring Association and as secretary and as chair of the Mentoring and Mentorship Special Interest Group of the American Education Research Association.

Laura Gail Lunsford is the Director of the Swain Center in the Cameron School of Business at UNC Wilmington. Previously, she was a tenured associate professor in psychology at the University of Arizona. Her scholarly interests focus on mentoring and leadership. She authored the *Handbook for Managing Mentoring Programs* and has published over 30 peer-reviewed articles, case studies and chapters on toxic leadership, leadership development, mentorship dysfunction, and optimizing mentoring relationships. Her work has appeared in journals such as *Mentoring & Tutoring*, *Journal of Higher Education Policy and Management,* and *To Improve the Academy.* She has presented at conferences sponsored by the European Mentoring and Coaching Council, American Psychological Association, Association for Psychological Science, American Educational Research Association, among others. The Department of Education, National Science Foundation, and the LUCE Foundation has funded her work. She was honoured with the 2009 International Mentoring Association's Dissertation Award.

Nora Dominguez is Director of the Mentoring Institute at the University of New Mexico (UNM), a professional consultant for the Office of Diversity at the Health Science Center at UNM (HSC-UNM), and President of the International Mentoring Association (IMA). Domínguez earned her bachelor degree in Accounting from the National Autonomous University of Mexico (UNAM), her MBA from the Autonomous Technological Institute of

Mexico (ITAM) and her PhD in Organizational Learning and Instructional Technologies from the University of New Mexico (UNM). Nora has more than 25 years of experience developing and implementing financial and organizational learning strategies, holding educational and management positions in banking and higher education institutions, and providing consulting and program evaluation services both in the United States and Mexico. She is member of several boards, including the International Standards for Mentoring Programmes in Employment (UK) and the Diversity Leadership Council (NM). Domínguez is also member of the Editorial Board for the *International Journal for Mentoring and Coaching* (Emerald, UK) and the *Student Learning through Mentored Scholarship* Journal (Sage, US); co-author of the book *Mentoring: Perspectivas Teóricas y Prácticas* (2010), and Editor of nine Mentoring Institute's Annual Conference Proceedings.

Julie Haddock-Millar is Associate Professor (Practice) of Human Resource Management and Development at Middlesex University Business School. She is a Visiting Professor at the International University of Monaco, teaching on the Executive MBA programme. Julie is a Senior Teaching Fellow with the Higher Education Academy, Chartered Member of the Chartered Institute of Personnel and Development and Advisory Member for the Harvard Business Review. She leads on the development of International Standards in Mentoring and Coaching Programmes (ISMCP) with the European Mentoring and Coaching Council. Her scholarly interests focus on mentoring, career transitions, professional development and Green Human Resource Management. Julie has acted as Principal Investigating Officer for a number of high profile mentoring programmes, including the UK Cabinet Office and First Division Association developmental mentoring programme, addressing diversity and educational transitions. She is currently Principal Investigating Officer for a global mentoring entrepreneurship research project, partnering with Youth Business International.

THE CONTRIBUTORS

Nahed Abdelrahman is a third-year doctoral student in Public School Administration at the Department of Educational Administration and Human Resources. In 2011, she received her Masters in Public Affairs from Lyndon Baines Johnson School of Public Affairs in the University of Texas at Austin. Her research interests center on education policy and principal preparation. She was selected as a Barbara Jackson Scholar from (2015–2017). She authored and co-authored several publications related to education policy such as *Arab Spring and Teacher Professional Development in Egypt, A Website Analysis of Mentoring Programs for Latina Faculty at the 25 Top-Ranked National Universities, Women and STEM: A Systematic Literature Review of Dissertation in Two Decades (1994–2014)*. She presented her research in conferences including in American Educational Research Association (AERA), University Council for Educational Administration (UCEA), Research on Women and Education (RWE), The Universality of Global Education Issues Conference. She plays leadership roles in higher education as she serves as the president of Graduate Representative Advisory Board and a committee member in two committees of the Graduate and Professional Student Council at Texas A&M University: Award Committee and Graduate Appeals Panel. She currently serves as the Assistant Editor of the *Mentoring and Tutoring Journal, Advancing Women in Leadership,* and *Dual Language Research and Practice*.

NOTES ON THE EDITORS AND CONTRIBUTORS

Vonzell Agosto is Associate Professor at the University of South Florida. Her research focuses on educator preparation, curriculum leadership, and anti-oppressive education. She has published in journals such as the *Journal of School Leadership*, *Teachers College Record*, and *Race, Ethnicity and Education*.

Vicki L. Baker is Associate Professor of Economics and Management at Albion College. Her research interests include doctoral education and the doctoral student experience, developmental networks, mentoring, the professoriate, faculty development, and liberal arts colleges. She earned her BS in Safety Engineering from the Indiana University of Pennsylvania; MBA from the Clarion University of Pennsylvania, and an MS in Management and Organisations and PhD in Higher Education from the Pennsylvania State University. Prior to joining the faculty at Albion College, Vicki was an instructor of Management and Organization at the Smeal College of Business. She also currently teaches for Penn State's World Campus undergraduate Business Administration programme.

Wendy Baker is a Director of the New Zealand Coaching & Mentoring Centre. She works with organisations in NZ, Australia and the Pacific who want to be more strategic in how they link mentoring and coaching to organisational objectives or business needs. Her professional background spans academia and business. She has successfully run mentoring programmes in a range of organisations and has continuing research interests in taking a coaching approach to feedback conversations. Wendy enjoys working with mentoring and coaching as positive interventions for supporting people to be the best they can be.

Makini Beck is Research Associate at the Rochester Institute of Technology. Her scholarship centers on mentoring women of color in academia as well as understanding the teaching practices and experiences of international teachers in urban schools. She has published her work in handbook chapters and peer reviewed journals such as *Mentoring & Tutoring: Partnership in Learning*, and *NASPA Journal* about Women in Higher Education.

Sadhana Bhide is the Global Head of the Barclays Alumni Programme at Barclays Bank plc. Her broad HR experience includes HR partner and change management roles in broadcast media, retail distribution and the financial service industries. She has worked in London, Paris and Tanzania. Sadhana graduated from Queen Mary, London, with a BSc (Hons) in Genetics, followed by postgraduate study in Human Resources Management at the University of the West of England, Bristol. Her dissertation on mentoring schemes at British Aerospace, provided Sadhana with her first opportunity to meet and collaborate with David Clutterbuck. Sadhana is passionate about international mentoring as a means to support multi-country working, especially in today's organisational environment where teams operate across virtual and real boundaries.

Vasudha B has worked in a variety of general management roles in the publishing and healthcare industries before moving to New Zealand to pursue a PhD in the School of Management, College of Business, Massey University. Her research interest is in the area of women and leadership and her PhD focuses on the experiences of workplace sponsoring among women in New Zealand. She has helped to deliver a Young Women in Leadership Programme at Massey for Year 12 female students in the Manawatū region and is a co-facilitator for the Strengths@Massey programme for new students at Massey University, Palmerston North.

Laura Bierema is Associate Dean and Professor, University of Georgia, College of Education, program of Learning, Leadership, and Organization Development. Dr. Bierema's research interests include workplace learning, career development, women's development, organization development, executive coaching, leadership, and critical human resource development. Dr. Bierema holds both bachelors and masters degrees from Michigan State University and a doctorate in adult education from the University of Georgia. She has published over 50 articles and six books. Dr. Bierema is a Cyril O. Houle Scholar in Adult and Continuing Education and Lilly Fellow. She is the recipient of the Richard A. Swanson Excellence in Research Award and four Academy of Human Resource Development's 'Cutting Edge' Awards. She is the 2009 recipient of the *Highly Commended Award* by the Emerald Literati Network Awards for Excellence; 2012 winner of the University of Georgia College of Education Russell H. Yeany, Jr. Research Award; 2012 recipient of the Sherpa Trailblazer of the Year Award in recognition of innovation application of the Sherpa Coaching Process; 2013 winner of the Academy of Human Resource Development's Outstanding Scholar Award; 2014 winner of the Academy of Human Resource Development's Book of the Year; and 2015 winner of the University, Professional, and Continuing Education Association Phillip E. Frandson Award for Literature.

Anna Blackman is Senior Lecturer for James Cook University in their College of Business, Law and Governance. She is the Course Co-ordinator for the Graduate Certificate in Australian Rural Leadership for the Australian Rural Leadership Foundation and is a Fellow and a Queensland Councillor for the Australian Human Resources Institute. Dr Anna Blackman's areas of expertise include business coaching effectiveness, Human Resource Management, Business Management and Wellbeing. She is specifically interested in building capacity with regional and rural businesses. Dr Blackman has worked in small business management for approximately eight years in Australia and has worked for a large multinational corporation in the UK.

Jennifer Boswell is Assistant Professor at the University of Houston-Victoria. She has served as the Assistant Editor of the *Mentoring and Tutoring Journal: Partnership in Learning* for six years and as the Assistant Editor of the *Advancing Women in Leadership Journal* for seven years. She also served as the Editor of the *Michigan Journal of Counseling: Research, Theory, and Practice* (Michigan Counseling Association). She earned her PhD in Counselor Education from Sam Houston State University. In her work, she practices mentoring techniques and teaches such. Her current research focuses on the mentoring needs of women in counselor education programs. Dr Boswell is a published author with an average of three papers per year and has made numerous presentations at state, national and international mental health conferences.

Tim Bright has over 25 years of management and consulting experience having lived and worked in the UK, Turkey, the USA, the Middle East and across Europe and Asia. He is a partner with OneWorld Consulting, based in Istanbul, and works with clients at all stages of the executive talent lifecycle. He delivers executive search projects, works as an executive coach, designs and supports in-company mentoring programmes and works with top leadership teams to help them become even more effective. OneWorld Consulting also provides customised outplacement. He has worked on the ground in over 20 countries and uses his diverse experience to add value to his clients. Tim began working as an executive coach in 1997, specialising in coaching senior executives and leadership teams, with the aim of raising their levels of awareness, and providing challenge and support as they reflect, achieving real behavioural change and improving results. He has designed and supported mentoring programmes with a number of clients in Turkey and internationally. Tim's clients include Adidas, Anadolu Group, Coca-Cola, Henkel, Microsoft, Sabanci Group, Siemens and Vodafone.

Kathleen Bury is the Chief Executive Officer for the Mowgli Foundation, an international and award-winning mentoring organisation, including the EMCC European Quality Award for their core program syllabus. Kathleen is a 'global nomad', having lived in the Middle East, Africa, Europe, UK, US and now Kenya. She has over 16 years of multicultural, start up and growth, for-profit and not-for-profit experience. She is a member of the Entrepreneurs Organisation East Africa Chapter and Global Philanthropists Circle. Her experience includes executive leadership, mentoring, coaching, stakeholder management, management consulting, market analysis, communications/marketing, knowledge management, process design, event management and writing. She holds a BA (Hons) degree in Business and Quality Management from the Nottingham Trent Business School and has participated in executive education courses at Wharton Business School, Columbia Business School, New York University Stern (NYU Stern) and INSEAD. When not working, Kathleen loves visiting her adopted elephants in Kenya and taking every opportunity to enjoy the African/safari plains.

Esther Cavett is an Executive and Career Coach and is a Senior Research Fellow at King's College, London. Trained in psychological coaching, she was previously a senior partner in a large City law firm and a professional musician. She has coached in private practice and with various coaching and counselling organisations, working with people in occupations ranging from business and law to education, charity and the arts. She writes regularly on diversity and coaching-related topics and has a special interest in the transfer of skills from one area of expertise to another.

Deirdre Cobb-Roberts is Associate Professor at the University of South Florida. Her research focuses on issues of equity and treatment in the history of American higher education, teacher preparation, and the role of social justice in education. She has a co-edited book and has published in several journals including the *History of Education Quarterly* and the *Journal of Teacher Education*.

Emily Cosgrove, co-founder of The Conversation Space, has worked with organisations, teams and individuals on a national and international level for 20 years. Her interest in powerful conversations began when she won young Business Person of the Year for mentoring in her first business. Through her experience of setting up and supporting innovative mentoring and leadership programmes in over 50 organisations, she has worked with thousands of mentors and coaches to bring learning conversations to life. Emily is a contributor to journals including *Coaching at Work*, *Training Journal* and her recent research won the *Roffey Park/HR Magazine* research competition. She has a specific interest and writes regularly on the internal mentoring space. She is a qualified Executive Coach-Mentor, Internal Mentoring Special Advisor to the Association of Coaching Supervisors and an active member of the EMCC. When not working, Emily can often be found recharging her batteries at Kenwood Ladies pond, swimming outdoors throughout the year.

Gloria Crisp is an Associate Professor at Oregon State University and Co-Editor of *New Directions for Institutional Research (NDIR)*. Her scholarship seeks to identify factors that promote academic success for students who attend community colleges and four-year broad access institutions. To date, her work has focused on developing a mentoring framework to explain how students who attend broad access institutions experience and receive various forms of mentoring support. Her survey instrument, the College Student Mentoring Scale (CSMS), is currently being used at institutions across the country and abroad to evaluate the effectiveness of mentoring relationships. Gloria's scholarship also explores other behaviors and experiences that support student success at accessible institutions, including co-enrolling at multiple institutions and enrolling in developmental education courses. She has a particular interest in work to understand and support the college experiences of Latina/o students and students attending Hispanic Serving Institutions (HSIs).

Gary M. Crow is Professor in the Department of Educational Leadership and Policy Studies and Executive Associate Dean of the School of Education at Indiana University (USA). His PhD is from the University of Chicago. He has also taught at Bank Street College, Louisiana State University, University of Utah, and Florida State University. He has also been a visiting faculty member at the University of Reading (England) and the University of Otago (New Zealand). His research interests include school leadership and school reform, leadership development and professional identities. Crow is currently conducting research on successful school principals and professional identities of school leaders in reform contexts. His most recent book is *The Principalship: New roles in a professional learning community* (with Matthews, published by Allyn and Bacon). He is also a co-editor of the *International Handbook on the Preparation and Development of School Leaders* (2008) and the *Handbook of Research on the Education of School Leaders* (2009). Articles authored by Crow have appeared in *Educational Administration Quarterly, Educational Management, Administration and Leadership (UK), Journal of Educational Administration (Australia)*, and *Journal of School Leadership*. Crow is a past president of the University Council for Educational Administration and founding editor of the *Journal of Cases in Educational Leadership*. He is also a recipient of the Roald Campbell Lifetime Achievement Award presented by the University Council for Educational Administration.

Mariola Czechowska-Fraczak is an executive coach, mentor and leadership advisor who brings almost 20 years of practical leadership and business experience from corporate environments in Eastern Europe. Her areas of expertise are leadership issues (around building high performing, emotionally intelligent teams); alignment and maintaining commitment along mission, vision, goals and values; and developing leaders as mentors. She is now the Founder and Managing Partner of Mind Partners – European Mentors and Coaches' Group. Prior to starting her independent career Mariola spent many years in corporate-management functions – general manager at Berthelsmann Music Group, Deputy Director for Young and Rubicam, and Deputy Director for Polish Television's Advertising Department. She also worked with White House representatives for the speech of two presidents (Polish and American) on the occasion of Polish access to NATO.

Leslie Dashew has worked with family businesses for over 30 years and is a pioneer in understanding and helping them to be harmonious and profitable. She is the managing partner of the Aspen Family Business Group, an internationally recognised advisor to families in business and has been recognised by her peers in the Family Firm Institute for her contributions to the field with one of their highest honours, The Richard Beckhard Award. Leslie has co-authored four books in the field including the most recent *The Keys to Success in Family Business*.

Erin L. Dolan is the Georgia Athletic Association Professor in Innovative Science Education in the Biochemistry & Molecular Biology Department at the University of Georgia. She teaches introductory biology and biochemistry, and her research group studies scalable ways of engaging students in science research and mentoring of undergraduate researchers in the life sciences. She has designed and led a wide range of professional development on active learning and mentoring, including intensive sessions for faculty to develop course-based undergraduate research experiences. She is principal investigator principal investigator or co-investigator on more than $6 million in grants, including one for CUREnet (http://curenet.cns.utexas.edu/), a network of people and programs integrating research experiences into undergraduate courses. She is also Editor-in-Chief of the leading biology education journal, *CBE - Life Sciences Education* (http://www.lifescied.org/).

Amanda Edwards is the Chief Operating Officer at the Mowgli Foundation. Amanda joined the Mowgli team after working for more than a decade in the corporate sector with Lloyds Banking Group where she gained commercial, project and operational experience across many leadership roles. During this time she led numerous strategic pieces of work for the Bank. This included leading on the commercial aspects of the launch of a new online comparison site, an unusually entrepreneurial venture for the organisation, where she negotiated contract and commercial deals with 52 insurers. She was also pivotal in the smooth transition of the merging of several functions during the Lloyds acquisition of HBOS group, leading on the restructuring of the sales and marketing functions within the group's insurance business, transitioning over 450 colleagues through a restructuring process. She is an experienced leader, mentor and coach, having led large operational areas, smaller specialist teams, cross location teams and multicultural teams. Within Mowgli, she has most recently led on the development of a strategy and design model for the replication of Mowgli's program and impact through the creation of a franchising network, a project critical to Mowgli's sustainability and scalability.

Jennybeth Ekeland is Senior Consultant and Program Director, responsible for professional mentoring, at AFF at NHH Norwegian School of Economics. She qualified as an Educational Psychologist at the University of Oslo and as Advanced Organizational Consultant at the Tavistock Institute, UK. She has more than 25 years of experience in organisational and leadership development. She currently works in executive mentoring and coaching, management, leadership and organisational development. Jennybeth is also author of the book *Mentoring. Lærende allianser i ledelse* (2014), and she is co-founder and vice-president of EMCC Norway.

Talia Esnard is Lecturer at the University of the West Indies. Her research interests include educational leadership, mentoring and networks, as well as female entrepreneurship in the context of the Caribbean. Her work has been published in several journals including the *Journal of Asian Academy and Management*, *Journal of Higher Education and Practice*, *Caribbean Curriculum*, and the *Journal of Educational Administration and History*.

Warrant Officer Viti Flanagan is an aircraft technician who was in the Royal New Zealand Air Force for 24 years. Viti was one of the first women in the engineering fields in the RNZAF and has featured in two books on women in aviation and been quoted in the New Zealand parliament. Viti now works as an active reservist managing the RNZAF's mentoring programme. As an active reservist, Viti researched and wrote the accreditation documents for the RNZAF's successful submission to the ISMPE in 2014. Viti is of Fijian, NZ Maori and European background and is married with two teenage sons. When not working as an active reservist, Viti runs her technical writing company.

Vanessa Fudge is a founder of coaching and consulting firm LeadingWell, a partner with AltusQ, a non-executive Director of MINDD.org and a member of the European Coaching and Mentoring Council. Vanessa was recently the author and lecturer in the Sydney Business School 'Applied Coaching Skills' Masters of Business Coaching degree. Vanessa trains and supervisors coaches to EMCC standards.

Vanessa is a registered Psychologist specialising in leadership coaching, mentoring program facilitation and organisational system dynamics; an Accredited Certified Meta Coach (ACMC) through the Institute of Neuro-Semantics; Organisational Development Resources (ODR) Practitioner and Train the Trainer; Certified Leadership Circle 360 Assessment coach, holds a Certificate IV in Workplace Training and a Bachelor of Science (Honours) Psychology from the University of New South Wales.

Judie Gannon is a Senior Lecturer in the International Centre for Coaching and Mentoring Studies (ICCaMS) at Oxford Brookes University. Originally a manager in the international hotel industry, Judie joined academia in 1994 after completing an MA in Industrial Relations (Warwick University). Her PhD (Oxford Brookes University 2007) explored the resourcing and development of managers in international hotel companies. She also completed a PG Cert in Coaching and Mentoring during this time and has supervised students on the Doctorate in Coaching & Mentoring over the last 7 years. Until 2015 Judie taught and researched in the Oxford School of Hospitality Management at Oxford Brookes University and developed and supported several mentoring schemes across different sectors and settings. Judie has written and presented academic and practitioner papers in the areas of international human resource management, management development, coaching and mentoring. She reviews for several high profile academic journals, is a member of the EMCC and CIPD, and serves on the editorial board of the *International Journal of Evidence Based Coaching & Mentoring*.

Bob Garvey is Visiting Professor at Sheffield Business School. He is one of Europe's leading academic practitioners in coaching and mentoring. Described as a 'thought leader', Bob offers a critical perspective on many aspects of coaching and mentoring practice. He has an impressive record of research, teaching and consultancy in a range of different national and international organisations and is in demand as a lively and sometimes controversial keynote speaker. He is widely published, particularly in the area of coaching and mentoring, and he is a Fellow of the Royal Society of Arts and a Fellow of the Higher Education Academy.

Hilary Geber (PhD, University of the Witwatersrand, Johannesburg) is an industrial and organisational psychologist and a qualified Results coach. She owns the mentoring and coaching consultancy Mentorfundi. She worked as an academic at the University of the Witwatersrand, Johannesburg in the Centre for Learning, Teaching and Development. She was also Programme Director of the Masters in Business and Executive Coaching at the Wits Business School and is a member of their College of Coaches. She has published extensively on cross-cultural and diversity mentoring in post-Apartheid South Africa. She is a member of the editorial board of the *International Journal of Evidence Based Coaching and Mentoring*.

Rodney K. Goodyear (PhD, University of Illinois at Urbana-Champaign) is a Professor at the University of Redlands as well as Emeritus Professor of Counseling Psychology, University of Southern California and was the 2015 President of the Society for the Advancement of Psychotherapy. A major theme of his scholarship has been supervision and training of counselors and psychologists. His book with Janine Bernard (*Fundamentals of Clinical Supervision*) is in its fifth edition and is arguably the most used supervision book in world. He was a member of the American Psychological Association's task group that developed the Association's supervision guidelines; and he received the American Psychological Association's 2015 award for Distinguished Lifetime Contributions to Education and Training.

Margaret Grogan is Dean of the College of Educational Studies, Chapman University, California. Originally from Australia, she received a Bachelor of Arts degree in Ancient History and Japanese Language from the University of Queensland. She taught high school in Australia, and was a teacher and an administrator at the International School of the Sacred Heart, Tokyo, where she lived for 17 years. After graduating from Washington State University with a PhD in Educational Administration, she taught educational leadership and policy at the University of Virginia and at the University of Missouri-Columbia and mentored many aspiring leaders. Among the various leadership positions she has held at her institutions and professional organisations, she served as Dean of the School of Educational Studies at Claremont Graduate University from 2008–12, Chair of the Department of Educational Leadership and Policy Analysis at the University of Missouri-Columbia, 2002–8, and President of the University Council for Educational Administration in 2003–4. She has also published many articles and chapters and has authored, co-authored or edited six books, including *Women and Educational Leadership* (with Charol Shakeshaft, 2011). Her current research focuses on women in leadership, gender and education, the moral and ethical dimensions of leadership, and leadership for social justice.

Ridwanah Gurjee is Senior Lecturer at the University of Central Lancashire (UCLan). Since 2001, she has taken a core role in co-ordinating the volunteering programme at the university and has been involved in developing the Community Leadership programme at Foundation, BA and Masters levels. Ridwanah has developed mentoring projects locally throughout the UK and, most recently, internationally, with UCLan Students and young people from the Agadir Orphanage Centre in Morocco. She is also part of the Lancashire Education Authority Governing Body for Deepdale Community Primary School and Preston Muslim Girls High School. She is on the Board of Directors for the International Mentoring Association, USA and Fellow of the Higher Education Academy. Ridwanah's research in mentoring stems from her values and purpose to make a difference in the lives of others.

Denise Harris has over 30 years' experience of working in the NHS. She originally qualified as an Occupational Therapist but has more recently worked within leadership development roles. Denise qualified as a Coach in 2008 and as a Coach Supervisor in 2010. She has a particular interest in coaching and mentoring within the NHS and how these can be used to support, enable and develop staff. She is also interested in the impact that a coaching approach can have on the effectiveness of clinical interventions. Denise is currently undertaking a PhD and is investigating the understanding, use and development of supervision in a health care organisation.

Eeva-Liisa Heinaro is currently Sales Director, Paper ENA, Finland and Scandinavia for UPM-Kymmene Oy, one of the biggest paper producers globally. She has extensive experience in business-to-business sales and strategic sales development. She was chairperson for Gaia Network 2012–15. During this time Rhea Challenge Mentoring program was developed at her initiative. She continues to run Rhea Challenge program, which will go into a new round in Fall 2016.

Andrew J. Hobson is Professor of Teacher Learning and Development and Head of Education Research at the University of Brighton, UK. He was previously Research Professor in Education at Sheffield Hallam University and has also been employed at the Universities of Nottingham and Leeds, the National Foundation for Educational Research, and as a teacher, middle leader and mentor in secondary and post-compulsory education. His research has focused on the nature and impact of support for the professional learning and development of teachers, and early career teachers in particular. He has particular interests in mentoring and teacher well-being, and is Editor-in-Chief of the *International Journal of Mentoring and Coaching in Education*. Professor Hobson coined the term 'judgementoring' (Hobson & Malderez, 2013; Hobson, 2016) and developed the ONSIDE Mentoring framework (Hobson, 2016), both of which are discussed in Chapter 21 of this volume.

Beverly J. Irby, Professor, Program Chair, and Associate Department Head for Educational Administration and Human Resource Development, College of Education and Human Development at Texas A&M University, is the Director of the Educational Leadership Research Center. Her primary research interests center on issues of social responsibility, including bilingual and English-as-a-second-language education, administrative structures, curriculum, and instructional strategies. She is the author of more than 200 refereed articles, chapters, books, and curricular materials for Spanish-speaking children. She has had in excess of $20,000,000 in grants. She was awarded, in 2009, the Texas State University System – Regent's Professor. Dr Irby has extensive experience working with undergraduate students for more than 25 years, and many of these students, including first-generation college students, ethnic minorities, and the economically disadvantaged, have obtained doctorates and received research/teaching awards under her mentorship. Dr Irby is the editor of the *Mentoring and Tutoring* journal.

Anna Jarzębska is a Recruitment Manager and Mentoring Program Coordinator at Sanofi Poland and an accomplished HR professional with over 17 years of experience in the different sectors. She is responsible for implementing recruitment standards and strategies that enable Sanofi Poland to recruit a high-performing and motivated workforce. Anna specialises in recruiting (education of hiring managers, providing the recruitment processes), development (mentoring) and employer branding. Anna has served as the Development Senior Specialist and HR Coordinator for the Volkswagen Bank in Poland and Volkswagen Bank GmbH in Germany. In these capacities, Anna was responsible for talent management, implementing international-development programs, creating AC standards employer branding and recruitment. Anna holds a MA in Psychology from SWPS University in Warsaw (Poland). She is a certified coach (ICC) and mentor (Mind Partners).

Malgorzata Jastrzebska is Director of HR&Admin in Sanofi Group Poland for 11 years. Professional with 25 years of experience in HR, combining perspective from consulting (CE Trust, E&Y) and business from different sectors (IFF Corp, PepsiCo, Coca-Cola, Sanofi). In Sanofi responsible for HR strategy for Poland, aligned with corporate HR strategy, personnel policy, building human capital and leadership capabilities to create Sanofi competitiveness. As Administration Head, assuring best possible work conditions, supervising facilities, car fleet and safety. She is leading whole HR function in Sanofi Group – Sanofi, Sanofi Pasteur, Sanofi-Genzyme up to Merial and Nepentes, as well as different activities – commercial operations and industrial affairs. She holds a MA in Psychology From Warsaw University (Poland) and is a certified coach (International Coach Federation) and Mentor (Mentors' Academy of Mind Partners).

W. Brad Johnson is Professor of Psychology in the Department of Leadership, Ethics and Law at the United States Naval Academy, and a Faculty Associate in the Graduate School of Education at Johns Hopkins University. A clinical psychologist and former Lieutenant Commander in the Navy's Medical Service Corps, Dr Johnson served as a psychologist at Bethesda Naval Hospital and the Medical Clinic at Pearl Harbor, where he was the division head for psychology. He is a fellow of the American Psychological Association and recipient of the Johns Hopkins University Teaching Excellence Award. Dr Johnson is the author of numerous publications, including 13 books, in the areas of mentoring, professional ethics, and counseling. His most recent books include *Athena Rising: How and Why Men Should Mentor Women* (2016, with David Smith), *On Being a Mentor (2015)*, and *The Elements of Mentoring* (2008, with Charles Ridley).

Stella S. Kanchewa, PhD, received her doctorate in Clinical Psychology from the University of Massachusetts Boston. Her research interests include factors related to risk and resiliency within the developmental trajectories of children and youth. This includes psychopathology and relationships with non-parental adults, as well as prevention and intervention programs with a specific focus on youth mentoring relationships.

Zorka Karanxha is Associate Professor at the University of South Florida. Her research examines issues of educational leadership preparation for social justice, education law, and charter schools. She has published in *Educational Administration Quarterly*, *Journal of Research in Educational Leadership*, and many other journals.

Moyra Keane, is an Educational Developer, senior lecturer and researcher in Johannesburg. She coordinates and teaches on postgraduate courses, presents workshops and courses for academic staff. These include Research Writing, Postgraduate Supervision, and Teaching in Higher Education. She coordinates the PGDipE(HE), runs a mentoring programme for staff, and supervises post-graduate students. She is a qualified coach. Her research interests are in indigenous knowledge, decolonisation, participative research, and the Scholarship of Teaching and Learning.

Paula King is a psychologist and leadership coach. She is registered with the British Psychological Society on the Register of Competence in Psychological Testing, a European Accredited Coaching Supervisor and a member of the Society for Coaching Psychology. Paula holds an MSc in Coaching, Mentoring and Organisational Development from Portsmouth University and is President of the European Mentoring and Coaching Council in Ireland

(EMCC IE). She is also a European Council Member of the EMCC, working with this organisation promoting standards and ethics in the coaching profession. She has been recently appointed by the Minister for Health to the Healthy Ireland Board due to her interest and work in the area of Coaching and Mental Health and Wellbeing. Paula's current clientele consists of leaders with influence, CEOs, politicians and members of the media. She brings genuine warmth to her coaching interventions whilst consistently assisting her clients to achieve goals, which may have seemed unachievable, through an empathic and challenging approach.

Terezia Koczka is a Director of the coaching consultancy firm KEY Coaches Ltd, UK (www.keycoach.co.uk) who provides leadership coaching, leadership-development programs and change consulting for a wide range of private and corporate clients. She holds an MBA from Heriot-Watt Business School, Edinburgh. Terezia has a wide range of experiences in leadership development, design and management of large-scale change programmes and executive coaching. With over 20 years' international experience as executive coach and the founding president of European Mentoring and Coaching Council (EMCC) Hungary, she played a leading role in developing the emerging profession of coaching and mentoring in Hungary. She is the Professional Excellence Director of EMCC UK. She contributes to the profession by translating coaching books from English to Hungarian. She is visiting lecturer at Budapest University of Technology and Economics MBA programme.

Kathy E. Kram is the R.C. Shipley Professor in Management Emerita at Boston University. Her primary interests are in the areas of adult development, relational learning, mentoring and developmental networks, leadership development, and change processes in organisations. In addition to her book, *Mentoring at Work*, she has published in a wide range of journals. She is co-editor of *The Handbook of Mentoring at Work: Theory, Research and Practice* with Dr Belle Rose Ragins, and a founding member of the Center for Research on Emotional Intelligence in Organizations (CREIO). She served as a member of the Board of Governors at the Center for Creative Leadership from 2002 to 2009. Her new book *Strategic Relationships at Work: Creating Your Circle of Mentors, Sponsors and Peers for Success in Business and Life* was co-authored with Prof Wendy Murphy (Babson College). Dr Kram is currently collaborating on two new projects: a book on peer coaching, and a study of the transition into retirement.

Rafael Lara-Alecio is Regent's Professor and Director of Bilingual Programs in the Department of Educational Psychology at Texas A&M University. He is also the Director of the Center for Research and Development in Dual Language and Literacy Acquisition. His primary areas of research are in assessment, evaluation, and bilingual content instruction. He co-authored a pedagogical theory and model for transitional English bilingual classrooms. Dr Lara-Alecio has served as PI of multiple US DOE funded projects, and has managed a total of $38,000,000 in grant funds. Dr Lara-Alecio has mentored numerous undergraduate and graduate students across the department, college and university. Many of these students, including first-generation college students, ethnic minorities, and the economically disadvantaged, have obtained their doctorates under his mentorship.

Sally Lawson is a PhD student in the Business School, York St John University (UK). From an environmental career, she retrained to work as an occupational therapy practitioner, moving into service management and most recently project management in health and care. This enabled her to focus on innovative integration projects, including developing and delivering a novel mentoring-focused development programme for non-medical neuro practitioners. Based on this project, and continuing a partnership and outcomes approach, she is currently completing her PhD on Mentoring in specialist workforce development: a realist evaluation for submission in 2017.

Hoang Anh Thi Le is the Head of Mentoring for Youth Business International, a global network of not-for-profit organisations which help underserved entrepreneurs to start and grow sustainable businesses. In her role, Hoang Anh is responsible for building, coordinating and supporting the YBI global mentoring network which encompasses over 15,000 volunteer business mentors. She works to improve the effectiveness of member organisations to deliver quality mentoring services to young entrepreneurs and has commissioned Middlesex University to conduct a piece of global research to study how volunteer business mentoring assists young entrepreneurs in their journey to enterprise. Hoang Anh pioneered YBI's flagship mentoring programme build methodology and has supported a number of YBI's members to build and launch sector leading mentoring programmes. Hoang Anh passionately believes in the power of mentoring; she has greatly benefitted from being a mentee and is an active mentor to young women in her local community in London. Hoang Anh is currently completing a Post Graduate Certificate in Coaching and Mentoring at York St John University.

Joanne Leck joined the Telfer School of Management, University of Ottawa, Ontario Canada, in 2000 as a professor of human resource management and organisational behaviour. Dr. Leck obtained a B.Math from the University of Waterloo in 1980, an MBA in 1987 and PhD in 1992 from McGill University. Her thesis examined the effectiveness of employment equity programs and issues related to managing diversity. Dr. Leck's earliest work was an extension of her dissertation, where she continued to research employment and pay equity. After interviewing women who broke the glass-ceiling, she became increasingly aware of another problem women face in the workplace, namely bullying and harassment. As these working conditions may dissuade women from advancing in their careers, she turned her attention to this area of research. Most recently, she has been investigating how mentoring can not only protect women from any adverse forces but also provide them with the psychosocial and career support they need to advance.

Jane Lewes is a specialist in developing and delivering work-based learning programmes for diverse groups and organisations in private, public and third sectors across Europe. Jane works largely in 'non-traditional' learning environments using interactive methods that encourage and empower people to take responsibility for their own development. Jane led the team that designed and delivered the acclaimed Birmingham Apprenticeship Scheme, coaching and mentoring to support the retention of young adults in their work placements. Jane's publications include: *Mentoring for Business Success*, Welsh Assembly Government; *Change Facilitator Toolkit*, London Guildhall University; *The Good Mentee Guide*, Welsh Assembly Government; *Coaching for High Performance*, Management Centre Europe; *Coaching and Mentoring: A manager's toolkit to support employability*, Birmingham City Council and *Dialogi: Question your way to great results!* The Learning Consultancy.

Petra Lockhart is a senior L & D executive who has worked for a number of international organisations, primarily focusing on organization and people development, leadership, change, mentoring and the Consumer Experience. Her passion is to lead, develop and inspire both individuals and teams to reach their full potential, thus supporting organisations to achieve their strategic objectives, whilst having fun at work!

Lockhart's work with the global Mentoring at Swarovski program has been recognised in the industry press and used as case study at the Coaching at Work conference in 2015. Petronella continues to progress her passion for people and learning with enthusiasm and application.

Fiona McInnes-Craig is the Founder and Managing Director of Thresholds Ltd. She established Thresholds in 2000 to provide coaching and career development programmes for women and other groups who are under-represented in leadership and management roles. Her 'Women At A Threshold' programme for the Ministry of Defence was shortlisted for a national award and gave the company wider exposure in the public sector. This led very quickly to similar programmes across central government departments, most notably 'Crossing Thresholds', a year-long career mentoring programme for women and BME staff. Since 2006, nearly 2000 mentoring partnerships have completed or are underway. On average 75% of participants get promoted or move to more satisfying jobs within a year.

David Megginson is Emeritus Professor of HR Development at Sheffield Hallam University in the UK. His PhD was from Lancaster, his MSc from UMIST and his BSc from Bristol University. He is a Chartered Fellow of the Chartered Institute of Personnel and Development, UK. He co-founded (with David Clutterbuck) the European Mentoring and Coaching Council (EMCC), and is currently an Ambassador for EMCC in Europe and Honorary Vice-President of EMCC UK. David has engaged in research over many years on coaching, mentoring, CPD and self-development. He has written five books with David Clutterbuck, *Techniques for Coaching and Mentoring, Mentoring in Action, Mentoring Executives and Directors, Making Coaching Work: Creating a Coaching Culture and Further Techniques for Coaching and Mentoring*. Recent books also include *Learning from Burnout* (with Tim Casserley - 2009), *Coaching and Mentoring: Theory and Practice* (with Bob Garvey and Paul Stokes - 2009). David has also lectured internationally in this field and is a popular speaker at many coaching conferences across Europe.

Lis Merrick's career in mentoring and coaching follows a successful career in Human Resources with senior posts for Merrill Lynch, European Investment Banking and The Thomas Cook Group. She is Managing Director of Coach Mentoring Limited, the ISMCP Accreditation Chair (EMCC International Standards for Mentoring and Coaching Programmes) a Visiting Fellow of the Coaching and Mentoring Research Unit at Sheffield Business School and the EMCC (European Mentoring and Coaching Council) UK President. She was voted 'Mentoring Person of the Year 2011/12' by Coaching at Work magazine in the UK. Her experience in mentoring programme design and development is now nationally acclaimed in the UK, with over 100 mentoring programmes to her name internationally. Lis writes and speaks at conferences about mentoring and coaching regularly and this work also informs her practice as an executive coach and designer of mentoring and coaching programmes. Her expertise and research is predominantly in the field of designing mentoring and coaching programmes with regard to talent management, coaching and mentoring women and supervision in mentoring. Lis's research and interests in 2016/17 are particularly focused around coaching women in their careers for a book for the Open University Press.

Lis works as an Executive Coach and consultant in coaching and mentoring on a global basis and has over 25 years' experience of working in cross-cultural environments. She lectures at Sheffield Business School on the MSc Coaching and Mentoring. Lis holds an MBA and an MSc in Coaching and Mentoring from Sheffield Business School.

Maria da Graça Nicoletti Mizukami holds a degree in Education from São Paulo State University and a doctorate in Social Sciences from the Catholic University of Rio de Janeiro. She carried out postdoctoral research at Santa Clara University, California, USA. She teaches in the Graduate Education Program of the Federal University of São Carlos, São Paulo and the Education, Art, and Cultural History of Presbyterian Mackenzie University, São Paulo, SP – Brazil. Her research interests are knowledge base for teaching, professional development of teachers, pedagogical practices and teaching cases.

Catherine Mossop is President of Sage Mentors Inc., Toronto, Ontario Canada. She has deep expertise in supporting organisations in finding ways to capitalise on their talent and deliver better outcomes by building coaching and mentoring capacity inside organisations, and coaching and mentoring for employee remediation and career management. Over her 30-year career, Catherine has worked with multi-faceted organisations in the public, private and 3rd sectors and has designed award-winning mentoring programs that have had measurable social, economic and organisational impact.

Catherine is a contributing author: Mentoring and the World of Work in Canada, 2003, Fondation d'entrepreneurship du Quebec; and *Developing Successful Diversity Mentoring Programmes, An International Casebook*, 2012, Editors: Clutterbuck, D, Posluns, K., McGraw Hill. She has produced many mentoring guides for mentors and mentees, and produced several film-quality videos to support mentor development.

Catherine is a Fellow Certified Management Consultant, a Certified Human Resources Leader; and an alumnus of the Governor General Canadian Leadership Conference.

Carol A. Mullen, PhD, is a tenured full professor of Educational Leadership at Virginia Tech. A US Fulbright Scholar, she conducted her work in China, selected for her expertise in mentoring and learning innovation. This Past President of National Council of Professors of Educational Administration is an award-winning teacher, supervisor, and scholar in mentoring, leadership, and diversity. Dr Mullen has received the 2016 Jay D. Scribner Mentoring Award and the 2015 *Educational Administration Quarterly* Service Award for Outstanding Editorial Board Service, both from the University Council for Educational Administration. Additionally, she received the 2016 Charles Clear Research Award from the Virginia Educational Research Association. She serves as a Plenary Session Representative for the University Council for Educational Administration. She has authored over 200 journal articles and book chapters and authored, edited, or co-edited 21 books, including *Creativity and Education in China: Paradox and Possibilities for an Era of Accountability* (Routledge, 2017), *Education Policy Perils: Tackling the Tough Issue* (Routledge, 2016) and *The SAGE Handbook of Mentoring and Coaching in Education* (Sage, 2012). She is the former Director of the School of Education and Associate Dean for Professional Education of the College of Liberal Arts and Human Sciences. Previously, for many years she served as Department Chair at The University of North Carolina at Greensboro.

Eileen Murphy (MCIPD, BSc Econ, MBA), is an associate of the Learning Consultancy with over 20 years' experience of providing training, facilitation and organisational-development consultancy for the voluntary and public sectors in Wales. Eileen's areas of expertise include coach/mentoring, evaluation and measuring service outcomes, leadership development, performance management and project management. Eileen's focus is on supporting managers, staff and organisations to provide the best services possible for service users. Eileen was a member of the team that delivered the work-based coach/mentoring programme aimed at supporting and retaining young adults in employment. Eileen's recent in-house publications include: *Engage Mid-Term Evaluation* (July 2015, GAVO Newport), *Valleys Voice Mid-Term Evaluation* (July 2015, GAVO Newport) and *CREA8 Project Case-studies* (January 2015, SMT Merthyr Tydfil).

Donnel Nunes is the Program Director of a group of learning centres that provide specialized instruction and socio-emotional supports to students and their families in Hawaii. He is the principal owner of PVA Knowledge Group, a family-learning consultancy, a member of Coaching and Mentoring International (CMI), and a licensed mental-health counselor. He is also a former lecturer and current PhD Candidate in the Educational Psychology Department at the University of Hawaii, Manoa. His research interests focus on familial mentoring relationships. He regularly presents at state, national, and international conferences on topics related to education, mental health, parent/child engagement, and mentoring relationships between family members.

Mikaela Nyström is Managing Director and owner of 4L.com Oy (www.4l-consulting.com). She coaches executive leaders and teams in global companies. She has been creating and delivering mentoring programs since 1988 and is a true believer in the impact of mentoring as a great learning alliance. Mikaela has been designing with the Gaia Rhea Challenge Project team, the Rhea Challenge Mentoring process and has also been the facilitator of the Rhea Challenge kick-off and closing sessions with the mentees and the mentors. She will continue to co-create and facilitate Gaia Rhea Challenge into the new round, Fall 2016.

Rose Opengart, PhD, is currently an Associate Professor of Management at Dalton State College. Dr Opengart has taught a variety of management-related courses and has worked in HR in multiple industries including manufacturing, non-profit, and academia. She holds a PHR, professional human resources certification and has received awards for course development, teaching and publishing. She earned her PhD in Human Resources & Organizational Development from The University of Georgia. Dr Opengart's research interests include emotional and cultural intelligence, women's career development and mentoring.

Farah Palmer is the Director of the Māori Business and Leadership Centre and a Senior Lecturer in the School of Management, College of Business, Massey University. Her teaching and research interests are in sport sociology, sport management, leadership and governance as they relate to Māori and women in particular. She has helped to deliver a Young Women in Leadership Programme at Massey for Year 12 female students in the Manawatū and Auckland regions, and helped establish a Māori Mentoring and Leadership Programme in the Massey Business School.

Matteo Perchiazzi is the Director and founder of SIM – Italian School of Mentoring (since 2010), the President and Founder of Sport Association 'Mentor – Net'. SIM is the Italian partner of CMI Clutterbuck (Coaching and Mentoring International). Perchiazzi is a member of the 'board EMCC International' for the definition and determination of the mentoring standard. He is now founding the Publishing Company of the 'Italian Mentoring School' to promote mentoring culture in Italy. Since 1998 Perchiazzi has been involved in the first Italian research about Mentoring, called 'Cameo, and applied Mentoring "training, research and consulting"' in every sector: businees and Sme's, school and university, social filed and sports, public administrations, big organizations, disabilities in labour market till NATO training mission in Afghanistan.

He's an author and writer about Mentoring with many specialist and scientific articles, and the following books: 'Telemaco e il Manager. Strumenti per il Mentoring nelle organizzazioni, Edizioni SIM – Scuola Italiana di Mentoring, Florence, in press. 'Apprendere il Mentoring. Manuale operativo per la formazione dei Mentor, Edizioni Transeuropa, 2009. Batini, G. Del Sarto, M. Perchiazzi, 'Raccontare le competenze', Transeuropa Edizioni, 2007.

Patricia Pérez is a certified coach, member of the AAPC (Professional Coaches Association in Argentina). She has a Bachelor degree in Education from the PUC-SP in Brazil; with post-graduation diplomas in HR and NGO's Management in Argentina. She is also graduated from the School of Social Psychology '*Dr. Enrique Pichón Riviere*'. In 2011 Patricia founded SKEYLLS in order to contribute to the mutual growth of organisations and people through the development of key skills. Patricia led the start-up of a Swiss foundation in Argentina (*Fondation Forge*), and was its Executive Director for 5 years, and previously performed as Junior Achievement Argentina's Development Director. She has 7 years of experience as a coach. She is fluent in Spanish, English and Portuguese, since she lived in Buenos Aires, New York and Sao Paulo.

Jeffrey D. Peterson served as an Army officer for 28 years and currently serves as the Chair for the Study of Officership at the Simon Center for the Professional Military Ethic, West Point, NY. As an Army officer, he served in multiple operational leadership roles. He holds a BS from the United States Military Academy, an MBA from the MIT Sloan School of Management, and a PhD in Policy Analysis from the RAND Graduate School.

Ana Oliveira Pinto is a certified Portuguese Executive Coach and Consultant in Change Management and Executive & Talent Development. With 20 years' experience, Ana works in Portugal and internationally, namely in Europe, South America and Africa and across a wide range of sectors: Health, IT, Finance, Pharmaceuticals, FMCG, Manufacturing, Consultancy, Telecommunications and Retail. Ana is passionate about supporting the development of high potential women and women in middle/senior management in advancing to top leadership roles. Over the last 8 years, Ana has developed a particular specialism in designing and implementing mentoring programmes, namely internal mentoring programmes for companies, as well as cross-mentoring programmes for volunteer organisations.

Kirsten M. Poulsen is Managing Director of KMP + House of Mentoring, External Professor at Copenhagen Business School and co-founder and former president (2007–2009) of the European Mentoring and Coaching Council in Denmark. A major theme in her work is enhancing the quality of organisational mentoring programmes at all levels of the organisation. With this as an aim, Kirsten has authored tools and concepts for designing and evaluating mentoring programs, as well as for training, supporting and supervising mentors and mentees. With the Mentor + Game (the 10 situational mentor roles) she has, at the end of 2016, trained more than 7,000 mentors and mentees internationally.

Through KMP + House of Mentoring, Kirsten delivers tailor-made mentoring programs globally for talent and leadership development – and increasingly also through virtual seminars. Kirsten is the author of several books and numerous articles on mentoring, career navigation, leadership and talent development; she has more than 25 years of international experience as a management consultant and holds an MBA from IESE Business School, Barcelona, Spain.

Laura Rana worked with Youth Business International as a Monitoring, Evaluation and Learning (MEL) Advisor from January 2013 to January 2016, following five years' previous experience in MEL, in a variety of overseas- and UK-based roles, with a particular focus on livelihoods and youth. She now leads the equivalent of the MEL team at the British Red Cross. On a personal level, Laura is a great believer in the power of mentoring, having benefitted from two transformational mentoring relationships. She is currently exploring opportunities to take on the role of mentor, so she can 'pay it forward!'

Roxanne B. Reeves is a part-time professor at the faculty of Leadership Studies–Renaissance College, at the University of New Brunswick, Canada. She is a recent PhD graduate, a former ANBLH fellow, and a MITACS doctoral fellowship recipient. She has extensive international experience and has worked in Colombia, Italy and Japan. While living in Japan, Dr Reeves was president of the Cross-Cultural Association.

She has presented and published her work at the provincial, national and international levels. Her work has appeared in, for example, the *International Journal of Coaching and Mentoring* and the *International Journal of Evidence Based Coaching and Mentoring* and in F. Kochan, and A. Green's (Eds.), *Uncovering the Hidden Cultural Dynamics in Mentoring: Perspectives in Mentoring Series*.

Dr Reeves was honoured with the 2014/2016 International Mentoring Association's Dissertation Award. Her research, an article-based dissertation, (a) investigated corporate/workplace mentorship for high-potential employees within the corporate setting; (b) evaluated cross-cultural mentorship as it pertains to newcomer immigrant entrepreneurs; and (c) comprehensively critiqued literature on cross-cultural mentoring. As a consultant, she helps executives and managers with their future workforce requirements by assisting efforts to find, train, and retain the best possible people.

Melissa Richardson is Managing Director of Art of Mentoring, a mentoring programme consultancy based in Australia. Melissa is one of Australia's experts in coaching and mentoring, having worked in the field for twenty years. She has designed and implemented mentoring programmes across public and private sector organisations, specialising in programmes for membership organisations and in virtual mentoring.

She is also an executive coach and coaching supervisor, working with senior leaders and helping coaches and mentors develop their professional practice. Her qualifications include a Master's degree in Organisational Coaching as well as post-graduate qualifications in Strategic Marketing, Coaching Supervision and Counselling.

Aline Maria de Medeiros Rodrigues Reali is Graduate and Doctor in Psychology (São Paulo University). She is a Category 2 Researcher at CNPq (National Council of Technological and Scientific Development, Brazil) and Full Professor in the Pedagogical Theories and Practices

Department and the Graduate Education Program of the Federal University of São Carlos, São Paulo, Brazil. Her research interests are professional development of teachers, teachers' continuing education, and online mentoring and teacher education.

Jean E. Rhodes is the Frank L. Boyden Professor of Psychology and the Director of the MENTOR/UMass Boston Center for Evidence-Based Mentoring. Rhodes has devoted her career to understanding and advancing the role of intergenerational relationships in the social, educational, and career development of disadvantaged youth. She has published three books (including *Stand by Me: The Risks and Rewards of Mentoring Today's Youth*, Harvard University Press), four edited volumes, and over 100 chapters and peer-reviewed articles on the topics related to positive youth development, the transition to adulthood, and mentoring. Rhodes is a Fellow in the American Psychological Association and the Society for Research and Community Action, and Distinguished Fellow of the William T. Grant Foundation. She serves as Chair of the Research and Policy Council of MENTOR: The National Mentoring Partnership, is a member of the John D. and Catherine T. MacArthur Foundation Research Network on Connected Learning and sits on the advisory boards of many mentoring and policy organisations.

Tony Rousmaniere is a Psychologist in Seattle at the Clinical Faculty at the University of Washington and in private practice. He provides training and supervision in Intensive Short-Term Dynamic Psychotherapy to clinicians in the United States, Europe, and Australia. Dr Rousmaniere's research focus is clinical supervision. He is the co-editor of *Using Technology to Enhance Counseling Training and Supervision: A Practical Handbook* (American Counseling Association Press) and the forthcoming edited volume *The Cycle of Expertise: Using Deliberate Practice in Supervision, Training, and Independent Practice* (Wiley Press). More about Dr Rousmaniere can be found at www.drtonyr.com.

Diane M. Ryan is Director of the Eisenhower Leader Development Program and Acting Deputy Department Head in the Department of Behavioral Sciences and Leadership at the United States Military Academy, West Point, NY. During her 28 year career as an Army officer she has served in multiple operational leadership roles both stateside an abroad. Presently she teaches and conducts research on leadership and leader development. COL Ryan holds a BA in Psychology from the College of the Holy Cross, an MS in International Relations from Troy University, an MSS in Strategic Studies from the US Army War College, and a PhD in Psychology from North Carolina State University.

Akram Sabbagh is a Partner and Senior Coach with AltusQ Australia. With over 30 years of business and coaching experience behind him, Ak works with leaders and teams at the Board, Senior Executive, and Management levels in the Corporate market. In the Emerging Markets sector he works with Partners, Directors and Business owners on their professional, personal and commercial Growth.

Based in Western Australia, he has coached in a wide range of sectors including Government, Banking & Finance, Property, Bio-technology, Engineering and Construction, Advertising, IT, and Manufacturing.

Together with fellow AltusQ Partner Vanessa Fudge, Ak has developed QMentor – a Corporate Mentoring 'white label' program which is being used within a number of corporations and industry bodies across Australia and internationally.

Chandana Sanyal is Senior Lecturer in Human Resource Management and Development at Middlesex University Business School. She has over 17 years of experience of working as a human resource development practitioner. She made a transition from practice to academia after completing an MA in Human Resource Management at Middlesex University in 2009. Her areas of specialisation include individual, team and organisational learning, professional practice, organisational behaviour, coaching, mentoring and action learning. Chandana has led and collaborated on a number of mentoring programmes including the International Professional Mentoring Programme within the Business School. She is one of the Research Consultants, working with Youth Business International to evaluate their global entrepreneurial mentoring programme and has published widely in the areas of mentoring and professional development. She is a Fellow of the Higher Education Academy and Chartered Institute of Personnel and Development and a member of the European Mentoring and Coaching Council.

Sarah E. O. Schwartz is an Assistant Professor of Psychology at Suffolk University in Boston. She holds a doctorate in Clinical Psychology from the University of Massachusetts Boston and a Master degree in Education from the Harvard Graduate School of Education. Her research focuses on positive youth development, with a particular interest in relational interventions and youth mentoring.

Faith Sears is studying English and Political Science at the University of New Mexico and works in early childhood development and education. She co-founded a city wide youth poetry team in her hometown and has had her research published in the International Journal of Genetic Engineering. Faith has worked in the mentoring field as a research assistant for the Mentoring Institute and the International Mentoring Association. She will work with Teach for America in 2017, where she hopes to continue her work in mentoring.

Regina Maria Simões Puccinelli Tancredi is a graduate in Mathematics (São Paulo State University) and a Doctor in Education from the Federal University of São Carlos, Brazil. She teaches in the Graduate Education Program of the Federal University of São Carlos, São Paulo and the Education, Art, and Cultural History of Presbyterian Mackenzie University, São Paulo, SP – Brazil. Her research activities are teachers' and other educational agents' development, teaching and learning processes, and educational public policy.

Aimee LaPointe Terosky is Assistant Professor of Educational Leadership at Saint Joseph's University in Philadelphia, PA. Her research focuses on higher education and K-12 settings with a concentration on teaching, learning, career management, faculty development, instructional leadership, and educational or professional experiences of girls/women. Aimee received her BS in Secondary Education (social studies) from The Pennsylvania State University, her MA in School Leadership from Villanova University, and her EdD in Higher and Postsecondary Education from Teachers College, Columbia University. Prior to joining Saint Joseph's University, Aimee was the assistant principal of Public School #334 in New York City and an adjunct professor in the Higher and Postsecondary Education program at Teachers College, Columbia University.

Fuhui Tong is Associate Professor in the Department of Educational Psychology at Texas A&M University (TAMU). She is also the Associate Director of the Center for Research and Development in Dual Language and Literacy Acquisition (CRDLLA). Her primary expertise is bilingual/ESL education, second-language acquisition, longitudinal-data analyses, and program evaluation. She has authored/co-authored more than 30 peer-reviewed journal publications, more than 15 book chapters, more than 20 technical reports, and numerous refereed and invited presentations disseminating research findings related to high-need students' school performance. Dr Tong was the recipient of the 2015 AERA Bilingual Research SIG Early Career Award. She has extensive experiences mentoring undergraduate and graduate students. She has served as a faculty advisor/mentor for the undergraduate research scholar program at TAMU, and for the undergraduate students' research initiative in the College of Education and Human Development for three consecutive years. The majority of these students are underrepresented, including ethnic minorities and the economically disadvantaged.

Mariano Ulanovsky is a certified coach (*Esc. Arg. de PNL y Coaching*). He is a lawyer, graduated with honors at the University of Buenos Aires. He has several post graduate diplomas on HR. In 2011 Mariano founded SKEYLLS in order to contribute to the mutual growth of organisations and people through the development of key skills. Mariano has more than 8 years of experience as a partner in Levin Global; led the start-up of the office in Monterrey and performed as Mexico country manager and global director for HR. He also has 10 years of experience as Education Director and COO at Junior Achievement Argentina. He has lived in Buenos Aires, Monterrey, Mexico City and New York City, and is fluent in Spanish, English, Portuguese and Italian.

Ann Unterreiner is a Learning Specialist at Arizona State University, Office of Student Athlete Development in addition to being an Independent Research Scholar academic. Her research addresses issues of equity, professional identity in career transition and mentorship of women faculty in institutions of higher education. Publications and chapters she authored can be found in *Globalisation, Education and Social Justice* (volume 10) and journals such as *NASPA Journal About Women in Higher Education, Education and Society and Mentoring & Tutoring: Partnership in Learning*.

Åse Velure is an independent senior consultant who was at AFF at NHH Norwegian School of Economics from 2005 to 2015 and is now on a networking agreement with AFF. She holds a degree in business administration from the NHH Norwegian School of Economics and a Master's in organisational psychology. Åse has been working as a consultant within organisational and leadership development since 2001. Her main areas are within management-team development, executive coaching and supporting management in organisational processes. She was AFF lead in the Statoil Mentoring programme from 2006 until its close, and she has been running similar in-house programmes for other customers.

Rebecca Viney has been a General Practitioner (GP) and a medical educationalist for 24 years. In addition, she appraises GPs for revalidation. Her educational work has focused on retaining, supporting and developing the medical workforce, both nationally and London-wide. In 2008, she designed and launched the first London-wide mentoring service for doctors and dentists in transition. It won a major national award for the best learning and development strategy. Under her leadership from 2008 to 2014 the service flourished. Over 2,000 doctors and dentists applied to be mentored and over

600 doctors and dentists were substantively trained as coaches and mentors. Rebecca was educated in the UK, USA and Belgium. She studied fine-art painting for six years before medicine.

Ke Wu is Associate Professor in the Department of Mathematical Science at the University of Montana. Her research interests include statistical modeling in education, STEM learning, and multicultural curriculum. Her publications appear in a variety of journals such as *Journal for Research in Mathematics Education* and *Mentoring & Tutoring: Partnership in Learning*.

Brad Wuetherick is the Executive Director, Learning and Teaching in the Office of the Provost and Vice-President Academic and Centre for Learning and Teaching at Dalhousie University in Halifax, Canada. Brad is also an Associate Member of the Centre for Higher Education Research and Evaluation at Lancaster University in the UK. He also served from 2014–16 as Vice-President (Canada) on the Board of the International Society for the Scholarship of Teaching and Learning. Brad's areas of scholarly focus include undergraduate research, mentorship, academic development, threshold concepts, academic analytics, the scholarship of teaching and learning, and change in higher-education teaching and learning.

Jeffrey Yip is Assistant Professor in Organizational Psychology at Claremont Graduate University. He is also the founding director of the Talent Science Lab – a group focused on organizational and talent management research. Dr Yip's research is in the areas of mentoring, leadership, and career development. His work has been published in academic journals such as the *Academy of Management Annals*, the *Journal of Applied Behavioral Science*, and the *International Journal for Selection and Assessment*. A Fulbright scholar, Jeffrey received his PhD in Organizational Behavior from Boston University and a Masters in Human Development and Psychology from Harvard University.

Jeff Zimmerman, PhD, ABPP is a licensed psychologist. He has been in independent practice for approximately 35 years. For 22 years he was managing partner of an interdisciplinary multi-office group mental-health practice. Throughout his career he has served as a supervisor and mentor. When serving as an organisational consultant he works with systems that are seeking to develop excellence in their employees and consistency in management style and service delivery. He is the 2017 President of the Society for the Advancement of Psychotherapy, Division 29 of The American Psychological Association. He is a past President of the Connecticut Psychological Association. Among other honors, in 2016 Dr Zimmerman was awarded Distinguished Fellowship in the National Academies of Practice (NAP) and the Psychology Academy as a Distinguished Practitioner and Fellow. Dr Zimmerman received his doctorate in Clinical Psychology from the University of Mississippi (1980).

Acknowledgements

We would like to thank the key members of our support team, Associate editors Chandana Sanyal and Kelly Amber, who devoted many hours to keeping this complex project on track. We are also grateful to SAGE editor Matthew Oldfield, for his patience and constant practical guidance.

The Editors

Introduction

David A. Clutterbuck, Frances Kochan,
Laura Gail Lunsford, Nora Dominguez
and Julie Haddock-Millar

The concept we call mentoring has been around for thousands of years. Yet, only in the past 35 years, with the widespread emergence of mentoring programmes (as opposed to ad hoc individual, informal mentoring relationships) has this phenomenon attracted significant attention from researchers, policy-makers, wider professional bodies and employer organisations. In that short period, mentoring has evolved into multiple forms and affected every branch of society from education to sport, from business to the military and from the highly privileged and economically powerful to the desperately underprivileged and disempowered. Mentoring has become an essential vehicle for change in all of these areas, positively affecting the lives of tens of millions of people.

This book attempts to reflect the diversity of perspectives on mentoring from an international lens. Our aim is to help the many stakeholders in mentoring better understand underlying foundations, the definitions, the practice and the evidence for how and why mentoring works, how it can best be encouraged and supported and future possibilities for its development, implementation and study. We present this evidence in two main forms. First, in the form of scholarly analysis of the literature relating to common themes and issues in mentoring. Second, we present case studies that illustrate how mentoring programmes and relationships evolve and function in a wide variety of environments.

A useful way of looking at mentoring is to view it through the following lenses:

- *Mentoring philosophy* relates to the mental constructs, values and assumptions that define our expectations of a mentoring relationship. These appear to be shaped by many factors, in particular, by culture and powerful interest groups within cultures. For example, in Kochan and Pascarelli's (2003) review of mentoring programmes funded by state or national governments, aimed mainly at disadvantaged or excluded groups, found that culture appears to have an impact on 'how projects were funded,

their purposes, and the level of control exerted over them by the funding source' (2003: 418).
- *Mentoring context* relates to the sphere of activity in which mentoring takes place. Principal amongst these are education, business and the professions, societal change and sport. In any given context, there are multifaceted dimensions that influence the way in which mentoring is perceived, supported and delivered (Allen et al., 1997; Janssen et al., 2015; Jones and Corner, 2012; Kram and Yip, 2011).
- *Mentoring application or practice* relates to the particular group of people, within a given context, who are designated as the intended beneficiaries of mentoring and the expected outcomes. This may, of course, include both mentors and mentees, as mentors tend to learn from the relationship as well (Ghosh and Reio, 2013).
- *Mentoring dynamics* refers to what happens within the mentoring relationship. Clearly, these dynamics will be influenced by the previous three lenses, but researchers have attempted to extract generic patterns of the evolution of an effective mentoring relationship. Themes relevant to this lens include how mentor and mentee initiate the relationship and build rapport (or fail to do so), the degree of mutual respect, the processes of knowledge sharing and giving advice, the role of the mentor as role model and how mentor and mentee move on from the relationship once it has run its course (Clutterbuck, 1984, 2004; Haddock-Millar et al., 2015; Lunsford, 2016a, 2016b; Missirian, 1982).
- *The mentoring conversation* is about the nature and structure of the learning dialogue. Generally less well researched than the mentoring dynamics, this topic relates to how the mentor helps the mentee with the quality of their thinking through insight-provoking questions and a conversation structure that holds back from problem-solving until mentor and mentee have explored sufficiently just what the problem really is. Several scholars have identified a set of skills for mentors based on the mentors' ability to engage the mentee in reflective learning leading to change (Brockbank and McGill, 2006; Rodenhauser et al., 2000).
- *The mentoring programme* provides the structure within which mentoring relationships can be created and supported. Studies have examined issues of programme design, programme management, measurement of outcomes, selection and matching of participants and the influence of organisational environment or culture and the role of key stakeholders within the programme (Cranwell-Ward et al., 2004; Eby et al., 2008; Klasen and Clutterbuck, 2002; Merrick, 2009).

MENTORING PHILOSOPHY

As noted in a number of the chapters in this book, mentoring traces its origins in Greek mythology, some 4,000 years ago. While modern philosophies of mentoring derive from the dialogues between Odysseus and the Goddess Athena (and subsequently between Athena and Odysseus' son, Telemachus), it is easy to forget that the world in which Homer and his (or her – no-one knows for sure!) characters existed was a very different place from ours. It was one where slavery, horrific violence and bloodlust were the norm. Thus, we need to exercise great care in how we interpret and draw legitimacy for more modern interpretations of mentoring from ancient history.

Athena was a complex character. It is perhaps not surprising that different cultures have chosen to emphasise different characteristics of her role as mentor. In North America, where the formalisation and corporatisation of mentoring appears to have begun in the early 1980s, researchers and practitioners seized upon her role as the protector and champion of Odysseus and his son – hence the use of the term protégé (someone who is protected). Athena had a cloak of invisibility (an *aegis*), which she used to shield Odysseus from his enemies. Thus, the concept of a mentor as a more senior, more powerful person, who uses their influence on behalf of a more junior favourite, is deeply embedded in US literature, research and practice. We see here echoes of Athena's role as Goddess of Martial Arts – heroic, action-oriented and potent.

In Europe, and especially northern Europe, the emphasis has been upon a different aspect and role of Athena – her primary persona as the Goddess of Wisdom. In this role, Athena engages in learning dialogue with Odysseus and Telemachus, causing them to reflect upon and learn from their experiences and develop wisdom of their own. She is both philosopher and sage, raising their self-awareness, increasing the depth of their thinking and helping them to develop qualities, such as humility and mindfulness (hence the term 'mentee').

It is tempting to see these contrasting constructs in terms of the United States' cultural pre-occupation with power and particularly individual power; and in terms of European cultures being more inclined to the worlds of philosophy, psychology and the exploration of the mind, along with having more of a balance between individualism and collectivism in cultural norms. This is, however, conjecture and there are considerable divergences in culture between European countries. It is also easy to talk about 'sponsorship mentoring' and 'developmental mentoring' as clearly defined and distinct constructs, and there is empirical evidence to support this (Clutterbuck, 2007). However, the melting pot of transatlantic exchange of ideas means that these distinctions are rarely completely clear!

Despite our best attempts, in this volume we have not been able to explore extensively mentoring-like constructs that come from cultures other than from the West. However, it would be culturally arrogant to assume that the mentor role is unique to the Graeco-Roman culture and its inheritors in Europe and North America. Many cultures, on all inhabited continents, have philosophical traditions that include the role of a wise companion, who joins a younger person on their journey towards maturity and wisdom of their own. Sage, guru, elder – all have similar elements, including the use of metaphor or narrative, and the posing of questions that provoke reflection and insight.

THE MENTORING CONTEXT

The editors and their collaborative networks have been involved with hundreds of mentoring programmes around the world, as researchers, consultants or both. There has been little exploration of how, or whether, context significantly affects the design or implementation of mentoring programmes or the nature of mentoring relationships. There have been numerous studies, however, in each of the four principal areas of education, business, societal change and sport. Chapter 3 explores a variety of issues relating to mentoring in education and several of our case studies illustrate mentoring in practice within educational settings. Chapter 17, for example, focuses on higher education and Chapter 18 on mentoring teachers. The literature includes numerous case studies from primary to tertiary education (Fletcher and Mullen, 2000). Mentoring in business has been another major area for research within contexts such as professional services (e.g. Wallace, 2001), manufacturing (e.g. Cutler, 2003; Scandura, 1992) and entrepreneurship/small business support (for example, the case study in this volume of the Mowgli project and Chapter 19 on mentoring immigrant entrepreneurs). Mentoring in the context of societal change includes issues ranging from supporting immigrant women in Canada and Denmark (Cruz, 2012; Moller-Jensen, 2012) to movements aimed at young people at risk, such as Big Brothers Big Sisters (Grossman and Tierney, 1998). Chapter 16 examines the literature relating to mentoring for disadvantaged youth. Mentoring in sport is less well-defined as a concept and it tends to focus on developing resilience and focus, rather than specific skills (Pastore, 2003; Weaver and Chelladurai, 1999).

Within the literature and within practice, there is a discussion about the extent to which learning from one of these contexts is transferrable to another and whether these different contexts share common predictors of mentoring efficacy. There is little evidence from which to draw clear conclusions. An indication that there may be significant differences comes from empirical studies and scholarly discussions comparing the worlds of business and sport. Katz (2001) identified two key contextual differences, which suggest caution in the use of sports metaphors in business. Among these differences are:

- Sports competition is about winning or losing, or relative position (i.e. runner-up or also ran); in business, competitors frequently collaborate to achieve goals where their interests overlap.
- Sports people tend to train hard for short periods of exceptional effort; in business, performance is usually judged by consistent, long-term levels of effort and attention. The military and emergency services can be seen as operating in a space between these two contexts.

Context may also include environmental factors, such as the developmental climate in an organisation or in society. It can be predicated that an organisational climate, which is hostile to learning conversations and taking work time for self-development, would be less supportive of mentoring than one where the opposite climate exists. However, a counter-proposition would be that in a hostile developmental climate, people would attach greater value to strong and caring developmental relationships, although these might happen informally rather than formally. Another unanswered question in this poorly explored area is whether hostile developmental climates lead to greater emphasis on transactional mentoring functions and sponsorship, while positive developmental climates give rise to more reflective, more person-centred and socio-emotional behaviours within the mentoring dyad. Failure to take context sufficiently into account undermines the credibility of much academic research in the field of mentoring (Clutterbuck, 2003). The context of being a mentor to a direct report, while informed by the literature on leader-member exchange (Scandura and Schriesheim, 1994), is radically different from mentoring by someone outside the direct reporting line. Similarly, peer mentoring or reverse mentoring introduces different power dynamics than 'standard' hierarchically based mentoring (Lunsford, 2016c, Marcinkus Murphy, 2012).

MENTORING DYNAMICS

There have been several studies exploring the mentoring cycle, and in particular, the concept of phases within the context of the mentoring relationship. The earliest empirical investigation of mentoring dynamics was Kram's seminal qualitative study of a small number of informal sponsorship mentoring dyads (1980, 1983, 1985). Kram (1980) explored what these mentors did, identifying a number of functions, which she divided into two categories – socio-emotional and career-oriented. She also mapped out a typical evolution of a mentoring relationship, with four stages from initiation to redefinition. Clutterbuck (2007) validated a model of mentoring dynamics drawing upon a broader overview of mentoring (Clutterbuck, 1985) in the context of formal, developmental mentoring. This was one of few studies that explored relationship dynamics simultaneously from the perspective of mentors and mentees, investigating expectations, behaviours and outcomes from their own and each other's perspective. It is also one of the few longitudinal studies in mentoring, sampling 80 dyads over a 12-month period, and one of the few to include both qualitative and quantitative analysis. Clutterbuck also proposed a five-stage model of relationship phases for formal, developmental mentoring. While the Kram (1980) and Clutterbuck (1985) models have much overlapping, they differ in ways that might be expected from the contrast between informal, sponsorship mentoring and formal, developmental mentoring. Furthermore, the degree of change in modern society influences the dynamics of the mentoring relationship within the context of the mentoring cycle is an area of opportunity. For example, the rapid evolution of ICT is seen as a process to overcome spatial and temporal divides, however, the degree to which this influences the relationship is unclear. Chapter 8 examines the mentoring cycle from various perspectives, both philosophical and contextual.

Other studies have examined specific aspects of the interactions between mentor and mentee. For example, Aryee et al. (1996) explored the role of mentee ingratiation behaviours on relationship dynamics, using participant samples drawn from mentoring dyads in Hong Kong. Hale (2000) examined the dynamics of matching within mentoring pairs. Turban and Lee (2007) developed hypotheses about the role of personality in the mentoring relationship, suggesting that different personality traits may have greater utility at different points in the evolution of the relationship.

Part of the problem in gaining clarity about mentoring dynamics in the concept is difficult to define. If we assume that mentoring dynamics are recurrent patterns that occur within a particular mentoring context, then any attempt to establish a generic dynamic is likely to fail. Moreover, as Turban and Lee (2007) suggest, the dynamics of the relationship are likely to change as the dyad evolves through the different stages of its life cycle. For example, the early stages of a mentoring relationship, called initiation by Kram (1980) and rapport building by Clutterbuck (2004), may require different behaviours and competences on the part of both mentor and mentee, compared to those when the relationship is in full flow.

It is interesting that one of the main functions of a mentor identified by both Kram (1980) and Clutterbuck (2004), and by other researchers, is that of a role model. Yet the few studies that directly address the dynamic of role modelling in mentoring tend to separate out role modelling and mentoring. They also view role modelling as a passive activity. Clutterbuck (1998) argues that being a role model and using role models are learnable skills.

Another key area of dynamics in the literature relates to mentor and mentee benefits (e.g. Burke et al., 1994; Ragins and Scandura, 1999; Schulz, 1995). Again, these tend to be heavily influenced by context and philosophy as they influence the expectations of the mentoring relationship by the participants. For example, learning by the mentor may depend on whether he or she perceives the purpose of the relationship as passing on their knowledge and experience, or as a mutual, perhaps intergenerational, exchange of perspectives and learning.

THE MENTORING APPLICATION

The purpose of the mentoring relationship or programme has relevance to context. In education, the purpose might relate to the prevention of bullying of schoolchildren through helping young minority 18 year olds transition into, and stay within, higher education, to helping researchers in universities gain academic tenure. In business, the purpose may range from induction of new hires to helping with each of the key transitions in the leadership pipeline (managing self, managing others, managing managers, managing functions and so on). Overlaying each and any of these may be other purposes, such as addressing gender inequalities or achieving a change in corporate culture.

Each purpose or application will imply different demands of the mentoring relationship and process. For example, what would be an appropriate meeting place for an executive mentoring programme may not be suitable for a programme aimed at supporting inner city teenagers at risk.

Different applications may also require different methods of evaluation. For example, it may require a different type of approach to determine success dependent upon how one defines success. If success is the quality of relationships or the number of mentors who advance in their careers as a result of the relationship, the type of data gathered and the approach used to garner it would differ. Approaches may also differ depending on the purposes of the evaluation. It is easy in examining these issues to lose sight, amongst all the data, of where mentoring is intended to focus – on the mentee or protégé initially, and to a lesser extent on the mentor. It can be argued (and the editors' 'passionate belief') that if mentoring does not achieve significant change in the mentee's sense of identity and connectedness with the world around them, it is but a pale shadow of what it could be. When mentoring is aimed at specific groups, which are subject to some form of disadvantage, inequity or difficulty in participating fully in society – for example, by virtue of ethnicity, sexual preference, disability, age or religion – many complexities are introduced that may lead to more transactional, less empowering conversations with a mentor from a more privileged group. Chapter 21 analyses some of the learning about effectiveness in mentoring programmes and relationships aimed at diverse populations.

THE MENTORING CONVERSATION

A useful metaphor for the mentoring conversation is shown in Figure I.1. Effective mentors help the mentee understand their inner world, fostering their ability to become more self-aware of their emotions, strengths, weaknesses, values, aspirations, fears, self-limiting beliefs and so on. They also help them gain a better understanding of the world around them and particularly the systems of which they are a part. Discussions often focus around some aspect of how the mentee is influenced by or influences these people and systems.

The structure of a mentoring conversation is yet another relatively neglected area

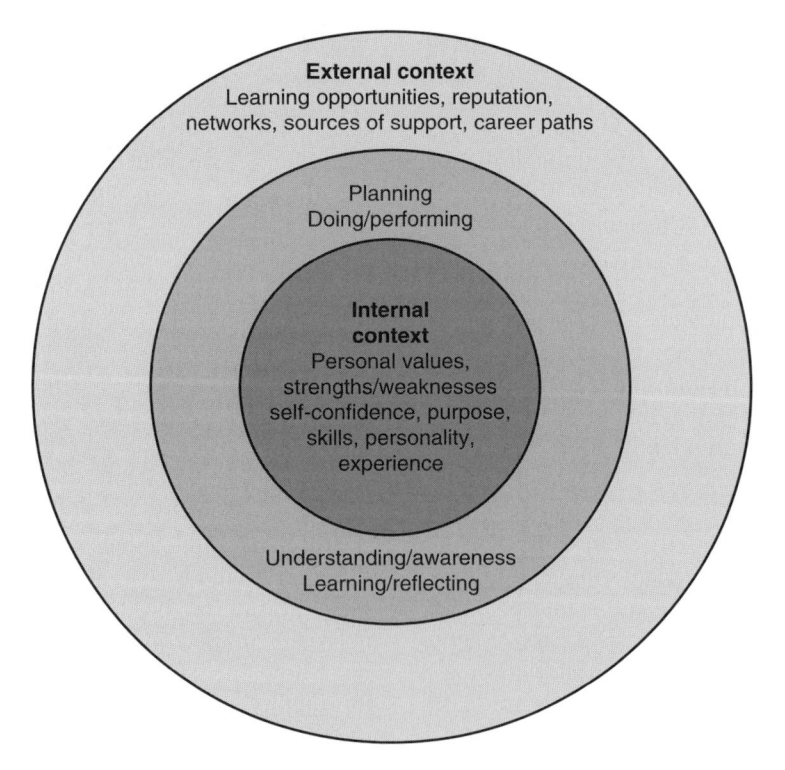

Figure I.1 The developmental conversation

of research. From observations of hundreds of effective and less effective mentoring sessions, Clutterbuck (1985, 2014) identified a repeated pattern in conversations that were seen as purposeful, helpful, insight-provoking and leading to further reflection or action by the mentee. It is important to note that these observations were not carried out under controlled experimental conditions and took place within the meta-context of developmental mentoring programmes in a variety of public, private and not-for-profit sectors. While no significant deviation was observed between sub-contexts, such as level in the organisation, hierarchy gap, programme purpose and so on, no research was carried out to compare and contrast within those contexts. Nonetheless, the consistency of conversation structure was sufficiently high to give it face validity as a generic template for an effective mentoring conversation in the context of employment. In addition, no attempt was made to compare and contrast with conversations within sponsorship mentoring relationships, where the power dynamics might be expected to lead to different conversational dynamics.

Clutterbuck, over a 10-year period, made the following observations in effective mentoring conversations:

- The mentor started by creating an appropriate atmosphere for learning dialogue – for example, paying attention to the surroundings and ensuring that both mentor and mentee were in as relaxed and creative a mind-frame as possible. Ineffective mentors tend to jump straight in.
- Mentor and mentee spent most of the session time clarifying the issue brought by the mentee, until both parties understood it more clearly. Ideas for solutions may arise, but become part of the background information, rather than the main focus of attention. Frequently, this part of the conversation changes perceptions about what the issue is. The mentor holds back on giving advice and/or sharing their own experience, allowing the mentee to access their own knowledge and creative thinking. Ineffective mentors got the 80/20 rule the wrong way round when it came to who spoke most!
- The mentor summarised at an appropriate point, to clarify both parties' understanding and invite the mentee to question whether the summary was accurate. (They will typically have given mini-summaries as the conversation evolved.) Ineffective mentors fail to make the summarising process a joint activity.
- The mentor reinforced the mentee's self-belief and confidence. Ineffective mentors launched straight into solutions, if they had not already done so.
- The mentor helped the mentee identify and evaluate solutions or ways forward that are congruent with their values. The outcome may simply be to take away some questions, which the mentee needs to explore more deeply outside the session. Ineffective mentors tend to nudge the mentee towards solutions that fit the mentor's; or they may feel that they have not done a good job if the mentee does not come away with a clear solution.
- Finally, effective mentors encouraged the mentee to summarise what they had learned and what they intended to do differently as a result. Ineffective mentors summarised again and took the monkey back on their own shoulders.

While the primary responsibility for guiding the mentoring conversation rests with the mentor, the mentee also has a role to play. Successful mentoring relationships are a two-way, dynamic process, and functional, relational skills and capabilities are necessary to sustain an effective relationship (Colley, 2013; Haddock-Millar et al., 2015). If it is to be a genuine learning dialogue, the mentee has to be able to engage with a conversation that is exploratory, self-directing, open to questioning assumptions about oneself and one's environment and sometimes painful. We lack reliable data – or even a hypothetical framework – for exploring how mentoring conversations can be enhanced or limited by the dialogic competence of mentor and mentee.

THE MENTORING PROGRAMME

The mentoring programme provides structure to what would otherwise be an ad hoc, informal arrangement. Among the issues explored in an increasingly extensive, though mainly non-empirical literature, include, inter alia:

- Balancing formality and informality to gain the appropriate level of support, without making the process bureaucratic. This is a significant challenge because informal selection and matching may marginalise people who do not fit the idealised model of a good mentee or mentor
- The role of the programme manager/co-ordinator
- Cross-cultural issues in mentoring
- Aligning individual and organisational outcomes
- Boundaries and overlaps between mentoring and coaching
- Supervision in mentoring
- The amount of support participants need after training
- Measuring the effectiveness of mentoring programmes
- The appropriate duration of a mentoring programme (like relationships, do they naturally run their course?)
- The role of mentoring in culture change

The importance of research and case studies in mentoring programme management lies in its impact on raising the quality and impact of mentoring relationships, both with regard to the participants and to the wider society. The many experts, who contributed to the International Standards for Mentoring Programmes in Employment have contributed significantly to this. Chapter 12 focuses specifically on mentoring programmes and evolving perceptions of good practice, while Chapter 13 explores how to measure the effectiveness of mentoring programmes.

OUR AIM IN THIS BOOK

This book aims to present a comprehensive view of mentoring, capturing all the aspects describes in this introduction. It is a unique blend of research and practice that we believe will be of value to all those who engage in this endeavour and seek to understand it from a researcher's lens.

This book seeks to examine mentoring from all of the perspectives described. It is organised into four major parts. Part I, 'The Landscape of Mentoring', presents research on mentoring and examines it from a variety of foci that align with the 'lenses' described above. There are eight chapters. Part II, 'The Practice of Mentoring', enabled us to understand how mentoring works from a variety of perspectives, drilling down on specific aspects within the practice of mentoring such as the design of effective mentoring programmes, the role of the key stakeholders in supporting mentoring interventions and the effective mentor, mentee and mentoring relationship. The contributors to the chapters often incorporate their own reflections and experiences as practitioners and academics. The 12 chapters in Part III, 'The Context of Mentoring', highlight how mentoring is influenced by the cultural and organisational environment. Part IV, 'Case Studies of Mentoring Around the Globe', shows mentoring in practice through the presentation of case studies.

Each section begins with an overview of the chapters within it. Each section ends with a chapter that seeks to capture the essence of the research in the section by reporting on consistency in findings, lessons learned and reflections on issues requiring further examination and study.

As a team of editors, we have attempted to capture as much of the diversity of philosophy, context, application, dynamics, conversation and programme as possible. Our intention has been to assure that this book has value both for academic scholars and for mentoring practitioners. We have also encouraged the contributors in this book to identify and comment upon potential areas for future research and development of good practice. Although there is always much more to learn, we hope this *Handbook* will provide an important resource to you, our readers, and to the world of practice and scholarship and that it will foster further dialogue and additional research and study on this important topic.

REFERENCES

Allen, T.-D., et al. (2004) 'Career benefits associated with mentoring for proteges: a meta-analysis', *Journal of Applied Psychology*, 89(1): 127.

Aryee, S., Wyatt, T. and Stone, R. (1996) 'Early career outcomes of graduate employees: the effect of mentoring and ingratiation', *Journal of Management Studies*, 33(1): 95–118.

Brockbank, A. and McGill, I. (2006) *Facilitating Reflective Learning Through Mentoring and Coaching*. London: Kogan Page Publishers.

Burke, R.J., McKeen, C.A. and McKenna, C. (1994) 'Benefits of mentoring in organizations: the mentor's perspective', *Journal of Managerial Psychology*, 9(3): 23–32.

Chandler, D.E., Kathy, E.K. and Jeffrey, Y. (2011) 'An ecological systems perspective on mentoring at work: A review and future prospects', *The Academy of Management Annals*, 5(1): 519–70.

Clutterbuck, D. (1984) *Everyone Needs a Mentor*. Hyderabad: Universities Press.

Clutterbuck, D. (1998) *Learning Alliances*. Wimbledon: Chartered Institute of Personnel and Development.

Clutterbuck, D. (2003) 'The problem with research in mentoring', *The Coaching and Mentoring Network* (http://www.coachingnetwork.org.uk/information-portal/articles/ViewArticle.asp?artId=82).

Clutterbuck, D. (2004) *Everyone Needs a Mentor: Fostering Talent in Your Organisation*. London: CIPD Publishing.

Clutterbuck, D. (2007) *A Longitudinal Study of the Effectiveness of Developmental Mentoring*. Thesis submitted to King's College, University of London, London.

Cranwell-Ward, J., Bossons, P. and Gover, S. (2004) *Mentoring: A Henley Review of Best Practice*. London: Palgrave Macmillan.

Cruz, P. (2012) 'Integrated women's mentorship program', in D. Clutterbuck, K.M. Poulse and F. Kochan (eds), *Developing Successful Diversity Mentoring Programmes: An International Casebook*. Maidenhead: McGraw-Hill Education, pp. 96–9.

Cutler, G. (2003) 'Innovation mentoring at Whirlpool', *Research Technology Management*, 46(6): 57–8.

Eby, L.T., Allen, T.D., Evans, S.C., Ng, T. and DuBois, D.L. (2008) 'Does mentoring matter? A multidisciplinary meta-analysis comparing mentored and non-mentored individuals', *Journal of Vocational Behavior*, 72(2): 254–67.

Fletcher, S. and Mullen, C.A. (eds) (2000) *Sage Handbook of Mentoring and Coaching in Education*. Los Angeles: Sage.

Ghosh, R. and Reio, T.G. (2013) 'Career benefits associated with mentoring for mentors: a meta-analysis', *Journal of Vocational Behavior*, 83(1): 106–16.

Grossman, J.B. and Tierney, J.P. (1998) 'Does mentoring work? An impact study of the Big Brothers Big Sisters program', *Evaluation Review* 22(3): 403–26.

Haddock-Millar, J., Rigby, C. and Sanyal, C. (2015) 'Supporting education and career transitions in the financial and accountancy sector', *Business Education and Accreditation,* 10(1): 112.

Hale, R. (2000) 'To match or mis-match? The dynamics of mentoring as a route to personal and organisational learning', *Career Development International*, 5(4/5): 223–34.

Janssen, S., Mark, V. and Menno, DT Jong. (2015) 'Informal mentoring at work: A review and suggestions for future research', *International Journal of Management Reviews*.

Jones, R. and James, C. (2012) 'Seeing the forest and the trees: A complex adaptive systems lens for mentoring', *Human Relations*, 65(3): 391–411.

Katz, N. (2001) 'Sports teams as a model for workplace teams: lessons and liabilities', *Academy of Management Executive*, 15(3): 56–67.

Klasen, N. and Clutterbuck, D. (2002) *Implementing Mentoring Schemes: A Practical Guide to Successful Programmes*. London: Butterworth-Heinemann.

Kochan, F. and Pascarelli, J. T. (2003) 'Culture, context, and issues of change related to mentoring programs and relationships', in F. Kochan and J. Pascarelli (eds), *Global Perspectives on Mentoring: Transforming Contexts, Communities, and Cultures*. Greenwich: Information Age, pp. 417–28.

Kram, K.E. (1980) *Mentoring processes at work: Developmental relationships in managerial careers.* Unpublished doctoral dissertation, Yale University, New Haven.

Kram, K.E. (1983) 'Phases of the mentor relationship', *Academy of Management Journal*, 26(4): 608–25.

Kram, K.E. (1985) *Mentoring at Work: Developmental Relationships in Organizational Life*. Glenview: Scott Foresman.

Lunsford, L.G. (2016a) 'Supporting the beginning, middle, and end', in L.G. Lunsford, *A Handbook for Managing Mentoring Programs: Starting, Supporting, and Sustaining Effective Mentoring*. New York: Routledge, pp. 97–113.

Lunsford, L.G. (2016b) 'Promoting learning conversations', in L.G. Lunsford, *A Handbook for Managing Mentoring Programs: Starting, Supporting, and Sustaining Effective Mentoring*. New York: Routledge, pp. 114–27.

Lunsford, L.G. (2016c) 'Mentors as friends', in M. Hojjat and A. Moyer (eds), *The Psychology of Friendship*. Oxford: Oxford University Press, pp. 141–156.

Marcinkus Murphy, W. (2012) 'Reverse mentoring at work: fostering cross-generational learning and developing millennial leaders', *Human Resource Management*, 51(4): 549–73.

Merrick, L. (2009) 'How to set up a mentoring programme', *Coaching at Work*, 3(4): 52–4.

Missirian, A.K. (1982) The corporate connection: *Why executive women need mentors to reach the top*. NJ: Prentice Hall.

Moller-Jensen, E. (2012) 'Mentoring immigrant women into employment and into society', in D. Clutterbuck, K.M. Poulse and F. Kochan (eds), *Developing Successful Diversity Mentoring Programmes: An International Casebook*. Maidenhead: McGraw-Hill Education, pp. 90–5.

Pastore, D.L. (2003) 'A different lens to view mentoring in sport management', *Journal of Sport Management*, 17(1): 1–12.

Ragins, B.R. and Scandura, T.A. (1999) 'Burden or blessing? Expected costs and benefits of being a mentor', *Journal of Organizational Behavior*, 20(4): 493–509.

Rodenhauser, P., Rudisill, J. R., and Dvorak, R. (2000). Skills for mentors and protégés applicable to psychiatry. *Academic Psychiatry*, 24(1): 14–27.

Scandura, T.A. (1992) 'Mentorship and career mobility: an empirical investigation', *Journal of Organizational Behavior*, 13(2): 169–74.

Scandura, T.A. and Schriesheim, C.A. (1994) 'Leader-member exchange and supervisor career mentoring as complementary constructs in leadership research', *Academy of Management Journal*, 37(6): 1588–602.

Schulz, S.E. (1995) 'The benefits of mentoring', *New Directions for Adult and Continuing Education*, 1995(66): 57–67.

Turban, D.B. and Lee, F.K. (2007) 'The role of personality in mentoring relationships: formation, dynamics, and outcomes', in B.R. Ragins and K.E. Kram (eds), *The Handbook of Mentoring at Work: Theory, Research, and Practice*. Thousand Oaks: Sage, pp. 21–50.

Wallace, J.E. (2001) 'The benefits of mentoring for female lawyers', *Journal of Vocational Behavior*, 58(3): 366–91.

Weaver, M.A. and Chelladurai, P. (1999) 'A mentoring model for management in sport and physical education', *Quest* 51(1): 24–38.

PART I

The Landscape of Mentoring: Past, Present, and Future

Frances Kochan

The first section of Part I of this edition of the *Sage Handbook of Mentoring*, as titled, presents us with the landscape of mentoring. A landscape is defined as something that has or represents distinctive features of something. Indeed, the authors of the chapters in this section present an in-depth overview and analysis of the historical, foundational, structural, cultural, individual, organizational, and societal features of mentoring. Their findings are grounded in a comprehensive overview of the literature which presents a view of the past, an examination of the present status of practice and research, the tensions and conflicts inherent in the field, and the direction mentoring is or should be going in the future.

A landscape is also defined as a portion of a territory that can be viewed at one time from one place. Although each of the chapters in this section presents a singular view of a topic from a unique perspective, there are some major themes that run through them, like a stream flowing across a plain.

The first theme is that mentoring has a long history and, although there is some disagreement about its historical roots, there is agreement that it has theoretical, sociological, cultural, and philosophical aspects that mold and determine the manner in which it is conceived and practiced. The authors remind us that although these underlying foundations are sometimes unrecognized or misunderstood, it is essential that we acknowledge and study them as this enhances our ability to foster strong mentoring endeavors and create changes when they are necessary.

A second theme is that a single definition of mentoring eludes us and perhaps it always will. Further, the authors suggest that since the foundations and values upon which mentoring is built are dependent upon diverse understandings, mores, and beliefs, it is plausible that a single definition may be inappropriate. However, there is broad agreement that mentoring is relational and developmental and that it includes phases and transitions.

It can be formal or informal and, although each relationship is unique, an essential element is having a high level of trust between and among those involved.

There is also a general consensus that a key factor in all mentoring relationships and programs is the degree of control held by the mentor and mentee within the relationship. This factor impacts the extent to which those involved can be open and honest with one another, the degree of trust between them, and the level of transformation and change that will occur. The degree of control is also closely related to the foundational values upon which the relationship is formulated, the purposes of the relationship, and the context within which it operates.

A third theme, which overlaps with the other two themes, is that the practice of mentoring, like its definition, varies, and the models it uses are expanding. These models vary from a didactic teaching/learning model, which is controlled primarily by the mentor, to models that include multiple mentors and multiple experiences, such as mentoring circles, which may occur as continuous processes over time and place and, in some situations, may include the role of mentor and mentee being fluid and changing. Additionally, the authors note that technology is fostering new models and opportunities for mentoring across time and space and that new technologies may usher in models that have not as yet been conceived.

Another recurring theme within these chapters is that mentoring can and does positively impact and benefit individuals, organizations, and societies. However, the authors stress that mentoring relationships can die and fail as well as grow and flourish. This is largely dependent on the quality of the relationships involved, the degree of skill and caring on the part of the mentor, the willingness of the mentee to engage in the process, the openness to change and transformation that exists within those involved, and the context within which they are operating. The authors note that it is essential that mentors, in particular, be aware of unseen and underlying motives and nuances within the relationship and context. They also suggest that those involved be sensitive to the underlying assumptions and purposes of the relationship, continually assess the degree to which the relationship is succeeding in achieving these purposes, identify those elements that are serving to hinder it, and develop processes and strategies that can be implemented to overcome these barriers. The authors also emphasize that it is vital that mentors are skillful in displaying attitudes of caring and that they have the ability to listen and respond with empathy.

Although we may admire a landscape, it changes with the time of day and seasons and other natural events. We often engage in changing these surroundings, too, through varied activities such as planting flowers or trees or building a bridge. Likewise, a final theme presented by the authors of these chapters is that while some areas of mentoring appear to be changing naturally, some need to be tended to and transformed in order to enhance the field of practice and research. They remind us that while it is important to examine, understand, and, at times, honor the past and the present, it is also important to recognize the weaknesses which must be addressed and seek new possibilities to enrich the mentoring process.

One of the primary themes within this need for change is that, although there is a growing body of research and literature on mentoring, much remains to be learned. The authors recommend that the field engage in a deeper exploration of topics seldom studied. These include: conducting more in-depth analyses of the foundational aspects of mentoring; delving more deeply into the benefits of mentoring to the organization; examining and finding solutions and alternatives to the tensions in mentoring; fostering new directions and possibilities for the mentoring process; investigating cultural, contextual, and personal differences between and among those engaged in mentoring; inquiring into the role of technology and its influence on the mentoring process; assessing the role of generational place and values in the process; and establishing a more comprehensive set of best practices for the field. In addition to expanding the topics examined, there appears to be agreement that there must be an increase in the rigor of research on the mentoring topic in general.

The landscape of mentoring appears to have a firm foundation. It includes a rich variety of relationships and programs with expanding possibilities for future growth and development. This section of the *Sage Handbook of Mentoring* gives us a view of the past and present and provides a path for us to forge the future as this landscape changes and expands. I am sure you will find it useful and informative.

Philosophical Origins of Mentoring: The Critical Narrative Analysis

Bob Garvey

INTRODUCTION

Mentoring is, according to many writers (Clutterbuck, 1992; Eby et al., 2007; Garvey, 1994; Lean, 1983; Starr, 2014), as 'old as the hills'. This is probably because Mentor is a character in the Ancient Greek poem, Homer's *'The Odyssey'*. However, many writers over the years (Anderson and Lucasse Shannon, 1988/1995; Brounstein, 2000; Starr, 2014; Tickle, 1993) have drawn on elements in the poem uncritically, perhaps to give credibility to the supposed antecedents of their arguments. The 'old as the hills' discourse is employed to, perhaps, justify mentoring against an illustrious historical lineage or as a counter to the 'it's new and untried' arguments made by mentoring's critics: the 'old as the hills' argument gives mentoring an historical gravitas, but this is perhaps a false interpretation, or at least one that does not accord with today's values.

For example, these authors rarely explore the sometimes negative or the confusing elements in the poem and arguably draw on romanticised notions of the past. Such elements may include, for example, the violence within the original story (Garvey and Megginson, 2004), the failure of the original mentor (Colley, 2002), the cross-gender issues (Harquail and Blake, 1993) or the male dominated stereotypes within the story (Colley, 2002) and the fact that the original mentor was not very good (Colley, 2002)! This is an omission because uncritical interpretations can only offer a false philosophical foundation.

Over the centuries, the influences on mentoring, as a concept and practice, have been multiple and varied. Claims are made that models such as the knight and the squire (Purkiss, 2007) or the medieval craftsman and apprentice (Gay and Stephenson, 1998) are essentially mentoring models. These accounts or claims are rarely submitted to critical scrutiny with idealised versions of the past being promoted as the positive model of learning and development.

Mentoring, it is agreed among some scholars (Lee, 2010; Roberts, 2000), really started to develop as a concept in early eighteenth century Europe based on Fénelon's (1699) work.

Later the term 'mentoring' found its way into US led research in the twentieth century (Levinson et al., 1978; Sheehy, 1974). Since then, there have been many variations all with their underpinning philosophies and associated practices. Mentoring, it is argued, has become a major social phenomenon.

CRITICAL NARRATIVE ANALYSIS

People live their lives through narratives. As Edwards and Usher point out:

> Through narratives, selves and worlds are simultaneously and interactively made. The narrator is positioned in relation to events and other selves, and an identity conferred through this. Positioning oneself and being positioned in certain discourses, telling stories and being 'told' by stories, becomes therefore the basis for personal identity. Narratives are unique to individuals, in the sense that each tells their own story, yet at the same time culturally located and therefore trans-individual – we are told by stories. (Edwards and Usher, 2000: 41)

The author, Salman Rushdie, goes further:

> Those who do not have the power of the story that dominates their lives – power to retell it, rethink it, deconstruct it, joke about it, and change it as times change – truly are powerless because they cannot think new thoughts. (Rushdie, 1991)

Rushdie's call is to unpick the narrative and view it from many positions; to think critically about it to have 'power' over one's own story. In mentoring, there are many stories and many interpretations of these stories. Some of these interpretations have become part of a dominant narrative of mentoring to which many writers subscribe for various reasons. However, there are alternative interpretations and this is the basis of this chapter.

ANCIENT HISTORICAL BACKGROUND

It is clear that there are many potential positive interpretations to draw on in Homer's poem. For example, Lean (1983) highlights the cross-gender element of the poem as a positive aspect; Anderson and Lucasse Shannon (1988/1995) position mentoring as an intentional, nurturing, insightful, supportive and protective process; Tickle (1993) emphasises trust, wisdom, advisor and role model; and Garvey (1994) raises the idea that an individual may have several mentors in challenging and supportive relationships, knowledge is exchanged, time is invested, positive interventions may happen in mentoring and trust is key along with a fostering of independence. Higgins and Kram (2001), whilst not directly drawing on the Ancient narrative, support Garvey's 'several mentors' argument and raise the issue of mentoring as a developmental network of relationships reminiscent of the multiple relationships enjoyed by Telemachus as part of his development. Brounstein (2000) stresses developing independence while Starr (2014) links the story to a relationship of support, help and guidance between an elder to a younger person or 'passing down wisdom'. Smith and Alred (1993: 103) suggest that mentoring is a civilising process and that Mentor is a stand in for Odysseus making Mentor 'personify the kingly quality of wisdom'. Others, Eby et al. (2007) for example, accept the ancient link on the basis that many writers make the same link and, by implication, suggest that this gives credibility.

These are interpretations to which many would adhere. However, these interpretations also create a philosophy of mentoring to suit modern times. This philosophy is about care, support, experiential learning and challenge, wisdom and development. However, whilst these interpretations of the ancient poem are made in the context of today to suit a modern philosophy of learning, they bear little resemblance to the narrative of the ancient time. Then there was a different philosophy.

One based on the subjugation of women in a male dominated and violent society.

There are many elements that support this alternative, contextually based interpretation. These elements include, for example, the violence within the original story (Garvey and Megginson, 2004), the failure of the original mentor (Colley, 2002), the cross-gender issues (Harquail and Blake, 1993) or the male dominated stereotypes within the story (Colley, 2002). To exclude these negative elements is an omission because uncritical interpretations can only offer a false philosophical foundation. As Roberts states:

> [I]t appears that mentoring has (...) essential and contingent attributes (...). This (....) is properly open to falsification. Falsification in this context refers back to the assertion that such essential and contingent attributes will be determined by how the varied authors perceive and experience mentoring: within a phenomenological design, it would be unwise to expect total agreement in claims of mentoring's essential attributes. Different schemas will prompt different descriptions, and such may change over time, although they may not always be inconsistent ones. (...) The essential and contingent attributes (...) may be falsified or modified by a study adopting the same approach at a different point in time. (Roberts, 2000: 163)

So what are the falsifying narratives within Homer's poem?

First, the context of the time in which the original narrative was written needs consideration because what was 'normal' then is probably abnormal now!

Historians find it difficult to position Homer in a time line and estimates of his time are around 252 years apart! However, in general terms, Ancient Greece was a collection of states governed by rich landowners under an oligarchy system. There were many warring factions within these states. Men were often trained in the military but there were exceptions and these exceptions were men who spent their time in politics, farming, in the theatre or partying. It is thought that women had a subjugated role to men and were expected to live their lives in domestic activities and duties. They were not involved in politics or partying, and although often confined to the household, they were, however, priestesses in the temples. Sports and games were also common pastimes but women were not allowed to participate. In this ancient society, individuals had a clear view of their function and 'place' in the hierarchy. An exception was found in the treatment of women in Sparta. There, women were given far more freedom and Spartan women were trained in sports and the martial arts. Some historians believe that this was based on the misogynistic belief that strong women meant strong babies – an exploitative philosophy.

Set in Ithaca, the subtheme of Homer's poem revolves around King Odysseus' son, Telemachus. Odysseus is away fighting the Trojan wars and his son is left in the care of a member of the court, Mentor. The name 'Telemachus' means 'far from the battle' and this places Telemachus as weak and in need of protection. The clear power differential between Mentor and Telemachus is not fully explored in modern interpretations of mentoring but it is raised by Colley (2002) for example. Colley is discussed later.

Whilst Telemachus was born to be King, Homer placed him in a difficult context for which he was not equipped. During the King's absence, a large number of suitors positioned themselves in the court to take over the throne through Queen Penelope and to divest Telemachus (and Odysseus) of his power and wealth. Athene, sent by Zeus to restore order, first appeared to Telemachus, not as a woman but as Mentes, Chief of the Taphians. Later, she took the form of Mentor and then later Telemachus himself.

The guise in which she appeared was a strategic and shrewd choice. First, both Mentes and Mentor were Odysseus' companions and second, they were male and more likely to be accepted by Telemachus than a domestic, servile female. Athene appeared in the form of Telemachus to recruit sailors for a voyage in search of Odysseus. In effect, she substituted herself for him and intervened on his behalf. Here, another modern interpretation is shown to be false (see below Gibb and Megginson, 1993). The modern interpretation of Mentor fostering independence is shown to be a false interpretation because, as shown above in the original story, Mentor does intervene on Telemachus' part. The philosophic model of developing independence and generous altruism are therefore rather flimsy interpretations.

Mentes suggests that Telemachus embarks on a voyage to look for Odysseus. There are many adventures along the way but eventually Odysseus and Telemachus are reunited and join forces in a brutal and bloody act of revenge on the suitors and female members of the court.

It is interesting that few writers visit the aspect of gender or violence. An example of the merciless violence against the women and men alike is as follows:

> Now the thoughtful Telemachos began speaking among them: 'I would not take away the lives of these creatures by any clean death, for they have showered abuse on the head of my mother, and on my own head too, and they have slept with the suitors'. So he spoke, and taking the cable of a dark-prowed ship, fastened it to the tall pillar, and fetched it about the round-house; and like thrushes, who spread their wings, or pigeons, who have flown into a snare set up for them in a thicket, trying to find a resting place, and meeting death where they had only looked for sleep; so their heads were all in line, and each had her neck caught fast in a noose. So that their death would be most pitiful. They struggled with their feet for a little, not for very long. They took Melanthios along the porch and the courtyard. They cut off, with pitiless bronze, his nose and his ears, tore off his private parts and gave them to the dogs to feed on raw, and lopped off his hands and feet, in fury of anger. (Lattimore, 1965: vs 461–75)

Given the context at the time, this cruel violence would probably have been normal. However, it is not what we would consider today as the philosophy of mentoring that emphasises caring support!

Overall, this narrative of a caring nurturing mentor, as is portrayed in many modern texts, is challenged. *The Odyssey* is a model of Ancient Greek male development. It is based on hierarchy, paternalism, macho violence and control.

Colley (2002) argues that, Athene, born from Zeus' head is the 'embodiment of male rationality' (2002: 4). This is a particular type of wisdom that assumes male dominance and aggression. She is not the typical Ancient Greek passive woman but rather she performs key functions of 'advising, role modelling, advocating, raising the young man's self-esteem' (2002: 4) without any kind of emotional attachment. It is also rarely raised in mentoring texts that Athene was needed because Mentor had left the royal household in utter chaos (Colley, 2002). The household was ravaged by rampaging suitors vying for Queen Penelope's attention and hoping to relieve Telemachus of his wealth. Roberts (1998) argues that, far from being the 'counsellor, teacher, nurturer, protector, advisor and role model', as portrayed in much literature on mentoring, Mentor in *The Odyssey* was 'little more than an old friend of King Odysseus (…) quite simply, Homer's Mentor did not mentor' (1998: 19).

Another example of a mistakenly positive interpretation of the poem is in Gibb and Megginson (1993). Here they interpret Athene's actions rather heroically when they state:

> And, even though being a goddess gave her access to formidable power in Homer's world, Athene/Mentor was judicious about how she employed it. In what might have been a glorious denouement for her, when Odysseus and Telemachus confront their usurpers at the close of The Odyssey, Athene did not: (…) 'throw all her powers in, to give him victory, but continued to put the strength and courage of both Odysseus and Telemachus on trial, while she herself withdrew, taking the shape of a swallow and darting aloft to perch on the smoky beam of the hall' (Rieu, 1946: 334). While we would not suggest that modern mentors attempt similar feats, the story clearly places the mentor where we would want her – looking on and encouraging the protégé. (Gibb and Megginson, 1993: 42)

This quote is an example of very laudable qualities being heaped on Athene (Mentor), providing a powerful underpinning philosophy – mentoring enables independence or the Mentor knows best when to leave the Mentee to fend for him or herself. However, in the final bloody battle, Odysseus and Telemachus are hopelessly outnumbered by the heavily armed suitors but Athene comes to the rescue from her 'perch on the smoky beam of the hall'. Homer describes the scene in graphic and precise detail in several subsequent verses in the poem and Athene employs her Godly powers from the rafters to make certain that in two assaults the suitors miss their mark. She did not relinquish control and allow her protégé to do it by himself as Gibb and Megginson (1993) suggest, she engineered the outcome in order to meet her Father's requirements. Athene was playing to another's agenda and whilst it may be argued that it was also Telemachus' agenda, he was not freely engaged in that choice.

Athene's God-given task to maintain Ithaca as a strategic centre for Zeus' purposes is completed through macho, violent prowess. Power, through the male line is re-established in Ithaca. Athene is not a standard woman. Not the kind, trusting, selfless, caring and avuncular figure of Mentor. She is the powerful, artful, cunning and aggressive male. Therefore, modern presentations of Mentor are shown to be a modern creation to suit modern purposes. If we root mentoring in Ancient Greece, the traditionally claimed foundation of mentoring, we have a choice to accept the romanticised and mythical interpretations of today or see it for what it was – a story of male dominance that reflected and reinforced the misogyny of an ancient time.

In this sense, Friedrich Nietzsche's comment in the essay, The Use and Abuse of History (2010), that there is a 'malignant historical fever' (2010: 1), is justified. Nietzsche believed that studying history is a worthless activity because past knowledge should serve both the present and the future – history should not become abstract and devoid of the context that gave it life. This is a central point. This does not mean that we should not look at the antecedents of, for example, mentoring, but the interpretations need to be made against the background of context. The modern interpretations of *The Odyssey* are selective and idealised to suit a purpose, arguably, that mentoring is as 'old as the hills', tried and tested, and therefore, good; Mentor is positioned in the narrative as kindly, caring supportive, developmental and good. A more accurate reading is that he was a bumbling idiot who had to be bailed out by a higher authority for the good of the strategic stronghold of Ithaca.

If the ancient historical narrative is falsified, where else might we find an underpinning narrative philosophy of mentoring?

THE KNIGHT AND SQUIRE

In Purkiss (2007), there is a strong link between evangelical Christianity, knights and squires, mentoring and developing manhood. This is a narrative, which positions mentor quite firmly as a role model who teaches and advises. The premise being that there is a 'vacuum of authentic manhood' (2007: 8) and this is the cause of many social ills. Mentoring is positioned as the agent in a life process with an underpinning philosophy of developing the 'modern knight'. This model of mentoring is based on a romanticised notion of historic chivalry. While this includes quite honourable ideas of respect, both giving it and commanding it, discipline, courage and integrity, the model is heavily laced with medieval metaphors of beautiful maidens waiting for knights in shining armour to 'rescue' them – another romanticised interpretation of history. To continue Nietzsche's argument, this philosophic underpinning does not reflect the context from which it is derived.

In medieval history, the knight was a military officer, often attached to the nobility and therefore was likely to be a rich landowner. The knight would be expected to perform a militaristic exploit in order to earn the title. It was in the late Middle Ages that training to be a knight became common. The trainee or squire would have knighthood bestowed upon him through a religious ceremony and this marks the association between knighthood and Christianity. The knight would then fight, either under his own banner or of another landowner. However, these times should not be romanticised into a modern mentoring model. It was brutal time – a time of feudalism, gross injustice, disease and poverty.

The relationship between knight and squire is of interest. The first step to become a squire was to act as a page for a period of about seven years until reaching the age of about 14 years. A squire was expected to acquire certain skills such as horsemanship, musicianship, agility and strength as well as understand and enact codes of chivalry and court etiquette. The squire was also expected to attend to the needs of a knight such as tend to horses, carry messages, care for weaponry, attend to the knights clothing and help in the kitchen. All this seems reasonable, however, with reference to the knight in Chaucer, Sir John Hawkwood, Jones (2015) argues that, rather than the noble warrior and paragon of Christian virtue, the knight was simply a mercenary, who basically ran protection rackets! Saul states:

> For many, chivalry evokes images of knights in shining armour, menfolk competing for attention of a fair lady, pennons and streamers fluttering from castle battlements. Much of this picture is a product of the nineteenth-century romanticisation of the Middle Ages (…). Its roots lay in an idealised view of the medieval past, which grew up in reaction to the horrors of the grim industrialisation of the time. (Saul, 2011: vii)

Saul's book goes on to explore the horrific treatment of non-combatants in war and the brutality to the losers in battles. In essence, chivalry was a façade and there is no reason to assume that the lower orders of pages and squires were treated well, after all, they were being prepared to participate in the same savagery of battle as their knights.

So again, we find a misogynistic and violent link to mentoring activity smoothed over to suit a particular modern narrative about mentoring. A male dominated narrative of paternalistic care with the agenda being with the mentor or the holder of power. If this historical narrative can also be falsified, where else might we find an underpinning narrative philosophy of mentoring?

THE APPRENTICESHIP MODEL

Gay and Stephenson (1998) associate mentoring with the medieval master craftsman model. This included the concept of 'tied' to a craftsperson for a period of time in order to reach a 'significant level' of 'development' and proficiency in a trade. Whilst they adopt these concepts as part of their model, they suggest that this model may be an element of a developing continuum in mentoring practice.

The origins of the apprenticeship are again found in medieval times. Similar to the page, squire and knight relationship, a young person would be formally bound to a trade's person for a period of time. This would, in theory at least, provide training to develop certain trade skills and ensure a supply of suitably qualified labour.

In England in 1601, the system was extended to force the children of the poor into apprenticeship. Those under 21 years old refusing to be apprenticed were imprisoned. The order could only be overturned by a Justice but in practice, writings from the time suggest that only about 50 per cent of apprentices actually completed the indenture. Some apprentices were ill-treated, some ran away, some became ill or the master became ill and some died. There was an expectation that the parents would pay a fee to the 'master'. It was fairly usual for an apprentice to be paid small sums of money but more common for them to have lodgings. Despite the Guild system, which helped to regulate apprenticeships and ensure fair play, the nature of the relationship was hard to control and in effect, apprenticeships exploited children under the law as a form of cheap labour. Again, this model of mentoring, to which some modern writers link mentoring practice, is also shown to be idealised. In many ways, it is the same male dominated model where power is not with the mentee but with a third party. Learning, in some cases, may have taken place but with a 50 per cent drop-out rate, something was not right with the system. It is therefore curious that modern writers want to make this link to the past uncritically.

If, like the previous links to mentoring the historical narrative can also be falsified, where else might we find an underpinning narrative philosophy of mentoring?

THE FÉNELON NARRATIVE

In his seminal work, 'Les Aventures de Telemaque', Fénelon developed the themes of *The Odyssey* to create what Clarke (1984) considers to be an educational treatise. He argues that the term 'mentoring' started in France and quickly migrated to England so that 'by the early eighteenth century (...) Mentor had entered both French and English as a common noun'.

Roberts argues that the term 'mentor' was not present in the English language until 1750 (2000: 162), which suggests that the previously mentioned historical references are wrongly associated by terminology alone!

Lee (2010) argues that Fénelon is the true source of the word 'Mentor' and 'not Homer'. The word 'mentor' is used extensively in eighteenth century texts, where it is often capitalised, in reference to Fénelon's character, Mentor.

Fénelon is a substantial case history of human development. It provides the basis for the development of a mentoring philosophy that we might recognise in today's world. For example, Fénelon demonstrates that all life's events are potential learning experiences. He shows us through Mentor that the observation of others' behaviour can provide both positive and negative experiences. He suggests that both pre-arranged or chance happenings, if fully explored with the support and guidance of a mentor, provide opportunities for the learner to quickly acquire a high level understanding of 'the ways of the world' – the beginnings of Kram's (1985) 'psychosocial function'.

His objective in writing the work was outlined in his letter to Father Le Tellier (1710), in *Oeuvres de Fenelon*:

> As for 'Telemaque', it is a fabulous narration in the form of an heroic poem like those of Homer and of Virgil, into which I have put the main instructions which are suitable for a young prince whose birth destines him to rule (...). In these adventures I have put all the truths necessary to government, and all the faults that one can find in sovereign power. (Fénelon, 1835: 653–4)

Fénelon believed in the idea of the 'disinterested love of God' (Riley, 1994). In essence, this is love without 'fear of punishment' or the 'hope of reward' (Riley, 1994). He applies this philosophy to the character Mentor who is the 'true hero', and 'the moral educator' in the story (Riley, 1994). This is the beginning of the idea of the selfless, altruistic and generous educator – the educator who gives of their experience without motive.

Fénelon's view of adult development was in many ways revolutionary in the context of the time and was heavily criticised in 'two thick volumes of hostile criticism' (Hubert and Hubert, 1997: 6). Some people of the time interpreted it as a threat to the then Christian belief of the divine right of Kings for example and perhaps even more threatening, 'Telemaque' showed that a monarchy and a republic could coexist with the proviso that monarchs were educated and developed into the role!

Roberts (1998) argues that Fénelon's Mentor is androgynous and therefore has the qualities of both male and female:

> Fénelon's Mentor demonstrates the ability to proffer calm advice, admonish with reason, nurture and guide, empathise, display aggression in the protection of his charge and consideration of ending the mentoring relationship (…). Both stereotypically masculine and stereotypically feminine personality traits seem apparent in Mentor's behaviour towards his charge; after all, Fénelon's Mentor was half-male and half-female. (Roberts, 1998: 19)

The following extracts from the Hawkesworth translation (1741; republished in 1808) are briefly discussed here in order illustrate some mentoring qualities, skills and behaviours. These provide insights into the underpinning of the modern philosophies of mentoring that Fénelon created.

Mentor regularly challenges Telemachus by the use of reflective questions; a well identified counselling technique. 'Are these then', said he, 'Telemachus, such thoughts as become the son of Ulysses?' (1808: 10).

Mentor is also very supportive of Telemachus in that he does not reproach him for error. This is a clear example of a mentor providing the supportive environment for an individual to learn where the fear of failure is removed.

> 'My dear Mentor', said I, (Telemachus) 'why did I reject your advice? What greater evil can befall me than a confidence in my own opinion, at an age which can form no judgement of the future, has gained no experience from the past, and knows not how to employ the present?' (…) Mentor replied with a smile, 'I have no desire to reproach you with the fault you have committed'. (Fénelon, 1808: 12)

Fénelon treats us to a view of one of the benefits of mentoring for a mentee when he shows that Telemachus is clearly very impressed by Mentor's personal qualities and intellect: 'The candour and magnanimity of Mentor gave me great pleasure; but I was transported with wonder and delight at the stratagem by which he delivered us' (1808: 13).

Mentor displays calmness and great assertive powers in the face of adversity: 'But, just at this dreadful crisis, Mentor, with all the calmness of security, demanded audience of the king (…). At this moment there appeared in the eyes of Mentor somewhat that intimidated the fierce, and overawed the proud' (1808: 15–17).

Fénelon, gave the character Mentor charismatic leadership qualities that enabled people to tackle and overcome great difficulties with confidence. Fénelon's Mentor was inspirational: 'I listened attentively to this discourse of Mentor; and, while he spoke, I perceived new courage kindle in my bosom' (1808: 24).

Additional to these exceptional attributes, Mentor also placed Telemachus in learning situations so that the young man could learn by observation. The following extract is an example of Mentor's wisdom in using a reflective discussion to enable Telemachus to draw out the learning points from a previous experience.

> 'Happy are the people', said Mentor, 'who are governed by so wise a king! They flourish in perpetual plenty, and love him by whom that plenty is bestowed. Thus, O Telemachus! ought thy government to secure the happiness of thy people, if the gods shall at length exalt thee to the throne of thy father. The tyrants who are only so licentious to be feared, and teach their subjects humility by oppression, are the scourges of mankind: they are, indeed, objects of terror; but as they are also objects of hatred and detestation, they have more to fear from their subjects than their subjects can have to fear from them'. (Fénelon, 1808: 22)

And here Telemachus sums up his learning:

> Mentor then called my attention to the cheerfulness of plenty, which was diffused over all Egypt; a country which contained twenty-two thousand cities. He admired the policy with which they were governed: the justice which prevented the oppression of the poor by the rich; the education of the youth, which rendered obedience, labour, temperance, and the love of arts, or of literature, habitual; the punctuality in all the solemnities of religion; the public spirit; the desire of honour; the integrity to man, and the reverence to the gods, which were implanted by every parent in every child. He

long contemplated this beautiful order with increasing delight, and frequently repeated his exclamation of praise. 'Happy are the people who are thus wisely governed!' (Fénelon, 1808: 24)

Here, Telemachus is reflecting on his experience with Mentor and is clearly learning about leadership: 'Nor shall I forget, if the gods hereafter place me upon a throne, so dreadful a demonstration that a king is not worthy to command, nor can be happy in the exercise of his power' (1808: 41).

Louis XIV saw 'Telemaque' as 'an attack on his faults' (Riley, 1994). Even more annoying for Louis was the idea that the real hero in the tale was Mentor, the personification of wisdom and not the young prince. Perhaps Fénelon is suggesting that the educator has status? Further, the very suggestion that it would be possible to develop the abilities of kingship rather than be born to them was too challenging for Louis and Fénelon was banished for his efforts. However, 'Telemaque' became a best seller in Fénelon's own life time across France and England (Hubert and Hubert, 1997).

Fénelon's narrative was not something that was rooted in its time; it was ahead of its time. It was a piece of innovative and original thinking which dominated the development of educational thinking in both France and England beyond the eighteenth century. This did not stop the Dadaist writer, Aragon writing a satire of Fénelon in 1922, thus adding another interpretation of mentoring into the mix. An interpretation that placed the development of Telemachus as an element of bourgeois capitalism, where Telemachus is simply an instrument of utility and fit only for capitalist exploitation.

However, the Fénelon narrative provides some insight into the process of mentoring mainly from both the mentor's and the mentee's perspective and helps to provide some of the discourses about mentoring in today's understanding of mentoring. This includes:

- Fostering independence and self-efficacy
- Support and challenge
- Experiential learning
- Developing values and virtue
- Psychosocial development
- Trust and emotional commitment
- Altruism

It is unsurprising then that Telemaque was greatly admired by the educational philosopher Rousseau and finds itself placed as core element in his seminal text on moral and political education, *Emile*. In *Emile*, Telemaque is the only book given to the main character, Emile, as a guide for his developmental journey (Riley, 1994). The French philosopher, Montesquieu (Lee, 2010), attracted by the republican philosophy in the work, was also greatly influenced by Fénelon.

To further highlight the impact of Fénelon, another writer in the eighteenth century, Caraccioli (1760) gives credit to Fénelon: 'The word "mentor" signifies the fame as Governor, and has become famous since the elegant Fénelon made use of it in his Telemachus' (1760: xix).

Caraccioli wrote *Veritable le Mentor ou l'education de la noblesse* in French in 1759 and it was translated into English in 1760 to become *The True Mentor*, or, an *Essay on the Education of Young People in Fashion*. This is a treatise on education and how to mentor. The philosophical underpinnings in Caraccioli are clear: 'True genius is stifled by a cumbrous load of dry rules, and an austere, pedantic and formal manner of education' (1760: vii).

Based on Fénelon, Caraccioli suggests that Mentor is personification of wisdom with a highly developed self-knowledge. A mentor acts from principle and not self-interest, and draws on experience to tackle serious issues and is sought out rather than seeks mentees. Caraccioli's (1760) model of mentoring leads to 'awareness' and this is described as the overall purpose of mentoring. Caraccioli also contributed two further concepts, first, a mentor needs an experienced and successful mentor as a guide. In modern parlance this maybe thought of as 'supervision'. In the second, Caraccioli links mentoring to the phases of life, with which some modern discourses on mentoring concur (see, for example, Allen and Eby, 2007; Alred and Garvey, 2010; Kram, 1983; Levinson et al., 1978). However, Caraccioli, unlike Fénelon, who tends to emphasise the act of mentoring as an educational process, attributes power in the relationship to Mentor.

A further eighteenth century link to Fénelon is found in *The Female Mentor* by Honoria published in three volumes in English in 1793 and 1796. Honoria was the female mentor's daughter and the link to Fénelon is made in the introduction – 'Telemachus was a favourite book in our society' (1793: v). This is an account of, what started as an educational group for young girls and developed into a learned society. Fénelon was the basis of the educational philosophy and is constantly referenced throughout the work. There is even a chapter dedicated to his life. The accounts in the books were 'founded on truth and nature, and intended to promote the cause of religion and virtue' (1793: vi).

There are other models of mentoring presented during the eighteenth century, for example, in 1750, Lord Chesterfield (1838), in a letter to his son describes the developmental process as 'the friendly care and assistance of your mentor'. Lord Byron (1821, 1829, 1843) used the term 'Mentor' in some of his poems where mentor is described as 'tolerant', 'stern' and 'friendly'.

Mentor then, or perhaps mentoring, is a social construction created in eighteenth century literature. It is presented as a principled activity and as one that may facilitate learning and development within a caring, supportive and challenging relationship.

Many of these principles, outlined above, are also found in more modern discourses on mentoring, for example, Appelbaum et al. (1994), Barnett (1995), Garvey et al. (1996), Garvey and Galloway (2002), Johnson et al. (1999), Kellar et al. (1995), Lantos (1999), Nelson and Quick (1985), Pegg (1999) and Tabbron et al. (1997).

Clearly the religious connection to mentoring continues to find its way into modern mentoring narratives, particularly the notion of 'virtue', doing good and altruism but there are other philosophies that may claim part of the mentoring story and these are discussed in the next section.

ASSOCIATIVE MODERN PHILOSOPHIES

A 'love' relationship

Probably the first to mention mentoring in the USA was Levinson et al. (1978) in the seminal work *The Seasons of a Man's Life*. Levinson et al. state:

> The mentor relationship is one of the most complex, and developmentally important, a man can have in early adulthood (…). No word currently in use is adequate to convey the nature of the relationship we have in mind here (…). The term 'mentor' is generally used in a much narrower sense, to mean teacher, adviser or sponsor. As we use the term, it means all these things, and more. (Levinson et al., 1978: 97)

Levinson et al. (1978) suggest that mentoring is a trusting, developmental relationship between two people and it is positioned as essential in enabling people to make life transitions more quickly and with reduced problems.

There is no discussion in the work about the term 'mentor' and its origins but there is some link to the eighteenth century narrative when they state that 'mentoring is best understood as a form of love relationship' and as such 'it is a difficult one to terminate' (Levinson, et al., 1978: 100).

In her research into the 'loving' aspect of mentoring, Bennetts (1995) found that the word 'love' was used in a holistic way; for some, it was used as a part of their spiritual philosophy, but for others, it was a mixture of both. Bennetts (1995) also included in her analysis a strong emotional attraction which led to being 'in love'.

> Some individuals handled that aspect of the relationship by remaining silent and never mentioning it to their mentors or learners, and some individuals made it explicit and the relationship became sexual. (Bennetts, 1995: 11)

However, in every case the relationship was conducted with integrity and was not based on the abuse of power. She also noted that 'it would be too simplistic to think that these were ordinary romances. They were described in the same way for both opposite and same sex partners, regardless of their previous chosen sexuality' (1995: 11). Torrance (1984) supports this finding:

> Those who organise and foster mentor programs should also recognise that the mentor relationship may in time become one of friendship, teacher, competitor, lover or father figure. If the relationship is a deep and caring one (and this seems to be a major characteristic of a genuine mentor relationship), any of these relationships may evolve. However, because of the caring nature, the outcomes are not likely to be harmful. However, this may be a necessary risk. (Torrance, 1984: 5)

In the context of US inter-racial mentoring, Calafell (2007) sees that mentoring is about resistance and this 'consists of loving the unlovable and affirming their humanity. Loving Black people in a society that is so dependent on hating Blackness constitutes a highly rebellious act' (Collins, 2004: 250). The altruistic and rebellious narrative line can be traced to Fénelon's narrative of 'virtue' in mentoring and further, the rebellious nature of Fénelon himself in his original thought. If mentoring is about development, development is a challenging business in which one makes oneself vulnerable. Lawrence-Lightfoot argues that the act of vulnerability 'is an act of trust and respect' (1999: 93).

It is clear that 'love' as a concept may manifest in mentoring relationships. Love is a complex notion and one that can have many meanings. In some cases, it may be a motive for a mentor to participate or a mentee to continue, in others it has the potential to create difficulties (see, for example, Hurley and Fagenson-Eland (1996) or Lobel et al. (1994) for more discussion).

Adult development versus utility

The adult development philosophical narrative is one which stresses the importance of relationships and environments (Garvey and Williamson, 2002). Levinson et al. (1978) argue that mentoring relationships as critical in helping age related transitions. Their model is a mentor who is half-a-generation older and more experienced. Levinson et al. (1978) is often interpreted as a model where the mentor shares experience and develops autonomy, self-awareness, leadership and, notably, accelerates career progression. Arguably, it was the Levinson model that dominated the early to late 1980s in the US with publications such as *Everyone who makes it has a mentor: interviews with FJ Lunding, GL Clements and DS Perkins* (Collins, 1978); *Mentoring in managerial careers* (Clawson, 1980) and in the UK; *How much does career success depend upon a helping hand from above?* (Clutterbuck, 1982). Here, mentoring is positioned as central to an individual's career progression.

These examples perhaps, mark a shift away from the value-based and altruistic model of Fénelon towards a model of utility reminiscent of Aragon's Dadaist perspective raised above. Development here is not for its own sake but for a purpose often independent of the individual and this takes us into the realms of the managerialist narrative of practical utility and goals.

The philosopher Kant would argue that a utility-based view of people is fundamentally immoral and, arguably at least, Kant's view prevails when modern writers consider the utility of mentoring above all else.

An example of this is found in the two decades of mainly functionalist research in the USA that aims to 'prove' mentoring has practical application. Thus, these researchers are joining the managerialist agenda of 'rational pragmatism' (Garvey and Williamson, 2002) where practical application and efficiencies rule the narrative. Gill and Johnson (2010) argue that the managerialist philosophy dominates most capitalist societies. Therefore, it is not surprising that the philosophies of utility, pragmatism and measurement should find their way into the mentoring narrative.

However, as Eby and Allen (2008) point out, the extant scholarship on mentoring shows that there are clearly very different populations of mentoring activity ranging from the youth to young adults in college and workplaces. These contexts will inevitably create their own versions of mentoring and similar to the historical point made earlier, the context in which mentoring happens influences underpinning philosophy, purpose and practice.

Social control

One purpose is social control. This is often dressed up in a different narrative: a Fénelon influenced narrative.

In the UK during the late 1990s, there was a flurry of government sponsored mentoring activity (Colley, 2003) aimed at reducing offending rates among young people and increasing employment opportunities. The fast food chain McDonalds, also contributed financially to these initiatives. However it is presented, commercial interests may have played a part in this seemingly generous act.

This type of social agenda mentoring, a concept borrowed by the British Government from the US with schemes such as Big Brothers and Big Sisters, on the surface at least had a value-based altruistic model of mentoring behind the initiatives. However, neither business nor governments invest money without an expectation of some kind of return. Freedman (1999), commenting on the Big Brothers and Big Sisters youth mentoring scheme, described it as 'fervor without infra-structure'. His argument was that government funded youth mentoring projects had strong political motivations. These projects took advantage of widespread middle class fears of the disruptive potential of young people, particularly, Hispanic and African Americans. Mentoring provided a visible solution to these perceived social problems. Freedman saw this as an 'heroic conception of social policy' (1999: 21), crusade like, and the American middleclass would rescue and save the Black and Latino underclass with mentoring.

It is important here to separate the motives of business and politicians from those volunteers who participated in their thousands across the UK and the US in mentoring programmes. These people no doubt had humanistic motivations to do 'virtuous' things and to enable 'virtue' in others. However, the version of 'virtue' may not always accord with the potential mentees.

Colley (2003) notes that these US schemes and the burgeoning UK schemes focussed primarily on the 'at risk' category of young people. Dondero (1997) justifies the use of mentoring in this context by drawing on the 'old as the hills' association and by emphasising utility. However, what is offered is another romanticised idealistic model of mentoring (reminiscent of those discussed previously who make specific historic links to mentoring) in the statement: 'Mentoring is an old idea that works (...) Adult mentors serve as beacons of hope for young people adrift in an uncertain world' (Dondero, 1997: 881).

Despite this seemingly value driven, altruistic version of mentoring, there is still an agenda behind these models which is with someone other than the mentee. While Grossman and Tierney (1998) in the US and Colley (2003) in the UK show that youth mentoring can make a positive difference to the mentee, if the goals are prescribed by the scheme or funders, there is far less success. Arguable at least, this suggests a flawed philosophy or one that some mentees see through. The real agenda is economic prosperity for a nation but with the responsibility for it being firmly placed on the young person through so called 'empowering' agendas. The standard by which the 'at risk' are judged is generally alien to them and based on a paternalistic view of what is right. Further, this paternalistic view positions the 'at risk' in a narrative that has the potential to replicate itself through mentoring; the mentor is positioned in the hierarchy as the overseer and therefore, potentially at least, an agent of social control imposed, Zeus like, from a 'higher' authority.

Becoming human

An alternative to the social control model is the 'becoming human' philosophy of mentoring. This philosophy is often located within the 'caring professions', for example, nursing. Parse (1998) argues that this philosophy provides a logical framework to underpin a mentoring programme. The philosophy of human becoming is about co-creation. The mentor and the mentee together create meaning and they develop creatively by recognising that there are choices to be made and that there is personal responsibility for that choice. This philosophy does not reduce human relationships to stages, phases, rules and ciphers. Instead, the belief is that people live and work in a series of paradoxical patterns (see, Garvey and Alred [2001] for an account of mentoring and the tolerance of complexity) at the same time as attempting to progress their individual hopes and dreams. It invites people to imagine who they would like to be and to identify the mentors that may help them to develop into that person. Parse states: 'In a human becoming approach persons are considered to be indivisible, unpredictable, and ever-changing. Therefore, mentoring is a process of being with another and coming to know rather than focusing on a preordained outcome' (1998: 319).

A human becoming philosophy could also be challenged as romantic or idealistic. However, it is the managerialist discourse (see below) that is most likely to claim that the human becoming philosophy is romanticised because, as a philosophy it is at odds with the discourse of 'rational pragmatism', utility and functional efficiency. However, to its credit, the human becoming philosophy offers an alternative model of mentoring that reduces the power differentials and offers a more egalitarian model and perhaps one that is more in line with Fénelon's philosophy of learning.

Radical humanism

Many mentoring programmes exist across the developed world within organisational settings, both in the private and public sector. Advocates of a learning and development culture (Barnett et al., 2013; Garvey and Williamson, 2002; Webster-Wright, 2010) argue for greater autonomy, empowerment and increased democracy. They also argue for flatter and less hierarchical organisations. They see this philosophy as central to facilitating learning.

However, as argued above, the managerialist philosophy is a dominant model within developed economies. This discourse sets out to establish what 'good practice' in management is all about. This includes reductionist, cause and effect thinking, taking action on the reductionist argument, creating objectives, valuing individualism and locating measurement as a key driver of activity and performance. It is a 'technical' discourse that creates practices and behaviours that reduce humanity to codes and ciphers.

Porter (1995) argues that numbers are the 'most pervasive forms of power in modern democracies' (1995: 45). He further argues that the managerialist agenda often links objectivity and numbers but this creates an environment where there is a lack of trust, leadership is weak and private negotiation is morally suspect. Amabile (1997) argues that measurement driven management is a form of social coercion as people are excluded and differentiated by measurement.

Another aspect of the managerialist discourse is its preoccupation with change. It argues that the pace of change has accelerated. It creates slogans such as 'change is the only constant' or 'change, change or be changed'. While there has been change in people's lives due to technological advances and political initiatives, this has also brought increased competition. This offers both opportunity and threats and it could be argued that the change discourse is simply a way to manipulate people and scare them into compliance. Here, the change discourse becomes a piece of social engineering aimed at achieving control and giving increased power to the owners of the discourse.

Shearing (2001) argues that the managerialist discourse is a function of globalisation and globalisation has delivered 'neofeudalism' to most developed economies. This is a system reminiscent of medieval times, as described earlier in this chapter. In essence, 'Barons' who control the discourse in modern society have created localised 'fiefdoms', where rules are created and enforced and powerbases established. In this globalised society, power is vested in a few Barons and a new leadership model has developed – the powerful and greedy model of leadership. Lasch (1995) described these new elites in the global economy as having abdicated fundamental social or political responsibility within the societies they inhabit and yet they pass judgement on the rest of us and influence political decision making and economic policy. These Barons call for deregulation and freedom at the same time as imposing greater regulation of those they control (Saul, 1997).

It is no accident, for example, that in the UK we now have a distinction between the 'deserving poor' and the 'undeserving poor' and, I quote the recent former UK Prime Minister, David Cameron, when he talks of 'hardworking families', the subtext being the rest are not! No mention of the few who control what goes on and the ever widening poverty gap! This is all part of a dominating and controlling discourse.

Mentoring (see Carden, 1990) is not immune from this discourse and it too could be viewed as instruments of surveillance aimed at extracting compliance under the discourse of learning, 'risk' reduction, social change or performance improvement. Mentoring, could, therefore, be viewed as part of a traditional managerialist narrative where control and power is vested in the management process (see Beech and Brockbank, 1999). Mentoring, located in this setting becomes, therefore, subject to power dynamics of the managerialist philosophy.

A radical humanist perspective on mentoring in general goes below the surface of these power dynamics because it locates mentoring within a social justice agenda. Rather like the exponents of mentoring within the social settings discussed above, those who engage with mentoring with this background narrative value mentoring for its own sake, see it as an important contribution to humanity. They move beyond utility and commodification – the power house of managerialism. Therefore, there is a tension between the two philosophies.

Within a radical humanist philosophy, mentoring is operated with the concept of co-creation, co-learning, mutuality and celebrates the development of people for its own sake and not for an external purpose. Diversity is valued and challenge is a necessary element akin to the Fénelon philosophy of mentoring.

However, Darwin (2000) points out that within the tradition of utility-based research (of which there is a great deal on mentoring (see Garvey et al., 2014), having a mentor leads to career progression and a higher income. Finding a mentor in the 'everyone who makes it has a mentor' tradition becomes socially desirable and functionally sensible. But, 'making it' is not commonly found in lower socioeconomic groups. Arguably, it is this observation that leads to the development and rapid expansion of social and educational mentor programmes on both sides of the Atlantic. We have yet to see how these may develop.

From a radical humanist perspective, what is clear is that the philosophy of 'meritocracy', so strongly associated with the narrative of managerialism, is perhaps a myth, culturally created within a capitalist narrative which states that 'making it' will come by working hard and getting a mentor. Perhaps it is time to rethink our version of capitalism if we are really to make strides in becoming a humane society (see Hutton, 2011).

Person centeredness

The Rogerian philosophy of person centeredness is also associated with mentoring both historically (before Rogers coined the term) and in recent times. The humanity of this approach is made clear in the following: 'the human organism toward the more complete development of awareness (…) toward increased order and interrelated complexity (…) in the direction of wholeness, integration, and a unified life' (Rogers, 1980: 124–8).

Kass et al. (2014) argue that this philosophic underpinning within mentoring consists of a self-regulated individual who is mindfully aware of self and others by developing a 'critical analysis and intellectual understanding' of humanity. The philosophy is about compassion, empathy and growth and includes the 'capacity for altruistic love', security in existential attachment and resilience. This appears to relate to the quite basically expressed eighteenth century view of mentoring with its purpose being the development of self-efficacy.

CONCLUSION

In modern literature, many writers claim that the origins of mentoring are in Ancient Greece. Whilst Mentor was a character in an Ancient epic poem, the association to mentoring as we know it today is shown to be a false one – there are too many problems with the violent, misogynistic context of the time, the purpose and practice of the mentoring, gender issues and elaborate modern misinterpretations. Further associations with other dyadic relationships from history, for example, Knight and Squire or master and apprentice, are also shown to be false for similar contextual reasons. These examples are part of the 'old as the hills' association that appears to be very common in the literature (Table 2.1).

A more accurate link to the underpinning philosophy of some modern versions of mentoring are traceable to Fénelon. It is here that we have the caring, supportive, challenging educational relationship between two people.

In fairly recent times, this model has been appropriated by politicians and businesses. However, while the rhetoric of the Fénelon model is often present, the agenda is commonly with a third party outside of the relationship. This presents a moral challenge to mentoring.

The philosophies of 'human becoming', 'person centeredness' and 'radical humanism' offer a real alternative to the managerialist narrative, which dominates most capitalist societies. Whether this alternative is actually achievable is open to debate. The lessons of the 2008 global crash do not seem to have been learned and the exploitative, controlling managerialism based on competitive rather than collaborative models seem to persist. Whether this changes or not is a matter of time and political will. There are those within the modern day mentoring movement who work tirelessly to make positive change happen for the individuals they represent. Perhaps this is the best we can hope for – time will tell.

Table 2.1 Underpinning philosophies

Philosophies of mentoring	Description	Authors cited
'Old as the hills'	A link to historical antecedents	Anderson and Lucasse Shannon (1988/1995); Brounstein (2000); Clutterbuck (1992); Eby et al. (2007); Garvey (1994); Gay and Stephenson (1998); Lean (1983); Purkiss (2007); Starr (2014); Tickle (1993)
Human development	Fostering independence and self-efficacy; Support and challenge; Experiential learning; Developing values and virtue; Psychosocial development; Trust and emotional commitment; Altruism	Fénelon, early 18C; Caraccioli, mid 18C; Honoria, late 18C; Allen and Eby (2007); Alred and Garvey (2010); Appelbaum et al. (1994); Barnett (1995); Garvey et al. (1996); Garvey and Galloway (2002); Johnson et al. (1999); Kellar et al. (1995); Kram (1983); Lantos (1999); Levinson (1978); Pegg (1999); Nelson and Quick (1985); Tabbron et al. (1997)
Love relationship	A complex emotional bond	Bennetts (1995); Calafell (2007); Collins (2004); Hurley and Fagenson-Eland (1996); Lawrence-Lightfoot, (1999); Levinson et al. (1978); Lobel et al. (1994); Torrance (1984)
Adult development versus utility managerialism	Human relationships, environments and power	Beech and Brockbank (1999); Clawson (1980); Collins (1978); Clutterbuck (1982); Darwin (2000); Fénelon, early 18C; Garvey and Williamson (2002); Garvey et al. (2014); Gill and Johnson (2010); Hutton (2011); Kant, 19C; Lasch (1995); Levinson, et al. (1978); Saul (1997); Shearing (2001)
Social control	A government lead social agenda aimed at dealing with those 'at risk' – managerialism through society	Colley (2003); Dondero (1997); Freedman (1999); Grossman and Tierney (1998)
Becoming human	Located in caring professions – addressing one's humanity, co-creation, addressing individual hopes and dreams	Garvey and Alred (2001); Parse (1998)
Radical humanism	Social justice, value human beings for their own sake and not as instruments of utility	Barnett et al. (2013); Carden (1990); Garvey and Williamson (2002); Webster-Wright (2010)
Person centeredness	Self-regulated and aware people, altruism, resilience and self-efficacy	Kass et al. (2014); Rogers (1980)

REFERENCES

Allen, T.D. and Eby, L.T. (2007) 'Common bonds: an intergrative view of mentoring relationships', in T.D. Allen and L.T. Eby (eds), *Blackwell Handbook of Mentoring: A Multiple Perspectives Approach*. Oxford: Blackwell, pp. 397–420.

Alred, G. and Garvey, B. (2010) *The Mentoring Pocket Book*, 3rd edn. Alresford: Management Pocket Books.

Amabile, T. (1997) 'Motivating creativity in organizations: on doing what you love and loving what you do', *California Management Review*, 40(1): 39–58.

Anderson, E.M. and Lucasse Shannon, A. (1988/1995) 'Toward a conceptualisation of mentoring', in T. Kerry and A.S. Shelton Mayes (eds), *Issues in Mentoring*. London: Routledge.

Appelbaum, S.H., Ritchie, S. and Shapiro, B. (1994) 'Mentoring revisited: an organizational behaviour construct', *International Journal of Career Management*, 6(3): 3–10.

Barnett, B. (1995) 'Developing reflection and expertise: can mentors make the difference?', *Journal of Educational Administration*, 33(5): 45–59.

Barnett, R., Nygaard, C., Branch, J. and Holtham, C. (eds) (2013) *Learning in Higher*

Education: Contemporary Standpoints. Faringdon: Libri Publishing.

Beech, N. and Brockbank, A. (1999) 'Power/knowledge and psychosocial dynamics in mentoring', *Management Learning*, 30(1): 7–25.

Bennetts, C. (1995) 'Interpersonal aspects of informal mentor/learner relationships: a research perspective', in paper in proceedings at the *European Mentoring Centre* Conference, London, 10 November (www.emccouncil.org).

Brounstein, M. (2000) *Coaching and Mentoring for Dummies*. Newtonville: IDG Books Worldwide, Inc.

Byron, L. (1821) *The Curse of Minerva: A Poem*, 5th edn. Paris: Galignani.

Byron, L. (1829) *Childe Harold's Pilgrimage*. Brussels: Du Jardin-Sailly Brothers.

Byron, L. (ed.) (1843) *Thomas Moore, The Works of Lord Byron in Four Volumes*. Philadelphia: Carey and Hart, Vol. III, p. 187.

Calafell, B.M. (2007) 'Mentoring and love: an open letter', *Cultural Studies Critical Methodologies*, 7(4): 425–41.

Caraccioli, L.A. (1760) *The True Mentor, or, an Essay on the Education of Young People in Fashion. Kings Arms in Paternoster Row*. London: J. Coote.

Carden, A. (1990) 'Mentoring and adult career development', *The Counselling Psychologist*, 18(2): 275–99.

Chesterfield, P.D.S. (1838) *The works of Lord Chesterfield*, First Complete American Edition, including Letters to his Son to which is prefixed an original life of the author. New York: Harper and Brothers, p. 331.

Clarke, P.P. (1984) 'The metamorphoses of mentor: Fenelon to Balzac', *The Romanic Review*, IV: 199–211.

Clawson, J.G. (1980) 'Mentoring in managerial careers', in C.B. Derr (ed.), *Work, Family and Career*. New York: Praeger, pp. 144–65.

Clutterbuck, D. (1982) 'How much does career success depend upon a helping hand from above?', *International Management*, 37: 17–19.

Clutterbuck, D. (1992) *Everyone Needs a Mentor*. London: IPM.

Colley, H. (2002) 'A "Rough Guide" to the history of mentoring from a Marxist feminist perspective', *Journal of Education for Teaching*, 28(3): 247–63.

Colley, H. (2003) *Mentoring for Social Inclusion: A Critical Approach to Nurturing Relationships*. London: RoutledgeFalmer.

Collins, E.G.C. (ed.) (1978) 'Everyone who makes it has a mentor: interviews with F.J. Lunding, G.L. Clements and D.S. Perkins', *Harvard Business Review*, 56(4): 89–101.

Collins, P.H. (2004) *Black Sexual Politics: African Americans, Gender, and the New Racism*. New York: Routledge.

Darwin, A. (2000) 'Critical reflections on mentoring in work settings', *Adult Education Quarterly*, 50(3): 197–211.

Dondero, G.M. (1997) 'Mentors: beacons of hope', *Adolescence*, 32(128): 881–6.

Eby, L.T. and Allen, T.D. (2008) 'Moving towards interdisciplinary dialogue in mentoring scholarship: an introduction to the Special Issue', *Journal of Vocational Behavior*, 72(2): 159–67.

Eby, L., Rhodes, J.E. and Allen, T.A. (2007) 'Definition and evolution of mentoring', in T. Allen and L. Eby (eds), *The Blackwell Handbook of Mentoring*. Malden: Blackwell Publishing, pp. 7–20.

Edwards, R. and Usher, R. (2000) 'Research on work, research at work: postmodern perspectives', in J. Garrick and C. Rhodes (eds), *Research and Knowledge at Work*. London: Routledge, pp. 45–6.

Fénelon, F.S. de la M. (1808/1699) *The Adventures of Telemachus* (2nd edn in English), Vols 1 and 2, trans. J. Hawkesworth. London: Union Printing Office.

Fénelon, F.S. de la M. (1835/1994) 'Oeuvres de Fenelon', Vol. III, in P. Riley, *Fenelon: Telemachus*. Cambridge: Cambridge University Press.

Freedman, M. (1999) *The Kindness of Strangers: adult mentors, urban youth and the new voluntarism*. Cambridge, Cambridge University Press

Garvey, B. (1994) 'Ancient Greece, MBAs, the Health Service and Georg', *Education and Training*, 36(2): 18–26.

Garvey, B. and Alred, G. (2001) 'Mentoring and the tolerance of complexity', *Futures*, 33(6): 519–30.

Garvey, B. and Galloway, K. (2002) 'Mentoring in the Halifax, a small beginning in a large organization', *Career Development International*, 7(5): 271–9.

Garvey, B. and Megginson, D. (2004) 'Odysseus, Telemachus and Mentor: stumbling into, searching for and signposting the road to desire', *The International Journal of Mentoring and Coaching,* 2(1): 16–40.

Garvey, B., Stokes, P. and Megginson, D. (2014) Coaching and Mentoring theory and practice. (2nd Edition) UK: Sage.

Garvey, B. and Williamson, B. (2002) *Beyond Knowledge Management: Dialogue, Creativity and the Corporate Curriculum.* Harlow: Pearson Education.

Garvey, B., Alred, G. and Smith, R. (1996) 'First person mentoring', *Career Development International,* 5(1): 10–14.

Gay, B. and Stephenson, J. (1998) 'The mentoring dilemma: guidance and/or direction?', *Mentoring and Tutoring,* 6(1–2): 43–54.

Gibb, S. and Megginson, D. (1993) 'Inside corporate mentoring schemes: a new agenda of concerns', *Personnel Review,* 22(1): 40–54.

Gill, J. and Johnson, P. (2010) *Research Methods for Managers,* 4th edn. London: Paul Chapman.

Grossman, J. B. and Tierney, J.P. (1998) 'Does Mentoring Work? An Impact Study of the Big Brothers Big Sisters Program', *Public/Private Ventures Evaluation Review,* 22(3): 403–426

Harquail, C.V. and Blake, S.D. (1993) *UnMasc-ing Mentor and Reclaiming Athena: Insights for Mentoring in Heterogeneous Organizations.* Standing Conference on Organizational Symbolism, Collbato, Barcelona, Spain, Paper 8

Higgins, M.C. and Kram, K.E. (2001) 'Reconceptualizing mentoring at work: a developmental network perpective', *Academy of Management Review,* 26(2): 264–88.

Honoria (1793) *The Female Mentor or Select Conversations,* Vols 1 and 2. London: The Strand: T. Cadell.

Honoria (1796) *The Female Mentor or Select Conversations,* Vol. 3. London, The Strand: T. Cadell.

Hubert, R.R. and Hubert, J.D. (1997) (trans) *The Adventures of Telemachus by Louis Aragon.* Boston: Exact Change.

Hurley, A.E. and Fagenson-Eland, E.A. (1996) 'Challenges in cross-gender mentoring relationships: psychological intimacy, myths, rumours, innuendoes and sexual harassment', *Leadership and Organization Development Journal,* 17(3): 42–9.

Hutton, W. (2011) 'Good capitalism does exist. And it's more crucial now than ever', *The Observer,* 2 October 2011 (http://www.theguardian.com/commentisfree/2011/oct/02/will-hutton-ed-miliband-new-capitalism).

Johnson, S.K., Geroy, G.D. and Griego, O.V. (1999) 'The mentoring model theory: dimensions in mentoring protocols', *Career Development International,* 4(7): 384–91.

Jones, T. (2015) *Chaucer's Knight: The Portrait of a Medieval Mercenary.* London: Methuen.

Kass, J.D., Baxter, J. and Lennox, S. (2014) 'Mentoring person-centered spiritual maturation: a quasi-experimental mixed methods study of a contemplative self-inquiry curriculum', *Journal of Humanistic Psychology,* 55(4): 474–503.

Kellar, G.M., Jennings, B.E., Sink, H.L. and Mundy, R.A. (1995) 'Teaching transportation with an interactive method', *Journal of Business Logistics,* 16(1): 251–79.

Kram, K.E. (1983) 'Phases of the mentor relationship', *Academy of Management Journal,* 26(4): 608–25.

Kram, K.E. (1985) *Mentoring at Work: Developmental Relationships in Organizational Life.* Glenview: Scott, Foresman.

Lantos, G. (1999) 'Motivating moral corporate behaviour', *Journal of Consumer Marketing,* 16(3): 222–33.

Lasch, C. (1995) *The Revolt of the Elites and Betrayal of Democracy.* New York: Norton.

Lattimore, R. (1965) *The Odyssey of Homer.* New York: Harper Perennial

Lawrence-Lightfoot, S. (1999) *Respect: An exploration.* Cambridge: Perseus.

Lean, E. (1983) 'Cross-gender mentoring: downright upright and good for productivity', *Training and Development Journal,* 37(5): 61–5.

Lee, A.W. (ed.) (2010) Authority and influence in eighteenth-century British literary mentoring, in *Mentoring in Eighteenth-Century British Literature and Culture.* Farnham: Ashgate Publishing Company, pp. 1–17.

Levinson, D.J., Darrow, C.N., Klein, E.B., Levinson, M.H. and McKee, B. (1978) *The Seasons of a Man's Life.* New York: Knopf.

Lobel, S.A., Quinn, R.E., St Clair, L. and Warfield, A. (1994) 'Love without sex: the impact of psychological intimacy between men and women at work', *Organizational Dynamics,* 23(1): 5–16.

Nelson, D.L. and Quick, J.C. (1985) 'Professional women: are distress and disease inevitable?', *Academy of Management Review,* 10(2): 206–18.

Nietzsche, F. (2010) *The Use and Abuse of History,* (New Edition). London: Createspace.

Parse, R.R. (1998) *The Human Becoming School of Thought: A Perspective for Nurses and Other Health Professionals.* Thousand Oaks: Sage.

Pegg, M. (1999) 'The art of mentoring', *Industrial and Commercial Training,* 31(4): 136–41.

Porter, T.M. (1995) *Trust in Numbers.* Princeton: Princeton University Press.

Purkiss, J. (2007) *Squires to Knights: Mentoring our Teenage Boys.* self-published in USA, Xulonpress.

Rieu, E.V. (1946) (trans) *The Odyssey.* Harmondsworth: Penguin Books.

Riley, P. (1994) *Fenelon: Telemachus.* Cambridge: Cambridge University Press.

Roberts, A. (1998) 'The Androgynous Mentor: bridging gender stereotypes in mentoring', *Mentoring and Tutoring,* 6(1–2): 18–30.

Roberts, A. (2000) 'Mentoring revisited: a phenomenological reading of the literature', *Mentoring and Tutoring,* 8(2): 145–70.

Rogers, C.R. (1980) *A Way of Being,* 3rd edn. Boston: Houghton-Mifflin.

Rushdie, S. (1991) '1,000 days "trapped inside a metaphor"', Columbia University Speech on 12 December: *The New York Times,* 15 December 2015 (https://www.nytimes.com/books/99/04/18/specials/rushdie-address.html).

Saul, J.R. (1997) *The Unconscious Civilization.* Ringwood: Penguin.

Saul, N. (2011) *For Honour and Fame: Chivalry in England 1066–1500.* London: Bodley Head.

Shearing, C. (2001) 'Punishment and the changing face of the governance', *Punishment and Society,* 3(2): 203–20.

Sheehy, G. (1974) *Passages: Predictable Crises of Adult Life.* New York: E.P. Dutton.

Smith, R. and Alred, G. (1993) 'The impersonation of wisdom', in D. MacIntyre, H. Hagger and M. Wilkin (eds), *Mentoring: Perspectives on School Based Teacher Education.* London: Kogan Page, pp. 103–16.

Starr, J. (2014) *The Mentoring Manual: A Step by Step Guide to Becoming a Better Mentor.* Harlow: Pearson Education.

Tabbron, A., Macaulay, S. and Cook, S. (1997) 'Making mentoring work', *Training for Quality,* 5(1): 6–9.

Tickle, L. (1993) 'The wish of Odysseus? New teachers' receptiveness to mentoring', in D. MacIntyre, H. Hagger and M. Wilkin (eds), *Mentoring: Perspectives on School Based Teacher Education.* London: Kogan Page, pp. 190–205.

Torrance, E.P. (1984) *Mentor Relationships; How they Aid Creative Achievement, Endure, Change and Die.* New York: Brearly Ltd.

Webster-Wright, A. (2010) *Authentic Professional Learning: Making a Difference Through Learning at Work.* London: Springer.

Critical Issues on Democracy and Mentoring in Education: A Debate in the Literature[1]

Carol A. Mullen

OVERVIEW: SCOPE OF MENTORING RESEARCH

The purpose of this review of the scholarly literature on mentoring is to spark debate about democratic tensions in research on higher education. Focusing primarily on this tension (instead of trying to exhaust the mentoring literature), I describe some democratic perspectives on critical contemporary issues. The 'Background' section sets the stage with a series of tensions between democratic (e.g. alternative) and nondemocratic (e.g. traditional) mentoring. This analysis of mentoring is anchored in education.

Democracy refers in this writing to the common good and the collective participation of citizens in creating a better world focused on such core values as equality, justice, and freedom. Apple (2014), the critical educator, has made the useful, if not provocative, distinction between a 'thick democracy' and a 'thin democracy', with respect to values and actions, and trends and movements that either strengthen or erode a democracy, respectively (2014: xx, 193). Thus, the full participation by citizens in education is vital for helping to ensure a thick democracy, that is, a strong and healthy public sphere.

Progressivism and traditionalism are contrasting epistemological viewpoints underpinning some of the perspectives articulated herein. While the approach taken is that these philosophies are opposing, my caveat is that they should not be seen as absolutes that are somehow completely dissimilar. For example, democratic and nondemocratic epistemologies alike conceive of human development and learning as essential to the viability of the professions and the workplace.

Democratic and nondemocratic mentoring constitute a prevailing source of tension in the mentoring literature in education (Browne-Ferrigno and Muth, 2004; Schunk and Mullen, 2013). As described in this writing, the theories of informal and formal mentoring are highlighted as part of this mix, along with identical pairing and diverse mentoring, mentoring and coaching, mentoring and induction, face-to-face and e-mentoring, and self-regulated and other-directed mentoring.

This chapter is organized around the review methods used, with emphasis on the existing and known 'tensions' and 'new' tensions upon which readers might focus.

METHODS: LITERATURE REVIEW STRATEGIES

The educational literature searched spanned the period 2000 to 2015, highlighting the present day and thus qualifying as contemporary. Also, the literature reviewed focused on education but also incorporated business in relation to empirical studies and case studies pertinent to democratic and nondemocratic models.

Databases were examined to review the literature, yielding full-text articles, academic books, and book chapters. Within these parameters, influential sources in mentoring – scholarly reviews, current articles and book chapters, and handbooks and a book series – were highlighted.

The review of the literature involved searches of databases for full-text journal articles and academic books, specifically ERIC from WorldCat and Education Research Complete from EBSCOhost. Subject terms (key descriptive words) used for extracting and extrapolating democratic and nondemocratic concepts included *education*, *educational leadership*, *educational psychology*, *social sciences*, *higher education*, *management*, *culture*, *teaching*, *minority*, *ethnicity*, *women*, *global*, and *international*.

In the broad area of mentoring, 433,270 library holdings (e.g. articles, books) were identified. In the specific area of mentoring in education, 255,481 holdings were extracted. Honing these results to align with the parameters of published empirical studies and case studies, 80,857 journal articles and 26,208 books were identified. Within the 62 selected works (books and articles), the key words were typed into the 'find' function of a Word program, allowing for greater precision in the analysis.

As stated with respect to the results, weighted attention was given to: (1) published scholarly reviews of the mentoring literature (e.g. Ehrich et al., 2004; Huizing, 2012; Mullen, 2013; O'Neill, 2002; Schunk and Mullen, 2013); (2) articles appearing in the premier international mentoring journal (i.e. *Mentoring and Tutoring: Partnership in Learning*); (3) classic, influential works in mentoring (e.g. Kram, 1983, 1985/1988; Noe, 1988); and (4) compendium books on mentoring from an interdisciplinary perspective in education and business (e.g. Allen and Eby, 2007; Fletcher and Mullen, 2012; Kochan et al., 2014), as well as the current book series Perspectives on Mentoring (International Mentoring Association, n.d.).

BACKGROUND: A SURVEY OF THE TERRAIN

Definition of mentoring

The traditional definition of mentoring refers to a one-way, long-term teaching relationship in a one-to-one situation whereby knowledge and wisdom are imparted by the expert to the mentee. The protégé, typically younger and less experienced, receives career support and psychosocial (e.g. emotional, cognitive) benefits. Mentorship historically involves training youth or adults in skills building and knowledge acquisition, both inside and outside education (Merriam, 1983; Mullen, 2005).

Over time, this definition has gained complexity in meaning and scope – some researchers consider its current status confusing and fragmentary rather than varied and fluid. The term reflects variability in the mentoring literature and new ways of thinking about the mentoring process, with traditional associations losing traction.

Current definitions of mentoring range from a personal relationship to an educational process, an organizational or a cultural context, or a systemic reform strategy that builds the capacity of individuals and groups (Allen and Eby, 2007; Kochan et al., 2014; Mullen, 2005), including virtual and online global communities (Huizing, 2012; Kochan and Pascarelli, 2012). This form of learning can occur on a voluntary basis, connecting people with the values, attitudes, understandings, and skills that infuse the professions and clinical practice (Ehrich et al., 2004; Kram, 1985/1988). Having a ripple effect, mentors not only impart knowledge and wisdom but also commit to a *multiplying investment* in their mentees (Moerer-Urdahl and Creswell, 2004; Mullen, 2013).

Mentoring activity involves nurturing, advising, befriending, and instructing, with mentors serving as advocates, advisors, and promoters (Kram, 1985/1988; Schunk and Mullen, 2013). Mentors who are veteran teachers and school principals, for example, shoulder this intense work; seasoned school practitioners shape how novices learn through initial and ongoing professional development (Browne-Ferrigno and Muth, 2004; Mullen and Hutinger, 2008; Portner, 2002).

Inherited tensions in mentoring

Traditional mentoring theories – technical/functionalist in form – are inheritances of apprenticeship learning and systems thinking (Mullen, 2013). The root of mentor is men, meaning to counsel, and protégé refers to the need for mentors to protect. Apprenticeships in the Middle Ages occurred through the trades and mostly benefitted males. These continue to be a required career step in Germany, for example. Alternative expressions of traditional apprenticeships include cascade mentoring wherein more senior students mentor more junior students such as in a research laboratory setting wherein students who are more advanced and less advanced academically guide their more junior counterparts (Feldon et al., 2015). Another example of the alternative apprenticeship model is the whole-community apprenticeship; such an offering for preservice teachers has been documented in Britain (Cain, 2007).

Mentoring theory has roots in a range of disciplines, primarily social psychology, learning theory, adult theory, organizational development, and systems thinking (Schunk and Mullen, 2013). Professionals in schools, universities, businesses, and other settings enact technical mentoring – a needs-based, short-term solution involving the transfer of know-how to apprentices (Darwin, 2000; Mullen, 2005). Scientific management, technical efficiency, bureaucratic leadership, and skills-based learning – what Crow (2012) describes as a 'functionalist perspective of mentoring' (2012: 232) – pervade the professions. The historical and originating antecedents of mentoring set the stage for activism and change.

Mentoring tensions alive in the literature

With the proliferation of mentoring research in the education field, a series of tensions has become more evident. For the sake of brevity, contrasting viewpoints suggest different epistemologies and ideologies. Progressivism expressed in democratic attitudes and environments interrogates power, hierarchy, authority, rank/status, privilege, and other barriers to social justice in the workplace. The pushback idea is that social, relational, and organizational inequities reinforce patriarchal values and the unfair treatment of females and minorities – structurally and interpersonally limiting their access to the power grid of organizations and networks (Darwin, 2000; Mullen, 2013).

Barrier transcendence can be construed as a critical feminist framing in which consciousness, activism, and agency are valued. Using this concept, Murakami and Núñez (2014) describe the facilitation of hegemonic counter narratives for fostering cultural and organizational change and particular attitudes and behaviors. In the Hispanic-serving institution they describe, ethnic female faculty members report their pursuit of cultural change on multiple levels, their overlapping agendas involve dismantling systemic barriers while pursuing identity development and academic goals.

Feminism in the mentoring literature has grown out of a deep-seated political reaction to authoritarianism that is historically, organizationally, and societally rooted. In Crow's (2012) lexicon, the progressive construct is named *critical constructivism*, which, as he explains, 'blends the understanding of learning as a co-constructed endeavour between mentor and protégé in which both are active participants with a critical activism in which this understanding is used to influence changes in the practice of leadership' (2012: 233). Either way, democratic mentoring upholds the importance of criticality and co-construction of participants' life-worlds so that technocratic orientations to education do not overshadow values and beliefs, as well as motivations and identities (Crow, 2012).

Categorized herein as *nondemocracy*, authoritarianism upholds the authority and importance of the status quo and is devoid of relational caring and humanism (Hansman, 2003), or put another way, is dismissive of the psychosocial (i.e. psychological and social/environmental) function that Kram (1985/1988) identified as critical to the mentoring relationship. Negating a critical view of socialization through the transmission of knowledge and skills, hegemonic Euro-Western epistemologies do not recognize the influence of bias, prejudice, and reductionism in the treatment of complex, let alone perplexing, issues in academia (Lloyd-Jones, 2014; O'Neill, 2002).

The six primary mentoring tensions to be covered follow next: informal and formal mentoring, identical and diverse mentoring, mentoring and coaching, mentoring and induction, face-to-face and e-mentoring, and self-regulated and other-directed mentoring (Table 3.1).

Informal mentoring versus formal mentoring

For decades, informal and formal mentoring have been contrasted by mentoring researchers. Informal mentoring, characterized as traditional mentoring, is considered the classic, familiar case, whereby mentor (e.g. professor) and mentee (e.g. student) encounter each other spontaneously and naturally – in this context, the mentoring is left to chance (Allen and Eby, 2007; Mullen, 2007).

In contrast, formal mentoring occurs in intentional and planned ways (Ehrich et al., 2004; Fletcher and Mullen, 2012; Mullen, 2008; Single, 2008). It has been countered that formal mentoring may not be adequate in leadership mentoring contexts. Accordingly, based on the study of clinical practice, Browne-Ferrigno and Muth (2004) report that principals are not simply being inducted

Table 3.1 Primary mentoring tensions in the scholarly literature

Mentoring tensions	Key associated dimensions
Informal mentoring and formal mentoring	Spontaneous versus planned interactions
Identical mentoring and diverse mentoring	Matched versus mixed demographics and interests
Mentoring and coaching	Transformative versus socialized development
Mentoring and induction	Developmental versus one-way learning
Face-to-face and e-mentoring	In-person versus electronic interaction
Self-regulated mentoring and other-directed mentoring	Self-directed versus extrinsic learning

into the administrative leadership profession through role socialization. The point being argued is that the induction process is in itself insufficient, as is the professional development involved; the call is for transformation, described as 'a new professional self-concept grounded in confidence about leading schools' (Browne-Ferrigno and Muth, 2004: 471).

Leadership mentoring (originally coined *mentoring leadership* by Mullen and Lick, 1999) is postulated to effect change in relationships, organizations, and systems. As Browne-Ferrigno and Muth (2004) explain, regardless of whether the context is formal or informal, peer-based collegiality replaces 'traditional power roles (e.g. teacher-student, superior-subordinate)' and fosters goal setting, problem identification and solving, trust building, and more (2004: 470; also, Schunk and Mullen, 2013). The democratic mentoring implied in the leadership mentoring/mentoring leadership construct educates mentees to question traditional scripts of learning and rewrite them. These scripts are anchored in predefined activities and prescribed ways of thinking about mentoring (e.g. teachers teach authoritatively; learners learn unquestioningly). Huizing (2012) reports that group mentoring is vital to this change process wherein peers rely on each other for social support, as well as academic and political capital, which can take such forms as advocacy and protection within stymied workplaces.

From a broad perspective, democratic theories that critique nondemocratic stances are relevant to the mentoring of education practitioners and, in turn, the mentoring they do. Leadership mentoring can be adapted to this broader framework of mentoring for describing interactions, dynamics, and barriers within educational and societal contexts. Adult learning principles inform these models (Hansman, 2003), as do systems thinking (Lick, 1999) and instrumental thinking (Cain, 2007).

Based on research (Schunk and Mullen, 2013), informal mentoring may offer greater benefits than formal mentoring, although this remains an unresolved issue. Protégés with informal mentors reported that their mentors provided more career and psychosocial functions; they also reported greater satisfaction with their mentors and more compensation.

Reddick and Young (2012) enter the debates in the literature over informal and formal mentoring from a social justice perspective. When it comes to 'developing and supporting scholars of color', they argue, 'diversifying the pipeline of faculty and leaders in K-12 and higher education will not happen by chance' (2012: 413–14). Based on the research Reddick and Young cite, they believe 'it will require a comprehensive effort' (2012: 413), advocating for a concerted mentoring support for graduate students of color before, during, and beyond their programs.

Identical mentoring versus diverse mentoring

Formal programs often match participants based on similarities in demographics (e.g. age, gender), disciplines, and interests (Mullen, 2008). Yet a key question in the mentoring literature is whether same-gender or same-race mentoring makes a difference for mentees. Gender and ethnic minority status are considered by many researchers to potentially influence the effectiveness of mentoring, with females and members of minority groups experiencing fewer benefits (Sedlacek et al., 2007).

Schunk and Mullen (2013) asked whether such effects, if obtained, arise from gender and ethnicity as such or from other differences in dyadic composition (e.g. whether female protégés gain more from female than male mentors). Mentoring research studies do not seem to support disadvantages in mixed race and gender dyads (Allen and Eby, 2003; Johnson, 2016), and some studies have actually found benefits of cross-gender dyads (Noe, 1988; Ragins and Cotton, 1999). Research on minority status shows that mentoring experiences may be different for such members (Lloyd-Jones, 2014; Sedlacek et al., 2007). Although some ethnic minority protégés report a preference for ethnically similar mentors, cross-ethnicity dyads seem to be equally effective (Johnson, 2016).

Concerning ongoing debates about race and gender (the most accentuated demographic variables in the mentoring research), Schunk and Mullen (2013) conclude that the quality of the mentoring interactions is probably more influential than demographic configurations, although the research is inconclusive. They explain that there were no differences reported in the quality of mentors in same-gender versus cross-gender relationships nor between mentors in formal versus informal relationships. Duration of the mentoring relationship was important for reported benefits in formal mentoring relationships but not in informal ones. Given this perceived weakness in formal mentoring, sustainability receives attention in research on formal mentoring programs (e.g. Mullen, 2008).

Mentoring versus coaching

Mentoring is aligned with a critical-constructivist, or democratic, perspective with five areas of emphasis: the construction and negotiation of experience; communities of membership; active, transformative learning; multiple identity formation and integration; and leadership, policy, or other impactful spheres of responsibility (Crow, 2012).

Nonetheless, mentoring is often confused with coaching; these types of learning have even been viewed as interchangeable (Mullen, 2013). Peer coaching, like mentoring, is a nonjudgmental and nonevaluative approach to professional development – some researchers think of peer coaching as a type of mentoring, whereas others see the exact reverse. Perhaps because it is amenable to quick results, skills development, and instrumental learning, peer coaching has become especially popular in school systems (Becker, 2010). This type of professional learning has a managerial quality – traditionally, it focuses on short-term goals and one-way exchange. Observations of performance are combined with practical work and other types of guided intervention, such as lesson development.

Single (2008) describes coaching as a secondary function supporting formal faculty mentoring programs that has allowed for regular, necessary interventions for success. In her study of a formal mentoring program, mentors indicated that they were motivated by the program coordinator's reminders for mentors to meet with their mentees and deliver the expected content and feedback.

Coaching is being formulated as more than just a structured apprenticeship – that is, a reform strategy that socializes newcomers into the profession (Cox et al., 2014; Fletcher and Mullen, 2012). Coaches are typically contracted as practitioner-experts and focus on helping individuals or groups become more fully functioning and effective. Developmental coaching relies on stories to diagnose teachers' issues in a way that is meaningful to education and life. Team coaching, as named by David Clutterbuck, draws upon democratic principles (e.g. open dialogue, collective learning, interrogation of assumptions) within interactive group environments; other types of coaching are behavioral, psychodynamic, person-centered, and solution-focused (Cox et al., 2014).

A new type of mentoring known as 'reverse mentoring' (Murphy, 2012) formalizes the informal reciprocity that has occurred for years whereby older professionals are mentored by their younger counterparts. Although the concept has yet to be tested empirically, it has been initiated with case study research whereby faculty have learned about instructional technology integration from their mentors (college students) (see Murphy, 2012).

In reverse mentoring arrangements, mentors use their knowledge of technology (e.g. how to become part of a global online community), the latest research on a subject, diversity, and other trends to educate professionals who, in turn, offer knowledge of career planning, interpersonal skills development, and organizational issues, such as how to navigate a business or education context. Such an exchange helps prepare the millennial workforce as leaders, and, given the looming retirements of baby boomers, to expedite this process.

Mentoring versus induction

Mentoring and induction, while also treated as interchangeable concepts, is another distinguishing tension. Some researchers (e.g. Wong, 2004) see mentoring (and coaching) as elements of induction theories and programs. Along these lines, site-based, effective induction programs incorporate the mentoring of new teachers in a 'highly organized and comprehensive staff development process' for two to five years (Wong, 2004: 107). Induction, like coaching, involves one-way learning focused on content mastery and the expected outcomes of the coachee's development (Portner, 2002).

It has been argued that mentoring is more theory steeped and developmentally oriented than coaching and induction (Mullen, 2013). Whether traditional or progressive in form, the relationship is longer term and sustained, and the learning is intrinsically focused, with feedback geared toward self-learning. Browne-Ferrigno and Muth (2004) report that mentoring is a developmental theory that promotes growth of the mentee as a whole person or transformation of a community; the growth patterns are not unidirectional or limited to one-way development. Further, mentees and mentors alike are situated as learners and comentors, and sometimes as change agents.

Face-to-face versus e-mentoring

As Huizing's (2012) review of the mentoring literature confirms, 'The world of technology is changing the way that individuals – both inter-culturally and cross-culturally – interact' (2012: 52). Peg Boyle Single conducted pioneering studies in e-mentoring (i.e. virtual, telementoring, online) contexts. Results indicate that e-mentoring supports the development of job-related and interpersonal skills (Single and Single, 2005). While there are benefits and drawbacks to formal and informal mentoring online, in the virtual environment the success of mentoring relies on the commitment and training of mentees (e.g. adult learners) to learn remotely (Kasprisin et al., 2008).

E-mentoring has typically been used as a supplement to face-to-face mentoring. Its numerous advantages include providing more-frequent communication, reducing time for personal meetings, offering a venue for developing a relationship, and exploring issues in a less-threatening manner (Johnson, 2016). But this reality is rapidly changing. Traditional mentoring is being augmented with technology, especially the internet and social media outlets (e.g. Facebook, Twitter). Greater reliance on digital tools in mentoring is likely occurring, but more research is needed to settle the accuracy of this claim.

Historically, informal mentoring advantaged white males, but even white males often did not have the opportunity to experience that initial spark with a potential mentor, whether in education or medicine (Single, 2008). As noted, formal mentoring constraints involve access (i.e. lack thereof) for marginalized groups. Similarly, access for diverse populations may be problematic in the digital era, where, for example, new technologies are not affordable or available.

More females, minorities, and other underrepresented groups are discovering non-traditional, creative ways to be mentored; however, this is not simply a quiet process of creativity, as this discovery tends to necessitate creative political struggle with dominant forces and within contexts of ill-conceived socialization processes and patterns, making social isolation and systemic barriers a seemingly permanent fixture of reality (Lloyd-Jones, 2014; Murakami and Núñez, 2014). Formal mentoring does not always attract these populations in academia, reports Single (2008), because of the 'spontaneous supports' effective informal mentoring facilitates and because formal programs can carry the stigma of being 'remedial', thus 'potentially harmful to [one's] advancement' (2008: 215).

Self-regulated mentoring versus other-directed mentoring

Self-regulated learning is regulated during the mentoring experience where goals are stated and achieved and development is structured and deepened (Sitzmann and Ely, 2011). Mentees are expected to internalize healthy messages as lifelong learners and to pay forward what they are learning. They psychologically and socially develop by using an array of strategies such as goal setting and refinement, self-monitoring of progress, and self-evaluative reflection on feedback. These are supported through the interaction with a mentor and within a larger social system (Schunk and Mullen, 2013).

When mentoring is done well, we might expect that self-regulated learning (referred to as 'self-regulated mentoring' in Mullen [2011a]) would play a prominent role before, during, and after mentor-protégé interactions. A primary goal of mentoring is to help protégés function independently (Allen and Eby, 2007). This developmental outcome of the mentoring relationship or process is in keeping with Kram's (1983) seminal study that identified separation from the mentor as one of four expected mentoring phases (initiation, cultivation, separation, and redefinition).

However, mentoring in which mentees remain dependent on their mentors – such as for motivation to do their work, set or meet goals, maintain positive attitudes, and utilize resources effectively (Mullen, 2011a; Schunk and Mullen, 2013) can be labelled other-directed. These activities, while important *during* mentoring interactions (Johnson, 2016), are likely clutches following mentoring. It is not unusual, however, for mentees to struggle with separation and redefinition. Ideally accepting responsibility for mentoring themselves and taking on the identity of mentor, mentees who have redefined themselves have committed to the process and probably trusted in it. Like the other phases of mentoring, the redefinition phase was 'storied' in Zachary and Fischler's (2014) business context; within its workplace parameters, career goals were met and corporate promotion was achieved by the mentee turned mentor.

DISCUSSION: DEMOCRATIC CONCEPTS AND STUDIES IN MENTORING

Democratic concepts and studies in contemporary mentoring research focus on collaborative mentoring, mentoring circles, multiple-level comentoring, and cultural mentoring, although these models have various names in the literature, such as multiple mentoring. What follows are results from studies illustrating particular concepts. Empirical evidence validating mentoring concepts is included.

Collaborative mentoring

Also known as relationship comentoring, collaborative mentoring is a proactive force that unites individuals or groups in a reciprocal, mutual exchange and dynamic context for learning. This theory is founded upon feminist postmodern values that are aligned with a transcendence of status and power differences and diversity that incorporates women and minorities (Bona et al., 1995). A goal is to mobilize social equality among individuals of various statuses and ability levels, enabling productive synergy and solidarity (Mullen, 2000).

The collaborative mentoring theory has been validated through case studies ranging from schools to universities to partnerships and within educational leadership and teacher education programs (Fletcher and Mullen, 2012; Mullen and Lick, 1999). Researchers have shown collaborative mentoring to be vital to the professional partnership of professors and teachers who are paired within codirectional mentoring (Mullen, 2000). Action research study of classrooms and schools has been mutually conducted, and mentoring duties and processes equally shared.

In Florida, a peer assessment of a school-university team's inquiry into purposeful collaboration, known as the Partnership Support Group (PSG), concluded that the collective experience had mostly proven successful (Mullen and Lick, 1999). Strengths included shared leadership, appreciative understanding, and structured inquiry; areas needing further support and development were conflicting responsibilities, uneven commitment, and variation in skill. Huizing (2012) describes this Florida example among others and notes that the PSG model is the most researched model.

Critical mentoring theorists link issues of identity and voice, and struggle and power to mentoring models. When the mentoring experience is democratic, mentees and mentors alike can receive positive messages about their race, gender, or other identifications; when the experience is alienating, mentees have reported profound anxiety (see Irby, 2014). The stress can be worse for mentees who are persons of color. The expectation that, for example, they will simply absorb the values of the dominant culture and subjugate their own cultural values and beliefs is an issue. Another issue is the exploitation of their unique identity, as in the case of token representation on university committees.

According to an autoethnographic comentoring study (Mackey and Shannon, 2014), female, ethnic, and first-generation scholars must be vigilant about their core identities throughout the mentoring process. They should protect themselves from others' 'self-serving agendas' and 'false identities that go unchallenged' (2014: 341). Examples include suspending one's ethnic identity to fit into higher education and covering up or hiding components of one's identity, and the resultant stress and denial. Mentees are guided to 'consciously examine external constructs of identity assigned to them by others and assess for themselves if these constructs match the core self' (2014: 341). Identity development is a multifaceted, challenging concept and a growing area of mentoring research to which historically underrepresented groups are contributing (Irby, 2014; Reddick and Young, 2012).

Mentoring circles

An influential alternative conception of mentoring is Kram's (1985/1988) relationship constellation, also known as a mentoring mosaic (Tharp and Gallimore, 1995/1988) or mentoring circle (Darwin and Palmer, 2009). Even though the concept of network mentoring was articulated more than 30 years ago, it is more recently impacting educational studies. The mentoring mosaic/circle theory posits that peer interaction is based on shared interests; members tap each other's strengths and qualities and collaborate beyond disciplinary borders.

This network has been empirically assessed. Mentoring circles can be indispensable for compensating for the dissatisfactions of traditional mentoring and facilitating team projects (Darwin and Palmer, 2009; Mullen, 2005). Indeed, if mentoring is defined more as a learning process than an activity performed by an individual, then mentoring mosaics can provide nurturing, advising, befriending, and instructing from subject specialists, counselors, advocates, and so forth. The camaraderie, interdependence, identity formation, and ownership of this model places value on *how* learning is achieved, not just *what* is learned (Schunk and Mullen, 2013).

Because of the process-based nature of work by participants in mentoring circles, Darwin and Palmer's (2009) Australian study of three higher education mentoring circles found that the use of themes for guiding conversation and propelling motivation, such as 'promotion and collaborative research', increases the chances of success for faculty-led mentoring as does storytelling around career paths, frustrations, and barriers, in addition to cross-disciplinary membership (2009: 132).

Group approaches to comentoring guide the structuring of activity settings, enabling organizations to change and practitioners to be professionally prepared (Tharp and Gallimore, 1995/1988). Tharp and Gallimore's mentoring mosaic theory was founded upon John Dewey's notion of activity settings as crucial for students' experiential growth and Lev Vygotsky's social-psychological theories of learning and instruction (see Fletcher and Mullen, 2012).

The mosaic learning innovation has had discernible impact. In a decade-long intervention that ended in 1983 and spanned three US states, 3,000 students, representing many diverse cultures and languages, participated in the Kamehameha Early Education Project (KEEP). This interdisciplinary school literacy program fostered the opportunity for teachers to create and study meaningful contexts that drive instruction. Teacher-student instructional conversation and role modeling assisted at-risk ethnic children (e.g. native Hawaiians) with new learning. The activity setting contained independent stations (e.g. listening-skills center) designed to harness peer learning. Results indicate that cognitive thought and language development dramatically improved as the young apprentices took part in structured learning activities with teachers and peers. The classroom teachers also learned how to better engage students with 'assisted performance' (Mullen, 2013).

The KEEP program inspired other marginalized ethnic groups, including Latino Americans in Los Angeles and Native Americans in Arizona (Tharp and Gallimore, 1995/1988), as well as a school project in Israel (Almog and Hertz-Lazarowitz, 1999). In the Israeli context, a peer learning community program targeted the support of teacher activism using advanced technologies and interdisciplinary curricula. Sociocultural learning occurred in 12 group sessions; participants worked in teams, combated isolation, and transferred cognitive learning and mentoring skills to their schools (Almog and Hertz-Lazarowitz, 1999; Mullen, 2013).

Mentoring needs, abilities, and resources are essential to sociocultural mentoring. These components have been used to identify aspects of mentoring that best nurture mentees at a particular time. For example, mentor pairing with respect to similarities in gender, ethnicity, age, and discipline (Wilson et al., 2002) diminishes when groups have been configured to reflect diversity. Some ethnic minority students may feel that ethnic mentors would be ideal but have nonetheless drawn strength from diverse mentors. Female students generally prefer female mentors, perceiving an opening for personal contact (Wilson et al., 2002). But, they have also benefited from mixed-gender groups led by male mentors. Peer mentoring within mosaics promotes positive synergy, the exchange of ideas and experience, critical self-awareness, knowledge of international work, and enhanced social skills and leadership capacity (Bona et al., 1995).

Proliferating examples of the mosaic mentoring model are an outgrowth of critical democratic frameworks. Dynamic mentoring mosaics have enabled culturally ethnic, female, international, and immigrant students to generate new ways of working within cultures of collaboration. A longitudinal example reported in the educational psychology literature is that of the Writers in Training (WIT), a faculty-led higher education mosaic (Mullen, 2011a; Schunk and Mullen, 2013). Studied for the seven years it existed at the University of South Florida, USA, Carol Mullen initiated this informal mentoring of a diverse group of graduate students (school practitioners and higher education professionals) to undertake the dissertation process as a team unhindered by the norms of coursework and dyadic mentoring practices.

To elaborate, the WIT collaborative sponsored critical thinking, quality writing, and peer mentoring. A learning enterprise that operated outside the formal structure of the university's bureaucracy, it was continually adapted to build strength, confront challenges, and diversify its membership. Data for the study of this collaborative were systematically collected and analyzed through audiotaped conversations with 20 members from the group sessions and with individuals. Members reported having gained confidence in conducting research and with their professional identity development as a scholar practitioner.

Multiple-level comentoring

Multiple-level comentoring theory underscores the importance of facilitating comentoring at various levels of an organization via school-based focus teams, study groups, and leadership (Kochan, 2002; Lick, 1999). The idea is that serious research and inquiry aimed at reform initiate a mentoring process not limited to classrooms or certain groups. Entire social cultural systems must be deliberately reshaped and teacher resistance transformed so that all students can succeed.

Collaborative mentoring facilitates interdependence, commitment, and empowerment, as well as participative leadership and involvement. Principals and teaching staff decide what changes are necessary; they spearhead and monitor them, generating synergistic comentoring that activates change vertically and horizontally (Mullen and Hutinger, 2008). Systems thinking, change management, instrumental methods, and comentoring techniques are all embedded functions. Entire systems are the target of change, meaning that the reforms can be sponsored or initiated by outsiders (e.g. school boards). Ownership of the change process is accentuated by stakeholder buy-in and planned transitions.

Design scripts adapted from change management theorists and coaching experts (e.g. David Clutterbuck, Dale Lick, Hal Portner) guide this mentoring theory. Multiple-level comentoring outcomes have resulted from whole-faculty study group interventions. This site-based model is a type of learning community implemented in many schools across North America and the United Kingdom (Clauset et al., 2008). The teachers study strategies for impacting student achievement. Systems-level study groups rely on teacher participation in multiage, teacher-led, student learning, faculty study, learning, grade-level, and specialist (e.g. reading) teams.

Curricular innovations and assessments, as well as standards-driven test results, guide teacher study groups. The participants identify student needs based on data, address deficiencies in learning, and generate pedagogical solutions (Clauset et al., 2008; Hutinger and Mullen, 2007). Richardson (2007) reports that teacher teams in a secondary school in Michigan identified outcomes for courses, created common assessments, and monitored student progress. Curricular outcomes were calculated by observing the impact of instructional strategies on student learning.

Other researchers who have studied teacher professional development affirm that participation in faculty study groups affords teachers an opportunity to focus on student needs and school improvement goals in a supportive context (Hutinger and Mullen, 2007; Tallerico, 2005). Analysis of student data has, for example, justified the teaching of higher-order thinking skills. Administrators, teachers, and counselors have all upheld principles that guide study groups: students come first, everyone participates, leadership is shared, responsibility is equal, and work is public (Clauset et al., 2008).

An elementary school in Florida undergoing mandated whole-school mentoring change served as a case study. At the completion of the school year, more than

90 percent of teachers (61 in total) involved in the study group felt confident about assisting their colleagues in analyzing student data and improving instruction (Hutinger and Mullen, 2007). Additionally, the majority reported that the group process provided professional development. Although the teachers expressed positive outcomes overall, their initial feedback suggested variance in emotion and receptivity due to the resistance perceived from colleagues and insufficient time to complete tasks. Such cautionary messages qualify the assertion that multiple-level mentoring interventions can be wholly positive.

Cultural mentoring

Mentoring researchers are beginning to formulate the importance of culture and present guidelines for promoting socialization and success in mentorships. Cultural mentoring fosters cross-cultural, transcultural, and transnational relationships in international spaces. In such contexts, more than one country or culture is included in a process or enterprise.

A global democratic perspective is the worldview informing Frances Kochan's research on international perspectives on mentoring (e.g. Kochan and Pascarelli, 2003; Kochan et al., 2014). Such cultural mentoring perpetuates the core values as equality, justice, and freedom, which has the potential to broaden otherwise limited approaches to socialization. When alterative voices from around the world are heard, a ripple effect can occur, changing the narrow-minded parochialism and the regionalism inherent in hegemonic, transmissive learning models.

Personal professional knowledge enables scholars to explore intersections between culture and mentoring and integrating cultural values into mentoring initiatives, 'particularly when those values are not the primary ones held by those in the larger society' (Kochan et al., 2014: 209). Another goal of cultural mentoring is to develop 'culturally appropriate and respectful' programs to benefit groups that are excluded from, or marginalized within, organizations or societies (Kochan et al., 2014: 209). Within this model, participants engage with unfamiliar contexts, build bridges across cultures, and foster sensitivity to diversity.

In a basic sense, culture involves shared patterns of behaviors and interactions, cognitive constructs, and affective understanding for which socialization is the teacher. As Kochan et al. (2014) explain, *culture* originally meant the cultivation of the soul or mind, referring to a unique or authentic identity – the expression of the self – typically a self that is growing and changing while anchored in core values. It is believed that culture – the complex whole for which values, cultures, and traditions are transmitted (Kochan and Pascarelli, 2012; Kochan et al., 2014) – shapes communities and affects many lives.

It has been documented that culture greatly influences the socialization of minorities in the academy wherein the dominant culture favors mainstream groups and their access to the power grid and influence over it (Mackey and Shannon, 2014; Reddick and Young, 2012). Thus, personal identity development is a cultural issue for underrepresented populations, and generational differences also have an effect – people's generations shape how they see the world and their expectations for mentoring relationships (Fletcher and Mullen, 2012). Identities depicted in cultural mentoring are personal and relational, as well as shared and societal. Kochan et al. (2014) describe identity fraught with tension from such obstacles as generationally entrenched teachers or learners. Another barrier in cultural mentoring is the balkanized practice of organizations that block continuity and creativity in the role development of professionals or scholars of color (Reddick and Young, 2012).

In cultural mentoring within virtual contexts involving high school teachers, educators, and professors in an online mentoring program, it was reported that organizational culture cannot exist solely in virtual time to be successful (Kochan et al., 2014). Real-time interaction seems necessary. Personalizing the mentoring interaction using digital or video recording is one way to nurture a bonding experience that may include fellowship.

Cultural mindfulness of one's environment – such as workplace dynamics, external forces, and socializing variables – also influences cultures of mentoring (Kochan et al., 2014). A primary purpose of productive mentorships fosters awareness of environmental conditions. Because obstacles should be confronted for mentoring to develop at the expected levels, cultural competency must be upheld. This benchmark involves understanding and respect for other cultures and the broadening of one's world to reflect culturally different values and beliefs. One such conduit is 'cultural dialogue' within groups steered to comprehend democratic issues, such as 'inequities and disparities' in schooling and society (Mullen et al., 2014: 1145). Mullen et al. (2014) found in their cultural dialogic work with graduate classes of aspiring school leaders that 'No matter the lead questions asked' – such as what are tacit values and beliefs transmitted in particular leaders' communications and interactions? – 'consciousness-raising' is a goal (2014: 1155).

On the topic of cultural mentoring, when mentoring is mandated or forced this can disturb cultural balances. The oxymoronic concept coined 'mandated mentoring' disrupts the volunteerism and essence – what many have coined 'spirit' – of mentoring (Mullen, 2011b). It can fuel the resentment of those required to mentor and members from underrepresented groups obligated to join mentoring arrangements (Kochan et al., 2014; Single, 2008). School cultures struggle with mentoring neophytes for whom acceptance and support can be an issue. The more distant the authority (such as a governing agency), the more amplified the organizational problems and human struggles. Study of top-down forces (e.g. technocratic policies) helps illuminate the dynamics that limit empowerment and creativity in mentoring and uncover new ways forward (Kochan et al., 2014; Mullen, 2011b).

The international scope of mentoring contexts (depicted in, for example, Kochan et al., 2014) reaches beyond the taken-for-granted worldview and the hypothetical. When a national context is presumed in the mentoring research – perhaps particularly noticeable in research coming out of the United States – this is debatably insular and thus restrictive. Mentoring programs and processes have been opened up to the world and Africa, Australia, Canada, Finland, India, Ireland, Korea, Scotland, Sweden, the United Kingdom, and more are all being studied (Fletcher and Mullen, 2012; Kochan et al., 2014; Schunk and Mullen, 2013). The programs reflect a wide array of cultural dynamics and issues, and the studies themselves have such quality controls as reflection, assessment, and longitudinal analysis.

In an alternative worldview that incorporates the lens of cultural mentoring, the globally engaged workplace – or, more broadly, learning environment – is one in which leadership, decision making, and power are shared experiences that can help bridge differences between and among cultures. There is an idealism afoot in the literature.

CONCLUSION

Future research is needed to address the six primary tensions of mentoring in education (e.g. informal mentoring versus formal mentoring), with particular relevance for mentoring theory and practice in different cultural contexts.

The eight recommendations being made in this section could help guide readers with their own research into mentoring theory and practice, as well as with contributions to their disciplines, professions, and workplaces.

First, as mentoring researchers and practitioners, we simply need to know more about these primary tensions in order to better understand their influence on mentoring research and practice: informal and formal mentoring, identical and diverse mentoring, mentoring and coaching, mentoring and induction, face-to-face and e-mentoring, and self-regulated and other-directed mentoring.

Second, alternative conceptualizations are called for to deepen or develop explorations of scholar and educator development, as well as teacher and administrator preparation.

Third, culturally relevant concepts and research show promise, with emerging study of diversity in mentoring, innovations in virtual settings, and perspectives on culture and mentoring in the global age. The vision and goal of reimagining mentoring within transnational and transcultural contexts is potentially powerful. Research in this area is anchored in the assumption that more than one country or culture must be involved in the process, benefits, and outcomes of mentoring for its potential to be realized globally. Research issues and cultural dissonance must be openly shared. New concepts and research in mentoring (e.g. collaborative mentoring) can initially lack balance, overstating positive outcomes.

A fourth recommendation is that much academic mentoring occurs outside of formal and workplace contexts, such as during spontaneous sessions between mentor and mentee where shorter, rapid exchanges may be more the norm than lengthy discussion. Evidence is needed for how mentoring processes may evolve in these and other types of unplanned settings.

Importantly, mentoring research has primarily focused on benefits to individual mentees. However, increasingly attractive alternative mentoring formats include multiple mentors, group mentoring, peer mentoring, and e-mentoring, all of which may help broaden the appeal of mentoring among diverse populations. Thus, a fifth recommendation is for more study of the processes that transpire during peer mentoring. Perceptions of the credibility of peer mentors could enhance understanding of its operation. Related to this research direction, educating about the role, process, quality, and benefits of mentoring is crucial, in part because it can be overlooked, misunderstood, or even mistaken for coaching or another form of learning.

Additionally, mentoring is happening much more electronically, but, to date, there is little empirical research on its effects. Research in this area continues to be scarce, especially where online mentoring models are concerned, thus, it has been thought that judgements of its effectiveness have been premature (see, for example, Fletcher and Mullen, 2012). Although Single and Single (2005) found benefits of e-mentoring, a sixth recommendation is for researchers to discover how mentoring and self-regulation operate in support of mentees' motivation and progress toward goals and identity development.

The future will introduce significant change. According to Huizing (2012), this is expected given the reliance on innovative technologies, including 'online networking resources such as Facebook' and the new models allowing 'group mentoring to occur in a real-time or asynchronous method with little structural development on the part of mentors' (2012: 52). 'Little structural development' is likely problematic, though, for mentees who depend on extrinsic structure and a strong mentoring hand. Hence, insights are needed about the effectiveness of online mentors for sharing their expertise and ensuring that pedagogical learning is mediated and supported as well as understood (Fletcher and Mullen, 2012). An unresolved question is how digital technology use may be changing the very nature of mentoring and its psychosocial and career functions, and thus, expectations for support.

As Schunk and Mullen (2013) have reported, most mentoring research in education and business has tested predictions in traditional settings and directed attention to job-related skills developed face-to-face during the cultivation phase (see Kram, 1983). Little research exists about Kram's (1983) other phases known as separation and redefinition, during which time mentees' learning should enhance their self-directed learning capabilities and build their relational networks. Researchers have yet to explore ongoing dynamic mentor-mentee interactions that happen before, during, and after mentoring, and beyond self-studies. Thus, a seventh recommendation calls for in-depth knowledge of these 'neglected' learning phases and about the role of dialogue in conversations. Learning conversations are a crucial part of mentoring and light needs to be shed on what occurs during these complex exchanges and to what end.

Finally, the sheer amount of mentoring literature on peer-based, collaborative, and cultural mentoring suggests that many researchers not only take the study of mentoring seriously but also that participants have taken mentoring into their own hands. On the one hand, the ownership and empowerment suggested by the proliferating philosophies beyond limited meanings and initiatives of mentoring (such as the self-powering socialization of mentees) has introduced new dimensions in the mentoring equation.

On the other hand, a question worth investigating across disciplines involves the extent to which mentors' workloads affects the guidance they can afford mentees. An eighth recommendation is for close study of the increased workloads of faculty mentors and the effects on informal and formal mentoring. How are the workloads of faculty mentors changing and what tasks are crowding the time needed for mentoring? How can advocacy for quality mentoring be articulated in the mission of professions and institutions and be reflected in faculty mentors' workloads?

The role (and duty) of organizations in protecting quality mentoring is undermined when work duties interfere with the time that mentors can devote to their mentoring relationships and with the expected progress of mentees (Mullen, 2005). As the cautionary empirical tale about primary mentoring relationships in the STEM field of Feldon et al. (2015) underscores, the primary mentoring relationship – and the modelling, coaching, and facilitating it provides for skills and identity development – is essential to the success of mentees in academic and professional settings, even where alternatives, such as multiple mentoring, are successfully pursued as supplemental.

Readers can benefit from the new ways of thinking about mentoring and approach mentoring as important, life-changing work. Academies, schools, businesses, and organizations can support the learning enterprise by becoming more attuned to the intense commitment expert mentors make on the journey with mentees.

Note

1. A key source is Mullen (2013) in the development of this writing and examples cited.

REFERENCES

Allen, T.D., and Eby, L.T. (2003) 'Relationship effectiveness for mentors: Factors associated with learning and quality', *Journal of Management,* 29(4): 469–86.

Allen, T.D. and Eby, L.T. (eds) (2007) *The Blackwell Handbook of Mentoring: A Multiple Perspectives Approach*. Malden: Wiley-Blackwell.

Almog, T. and Hertz-Lazarowitz, R. (1999) 'Teachers as peer learners: professional development in an advanced computer learning environment', in A.M. O'Donnell and A. King (eds), *Cognitive Perspectives on Peer Learning*. Mahwah: Erlbaum, pp. 285–311.

Apple, M.W. (2014) *Official Knowledge: Democratic Education in a Conservative Age*, 3rd edn. New York: Routledge.

Becker, J.M. (2010) *Peer Coaching for Improvement of Teaching and Learning*. Teachers Network (http://teachersnetwork.org/tnli/research/growth/becker.htm).

Bona, M.J., Rinehart, J. and Volbrecht, R.M. (1995) 'Show me how to do like you: co-mentoring as feminist pedagogy', *Feminist Teacher*, 9(3): 116–24.

Browne-Ferrigno, T. and Muth, R. (2004) 'Leadership mentoring in clinical practice: role socialization, professional development, and capacity building', *Educational Administration Quarterly*, 40(4): 468–94.

Cain, T. (2007) 'Mentoring trainee music teachers: beyond apprenticeship or reflection', *British Journal of Music Education*, 24(3): 281–94.

Clauset, K.H., Lick, D.W. and Murphy, C.U. (eds) (2008) *Schoolwide Action Research for Professional Learning Communities: Improving Student Learning Through the Whole-Faculty Study Groups Approach*. Thousand Oaks: Corwin.

Cox, E., Bachkirova, T. and Clutterbuck, D.A. (2014) *The Complete Handbook of Coaching*, 2nd edn. Thousand Oaks: Sage.

Crow, G.M. (2012) 'A critical-constructivist perspective on mentoring and coaching for leadership', in S. Fletcher and C.A. Mullen (eds), *The SAGE Handbook of Mentoring and Coaching in Education*. Thousand Oaks: Sage, pp. 228–42.

Darwin, A. (2000) 'Critical reflections on mentoring in work settings', *Adult Education Quarterly*, 50(3): 197–211.

Darwin, A. and Palmer, E. (2009) 'Mentoring circles in higher education', *Higher Education Research and Development*, 28(2): 125–36.

Ehrich, L.C., Hansford, B. and Tennent, L. (2004) 'Formal mentoring programs in education and other professions: a review of the literature', *Educational Administration Quarterly*, 40(4): 518–40.

Feldon, D.F., Maher, M.A., Hurst, M. and Timmerman, B. (2015) 'Faculty mentors', graduate students', and performance-based assessments of students' research skill development', *American Educational Research Journal*, 52(2): 334–70.

Fletcher, S. and Mullen, C.A. (eds) (2012) *The SAGE Handbook of Mentoring and Coaching in Education*. Thousand Oaks: Sage.

Hansman, C.A. (2003) 'Power and learning in mentoring relationships', in R. Cervero, B. Courtenay and M. Hixson (eds), *Global Perspectives*: Vol. III. Athens: University of Georgia, pp. 102–22.

Huizing, R.L. (2012) 'Mentoring together: a literature review of group mentoring', *Mentoring and Tutoring: Partnership in Learning*, 20(1): 27–55.

Hutinger, J.L. and Mullen, C.A. (2007) 'Supporting teacher leadership: mixed perceptions of mandated faculty study groups', in S. Donahoo and R.C. Hunter (eds), *Teaching Leaders to Lead Teachers: Educational Administration in the Era of Constant Crisis*, Vol. 10. Oxford: Elsevier, pp. 261–83.

International Mentoring Association (IMA) (n.d.) *Perspectives on Mentoring Book Series*. (sponsored by Information Age Publishing) (http://www.infoagepub.com/series/Perspectives-on-Mentoring).

Irby, B.J. (2014) 'Advancing women of color in the academy: research perspectives on mentoring and strategies for success', *Mentoring and Tutoring: Partnership in Learning*, 22(4): 265–389.

Johnson, W.B. (2016) *On Being a Mentor: A Guide for Higher Education Faculty*, 2nd edn. Mahwah: Erlbaum.

Kasprisin, C.A., Single, P.B., Single, R.M., Muller, C.B. and Ferrier, J.L. (2008) 'Improved mentor satisfaction: emphasizing protégé training for adult-age mentoring dyads', *Mentoring and Tutoring: Partnership in Learning*, 16(2): 163–74.

Kochan, F.K. (ed.) (2002) *The Organizational and Human Dimensions of Successful Mentoring Programs and Relationships*. Greenwich: Information Age.

Kochan, F.K. and Pascarelli, J.T. (eds) (2003) *Global Perspectives on Mentoring: Transforming Contexts, Communities, and Cultures*. Greenwich: Information Age.

Kochan, F.K. and Pascarelli, J.T. (2012) 'Perspectives on culture and mentoring in the global age', in S. Fletcher and C.A. Mullen (eds), *The SAGE Handbook of Mentoring and Coaching in Education*. Thousand Oaks: Sage, pp. 184–98.

Kochan, F.K., Kent, A.M. and Green, A.M. (eds) (2014) *Uncovering the Cultural Dynamics in Mentoring Programs and Relationships: Enhancing Practice and Research*. Charlotte: Information Age.

Kram, K.E. (1983) 'Phases of the mentor relationship', *Academy of Management Journal*, 26: 608–25.

Kram, K.E. (1985/1988) *Mentoring at Work: Developmental Relationships in Organizational Life*. Lanham: University Press of America.

Lick, D.W. (1999) 'Multiple level comentoring: moving toward a learning organization', in C.A. Mullen and D.W. Lick (eds), *New Directions in Mentoring: Creating a Culture of Synergy*. London: Falmer, pp. 202–12.

Lloyd-Jones, B. (2014) 'African-American women in the professoriate: addressing social exclusion and scholarly marginalization through mentoring', *Mentoring and Tutoring: Partnership in Learning*, 22(4): 269–83.

Mackey, H. and Shannon, K. (2014) 'Comparing alternative voices in the academy: Navigating the complexity of mentoring relationships from divergent ethnic backgrounds', *Mentoring and Tutoring: Partnership in Learning*, 22(4): 338–53.

Merriam, S.B. (1983) 'Mentors and protégés: a critical review of the literature', *Adult Education Quarterly*, 33(3): 161–73.

Moerer-Urdahl, T. and Creswell, J. (2004) 'Using transcendental phenomenology to explore the "ripple effect" in a leadership mentorship program', *International Journal of Qualitative Methods*, 3(2): 1–28.

Mullen, C.A. (2000) 'Constructing co-mentoring partnerships: walkways we must travel', *Theory Into Practice*, 39(1): 4–11.

Mullen, C.A. (2005) *The Mentorship Primer*. New York: Peter Lang.

Mullen, C.A. (2007) 'Naturally occurring student–faculty mentoring relationships: a literature review', in T.D. Allen and L.T. Eby (eds), *The Blackwell Handbook of Mentoring: A Multiple Perspectives Approach*. Malden: Wiley-Blackwell, pp. 119–38.

Mullen, C.A. (ed.) (2008) *The Handbook of Formal Mentoring in Higher Education: A Case Study Approach*. Norwood: Christopher-Gordon.

Mullen, C.A. (2011a) 'Facilitating self-regulated learning using mentoring approaches with doctoral students', in B. Zimmerman and D.H. Schunk (eds), *Handbook of Self-Regulation of Learning and Performance*. New York: Routledge, pp. 137–52.

Mullen, C.A. (2011b) 'New teacher mentoring: a mandated direction of states', *Kappa Delta Pi Record*, 47(2): 63–7.

Mullen, C.A. (2013) 'Mentoring theories for educational practitioners', in B.J. Irby, G. Brown, R. Lara-Alecio and S. Jackson (eds), *The Handbook of Educational Theories*. Charlotte: Information Age, pp. 959–67.

Mullen, C.A. and Hutinger, J.L. (2008) 'The principal's role in fostering collaborative learning communities through faculty study group development', *Theory Into Practice*, 47(4): 276–85.

Mullen, C.A. and Lick, D.W. (eds) (1999) *New Directions in Mentoring: Creating a Culture of Synergy*. London: Falmer.

Mullen, C.A., Young, J.K. and Harris, S. (2014) 'Cultural dialogue as social justice advocacy within and beyond university classrooms', in I. Bogotch and C. Shields (eds), *International Handbook of Educational Leadership and Social [In]Justice*, Vol. 2. New York: Springer, pp. 1145–68.

Murakami, E.T. and Núñez, A.M. (2014) 'Latina faculty transcending barriers: peer mentoring in a Hispanic-serving institution', *Mentoring and Tutoring: Partnership in Learning*, 22(4): 284–301.

Murphy, W.M. (2012) 'Reverse mentoring at work: fostering cross-generational learning and developing millennial leaders', *Human Resource Management*, 51(4): 549–74.

Noe, R.A. (1988) 'An investigation of the determinants of successful assigned mentoring relationships', *Personnel Psychology*, 41(3): 457–79.

O'Neill, R.M. (2002) 'Gender and race in mentoring relationships: a review of the literature', in D.A. Clutterbuck and B.R. Ragins (eds), *Mentoring and Diversity: An International Perspective*. London: Butterworth-Heinemann, pp. 1–22.

Portner, H. (2002) *Being Mentored: A Guide for Protégés*. Thousand Oaks: Sage.

Ragins, B.R. and Cotton, J.L. (1999) 'Mentor functions and outcomes: a comparison of men and women in formal and informal mentoring relationships', *Journal of Applied Psychology*, 84(4): 529–50.

Reddick, R.J. and Young, M.D. (2012) 'Mentoring graduate students of color', in S. Fletcher and C.A. Mullen (eds), *The SAGE Handbook of Mentoring and Coaching in Education*. Thousand Oaks: Sage, pp. 412–29.

Richardson, J. (2007) 'Dynamic groups: teachers harness the power of professional learning communities', *The Learning Principal*, 2(6): 1, 6–7.

Schunk, D.H. and Mullen, C.A. (2013) 'Toward a conceptual model of mentoring research: integration with self-regulated learning', *Educational Psychology Review*, 25(3): 361–89.

Sedlacek, W.E., Benjamin, E., Schlosser, L.Z. and Sheu, H. (2007) 'Mentoring in academia: considerations for diverse populations', in T.D. Allen and L.T. Eby (eds), *The Blackwell Handbook of Mentoring: A Multiple Perspectives Approach*. Malden: Blackwell, pp. 259–80.

Single, P.B. (2008) 'A campuswide faculty mentoring program: putting research into practice', in C.A. Mullen (ed.), *The Handbook of Formal Mentoring in Higher Education: A Case Study Approach*. Norwood: Christopher-Gordon, pp. 213–34.

Single, P.B. and Single, R.M. (2005) 'E-mentoring for social equity: review of research to inform program development', *Mentoring and Tutoring: Partnership in Learning*, 13(2): 301–20.

Sitzmann, T. and Ely, K. (2011) 'A meta-analysis of self-regulated learning in work-related training and educational attainment: what we know and where we need to go', *Psychological Bulletin*, 137(3): 421–42.

Tallerico, M. (2005) *Supporting and Sustaining Teachers' Professional Development: A Principal's Guide*. Thousand Oaks: Corwin.

Tharp, R.G. and Gallimore, R.G. (1995/1988) *Rousing Minds to Life: Teaching, Learning, and Schooling in Social Context*. New York: Cambridge University Press.

Wilson, P.P., Pereira, A. and Valentine, D. (2002) 'Perceptions of new social work faculty about mentoring experiences', *Journal of Social Work Education*, 38(2): 317–33.

Wong, H.K. (2004) 'Producing educational leaders through induction programs', *Kappa Delta Pi Record*, 40(3): 106–11.

Zachary, L.J. and Fischler, L.A. (2014) *Starting Strong: A Mentoring Fable*. San Francisco: Jossey-Bass.

Critical Issues in Mentoring Research

Julie Haddock-Millar

INTRODUCTION

Research into the activity of mentoring has grown at a significant rate in the last 20 years (Allen et al., 2008; Janssen et al., 2015), as has the range of inter-disciplinary subjects associated with mentoring, such as business, education, entrepreneurship, nursing and psychology (De Four-Babb et al., 2015; Kochan, 2013; Laukhuf and Malone, 2015; Underhill, 2006).

The review of Allen et al. (2008), on organisational mentoring literature – consisting of 207 individual research studies, published in 60 different journals – acknowledged the growing interest and research on the topic of mentoring. The authors attributed this to the increasing recognition that formal and informal mentoring is associated with behavioural, attitudinal and career benefits for mentees and mentors (Allen et al., 2004; Eby et al., 2008). Additionally, over the last 10 years, there have been an increasing number of evaluations of mentoring research processes and practices (Allen et al., 2008; Bozeman and Feeney, 2007; Janssen et al., 2015; Kammeyer-Mueller and Judge, 2008; Underhill, 2006). A broad range of mentoring studies are explored in this chapter within the context of identifying the critical issues involved in assuring the quality of mentoring research.

Purpose and overview

The aim of this chapter is to provide an in-depth analysis of the critical issues related to the quality of research processes and strategies used in contemporary inter-disciplinary scholarly literature in mentoring. Further, it seeks to expand researcher and practitioner perspectives about these issues, which will ultimately enhance the research about, and practice of, mentoring.

The chapter begins with an outline of the process used to identify critical issues in assuring quality in mentoring research. This is followed by a discussion of each of the eight critical issues identified through this process, referring to specific studies that illustrate the degree to which quality is achieved. The final section posits the way ahead for mentoring research.

Critical issues in mentoring research

It is not possible to identify, review, and then discuss in detail the hundreds of scholarly articles, dissertations and books available on the subject of mentoring. Instead, I searched for some general themes from a bounded set of resources to identify the critical issues in mentoring research. The process I adopted was the following:

- Reviewed all mentoring articles published within the last five years in five journals with a strong mentoring focus, including: *International Journal of Coaching and Mentoring, International Journal of Evidence-Based Coaching and Mentoring, International Journal of Mentoring in Education, Journal of Vocational Behavior* and *Mentoring and Tutoring: Partnership in Learning.*
- Through the back chaining process, I identified 20 further studies that provided a critical insight into methodological limitations.
- Reviewed 10 widely published textbooks on the subject of mentoring, with a view to identifying common issues related to the quality of mentoring research.
- Identified a sample of articles that illustrated a cross-section of methodological approaches and limitations.
- Selected a list of critical issues in mentoring, identified through this review process and incorporated them into this chapter.

Critical areas in mentoring research

Overall, the literature appears to call for the further development and refinement of mentoring research in eight critical areas:

- Defining the mentoring concept as a theoretical basis for research

- Identifying mentoring programme aims, objectives and operational components
- Understanding context and the connectedness between multiple factors
- Proving cause-and-effect
- Developing cross-cultural comparative studies
- Engaging in the utilisation of multiple and varied research methods
- Enhancing methodological rigour
- Addressing the 'so what' question

The sections that follow summarise each critical issue and explain why each is important in advancing knowledge, understanding and mentoring practice through the continual improvement of the quality of mentoring research. I draw on specific studies and examples to illuminate some of the concerns.

DEFINING THE MENTORING CONCEPT AS A THEORETICAL BASIS FOR RESEARCH

Perhaps the most critical review of mentoring theory and research was carried out by Bozeman and Feeney (2007). They 'nominate mentoring as an outstanding illustration of limited progress in theory for a topic that is obviously important and amenable to convenient measurement … there has been too little attention to core concepts of theory' (2007: 719). This problem was also noted by Janssen et al. (2015) in their literature review of informal mentoring at work, and is echoed by multiple authors including Allen et al. (2004), Gershenfeld (2014), and Janssen et al. (2015).

The most troublesome issue related to theory building appears to be that many studies do not provide a definition of the concept. The consequence of this is that mentoring research can be confused with neighbouring theories such as training, coaching and socialisation. Let us consider a number of different mentoring definitions:

- 'Offline help from one person to another in making significant transitions in knowledge,

work or thinking' (Megginson and Clutterbuck, 1995: 13).
- 'Mentoring is a long-term relationship between a senior, more experienced individual (the mentor) and a more junior, less experienced individual (the protégé)' (Eby and Allen, 2002: 456).
- 'Mentoring is defined as a developmental relationship that involves organizational members of unequal status or, less frequently, peers' (Bozionelos, 2004: 5).
- 'Mentoring has one clear purpose, the learning and development of an individual, a process that involves change, in this case social change' (Brockbank and McGill, 2006: 9).

Whilst we may not subscribe to any of the aforementioned definitions, we can probably agree that over the last 20 years, views on mentoring have changed to encompass a much broader perspective than the traditional US-centric protégé/mentor dyad. Clutterbuck (2003) notes that clarifying the mentoring concept in mentoring research is vital because failure to do so makes it difficult, if not impossible, to replicate the study, make direct comparisons between studies or draw meaningful conclusions about the mentoring relationship.

IDENTIFICATION OF MENTORING PROGRAMME AIMS, OBJECTIVES AND OPERATIONAL COMPONENTS

In addition to clarifying the definition of mentoring, the research indicates that it is also essential to clarify the aim and specify objectives and operational components of the mentoring programme. Logically, if one of the purposes of the evaluation of the mentoring programme is to understand the extent to which the objectives have been achieved, it is important to articulate the aims and objectives clearly at the outset of programme development and implementation.

Programme components are generally developed to meet programme goals and purposes. These components are varied across programmes (Long et al., 2012) and these components can have a serious impact on programme success. Allen et al. (2008) identified a clear lack of explicit programme operational components, such as participants' profile, training, duration and frequency of mentoring within programme descriptions and within research studies. Examining this issue, Gershenfeld's (2014) review of 20 published studies on undergraduate mentoring programmes in the US from 2008 to 2012 found a clear lack of identification of explicit programme operational components, including, for example, participant profile, role, training, duration and frequency of mentoring.

Not identifying components such as the aims and objectives of the programme when conducting research on it makes it difficult to understand the extent to which the participants' outcomes relate to the overall purpose of the mentoring programme (Clutterbuck, 2004). Additionally, the inclusion of such detail is important because failure to do so, results in the inability to compare studies on a like-for-like basis.

Brondyk and Searby (2013) deal with the importance of these elements in assuring best practices in mentoring. Although the article identifies the complexities of mentoring in higher education and primary and secondary school education, their recommendations have implications for mentoring in general. The authors suggest that best practice involves assuring that mentoring programmes achieve their intended consequences. This, of course, necessitates having a clear delineation of the purposes of the programme or relationship. The authors acknowledge the importance of understanding what is being done well and what needs to improve in mentoring specific to different contexts. The importance of context will be discussed next.

UNDERSTANDING CONTEXT AND THE CONNECTEDNESS BETWEEN MULTIPLE FACTORS

Arguably, there has been little attention in the literature and practice paid to the broader context of mentoring (Chandler et al., 2011; Jones and Corner, 2012); for example, there is a greater emphasis on functional approaches that examine instrumental mentor/protégé motivations, with little focus on relational or affiliative mentee/mentor motivations (Ragins, 2011; Ragins and Verbos, 2007). A number of researchers have explored and recommended the need for further in-depth description and appreciation of context, acknowledging the degree to which multiple factors can influence and impact the study of mentoring (Allen et al., 1997, 2008; Janssen et al., 2015; Jones and Corner, 2012). These factors are important in understanding the influence and impact of developmental networks, organisational structure and culture. Kochan's (2013) paper presented a theoretical model of culture from which a conceptual framework was built that can be used to conduct a cultural analysis within the context of the development and implementation of mentoring programmes.

Kochan provides a working scenario, in which a mentoring programme can be developed, examined, implemented and evaluated from a cultural perspective (2013: 422–4). This type of analysis is important as it acknowledges that the success or failure of mentoring programmes is dependent upon a multitude of issues, including cultural aspects inherent within the individual, organisation, programme design and processes and society.

Chandler et al. (2011) reviewed the mentoring literature from an ecological perspective. They recommend that researchers need to adopt different methodological approaches that facilitate our understanding of multiple levels of analysis. This includes the ontogenic system (individual) microsystem (developmental networks and organisational context) and societal marcosystem (societal influences such as technology and culture). Adopting this approach requires us to consider mentoring from a reciprocal, interdependent perspective, considering the connectedness between the individual and the environmental system. Research to-date focuses on the ontogenic individual-level and microsystem dyadic-level, examining specifics such as gender, race, informal versus formal mentoring and behaviours by individuals, but tends not to focus on the organisational or societal levels (Blickle et al., 2009).

Similarly, the literature review of informal mentoring at work by Janssen et al. (2015) suggests that the context of mentoring is important in understanding mentees developmental networks as a means of considering influences outside of the mentor-protégé relationship. This extends to individuals, groups and the organisational context, acknowledging the influence of the ecosystem of the protégés and the impact this may have on the mentoring processes between mentor and protégé (Chandler et al., 2011; Kram and Ragins, 2007).

Waterman and He's (2011) literature review of 14 mentoring studies examining teacher retention between 2005 and 2010 makes a number of suggestions in regards to the design and evaluation of future mentoring programmes. First, in recognising the complexity of mentoring relationships, attempts to establish linear connections between two phenomena such as mentoring and retention is challenging. Instead, they suggest a more contextual approach, which takes into account broader personal needs in interactional capacities is more useful in understanding value. This point is not that dissimilar from Janssen et al. (2015), who suggest that the degree to which positive outcomes related to mentoring are a direct result of mentoring activities is unclear and that there is a lack of studies addressing the multiple aspects, including, amongst others, interactions and temporal influences. Second, the importance of holistic process evaluation, rather than programme evaluation, is important in establishing the degree to which other actors influence professional development and ultimately, retention. Finally, evaluating the same mentoring programme from different paradigms would facilitate greater insight for those engaged in design, development and evaluation.

A final issue of importance related to context was explored through Waterman and He's (2011) literature review that found a dominance of quantitative approaches to research. Of the 14 studies the authors reviewed, five were quantitative, and of the seven that adopted a mixed method approach, quantitative data dominated, with qualitative data being very much secondary. This focus on quantitative data, although valuable, can also neglect the deep exploration of features within the mentoring process that help explain the significance of context (Kapadia et al., 2007).

However, one study, which provides interesting insights into context, exploring the experiences of female academics was conducted by Esnard et al. (2015). The authors chose to use narrative stories to facilitate the personal reflections of seven multicultural network members – including the authors – describing their experiences of collaboration and mentoring within the network. Mentoring networks are regarded as an important developmental aspect for women of colour, addressing both gender and race issues (Davis et al., 2012; Johnson-Bailey and Cervero, 2008; Ragins et al., 1998). The focus of the research was the examination of the processes and structures of the peer mentoring network and how this influences relationships and outcomes. There were clear benefits for the group participants. At the relational level, the central interest in multicultural issues became the glue that held the group together, creating a shared sense of identity and enabling voice. What was less clear was the extent to which interconnected networks, organisational and societal norms influenced the mentoring experiences of the network members.

The exploratory study of De Four-Babb et al. (2015) analysed the stories of eight non-tenure-track academics belonging to an international peer mentoring group, described as a 'professional learning community' (2015: 77). Careers of non-tenure-track academics are subject to increasing interest (Anderson, 2007; Basten, 2012; Goldman and Schmalz, 2012; Hoyt, 2012; Wolfinger et al., 2009). The narrative stories of the academics were analysed to understand their experience as 'outsider' academics in relation to tenure track, geographic transition and academic trajectory. Included within the analysis was the lived experience and narrative stories of the three authors. Informal peer mentoring groups are identified as having a supportive role in academic career development and can mitigate intellectual poverty experienced by 'outsiders'. What is unclear in the article is the extent to which contextual factors such as organisational structure and culture influence the peer mentoring affiliations, enabling and/or constraining professional development. It would be helpful to understand the organisational microsystem and broader societal macrosystem (Chandler et al., 2011).

Exploring the connectedness between the ontogenic system, microsystem and macrosystem enhances our ability to understand the ecological perspective (Chandler et al., 2011). Examining mentoring and the relationship between multi-dimensional outcomes would also be helpful in determining construct validity and relevance (Janssen et al., 2015; Ragins, 2011; Ragins and Verbos, 2007). More research needs to be done in this area in order to garner a deeper understanding of the mentoring process within its contextual framework.

PROVING CAUSE-AND-EFFECT

Mentoring literature has been criticised for its instrumental and functional emphasis, which is often focused on findings and outcomes (Bozeman and Feeney, 2007), rather than to understanding the causal explanations involved in these relationships and programmes. The literature review of 24 past mentoring studies of informal mentoring at work by Janssen et al. (2015) argues that the degree to which studies are able to prove cause-and-effect relationships is questionable. These authors suggest that the relationship between positive outcomes and mentoring activities is unclear and there is little understanding of the underlying developmental mechanisms that cause mentoring outcomes. This is, in part, due to the lack of studies addressing the multi-aspects of mentoring including, amongst others processes, interactions, context and temporal influences.

Examples of the lack of attention to the connection between outcomes and processes are numerous. For example, Collins et al. (2014) explored the experiences of eight women academics – including the author's – belonging to a women's peer mentorship group. The particular focus was on career pathways into academia, a subject that has been widely researched from a variety of perspectives (Kamvounias et al., 2008; McCormack and West, 2006; Walkington et al., 2008; Wasburn, 2007). Each group member wrote an autobiographical narrative account of their experience relating to 'pathways to academia, experience of academia, and future career aspirations' (Collins et al., 2014: 98). All group members working in the sector secured a promotion to higher-level academic positions. While the authors claim that the mentoring model turned out to be effective in reaching the participants career aspirations, cause and effect is not entirely transparent. For example, there was no indication as to what extent wider interconnected developmental relationships influenced this success.

Jones' (2012) longitudinal study investigated the learning outcomes of 48 mentees and mentors in formal mentoring dyads in a Healthcare Trust. Semi-structured interviews were conducted over a 17-month period during the beginning, middle and end stages of their mentoring relationship. One of the most significant limitations noted was the difficulty in making a direct link between the impact of mentoring and the participants' wider network, including, amongst others, managers, colleagues and tutors.

Similarly, Laukhuf and Malone's (2015) phenomenological study of 22 women entrepreneurs was not able to identify the extent to which immediate and wider networks facilitated mentee development. The authors used interviews to understand the participants' lived experience and perceived value of the mentoring intervention (Creswell, 2012; Marshall and Rossman, 2014). The study did show that the mentoring was of benefit to the women entrepreneurs. It was also noted that many women entrepreneurs rely on family and friends for guidance and support, but the degree to which the wider networks facilitated development was absent.

There appears to be little research that delves deeply into cause and effect in mentoring endeavours. Further focus on this issue would help us to better understand the connectedness between the individual and the environmental system, shifting from the ontogenic system and microsystem to understanding the influence and impact of the macrosystem (Chandler et al., 2011).

DEVELOPING CROSS-CULTURAL COMPARATIVE STUDIES

US literature and Western culture tends to dominate mentoring literature reviews (Allen et al., 2008). This Western bias was also a feature of Terrion and Leonard's (2007) literature review of 54 student peer mentoring programmes in which the majority of these studies were in Canadian and US universities. The authors suggested that cross-cultural comparative studies would enhance our understanding of the characteristics of effective mentors in other cultures and contexts. Because of this, many mentoring studies assume that the aim of the relationship is development of leadership attributes but recent studies indicate that the concept of leadership is culturally dependant. For example, in African culture, respect, caring for others, sharing and cooperation may differ to that of Western cultures (Kochan, 2013).

Closely related to this issue is the way in which issues connected to culture are defined. Reeves (2015) recent review of cross-cultural mentoring across 123 articles identified the need for construct clarification and use of consistent terminology related to cultural concepts. One of the most significant issues was the inconsistent use of terminology. This is illustrated by the similar use of *cross-cultural* and *inter-cultural* mentoring. Cross-cultural mentoring is described as the 'means to compare and contrast two cultural groups', and intercultural 'is what happens when the two or more culturally-different groups come together, interact, and communicate' (2015: 11). The terminology is used interchangeably in the articles reviewed, which can cause difficulty in developing a significant body of literature, providing direct comparison. More recently, the term pan-cultural has also been used to describe mentoring across cultures, acknowledging the societal differences which may influence the way in which mentoring may occur.

In the societal macrosystem, Chandler et al. (2011) identify the need to examine mentoring across cultures and in multicultural contexts, acknowledging the shift in extra-organisational platforms such as Facebook and LinkedIn that connect individuals, groups and organisations. Here, in-depth studies are needed to understand mentoring across cultures, particularly with advances in technology and the enhanced ability to facilitate global mentoring systems.

MULTIPLE AND VARIED RESEARCH METHODS

Broadly, mentoring studies can be grouped into three categories: literature reviews, concept papers and empirical research. Literature reviews consist of critical, integrative, literature and mapping analyses. Concept papers explore hypotheses, evaluate literature and philosophical underpinnings. Several literature reviews, focused on varied aspects of mentoring, have been published in a variety of peer reviewed journals over the last 10 years. Journals include the *Academy of Management Annals* (Chandler et al., 2011), *Administration and Society* (Bozeman and Feeney, 2007), *International Journal of Mentoring and Coaching* (Reeves, 2015); *International Journal of Management Reviews* (Jansse et al., 2015), *Journal of Vocational Behavior* (Allen et al., 2008; Kammeyer-Mueller and Judge, 2008; Underhill, 2006), *Mentoring and Tutoring: Partnership in Learning* (Huizing, 2012; Long, et al., 2012; Terrion and Leonard, 2007; Waterman and He, 2011), *Research in Higher Education* (Crisp and Cruz, 2009), *Review of Educational Research* (Gershenfeld, 2014; Jacobi, 1991) and the *International Journal of Mentoring and Coaching in Education* (Brondyk and Searby, 2013).

In particular, Waterman and He's (2011) article highlighted mentoring research and evaluations carried out in the USA since 2005 regarding the effectiveness of mentoring programmes for new teacher retention. Huizing's (2012) article presented a literature review of peer-reviewed articles and dissertations that contribute to the theory of research of group mentoring. Brondky and Searby's concept paper describes the complexity that underlies best practices in mentoring research. The purpose of their article is to begin to develop and identify research-based best practices in mentoring education. Kochan's (2013) article presented a theoretical model of culture from which a conceptual framework was built.

Empirical research consists of qualitative, quantitative, mixed method and case study reviews. Qualitative mentoring research adopts a range of approaches, techniques and data collection methods including, amongst others: participatory action research exploring peer group mentoring narrative stories (Collins et al., 2014); longitudinal qualitative case study, semi-structured interviews with mentees and mentors (Jones, 2012); phenomenological study, investigating the lived experience of the participants through interviews (Laukhuf and Malone, 2015); narrative enquiry to make sense of the lived experience (De Four-Babb et al., 2015); in-depth, semi-structured interviews and focus groups (Zambrana et al., 2015); structured interviews (Lakind et al., 2015); interpretative involving day long reviews with discussion and focus groups (Ivey et al., 2013); and reflective narratives (Esnard et al., 2015; Jones and Brown, 2011).

Qualitative data, in particular, can enhance our understanding of the role of mentoring in different contexts and content domains. This is particularly important as mentoring has become a global, boundary-less phenomenon, facilitated by increasing use of technology to facilitate workplace mentoring.

Examining the literature, Bozeman and Feeney (2007) found that the vast majority of mentoring research is quantitative. In their research review, over 90 per cent used survey-based methods and less than 20 per cent triangulated multiple data sources. Quantitative mentoring research adopts a much more narrow range of approaches than qualitative research, techniques and data collection methods include: mentor triad questionnaire using a Mentor Self-Efficacy Scale (Ferro et al., 2013); mentee questionnaire based on the mentor behaviour scale (Brodeur et al., 2015); protégé questionnaire, using t-test (Bouquillon et al., 2005); mentee questionnaire (Baranik et al., 2010); protégé-mentor dyad questionnaire using polynominal regression analyses (Mitchell et al., 2015); and mentee questionnaire using correlations, cross-tabulations and binary logistic regression (Roszkowski and Badmus, 2014).

Mixed method mentoring research adopts a range of approaches, techniques and data collection methods including, amongst others, questionnaires, focus groups and interviews (Flavian and Kass, 2015); questionnaires, semi-structured individual and focus-group interviews, contributions in workshops and observations (Ruru et al., 2013); questionnaire and semi-structured interview (Johns et al., 2012); and observation, archival documents, audio/video data and interviews (Sempowicz and Hudson, 2012).

Examples of mixed-method approaches demonstrate variation in the methodological approaches used. For example, the research of Zambrana et al. (2015) examined mentoring experiences of 58 underrepresented minority faculty at 22 research-extensive institutions, utilising in-depth interviews and focus groups. The research of Brodeur et al. (2015) involved the construction and validation of a tool to measure the supportive behaviours of mentors participating in school-based mentoring programmes. Kammeyer-Mueller and Judge (2008) conducted a quantitative research synthesis, focusing on estimating multivariate analytical paths between mentoring and career outcomes. Johns et al. (2012) exploratory research triangulated quantitative and qualitative research to better understand the impact of a group-mentoring model in an Australian university.

Multiple methods and data sources provide the opportunity to collect different types of data and enable triangulation through the comparison of data sources and potentially increases the external validity of the research. Notwithstanding the aforementioned, Chandler et al. (2011) identified at least six recent studies that combine quantitative and qualitative methods, consider multiple sources of data and/or involve multiple data-collection points over time (Cotton et al., 2011; Gentry et al., 2008; Higgins et al., 2010; Shen, 2010; Singh et al., 2009a, 2009b).

At the ontogenic level, Chandler et al. (2011) suggest that researchers need to develop multi-method approaches that explore the inter-connectedness of influences such as education, individual competence, ethnicity, race and gender (Allen et al., 1997; Cole, 2009). In examining the microsystem, it is suggested that a qualitative research approach can be best used to consider group characteristics, functions and processes, particularly in regard to the distinction to dyadic mentoring relationships, including a constellation of relationships beyond. This extends to the organisational microsystem, where structure and culture influence mentoring programmes in varying degrees (Noe et al., 2002).

Overall, the need to adopt varied research methods, which support the ecological perspective, underlies the review of mentoring literature.

ENHANCING RIGOUR

A number of studies have criticised mentoring research for its lack of rigour. These criticisms focused primarily upon the use of single data collection points, the lack of longitudinal studies and small sample sizes (Allen et al., 2008; Bozeman and Feeney, 2007; Gershenfeld, 2014). Bozeman and Feeney (2007) suggest that lack of longitudinal studies, single data point collection studies and limited sample sizes illustrate the extent to which advancement in the field of mentoring research is limited. Allen et al. (2008) found that mentoring research uses fewer longitudinal methodological designs than organisational and management research. This is significant because mentoring studies are often concerned with identifying beneficial outcomes, but a single point in time of analysis provides little evidence of development over time; the primary purpose of longitudinal design is to examine changes over time, which is arguably more suitable in this regard.

As noted in the first section on defining mentoring, while definitions differ, all agree that mentoring is a developmental relationship. Thus, an expectation might be that the mentee experiences significant change and gain greater insight through enhancing the quality of their thinking. If this is the case, then the examination of change over time is important in order to determine longer-term development. A single data collection point is a deeply inadequate method to approach the evaluation of mentoring relationships, where a longitudinal method facilitotes analysis over time.

Ferro et al. (2013) evaluated the measurement properties of a newly created Mentor Self-Efficacy Scale. The purpose of the scale is to better understand 'mentors' levels of confidence in their knowledge and ability to provide support and guidance for children in ... community relationships' (2013: 147). In the first round of questionnaires, 249 triads participated. In the second round of questionnaires, 151 of the original 249 participated. There were several methodological limitations recognised in the study. First, data were only collected from mentors in current relationships, not those that were terminated; this is a missed opportunity to understand what led to the termination and whether or not there was a causal link with knowledge and ability to provide support and guidance. Second, data were not collected from subsequent follow-up periods. Therefore, the impact on mentor self-efficacy of their growing experience and longer-term relationships is unknown.

Mitchell et al. (2015) examined the antecedents and outcomes of perceived similarity in mentoring relationships. Their sample consisted of 82 protégé-mentor dyads from two large US universities, consisting of both informal and formal mentoring relationships. The most significant limitation within the context of this chapter is that the study was not longitudinal, further research would help to identify direction of causality between associations found. Allen et al. (2008) similarly found the lack of longitudinal methodological designs to be a concern, particularly as a significant number of studies measure a single point in time, providing minimal, if any evidence of development over time.

Johns et al. (2012) explored academics' perceptions, motivations and barriers for participation in the Women's Group Mentoring Programme (WGMP) in an Australian university. The WGMP is defined as a 'specific corporate product' (2012: 74). Thirty-three participants completed a survey and 11 then participated in follow-up interviews. The results raised a number of concerns around programme branding. This type of pragmatic approach is useful in supporting others embarking on the development of mentoring programmes. From a methodological perspective, the sample size was small and the research focused on one voluntary corporate programme, which raises issues around external validity.

There have been a number of literature reviews of mentoring in the educational context (Brondyk and Searby, 2013; Gershenfeld, 2014; Long et al., 2012; Terrion and Leonard, 2007; Waterman and He, 2011), specifically in the areas of peer mentoring, teacher attrition and retention and peer mentoring. Gershenfeld's (2014) review summarised 20 published studies on undergraduate mentoring programmes in the US from 2008 to 2012. The review acknowledges and builds on two previous reviews conducted by Jacobi (1991) and Crisp and Cruz (2009). Gershenfeld (2014) acknowledges the methodological progress made since the previous two reviews, particularly in respect of the use of theory or conceptual frameworks, present in 70 per cent of the mentoring studies reviewed. However, considerable progress is still needed if we are to improve internal and external validity of mentoring research. The literature review classified the 20 mentoring studies using the Levels of Evidence-Based Intervention Effectiveness (LEBIE), developed by Jackson (2009). The LEBIE framework was developed to assess methodological rigor of social service interventions and was used to establish the level of research, from Level 1, *Superior Intervention*, to Level 5, *Concerning Intervention*. Over 70 per cent of studies reviewed, were either Level 4 (*Emerging Intervention*) or Level 5, the lowest classification. The consequence of receiving the lowest score on the LEBIE classification scale was that 'there was no conclusive evidence that mentoring programmes had impact on the desired outcomes' (2009: 385). The drivers of the classification were two-fold; first, a single point of data collection and, second, no comparison group, showing little evidence of positive change to participants as a result of mentoring.

There are a number of practical implications involved in increasing methodological rigour in mentoring resources including such things as financial costs and time. However, if we are to illustrate the impact and value of mentoring practice, longitudinal research should be given serious consideration.

THE 'SO WHAT' QUESTION

The final critical issue in mentoring research is dealing with the 'so what' question. The 'so what' question concerns the degree to which mentoring research contributes to the existing body of knowledge and practice, theoretical and empirical. This is particularly relevant for others researching in the field and for the organisation investing in mentoring programmes (Clutterbuck, 2013).

There are different ways in which we can address the 'so what' question. Among these are:

- How does the study contribute to the existing body of knowledge?
- What are the implications in relation to mentoring as a concept?
- What are the implications of the findings for the future design, implementation and evaluation of mentoring programmes?

- What are the implications for key stakeholders invested in mentoring programmes: organisations, programme teams, mentees and mentors?
- Does it enable programme managers to design, implement and evaluate more effective programmes?
- Does it assist participants in building strong, more effective mentoring relationships?
- What are the implications in respect of mentoring methods, techniques and processes?
- What are the implications from a methodological perspective?
- What are the implications for future research agendas?

Broadly, it is important to think about the contribution research makes to the continual development of theory and practice. It is not one or the other; it is connectedness between theory and practice that will address many of the criticisms discussed in this chapter.

THE WAY AHEAD FOR MENTORING RESEARCH

In this chapter, I have provided an in-depth analysis of the quality of contemporary interdisciplinary scholarly literature in mentoring; exploring trends in the use of different research methodologies and identifying critical issues in mentoring studies.

Research can help to develop knowledge and understanding and the practice of mentoring, but only if the research is explicitly reported. This includes defining the mentoring concept and relationship; identifying the aim, objectives and operational components of the programme; recognising the context and influencing factors; and explicitly describing the methodology and study protocol. In addition to this, there is a need to continue to be more creative and take a longer-term view in our approaches to methodology, including longitudinal research, mixed method research and exploring multiple levels of analysis. From a pragmatic perspective, mentoring practitioners and researchers need to address the 'so what question'. This will assist organisations, programme developers, managers, evaluators, researchers and participants to understand the practical implications of the results.

There is a clear opportunity for greater collaboration between academics and practitioners in the design and analysis of research. An evaluation strategy is a necessary and important aspect of any mentoring programme. This can be supported by a strong theoretical foundation that will ultimately improve the quality of research and practice.

REFERENCES

Allen, T.D., Eby, L.T., O'Brien, K.E. and Lentz, E. (2008) 'The state of mentoring research: A qualitative review of current research methods and future research implications', *Journal of Vocational Behavior*, 73(3): 343–57.

Allen, T.D., Eby, L.T., Poteet, M.L., Lentz, E. and Lima, L. (2004) 'Career benefits associated with mentoring for protégés: a meta-analysis', *Journal of Applied Psychology*, 89(1): 127–36.

Allen, T.D., Poteet, M.L. and Burroughs, S.M. (1997) 'The mentor's perspective: a qualitative inquiry and future research agenda', *Journal of Vocational Behavior*, 51(1): 70–89.

Anderson, V. (2007) 'Contingent and marginalised? Academic development and part-time teachers', *International Journal for Academic Development*, 12(2): 111–21.

Baranik, L.E., Roling, E.A. and Eby, L.T. (2010) 'Why does mentoring work? The role of perceived organizational support', *Journal of Vocational Behavior*, 76(3): 366–73.

Basten, F. (2012) 'Through the looking glass: a narrative of non-change', *Educational Action Research*, 20(1): 95–111.

Blickle, G., Witzki, A.H. and Schneider, P.B. (2009) 'Mentoring support and power: a three-year predictive field study on protégé networking and career success', *Journal of Vocational Behavior*, 74(2): 181–9.

Bouquillon, E.A., Sosik, J.J. and Lee, D. (2005) '"It's only a phase": examining trust, identification and mentoring functions received across the mentoring phases', *Mentoring and Tutoring: Partnership in Learning*, 13(2): 239–58.

Bozionelos, N. (2004) 'Mentoring provided: relation to mentor's career success, personality, and mentoring received', *Journal of Vocational Behavior*, 64(1): 24–46.

Bozeman, B. and Feeney, M.K. (2007) 'Toward a useful theory of mentoring a conceptual analysis and critique', *Administration and Society*, 39(6): 719–39.

Brockbank, A. and McGill, I. (2006) *Facilitating Reflective Learning Through Mentoring and Coaching*. London: Kogan Page Publishers.

Brodeur, P., Larose, S., Tarabulsy, G., Feng, B. and Forget-Dubois, N. (2015) 'Development and construct validation of the mentor behavior scale', *Mentoring and Tutoring: Partnership in Learning*, 23(1): 54–75.

Brondyk, S. and Searby, L. (2013) 'Best practices in mentoring: complexities and possibilities', *International Journal of Mentoring and Coaching in Education*, 2(3): 189–203.

Chandler, D.E., Kram, K.E. and Yip, J. (2011) 'An ecological systems perspective on mentoring at work: a review and future prospects', *The Academy of Management Annals*, 5(1): 519–70.

Clutterbuck, D. (2003) 'The problem with research in mentoring', *The Coaching and Mentoring Network* (http://www.coachingnetwork.org.uk/information-portal/articles/ViewArticle.asp?artId=82).

Clutterbuck, D. (2004) *Everyone Needs a Mentor: Fostering Talent in Your Organisation*. London: CIPD Publishing.

Cole, E.R. (2009) 'Intersectionality and research in psychology', *American Psychologist*, 64(3): 170–80.

Collins, A., Lewis, I., Stracke, E. and Vanderheide, R. (2014) 'Talking career across disciplines: peer group mentoring for women academics', *International Journal of Evidence Based Coaching and Mentoring*, 12(1): 92–108.

Cotton, R.D., Shen, Y. and Livne-Tarandach, R. (2011) 'On becoming extraordinary: the content and structure of the developmental networks of major league baseball hall of famers', *Academy of Management Journal*, 54(1): 15–46.

Creswell, J.W. (2012) *Educational Research: Planning, Conducting, and Evaluating Quantitative and Qualitative Research*. Boston: Pearson Education.

Crisp, G. and Cruz, I. (2009) 'Mentoring college students: a critical review of the literature between 1990 and 2007', *Research in Higher Education*, 50(6): 525–45.

Davis, D.J., Chaney, C., Edwards, L., Thompson-Rogers, G.K. and Gines, K.T. (2012) 'Academe as extreme sport: black women, faculty development, and networking', *Negro Educational Review*, 62/63(1–4): 167–87.

De Four-Babb, J., Pegg, J. and Beck, M. (2015) 'Reducing intellectual poverty of outsiders within academic spaces through informal peer mentorship', *Mentoring and Tutoring: Partnership in Learning*, 23(1): 76–93.

Eby, L.T. and Allen, T.D. (2002) 'Further investigation of protégés' negative mentoring experiences patterns and outcomes', *Group and Organization Management*, 27(4): 456–79.

Eby, L.T., Allen, T.D., Evans, S.C., Ng, T. and DuBois, D.L. (2008) 'Does mentoring matter? A multidisciplinary meta-analysis comparing mentored and non-mentored individuals', *Journal of Vocational Behavior*, 72(2): 254–67.

Esnard, T., Cobb-Roberts, D., Agosto, V., Karanxha, Z., Beck, M., Wu, K. and Unterreiner, A. (2015) 'Productive tensions in a cross-cultural peer mentoring women's network: a social capital perspective', *Mentoring and Tutoring: Partnership in Learning*, 23(1): 19–36.

Ferro, A., DeWit, D., Wells, S., Speechley, K.N. and Lipman, E. (2013) 'An evaluation of the measurement properties of the Mentor Self-Efficacy Scale among participants in Big Brothers Big Sisters of Canada community mentoring programs', *International Journal of Evidence Based Coaching and Mentoring*, 11(1): 146–60.

Flavian, H. and Kass, E. (2015) 'Giving students a voice: perceptions of the pedagogical advisory role in a teacher training program', *Mentoring and Tutoring: Partnership in Learning*, 23(1): 37–53.

Gentry, W.A., Weber, T.J. and Sadri, G. (2008) 'Examining career-related mentoring and managerial performance across cultures: a multilevel analysis', *Journal of Vocational Behavior*, 72(2): 241–53.

Gershenfeld, S. (2014) 'A review of undergraduate mentoring programs', *Review of Educational Research*, 84(3): 365–91.

Ghosh, R. (2014) 'Antecedents of mentoring support: a meta-analysis of individual, relational, and structural or organizational factors', *Journal of Vocational Behavior*, 84(3): 367–84.

Goldman, K.D. and Schmalz, K.J. (2012) 'Adjunct teaching part-time professorial possibilities, provisions, and provisos', *Health Promotion Practice*, 13(3): 301–7.

Higgins, M., Dobrow, S.R. and Roloff, K.S. (2010) 'Optimism and the boundaryless career: the role of developmental relationships', *Journal of Organizational Behavior*, 31(5): 749–69.

Hoyt, J.E. (2012) 'Predicting the satisfaction and loyalty of adjunct faculty', *The Journal of Continuing Higher Education*, 60(3): 132–42.

Huizing, R.L. (2012) 'Mentoring together: a literature review of group mentoring', *Mentoring and Tutoring: Partnership in Learning*, 20(1): 27–55.

Ivey, P., Geber, H. and Nänni, I. (2013) 'An innovative South African approach to mentoring novice professionals in biodiversity management', *International Journal of Evidence Based Coaching and Mentoring*, 11(1): 85–111.

Jackson, K.F. (2009) 'Building cultural competence: a systematic evaluation of the effectiveness of culturally sensitive interventions with ethnic minority youth', *Children and Youth Services Review*, 31(11): 1192–8.

Jacobi, M. (1991) 'Mentoring and undergraduate academic success: a literature review', *Review of Educational Research*, 61(4): 505–32.

Janssen, S., Vuuren, M. and Jong, M.D. (2015) 'Informal mentoring at work: a review and suggestions for future research', *International Journal of Management Reviews*: doi: 10.1111/ijmr.12069.

Johns, R., McNamara, J. and Moses, Z. (2012) 'Marketing and branding implications of a corporate service program: the case of women's group mentoring', *International Journal of Evidence Based Coaching and Mentoring*, 10(1): 74–88.

Johnson-Bailey, J. and Cervero, R.M. (2002) 'Cross-cultural mentoring as a context for learning', *New Directions for Adult and Continuing Education*, 2002(96): 15–26.

Jones, J. (2012) 'An analysis of learning outcomes within formal mentoring relationships', *International Journal of Evidence Based Coaching and Mentoring*, 10(1): 57–73.

Jones, R. and Brown, D. (2011) 'The mentoring relationship as a complex adaptive system: finding a model for our experience', *Mentoring and Tutoring: Partnership in Learning*, 19(4): 401–18.

Jones, R. and Corner, J. (2012) 'Seeing the forest and the trees: a complex adaptive systems lens for mentoring', *Human Relations*, 65(3): 391–411.

Kammeyer-Mueller, J.D. and Judge, T.A. (2008) 'A quantitative review of mentoring research: test of a model', *Journal of Vocational Behavior*, 72(3): 269–83.

Kamvounias, P., McGrath-Champ, S. and Yip, J. (2008) '"Gifts" in mentoring: mentees' reflections on an academic development program', *International Journal for Academic Development*, 13(1): 17–25.

Kapadia, K., Coca, V. and Easton, J.Q. (2007) *Keeping New Teachers: A First Look at the Influences of Induction in the Chicago Public Schools*. Chicago: Consortium on Chicago School Research, University of Chicago.

Kochan, F. (2013) 'Analyzing the relationships between culture and mentoring', *Mentoring and Tutoring: Partnership in Learning*, 21(4): 412–30.

Kram, K.E. and Ragins, B.R. (2007) 'The landscape of mentoring in the 21st century', in B.R. Ragins and K.E. Kram (eds), *The Handbook of Mentoring at Work: Theory, Research and Practice*. Thousand Oaks: Sage, pp. 659–92.

Lakind, D., Atkins, M. and Eddy, J.M. (2015) 'Youth mentoring relationships in context: mentor perceptions of youth, environment, and the mentor role', *Children and Youth Services Review*, 53: 52–60.

Laukhuf, R.L. and Malone, T.A. (2015) 'Women entrepreneurs need mentors', *International Journal of Evidence Based Coaching and Mentoring*, 13(1): 70–86.

Long, J.S., McKenzie-Robblee, S., Schaefer, L., Steeves, P., Wnuk, S., Pinnegar, E. and Clandinin, D.J. (2012) 'Literature review on induction and mentoring related to early career teacher attrition and retention', *Mentoring and Tutoring: Partnership in Learning*, 20(1): 7–26.

Marshall, C. and Rossman, G.B. (2014) *Designing Qualitative Research*, 6th edn. Thousand Oaks: Sage.

McCormack, C. and West, D. (2006) 'Facilitated group mentoring develops key career competencies for university women: a case study', *Mentoring and Tutoring*, 14(4): 409–31.

Megginson, D. and Clutterbuck, D. (1995) *Mentoring in Action: A Practical Guide for Managers*. London: Kogan Page.

Mitchell, M.E., Eby, L.T. and Ragins, B.R. (2015) 'My mentor, my self: antecedents and outcomes of perceived similarity in mentoring relationships', *Journal of Vocational Behavior*: doi: 10.1016/j.jvb.2015.04.008.

Noe, R.A., Greenberger, D.B. and Wang, S. (2002) 'Mentoring: what we know and where we might go', *Research in Personnel and Human Resources Management*, 21, 129–74.

Ragins, B.R. (2011) 'Relational mentoring: a positive approach to mentoring at work', in K.S. Cameron and G.M. Spreitzer (eds), *The Oxford Handbook of Positive Organizational Scholarship*. New York: Oxford University Press, pp. 519–36.

Ragins, B.R., Townsend, B. and Mattis, M. (1998) 'Gender gap in the executive suite: CEOs and female executives report on breaking the glass ceiling', *The Academy of Management Executive*, 12(1): 28–42.

Ragins, B.R. and Verbos, A.K. (2007) 'Positive relationships in action: relational mentoring and mentoring schemas in the workplace', in J.E. Dutton and B.R. Ragins (eds), *Positive Relationships at Work: Building a Theoretical and Research Foundation*. Mahwah: Lawrence Erlbaum, pp. 91–116.

Reeves, R.B. (2015) 'What is cross-cultural mentoring? An integrative literature review and discussion of the term cross-cultural mentoring', *International Journal of Mentoring and Coaching*, XIII(1): 2–20.

Roszkowski, M.J. and Badmus, P.F. (2014) 'Mentee's interest in becoming a peer mentor as a function of perceived quality of the mentorship experience', *International Journal of Evidence Based Coaching and Mentoring*, 12(1): 123–37.

Ruru, D., Sanga, K., Walker, K. and Ralph, E. (2013) 'Adapting mentorship across the professions: a Fijian view', *International Journal of Evidence Based Coaching and Mentoring*, 11(2): 70–92.

Sempowicz, T. and Hudson, P. (2012) 'Mentoring pre-service teachers' reflective practices towards producing teaching outcomes', *International Journal of Evidence Based Coaching and Mentoring*, 10(2): 52–64.

Shen, Y. (2010) *Developmental Networks of Expatriates: The Antecedents, Structure, and Outcomes*. Boston: Working Dissertation, Boston University.

Singh, R., Ragins, B.R. and Tharenou, P. (2009a) 'What matters most? The relative role of mentoring and career capital in career success', *Journal of Vocational Behavior*, 75(1): 56–67.

Singh, R., Ragins, B.R. and Tharenou, P. (2009b) 'Who gets a mentor? A longitudinal assessment of the rising star hypothesis', *Journal of Vocational Behavior*, 74(1): 11–17.

Terrion, J.L. and Leonard, D. (2007) 'A taxonomy of the characteristics of student peer mentors in higher education: findings from a literature review', *Mentoring and Tutoring*, 15(2): 149–64.

Underhill, C.M. (2006) 'The effectiveness of mentoring programs in corporate settings: a meta-analytical review of the literature', *Journal of Vocational Behavior*, 68(2): 292–307.

Walkington, J., Vanderheide, R. and Hughes, R. (2008) 'Empowering university women through a group mentoring relationship', *The International Journal of Mentoring and Coaching [E]*, 4(1): 83–93.

Wasburn, M.H. (2007) 'Mentoring women faculty: an instrumental case study of strategic collaboration', *Mentoring and Tutoring*, 15(1): 57–72.

Waterman, S. and He, Y. (2011) 'Effects of mentoring programs on new teacher retention: a literature review', *Mentoring and Tutoring: Partnership in Learning*, 19(2): 139–56.

Wolfinger, N.H., Mason, M.A. and Goulden, M. (2009) 'Stay in the game: gender, family formation and alternative trajectories in the academic life course', *Social Forces*, 87(3): 1591–621.

Zambrana, R.E., Ray, R., Espino, M.M., Castro, C., Cohen, B.D. and Eliason, J. (2015) '"Don't leave us behind": the importance of mentoring for underrepresented minority faculty', *American Educational Research Journal*, 52(1): 40–72.

A Research Analysis of the Underpinnings, Practice, and Quality of Mentoring Programs and Relationships

Nora Dominguez

INTRODUCTION

Organizations around the globe, particularly those in the United States, are experiencing an increase in the complexity of business and organizational processes and procedures. They are at great risk of losing key intellectual capital, competitive advantages, and effectiveness due to massive retirement waves, high turnover rates, and attrition of the younger workforce (Marquardt, 1995; Pink, 2005). Many corporations, businesses, governmental, health, educational, military, educational, and service-focused non-profit organizations implemented mentoring programs in response to these challenges. Such programs prove to be effective strategies for increasing personnel retention and satisfaction, accelerating the development of leadership, and reducing the learning curve in response to a more demanding, competitive, and global market place (Hegstad, 1999; Jossi, 1997; Murray, 2001).

The increasing popularity and proliferation of mentoring programs in the workplace and academic settings 'makes imperative the understanding of the several issues that should be taken into consideration when designing and executing formal mentoring programs' (Allen et al., 2009). One of the ways to understand these issues is to delve into the purposes and foundations of mentoring, the most effective practices employed, the benefits and values, and the new directions in the field. The purpose of this chapter is to provide this foundational information from a review of the literature examining the origins and foundations of mentoring, mentoring practices, outcomes and value, and possibilities for its future applications.

The chapter begins with an explanation of the methodology used to engage in this search and analysis. This is followed by an overview of the origins of mentoring, definitional issues, and a summary about theoretical underpinnings of the field. The next part of the changer focuses upon the practice of mentoring. The final part of the chapter focuses upon issues of quality in mentoring and the problems and possible solutions in the literature about how to ensure that mentoring endeavors set and met high standards.

METHODOLOGY

In this study, the researcher used grounded theory and qualitative research synthesis methodologies to inductively analyze data in an iterative process to discover concepts and generate explanations of phenomena (Creswell, 1998; Glaser and Strauss, 1967; Strauss and Corbin, 1998). The researcher examined aggregated data from 588 articles in adult mentoring and 500 books in a search for a general overview of the literature. After achieving a saturation point determined by the familiarity with authors and publications, 25 books and 80 qualitative studies were selected based on the following criteria: (i) seminal work: the publication is considered by others as seminal work in the field; (ii) authority: the author has more than a single publication on the topic; (iii) most cited: the publication has been quoted by others; (iv) date of publication: most recent work has been included. Qualitative research synthesis methodologies were used to summarize this large body of information, aimed at making sense of diverse findings of multiple studies and present a cumulative picture of the state of knowledge for both theory development and practice (Cooper, 2010; DeWitt-Brinks, 1992).

HISTORICAL, DEFINITIONAL, AND THEORETICAL ORIGINS OF MENTORING

An historical account is essential in order to identify patterns in the evolution of an emerging field; therefore, a deep understanding of the mentoring phenomena requires the analysis of its origins and evolution. This section deals with this issue from an historical, definitional, and theoretical perspective. It begins with a description of the history of mentoring followed by issues related to its definition. The section concludes with a presentation of the theoretical underpinnings of mentoring.

Historical overview of mentoring

The review of the selected literature showed very little research into historical accounts of mentoring. Most studies merely alluded to Homer's tale, *The Odyssey*, often citing this play as the original source of the field, in which Mentor, Odysseus's best friend, is entrusted with the education and guidance of his son Telemachus. This story provides us with examples to identify mentoring relationships through the role of Athena's role, goddess of wisdom, who impersonates *Mentor* and exhibits behaviors such as tutoring, role modeling, advising, and inspiring. However, mentoring senior-junior pairs existed in prior eras and mentoring behaviors can be recognized in ancient cultures' literary works such as those displayed by patriarchal figures exhibiting discipleship functions (Carruthers, 1993).

From the earliest cultures to the Medieval Age and the Renaissance, mentoring represented the formal system for the education among royal classes in monarchical regimes, demonstrated by the relationships between *Magistrates* and their young *Princes*. The relationships between Aristotle and Alexander the Great or Merlyn and King Arthur, offer historic examples of such relationships. Moreover, the roles of *Maecenas* and *Patrons* contributed to the development of the arts and sciences, not only by providing protection and financial assistance, but by advising and counseling, and becoming confidants to their protégés. Historic instances of such relationships include Hayden and Beethoven, Freud and Jung, and Gertrude Stein and Ernest Hemingway, etc. (Lee, 2010).

Several accounts of the word *mentor* also appeared in epistolary collections aimed at providing moral and spiritual advice to a youthful audience (Lee, 2010); however, according to Grassinger et al. (2010), the popularity of the term is credited to the publication of Fénelon's work, *Les Aventures de Telemaque*, in 1699, when the word mentor came into general use in France and England as a common noun, being used to describe a wise, kind, selfless, caring, and trusted advisor, while representing a 'powerful and emotional interaction between an older and a younger person' in which the elder imparted to the younger experience, knowledge, and expertise (Merriam, 1983: 163).

This type of relationship is known as the apprenticeship model. Many articles point to the apprenticeship model as antecedent of the modern concept of mentoring (Bolton, 1980; Jones and Vincent, 2010; Mullen, 2000; Ragins and McFarlin, 1990; Wildman et al., 1992). In the pre-industrial era, apprenticeship relationships also mirrored the one between mentor and protégé; these relationships were conceived as a cultural and communal institution for the transmission of knowledge, competence, and expertise (Snell, 1996). In this sense, masters and mentors transmitted the established canon through lessons, stories, and example (Gray and Gray, 1986). The apprentice learned tasks, processes, and skills from the master; the master imparted an understanding of the purposes, values, and attitudes for a better use of those skills, while also becoming a role model for the protégé. The novice often watched the expert's work and used the same process in his/her own work, a concept now known as 'shadowing' (Charland, 2005).

Apprenticeship relations are also considered the precursors of employer-employee relationships in the industrial society, while the medieval concepts of the tutor (guard, custodian, defender), the preceptor (teacher, tutor), and monitor (in-school advisor, admonisher) might be considered the transitional figures of mentors into our modern scholarly system. Clutterbuck and Lane (2004) mention the medieval concept of apprenticeship, its relationship with mentoring, the elitist process of selecting protégés, and the apprenticeship model in which the mentor acts as master. In addition, they make reference to the linguistic and syntactic origin of the word *mentor* to define a mentor as one who makes another think and a mentee as someone who is instigated to think.

Formal academic training and highly impersonal relationships between teachers and students, trainers and trainees, and employers and employees, gradually replaced the traditional apprenticeship model – the personalized instruction of the novice until mastery is achieved and the long-term and nurturing relationship between master and apprentice. The essence of mentoring, the bonding of relationship, the individualized development, and the identity shared by mentor and protégé were displaced by standardized education ruled by institutional goals (Jacobi, 1991; Noller, 1982).

Stone (2007) makes a brief account of the apprenticeship model through the ages and states that it has been replaced with vocational training and discusses the role of mentors in organizations. Johnson describes the faculty-student relationship as 'a useful and career-enhancing academic apprenticeship' (2007b: 194), while Mullen (2000) refers to the model as a hierarchical arrangement of mentoring that historically occurred in conjunction with formal schooling. Campbell (2007) recommends the combination of a modified apprenticeship model that incorporates vertical integration of research teams as *best practices* for student-faculty mentoring programs; however, it does not provide data to validate the effectiveness of this model.

In the twentieth century, formal mentoring approaches seemed to resurface in 1931 when 'The Jewel Tea Company paired each MBA who entered the firm with a senior manager during the newcomer's early-career period' (Douglas, 1997: 75). Soon after, the work of Daniel J. Levinson, *The Seasons of a Man's Life* (1978), was written. His study of the mentoring relationships of 40 men demonstrated the importance of a mentor in the lives and professional careers of young adults, which fostered a resurgence of interest in mentoring. Levinson defined a good mentor as someone who serves as a guide, teacher, and sponsor in the transition of a young man into the adult world. Despite this important role, Levinson emphasized that the limited quantity and poor quality of mentoring relationships in educational institutions and work organizations as an impediment to constructive social change. After Levinson's study, a multitude of studies of formal and informal mentoring relations in academic and workplace settings were developed, ushering in the modern era of mentoring.

This investigation into the historical foundations of mentoring indicate that there is a lack of well-developed historical accounts in the empirical research related to this important topic (Ragins and McFarlin, 1990). Consequently, further analysis of mentoring antecedents is recommended as a way to increase our understanding of the initiation of mentoring and its relation with modern mentoring theories, lessons learned, and transference to improve formal mentoring programs.

Mentoring definitions

Most scholars agree that there is no single, accepted definition of mentoring. Additionally, multiple scholars have claimed that the failure to provide an operational definition of mentoring continues to prevent the evolution of mentoring research (Crosby, 1999; Jacobi, 1991; Merriam, 1983). Early warnings resulted in a proliferation of mentoring definitions; however, problems arise in comparing studies when scholars focus on different aspects of the mentoring relationship, various degrees of psychosocial versus career support offered, and/or the specific functions/activities provided by mentors (Eby et al., 2007).

Despite these issues, there are common elements, which are inherent in the mentoring processes that help to define it. Most authors agree that mentoring is a *relationship*, implying a degree of emotional or intellectual connection and involvement. This particular relationship is *developmental* – established for the growth, learning, and/or advancement of the mentee; *reciprocal* – for the benefit of each of parties, and *dynamic* – constantly changing and progressing; it involves a *process* to achieve positive outcomes – emotional or instrumental purposes of the relationship; and engagement in mentoring *activities or functions* are the means to achieve the desired outcomes (Eby et al., 2007; Johnson et al., 2007; Spencer, 2007).

Although there appear to be commonalities in mentoring definitions, some researchers ponder the risks of either defining or not defining the mentoring construct in empirical studies (Johnson et al., 2007; Scandura and Pellegrini, 2007; Spencer, 2007). Johnson et al. (2007) emphasize that not providing a definition may result in studying different phenomena in a single study, while over-defining limits the possibility of discovering new elements in the research. Therefore, he recommends that researchers clarify the type of the relationship they are studying, but limiting the use of too ambiguous or highly constrained definitions that could prevent the generalization of studies (Johnson, 2007b).

Because of the proliferation of mentoring definitions, many contemporary authors concur that major defining problems appear when the definition does not provide enough elements to differentiate mentoring from other developmental relationships (Johnson et al., 2007). Kram (1985) proposes a model to distinguish developmental relationships in the workplace by evaluating the degree of career support versus the degree of psychosocial support provided. Lankau et al. (2006)

add to this schema in the differentiation of developmental relationships in the workplace based on the instrumental or relational purposes of the learning context and their ability to develop cognitive capital, relational capital, leadership development, or diversity competence. Eby et al. (2007) differentiate developmental relationships based on the participants in the relationship. In their model, they analyze relationships among mentor-protégé, role model-observer, supervisor-subordinate, and coach-client in the workplace; and, teacher-student, and advisor-advisee in academic settings. They segregate these interpersonal relationships in terms of: (i) the primary scope of influence; (ii) the degree of mutuality; (iii) the formality or informality of the relationship; (iv) the relational closeness; (v) the required interaction; and (vi) the power distance among participants.

Clutterbuck (2007) differentiates the American from the European perspective of mentoring, asserting that the European model is developmental and non-directive in nature, while the American sponsorship functions add a directedness component. He also distinguishes mentoring from coaching in terms of the focus on performance or career goals. He proposes a cross-matrix to map these differences, generating four types of developmental relationships in the workplace: (i) sponsorship mentoring (directive-career oriented); (ii) developmental mentoring (non-directive-career oriented); (iii) executive/developmental coaching (non-directive-performance oriented); and (iv) traditional coaching (directive-performance oriented). Clutterbuck (2007) also cautions about the risks of using the number of functions or activities provided in a mentoring relationship as the metric for relationship quality, questioning the effectiveness of narrow research perspectives that have overvalued the efficacy of mentoring functions. The variation in mentoring definitions may flow from foundational differences in the theoretical framework used for its conceptualization, purposes, and proposed outcomes (Kochan, 2013). We now turn to these frameworks to help clarify the issues involved.

Theoretical frameworks of mentoring

Dominguez and Hager (2013) initiated a study of theoretical frameworks of mentoring by classifying them in three categories: learning, developmental, and social. This section builds upon this work and examines the manner in which these theories have been used as a foundation for the development of mentoring programs and relationships and practices.

Learning theories

Learning theories have been used to explain mentoring relationships as a phenomenon and/or to enhance parts of the mentoring process (Allen et al., 2003; Clutterbuck, 1998; Lankau and Scandura, 2002; Zachary and Daloz, 2000). One of these, adult learning theory, has made a unique contribution to our understanding of the learning process of adults in mentoring relationships. From this theory, we know that the adult learner is self-directed, has a great deal of past experiences to draw upon for learning, learns new social roles from role models, approaches learning with a purpose in mind, and has internal motivators for learning (Marquardt and Waddill, 2004; Merriam, 2001).

Mentoring adults is a learner-focused process in that adults tend to be proactive in defining what their goals in the mentoring relationship are and can largely carry out tasks and assignments on their own. Mentors provide support and guidance and can share their experiences with the mentee to help them understand how to navigate their organizational/social role, locate resources, become aware of their own learning styles, and understand their development over time (Zachary and Daloz, 2000). Zachary and Fischler (2009) claim that our knowledge about adult learning has provided a shift in the mentoring paradigm from the traditional authority figure of the mentor to a facilitator role where both mentor and mentee engage in a learning process and gain greater knowledge and understanding

Of particular importance in adult learning theory is the concept of *self-directed learning*. Ideally, a primary goal for mentors is to assist and encourage learners in such a way that they will become confident in taking control of their own learning. Mentors may start with showing mentees organizational processes step-by-step, but eventually they want their mentees to be able to work autonomously, set personal learning objectives, develop strategies, find resources, and evaluate their own learning. While the responsibility is shared in the mentoring relationship, accepting ownership and accountability provides a means for the development of autonomy, which is essential to advancing in the organization and in developing the mentee personally and professionally in a continuous process of acquiring mastery and becoming a life-long learner (Daloz, 1999).

Behaviorist theories claim that repetition and reinforcement affect learning behavior. In the workplace, the success of a mentoring relationship is usually measured by changes in salary, promotions, or new competencies acquired. In academic settings, positive outcomes of mentoring relationships result in higher GPAs, retention and graduation rates of students, as well as production and tenure achievement for faculty members. In this perspective, mentors model desired behaviors and competencies providing constructive feedback and rewarding productive performance (pointing out/praising successes and correcting/discussing failures/deficiencies).

Cognitivist theories place emphasis on brain and memory functions. The way the brain works to make sense of the inputs it receives and translates them into understandable knowledge is important to learning, and how the brain stores information and past experiences aids in determining future behavior. This theory suggests that mentors must adapt their practice based on the mentee's learning preferences. Mentors using this theoretical framework engage in discussing past experiences with mentees and guide them to make connections between actions that produced desired results and those that did not, while establishing goals that are suitable to the mentee's developmental stage.

Constructivist theories establish that we create knowledge from our experiences and then base our actions on that knowledge. Learning occurs when we compare our experiences of the world to our past knowledge base and re-evaluate/reconstruct our knowledge as a consequence. Mentoring encourages reflective practice (critical reflection) in order to point out/understand successes and failures so that mentees can learn from past experiences, develop self-awareness, and alter their behavior in the future.

Transformative learning is 'the process of affecting change in a frame of reference' (Mezirow, 1997: 5). Specifically, transformative learning theory (TLT) assumes that adults have developed through their life experiences, frames of reference and points of view. TLT agrees that most adults' frames of reference have been uncritically acquired as conditioned responses and as the result of cultural assimilation. According to Mezirow (1997), transformative learning occurs when adults critically explore their assumptions by engaging in task-oriented problem solving (objective reframing) or self-reflection to assess their own ideas and beliefs (subjective reframing) that leads to the growth in changes in points of view (meaning schemes transformations), and/or a transformation of a habit of mind (perspective transformation, a world view shift). In mentoring relationships, the process of critical reflection and dialogue are assumed to be transformational in nature (Clutterbuck and Lane, 2004; Daloz, 1999; Mullen and Noe, 1999), whether it is through the engagement in a mutual process to cope with disorienting dilemmas or throughout the accumulation of changing schemes – a product of the interaction of mentors and mentees.

Social learning theory (also called social cognitive theory) (Bandura, 1977) explains how people learn through modeling/imitation and provides insights into the role modeling functions of mentors. Through continuous interaction, a mentor sets behaviors for newcomers into the organizational life. In this socialization process, the mentee defines the social context to establish productive and rewarding interactions by adopting attitudes accepted in the system. A mentor models not only conventional behaviors, but also desirable competencies and skills in an acculturation process. 'It is also a non-conscious process when the mentor may be unaware of setting an example for the protégé, and the protégé may be unaware of tacit knowledge gained from the mentorship' (Chao, 2007: 183). Social learning also explains the identification process between mentor and mentee, essential for building a relationship. When affinity is discovered or created, the mentoring pair or group has a ground base for professional socialization, the acquisition of competences, and appropriate professional behaviors in a learning partnership.

Vygotsky's *theory of proximal development* provides the mentors with a set of strategies to promote mentees' learning. Through a scaffolding process, mentors assign tasks, provide information, motivate, give feedback, challenge, and offer confirmation to their mentees in a process to develop the mentee's identity, competencies, confidence, and self-efficacy (Bearman et al., 2007: 183). 'Through acceptance and confirmation from the mentor, the protégé feels free to experiment with new behaviors and take risks in achieving his or her goals' (Ramaswami and Dreher, 2007: 219). As an extension of the scaffolding process, theory of cognitive apprenticeship was mentioned as an analogy to mentoring relationships among faculty and students (Johnson, 2007a), but none of the authors provided a description of the theory and/or its relationship with or to adult mentoring.

Developmental theories

One of the most cited developmental theories is Levinson's stages model, also known as *career stage* or *life stage theory*. Based on Freud, Jung, and Erikson's developmental theories, Levinson (1978) defines two key periods in men's life cycle: a stable period in which a person makes important decisions in life and a transitional period in which a person changes life commitments and beliefs. Through a succession of stable and transitional periods, a male travels across defined life structural, not biological, stages into adulthood.

Subsequent work on mentoring has been built on Levinson's theory. Mentoring has been seen as the practical means to support people in career and adulthood transitions. Kram's (1983) theory of mentoring phases takes into account Levinson's career stages to define the role of mentors and protégés. For Kram, the variations in mentoring relationships are related to the career stage and the developmental tasks needed at each stage: 'While the primary functions of each type of relationship do not change, the content of what is discussed and how that content is shared differs at successive career stages' (1983: 143). Kram concludes that organizations should 'encourage contact among individuals who have the potential to meet important relationship [and professional] needs at a particular career stage' (1983: 180).

Constructive developmental theory (Kegan, 1982, 1994; Kegan and Lahey, 2001) is a model of adult development based on the idea that human beings naturally progress over a lifetime through five stages. The first two stages comprise childhood and adolescence, while stage three, the socialized mind–dependence – marks the transition into adulthood in which individuals recognize others' points of view and are able to empathize with others, but avoid conflict for fear of losing their esteem. Stage four, the self-authoring mind–independence – marks the development of value systems, views about the world, sense of responsibility, self-esteem, and ownership in constructing one's own life. In stage five, the self-transforming mind–interdependence – individuals are able to delineate the limits of their own value systems, are able to deal with ambiguities and perceive polarities, are more concerned with larger systems, and have developed resilience and humility to move beyond ego. Each stage demands different competencies from the mentor and the development of different activities.

Social theories

Socialization theories have focused on understanding the role of mentors as key agents in providing information and role modeling behaviors to facilitate a protégé's acculturation and assimilation into the new environment (Allen et al., 1999; Chao, 2007; Ostroff and Kozlowski, 1993), providing positive mentoring outcomes, such as career advancement and satisfaction in the workplace. These outcomes are the result of an increased sense of belonging to the organization, a better understanding of tacit and implicit organizational rules and practices, connectedness, less stress, and commitment (Clutterbuck and Megginson, 1999; Johnson, 2002, 2007a; Johnson and Ridley, 2008; Kram, 1983; Kram and Hall, 1989). However, successful organizational socialization depends on the protégés 'choices of role models and the quality of observations and interactions with these models' (Chao, 2007: 184), as well as individual socialization needs (Scandura and Prellegrini, 2007).

The socialization process has also been studied from the perspectives of gender, sexual orientation, and race in organizations. Most research in this area has focused on diversity issues and stereotypes of roles that constitute a barrier for minorities to advance into the organizational culture. Despite the number of articles published in this area, most researchers acknowledge the need for further studies in regards to the influence of mentors in dealing with and alleviating diversity issues (Clutterbuck, 2000; Johnson, 2002; Ragins, 1997).

Human and social capital theories explain the dialectic process of how a mentor's human capital contributes to the reproduction of the human capital variables of their mentees (Ramaswami and Dreher, 2007; Stone, 2004; Zachary, 2005). According to Ramaswami and Dreher, human capital 'deals with the acquisition of knowledge, skills, and abilities that ultimately enhance the protégé's job performance' (2007: 215). Human capital is therefore generated in mentoring relations through multiple activities or functions, such as providing challenging assignments, sponsorship, exposure and visibility; coaching, protection, and friendship. Interactions between mentors and mentees create individual cognitive and affective responses, which are translated into behavioral responses that subsequently produce individual and organizational outcomes.

Social exchange theories describe cost-benefit as a motivator to participate in a mentoring relationship. In general, this theory describes a reciprocity process between members of an organization and the organization itself. If the individual perceives support to his/her own development of skills, feels valued by the organization, and foresees career opportunities, then the individual will effectively increase performance, develop loyalty, and remain committed to the achievement of organizational goals (Dougherty et al., 2007). Additionally, participants will enter into relationships in which rewards will outweigh the costs; therefore, social exchange has also been used to explain the natural process of the informal mentoring relationship (Ragins and Scandura, 1999).

Leader-member exchange theory explains how leaders use their position power and access to organizational resources as a transactional strategy to achieve organizational results (Scandura and Schriesheim, 1994). Many researchers question the true nature of mentoring relationships among supervisor-subordinate members due to the contractual and positional aspects of the relationship. However, from the perspective of *Leader-Member Exchange* theory, such relationships, if based on trust, mutual respect, and support can still be described as mentoring relationships (Godshalk and Sosik, 2007).

Social network theory – multiple research articles have focused on investigating the nature, amount, and quality of support provided by mentors (Young and Perrewe, 2000), leading to the idea that a single mentor might not be able to satisfy all developmental needs of a protégé and that protégés might choose to acquire information and model their behaviors from multiple sources (Chao, 2007; Ragins and Kram, 2007). Therefore, Kram (1983) suggested the establishment of a constellation of mentoring relationships, and more recently, has introduced the idea of developmental mentoring networks (Higgins and Kram, 2001). Higgins and Kram (2001) define a developmental network as:

> The set of people a protégé names as taking an active interest in and action to advance the protégé's career by providing developmental assistance ... [through] two types of support: (1) career support, such as exposure and visibility, sponsorship, and protection, and (2) psychosocial support, such as friendship, counseling, acceptance, and confirmation, and sharing beyond work.
> (Higgins and Kram, 2001: 268)

According to Higgins and Kram (2001), the greater the diversity of the network in terms of range (number of different social systems), density (connectedness of members of the network), and the relationship strength (measured by the frequency of communication and level of emotional engagement), the greater the personal learning, the organizational commitment, and work satisfaction. These authors suggest developing empirical research projects to validate their propositions with diverse populations, a variety of settings, and implications for the design of formal mentoring programs.

Applying theory to practice

Godshalk and Sosik (2007) state 'theoretical frameworks provide pathways for researchers to build upon knowledge that can be advanced in a verifiable manner. They are not just theories, but rather blueprints for what is currently known about relationships among constructs that define a field' (2007: 168). In this section, several frameworks for mentoring research have been examined, identifying the most frequent concepts to explain adult mentoring. It is hoped that it will contribute to the overall mentoring theory by providing the theoretical foundation for future empirical work to extend our understanding of new forms of mentoring relationships, while taking into account the context and characteristics of participants and also enhance individual and group capacity to develop and implement mentoring programs.

PRACTICE OF MENTORING

The practice of mentoring is related to the theoretical model used, which is, in turn, related to the definition of mentoring that guides the endeavor and those involved in it. The success of mentoring relationships is contingent on a number of factors that shape their nature, purpose, and outcomes. This section examines these factors. It examines the functions and competencies of mentoring and the benefits and outcomes, as studied and identified in the literature.

Mentoring functions

The study of mentoring functions is attributed to the seminal work of Kram (1983), who summarized the multiple activities performed by mentors in two broad categories: career functions and psychosocial functions. This seminal work has produced a great interest among the mentoring community of researchers. For Kram (1983, 1985), career or vocational functions include those aspects of the relationship that enhance career advancement, such as providing information, challenging assignments, exposure, visibility, and protection. Psychosocial functions are those aspects that enhance a sense of competence, identity, and effectiveness in a professional role, such as emotional support, counseling, confirmation, acceptance, and friendship. Multiple empirical studies have supported these functions (Noe, 1988; Ragins and McFarlin, 1990).

Further research has proposed minor changes and/or additions to Kram's model; for example, Scandura (1992) proposed role modeling as a separate function. Because it involves behaviors that affect both career and psychosocial functions, it does not require action or active involvement of the mentor, but rather an active observation of the protégé to identify and emulate valued behaviors in the system – mainly identification with the mentor's characteristics that are trusted, respected, and held in high regards. A mentor's influence entails displaying role model behaviors through exemplary personal achievements, character, and/or behavior, and which is meant to inspire stimulation and motivation for high performance (Godshalk and Sosik, 2007).

In an attempt to measure the influence of mentoring functions to benefits and outcomes, sometimes in particular populations, several scales have been developed (Dreher and Ash, 1990; Noe, 1988; Scandura and Ragins, 1993). These instruments have been validated mainly in protégés populations. Scandura and Pellegrini (2007) suggest the need for comparison and validation of the scales from mentor and mentee perspectives in emerging mentoring models, within positive and dysfunctional mentoring relationships, longitudinal research to evaluate the phenomena over time, and extension of the scales to include additional items and better operationalize different functions in multiple settings.

From the analysis of mentoring functions, it appears to be important to differentiate the types of skills that are actually developed as a result of the interaction between the mentor-mentee and the relative importance of these skills across disciplines. A deeper analysis of academic functions is suggested to better understand the role of mentors and the ways in which mentoring differentiates from other developmental relationships and functions in academic settings.

Due to the proliferation of studies and theoretical frameworks drawing conclusions from defined mentoring functions, it is important to remember Clutterbuck's (2007) caution about the risks of equating the quantity of mentoring functions with the quality of the relationship. He recommends the development of specific measurements to evaluate the quality of the relationship as a predictor of the efficacy and effectiveness of mentoring relationships.

Mentoring competencies

The topic of mentoring competencies has not been extensively explored in empirical studies; most of the data available comes from books, and validation of assertions is scarce. This has resulted in a long list of mentor characteristics that can be categorized in four large areas of competencies: instrumental behaviors, relational behaviors, personal characteristics, and negative characteristic. Instrumental behaviors include competencies such as professional and communication skills, the ability to assign challenging activities, being open to learning and having business and strategic focus, and being direct, realistic, practical, and knowledgeable.

Relational behaviors include emotional and psychosocial characteristics, such as being positive, respectful, supportive, honest, and caring. Among personal characteristics, being successful, experienced, powerful, and serving as a positive role model were the most common attributes mentioned.

In the area of negative characteristics, being demanding, distant, stressed, inconsistent, and vindictive were some of the attributes found in the literature, just to mention a few. These long lists of positive and negative characteristics have not led to a structured, evidence-based framework of mentoring competencies, except for the few following attempts.

According to Darwin (2004), women, peers, and mentors close to the protégés are frequently described as nurturing mentors, while men in management positions are described by their mentees as competent. In addition, he points out that even mentors with volatile characteristics are a source of learning for mature protégés who are able to observe the flaws in their mentors and avoid those behaviors. Nurturing, authentic, and approachable mentors better satisfy psychosocial needs, whether inspirational or volatile. Hard-working mentors are more suitable to satisfy instrumental needs of their protégés.

Clutterbuck (2004a) defines competence as the ability to perform a task in a consistent manner, emphasizing the need for situational mentors – those who are able to respond to the mentees' needs. He also identifies the need for mentors to develop general competences, including: (i) the ability to establish rapport; (ii) define, plan, take action, and collaborate with the mentee in achieving goals; (iii) sustain commitments, provide challenge, help the mentee to become autonomous, and cope with failure; and (iv) come to closure, redefine the relationship, and move on. Clutterbuck (2004a) provides a model of five pairs of behavioral competences for mentors to include: (i) self-awareness – behavioral awareness; (ii) communicating – conceptualizing; (iii) sense of proportion/ humor – business and professional savvy; (iv) interest in developing others – committed to own learning; and (v) goal clarity – relationship management.

Mentees' competences have been less studied because there is a perception that protégés engage in a mentoring relationship precisely to develop their own competences. However, under the assumption that mentoring relationships succeed when both parties actively contribute to their development, Clutterbuck (2004b) suggests the need of basic abilities to establish rapport and a minimum of communication skills in the mentee to initiate a mentoring relationship, also providing five pairs of desirable mentee competencies: (i) articulating/questioning – listening; (ii) open minded – reflecting; (iii) challenge – be challenged; and (iv) focused/proactive – openness and honesty. The only general agreement across the literature is the need for both mentor and mentees to be able to offer and receive feedback, along with listening and communication skills (Finkelstein et al., 2003; Johnson, 2007a; Mullen, 2005). Lately, Searby (2014) has proposed a framework to evaluate the protégé's mentoring mindset, defined as the visible 'attitudes, behaviors, and competencies that enable the protégé to embrace the mentoring process and maximize the benefits of the mentoring relationship' (2014: 265). For this researcher, a protégé who shows proactive behaviors, learning and goal orientations, and relational and reflective attitudes, possesses a mentoring mindset.

Mentoring benefits and outcomes

Kram (1983) situated mentoring within a theoretical framework and this helped to stimulate countless studies and research into causes and effects of mentoring. She outlined the two basic branches of mentoring in workplace settings: career and psychosocial. The two have different roots and outcomes, with career predicting success in compensation and advancement, and psychosocial leading to increased satisfaction with the mentor-mentee relationships. These outcomes have been tested profusely, being the only area of adult mentoring research where a quantitative meta-analysis study has been performed (Allen et al., 2009).

The meta-analysis of Allen et al. (2004) studied protégés' objective (compensation) and subjective career outcomes (career satisfaction, expectations of advancement, career commitment, job satisfaction, and intention to stay). Their research analyzed 43 studies that compared outcomes across protégés and non-protégés and those that correlate mentor functions with protégé outcomes. They found support to general claims associated with the benefits of mentoring, with the caveat of a small effect associated with objective career outcomes.

Multiple studies, in addition to the 43 analyzed in Allen's meta-analysis, have focused not only on the positive career outcomes for the protégé, but also the psychosocial benefits of mentoring (Chao, 1997; Dreher and Ash, 1990; Fagenson, 1989; Kirchmeyer, 1998; Koberg et al., 1994), and less studied, the benefits for the mentor (Eby et al., 2010; Wanberg et al., 2007).

Despite all the evidence in favor of mentoring, researchers warn against making causal conclusions due to many methodological issues in existing studies. Among these are lack of consistency in the definition of the mentoring construct, lack of agreement in the conceptualization of formal versus informal mentoring, differences in the goals and objectives among programs, and differences among the phenomena in study, such as validation of behavioral, affective, and/or relational benefits (Lockwood, Evans and Eby, 2007). Longitudinal studies rather than retrospective studies, as well as those that focus on differentiating qualitative aspects of the mentoring relations, have been cited as strategies to alleviate these issues (Johnson, 2010).

Very little research has been performed regarding the benefits of mentoring for an organization (Richard et al., 2002; Seibert, 1999), and the existing research has heavily focused on subjective outcomes such as commitment and socialization, with a lower focus on objective outcomes such as productivity, performance, and return on investment.

However, there is a general perception of the positive benefits associated with mentoring that has resulted in the proliferation of formal mentoring programs in academic and workplace settings alike.

Of less interest to researchers has been the evaluation of negative outcomes in a mentoring relationship. Apparently, Merriam's (1983) assertion in regards to the biases in favor of the experiences is still prevalent as only eight studies were found addressing dysfunctional mentoring relationships. For Scandura and Pellegrini (2007), there are two different types of negative experiences: marginal mentoring relationships in which the negative experiences reduce the effectiveness of the relationship and dysfunctional relationships where the relationship is not beneficial for any of the participants. Dysfunctional relationships are likely to terminate, while marginal ones might continue (Ragins et al., 2000).

Potential problems leading to marginal or dysfunctional mentoring relationships are the lack of time and training of the mentor, personality and/or professional mismatch, lack of organizational support, and general incompatibility (Scandura and Pellegrini, 2007). Eby et al. (2010) identified a continuum of relational problems from low to high severity including superficial interactions, unmet expectations, jealousy, sabotage, betrayal, overdependence, and negative interactions. Negative outcomes that distress performance and work attitudes might deter a participant's career progress and have negative consequences for the organization.

The review of the literature on mentoring outcomes and benefits confirmed Kram's (2004) assertions that outcomes achieved in a mentoring relationship are highly dependent on factors such as the context, the purposes and objectives of establishing a relationship, the type and length of the relationship, and the values and competencies of the participants. This means that those developing and implementing such programs must be attentive to these features and processes. The lack of extensive research on this topic also points to the need for further exploration into this important topic.

ELEMENTS OF HIGH QUALITY MENTORING PRACTICES

The success of a mentoring program has been studied from theoretical perspectives, but evidence-based guidance is scarce (Miller, 2007). The following is an attempt to capture evidence-based elements of mentoring practice that research suggests fosters mentoring success. This section begins with a discussion of the issues related to developing and implementing high quality practices in mentoring. This is followed by a review.

Best-practice versus good practice

The term 'best practice' is a slippery one. There are many ways to approach defining the components of a 'best practice'. In general, the term refers to responsiveness, due diligence, and overall effectiveness. 'Best practice' defines a practice, process, or activity that has been shown through evaluation and research to be most effective in producing a desired outcome. Best practices promote specific actions (or ways of doing things) that will help individuals adhere to the standards of the organization. However, what may constitute a best practice for one program (e.g. mentoring young professionals) may not be relevant for another (e.g. mentoring undergraduate students). For this reason, practical definitions are provided for these terms before looking at more specific applications.

A standard, sometimes referred to as a 'best practice' or as a way of measuring 'best practice', in general is defined by a performance goal (Dean, 1990). Standards are overall goals or achievements that organizations strive to meet with the idea that adhering to these standards will help to further the mission or purpose of the organization. *Standards* can be based on previous research or successful practices that have been reproduced over time. *Competencies*, sometimes examined as part of 'best practice', refer to the knowledge, skills, and abilities that allow a person to perform a specific task or excel in a certain area. Individuals may need to display several concrete competencies in order to carry out the 'best practices' of their organization.

'Best practices', standards, and competencies can be seen in terms of an organizational hierarchy. A program's standards or overall goals can be achieved through the use of 'best practices'. In turn, 'best practices' can only be used if the individuals in the program have competencies that allow them to understand and carry out specific actions relevant to the 'best practices' (Roybal, 2001).

Brondyk and Searby (2013) have studied the complexity of defining 'best practices' in mentoring, acknowledging the need of 'evidence of effectiveness and generalizability in order for something to be considered a best practice' (2013: 196); however, 'the complexity of both the practice of mentoring and the term "best practices" make it difficult to draw broad conclusions on what is working well in mentoring' (2013: 197). Consequently, while the term 'best-practice' is common and highly used in the literature, there is still the assumption that those practices would carry equally if applied to different contexts and programs with differing purposes, processes, and goals, which has not been empirically demonstrated. Therefore, in this section, the concept of 'good practice' will be used to identify the measurable components of practice that include results substantiated by credible evidence to improve outcomes and achieve goals, identifying a general convergence in the literature on what standards and good practices are present in successful mentoring relationships and programs (Higgins and Kram, 2001; Mullen, 2009), including the standards defined by international organisms such as the International Mentoring

Association (IMA) and the International Standards for Mentoring Programmes in Employment (ISMPE) that lead to good practices.

ELEMENTS OF GOOD PRACTICES IN MENTORING

Mentoring good practices seem to unfold in two different areas: general project/program management topics such as the need for assessment, planning, implementation, and evaluation of the program, and the particular areas of mentoring relationships, including critical aspects such as matching processes and training of participants. An outline of the most common program management good practices follows.

Project and program management

In her work, Zachary (2005) emphasizes the need to create a mentoring culture and practice within organizations. Starting with an assessment of the organizational culture, measuring its readiness, opportunities, and support, Zachary suggests the identification of key people as critical in planning and implementing a mentoring schema. Grounded in the organizational infrastructure and aligning mentoring goals with the organizational ones, mentoring programs increase their chances to succeed. Across all stages of the mentoring program's life, accountability factors, that is, the process of setting goals, clarifying expectations, defining roles and responsibilities, monitoring progress, and measuring results through formative and summative processes of gathering feedback and communication of the value and visibility of the program across the organization, are the most acute factors for effectiveness and success.

For Mullen (2007), most successful mentoring programs exhibit one or more of the following characteristics: (i) high-potential pairings: protégés who are assigned to mentors are carefully selected on the basis of their likelihood of benefiting from the process and their potential to contribute to the organization; (ii) regulated relationships: mentorships are given guidelines (meeting frequency, certain subjects to cover) by an overseeing advisory figure; and (iii) evaluation: some form of assessment will be made by the organization to see if particular aims have been met.

Kochan (2002) identified three primary elements in developing and managing successful mentoring programs: (i) taking a systemic view; (ii) attending to organizational structures; and (iii) developing support systems. Strategies for taking a systemic view include being attentive to the context by examining and dealing with elements that might hinder and facilitate program success, connecting mentoring program goals to organizational goals, and addressing the individual needs of the mentoring pair of dyad. The element of attending to organizational structures emphasizes the need to include and involve others in continuous planning and assessment, preparing mentors and mentees for their roles and responsibilities, and providing appropriate financial and human resources. The last element in fostering program success, providing support systems, involves assuring that there is appropriate program coordination, guiding the pairing and functioning of mentoring relationships, and providing incentives and recognition for participation.

Sontag et al. (2007) propose a six-step process in launching a mentoring program: (i) the sponsor meeting; (ii) the implementation team planning sessions: omination and recruitment of mentors and mentees; (iii) interviews with mentors and mentees: a matching process based on goals and competences; (iv) mentor and mentee orientation and launch; (v) check points at two, four, and eight months; and (vi) program closure and evaluation (2007: 600–3).

Campbell (2007) suggests including mentoring functions as part of job descriptions and limiting the number of protégés assigned per mentor. In regards to the matching process, he suggests emulating naturally occurring mentor relationships and matching dyads in terms of affinity and having an adequate representation of gender and ethnicity mentors. Related to training, he recommends basic mentoring information through readings, lectures, small discussions, email list servers, and monthly meetings with mentors. He suggests providing a set of ground rules regarding power and boundaries in the relationship, added with regular conversation on the nature and objectives of the relationship. The good practices proposed regarding frequency is left to the participants but encourages the establishment of regular meetings. Campbell's (2007) general program management recommendations call for the need for careful planning, recruitment, gathering institutional support, anticipating data collection and assessment, and gaining institutional support to address organizational barriers such as time and space allocations.

In a review of multiple mentoring programs, Finkelstein and Poteet (2007) found that the perception of organizational support plays a role in preventing negative mentoring behaviors by promoting a culture that models positive behaviors. They recommend finding leadership sponsors in the organization to support the program in three areas: becoming mentors, influencing the organizational reward system, and changing the organizational structure to support mentoring programs. Setting clear program objectives seems to be important due to findings linking programs designed to promote careers as producing greater satisfaction. These objectives must be aligned with organizational strategic plans and clearly communicated.

Of critical importance is the selection of mentors and mentees using a combination of skill-based, motivation-based, and personality-based characteristics, as well as being careful in using volunteers due to lack of evidence of its benefits. They recommend against random assignments and caution in regards to the degree of input of participants in the matching process due to the existence of moderators pointing in different directions. In terms of the race, gender, and ethnicity, they found contradictory strategies, some in favor of matching by similarity and others promoting diversity. They conclude that these strategies have to be aligned with the programmatic purposes and the organizational culture. They propose the use of multiple mentors or groups to overcome multiple factors when matching, selection of factors based on programs objectives, and at least assigning one mentor based on similarity to overcome problems surrounding the matching process. Training and setting clear expectations are recommended as precursors to participation and success of the program. Even though they recommend assessment, they do not suggest procedures or criteria to evaluate the program.

Allen et al. (2009) warn that one-size-fits-all strategies to design mentoring programs do not work and that organizations must consider the several issues in designing mentoring programs to tailor strategies to their needs, objectives, and culture. Overarching guideless suggest the critical need to establish specific objectives for the program and alignment with organizational values and mission. These general programmatic recommendations are later translated into good practices for managing the relationship.

Many other authors (Allen et al., 2009; Campbell, 2007; Finkelstein and Poteet, 2007; O'Brien et al., 2007; Sontag et al., 2007) propose several processes for the effectiveness of mentoring programs. Finally, the IMA (2014), and the ISMPE (2015) have developed sets of standards for the effectiveness of mentoring programs. Those practices and standards had defined and captured what the research says about good practice and are important resources for those wishing to develop high quality programs.

Managing the mentoring relationship

Similar principles established for the organization are also essential for the mentoring relationship. Mentoring dyads are recommended to prepare for the relationship, working together in preparing the relationship, negotiating goals, boundaries and expectations, establishing mechanisms to measure progress and accountability, enabling the relationship, and coming to closure. Zachary (2005) offers with great detail, a set of strategies for mentors and mentees, a large amount of checklists, assessments, and tools, with emphasis in the development of two competences for mentors: the ability of providing feedback and facilitation skills for mentors and the ability of acting on feedback and listening skills for mentees.

Most of the research in regards to managing the mentoring relationship delves into a deep understanding of the mentoring phases, and the factors that influence the effectiveness of the mentoring relationship; for details in this topic, please refer to Chapter 10.

CONCLUSION

Research on formal adult mentoring has greatly increased over the last few decades, necessitating a systematic review of the literature to identify best practices. This study outlined the development of the field of mentoring over the past three decades, revealing an organized framework of the theory and practice of formal adult mentoring in academic and workplace contexts. It also provided a review of good practices for creation and maintenance of exemplary formal adult mentoring programs.

The systematic review of books and articles published in peer-reviewed journals provided two things missing for understanding mentoring and for creating and maintaining exemplary formal adult mentoring programs. It arrives at an organized historical framework of the theory and practice of adult mentoring in academic and workplace contexts and also yields an outline of the elements of mentoring good practices. By providing a picture of the state of development in mentoring research and identifying gaps in the literature, it creates a basis to develop a research agenda for the future, which will enrich the field and our understanding of mentoring programs, processes, and relationships.

REFERENCES

Allen, T., Cobb, J. and Danger, S. (2003) 'Inservice teachers mentoring aspiring teachers', *Mentoring and Tutoring: Partnership in Learning*, 11(2): 177–82.

Allen, T., Eby, L., Poteet, M., Lentz, E. and Lima, L. (2004) 'Career benefits associated with mentoring for protégés: a meta-analysis', *Journal of Applied Psychology*, 89(1): 127–36.

Allen, T., Finkelstein, L. and Poteet, M. (2009) *Designing Workplace Mentoring Programs: An Evidence-Based Approach*. Chichester and Malden: Wiley-Blackwell.

Allen, T., McManus, S. and Russell, J. (1999) 'A newcomer socialization and stress: formal peer relationships as a source of support', *Journal of Vocational Behavior*, 54(3): 453–70.

Bandura, A. (1977) 'Self-efficacy: toward a unifying theory of behavioral change', *Psychological Review*, 84(2): 191–215.

Bearman, S., Blake-Beard, S., Hunt, L. and Crosby, F.J. (2007) 'New directions in mentoring', in T. Allen and L. Eby (eds), *The Blackwell Handbook of Mentoring: A Multiple Perspectives Approach*. Malden: Blackwell Publishing Ltd, pp. 375–96.

Bolton, E. (1980) 'A conceptual analysis of the mentor relationship in the career-development of women', *Adult Education*, 30(4): 195–207.

Brondyk, S. and Searby, S.B.L. (2013) 'Best practices in mentoring: complexities and possibilities', *International Journal of Mentoring and Coaching in Education*, 2(3): 189–203.

Campbell, C. (2007) 'Best practices for student-faculty mentoring programs', in T. Allen and L. Eby (eds), *The Blackwell Handbook of Mentoring: A Multiple Perspectives Approach*. Malden: Blackwell Publishing Ltd, pp. 325–44.

Carruthers, J. (1993) 'The principles and practices of mentoring: strategies for workplace mentoring', in B. Caldwell and E. Carter (eds), *The Return of the Mentor*. London: Falmer Press, pp. 9–24.

Chao, G. (1997) 'Mentoring phases and outcomes', *Journal of Vocational Behavior*, 51(1): 15–28.

Chao, G. (2007) 'Mentoring and organizational socialization: networks for work adjustment', in B. Ragins and K. Kram (eds), *The Handbook of Mentoring at Work*. Thousand Oaks: Sage, pp. 179–96.

Charland, W. (2005) 'The youth arts apprenticeship movement: a new twist on an historical practice', *Art Education*, 58(5): 39–47.

Clutterbuck, D. (1998) *Learning Alliances: Tapping Into Talent*. London: Institute of Personnel and Development.

Clutterbuck, D. (2000) *Mentoring for Diversity*. Oxford: Butterworth-Heinemann.

Clutterbuck, D. (2004a) 'Mentor competences: a field perspective', in D. Clutterbuck and G. Lane (eds), *The Situational Mentor: An International Review of Competencies and Capabilities in Mentoring*. Burlington: Gower Publishing Limited, pp. 42–56.

Clutterbuck, D. (2004b) 'What about mentee competences?', in D. Clutterbuck and G. Lane (eds), *The Situational Mentor: An International Review of Competencies and Capabilities in Mentoring*. Burlington: Gower Publishing Limited, pp. 72–82.

Clutterbuck, D. (2007) 'An international perspective on mentoring', in B. Ragins and K. Kram (eds), *The Handbook of Mentoring at Work*. Thousand Oaks: Sage, pp. 633–56.

Clutterbuck, D. and Lane, G. (eds) (2004) *The Situational Mentor: An International Review of Competencies and Capabilities in Mentoring*. Burlington: Gower Publishing Limited.

Clutterbuck, D. and Megginson, D. (1999) *Mentoring Executives and Directors*. Oxford: Butterworth-Heinemann.

Cooper, H. (2010) *Research Synthesis and Meta-Analysis: A Step-By-Step Approach*, Vol. 2. Los Angeles: Sage.

Creswell, J. (1998) *Qualitative Inquiry and Research Design: Choosing Among Five Traditions*. Thousand Oaks: Sage.

Crosby, F. (1999) 'The developing literature on developmental relationships', in A. Murrell, F. Crosby and R. Ely (eds), *Mentoring Dilemmas: Developmental Relationships Within Multicultural Organizations*. Mahwah: Lawrence Erlbaum, pp. 3–20.

Daloz, L. (1999) *Mentor: Guiding the Journey of Adult Learners*. San Francisco: Jossey-Bass.

Darwin, A. (2004) 'Characteristics ascribed to mentors by their protégés', in D. Clutterbuck and G. Lane (eds), *The Situational Mentor: An International Review of Competencies and Capabilities in Mentoring*. Burlington: Gower Publishing Limited, pp. 1–15.

Dean, P. (1990) 'Using standards to improve performance', *Australian Journal of Educational Technology*, 6(2): 75–91.

DeWitt-Brinks, D. (1992) 'Listening instruction: a qualitative meta-analysis of twenty-four selected studies', in *Annual Meeting of the International Communication Association*. Miami: EDRS, pp. 5.

Dominguez, N. and Hager, M. (2013) 'Mentoring frameworks, synthesis and critique', *International Journal for Mentoring and Coaching in Education*, 2(3): 171–88.

Dougherty, T., Turban, D. and Haggard, D. (2007) 'Naturally occurring mentoring relationships involving workplace employees', in T. Allen and L. Eby (eds), *The Blackwell Handbook of Mentoring: A Multiple Perspectives Approach*. Malden: Blackwell Publishing Ltd, pp. 139–58.

Douglas, C. (1997) *Formal Mentoring Programs in Organizations: An Annotated Bibliography*. Greensboro: Center for Creative Leadership.

Dreher, G. and Ash, R. (1990) 'A comparative-study of mentoring among men and women in managerial, professional, and technical positions', *Journal of Applied Psychology*, 75(5): 539–46.

Eby, L., Butts, M., Durley, J. and Ragins, B. (2010) 'Are bad experiences stronger than good ones in mentoring relationships? Evidence from the protégé and mentor perspective', *Journal of Vocational Behavior*, 77(1): 81–92.

Eby, L., Rhodes, J. and Allen, T. (2007) 'Definition and evolution of mentoring', in T. Allen and L. Eby (eds), *The Blackwell Handbook of*

Mentoring: A Multiple Perspectives Approach. Malden: Blackwell Publishing Ltd, pp. 7–20.

Fagenson, E. (1989) 'The mentor advantage – perceived career job experiences of protégés versus non-protégés', *Journal of Organizational Behavior*, 10(4): 309–20.

Finkelstein, L. and Poteet, M. (2007) 'Best practices for workplace formal mentoring programs', in T. Allen and L. Eby (eds), *The Blackwell Handbook of Mentoring: A Multiple Perspectives Approach*. Malden: Blackwell Publishing Ltd, pp. 345–68.

Finkelstein, L., Allen, T. and Rothen, A. (2003) 'An examination of the role of age in mentoring relationships', *Group and Organization Management,* 28(2): 249–81.

Glaser, B. and Strauss, A. (1967) *The Discovery of Grounded Theory: Strategies for Qualitative Research*. Chicago, IL: Aldine.

Godshalk, V. and Sosik, J. (2007) 'Mentoring and leadership: standing at the crossroads of theory, research, and practice', in B. Ragins and K. Kram (eds), *The Handbook of Mentoring at Work: Theory, Research, and Practice*. Thousand Oaks: Sage, pp. 149–68.

Grassinger, R., Porath, M. and Ziegler, A. (2010) 'Mentoring the gifted: a conceptual analysis', *High Ability Studies,* 21(1): 27–46.

Gray, W. and Gray, M. (eds) (1986) *Mentoring: Aid to Excellence in Education, the Family and the Community: Proceedings of the First International Conference on Mentoring*. Vancouver: International Association for Mentoring.

Hegstad, C. (1999) 'Formal mentoring as a strategy for human resource development: a review of research', *Human Resource Development Quarterly*, 10(4): 383–90.

Higgins, M. and Kram, K. (2001) 'Reconceptualizing mentoring at work – a developmental network perspective', *Academy of Management Review*, 26(2): 264–88.

International Standards for Mentoring Programs in Employment (ISMPE) (2015) *The International Standards for Mentoring Programmes in Employment: Self-Assessment Guide*. London: ISMPE. [Unpublished pdf file.]

International Mentoring Association (IMA) (2014) *Mentoring Program Standards: Accreditation Scoring Guide*. Albuquerque: IMA. [Unpublished pdf file.]

Jacobi, M. (1991) 'Mentoring and undergraduate academic success: A literature review', *Review of Educational Research*, 61(4): 505–32.

Johnson, W. (2002) 'The intentional mentor: strategies and guidelines for the practice of mentoring', *Professional Psychology-Research and Practice*, 33(1): 88–96.

Johnson, W. (2007a) *On Being a Mentor: A Guide for Higher Education Faculty*. New York: Lawrence Erlbaum Associates.

Johnson, W. (2007b) 'Student-faculty mentorship outcomes', in T. Allen and L. Eby (eds), *The Blackwell Handbook of Mentoring: A Multiple Perspectives Approach*. Malden: Blackwell Publishing Ltd, pp. 189–210.

Johnson, W. and Ridley, C. (2008) *The Elements of Mentoring*. New York: Palgrave Macmillan.

Johnson, W., Rose, G. and Schlosser, L. (2007) 'Student-faculty mentoring: theoretical and methodological issues', in T. Allen and L. Eby (eds), *The Blackwell Handbook of Mentoring: A Multiple Perspectives Approach*. Malden: Blackwell Publishing Ltd, pp. 49–70.

Jones, A. and Vincent, J. (2010) 'Collegial mentoring for effective whole school professional development in the use of IWB technologies', *Australasian Journal of Educational Technology*, 26(4): 477–93.

Jossi, F. (1997) 'Mentoring in changing times', *Training and Development*, 51(8): 50–4.

Kardos, S. and Johnson, S. (2010) 'New teachers' experiences of mentoring: the good, the bad, and the inequity', *Journal of Educational Change*, 11(1): 23–44.

Kegan, R. (1982) *The Evolving Self: Problem and Process in Human Development*. Cambridge: Harvard University Press.

Kegan, R. (1994) *In Over Our Heads: The Mental Demands of Modern Life*. Cambridge: Harvard University Press.

Kegan, R. and Lahey, L.L. (2001) 'Adult leadership and adult development: a constructionist view', in B. Kellerman (ed.), *Leadership: Multidisciplinary Perspectives*. Englewood Cliffs: Prentice-Hall, pp. 199–230.

Kirchmeyer, C. (1998) 'Determinants of managerial career success: evidence and explanation of male/female differences', *Journal of Management*, 24(6): 673–92.

Koberg, C., Boss, R., Chappell, D. and Ringer, R. (1994) 'Correlates and consequences of protégé mentoring in a large hospital', *Group and Organization Management*, 19(2): 219–39.

Kochan, F. (2002) 'Examining the organizational and human dimensions of mentoring: a textual data analysis', in F. Kochan (ed.), *The Organizational and Human Dimensions of Successful Mentoring Programs and Relationships*. Greenwich: Information Age Publishing, pp. 269–86.

Kochan, F. (2013) 'Analyzing the relationships between culture and mentoring', *Mentoring and Tutoring: Partnership in Learning,* 21(4): 412–43.

Kram, K. (1983) 'Phases of the mentor relationship', *Academy of Management Journal,* 26(4): 608–25.

Kram, K. (1985) *Mentoring at Work: Developmental Relationships in Organizational Life*. Glenview: Scott Foresman.

Kram, K. (2004) 'Foreword', in D. Clutterbuck and G. Lane (eds), *The Situational Mentor: An International Review of Competences and Capabilities in Mentoring*. Burlington: Gower, pp. xi–xiv.

Kram, K. and Hall, D. (1989) 'Mentoring as an antidote to stress during corporate trauma', *Human Resource Management*, 28(4): 493–510.

Lankau, M. and Scandura, T. (2002) 'An investigation of personal learning in mentoring relationships: content, antecedents, and consequences', *Academy of Management Journal*, 45(4): 779–90.

Lankau, M., Carlson, D. and Nielson, T. (2006) 'The mediating influence of role stressors in the relationship between mentoring and job attitudes', *Journal of Vocational Behavior*, 68(2): 308–22.

Lee, A. (2010) *Mentoring in Eighteenth-Century British Literature and Culture*. Burlington: Ashgate Publishing Limited.

Levinson, D. (1978) *The Seasons of a Man's Life*. New York: The Random House Publishing Group.

Lockwood, A.L., Carr Evans, S. and Eby, L.T. (2007) 'Reflections on the benefits of mentoring', in T. Allen and L. Eby (eds), *The Blackwell Handbook of Mentoring: A Multiple Perspectives Approach*. Malden: Blackwell Publishing Ltd, pp. 233–6.

Marquardt, M. (1995) *Building the Learning Organization: A Systems Approach to Quantum Improvement and Global Success*. New York: McGraw Hill.

Marquardt, M. and Waddill, D. (2004) 'The power of learning in action learning: a conceptual analysis of how the five schools for adult learning theories are incorporated within the practice of action learning', *Action Learning: Research and Practice,* 1(2): 185–202.

Merriam, S. (1983) 'Mentors and protégés: a critical review of the literature', *Adult Education Quarterly*, 33(3): 161–73.

Merriam, S. (ed.) (2001) *The New Update on Adult Learning Theory: New Directions for Adult and Continuing Education*, Vol. 89. San Francisco: Jossey-Bass.

Mezirow, J. (1997) 'Transformative learning: theory to practice', *New Directions for Adult and Continuing Education*, 74(Summer): 5–12.

Miller, A. (2007) 'Best practices for formal mentoring', in T. Allen and L. Eby (eds), *The Blackwell Handbook of Mentoring: A Multiple Perspectives Approach*. Malden: Blackwell Publishing Ltd, pp. 307–24.

Mullen, C. (2000) 'Constructing co-mentoring partnerships: walkways we must travel', *Theory Into Practice,* 39(1): 4–11.

Mullen, C. (2005) *Mentorship Primer*. New York: Peter Lang Publishing.

Mullen, C. (2007) 'Naturally occurring student-faculty mentoring relationships: a literature review', in T. Allen and L. Eby (eds), *The Blackwell Handbook of Mentoring: A Multiple Perspectives Approach*. Malden: Blackwell Publishing Ltd, pp. 119–38.

Mullen, C. (2009) *The Handbook of Leadership and Professional Learning Communities*. New York: Palgrave Macmillan.

Mullen, E. and Noe, R. (1999) 'The mentoring information exchange: when do mentors seek information from their protégés?' *Journal of Organizational Behavior*, 20(2): 233–42.

Murray, M. (2001) *Beyond the Myths and Magic of Mentoring: How to Facilitate an Effective Mentoring Process*, New and Revised Edition. San Francisco: Jossey-Bass.

Noe, R. (1988) 'An investigation of the determinants of successful assigned mentoring relationships', *Personnel Psychology*, 41(3): 457–79.

Noller, R.B. (1982) 'Mentoring – a renaissance of apprenticeship', *Journal of Creative Behavior,* 16(1): 1–4.

O'Brien, K., Rodopman, O. and Allen, T. (2007) 'Reflections on best practices for formal mentoring programs', in T. Allen and L. Eby (eds), *The Blackwell Handbook of Mentoring: A Multiple Perspectives Approach*. Malden: Blackwell Publishing Ltd, pp. 369–72.

Ostroff, C. and Kozlowski, S. (1993) 'The role of mentoring in the information gathering processes of newcomers during early organizational socialization', *Journal of Vocational Behavior,* 42(2): 170–83.

Pink, D. (2005) *A Whole New Mind: Moving from the Information Age to the Conceptual Age*. New York: Penguin Group.

Ragins, B. (1997) 'Antecedents of diversified mentoring relationships', *Journal of Vocational Behavior*, 51(1): 90–109.

Ragins, B., Cotton, J. and Miller, J. (2000) 'Marginal mentoring: the effects of type of mentor, quality of relationship, and program design on work and career attitudes', *Academy of Management Journal,* 43(6): 1177–94.

Ragins, B. and Kram, K. (eds) (2007) *The Handbook of Mentoring at Work: Theory, Research, and Practice*. Los Angeles: Sage.

Ragins, B. and McFarlin, D. (1990) 'Perceptions of mentor roles in cross-gender mentoring relationships', *Journal of Vocational Behavior*, 37(3): 321–39.

Ragins, B. and Scandura, T. (1999) 'Burden or blessing? Expected costs and benefits of being a mentor', *Journal of Organizational Behavior,* 20(4): 493–509.

Ramaswami, A. and Dreher, G. (2007) 'The benefits associated with workplace mentoring relationships', in T. Allen and L. Eby (eds), *The Blackwell Handbook of Mentoring: A Multiple Perspectives Approach*. Malden: Blackwell Publishing Ltd, pp. 211–32.

Richard, O., Taylor, E., Barnett, T. and Nesbit, M. (2002) 'Procedural voice and distributive justice: their influence on mentoring career help and other outcomes', *Journal of Business Research*, 55(9): 725–35.

Roybal, K. (2001) *Standards, Best Practices, and Competencies from a Mentoring Perspective*. New Mexico: Mentoring Institute. [Unpublished literature review.]

Scandura, T. (1992) 'Mentorship and career mobility: an empirical investigation', *Journal of Organizational Behavior*, 13(2): 169–74.

Scandura, T. and Pellegrini, E. (2007) 'Workplace mentoring: theoretical approaches and methodological issues', in T. Allen and L. Eby (eds), *The Blackwell Handbook of Mentoring: A Multiple Perspectives Approach*. Malden: Blackwell Publishing Ltd, pp. 71–92.

Scandura, T. and Ragins, B.R. (1993) 'The effects of sex and gender role orientation on mentorship in male dominated occupations', *Journal of Vocational Behavior,* 43(3): 251–65.

Scandura, T. and Schriesheim, C. (1994) 'Leader-member exchange and supervisor career mentoring as complementary constructs in leadership research', *Academy of Management Journal,* 37(6): 1588–602.

Searby, S.B.L. (2014) 'The protégé mentoring mindset: a framework for consideration', *International Journal of Mentoring and Coaching in Education*, 3(3): 255–76.

Seibert, S. (1999) 'The effectiveness of facilitated mentoring: a longitudinal quasi-experiment', *Journal of Vocational Behavior*, 54(3): 483–502.

Snell, K. (1996) 'The apprenticeship system in British history: the fragmentation of a cultural institution', *History of Education*, 25(4): 303–21.

Spencer, R. (2007) 'It's not what I expected: a qualitative study of youth mentoring relationship failures', *Journal of Adolescent Research*, 22(4): 331–54.

Sontag, L., Vappie, K. and Wanberg, C. (2007) 'The practice of mentoring: MENTTIUM Corporation', in B. Ragins and K. Kram (eds), *The Handbook of Mentoring at Work: Theory, Research, and Practice*. Thousand Oaks: Sage, pp. 593–616.

Stone, F. (2004) *The Mentoring Advantage: Creating the Next Generation of Leaders*. Chicago: Dearborn Trade Publishing.

Stone, F. (2007) *Coaching, Counseling and Mentoring: How to Choose and Use the Right Technique to Boost Employee Performance*. New York: American Management Association.

Strauss, A. and Corbin, J. (1998) *Basics of Qualitative Research Techniques and Procedures for Developing Grounded Theory*. London: Sage.

Wanberg, C., Welsh, E. and Kammeyer-Mueller, J. (2007) 'Protégé and mentor self-disclosure: levels and outcomes within formal mentoring dyads in a corporate context', *Journal of Vocational Behavior*, 70(2): 398–412.

Wildman, T., Magliaro, S., Niles, R. and Niles, J. (1992) 'Teacher mentoring – an analysis of roles, activities, and conditions', *Journal of Teacher Education*, 43(3): 205–13.

Young, A. and Perrewe, P. (2000) 'What did you expect? An examination of career-related support and social support among mentors and protégés', *Journal of Management*, 26(4): 611–32.

Zachary, L. (2005) *Creating a Mentoring Culture: The Organization's Guide*. San Francisco: Jossey-Bass.

Zachary, L. and Daloz, L. (2000) *The Mentor's Guide: Facilitating Effective Learning Relationships*. San Francisco: Jossey-Bass.

Zachary, L. and Fischler, L. (2009) *The Mentee's Guide: Making Mentoring Work for You*. San Francisco: Jossey-Bass.

Developmental Networks: Enhancing the Science and Practice of Mentoring

Jeffrey Yip and Kathy E. Kram

Historically, mentoring has been conceived of as a transformative relationship in which an experienced person helps a less experienced person realize their personal and professional goals (Kram, 1985; Levinson, 1978). It has also been traditionally perceived of as a dyadic relationship between a mentor and a protégé. Yet, research indicates that a single mentor is not sufficient to meet a person's developmental needs, particularly in today's volatile, uncertain and fast-paced work environment (Baugh and Scandura, 1999; Murphy and Kram, 2014). The people who are actively involved in helping others to develop, generally include both formal and informal mentors from a variety of sectors and settings. This suggests that mentoring occurs across multiple developmental relationships in a constellation that has been described as a developmental network (Higgins and Kram, 2001).

In this chapter, we review research on mentoring as a developmental network and provide suggestions for future research. In particular, we examine how research on developmental networks can enhance the understanding of mentoring through a focus on mentoring functions as they occur across multiple developmental relationships. A person's developmental network may include one or more formal mentors and may also include other developmental partners, such as a boss who provides developmental opportunities, a junior colleague or subordinate who has deeper expertise of value to the person, or a family member who provides personal and professional counsel. A particular developmental network is defined by the person who is common to all of the relationships. Defined as the 'focal person', this individual defines members of the developmental network by enlisting and/or acknowledging the help they provide. Those involved in supporting the individual are described as developers and their individual interactions with the focal individual as developmental relationships.

This chapter begins with a review of current research on developmental networks and its contributions to the mentoring literature. The second section presents a description of methods that scholars and practitioners have used to collect and analyze data on developmental networks. The third section describes organizational applications using a developmental network approach to mentoring. The chapter concludes with recommendations for future research and a discussion on the role of developmental networks within a broader mentoring ecology.

DEVELOPMENTAL NETWORKS AND MENTORING

A significant body of research has established that people learn and develop with the support of multiple developmental relationships (Chandler et al., 2011; Dobrow et al., 2012; Kram, 1985). In her early research on workplace developmental relationships, Kram (1985) found that mentoring functions, such as coaching, sponsorship, and personal counsel, are not exclusive to traditional mentoring, but rather that they can be found in a variety of developmental relationships with peers and developers from different social spheres. The constellation of these developmental relationships are what Higgins and Kram (2001) define as a developmental network: 'people a protégé names as taking an active interest in and action to advance the protégé's career by providing developmental assistance' (Higgins and Kram, 2001: 268).

The characteristics of developmental networks are an extension of Kram's (1985) study of mentoring and developmental relationships in organizations. Grounded in qualitative interviews with managers and their direct reports, Kram found that developmental relationship functions converged into two, broad categories: career and psychosocial functions. Career functions of mentoring include coaching, sponsorship, exposure and visibility, protection, and the provision of challenging assignments. Psychosocial functions involve role modeling, acceptance and confirmation, counseling, and personal friendship. These primary developmental functions have been empirically validated in numerous studies (Noe, 1988; Ragins and McFarlin, 1990; Scandura and Ragins, 1993). In addition, researchers have demonstrated that higher levels of these functions are associated with positive protégé outcomes (Allen et al., 2004; Chandler et al., 2011; Wanberg et al., 2003).

In recent years, another set of functions has been identified as relational functions (Ragins and Verbos, 2007). These go beyond the basic career and psychosocial functions, first defined by Kram (1985), to include a number of functions that enhance the quality and closeness of such developmental relationships. For example, Ragins (2012) developed a relational mentoring index (RMI) that included the following functions: personal learning and growth, inspiration, self-affirmation, reliance on communal norms, shared influence and respect, and trust and commitment (Ragins, 2012). In an in-depth qualitative study of professional developmental networks, Janssen et al. (2013) identified five relational functions occurring within developmental networks: intimacy, self-disclosure, emulation, genuine interest, and caring.

Integrating perspectives from social network research (Burt, 1992; Granovetter, 1973) and two decades of research on dyadic mentoring relationships and associated developmental functions, Higgins and Kram (2001) developed a typology of developmental networks based on two primary dimensions: (1) strength of developmental tie, and (2) diversity of network, which included range (the number of social systems from which relationships stem) and density (degree of connectedness of developers). This typology offered a new lens on how multiple developmental relationships might enhance individual outcomes related to personal and professional development.

The strength of a person's developmental networks has since been found to predict important job outcomes such as career

Table 6.1 Example of a name generator

Think about the people who *currently (in the last year)* have taken an *active interest* and *action* to advance your career by assisting you with your personal and professional development. Think broadly, these may be people from your work or outside of work (e.g. mentors, coaches, family members, peers, professional contacts, friends, etc.).
In *order of importance*, please list their first names or initials in the space below:

---

advancement (Murphy and Kram, 2010), number of job offers (Higgins, 2001), optimism (Higgins et al., 2010), job satisfaction (Higgins and Thomas, 2001; Murphy and Kram, 2010), organizational commitment (Higgins and Thomas, 2001), and a strong sense of professional identity (Dobrow and Higgins, 2005). Further, developmental networks have been found to be a stronger predictor of individual's career outcomes than dyadic relationships such as traditional mentoring or coworker relationships (Higgins and Thomas, 2001). This suggests that people will achieve better outcomes when they rely on a small network of developmental relationships, rather than on one strong dyadic relationship such as traditional mentoring or supervisory support.

ASSESSING DEVELOPMENTAL NETWORKS

Developmental networks can be assessed both qualitatively and quantitatively through a network elicitation approach, consistent with methods used in social network analysis (Cummings and Higgins, 2006). The method involves a three step procedure including a *name generation* process, a *name interpretation* process, and a *network structure*. We describe these steps, with examples below. It should be noted that these methods have been useful for both research and educational purposes.

Step 1. Name generator

The first step in collecting data on a person's developmental network is to elicit the names of people within the respondent's developmental network. This is done through a survey or interview with the protégé. It is important to note that developers are those who the protégé considers to be providing developmental support. While this might be perceived as a one-sided approach, it is the protégé's perspective that matters, as he or she is the recipient of developmental support. Table 6.1 presents an example of this approach, commonly used in research on developmental networks (e.g. Dobrow and Higgins, 2005; Higgins and Thomas, 2001; Murphy and Kram, 2010).

Step 2. Name interpreter

The second step of name interpretation involves questions about people within the developmental network and their relationship with the focal respondent. The purpose of this questioning is to obtain both the characteristics of developers and the nature of their developmental relationship with the respondent. This data can be analyzed at the dyadic level for specific relationships, or at an aggregate level as a measure of network content. Table 6.2 provides examples of name interpreter questions. These questions have been used in prior research on developmental networks (Cummings and Higgins, 2006; Higgins, 2001).

Step 3. Network structure

The final step in a developmental network assessment analysis is a move towards understanding the structural properties of a person's developmental networks. This can be done in a visual manner, by asking respondents to draw lines representing relationships

Table 6.2 Example of name interpreter questions

Construct	Question
1. Length of relationship	How many years have you known this person?
2. Social arena (Higgins, 2001)	Please indicate one of the following that best describes your relationship with each person: • Family member • Community member • Friend outside of your organization • Coworker from your organization • Professor/teacher • Someone you worked for • Coworker from a previous employer
3. Frequency of contact	How often do you communicate with this person? • Less than once a month • Once or twice a month • Three to five times per month • A few times a week • Daily
4. Psychological closeness	How close do you feel to this person? • Very close • Close • Less than close • Distant
5. Psychosocial support (Cummings and Higgins, 2006)	Please indicate the extent to which the person does the following: • Is a friend of yours • Cares and shares in ways that extend beyond the requirements of work • Counsels you on work and non-work related matters Items are assessed on a seven-point scale (1, never, not at all, to 7, the maximum extent possible)
6. Career support (Cummings and Higgins, 2006)	Please indicate the extent to which the person does the following: • Provides you with opportunities that stretch you professionally • Creates opportunities for visibility for you • Opens doors for you professionally Items are assessed on a seven-point scale (1, never, not at all, to 7, the maximum extent possible.

between respondents or circles to group respondents who are connected to each other through a shared community (McCarty et al., 2007). A more typical approach would be to ask respondents to fill out a network matrix, a common method in social network research (Burt, 1992). An example of this matrix is provided in Table 6.3.

A developer data matrix such as the example in Table 6.3 allows for subsequent analyses on network structure and patterns of relationships between developers. It complements traditional analyses of mentoring relationships, which generally look at the developmental functions provided in each relationship, as well as the outcomes to both parties and the organization in which the relationships are embedded. So, for a given individual, each developmental relationship is examined in terms of the functions it provides and the benefits that accrue to the developer and to the protégé. The data matrix offers additional insight by examining the relationships between developers and how these interactions may affect the focal person through coordinated support amongst developers in his or her network. This additional insight might enhance a protégé's actions in relationships with developers. For example, the protégé could grant permission

Table 6.3 Example of a matrix

	a.	b.	c.	d.	e.	f.
a.						
b.						
c.						
d.						
e.						
f.						

Use the grid to indicate if, and how well, these people know each other. Indicate 1 if the two individuals know each other and 0 if they do not know each other.

for developers to discuss aspects of his or her career development with each other, or convene a meeting of the group at strategic moments when multiple perspectives would be helpful to decision-making.

Analyzing developmental networks

The data collected through the assessment process described earlier can be used for both developmental and research purposes. For developmental purposes, such as teaching, mentoring, and coaching, protégés can be guided to use the steps outlined above to map out their developmental network and coached to reflect on characteristics of their developmental network based on the dimensions that we describe in this section. While it is possible to follow the outlined steps to reflect on one's developmental network, without the guidance of a coach or mentor, it is more often beneficial to be engaged in a guided reflection with another person.

For research purposes, data collected across multiple individuals can be aggregated and computed through UCINET (Borgatti et al., 2002, 2013) for moderate-to-large samples or compared qualitatively across cases for smaller samples (e.g. Janssen et al., 2013; Richardson and McKenna, 2014; Shen and Kram, 2011). UCINET is a computer program that analyzes the dimensions of networks described below. Whether the analyses are done by individuals, for developmental purposes, or analyzed across individuals for research purposes, the relevant constructs to consider are the same. These constructs include the following.

Network size

The size of a developmental network refers to the number of people who an individual can name as actively supporting them in their personal or professional development. Prior research has identified that the size of a person's developmental network is positively associated with outcomes of job satisfaction (Higgins and Thomas, 2001; van Emmerik, 2004) and performance (Peluchette and Jeanquart, 2000).

However, bigger is not always better. In fact, at some point, it appears that diminishing returns set in. When an individual has many developers, it is difficult to find the time to deepen the quality of multiple relationships (Higgins, 2007; Higgins and Kram, 2001; Murphy and Kram, 2014). There is clearly a balance to achieve between depth of relationships and breadth of relationships. It appears that more often than not, individuals seem to be satisfied if they have three to five close relationships in their developmental network at a given time (van Emmerik, 2004).

Strength of ties

In social network research, the strength of tie refers to a 'combination of the amount of time, the emotional intensity, the intimacy (mutual confiding), and the reciprocal services which characterize the tie' (Granovetter, 1973: 1361). In the context of developmental networks, the strength of tie refers to the quality of the developmental relationship between developer and protégé. The strength of tie can be measured along a number of dimensions, including psychological closeness (Cummings and Higgins, 2006; van Emmerik, 2004), frequency of communication (Cummings and Higgins, 2006; van Emmerik, 2004), or levels of career and psychosocial support (Murphy and Kram, 2010).

As with size of network, there is not an ideal number of strong ties and weak ties. Most scholars working in this area have suggested that the ideal balance of strong and weak ties depends on the personal and professional goals of the focal person, as well as their learning style and various personality factors (Higgins, 2007; Yan et al., 2015).

Range and homophily

The concept of range refers to the diverse social identities represented by members within a developmental network. For example, a high range developmental network would consist of members from one's organization, from other organizations, family members, and members of the community. In contrast, a low range, or a homophilous developmental network, is one that might consist of developers from similar communities and backgrounds. Given the nature of today's workforce, an important part of range is diversity in terms of race, gender, ethnicity, national origin, and age (Ragins and Kram, 2007; Shen and Kram, 2011; Trau, 2015; van Emmerik, 2004). A final source contributing to range would be the functional areas within a particular work context that developers come from.

Each type of diversity, including role and cultural diversity, that is represented in a developmental network offers the possibility of new ideas and perspectives that can enhance the focal person's knowledge, understanding, skills development, and preparedness for future opportunities that may appear. When developmental networks are low range, it is possible that the focal individual does not have access to thought provoking ideas that foster learning, risk taking, and other growth-enhancing actions (Higgins, 2007; Shen and Kram, 2011).

Network reachability

The concept of reachability refers to access to high status members within a developmental network and varies by how status is defined within a particular context. For example, in a national study of job seekers in the United States, McDonald et al. (2009) assessed network reachability through the occupational prestige (using the standard international occupational prestige scale) of occupations represented in the job seeker's network. The concept of reachability has not been theorized or examined to date in research on developmental networks. Yet, it is a valid network construct, developed in research on social capital (Lin, 2002).

We propose that the concept of reachability will be particularly useful in examining the role of sponsorship and access to expert knowledge in developmental networks. For example, reachability will be important for the individual who wants to advance to senior executive status within a particular organization. Without such access over time, it is unlikely that the individual will experience sufficient sponsorship at critical moments that would provide access to necessary interim positions and networking opportunities to garner the support for further advancement.

Network density represents the extent to which a network is closely knit. It refers to the interconnectedness of ties within a network and is measured by dividing the total number

Dense developmental network   Sparse developmental network   Mentoring subgroups

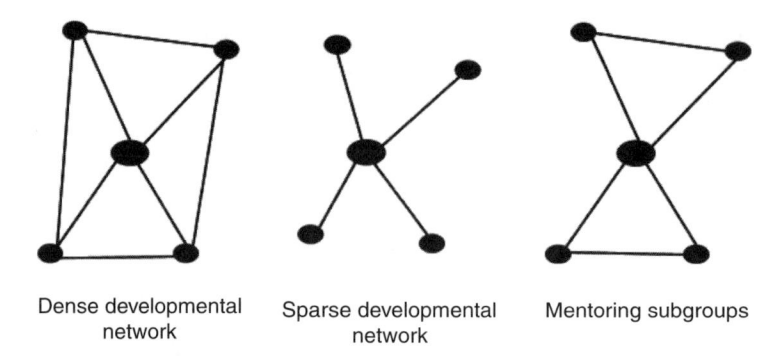

Figure 6.1 Differences in network density

of identified relationships between network members by the total possible number of ties (Wasserman and Faust, 1994). In research on elite MBA graduates, Dobrow and Higgins (2005) found a negative association between the density of their developmental network and the outcome of professionally identity exploration. This can be a negative for individuals who aspire to change careers or organizations, as developers who know each other well may have similar perspectives and similar contacts, thus making it difficult to discover new opportunities that are more distant from the current context.

A dense network is one that is characterized by strong connections between developers. While this is characteristic of a strong support network, it can have the unintended consequence of reinforcing similar perspectives. In contrast, a sparse developmental network is one where developers are not connected and are likely to be from different social spheres. One type of network is not better than the other. What matters are the developmental goals of the focal person. This contingency approach suggests that dense networks are preferable for the individual whose goals include advancing within a prescribed context where the developers can coordinate their efforts to help the person succeed (Higgins, 2007). If an individual is seeking to change course—inside or outside a given organization or career—a sparse network is likely to be more helpful, exposing the individual to new information from multiple perspectives. A hybrid network, that is neither dense nor sparse, is likely to be comprised of one or more mentoring subgroups, where some developers are connected to others. Examples of these subgroups could be developers who are within the same organization, or friends who are part of the same community. The differences by network density in developmental networks is illustrated in Figure 6.1.

Multiplexity

This refers to the extent to which two actors in a network are connected through more than one kind of relationship (Wasserman and Faust, 1994). In the context of developmental networks, multiplexity refers to the occurrence of multiple developmental functions within one relationship. For example, a developmental relationship that involves both sponsorship and coaching from the same person can be referred to as a multiplex relationship. The developer provides both developmental functions to the focal person. In contrast, a non-multiplex relationship is one that is limited to a single developmental function. In research on the developmental networks of Baseball Hall of Fame Members, Cotton et al. (2011) found that baseball professionals with extraordinary career achievements had developmental networks consisting of greater numbers of multiplex relationships than other players.

It is generally the case that multiplex relationships are characterized by greater tie strength than relationships that only provide one developmental function (Cotton et al., 2011; Yan et al., 2015). Accordingly, these stronger ties are characterized by greater intimacy and deeper learning opportunities. They are what positive organizational scholarship scholars define as high quality connections, which lead to increases in self-esteem, sense of empowerment, new knowledge and skills, and the desire for more connection (Dutton and Heaphy, 2003; Dutton and Ragins, 2007). For example, a developer who offers challenging assignments and sponsorship, as well as affirmation, friendship, and/or role modeling, is likely to know the protégé better than if they only provide challenging assignments. When the relationship is deep in familiarity and mutual respect, both individuals have greater opportunities to learn and benefit more fully from the connection (Fletcher and Ragins, 2007).

DEVELOPMENTAL NETWORKS IN PRACTICE

It has been over a decade since the developmental network perspective has been part of the discourse about mentoring (Dobrow et al., 2012; Higgins and Kram, 2001). Yet, we are only beginning to see its application in various settings such as healthcare (DeCastro et al., 2013), public administration (Kim, 2014), higher education (De Janasz and Sullivan, 2004), and with entrepreneurs (Gruber-Mücke and Kailer, 2015). For the most part, the idea of mentoring as a small network of developers, in contrast to a single relationship, is beginning to take hold as part of education and training opportunities on the subject of mentoring. In particular, organizations have begun to experiment with alternatives to formal dyadic mentoring programs, and initiating programs such as group mentoring and mentoring circles, where developmental networks are formed in support of the development of a target group of employees (Emelo, 2011; Murphy and Kram, 2014).

In essence, initiatives such as group mentoring and mentoring circles facilitate the formation of multiple and overlapping developmental networks, with a group of protégés connected to multiple developers. These mentoring alternatives vary in design: some include a group of peers only, some include one or two senior members who serve as mentors to the group of peers, and some include equal numbers of junior and senior members. The particular design depends on the specific objectives of the initiative and the resources available.

In higher education, for example, in MBA and undergraduate classrooms, faculty have taken a developmental network approach to learning (Burt and Ronchi, 2007; Whiting and de Janasz, 2004). Students are invited to reflect on their experiences with mentors as well as their current developmental networks. Using one of the assessment tools now available (Higgins, 2004; Murphy and Kram, 2014), students have the opportunity to assess whether their current developmental network aligns with their current personal and professional goals. Most often they identify a gap in shared reflection exercises with their classroom peers. The outcome of this work is an action plan for inviting new developers into their developmental network and perhaps letting go of one or more relationships that are no longer vital or relevant to their ongoing learning and development. This same kind of education and training practice has been introduced in leadership education offered within corporate settings, as well as in leadership development programs offered by external centers for leadership development (Bossen and Yost, 2013; George et al., 2011).

In organizational settings and in business education, developmental networks are also referred to as a person's 'personal board of advisors' (Yan et al., 2015). In doing so, protégés are encouraged to consider potential developers (advisors) both inside and outside their organization. Self-assessment and action planning activities are substantially enhanced by the introduction of material on different types of developmental relationships including mentors, sponsors, coaches, reverse mentors, and mentoring circles (Murphy and Kram, 2014). This information expands individuals' understanding of the alternatives to traditional mentoring relationships and makes it more likely that they will enlist a wider range of developers in to their developmental networks. We have begun to work with executive coaches as well, as when they bring a developmental network perspective to their one-to-one work with clients, they can encourage them to assess their current system of support, and to consciously plan how to enlist others with whom they can develop reciprocally rewarding connections.

In order for individuals to be able to leverage learning about different types of developers, and the developmental network perspective more generally, they will need the relational skills to initiate, nurture, and maintain or transform ongoing relationships (Schein, 2010, 2013). An understanding of the potential of a developmental network that is aligned with personal goals is only a first step. Self-assessment and shared reflection must be combined with skill practice in deep listening, empathy, self-disclosure, giving and receiving constructive feedback, and self-management (Pearce, 2007; Sigetich and Leavitt, 2008). Most recently, such relational skill training has been combined with a diversity lens so that individuals develop the capacity to build relationships that can cross gender, racial, and ethnic boundaries (Holvino, 2010; Wasserman and Blake-Beard, 2010).

Finally, and perhaps most obviously, are the formal mentoring programs that have been around now for several decades. Before concluding our review of developmental networks in practice, it is important to consider mentoring programs that have been incorporated into organizations, associations, and other agencies for several decades. While these have produced some good results in terms of increased satisfaction, commitment, and compensation (Allen et al., 2004) it is our view that the primary focus on matching dyadic relationships may be limiting the impact of these initiatives. Such formal programs have tended to emphasize the one special mentoring relationship, rather than a small network of developers (perhaps including a formally assigned mentor as one of these). However, in recent years, there are several instances of such programs modifying their education and training infrastructure to emphasize the fact that the formally assigned relationship is one of several that participants should cultivate (Blood et al., 2015). Here, the message becomes that the matched relationship is one where participants can practice and develop the relational skills to bring to other relationships that have developmental potential.

Perhaps most importantly, a number of organizations are beginning to conceptualize formal mentoring programs as mentoring circles – groups of eight to 10 participants whose primary purpose is to support the learning and development of its members. Sometimes these groups are comprised of peers, and sometimes they include one or more senior mentors to guide the group in its learning process (Murphy and Kram, 2014). The design is based on the premise that individuals will enhance their developmental networks by participating with peers (and potentially seniors) in an ongoing group characterized by support, confidentiality, positive regard, and effective helping behaviors.

In essence, the mentoring circle program touts the foundational idea of having multiple developers, many of whom may come from this particular mentoring circle. The (usually) year-long experience of monthly meetings provides members with the skills and experiences to continue building developmental relationships, even after the program ends. Examples of these are evident today at Sodexo, Boston Scientific, and Brigham and Women's hospital in Boston, where physician mentors are meeting in year-long mentoring circles to enhance their skills in developing others, including their peer physicians (Tsen et al., 2012). Other examples include peer-advisory groups, such as those hosted by the Young Presidents Organization, for professionals at similar levels within an organization, and peer coaching groups in business schools (Parker et al., 2014).

DIRECTIONS FOR FUTURE RESEARCH

Developmental networks represent a paradigm shift in the study and practice of mentoring: from mentoring dyads to mentoring as a constellation of developmental relationships. This shift requires new methods and suggests new questions that can be examined by mentoring scholars. The following are some potential areas for future research:

1 *Distributed mentoring*. With a focus on developmental networks, researchers could examine how mentoring occurs as a distributed function across multiple developers. This would enable researchers to examine the distributed and sometimes coordinated characteristics of mentoring occurring in multiple mentor situations, such as developmental networks initiatives in professional education (Johnson, 2014) or group mentoring, often involving multiple peers in a formal mentoring initiative (Hooker et al., 2014; Huizing, 2012). In particular, group mentoring has been found to be more effective than traditional dyadic mentoring medicine in the training of physicians (DeCastro et al., 2013). Research from a developmental network perspective could unpack the mechanisms behind this.
2 *Diversified mentoring*. Issues of social inclusion and diversity are important and longstanding concerns in mentoring research (Clutterbuck and Ragins, 2002; Kochan and Pascarelli, 2012). In particular, findings have established that women face systemic social barriers in access to mentors (Ragins and Cotton, 1991). These dynamics can be explored further through a developmental network perspective. In particular, the long-standing concern about 'old boys networks' in organizations (Kanter, 1977) could be examined through a closer inspection of gender differences and dynamics in the developmental networks of men and women in management. More broadly, research on social identity dynamics within developmental networks could help advance what Ragins (1997) describes as diversified mentoring – relationships 'comprising mentors and protégés who differ on the basis of race, ethnicity, gender, sexual orientation, class, religion, disability, or other group memberships associated with power in organizations' (Ragins, 1997: 482). We have yet to understand how different patterns of diversity in social group membership amongst developers impact the support and development of a focal individual.
3 *Individual differences and developmental networks*. Prior studies on developmental networks have focused primarily on the consequences of developmental networks for wellbeing and career success (Dobrow et al., 2012; Seibert et al., 2001). Building on these studies, there is need for further research on the antecedents to developmental networks, and in particular, the role of individual differences in predicting the composition and content of a person's developmental network. Individual differences, such as personality, developmental position, gender, and proactivity, have been proposed as important antecedents (Chandler et al., 2010; Dougherty et al., 2008) and have yet to be empirically examined.
4 *Attachment dynamics within developmental networks*. Research on dyadic mentoring processes have drawn substantive insights from attachment theory: a theory that examines how and why people seek (or avoid) close relationships (Bowlby, 1973; Germain, 2011). More specifically, studies have examined the influence of individual attachment styles on mentoring processes such as feedback seeking (Wu et al., 2014), feedback acceptance (Allen et al., 2010), and the willingness to mentor (Wang et al., 2009). Attachment styles refer to a person's internal working models of relationships and comprise three different categories: anxious, avoidant, and secure attachment (Bowlby, 1973; Fraley, 2002). By focusing on the context of developmental networks, researchers interested in attachment

dynamics could study the conditions where convergence (or divergence) of attachment styles, across multiple relationships, could be developmentally beneficial. For example, one could examine the strength of attachment security within a developmental network by considering not only individual differences in attachment style, but by looking at levels of agreement in the attachment styles of developers within the network.

5   *Organizational interventions*. With this relatively new understanding of mentoring as a developmental network, it seems critical to bring this in to organizational settings where dyadic mentoring has been a significant tool for employee and leadership development for at least two decades (Allen et al., 2009). Rather than encouraging individuals to form a single dyadic relationship (often assigned through a formal program sponsored by the human resource HRM or talent management function), a new mindset on mentoring encourages individuals to look at their current developmental networks and consider how these could be strengthened through proactive planning and action designed to invite potential developers to take an interest in their learning and development. Such initiatives might be initiated in the context of a leadership development program, a mentoring training program, or as part of a mentoring circle initiative in which every member of the circle is encouraged to examine and strengthen their development networks. Accordingly, this opens up opportunities for research into the effectiveness of such interventions.

6   *Organizational cultures and developmental networks*. An organization's culture can shape the career orientation of its employees, with consequences on developmental relationships (Hall and Yip, 2014). Developmental networks can be a unique window to examine this dynamic. For example, we hypothesize that the effectiveness of developmental network interventions would be moderated by an organization's career culture. More specifically, in cultures that value relationship building, learning, and reflection as part of the everyday work of organizational members, the idea of periodically examining and re-building developmental networks will be considered an important and valued activity. In contrast, this same idea will be viewed less favorably (and as a distraction from the work itself) in a highly results oriented, hierarchical culture, in which learning, and relational learning in particular, are not valued (Murphy and Kram, 2014).

7   *Evaluation of mentoring programs*. The methodological tools of network analysis could be used to strengthen the understanding and evaluation of mentoring programs. In particular, a promising avenue of research would be to examine how dyadic mentoring relationships influence the broader composition of a protégé's developmental network. This could elucidate how the benefits of traditional mentoring extend beyond the dyad. For example, in a longitudinal quasi-experimental study, Srivastava (2015) found changes in the network composition of participants in a traditional mentoring program and gender differences in the benefits that participants derive from these changes.

SITUATING DEVELOPMENTAL NETWORKS IN A MENTORING ECOLOGY

Mentoring relationships do not occur in a vacuum, but rather in a relational ecosystem comprised of multiple relationships, shaped by broader cultural norms and beliefs about mentoring. Developmental networks are situated within this ecosystem, comprised of dyadic mentoring relationships, and nested within a broader ecology of beliefs and practices about mentoring. The dynamic nature of these nested relationships suggests an ecological systems perspective on mentoring (Chandler et al., 2011) – a perspective that proposes that traditional dyadic mentoring and developmental networks are not exclusive, but rather co-existing relational systems.

In contrast to an input-output model of mentoring, an ecological perspective suggests a consideration of mentoring as a property of a whole system, rather than an exchange that occurs between individuals. For example, a person may be engaged in a formal mentoring relationship, but may also be receiving mentoring support from peers

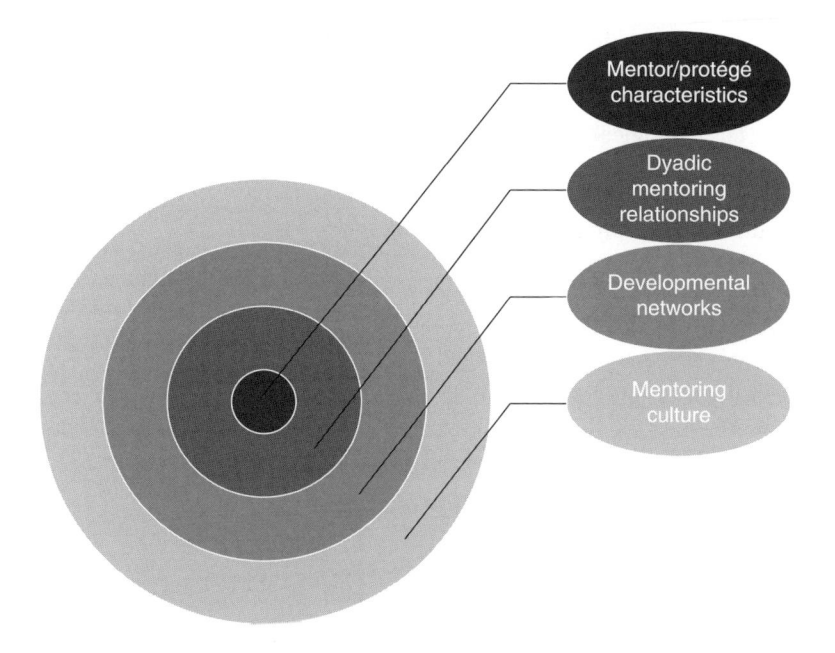

Figure 6.2 Levels of analysis in mentoring research

and family members, whose mentoring may be influenced by their role and the social context that they are nested within. At one level, these relationships are nested within a person's developmental network; at another level, these developmental relationships are nested within a broader social and cultural ecology. Figure 6.2 illustrates these broad nested systems in context.

Figure 6.2 illustrates our proposed framework for understanding the role of developmental networks within a mentoring ecology. As represented in the model, mentoring relationships are nested within developmental networks, which, in turn, are nested in broader cultural beliefs and practices about mentoring. This model is an extension of Bronfenbrenner's (1979) ecological systems theory: a theory that suggests that human development and relationships are not isolated, but rather occur within multiple reciprocal systems. As Bronfenbrenner notes, 'The understanding of human development demands more than the direct observation of behavior on the part of one or two persons in the same place; it requires examination of multi-person systems of interaction not limited to a single setting and must take into account multiple setting' (Bronfenbrenner, 1979: 21).

Research on developmental networks can inform and open up new ways of examining mentoring as an ecological system. In particular, developmental networks provide a link to examine how macrosystems (such as culture) can influence the composition, structure, and interaction across developers within a developmental network. This dynamics offers promise for future research in mentoring. For example, through research on developmental networks, it is possible to examine how people are shaped by diverse cultural influences, represented by relationships with developers from different cultures. Research by Mao and Shen (2015), for example, examines the process of cultural identity change in expatriates through the lens of expatriate developmental networks. At a broader level, research on developmental networks has also revealed how macro-level institutional logics influence the composition of developmental networks within particular industries (Cotton, 2013).

In practice, an ecological approach to mentoring requires more than the selection, training, and assignment of competent mentors in a formal mentoring program – this is a common practice in organizations. Instead, an ecological approach to mentoring is about creating environments for developmental networks to thrive – where people are engaged in multiple and diverse developmental relationships, in addition to relationships with formal mentors. As prior research has shown, informal mentoring is a stronger predictor of mentoring outcomes over formal mentoring (Eby et al., 2013; Ragins and Cotton, 1999). Further, organizational support for mentoring has been found across studies to be an important predictor of mentoring success (Ghosh, 2014).

CONCLUSION

In conclusion, our chapter has described how research on developmental networks can enhance the science and practice of mentoring beyond traditional dyadic relationships. Research on formal mentoring relationships suggests that a single mentor is not sufficient to meet a person's developmental needs (Baugh and Scandura, 1999; Higgins and Thomas, 2001; De Janasz and Sullivan, 2004). As a complement to research on formal and dyadic mentoring relationships, a developmental network perspective offers an expanded understanding of how mentoring functions occur across multiple developmental relationships and how the composition and structure of these relationships influence outcomes related to learning and performance. By considering mentoring as a relational system involving multiple developers, a developmental network perspective opens up new approaches to further the science and practice of mentoring.

REFERENCES

Allen, T.D., Eby, L.T., Poteet, M.L., Lentz, E. and Lima, L. (2004) 'Career benefits associated with mentoring for protégés: a meta-analysis', *Journal of Applied Psychology*, 89(1): 127–36.

Allen, T.D., Finkelstein, L.M. and Poteet, M.L. (2009) *Designing Workplace Mentoring Programs: An Evidence-Based Approach*. Malden: Wiley-Blackwell.

Allen, T.D., Shockley, K.M. and Poteat, L. (2010) 'Protégé anxiety attachment and feedback in mentoring relationships', *Journal of Vocational Behavior*, 77(1): 73–80.

Baugh, S.G. and Scandura, T.A. (1999) 'The effect of multiple mentors on protégé attitudes toward the work setting', *Journal of Social Behavior and Personality*, 14(4): 503–21.

Blood, E.A., Trent, M., Gordon, C.M., Goncalves, A., Resnick, M., Fortenberry, J.D., Boyer, C.B., Richardson, L. and Emans, S.J. (2015) 'Leadership in adolescent health: developing the next generation of maternal child health leaders through mentorship', *Maternal and Child Health Journal*, 19(2): 308–13.

Borgatti, S.P., Everett, M.G. and Freeman, L.C. (2002) *UCINET for Windows: Software for Social Network Analysis*. Harvard: Analytic Technologies.

Borgatti, S.P., Everett, M.G. and Johnson, J.C. (2013) *Analyzing Social Networks*. London: Sage.

Bossen, M. and Yost, P. (2013) 'Building a board of learning advisors', in C.D. McCauley, D.S. DeRue, P.R. Yost and S. Taylor (eds), *Experience-Driven Leader Development*. San Francisco: John Wiley and Sons, Inc., pp. 259–64.

Bowlby, J. (1973) *Attachment and Loss: Volume 2. Separation: Anxiety and Anger*. New York: Basic Books.

Bronfenbrenner, U. (1979) *The Ecology of Human Development: Experiments by Nature and Design*. Cambridge: Harvard University Press.

Burt, R.S. (1992) *Structural Holes: The Social Structure of Competition*. Cambridge: Harvard University Press.

Burt, R.S. and Ronchi, D. (2007) 'Teaching executives to see social capital: results from a field experiment', *Social Science Research*, 36(3): 1156–83.

Chandler, D.E., Hall, D.T. and Kram, K.E. (2010) 'A developmental network and relational savvy approach to talent development: a low-cost alternative', *Organizational Dynamics*, 39(1): 48–56.

Chandler, D.E., Kram, K.E. and Yip, J. (2011) 'An ecological systems perspective on mentoring at work: a review and future prospects', *Academy of Management Annals*, 5(1): 519–70.

Clutterbuck, D. and Ragins, B.R. (2002) *Mentoring and Diversity: An International Perspective*. Oxford: Routledge.

Cotton, R.D. (2013) 'Going global: the historical contingency of baseball hall of famer developmental networks', *Career Development International*, 18(3): 281–304.

Cotton, R.D., Shen, Y. and Livne-Tarandach, R. (2011) 'On becoming extraordinary: the content and structure of the developmental networks of Major League Baseball Hall of Famers', *Academy of Management Journal*, 54(1): 15–46.

Cummings, J. and Higgins, M.C. (2006) 'Relational instability at the core: support dynamics in developmental networks', *Social Networks*, 28(1): 38–55.

DeCastro, R., Sambuco, D., Ubel, P.A., Stewart, A. and Jagsi, R. (2013) 'Mentor networks in academic medicine: moving beyond a dyadic conception of mentoring for junior faculty researchers', *Academic Medicine: Journal of the Association of American Medical Colleges*, 88(4): 488–96.

De Janasz, S.C. and Sullivan, S.E. (2004) 'Multiple mentoring in academe: developing the professorial network', *Journal of Vocational Behavior*, 64(2): 263–83.

Dobrow, S.R. and Higgins, M.C. (2005) 'Developmental networks and professional identity: a longitudinal study', *Career Development International*, 10(6/7): 567–83.

Dobrow, S.R., Chandler, D.E., Murphy, W.M. and Kram, K.E. (2012) 'A review of developmental networks: incorporating a mutuality perspective', *Journal of Management*, 38(1): 210–42.

Dougherty, T.W., Ha Cheung, Y. and Florea, L. (2008) 'The role of personality in employee developmental networks', *Journal of Managerial Psychology*, 23(6): 653–69.

Dutton, J. and Heaphy, E. (2003) 'The power of high quality connections', in K. Cameron J. Dutton and R. Quinn (eds), *Positive Organizational Scholarship: Foundations of a New Discipline*. San Francisco: Berrett-Koehler, pp. 263–78.

Dutton, J. and Ragins, B.R. (2007) *Exploring Positive Relationships at Work: Building a Theoretical and Research Foundation*. Malwah: Lawrence Erlbaum Associates.

Eby, L.T., Allen, T.D., Hoffman, B.J., Baranik, L.E., Sauer, J.B., Baldwin, S., Morrison, M.A., Kinkade, K.M. ... and Evans, S.C. (2013) 'An interdisciplinary meta-analysis of the potential antecedents, correlates, and consequences of protégé perceptions of mentoring', *Psychological Bulletin*, 139(2): 441–76.

Emelo, R. (2011) 'Group mentoring: rapid multiplication of learning', *Industrial and Commercial Training*, 43(3): 136–45.

Fraley, R.C. (2002) 'Attachment stability from infancy to adulthood: meta-analysis and dynamic modeling of developmental mechanisms', *Personality and Social Psychology Review*, 6(2): 123–51.

George, W.W., George, B., Baker, D. and Leider, R.J. (2011) *True North Groups: A Powerful Path to Personal and Leadership Development*. San Francisco: Berrett-Koehler.

Germain, M.L. (2011) 'Formal mentoring relationships and attachment theory: implications for human resource development', *Human Resource Development Review*, 10(2): 123–50.

Ghosh, R. (2014) 'Antecedents of mentoring support: a meta-analysis of individual, relational, and structural or organizational factors', *Journal of Vocational Behavior*, 84(3): 367–84.

Granovetter, M.S. (1973) 'The strength of weak ties', *American Journal of Sociology*, 78(6): 1360–80.

Gruber-Mücke, T. and Kailer, N. (2015) 'Developmental networks and entrepreneurial competence development: a survey of active and former junior entrepreneurs', in A. Fayolle, P. Kyro and F. Linan (eds), *Developing, Shaping and Growing Entrepreneurship, Series Developing, Shaping and Growing Entrepreneurship*. London: Edward Elgar, pp. 150–75.

Hall, D.T. and Yip, J. (2014) 'Career cultures and climates in organizations', in B. Schneider and K. Barbera (eds), *The Oxford Handbook of Organizational Climate and Culture*. Oxford: Oxford University Press, pp. 215–34.

Higgins, M.C. (2001). 'Changing careers: The effects of social context', *Journal of Organizational Behavior*, 22(6): 595–618.

Higgins, M.C. (2004) *Developmental Network Questionnaire*. Boston: Harvard Business School Publishing.

Higgins, M.C. (2007) 'A contingency perspective on developmental networks', in J. Dutton and B.R. Ragins (eds), *Exploring Positive Relationships at Work: Building a Theoretical and Research Foundation*. Hillsdale: Lawrence Erlbaum Associates, pp. 207–24.

Higgins, M.C. and Kram, K.E. (2001) 'Reconceptualizing mentoring at work: a developmental network perspective', *Academy of Management Review*, 26(2): 264–88.

Higgins, M.C. and Thomas, D.A. (2001) 'Constellations and careers: toward understanding the effects of multiple developmental relationships', *Journal of Organizational Behavior*, 22(3): 223–47.

Higgins, M., Dobrow, S.R., and Roloff, K.S. (2010) 'Optimism and the boundaryless career: The role of developmental relationships', *Journal of Organizational Behavior*, 31(5): 749–69.

Holvino, E. (2010) 'Intersections: the simultaneity of race, gender, and class in organization studies', *Gender, Work, and Organization*, 17(3): pp. 248–77.

Hooker, C., Nakamura, J. and Csikszentmihalyi, M. (2014) 'The group as mentor', in M. Csikszentmihalyi (ed.), *The Systems Model of Creativity*. Dordrecht: Springer Netherlands, pp. 207–25.

Huizing, R.L. (2012) 'Mentoring together: a literature review of group mentoring', *Mentoring and Tutoring: Partnership in Learning*, 20(1): 27–55.

Janssen, S., van Vuuren, M. and de Jong, M.D. (2013) 'Identifying support functions in developmental relationships: a self-determination perspective', *Journal of Vocational Behavior*, 82(1): 20–9.

Johnson, W.B. (2014) 'Mentoring in psychology education and training: a mentoring relationship continuum model', in W.B. Johnson and N.J. Kaslow (eds), *The Oxford Handbook of Education and Training in Professional Psychology*. New York: Oxford University Press, pp. 272–90.

Kanter, R.M. (1977) *Men and Women of the Corporation*. New York: Basic Books.

Kim, S.E. (2014) 'The mentor-protégé affinity on mentoring outcomes: the mediating effect of developmental networking', *International Review of Public Administration*, 19(1): 91–106.

Kochan, F. and Pascarelli, J.T. (2012) 'Perspectives on culture and mentoring in the global age', in S.J. Fletcher and C.A. Mullen (eds), *The Sage Handbook of Mentoring and Coaching in Education*. Los Angeles: Sage, pp. 184–98.

Kram, K.E. (1985) *Mentoring at Work: Developmental Relationship in Organizational Life*. Glenview: Scott Foresman. [Reprinted by University Press of America, Lanham, 1988.]

Levinson, D.J. (1978) *The Seasons of a Man's Life*. New York: Random House LLC.

Lin, N. (2002) *Social Capital: A Theory of Social Structure and Action*, Vol. 19. Cambridge: Cambridge University Press.

Mao, J. and Shen, Y. (2015) 'Cultural identity change in expatriates: a social network perspective', *Human Relations*, 68(10): 1533–56.

McCarty, C., Molina, J.L., Aguilar, C. and Rota, L. (2007) 'A comparison of social network mapping and personal network visualization', *Field Methods*, 19(2): 145–62.

McDonald, S., Lin, N. and Ao, D. (2009) 'Networks of opportunity: gender, race, and job leads', *Social Problems*, 56(3): 385–402.

Mitchell, M.E., Eby, L.T. and Ragins, B.R. (2015) 'My mentor, my self: antecedents and outcomes of perceived similarity in mentoring relationships', *Journal of Vocational Behavior*: doi: 10.1016/j.jvb.2015.04.008.

Murphy, W. and Kram, K.E. (2010) 'Understanding non-work relationships in developmental networks', *Career Development International*, 15(7): 637–63.

Murphy, W. and Kram, K.E. (2014) *Strategic Relationships at Work: Creating Your Circle of Mentors, Sponsors, and Peers for Success in Business and Life*. New York: McGraw-Hill.

Noe, R. (1988) 'An investigation of the determinants of successful assigned mentoring relationships', *Personnel Psychology*, 41(3): 457–79.

Parker, P., Kram, K.E. and Hall, D.T. (2014) 'Peer coaching: an untapped resource for development', *Organizational Dynamics*, 43(2): 122–9.

Pearce, W.B. (2007) *Making Social Worlds: A Communication Perspective*. Malden: Blackwell Publishing.

Peluchette, J.V. and Jeanquart, S. (2000) 'Professionals' use of different mentor sources at various career stages: implications for career success', *Journal of Social Psychology*, 140(5): 549–64.

Ragins, B.R. (1997) Diversified mentoring relationships in organizations: A power perspective. *Academy of Management Review*, 22(2): 482–521.

Ragins, B.R. (2012) 'Relational mentoring: a positive approach to mentoring at work', in K. Cameron and G. Spreitzer (eds), *The Oxford Handbook of Positive Organizational Scholarship*. New York: Oxford University Press, pp. 507–18.

Ragins, B.R. and Cotton, J.L. (1991) 'Easier said than done: gender differences in perceived barriers to gaining a mentor', *Academy of Management Journal*, 34(4): 939–51.

Ragins, B.R. and Cotton, J.L. (1999) 'Mentor functions and outcomes: a comparison of men and women in formal and informal mentoring relationships', *Journal of Applied Psychology*, 84(4): 529–50.

Ragins, B.R., and Kram, K.E. (2007) *The Handbook of Mentoring at Work: Theory, research, and Practice*. Sage.

Ragins, B.R. and McFarlin, D. (1990) 'Perceptions of mentor roles in cross-gender mentoring relationships', *Journal of Vocational Behavior*, 37(3): 321–39.

Ragins, B.R. and Verbos, A.K. (2007) 'Positive relationships in action: relational mentoring and mentoring schemas in the workplace', in J.E. Dutton and B.R. Ragins (eds), *Exploring Positive Relationships at Work: Building a Theoretical and Research Foundation*. Mahwah: Lawrence Erlbaum Associates, Inc., pp. 91–116.

Richardson, J. and McKenna, S. (2014) 'Towards an understanding of social networks among organizational self-initiated expatriates: a qualitative case study of a professional services firm', *The International Journal of Human Resource Management*, 25(19): 2627–43.

Scandura, T. and Ragins, B.R. (1993) 'The effects of sex and gender role orientation on mentorship in male-dominated occupations', *Journal of Vocational Behavior*, 43(3): 251–65.

Schein, E. (2010) *Helping: How to Offer, Give, and Receive Help*. San Francisco: Berrett-Koehler.

Schein, E. (2013) *Humble Inquiry: The Gentle Art of Asking Instead of Telling*. San Francisco: Berrett-Koehler.

Shen, Y. and Kram, K.E. (2011) 'Expatriates' developmental networks: network diversity, base, and support functions', *Career Development International*, 16(6): 528–52.

Seibert, S.E., Kraimer, M.L. and Liden, R.C. (2001) 'A social capital theory of career success', *Academy of Management Journal*, 44(2): 219–37.

Sigetich, A. and Leavitt, C. (2008) *Play to Your Strengths*. Franklin Lakes: Career Press.

Srivastava, S.B. (2015) 'Network intervention: assessing the effects of formal mentoring on workplace networks', *Social Forces*, 94(1): 427–52.

Trau, R.N. (2015) 'The impact of discriminatory climate perceptions on the composition of intraorganizational developmental networks, psychosocial support, and job and career attitudes of employees with an invisible stigma', *Human Resource Management*, 54(2): 345–66.

Tsen, L.C., Borus, J.F., Nadelson, C.C., Seely, E.W., Haas, A. and Fuhlbrigge, A.L. (2012) 'The development, implementation and assessment of an innovative faculty mentoring leadership program', *Academic Medicine*, 87(12): 1757–61.

van Emmerik, I.J.H. (2004) 'The more you can get the better: mentoring constellations and intrinsic career success', *Career Development International*, 9(6): 578–94.

Wanberg, C.R., Welsh, E.T. and Hezlett, S.A. (2003) 'Mentoring research: a review and dynamic process model', *Research in Personnel and Human Resources Management*, 22: 39–124.

Wang, S., Noe, R.A., Wang, Z.M. and Greenberger, D.B. (2009) 'What affects willingness to mentor in the future? An investigation of attachment styles and mentoring experiences', *Journal of Vocational Behavior*, 74(3): 245–56.

Wasserman, I. and Blake-Beard, S. (2010) 'Leading inclusively: mindsets, skills, and actions for a diverse, complex world', in K. Bunker, D.T. Hall and K.E. Kram (eds), *Extraordinary Leadership: Addressing the Gaps in Senior Executive Development*. San Francisco: John Wiley, pp. 197–212.

Wasserman, S. and Faust, K. (1994) *Social Network Analysis: Methods and Applications*. Cambridge: Cambridge University Press.

Whiting, V.R. and de Janasz, S.C. (2004) 'Mentoring in the 21st century: using the internet to build skills and networks', *Journal of Management Education*, 28(3): 275–93.

Wu, C.H., Parker, S.K. and de Jong, J.P. (2014) 'Feedback seeking from peers: a positive strategy for insecurely attached team-workers', *Human Relations*, 67(4): 441–64.

Yan, S., Cotton, R. and Kram, K.E. (2015) 'Assembling your personal board of advisors', *MIT Sloan Management Review*, 56(3): 81–90.

Ethical Considerations for Mentors: Toward a Mentoring Code of Ethics

W. Brad Johnson

Mentoring relationships are personal and reciprocal relationships in which a more seasoned professional acts as a guide, role model, teacher, and sponsor of a less experienced (often younger) student or junior professional. A mentor provides the mentee with knowledge, advice, counsel, challenge, and support in the mentee's pursuit of becoming a full member of a particular profession (Johnson, 2016). In organizational settings, the mentor teaches the mentee about his or her job, introduces the mentee to contacts, orients the mentee to the organization and its culture, and often addresses social and personal issues that arise on the job (Allen et al., 2009). As Belle Ragins and Kathy Kram (2007) observed: 'At its best, mentoring can be a life-altering relationship that inspires mutual growth, learning, and development. Its effects can be remarkable, profound, and enduring; mentoring relationships have the capacity to transform individuals, groups, organizations, and communities' (2007: 3).

Considerable research has largely confirmed Kram's (1985) discovery that effective mentors tend to provide two broad categories of mentoring functions (Ragins and Kram, 2007). *Career functions* (e.g. coaching, sponsorship, challenge) involve behaviors aimed at assisting the mentee to prepare for career advancement and success. *Psychosocial functions* (e.g. acceptance, friendship, counseling) build on interpersonal bonds and are designed to bolster the mentee's personal growth, self-efficacy, and professional identity. Moreover, mentoring relationships are defined by several qualities that tend to distinguish them as unique developmental relationships (Allen et al., 2009; Johnson, 2016). For instance, mentoring relationships are often enduring and reciprocal/collegial personal relationships. Yet, while increasingly mutual, they are by definition asymmetrical, and there is typically a power imbalance inherent to the relationship. Mentors serve as role models committed to a transformation in the mentee's identity, and they provide a safe space for self-exploration and tailor their mentoring behaviors to the unique developmental needs of the mentee.

Research bearing on the efficacy and outcomes associated with good mentoring relationships is also quite consistent in aggregate. Meta-analytic reviews reveal that a strong mentor is associated with a host of career benefits including more rapid career advancement, higher rates of compensation, enhanced professional identity development, greater career and organizational commitment, and greater job and career satisfaction (Allen and Eby, 2003; Eby et al., 2008; Kammeyer-Mueller and Judge, 2008; Underhill, 2005). Reflecting on the outcome evidence bearing on mentoring relationships, Sternberg (2002) reflected that a mentor, 'inspires one, reveals new ways of understanding professional and personal matters, and motivates one to transcend who one is to become a different kind of professional and perhaps, person' (2002: 68). It comes as little surprise that institutions and organizations increasingly call on their more accomplished citizens to become intentional and deliberate mentors for junior personnel (Johnson, 2014; Kaslow and Mascaro, 2007).

In addition to these outcomes and benefits, mentoring relationships should also serve as an essential route for the transmission of values, ethical principles, and cultural mores of various professions. For centuries, mentors have sought to serve as models of the bedrock moral virtues and ethical principles necessary for upright professional conduct for their mentee/apprentices (Johnson and Ridley, 2008a; Moberg and Velasquez, 2004). Intentional mentoring encourages novices to strive for excellence and care for the ethical commitments and fundamental aspirations of their profession. In this way, mentoring experiences can contribute to the strength of professions across generations and the welfare of the communities they serve (Nakamura and Shernoff, 2009). However, values-based and ethically astute mentoring is neither easy to practice nor universal in execution.

There is good evidence that mentors sometimes are disrespectful, harassing, coercive, neglectful, relationally incompetent, and prone to model unethical behavior (Braxton et al., 2011). It is imperative, therefore, that the field of mentoring pay greater attention to the foundational competencies of both effective and *ethical* mentorship (Forehand, 2008; Johnson, 2003).

This chapter provides a review and consolidation of scholarship on mentoring, professional ethics, and fiduciary relationships. It summarizes the most salient and consistent ethical concerns and tensions confronting mentors across organizations and mentoring contexts. The author frames mentorship as a fiduciary relationship in which mentors own a fundamental obligation to simultaneously avoid harm to the mentee and to promote the mentee's best interests whenever possible. A preliminary Mentoring Code of Ethics is proposed. The Code includes a preamble followed by several general *ethical principles* for mentors highlighting key aspirational ethical/moral commitments to abide by when serving in the mentor role. These principles are framed so as to be applicable across professions, organizations, and mentoring contexts.

MENTORING RELATIONSHIPS ARE COMPLEX, FLUID, AND SOMETIMES DYSFUNCTIONAL

In 1978, developmental psychologist Daniel Levinson and his colleagues conducted a sweeping and often-cited study of seasons of adult development (Levinson et al., 1978). Across professions, Levinson discovered that mentoring relationships were often pivotal to subsequent career success: 'the mentor relationship is one of the most complex and developmentally important a [person] can have in early adulthood' (1978: 97). But mentoring relationships are also fertile ground for ethical tensions and dilemmas

(Johnson, 2002, 2016; Johnson and Nelson, 1999; Rosenberg and Heimberg, 2009). Mentorships are often long in duration, gradually more intimate and emotionally bonded, and they are often characterized by numerous overlapping roles. Moreover, strong mentoring relationships often begin informally, driven by interpersonal 'chemistry' or attraction (e.g. shared interests, proximity, perceived similarity) and the most highly rated mentoring relationships are described as reciprocal, mutual, and increasingly collegial by the participants. Although mentors often hold considerable power vis-à-vis the mentee, the friendship component of mentoring can cause the mentor to lose sight of his or her fiduciary obligations to the mentee. For all of these reasons, mentoring relationships are often complex. On occasion, they place both parties at risk of harm – whether intentional or inadvertent.

In addition to the myriad roles and interpersonal complexity common of mentoring relationships, these developmental relationships are always evolving with concomitant changes to relational dynamics such as perceived intimacy, trust, implicit expectations, and degree of mutuality. Dating to the original work of Levinson and colleagues (Levinson et al., 1978), there has been some appreciation for the fact that mentoring is not easily defined merely by virtue of the formal roles served by the mentor, but more by the fundamental character and quality of the relationship itself and the functions received by the mentee. Johnson (2014, 2016) has provided a mentoring relationship continuum (MRC) model as a way to conceptualize mentoring as a relationship *quality*, rather than a *category*. Any developmental relationship may be placed on a continuum defined by degree of involvement, relational reciprocity, emotional connection, and genuine collaboration. As a developmental relationship (e.g. managerial, supervisory, academic advisory) moves along the continuum from one end (formal, hierarchical, focused exclusively on skill development) to the other (a rich developmental relationship characterized by greater mutuality and relational mentoring), the senior member of the dyad begins to offer a range of both career and emotional or psychological functions, the relationship becomes increasingly reciprocal, and the senior member (mentor) becomes more invested in the mentee's broad success as a person and a professional (Johnson et al., 2014). The MRC model highlights the constantly evolving nature of most mentoring relationships and the fact that ethical obligations may take on the feel of moving targets as relational contours shift.

As a consequence of this complexity and fluidity, mentoring relationships occasionally become tense, problematic, and conflict-ridden (Eby et al., 2000; Johnson and Huwe, 2002). Survey research in graduate school contexts reveals that a not insignificant proportion of mentees report ethical maleficence on the part of graduate school mentors (Braxton et al., 2011). Patterns of problematic mentor behavior included disrespect, misappropriation of student work, harassment, and directed research fraud. In one large-scale study of nearly 700 new psychology doctorates, 17 percent reported negative aspects in the mentor-mentee relationship (Clark et al., 2000). The most common problems included: (1) mentor unavailability; (2) difficulty terminating the relationship; (3) feeling unable to meet the mentor's expectations; and (4) exploitation by the mentor. When mentorships become dysfunctional, it is safe to assume that the primary needs of one or both partners are not being met, the long-term costs outweigh the benefits (at least for one partner), or one or both partners is suffering distress as a result of them being in the relationship (Eby et al., 2000; Johnson and Huwe, 2002; Scandura, 1998).

TOP ETHICAL CHALLENGES FOR MENTORS

In this section of the chapter, I discuss eight primary areas of ethical tension and challenge for mentors. Each of these ethical issues requires thoughtful attention and consideration on the part of professionals who mentor. If anticipated and addressed appropriately, these challenges need not become ethical conflicts, nor lead to a rupture in the mentoring relationship. The top ethical challenges include: (1) level of relationship formality; (2) competence in the mentor role; (3) advocacy versus evaluation; (4) privacy and confidentiality; (5) intimacy, attraction and sexual feelings; (6) self-disclosure; (7) multiple relationships; and (8) equal access by diverse mentees.

Level of relationship formality

A hallmark of many professional relationships with clients, students, and others to whom professionals deliver services is the process of providing – using language the recipient of those services can understand – appropriate information beforehand about the nature of such services and what the recipient can reasonably expect (American Psychological Association, 2010). Termed *informed consent*, this process assumes a formal beginning and clear start date to the relationship. Eliciting informed consent from a prospective mentee might allow a mentor to describe the contours and boundaries of such relationships, the potential benefits as well as any realistic risks, and reasonable expectations for both the mentor and the mentee. Most would agree that in professional relationships generally, it is appropriate for the person receiving a service to be informed about the service, including the nature of the relationship with the professional, and that the client should be able to make autonomous decisions pertaining to it (Corey et al., 2015).

As logical and ethically appealing as it might be to fit mentoring relationships under the umbrella of professional helping relationships generally, with the associated expectation for a reasonable process of informed consent, the reality is that many long-term mentorships develop informally or organically without any discernable start date (Chao, 2009). Moreover, while many researchers point to the value of formal mentoring relationships (Allen et al., 2009; Underhill, 2005), others argue that informally evolved mentorships tend to produce more robust benefits and outcomes for mentees than those formally assigned in organized mentoring programs (Egan and Song, 2008; Ragins and Cotton, 1990). Many mentorships begin as a result of proximity, frequency of interaction, and attraction based on common interests and increasingly positive interactions. When mentoring relationships begin informally in academe or organizations, the relationships tend to be distinct from more formal developmental relationships in three ways (Chao, 2009): (1) *visibility*: informal relationships are often less visible, operating without formal recognition or monitoring; (2) *focus*: informal relationships often have a less specific focus and tend to encompass the general wellbeing of the mentee; and (3) *duration*: informal relationships are unconstrained in terms of variables such as frequency of meeting and expected duration of the relationship. Although surveys reveal that both prospective mentors and mentees prefer such informal or organizationally 'hands off' mentorship initiation, such informality makes it challenging for mentors to provide mentees with information at the outset that may be necessary to make an informed decision about starting or continuing in the relationship (Johnson and Nelson, 1999).

Competence in the mentor role

Increasingly, scholars and practitioners of mentoring are focusing on the acquisition, measurement, and maintenance of competence in the mentor role (Allen and Eby, 2007; Allen et al., 2009; Johnson, 2003, 2014). Competence is a multidimensional construct characterized by the attainment, maintenance, and preservation of critical knowledge, skills, and attitudes (Rubin et al., 2007). In a broad sense, competence in most professions is defined as, 'the habitual and judicious use of communication, knowledge, technical skills, clinical reasoning, emotions, values, and reflection in daily practice for the benefit of the individual and the community served' (Epstein and Hundert, 2002: 226). Excellent mentors weave together key character virtues, emotional and interpersonal abilities, and specific behavioral mentor competencies or skills in the execution of ethical and helpful mentorships.

Most professional ethics codes emphasize that professionals should provide services or engage with consumers only within the clear boundaries of their competence, based on education, training, supervised experience, and appropriate professional experience (APA, 2010). Although competence does not imply perfection, it does imply a clear ethical obligation that one has the necessary knowledge, skills, abilities, and values to provide effective services (Corey et al., 2015). In the case of mentoring, it is quite often the case that people learn 'by osmosis' or perhaps by experiencing a positive mentoring relationship as a mentee. Rarely are their formal educational and supervisory opportunities to develop, assess, and refine mentoring competencies. This places a significant ethical burden on the individual mentor to thoughtfully assess competence in the mentor role, ideally with input from others with expertise in mentoring abilities and practices.

Not all people – including those assigned as mentors in some programs – possess the competence to mentor (Johnson and Huwe, 2002). At times, a mentor may not have sufficient experience or expertise in the profession or the specific job to serve as an able guide to someone junior. At other times, a person may be quite skilled and experienced – even renowned – in his or her profession, yet manifest clear deficits in social skills and emotional awareness. Basic emotional intelligence characterized by self-awareness and accuracy in reading the emotional states of others is a key component of mentorship (Goleman, 1995). Additionally, assigned mentors may harbor malignant personality characteristics or unresolved emotional or mental health problems that pose significant challenges to prospective mentees.

A final ethical challenge bearing on mentoring competence is the obligation to maintain competence over time. At times, any professional may become impaired, meaning that previous competence is diminished or threatened by life events, life changes, or distress that accompanies them (Barnett, 2008; Johnson et al., 2013). If a mentor experiences problems with mentoring competence as a result of conflicts, relational problems, or phase-of-life difficulties – particularly if he or she can no longer work safely and helpfully with mentees – then it is incumbent upon that professional to suspend, limit, or discontinue mentoring activities.

Advocacy versus evaluation

As any mentoring relationship moves across the mentoring relationship continuum and involves greater trust, commitment, and mutuality, the relationship may take on many of the features of what Ragins labels *relational mentoring* (Fletcher and Ragins, 2007; Ragins, 2012). Strong relational mentorships are defined by these features: (1) *fundamentally reciprocal* – the relationship involves mutual influence, growth, and learning; (2) *fluid expertise and complementarity* – the dyad develops the ability to easily and authentically switch between learner and expert roles as appropriate; (3) *increasing vulnerability* – both parties must develop the ability to reveal shortcomings and developmental needs so that these can be addressed in a supportive way; (4) *extended range of intended outcomes* – relational mentoring may bolster not only career success but also stimulate a stronger sense of professional identity; and (5) *holistic approach* – relational mentoring acknowledges that high-quality mentoring can influence quality of life generally, not just work performance.

It should come as no surprise that as a mentoring relationship becomes more mutual, reciprocal and relational in character, mentors feel a pull to engage in greater advocacy, protection, and collegial friendship (Johnson, 2014). But in many mentoring contexts, mentors must simultaneously provide some evaluation or assessment of performance. Sometimes, these are high-stakes assessments (e.g. graduation, tenure, salary increase, promotion) with significant implications for both the mentee and the organization or profession. The ethical challenge here is strong advocacy born of mutuality on one hand and the professional requirement to safeguard the organization, the profession, and possibly the public (a mentee's future clients) on the other (Johnson, 2008, 2016). Managing this ethical tension is an inherent obligation of effective mentoring in many contexts and therefore a component of mentor competence. Excellent mentors carefully walk the line between advocacy and screening on behalf of the profession; nowhere is this ethical duty more acute than in professions in which the mentee will go on to interact with the public in positions of trust.

Privacy and confidentiality

From time to time, most mentors will struggle with ethical tensions and quandaries linked to whether to keep information disclosed to them by a mentee in confidence. In most professions, confidentiality is a time honored tradition. It may also have legal implications if the mentor is a lawyer, healthcare provider, or clergy member. Confidentiality refers to a general standard of professional conduct that requires professionals not to discuss information about those they serve with others, except under certain circumstances agreed to by both parties (Fisher, 2013; Koocher and Keith-Spiegel, 2008). Maintaining confidentiality is central to professionalism and inextricably linked to respect and trust (Johnson and Ridley, 2008a).

In the context of mentoring relationships, preserving confidentiality demonstrates respect for the mentee as well as discretion, respect, and trustworthiness on the part of the mentor. In many contexts, the mentoring relationship is perceived by the mentee as a safe space in which to address deeply personal concerns and to experiment with new ways of thinking and behaving. As a mentoring relationship moves across the MRC in the direction of relational mentoring, this implicit sense of trust in the mentor's discretion is likely to increase. Ethical tensions related to confidentiality may arise in contexts such as educational and professional training programs in which the mentor is obligated to render summative evaluations of the mentee or register concerns about competence with institutional administrators or credentialing authorities (Johnson, 2008).

Behnke (2014) recently called into question the validity of applying traditional conceptions of confidentiality – best understood in the context of professional-client relationships – to other varieties of relationships, such as mentorships. When discussing mentoring, it may be more appropriate to speak in terms of the ethical obligation to *protect privacy*. Whereas confidentiality pertains primarily to professional service-delivery – having clear legal and ethical foundations – privacy flows from the value of respect for persons more generally (Behnke, 2014). Both privacy and confidentiality share an interest in protecting people, but in most cases, mentors will not have a legal/ethical obligation to protect confidentiality as much as a broad ethical/professional interest in serving their mentee's best interests, including the safeguarding of any information shared with the mentor in private.

Intimacy, attraction, and sexual feelings

Those mentorships that endure over time, becoming increasingly relational and mutual in nature are likely to involve greater attachment, emotional depth, and intimacy. Feelings of closeness and connection in strong mentorships can inevitably lead to an increase in intimacy and commitment, a desire to promote the best interests of the other person. In Sternberg's triangular theory of love (Sternberg, 1986), any relationship defined by intimacy and commitment – and excluding any romance or sexual passion – is described as *companionate love*. Such love relationships are essentially long-term, committed friendships. Because it is not unusual for both mentors and mentees to report emotional intimacy and commitment in some mentorships, it is particularly important for mentors to ensure that romantic passion does not also enter the equation, creating potential risk for the mentee (Ragins, 2012).

Although emotional intimacy need not create ethical problems in a mentorship, the addition of romantic attraction and sexual feelings clearly require a thoughtful response on the part of the mentor. Survey research reveals that sexual and romantic attraction is not an uncommon experience among professionals who mentor. For instance, a survey of 483 psychologists in academic settings found that 93 percent of male and 64 percent of female professors experienced sexual attraction to students (Tabachnick et al., 1991).

Most often a concern in cross-gender mentorships, some mentors respond to feelings of attraction with shame and anxiety leading to abrupt termination of the mentorship and feelings of confusion and abandonment on the part of the mentee (Johnson and Huwe, 2002). In other cases, mentors may fail to manage their own romantic/sexual attraction to a mentee, resulting in the sexualizing of the mentorship, potential harm to the mentee, and subsequent loss of the mentoring value in the relationship (Hammel et al., 1996; Koocher and Keith-Spiegel, 2008). It is clear that mentors must find an appropriate balance between intimacy and professionalism while carefully managing their own experiences of attraction. Self-awareness, close consultative relationships with colleagues, persistent focus on one's fiduciary responsibilities to mentees, and a willingness to transition a mentee to a different mentor might all be elements of an ethical stance when attraction and sexual feelings begin to interfere with the work of mentorship.

Self-disclosure

Defined as revealing information – especially personal information – about oneself to a mentee, self-disclosure is considered a salient mentoring competency. Self-disclosure by an admired mentor can bolster a mentee's confidence, alleviate anxiety, and model professional problem-solving for a mentee (Johnson, 2014). In the hands of a seasoned and judicious mentor, the technique of self-disclosure – particularly when tailored to the mentee's current situation or developmental need – may offer poignant life and career lessons, provide examples to steer by, and reduce the trainee's chances of making similar mistakes. A struggling mentee might be deeply impacted and encouraged to discover that even an accomplished senior professional has struggled, even failed, in years gone by. Self-disclosure models self-awareness and a willingness to be authentic in the relationship. It can reinforce for the mentee that often, success does not come without a struggle.

Self-disclosure also enhances intimacy and communicates commitment and caring to a mentee. This may explain why mentees often rate self-disclosure as a key quality in a mentor (Johnson and Ridley, 2008b). A mentee suffering from self-doubt, performance anxiety, and hopelessness may be profoundly buoyed by examples from the mentor's own missteps and subsequent triumphs. Because self-disclosure is one element of increasing intimacy, a mentor must remain vigilant to evidence that self-disclosure is leading to dependency, undue intimacy, or romantic involvement. It is also vitally important for mentors to keep in mind that personal information disclosed to a mentee can never be retracted; it may also be shared by the mentee with others in the organization.

The ethical issue here involves assuring a prudent balance between self-disclosure in the service of encouraging and guiding the mentee and self-disclosure that becomes too personal, crossing boundaries that leads to a loss of professionalism. From an ethical/professional perspective, self-disclosure should only occur if – in the mentor's thoughtful opinion – the disclosure is likely to be helpful and useful in the career or personal development of the mentee. There are obvious boundary concerns when a mentor discloses merely for personal gratification.

Multiple relationships

A multiple relationship occurs when a professional in one professional role with a person simultaneously enters another role with that same person. As a general rule, professionals are instructed to avoid multiple relationships when feasible, particularly if there is a reasonable potential for the multiple relationship to impair the professional's objectivity, competence, or effectiveness in performing his or her professional functions (APA, 2010). While a laudable aspiration in most circumstances, quite often mentoring relationships are characterized by numerous overlapping roles and multiple relationships may be ubiquitous in many mentoring contexts. For instance, in academe, a faculty mentor may serve as a mentee's instructor, evaluator, research supervisor, and program advisor, and some of the most effective mentorships involve interaction during travel and at social gatherings, making multiple relationships an ever present ethical challenge (Biaggio et al., 1997; Johnson, 2002). Decision-making models for avoiding multiple relationships may be of limited utility when it comes to mentoring. For instance, these models often caution professionals to avoid entering into multiple roles if a significant power imbalance exists, the relationship is of long duration, or there is no clear termination point to the relationships (cf. Gottlieb, 1993). Naturally these are all features of mentorships (Johnson and Nelson, 1999). An alternative decision-making model for deciding to enter a multiple relationship with a mentee in academe was proposed by Blevins-Knabe (1992). She posed several questions mentors could use in multiple relationship decision-making: (1) Is the professor role negatively compromised? (2) Is the professor exploiting the student? (3) Is the professor increasing the likelihood of being exploited? and (4) Is the professor's behavior interfering with the professional roles of other faculty?

A significant ethical issue related to multiple relationships between mentors and mentees is the increasing risk of exploitation of the mentee – whether deliberate or inadvertent. When boundaries and caution about multiple roles are not honored, a mentee may be exploited sexually, emotionally, financially, or otherwise (Moberg and Velasquez, 2004; Tucker and Adams-Price, 2001). At times, exploitation may be quite subtle (e.g. using a mentee to get revenge on a colleague, requiring a mentee to perform menial research or administrative tasks, using a mentee to meet emotional needs). It is imperative that mentors are appropriately cautious about crossing boundaries and creating multiple roles with mentees. Always alert to avoiding exploitation of their mentees, mentors also appreciate the need for increasing collegiality and mutuality as a mentoring relationship endures and evolves.

Equal access by diverse mentees

A final ethical challenge for mentors is rooted in the general ethical principles of justice and fairness. Professionals recognize that justice and fairness entitle all individuals to access and benefit from the crucial advantages associated with mentoring (APA, 2010; Atkinson et al., 1991; Clark et al., 2000; Lunsford, 2012). Mentors must work consciously to ensure that their selection and engagement with mentees does not systematically exclude talented members of any demographic group. Here is a salient question for mentors: Do potential mentees have equal access to you as a mentor regardless of age, race, ethnicity, sex, sexual orientation, religion, disability, or attractiveness (Johnson, 2016)? If all of a mentor's mentees look exactly the same in a context in which diversity exists among junior personnel or students, then the most ethical response would be to honestly consider how to intentionally reach out to demographic groups not represented among one's current mentees.

The ethical challenge of equal access is inextricably linked with the ongoing challenge to monitor and update one's competence in the mentor role (Johnson, 2003; Schlosser and Foley, 2008). Competence includes attitudes, knowledge, and skills bearing on multicultural and cross-gender mentoring relationships (Hyers et al., 2012; Schlosser et al., 2011).

MENTORSHIPS ARE FIDUCIARY RELATIONSHIPS

Among the many benefits of mentoring is the inevitable transmission of professional values and practices across generations. Regardless of the mentor's intentionality as a role model in this regard, mentees will inherit key elements of a profession's culture of moral, ethical, and collegial mores directly from the person and behavior of the mentor (Nakamura and Shernoff, 2009). Ragins (2012) observed that, for better or worse, strong mentoring relationships will instill mental maps in mentees for what professionals do, as well as how mentoring relationships work. Framing these mental maps as *mentoring schemas*, Ragins believes these schemas, 'shape their [mentees] expectations, frame their experiences, and motivate their behaviors in mentoring relationships...Essentially, mentoring schemas are knowledge structures of what mentoring relationships look like' (2012: 523).

Because those who mentor are automatically exemplars of ethics, professionalism, interpersonal skill, and competency for mentees, they must be especially vigilant and thoughtful regarding both the implicit attitudes and explicit behaviors they communicate to mentees about how to 'be' ethical in one's discipline (Johnson, 2016). In this vein, Silva and Tom (2001) offered three *moral imperatives* for mentors to live by when serving in the mentor role. They include: (1) *embrace a moral stance* – accept the moral obligation to care for, and take responsibility for, your mentees. Moral mentors believe they are obligated to support and actively influence the growth of those they mentor; (2) *create a moral context* – develop a protected space in which mentees can take risks, experiment with professional behaviors, and receive unconditional encouragement and support; and (3) *engage in a pedagogy of the moral* – mentors must model and teach morally and ethically, be congruent in attitude and behavior, highlight ethical dilemmas and solutions for mentees, and model ethical/professional behavior.

Not only are mentors powerful models of professional ethics, mentoring relationships that persist over time often create a strong working alliance between the members, including some level of attachment on the part of the mentee (Gunn and Pistole, 2012; Huber et al., 2010). Attachment connotes an emotional bond that develops between mentor and mentee that results in greater proximity between the two and more protective functions from the mentor. As working alliance and attachment grow, there is a natural increase in deep – often implicit – psychological contracts in a mentorship

(Haggard and Turban, 2012). These reflect the individual mentee's belief regarding the terms and conditions of the relationship and obligations owed to the mentor in exchange for his or her guidance. Such implicit, unspoken contracts can leave the mentee vulnerable to exploitation.

For all of these reasons, Plaut (1993) emphasized that a mentoring relationship must always be considered a *fiduciary* relationship: 'a special relationship in which one person accepts the trust and confidence of another to act in the latter's best interest… the parties do not deal on equal terms…the fiduciary [mentor] must act with the utmost good faith and solely for the benefit of the dependent party' (1993: 213).

In nearly all cases, mentors hold some measure of power relative to mentees and therefore must place mentee's interests first in all decisions and actions.

In order to assist mentors in accepting and managing their fiduciary responsibility to mentees, and in order to support mentors in the work of meeting the ethical challenges and tensions described earlier in this chapter, I now offer a preliminary Mentoring Code of Ethics. Based on earlier efforts by the author to codify mentoring ethics (Johnson, 2003, 2016; Johnson and Nelson, 1999), and the ethics codes of various professions (American Counseling Association, 2014; APA, 2010), this ethical code may be useful for mentors working in a wide range of institutions and organizations. The code is distinct from the European Mentoring and Coaching Council's Code of Ethics (EMCC, 2008) in that it emphasizes mentoring relationships exclusively. It may serve as a template that can evolve and be modified as required for use in specific mentoring contexts. The Code provides the salient, foundational ethical principles that should guide a mentor's values, attitudes, and behaviors in relationships with mentees. The Code incorporates the ideal mentor attributes and ethical competencies discussed earlier in this article.

A MENTORING CODE OF ETHICS

Preamble

Mentors strive to work competently and thoughtfully, with the best interests of those they serve in mind. Mentors accept the fiduciary responsibility to always consider the potential effects of their actions on the mentee when making decisions in the mentoring relationship. They are committed to encouraging and promoting the career and personal development of those they mentor. In doing so, they recognize that they often serve many roles such as role model, teacher, coach, confidant, and colleague. This Mentoring Code of Ethics provides a common set of principles upon which mentors build their mentoring work. Mentors endeavor to align all of their mentoring activities with the following foundational moral principles.

Ethical principles for mentors

Adhering to general moral and ethical principles is an important first step in living out an ethical commitment. This section of the Mentoring Code of Ethics contains nine ethical principles for the practice of mentoring. These principles serve as the foundation for ethical mentor behavior and decision-making.

- *Beneficence*. Mentors strive to facilitate the growth and contribute to the welfare of their mentees. Mentors are obligated to promote mentees' best interests, to understand the unique needs of each mentee, and to be diligent in providing knowledge, wisdom, and developmental support.
- *Nonmaleficence*. Mentors work deliberately to avoid intentional or unintended harm to those they mentor. Mentors are careful to avoid neglect, abandonment, or exploitation of mentees and quick to intervene when a mentee's attempt to follow a mentor's guidance turns out badly. Mentors avoid boundary violations

(for example, romantic or sexual behavior) that are likely to harm mentees.
- *Autonomy*. Mentors endeavor to strengthen mentees' knowledge, maturity, and independence. Mentors work to facilitate rather than hinder mentees' ability to exercise autonomous judgment and reasoning. Mentors avoid promoting intellectual or relational dependency and encourage mentees to demonstrate creativity, progressive independence, and a sense of self as a professional.
- *Fidelity*. Mentors keep promises and remain loyal to those they mentor. Mentors are loyal to mentees above all else and work diligently to ensure that mentees receive what is due them in terms of attention, reward, support, and timely and honest evaluation. Mentors are honest in their feedback to mentees.
- *Justice*. Mentors ensure fair and equitable treatment of mentees regardless of variables such as race, ethnicity, gender, sexual orientation, and age. Mentors work to ensure equal access to mentoring for prospective mentees representing the full range of diversity present in the institution, organization, or other context.
- *Transparency*. In formal programs, mentors provide mentees with information necessary to make an informed decision about entering an assigned mentoring relationship. When mentorships begin informally, mentors encourage transparency and good communication about mutual expectations for the relationship.
- *Boundaries and multiple relationships*. Mentors are careful to honor boundaries in their relationships with mentees. They are cautious not to enter into a new relationship with the mentee if the new relationship (e.g. business, romantic) could compromise the value of the mentorship or if the new relationship could result in exploitation of the mentee. When the mentoring context creates unavoidable multiple relationships, the mentor is careful to discuss these overlapping roles with the mentee and to prevent harm to the mentee as a consequence of the multiple roles.
- *Privacy*. Mentors protect information shared with them in confidence by mentees. Mentors recognize that although mentor-mentee relationships are not privileged in the sense of legal protection, mentors always avoid revealing sensitive material disclosed by mentees in the course of the mentorship without the mentee's consent. If a disclosure of private information is necessary, such as to keep a mentee safe or to prevent harm to others (such as clients with whom a mentee works), then mentors attempt to discuss this exception to privacy with their mentees in advance of the disclosure.
- *Competence*. Mentors consistently work to establish and develop competence in the mentor role. These efforts may include training, continuing education, supervised experience, study, and consultation. If personal problems or conflicts create problems of competence in the mentor role, mentors seek collegial consultation and limit or suspend their mentoring activities as necessary.

CONCLUSION

Excellence in the mentor role requires both competence in delivering a number of distinct mentoring functions and careful adherence to salient ethical principles. The key ethical challenges for mentors and the proposed Mentoring Code of Ethics presented by the author naturally lead to several recommendations. First, it is imperative that organizational and institutional leaders tasked with screening and hiring decisions consider evidence of moral virtue and a track record of ethical behavior when considering applicants for mentoring roles. Second, the Mentoring Code of Ethics might naturally lend itself to mentor training and development efforts. Third, prospective mentees (e.g. students, junior personnel) should be made familiar with the ethical expectations of mentors such that they are empowered to discuss or report ethical concerns that may arise. As a corollary to this recommendation, it is important for mentees to understand and internalize their own ethical obligations as participants in reciprocal developmental relationships. Future scholarship and policy development should focus on a reasonable set of ethical guidelines for mentees. Finally, the proposed Mentoring Code of Ethics may be useful as a starting point for discussing concerns or adjudicating complaints about a mentor's behavior.

REFERENCES

Allen, T.D. and Eby, L.T. (2003) 'Relationship effectiveness for mentors: factors associated with learning and quality', *Journal of Management*, 29 (4): 469–86.

Allen, T.D. and Eby, L.T. (2007) The Blackwell Handbook of Mentoring: A Multiple Perspectives Approach. Malden: Blackwell.

Allen, T.D., Finkelstein, L.M. and Poteet, M.L. (2009) *Designing Workplace Mentoring Programs: An Evidence-Based Approach*. New York: Wiley-Blackwell.

American Counseling Association (ACA) (2014) *Code of Ethics*. Alexandria: American Counseling Association (http://www.counseling.org/knowledge-center/ethics).

American Psychological Association (APA) (2010) *Ethical Principles of Psychologists and Code of Conduct*. Washington, DC: American Psychological Association (http://www.apa.org/ethics/code/index.aspx).

Atkinson, D.R., Neville, H. and Casas, A. (1991) 'The mentorship of ethnic minorities in professional psychology', *Professional Psychology: Research and Practice*, 22 (4): 336–8.

Barnett, J.E. (2008) 'Impaired professionals: distress, professional impairment, self-care, and psychological wellness', in M. Herson and A.M. Gross (eds), *Handbook of Clinical Psychology*, Vol. 1. New York: John Wiley and Sons, pp. 857–84.

Behnke, S. (2014) 'Remedial and disciplinary interventions in graduate psychology training programs: twenty-five essential questions for faculty and supervisors', in W.B. Johnson and N.J. Kaslow (eds), *Oxford Handbook of Education and Training in Professional Psychology*. New York: Oxford University Press, pp. 356–76.

Biaggio, M., Paget, T.L. and Chenoweth, M.S. (1997) 'A model for ethical management of faculty-student dual relationships', *Professional Psychology: Research and Practice*, 28 (2): 184–9.

Blevins-Knabe, B. (1992) 'The ethics of dual relationships in higher education', *Ethics and Behavior*, 2 (3): 151–63.

Braxton, J.M., Proper, E. and Bayer, A.E. (2011) 'Professionalism in graduate teaching and mentoring', in J.C. Hermanowicz (ed.), *The American Academic Profession: Transformation in Contemporary Higher Education*. Baltimore: The Johns Hopkins University Press, pp. 168–90.

Chao, G.T. (2009) 'Formal mentoring: Lessons learned from past practice', *Professional Psychology: Research and Practice*, 40 (3): 314–20.

Clark, R.A., Harden, S.L. and Johnson, W.B. (2000) 'Mentor relationships in clinical psychology doctoral training: results of a national survey', *Teaching of Psychology*, 27 (4): 262–8.

Corey, G., Corey, M.S., Corey, C. and Callanan, P. (2015) *Issues and Ethics in the Helping Professions*, 9th edn. Stamford: Cengage Learning.

Eby, L.T., Allen, T.D., Evans, S.C., Ng, T. and DuBois, D.L. (2008) 'Does mentoring matter? A multidisciplinary meta-analysis comparing mentored and non-mentored individuals', *Journal of Vocational Behavior*, 72 (2): 254–67.

Eby, L.T., McManus, S.E., Simon, S.A. and Russell, J.E.A. (2000) 'The protégé's perspective regarding negative mentoring experiences: the development of a taxonomy', *Journal of Vocational Behavior*, 57 (1): 1–21.

Egan, T.M. and Song, Z. (2008) 'Are facilitated mentoring programs beneficial? A randomized experimental field study', *Journal of Vocational Behavior*, 72 (3): 351–62.

Epstein, R.M. and Hundert, E.M. (2002) 'Defining and assessing professional competence', *Journal of the American Medical Association*, 287 (2): 226–35.

European Mentoring and Coaching Council (EMCC) (2008) *EMCC Code of Ethics*. Marlborough: European Mentoring and Coaching Council (http://www.emccouncil.org/src/ultimo/models/Download/4.pdf).

Fisher, M.A. (2013) *The Ethics of Conditional Confidentiality: A Practice Model for Mental Health Professionals*. New York: Oxford University Press.

Fletcher, J.K. and Ragins, B.R. (2007) 'Stone center relational cultural theory', in B.R. Ragins and K.E. Kram (eds), *The Handbook of Mentoring at Work: Theory, Research, and Practice*. Thousand Oaks: Sage, pp. 373–99.

Forehand, R.L. (2008) 'The art and science of mentoring in psychology: a necessary practice to ensure our future', *American Psychologist*, 63 (8): 744–55.

Goleman, D. (1995) *Emotional Intelligence*. New York: Bantam.

Gottlieb, M.C. (1993) 'Avoiding exploitive dual relationships: a decision-making model', *Psychotherapy*, 30 (1): 41–8.

Gunn, J.E. and Pistole, M.C. (2012) 'Trainee supervisor attachment: explaining the alliance and disclosure in supervision', *Training and Education in Professional Psychology*, 6 (4): 229–37.

Haggard, D.L. and Turban, D.B. (2012) 'The mentoring relationship as a context for psychological contract development', *Journal of Applied Social Psychology*, 42 (8): 1904–31.

Hammel, G.A., Olkin, R. and Taube, D.O. (1996) 'Student-educator sex in clinical and counseling psychology doctoral training', *Professional Psychology: Research and Practice*, 27 (1): 93–7.

Huber, D.M., Sauer, E.M., Mrdjenovich, A.J. and Gugiu, P.C. (2010) 'Contributions to advisory working alliance: advisee attachment orientation and pairing methods', *Training and Education in Professional Psychology*, 4 (4): 244–53.

Hyers, L.L., Syphan, J., Cochran, K. and Brown, T. (2012) 'Disparities in the professional development interactions of university faculty as a function of gender and ethnic underrepresentation', *Journal of Faculty Development*, 26 (1): 18–28.

Johnson, W.B. (2002) 'The intentional mentor: strategies and guidelines for the practice of mentoring', *Professional Psychology: Research and Practice*, 33 (1): 88–96.

Johnson, W.B. (2003) 'A framework for conceptualizing competence to mentor', *Ethics and Behavior*, 13 (2): 127–51.

Johnson, W.B. (2008) 'Are advocacy, mutuality, and evaluation incompatible mentoring functions?' *Mentoring and Tutoring: Partnership in Learning*, 16 (1): 31–44.

Johnson, W.B. (2014) 'Mentoring in psychology education and training: a mentoring relationship continuum model', in W.B. Johnson and N.J. Kaslow (eds), *The Oxford Handbook of Education and Training in Professional Psychology*. New York: Oxford University Press, pp. 272–90.

Johnson, W.B. (2016) *On Being a Mentor: A Guide for Higher Education Faculty*, 2nd edn. New York: Routledge.

Johnson, W.B., Barnett, J.E., Elman, N.S., Forrest, L. and Kaslow, N.J. (2013) 'The competence constellation model: a communitarian approach to support professional competence', *Professional Psychology: Research and Practice*, 44 (5): 343–54.

Johnson, W.B. and Huwe, J.M. (2002) 'Toward a typology of mentorship dysfunction in graduate school', *Psychotherapy*, 39 (1): 44–55.

Johnson, W.B. and Nelson, N. (1999) 'Mentor-protégé relationships in graduate training: some ethical concerns', *Ethics and Behavior*, 9 (3): 189–210.

Johnson, W.B. and Ridley, C.R. (2008a) *The Elements of Ethics for Professionals*. New York: Palgrave McMillan.

Johnson, W.B. and Ridley, C.R. (2008b) *The Elements of Mentoring*. New York: Palgrave McMillan.

Johnson, W.B., Skinner, C.J. and Kaslow, N.J. (2014) 'Relational mentoring in clinical supervision: the transformational supervisor', *Journal of Clinical Psychology: In Session*, 70 (11): 1073–81.

Kammeyer-Mueller, J.D. and Judge, T.A. (2008) 'A quantitative review of mentoring research: a test of a model', *Journal of Vocational Behavior*, 72 (3): 269–83.

Kaslow, N.J. and Mascaro, N.A. (2007) 'Mentoring interns and postdoctoral residents in academic health sciences centers', *Journal of Clinical Psychology in Medical Settings*, 14 (3): 191–6.

Koocher, G.P. and Keith-Spiegel, P. (2008) *Ethics in Psychology: Professional Standards and Cases*, 3rd edn. New York: Oxford University Press.

Kram, K.E. (1985) *Mentoring at Work: Developmental Relationships in Organizational Life*. Glenview: Scott Foresman.

Levinson, D.J., Darrow, C.N., Klein, E.B., Levinson, M.H. and McKee, B. (1978) *The Seasons of a Man's Life*. New York: Ballentine.

Lunsford, L. (2012) 'Doctoral advising or mentoring? Effects on student outcomes', *Mentoring and Tutoring: Partnership in Learning*, 20 (2): 251–70.

Moberg, D.J. and Velasquez, M. (2004) 'The ethics of mentoring', *Business Ethics Quarterly*, 14 (1): 95–122.

Nakamura, J. and Shernoff, D.J. (2009) *Good Mentoring: Fostering Excellent Practice in Higher Education*. New York: Wiley.

Plaut, S.M. (1993) 'Boundary issues in teacher-student relationships', *Journal of Sex and Marital Therapy*, 19 (3): 210–19.

Ragins, B.R. (2012) 'Relational mentoring: a positive approach to mentoring at work', in K.S. Cameron and G.M. Spreitzer (eds), *The Oxford Handbook of Positive Organizational Scholarship*. New York: Oxford University Press, pp. 519–36.

Ragins, B.R. and Cotton, J.L. (1990) 'Mentor functions and outcomes: a comparison of men and women in formal and informal mentoring relationships', *Journal of Applied Psychology*, 84 (4): 529–30.

Ragins, B.R. and Kram, K.E. (2007) 'The roots and meaning of mentoring', in B.R. Ragins and K.E. Kram (eds), *The Handbook of Mentoring at Work: Theory, Research and Practice*. Los Angeles: Sage, pp. 3–15.

Rosenberg, A. and Heimberg, R.G. (2009) 'Ethical issues in mentoring doctoral students in clinical psychology', *Cognitive and Behavioral Practice*, 16 (2): 181–90.

Rubin, N.J., Bebeau, M., Leigh, I.W., Lichtenberg, J.W., Nelson, P.D., Portnoy, S., Smith, I.L. and Kaslow, N.J. (2007) 'The competency movement within psychology: an historical perspective', *Professional Psychology: Research and Practice*, 38 (5): 452–62.

Scandura, T.A. (1998) 'Dysfunctional mentoring relationships and outcomes', *Journal of Management*, 24 (3): 449–67.

Schlosser, L.Z. and Foley, P.F. (2008) 'Ethical issues in multicultural student-faculty mentoring relationships in higher education', *Mentoring and Tutoring: Partnership in Learning*, 16 (1): 63–75.

Schlosser, L.Z., Lyons, H.Z., Talleyrand, R.M., Kim, B.S.K. and Johnson, W.B. (2011) 'A multiculturally infused model of graduate advising relationships', *Journal of Career Assessment*, 38 (1): 44–61.

Silva, D. and Tom, A.R. (2001) 'The moral basis of mentoring', *Teacher Education Quarterly*, 28 (2): 39–52.

Sternberg, R.J. (1986) 'A triangular theory of love', *Psychological Review*, 93 (2): 119–35.

Sternberg, R.J. (2002) 'The teachers we never forget', *Monitor on Psychology*, 33: 68.

Tabachnick, B.G., Keith-Spiegel, P. and Pope, K.S. (1991) 'Ethics of teaching: beliefs and behaviors of psychologists as educators', *American Psychologist*, 46 (5): 506–15.

Tucker, R.C. and Adams-Price, C.E. (2001) 'Ethics in the mentoring of gerontologists: rights and responsibilities', *Educational Gerontology*, 27 (2): 185–97.

Underhill, C.M. (2005) 'The effectiveness of mentoring programs in corporate settings: a meta-analytical review of the literature', *Journal of Vocational Behavior*, 68 (2006): 292–307.

New Horizons for Mentoring Research: Exploring the Present and Past to Frame the Future

Beverly J. Irby, Jennifer Boswell, Nahed Abdelrahman, Rafael Lara-Alecio and Fuhui Tong

Buddha said, 'If you want to know your future, look to the past'. Just as Buddha indicated, we, too, found it important to look to the past to examine published literature on mentoring in order to create a clearer picture of what the future might hold for mentoring research. Mentoring has become a worldwide phenomenon that has been proliferated in publications for no less than 20 years. In fact, when searching Amazon, we found 1,741 books published on some aspect of mentoring, while there are 627 handbooks inclusive of mentoring noted. Additionally, since 1993, there has been a journal devoted specifically to mentoring, *Mentoring and Tutoring: Partnership in Learning* (M&T; originally published under the name, *Mentoring and Tutoring*), which is published by Routledge (Taylor & Francis); another that was founded in 2004 by the European Mentoring and Coaching Council (EMCC), entitled the *International Journal of Mentoring and Coaching* (IJMC), and an additional newer journal was initiated five years ago as the *International Journal of Mentoring and Coaching in Education* (IJMCE) published by Emerald Publishing. Though such publication formats on mentoring have flourished with concepts and processes of mentoring changing over time, the future of mentoring research is unknown. In order to help provide a glimpse into this future, we (i) examined published research methods and topics over the most recent five years in the three major journals on mentoring; (ii) provided an overview of the research; and (iii) presented insights into what the future of mentoring research might be.

METHOD FOR THE REVIEW

Scoping analysis

A scoping analysis was employed in this study. This type of analysis has been defined as a review within which broader topics have been addressed (Arksey and O'Malley, 2007). Scoping analysis has not been common in specific research to address questions or assess the quality of included data; but rather, it has been used to examine the key issues studied in a particular field or topic and map the available evidence (Ehrich et al., 2002). We sought to provide a comprehensive coverage of the available data on mentoring from the journals based on the intent of the chapter. We chose a scoping analysis for our method because we wanted to know what was predominant and broadly cast in the literature on *mentoring* published in the three major journals within the most recent five years.

Because our goal was to analyze what has existed in the literature from the three journals and to locate the gaps, we found the scoping analysis was appropriate; specifically, as in this analysis we included: (i) scanning the extent and the nature of research activity (Levac et al., 2010); (ii) summarizing and disseminating research findings and implications in order to make these results feasible for scholars (Valaitis et al., 2012); and (ii) addressing the gaps in the existing literature in mentoring in order to determine how the future of mentoring will be and how those gaps might be closed in the future. In conducting the scoping analysis, we followed five stages developed by Arksey and O'Malley (2007): (i) identified the research question(s); (ii) identified relevant studies; (iii) studied the selections; (iv) charted the data; and (v) collated and reported the results.

Stage 1. Identifying the scoping analysis research question(s)

The first step in the scoping analysis process was to identify the research questions. There were three research questions:

1 What primary methods did authors employ in published research in the three major journals focused on mentoring between 2010 and 2015?
2 What primary topics on mentoring were examined in published research in the three major journals focused on mentoring between 2010 and 2015?
3 What do these findings suggest about the future of mentoring research?

Stage 2. Identifying relevant studies

The second step in the process was to identify relevant studies. We decided to use the past five years, which would include the most recent publications on mentoring in the top three journals to determine what is published collectively in current literature and perhaps where the field might be moving. Therefore, we adopted a strategy to search through M&T, IJMCE, and IJMC in the time period between 2010 and 2015. For IJMCE, we analyzed all its four volumes including volume IV of 2015, because IJMCE was initiated in 2012. For M&T, we reviewed all 136 articles between 2010 and 2015, and we reviewed the 39 articles in the IJMC and the 59 articles in IJMCE. We screened a total of 234 peer-reviewed articles.

Refworks was utilized to store the articles and make the initial scan to determine the methodology that was used and the results found. Refworks is an online research management tool that is utilized to organize the documents and create instant citations and bibliographies (ProQuest, 2015). It is also useful when more than one researcher works on the same project, because it allows the researchers to screen documents separately and make decisions about the screened documents based on the study's inclusion and exclusion criteria. Refworks also enables the researchers to validate their findings through comparing the decision made by each one of the research team members (Refworks, 2015).

Themes were developed based on the topic discussed in each journal and then combined. In order to ensure that all articles were included in the scoping analysis, we developed a reference list and hand searched them in the process.

Stage 3. Study selection

We engaged in study selection by conducting two intensive screens of the abstract and then an optional screening of the full article as a third screen, if necessary, for a full understanding of the topic and findings. A fourth and final screening for the implication and discussion sections was conducted in order to identify the gaps and the future of mentoring based on the examined research.

Stage 4. Charting the data

The next step was to chart key items of the results obtained from the first and second screening. Ritchie and Spencer (1994) introduced charting as a technique to synthesize and interpret qualitative data by sorting the materials based on the key themes. The charted information included items as follows:

- Abstract of all articles that were published in the three journals 2010 and 2015
- The method of the studies (qualitative, quantitative, or mixed method)
- The major findings

Stage 5. Collating, summarizing, and reporting the results

In the final stage, we collated the results in spreadsheets. The research team met to have final discussions on the findings and to validate the results that each one found. An agreement was required on the themes and sub-themes of the search. Therefore, we discussed each theme in this final stage in order to make a final agreement about the themes and inclusion of articles within that theme. Next, we summarized the results. These findings are shared in the sections that follow.

FINDINGS

We report our findings to the research question. The first section deals with the types of research methods utilized in the past five years among the three mentoring journals. The second section is related to topics researched in mentoring in those journals. In the final section, we report future research directions based on the findings.

Type of methods employed

Commonalities in methods used by authors were evident across the three journals examined, and in Table 8.1, we have noted the different methods evident in each of the journals.

Upon review, qualitative approaches were the most prominently used by the researchers in the articles published in 128 articles in the three journals, M&T, IJMCE, and IJMC. The most commonly-used qualitative approaches were case study designs, phenomenology,

Table 8.1 Methods employed

	M&T	IJMCE	IJMC	Total
Quantitative	41	8	12	61
Qualitative	60	47	21	128
Mixed methods	6	4	5	15
Conceptual	12	0	0	12
Other	19	0	0	19
Total	138	59	38	235

M&T, *Mentoring and Tutoring; Partnership in Learning*; IJMCE, *International Journal of Mentoring and Coaching in Education*; IJMC, *International Journal of Mentoring and Coaching*.

and narrative inquiry. In the quantitatively-focused articles ($n = 61$), the authors used experimental designs, single subject design, and quasi-experimental designs. They used analyses such as structural equation modeling (SEM), ANOVA, MANOVA, multiple regression, and simple correlations. The authors of the published articles also reported mixed methods ($n = 15$), longitudinal designs ($n = 8$), action research ($n = 1$), meta-analyses ($n = 1$), mentoring scale development ($n = 1$), and literature syntheses ($n = 6$). Additionally, we found 12 conceptual articles among the three journals.

Major topics

The topics we determined to exist from the three major journals in mentoring were: (i) mentoring in academia; (ii) mentoring educators and students in schools; (iii) peer mentoring; (iv) mentoring programs and practices; (v) mentoring and diversity; and (vi) mentoring relationships. The following sections are results by topics from among the total 235 articles, with specific references to the related 166 articles that are exclusive to mentoring only; coaching and tutoring (68 articles) were not included for this particular analysis. Subcategories among the six topics are presented in italics.

Mentoring in academia (n = 39)

A large majority of the articles written from 2010 to 2014 in the three journals were centered on mentoring issues in the academic setting. General findings are that mentoring in academic settings leads to benefits in student success and an overall greater functionality of the university. Mentoring in higher education has been suggested in these articles collectively to be a significant factor in the professional development and retention of newer faculty members who have moved into higher education, particularly as much of the mentoring focuses on tenure and promotion issues. For students, mentoring also results in greater success academically, socially, and planning of careers. The articles can be divided into four topical sub-categories: (i) *mentoring issues in universities and academic organizational behavior* (i.e. Bean et al., 2014; Beane-Katner, 2014; Bristol et al., 2014; Dominguez and Hager, 2013; Lunsford, 2014; Millard and Korotov, 2014; Noufou et al., 2014; Searby, 2014); (ii) *mentoring needs and issues with faculty* (i.e. Cohen et al., 2012; Cureton et al., 2011; Diamond, 2010; Griffin and Beatty, 2010; Larose, 2013; Lunsford et al., 2013; Parker and McQuirter Scott, 2010; Pleschová and McAlpine, 2015; Reddick, 2012; Riebschleger and Cross, 2011; Rogers et al., 2010; Shobe et al., 2014); (iii) *mentoring needs and issues of students* (i.e. Behar-Horenstein et al., 2010; Charteris and Smardon, 2014; Creighton et al., 2010; de Haan and Sills, 2010; George and Mampilly, 2012; Grima-Farrell, 2015; Johnson and Harreld, 2012; Kendall and Smith-Jentsch, 2015; Langer, 2010; Larsen et al., 2015; Leidenfrost et al., 2011; Lunsford, 2012; Nganga, 2011; Rhodes and Fletcher, 2013; Schwartz and Holloway, 2014; Tenhunen and Leppisaari, 2010; Welfare et al., 2011; Welton et al., 2014); and (iv) *mentors personal professional growth, beliefs, and development* (i.e. Butler et al., 2013; George and Mampilly, 2012; Lejonberg et al., 2015; Sciarappa and Mason, 2014; Rekha and Ganesh, 2012; Stephens et al., 2014).

Mentoring educators and students in schools (n = 45)

The findings from 45 articles suggest six topical categories related to mentoring in schools. First, there is the topic of *mentoring teachers in training and in practice*, which has yielded increased job satisfaction, teacher retention, passion for social justice, development of critical pedagogies, and quality education (i.e. Ambrosetti et al., 2014; Asada, 2012; Bashan and Holsblat, 2012; Bullough, Jr., 2012; Catapano and Huisman,

2013; Clayton and Myran, 2013; D'Souza, 2014; Deutsch and Tong, 2011; Duckworth and Maxwell, 2015; Duncan and Stock, 2010; Eisenschmidt et al., 2013; Eriksson, 2013; Flavian and Kass, 2015; Flores et al., 2011; Frels et al., 2013; Grima-Farrell, 2015; Gut et al., 2014; Kass and Rajuan, 2012; LoCasale-Crouch et al., 2012; Long et al., 2012; Pogodzinski, 2012; Polly et al., 2015; Salter, 2015; Smith and Arsenault, 2014; Stanulis et al., 2014; Thurlings et al., 2012; Waterman and He, 2011; Wolffensperger, 2010; Wright et al., 2012; Wyatt and Arnold, 2012; Young and Cates, 2010). Another category is related to *principal mentoring and mentoring in principal preparation programs*, which was determined to improve instructional leadership (Parylo et al., 2012; Sciarappa and Mason, 2014; Searby, 2010). The third category is related to *mentors' knowledge and practices* (i.e. Achinstein and Davis, 2014; Barrera et al., 2010). The fourth category found concerns about the *mentoring of novice counselors* (Bickmore and Curry, 2013). The fifth category of articles in this section notes the opportunity for *mentoring of students* that bring about important impacts on the student and positive outcomes from the mentoring relationship, particularly related to improved student confidence, resilience, and satisfaction (i.e. Garza and Ovando, 2012; Holloway and Salinitri, 2010; Johnson et al., 2013; Kolar and McBride, 2011; Komosa-Hawkins, 2012; Larose et al., 2011; O'Shea et al., 2013; Thompson et al., 2013). The sixth subcategory of this topic is that of *role modeling and leadership development for female students* (i.e. Archard, 2012; Holmes et al., 2012).

Peer mentoring (n = 26)

In the 26 articles found on peer mentoring, there are six subcategories on the topic. First, *peer mentoring benefits both the mentor and mentee* (i.e. Bottoms et al., 2013; Brown et al., 2014; Douglass et al., 2013; Fleck and Mullins, 2012; Ward et al., 2012). Second, findings suggest that *peer mentors play a significant role in the academic success of the mentee* (i.e. De Four-Babb et al., 2015; Marshall et al., 2013). Third, *peer mentoring is commonly found in the university setting* and in faculty-to-faculty mentoring relationships (i.e. Bottoms et al., 2013; Esnard et al., 2015), student-to-student mentoring relationships (i.e. Douglass et al., 2013; Fleck and Mullins, 2012; Noufou et al., 2014; Outhred and Chester, 2013; Packard et al., 2014), and with non-traditional university students (Ward, 2012). Fourth, *trust is critical to peer mentoring* – on both sides of the mentoring relationship for the healthy development of a peer mentoring relationship (i.e. Cox, 2012; Holt and Lopez, 2014; Roach, 2014; Skaniakos et al., 2014; Ward, 2012). Fifth, specific *instruments were noted on how to assess peer mentoring* (i.e. Asada, 2012; Rivera-McCutchen and Panero, 2014; Wyatt and Arnold, 2012). Sixth, varying types of *peer e-mentoring* approaches were reported (i.e. Kendall and Smith-Jentsch, 2015; Tenhunen and Leppisaari, 2010; Thomas and Ensher, 2013).

Mentoring programs and practices (n = 24)

In the 24 articles on program and practices in the three major mentoring journals, six subcategories or subthemes were determined. First, it was found that there *is a need for ongoing development of research-based, developmental mentoring programs in higher education, K-12 settings, online settings, and in the workplace* (i.e. Barczyk et al., 2011; Brodeur et al., 2015; Crawford et al., 2014; Gallant and Gilham, 2014; Godden et al., 2014; Grima-Farrell, 2015; Huizing, 2012; Marcellino, 2011; Ness, 2013; O'Neill et al., 2011; Prywes, 2012; Stephens et al., 2014). Second, mentoring programs provide *experiential learning opportunities and promote reflection* for mentors and mentees regarding their relationships (i.e. Smith et al., 2013). Third, *positive experiences in mentoring programs were reflective of mentors' perceived satisfaction with the mentoring relationship* (Fair et al., 2011; Hughes et al.,

2010; Strapp et al., 2014). Fourth, mentoring programs in which there were *ongoing mentoring relationships where the mentor and mentee were in contact* often led to increases in the mentees' self-confidence (i.e. Choi and Lemberger, 2010; Griffiths and Armour, 2012; Mooney Simmie and Moles, 2011; Sandford et al., 2010). Fifth, *teachers mentoring teachers' programs* were beneficial for new educators by helping them to understand and navigate the educational setting (Feldhaus and Bentrem, 2015). Finally, related to *mentoring in the workplace*, most mentees reported positive experiences in the workplace but, in some cases, conflict occurred between the power of organizational structures and the performance of the mentees (i.e. Carter and Connage, 2007; Du Toit, 2006; Grace and Holloway, 2010).

Mentoring and diversity (n = 18)

Eighteen articles were published during the five-year period in the three journals about mentoring and diversity with four subtopics. In the vast majority of these articles, the authors argued that diversified cultures have significant impacts on higher education mentoring relationships and therefore have similar influence on public school mentoring and coaching relationships. In the first subcategory, it was argued by many authors that there were *challenges that face mentor-mentee relationships that are related to cultural differences* such as lack of organizational support and the unmatched attitudes of the mentees or mentoring processes (i.e. Chandler and Ellis, 2011; Lopez, 2013; Mackey and Shannon, 2014; Orland-Barak et al., 2013; Reddick, 2011). The second subcategory deals with the need to *better identify the varying aspects of culture and the role it plays in the mentoring relationship* (Aziz, 2011; Kochan, 2013; Lloyd-Jones, 2014; Meyer, 2015; Noufou et al., 2014; Parylo et al., 2012; Reddick, 2012). The third subcategory relates to mentoring relationships as they influence the professional and leadership development with *faculty of colo*r (i.e. Chang et al., 2014; Dancy II and Jean-Marie, 2014; Lloyd-Jones, 2014; Noufou et al., 2014; Reddick, 2012; Santamaria and Jaramillo, 2014; Tran, 2014), with the focus of those relationships being on psychosocial support, career skills, and expanding the faculty member's professional network. It was noted faculty of color experience isolation and many other formidable barriers to success, which leads to feelings of inferiority and anxiety. Different directions and possibilities that faculty of color, especially women faculty of color, could take in developing a professional network and community within higher education settings were suggested. The fourth subcategory, *gender and mentoring*, indicated that the results of the current body of mentoring research suggest that although gender was still a critical issue encountered by female mentors, it did not have a significant influence on coaching and mentoring competence. Mentoring appears to offer women a significant opportunity to be more engaged in academic life and helps them enhance their professional development through improving some soft skills such as interpersonal and leadership skills (Murakami and Nunez, 2014).

Mentoring relationships (n = 14)

Fourteen articles published in the three journals included in this scoping study focused specifically on mentoring relationships. There were four subtopics or categories identified under the topic or mentoring relationships. The first subcategory related to a *solid, trusting relationship* as important to mentoring outcomes and perceived effectiveness of the mentor (i.e. Bower and Hums, 2014; Dobie et al., 2010; Frels and Onwuegbuzie, 2012; Hargreaves, 2010; Jones and Brown, 2011; Peterson et al., 2010; Schwartz and Holloway, 2012; St. Jean and Audet, 2013). The second subcategory dealt with the *readiness of the mentor*; for example, the more a mentor was ready and willing to be a mentor, impacted the relationship and level of safety and trust of the mentee (i.e. Alhija and Fresko, 2014; Colvin and Ashman, 2010; Whitney et al., 2011).

The third subcategory or subtheme is related to *specific roles in the mentoring relationship* (roles as manager, mentor, and mentee, as well as service as a role model, advocate, developer of skills, challenger, and listener) (Adams and Slaven, 2011; Grace and Holloway, 2010). The fourth subcategory was promoted by Profetis (2015), who found that employing an *initiation phase in the mentoring process* strengthened the relationship between mentors and mentees, particularly in online mentoring.

NEW HORIZONS FOR MENTORING RESEARCH

Not only does what was published in the major three mentoring journals within the last five years point to the need for continuing study to address questions that still exist within the topics that have been recognized, but it also provides an important compass to steer researchers toward the future horizon dealing with topics and areas that have yet to be thoroughly examined. In general, our findings have led us to seven propositions.

Quantitative studies

First, as there were few substantive quantitative studies, we propose that there should be more of that type of study undertaken to help further understand the role of mentoring with various populations such as different K-12 student populations and diverse groups within higher education. With few quasi-experimental and virtually no experimental studies, we recommend such so that generalizations could be made to broader populations regarding mentoring.

Mentoring and cultural and linguistic diversity

Second, we advocate that more researchers focus on the relationship of mentoring and cultural and linguistic diversity. The literature contains a scant number of studies related to the combination of cultural and linguistic diversity and mentoring. Even in a general scan of the literature not included in the three journals, there are few studies related to mentoring such groups as English learners or bilingual teachers. The percentage of growth among school-aged Hispanic English learners in the United States increased rapidly from 2009 and 2013, from 10.9 million to 12.4 million – or 13.6 percent (National Center for Education Statistics, 2016). Thus, due to the sheer numbers of such learners in schools today, it would behoove the scholarly community to test and provide effective mentoring programs for the students and their teachers.

Seven typologies of mentoring

Third, we propose the further development of research related specific typologies of mentoring. There are seven that are not particularly noted in the literature or which did not include information published over the last five years. Included among these are (i) collaborative mentoring; (ii) topical mentoring; (iii) group mentoring; (iv) global mentoring; (v) situational mentoring; (vi) cultural mentoring; and (vii) virtual mentoring. For example, innovative *collaborative mentoring*, introduced in 2002 (Chaliès et al., 2008; Pololi et al., 2002), professes to help provide a supportive learning environment, but it was not explicitly discussed in the three journals. *Topical mentoring* is a new concept that we believe will become more important as the twenty-first century moves forward. By topical mentoring, we mean mentoring on specific information needed by individuals; for example, it could be technical information, workplace knowledge, or insight into a specific profession, institution, or sharing technical information, institutional knowledge and insight with respect to a particular occupation, profession, or work. This would be short-term mentoring based on immediate need. Third, there is little research that has been published on the significance of *group mentoring*. The significance of group mentoring relates to Irby's (2015) concept of *mentor capital*. She defined *mentor capital* as the professional and personal efficacy derived from the interactions of a dyad of people (and we add it could be with a group of people), particularly when there is mentoring of an individual(s) for professional growth. Professional and personal benefits for the mentor are that there is a satisfaction in seeing the mentee succeed and be productive. Additionally, there are opportunities for the mentor to also grow professionally through Bourdieu's concept of accumulated capacity (Bourdieu, 1986). For the mentee, the benefits are the productivity in performance and the enhancement of skills via the accumulated capacity. In all, the *mentor capital* has, in economic terms, specific returns on the investment of time of the mentor that is devoted to the mentee and is efficacious for both individuals. With group mentoring, there could be a multiplied effect on the investment. *Global mentoring*, not adequately present in the literature, should be studied for effectiveness. It has mainly been used with women in leadership and women in the sports arena (e.g. Global Mentoring Walk, 2016; Global Sports Mentoring Program [United States Department of State, 2016]) for the development of career trajectories. Also, largely absent from the literature is situational mentoring, which is similar to what we called topical mentoring, and what Derrick (2009) termed, 'flash mentoring'. According to Emelo (2010), *situational mentoring* is:

> [Q]uick hitting, short-term collaborative learning relationships that stimulate creative solutions. As with traditional mentoring, learners in situational mentoring engage advisers and experts for information, advice and feedback. Unlike traditional mentoring, learners in situational relationships look for collaborators who can give them specific advice on a single, targeted issue that requires a quick resolution. These compact micro-learning engagements are fast to set up and fast to shut down. (Emelo, 2010: 43)

Such mentoring is showing up in talent development and management programs, but was not found by this name in educational literature in the journals examined. The sixth typology is cultural mentoring. The Alberta Mentoring Partnership defined *cultural mentoring* as a 'focus is to share the customs, values and practices of a specific culture, tradition or group with the child, youth or group being mentored' (2014: 12). Although cross-cultural mentoring was noted in some of the articles reviewed, cultural mentoring was not. As the world grows more diverse, cultural mentoring could become more important. Furthermore, technological advances place the world at everyone's fingertips. The global culture must be considered in mentoring, and global cultural mentoring is on the horizon if not already here. One approach may be the use of a network of mentors. Such networks cannot be burdensome and may involve distant relationships through the use of technology and virtual platforms (Crocitto et al., 2005; Overman, 2004). The seventh typology we mention is virtual mentoring. According to Owen (2015), *virtual mentoring* is equated with 'distance mentoring, remote mentoring, tele-mentoring, cyber-mentoring and eMentoring. A virtual mentor works with a mentee using: synchronous tools: webinars, Voice Over Internet Protocol such as Skype and text chat; and asynchronous tools: emails, discussion forums, blog posts and comments on posts' (2015: 1). The concept of working face-to-face remotely and mentoring an individual in this manner and in real time is a needed area of research in mentoring. A fair amount of literature has emerged on how to conduct eMentoring, but not much is written in terms of research for virtual real-time mentoring.

Mentoring Millennials and GenXers

The fourth proposition emanates from the lack of research on mentoring with, and for, Millennials and GenXers. More than half of the employees in the world are Millennials. With Baby Boomers retiring and Generation Xers (term used for individuals born between early 1960s and early 1980s) being a smaller number than the Millennials (term generally considered born between early 1980s and 2004), there may not be sufficient numbers of mentors for the latter group. This situation calls for new strategies in mentoring to begin to take shape. There may be a need for *collaborative mentoring* in which the groups work with each other and mentor each other on specific job skills at which each group might be more adept – such as social media skills versus leadership skills. There may be a need for *topical mentoring* as change is coming about so rapidly and the topics may call for specific topics to be mentored – perhaps on a more short-term basis. *Group mentoring* may be used more widely as there are not sufficient mentors to match to the Millennials (Altus, 2015). *Virtual mentoring* may be appropriate in this context as Millennials are comfortable with technology, including texting and video conferencing (such as with Skype) (Owen, 2015). As factors such as body language and emotional connections may be lacking in such relationships, virtual mentoring is an area that needs much more development and exploration (Wallis et al., 2015). These differing types of platforms are structured for mentoring and differences between generations may require the development and investigation of training programs for mentors and mentees on how to work collaboratively and how to understand and value one another. Millennials, who tend to be dreamers, may require mentoring that establishes deeper reflective thoughts and actions (Beane-Katner, 2014; Myers and Sadaghiani, 2010; Trower, 2006). Generation Zers (born in the 2000 through 2010s) may be in early college now, and some are already in the workforce. They are digital technology savvy natives. This group has never been without mobile devices, but this group is a group of realists who like their work to be meaningful and engaging. Their high accessibility to technology and the internet may make them consider that coming in to the office is not realistic when they can finish tasks online instead. Therefore, *virtual mentoring* and technological access to the mentor may be more convenient to this group than face-to-face mentoring. Instant feedback, as that they have found in technology, may be required of the mentor.

Mentoring in succession planning

A fifth proposition is that there is a need to focus research on succession planning for leadership positions. Groves (2007) and Kim (2003) emphasized the importance of integrating mentoring relationships and succession planning in organizational workplace levels; however, nothing was found within these journals that dealt with succession planning at higher education or public school levels, or other workplace settings. The blending of mentoring and succession planning is hardly observed in governmental agencies due to the inability to show a preference of one individual over another (Reeves, 2010). A search in EBSCO yielded no references to mentoring, succession planning, and higher education or public schools. Mentoring for succession planning with Baby Boomers retiring is critical for the moment, but new jobs in technology for the future will require mentoring for roles that society has no idea even exists at this juncture in time. For example, it has been said that future workforce will be dealing with job roles in 3D printing (and ethical considerations for such; already guns can be produced with 3D printing),

DNA reading, environmental scientists, nanotechnology, privacy and cyber security, vertical farming, air bottling, water trading, and many more. The point is that there are jobs that no one even knows will exist. They are beyond imagination, and the type of mentoring needed may have to become what might be called *situational mentoring* – based on the job role and demand. The mentor may even be much younger than the mentee in such cases.

Ethics and mentoring

A sixth research recommendation or proposition is for researchers to consider adding to the literature in the area of ethics and mentoring. The topic of ethics in mentoring seems to be lacking as well in publications in the three journals. The University of Pittsburgh's Institute for Clinical Research Education (2016) noted that 'ethics involves the use of reasoned moral judgments to examine one's responsibility in any given situation. Mentors have the responsibility of teaching and role modeling the appropriate ethical behavior of academic professionals' (2016: para 1).

Mentoring as a discipline

With the topic of mentoring proliferating, the seventh proposition that we suggest is that mentoring becomes a discipline in its own right. Riggio (2013) indicated that there is not a clear answer as to what specifically defines an academic discipline. However, he did state that a discipline emerges with consensus. He stated, 'Consensus refers to shared agreement about: (1) a circumscribed knowledge base, (2) research methodology, (3) content and procedures for training, and (4) professional, scholarly journals and association(s)' (2013: 10). Mentoring is an *emergent discipline* as it (i) has a set of practices that define it; (ii) has a defined knowledge based with at least 20 years of published knowledge within a journal that is focused only on the topic of mentoring and within similarly-focused published books; (iii) has published studies using quantitative and/or qualitative methods grounded in the social sciences; (iv) has content and procedures for training; and (v) has professional, scholarly journals and associations. We promote this concept of mentoring as a discipline and more should be promulgated on this topic.

Conceptually, mentoring has been around since ancient times and much has been written about *what is* mentoring or on the present state of mentoring. However, it is critical for researchers and practitioners alike to understand that times are changing quickly and forward thinking regarding mentoring and mentors will be required over the next few decades.

CONCLUSION

Our review of the mentoring literature over the past five years from the leading journals in mentoring indicated that there are a broad range of topics that have been examined and a solid body of research has emerged in the field. However, there is still much to be accomplished. The field itself requires a clearer delineation and development. There are also many areas of research that need attention if the field is to continue to expand and assure relevancy in the years ahead. We hope that this review will further the rigor of future mentoring research. In addition, we hope that the proposals we have made for expanding the topical foci of these studies will be akin to providing fully-loaded brushes, which will enable researchers to paint the mentoring research horizon in rainbow colors.

Notes

1. All articles were reviewed from the journal, *Mentoring and Tutoring: Partnership in Learning*

(2010, Volume 18 through 2015, Volume 23, issues 1 and 2).
2. All articles were reviewed from the *International Journal of Mentoring and Coaching* (2010, Volume VIII through 2015, Volume XIII, including all issues of each).
3. All articles were reviewed from the journal, *International Journal of Mentoring and Coaching in Education* (2012, Volume 1 through 2015, Volume 4).

REFERENCES

Achinstein, B. and Davis, E. (2014) 'The subject of mentoring: towards a knowledge and practice base for content-focused mentoring of new teachers', *Mentoring and Tutoring: Partnership in Learning*, 22(2): 104–26.

Adams, C. and Slaven, F.J. (2011) 'Mentoring in two voices: an autoethnographic fugue', *International Journal of Mentoring and Coaching*, 9(2): 38–55.

Alberta Mentoring Partnership (2016) 'Alberta mentoring partnership'. (http://albertamentors.ca/).

Alhija, F.N. and Fresko, B. (2014) 'An exploration of the relationships between mentor recruitment, the implementation of the mentoring, and mentors' attitudes', *Mentoring and Tutoring: Partnership in Learning*, 22: 162–80.

Altus, J. (2015) 'Answering the call: how group mentoring makes a difference', *Mentoring and Tutoring: Partnership in Learning*, 23(2): 100–15.

Ambrosetti, A., Knight, B.A. and Dekkers, J. (2014) 'Maximizing the potential of mentoring: a framework for pre-service teacher education', *Mentoring and Tutoring: Partnership in Learning*, 22(3): 224–39.

Archard, N. (2012) 'Developing future women leaders: the importance of mentoring and role modeling in the girls' school context', *Mentoring and Tutoring: Partnership in Learning*, 20(4): 451–72.

Arksey, H. and O'Malley, L. (2007) 'Scoping studies: towards a methodological framework', *International Journal of Social Research Methodology*, 8(1): 19–32.

Asada, T. (2012) 'Mentoring novice teachers in Japanese schools', *International Journal of Mentoring and Coaching in Education*, 1(1): 54–65.

Aziz, R. (2011) 'The dance of diversity', *International Journal of Mentoring and Coaching*, 9(1): 3–17.

Barczyk, C., Buckenmeyer, J., Feldman, L. and Hixon, E. (2011) 'Assessment of a university-based distance education mentoring program from a quality management perspective', *Mentoring and Tutoring: Partnership in Learning*, 19(1): 5–24.

Barrera, A., Braley, R.T. and Slate, J.R. (2010) 'Beginning teacher success: an investigation into the feedback from mentoring of formal mentoring programs', *Mentoring and Tutoring: Partnership in Learning*, 18(1): 61–74.

Bashan, B. and Holsblat, R. (2012) 'Co-teaching through modeling processes: professional development of students and instructors in a teacher training program', *Mentoring and Tutoring: Partnership in Learning*, 20(2): 207–26.

Bean, N.M., Lucas, L. and Hyers, L.L. (2014) 'Mentoring should be the norm to assure success: Lessons learned from the faculty mentoring program, West Chester University, 2008–2011', *Mentoring and Tutoring: Partnership in Learning*, 22(1): 56–73.

Beane-Katner, L. (2014) 'Anchoring a mentoring network in a new faculty development program', *Mentoring and Tutoring: Partnership in Learning*, 22(2): 91–103.

Behar-Horenstein, L.S., Roberts, K.W. and Dix, A.C. (2010) 'Mentoring undergraduate researchers: an exploratory study of students' and professors' perceptions', *Mentoring and Tutoring: Partnership in Learning*, 18(3): 269–91.

Bickmore, D.L. and Curry, J.R. (2013) 'The induction of school counselors: meeting personal and professional needs', *Mentoring and Tutoring: Partnership in Learning*, 21(1): 6–27.

Bourdieu, P. (1986) 'The forms of capital', in J.G. Richardson (ed.), *Handbook of Theory and Research for the Sociology of Education*. New York: Greenwood Press, pp. 231–58.

Bottoms, S., Pegg, J., Adams, A., Wu, K., Risser, H.S. and Kern, A.L. (2013) 'Mentoring from the outside: the role of a peer mentoring community in the development of early career education faculty', *Mentoring and Tutoring: Partnership in Learning*, 21(2): 195–218.

Bower, G.G. and Hums, M.A. (2014) 'Examining the mentoring relationships of women working in intercollegiate athletic administration', *Mentoring and Tutoring: Partnership in Learning*, 22: 4–19.

Bristol, L., Adams, A.E. and Johannessen, G.G. (2014) 'Academic life-support: the self study of a transnational collaborative mentoring group', *Mentoring and Tutoring: Partnership in Learning*, 22(1): 396–414.

Brodeur, P., Larose, S., Tarabulsy, G., Feng, B. and Forget-Dubois, N. (2015) 'Development and construct validation of the mentor behavior scale', *Mentoring and Tutoring: Partnership in Learning*, 23(1): 54–75.

Brown, K., Nairn, K., van der Meer, J. and Scott, C. (2014) '"We were told we're not teachers… it gets difficult to draw the line": negotiating roles in peer-assisted study sessions (PASS)', *Mentoring and Tutoring: Partnership in Learning*, 22(2): 146–61.

Bullough, R.V.Jr. (2012) 'Mentoring and new teacher induction in the United States: a review and analysis of current practices', *Mentoring and Tutoring: Partnership in Learning*, 20(1): 57–74.

Butler, A., Whiteman, R., and Crow, G.M. (2013) 'Technology's role in transformational educator mentoring', *International Journal of Mentoring and Coaching*, 2(3): 233–48.

Carter, A. and Connage, T. (2007) 'A case study in evaluating behavioural change from a coaching programme', *International Journal of Mentoring and Coaching*, 5(1): 30–5.

Catapano, S. and Huisman, S. (2013) 'Leadership in hard-to-staff schools: novice teachers as mentors', *Mentoring and Tutoring: Partnership in Learning*, 21(3): 258–71.

Chaliès, S., Bertone, S., Flavier, E. and Durand, M. (2008) 'Effects of collaborative mentoring on the articulation of training and classroom situations: a case study in the French school system', *Teaching and Teacher Education*, 24(3): 550–63.

Chandler, D.E. and Ellis, R. (2011) 'Diversity and mentoring in the workplace: a conversation with Belle Rose Ragins', *Mentoring and Tutoring: Partnership in Learning*, 19(4): 483–500.

Chang, H., Longman, K.A. and Franco, M.A. (2014) 'Leadership development through mentoring in higher education: a collaborative autoethnography of leaders of color', *Mentoring and Tutoring: Partnership in Learning*, 22(4): 373–89.

Charteris, J. and Smardon, D. (2012) 'Dialogic peer coaching as teacher leadership for professional inquiry', *International Journal of Mentoring and Coaching in Education*, 3(2): 108–24.

Choi, S. and Lemberger, M.E. (2010) 'Influence of a supervised mentoring program on the achievement of low-income South Korean students', *Mentoring and Tutoring: Partnership in Learning*, 18(3): 233–48.

Clayton, J.K. and Myran, S. (2013) 'Content and context of the administrative internship: how mentoring and sustained activities impact the preparation', *Mentoring and Tutoring: Partnership in Learning*, 21(1): 59–75.

Cohen, L.M., Cowin, K., Ciechanowski, K. and Orozco, R. (2012) 'Portraits of our mentoring experiences in learning to craft journal articles', *Mentoring and Tutoring: Partnership in Learning*, 20(1): 75–97.

Colvin, J.W. and Ashman, M. (2010) 'Roles, risks, and benefits of peer mentoring relationships in higher education', *Mentoring and Tutoring: Partnership in Learning*, 18(1): 121–34.

Cox, E. (2012) 'Individual and organizational trust in a reciprocal peer coaching context', *Mentoring and Tutoring: Partnership in Learning*, 20(3): 427–43.

Crawford, L.M., Randolph, J.J. and Yob, I.M. (2014) 'Theoretical development, factorial validity, and reliability of the online graduate mentoring scale', *Mentoring and Tutoring: Partnership in Learning*, 22(1): 20–37.

Creighton, L., Creighton, T. and Parks, D. (2010) 'Mentoring to degree completion: expanding the horizons of doctoral protégés', *Mentoring and Tutoring: Partnership in Learning*, 18(1): 39–52.

Crocitto, M.M., Sullivan, S.E. and Carraher, S.M. (2005) 'Global mentoring as a means of career development and knowledge creation: a learning-based framework and agenda for future research', *Career Development International*, 10(6/7): 522–35.

Cureton, D., Jones, J. and Foster, W. (2011) 'The impact of mentoring on stress in higher education', *International Journal of Mentoring and Coaching*, 9(1): 18–45.

Dancy, E. II and Jean-Marie, G. (2014) 'Faculty of color in higher education: exploring the intersections of identity, impostership, and internalized racism', *Mentoring and Tutoring: Partnership in Learning*, 22(4): 354–72.

De Four-Babb, J., Pegg, J. and Beck, M. (2015) 'Reducing intellectual poverty of outsiders within academic spaces through informal peer mentorship', *Mentoring and Tutoring: Partnership in Learning*, 23(1): 76–93.

De Haan, E. and Sills, C. (2010). 'The relational turn in executive coaching'. *The Journal of Management Development*, 29(10): 845–51.

Derrick, K.S. (2009) *Flash Mentoring: Transferring Knowledge and Experience in a Busy World*. A presentation at ASTD 2009 International Conference and Exposition, Washington, DC (http://www.slideshare.net/KScottDerrick/flash-mentoring-transferring-knowledge-and-experience-in-a-busy-world-astd-2009-conference).

Deutsch, F.M. and Tong, T.L. (2011) 'Work-to-school mentoring: childcare center directors and teachers' return to school', *Mentoring and Tutoring: Partnership in Learning*, 19(2): 157–77.

Diamond, C.T.P. (2010) 'A memoir of co-mentoring: the "we" that is "me"', *Mentoring and Tutoring: Partnership in Learning*, 18(2): 199–209.

Dobie, S., Smith, S. and Robins, L. (2010) 'How assigned faculty mentors view their mentoring relationships: an interview study of mentors in medical education', *Mentoring and Tutoring: Partnership in Learning*, 18(4): 337–59.

Dominguez, N., and Hagar, M. (2013) 'Mentoring frameworks: synthesis and critique', *International Journal of Mentoring and Coaching in Education,* 2(3): 171–88.

D'Souza, L.A. (2014) 'Bridging the gap for beginning teachers: researcher as mentor', *International Journal of Mentoring and Coaching in Education*, 3(2): 171–87.

Du Toit, A. (2006) 'Creating a learning organisation within local government through a coaching approach', *International Journal of Mentoring and Coaching*, 5(1): 21–9.

Douglass, A.G., Smith, D.L. and Smith, L.J. (2013) 'An exploration of the characteristics of effective undergraduate peer-mentoring relationships', *Mentoring and Tutoring: Partnership in Learning*, 21(4): 219–34.

Duckworth, V. and Maxwell, B. (2015) 'Extending the mentor role in initial teacher education: embracing social justice', *International Journal of Mentoring and Coaching in Education*, 4(1): 4–20.

Duncan, H.E. and Stock, M.J. (2010) 'Mentoring and coaching rural school leaders: what do they need?', *Mentoring and Tutoring: Partnership in Learning*, 18(3): 293–311.

Ehrich, K., Freeman, G.K., Richards, S.C., Robinson, I.C. and Shepperd, S. (2002) 'How to do a scoping exercise: continuity of care', *Research Policy and Planning*, 20(1): 25–9.

Eisenschmidt, E., Oder, T. and Reiska, E. (2013) 'The induction program: teachers' experience after five years of practice', *Mentoring and Tutoring: Partnership in Learning*, 21(3): 241–57.

Emelo, R. (2010) 'In practice. Situational mentoring: microlearning in action', *Chief Learning Officer*, 9(7): 43.

Eriksson, A. (2013) 'Positive and negative facets of formal group mentoring: preservice teacher perspectives', *Mentoring and Tutoring: Partnership in Learning*, 21(3): 272–91.

Esnard, T., Cobb-Roberts, D., Agosto, V., Karanxha, Z., Beck, M., Wu, K. and Unterreiner, A. (2015) 'Productive tensions in a cross-cultural peer mentoring women's network: a social capital perspective', *Mentoring and Tutoring: Partnership in Learning*, 23(1): 19–36.

Fair, C.D., Decker, A.K. and Hopkins, K.E. (2011) 'To me it's like having a kid, kind of: analysis of student reflections in a developmental mentoring program', *Mentoring and Tutoring: Partnership in Learning*, 19(3): 301–17.

Feldhaus, C. and Bentrem, K. (2015) 'STEM mentoring and the use of the principles of Adult Mentoring Inventory', *International Journal of Mentoring and Coaching in Education*, 4(3): 213–35.

Flavian, H. and Kass, E. (2015) 'Giving students a voice: perceptions of the pedagogical advisory role in a teacher training program', *Mentoring and Tutoring: Partnership in Learning*, 23(1): 37–53.

Fleck, C. and Mullins, M.E. (2012) 'Evaluating a psychology graduate student peer mentoring program', *Mentoring and Tutoring: Partnership in Learning*, 20(2): 271–90.

Flores, B.B., Hernandez, A., Garcia, C.T. and Claeys, L. (2011) 'Teacher academy induction learning community: guiding teachers through their zone of proximal development',

Mentoring and Tutoring: Partnership in Learning, 19(1): 365–89.

Frels, R.K. and Onwuegbuzie, A.J. (2012) 'The experiences of selected mentors: a cross-cultural examination of the dyadic relationship in the school-based mentoring', Mentoring and Tutoring: Partnership in Learning, 20(2): 181–206.

Frels, R.K., Zientek, L.R. and Onwuegbuzie, A.J. (2013) 'Differences of mentoring experiences across grade span among principals, mentors, and mentees', Mentoring and Tutoring: Partnership in Learning, 21(1): 28–58.

Gallant, A. and Gilham, V. (2014) 'Differentiated coaching: developmental needs of coaches', International Journal of Mentoring and Coaching in Education, 3(3): 237–54.

Garza, R. and Ovando, M.N. (2012) 'Preservice teachers' connections of pedagogical knowledge to mentoring at-risk adolescents: benefits and challenges', Mentoring and Tutoring: Partnership in Learning, 20(3): 343–60.

George, M.P. and Mampilly, S.R. (2012) 'A model for student mentoring in business schools', International Journal of Mentoring and Coaching in Education, 1(2): 136–54.

Global Mentoring Walk. (2016) 'Global mentoring walk' (https://vitalvoices.exposure.co/global-mentoring-walk-2016).

Godden, L., Tregunna, L. and Kutsyuruba, B. (2014) 'Collaborative application of the Adaptive Mentorship© model: the professional and personal growth within a research triad', International Journal of Mentoring and Coaching in Education, 3(2): 125–40.

Grace, M. and Holloway, E. (2010) 'The mentoring triad: a relational structure for workplace mentoring', International Journal of Mentoring and Coaching, 8(1): 3–23.

Griffin, S.M. and Beatty, R.J. (2010) 'Storying the terroir of collaborative writing: like wine and food, a unique pairing of mentoring minds', Mentoring and Tutoring: Partnership in Learning, 18(2): 177–97.

Griffiths, M. and Armour, K. (2012) 'Mentoring as a formalized learning strategy with community sports volunteers', Mentoring and Tutoring: Partnership in Learning, 20(1): 151–73.

Grima-Farrell, C. (2015) 'Mentoring pathways to enhancing the personal and professional development of pre-service teachers', International Journal of Mentoring and Coaching in Education, 4(4): 255–68.

Groves, K.S. (2007) 'Integrating leadership development and succession planning best practices', Journal of Management Development, 26(3): 239–60.

Gut, D.M., Beam, P.C., Henning, J.E., Cochran, D.C. and Knight, R.T. (2014) 'Teachers' perceptions of their mentoring role in three different clinical settings: student teaching, early field experiences, and entry year teaching', Mentoring and Tutoring: Partnership in Learning, 22(3): 240–63.

Hargreaves, E. (2010) 'Knowledge construction and personal relationship: insights about a UK university mentoring and coaching service', Mentoring and Tutoring: Partnership in Learning, 18(2): 107–20.

Holloway, S.M. and Salinitri, G. (2010) 'Investigating teacher candidates' mentoring of students at risk of academic failure: a Canadian experiential field model', Mentoring and Tutoring: Partnership in Learning, 18(4): 383–403.

Holmes, S., Redmond, A., Thomas, J. and High, K. (2012) 'Girls helping girls: assessing the influence of college student mentors in an afterschool engineering program', Mentoring and Tutoring: Partnership in Learning, 20(1): 137–50.

Holt, L.J. and Lopez, M.J. (2014) 'Characteristics and correlates of supportive peer mentoring: a mixed methods study', Mentoring and Tutoring: Partnership in Learning, 22(5): 415–32.

Hughes, C., Boyd, E. and Dykstra, S.J. (2010) 'Evaluation of a university-based mentoring program: mentors' perspectives on a service-learning experience', Mentoring and Tutoring: Partnership in Learning, 18(4): 361–82.

Huizing, R.L. (2012) 'Mentoring together: a literature review of group mentoring', Mentoring and Tutoring: Partnership in Learning, 20(1): 27–55.

Irby, B.J. (2015) 'Mentor capital', Mentoring and Tutoring: Partnership in Learning, 23(1): 1–5.

Johnson, B.A. and Harreld, D.J. (2012) 'Nurturing independent learning in an undergraduate student in history: a faculty-student mentoring experience', Mentoring and Tutoring: Partnership in Learning, 20(3): 361–78.

Johnson, K.F., Gupta, A., Rosen, H. and Rosen, H. (2013) 'Improving reading comprehension through holistic intervening and tutoring during after-school with high risk minority elementary school students', *Mentoring and Tutoring: Partnership in Learning*, 21(4): 431–43.

Jones, R. and Brown, D. (2011) 'The mentoring relationship as a complex adaptive system: finding a model for our experience', *Mentoring and Tutoring: Partnership in Learning*, 19(4): 401–18.

Kass, E. and Rajuan, M. (2012) 'Perceptions of freedom and commitment as sources of self-efficacy among pedagogical advisors', *Mentoring and Tutoring: Partnership in Learning*, 20(2): 227–50.

Kendall, D.L. and Smith-Jentsch, K.A. (2015) 'The influence of protégé input to the match on mentoring processes: an experimental investigation', *International Journal of Mentoring and Coaching*, 13(1): 2–25.

Kim, S. (2003) 'Linking employee assessments to succession planning', *Public Personnel Management*, 32(4): 533–47.

Kochan, F. (2013) 'Analyzing the relationships between culture and mentoring', *Mentoring and Tutoring: Partnership in Learning*, 21(4): 412–30.

Kolar, D.W. and McBride, C.A. (2011) 'Mentoring at-risk youth in schools: can small doses make a big change?', *Mentoring and Tutoring: Partnership in Learning*, 19(2): 125–38.

Komosa-Hawkins, K. (2012) 'The impact of school-based mentoring on adolescents' social-emotional health', *Mentoring and Tutoring: Partnership in Learning*, 20(3): 393–408.

Langer, A.M. (2010) 'Mentoring nontraditional undergraduate students: a case study in higher education', *Mentoring and Tutoring: Partnership in Learning*, 18(1): 23–38.

Larose, S. (2013) 'Trajectories of mentors' perceived self-efficacy during an academic mentoring experience: what they look like and what are their personal and experimental correlates?', *Mentoring and Tutoring: Partnership in Learning*, 21(2): 150–74.

Larose, S., Cyrenne, D., Garceau, O., Harvey, M., Guay, F., Godin, F., Tarabulsy, G.M. and Deschénes, C. (2011) 'Academic mentoring and dropout prevention for students in math, science, and technology', *Mentoring & Tutoring: Partnership in Learning*, 19(4): 419–31.

Larsen, T., Van Hoye, A., Tjomsland, H.E., Holsen, I., Wold, B., Huezé, J., Samdal, O. and Sarrazin, P. (2015) Creating a supportive environment among youth football players: A qualitative student of French and Norwegian youth grassroots football coaches', *Health Education*, 115(6): 570–86.

Leidenfrost, B., Strassnig, B., Schabmann, A., Spiel, C. and Carbon, C.C. (2011) 'Peer mentoring styles and their contribution to academic success among mentees: a person-oriented study in higher education', *Mentoring and Tutoring: Partnership in Learning*, 19(3): 347–64.

Lejonberg, E., Elstad, E. and Christophersen, K.A. (2015) 'Mentor education: challenging mentors' beliefs about mentoring', *International Journal of Mentoring and Coaching in Education*, 4(2): 142–58.

Levac, D., Colquhoun, H. and O'Brien, K.K. (2010) 'Scoping studies: advancing the methodology', *Implementation Science*, 5(1): 1–9.

Lloyd-Jones, B. (2014) 'African-American women in the professoriate: addressing social exclusion and scholarly marginalization through mentoring', *Mentoring and Tutoring: Partnership in Learning*, 22(4): 269–83.

LoCasale-Crouch, J., Davis, E., Wiens, P. and Pianta, R. (2012) 'The role of the mentor in supporting new teachers: associations with self-efficacy, reflection, and quality', *Mentoring and Tutoring: Partnership in Learning*, 20(3): 303–23.

Long, J.S., McKenzie-Robblee, S., Schaefer, L., Steeves, P., Wnuk, S., Pinnegar, E. and Clandinin, D.J. (2012) 'Literature review on induction and mentoring related to early career teacher attrition and retention', *Mentoring and Tutoring: Partnership in Learning*, 20(1): 7–26.

Lopez, A.E. (2013) 'Collaborative mentorship: a mentoring approach to support and sustain teachers for equity and diversity', *Mentoring and Tutoring: Partnership in Learning*, 21(3): 292–311.

Lunsford, L.G. (2012) 'Doctoral advising or mentoring? Effects on student outcomes', *Mentoring and Tutoring: Partnership in Learning*, 20(2): 251–70.

Lunsford, L.G. (2014) 'Mentors, tormentors, and no mentors: mentoring scientists', *International Journal of Mentoring and Coaching in Education*, 3(1): 4–17

Lunsford, L.G., Baker, V., Griffin, K.A. and Johnson, W.B. (2013) 'Mentoring: a typology of costs for higher education faculty', *Mentoring and Tutoring: Partnership in Learning*, 21(2): 125–49.

Mackey, H. and Shannon, K. (2014) 'Comparing alternative voices in the academy: navigating the complexity of mentoring relationships from divergent ethnic backgrounds', *Mentoring and Tutoring: Partnership in Learning*, 22(4): 338–53.

Marcellino, P.A. (2011) 'Fostering sustainability: a case study of a pilot mentoring program at a private university', *Mentoring and Tutoring: Partnership in Learning*, 19(4): 441–64.

Marshall, J.H., Lawrence, E.C. and Peugh, J. (2013) 'College women mentoring adolescent girls: the relationship between mentor peer support and mentee outcomes', *Mentoring and Tutoring: Partnership in Learning*, 21(4): 444–62.

Meyer, M. (2015) 'Dialectical tensions experienced by diversified mentoring dyads', *International Journal of Mentoring and Coaching in Education*, 4(1): 21–36.

Millard, J.A., and Korotov, K. (2014) Do mental health stigma and gender influence MBAs' willingness to engage in coaching? *International Journal of Mentoring and Coaching in Education*, 3(3): 277–92.

Mooney Simmie, G. and Moles, J. (2011) 'Critical thinking, caring and professional agency: an emerging framework for productive mentoring', *Mentoring and Tutoring: Partnership in Learning*, 19(4): 464–82.

Murakami, E.T. and Nunez, A.M. (2014) 'Latina faculty transcending barriers: peer mentoring in a Hispanic-serving institution', *Mentoring and Tutoring: Partnership in Learning*, 22(4): 284–301.

Myers, K. and Sadaghiani, K. (2010) 'Millennials in the workplace: a communication perspective on millennials' organizational relationships and performance', *Journal of Business and Psychology*, 25(2): 225–38.

National Center for Education Statistics (2016) *Digest of Education Statistics*. Washington, DC: National Center for Education Statistics (https://nces.ed.gov/programs/digest/d14/tables/dt14_204.25.asp).

Ness, B.M. (2013) 'Supporting self-regulated learning for college students with Asperger syndrome: exploring the "strategies for college learning" model', *Mentoring and Tutoring: Partnership in Learning*, 21(4): 356–77.

Nganga, C.W. (2011) 'Emerging as a scholar practitioner: a reflective essay review', *Mentoring and Tutoring: Partnership in Learning*, 19(2) 239–51.

Noufou, O., Rezania, D. and Hossain, M. (2014) 'Measuring and exploring factors affecting students' willingness to engage in peer mentoring', *International Journal of Mentoring and Coaching in Education*, 3(2): 141–57.

O'Neill, D.K., Asgari, M. and Dong, Y.R. (2011) 'Trade-offs between perceptions of success and planned outcomes in an online mentoring program', *Mentoring and Tutoring: Partnership in Learning*, 19(2): 45–63.

O'Shea, S., Harwood, V., Kervin, L. and Humphry, N. (2013) 'Connection, challenge, and change: the narratives of university students mentoring young indigenous Australians', *Mentoring and Tutoring: Partnership in Learning*, 12(4): 392–411.

Orland-Barak, L., Kheir-Farraj, R. and Becher, A. (2013) 'Mentoring in contexts of cultural and political friction: moral dilemmas of mentors and their management in practice', *Mentoring and Tutoring: Partnership in Learning*, 21(1): 76–95.

Outhred, T. and Chester, A. (2013) 'Improving the international student experience in Australia through embedded peer mentoring', *Mentoring and Tutoring: Partnership in Learning*, 21(3): 312–32.

Overman, S. (2004) 'Mentors without borders expand your search for mentors beyond US shores', *HR Magazine*, 49(3): 83–8.

Owen, H.D. (2015) 'Making the most of mobility: virtual mentoring and education practitioner professional development', *Research in Learning Technology*, 23: 25566. (http://dx.doi.org/10.3402/rlt.v23.25566).

Packard, B.W., Marciano, V.N., Payne, J.M., Bledzki, L.A. and Woodard, C.T. (2014) 'Negotiating peer mentoring roles in undergraduate research lab settings'. *Mentoring and Tutoring: Partnership in Learning*, 22(5): 433–45.

Parker, D.C. and McQuirter Scott, R. (2010) 'From mentorship to tenureship: a storied inquiry of two academic careers in education', *Mentoring and Tutoring: Partnership in Learning*, 18(4): 405–25.

Parylo, O., Zepeda, S.J. and Bengtson, E. (2012) 'The different faces of principal mentorship', *International Journal of Mentoring and Coaching in Education*, 1(2): 120–35.

Peterson, S.M., Valk, C., Baker, A.C., Brugger, L. and Hightower, A.D. (2010) '"We're not just interested in the work": Social and emotional aspects of early educator mentoring relationships', *Mentoring and Tutoring: Partnership in Learning*, 18(2): 155–75.

Pleschová, G. and McAlpine, L. (2015) 'Enhancing university teaching and learning through mentoring: a systematic review of the literature', *International Journal of Mentoring and Coaching in Education*, 4(2): 107–25.

Pogodzinski, B. (2012) 'Considering the social context of schools: a framework for investigating new teacher induction', *Mentoring and Tutoring: Partnership in Learning*, 20(3): 325–42.

Polly, D., Algozzine, R., Martin, C.S. and Mraz, M. (2015) 'Perceptions of the roles and responsibilities of elementary school mathematics coaches', *International Journal of Mentoring and Coaching in Education*, 4(2): 126–41.

Pololi, L.H., Knight, S.M., Dennis, K. and Frankel, R.M. (2002) 'Helping medical school faculty realize their dreams: an innovative, collaborative mentoring program', *Academic Medicine*, 77(5): 377–84.

Profetis, G. (2015) 'The impact of our emotional states on life satisfaction and income', *International Journal of Mentoring and Coaching*, 13(5).

ProQuest (2015) *Reworks*. Ann Arbor: ProQuest (http://www.proquest.com/products-services/refworks.html).

Prywes, Y. (2012) 'Cognitive, behavioral, and affective learning outcomes of a coaching program', *International Journal of Mentoring and Coaching*, 10(1): 41–55.

Reddick, R.J. (2011) 'Intersecting identities: mentoring contributions and challenges for black faculty mentoring black undergraduates', *Mentoring and Tutoring: Partnership in Learning*, 19(3): 319–46.

Reddick, R.J. (2012) 'Male faculty mentors in black and white', *International Journal of Mentoring and Coaching in Education*, 1(1): 36–53.

Reeves, T.Z. (2010) 'Mentoring programs in succession planning', *State and Local Government Review*, 42(1): 61–8.

Refworks (2015) *Refworks*. Ann Arbor: ProQuest (https://www.refworks.com).

Rekha, K.N., and Ganesh, M.P. (2012). 'Do mentors learn by mentoring others?' *International Journal of Mentoring and Coaching in Education*, 1(3): 205–17.

Rhodes, C. and Fletcher, S. (2013), 'Coaching and mentoring for self-efficacious leadership in schools', *International Journal of Mentoring and Coaching in Education*, 2(1): 47–63.

Riebschleger, J. and Cross, S. (2011) 'Loss and grief experiences of mentors in social work education', *Mentoring and Tutoring: Partnership in Learning*, 19(1): 65–82.

Riggio, R.E. (2013) 'Advancing the discipline of leadership studies', *Journal of Leadership Education*, 12(3): 10–14.

Ritchie, J. and Spencer, L. (1994) 'Qualitative data analysis for applied policy research', in A. Bryman and R. Burgess (eds), *Analyzing Qualitative Data*. London: Sage, pp. 173–94.

Rivera-McCutchen, R. and Scharff Panero, N. (2014) 'Low-inference transcripts in peer coaching: a promising tool for school improvement', *International Journal of Mentoring and Coaching in Education*, 3(1): 86–101.

Roach, G. (2014) 'A helping hand? A study into an England-wide peer mentoring program to address bullying behavior', *Mentoring and Tutoring: Partnership in Learning*, 22(3): 210–23.

Rogers, C.B.H., McIntyre, M. and Jazzar, M. (2010) 'Mentoring adjunct faculty using the cornerstone of effective communication and practice', *Mentoring and Tutoring: Partnership in Learning*, 18(1): 53–9.

Salter, T. (2015) 'Equality of mentoring and coaching opportunity: making both available to pre-service teachers', *International Journal of Mentoring and Coaching in Education*, 4(1): 69–82.

Sandford, R.A., Armour, K.M. and Stanton, D.J. (2010) 'Volunteer mentors as informal educators in a youth physical activity program', *Mentoring and Tutoring: Partnership in Learning*, 18(2): 135–53.

Santamaria, L.J. and Jaramillo, N.E. (2014) '*Comadres* among us: the power of artists as informal mentors for women of color in academe', *Mentoring and Tutoring: Partnership in Learning*, 22(4): 316–37.

Schwartz, H.L. and Holloway, E.L. (2014) '"I become a part of the learning process":

mentoring episodes and individualized attention in graduate education', *Mentoring and Tutoring: Partnership in Learning*, 22(1): 38–55.

Schwartz, H.L. and Holloway, E.L. (2012) 'Partners in learning: a grounded theory study of relational practice between master's students and professors', *Mentoring and Tutoring: Partnership in Learning*, 20(1): 115–35.

Sciarappa, K. and Mason, C.Y. (2014) 'National principal mentoring: does it achieve its purpose?', *International Journal of Mentoring and Coaching in Education*, 3(1): 51–71.

Searby, L.J. (2010) 'Preparing future principals: facilitating the development of a mentoring mindset through graduate coursework', *Mentoring and Tutoring: Partnership in Learning*, 18(1): 5–22.

Searby, L.J. (2014) 'The protégé mentoring mindset: a framework for consideration', *International Journal of Mentoring and Coaching in Education*, 3(3): 255–76.

Shobe, M.A., Murphy-Erby, Y. and Sparks, J. (2014) 'Mentorship efforts to support part-time social work faculty members', *Mentoring and Tutoring: Partnership in Learning*, 22(5): 446–60.

Skaniakos, T., Penttinen, L. and Lairio, M. (2014) 'Peer group mentoring programmes in Finnish higher education: mentors' perspectives', *Mentoring and Tutoring: Partnership in Learning*, 22(1): 74–86.

Smith, C.S. and Arsenault, K. (2014) 'Mentoring as an induction tool in special education administration', *Mentoring and Tutoring: Partnership in Learning*, 22(5): 461–80.

Smith, E.R., Calderwood, P.E., Dohn, F.A. and Lopez, P.G. (2013) 'Reconceptualizing faculty mentoring within a community of practice model', *Mentoring and Tutoring: Partnership in Learning*, 21(2): 175–94.

St-Jean, E. and Audet, J. (2013) 'The effect of mentor intervention style in novice entrepreneur mentoring relationships', *Mentoring and Tutoring: Partnership in Learning*, 21(1): 96–119.

Stanulis, R.N., Brondyk, S.K., Little, S. and Wibbens, E. (2014) 'Mentoring beginning teachers to enact discussion-based teaching', *Mentoring and Tutoring: Partnership in Learning*, 22(1): 127–45.

Stephens, S., Doherty, O., Bennett, B. and Margey, M. (2014) 'The challenge of work-based learning: a role for academic mentors?', *International Journal of Mentoring and Coaching in Education*, 3(2): 158–70.

Strapp, C.M., Gilles, A.W., Spalding, A.E., Hughes, C.T., Baldwin, A.M., Guy, K.L., Feakin, K.R. and Lamb, A.D. (2014) 'Changes in mentor efficacy and perceptions following participation in a youth mentoring program', *Mentoring and Tutoring: Partnership in Learning*, 22(3): 190–209.

Tenhunen, M.L. and Leppisaari, I. (2010) 'Promoting growth entrepreneurship through e-mentoring', *The International Journal of Mentoring and Coaching*, 8(1): 48–66.

Thomas, A.M. and Ensher, E.A. (2013) 'The impact of prior mentoring and computer mediated communication', *The International Journal of Mentoring and Coaching*, 11(1): 8–27.

Thompson, R.B., Corsello, M., McReynolds, S. and Conklin-Powers, B. (2013) 'A longitudinal study of family socioeconomic status (SES) variables as predictors of socio-emotional resilience among mentored youth', *Mentoring and Tutoring: Partnership in Learning*, 21(4): 378–91.

Thurlings, M., Vermeulen, M., Bastiaens, T. and Stijnen, S. (2012) 'Investigating feedback on practice among teachers: coherence of observed and perceived feedback', *Mentoring and Tutoring: Partnership in Learning*, 20(4): 473–90.

Tran, N.A. (2014) 'The role of mentoring in the success of women leaders of color in higher education', *Mentoring and Tutoring: Partnership in Learning*, 22(4): 302–15.

Trower, C. (2006) 'Gen x meets theory x: what new scholars want', *Journal of Collective Bargaining in the Academy,* 0: Article 11.

United States Department of State: Bureau of Educational and Cultural Affairs (2016) 'Global sports mentoring program'. (https://eca.state.gov/programs-initiatives/sports-diplomacy/empowering-women-and-girls-through-sports/global-sports).

University of Pittsburgh, Institute for Clinical Research Education (2016) *Ethic in Mentoring*. Pittsburgh: University of Pittsburgh, Institute for Clinical Research Education (http://www.icre.pitt.edu/mentoring/ethics.html).

Valaitis, R., Martin-Misener, R., Wong, S.T., MacDonald, M., Meagher-Stewart, D.,

Austin, P. and Kaczorowski, J. (2012) 'Methods, strategies and technologies used to conduct a scoping literature review of collaboration between primary care and public health', *Primary Health Care Research and Development*, 13(3): 219–36.

Wallis, J.A.M., Riddell, J.K., Smith, C., Silvertown, J. and Pepler, D.J. (2015) 'Investigating patterns of participation and conversation content in an online mentoring program for northern Canadian youth', *Mentoring and Tutoring: Partnership in Learning*, 23(3): 228–47.

Ward, E.G. (2012) 'The intergenerational transmission of inspiration: reflections on the origin of a peer-mentoring project', *Mentoring and Tutoring: Partnership in Learning*, 20(1): 99–113.

Ward, E.G., Thomas, E.E. and Disch, W.B. (2012) 'Protégé growth themes emergent in a holistic, undergraduate peer-mentoring experience', *Mentoring and Tutoring: Partnership in Learning*, 20(3): 409–25.

Waterman, S. and He, Y. (2011) 'Effects of mentoring programs on new teacher retention: a literature review', *Mentoring and Tutoring: Partnership in Learning*, 19(2): 139–56.

Welfare, L.E., Sackett, C. and Moorefield-Lang, H. (2011) 'Student-faculty collaborative research: a qualitative study of experiences with the authorship determination process', *Mentoring and Tutoring: Partnership in Learning*, 19(2): 179–98.

Welton, A.D., Mansfield, K.C. and Lee, P.L. (2014) 'Mentoring matters: an exploratory survey of educational leadership doctoral students' perspectives', *Mentoring and Tutoring: Partnership in Learning*, 22(5): 481–509.

Whitney, S.D., Hendricker, E.N. and Offutt, C.A. (2011) 'Moderating factors of natural mentoring relationships, problem behaviors, and emotional well-being', *Mentoring and Tutoring: Partnership in Learning*, 19(1): 83–105.

Wolffensperger, Y. (2010) 'Caring mentoring for academic literacy: a case study of a teacher education college in Israel', *Mentoring and Tutoring: Partnership in Learning*, 18(3): 249–67.

Wright, S., Grenier, M. and Channell, K. (2012) 'Post-lesson observation conferencing of university supervisors and physical education teacher education students', *Mentoring and Tutoring: Partnership in Learning*, 20(3): 379–92.

Wyatt, M. and Arnold, E. (2012) 'Video-stimulated recall for mentoring in Omani schools', *International Journal of Mentoring and Coaching in Education*, 1(3): 218–34.

Young, R.W. and Cates, C.M. (2010) 'Listening, play, and social attraction in the mentoring of new teachers', *Mentoring and Tutoring: Partnership in Learning*, 18(3): 215–31.

PART II

The Practice of Mentoring

Julie Haddock-Millar

Section 2 of Part I of this edition of the *Sage Handbook of Mentoring*, as titled, presents us with the practice of mentoring. The practice of mentoring offers insight into the practical process to support and guide the many stakeholders involved in all aspects of mentoring. By definition, this section is expansive in nature, encompassing a diverse collection of perspectives and approaches to mentoring in practice. The authors of the chapters in this section present comprehensive accounts of the effective mentoring relationship, including the role of goals and emotional intelligence, the typical relationship phases or stages mentees and mentors traverse, the role of supervision in mentoring, the 'how to' guide for the design, delivery, and evaluation of effective mentoring programs, the alignment of individual and organizational outcomes, and the pivotal role key stakeholders play in ensuring the success of mentoring in action. The authors' accounts combine a comprehensive review of the literature, referring to key sources and case studies, supported by their reflective accounts, drawing on their knowledge and understanding as experienced practitioners and researchers in the field of mentoring practice. Despite the distinctiveness of each chapter, there are a number of themes that are consistent across several chapters.

The first theme is the degree to which research into the practice of mentoring considers the interactional nature of the mentoring relationship. It appears that a significant proportion of studies have only considered mentee-perspective accounts of the mentoring relationship. Going forward, research should compare and contrast mentee and mentor accounts to shine a light on the degree to which there is consistency in perceived functions and behaviors, as well as the extent to which mutual learning and growth impacts both parties from both a personal and professional perspective.

The second theme concerns the importance of recognizing the extent to which mentoring as a talent-development tool can have a positive impact on the organization and, in the case of formal mentoring programs, deliver competitive advantage. Similar to the first theme, the organizational perspective is often neglected. Bearing in mind the resources, energy, and commitment required to develop any formal mentoring program, it seems astounding that program evaluation would not consider the importance of identifying, demonstrating, and evidencing organizational learning and competitive advantage. Making the connection between individual- and organizational-level outcomes from a measurement perspective is complex and challenging; this might account for the lack of research into the practice and triangulation of multi-stakeholder outcomes. Various tools and techniques can be adopted; regardless of the strategy and approach adopted, the importance of transparency and clarity are emphasized.

The third theme is the changing nature of mentoring relationships within the context of the inner and outer ecosystem. People operate within an ecosystem, an ecosystem which has many layers and complexities where context can vary considerably. The *traditional* single-mentor model is the most common in the literature; however, practice tells us that people operate within a dynamic environment, forming a network of mentors that might be considered a constellation of mentoring relationships. The authors highlight the need to consider the global context of change and volatility which embraces developmental dialogues in different shapes and models. It is important to consider the extent to which the interconnected networks such as organizational and societal norms influence the mentoring experiences and how mentoring and support relationships develop and progress. In this regard the extent to which contextual factors, such as organizational, cultural, and structural, enable and/or constrain professional development is an important dimension to consider in the assessment of relationship progression.

The fourth theme relates to the skills and competencies of the mentee and mentor during different *phases* of the mentoring relationship and their impact on the perceived success of the relationship from different lenses. Equipping mentees and mentors to develop effective, meaningful relationships is a crucial stage in the design and development of most, if not all, mentoring programs; this is underscored throughout this section of the book. Two key areas are the emotional intelligence of the mentee and mentor and working with goals in mentoring. There is a link between the quality of mentoring relationships, clarity of goals, having a broad sense of purpose, and the emotional intelligence of the mentee and mentor. In the early stages of the relationship, developing mentee–mentor affinity is necessary to foster the necessary degree of openness, trust, and mutuality of learning. Affinity is not a term all participants might be familiar with, so it is important to use a common language which is easily understood by all. Similarly, the ability to work with purpose, either through goal-setting or the goal-free context, is necessary at the beginning of the relationship in order to establish direction. Rapport and purpose are two mainstays of an effective mentoring relationship. As the mentee and mentor transition through their relationship, constant re-focusing may be useful, and in some cases a necessity, where some dyads might begin to experience relationship droop. Relationship droop can occur when the dialogue tails off, surface issues have been addressed and the mentee and mentor run out of topics to talk about. Often there is a need to re-focus, re-frame the relationship, and delve into much deeper meaningful issues. Therefore, in relation to mentoring practice, developing mentees' and mentors' competence and capability to be able to transition through different phases of the mentoring relationship is a necessary requirement of the program framework.

Aligned to this is the role of mentoring supervisors who are able to provide mentors with essential support to help facilitate their relationships. Coaching supervision in the professional coaching community is viewed as a necessity; in the mentoring community mentor supervision has developed at a slower pace. However, we have seen the emergence of professional mentors, who have equal levels of training compared to their coach counterparts and significant experience relevant to the mentee, including context, industry, sector, and organization. Compared to coaching, the mentor supervisor fulfils a number of roles, specifically around continually developing mentor competence, but also a restorative one, helping mentors to maintain a sense of well-being and dealing with psychosocial issues that may be present in the mentor dialogue. In turn, this potentially increases mentee career success and satisfaction and the quality of service to mentees and/or the organization.

The practice of mentoring occurs in many different formats, approaches and contexts. Individuals and organizations responsible for mentoring-program development and management are often constrained by the pragmatics of design, delivery, evaluation, and dissemination. Notwithstanding the aforementioned, there is a wealth of good mentoring practice: informal and formal, charities, public-sector and private-sector, local, regional, and global. As practitioners and researchers, we are influenced by the powerful stories, narratives, and evidence which support the continual development of mentoring practice. I hope you will find this section of the *Sage Handbook of Mentoring* insightful and valuable for your mentoring practice and research.

The Effective Mentor, Mentee and Mentoring Relationship

Chandana Sanyal

INTRODUCTION

The aim of this chapter is to examine the various competency frameworks for mentors and mentees and consider the requirements for an effective mentoring relationship, exploring theoretical and empirical studies as well as conceptual models and frameworks. The chapter begins by outlining the behaviours, capabilities and characteristics of mentors and mentees, drawing on current literature (Cooper and Palmer, 2000; Clutterbuck, 2004, 2011; Brockbank and McGill, 2006; Allen and Eby, 2011). These are compared and contrasted, taking into account methodological issues such as the significance of context (Kram, 1983; Bierema and Merriam, 2002; Fowler and O'Gorman, 2005; Ghosh, 2012), purpose and type of mentoring (Kram, 1983 1985; Ragins and Cotton, 1999; Clutterbuck, 1998, 2015) and the fact that competences may evolve through the different phases of the mentor-mentee relationship (Merriam, 1983; Kram, 1983; Clutterbuck, 1998).

In addition, the author recognises the need to consider the complex adaptive system (Mitleton-Kelly, 1997; Lansing, 2003; Clutterbuck, 2012) in which the mentor-mentee relationship is established and developed. Next, the author examines the measures for the effectiveness of a mentoring relationship, with particular reference to how this might be useful in the initiation, support and measurement of mentoring outcomes. Finally, the author offers recommendations for future research.

AN EFFECTIVE MENTOR

It is important to consider the skills and capabilities that the role of a mentor requires to ensure that appropriate individuals are selected and supported within mentoring programmes. According to Cooper and Palmer

(2000, p. 55), '*it is evident that successful mentors are reported as employing a range of enabling strategies and skills within mentoring relationships.... it is important to consider the behaviours, qualities and characteristics of those who will be deemed suitable to provide this supportive role for others*'. Specific skills and attributes necessary to carry out the functions of a mentor have been highlighted by those who have experience of designing, implementing and evaluating mentoring programmes. These are characteristics such as strong interpersonal skills, organisational knowledge, exemplary supervision skills, technical competence, personal power and charisma, status and prestige, patience and risk taking, aptitude to develop and grow others and ability to share credit (Murray, 2002; Haddock-Millar and Sanyal, 2015). The mentor's interpersonal skills were highlighted as a key capability in an experimental three-phase study by Olian, Carroll, Giannantonio and Feren (1988) on 'What do Protégées look for in a mentor?', which concluded that mentees will more readily establish a relationship with individuals who are enjoyable to deal with because of their interpersonal style, who may be perceived as more instrumental to the career of protégés than those without such competencies.

Research studies on mentorship in specific sectors such as early-career teachers, medicine and academia have presented sets of competencies for mentors. A study of the role of effective teachers as mentors based on five case studies in Oregon, USA (Ackley and Gall, 1992) identified successful mentor skills as social process skills of interpersonal ease, listening, knowledge of educational content, demonstration/modelling and confidence building. Denmark and Podsen (2000) emphasise that a teacher mentor should be able to ask questions freely to be able to engage in an effective two-way conversation that is meaningful. According to Rodenhauser, Rudisill and Dvorak (2000), mentors in medicine serve as critical points of reference and provide some degree of guidance through education, collaboration, advice, sponsorship and friendship. Again, there is a clear emphasis here on relational competency as well as subject expertise. Similarly, Johnson's (2003) framework for conceptualising competence for mentors among graduate school faculty also advocates a set of virtues, abilities and skills with specific emphasis on relational capabilities to communicate empathy, respect and compassion to protégés. Finally, a more recent study (Abedin et al., 2012) on competences for research mentors of clinical and translational scholars also highlighted communication and managing the relationship as a key competence.

Therefore, as mentoring is defined as a '*relationship between two people with learning and development as its purpose*' (Megginson and Garvey, 2004, p. 2), a mentor must establish a person-centred approach grounded in core competencies such as congruence, unconditional positive regard and empathy, which are essential for humanistic learning (Rogers, 1983). A mentor is expected to embrace these over-arching principles to be able to engage in an effective mentoring relationship. Brockbank and McGill (2006) have identified a generic set of skills for mentors based on these principles to be able to engage the mentee in reflective learning leading to change. These are presented in clusters:

- Mentor presence – the mentor needs to be aware of non-verbal messages such as body language, facial expression and voice, which can deliver meaning quite independently of spoken communication.
- Listening and congruence – active listening requires observation of the mentee's non-verbal behaviour as well as listening to verbal messages, putting oneself in the frame of the mentee. This will require the mentor to be genuine and real, sharing feelings and attitudes as well as opinions and beliefs in a way that clearly takes ownership (i.e. I think…, I feel…).
- Restating, summarising and questioning – restating requires a process of disentangling to ensure

one's own views are not imposed on the mentee; questions have to be framed and discussed to empower the mentee to learn and develop; summarising key thoughts and discussion can provide clarity of key issues.
- Managing emotions – a mentor has to be aware of his or her own emotions and manage these alongside being in tune with the mentee's feelings. This will require a high level of emotional intelligence.
- Feedback – a mentor should give feedback in a way that the mentee accepts it, understands it and is able to use it.
- Challenge and confrontation – a mentor has to seek to raise consciousness in the mentee about any restriction or avoidance that blocks, distorts or restricts their learning. This should be through an appropriate challenge that raises the mentee's awareness and help them reframe situations.

Another perspective to appreciate the behaviours that a mentor needs to demonstrate is to focus on the types of assistance a mentor is expected to provide to a mentee. Shea (2001) identifies seven types of mentor assistance to encourage mentee development – help the mentee to shift context and envision a positive future or outcome; listen and be a sounding board when the mentee has a problem; pick up on underlying feelings related to the mentee's issues/problems; confront and challenge when appropriate; offer relevant information or suggest possible solutions; encourage explorations of options and bolster the mentee's confidence by delegating authority and providing new opportunities.

There is no doubt, therefore, that mentors who are friendly, honest, approachable, understanding, compassionate, dedicated, patient and act with integrity make 'good' mentors (Gray and Smith, 2000; Elzubeir and Rizk, 2001). The willingness to provide honest feedback is another important skill that effective mentors possess (Gray and Smith, 2000; Wright and Carrese, 2002). In addition to interpersonal skills, effective mentors also demonstrate a high level of expertise, including professional skills, organisation and communication skills and self-confidence (Gray and Smith, 2000; Elzubeir and Rizk, 2001; Wright and Carrese, 2002; McDowall-Long, 2004).

According to Clutterbuck (2004), there is a great deal of confusion about the skills and competencies of a mentor. He offers a conceptual set of competencies based on what mentors do and how they do it. The ten mentor competences are:

- Self-awareness – mentors need a high level of self-awareness in order to recognise and manage their own behaviour within the relationship.
- Communication competence – this requires use of multiple skills such as listening, observing non-verbal signals, keeping in tune with what the recipient is hearing, understanding; and adapting tone, voice, volume, pace and language accordingly.
- Sense of proportion/good humour – mentors need to feel at ease with themselves and their role in the organisation; humour and laughter can help to build rapport, release tension and develop multi-perspectives.
- Interest in developing others – effective mentors have an innate interest in achieving through others and in helping others recognise and achieve their potential.
- Goal clarity – mentors must have the ability to support mentees to identify what they want to achieve and to help them to set and pursue clear goals.
- Behavioural awareness – mentors must have reasonable insight into behaviour patterns of individuals and their interaction with groups; observation and reflective skills are required for this.
- Conceptual modelling – over time mentors need to develop a toolkit i.e. a portfolio of models and frameworks to help mentees understand the issues they face.
- Business and/or professional savvy – mentors must be able to reflect critically on experience to develop judgement, which they can share with mentees and also use to address mentee issues.
- Commitment to own learning – mentors have to take responsibility for their learning and become role models for self-managed learning.
- Relationship management – mentors should be confident and comfortable to manage the dynamics in the mentor-mentee relationship,

build a rapport and respond sensitively to mentees' needs and emotions.

Therefore, an effective mentor must have a blend of both functional and relational skills. Merriam (1983), in his empirical mixed method study within leading US corporations of the time such as Manhattan Bank, General Electric and Ogilvy-Mather Inc., emphasised that an effective mentor, apart from carrying out the functions of advising, guiding, supporting, protecting, directing, challenging, encouraging and motivating, must be able to develop and maintain an 'intense emotional relationship akin to parental love' with his or her mentee. This emphasis on relational capabilities with emotional intelligence as a core competence of a mentor is an area of current and future research.

AN INEFFECTIVE MENTOR

In practice not all mentors demonstrate the competencies discussed previously. Sometimes, mentors may volunteer to take on this role but not dedicate the time and commitment required; in some instances they may want to but are not able to manage conflicting priorities (Sanyal and Rigby, 2013). Others may have their own agenda, including own personal development, which can lead to the process becoming a paper exercise rather than a two-way dynamic learning process leading to development and change. Cooper and Palmer (2000) have placed mentor traits within two axes: enabling/disabling and facilitation/manipulation. While the behaviours for an enabling and facilitative role have been discussed above, they describe the following types of mentor as showing disabling and manipulative traits: a 'toxic mentor' who is not easily accessible, 'dumpers' who place protégés in challenging situations and then abandon them, 'blockers' who thwart mentees' needs either deliberately or unconsciously and 'destroyers' who 'tear down' their protégés and undermine them in private or public. Clutterbuck (2004) refers to such individuals as 'mentors from hell'. He suggests that such mentors might have an alternative agenda, transfer their own problems into the mentee's situation, take umbrage if the mentee is able to address their own solution and not be engaged in their own learning.

The sets of competencies, behaviours and skills discussed above illustrate that, to be effective as a mentor, one needs to be authentic, display strong emotional intelligence, be an excellent communicator and be sincerely committed to the development of others. However, these are generic competencies of a mentor and several contextual factors are likely to determine the emphasis a mentor may need to place on particular competencies or sets of competencies. These will be discussed in later sections.

AN EFFECTIVE MENTEE

Although there is no doubt that the role of mentoring is to help mentees develop themselves, it is still essential to consider the skills and behaviours of a mentee, as this can have substantial impact on the quality and type of help he or she receives (Clutterbuck, 2004). In their study, Singh, Ragins and Tharenou (2009) assessed the rising star hypothesis and proposed that individuals who are on the fast track to career success are more likely to gain mentors than others. Allen and Eby (2011) in their handbook on mentoring also suggest that mentors select their protégés based on their performance and potential; intuitively, mentors will be drawn to those who stand out for their talent and they will be more willing to invest their time when mentees use the time well and are open to feedback.

Therefore, literature appears to focus on what mentors are looking for in a mentee; for example, Zey (1984) highlights the following criteria:

- Intelligence – mentees must have the ability to identify and solve business problems.
- Ambition and enthusiasm – mentees must be able and ambitious, striving for career progression, willing to take on new or additional roles.
- Succession potential and hard work – mentors are likely to want a mentee who is capable of following in his or her footsteps and is willing to work hard for this i.e. actively seek challenging assignments.
- Strong interpersonal skills – mentees must be able to forge new alliances and demonstrate networking ability.

Where mentors seek such capabilities in a mentee, the context is usually sponsorship mentoring within an organisation aimed at 'high flyers' or 'future potentials'. However, mentoring is increasingly viewed as an individual learning and development tool for wider use directed at individuals with a wide range of abilities and needs, such as mentoring programmes for disaffected youths and people with learning disability, mentoring in the context of gender and sexual preference, mentoring for refugee and immigrant students and academic mentoring for students. Mentees on such programmes are unlikely to require the same criteria, although ownership of learning and personal commitment will be expected of all mentees irrespective of the type or context of the programme.

Thus, as mentoring is a two-way relationship, the mentee's capabilities and commitment are crucial for its success. According to Clutterbuck (2004), a 'good' mentee will take primary responsibility for arranging meetings and setting agendas, manage his or her own expectations of the relationship, be able to select and bring issues for discussion, be willing to challenge and be challenged, show respect, openness and good humour and fulfil obligations of the relationship not only to the mentor but also to any other third party such as his or her line manager or programme co-ordinator. He or she must also understand the purpose and organisational context of the mentoring programme, manage his or her own as well as the mentor's expectations and be clear about the positive outcomes for both parties. Therefore, a mentee is required to take the initiative, regularly reflect on the process, take responsibility for his or her own development and embrace change and new ideas (Allen et al., 2011; Clutterbuck, 2011).

AN INEFFECTIVE MENTEE

Not all mentees are fully engaged in the mentoring relationship. There may be numerous reasons for this, such as lack of commitment or interest in the process, or they may have been recruited on to a mentoring programme without fully understanding the context or being fully clear about expectations. In such cases, this can have a negative effect on the mentoring relationship in the first phase and can lead to an early closure. In other cases, a mentee may be keen to engage with the mentor but may lack confidence or may find it difficult to be at ease with his or her mentor. Here, self-confidence can be a valuable competency in a mentee; however, overconfidence verging on arrogance is unlikely to be appreciated by the mentor. A mentor can also help a mentee to build his or her confidence as a part of their development.

EFFECTIVE MENTORING RELATIONSHIP

Once started, a mentoring relationship tends to follow a common pathway of evolution (Kram, 1983; Merriam, 1983; Clutterbuck, 1998). However, how mentors and mentees are supported through each of these stages and the transition from one to the other may have a significant influence on the effectiveness of the mentoring relationship. This is dependent on a range of factors.

First, the affinity between the mentor and mentee will impact on the effectiveness of the relationship. This is referred to as 'rapport' or 'rapport building' in the mentoring literature (Clutterbuck, 1998, 2001; Megginson et al., 2006). The matching process within a mentoring programme attempts to address this by trying to ensure that mentors and mentees are paired to enable this rapport-building process. Thus, the matching process may consider race, age, gender, work experience, personal interests, mode of preferred communication etc. to support this. However, it will be up to the individual pairs to build on their mutual interest, motivation and commitment to establish a sustainable relationship throughout the mentoring programme and sometimes even beyond it. Training and support sessions can also help both mentors and mentees to consider behaviours and capabilities that will help them to maintain this relationship.

Second, both mentors and mentees must be clear about the 'purpose' of the mentoring exchange. If the goal of each mentoring exchange as well as the overall outcome of the mentoring intervention is clear, this will ensure that each mentor-mentee exchange delivers optimum value both for the mentor and the mentee. Therefore, the 'clarity of purpose' (Clutterbuck, 2001) or the 'working alliance' (Brockbank and McGill, 2006) to achieve the mentoring outcomes together is another essential factor in the effectiveness of a mentoring relationship. Several studies have discussed the need for 'expectations' to be shared early on in formal mentoring relationships to ensure both parties receive the support to achieve them and early alignment with perceptions and expectations between mentors and mentees can avoid problems with mismatch and misunderstanding later (Young and Perrewé, 2004). However, it is important to note that 'early' expectations and objectives may change with the mentee's increasing understanding of themselves and their environment and therefore an effective mentoring relationship will require regular review of mentoring expectations. Thus, 'goal clarity' will be a key competency for both mentors and mentees.

Third, the progress through the stages or phases of the mentoring relationship is likely to be dependent on the 'intensity of learning' (Clutterbuck, 1998) i.e. the quality of the learning exchange. The mentor-mentee conversations must be meaningful for both. The mentee should be able to 'learn' or at least gain relevant information which increases knowledge and understanding or sign posting for access to further information or networking opportunities. The mentor should get a clear sense that he or she is contributing to the mentee's learning and development. According to Jones (2013), sharing experiences, views and stories is the most influential way mentors and mentees learn. Consequently, mentoring conversation offers a social learning process by which both the mentors and the mentees acquire new information, attitude and behaviours (McDowall-Long, 2004). However, as sometimes the most significant mentoring outcomes may be realised long after the formal ending of the relationship and on some occasions personal development and growth may be difficult to attribute specifically to mentoring interventions, the most common measure of effective mentoring relationship, i.e. achievement of agreed outcomes, may not always be valid.

Finally, successful mentoring is a two-way, dynamic process where the functions of both the mentors and mentees are equally important. The number of functions may not always equate to the success of the relationship. Whether these functions are psychological, developmental or specifically career related, mentors and mentees will require both functional as well as relational skills and capabilities to sustain an effective mentoring relationship (Colley, 2003; Haddock-Millar and Sanyal, 2015).

KEY METHODOLOGICAL ISSUES FOR CONSIDERATION

As discussed above, research in the field of mentoring has tended to offer sets of generic competencies, skills and behaviours for mentors and mentees and the outcomes from mentoring relationships. Although this has enabled all professionals involved in mentoring programmes to identify, develop and support these skill sets, it is important to consider the contextual relevance of when, where and which competencies will or should apply. It is the purpose, functions, type and stage of mentoring which will determine the requirement of the competencies for mentors and mentees.

The context and purpose is an important factor. For example, although comparison is often made between the mentoring functions within education and industry (Ghosh, 2012), there are also overlaps. Anderson and Shannon (1988) argue that effective educational mentoring programmes must be grounded on a clear and strong conceptual foundation, particularly as, in education, a mentor may play several roles ranging from being a role model to a counsel, teacher, guide and a friend. Therefore, it is imperative to have an articulated approach to mentoring which includes an agreed definition of the mentoring relationship, the essential functions of the mentor role, the activities through which selected mentoring functions will be expressed and the dispositions or capabilities that mentors must exhibit if they are to carry out requisite mentoring functions and activities. Similarly in business mentoring, the mentor also plays multiple roles that serve the overarching purposes of supporting both career and psychosocial development of the mentee (Kram, 1983). Business mentors may be involved in personal and emotional guidance, coaching and advocating, as well as facilitation of learning and career advice of the mentees within the organisation (Fowler and O'Gorman, 2005). This will involve more than one mentoring function and hence requires an appropriate set of competencies. Therefore, it is important to recognise that the context may require emphasis on different sets of mentor competencies. For example, listening and congruence, giving feedback and interest in developing others may be a strong set of competencies in educational mentoring, whereas business savvy, conceptual modelling, challenge and confrontation may be more relevant for business mentors. Some common core mentor competencies, regardless of context, are self-awareness, communication competence, goal clarity and managing emotions.

Another difference to consider is the function or type of mentoring. Although traditionally mentoring has been defined as a relationship between an older, more experienced mentor and a younger, less experienced protégé for the purpose for helping and supporting the protégé's career (Levinson, 1978; Kram, 1985; Ragins, 1999; Wanberg et al., 2003), this is considered to be a US-centric definition where the mentee is a protégé i.e. someone who is sponsored and/or protected. In such 'sponsorship mentoring' (Kram, 1985), mentors have been able to oversee the career development of the mentee through facilitating their learning, offering advice and guidance, providing psychological support and promoting or sponsoring (Zey, 1984; Haddock-Millar and Sanyal, 2015). Thus, where mentoring is primarily about career development i.e. sponsorship mentoring, the essential competences for the mentor will focus on his or her interest in achieving through others and guiding the mentee to achieve career progression. Where the mentor is also the direct line manager or the boss i.e. in supervision mentoring, which is a sub-set of sponsorship mentoring, clearly one of the key competences here must relate to the relational aspect of how the mentor separates out the mentoring functions from the supervisory functions, avoiding or managing any potential for conflicting priorities. The mentee must demonstrate ambition and enthusiasm to succeed and be willing to work hard and forge new alliances through networking opportunity. In contrast, in a development mentoring programme, where the aim is to enhance learning and development, the mentee competencies will focus on commitment and willingness to learn and be challenged. For the mentor, the behavioural awareness and relationship management competencies will be the key to the success of the relationship.

A consideration for difference is the medium of mentoring i.e. a traditional mentoring (face-to-face) or e-mentoring (Bierema and Merriam, 2002; Hamilton and Scandura, 2003; Shpigelman et al., 2009). A face-to-face mentoring programme within a medium-size company, where line managers are the mentors, may require emphasis on a different set of competencies to an in-house e-mentoring programme set up in a multinational company where mentors and mentees are separated by different time zones and geographical boundaries. Here, communication competence and relationship management skills within the e-mentoring programme will need to be considered in the context of e-communication and telephone conversations. Hamilton and Scandura's (2003) study exploring the benefits and challenges of e-mentoring emphasises the need to develop 'electronic chemistry' in an e-mentoring relationship, particularly in the initial stage. Here, alongside computer literacy, the ability to personalise and emotionalise the media will require a lot of commitment and patience from both the mentor and mentee to move through the phases of the relationship. If mentor and mentee invest the time and engage in building the rapport, the relationship will move forward; otherwise, e-communication may become a challenge to the development of the relationship.

Moreover, the competencies required for both the mentor and the mentee may evolve as the relationship develops and matures. The early stage of mentoring will require emphasis on effective communication to build rapport; goal clarity will be essential to progress the relationship. Other competencies would come into play to sustain the relationship and achieving the mentoring outcomes. Purcell (2004) suggests that the initial opportunity to develop a mentoring relationship in person may be most effective. In an e-mentoring programme, video skyping conversations should be considered where possible to ensure visual cues can be exchanged as a part of the rapport-building process between mentors and mentees. Thus, multiple methods of communication are likely to maximise learning and achieve programme outcomes (Hegstad and Wentling, 2005). A mentee must be willing to engage and learn from the mentor as a first step and then build on this as the relationship progresses using the mentee competencies discussed earlier.

Finally, in establishing the effectiveness of mentors, mentees and the mentoring relationship, the researchers and authors so far appear to have taken a linear approach. However, today's fast changing organisations are characterised by complex behaviours that emerge as a result of often non-linear spatio-temporal interactions among a large number of component systems at different levels of the organisation. Mitleton-Kelly (1997) referred to these systems in organisations as the Complex Adaptive Systems. Lansing (2003) also suggests that complexities lurk within even extremely simple systems and therefore it may not be practical to know the outcome of interactions that are likely to be emergent and spontaneous. Therefore, this is more than likely to impact on the nature of relationships in organisations. More recently, Clutterbuck (2012) has also highlighted that organisations and their employees form a complex, adaptive system where the people and the organisations are constantly changing and so the relationships in these organisations are dynamic and constantly evolving. However, the phases and stages of mentoring models (Kram, 1983; Merriam, 1983; Clutterbuck, 1998) suggest that the individuals involved in the mentoring process will move from one stage of their relationship to another, which reinforces the notion of mentoring as a linear, quasi-parental relationship

(Colley, 2003). Similarly, the mentoring success and outcomes of the relationships do not appear to consider societal factors such as individual lifestyles or life histories and the impact these can have on the relationship. Thus, a mentor's or mentee's family circumstances, beliefs, religious practice or economic status are often not considered – when understanding the mentor-mentee relationship development. Furthermore, organisational antecedents such as organisational culture and structure will have an effect on the mentoring programme (Hegstad and Wentling, 2005). For example, where the culture supports the pursuit of personal power and influence, as in the US context, the behaviours by the mentor in helping the mentee to gain power would be an important competence and high levels of ambition might be a desirable quality in a mentee. In contrast, in a collectivist or less authoritarian culture, such competencies would be less relevant. Another cultural variation that may impact on the mentor-mentee relationship is that, if an organisational culture supports employee learning and development, a mentoring programme's likelihood of success increases; on the other hand, if an organisation is downsizing or experiencing turbulence, it may be difficult to locate suitable mentors.

The broader socio-economic and political agenda that has driven the formalisation of mentoring is obvious from the increasing range of contexts in which mentoring is offered today, such as in education to support students, in companies for staff development, in youth development programmes, as a part of diversity training and social inclusion. However, it is important to note that, in most situations, mentoring programmes operate within a complex, adaptive system where both internal organisational dynamical systems as well as external environmental factors will impact on behaviours, both individual and group, which in turn will affect the interaction between mentors and mentees. These circumstances will define the expected mentor and mentee behaviours and competences.

WHAT MEASURES NEED TO BE TAKEN FOR AN EFFECTIVE MENTOR-MENTEE RELATIONSHIP?

Design and development of mentoring programme

A robust and well-structured mentoring programme can go a long way to ensuring that mentor-mentee relationships are well matched, developed and sustained. There are a number of different frameworks which can be utilised to assist with the design and implementation of mentoring programmes. For example, the International Standards for Mentoring Programmes in Employment (ISMPE) provide a clear structure which can also be used to continually evaluate the effectiveness of the mentoring programmes. Generally, the stages of these programmes are:

- Project design involves clear scoping and identification of stakeholder aims, objectives and evaluation strategy.
- Criteria for recruitment of mentors and mentees are established and awareness-raising activities are undertaken prior to recruitment.
- Training or briefing for both mentors and mentees is provided. The ISMPE guidelines suggest that mentors and mentees be trained together to develop a shared understanding.
- Mentors and mentees are given an opportunity to express a preference for a partner based on brief biographical profiles before matching is undertaken.
- Once the matches are agreed and accepted, the mentoring begins.
- At the outset, throughout and at the end of the project, baseline, interim and final evaluations are undertaken to capture experiences and learning from all project stakeholders.
- Mentors and mentees receive some form of continuous support for at least the first 12 months of the relationship.

- Clear and planned endings are considered at the start; this will result in stronger positive recollection of the relationship.

Training and support for mentors and mentees

Many mentors volunteer to take on this role and others find themselves acting as mentor to contribute to an in-house mentoring programme. Where programmes are planned and structured in advance, there may be opportunity to train mentors on the skills discussed above. Clutterbuck (2004) advocates the need to motivate the mentor and help him or her to understand how he or she can contribute to the mentee's development. Workshops can be planned, designed and delivered to ensure that mentors are clear about the aims and objectives of the programme and understand the dynamic nature of mentoring, its stages and phases and the behaviours, capabilities and techniques required to be an effective mentor.

To be able to take responsibility for the mentoring relationship, a mentee training session or a workshop is also essential. Here, the aims and objectives of the mentoring programme as well as the expectations of both the mentor and mentee can be addressed. The skills and behaviours of a mentee can be explored through experiential, interactive learning activities to enable a mentee to understand how he or she can be effective in the relationship and achieve the required mentoring outcomes. Where possible and appropriate, mentors and mentees should be trained together as it provides a developmental opportunity for both joint understanding as well as building the mentoring relationship. This can help to strengthen the initial 'phase' of the relationship. In the case of e-mentoring programmes, online training material should be made available to both mentors and mentees.

Apart from initial training, some mentors and mentees may require ongoing support to develop and sustain the mentoring relationship during the mentoring programme. Here, the role of experienced learning facilitators with a clear understanding of the organisational context as well as individual capabilities can help and guide mentors and mentees to manoeuvre through the layers of complexities within the organisation to maintain effective mentoring relationships and achieve the required mentoring outcomes.

Role of a mentoring programme manager

Although both the mentors and the mentees must be fully engaged and committed to the mentoring for its success, the role of an effective programme manager or co-ordinator is essential within a professional mentoring programme. An effective mentoring programme manager can often make the difference between a failed mentoring relationship and a successful one, as he or she plays a critical role in the development and implementation of the mentoring programme. Key functions may include training participants, engaging key stakeholders, reporting to senior management and evaluating the programme. Therefore, the mentoring programme manager can be pivotal in managing the dynamic processes in recruiting, building and maintaining relationships with mentors, mentees and their line managers/tutors, as well as sponsors of the programme such as senior management and funding bodies.

Ongoing evaluation of mentoring relationships

The process of evaluation must be interwoven throughout the mentoring programme as part of both support and supervision processes, including continual monitoring of the mentoring relationships and their progress toward established goals, as well as capturing qualitative and quantitative data efficiently and accurately. This method of ongoing evaluation can help to address any arising issues with individual mentor-mentee pairs and thereby improve overall mentoring success. It can identify and meet the need for additional support for a mentee or a mentor as required, as well as resolving other resourcing and management issues within the programme. This enables an overview of the mentor-mentee relationship within a more complex adaptive system, rather than a linear approach which can be limiting to the growth and development of both individual relationships as well as the programme as a whole.

RECOMMENDATION FOR FUTURE RESEARCH

The current sets of mentor-mentee competencies are mainly conceptual; therefore, in-depth empirical studies on the effectiveness of these competencies and their impact on the mentoring relationship should be considered. Application of sets of competencies could be tracked through recruitment, selection and development of mentors and mentees as well as through the stages of the relationship to understand effectiveness and impact. Another potential area of research is a comparison of multiple case studies of traditional mentoring and e-mentoring to identify the similarities and differences in the competencies applied. The evolving nature of the required competencies through the development of the mentoring relationship could be another specific area of research. Mentoring research can also be further widened to study the impact of personal context such as socio-economic, religious and life histories on the capabilities of mentors and mentees as well as on the development and effectiveness of mentoring relationships. Similarly, how mentor and mentee competencies may vary according to context, purpose and type of mentoring could be another both interesting and useful area for further research. Finally, mentoring relationships should be studied in the context of the dynamic, complex systems in which mentoring programmes often operate to understand the key influences and drivers of an effective mentoring programme. In such an evolving system, how the competencies of a mentor and mentee may interact and influence behaviours of each other and the overall efficacy of the relationship will be another interesting and cutting-edge topic for future research.

REFERENCES

Abedin, Z., Biskup, E., Silet, K., Garbutt, J. M., Kroenke, K., Feldman, M. D., and Pincus, H. A. (2012). Deriving competencies for mentors of clinical and translational scholars. *Clinical and translational science*, *5*(3), 273–280.

Ackley, B., and Gall, M. D. (1992). Skills, strategies, and outcomes of successful mentor teachers. Conference Paper presented at the Annual Meeting of the American Educational Research Association (San Francisco, CA, April 20–24, 1991).

Allen, T. D., and Eby, L. T. (Eds.). (2011). The Blackwell handbook of mentoring: A multiple perspectives approach. Chichester: John Wiley and Sons.

Anderson, E. M., and Shannon, A. L. (1988). Toward a conceptualization of mentoring. *Journal of Teacher Education*, *39*(1), 38–42.

Bierema, L., and Merriam, S. (2002). E-mentoring: Using computer mediated communication to enhance the mentoring process. *Innovative Higher Education*, *26*(3), 211–227.

Brockbank, A., and McGill, I. (2006). Facilitating reflective learning through mentoring and coaching. London: Kogan Page Publishers.

Clutterbuck, D. (1998). Mentoring Diagnostic Kit. Buckinghamshire: Clutterbuck Associates.

Clutterbuck, D. (2001). Everyone needs a mentor: fostering talent at work (3rd Ed.). London: CIPD Publishing.

Clutterbuck, D. (2004). Everyone needs a mentor: fostering talent in your organisation (4th Ed.). London: CIPD Publishing.

Clutterbuck, D. (2011). Mentoring for diversity (e-resource). Buckinghamshire: Clutterbuck Associates.

Clutterbuck, D. (2012). How to harness the energy of the talent wave. People Management, October 2012. CIPD Publication.

Clutterbuck, D. (2015). How mentoring functions have become a dangerous distraction for research and practice in mentoring. Coaching and Mentoring International, posted on 16th March, 2015. Retrieved from https://coachingandmentoringinternational.org/ (accessed 21 September, 2016).

Cooper, A. M., and Palmer, A. (2000). Mentoring, preceptorship and clinical supervision: A guide to professional roles in clinical practice. New Jersey: Wiley-Blackwell.

Denmark, V. M., and Podsen, I. J. (2000). The mettle of a mentor. Teachers who mentor others need to explore seven competencies. *Journal of Staff Development*, *21*(4), 18–22.

Elzubeir, M. A., and Rizk, D. E. (2001). Identifying characteristics that students, interns and residents look for in their role models. *Medical Education*, *35*(3), 272–277.

Fowler, J. L., and O'Gorman, J. G. (2005). Mentoring functions: A contemporary view of the perceptions of mentees and mentors. *British Journal of Management*, *16*(1), 51–57.

Gray, M. A., and Smith, L. N. (2000). The qualities of an effective mentor from the student nurse's perspective: Findings from a longitudinal qualitative study. *Journal of Advanced Nursing*, *32*(6), 1542–1549.

Ghosh, R. (2012). Mentors providing challenge and support: Integrating concepts from teacher mentoring in education and organizational mentoring in business. *Human Resource Development Review*, 2012 Nov, 1–33d.o.i: 1534484312465608.

Haddock-Millar, J., and Sanyal, C. (2015). The role of a mentor in supporting early career academics: The relationship is more important than the label. In B. L. H. Marina (Ed.). *Mentoring away the glass ceiling in academia: A cultured critique*. Maryland: Lexington Books, 129–140.

Hamilton, B. A., and Scandura, T. A. (2003). E-mentoring: Implications for organisational learning and development in a wired world. *Organisational Dynamics*, *31*(4), 388–402.

Hegstad, C. D., and Wentling, R. M. (2005). Organizational antecedents and moderators that impact on the effectiveness of exemplary formal mentoring programs in Fortune 500 companies in the United States. *Human Resource Development International*, *8*(4), 467–487.

Johnson, W. B. (2003). A framework for conceptualizing competence to mentor. *Ethics and Behaviour*, *13*(2), 127–151.

Jones, J. (2013). Factors influencing mentees' and mentors' learning throughout formal mentoring relationships. *Human Resource Development International*, *16*(4), 390–408.

Kram, K. E. (1983). Phases of the mentor relationship. *Academy of Management Journal*, *26*(4), 608–625.

Kram, K. E. (1985). Mentoring at work: Developmental relationship in organisational life. Glenview, IL: Scott, Foresman and Co.

Lansing, J. S. (2003). Complex adaptive systems. *Annual Review of Anthropology*, *32*(1), 183–204.

McDowall-Long, K. (2004). Mentoring relationships: Implications for practitioners and suggestions for future research. *Human Resource Development International*, *7*(4), 519–534.

Megginson, D., and Garvey, B. (2004). Odysseus, Telemachus and Mentor: Stumbling into, searching for and signposting the road to desire. *International Journal of Mentoring and Coaching*, *2*(1), 2–10.

Megginson, D., Clutterbuck, D., Garvey, B., Stokes, P., and Garrett-Harris, R. (2006). Mentoring in action: A practical guide. *Human Resource Management International Digest*, *14*(7).

Merriam, S. (1983). Mentor and protégés: A critical review of the literature. *Adult Education Quarterly*, *33*(3), 161–173.

Mitleton-Kelly, E. (1997). Organisations as Co-evolving Complex Adaptive Systems, British Academy of Management Conference. 8–12 September 1997, London, UK.

Murray, M. (2002). Beyond the myths and magic of mentoring: How to facilitate an effective mentoring process.Chichester: John Wiley and Sons.

Olian, J. D., Carroll, S. J., Giannantonio, C. M., and Feren, D. B. (1988). What do protégés look for in a mentor? Results of three experimental studies. *Journal of Vocational Behavior, 33*(1), 15–37.

Ragins, B. R., and Cotton, J. L. (1999). Mentor functions and outcomes: a comparison of men and women in formal and informal mentoring relationships. *Journal of Applied Psychology, 84*(4), 529.

Ragins, B. R. (1999). Gender and mentoring relationships: A review and research agenda for the next decade. In Powell, Gary N. (Ed.). (1999). Handbook of gender and work, (pp. 347–370). Thousand Oaks, CA, US: Sage.

Rodenhauser, P., Rudisill, J. R., and Dvorak, R. (2000). Skills for mentors and protégés applicable to psychiatry. *Academic Psychiatry, 24*(1), 14–27.

Rogers, C. (1983). Freedom to learn for the Eighties. Columbus OH: Charles Merrin.

Sanyal, C., and Rigby, C. (2013). 'Does e-mentoring work? The effectiveness and challenges of an International Professional Mentoring Scheme', European and Mentoring Coaching Council 3rd Annual Research Conference, Dublin, Ireland.

Shea, G. (2001). Mentoring: How to develop successful mentor behaviors. Crisp Learning.

Shpigelman, C., Weiss, P. L., and Reiter, S. (2009). E-Mentoring for all. *Computers in Human Behaviour, 25*, 919–928, Elsevier Ltd.

Singh, R., Ragins, B. R., and Tharenou, P. (2009). Who gets a mentor? A longitudinal Assessment of the rising star hypothesis. *Journal of Vocational Behavior, 74*(1), 11–17.

Wanberg, C. R., Welsh, E. T., and Hezlett, S. A. (2003). Mentoring research: A review and dynamic process model. In J. J. Martocchio and G. R. Ferris (Eds.). Research in personnel and human resources management, Vol. 22, pp. 39–124. Oxford, England: Elsevier Science.

Wright, S. M., and Carrese, J. A. (2002). Excellence in role modelling: Insight and perspectives from the pros. *Canadian Medical Association Journal, 167*(6), 638–643.

Young, A. M., and Perrewé, P. L. (2004). The role of expectations in the mentoring exchange: An analysis of mentor and protégé expectations in relation to perceived support. *Journal of Managerial Issues*, 16(1), 103–126.

Zey, M. G. (1984). The mentor connection. Illinois: Irwin Professional Publishing.

The Mentoring Cycle

Julie Haddock-Millar

INTRODUCTION

The aim of this chapter is to explore the mentoring cycle and in particular the concept of phases within the context of the mentoring relationship. The chapter begins by outlining a number of models that describe how mentoring relationships develop over time, such as Kram (1980, 1983), Missirian (1982), Clutterbuck (1985, 2004), and Westland (2015). The mentee and mentor perspective is explored by understanding the experiences of each, through insight, during various stages of the relationship. Next, the author identifies a number of empirical studies that have 'tested' the models to better understand their application to specific contexts (Westland, 2015). The models are compared and contrasted in order to identify the challenges associated with the concept of the mentoring cycle. The author also considers factors that influence the mentoring cycle and the effectiveness of the mentoring relationship. Finally, the author considers the implications of the mentoring cycle from a number of perspectives: mentoring relationships, program design, training for mentees and mentors, and future research agendas for both researchers and practitioners.

PHASES OF THE MENTORING RELATIONSHIP

Literature explores mentoring from a number of different perspectives, approaches, models, modes, and contexts. The continuum includes the United States (US), European and African perspectives that broadly encompass sponsorship, developmental mentoring, and community mentoring (Clutterbuck, 2004; Geber and Nyanjom, 2009; Kochan, 2013). Approaches to mentoring include both informal and formal tactics differing in strategy, design, and ethos, as described by Pollock: *'informal mentors are distinct from formal mentors in that the duties and personnel are not assigned by the organization*' (Pollock, 1995, p. 144). Furthermore, formal mentoring consists of a structured program that establishes and supports mentoring relationships (Clutterbuck, 2004). Modes of mentoring include the ways in which relationships are facilitated, such as face-to-face, e-mentoring, telephone, and blended components (Haddock-Millar and Rigby, 2014a, 2014b; Haddock-Millar et al., 2015; Sanyal and Rigby, 2013a). The context of the mentoring relationship may vary and be applied to business, community, cross-cultural contexts, education, entrepreneurship, executive positions, finance, government, nursing, and psychology (Anderson, 2007; Clandinin, 2012; Collins et al., 2014; Crisp and Cruz, 2009; De Four-Babb et al., 2015; Goldman and Schmalz, 2012; Haddock-Millar and Rigby, 2014a, 2015; Laukhuf and Malone, 2015; Missirian, 1982; Sanyal and Rigby, 2013a, 2013b, 2013c; Underhill, 2006).

The mentoring cycle and/or phases of the mentoring relationship may exist regardless of perspective, approach, model, mode, and context. The mentoring cycle broadly refers to the way in which mentoring relationships change over time; in other words, how the mentee and mentor might interact as the relationship evolves (Chao, 1997). The majority of literature examining relationship changes may utilize the terminology of *phases* and *stages* rather than *cycles* (Clutterbuck, 2004; Kram, 1980, 1983, 1985; Missirian, 1982; Phillips, 1977; Westland, 2015). For consistency, the author adopts the term phases throughout this chapter.

Bozeman and Feeney's (2007) conceptual analysis and critique of mentoring theory and research suggests that Kram's (1980, 1983, 1985) work, particularly the *Academy of Management Journal* article (1983), remains the most frequently cited. Kram's article recognizes the ways in which mentoring relationships may change over time and the necessary observation of the mentee and mentor as their relationship unfolds (Clawson, 1979; Kram, 1980; Levinson et al., 1978; Missirian, 1982; Phillips, 1977). Kram's (1983) model is a useful starting point to consider how mentoring relationships develop from the perspective of the mentee and the mentor.

Kram (1980, 1983) model

Kram's (1980, 1983) empirical qualitative study explored eighteen mentee-mentor dyads in *informal* developmental relationships within a large US North Eastern public utility company. The mentees comprised eight male and seven female junior managers ranging in age from twenty-six through thirty-four, with an average service length of nine point two years' service in the company; the mentors were senior managers with an average service length of twenty-three years ranging in age from thirty-nine through sixty-three. The relationships were sponsorship-orientated and informal; they were initiated by the mentee and/or mentor rather than matched by the organization, which is typical of formal programs (Janssen et al., 2016). The relationships were unbounded in the sense that the mentee identified developmental mentors, people who had a personal interest in the mentee and his or her development (Kram, 1983). The relationships were not constrained by duration, as is often the case in formal mentoring programs (Janssen et al., 2016). The average length of the developmental relationships was five years. Kram (1983) held interviews with both mentees and mentors on two separate occasions and two primary developmental mentoring functions were identified: career functions and psychosocial functions. Career functions comprised aspects such as sponsorship, exposure and visibility: coaching, protection, and challenging assignments (Kram, 1983). Psychosocial functions included role modelling, acceptance and confirmation, counselling, and friendship (Kram, 1983).

Kram (1983) identified four mentoring relationship phases: *initiation, cultivation, separation*, and *redefinition*. The *initiation* phase occurs in the first six to twelve months and is characterized by admiration, respect, and fantasy. Over time the mentee feels '*cared for, supported and respected by someone who is admired and who can provide important career and psychosocial functions*' (p. 615). The *cultivation* phase lasts from two to five years. During this stage boundaries are clarified and the career and psychosocial functions have the greatest influence and impact as the bond and level of intimacy strengthens and the mentor takes more of an interventionist approach, which extends to counselling and friendship. During this phase both mentees and mentors report positive outcomes: mentees reported increased confidence and competence, particularly within their organizational context; some mentors reported a parental sense of satisfaction at seeing and hearing success and progress through support and nurturing. The *separation* phase signals changes in both the structure and psychology of the relationship: structural separation can occur through job role changes such as an internal promotion, while psychological separation occurs as the mentee experiences autonomy and independence and the relationship becomes less pivotal in his or her development. It is acknowledged that this can be a time that results in feelings of anxiety and loss as the form of the relationship changes. The final phase involves a period of *redefinition*; in Kram's (1983) examination of the eighteen relationships that embarked on the study, eight reached the final phase. In this phase the relationship dynamic changes, as greater informality occurs and prompts a shift toward friendship and peer conversation. Both the mentee and mentor experience changes as the protégé develops greater autonomy, competence, and self-confidence. Mentors might shift their focus and energies to new mentees, reflecting their growth in competence and generativity.

Missirian (1982) model

Missirian's (1982) empirical mixed method study is set in the context of leading corporations in the US, such as Manhattan Bank, General Electric, and Ogilvy-Mather, Inc. The purpose of the study was to explore whether mentoring was a significant part of career development for successful executive female managers. The study comprised ten protégé-mentor dyads in sponsorship and developmental relationships. It is important to note that Missirian describes mentoring as '*supportive relationships along a continuum*' (Missirian, 1982, pp. 86–87). The continuum comprises peer, coach, sponsor, and mentor. A mentor relationship is regarded as one that goes beyond the utility of sponsorship or career modelling. The protégés' length of service with their organization averaged twenty-two years, the lowest was nine and the highest was thirty-six years. The protégés varied in age between early twenties and sixties. Unlike Kram's (1980, 1983) study the relationships were initiated by mentors rather than protégés, and were sponsorship orientated and informal. Overall the mentors identified the protégés as individuals that possessed ability, performed above average, and had potential (Missirian, 1982, p. 40). The relationships were unbounded in the sense that mentees identified developmental mentors as individuals with personal interests in the protégés and their developments (Kram, 1983, p. 612). The relationships were not constrained by duration, and the average length of the relationships was ten to twelve years.

Missirian (1982) identified three mentoring relationship phases: *initiation, development*, and *termination*. In the *initiation* phase, the mentoring relationships are formed, and rapport is developed through feelings engendered by interaction. During this phase, the protégés feel a sense of potential fulfilment and of being '*moulded*' or '*created*' by their mentors. This sense is referred to as the 'Pygmalion' syndrome because biased expectancies could affect reality and create self-fulfilling prophecies (Rosenthal and Jacobson, 1968, 1992, p. 42). The next phase of *development* signals the period of greatest professional growth for the protégé and potentially the mentor. In this phase the protégé and mentor develop a relationship that fosters a bond of trust, sacrifice, and admiration. The mentor creates an environment of stretch, challenge, and creativity. Missirian (1982) found that the mentor takes on the role of teacher, sponsor, and protector by directing and shaping the protégé's experiences, and increasing responsibility and exposure to new practices. The mentor effectively publicizes the protégé's successes by instigating promotion opportunities and shielding the protégé from what the mentor might regard as unreasonable or unwarranted attacks. The mentees experience a stronger sense of self and develop their ability to retain creative individuality by accepting only organizational norms that are necessary to their career progression. The *termination* phase indicates a change in the role of the mentor in the relationship, which shifts toward com-peer, resource person, counsellor, and friend, and moves away from the pivotal sponsorship role. This involves a period of reflection, redefinition, and letting go. The protégé recognizes his or her own strengths and contribution to the relationship, and takes pride in his or her achievements.

Clutterbuck (1985, 2004) model

Clutterbuck (1985, 2004) suggests that developmental relationships, which might be formal (organizationally supported) or informal, broadly transition through five phases including *rapport building, direction setting, progress making, winding down,* and *moving on*. Clutterbuck's (1985, 2004) model was developed primarily in the context of a formal mentoring relationship. The first two phases are associated with the beginning of the relationship, the middle phase oversees progress making, and the final two phases involve dissolving the relationship. In the first phase, *rapport building,* the mentee and mentor engage in dialogue to understand if they are able to work productively together. Rapport is dependent upon a number of factors:

- "the perception of alignment and values, especially at a personal level;
- the degree of mutual respect;
- broad agreement on the purpose of the relationship." (Megginson et al., 2006).

Developing a high degree of rapport is essential in ensuring the positive development of the mentoring relationship. In organizational mentoring programs, participants can be re-matched if they feel rapport is not present in the early stage. Phase two is the *setting direction* stage. This involves setting goals, giving the relationship a sense of purpose, and working out what the short-term, medium-term, and long-term direction might be. Potentially, phases one and two can be accomplished in a few meetings and thus are regarded as taking place at the beginning of the relationship. Phase three is the *progression* stage, or *core* period. The mentee and mentor can shift to phase three fairly rapidly, possibly within a six-month period of commencing the relationship. The intensity of learning for both the mentee and mentor is greatest during this period of the relationship, with both the mentee and mentor experiencing learning and growth during this phase. As time progresses, the mentee leads the meetings and content while relying increasingly on his or her judgment. Clutterbuck (2004, p. 113) outlines a number of observations of mentors, describing the mentoring meeting during this phase:

- "establish a relaxed, yet business like atmosphere
- gain consensus on the purpose of the meeting
- explore the issues from the mentee perspective
- clarify and elucidate, challenge assumptions, stimulate analysis, draw on own experience
- build confidence/motivation; agree options for action/consideration; agree actions by both partners; agree milestones

- summarise
- outline agenda for next meeting".

Effective mentors are responsive to mentees' needs and help focus the mentee on developing pragmatic solutions by using a variety of techniques to support the mentee in the quality of his or her thinking. Phase four is the *winding up* stage. Here the mentee and mentor plan to close the relationship by reviewing and celebrating what has been achieved. The mentee has developed confidence, capability, and competence, and gained a greater insight to enable career success. The terminology of winding up rather than winding down is interesting; in Clutterbuck and Megginson's (2003) study of relationship endings, they found that relationships that drifted away were nearly always viewed as negative, while formal relationships that had a clear ending were nearly always viewed by the mentee and mentor as positive. *Winding up* suggests taking action, reviewing, and celebrating. Phase five is the *moving on* stage. This involves reformulating the relationship, whereby the mentee and mentor close the formal mentoring relationship and may move on to become friends and colleagues.

EMPIRICAL STUDIES TESTING THE MODELS

Pollock's (1995) empirical study was based on the models of Missirian (1982), Kram (1983), and Phillips (1977). The quantitative study explored protégés' retrospective perceptions of their mentors' behaviors during the mentoring relationship. The sample consisted of three hundred fifty-six protégés in enduring informal mentoring relationships with senior managers within their organization in the US. The mean length for the mentoring relationship was eight point four years, and eighty-nine percent of protégés reported relationships lasting three or more years. Data were collected through a survey. The results supported Kram's (1983) timeline around the phases of the mentoring relationship, particularly around the early, middle, and late part of the relationship. The psychosocial functions and specific aspects around stimulation and challenge were present early on, therefore supporting Missirian (1982) and Kram (1983). However, the mentoring functions differed considerably; the mentor utilized the full range of mentoring functions throughout the relationship, even from the initial stage of the relationship. Furthermore, there was no evidence of the *termination* stage where the mentor would retract functions, which suggests that further research of each stage is needed.

Chao (1997) adopted Kram's (1983, 1985) model for his longitudinal empirical study set in an engineering and managerial context. The quantitative study explored the link between mentoring phases, functions, and positive outcomes. The sample consisted of one hundred seventy-eight protégés in informal mentoring relationships within their organization in the US. The majority of participants were male ($N = 137$), with a mean age of thirty-six point nine years. Data were collected through a survey over a five-year period. Overall, Chao's (1997) study supported Kram's (1983) guidelines for each phase; the protégés broadly transitioned through the phases as outlined in the model, including the time frames detailed in Kram's (1983) qualitative study. However, there were some differences: in particular, the degree to which mentoring functions are heightened in the *cultivation* stage was not consistent. Psychosocial and career-related functions were heightened in the final stages, suggesting that the intensity of learning takes place in the latter stages of the mentoring relationship.

Bouquillon, Sosik, and Lee (2005) also adopted Kram's (1983) model for their empirical study set within industry and education in the US. The quantitative study explored how mentoring phases influence the dynamics and functions of the mentoring relationships, in particular the concepts of trust and identification. The sample consisted of eighty-eight protégés, half of which were in informal mentoring relationships, with the remaining half in formal mentoring relationships (pairings were assigned by the organization and the program was managed by the organization). The average length of the mentoring relationships was between thirteen and twenty-four months. The average age of protégés and mentors ranged from forties to fifties. Bouquillon, Sosik, and Lee (2005) found that the organizational context significantly moderated the mentoring relationships, particularly around the *core* and *redefinition* phases. In the educational setting, trust and identification were significantly stronger during these phases, where a peer-like friendship emerged. By contrast, the competitive and fast-paced environment in an industry setting dictates the acceleration of these aspects. Overall, their results diverged from Chao (1997), Missirian (1982), and Kram (1985). The primary reasons accounting for the divergence were the high degree of mentoring functions identified in the early stages of the mentoring relationship, including career development, role modelling, and psychosocial support. Differences are attributed to context and the dynamic nature of hi-tech industry.

Bullis and Bach's (2009) turning point analysis tested a number of mentoring relationship phase models including Kram (1983, 1985) and Missirian (1982). The empirical study, set within a Higher Education Institution (HEI) in the US, explored the experience of twenty-six mentee postgraduate students in an informal mentoring relationship with a professor. The majority of mentees were female. The purpose of the study was to inductively identify turning points in the relationships, how they develop over time, and the utility of phase models. The study involved two sets of interviews four months apart. The mentees identified one hundred ninety-eight turning points grouped into nine themes or significant turning points. The most significant aspect of the study in relation to Kram's (1983, 1985) model was observing how turning points identified by mentees diverged from those in the four-phase model: in particular, the mentoring relationship traversed through positive and negative cycles; therefore progression did not follow the linear, stable, ordered manner suggested by Kram (1983, 1985), Missirian (1982), and Chao (1997). The implications for mentoring program managers, organizational stakeholders, mentees, and mentors should be considered in order to maximize the opportunity for success.

In 2014, alongside two colleagues, the author designed, implemented, and evaluated a six-week e-mentoring scheme in partnership with Middlesex University and the Financial and Legal Skills Partnership (FLSP) (Haddock-Millar et al., 2015). We applied the Clutterbuck (2004) model as a framework to evaluate the degree to which the relationships developed over the six-week period. Our findings suggested that there is evidence to support the transitional developmental nature of the mentoring relationships, even over a six-week period. Before discussing the outcomes in relation to mentoring relationship phases in detail the author will first provide an overview of the project.

The FLSP is the 'skills champion' for the financial and legal sectors in the United Kingdom (UK); FLSP has a single goal: to proactively support the development of a skilled workforce in the UK's finance, accountancy, and legal sectors. In recent years FLSP has partnered with Brightside, a charity that aims to give every young person the advice or inspiration they need to get to where they want to be in life, to develop the online learning resources and online mentoring framework known as 'Get In Get On' (GIGO). In 2014, twenty-eight mentees and mentors from Middlesex University Business School and individuals from supportive organizations in the financial and legal sectors participated in the GIGO scheme. A set of core attributes is routinely outlined by employers as indicators of their needs and as ciphers of 'graduateness'. These relate to 'world of work' behavioral practices such as reliability, good time-keeping, confidence, and complex problem solving. Equally relevant 'soft skills' are also included, such as communication, team working, and a capacity to operate independently and demonstrate contextual sensitivity, which includes intercultural awareness.

Fourteen mentees commenced the program in 2014, each supported by a mentor from the accounting and finance sector. The pairs that completed the program reported a high degree of purpose and focus, supported by strong rapport. In all these mentoring pairs, mentees and mentors felt that the mentoring relationship had reached the maturity stage, having established and maintained rapport, set direction, progressed, and matured (Klasen and Clutterbuck, 2002). In the majority of these pairs the mentee was based in London and the mentor was based in Scotland; this demonstrates that the challenge of geographical distance can be overcome by e-mentoring (Hamilton and Scandura, 2003). Furthermore, the relationships were conducted entirely by email and the website platform that facilitated online discussion; the loss of visual cues and body language were not a barrier for the participants that completed the program (Bierema and Hill, 2005). When asked about the style of mentoring, mentees and mentors felt that the style adopted was predominantly that of a coach or facilitator (Klasen and Clutterbuck, 2002). The mentees felt sufficiently stretched and challenged, but simultaneously acknowledged the supportive style of the mentors. There is also evidence that the program offers the opportunity for both mentee and mentor to develop their respective professional practice: for mentees, the greatest opportunity is to learn from someone experienced in the sector, develop their knowledge of the sector, and raise awareness of roles and opportunities available to continually develop their work-related skills; for mentors, the greatest opportunity is to develop their mentoring capability and adaptability in a variety of dimensions including guiding, coaching, and facilitating learning.

Sanyal and Rigby's (2013a) empirical mixed method study explored the development of mentee-mentor relationships across international boundaries. Twenty-three mentees studying for a postgraduate qualification were recruited at Middlesex University. The mentors were predominantly human resource management professionals from a range of disparate organizations in India, some of which maintained global organizational responsibilities. Their mentoring program tested Clutterbuck's (1985, 2004) mentoring relationship phases model. The average duration of each relationship was approximately nine months and the methods of communication included email, telephone, Skype, and the occasional face-to-face meeting when mentors were visiting the UK. Of the twenty-three matches, eight reached maturity (involving seven to ten hours of communication), six relationships moved between rapport building and direction and did not shift to the progression stage (three to six hours of communication), and seven relationships struggled at the rapport stage (thirty to forty-five minutes of communication); two did not get past the introductory stage. High rapport was regarded as a key driver in the success of the mentoring relationships; however, to what degree this can realistically be built across geographical boundaries is open to debate. Expectations that differ regarding turnaround time, frequency of interactions, accountability, and responsibility for driving the meetings, agenda, and conversation are all components that influenced the development of the mentoring relationships; these expectations demonstrate the complexity and risks associated with the careful nurturing of a mentoring relationship.

Westland's (2015) empirical qualitative study set within a Higher Education Institution (HEI) in the UK explored eleven developmental relationships involving mentee and mentor dyads. The study reflected on the conceptual theoretical frameworks and phases of mentoring as described by Kram (1983) and Clutterbuck (1985, 2004). The formal mentoring pilot scheme paired more experienced academic researchers with less experienced academicians wishing to develop their research. The purpose of the study was to explore what happened within mentoring relationships, identify how they developed, and determine if distinguishing features, characteristics, and traits that differentiate 'successful' and 'unsuccessful' relationships could be identified. The longitudinal study was undertaken over the period of the pilot and the participants' 'lived' experiences were considered at four points in time, totalling sixty-seven interviews.

Although Westland (2015) does not suggest that the mentoring phases in the HEI program differ significantly from Kram (1983) and Clutterbuck (1985, 2004), he does identify the importance of an '*additional pre-mentoring phase which focuses attention to the need for participants to have prior knowledge and understanding of their role and responsibility in the process of mentoring and mentoring relationship development*' (Kram, 1983; Clutterbuck, 1985, 2004). Three types of mentoring relationships are presented and referred to as *progressive*, *flat-lining*, and *break-down*. Few relationships reached the final phases of either model, indeed three relationships *flat-lined* (faltered), two relationships were terminated, and one left the organization. A number of factors negatively influenced, inhibited, or caused dysfunction in the mentoring relationship, such as lack of time, lack of prioritization, mismatching of pairings, knowledge gaps creating a progression barrier between the mentee and mentor, and ease of meeting.

CHALLENGES

Overall the phase models fall into two categories, the sponsorship approach common with US mentoring relationships, and the developmental approach, which is more common in European mentoring relationships (Clutterbuck, 1985, 2004). Furthermore, the models were developed in the context of informal or formal mentoring programs; both approaches emphasize learning and development over time, particularly long periods of time in the case of Kram (1980, 1983) and Missirian (1982). As illustrated in the previous section, mentoring programs may have a much shorter duration than the lengthy periods described by Kram (1983) and Missirian (1982); this raises issues around the dynamics of the phases. Does, for example, the creation of a three-month, twelve-month, or a twenty-four-month program change the dynamics of the phases? Is it possible for mentees and/or mentors to transition through some or all of the phases in a shorter timescale than the models suggest? Do the mentees progress through the phases linearly or is it possible to transition between multiple phases? There are no definitive answers to these questions, not least because many empirical program evaluations only consider one perspective – that of the mentee. The extent to which the views of the mentee and mentor converge is often overlooked (Collins et al., 2014; De Four-Babb et al., 2015); is the triangulation of multiple views important in understanding what is happening in the mentoring relationship?

Both Kram's (1983) and Missirian's (1982) approaches have been criticized for their emphasis on stages, rather than participant needs and an explicit understanding of the occurrences of the mentoring sessions (Brockbank and McGill, 2006). In addition, the degree to which processes, interactions, context, and temporal influences may affect relationship development and positive outcomes is unclear (Janssen et al., 2016). Furthermore, there is an implicit assumption within the Kram (1983) and Missirian (1982) models that the phases in informal and formal mentoring might be the same, although in this case evidence is lacking. Brockbank and McGill (2006) suggest an alternative, cyclical mentoring model that can be used from functionalist to evolutionary mentoring; their model adapted from Page and Wosket (2013) for counsellors, outlines the five stages of the mentoring relationship: *contact*, *focus*, *space*, *bridge*, and *review*. Unlike Kram (1980, 1983), Missirian (1982), and Clutterbuck (2004), Brockbank and McGill's (2006) model can be mapped over time, or to one particular mentoring session applied in informal and/or formal mentoring program situations.

In the US approach, the parental/child analogy is dominant and associated with biological phases of development; this approach raises issues around collusion, defensiveness, anger, love, and vulnerability. In the European developmental approach the mentor draws on four different approaches, including *the coach*, *guardian*, *counsellor*, and *facilitator* (Brockbank and McGill, 2006); this enables the mentoring relationship to adopt a situational approach that may shift between directive and non-directive, as well as nurturing and challenging. Here, the degree to which the phases are discrete or overlapping can inform the different approaches, functions, and behaviors within the mentoring relationship.

The rapid evolution of ICT has been seized by many organizations and individuals participating in mentoring programs, as a way of extending the process of mentoring to overcome spatial and temporal divides. Much debate has ensued between them and they continue in an effort to determine whether the benefits of face-to-face traditional (or t-mentoring) is maintained, enhanced or diminished by the increasing range and modes of electronic communication now available for what is variously referred to as e-mentoring (Bierema and Merriam, 2002; Hamilton and Scandura, 2003; Shpigelman et al., 2009) and virtual mentoring (Bierema and Hill, 2005; Zey, 2011). The degree to which technology influences the dynamics of the phases in mentoring relationships is yet to be fully explored from both the mentee and mentor perspective.

FUTURE RESEARCH AGENDAS

There are numerous opportunities to further research the complexities of the mentoring relationship from both the mentee and mentor perspective. Overall, studies tend to focus on relationships regarded as successful, or with positive outcomes. For example, Chao's (1997) study only explored the positive outcomes of the mentoring relationship. Negative associations with the latter phases of the mentoring relationship could significantly impact the perceived value of the relationship interactions; it is therefore necessary to explore both positive and negative outcomes to fully understand and appreciate mentoring relationship implications from a variety of perspectives, as well as fully understand what, if any, outcomes are associated with specific phases.

Reports from literature display the numerous benefits of informal and formal mentoring, including behavioral, attitudinal, and careers gains for mentees and mentors (Allen et al., 2004; Eby et al., 2008; Ferro et al., 2013; Parsloe and Wray, 2000; Ragins, 2011). There are numerous factors that influence the effectiveness of mentoring relationships. The vast majority of research to date focuses on the ontogenic individual-level and microsystems dyadic-level, examining specifics such as gender, race, informal vs. formal mentoring, and behaviors by individuals (Blickle et al., 2009; Chandler et al., 2011). What is also important to consider is the extent to which interconnected networks such as organizational and societal norms influence the mentoring experiences and how the relationship progresses. For example, mentoring networks are regarded as an important developmental aspect for women of color, addressing gender, race, and those experiencing the feeling of an 'outsider' (De Four-Babb et al., 2015; Esnard et al., 2015; Johnson-Bailey and Cervero, 2002; Jones, 2012; Laukhuf and Malone, 2015; Ragins et al., 1998).

The extent to which contextual factors, such as organizational, cultural, and structural, enable and/or constrain professional development is an important dimension to consider in the assessment of mentoring relationship progression (De Four-Babb et al., 2015). Bouquillon, Sosik, and Lee (2005) also suggest that more research is needed to understand the nature of different contexts, such as the contrast between the highly competitive, fast-paced, dynamic hi-tech environment and the collegiate education environment (although some academics may take issue with this distinction). The context may influence the degree to which learning, career, and personal development is accelerated, which may have a direct implication on the phases of the mentoring relationship. Chandler, Kram, and Yip (2011) identify that little testing or systematic examination of the organizational context influencing formal and informal mentoring programs is found in the literature. Kram (1985) suggests that context is characterized by culture and beliefs, hierarchy, reward systems, task designs, and performance management systems (Chandler et al., 2011, p. 545). Program design factors influence the success of the mentoring relationship to the extent that they can facilitate or hinder the relationship. Future research should examine the influence of organizational context on mentoring relationships and understand the degree to which the microsystem plays a part in the relationship development and outcomes.

Bullis and Bach (2009) suggest that turning point events in mentoring relationships should be explored over the entire course of the relationship. Longitudinal research can enable researchers and practitioners to better understand the development of mentoring relationships over time. From the perspective of the practitioner, mentees and mentors can be supported at key points in their relationship. From the perspective of the researcher, this will enable the further conceptualization of mentoring relationship transition, effectively developing new knowledge in continually broadening contexts and situations.

Janssen et al. (2016) go further and question whether or not the mentoring phase models (Clutterbuck, 1985, 2004; Kram, 1983; Missirian, 1982) are valid in modern work contexts. Modes of mentoring have changed over the years from face-to-face, virtual, and blended mentoring. As was identified in the previous section, rapid changes in technology have removed geographical boundaries and career mobility has increased; organizations with a global footprint value fluidity and mobility and actively encourage employees to develop a more global mindset. Future research should examine the depth and quality of virtual mentoring and blended mentoring relationships in order to understand when and how distinct transitions take place.

Some studies in the past have only considered the protégé/mentee retrospective accounts of the mentoring relationship (Bouquillon et al., 2005; Pollock, 1995). Future research should consider the interactional nature of the mentoring relationship, comparing and contrasting mentee and mentor accounts to shine a light on the degree to which there is consistency in perceived functions, behaviors, and outcomes.

These suggestions for future research are important since organizations and individuals invest time and resources into mentoring schemes, and providing insight into the development and transition of mentoring relationships can assist in supporting the participants. Due to this, in-depth empirical longitudinal studies are needed; such studies will explore mentoring relationships throughout the entire course from all perspectives and will assist in understanding developmental patterns; this applies to all approaches, modes, and mentoring contexts.

LEARNING OUTCOMES

- Understand how successful mentoring relationships develop over time
- Compare and contrast different mentoring relationship models
- Identify the challenges across the spectrum of models
- Understand the implications of the mentoring relationship phases from multiple perspectives
- Understand potential for future research agendas

REFERENCES

Allen, T. D., Eby, L. T., Poteet, M. L., Lentz, E., and Lima, L. (2004). Career benefits associated with mentoring for protégés: a meta-analysis. *Journal of Applied Psychology*, *89*(1), 127.

Anderson, V. (2007). Contingent and marginalised? Academic development and part-time teachers. *International Journal for Academic Development*, *12*(2), 111–121.

Bierema, L., and Merriam, S. (2002). E-mentoring: Using computer mediated communication to enhance the mentoring process. *Innovative Higher Education*, *26*(3), 211–227.

Bierema, L., and Hill, J. R. (2005). Virtual Mentoring and HRD. *Advances in Developing Human Resources*, *7*(4), 556–568.

Blickle, G., Witzki, A. H., and Schneider, P. B. (2009). Mentoring support and power: A three year predictive field study on protégé networking and career success. *Journal of Vocational Behavior*, *74*(2), 181–189.

Bouquillon, E. A., Sosik, J. J., and Lee, D. (2005). 'It's only a phase': examining trust, identification and mentoring functions received across the mentoring phases. *Mentoring and Tutoring: Partnership in Learning*, *13*(2), 239–258.

Bozeman, B., and Feeney, M. K. (2007). Toward a useful theory of mentoring: A conceptual analysis and critique. *Administration and Society*, *39*(6), 719–739.

Brockbank, A., and McGill, I. (2006). *Facilitating reflective learning through mentoring and coaching*. London: Kogan Page Publishers.

Bullis, C., and Bach, B. W. (2009). Are mentor relationships helping organizations? An exploration of developing mentee-mentor-organizational identifications using turning point analysis. *Communication Quarterly*, *37*(3), 199–213.

Chandler, D. E., Kram, K. E., and Yip, J. (2011). An ecological systems perspective on mentoring at work: A review and future prospects. *The Academy of Management Annals*, *5*(1), 519–570.

Chao, G. T. (1997). Mentoring phases and outcomes. *Journal of Vocational Behavior*, *51*(1), 15–28.

Clandinin, D. J. (2012). Literature review on induction and mentoring related to early career teacher attrition and retention. *Mentoring and Tutoring: Partnership in Learning*, *20*(1), 7–26.

Clawson, J. (1979). *Superior-subordinate relationships for managerial development*. Doctoral dissertation, Harvard Business School, Boston, MA.

Clutterbuck, D. (1985). *Everyone needs a mentor*. London: Universities Press.

Clutterbuck, D. (2004). *Everyone needs a mentor: Fostering talent in your organisation*. (4th edn) London: CIPD Publishing.

Clutterbuck, D., and Megginson, D. (2003). Winding up and winding down: A mentoring relationship. Retrieved from: www.clutterbuckassociates.com (03.01.2016).

Collins, A., Lewis, I., Stracke, E., and Vanderheide, R. (2014). Talking career across disciplines: Peer group mentoring for women academics. *International Journal of Evidence Based Coaching and Mentoring*, *12*(1), 92–108.

Crisp, G., and Cruz, I. (2009). Mentoring college students: A critical review of the literature between 1990 and 2007. *Research in Higher Education*, *50*(6), 525–545.

De Four-Babb, J., Pegg, J., and Beck, M. (2015). Reducing intellectual poverty of outsiders within academic spaces through informal peer mentorship. *Mentoring and Tutoring: Partnership in Learning*, *23*(1), 76–93.

Eby, L. T., Allen, T. D., Evans, S. C., Ng, T., and DuBois, D. L. (2008). Does mentoring matter? A multidisciplinary meta-analysis comparing mentored and non-mentored individuals. *Journal of Vocational Behavior*, *72*(2), 254–267.

Esnard, T., Cobb-Roberts, D., Agosto, V., Karanxha, Z., Beck, M., Wu, K., and

Unterreiner, A. (2015). Productive tensions in a cross-cultural peer mentoring women's network: A social capital perspective. *Mentoring and Tutoring: Partnership in Learning*, *23*(1), 19–36.

Ferro, A., DeWit, D., Wells, S., Speechley, K. N., and Lipman, E. (2013). An evaluation of the measurement properties of the Mentor Self-Efficacy Scale among participants in Big Brothers Big Sisters of Canada Community Mentoring Programs. *International Journal of Evidence Based Coaching and Mentoring*, *11*(1), 146–161.

Geber, H., and Nyanjom, J. A. (2009). Mentor development in higher education in Botswana: How important is reflective practice? *South African Journal of Higher Education*, *23*(5), 894–911.

Goldman, K. D., and Schmalz, K. J. (2012). Adjunct teaching part-time professional possibilities, provisions, and provisos. *Health Promotion Practice*, *13*(3), 301–307.

Haddock-Millar, J., and Rigby, C. (2014a). Blended approaches to mentoring programmes. *International Association of Mentoring, 26th International Conference: Learn, Share and Grow*. Phoenix, AZ, USA.

Haddock-Millar, J., and Rigby, C. (2014b). Mentoring for employability in the context of race, culture and socio-economic diversity: Public Sector Developmental Mentoring Scheme. *University Forum for Human Resource Development, 15th International Conference: HRD Research and Practice across Europe*. Edinburgh, UK.

Haddock-Millar, J., Rigby, C., and Sanyal, C. (2015). Supporting education and career transitions in the financial and accountancy sector. *Business Education and Accreditation*, *10*(1), 112. Institute for Business and Finance Research.

Hamilton, B. A., and Scandura, T. A. (2003). E-mentoring: Implications for organisational learning and development in a weird world. *Organisational Dynamics*, *31*(4), 388–402.

Janssen, S., Vuuren, M., and Jong, M. D. (2016). Informal mentoring at work: A review and suggestions for future research. *International Journal of Management Reviews*, *18*(4), 498–517.

Johnson-Bailey, J., and Cervero, R. M. (2002). Cross-cultural mentoring as a context for learning. *New Directions for Adult and Continuing Education*, *2002*(96), 15–26.

Jones, J. (2012). An analysis of learning outcomes within formal mentoring relationships. *International Journal of Evidence Based Coaching and Mentoring*, *10*(1), 57–73.

Klasen, N., and Clutterbuck, D. (2002). *Implementing mentoring schemes: A practical guide to successful programs*. Oxford: Elsevier.

Kochan, F. (2013). Analyzing the relationships between culture and mentoring. *Mentoring and Tutoring: Partnership in Learning*, *21*(4), 412–430.

Kram, K. E. (1980). *Mentoring processes at work: Developmental relationships in a managerial career*. Unpublished doctoral dissertation, Yale University, New Haven, CT.

Kram, K. E. (1983). Phases of the mentor relationship. *Academy of Management Journal*, *26*(4), 608–625.

Kram, K. E. (1985). *Mentoring at work: Developmental relationships in organizational life*. Glenview, IL: Scott Foresman.

Laukhuf, R. L., and Malone, T. A. (2015). Women entrepreneurs need mentors. *International Journal of Evidence Based Coaching and Mentoring*, *13*(1), 70–86.

Levinson, D. J., Darrow, C. N., Klein, E. B., Levinson, M. A., and McKee, B. (1978). *Seasons of a man's life*. New York: Knopf.

Megginson, D., Clutterbuck, D., Garvey, B., Stokes, P., and Garrett-Harris, R. (2006). *Mentoring in action: A practical guide for managers*. London: Kogan Page.

Missirian, A. K. (1982). *The corporate connection: Why executive women need mentors to reach the top*. Englewood Cliffs, NJ: Prentice Hall.

Page, S., and Wosket, V. (2013). *Supervising the counsellor: A cyclical model*. London: Routledge.

Parsloe, E., and Wray, M. (2000). *Coaching and mentoring: Practical conversations to improve learning*. London: Kogan Page.

Phillips, L. L. (1977). *Mentors and protégés: A study of the career development of women managers and executives in business and industry*. Los Angeles, CA: University of California.

Pollock, R. (1995). A test of conceptual models depicting the developmental course of informal mentor-protégé relationships in the workplace. *Journal of Vocational Behavior*, *46*(2), 144–162.

Ragins, B. R. (2011). Relational mentoring: A positive approach to mentoring at work. *The Handbook of Positive Organizational Scholarship*, Oxford University Press, 519.

Ragins, B. R., Townsend, B., and Mattis, M. (1998). Gender gap in the executive suite: CEOs and female executives report on breaking the glass ceiling. *The Academy of Management Executive*, *12*(1), 28–42.

Rosenthal, R., and Jacobson, L. (1968). *Pygmalion in the classroom*. New York: Holt, Rinehart and Winston.

Rosenthal, R., and Jacobson, L. (1992). *Pygmalion in the classroom*. New York: Irvington.

Sanyal, C., and Rigby, C. (2013a). Does e-mentoring work? The effectiveness and challenges of an international professional mentoring scheme. *European and Mentoring Coaching Council 3rd Annual Research Conference*. Dublin, Ireland.

Sanyal, C., and Rigby, C. (2013b). Does e-mentoring enhance the employability attributes of mentees? An action research within an international professional mentoring scheme. *Association of Business School Annual Learning and Teaching, Innovation and Student Experience*. London, United Kingdom, Nottingham Trent University.

Sanyal, C., and Rigby, C. (2013c). Does e-mentoring enhance the employability attributes of mentees? An action research within an International Professional Mentoring Scheme. *Higher Education Academy Annual Conference, Powerful Partnership: Defining Learning Experience*. York, United Kingdom Warwick University.

Shpigelman, C., Weiss, P. L., and Reiter, S. (2009). E-mentoring for all. *Computers in Human Behavior*, *25*(4), 919–928.

Underhill, C. M. (2006). The effectiveness of mentoring programs in corporate settings: A meta-analytical review of the literature. *Journal of Vocational Behavior*, *68*(2), 292–307.

Westland, P. R. (2015). *Insights into the determinants of successful dyadic mentoring relationships in higher education*. Doctoral dissertation, Sheffield Hallam University, Sheffield, UK.

Zey, M. G. (2011). *The mentor connection*. Homewood, IL: Dow Jones-Irwin.

Working with Goals in Mentoring

David A. Clutterbuck and David Megginson

Goals do not exist in abstract; they are part of a process of change. A linear view of change assumes that it is important to identify what we want (goal setting), to make plans about how we will get there (goal pursuit) and to take steps to implement the goal (goal management) – with goal management including ways of maintaining motivation and momentum. The outcome of the process should also be a measurable change. There is relatively high expectation of predictability at each stage. By contrast, a systemic approach takes the perspective that goals are messy (unfixed or abstract) and evolutionary (adaptive to internal and external change). In this chapter, we explore the complexity of goal setting, pursuit and management in the context of mentoring, through the lens of both the practical experience of mentors and the evidence base of a portfolio of theoretical constructs and research.

WHAT DO WE MEAN BY A 'GOAL'?

The term goal is often used interchangeably with objective, mission, and other words. What these all have in common is an orientation to the future and to achieving a particular outcome, which may be very specific (to lose two kilos in weight, gain a distinction in an exam) or relatively unspecific (to survive, to be a good mother to my kids). Also implied in all these terms is that the desired future status or change is recognisable. Change of course may be from a current situation to a different, more desirable situation; or it may be to maintain as far as possible an existing situation in the face of change in the external environment.

Another term often used alongside goal is 'success'. In ad hoc experiments over 20 years, one of us has asked groups of mentoring workshop participants to define success as concisely as possible. In most cases, people quickly divide into two camps. One camp uses words such as 'achieving your goals'; the other uses words relating to happiness, contentment and self-fulfilment. In subsequent discussion, it emerges that both of these perspectives are valid, to a point, but that in combination (for example, 'achieving what you value') they are much more meaningful and relevant. (There may, however, be a generational aspect emerging. Amongst more than 100 graduating student mentees at Aarhus University, repeating the same experiment, over 90% opted for success in terms of being, rather than achieving, while their mentors from previous generations followed the expected 50/50 split.)

General definitions of goals include:

- 'The object of a person's ambition or effort; a destination; an aim' (Oxford English Dictionary)
- 'A boundary or limit' (Elliot and Fryer, 2008); 'obstacle or hindrance' i.e. a difficulty to be overcome through striving (Old English derivation)

These two very different perspectives have significant implications for coaching. Both imply finite outcomes, but the former less than the latter.

Virtually all of the research and literature on goals within the world of coaching and mentoring comes from a coaching perspective. In this chapter, therefore, we draw substantially on the coaching literature, not least because developmental coaching and developmental mentoring are frequently confused or conflated (Garvey, 2011). Within the coaching literature, there is much discussion of what goals are like (with a heavy emphasis on the need for them to be SMART – specific, measurable, achievable, realistic, time-bound (Doran, 1981), but not much on what goals are. It is assumed that a goal in sports is essentially the same as one in business, but there has been little or no investigation as to whether this is indeed the case. There is also little distinction between or investigation into the relationship between goals as ends or desired outcomes and goals as waypoints. The general literature on goals in coaching and mentoring can be described as simplistic.

However, more recently scholars have described it in much more complex, nuanced terms.

Grant (2006) points out that goals can be very different in nature and intent. They may be:

- Distal or proximal (long term and therefore often 'fuzzy', or short term and specific)
- Outcome focused (concrete) or abstract
- Avoidance or approach based – i.e. to prevent an undesirable outcome or enhance the possibility of achieving a desired one
- Performance or learning oriented. Performance goals typically involve some level of competition and or targets, with the motivation being primarily externally driven. Learning or mastery goals tend to be associated more with internal or intrinsic motivation (Sarrazin et al., 2002)
- Complementary or competing – studies in a wide variety of fields show that, when goals are congruent, achievement potential is enhanced; however, goal conflict leads to reduced performance (e.g. Asare et al., 2009; Pressau et al., 2011)
- Conscious or unconscious – we may not be aware of some of our strongest goals
- Self-concordant or self-discordant – the extent to which the goal aligns with our intrinsic interests, values and motivations
- Ordinate or subordinate – is a goal wide and closely associated with deeply held values, or a link in the chain towards achieving such a goal?

We can also observe (David et al., 2013, p. 30) that goal *progress* may be mitigated by a variety of factors, including:

- Motivation (level of importance attached to the outcome)
- Contextual awareness (for example, the quality and level of realism the person has with regards to systemic factors that influence goal achievability)
- Whether the goal is theirs alone or shared with others
- How clear they are about the goal and what achieving it would mean for them or for others
- Measurability – how they will know the goal has been achieved
- Stability – is it a fixed or moving target?
- Link to personal values
- Previous experience of goal pursuit and how this affects their self-belief with regard to achievability and/or effort v reward

WHAT DO THE GOAL THEORISTS HAVE TO SAY?

It's important to start this section with the observation that, with few exceptions, researchers working in the field of goal management have not derived their results from an exploration of the coaching context. Two main bodies of study underpin our understanding of goals generally: goal theory, built especially on the work of Edwin Locke and Gary Latham; and self-determination theory, derived from the work of Ed Deci and Richard Ryan. Other relevant literature comes from the field of career management.

While there is a history of research into goal setting and goal management going back over 100 years, the pivotal point was probably Ryan's studies of conscious goals, published in 1970 (Ryan, 1970). Locke and Latham (1990) built on Ryan's work and also on work by motivational theorists (Maslow, 1954; Fishbein and Ajzen, 1975; Bandura, 1986), firstly, by establishing a positive relationship between goal difficulty (or complexity) and performance.

They subsequently defined goal content in terms of two key factors: specificity (precision, clarity and measurability) and difficulty (the amount of effort needed to achieve it). They maintained that specific goals focus attention and encourage people to plan how they will achieve the desired outcome, and that an appropriate level of challenge provides the motivation to pursue the goal. After two decades of research generally reinforcing their conclusions, but introducing a number of caveats, they summarised their observations as follows: 'So long as a person is committed to the goal, has the requisite ability to attain it, and does not have conflicting goals, there is a positive, linear relationship between goal difficulty and task performance' (Locke and Latham, 2006, p265).

In recent years, however, the theory has come under increasing criticism as overly simplistic. Lisa Ordonez and her colleagues identified a number of problems, which we summarise here. Firstly, they detailed cases of 'the hazards of indiscriminate goal setting', describing how 'the use of goal setting can degrade employee performance by narrowing focus to neglect important but non-specified goals, motivating risky and unethical behaviors, inhibiting learning, corroding organizational culture, and reducing intrinsic motivation ... in many situations, the damaging effects of goal setting outweigh its benefits' (Ordonez et al., 2009, p6).

Taking each of these concerns in turn:

- Focusing on specific, narrow goals

This induces 'inattentional blindness' – a tendency to miss important information or opportunities because the conscious mind does not acknowledge them. In the context of career self-management, Ibarra (2005) identifies that too narrow a focus on career next steps may reduce the chances of career advancement.

- Increased risk taking

Ordonez et al. state that 'goal setting distorts risk preferences' (p9). They point to studies of negotiation, which found that 'negotiators with goals are more likely to reach an inefficient impasse (i.e. failure to reach a reasonable agreement) than are negotiators who lack goals' (Galinsky et al., 2002). Prospect theory says that decision makers become more risk seeking in the domain of losses. In all three experiments, Larrick et al. (2009) compared a 'do your best' condition with a 'specific, challenging goal' condition. The goal condition consistently increased risky behaviour in both negotiation and decision-making tasks. Other literature from our own desk studies supports this conclusion – most dramatically, Kayes' account of what he calls 'goal blindness' leading to fatal results when climbers approach their goal in reaching the summit of Everest (Kayes, 2006).

- Unethical behaviour

This arises when people become overly goal focused, especially if they are going to narrowly miss a goal – in which case, they tend to cheat (Schweitzer et al., 2004). Ordonez and her colleagues conclude that 'aggressive goal setting within an organisation increases the likelihood of creating an organizational climate ripe for unethical behaviour' (p10).

- Goals inhibit learning

'An individual who is narrowly focused on a performance goal will be less likely to try alternative methods that could help her learn how to perform a task' (p11).

- Focus on individual goals

According to Mitchell and Silver (1990), a focus on individual goals can undermine collective performance.

- High emphasis on goal setting and goal achievement

This may increase extrinsic motivation at the expense of intrinsic motivation (Rawsthorne et al., 1999). How goals affect people's performance on tasks and their engagement with tasks is influenced by whether they are achievement oriented or mastery (learning) oriented (Elliot and Harackiewicz, 1994). Say Ordonez and her colleagues: 'Managers may think that others need to be motivated by specific, challenging goals more often than they actually do' (p11).

- Stretch goals

These are promoted strongly by some companies, such as General Electric, but they come in for a lot of criticism. Stretch goals are goals that seem impossible, but which galvanise people into radical new thinking. The classic example is President Kennedy's promise to put a man on the Moon within 10 years. The idea is highly seductive and a handful of well-publicised corporate examples suggest that talented employees should seek out stretch goals for themselves and join projects based on stretch goals. The reality, however, is that stretch goals – as typically created and managed – often don't deliver and are more likely to result in disappointment and derailing (Sitkin et al., 2011). It seems that the conditions in which organisations are most likely to make stretch goals work are when people are buoyed up by previous success and when they have sufficient slack in terms of resources to invest in pursuing unconventional ideas. Without these conditions, the likely outcome is failure and reduced motivation to innovate. Brim and Liebnau (2011), in a comment based on analysis of data from Gallup employee surveys, claim that stretch goals that do not align closely with self-identity can do more harm than good and that a 'slight shift' approach to developmental goals is more productive and increases employee engagement.

- Demotivation

Ordonez and her colleagues also point out that, while stretch goals can increase short-term performance, they also lead people into increased self-doubt about their future performance (Mussweiler and Strack, 2000).

Other research in the same genre shows that:

- People find it difficult to cope with multiple goals. They either pursue a few narrow goals at the expense of others (Shah et al., 2002), or sacrifice quality for quantity (Gilliland and Landis, 1992).
- Outcome goals can reduce performance (Winters and Latham, 1996).
- Learning goals are often more effective than performance goals – for example, when the task is too complex for the skills level of the performer (Midgley et al., 2001). Learning goals are associated with greater intrinsic motivation (Sarrazin et al., 2002), task engagement (Deci and Ryan, 2002) and collaboration within teams (Kristof-Brown and Stevens, 2001).
- Studies of corporate behaviour find no evidence that companies that engage in extensive strategic planning and SMART goal setting are any more successful than those that do not (Abrahamson and Freedman, 2013).

- Anne McKee's (1991) study of SMART goals shows that only 25% of people are motivated by them, 25% prefer to work to an image of desired vision, 25% are focused on the steps towards the goal, rather than the goal itself – and 25% don't plan at all. In all but the first group, SMART goals induced stress and reduced motivation, creativity and resilience.

Self-determination theory takes a broader perspective on goals. It assumes that people engage with their environment in ways that promote mastery, connectedness and empowerment (also called competence, relatedness and autonomy – Deci and Ryan, 1985). Motivation to pursue a goal occurs along a spectrum of controlled (extrinsic) or autonomous (intrinsic). Controlled motivation occurs when someone else is pulling the strings, so behaviour is motivated either by a reward they hold out, or by the threat of punishment. Introjected goals are partially internalised motivations, based, for example, on feelings of shame, guilt or anxiety. It's about what you 'ought' to do and how we apply internal sanctions to moderate our own behaviour in line with external expectations.

Identified autonomous motivation occurs when external values become internally normalised. They may have been acquired from other people, but you accept them as congruent with your own goals and needs. With integrated autonomous motivation, the values, behaviours or goals become integral to your own identity – with who you are, what gives your life meaning and how you achieve self-respect.

People also tend to adopt aspirations, which are either extrinsic or intrinsic (Kasser and Ryan, 1993). Extrinsic motivations include becoming rich, famous (or infamous) or trendy; intrinsic motivations include personal growth and contributing to the community. The former tend to have lower levels of overall well-being, feel less autonomous and less connected. People focused on extrinsic aspirations and goals also tend to be less successful on both learning and performance measures (Vansteenkiste et al., 2004).

Closely allied to the Deci and Ryan concept of competence or mastery is the work of Carol Dweck (2006), who found that people's mindsets towards goals determined behaviour. People who focus upon winning and upon achieving clear outcomes are described as having a fixed (achievement) mindset. They tend to assume that intelligence is something very basic and unchanging about a person and that you can learn new things, but not change how smart you are. People who focus on effort, who enjoy learning for its own sake and measure success on the effort they invest, are described as having a growth (mastery) mindset. The latter are more successful in recovering from failure and setbacks and learning from experience. People with fixed mindsets are more likely to cheat to achieve a goal and/or to hype up their achievements.

The third corner of the Deci and Ryan trilogy is relatedness or connectedness. This concerns the need people feel for close personal relationships with others. In the workplace, studies of employee engagement support the view that performance and intention to quit are related to quality of relationships with key colleagues (Saks, 2006). Goal-related behaviour may therefore be influenced by the quality of the relationship between coach and coachee, and between coachee and key stakeholders, such as their boss. Highly effective working relationships are associated with a high degree of mutual support for each other's autonomy (Deci et al., 2006).

An element missing from much of the goal-focused literature, both practitioner and academic, is the systems dimension. The centre of attention is the client and their ability to find their own solutions. Understanding of context is seen as significant only so far as it helps to resolve the immediate problem. Yet there is a growing literature that suggests long-term change can only be realised by addressing the systems – both internal and external – that influence assumptions and behaviours. Pryor and Bright (2011) point out that, while both linear and systemic processes involve feedback, in linear systems the focus is on the goal itself, and in complex adaptive systems the focus is on responding to feedback and amending goals. Success may be defined in terms of the wider system rather than a specific achievement. (For example, achievement of this year's profit target may be a linear goal, but survivability of the business requires a more systemic perspective.) They propose that the nature of goals and goal setting needs to be adjusted to take into account the speed of change of the environment. Simple problems in a slowly changing environment may best be tackled through SMART performance goals. Simple problems in a rapidly changing environment require goals that emphasise learning and are revisable in response to systemic change. Complex problems in a slowly changing environment require a focus on learning goals rather than performance goals. And complex goals in a rapidly changing environment are best served with fuzzy goals, supported by multiple, adjustable micro-goals.

Another general criticism of goal research is that there is a high reliance on laboratory studies, which are not replicable in the messy, more complex environment of the outside world (Tubbs, 1986).

In summary, the literature on goals and goal-related behaviour provides a complex picture of why and how people set and pursue goals, and the probability of achieving those goals. By contrast, as we now explore, the coaching literature has tended to adopt a much more simplistic approach and has evolved largely independently of motivational theory.

WHAT DOES THE COACHING LITERATURE SAY?

The concept of goals and goal pursuit is embedded in many – if not the vast majority of – definitions of coaching. For example:

> Typically coaching is a goal-focused activity; clients come to coaching because there is a problem they need or want to solve or a goal they want to attain, and they are looking for help in constructing and enacting solutions to that problem. (Passmore et al., 2013, p16)

> To help the client achieve a mutually identified set of goals to improve his or her professional performance and personal satisfaction and, consequently, to improve the effectiveness of the client's organization within a formally defined coaching agreement. (Kilburg, 2000, p142)

However, not all definitions of coaching place goals so centrally. Indeed, Kilburg says goals should only be set halfway through the coaching process, and he has little to say for good or ill about goals compared with his analysis of other parts of the coaching process.

To many people, the GROW model (Goal, Reality, Options, Will) is synonymous with coaching, although it is actually only a model of a coaching conversation. It was promoted in the 1980s by John Whitmore (1996), who now points out that 'GROW is simply a questioning tool'. Nonetheless, many schools of coaching teach that the first step in a coaching conversation is to define the goal as precisely as possible. A later model (Downey, 2014) offers TGROW, in which the T stands for Topic – i.e. establish first generally what the coachee wishes to talk about. In practice, the topic phase and the goal-setting phase tend to be merged within a coaching conversation. Starr describes the process as creating 'a sense of direction and purpose for the conversation, so that as the coach you know where you need to be heading' (Starr, 2008, p127).

A brief Google search on GROW quickly reveals claims of how simple the GROW model is to apply. For example:

> The GROW Model has become very well known in the business area and has also been adopted by many life coaches. It provides an effective, structured methodology, which both helps set goals effectively and is a problem solving process. It is easily understood, straightforward to apply and very thorough. Its simplicity means that it can be used by anyone without special training (http://www.thegrowmodel.com).

Even where research data question the efficacy of the GROW model, practitioners can be reluctant to let go of this safety net. For example, Scoular and Linley (2006) observed a series of 120 coaching sessions, between previously unintroduced coaches and coachees, with half of the coaches being instructed to use the GROW model and half told not to. Self-report from both coach and coachee was used as a measure of effectiveness. The data revealed no difference in quality of outcome between the two groups. It did, however, find that coach and coachee differed on temperament, as defined by MBTI self-assessment, and outcome scores were significantly higher – an outcome they suggest may relate to the effects of difference in perspective between coach and coachee. Rather than question the utility of the GROW model, however, the authors posited:

> Two factors may have led to these surprising results. First, some coaches commented in their post-coaching evaluation questionnaires that they felt unethical not using this key element, so sought through listening to impute the goal the coachee was working towards, and coach against that. Secondly, they felt they may simply have been trying even harder: listening more acutely, and in general straining every muscle to help the coachee nevertheless benefit from the session... Goal-setting remains important whether explicit or imputed and should still be regarded as best practice in business coaching. (p10–11)

However, a different view is expressed by Pemberton (2006), who says:

> It is usual in coaching books to talk about the importance of goal setting. Define the goal at the start and the rest will follow. Decide that you want to be promoted in a year and a clear path of action will emerge ...This presupposes that the person is clear about their goal at the start, which they often aren't ... Meaningful goals, i.e. the ones the individual really connects with so that they are committed to action, emerge from skilled conversations, and often late in those conversations. What the coachee does know, even if they are unarticulated, are their values. Their values shape what they believe is possible for themselves, what they are willing to do and how they approach it. (Pemberton, 2006, p36)

A similar polarisation of views can be seen amongst academic literature. Grant (2006) firmly places goal setting and action planning as central to the coaching process. Ives and Cox (2012) examine the concepts and practice of goal-focused coaching (GFC). They point out that, although much reference is made to goal focus in coaching, relatively little research has been carried out. They depict goal-focused coaching as a genre, arguing that:

> GFC we identify as being essentially about raising performance and supporting action, rather than addressing feelings and generating deep reflection. We suggest that GFC primarily aims for level of operational change, rather than psychological restructuring (Hall and Duval, 2004) and looks primarily to make small, incremental improvements (Jackson and McKergow, 2008). According to this conception, its foremost intention is to promote immediate enhancement of productivity, rather than transformation of the coachee. (Ives and Cox, 2012, p2)

This places goal-focused coaching at one end of the spectrum of coaching outlined by Hawkins and Smith (2006, p24) of skills, performance, development and transformation. Hawkins and Smith argue that a coach's ability to work at various points on the spectrum is linked to their relative personal maturity.

Ives and Cox further describe GFC as 'a self-regulation tool', 'about discrepancy management, crafting the careful balance that is required to achieve optimum goal-oriented motivation' and having a 'relative disinterest in directly addressing underlying motives or resolving issues'.

Other coaching literature positions goal setting and goal pursuit as less urgent within the coaching relationship or conversation. An immediate observation is that most models of coaching don't place goal setting at the beginning of the process.

In a survey of 200 US coaches by Kaufmann and Coutu (2009), it emerged that all but eight said that goals often changed during the course of a coaching assignment.

Goals shifted to be more congruent with clients' new insights about what they really needed and wanted. Among comments from respondents:

- 'Over time the focus often becomes more strategic and discretionary rather than so immediate and results driven'.
- 'At first the client wants to focus on "doing something". As coaching continues, the focus moves to the "quality of life" and the "passion of life" and "living their most authentic life"'.
- 'As trust and new skills take root, coaching often moves to address underlying beliefs and attitudes for deeper, more lasting change'.
- 'As the coachee becomes more self-aware and understands more clearly how his/her behaviours impact others, the focus of the work changes, and we work on more in-depth issues'.

David et al. (2013) found that goal orientation among coaches differed geographically. In a survey of 184 coaches in Europe and North America, they observed differences in how coaches regarded goals and goal setting in the context of region, education and experience. A questionnaire designed to measure goal orientation, which sampled goal-related behaviour from first meeting to final evaluation, contained the following nine items:

- I set goals with my coachees at the start of a coaching assignment
- At the start of a coaching assignment we set goals for the whole assignment
- In subsequent coaching sessions we refer back to the goals set at the start
- We determine when to finish a coaching assignment by checking whether goals have been achieved
- The goals help us to decide whether the coaching is appropriately focused
- Goals remain the same throughout the coaching assignment
- We set goals for each coaching session
- The goals are central to deciding the effectiveness of the coaching
- We have purposeful conversations without setting goals (reverse scored)

Amongst the significant conclusions of this analysis was that, while US coaches showed no obvious correlation between experience and goal orientation, European coaches tended to become less goal oriented as they grew in experience. The authors suggest that this difference may be related to the traditions of coaching in the two continents, with Europe drawing more deeply on psychological orientations. Another possibility is that coaches in the US are more often working at the skills and performance end of Hawkins' spectrum and those in Europe at the developmental and transformational end of the spectrum. These and other theories have yet to be tested!

In workshops and interviews with coaches and their clients, we also attempted to gather experiences relating to goals and goal management. Here are some of the illustrative quotes that emerged from coaches:

- Goals over-privilege the sponsor's agenda at the price of the coachee's agenda
- Goal setting is an unconsidered routine
- Goals encourage 'do more' in a society where 'do less' may be more valuable
- Goals serve the coach's need for clarity and control
- Clients may not be ready to set goals (or may have moved beyond them)
- Goals can be used as an excuse to avoid the painfully beneficial
- Goals save coach from having to be fully present

And from clients:

- Over-goaled (NHS Chief Executive)

'I already have 13 organisations setting me goals, I don't need a 14th'.

- Emergent (Head of major institution)

'I don't know what I want to address yet – by the time I do, the goal will be a thing of the past'.

- SMART is too late (Manufacturing company MD)

'If I can set SMART goals don't you think I would have sorted it? It's the messy, wicked issues I want to look at'.

- Stakeholder conflicts (Newly promoted CEO)

'I know what my predecessor wants for me to achieve through the coaching, but I disagree – that is his way: I have mine'.

Of course, there were also many examples of positive experiences from goal emphasis within coaching. What our interviews and focus groups gave us was a clear understanding that the assumption that goals should *always* be central to the coaching conversation was inaccurate and sometimes unhelpful or even dangerous. This led us to explore why people came to coaching. Many of the reasons shared with us by coaches and clients did not fit the mode of 'needing an immediate solution'. Instead, clients:

- Came with a situation, which they only partly understood, or had only partly thought through. What they required from the coach was help in clarifying their internal and external context, so that they could work out what their goal was. Once they knew what they wanted, they were often smart enough and motivated enough to pursue the goal on their own. In other words, the role of the coach was to help them establish the goal, rather than work with a goal they brought to the table.
- Wanted an opportunity to be challenged on their thinking. They already had a goal and a plan for achieving it, but they wanted the reassurance of testing it against their values and other, external criteria; or to identify any blind spots in their thinking.
- Sought values clarification rather than goal achievement.

In our book *Beyond Goals* (David et al., 2013), we invited some of the leading authorities on goals and motivation theory to contribute chapters on goals in coaching from the perspective of their research. Most of these contributors were also coaches in their own right. Amongst significant themes that emerged from these chapters were the following:

- Robert Kegan, writing with David and Congleton (Kegan et al., 2013), relates client goals to their level of adult maturity. At an early stage of development, a coachee perceives the world through what Kegan calls 'the socialised mind', in which behaviours and values are driven by the need for the esteem of other people. Many people transcend this limiting world view to the point where they regard the world from a 'self-authoring' standpoint, in which values are internally generated and satisfaction comes from achievements that accord with those internalised values, as judged by the coachee, rather than by others. This perspective also has its limitations, which a relatively small proportion of people overcome by evolving into a third mindframe, which takes a more systemic view of the interaction between self and others. The goals people hold and how they work towards those goals are likely to be substantially different between people at different stages of adult development. Otto Laske, a disciple of Kegan, has explored the relationship between coach and client in similar terms. He concludes that:

> Most coaches do not know who their client is developmentally. Most coaches also don't know their own adult-developmental profile and thus have only a fuzzy notion of what coachees they can do more harm than good for. As a result, coaches are less effective than they could be, especially in coaching executives at high levels of organizational responsibility. (Laske, in press)

- Richard Boyatzis' intentional change theory is based on the proposition that goal setting works best when supported by mindful reflection on what matters most to the individual. When goals are linked to the Ideal Self, the change process is better grounded in 'intrinsic motivation, personal passion, resonant meaning and belief in possibility – this enables people to be more resilient and robust during work on development and change' (Boyatzis and Howard, 2013, p215; Boyatzis, 2008). Goal setting is not helpful, they conclude, when goals do not align with the individual's own authentic values and vision, result from extrinsic requirements that activate the 'ought self', or when they are inconsistent with the individual's learning style or planning style.

WHAT DOES THE MENTORING LITERATURE SAY?

Although there is much overlap between coaching and mentoring, the nature of the goals set may be dissimilar. Dubrin (2005) suggests that goals set in coaching are more likely to be linked to the organisation's mission, while goals set in mentoring may be more focused on personal or career. Other authors propose a strong link between organisational goals and mentee goals (Wunsch, 1994). Clutterbuck (2007) finds that programme goals influence the quality and outcome of mentoring relationships. It is logical that a programme created for a specific business purpose (such as retention of high flyers, or supporting corporate diversity objectives) will influence both who seeks to take part and the goals they set.

In tune with the mainstream practitioner literature in coaching, Zachary and Fischler (2011) advocate that the first step in mentoring is to define a goal and, second, to track progress towards it. This perspective is echoed in a variety of other sources. For example, Green and Puetzer (2002) describe a highly organised, structured approach to mentoring in the training of new nurses. (It could be argued that they are actually documenting a form of instruction, rather than mentoring.) Says Noe (1988): 'The protégé must interact with the mentor to discuss problems [and] set personal and work-related goals'. Black et al. (2004) distinguish between short-term and long-term goals, but see both as an issue for the initiation or early stages of the relationship.

As with the coaching literature and the general literature on goals, there is a contrasting perspective. Clutterbuck (2007) compared goal clarity and commitment to a specific goal at the start of a developmental relationship with four categories of outcome – career, learning, enabling and emotional – and with perceived quality of relationship, from both mentor and mentee perspectives in a sample of 80 matched pairs. No statistically significant correlation was found between having initial clear goals or commitment to initial goals and either outcomes or relationship quality. There was, however, a moderate correlation with having a broad sense of purpose for the relationship.

McCarthy (2014, p45) suggests that mentors should 'ask themselves whether a goal is the right thing for the client at this point in time. A goal may emerge from an exploration of where the client is and wants to be. However, the client may not yet be ready to commit to change'.

Clutterbuck and Megginson (2009) and Garvey and Stokes (2009) warn of the danger of collusion, where a client goes through the mechanics of goal setting to keep the coach happy, using it to avoid more meaningful or challenging discussions, which could hold opportunities for genuine, although perhaps temporarily uncomfortable, transformational learning. Warning signs are goals being chosen too quickly or being too easily attainable.

Garvey and Alred (2001, p523) add further that the organisational environment can influence the kind of goals chosen, or whether the relationship is goal focused:

> Mentoring is an activity that addresses a combination of short, medium and long-term goals, and concerns primarily "ends" as well as "means". Hence, mentoring is severely challenged in an unstable environment. It may become focused exclusively on short-term goals, disappear or be displaced by friendships between people sharing a common difficult fate.

PRACTICAL APPROACHES FOR MENTORS

So how are we to make sense of this somewhat contradictory evidence base in both coaching and mentoring? Three areas we have found helpful for discussion are:

- How can mentors approach contracting with clients and the conduct of the mentoring conversation without falling into simplistic assumptions about the mentee's goals and how they should be managed?
- How can mentors build their capacity to work with goal emergence and goal evolution?

- Can mentoring be effective in a goal-free context and, if so, what can mentors do to become comfortable and effective in this context?

Starting the mentoring relationship

In the initial contracting stage, it is usual for mentors to set expectations relating to the non-directiveness of their role, the logistics of relationship management and so on. Discussion about expectations with regard to goals is equally important and may include:

- A brief explanation of the nature of goals, how mentoring may address them, and how they may evolve and change over time
- Clarification about where existing goals come from
- Goal ownership (are they internally or externally generated?)
- Goal evaluation (how will we know a goal has been achieved and how will we know it was worthwhile pursuing?)

Given that many mentors will be familiar with SMART goals, a pragmatic approach may be to compare and contrast the standard interpretation with that suggested by Winter (2010): Situational, Multi-faceted, Adaptable, Risk-taking, Transformational.

A consequence of this discussion is that both mentor and mentee can agree that goals can and should be challenged and reviewed.

Exploring the origins of presented goals may be an unfamiliar concept for the mentee, especially if they are at the socialised mind stage of Kegan's model of adult development. Useful questions a mentor can employ include:

- Why this goal, now?
- From what set of values does this goal originate? (Your own, deeply held beliefs about what is important? A requirement of the organisation, or the coachee's boss? A general assumption about what is important?) Path-goal theory predicts that bosses strongly influence direct reports' goals and how they approach them (House, 1971)
- What does achieving this goal represent to you in terms of your sense of identity and self-worth?
- Is the purpose of this coaching relationship more about helping you work out what your goals are, or about helping you achieve the goals that you already have?

It can also be helpful to position the presented goal within a goal hierarchy, in which the highest level is personal purpose. The questions 'In service of what?' or 'What larger, longer-term outcome will achieving this goal enable?' can help the mentee establish how the presented goal relates to wider desired outcomes (or that it doesn't; in which case, what is making them pursue it?). Similarly, questioning whether the goal is stimulated by a need for avoidance or an attraction to a positive outcome can stimulate reflection on the part of the mentee.

Where goals are set overtly or under the influence of a third party or sponsor, it may also be necessary to have a similar, expectations-setting conversation. A boss or sponsor, in particular, may have his or her own views about what mentoring should achieve and therefore about the goals that should be set. These views will be rooted in their perceptions of the mentee and the mentee's performance and may reflect a different set of values and priorities to those of the mentee. A simplistic endorsement of the boss' goal expectations may therefore either distort the natural development of the mentoring conversation and/or result in disappointment for one or both parties. Equally, it is important for the mentor to avoid entangling their own goals with those of the mentee. As Hawkins and Smith (2006, p41) express it, the 'tendency for an untrained mentor is to see the transition of the mentee solely through the lens of their own journey through a similar transition'.

Goal evaluation may not be as simple as it appears, either. The simplest measures may not reflect the most important outcomes of coaching and these may not occur until some time after the assignment has formally ended.

Clutterbuck (2007) identifies four categories of measurable outcome, which can form the basis of the mentoring relationship: career progress, learning/personal development, enabling (e.g. having a more effective personal development plan, or more effective networks for career and personal development) and emotional (e.g. greater self-belief or self-confidence). In a 12-month formal mentoring relationship, career goals, in particular, may not have been achieved.

There is also the largely unexplored issue of mentor goals. If mentoring is a form of developmental alliance (Clutterbuck, 1998) in which both parties have learning goals, it makes sense for both parties' goals to be articulated. In this way, the mentee can exhibit supportive behaviours towards the mentor, contributing to the quality of the relationship (Aryee et al., 1996).

Building capability to work with goal emergence and evolution

When does a goal become a goal? Mentees often bring to mentoring a complex cauldron of unstructured and unarticulated concerns, which may or may not be interdependent. An analogy we have found useful is 'itch – question – goal'.

Stimulus	Response	Process
Goal	Score	Keep going until you have a result
Question	Better question	You can stop at any point; pick up again at any time
Itch	Scratch	Decide whether to acknowledge or ignore it

In this analogy, an itch is an unarticulated sense of discomfort. The sensation of itching arises in the cingulum, an area of the brain associated with emotions, such as disgust. Pain, by contrast, is recorded in the sensorimotor cortex (Geiler and Walter, 2008). Mentors have many tools and techniques available to them to elicit this kind of information – not least, just listening to the mentee sharing their narrative. However, focusing down too soon on a specific goal is likely to prevent this relatively unstructured exploration.

If we choose to acknowledge an 'itch', we are primed to respond either instinctively or with curiosity – 'what is making me feel dissatisfied, uncomfortable, unfulfilled or uneasy?'. Having postulated a cause, we can explore what, if anything, we want to do about it. If we decide that some form of action is needed, then a conscious goal is likely to emerge of its own volition. In our use of this analogy, we have found that it often brings the mentee back around to a version of their presented goal. However, they now understand that goal more clearly and are better able to relate it to and integrate it with other goals they hold.

Once a goal or a purpose has been clearly articulated and owned, the mentor's role can place more emphasis on goal pursuit – how the client will make progress towards desired outcomes. The challenge now becomes how to create the right balance for the particular mentee and their circumstances between focus on the goal and focus on the systems that influence (and may possibly mutate) it. Critical questions include:

- What influences are likely to make this goal more or less achievable? (These may include, for example, support from their boss and colleagues, or pressure on time.)
- How will you obtain appropriate feedback to sustain momentum towards your goal? (Contracting for frequent feedback from others within the influence system may be important. Anecdotal evidence from case study suggests that bosses may not notice behavioural change in direct reports unless they contract to be mindful of it.)
- When and how shall we re-assess the goal in relation to changes in your understanding of yourself, your purpose and your understanding of what is happening around you?

Mentees may place themselves under pressure (internally or externally generated) to firm up goals before they have sufficient contextual understanding. The challenge for the mentor is that the mentee's anxiety around not having a solution can make it difficult for them to reflect and to think creatively, and this can become a vicious circle. Useful areas to explore here include:

- How clear are you about what you still have to find out, in order to be clear about what you want and why?
- What other conversations do you still need to have with other people and with yourself about this?
- What strategies do you now have to manage your anxieties about this issue?
- What would happen, if you let go of the need for a specific goal right now?
- How might you use your current uncertainty to develop new and more flexible options for the future?

An awareness of the mentee's goal orientation (achievement or mastery) can also be helpful here. Lunsford (2011) found that people with a learning goal orientation are more likely to have a mentor. Godshalk and Sosik (2003) observed that protégés with high levels of learning goal orientation received more psychosocial support than others, as well as greater career development and career satisfaction. Interestingly, the goal orientation of the mentor was also a factor. Other studies suggest that mentors can help mentees acquire more of a learning goal orientation or growth mindset (Seijts et al., 2004).

Mentoring in a goal-free context

One of the differences between dialogue and discussion is that dialogue creates new meaning, while discussion simply shares existing perspectives. Mentoring is primarily an instrument of dialogue. When we talk of goal-free mentoring, we do not mean that it is aimless or lacking direction – dialogue always has purpose. What's at issue is the relative balance between a focus on learning, from which unexpected outcomes are likely to emerge, and a focus on outcomes, in which any learning that occurs is incidental to the conversation. We propose that all effective mentoring that is not directed towards simple skills acquisition or short-term performance improvement will have periods in which a learning focus predominates and others in which an outcomes focus is desirable. A series of mentoring conversations therefore becomes an iteration between ever-deepening awareness of self and environmental context, and mindfully pursuing actions that lead to greater alignment between what the client wishes to achieve and who they want to become. In this intricate dance, the mentee calls the tune and takes the steps – the mentor's role is to adjust the tempo and intensity of the music according to their lead.

It is in the learning-predominant periods that mentoring can be goal-free and has the greatest potential to be liberating. Shapiro (2010) documents how freeing oneself from the constraints of goals – even temporarily – contributes to increased well-being, satisfaction and fulfilment. Among his guidelines is to replace goals and resolutions with themes, 'to do lists' with 'could do lists' and to seek opportunities to turn personal inadequacies and boundaries into unique qualities that you can use to advantage. In essence, by accepting the need for goal-free mentoring at least some of the time, mentoring can be more holistic and hence more beneficial than simply a means of helping someone achieve a short-term goal.

CONCLUSION

The sheer complexity of how goals evolve, transmute and relate to what is happening within both the mentee and their external environment tell us that working with goals requires both skill and insight on the part of the mentor and, arguably, of the mentee. There are many potentially fruitful areas of research into goal management in mentoring. Among them, the circumstances in which SMART or specific goals are helpful and unhelpful, how the mentor's assumptions and influence may shape the mentee's goal formation, and what constitutes an effective process of goal review.

REFERENCES

Abrahamson, E and Freedman, DH (2013) *A Perfect Mess: The Hidden Benefits of Disorder*, Hachette, London.

Aryee, S, Wyatt, T and Stone, R (1996) Early career outcomes of graduate employees: The effect of mentoring and ingratiation, *Journal of Management Studies*, 33(1), 95–118.

Asare, SK, Cianci, AM and Tsakumis, GT (2009) The impact of competing goals, experience, and litigation consciousness on auditors' judgments, *International Journal of Auditing*, 13(3), 223–236.

Bandura, A (1986) *Social Foundations of Thought and Action: A Social-Cognitive View*, Prentice Hall, Englewood Cliffs, NJ.

Black, LL, Suarez, EC and Medina, S (2004) Helping students help themselves: Strategies for successful mentoring relationships, *Counselor Education and Supervision*, 44(1), 44–55.

Boyatzis, RE (2008) Leadership development from a complexity perspective, *Consulting Psychology Journal*, 60(4), 298–313.

Boyatzis, RE and Howard, A (2013) When Goal Setting Helps and Hinders Sustained, Desired Change. In David, S, Clutterbuck, M and Megginson, D (Eds) *Beyond Goals: Effective Strategies for Coaching and Mentoring*, 211–228, Gower, Aldershot.

Brian, Brim JB and Liebnau, D (2011) Does setting major development goals work?, *Gallup Management Journal*, http://www.gallup.com/businessjournal/150485/Setting-Major-Development-Goals-Work.aspx accessed December 2011.

Clutterbuck, D (1998) *Learning Alliances*, CIPD, Wimbledon.

Clutterbuck, D (2007) *A longitudinal study of the effectiveness of developmental mentoring*, Doctoral thesis, King's College London, London.

Clutterbuck, D and Megginson, D (2009) Client Focused Techniques. In Megginson, D and Clutterbuck, D, *Further Techniques for Coaching and Mentoring*, 129–193, Butterworth-Heinemann, Oxford.

Cury, F, Elliot, A, Sarazzin, P, Da Fonsesca, D and Rufo, M (2002) The trichotomous achievement goal model and intrinsic motivation: A sequential mediational analysis. *Journal of Experimental Social Psychology*, 38(5), 473–481.

David, S, Clutterbuck, D and Megginson, D (2013) *Beyond Goals: Effective Strategies for Coaching and Mentoring*, Gower, Aldershot.

Deci, EL and Ryan, RM (1985) *Intrinsic Motivation and Self-Determination in Human Behavior*, Plenum Press, New York.

Deci, EL, La Guardia, JG, Moller, AC, Scheiner, MJ and Ryan, RM (2006) On the benefits of giving as well as receiving autonomy support: Mutuality in close friendships, *Personality and Social Psychology Bulletin*, 32, 313–327.

Doran, GT (1981) There's a S.M.A.R.T. way to write management's goals and objectives, *Management Review*, 70(11), 35–36.

Downey, M (2014) *Effective Modern Coaching*, LID, London.

Dubrin, AJ (2005) *Coaching and Mentoring Skills*, Pearson/Prentice Hall, Upper Saddle River, NJ.

Dweck, C (2006) *Mindset: The New Psychology of Success*, Ballantine Books, New York.

Elliot, AJ and Fryer, JW (2008) The Goal Construct in Psychology. In Shah, JY and Gardner, WL (Eds), *The Handbook of Motivation Science*, 235–250, The Guildford Press, New York.

Elliot, AJ and Harackiewicz, JM (1994) Goal setting, achievement orientation, and intrinsic motivation: A mediational analysis, *Journal of Personality and Social Psychology*, 66(5), 968–980.

Fishbein, M and Ajzen, I (1975) *Belief, Attitude, Intention and Behavior: An Introduction to Theory and Research*, Monograph http://worldcat.org/isbn/0201020890

Galinsky, AD, Mussweiler, T and Medvec, VH (2002) Disconnecting outcomes and evaluations: The role of negotiator focus, *Journal of Personality and Social Psychology*, 83(5), 1131–1140.

Garvey, R (2011) *A very short, fairly interesting and reasonably cheap book about coaching and mentoring*, Sage, London.

Garvey, R and Alred, G (2001) Mentoring and the tolerance of complexity, *Futures* 33(6), 519–530.

Garvey, R and Stokes, P (2009) The goal assumption: A mindset in organisations. In Casserley, T, Garvey, R, Stokes, P and Megginson, D, *Coaching and mentoring: Theory and practice*, Sage, London.

Geiler, U and Walter, B (2008) Scratch this! *Scientific American Mind*, June/July 52–59.

Gilliland, SW and Landis, RS (1992) Quality and quantity goals in a complex decision task: Strategies and outcomes, *Journal of Applied Psychology*, 77(5), 672–681.

Godshalk, VM and Sosik, JJ (2003) Aiming for career success: The role of learning goal orientation in mentoring relationships, *Journal of Vocational Behavior*, 63(3), 417–437.

Grant, AM (2006) An integrative goal-focused approach to executive coaching. In Stober, D and Grant, AM (Eds), *Evidence-based Coaching Handbook*, 153–192, New York, Wiley.

Green, MT and Puetzer, M (2002) The value of mentoring: A strategic approach to retention, *Journal of Nursing Care Quality*, 1–22.

Hall, LM and Duval, M (2004) *Meta-coaching: Coaching Change*, Vol 1, Neurosemantic Publications, Clifton, CO

Hawkins, P and Smith, N (2006) *Coaching, Mentoring and Organizational Consultancy*, Open University Press, Maidenhead.

House, RJ (1971) A path goal theory of leader effectiveness, *Administrative Science Quarterly*, 321–339.

House, RJ and Mitchell, TR (1974) Path-goal theory of leadership, *Journal of Contemporary Business*, 81–97.

Ibarra, H and Lineback, K (2005) What's your story? *Harvard Business Review*, 83(1), 64–71.

Ives, Y and Cox, E (2012) *Goal-Focused Coaching: Theory and Practice*, Routledge, London.

Jackson, PZ and McKergow, M (2008) *The Solutions Focus: Making Coaching and Change Simple*, Nicholas Brealey, London.

Kasser, Tim and Richard M. Ryan (1993) A dark side of the American dream: correlates of financial success as a central life aspiration. *Journal of Personality and Social Psychology*, 65(2), 410–422.

Kaufmann, C and Coutu, D (2009) The realities of executive coaching, *Harvard Business Review*, 87(1), 91–97.

Kayes, DC (2006) *Destructive Goal Pursuit: The Mount Everest Disaster*, Palgrave Macmillan, Basingstoke.

Kegan, R (1982) *The Evolving Self*, Harvard University Press, Cambridge, MA.

Kegan, R, Congleton, C and David, S (2013) The Goals Behind the Goals: Pursuing Adult Development in the Coaching Enterprise. In David, S, Clutterbuck, M and Megginson, D (Eds). *Beyond Goals: Effective Strategies for Coaching and Mentoring*, Gower, Aldershot. 229–243.

Kilburg, RR (2000) *Executive Coaching: Developing Managerial Wisdom in a World of Chaos*, American Psychological Association, Washington, DC.

Kristof-Brown, AL and Stevens, CK (2001) Goal congruence in project teams: Does the fit between members' personal mastery and performance goals matter? *Journal of Applied Psychology*, 86(6), 1083–1095.

Larrick, RP, Heath, C and Wu, G. (2009) Goal-induced risk taking in negotiation and decision making, *Social Cognition*, 27(3), 342–364.

Laske, O (2015) What coaches should want to know about their clients, *International Journal of Mentoring and Coaching* (in press).

Locke, EA and Latham, GP (1990) *A Theory of Goal Setting and Task Performance*, Prentice-Hall, Englewood Cliffs, NJ.

Locke, EA and Latham, GP (2006) New directions in goal-setting theory, *Current Directions in Psychological Science*, 15(5), 265–268.

Lunsford, LG (2011) Development of the Arizona Mentoring Inventory, Mentoring Institute, University of New Mexico, Albuquerque, NM, 26–28.

Maslow, A (1954) *Motivation and Personality*, Harper and Row, New York.

McCarthy, G (2014) *Coaching and Mentoring for Business*, Sage, London.

McKee, A (1991) *Individual differences in planning for the future*, unpublished PhD dissertation, Case Western Reserve University.

Midgley, C, Kaplan, A and Middleton, M (2001) Performance-approach goals: Good for what, for whom, under what circumstances, and at what cost? *Journal of Educational Psychology*, 93(1), 77–86.

Mitchell, TR and Silver, WS (1990) Individual and group goals when workers are interdependent: Effects on task strategies and performance, *Journal of Applied Psychology,* 75(2), 185–193.

Mussweiler, T and Strack, F (2000) The 'relative self': Informational and judgmental consequences of comparative self-evaluation, *Journal of Personality and Social Psychology,* 79(1), 23–38.

Noe, RA (1988) An investigation of the determinants of successful assigned mentoring relationships, *Personnel Psychology,* 41(3), 457–479.

Ordonez, LD, Schweitzer, ME, Galinsky, AE and Bazerman, MH (2009) Goals gone wild: The systematic side effects of overprescribing goal setting, *Academy of Management Perspectives,* 23(1), 6–16.

Passmore, J, Petersen, G and Friere, T (2013) *The Wiley-Blackwell Handbook of the Psychology of Coaching and Mentoring,* Wiley, Chichester.

Pemberton, C (2006) *Coaching to Solutions,* Routledge, Abingdon.

Pressau, J, Francis, JJ, Campbell, NC and Sniehotta, FF (2011) Goal conflict, goal facilitation, and health professionals' provision of physical activity advice in primary care: An exploratory prospective study, *Implementation Science* 6(73) www.implementationscience.com/content/6/1/73

Pryor, RGL and Bright, JEH (2011) *The Chaos Theory of Careers: A New Perspective on Working in the Twenty-First Century,* Routledge, New York.

Rawsthorne, Laird J. and Andrew J. Elliot (1999) Achievement goals and intrinsic motivation: A meta-analytic review. *Journal of Personality and Social Psychology Review,* 3(4), 326–344.

Ryan, TA (1970) *Intentional Behaviour,* Ronald Press, New York.

Saks, AM (2006) Antecedents and consequences of employee engagement, *Journal of Managerial Psychology,* 21(7), 600–619.

Sarrazin, P, Vallerand, R, Guillet, E, Pelletier, L and Cury, F (2002) Motivation and dropout in female handballers, *European Journal of Social Psychology,* 32(3), 395–418.

Scoular, A and Linley, A (2006) Coaching, goal setting and personality type: What matters? *The Coaching Psychologist,* 2(1), 9–11.

Schweitzer, ME, Ordonez, L and Douma, B (2004) Goal setting as a motivator of unethical behaviour, *Academy of Management Journal,* 47(3), 422–432.

Seijts, GH, Latha, GP, Tasa, K and Latham BW (2004) Goal setting and goal orientation: an integration of two different related literatures, *Academy of Management Journal,* 47(2), 227–39.

Shah, YJ, Friedman, R and Kruglanski, AW (2002) Forgetting all else: On the antecedents and consequences of goal shielding, *Journal of Personality and Social Psychology,* 83(6), 1261–1280.

Shapiro, SM (2010) *Goal-free Living: How to Have the Life You Want Now!,* John Wiley and Sons, Oxford.

Sitkin, BS, See, KE, Miller, CC, Lawless, MW and Carton, AM (2011) The paradox of stretch goals: Organizations in pursuit of the seemingly impossible, *Academy of Management Review,* 36(3), 544–566.

Starr, J (2008) *Brilliant Coaching,* Pearson, London.

Tubbs, M (1986) Goal setting: A meta-analytic examination of the empirical evidence, *Journal of Applied Psychology,* 71(3), 474–83.

Vansteenkiste, M, Simons, J, Lens, W, Sheldon, KM and Deci, EL (2004) Motivating learning, performance and persistence: The synergistic effects of intrinsic goal contents and autonomy-supportive contexts, *Journal of Personality and Social Psychology,* 87, 246–60.

Whitmore, Sir J (1996) *Coaching for performance* (2nd ed.), Nicholas Brearley, London.

Winter, DA (2010) *How Smart is Smart?* http://careersintheory.wordpress.com/how-smart-is-smart, July

Winters, D and Latham, GP (1996) The effect of learning versus outcome goals on a simple versus a complex task, *Group and Organization Management,* 21(2), 236–250.

Wunsch, M. A. (1994) New directions for mentoring: An organizational development perspective, *New Directions for Teaching and Learning,* 57: 9–13.

Zachary, LJ and Fischler, LA (2011) Begin with the end in mind: The goal driven mentoring relationship, *T + D* January, 50–53.

Design of Effective Mentoring Programmes

Lis Merrick

HISTORICAL CONTEXT OF PROGRAMME DESIGN

The first formalised mentoring started in 1904 in New York, when a court clerk called Ernest Coulter was concerned about the number of boys coming through his courtroom. He realised that mentors could help many of these boys stay out of trouble, and that was the beginning of the Big Brothers movement (Beiswinger, 1985). At approximately the same time, the Ladies of Charity Group was befriending girls who had come through the New York Children's Court. This group would later become Catholic Big Sisters. In 1977, Big Brothers Association and Big Sisters International joined forces and became Big Brothers Big Sisters of America and they are still going strong today (DuBois and Karcher, 2013; Park et al., 2016; Tierney et al., 1995).

Garvey (2011) brings the history of mentoring to life with his tracking of mentoring from Homer's Odyssey through to the more modern-day concept of mentoring in Levinson (1978) and Sheehy (1976). However, it was really Kram (1983) and Zey (1993) who put formal mentoring into the public eye with their in-depth research on corporate mentoring programmes in the USA, which considered how to design a programme. Clutterbuck (1985) brought the modern concept of mentoring to Europe in his first version of *Everybody Needs a Mentor*, a book that had been inspired by his time in the USA. During the 1980s and 1990s, formal mentoring grew in popularity in both the corporate and public sectors in most of the wealthy industrialised nations of the world. Garvey's (2011) research on historical mentoring links it with cognitive development, emotional development, leadership and social integration, all of these being routed in an experiential learning philosophy. Over the last thirty years these themes have expanded to include transition, change, facilitated reflection and the acquisition of wisdom and knowledge.

At the present time, few large organisations have not dabbled with mentoring in some way or another and it is also used extensively in education and government globally (De Four-Babb et al., 2015; Esnard et al., 2015; Jones, 2012; Mitchell et al., 2015).

THE MENTORING DISCOURSES

Before examining the key frameworks for designing a mentoring programme, let us consider what we mean by 'mentoring'. There has been so much debate over the years as to what is mentoring and/or coaching: how are we defining the 'mentoring' used within the 'mentoring programme'? Mentoring can take place in so many different contexts, circumstances and modes; it makes an overall definition of mentoring for a programme very difficult to identify.

Many of us are familiar with developmental mentoring and align our thinking with the definition suggested by Megginson and Clutterbuck (1995, p.13): 'Off-line help by one person to another in making significant transitions in knowledge, work or thinking'. Clutterbuck (1985), Parsloe (1992) and Caruso (1992) have drawn similar conclusions on the role of a mentor being that of giving advice and direction, providing support and encouragement and acting as a critical friend and confidante. However, there is another school of thought, which is characterised by Zey's (1993) research in the US and reinforced by Kram (1983), in which Zey (1993, p.7) defines a mentor as: 'A person who oversees the career and development of another person, usually a junior, through teaching, counselling, providing psychological support, protecting and at times promoting or sponsoring'. At first glance this definition may seem inappropriate in a more egalitarian UK or European culture, but it is actually very prevalent in many corporate contexts globally. So what are the differences in practice?

The benefits accrued by the mentor in a sponsorship relationship include: helping the mentor to perform their job and contributing to the increase in the mentor's reputation (a form of empire building) and the mentee can contribute to the stock of knowledge the mentor requires to maintain their position in the organisation. In developmental mentoring the mentor can improve their communication, management and coaching skills, stimulate their own learning – a two-way learning relationship – improve their own processes and performance, gain insights into relationships with other people, have an opportunity to be challenged and take time out to reflect and renew focus on their own career and development. In both types of mentoring the

Figure 12.1 Differences between sponsorship and developmental mentoring

Sponsorship Mentoring	*Developmental Mentoring*
• The mentor is more influential and hierarchically senior. • 'The mentor gives, the protégé receives and the organization benefits' (Scandura et al., 1996). • The mentor actively champions and promotes the cause of the protégé. • The mentor gives the protégé the benefit of his or her wisdom. • The mentor steers the protégé through the acquisition of experience and personal resources. • The primary outcome or objective is career success. • Good advice is central to the success of the relationship. • The social exchange emphasises loyalty.	• The mentor is more experienced in issues relevant to the mentee's learning needs (perhaps life in general). • A process of mutual growth. • The mentor helps the mentee do things for him or herself. • The mentor helps the mentee develop his or her own wisdom. • The mentor helps the mentee towards personal insights from which they can steer their own development. • The primary outcome or objective is personal development, from which career success may flow. • Good questions are central to the success of the relationship. • The social exchange emphasises learning.

mentee's development provides the mentor with a feeling of pride and a sense of contributing to the organisation. Having an understanding of both these schools of mentoring can be very helpful, not only in designing your programme and preparing, matching and supporting participants, but in understanding some of the evaluation outputs you are analysing later on.

In formal mentoring programme design, generally a developmental approach is requested in a European context. Two definitions that reflect the model of developmental mentoring are:

- To help and support people to manage their own learning in order to maximise their potential, develop their skills, improve their performance and become the person they want to be (Parsloe and Wray, 2000).
- The role of the mentor is one of support to the mentee. The mentor will listen and give advice and guidance, when it is appropriate. Mentoring focuses on developing capability by working with the mentee's goals to help them realise their potential. The mentee is responsible for their learning and development and setting the direction and goals for the relationship. The flow of learning is two-way in a mentoring relationship and the mentor often gains as much as the mentee (Merrick, 2005).

It is inevitable that some formal developmental mentoring relationships will lead to longer-term, close relationships that will evolve into some form of informal sponsorship. The problem is that this can damage the core mentoring programme by creating expectations that this will be a normal outcome from the relationship, or the programme itself. I have found that senior leaders in some organisations are keen to shift their mentoring relationships in this direction in order to speed up the progression of talent; in this scenario mentoring of talent becomes a blended approach between the two forms of mentoring. This situation should not cause any great difficulties, providing that it does not cause noticeable inequalities in the way that different mentors support their mentees in the same organisation and the relationships retain a primarily developmental basis.

Therefore, in Talent Mentoring programmes, organisations often opt to go for a hybrid of the two forms of mentoring. Alongside Paul Stokes, I have explicitly examined sponsorship mentoring behaviours within mentoring programmes – see Figure 12.2 'The Talent Mentoring Wheel' (Merrick and Stokes, 2008, EMCC International Conference). However, it is critical to obtain organisational stakeholder, mentor and mentee buy-in to the mix of sponsorship/developmental mentoring that you utilise; otherwise you risk some mentoring pairs following a different mentoring path to their colleagues.

The Talent Mentoring Wheel is a practical tool to use when deciding how much of each element of mentoring to introduce into your programme. All Talent Mentoring programmes will normally expect an element of the emotional components of: role modelling, acceptance and confirmation, professional friendship and counselling (or just being a good sounding board). However, the inclusion of the career functions tends to be more widely debated by the key stakeholders, who need to consider the spectrum of support they are comfortable that the mentor provides in terms of: increasing the exposure and visibility of their mentee, coaching, providing or suggesting challenging assignments to them and organisational politics. Organisations tend to be more black and white about whether the mentor is a sponsor or not and whether they will be allowed to have the mentee under their wing in a protective way. However, many organisations are unable to stop senior, influential mentors from both sponsoring and providing a large degree of organisational immunity to the mentee.

The Talent Mentoring Wheel framework was developed after supporting and evaluating a number of mentoring programmes where some 'interesting' outcomes emerged from the mentoring. Schemes that were set up with a purely developmental bias quickly gathered momentum and turned into massive

Figure 12.2 The Talent Mentoring Wheel
(Merrick and Stokes, 2008)

sponsorship opportunities for some privileged mentees, or protégés as they became. I now use the Wheel very routinely as a discussion tool when agreeing with the programme champion, stakeholders and participants what they would like their mentoring to look like. It provides a great way to facilitate honest conversations to discuss the outcomes from mentoring that the organisation is seeking. It also provides a universal framework to eradicate some of the culturally led discourses identified in mentoring by Clutterbuck and Megginson (1999). See Figure 12.3, which illustrates the different approaches to executive mentoring adopted by different global cultures.

FRAMEWORK TO DESIGN A MENTORING PROGRAMME

Once the definition has been clarified, the designer can consider some of the published approaches to best programme design. Megginson et al. (2006) have tried to position mentoring programmes within a taxonomy of layers of mentoring, ranging from mentoring moments (key transition points within a mentoring conversation), through to techniques, episodes, relationships and, finally, culture. We can also view a mentoring programme as impacted by and related to the organisational culture and it can be seen as an artefact of the culture (Schein, 2010). In my 2013 review of best practice in mentoring programmes, I considered the following: Cranwell-Ward et al. (2004), Megginson et al. (2006), Klasen and Clutterbuck (2002), Sontag et al. (2007) and Merrick (2009). All these approaches have identified key steps that mentoring programme designers should consider. These are shown in Figure 12.4 below:

Although these approaches do differ, they mostly have a very similar practical approach to identifying process, preparing participants, matching, supervision, evaluation and

Figure 12.3 Characteristic approaches to executive mentoring by country

Country	Goals	Style of Relationship	Features in Scheme
USA	Sponsorship Promoting career	Paternalistic	Senior director taking up causes of younger high flyer
France	Insight Analysis of life purpose	Commitment to sharing values	Scheme-created outside companies
Netherlands	Mutual support Learning Networking	Informal Egalitarian Peer mentoring Universal	Recognising benefits for mentor and mentee Personal and professional
Sweden	Perpetuate culture	Share understanding Exchange knowledge	Strong sponsorship from HR and CEO
Britain	Insight Learning Support	Individualistic, charismatic mentor shares insights and challenges mentee	Ad hoc Diversity of opportunities

(Clutterbuck and Megginson, 1999)

Figure 12.4 Comparison of stepped approaches to designing a mentoring programme

Author	Number of Steps	Description of Steps
Cranwell-Ward et al. (2004)	6	• Identifying and influencing key stakeholders • Marketing the scheme • Matching • Training participants • Maintaining, concluding and developing the scheme • Evaluation and review of the scheme
Megginson et al. (2006)	7	• Scheme purpose • Evaluation • Recruitment and selection • Training and development • Matching • Supervision • Standards
Klasen and Clutterbuck (2002)	4	• Implementation proposal • Training • Evaluation • Problem solving
Sontag et al. (2007)	8	• Sponsor meeting • Implementation team planning • Nominate and recruit mentors/mentee • Interview mentors/mentee • Match mentors/mentees • Mentee and mentor orientation and launch session • 2/4/8-month checkpoint meetings
Merrick (2009)	9	• Programme close and evaluation • Rationale for a programme • Influencing stakeholders • Clear recruitment strategy • Communication and publicity • Preparing the participants • Matching process • Supporting the programme • Review and evaluation • Role of the mentoring co-ordinator

(Stokes and Merrick, 2013, p.199)

review. I will now use these recognised steps to examine some of the reported good practice in setting up a mentoring programme.

Clarifying programme purpose

When thinking about what the requirement is for mentoring and how it is going to add value or contribute strategically to the organisation, it is essential to identify what the business and organisational objectives are to be satisfied by the mentoring programme and what outputs or success factors you are seeking to obtain. Mentoring today is required to be much smarter with regard to evaluation and its value as a cost-effective way of development needs to be evident and justified from the beginning of the programme's inception. As mentoring programmes require resourcing in terms of people, finance and time, it is very important to have a clear understanding of what it is actually setting out to do and what the measurable success factors are. Mentoring can be used for so many purposes: talent management, new entrants and on-boarding, graduates, leadership development, diversity, mentoring women, maternity programmes, knowledge management, support through professional qualifications, small businesses, setting up a business, developing entrepreneurship, change and culture management, preparing for retirement and just finding out what is going on in different parts of an organisation by reducing silos.

Influencing stakeholders

As identified in Stokes and Merrick (2013), the importance of senior management commitment to the success of a mentoring programme is recognised by: Klasen and Clutterbuck (2002), Cranwell-Ward et al. (2004), Megginson et al. (2006) and Garvey et al. (2009). Klasen and Clutterbuck (2002, p.190) go as far saying that 'unqualified support is needed from all those involved', whilst Cranwell-Ward et al. (2004) point to the dangers of not involving senior stakeholders. The use of mentoring champions to support different types of mentoring has also increased significantly and plays a valuable role in ensuring the success of a programme. They need enthusiasm for mentoring and a sound reputation for developing people, maintaining confidentiality and an understanding of the culture; otherwise their reputation can damage a fledgling scheme. They can be responsible for a range of activities from being the guardian of the scheme, to sitting on a programme steering committee, helping with training and matching and recruiting participants. Cranwell-Ward et al. (2004) emphasise how instrumental this can be in gaining line management's acceptance of the mentoring programme. Klasen and Clutterbuck (2002) see the role of the champion as perhaps the most important in the design and implementation stage. They stress that the champion should be at a fairly high level in the organisation, to possess enough clout and experience to get things done.

A note of caution around utilising senior stakeholders and champions in programme development; Garvey et al. (2009) note that placing a lot of emphasis on senior stakeholder commitment can bring with it the pressure that attends a formal launch of an initiative within an organisation, which can raise expectations too high in terms of what mentoring as a process can achieve within an organisational context. This is echoed by Gibb (1994), who warns a formal approach to scheme design can be accompanied by functionalist assumptions about cause and effect and the importance of senior management control within organisations. He characterises such formal schemes as systematic mentoring, contrasting with process mentoring, which he describes as being driven by 'a concern to see mentoring as a relationship continually negotiated between partners, rather than defined at the beginning by an external source or the demands of a highly structured system' (p.54). Process mentoring seems to be a close fit with what Garvey et al. (2009) refer to as the organic approach to mentoring scheme design, which is more low-key, emphasising a longer-term, more gradual approach to nurturing mentoring within an organisational context. In my view and experience of working on over ninety mentoring programmes globally, organised mentoring should reflect the more natural characteristics of informal mentoring. However, there needs to be a loose structure of good practice to ensure the mentoring holds together and the relationships have a 'catalyst' to start them off, plus ongoing support to keep the focus and energy in the relationship.

Clear recruitment strategy

The next step is to identify the mentee or client target group and potential mentor population and invite them to participate on a voluntary basis. In my experience, voluntarism is a key factor in making your mentoring more successful. Programmes vary in terms of the formality of the recruitment process, but making participation compulsory or 'politically correct' for individuals or key talent can turn your mentoring programme into a competition to obtain the most senior sponsor in the organisation. How the programme is being communicated to the rest of the organisation is important. Communicate a clear programme outline to anyone you are interested in recruiting, to include the benefits of their involvement, but also communicate with line managers and other stakeholders so there is complete transparency. Ensure individuals understand what is expected of them within a formal programme. Are there events they need to commit to? Do they realise approximately how much time that participation in a relationship will take? Without this transparency, potential participants can make erroneous assumptions about who mentoring is for and the agendas of the various stakeholders involved. This can lead to accusations of favouritism or an assumption that mentoring is remedial; thus, managing impressions of the scheme is vital.

Matching

Certainly, in my experience, matching in mentoring programmes can present a number of challenges. Following Blake-Beard et al. (2007), I use the 'hunch' method (making matches based on personal assessment of compatibility of the dyad) most frequently. This seems particularly useful in small schemes where there is personal knowledge of the mentors and mentees through recruitment, selection and training (Megginson and Stokes, 2004). Blake-Beard et al. (2007) make connections with several studies that examine formal mentoring schemes. From their analysis, they are able to identify several common challenges when matching, in their terminology, mentors with protégés in formal mentoring programmes. These challenges include:

- Dealing with anticipation, awkwardness and anxiety at the orientation stage
- The under-utilisation of data and participant choice
- Costs of a poor match – reputational risk
- Making sure that matches support programme intent e.g. cross-fertilisation.

In larger schemes, the designer has the option (if budget is available) to use one of the many matching systems on the market, or more of a self-service approach. It is a question of weighing up the options and making the best decision around approach considering the budget/resources at their disposal.

TRAINING OR EDUCATING THE MENTORS AND MENTEES

Research has demonstrated that relationships are three times more likely to succeed if formal training of mentors and mentees has taken place (Klasen and Clutterbuck, 2002). As well as mentoring skills development, training provides the opportunity to raise concerns and questions prior to the relationship commencing. As a minimum, this preparation should encompass the programme purpose, objectives and process, roles and responsibilities of mentor and mentee, contracting, agreeing expectations and boundaries, a 'no fault' separation clause, skills and techniques (with an opportunity to practise in a safe environment) and the understanding of the life cycle of a relationship. If you are in the nice position of having more time and resources to prepare mentors and mentees, then you can cover rapport building, goal setting, learning styles, competences of a mentor and mentee, reflection and learning logs and not rush the skills practice element.

In my experience I would recommend there is some preparation – even if it is a short briefing, it will make a huge difference to the programme success. A one-day interactive workshop for participants makes for effective training, with time for practising mentoring skills in a safe environment with feedback. If this is not feasible, then a half-day workshop can also be very effective. In the current climate, most organisations opt for a half day of preparation but follow this up with group support three or four months later. The biggest mistake you can make is not preparing mentors or mentees in any way and letting them 'make it up' as they go along, especially when you do not cover the principles of a mentoring agreement between mentor and mentee, the most important 'safety net' in their relationship. Nowadays much of this training/education is conducted virtually through interactive webinars.

What should you do if you only have budget to work with the mentors or the mentees and not both? Then I suggest you work with the mentees; having a skilled mentee who is in the driving seat in the relationship and knows what they want from the relationship and how to use it appropriately has more of a positive impact on the relationship. Or consider a workshop with mentors and mentees being prepared together – in some situations that is even more effective than preparing them separately and can be useful when considering matching.

Some other key aspects to consider in your participant preparation:

- Will **e-mentoring** be a large component of the programme? In which case time needs to be spent in exploring electronic rapport building, how to communicate effectively and the challenges and advantages when face-to-face communication is not possible.
- **Cultural differences** between participants, how to recognise these and value them and ensure they don't impact on the effectiveness and outcomes of the relationship.

SUPPORT AND SUPERVISION IN THE MENTORING PROGRAMME

A key element in mentoring scheme design is supervision and ongoing support for participants. Supervision in formal mentoring programmes is a form of supervision that has been minimally researched and there is little evidence of good practice in programmes globally, although this situation is beginning to change and more programmes are investing in both individual and group supervision. My initial research from the JIVE Mentoring Programmes 2001 to 2003 (Merrick and Stokes, 2003) revealed the following common functions of mentor supervision in programmes as understood by the mentors:

- Being a mentor to the mentors,
- Being able to explore techniques and help with problems,
- An opportunity to reflect on own practice,
- To support a mentor who feels out of their depth,
- As a mark of good practice for the profession,
- To support with ethical issues,
- To be available for the mentor as an emotional safety valve.

This echoes Barrett's (2002) work in mentoring, which puts forward the following **benefits** of **being supervised:**

- Preventing personal burn-out,
- A celebration of what I do,
- Demonstrating skill/knowledge,
- Helping me to focus on my blind spot(s),
- Discovering my own pattern of behaviours,
- Developing skills as a mentor,
- A quality control process; and
- Providing a different angle on an issue.

So, apart from Barrett (2002), there has been little attention focused on mentoring supervision in the literature. However, the widening notion of supervision in other professions has coincided with increasing interest in how mentors might be developed. This interest prompted Paul Stokes and myself to develop a heuristic, which linked together the needs of the mentoring supervisee with their development as a mentor (see Figure 12.5).

The four stages of mentor development can be used as a device for mentoring practitioners to aid reflection on their own practice and the heuristic offers a brief description of each stage, summarising the benefits and challenges and the role and responsibilities of the supervisor.

The novice mentor

A novice mentor is someone who may be new to mentoring. This does not mean that

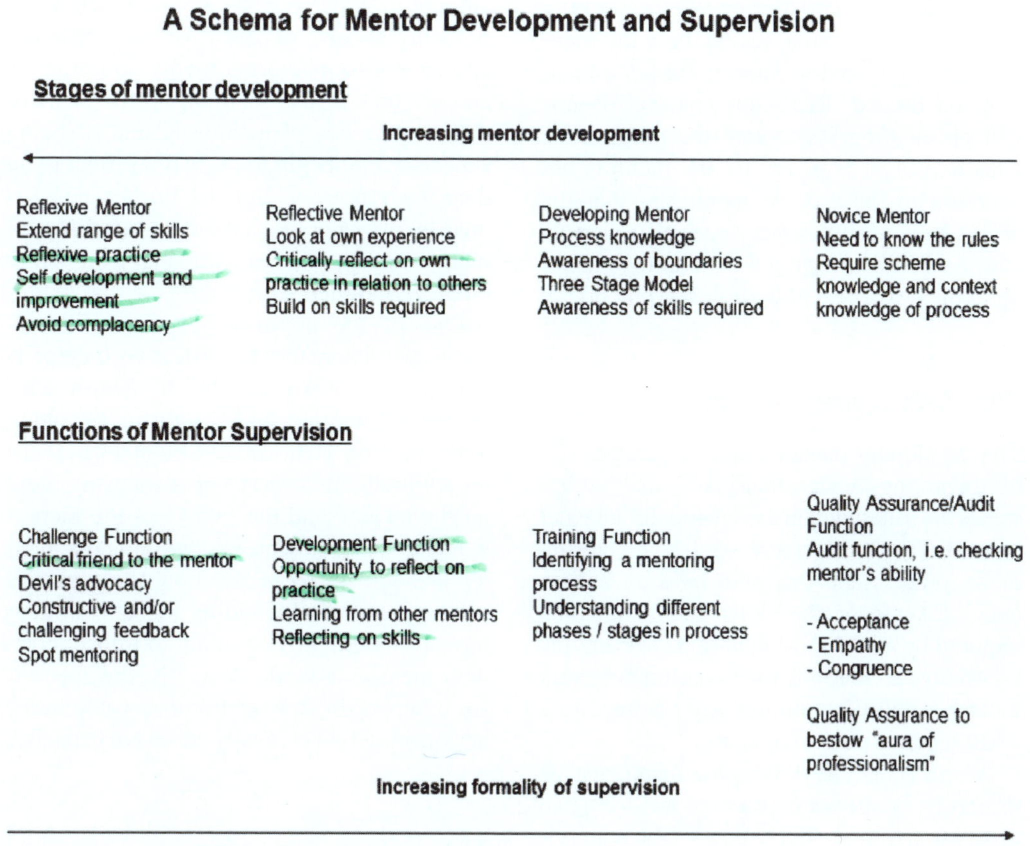

A Schema for Mentor Development and Supervision

Stages of mentor development

Increasing mentor development →

Reflexive Mentor	Reflective Mentor	Developing Mentor	Novice Mentor
Extend range of skills	Look at own experience	Process knowledge	Need to know the rules
Reflexive practice	Critically reflect on own practice in relation to others	Awareness of boundaries	Require scheme knowledge and context
Self development and improvement	Build on skills required	Three Stage Model	knowledge of process
Avoid complacency		Awareness of skills required	

Functions of Mentor Supervision

Challenge Function	Development Function	Training Function	Quality Assurance/Audit Function
Critical friend to the mentor	Opportunity to reflect on practice	Identifying a mentoring process	Audit function, i.e. checking mentor's ability
Devil's advocacy	Learning from other mentors	Understanding different phases / stages in process	
Constructive and/or challenging feedback	Reflecting on skills		- Acceptance
Spot mentoring			- Empathy
			- Congruence
			Quality Assurance to bestow "aura of professionalism"

Increasing formality of supervision →

Figure 12.5 A schema for mentor development and supervision

(Bachkirov et al., 2011)

they are untrained or unskilled, but that they have relatively little experience as a mentor of participating in a live, dynamic human mentoring process. Whilst there will be a number of development agendas for the novice mentor, one of the important functions of the supervisor at this stage is to ensure that mentoring is operating in a way that is congruent with the aims of the programme. This 'quality assurance'/audit function has two main purposes: to check the mentor's ability as a mentor i.e. are they using the key skills of acceptance, empathy and congruence with their mentee, and to bestow scheme credibility in the eyes of its sponsors.

With this level of mentor development, most supervision occurs through running small focus group activity for the mentors at regular intervals during the mentoring programme duration to review how the mentoring is going and to provide further education. Facilitated discussion in these groups will check progress around the programme aims and objectives, ensure the mentors are adhering to the type of mentoring that the programme is advocating and have a largely educative input to equip the mentors to move up to the next stage of their development.

The developing mentor

The developing mentor has some experience of mentoring 'under their belt' and understands the 'rules' within their particular scheme/context. They can use a recognised mentoring model/process and they will have an awareness of some of the skills and behaviours required by an effective mentor. However, this knowledge is basic and their comfort zone as a mentor is still fairly limited and confined to a small repertoire of behaviours.

At this stage, the developing mentor needs to start to identify other ways of mentoring so as to expand their effectiveness. The supervisor may therefore need to pay more attention to supporting the mentor in their process development and in recognising the dynamics within a mentoring relationship. Some schemes, where it is feasible, provide one-to-one supervision using the scheme organiser or bringing in an external supervisor. Challenges with this level of supervision can include the capability of the organiser, particularly if working with the mentor on a one-to-one basis, and the availability of the mentor to participate in the supervision. Due to logistical and budgetary constraints most formal programmes still use small focus group activity to supervise mentors at this stage, or begin to bring in peer discussion and reflection.

The reflective mentor

The reflective mentor is someone with a fair amount of experience as a mentor. They are probably aware of most of the different approaches to mentoring theory and practice and are now in the position, on the basis of their experience of mentoring and of being supervised, to begin to critically reflect upon their own practice and to further develop their skills and understanding of different mentoring approaches, drawing from other mentors and their supervisor.

One of the important aspects of effective supervision for the reflective mentor is that the supervisor is able to demonstrate emphatic attention and insightful reflection to the mentor. There are two changes in focus here. Firstly, the supervisor is focusing more on the mentee and the 'work' of the mentor whilst at the same time encouraging the mentor to begin to recognise how the mentor's own experiences (including those as a mentor/supervisee) are beginning to impact upon their mentoring work. Secondly, the supervisor is supporting the mentor to develop his or her own internal critically reflexive capacity.

The reflexive mentor

The reflexive mentor is someone with considerable experience as a mentor and may even be a mentor supervisor. They have developed sufficient self-awareness to critically reflect upon their own practice and to identify areas for their own development, as well as being more competent in detecting and using their own feelings within mentoring conversations to inform their practice. They are, however, astute enough to recognise that there is nevertheless a need to continue with their development and to understand the dangers that lie in complacency in terms of rigidity of approach. In this sense, the reflexive mentor needs supervision to assure the quality of their helping skills and to prevent blind spots or damage being done through arrogant or careless interventions. For the effective supervision of a reflexive mentor, the supervisor would need to be a highly competent, flexible and experienced mentor themselves as the range of supervision required might range from very gentle support when a problem occurs, as a 'spot mentoring' transaction, or conversely adopting a strong critical position in order to challenge the potentially complacent mentor supervisee.

The mentees also benefit from regular group support during the programme to ensure they are using their mentors in the most effective manner and to give them a safe space in which to reflect on the process of mentoring they are experiencing. Developing mentees is critical in producing a skilled mentee who is in the driving seat and can get the most out of their mentoring experience.

REVIEW AND EVALUATION

There is a paucity of research around the evaluation of mentoring programmes. I believe this is mainly because of the perceived lack of tangible, quantitative evaluation that is feasible in some programmes. The evaluation of a mentoring programme should be planned as part of the initial design whilst it is being set up and the programme outputs and success factors agreed. Mentoring programmes should be continually assessed to provide formative evaluation, which can be used to review the design and future implementation of the programme. In addition, summative evaluation should be completed at the end of each cycle of the programme. Evaluation should be conducted at programme and relationship level and focus on both process and outputs.

Some of the aspects to evaluate include:

- Programme and relationship processes,
- Selection criteria,
- Proportion of successes/failures,
- The training/briefing,
- Programme support/supervision,
- Meeting frequency/relevancy/value; and
- The learning acquired.

In addition, how the programme impacts on the retention, promotion and performance of individuals and some of the less tangible aspects such as self-confidence and self-belief can all be measured. This can all feed into the organisational perspective, as well as results observed by key stakeholders since the introduction of the mentoring programme.

Both formative and summative evaluation of mentoring schemes is useful to inform the design and future development of formal programmes. However, it is difficult to review what is basically a private developmental relationship between two people and ascertain sufficient information about the activities of and benefits from the mentoring pair to satisfy the organisation's expectations and to obtain resources for future mentoring. Cranwell-Ward et al. (2004, p.136) suggest that, in order to position mentoring as part of the mainstream of organisational development, a rigorous evaluation process is a key tool, which needs to be in place at the outset of the scheme. Klasen and Clutterbuck (2002) reinforce this message, whilst MacLennan (1995, p.264) considers that, if a mentoring system you set up is not systematically evaluated, monitored and shown to be effective, it will be dropped by design or default. However, Cranwell-Ward et al. (2004) and Klasen and Clutterbuck (2002) stress how intangible many mentoring outcomes can be, which is quite a challenge for the evaluator.

Some of the tools you can use as part of your evaluation process, particularly to collect some of the more intangible outputs from mentoring, include:

- Feedback from participants through focus groups;
- Qualitative interviews and questionnaires;
- Information taken from appraisal and performance management systems and employee attitude surveys;
- Exit interviews;
- Assessment against objectives set at the beginning of a mentoring relationship;
- 360-degree feedback; and
- Employee retention rates.

Obviously, the budget available for evaluation will dictate how much resource can be ploughed into evaluation. However, assessing whether the programme has met its original objectives and perhaps had other beneficial consequences is key. It must also ensure the needs of the stakeholders are being met and key sponsors are motivated to continue supporting the programme with justification for continued funding/resources. This is absolutely critical for the programme to continue.

The role of the mentoring co-ordinator, or programme manager, is covered in detail in Chapter 16 of this book, titled 'The Role of the Mentoring Program Co-ordinator'.

FUTURE IMPLICATIONS FOR MENTORING PROGRAMME DESIGN

Global mentoring

One of the biggest dilemmas for mentoring programmes in multinational companies is the requirement for consistency across borders, both geographical and divisional, but with the ability to be able to satisfy local needs. As Clutterbuck and Merrick (2014) suggest, many multinational mentoring programmes have failed because of perceived cultural imperialism on the part of the international headquarters. They recognise good practice as:

- Designing the programme(s) or the corporate approach to mentoring with input from a wide range of sources, and particularly from local HR and line managers;
- Recognising that, in countries that speak the same language, the context of mentoring may be very different (trying to impose a US approach on the United Kingdom, or vice versa, is likely to meet resistance);
- Openly acknowledging the impact of culture on the style of mentoring and including relevant cultural awareness elements in any training and supporting information resources;
- Designing training content and support materials with a core of common elements (definitions, skills, emphasis on learning dialogue) and a more flexible approach to case studies, role plays/ real plays, links with local mythology and social mores;
- Educating local HR professionals so that they can become champions for mentoring and identify opportunities to support regional/international programmes and to launch local programmes aimed at specific, local issues;
- Clarifying other important contextual factors – for example, the qualities associated with effective leadership are not universal and there are significant differences between cultures, which may need to be taken into account; and
- Wherever possible, rooting the mentoring story in the mythology or religious beliefs of the country. Islam, Buddhism, Christianity and other religions all exemplify learning dialogue, as do many of the stories told to children in East Africa and in Asia-Pacific cultures.

Second-wave mentoring

Clutterbuck and Merrick (2014) also name the reinvention and reinvigoration of both corporate and community mentoring programmes in the light of experiential learning.

One driver of this movement has been the desire by organisations, which have been relatively early adopters of supported mentoring, to learn from their own and other people's experiences. What has gained the description 'second-wave mentoring' has a number of other drivers. Clutterbuck and Merrick (2014) identify these as:

- The desire to make mentoring available to much wider audiences. This in turn puts pressure on programme managers to find lower-cost solutions, without sacrificing quality. However, many attempts to do mentoring on the cheap – especially by using off-the-peg online solutions – have failed to deliver the quality required. In particular, they have tended to push mentoring towards shallow, transactional skills and knowledge transfer, rather than longer-term deep personal change;
- The need to link mentoring more closely with talent management and succession planning;
- More critical questioning by enterprise leaders as to the outcomes of mentoring for participants and for the organisation, leading to a need for more effective measurement processes;
- Increased frustration in developmental mentoring programmes, when mentors relapse into sponsoring behaviours;
- Rejection of formal programmes (as currently practised) by some minority groups;
- Disparity between programmes in terms of failure rates, leading to re-examination of matching and re-matching processes; and
- The impact of the International Standards for Mentoring Programmes in Employment*, which have begun to set expectations of what a good-practice mentoring programme looks like.

*The International Standards for Mentoring Programmes in Employment have become The International Standards for Coaching and Mentoring (ISMCP) and are now part of the European Mentoring and Coaching Council (EMCC) Standards for Mentoring and Coaching Programmes, with effect from 2016.

ISMCP has been developed to support the maintenance and development of effective mentoring or coaching within the workplace and the broader working environment.

The intent is to provide a framework of standards that is both consistent in values yet evolving in line with broader developments in mentoring and coaching. The EMCC aims to develop the Standards continuously, incorporating changes that reflect the wider range of innovations in application and method of mentoring and coaching, and the diversity of approaches arising from different cultures. The ISMCP are a set of six principles upon which to base good mentoring or coaching programme practice. Six Core Standards have been identified, comprising:

1 Clarity of Purpose
2 Stakeholder Training and Briefing
3 Processes for Selection and Matching
4 Processes for Measurement and Review
5 Maintains High Standards of Ethics and Pastoral Care
6 Administration and Support

Mentoring for knowledge management

With the importance of intellectual capital, the knowledge and skills of the workforce of an organisation are viewed by many as the organisation's most valuable asset. Mentoring is now increasingly recognised as an incredibly powerful tool in facilitating the transition from 'knowing' work experience to actually becoming 'wisdom' or 'knowledge in action' which can be applied in the workplace. Whereas most formal training programmes tend to have little impact longer term, learning by doing and mentoring develops a deeper and more profound level of knowledge and eliminates the Knowing-Doing Gap identified by Pfeffer and Sutton (1999). They have identified a gap between knowledge an organisation possesses and the organisation actually using it or putting it into action.

The rationale behind the majority of mentoring programmes is to develop the mentee in order for them to maximise their potential. Any organisation that designs a programme so that both the development of the mentee and the goals of the organisation coincide can be called a 'mentoring organisation' (Garvey and Williamson, 2003, p.87). In designing programmes to enhance an organisation's knowledge productivity, it is possible to identify strategic learning and knowledge alliances, whereby the employees benefit from sharing knowledge and can deepen their knowledge and expertise in specific topics by formalising mentoring relationships.

So these are the types of mentoring that can be used to enhance knowledge productivity most successfully:

- Role model mentoring – The mentor is generally older and more experienced than the mentee, who can then look up to them as a role model and guide.
- Peer mentoring – Employees with similar experience levels take on the roles of mentor and mentee. Peer relationships tend to provide higher quality exchanges, greater reciprocity and greater continuity over time.
- Peer co-mentoring or reciprocal peer mentoring – This is where the roles of mentor and mentee are formally exchanged between the two individuals in the relationship, beneficial where both parties have relevant knowledge to share.
- Group peer mentoring – Informal, supportive group meeting using mentoring techniques, similar to action learning.
- Reverse mentoring – Where a more junior individual is the mentor to a more senior mentee. Can be useful where the mentor has specific skills or knowledge in a subject unknown to the mentee.

So programme designers who can assess potential tacit knowledge flows, create transparency around knowledge movement intent and identify the most effective mentoring form will create a very effective knowledge management intervention.

Mentoring in a VUCA world

Possessing adaptive capacity is a prerequisite for organisations operating in a VUCA world – volatile, uncertain, complex and ambiguous. Individuals must be able to assess their environment, embrace the changes that are occurring and modify people and organisational behaviour. It is the ability to navigate uncertainty, complexity and ambiguity that creates the adaptive capacity that is one of the most important predictors of performance and it is the creative, continuous learners who are the leaders of this successful performance. A recent move in supporting leaders has been to develop their *contextual intelligence.* Sternberg (1988) used the term 'contextual intelligence' as a synonym for his concept of *practical intelligence.* He described it as the ability to apply intelligence practically, which includes considering social, cultural and historical backgrounds. Individuals who have a high level of contextual intelligence easily adapt to their surroundings, can fit into new surroundings easily and can fix their surroundings when they perceive it to be necessary.

This concept focuses on principles of tacit-based learning, synchronicity and time orientation: all competencies that can be developed easily through mentoring. It can be broken down into the following areas and an awareness created during both the initial briefing/training and ongoing mentor supervision sessions to improve greatly the *contextual intelligence* of the mentee and the mentor.

Tacit knowledge – using vicarious experiences and analogical reasoning

Mentoring is a catalyst for the movement of tacit knowledge between people. Most simply, it comes from trial-and-error experiences, which are then analysed and decisions made in light of the outcomes. Analogical reasoning comes in when that experience doesn't exist but the mentor can support the mentee in comparing similarities in different situations and recognising trends. Having an experienced mentor to create the reflective space to develop informed analogical inference is immensely beneficial and, in terms of leadership development, it is key that leaders develop the ability to facilitate their own wisdom from vicarious experiences using analogical reasoning. Mentors and mentees really need to comprehend these processes in order to enjoy effective mentoring in any programme seeking to support leadership growth or managing/coping with change.

Synchronicity – understanding events that occur coincidentally, but result in a meaningful connection

Synchronicity can result from that reflective space developed by the mentor. It is not necessarily for the mentor to make the connections (although there is a linkage here with passing on tacit knowledge), but rather the mentor having the ability to use their challenge and listening skills to support that fresh insight around seemingly random connections within the mentee's context.

Time orientation – 3D thinking, 'time warping' and 'time chunking'

Successful leaders/mentors hold a frame of time reference that relates to the past, present and future. This 3D model of thinking of contextual intelligence takes into consideration hindsight, foresight and insight. 'Time warping' is where the mentor is able to 'manipulate' the past and future by making them seem closer to the present. Both familiarity with mentoring techniques used to review the past and a solutions-focused approach can aid a mentor with managing this aspect. Finally, 'time chunking', a tool to help the mentee be aware of creating a future with a higher priority or importance for a particular chunk of time, e.g. these are my key goals in the next three months, is a further effective way of supporting a mentee operating in a chaotic environment.

Organisations that emphasise *contextual intelligence* in both mentor and mentee briefings and build on this practice through supervision will develop not only effective mentoring outcomes for the relationships involved but also support the creation of an adaptive leadership paradigm within any VUCA environment. This is a new and exciting theme, which organisations are keen to embrace as they develop their mentors.

CONCLUSION

Looking to the future for mentoring programme design, some of the themes that Clutterbuck and Merrick (2014) have extrapolated from a wide variety of organisations include:

- Greater integration between different mentoring programmes in the same organisation;
- Clarification of the different interpretations of mentoring within the same organisation;
- Greater consideration of the differences in expectations of mentoring from diverse cultures; and
- A greater use of social media to change how mentoring is delivered.
- A key issue now emerging for many companies is the extent to which employees (and particularly talented employees) can be supported in developing dynamic networks of mentors. In these networks, there may be one or two close mentoring relationships focused on medium to long-term career development, several medium-term relationships focused on development of specific (leadership) competencies, and *ad hoc* short-term relationships focused on transfer of skills or knowledge.

The limitations of a single-mentor model for mentoring have often been identified. The chosen mentor might not represent the best, most current practices, might restrict the mentee's network of contacts and a flawed pairing might undermine the mentee's confidence. The alternative to one-on-one mentoring is a constellation of relationships and a range of mentoring experiences – from formal arrangements with assigned individual mentors or mentoring teams, to informal mentoring by senior colleagues, to opportunities for peer mentoring and reverse mentoring. The most effective mentoring programmes will provide multiple opportunities for mentoring and therefore also increase the quantity of knowledge to be transferred through the network.

I believe this is the dawn of a new period for mentoring programme design. The abundance of theory and knowledge that is available to inform programme designers in good practice and the global context of change and volatility that embraces developmental dialogues in different shapes and modes provides a receptive and encouraging backdrop on which the designer can craft their finest designs.

REFERENCES

Bachkirov, T. Jackson, P. & Clutterbuck, D. (2011). *Coaching and Mentoring Supervision Theory and Practice*. England: Open University Press.

Barrett, R. (2002). Mentor supervision and development – exploration of lived experience. *Career Development International.* 7(5): 279–283.

Beiswinger, G.L. (1985). One to one: The story of the Big Brothers/Big Sisters movement in America. Philadelphia: Big Brothers/Big Sisters of America.

Blake-Beard, S.D., O'Neill, R. and McGowan, E.M. (2007). Blind Dates? The Importance of Matching in Successful Formal Mentoring Relationships, pp.617–632, in Ragins, B.R. and Kram, K.E. (2007) (eds.), *The Handbook of Mentoring at Work: Theory, Research and Practice*. London: Sage.

Caruso, J.A. (1992). *How to Win at Everyday Negotiations*. Caruso Leadership Institute, University of Chicago Booth School of Business.

Clutterbuck, D. (1985). *Everybody Needs a Mentor: How to Foster Talent Within the Organisation*. Vanersborg: Oduate Forlag AB.

Clutterbuck, D. and Megginson, D. (1999). *Mentoring Executives and Directors*. London: Butterworth.

Clutterbuck, D. and Merrick, L. (2014). Where next in coaching and mentoring?, pp. 197–208, in Rebecca Norman-Hochman (ed.), *Mentoring and Coaching for Lawyers: Building Partnerships for Success*. London: Globe Law and Business.

Cranwell-Ward, J., Bossons, P. and Gover, S. (2004). *Mentoring: A Henley Review of Best Practice*. London: Palgrave Macmillan.

De Four-Babb, J., Pegg, J. and Beck, M. (2015). Reducing intellectual poverty of outsiders within academic spaces through informal peer mentorship. *Mentoring and Tutoring: Partnership in Learning.* 23(1): 76–93.

DuBois, D.L. and Karcher, M.J. (eds.). (2013). *Handbook of Youth Mentoring*. Washington DC: Sage Publications.

Esnard, T., Cobb-Roberts, D., Agosto, V., Karanxha, Z., Beck, M., Wu, K. and Unterreiner, A. (2015). Productive tensions in a cross-cultural peer mentoring women's network: A social capital perspective. *Mentoring and Tutoring: Partnership in Learning.* 23(1): 19–36.

Garvey, B. (2011). *A Very Short, Fairly Interesting and Reasonably Cheap Book about Coaching and Mentoring*. London: Sage.

Garvey, B., Stokes, P. and Megginson, D. (2009). *Coaching and Mentoring Theory and Practice*. London: Sage.

Garvey, B. and Williamson, B. (2003). *Beyond Knowledge Management*. Harlow, England: Pearson Education.

Gibb, S. (1994). Inside corporate mentoring schemes: The development of a conceptual framework. *Personnel Review.* 23(3): 47–60.

Jones, J. (2012). An analysis of learning outcomes within formal mentoring relationships. *International Journal of Evidence Based Coaching and Mentoring.* 10(1): 57–72.

Klasen, N. and Clutterbuck, D. (2002). *Implementing Mentoring Schemes: A Practical Guide to Successful Programmes*. London: Butterworth-Heinemann.

Kram, K.E. (1983). Phases of the mentor relationship. *Academy of Management Journal.* 26(4): 608–625.

Levinson, D.J., Darrow, C.N., Klein, E.B., Levinson, M.H. and McKee, B. (1978). *The Seasons of a Man's Life*. New York: Knopf.

MacLennan, N. (1995). *Coaching and Mentoring*. Aldershot: Gower.

Megginson, D. and Clutterbuck, D. (1995). *Mentoring in Action*. London: Kogan Page.

Megginson, D., Clutterbuck, D., Garvey, B., Stokes, P. and Garrett-Harris, R. (eds.). (2006). *Mentoring in Action*. London: Kogan Page.

Megginson, D. and Stokes, P. (2004). Mentoring for export success, pp. 265–285. In Stewart, J. and Beaver, G. (eds.) *HRM in Small Organisations: Research and Practice*. London: Routledge.

Merrick, L. (2005). Lecture on Mentoring (June), Sheffield Business School.

Merrick, L. (2009). How to set up a mentoring programme. *Coaching at Work*. 3(4): 52–54.

Merrick, L. and Stokes, P. (2003). Mentor development and supervision: A passionate joint inquiry. *International Journal of Mentoring and Coaching (E-journal)*. 1(1).

Merrick, L. and Stokes, P. (2008). Mentoring for Talent Management, Conference Paper presented at the 15th European Mentoring and Coaching Council, Amsterdam.

Mitchell, M.E., Eby, L.T. and Ragins, B.R. (2015). My mentor, my self: Antecedents and outcomes of perceived similarity in mentoring relationships. *Journal of Vocational Behavior*. 89: 1–9.

Park, H., Yoon, J. and Crosby, S.D. (2016). A pilot study of Big Brothers Big Sisters programs and youth development: An application of critical race theory. *Children and Youth Services Review*. 61: 83–89.

Parsloe, E. (1992). *Coaching, Mentoring, and Assessing: A Practical Guide to Developing Competence*. London: Kogan Page.

Parsloe, E. and Wray, M. (2000). *Coaching and Mentoring*. London: Kogan Page.

Pfeffer, J. and Sutton, R. (1999). *The Knowing-Doing Gap*. Boston: Harvard Business School Press.

Schein, E.H. (2010). *Organisational Culture and Leadership*. San Francisco, California: Jossey-Bass.

Sheehy, G. (1976). *Passages: Predictable Crises of Adult Life*. New York: Dotton.

Sontag, L.P., Vappie, K. and Wanberg, C.R. The Practice of Mentoring, MENTTIUM Corporation, pp.593–616. In Ragins, B.R. and Kram, K.E. (2007). (eds.). *The Handbook of Mentoring at Work: Theory, Research and Practice*. London: Sage.

Sternberg, R. (1988). *The Triarchic Mind: A New Theory of Human Intelligence*. New York, NY: Viking.

Stokes, P. and Merrick, L. Designing Mentoring Programmes for Organisations, pp.197–216. In Passmore, P., Peterson, D.B. and Freire, T. (2013). (eds.). *The Psychology of Coaching and Mentoring*. Hoboken, NJ: Wiley-Blackwell.

Tierney, J.P., Grossman, J.B. and Resch, N.L. (1995). Making a difference: An impact study of big brothers/big sisters. Philadelphia: Public/Private Ventures.

Zey, M.G. (1993). *The Mentor Connection*. New Jersey: Transaction Publishers.

A Case Study of the Operations and Perceived Attributes of Successful Multi-Country Mentoring Programmes

Sadhana Bhide

There is a wealth of information about mentoring programmes tailored to a specific industry, profession, geographical location or career experience such as expatriation, organisational change, or working remotely. For the purposes of this case study, mentoring is defined as 'off-line help by one person to another in making significant transitions in knowledge, work or thinking' (Clutterbuck and Megginson, 1999).

Over the past thirty years, there have been two significant drivers that have contributed to the growth in multi-country mentoring in organisations. In the 1990s, increasing globalisation and workforce demographic trends resulted in many organisations becoming more diverse in terms of gender, race, ethnicity and nationality (Cox, 1991). This led to the management of cultural differences moving to the top of the agenda, highlighting the need for individuals to understand how the benefits of diversity can support the success of the organisation. The second contributing factor was the digital revolution over the same period of time (Kaufman, 2012). This fundamentally changed the way in which people interact and the speed of communications, resulting in mentoring meetings taking place virtually, over email and via conference calls, as well as through face-to-face interactions. Mentoring programmes are a cost-effective and sustainable method of supporting colleagues in this type of environment, where the mentor and mentee are based in different countries (Atkinson and McKay, 2007).

However, it has been noted that there is an absence of data about international multi-country mentoring programmes to draw upon, both empirical and theoretical, and limited information about best practice, successes and learning. Crocitto, Sullivan and Carraher's (2005) research in this area also identified that theory has not kept pace with the rate of change from increased globalisation and technological advances. This study explored the implementation of multi-country mentoring programmes in order to identify the roles of those involved, the manner in which these programmes operated and the elements respondents perceived of as being necessary for these mentoring programmes to succeed. No restrictions or specific criteria were placed on which type of organizations would participate, as the aim was to gather a broad and rich view of experiences of individuals from different kinds of organisations and institutions.

SURVEY METHODOLOGY

The survey comprised thirty-six questions, of which ten included multiple choice options and five were open-ended questions to enable respondents to share detail and opinion. The remaining twenty-one questions were requests for facts about the individual, the organisation and the mentoring programme.

The survey was distributed using an online tool (Survey Monkey) and respondents were invited to complete the survey by direct invitation to selected contacts of the author of the case study and book (Sadhana Bhide and David Clutterbuck). Survey respondents were determined based on the following criteria:

- their current role should relate to management of mentoring programmes or be within HR and/or learning functions;
- their role remit should include awareness of or direct responsibility for mentoring programmes across multiple countries. It should also be noted that participants were invited to complete the survey regardless of their actual location, in order to gain data and views from different countries about local custom and practice.

The survey was sent to 134 individuals and 110 responses were received, giving a response rate of 82%.

PROFILE OF SURVEY PARTICIPANTS

One hundred and ten respondents from 92 organisations took part in the survey. Where respondents came from the same organisation, the responses were consolidated to produce one response for the organisation (i.e. there were nine separate respondents from different business divisions of Barclays, which were consolidated into one response).

Table 13.1 presents the types of organisations represented. The organisations were grouped into broad industry sectors with the majority of respondents working in professional services (35.5%), followed by financial services (16.4%). These two types of organisations tend to have large employee populations and also operate in global markets. Other major industry sectors included: charity and education (6.4%); IT services (4.5%); pharmaceutical, media and fast-moving consumer goods (2.7% each); and the National Health Service, manufacturing and legal (1.8% each). Other survey participants came from a variety of industry sectors; however, each represented less than 1% of the total number of respondents. A full breakdown of the industry groupings is referenced in the appendix.

The number of individuals employed by each organisation varied widely across the survey respondents, ranging from small to medium-sized enterprises (SMEs) with up to 250 employees, to very large organisations with over 100,000 employees. A large proportion (35.5%) of survey participants worked in or with organisations with between 0 and 100 employees globally. It is worth noting that nine respondents were independent consultants, who worked with a large number of different organisations by providing consulting services covering coaching, providing expertise around design and creation of mentoring programmes. They shared their experience as part of the survey. This may have had a small impact on the survey results; however, it did not materially affect trends or lessen the quality of the data.

As this survey focused on international mentoring, it was critical to understand the global presence of the organisations in the survey. Forty-seven out of the 110 respondents

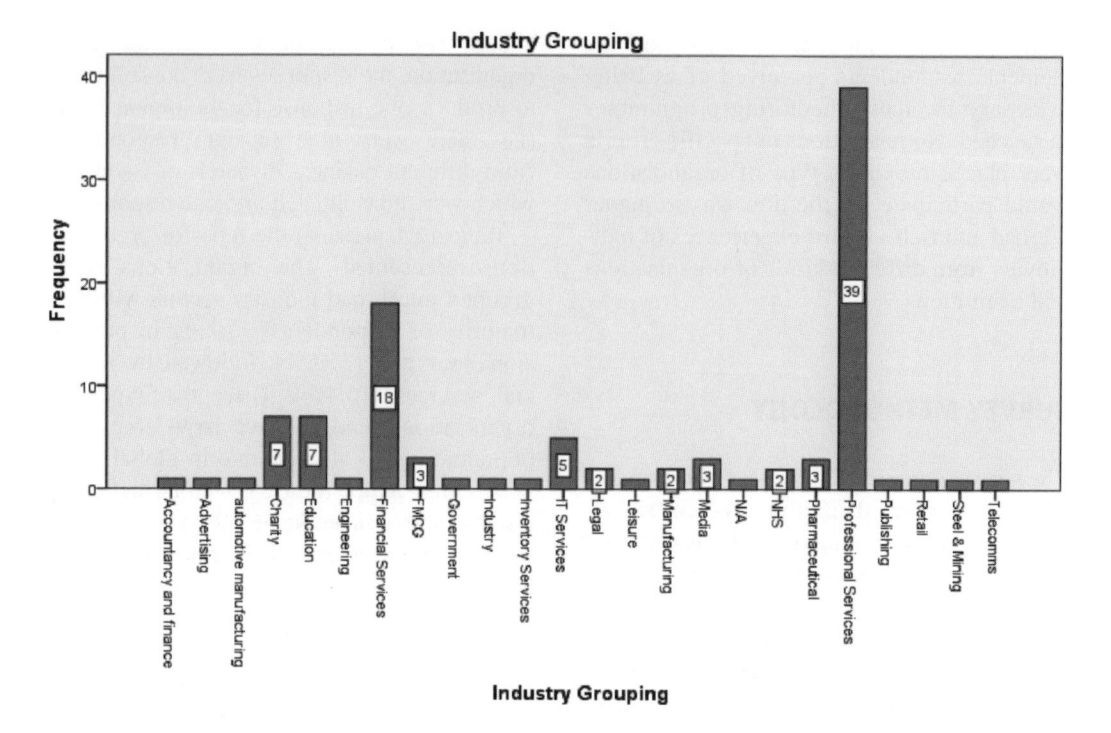

Table 13.1 Industry grouping (survey options)

worked in organisations that operated in up to 10 countries. Eleven organisations operated in 11 to 50 countries. Ten organisations operated in 150 to 200 countries.

The general profile of the survey respondents can be summarised as predominantly from the private sector, in a professional or financial services industry and with a significant global presence in 10 countries, with a smaller number operating in a greater number of countries. The number of colleagues employed varied considerably, ranging from 100 to over 100,000, with an average of 75,000. That gave us sufficient variety of organisation size, scale and geographical presence to explore international mentoring programmes.

SURVEY FINDINGS

The findings from the survey are presented in the sections that follow. Each section includes survey results and issues that need further examination and study. The first section deals with programme operations and participant roles.

Programme operations and roles of the survey participants

Three topics were examined in the area of me operations: overall management; span of involvement; and programme participants. In order to determine the manner in which programmes were managed and the role of the participants responding, we asked 'Do you have full or part responsibility for international mentors?'. Of the total 107 respondents who answered the specific question, there was almost a 50% split between those who reported that they did have full responsibility and those who reported that they did not.

The large majority of respondents (61%) have a job title related to a Human Resources role (HR), 28% hold a senior management level role and the remaining 12% have neither a HR nor a senior management level role. It is assumed that this last category consists of individuals who may fulfil a supporting or administrative type role, or have acted in a consultant capacity to design and launch a programme, but are not engaged in the daily management or future development of programmes. It is not surprising that the majority of respondents work in HR, as mentoring programmes are often managed by individuals in this role.

Further research would be helpful to seek to determine the level of theoretical and practical knowledge these individuals have about mentoring and the personal and job-related experiences they have had in mentoring. Another area to consider is whether the management of such programmes should always sit within HR. It would also be of value to determine the role of those individuals who do not have full responsibility, and how this links to mentoring programmes at their organisation. The next natural question is to understand how the role seniority and area of expertise impact the selection of these individuals as managers of mentoring programmes.

Span of responsibility

The next area of programme operations dealt with the span of responsibility that participants had for the mentoring programmes within their organisations. Seventy-four per cent of the respondents confirmed that they worked with or managed one international mentoring programme and the remaining 26% had a portfolio of international mentoring programmes. With regards to programme management, there was a blend of responses to whether the programmes were managed from one central centre of expertise or multiple locations. A number of organisations manage their programmes on a country by country basis.

From this finding, it can be assumed that organisations apply a blended approach to managing multi-country mentoring programmes on an international scale, particularly for a large organisation with a centralised approach. This is likely to be because programmes will need to adapt to local country and legislative requirements, e.g. data privacy, to navigate across multiple cultural preferences and styles and to integrate effective mentoring relationships into a typical working pattern.

The third issue within operations dealt with how mentees were selected and trained. They are matched with mentors either via a self-select approach or selection methods managed by the programme team. Most of the organisations surveyed confirmed that the matching process is handled by the core programme team, usually HR and senior leadership. The reasons behind this 'intelligent' matching approach are to support business requirements, to develop individuals and for mentor skills and experience to be utilised effectively. The selection criteria to be a mentor or mentee is not known. Frequently used criteria are 'high-potential' colleagues at the leader or manager level, entry-level colleagues needing mentors to support them in role, or colleagues newly promoted.

Training is managed via a combination of face-to-face or virtual workshops and supporting materials available online. The training covers the subjects of managing confidentiality, conflicts and developing cultural awareness to support understanding within the mentoring relationship.

Thirty-nine per cent of the respondents indicated that promoting cultural awareness is an important part of a multi-country mentoring programme, but that this is an area that could benefit from further research. They also indicated it would be helpful to have additional information and research into high-quality training and measurement of success.

Elements to foster programme success

Respondents were asked to identify elements that would be contained in a framework to foster programme success. In addition to the training, discussed within the management section, they identified four programme areas: clear communication and management plans; support systems; technology; and maintaining mentors.

Communications

Respondents indicated that having a clear communication and engagement plan is critical to the success of the programme. Communication is likely to be conducted via multiple channels such as internal colleague communications, sharing success stories from mentors and mentees where appropriate and providing updates to HR and business sponsors and stakeholders.

Communication is vital to the success of the scheme and the most important type of communication is between mentor and mentee in order for both parties to trust and respect the mentoring relationship, followed by stakeholder engagement. Thirty-two per cent of respondents deemed communication issues to be significant. With multi-country mentoring, it is likely that the mentor and mentee are from different countries and/or cultures, which can mean there may be misinterpretation, lack of understanding, or that it takes a longer period of time to establish the mentoring relationship. These issues may, in the long term, create a negative impression of the scheme, which has an impact on attracting and retaining mentors, encouraging mentees to use the scheme and sponsorship from senior management. It is expected that the mentor training will cover best practice and offer guidance on how to manage communication issues through examples, case studies, or hearing from other mentors and mentees.

Other stakeholders (i.e. the country leadership and the HR community) also require strong communication networks. They need regular updates as to the scheme, its development and success in order to be ambassadors for the scheme and to share feedback as participants.

Survey participants were asked to rate the significance of ensuring that there is sufficient inter-cultural understanding and 82% of respondents rated this as significant. This is to be expected as the success of the programme depends on the mentor having sufficient experience and exposure to cultures other than their own in order to be a mentor. Communication is vital when factoring in the programme objectives of developing cultural awareness. It is important to have guidelines to set expectations for both parties of the mentoring relationship and to ensure there is a clear, shared mutual understanding. This will support the success of the relationship by overcoming differing perceptions of the objectives of the mentoring relationship. Possible explanations for this are level of familiarity with mentoring relationships, the maturity of the participants in this kind of management style and the maturity of the organisation.

Support from the HR community and leadership

Seventy per cent of survey participants confirmed that having a consistent level of programme quality was significantly important. This programme quality is dependent upon the support of key stakeholders. Mentoring is valued and appreciated by many; however, it is not always a priority when there are competing and often conflicting demands from work and home responsibilities. Survey participants identified support from key stakeholders within the organisation as significantly important because it generates strong engagement and advocacy for the mentoring programme. Twenty-six per cent of respondents deemed HR buy-in as significantly important and 33% of respondents confirmed the same for regional leadership.

The HR community may have multiple roles, including programme management, facilitating the matching process and promoting the scheme to the rest of the organisation. Regional leaders are also viewed as key stakeholders who act as ambassadors for the programmes, often by being a mentor, or by becoming a key influencer through endorsing and publically championing the scheme. Without support from these two groups, it may be challenging for programme managers to achieve colleague engagement and buy-in.

Respondents also indicated that one of the key elements to success of the programme is building advocacy from participants, both mentors and mentees. This support seems to be dependent on a positive experience within the mentoring relationship. Alongside this, maintaining programme momentum is equally important, with 78% of survey participants rating this as significant. This is because regular mentor/mentee sessions are required to foster a strong relationship and trust and openness, and to develop a communication style between the two individuals to have successful conversations. So it appears that communication and advocacy are interrelated.

Technology

Technology to support multi-country mentoring programmes was deemed to be 'most significant' by 27% of respondents. Responses were approximately 22% each for the rating scale points of 3 and 4. This infers that respondents believe technology is important to the success of the scheme. This is expected as mentor and mentee are unlikely to be in the same location, time zone, or department. If meetings can be managed through virtual forms, e.g. video chat, calls or email, it will make it easier to maintain regular communications, which enables a successful mentoring relationship. For most individuals, a 'digital-first' approach is common for both work and personal activities (Barclays Bank plc, 2016).

Therefore, there is an expectation to have solutions where appropriate, for example to manage administrative processes, provide access to documentation and training and to facilitate contact between mentor and mentee simply and easily. Technology should not detract from the quality of the relationship, i.e. the discussion between mentor and mentee; it should support it through enabling the discussion to occur in the first place. It is likely that most mentors would recommend other resources to support a topic under discussion, e.g. books, articles or reports, which can be shared and reviewed virtually.

Recruiting and keeping mentors

Fifty-seven percent of the respondents agreed that recruiting and keeping mentors was significantly important to programme success. It was hypothesised that more significance would be attributed to keeping mentors. For mentors, it was expected that potential, perceived challenges would be mainly around time commitments. As mentors tend to be chosen by the programme facilitators, it is likely to be on that basis that they will have the necessary knowledge and experience of multi-country working. The skills to be a mentor would be enhanced by the programme training. For the mentor, the benefits would be developing their skill set, building a broader network and gaining personal satisfaction from the mentor/mentee relationship. If mentors participate in the programme on a volunteer basis, it may only be for a certain timeframe if there are conflicts with other work priorities. Since it seems likely that programme objectives need to have a strong supply of mentors to meet demand, the response from these participants indicates that this does not mean that they need to be the same group of people, but rather a pool of individuals to call upon who have the skills and experience needed.

Return on investments

A final issue addressed by the survey was to determine the degree to which organisations expected a return on their investment (ROI) from the mentoring programmes implemented. The survey authors define this as important as it is felt to be a predicator of how the mentoring programmes are perceived and valued and how much resource is allocated to the programme. Mentoring programmes can be a low-cost investment for organisations using existing resources and infrastructure to set up and manage a programme (Clutterbuck, 2014).

All survey participants were asked to rate the significance of demonstrating ROI, with 68% deeming this to be significant. The survey did not explore what ROI was deemed to be and it is assumed that this will vary; however, typical examples include: improved performance of individuals, personal development of individuals and impact on commercial performance through individual actions. Integrating a centrally managed mentoring programme into other HR and business priorities was rated as significant by 31% of the survey respondents. Interestingly, the spread of responses to this question over a 5-point scale, with 1 being the least significant and 5 being the most significant, was approximately 20% per point for the ratings of 2, 3, and 5. The first assumption is that multi-country mentoring schemes are created and launched in response either to colleague requests or an identified need or gap as multi-country working becomes the norm. It may be an activity that has emerged through informal mentor/mentee relationships and the organisation has decided to formalise the activity.

It is an area worth further investigation as it suggests a number of reasons as to how such schemes are valued within different types of organisations. An earlier question in the survey about having buy-in from HR and regional leadership shows that 50% of respondents deem this to be significant, which does not seem to tally with how such schemes are aligned to the broader HR and business priorities. Reasons may include the following: employers see multi-country mentoring as important over and above HR and business priorities and the programme is so well established that in itself it is a priority for HR and the business; employee demand is high and therefore the programme will run regardless of the HR and business priorities; or the programme runs in isolation from other activities and only when there is a clearly defined need.

SUMMARY

The purpose of this survey was to gather broad and rich insights from a wide variety of organisations as to how multi-mentoring programmes are managed and operated and the elements and strategies that respondents viewed as important in mentoring programme success. Common themes from the survey are:

- Programmes are usually centrally managed by HR, with mentor/mentee matching carried out by the core programme team
- Multi-country mentoring schemes are viewed as important within a variety of organisations as a means to develop understanding of different culture and country practices
- Sponsors for the programme tend to be from senior leadership and HR
- Key criteria to a successful mentoring relationship should include training for mentors to help them prepare and regular and frequent communication between mentor and mentee
- Internal support and advocacy for the programme from upper-level management is essential
- Communication issues should be addressed early on as they can impede the mentoring relationship
- Technology is essential to enable virtual meetings, to automate administration where possible and to create a library of resources
- Mentors may choose to participate in a formal programme for varying periods of time

Multi-country mentoring programmes should align with broader HR and business priorities; however, the survey results demonstrate that this is not always deemed to be of high significance

CONCLUSION

In addition to the previously suggested studies, we recommend that further research be conducted on how international mentoring programmes function, the elements that might foster their success and the use of ROI and feedback from mentors and mentees to assess the success of programmes. It would be interesting to understand how organisations are developing programmes through enablers such as technology to support regular and high-quality mentoring conversations. All of these elements contribute to a better quality of programme. It is also important to understand how the mentoring programme is perceived, understood and valued by the wider organisation. Finally, the issue of how ROI is considered and perceived in the development, adoption and continuation of programmes and how assessment processes may enhance this area would be helpful.

REFERENCES

Atkinson, R.D. and McKay, A.S. (2007) Digital prosperity: understanding the economic benefits of the information technology revolution. Available at SSRN 1004516. Retrieved from https://papers.ssrn.com/sol3/papers.cfm?abstract_id=1004516 (accessed 13 January, 2017).

Clutterbuck, D. and Megginson, D. (1999) *Mentoring Executives and Directors* p. 3; Butterworth – Heinneman, ISBN: 0 7506 3695.

Clutterbuck, D. (2014) Building a mentoring capability in a newly-merged multi-national company, posted on 3rd December 2014, at https://www.davidclutterbuckpartnership.com/building-a-mentoring-capability-in-a-newly-merged-multinational-company/

Cox, T. (1991) The Multicultural Organisation, *Academy of Management Executive*, 5(2), 34.

Crocitto, M.M., Sullivan, S.E. and Carraher, S.M. (2005) Global mentoring as a means of career development and knowledge creation: A learning-based framework and agenda for future research, *Career Development International*, 10(6/7), 522–535.

Kaufman, M. (2012) The Internet Revolution is the New Industrial Revolution, *Forbes/Entrepreneurs*, 5 p. posted on 5 October 2012, at http://www.forbes.com/sites/michakaufman/2012/10/05/the-internet-revolution-is-the-new-industrial-revolution/#704d36865905

Supporting the UK to become one of the most digitally savvy nations on earth, Barclays Bank plc, retrieved at https://www.home.barclays/news/2016/03/digital-revolution.html, accessed 9 March 2016.

APPENDIX 1– MULTI-COUNTRY MENTORING SURVEY

You and your organisation

1. What is your name (this allows us to track unique survey responses; your individual data will not be shared with anyone)
2. Please add a contact email address (this will be used to send you the outputs of the survey; it will not be shared with any other parties)
3. What is the name of your organisation (division if applicable)?
4. What is its sector?
5. Roughly how many employees does it have globally?
6. Roughly how many countries does it operate in?
7. Do you have part or full responsibility for international mentoring programmes? (yes/no)
8. What is your job title?
9. Are you willing to be interviewed to expand on this questionnaire? (yes/no)

Your mentoring programmes

10. Are you responding in respect of:
    - one international mentoring programme?
    - a portfolio of international mentoring programmes?

(You are encouraged to complete the survey more than once for different programmes or separately from both portfolio and single-programme perspectives.)

11 Do the following apply to your organization? (yes/no)
   - We manage our international mentoring programmes from one location
   - We manage our international mentoring programmes from several regional locations
   - We manage our international mentoring programmes country by country
   - We manage our international mentoring programmes division by division
   - We have a centralised advisory resource on mentoring to support initiatives wherever they occur
12 Mentoring strategy for your organisation
   - We have a consistent and coherent strategy for managing mentoring around the world
   - We encourage regions and countries to create their own mentoring strategies and programmes
   - Mentoring strategy is closely linked with strategies for:
     Talent management
     Diversity management
     Succession planning
     Transfer of know-how

Definition of mentoring in your organisation

13 We have a clear and consistent definition of mentoring, which we apply in all regions and cultures (yes/no)
14 We have a number of different definitions of mentoring (yes/no)
15 We have a multiplicity of mentoring programmes, with wide variations in approach (yes/no)
16 We have senior-management champions for mentoring around the world (yes/no)

About your mentoring programmes

17 We have a consistent training programme internationally for mentors (yes/no)
18 We have a consistent training programme internationally for mentees (yes/no)
19 We encourage regional and national programme managers to adjust training content to the local culture (yes/no)

20 When mentors and mentees are in different countries, training includes (yes/no)
   - Education in virtual mentoring (by telephone, email, etc.)
   - Cultural awareness
   - Other (please specify)
21 Mentoring relationships
   - Selection and matching of participants is supported by a central database
   - Selection and matching of participants is supported regionally/locally
   - We monitor the progress of mentoring relationships centrally
   - We monitor the progress of mentoring relationships regionally/locally
   - We don't monitor the progress of mentoring relationships
22 We monitor the quality and impact of mentoring programmes:
   - Always
   - Sometimes
   - Never
23 We benchmark our mentoring programmes internationally against:
   - Each other
   - Other multinational companies' programmes
   - The International Standards for Mentoring Programmes in Employment
24 Our international mentoring programmes have had a significant impact on:

   (yes/no)

   - Talent management
   - Diversity management
   - Succession planning
   - Transfer of know-how
   - Developing an international corporate culture
   - Other (please specify)
25 We train mentoring programme managers in their role (yes/no)
26 We have structures to promote sharing of mentoring good practice between mentoring programmes within the company (yes/no)
27 We support mentoring programmes with an online platform of information and processes (yes/no)
28 We support mentoring-programme participants with follow-on education (yes/no)
29 We support mentors with professional supervision (yes/no)

About multi-country mentoring

30 How significant a challenge is each of the following? (Rating scale of 1 to 5, with 1 being least significant and 5 being most significant)
   - Ensuring people in different countries have the same expectation of mentoring
   - Achieving a good and consistent level of buy-in and engagement from participants in each country
   - Achieving a good and consistent level of buy-in and engagement from leadership in each region or country
   - Achieving a good and consistent level of buy-in and engagement from the HR community
   - Recruiting mentors
   - Keeping mentors
   - Ensuring sufficient inter-cultural understanding/competence
   - Achieving a consistent level of programme quality
   - Maintaining the momentum of mentoring relationships
   - Maintaining the momentum of mentoring programmes
   - Effectiveness of matching
   - Measuring impact/demonstrating return on investment
   - Integrating mentoring with other HR and business priorities
   - Technology to support multi-country mentoring

31 Communication issues. What other challenges are you aware of?
32 Can you tell us a bit more about your programme(s), in particular:
   - Who is it aimed at?
   - How do you select and match participants?
   - How do you educate and support participants?
   - What do you do to gain buy-in from HR and line management?
   - How do you monitor outcomes?
   - How do you ensure confidentiality of mentoring conversations?
   - How do you manage potential conflicts of interest (e.g. using the mentor's knowledge of the mentee in promotion decisions)?

About your programme

33 What cross-cultural issues have arisen in your programme(s) and how have you dealt with them?
34 What have you done to address the challenges you see as most significant?
35 What are the most important lessons you have learned about multi-country mentoring?
36 Where could further research most usefully be focused?

Organizational Contexts: Aligning Individual and Organizational Outcomes

Vicki L. Baker

In their article 'Organizational Benefits of Mentoring', Wilson and Elman (1990) acknowledged the benefits of mentoring to the protégé and to the mentor, but lamented that the 'benefits that accrue to the organization that encourages mentoring within its ranks are referred to less often' (p. 88). Twenty-five years later, the organizational context and benefits of mentoring remain under-studied despite the proliferation of organizations in business, higher education, healthcare, and not-for-profit sectors relying on formal mentoring programs as a means of attracting and retaining a diverse, talented workforce.

In my prior work (Baker, 2015), I argued that mentoring scholars and practitioners need to deliberately examine the connection between individual and organizational outcomes to inform the next generation of mentoring research and practice. Not only would such an approach allow for a more specific identification and examination of the outcomes that can be achieved at these two levels, but it would provide a framework with which to develop, implement, and assess the effectiveness of such efforts.

The focus of this chapter is on the organizational contexts in which mentoring occurs, with a particular focus on formal mentoring programs. I provide an overview of the formal mentoring literature, followed by a discussion of the human resource framework, *alignment*, which I offer as a tool that individuals and organizations can use to achieve positive outcomes at both the individual and organizational levels. Such a framework can provide insights into the development and assessment of formal mentoring programs. I then illustrate how the alignment framework informed the development of a pilot formal mentoring program at Shape Corporation, in Grand Haven, Michigan.

FORMAL MENTORING PROGRAMS: CONTEXTS, BENEFITS, DRAWBACKS, AND BEST PRACTICES

In the following section I provide an overview of the literature on formal mentoring programs. I organize this review by focusing on five primary areas: (a) organizational purposes of mentoring programs, (b) contexts in which formal mentoring occurs, (c) benefits of formal mentoring programs, (d) drawbacks of formal mentoring programs, and (e) effective practices. To begin, I include a working definition of formal mentoring (Finkelstein and Poteet, 2007) to create a common language within this chapter, 'A formal mentoring program occurs when an organization officially supports and sanctions mentoring relationships. In these programs, organizations play a role in facilitating mentoring relationships by providing some level of structure, guidelines, policies, and assistance for starting, maintaining, and ending mentor–protégé relationships' (p. 345).

Purposes

Organizations rely on formal mentoring programs to support a variety of purposes (and corresponding outcomes). One of the primary purposes of workplace mentoring that has received a great deal of attention in the literature is employee and career development (Ehrich et al., 2004; Gaskill, 1993; Hegstad, 1999). Mentoring programs that are designed to support the overall development of the protégé can support growth and engagement, decrease negative work behaviors such as absenteeism and turnover, and help support future career growth.

Another important purpose for workplace mentoring is leadership development (Dziczkowski, 2013). Such efforts entail the identification of high potentials with the goal of supporting their leadership development, including business acumen, leadership skills, and overall learning for the intended role(s) they are to assume in their respective organization (Day, 2001). Initiatives that target high potentials are an effective human resource strategy, which garners personal attention and helps to nurture internal talent. Such efforts also allow individuals to advance quickly in an organization when focusing on skill development (Groves, 2007).

Diversity mentoring is also an important purpose of organizational mentoring initiatives. Research shows that a diverse workforce is more innovative and creative (Clutterbuck and Ragins, 2002; Megginson, 2006), and such efforts support a greater cultural awareness by organizational employees and help to attract and retain a more diverse workforce.

Contexts

Mentoring has proven to be a high-impact practice, when all parties take responsibility for the relationship. Such programs have been studied in various contexts with the majority of those practices (or at least published research) occurring in the fields of **business**, **higher education**, and **healthcare**.

Business

The business sector has long realized the importance of mentoring as a critical human resource development tool. In his article, Grossman (2012) shared an alarming statistic from a 2010 Corporate Leadership Council of the Corporate Executive Board survey, in which 880 high potential employees were surveyed. Over 25% of these high potential employees noted their intent to leave their current employer within 12 months, with 64% noting that their current employment experiences had little impact on their development. Grossman offered 14 ways to retain valued employees, which included more formalized mentoring experiences that cover developing leader attributes and aligning individual and company needs.

Businesses are also not just engaging in the traditional mentoring where a more senior colleague is paired with a junior colleague, which characterizes a top-down approach to career development. Leslie Kwoh (2011) revealed that the notion of reverse mentoring is breaking into the mainstream in tech and advertising firms:

> The idea is that managers can learn a thing or two about life outside the corner office. But companies say another outcome is reduced turnover among younger employees, who not only gain a sense of purpose, but also a rare glimpse into the world of management and access to top-level brass. (online, para 3)

Younger employees are 'schooling' senior executives in the areas of technology, social media, and the latest workplace trends. The reverse mentoring practice was originally championed by Jack Welch at GE. Fast-forward to today, and that practice is even more prevalent in organizations including Facebook and Twitter. Such efforts are also more prevalent in the United Kingdom and are associated with a variety of diversity objectives, one being the creation of a more diverse cabinet office. Two-way mentoring in the UK is characterized as more of a two-way exchange compared with the conceptualization in the United States.

Higher education

Mentoring research and practice in higher education predominantly focuses on two areas – faculty to student mentoring (undergraduate and graduate) and faculty member to faculty member. Undergraduate students who are mentored are more likely to persist and stay in college, see improvements in academic performance, experience a greater overall satisfaction related to college, and be more successfully socialized into a disciplinary community (Crisp and Cruz, 2009). The faculty mentor who supports the student also experiences important outcomes such as career enrichment, intrinsic rewards witnessing someone else's development, and support for research and teaching (Jacobi, 1991; Lopatto, 2003). At the graduate student levels, more intense relationships are likely to form between a student and programmatic faculty members. Some faculty may turn into mentors or other developmental relationships. While formal mentoring can, and does, occur as a result of academic departments, mentorships in graduate education happen more organically and are driven by the student and faculty members. In fact, research at the graduate student level revealed that perceptions of the ideal mentor are influenced to some extent by major socio-cultural factors, but individual differences appear to be the primary driver (Rose, 2005).

Faculty-to-faculty mentoring research and practices focus almost exclusively at the early career faculty stage. Such relationships serve as important socializing agents for early career faculty (Cawyer et al., 2002) and help manage the challenges associated with the tenure and promotion process (Austin and Rice, 1998). More recently, scholars and practitioners have encouraged faculty members to create networks of support relationships given the varied and sometimes conflicting challenges they face early in their career as they work to earn tenure (Darwin and Palmer, 2009; De Janasz and Sullivan, 2004). Such a network of supportive relationships can provide a greater diversity of access to social capital and career as well as psychosocial support.

Healthcare

In an article published in the *Healthcare Executive*, Hollister (2000) noted the importance of role models and leadership development. Such support, according to Hollister, is of particular importance in healthcare given the large numbers of managers opting to leave the industry. Hollister suggested mentoring as a means of providing much-needed development and support for the mentor and protégé. Others argue for the importance of mentoring to current and aspiring physicians. Organizations including the American College of Physicians (ACP) offer a formal mentoring program in which rising physicians can seek the support of a veteran physician mentor. Interested protégés and mentors can sign up to receive support ranging from mock residency interviews to networking opportunities. Other noteworthy programs include Carolina Covenant, in which low-income aspiring healthcare professionals receive mentorship from area physicians, and Children's Hospital of Los Angeles, which provides mentoring opportunities for high school students on lab techniques or newly graduated nurses receive mentorship from veteran nurses.

Benefits

Given the rise of formal mentoring programs in various organizational contexts, both domestically and abroad, more researchers and practitioners are examining such forms of support to determine if formal mentoring programs are worth the allotted resources, and researchers are finding that they are (Ensher and Murphy, 2011). When reviewing the benefits of formal mentoring programs, however, researchers once again examine them from the individual perspective by noting critical outcomes realized by the protégé and/or the mentor. The most commonly cited benefits to the protégé include organizational commitment, career involvement, and job satisfaction (Allen et al., 2004; Chun et al., 2012; Eby and Lockwood, 2005). Mentor-specific outcomes include increased self-esteem, professional and personal rejuvenation, and leadership and management development (Haggard et al., 2011). Trust and shared values, however, are important foundational elements necessary for both protégés and mentors (Wang et al., 2010).

Furthermore, based on a review of the literature, many organizations are focusing their formal mentoring efforts on targeted populations of employees as a means of diversifying and supporting key organizational members. For example, Egan and Rosser (2004) sought to study the impact of high and low facilitation of formal mentoring programs on three career outcomes for women in the healthcare field. Those outcomes were job satisfaction, organizational commitment, and job performance. Findings revealed increases on all three career outcomes for the females in both the high- and low-facilitated formal mentoring programs and even more so for those females in the highly facilitated mentoring programs. Gant and Houston-Philpot (2006) examined the outcomes of a formal mentoring pilot program for women at Dow Chemical Corporation to enhance career progress and retention for female engineers. This same pilot program was replicated in Kentucky at two manufacturing locations. The goals of the pilot mentoring program included countering the influences of negative mentoring, skill enhancement, and the promotion of mentoring relationships. All goals were achieved and female participants felt their expectations were met or exceeded as a result of their participation.

Very few studies, however, account for the organizational perspective when discussing the benefits (or drawbacks) of formal mentoring programs. Even fewer make the connection between individual- and organizational-level outcomes. One of the few studies I was able to find includes the work of Allen, Smith, Mael, O'Shea, and Eby (2009). They examined the relationship between the proportions of individuals mentored within an organization, and organization-level benefits, including organizational performance and citizenship behaviors. Study results revealed support for organizational-level job satisfaction, citizenship behaviors, and learning, to overall organizational performance: 'Our findings indicate that considering the organizational level of analysis in mentoring research has the potential to improve our understanding of how and why mentoring relates to organizational performance' (p. 1123). However, it is important to note that one reason for the lack of research in this area is due to the complexity associated with measuring organizational outcomes and identifying whether the outcomes of interest are at the team/group, functional, or organizational

Drawbacks

While a great deal of research on formal mentoring programs focuses on the benefits of such efforts, scholars have also highlighted the drawbacks of formal mentoring programs. Once again, however, that focus is almost predominantly at the individual level (e.g. protégé or mentor), with little research that examines drawbacks from the organizational perspective.

When considering the perspective of the protégé, such drawbacks may include unrealistic expectations (Allen et al., 2006a; Blake-Beard, 2001; Eby and Allen, 2002; Eby and Lockwood, 2005), overall negative experiences (Eby et al., 2000), and role conflict with an existing supervisor or boss (Murray and Owen, 1991). Mentors also report negative assessments as a result of their participation in formal mentoring programs. Those assessments include loss of reputation (Ragins and Scandura, 1999), challenging protégé assignments (Eby and McManus, 2004), too much of a time commitment (Eby et al., 2008), and overall negative experiences when there is a lack of organizational and management support for the mentoring program (Parise and Forret, 2008). It is important to note that research supports the claim that bad mentoring experiences outweigh positive experiences regarding intent to stay in a mentoring relationship (Eby et al., 2010). Lastly, drawbacks for the organization also exist and include lack of overall support to create a formal mentoring program, logistical and coordination challenges, and sustainability, among other concerns (Douglas and McCauley, 1999; Ehrich et al., 2004).

There is also a related literature that compares the effectiveness and value of formal versus informal mentoring relationships. For example, Ragins and Cotton (1999) found that protégés of informal mentors said they viewed mentors as more effective and they experienced greater compensation as compared with their formally mentored peers. Chao, Walz, and Gardner (1992) also found that informally mentored individuals reported greater career-related support from their mentors, higher salaries, and overall more favorable outcomes as compared with those in formal mentorships. Despite the possible drawbacks and differences in outcomes achieved for formal versus informal mentorships, formal mentoring programs can be effective when guidelines and a working structure are developed to support the program. I address these features in the next section.

EFFECTIVE PRACTICES OF FORMAL MENTORING PROGRAMS

While formal mentoring programs vary in terms of goals, length, levels of participation, and purpose, researchers and practitioners have revealed best practices that can (and should) serve as the foundation with which to build an effective formal mentoring program, regardless of organizational context (please refer to Chapter 12 in this book, Design of Effective Mentoring Programmes, by Lis Merrick). When such foundational elements are present, overall effectiveness and protégé and mentor satisfaction increases.

In their chapter, Finkelstein and Poteet (2007) revealed the effective practices they identified from a review of the literature. First and foremost was the need for a visible organizational commitment to the mentoring program starting at the executive leadership level. Such a commitment was a key contributor to the success of exemplary mentoring programs in Fortune 500 companies (Hegstad and Wentling, 2004). A commitment is present and illustrated in a variety of ways including adequate resources to support the program, leadership serving as possible mentors, including recognition for participation in organizational reward structures, and accountability for both mentors and protégés related to their participation.

Second, Finkelstein and Poteet (2007) noted the importance of explicit program objectives and intended outcomes. Such factors will influence the structure of the program, help provide guidance as to who is (or should be) eligible for participation, and enable key leaders to determine the types and amount of resources needed to support the program. Such clarity also supports better communication and guidance to the protégé and mentor in terms of overall expectations and behaviors (Allen et al., 2006b).

Participant selection was the third component of formal mentoring programs examined by Finkelstein and Poteet (2007). Actual practice varies by organization – some formal mentoring programs allow for an *open call* in which individuals self-select (protégés and mentors), while other programs seek nominations for individuals who will most benefit through participation (protégés and mentors). Additionally, such programs have been used as important succession planning tools to prepare those individuals identified to assume new leadership positions within an organization (Groves, 2007). Regardless of the approach an organization pursues when selecting individuals to participate in a formal mentoring program, the primary driver should be the objectives and intended outcomes of the program.

The fourth best practice noted by Finkelstein and Poteet (2007) related to participant (and participation) guidelines. Such explicit details provide much needed guidance about program goals, objectives, and intended outcomes as well as expected behaviors of protégés and mentors. Ideas addressed as part of participant guidelines can (and should) include details about (a) the matching process with input from the protégé and mentor (e.g. why an individual was selected, critical matching characteristics, etc.), (b) orientation and training for both the protégé and mentor, (c) the overall structure of the relationship (e.g. setting expectations about the degree and extent of engagement in the mentorship for the protégé *and* mentor), and (d) the duration of the mentorship (as it relates to the formal mentoring program).

The fifth and final guideline addressed the importance of monitoring and evaluation (Finkelstein and Poteet, 2007). Monitoring is a process whereby those responsible for the administration of the formal mentoring program engage in regular 'check ins' with the mentoring pairs. Monitoring allows program administrators to identify issues within the mentorship as well as identify those that are successful as a means of recreating such effectiveness in other dyads (Gaskill, 1993; Ragins et al., 2000). While monitoring allows program administrators to identify challenges (and positive outcomes) in process, program evaluation is still a necessary tool and effective practice to ensuring a high-quality formal mentoring program from start to finish. Some organizations engage in evaluation upon the completion of a formal mentoring program, while others engage in formal evaluation at the mid-point and completion points of the program (Baugh and Fagenson-Eland, 2007).

Formal mentoring programs that account for the above components serve as strong models displaying how an organization can effectively support the human resources of the organization. Such programs often result in strong outcomes at the individual level (e.g. for the protégé and mentor), with probable outcomes achieved at the organizational level such as reduced turnover and absenteeism. Yet, attention to the connection between individual and organizational level outcomes – at the planning stages of development through implementation and evaluation – is often neglected, given we lack a framework to serve as a tool that supports such consideration. In the following section, I will provide an overview of the human resource framework of alignment to serve such a purpose.

ALIGNMENT: A HUMAN RESOURCES FRAMEWORK

Organizations expend a great deal of energy and resources on developing, supporting, and evaluating formal mentoring programs. And researchers have revealed that such programs, when meeting the effective practices criteria noted above, result in professional (and personal) gains for the participating protégés and mentors. Yet, Friday and Friday (2002) noted an important observation: 'Most [organizations] have not strategically aligned their mentoring programs with their long-term objectives and strategic positioning of their organizations … therefore, ideally, a company that seeks to maximize the potential benefits of mentoring should create a corporate level mentoring strategy prior to implementing a formal mentoring program' (p. 152).

Such a strategy will align the organization's standardized mentoring process (and corresponding formal mentoring program) with the organization's long-term, strategic goals and vision, thereby contributing to the long-term effectiveness of the mentoring program and overall competitive advantage of the organization.

One tool that I proposed in my prior work (Baker, 2015) to support the connection between individual- and organizational-level outcomes is the human resources framework of *alignment* proposed by Gratton and Truss (2003). Alignment is a three-dimensional people strategy that allows for a more fluid, deliberate, and strategic connection among micro, macro, and implementation considerations. When human resource policies and practices support people strategies (e.g. formal mentoring programs) and those policies and practices complement organizational goals and objectives, a greater competitive advantage is achieved.

Vertical alignment, the first dimension of the alignment framework, is a macro-level consideration that focuses on the connection between an organization's people strategy and business goals. Given the changing career landscape, a one-size-fits-all people strategy is antiquated in today's professional environment. As such, people strategies should vary based on organizational circumstances and must align with organizational goals and aims. This point rests on one critical assumption – the presence of a clear direction and goals at the organizational (i.e. business goals) and human resource (i.e. people strategy) levels: 'A strong linkage is needed between the overall vision of the organization that is held in the minds of the senior executives and the aims, objectives, and underlying philosophy of the organization's approach to managing people' (p. 75).

The second dimension of the alignment framework is *horizontal* alignment. A micro-level consideration, horizontal alignment accounts for the degree to which personnel policies support (or hinder) individual performance. *Policy*, not practice, is at the core of horizontal alignment, given the need for organizations to have consistent, clearly articulated human resource policies, which relate to one another within an organizational context. The focus on policy highlights the importance of developing and articulating clear HR policies and corresponding messages to employees. Horizontal alignment also provides insights into connections between and among other developmental interventions such as coaching. Alignment allows for a more deliberate integration of such supports.

The third, and final, dimension of the alignment framework is *implementation* – the action component of the framework. Implementation includes both the employee experience, as related to HR policies and behaviors, and the behaviors and attitudes of managers and supervisors. In other words, all employees must be engaged in the high-impact practice and support the achievement of individual- and organizational-level outcomes in order for employee development strategies, such as formal mentoring programs, to result in the intended gains.

I would be remiss in my discussion of alignment if I did not at least briefly discuss the notion of disalignment. While the ideas presented in this chapter, particularly in the case study that follows, support the notion of agreement between the organizational goals and values with those of the mentors and protégés, there are instances when there is a disconnect or disalignment between these two constituents. For example, an organization's primary goal may be career development as a retention tool; however, the participating protégé may engage in formal mentoring with the goal of using the skill development to leverage a position with a new organization.

In the following section I provide an example of a pilot formal mentoring program that was developed and implemented at Shape Corporation in Grand Haven, Michigan. I, along with Doug Peterson (Vice President of Human Resources), developed a formal mentoring program using the alignment framework as a tool. Details are provided below.

SHAPE CORPORATION: A PILOT MENTORING PROGRAM

In 1974 five gentlemen in the Midwest founded a company housed in a rented building behind a trucking company. The first part they made was for a toolbox and their first big order was shelving for the office furniture industry. Fast-forward to 2015 and this business is now a global corporation with four sister companies and over 3,200 employees worldwide. Shape Corporation is a full-service supplier engaged in the design, engineering, testing, and manufacturing of metal and plastic solutions primarily in the automotive industry in North America, Europe, and Asia. Shape Corporation is recognized globally as a pioneer and innovator in advanced custom roll forming and injection molding that can be found in automotive, office furniture, medical, and agricultural uses. In 2013, global sales were between $500–510 million with projected global sales of $1 billion by 2020. Maintaining that kind of growth, while still maintaining the core company values and a 'family business feel' is every founder's dream. Yet, their desire to still have that 'family feel' that the company was founded on has been a challenge as they experience the domestic to global growing pains.

I began working with Shape Corporation in early 2014 as part of the Michigan Colleges Alliance (MCA)[1] in which a group of faculty members were assembled to help develop content for what was to become the Global Leadership Development Program (GLDP). This was Doug Peterson's idea in response to an imminent challenge Shape is soon to face. When Shape is primed to hit the billion dollar sales mark, the majority of the leadership council members (LC) will be retiring, leaving a void in terms of institutional memory and a collective of 175 years of experience and knowledge. Many members of the LC spent their careers at Shape. Doug was seeking to create a custom Shape program designed to help develop the next generation of leaders. With the blessing of the LC, the faculty team from the MCA embarked on the inaugural GLDP, with a group of 23 high potentials, which is currently underway.

As part of this work, Doug sought my advice regarding the Shape Corporate mentoring program that was in progress. While a helpful human resource support for Shape employees, the program, upon review, was more of a coaching program in my opinion, rather than a true mentoring program. Furthermore, Shape was missing a critical opportunity to link a formal mentoring program to their core values and goals, thus resulting in greater organizational *and* individual outcomes. Therefore, we developed the pilot mentoring program using the alignment framework.

Vertical alignment

I return to the components that make up vertical alignment, which are the organization's people strategy and business goals.

Step 1: Business goals

My first question to Doug was, 'why have a mentoring program?' To which Doug responded, 'to reinvigorate the Shape family culture'. This was of critical import to the LC members, given that this fundamental and founding value was challenging to maintain, as a result of the growth Shape was and is currently experiencing in a relatively short period of time.

I then prompted Doug to think about how a mentoring program could help facilitate the achievement of this larger goal as well as smaller, short-term goals at the *organizational level* that supported the larger goal of reinvigorating the Shape Family culture. At the onset of this discussion and program development, we kept our focus on the organizational level to ensure that a formal mentoring program was achieving what was intended, and that such outcomes would result in visible gains. Some short-term goals were to: (a) create more opportunities for employees and supervisors to engage in career growth discussions outside of the traditional performance appraisal periods, (b) provide additional human resources for Shape employees (e.g. to have non-direct supervisor supports), (c) design built-in opportunities for both protégés and mentors to enhance current skill sets, which would result in increased knowledge and expertise to support their immediate business units and the company at large, and (d) to develop an overall strategy to grow their talent, of which the mentoring program would be a component. Additionally, such a program, if developed and implemented correctly, could serve as an important recruitment and retention tool, which was critical for Shape given they are in direct competition with other large manufacturers for top talent.

Step 2: People strategy

We then turned our attention to *individual-level* outcomes or the people strategy currently employed at Shape. This led us to think about what the Shape people strategy is and how it could be enhanced with the inclusion of a formal mentoring program. I encouraged Doug to think about a 'tailored' mentoring program that would include some standardization such as how mentorship assignments were made, or the frequency and length of the meetings. In addition, to achieve a more custom formal mentoring program, we created goals, structures, and outcomes on a per-employee group level that we believed would meet employees' needs, positional realities, and career paths (e.g. managerial, shop floor, administration, etc.). This led us to decide that the pilot mentoring program needed to pull protégés and mentors from various organizational levels and divisions as a means of helping Shape develop a formal mentoring program that had an impact throughout the organization *and* that was visible and available to all employees as the formal program progressed.

Horizontal alignment

Step 3: Connecting people policies

Horizontal alignment focuses on policy, not practice, and is based on the assumption that an organization has consistent, clearly articulated human resource policies that relate to one another within an organizational context. I asked Doug to think about and discuss with me the key personnel policies that could be enhanced and complemented by the inclusion of a formal mentoring program. Some of the obvious were performance appraisal policies and the coaching program in process. I also asked if, or to what extent, a formal mentoring program would contradict, appear redundant, or result in a perceived burden to employees given the presence of an already existing strong employee development strategy. Between Doug and myself, we were thoughtful and deliberate about how, and in what ways, a formal mentoring program would enrich Shape's employee development strategy and we prepared talking points that would make clear those connections (in writing, and in practice) as we worked through the key components of the formal mentoring program, which I note below.

Step 4: The result

While implementation is the third component of alignment, I first share with you the end result of our efforts, which provide details about what the program looks like, and then I will share details about the implementation efforts. After working through the components and key considerations of vertical and horizontal alignment, we developed the following:

- A year-long pilot formal mentoring program,
- We would accept 10 mentoring dyads across various employee and divisional levels,
- We would require joint monthly meetings, that were approximately 1 hour in length (but allow dyads to meet more frequently if deemed appropriate or necessary),
- After each meeting, a joint 1-page summary of the meeting was required; the summary needed to include goals and action steps for the next month, quarter, etc.,
- We would build in a 6-month or mid-point check-in with mentors and protégés to determine how the program was progressing. We would also assess the program at the end of the year.

Additionally, we agreed that interested protégés would apply to participate in the pilot program, and our hope was that selection and participation would bring a level of prestige for the high-performing employees within Shape. We also limited the pilot program to 10 mentoring dyads to ensure a successful launch, with the hopes of expanding the program in the future. Given our desire to monitor the program closely and not fail due to overextending resources, we agreed 10 dyads was manageable, but expansive enough to represent divisional and positional levels in the organization.

We created a short mentoring application in which we asked interested protégés to discuss their career goals, to think about how a mentoring program might support those goals, to identify a possible mentor(s) who they felt could support their efforts, and to identify any possible resources that might be needed at the point of completing the application to ensure a successful start. We assembled a steering committee consisting of individuals across the Shape organization, who represented various levels of management and functional areas, to review the applications, to select candidates, and to think about appropriate mentor assignments based on the intended goals outlined by protégés in the application. I, as a non-Shape person, was included on the steering committee to ensure that all participants would have at least one person that was a resource outside of Shape in the instance there was a challenging situation and a person wanted to remain anonymous. Doug then reached out to mentors to invite them to participate.

IMPLEMENTATION

Training and establishing the mentorships

To kick off the formal mentoring program, a training session was scheduled. That session included time in which both mentors and protégés were present together. Individuals were informed about the big picture of Shape's employee development strategy, why and in what ways a formal mentoring program supported those efforts, and the goals of the mentoring program at the organizational level. Individuals were introduced to members of the Steering Committee and informed about their selection into the program. Details about the mentoring pilot logistics and broad expectations were communicated (e.g. frequency of meetings, details about formal monthly reports, etc.), and participants were also informed about available monetary resources to support any additional training (e.g. to attend seminars) that would be needed to achieve individual goals. We also consistently informed protégés and mentors that the mentoring program was the primary responsibility of the protégés. We expected them to drive the communication with mentors, to initiate scheduling of meetings, develop first drafts of monthly reports, and to assess achievement of interim goals.

We also felt it important to host separate sessions for protégés and mentors to discuss expectations of participation in the program and to finalize the needs assessment activity that was requested upon their selection into the program. For protégés specifically, we asked them to think about and answer the following questions: In what area(s) do I need support? What are my expectations from this working relationship? What is my work/collaboration style? What kinds of support do I expect from my mentor? What value added do I bring to the relationship? What are my goals for the mentorship? How will I ensure that the goals are being achieved?

Protégés were encouraged to develop interim goals and other performance metrics as a way of demonstrating personal agency over the process. To conclude the protégé session, I asked them to discuss any possible concerns, anticipated challenges, or any other issues that might be on the forefront of their minds as they embarked in this year-long pilot program. It is important to note that Doug left the room at this time, which I believe is an important and symbolic gesture. Our sincere hope was, and is, to create a program in which individuals feel their voices and concerns are heard. Throughout the pilot (and beyond) we want the mentorships to result in open and honest communication, but know that such trust and respect takes time to develop. Therefore, both protégés and mentors need an outlet or resource that was perceived to not be a direct threat to their advancement within Shape. Therefore, I served that role and continue to do so.

Upon completion of the protégé training session we conducted a training session with mentors. We provided additional details about their expectations for engaging in the program. To that end, we asked them to think about and write down responses to the following questions: (a) What kind(s) of support are you able/willing to provide? (b) What is your preferred method of contact? (c) How often (and for how long) are you willing to meet? (d) What is your work style/approach to collaboration? (e) What skills can you develop as a result of serving as a mentor? and (f) How does your participation in the mentoring program support you/your career goals? Rather than create a program in which the protégé is the only explicit benefactor, we wanted to make it clear that mentor selection and participation was also a testament to the skills, knowledge, and expertise at the managerial and upper leadership levels within Shape. Participation could also support mentors' skill enhancement and be used as an opportunity outside of performance appraisal time to assess areas of need and opportunities for growth (and provide an explicit opportunity to address needs). As with the protégé training session, I asked mentors to discuss any reservations, concerns, or perceived challenges related to their participation or the overall program.

In the joint session, as well as individual sessions, individuals were told that we expected them to meet within two weeks of the training, and to review the responses to the needs assessment questions. Our hope in requiring this meeting and establishing guidelines for this initial meeting was that the dyads would begin to develop 'working rules' for the relationship until more rapport and trust could be established. We also encouraged them to collaboratively pull from the information contained in the individual needs assessments to develop long-term and short-term goals for the mentorship as well as to define what success looked like in the context of this mentorship. We required each mentorship to submit a 1-page overview of the outcomes of this meeting and to outline their action plan for the year-long program. I, along with members of the Steering Committee, reviewed those submissions.

Monitoring and evaluation

Doug and I scheduled a mid-point check-in with protégés and mentors to assess how the mentorship program was progressing. We did not hold a joint session at the mid-point; rather, we held hour-long sessions with the protégés and mentors separately. Once again, Doug was not present at the protégé meeting, and instead I moderated the discussion and took notes. Overall, the protégés were pleased with the program, but did offer insights into how the program could be improved (e.g. developing some Shape-specific best practices) and what was needed for the duration of their time in the program. They suggested that more frequent meetings should happen early in the program to build more momentum and trust early. Monthly meetings did not allow for that to happen as quickly as necessary at the start, given the length of the program. As a result, many protégés requested to extend the length of the program to compensate for the early 'growing pains' that occur at the start of any new relationship. Protégés also felt it important to meet with mentors outside of the Shape confines to develop trust and feel more comfortable. Some protégés also suggested their mentors needed better training on how to be a mentor. While the mentors were meeting the required expectations, some protégés felt the interactions were too mechanical rather than organic. Protégés sought a greater investment from mentors and suggested mentors also create goals for the relationship. I concluded the session by asking the protégés to discuss any needed supports moving forward or feedback that I could share with Doug beyond what was discussed. I ended the session by suggesting that they, along with their mentors, review the goals established at the beginning of the mentorship to determine if those are still the right goals and, if yes, progress to goal achievement; if no, to take time at the next meeting to re-establish goals jointly for the remainder of the program and beyond. As part of that process, they were encouraged to identify performance metrics that would allow the dyads to measure success (as defined by the mentor and protégé).

I followed a similar format with the mentors. I first asked how the program was progressing from their perspective. The biggest concern communicated was the fear that the objectives established between the pairs at the start of the program might be 'too weak'. The mentors wanted to be sure that the goals were challenging while achievable, and met the needs of the protégés. Yet, they wanted to ensure those goals would also result in visible outcomes at the business unit and organizational levels. Mentors also shared experiential stories with me regarding what they thought their protégé would do, and they either did or did not follow through. Once the mentors shared their thinking, I communicated the feedback in a theme format, from the protégés. I used that as an opportunity to provide more training to the mentors about how to engage with and communicate with protégés. For example, I told them that if they thought a protégé should behave in a certain way or they expected a protégé to ask a certain question but they did not, that was an opportunity for the mentor to explain what he/she expected to happen and what the protégé could learn from that dialogue. I also suggested, similar to what was communicated with protégés, a formal review of the goals and objectives established at the beginning to determine if the goals were appropriate or not and to adjust accordingly; to redefine what success looked like in the context of the mentorship.

I typed up the notes in a summary format from both sessions and shared with Doug. He then communicated the feedback with members of the Steering Committee. At that time, adjustments and action steps related to the feedback were taken (e.g. for the protégés who requested additional time, that was granted with the permission of the mentor). Other feedback shared will inform revisions to the next iteration of the formal mentoring program. The final assessment will be scheduled for October, 2015, including an evaluation similar to the training session that was scheduled at the start of the pilot program. As part of that program, we will host a joint session and then individual sessions with protégés and mentors. Each dyad will provide an assessment of their own progress, give feedback on the overall experience, and talk about how their participation benefitted their growth and Shape as a company.

CONCLUSION

Mentoring can be an important organizational tool to support employee development for protégés and mentors. In this chapter, I argue that mentoring can also provide a critical competitive advantage for organizations, yet this consideration is often neglected in research and practice. Alignment, as a framework, can support the development of a more comprehensive and strategic organizational and individual effort given the macro, micro, and implementation considerations. As evidenced in the case study example of Shape Corporation, alignment allows for a review and accounting of the right questions and of current and needed resources, and supports the monitoring and evaluations processes. For the organizations that can create such synergies through their mentoring initiatives, greater outcomes at all levels can be achieved.

Note

1. A group of 15 independent colleges and universities in the state of Michigan.

REFERENCES

Allen, T. D., Eby, L. T., and Lentz, E. (2006a). The relationship between formal mentoring program characteristics and perceived program effectiveness. *Personnel Psychology*, *59*(1), 125–153.

Allen, T. D., Eby, L. T., and Lentz, E. (2006b). Mentorship behaviors and mentorship quality associated with formal mentoring programs: Closing the gap between research and practice. *Journal of Applied Psychology*, *91*(3), 567.

Allen, T. D., Eby, L. T., Poteet, M. L., Lentz, E., and Lima, L. (2004). Career benefits associated with mentoring for proteges: A meta-analysis. *Journal of Applied Psychology*, *89*(1), 127.

Allen, T. D., Smith, M. A., Mael, F. A., O'Shea, P. G., and Eby, L. T. (2009). Organization-level mentoring and organizational performance within substance abuse centers. *Journal of Management*, *35*, 1113–1128.

Austin, A. E., and Rice, R. E. (1998). Making tenure viable: Listening to early career faculty. *American Behavioral Scientist*, *41*(5), 736–754.

Baker, V. L. (2015). People strategy in human resources: Lessons for mentoring in higher education. *Mentoring and Tutoring: Partnership in Learning*, *23*(1), 6–18.

Baugh, S. G., and Fagenson-Eland, E. A. (2007). Formal mentoring programs: A 'poor cousin' to informal relationships? In B. R. Ragins and K. E. Kram (Eds.), *The handbook of mentoring at work: Theory, research, and practice* (pp. 249–272). Los Angeles, CA: Sage.

Blake-Beard, S. D. (2001). Taking a hard look at formal mentoring programs: A consideration of potential challenges facing women. *Journal of Management Development*, *20*(4), 331–345.

Cawyer, C. S., Simonds, C., and Davis, S. (2002). Mentoring to facilitate socialization: The case of the new faculty member. *International Journal of Qualitative Studies in Education*, *15*(2), 225–242.

Chao, G. T., Walz, P., and Gardner, P. D. (1992). Formal and informal mentorships: A comparison on mentoring functions and contrast with nonmentored counterparts. *Personnel Psychology*, *45*(3), 619–636.

Chun, J. U., Sosik, J. J., and Yun, N. Y. (2012). A longitudinal study of mentor and protégé outcomes in formal mentoring relationships. *Journal of Organizational Behavior*, *33*(8), 1071–1094.

Clutterbuck, D., and Ragins, B. R. (2002). *Mentoring and diversity: An international perspective*. Boston, MA: Butterworth Heinemann.

Crisp, G., and Cruz, I. (2009). Mentoring college students: A critical review of the literature between 1990 and 2007. *Research in Higher Education*, *50*(6), 525–545.

Darwin, A., and Palmer, E. (2009). Mentoring circles in higher education. *Higher Education Research and Development*, *28*(2), 125–136.

Day, D. V. (2001). Leadership development: A review in context. *The Leadership Quarterly*, *11*(4), 581–613.

De Janasz, S. C., and Sullivan, S. E. (2004). Multiple mentoring in academe: Developing the professorial network. *Journal of Vocational Behavior*, *64*(2), 263–283.

Douglas, C. A., and McCauley, C. D. (1999). Formal developmental relationships: A survey of organizational practices. *Human Resource Development Quarterly*, *10*(3), 203–220.

Dziczkowski, J. (2013). Mentoring and leadership development. *The Educational Forum*, *77*(3), 351–360.

Eby, L. T., and Allen, T. D. (2002). Further investigation of protégés' negative mentoring experiences patterns and outcomes. *Group and Organization Management*, *27*(4), 456–479.

Eby, L. T., Butts, M. M., Durley, J., and Ragins, B. R. (2010). Are bad experiences stronger than good ones in mentoring relationships? Evidence from the protégé and mentor perspective. *Journal of Vocational Behavior*, *77*(1), 81–92.

Eby, L. T., Durley, J. R., Evans, S. C., and Ragins, B. R. (2008). Mentors' perceptions of negative mentoring experiences: Scale development and nomological validation. *Journal of Applied Psychology*, *93*(2), 358.

Eby, L. T., and Lockwood, A. (2005). Protégés' and mentors' reactions to participating in formal mentoring programs: A qualitative investigation. *Journal of Vocational Behavior*, *67*(3), 441–458.

Eby, L. T., and McManus, S. E. (2004). The protégé's role in negative mentoring experiences. *Journal of Vocational Behavior*, *65*(2), 255–275.

Eby, L. T., McManus, S. E., Simon, S. A., and Russell, J. E. (2000). The protégé's perspective regarding negative mentoring experiences: The development of a taxonomy. *Journal of Vocational Behavior*, *57*(1), 1–21.

Egan, T. M., and Rosser, M. H. (2004, March). Do formal mentoring programs matter? A longitudinal randomized experimental study of women healthcare workers. In *Proceedings of the 2004 Academy of Human Resource Development Conference* (pp. 226–233).

Ehrich, L. C., Hansford, B., and Tennent, L. (2004). Formal mentoring programs in education and other professions: A review of the literature. *Educational Administration Quarterly*, *40*(4), 518–540.

Ensher, E. A., and Murphy, S. E. (2011). *Power mentoring: How successful mentors and protégés get the most out of their relationships*. San Francisco, CA: Jossey-Bass.

Finkelstein, L. M., and Poteet, M. L. (2007). Best practices in formal mentoring programs in organizations. In T. Allen and L. Eby (Eds.), *The Blackwell handbook of mentoring* (pp. 345–368). Oxford: Blackwell Publishing.

Friday, E., and Friday, S. S. (2002). Formal mentoring: Is there a strategic fit? *Management Decision*, *40*(2), 152–157.

Gant, G., and Houston-Philpot, K. R. (2006). Mentoring partnership program for women. *Women in Engineering ProActive Network*, 11–16.

Gaskill, L. R. (1993). A conceptual framework for the development, implementation, and evaluation of formal mentoring programs. *Journal of Career Development*, *20*(2), 147–160.

Gratton, L., and Truss, C. (2003). The three-dimensional people strategy: Putting human resources policies into action. *The Academy of Management Executive*, *17*(3), 74–86.

Grossman, R. J. (2012). The care and feeding of high-potential employees. *Human Resource Management International Digest*, *20*(1).

Groves, K. S. (2007). Integrating leadership development and succession planning best practices. *Journal of Management Development*, *26*(3), 239–260.

Haggard, D. L., Dougherty, T. W., Turban, D. B., and Wilbanks, J. E. (2011). Who is a mentor? A review of evolving definitions and implications for research. *Journal of Management*, *37*(1), 280–304.

Hegstad, C. D. (1999). Formal mentoring as a strategy for human resource development: A review of research. *Human Resource Development Quarterly*, *10*(4), 383.

Hegstad, C. D., and Wentling, R. M. (2004). The development and maintenance of exemplary formal mentoring programs in Fortune

500 companies. *Human Resource Development Quarterly*, *15*(4), 421–448.

Hollister, L. R. (2000). The benefits of being a mentor. *Healthcare Executive*, *16*(2), 49–50.

Jacobi, M. (1991). Mentoring and undergraduate academic success: A literature review. *Review of Educational Research*, *61*(4), 505–532.

Kwoh, L. (2011, March 7). Reverse Mentoring Cracks Workplace: Top Managers Get Advice on Social Media, Workplace Issues from Young Workers. *The Wall Street Journal.* Retrieved from http://onlineWsj.com/article/SB10001424052970203764804577060051461094004.html

Lopatto, D. (2003). The essential features of undergraduate research. *Council on Undergraduate Research Quarterly*, *24*, 139–142.

Megginson, D. (2006). Mentoring in action: A practical guide. *Human Resource Management International Digest*, *14*(7).

Murray, M., and Owen, M. A. (1991). *Beyond the myths and magic of mentoring*. San Francisco: Jossey-Bass.

Parise, M. R., and Forret, M. L. (2008). Formal mentoring programs: The relationship of program design and support to mentors' perceptions of benefits and costs. *Journal of Vocational Behavior*, *72*(2), 225–240.

Ragins, B. R., Cotton, J. L., and Miller, J. S. (2000). Marginal mentoring: The effects of type of mentor, quality of relationship, and program design on work and career attitudes. *Academy of Management Journal*, *43*(6), 1177–1194.

Ragins, B. R., and Cotton, J. L. (1999). Mentor functions and outcomes: A comparison of men and women in formal and informal mentoring relationships. *Journal of Applied Psychology*, *84*(4), 529.

Ragins, B. R., and Scandura, T. A. (1999). Burden or blessing? Expected costs and benefits of being a mentor. *Journal of Organizational Behavior*, *20*(4), 493–509.

Rose, G. L. (2005). Group differences in graduate students' concepts of the ideal mentor. *Research in Higher Education*, *46*(1), 53–80.

Wang, S., Tomlinson, E. C., and Noe, R. A. (2010). The role of mentor trust and protégé internal locus of control in formal mentoring relationships. *Journal of Applied Psychology*, *95*(2), 358.

Wilson, J. A., and Elman, N. S. (1990). Organizational benefits of mentoring. *The Executive*, *4*(4), 88–94.

Measuring the Effectiveness of Mentoring Programmes

Eileen Murphy and Jane Lewes

INTRODUCTION

The aim of this chapter is to discuss the purpose of evaluating the effectiveness of mentoring programmes, put forward case studies of good practices and suggest generic templates to support programme evaluation.

By establishing specific programme expectations or outcomes there is a greater chance of being able to develop a robust evaluation plan to assess programme effectiveness. Without clear outcomes and related indicators, there is little possibility of measuring effectiveness. It is important to recognise that to measure achievement of outcomes we must have baseline data.

Evaluation plans must form part of the initial mentoring programme plan with clear information about the scope of the evaluation. Effectiveness can be measured from the perspectives of Policymakers/Paymasters, Providers and Participants, and these stakeholders are likely to have diverse expectations.

As such, the evaluation plan must use relevant indicators to measure the effectiveness of the programme and mentoring relationships from different stakeholders' perspectives. Effective evaluation can establish if what the mentoring programme offers meets the established needs and expectations of the Policymakers/ Paymasters, Providers and Participants.

Effective evaluation plans can be established by using evaluation models and frameworks. This chapter explores a number of the models that can give structure to our evaluation plans: Programme Logic Models, Theory of Change, Kirkpatrick, and Phillips. If you are clear about the outcomes from the mentoring programme, you can establish the purpose of the evaluation and then design your evaluation plan.

The chapter will examine national and international standards that can be used to benchmark mentoring programmes, establish quality standards for programmes and support training and mentor practice.

THE IMPORTANCE OF CONTEXT

Mentoring is a planned, goal-oriented, results-focused, development intervention for individuals and organisations (Lewes, 2014). Mentoring programmes that lack specific aims, expectations, or articulated outcomes are rendered impotent in their planning and delivery and offer little or no possibility for evaluating effectiveness.

Contexts influence the reasons (and outcomes) for which mentoring programmes are established. Too often mentoring programmes are designed without a clear understanding of the expected outcomes. It is critical from the outset, therefore, to identify the aims and expected outcomes of a mentoring programme and each mentoring relationship so as to be able to confirm the validity of measuring and evaluating its outcomes, effectiveness and impact (NCWIT, 2011). Formal mentoring programmes have both individual and organisational outcomes (Lunsford, 2016).

There are two levels of contexts that are important to consider. Government, funders, and other organisations set the macro outcomes for a programme (Bronfenbrenner, 1979). At a micro level (Bronfenbrenner, 1979), outcomes are identified during the Setting Direction phase of each individual mentoring relationship (Clutterbuck, 2005).

Below are good examples of how the macro levels influence mentoring programmes. Each example provides a clear framework against which judgments could be made about the overall effectiveness of the programme.

- **Islington Housing Services,** who introduced a structured and accredited mentoring programme to support the delivery of its PASP (Positive Action Staff Placements) scheme, introduced this scheme to help redress the dearth of women, people with disability and people from the black and ethnic minority community holding senior management posts within the service (Ebbasi, 2002).
- **Birmingham City Council's** Birmingham Apprenticeship Scheme was set up to support a defined number of young adults (17-24) into sustained employment. A practical mentoring programme was delivered to employers to help them to develop genuine mentoring relationships with young people for whom they were providing the possibility of achieving permanent employment (Chisholm, 2011).
- **University Hospital Birmingham NHS Foundation Trust, Learning Hub** used a structured mentoring approach to help achieve its primary purpose, which was to offer integrated support provision within the Learning Hub. This yielded benefits both to healthcare providers as well as unemployed people who were making the transition into employment (Herdman, 2010).
- **Aarhus BSS Mentor100 (Aarhus University)** is a structured 9-month mentoring programme that focuses on master students' employability. The mentors are active alumni from the business community, who support students on their career paths. After 7 years with the programme a thoroughly effective measuring process was initiated, which showed that 78% of the mentees felt more aware of their personal and professional competencies and 64% obtained a better understanding of the labour market and work life. Another 64% reported they now had a wider perspective on their career options (Hejlsvig, 2016).

Therefore, to measure the effectiveness of the mentoring programme, its evaluation plan needs to be part of the initial programme plan, including the design of any supporting training and development. The evaluation criteria must be built into the programme design to gather data on the effectiveness of mentoring.

EVALUATING PROGRAMME EFFECTIVENESS FROM THE PERSPECTIVES OF ALL STAKEHOLDERS

The starting point for measuring effectiveness is to agree the scope of the evaluation. The different stakeholders involved in the mentoring programme will be interested in different measures. For evaluations to have maximum influence on change, the engagement of stakeholders, especially the users and 'influencers' of the evaluation, needs to be encouraged (Kusters et al., 2011). Engaging different stakeholders at the design stage of the evaluation adds value by providing perspectives on what will be considered a credible, high-quality and useful evaluation and increases the utilisation of the findings for the purpose of continuous improvements. Involving stakeholders in the process of an evaluation can lead to better data, better understanding of the data and more appropriate recommendations. After the evaluation, there is likely to be better uptake of findings (Gujit, 2014, p. 2).

As Patton argues, research on evaluation demonstrates that intended users are more likely to use evaluation findings if they understand and feel ownership of the evaluation process (Patton, 2008, Chapter 3).

The questions we should ask are: What should we be measuring to judge the effectiveness of mentoring programmes? And from whose perspective – Paymasters, Policymaking, Providers or Participants? The involvement of these stakeholder groups is shown in the following model (see Figure 15.1):

From a study of this model, it is clear that each stakeholder group will, almost inevitably, have a different set of expectations about a mentoring programme and therefore

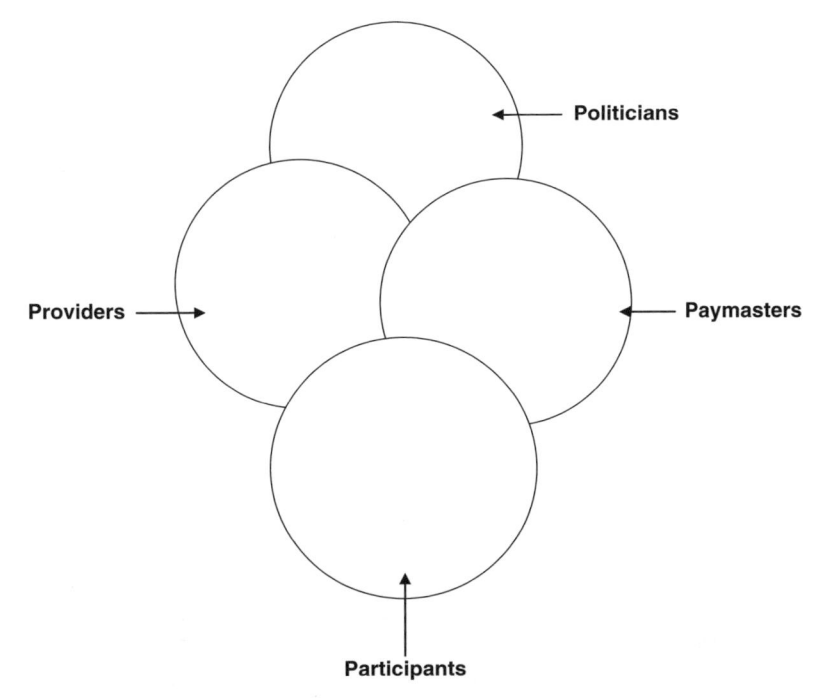

Politicians: Those with the agenda for driving through the programme, and the clout to ensure it happens.
Paymasters: Those who are providing the financial and material resources to support the programme.
Providers: Those who are appointed to lead the programme (the mentors).

Participants: Those who are most involved in the programme and who will be most directly affected by it (the learners or mentees).

Figure 15.1   Stakeholders' group

Source: Lewes, M.J. (2000). Monitoring and Evaluating Change. London, UK: London Guildhall University

may well wish to measure and evaluate its effectiveness against diverse indicators. It is important, therefore, to identify the diverse expectations of each stakeholder group to ensure relevant indicators are selected to evaluate the overall effectiveness of the mentoring programme. Indicators will be more relevant if we better understand the stakeholders' perspectives (Better Evaluation, 2014).

Paymasters and Policymakers

Thus, for *Paymasters* and *Policymakers*, judgements about overall effectiveness (including value for money) will usually be made as a response to the *How many…?*, *How much…?*, etc. questions and will rely largely on quantitative data to form those judgements.

Providers and Participants

For providers (Mentors) and Participants (Mentees), judgements about overall effectiveness will focus on the softer outcomes and questions such as *How does the mentee feel about…? How confident…? How willing….? To what extent….?* etc. will rely largely on **qualitative** data to form those judgements.

In any quality mentoring programme, the qualitative data can be captured from the outset, e.g. using notes of regular meetings to ask questions: *What has gone well? and What will we do differently next time?*

There are differences of opinion on what needs to be included in the evaluation of mentoring programmes, with variation in the terms used to describe what will be assessed. Karcher et al. (2006) stated 'the diversity of mentoring programs is both a strength and a liability for the establishment of a well-defined research base on the effectiveness of mentoring' (p. 710). They propose a framework that evaluates: Contexts – location of meeting, Structure – nature of mentor/mentee relationship, i.e. 1:1 group mentoring, adult/youth, and Goals – activities that occur in the match. Although their assessment is useful and accurate, the model presented lacks depth as it does not look at the outcomes of the relationship or the programme.

Evaluating the effectiveness of mentoring programmes from the perspectives of mentees and mentors requires a logical model for evaluation of inputs, outputs and outcomes. There will be differences between *formal* (often sponsored by an organisation) and *informal* mentoring relationships as the latter may have formed spontaneously and therefore is unlikely to be set within a programme. In making this distinction, however, we would take into account Clutterbuck's (2012) argument that:

> One of the paradoxes of formal mentoring programmes is that the essence of the relationship is its informality – the ability to discuss in private a wide range of issues that will help the mentee cope with and learn from issues he/she encounters, putting aside any power or status differences that might operate outside the relationship. So the idea of measurement and review is, on the face of it, to some extent at odds with the need to retain a high degree of informality and ad hoc responsiveness. (p. 1)

When evaluating the effectiveness of the programme from the mentee's perspective, include: the context from the programme (what mentees should be getting from the programme), the mentee's goals, their end achievements and an evaluation of the relationship.

Straus et al., found that: 'successful mentoring relationships were characterised by reciprocity, mutual respect, clear expectations, personal connections, and shared values. Failed mentoring relationships were characterized by poor communication, lack of commitment, personality differences, perceived (or real) competition, conflicts of interest, and the mentor's lack of experience' (2013: 82).

Eby et al., (2008) found 'in terms of workplace mentoring larger gains may be likely in terms of enhancing helping behaviour, situational satisfaction and attachment, and interpersonal relationships, whereas smaller gains might be likely in terms of enhancing job performance' (p. 264).

When evaluating from the mentor's perspective the evaluation needs to address the achievements from the relationship and the performance of the mentor to aid their continuing professional development. This is where national/international standards (with the possibility of accreditation) can play an effective role.

We can measure the effectiveness of formal and informal relationships, sponsored and spontaneous. The data collection methods may be different but the value of gathering information to aid improvements is the same. Clutterbuck (2012) argues that a certain amount of measurement gives us the foundation on which the informal relationship can grow and enable the mentor and mentee to build the relationship. Measurement can also show programme organisers areas for improvement.

Mentoring promotes reflective practice and learning. Reflective practice – 'a means of having a dialogue with yourself, asking the right questions at the right time, in order to discover the truth of yourself and your life. What really happened? Why did it happen? What did it do to me? What did it mean to me?' – Warren Bennis (2001, p. 61). These are key questions for reflective practice, but also key to self-evaluation for the mentor and the mentee. The success of a mentoring relationship can be assessed by the nature of the relationship and how well it benchmarks with mentor standards (relationship outputs).

Setting of relationship outcomes takes place at the Mentee Learning Agreement and Goal Setting stages of the mentoring sessions. Mentees and mentors are stakeholders and should be part of the design of the evaluation framework. In addition, the mentor and mentee will furnish the programme manager with a rich source of data. Mentees who have been well mentored know it.

To make evaluation manageable we must identify indicators for each constituent under evaluation: the output = mentoring sessions, the indicators = how often does the mentee need to attend sessions for performance to improve? Or how many mentees have an action plan?

To assess whether outcomes have been achieved requires us to monitor the outcome indicators. We address indicators later in the chapter. To identify the diverse expectations of each stakeholder group the evaluation plan must include appropriate indicators to judge the different aspects of the mentoring programme. This will give a more holistic picture of overall programme effectiveness.

USING EVALUATION MODELS TO MEASURE PROGRAMME EFFECTIVENESS

Overall purpose of evaluation

The questions to answer when designing a measurement of effectiveness are:

- who is driving the evaluation?
- is the evaluation for accountability or learning or both?
- what aspects need to be covered: programme, mentor/mentee relationship, achievement of goals by mentee? This will determine the indicators, the data collection methods and the report.

Before designing an evaluation plan we must be clear about the purpose of the evaluation. In writing this chapter, we have adopted Scriven's definition that evaluation determines the worth, merit or value of something (Scriven, 1991, p. 139). There are generally two key reasons to evaluate: to be accountable and to learn. Traditional outcome evaluation that focuses on accountability is externally driven, where the audience for the report is traditionally external and the organisation has little engagement with the findings. York (2003) argues that evaluations undertaken at the end of the funding have low potential for learning.

York promotes evaluation for the purpose of learning (2003) and advocates evaluation that:

- focuses on planning
- is determined by all **stakeholders**
- involves self-evaluation
- shares learning with the internal audiences (e.g. programme staff and managers)
- happens on an ongoing basis.

Blewden (2009) suggests that evaluation for learning requires a shift in focus from:

- what went wrong versus what works
- problem-focused versus solution-focused
- evaluation as an 'add-on' versus evaluation as ongoing and integrated. This means building evaluation into the project plan and throughout the delivery of the mentoring programme, rather than as an activity conducted at the end of a funding cycle, e.g. at the end of year 1 (Blewden, 2009, p. 7–9).

Evaluation purpose leads to design

To measure effectiveness it is essential to identify the purpose for which the information is required. Common reasons for carrying out evaluations include (Murphy, 2015):

- to improve programme design
- to improve internal systems and procedures
- to improve mentor training
- to enhance the outcomes of mentees
- to promote the programme
- to recruit future mentees and mentors
- to attract further funding
- to share learning internally and externally
- to communicate with stakeholders.

Evaluation models

There are many evaluation models to choose from when designing the evaluation of your mentoring programme (Stufflebeam and Coryn, 2014). The models we focus on in this chapter have been chosen because they:

- offer a structured and practical approach
- engage different stakeholders' need for data
- include a focus on outcomes and the assessment of changes due to the programme
- balance evaluation for learning with accountability
- enable a participatory approach.

We will cover the University of Wisconsin's Logic Model (2010), Kirkpatrick (1959) and Phillips (1991).

Using an evaluation model can assist in the development of a robust evaluation framework. One useful model being presented by Glenaffric Ltd (2007) has six steps:

1. Identify Stakeholder – Stakeholder Analysis
2. Describe Project and Understand Programme – Logic Model
3. Design Evaluation – Evaluation Plan
4. Gather Evidence – Evaluation Data
5. Analyse Results – Coding Frame
6. Report Findings – Evaluation reports

The University of Wisconsin's Logic Model (2010) (shown in Figure 15.2) can be used to describe the programme's constituent parts and aid in the construction of a comprehensive evaluation framework. Using a model to help design an evaluation framework means the measures can be matched to the programme. The measures chosen can be selected to describe success: success for the programme, the mentee and the mentor.

All aspects of the Logic Model Inputs – Process – Outputs – Outcomes – Impact can be measured and evaluated. The model below (see Figure 15.2) includes Participation, which evaluates the effectiveness of mentoring programmes. We argue that stakeholder involvement in determining the outcomes, the indicators and data collection is essential. Multilevel Logic Models can be drawn to cover government/funder, organisation and relationship programmes.

The inputs and outputs are the programme's response to the identified need, whilst the outcomes show the results of the programme. Evaluation provides the evidence about the effectiveness of the programme and its

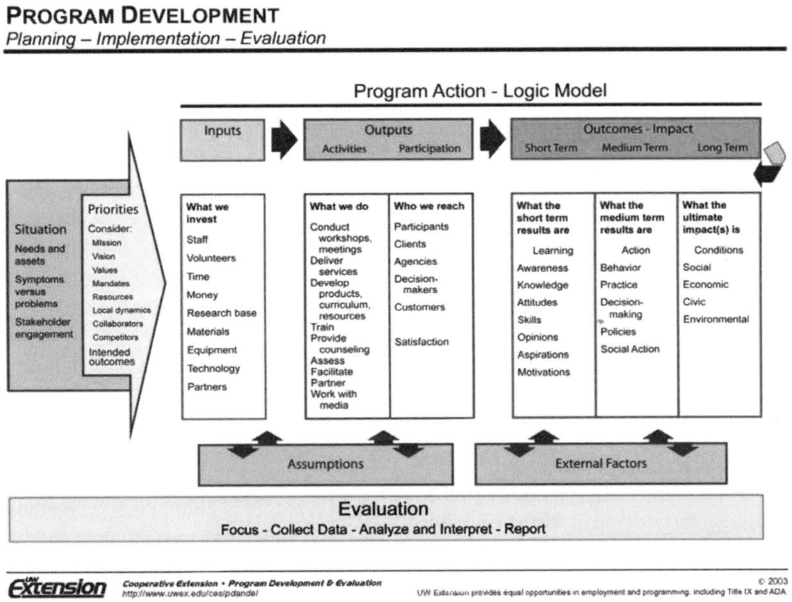

PROGRAM DEVELOPMENT
Planning – Implementation – Evaluation

[Logic Model diagram: Program Action - Logic Model with columns for Inputs, Outputs (Activities, Participation), Outcomes-Impact (Short Term, Medium Term, Long Term), with Situation/Priorities arrow on left, and Assumptions/External Factors/Evaluation boxes below]

Figure 15.2   Logic Model

Source: Programme Logic Model, University of Wisconsin. (2010). [Model]. Retrieved from http:// www.uwex.edu/ces/pdande/evaluation/evallogicmodel.html

constituent parts. Using the above model to develop our evaluation framework recognises that some mentee outcomes are short term, i.e. increased awareness and increased motivation, whilst others will be medium term, i.e. changes in decision-making or behaviour. Long-term outcomes are the same as impact.

To evaluate outcomes there needs to be a baseline assessment. At the relationship stage this forms part of the mentor–mentee agreement and goal setting. The initial goal may be broad (e.g. to get a job); it is a mark of an effective mentoring relationship for the mentee to identify a more focused goal (e.g. to get a job in Customer Services) as the relationship develops.

Clutterbuck (2012) puts forward a matrix that sets out to measure process and output from the scheme (programme) and the relationship. This matrix has strengths as it recognises that measurement of programme and relationship effectiveness are different but interconnected. The matrix does not address outcomes and therefore does not provide a full framework for measuring the effectiveness of mentoring.

We would argue that a comprehensive evaluation framework will help assess whether:

- money and resources are being well invested (**programme inputs**)
- the mentor is well trained and is performing against mentoring standards and within organisational guidelines (**relationship inputs**)
- the processes (supporting training programmes, matching processes, management of the programme) are effective and efficient (**process outputs**)
- mentees are engaged and express how satisfied they are with the mentoring (**relationship outputs**)
- the programme is achieving its aims and outcome, and to what extent (**programme outcomes**), e.g. better retention of staff, improved performance, increased employability, reduced college drop-out
- the mentee has succeeded in addressing their goals and made positive changes (**relationship outcomes**), e.g. increased knowledge, improved motivation, reduction in risky behaviour.

When measuring effectiveness, we are trying to assess whether the changes happening are in fact the result of mentoring. Theory of Change offers more than the Programme Logic Model as it includes cause. Theory of Change explains why and how the expected outcome will come about. To build a theory of change around a mentoring programme, stakeholders must be clear about the expected outcomes. We would argue this is essential in any plan to evaluate mentoring.

A further advantage of Theory of Change as a framework is the inclusion of indicators in the model. These identify the signs that should appear if the expected outcome is being achieved. Measuring the current status of the mentees (target population) on each indicator will give a baseline that can be used to measure successful change.

Measuring effectiveness requires programme designers to really understand the needs analysis, including the needs of potential mentees, understanding what mentoring offers and identifying potential outcomes. Without a true assessment of what mentoring offers, programmes may tend to be ill designed. Programme designers have to really understand what the needs are and why they exist, e.g. why do young adults struggle to settle into a new work environment, driving them to leave the programme? Why do new managers struggle with their confidence, preventing them from delegating and supervising effectively?

Outcomes that are too broad and vague lead to poorly defined activities and unrealistic evaluation plans and measurement strategies. Timescales for change are important to consider when building the evaluation plan. We need to understand when the target population is likely to achieve the changes identified in the indicators.

Donald Kirkpatrick's Training Evaluation Model was developed in 1959 and has been used widely. The original model identified four levels in the evaluation process:

1. The basic level of satisfaction or reaction measures how the individual initially reacted to the learning experience. Areas for evaluation questions could include: Facilitator (mentor) expertise, relevance of topic, quality of materials, or venue and domestic arrangements. The purpose of measuring initial reaction is to identify positive aspects as well as areas for improvement.
2. The second level attempts to capture the extent to which the learner's (mentee's) knowledge has increased as a result of the intervention. For this level the areas to be explored include: *Before* and *After* questions, as well as questions about the *fit* of the learning objectives with the learner's own needs.
3. Level three enables changes in learners' behaviour (including workplace performance), values and attitudes to be measured. Learning facilitators (mentors) need to monitor evidence of changes in behaviour on an ongoing basis.
4. Level four is about devising methods to measure sustainable change against the original performance (mentoring) goals. Obviously, in order to be assured of a sustainable change in performance (including values and attitudes), it is necessary to allow some time to elapse.

Phillips (1991) added a fifth level to Kirkpatrick's Model, the Return on Investment (ROI) as shown in Figure 15.3.

Level 1: SATISFACTION: *To what extent did the mentee enjoy the mentoring experience?*
Level 2: LEARNING: *To what extent was there transfer of knowledge/skills?*
Level 3: OUTCOMES: *To what extent were there behavioural changes as a result of the mentoring?*
Level 4: RESULTS: *To what extent did the mentoring have a sustainable impact on performance?*
Level 5: ROI: *To what extent did mentoring provide a positive return on investment?*

In *macro* mentoring programmes this level is sometimes not addressed in the evaluation plan. The evaluation of ROI attempts to measure the benefits of the learning intervention (mentoring) against its costs (both direct and indirect). In purely monetary terms this results in an ROI formula, which is:

ROI = (financial benefit from intervention − total cost of intervention)/(total cost of intervention) × 100%

In 2010, the Kirkpatrick organisation enhanced the original model to highlight the critical role of the Learning Facilitator (Mentor)

KIRKPATRICK AND PHILLIPS EVALUATION MODEL

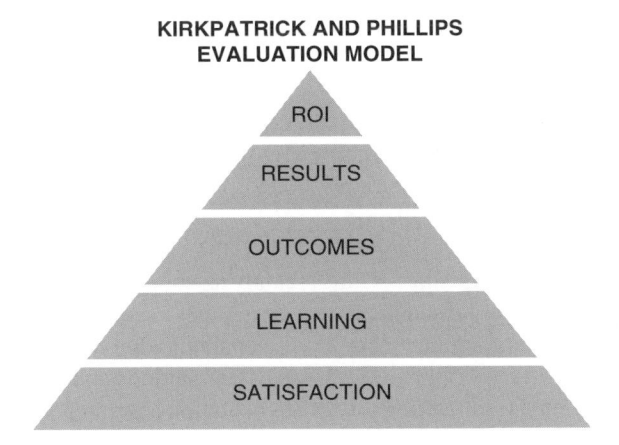

(Pyramid from bottom to top: SATISFACTION, LEARNING, OUTCOMES, RESULTS, ROI)

Figure 15.3 Evaluation model

Source: Handbook of Training Evaluation and Measurement Methods (3rd ed.), by J. J. Phillips, 1997a, (p. 43). Boston: Butterworth-Heinemann

in monitoring, capturing and responding to 'valuable actionable intelligence' (see Figure 15.4) (Dewhurst et al., 2015, p. 15).

IDENTIFYING BEHAVIOURAL OUTCOMES

When scoping the evaluation, selection of the outcomes will depend on the nature of the programme, the expectations of funders and meaningfulness to the mentees. It is important to be realistic but ambitious. There are many examples of programmes that have been set up to fail by expecting unrealistic outcomes. Outcomes should relate to changes that can come about during the lifetime of the programme.

Eby et al. (2008) focused their research on three major areas of mentoring research – youth, academic and workplace. They investigated

LEVEL 1 REACTION
• Engagement
• Relevance
• Customer satisfaction

LEVEL 2 LEARNING
• Knowledge
• Skills
• Attitude
• Confidence
• Commitment

LEVEL 3 BEHAVIOR (Monitor & Adjust: Monitor, Reinforce, Encourage, On-the-job learning, Reward)

LEVEL 4 RESULTS
• Leading indicators
• Desired outcomes

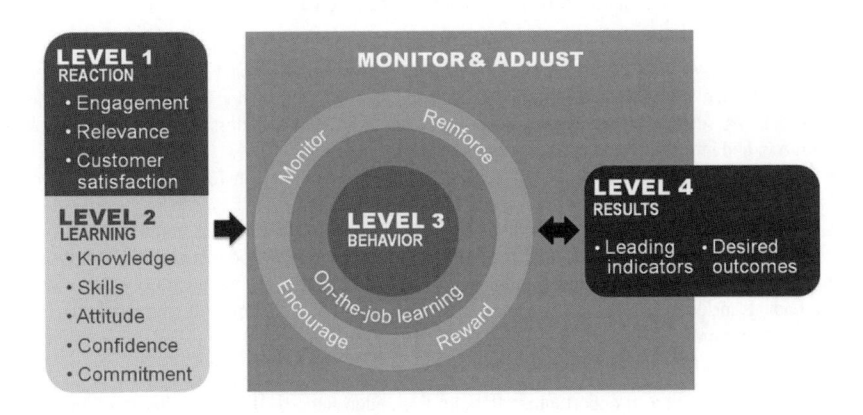

Figure 15.4 The new world Kirkpatrick Model

Source: Dewhurst, Harris, Foster-Bohm & Odell. (2015). Applying the Kirkpatrick model to a Coaching Program. *Journal of Training and Development*, Australian Institute of Training and Development. Sydney, NSW, Australia

whether outcomes vary by type of relationships. Mentoring was associated with a range of positive outcomes – behavioural, attitudinal, health, relational, motivational and career. There were some differences found across mentoring types. 'Despite the widespread study of mentoring and its prevalence in community, academic, and organisational contexts, research has progressed within its own disciplinary silos. As a consequence there is little cross-disciplinary communication among mentoring scholars' (p. 254).

DuBois and Karcher (2005) wrote that mentoring at different developmental stages tended to meet different purposes. Youth mentoring was often aimed at reducing risky behaviour or improving social or academic functioning; whilst academic mentoring targeted student retention, academic performance and adjustment to college life. Kram (1985) stated that workplace mentoring aimed to enhance employees' potential and career development.

These goals appear to be driven by government policy, funders, or organisations. Evaluation of these goals alone would miss out on evaluating mentee-led outcomes. These softer outcomes may have a more long-term effect moving across the developmental stages. It is necessary to identify and access these chains of outcomes (Programme Logic Model [University of Wisconsin, 2010]) to measure short-, medium- and long- term effects and to test the hypothesis put forward by the programme, e.g. improved motivation leads to staff retention.

Eby et al. (2008) caution us not to overestimate the potential effect of mentoring. Their analysis suggests we should temper what are sometimes seemingly unrealistic expectations about what mentoring can offer to mentees, institutions and society. We would argue expectations are not necessarily unrealistic, but not clearly defined.

'**Christopher Columbus** – He didn't know where he was going when he set off;

He didn't know where he was when he got there;

He didn't know where he had been when he got back' – Anon.

Expected outcomes depend on the nature of the programme the mentee is engaged with. However, from the mentee's perspective, the goals established at the beginning of the relationship should be mentee driven. When measuring the effectiveness of the programme we must include those outcomes that are mentee led.

Case Study: The Connections to Opportunities Pilot Project Workplace Post Employment Support, Final Research Report March 2010

The research hypothesis was that mentoring at the workplace had a positive impact on participating organisations, increased employee retention, reduced recruitment costs, and improved productivity. The research also looked at the outcomes for mentees, sustained employment, breaking cycles of habitual worklessness, enhancing employability, raising aspirations, and improving employee engagement in the workplace.

For Job Seekers Allowance, a UK based benefit scheme, claims retention rates at 13 weeks were 93.1% compared with 73% at a national level, 91.1% at 26 weeks, and 60% at national level.

The research asked mentors for feedback on the evidence of Employability Essentials (three critical behaviours) in their mentees; 80% saw improved **motivation** and **self-confidence** and 76% had **increased self-reliance**.

At a programme level the research looked at the impact on worklessness and barriers to sustained employment. Some of the findings include: 75% mentors reported increased aspirations, engagement, and motivation as a result of taking part in the programme. Two-thirds of mentees felt mentoring had helped them keep their jobs and provided them with valuable skills, experience, and confidence.

Herdman, J. (2010). Connection to opportunities [Interim Evaluation Report]. University Hospital Birmingham NHS Foundation Trust. Leicester, UK: Logiktree Associates

MEASURING THE EFFECTIVENESS OF MENTORING PROGRAMMES

The following quotes, collected during the research process, demonstrate some of the outcomes of the BAS programme for a selection of mentees.

"Before the course I was quiet, and didn't come out of my shell, but now I started thinking on my feet when customers call asking for quick answers or resolutions to problems. I feel better under pressure and my confidence in my work has increased. I have also improved my relationships with my colleagues and my ways of working. BAS is a good introduction for young people starting work."
   -Apprentice

"I am enjoying being an apprentice at the Birmingham Hippodrome; and I am constantly learning new things each day. I am very pleased I was given the chance to be an apprentice within the company. Definitely enjoying it."
   -Apprentice

"I am building a secure future here – the BAS programme and my learning programme are providing me with the push I need to build my confidence and get on."
   -Apprentice

"The apprentice scheme has allowed me the opportunity to gain new skills in the workplace and given me the chance to start a career in a friendly and warm environment. Without this opportunity, I believe that I would have found it hard to get into work."
   -Apprentice

"Being a part of the scheme has taught me to look at work from a different angle. It's not about money, it's about learning to help develop my skills for future employment."
   -Apprentice

Gathered by Chisholm, J. (2011) in research for Birmingham Apprenticeship Scheme Final Report. Birmingham UK: Birmingham City Council

---

The following quote gives examples of outcomes of the programme from the Principal Learning Facilitator's perspective:

"A great example of how a structured approach to coaching and mentoring in the workplace provides a range of tools and techniques to promote positive and sustainable learning outcomes for non traditional learners."

Principal Learning Facilitator

Chisholm, J. (2011). Birmingham Apprenticeship Scheme Final Report. Birmingham, UK: Birmingham City Council

---

Where the measurement of effectiveness relates to impact on society, longitudinal studies would need to be conducted to follow mentees beyond the end of programmes to assess sustainable impact.

Making behavioural outcomes measurable

To make it possible to measure achievement, programme designers must identify indicators.

It is these indicators that are monitored to assess whether the outcomes have been achieved or not. It is easy to turn these indicators into questions to judge the effectiveness of the mentoring. It is important to establish both quantitative and qualitative indicators to monitor mentoring effectiveness as the discussion is about human interaction. Indicators are about relevance, quality and quantity.

Template for programme evaluation for organisations, mentors and learners

Below is a generic evaluation plan for a workplace mentoring programme. Table 15.1 shows the different indicators that could be used to gather evidence of the effectiveness of the Programme, the Process and the Mentoring Relationship.

When evaluating changes that arise from mentoring it can be difficult to establish whether those changes would have arisen without mentoring or whether they are from a combination of activities and good practice. There should be different indicators at the start, middle and end of the relationship, recognising that there is a chain of outcomes.

Standards of behaviour should be built into the programme by the organisation and effective mentors will have the skills and behaviours required to perform well.

USING BENCHMARKS TO EVALUATE MENTORING EFFECTIVENESS

Mentoring standards (both national and international) have been developed. We present a selection of these standards and suggest practitioners could use them to benchmark their mentoring programmes, establishing quality standards for programmes, supporting training and mentor practice. Table 15.2 shows the different indicators that could be used to gather evidence of the progress towards outcomes.

International and national standards and benchmarks for mentoring have been introduced over time and are being increasingly used to define and describe recognised best practices. What follows is by no means an exhaustive catalogue of all mentoring standards, but a selection from the UK, Europe and USA.

National Occupational Standards for Coaching and Mentoring – UK

The National Occupational Standards (NOS) for Coaching and Mentoring, which

Table 15.1 Evaluation plan: output indicators

Outputs	Suggested Indicators	Suggested Data Collection Methods	Schedule
Programme Outputs	How many people attended training? How effective was the training? Has the mentee been assigned a mentor? Number of new matches	Training evaluation form Register	
Process Outputs	Frequency of meetings?	Diary/timetable	
Relationship Outputs	Quality of meetings? How many mentees have an action plan? Have they developed sufficient trust? Are there notes from the meetings? Is there a clear sense of direction to the relationship? What's going well for the mentor? What's going well for the mentee?	Satisfaction survey Action plan Self-reflection Notes of meetings Notes of meetings/Action plan Self-reflection Self-reflection	

Source: Murphy, E. (2015). Measuring and Evaluating Outcomes [PowerPoint slides].

Table 15.2 Evaluation plan: outcome indicators

We have established that Programme outcomes can be at three different levels: *Participant* outcomes (mentor/mentee), *Provider* outcomes and *Policymaker/Paymaster* outcomes. Outcome indicators have to relate directly to the expected outcome of the programme; therefore, it is difficult to establish generic indicators relevant to all programme types. The following is an example of a workplace mentoring programme.

	Indicators	Suggested data collection methods Schedule for baseline and ongoing measurement
Expected programme outcomes	How well has programme met its stated outcomes? Retention rates in organisation? College readiness? Levels of confidence? Attainment of Employability Essentials	Interviews/survey HR stats College stats Mentee survey Observation/self reflection
Expected relationship outcomes	Level of rapport Level of trust Have mentor and mentee met the goals they set? How well mentee is achieving action plan Progress towards goals Increased competence of the mentees in critical areas	Self-reflection by mentee and mentor Action plan and notes of meetings Feedback from mentee and mentor Action plan, notes of meeting Feedback from third party, mentor and self-reflection by mentee

Source: Murphy, E. (2015). Measuring and Evaluating Outcomes [PowerPoint slides].

identify the skills, knowledge and understanding needed by those who deliver coaching and mentoring were updated in 2012, having been extensively revised to ensure they reflect the needs of those who deliver coaching and mentoring functions in their role.

NOS are statements of the standards of performance individuals must achieve when carrying out functions in the workplace, together with specifications of underpinning knowledge and understanding. NOS can usually be applied across a wide range of roles, settings, levels of responsibility and contexts. Typically, they might describe current best practice, highlight values and principles associated with a role and benchmark achievable levels of attainment for individuals carrying out a role or part of a role.

NOS are:

- **National** – because they can be used in every part of the UK where the functions are carried out
- **Occupational** – because they describe the performance required of an individual when carrying out functions in the workplace
- **Standard** – because they are statements of effective performance agreed by representative samples of employers and other key stakeholders and approved by the UK NOS Panel.

As nationally recognised standards, NOS are being used in a number of ways, including:

- to inform the content of vocational and professional qualifications
- to inform the content of training programmes
- to form the basis of company/organisation competency frameworks
- to form the basis of a range of vocational qualifications
- to inform licences to practice with industries
- to raise skill levels and improve business productivity
- to form the basis of all types of human resource management and development, including:
- for workforce planning, performance appraisal and job descriptions
- to provide workplace coaching and assist reflective practice
- to ensure continuing professional development.

There is potential to use the UK National Occupational Standards as a benchmark to measure effectiveness of mentoring practice. A number of the standards refer to evaluation and reflection. One of these standards, Establishing and building relationships with the client, includes recognising how the mentor's values, behaviours, attitudes and emotional awareness affects mentoring relationships. The mentor must adhere to the organisation's professional standards of practice.

Standards of behaviour should be built into the programme by the organisation, and effective mentors will have the skills and behaviours required to perform well. These can be used as indicators or relationships outputs.

One Unit from the National Occupational Standards for Coaching and Mentoring (Learning and Skills Improvement Service, 2012) is 'review and evaluate the coaching or mentoring process' (p. 42). Mentors should be clear of the stakeholder objectives and goals of the programme. Mentors should also be aware of how they are expected to record outcomes of the relationship and to contribute to the evaluation.

The International Standards for Mentoring Programmes in Employment (ISMPE) – International

The purpose of the ISMPE is to provide a consistent and globally accepted benchmark of good practice in mentoring programme management to ensure that mentoring programmes are:

- well designed
- well managed
- significantly contributing to the development of participants and the effectiveness of the organisation.

Organisations considering a formal benchmark/ assessment against the ISMPE benefit by:

- legitimising their mentoring programme against a recognised standard
- strengthening and improving the mentoring programme through a rigorous assessment
- continuing to build the business case for mentoring within the organisation
- identifying opportunities to promote mentoring as a key people development activity within the organisation.

ISMPE standards have been generated to fill a gap in the evaluation of mentoring programmes with particular emphasis on programmes in adult employment and development. Six Core Standards have been identified, as follows:

1. Clarity of Purpose
2. Stakeholders' Training and Briefing
3. Processes for Selection and Matching
4. Effective Processes for Measurement and Review
5. Maintains High Standards of Ethics and Pastoral Care
6. Supports Participants Throughout the Process/ Systems of Programme Administration.

Core Standard 4 includes performance indicators designed specifically to enable *Providers* and *Participants* with a means of ensuring ongoing monitoring and evaluation of programmes. The programme is measured sufficiently frequently and appropriately to:

- identify problems with individual relationships
- make timely adjustments to programme
- provide a meaningful cost-benefit analysis and impact analysis.

The International Institute for Coaching and Mentoring (IIC&M)

The mission of the IIC&M is to increase the level of professionalism across the globe by ensuring that all coaching and mentoring training establishments are measured in terms of standards and ethics and core competencies and meet those requirements consistently (www.iicandm.org).

IIC&M's professional standards are set out under the following:

1 Client Care
2 Personal Professional Conduct
3 Professional Relationships

As a relatively recently established organisation, IIC&M does not yet provide evidence of the application of their standards to the evaluation of mentoring programmes. Reference to the organisation's key purposes does not include any direct guidance on providing information about evaluating the effectiveness of mentoring interventions.

European Mentoring and Coaching Council (EMCC) – UK and Europe

EMCC is a leading professional organisation that is composed of the best-known thinkers and practitioners in coaching and mentoring today. It is now the biggest network of its type in Europe, bringing together those in the coaching and mentoring community, including:

- managers using coaching
- users and buyers of external and internal coaching services
- providers of coaching and mentoring services
- researchers into coaching and mentoring
- coaching and mentoring training providers.

EMCC promotes best practice to ensure the highest possible standards are maintained in the coaching/mentoring relationship.

EMCC offers the opportunity for coaches/mentors to gain accreditation across four levels:

- foundation
- practitioner
- senior practitioner
- master practitioner.

Its Competence Framework is described within eight Coaching/Mentoring competence categories:

1. Understanding Self

Demonstrates awareness of own values, beliefs and behaviours, recognises how these affect their practice and uses this self-awareness to manage their effectiveness in meeting the client's and, where relevant, the sponsor's objectives.

2. Commitment to self-development

Explores and improves the standard of their practice and maintains the reputation of the profession.

3. Managing the Contract

Establishes and maintains the expectations and boundaries of the coaching/mentoring contract with the client and, where appropriate, with sponsors.

4. Building the Relationship

Skilfully builds and maintains an effective relationship with the client and, where appropriate, with the sponsor.

5. Enabling Insight and Learning

Works with the client and sponsor to bring about insight and learning.

6. Outcomes and Action Orientation

Demonstrates approach, and uses the skills, in supporting the client to make desired changes.

7. Use of Models and Techniques

Applies models and tools, techniques and ideas beyond the core communication skills in order to bring about insight and learning.

8. Evaluation

Gathers information on the effectiveness of their practices and contributes to establishing a culture of evaluation of outcome.

The eighth category of competence, Evaluation, is set out as follows in Table 15.3:

Table 15.3 EMCC competence framework

Category	Foundation Capability Indicators	Practitioner Capability Indicators	Senior Practitioner Capability Indicators	Master Practitioner Capability Indicators
Gathers information on the effectiveness of their practices to establish a culture of evaluation of outcomes	Evaluates outcomes with client (and stakeholders [if relevant]) Monitors and reflects on the effectiveness of the whole process Requests feedback from client on coaching/mentoring Receives and accepts feedback appropriately	Uses a formal feedback process from the client Has own processes	Establishes rigorous evaluation process with clients and stakeholders	Critiques diverse approaches to evaluation of coaching/mentoring Participates in building knowledge on evaluating coaching/mentoring Uses knowledge gained to comment on themes, trends and ideas related to evaluation process, coaching/mentoring processes and client themes

Investors in People (IiP) – UK

IiP is a nationally recognised framework that helps organisations to improve their performance and realise their objectives through the effective management and development of their people, see Figure 15.5 below.

The Standard is based on three key principles:

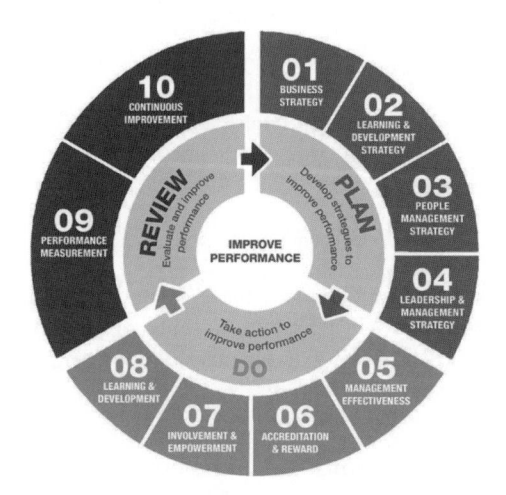

Figure 15.5 Investors in people framework

Source: Investors in People (2015), London, UK. Retrieved from: https://www.investorsinpeople.com

- **Plan** – Developing strategies to improve the performance of the organisation
- **Do** – Taking action to improve the performance of the organisation
- **Review** – Evaluating the impact on the performance of the organisation

Developing strategies to improve the performance of the organisation

An Investor in People develops effective strategies to improve the performance of the organisation through its people.

1. Business Strategy – The strategy for improving the performance of the organisation is clearly defined and understood
2. Learning and Development Strategy – Learning and Development is planned to achieve the organisation's objectives
3. People Management Strategy – Strategies for managing people are designed to promote equality of opportunity in the development of the organisation's people
4. Leadership and Management Strategy – The capabilities that managers need to lead, manage and develop people effectively are clearly defined and understood

Taking action to improve the performance of the organisation

An Investor in People takes effective action to improve the performance of the organisation through its people.

1 Management Effectiveness – Managers are effective at leading, managing and developing people
2 Recognition and Reward – People's contributions to the organisation are recognised and valued
3 Involvement and Empowerment – People are encouraged to take ownership and responsibility by being involved in decision-making
4 Learning and Development – People learn and develop effectively

Evaluation of the impact on the performance of the organisation

An Investor in People can demonstrate the impact of its investment in people on the performance of the organisation.

1 Performance Measurement – Investment in people improves the performance of the organisation
2 Continuous Improvement – Improvements are continually made to enhance the way people are managed and developed

CONCLUSION

If evaluation is about learning and accountability and mentoring is a goal-oriented, results-focused intervention (Lewes, 2014), then we should use the findings from our evaluations to enhance future results and implement more effective mentoring programmes. Evaluation should lead to improvements in the mentoring programme and the relationships, and stimulate shared learning. The evaluation process should be viewed as part of broader evaluative practices, informing decision-making for change (Kusters et al., 2011).

However, an area that is often missed when measuring effectiveness of programmes is *taking the next step* of using the evaluation data to propose and make changes to processes, procedures, future programme design and the training and support offered to mentors. For evaluations to matter we need to establish how the key findings will influence change at various levels, and think through a pathway of change (Kusters et al., 2011).

For evaluation to be valuable it must lead to improvements in all aspects of mentoring. Therefore, when measuring the effectiveness of mentoring programmes we recommend the implementation of a comprehensive evaluation framework. This will discover whether resources have been well invested, the mentor is performing well, the processes are effective and efficient, mentees are engaged and satisfied with the mentoring, the programme is achieving its aims and outcomes and the mentee has succeeded in addressing their goals and made positive change.

It is important that when measuring effectiveness we include both quantitative and qualitative **indicators**. In addition, it is important to remember that behavioural outcomes may occur in the short, medium and long term, and this chain of outcomes must be built into the evaluation plan.

In terms of next steps, there is need for more investment in longitudinal studies to assess the long-term impact of mentoring programmes. Where the measurement of effectiveness relates to impact on society, longitudinal studies would need to be conducted to follow mentees beyond the end of their programmes to assess sustainability and transportability of the mentoring programme (Stufflebeam, 2007).

REFERENCES

Bennis, W. (2001). *On Becoming a Leader*. London, UK: Random Century Group.
BetterEvaluation. (2014). *Rainbow Evaluation* [Pdf]. Retrieved from www.betterevaluation.org

Big Brothers Big Sisters. (2013). Youth outcomes report summary [Summary report]. Retrieved from: www.bbbs.org

Blewden, M. (2009). Evaluation for learning [Website]. Retrieved from http://www.philanthropy.org.nz

Bronfenbrenner, U. (1979). *The Ecology of Human Development: Experiments by Nature and Design*. Cambridge, Massachusetts and London, England: Harvard University Press, p. 22 and 26.

Chartered Institute of Personnel and Development. (2008). Developing coaching capability tool [Website]. Retrieved from www.cipd.co.uk ' Resources ' Practical Tools.

Chartered Institute of Personnel and Development. (2012). Coaching: The evidence base research report [Report]. Retrieved from http://www.cipd.co.uk/hr-resources/research/coaching-evidence-base.aspx

Chisholm, J. (2011). Birmingham Apprenticeship Scheme Final Report [Report]. Birmingham, UK: Birmingham City Council.

Clutterbuck, D. (2012). *Evaluating mentoring, measurement, and review in mentoring* [Pdf]. Retrieved from https://www.davidclutterbuckpartnership.com/wp-content/uploads/Evaluating-Mentoring.pdf

Developing a Logic Model, University of Wisconsin. (2010). Extension cooperative extension, program development and evaluation [Powerpoint presentation]. Retrieved from http://pde.osu.edu/program-resources/extension-program-logic-model

Dewhurst, D., Harris, M., Foster-Bohm, G., and Odell, G. (2015). Applying the Kirkpatrick to a coaching program. *Training and Development*, 42(1), 14.

DuBois, D.L. and Karcher, M.A. (Eds.). (2005). *Handbook of Youth Mentoring*. London, England: Sage.

Ebbasi, M. (2002). *Positive Action Staff Placement Scheme*. London, England: London Borough of Islington.

Eby, L.T., Allen, T.D., Evans, S.C., Ng, T., and Dubois, D. (2008). Does mentoring matter? A multidisciplinary meta-analysis comparing mentored and non-mentored individuals. *Journal of Vocational Behavior*, 72, 254–267.

European Mentoring and Coaching Council. (2009). Competence framework [Website]. Retrieved from www.emccouncil.org

Glenaffric Ltd. (2007). JISC. Six steps to effective evaluation: A handbook for programme and project managers [Pdf]. Retrieved from https://www.jisc.ac.uk/media/.../programmes/.../SixStepsHandbook.pdf

Guijt, I. (2014). Participatory Approaches, Methodological Briefs: Impact Evaluation 5, UNICEF Office of Research, Florence.

Herdman, J. (2010). The Connections to Opportunities Pilot Project Workplace Post Employment Support [Final Research Report]. Leicester, UK: Logiktree Associates Ltd.

Herdman, J. (2010). Connection to Opportunities [Interim evaluation report]. University Hospital Birmingham NHS Foundation Trust. Leicester, UK: Logiktree Associates Ltd.

International Institute for Coaching and Mentoring IIC&M. (1999). [Website]. Retrieved from www.iicandm.org

International Standards for Mentoring in Employment. (2001). [Website]. Retrieved from: www.ismpe.com

Investors in People Framework Summary. (2015). [Website]. Retrieved from https://www.investorsinpeople.co.uk

Investors in Young People Scotland. (2012). [Website]. Retrieved from http://investorsinpeople.scot/accreditation/investors-in-young-people

Karcher, M., Kupermins, G.P., Portwood, S.G., Sipe, C.L., and Taylor, A.S. (2006). Mentoring programs: A framework to inform program development, research and evaluation. *Journal of Community Psychology*, 34(6), 709–725.

Kirkpatrick, D.L. (1959). Techniques for evaluating training programs. *Journal of American Society of Training Directors*, 13(3), 21–26.

Kram, K.E. (1985). *Mentoring at work: Developmental relationships in organizational life*. Glenview, IL: Scott Foresman.

Kusters, C.S.L., van Vugt, S., Wigboldus, S., Williams, B., and Woodhill, J. (2011). *Making evaluations matter: A practical guide for evaluators*. Centre for Development Innovation, Wageningen University and Research Centre, Wageningen, The Netherlands.

Lewes, M.J. (2014). *Coaching and mentoring: A toolkit to promote employability*. Birmingham, UK: The Learning Consultancy.

Murphy, E. (2015). Measuring and Evaluating Outcomes [PowerPoint slides].

National Centre for Women and Information Technology. (2011). Retrieved from www.ncwit.org

National Occupational Standards for Coaching and Mentoring. (2012). Learning and skills improvement service. Retrieved from http://nos.ukces.org.uk/Pages/index.aspx

Patton, M.Q. (2008). *Utilization-focused evaluation*: (4th ed.). Thousand Oaks, CA: Sage. Retrieved from www.sagepub.com/books/Book229324#tabview=toc

Phillips, J. (1991). *Handbook of training evaluation and measurement methods* (3rd ed.). Boston, MA: Butterworth-Heinemann.

Programme Logic Model, University of Wisconsin. (2010). [Model]. Retrieved from http://www.uwex.edu/ces/pdande/evaluation/evallogicmodel.html

Scriven, M. (1991). *Evaluation thesaurus*. Newbury Park, CA: Sage.

Straus, S.E., Johnson, M.O., Marquez, C., and Feldman, M.D. (2013). Characteristics of successful and failed mentoring relationships: A qualitative study across two academic health centres [Article]. Retrieved from http://www.ncbi.nlm.nih.gov/pubmed/23165266

Stufflebeam, D.L. (2007). CIPP Evaluation Model Checklist. Western Michigan University Evaluation Centre.

Stufflebeam, D.L. and Coryn, C.L.S. (2014). *Evaluation theory, models, and applications* (research methods for the social sciences). San Francisco, CA: John Wiley and Sons.

York, P.J. (2003). Learning as we go: Making evaluation work for everyone [Briefing Paper]. New York, NY: TCC Group.

The Role of the Mentoring Programme Co-ordinator

Terezia Koczka

INTRODUCTION

The importance of a dedicated programme co-ordinator should not be under-estimated; indeed, one of the most common reasons for the failure or poor management of mentoring schemes is the lack of ownership and accountability for key activities and priorities. The literature review shows that, while having a programme champion, manager or co-ordinator seems to be one of the key mentoring programme success factors, there is very little, if any, empirical research examining the role and responsibilities of the mentoring programme co-ordinator.

This chapter will begin with an overview of some of the aspects that influence mentoring programme management, including issues such as context and diversity. The main section of the chapter focuses on the roles and responsibilities of the programme co-ordinator, aligned to the stages of mentoring programme management. Taking a practical approach, the author will refer to a number of frameworks to illuminate specific aspects of the role. Next, the author will explore the skills and competences of the programme co-ordinator and the challenges and risks associated with the role will be identified. Following this, the author presents two case studies that incorporate the reflections of two programme co-ordinators operating very different mentoring schemes. They begin by outlining their programmes, followed by the identification of key lessons learned. Finally, the chapter will conclude by recognizing and acknowledging a number of future research opportunities.

There is a debate over the merits of formal (planned) and informal (unplanned) mentoring. The degree to which formal or informal mentoring initiatives deliver individual, organizational and societal benefits is contested. For the purpose of this chapter, the author will focus on the role of the programme co-ordinator in relation to formal programmes. That is, programmes that have a recognized structure and series of processes designed to create effective mentoring relationships, including the evaluation of the impact of mentoring from a multi-stakeholder perspective. The content of this chapter is drawn primarily from text books, practice examples, reflections of programme co-ordinators and anecdotal evidence.

MENTORING PROGRAMME MANAGEMENT INFLUENCES

The nature of mentoring has changed in recent years and the environment within which mentoring takes place as a tool to support learning and development has transformed. Mentoring can be found in almost every professional setting and each setting has its own unique characteristics. Within the professions there are numerous conceptualizations of mentoring, which address multiple issues, such as:

- Mentoring to develop leadership competence (Kim, 2007)
- Mentoring to address gender imbalance (Yedidia and Bickel, 2001)
- Mentoring for employability (Haddock-Millar et al., 2014)
- Strategies for overcoming advancement in the context of disability (Jones, 1997)
- Mentoring to address teaching retention (Waterman and He, 2011)
- Minority mentoring in STEM fields (Carroll and Barnes, 2015)
- E-mentoring for HR professionals in India (Sanyal and Rigby, 2013)

The role of programme co-ordinator is influenced by numerous contextual elements: individual, organizational and societal cultures, the nature of organizations, approaches to mentoring, the nature and purpose of the programme, how a specific mentoring programme has been initiated/supported/championed, the location and environment in which the given programme takes place, the structure of the programme, the support and acceptance of mentoring as a learning concept, the time allocated for the role, whether it is a full-time, part-time or volunteer role, the available technological support, etc. Gibb and Megginson (1993) suggest that the context within which a mentoring scheme operates influences the scheme tremendously; therefore the adaptation of the programme framework to suit its context is a critical success factor. Mentoring relationships operate within a context, which for formal mentoring programmes involves the culture and/or the climate of the organization, the structure and purpose of the scheme and the background of the mentor and the mentee. It is widely acknowledged that multiple factors can influence mentoring programme success and both mentees' and mentors' expectations and behaviours are influenced by context (Allen et al., 2008; Kochan, 2013; Ragins and Kram, 2007). In contemporary society it is widely accepted that individuals, groups and organizations operate within a complex adaptive system, whereby multiple influences coalesce, bringing about a constant state of change (Lansing, 2003; Mitleton-Kelly, 1997). The challenge for the mentoring programme co-ordinator is to provide ways of describing what the concept of mentoring means in its specific context.

This is particularly evident in global, transnational and international mentoring programmes, which require a great deal of forethought and appreciation of local and regional cultures and circumstances. It is possible to design a corporate policy and/or individual mentoring programmes centrally and implement them across borders. However, the degree to which the programmes are successful is dependent on a number of factors, which encompass issues such as cultural diversity (Clutterbuck, 2014). Good mentoring programme management practice appears to involve:

- Input from a wide range of sources, particularly from the local human resource management function and line managers, when designing the mentoring programme.

- Recognizing that, even in countries that speak the same language, the context of mentoring may be very different.
- Openly acknowledging the impact of culture on the style of mentoring and including relevant cultural awareness elements in any training and supporting information resources.
- Designing training content and supporting material with a core of common elements (definitions, skills, emphasis on learning dialogue, etc.) and a more flexible approach to case studies, role plays/real plays, links with local mythology and social mores.
- Educating local human resource management professionals so that they can become champions for mentoring.
- Clarifying other important contextual factors, for example the local qualities associated with effective leadership.
- Wherever possible, rooting the mentoring 'story' in the mythology or religious beliefs of the country.
- Considering specific cultural issues, such as how people learn, how people relate to authority, concerns of loss of face, how people connect to the world around them, issues of family, masculinity/femininity, collectivism versus individualism, how people in different cultures cope with ambiguity and risk.

The degree to which a mentoring programme is centralized or decentralized also influences the role of the programme co-ordinator. In the case of a *centralized* mentoring programme, all activities (such as process or goal definition, gaining organizational commitment, identifying and engaging stakeholders, programme administration, budget management, marketing, training and support, review and evaluation, continuous programme development) are developed and handled by a central department, usually by human resources or learning and development. In this scenario, a single programme co-ordinator might be appointed to design, implement and evaluate the programme. In the case of a *decentralized* mentoring programme the key policy decision on the minimum standards and guidance (such as policy definition, definition of operating guidelines, set quality standards and pro formas, agreeing partners, funding, overall marketing, administration, liaison/support to local programmes, limited training delivery, overall review/evaluation, continuous programme development) are made centrally. The implementation of the mentoring programme is executed by a local group or organization, where a local programme co-ordinator with local knowledge might be appointed into the role.

The role and responsibilities of the programme co-ordinator

The role of the programme co-ordinator is to manage the entire scheme including the development of support mechanisms, to act as the main point of contact for all stakeholders within and associated with the scheme, to be the link between the programme and top management and to troubleshoot relationships (Clutterbuck, 2001; Klasen and Clutterbuck, 2002). The duties and responsibilities of the programme co-ordinator will vary slightly between contexts, organizations, the type of programmes and the scope of the programme. Murray (2001, p. 151) sees the nature of the programme co-ordinator role as '*relationship managers who see that the needs of the mentor, protégé and organisation are met*'. She proposes a sample job description for a co-ordination team in a small organization, which includes the tasks of planning and designing the process, creating and executing a communication plan, maintaining a mentor pool, assisting with development goals, negotiating the agreement, conducting group meetings, conducting mentor orientation, conducting protégé orientation and maintaining records.

In Klasen and Clutterbuck's (2002) review of numerous mentoring schemes in the UK and Europe, they found that schemes designate one person, usually in full-time employment, to be responsible for co-ordinating the design and implementation. In larger schemes, the organization is more likely to involve a team. They advise that an implementation team might consist of a programme champion, programme co-ordinator, external consultant or adviser, training and developmental specialist, relationship supervisors, evaluation experts and administration staff. An alternative model might have a single co-ordinator, who draws in the services of other people, normally human resource management staff, to do specific tasks such as: recruitment and selection, media and advertising, participant training and programme evaluation. One way to identify and analyse the role of the programme co-ordinator is to identify each phase of the mentoring programme and consider the responsibilities of the programme co-ordinator specific to each phase. The phases of a typical formal mentoring programme can be divided into three sections: Phase 1, striving for mentoring; Phases 2 and 3, preparation of the implementation proposal and design of the mentoring programme; and Phases 4 and 5, implementation and evaluation of the mentoring programme. Figures 16.1 to 16.3 summarize typical mentoring programme phases, broadly encompassing design, implementation and evaluation. The figures are based on the work of Cranwell-Ward, Bossons and Gover, 2004; Klasen and Clutterbuck, 2002; and Mentoring Programme Co-ordinator Guidelines, CGIAR.

Phase 1: Striving for mentoring

Figure 16.1 outlines Phase 1, striving for mentoring, providing a checklist for the programme co-ordinator. The mentoring programme champion will carry out a comprehensive analysis and provide the appropriate direction for the scheme. Later, very often, the role of the programme champion will evolve into that of the programme co-ordinator. Senior management support is vital, as their attitudes and behaviour are extremely powerful determinants of the evolution of the programme for better or worse.

In this initial phase, the programme co-ordinator will define the 'mentoring' within the context of the organization and identify how it is different from any other types of personal development. This is important because participants and stakeholders need to understand what it is that is different about the learning interventions versus alternative interventions. The specific target group will need to be identified and choices need to be made about the exclusive or inclusive nature of the programme. For example, is the aim of

Figure 16.1 Phase 1 Striving for mentoring

		Shaping initial thoughts
	Step to be taken	Explanation/Notes
1	Definition	Definition of the term 'mentoring' within the context of the organization. How it is different from any other types of personal development?
2	Recipients	Who will the programme be aimed at? Is there any specific target group or is it open to everyone?
3	Type of programme	Definition of the type and model of the programme: • Formal, semi-formal or informal • Centralized or decentralized • Peer mentoring or hierarchical • Is a cross-company mentoring programme appropriate?
4	Keeping on track	Definition of standards for the programme – creating them for the programme or using externally written standards (for example ISMPE)
5	Objectives with clear outcomes	Definition of the objectives and outcomes for the organization as a whole and for all stakeholders. How will mentoring assist in achieving business objectives?
6	Scope of the programme	What will it include and not include? How many pairs will the programme be able to support?

the programme to support women into senior leadership positions? Is the aim of the programme to support black and ethnic minorities and their wider employability? Is the aim of the programme to support early career entrants to address issues concerning retention and attrition? The aim of the programme will often dictate the specific target group, in addition to the organizational objectives and outcomes at the micro and macro level. The programme co-ordinator will need to define the type and model of the scheme. For example, is the scheme formal, semi-formal or informal; centralized or decentralized; peer mentoring or hierarchical?

One of the programme co-ordinator's key steps is to assemble a team of people that will support the design, implementation and evaluation of the scheme. More specifically, the team will prepare the implementation proposal and conduct the necessary research, identifying key stakeholders and gaining organizational commitment, marketing, design and development, maintenance, conclusion and further development and evaluation and review (Hatting et al., 2005).

Phases 2 and 3: Preparation of the implementation proposal and design of the mentoring programme

Phases 2 and 3 involve the preparation of the implementation proposal and design of the mentoring programme. Figure 16.2 outlines

Figure 16.2 Phases 2 and 3 Preparation and design of the proposal

		Planning the mentoring programme
Step to be taken		Explanation/Notes
1	Process mapping	• Stages of the programme • How will people be involved? • How will the programme be reviewed by the programme co-ordinator?
2	Roles and responsibilities	• Create role description for participants (mentors, mentees, administration support, programme co-ordinator, supervisors and volunteers)
3	Marketing	• Prior to implementation, provide organizational members with an overview about the forthcoming programme and invite feedback • Define the programme publication strategy and tools • Gain commitment from volunteers • Provide information about logistical issues: date of the selection process, how to apply, start date of the programme, etc. • Provide the contact details of the implementation team
4	Selecting and recruiting	• Based on role description, define the selection criteria • Recruit the implementation team (the number of staff depends on the number of mentors and mentees) • Define mentee and mentor recruitment and selection approach, including processes and criteria
5	Training	• Clarify financial budget and time allocation • Identify who will be the recipient of training • Design of the training programme; the content determinants are relevance and quality • Identify who will deliver the training (internal and/or external) • Identify the logistics for training delivery
6	Matching mentees and mentors	• Supporting processes and materials might include: • Asking mentors and mentees to indicate their preferences on career experience, age, gender, ethnicity and interest • Mentor and mentee application forms • Learning styles, communication styles and personality questionnaires
7	Mentoring agreements	Written or verbal agreement (depending on the decision of the mentoring pairs) can be useful by outlining and managing expectations

the key steps to be considered by the programme co-ordinator. Embarking on the research campaign, the programme co-ordinator needs to obtain information on the organizational readiness for mentoring, the organizational need for mentoring, the benefits of the mentoring programme and the potential objections and barriers to the programme. The purpose of the research is to evaluate the fit between the organization and the mentoring programme and gather evidence that corroborates the arguments in favour of the programme implementation. The preparatory research provides a framework for design and implementation and enables the programme co-ordinator to evaluate the risk to their reputation associated with pressing ahead with the programme. The notion of alignment is integral to the development of formal mentoring programmes. Baker (2015) identified three types of alignment that account for both individual and organizational factors which have the potential to improve the efficacy of mentorships and the intended outcomes of these relationships. *Vertical* alignment is associated with the connection between people strategy and business goals; *horizontal* alignment is the connection among individual human resource management and development interventions; *implementation* is the degree to which action is taken to put the people strategy into effect. Viewing alignment through multiple lenses in order to consider the extent to which the mentoring programme is aligned to different levels and aspects of the organization is important in the context of design and implementation. Key aspects the programme co-ordinator will need to address in the design and implementation of the proposal include:

1. Identification of the main purpose and the subsidiary objectives of the mentoring programme: why it is needed? What is the aim of the programme? What are the objectives? Who will be the participants – mentees and mentors?
2. Identification of the value of the programme to the business: why should the organization support the programme? What benefits (direct and indirect) does the programme bring to the organization? How will the programme contribute to the business objectives? How will the programme raise the organization's profile in the eyes of the stakeholders? Why is mentoring better suited to addressing the business need than other development approaches? What are the benefits for line managers, mentors and mentees?
3. Identification of the viability of the programme within the company: will the organization be able to sustain the mentoring programme? How will the mentoring programme fit and support the company culture? Will the programme co-ordinator be able to recruit sufficient mentors and mentees?
4. Identification of resources needed to effectively deliver the programme: human, spatial, temporal and material resources needed to design, implement and evaluate the programme; the budget required to cover the expenses associated with the programme.
5. Estimate costs and returns, providing quantitative information on both costs and returns associated with the programme. The difficulty in calculating financial returns varies depending on many factors, for example the objective of the programme, costs saved on any other types of inappropriate development activities, cost saved on recruitment and the enhanced retention of key staff, increased income from sales and productivity gains.
6. Design of the implementation strategy: identification of the timeframe of the programme, the individual stages of design and implementation, communication plan, who will be involved in design and implementation phase, the role of the steering committee, subject experts, advisers, etc.
7. Measurements of objectives: what are the objectives? How are they to be measured? What evaluation criteria will be applied? When will the evaluation take place? What methods will be used?
8. Risk factors and contingency plan: describe a worst case scenario (what could go wrong), what to do to put things right, and how to prevent potential pitfalls from occurring.
9. Recommendations: type of mentoring model, formal or informal programme, the development of a pilot programme, optimum time to launch the programme.

Phases 4 and 5: Implementation and evaluation of the mentoring programme

The final phases involve the implementation and evaluation of the mentoring programme. Figure 16.3 outlines the key steps the programme co-ordinator needs to follow. One of the most important aspects of implementation is the need to be flexible and adaptable. Even with the best laid plans, something will change as dictated by the nature of organizations and context. Nothing is static; the environment within which organizations operate is constantly changing, from both an external and internal perspective. Involving others at every stage, seeking advice and reflecting on feedback and suggestions will facilitate the necessary changes to the original plan (Klasen and Clutterbuck, 2002).

Within Phases 4 and 5, a typical mentoring programme will consist of the following steps:

1 Founding the implementation team (programme champion, programme co-ordinator, external consultant or specialist adviser, training, learning and development team, relationship supervisors, evaluation experts and administration staff).
2 Marketing: providing information and inviting feedback.
3 The statement of strategic objectives and long-range plans, creating a business case for the mentoring programme.
4 Outlining the parameters of the mentoring programme.
5 Drawing up a recruitment plan, selecting and recruiting.
6 Training of mentees and mentors.
7 Matching mentees and mentors.
8 Drawing up mentoring agreements.

Figure 16.3 Phases 4 and 5 Implementation and evaluation of the mentoring programme

	Ensuring a smooth progression	
Step to be taken		Explanation/Notes

1	Implement the mentoring agreement	• Monitor and encourage the mentors and mentees, e.g. answer questions, comment positively on any mentoring you observe, share ideas tried by other pairs, pass on interesting articles, identify and solve problems as they come up
		• Troubleshooting/monitoring relationships (apply 'no-fault opt-out clause' and emphasize it from the very start of the programme). If pair clearly cannot succeed, rematch the participants, using alternatives
		• Practical meeting management
		• Continue to help mentors and mentees improve their skills by:
		  - Organizing or letting participants know of other training events that may be of interest;
		  - Circulating information to participants and observers;
		  - Monitoring the pairs on a regular basis, providing information and encouragement as needed
		• Collect evaluation data on training and general impressions for analysis and programme adjustment

	Closing and evaluating the programme	
Step to be taken		Explanation/Notes
1	Ending the programme	• Work out the best way to say 'goodbye' (formal ending, involve all stakeholders) • Consider mentees and mentors that may wish to continue • Give recognition for involvement
2	Review and evaluation	• Evaluate the programme outcomes and success criteria for the organization and other stakeholders • Identify the value of the programme from a multi-stakeholder perspective
3	Future programme development	• What are the lessons learned for future programme development? • What will change as a result of the learning?

9 Implementing the agreement.
10 Supervising the relationships.
11 Ongoing evaluation of the mentoring programme.

All of the steps outlined above are usually carried out by the mentoring programme co-ordinator in consultation with key organizational stakeholders. For example, the mentoring programme co-ordinator will need to decide who will participate in the scheme; this will not be done in isolation. Several principles may influence this decision, including eligibility criteria, credibility, availability, commitment and motivation. The programme co-ordinator will be responsible for ensuring both mentees and mentors receive the appropriate training to ensure they have the right skills, knowledge and understanding to embark on their mentoring relationship. Often, in the context of training, issues might arise concerning values, power, ownership and responsibility. It is important for the programme co-ordinator to encourage open and honest dialogue within the climate of mutual learning and discovery. This is where learning and development can be maximized by all parties. The matching process is a crucial aspect of programme delivery. The programme co-ordinator will need to decide on the criteria for matching, typically taking into account factors such as mentee and mentor rapport, the balance between similarity and difference and the degree of choice (Megginson et al., 2006). There is no 'perfect' answer; it is important to re-visit the purpose of the scheme as this should permeate through all aspects of the programme, including matching.

A key stage that is often under-estimated is the need to fully evaluate the impact of the programme. The mentoring programme needs some system of ongoing feedback and evaluation in order to know whether the mentoring relationships are functioning effectively and successfully. Clutterbuck (2014) suggests that mentoring measurements fall into four categories: relationship process, programme process, relationship outcomes and programme outcomes. As the mentoring relationship progresses, the programme co-ordinator will want to understand what further support is needed, if any, to support the mentoring relationships. This might consist of skills training or general encouragement to participants. Good practice typically involves a short survey of participants, followed by a review session. At the end of a relationship, assuming that the relationship achieves formal closure, it is useful for both the mentee and mentor to review the learning and progress compared to the original expectations, the lessons learned and how they can be used in future developmental relationships. Assuming the programme specifies an end to the formal mentoring relationship, the outcomes can be measured against the original goals agreed. A mentoring programme co-ordinator recently described the process involved in evaluating her multi-organizational mentoring scheme and the benefits for stakeholders:

> In my experience, the evaluation process is frequently neglected and rarely mapped from the outset of a project. The choice of evaluation approach and tools used is always open to debate. However, from my point of view, as members of the project team, what is beyond question is that the development of an evaluation strategy from the outset enabled the project team to improve the management and delivery of the programme during the second iteration, to enhance the experience of the participants, and in turn capture legitimate evidence of process, progress and impact. These improvements in process and practice were a direct result of constant discussion, reflection and action.

> Questionnaires are helpful in identifying numerical trends and surfacing similarities and differences across the participant group. One to one interviews provide the ideal opportunity to probe participants about their experience and delve more deeply into the complexities of their mentoring relationship. The process of appreciative inquiry illuminated many positive aspects of the project that might not otherwise have been surfaced by other data collection methods. I would argue that without the multi-layered evaluation approach, the project team would not have been able to identify participant, programme and organizational learning.

The skills and competencies of an effective programme co-ordinator

There are a vast number of skills and competencies cited in relation to effective programme co-ordinators; however, there is no definitive list (Klasen and Clutterbuck, 2002). What is presented in this section are some of the key skills and competencies necessary to deliver effective mentoring programmes.

Although not essential, it is beneficial to appoint a programme co-ordinator who has substantial experience of mentoring, ideally having run schemes in a variety of contexts. The role and responsibilities may vary across each scheme and organization. Setting up, sustaining and evaluating a formal mentoring scheme can be an immense task that requires a huge amount of energy, thought, preparation, determination and resilience. Experience is often invaluable in foreseeing potential issues and challenges and being able to act quickly to resolve any problems that might occur over the course of the scheme.

One of the most important roles of the programme co-ordinator is to manage stakeholder needs and expectations. This includes senior management, line managers, mentors, mentees and the programme team, if applicable. Obtaining senior leadership and management buy-in to the scheme is an essential criterion for any formalized mentoring scheme; therefore being able to garner the support of others is crucial. Depending on the organizational climate, this can require a significant level of persuasion, influence and insight. Being able to purposively describe the benefits and potential impact of a scheme is a good starting point. The programme co-ordinator will communicate with each stakeholder on a regular basis at various intervals through different methods. This will require a high level of verbal and written language skills and the ability to produce a range of documentation, albeit assistance may be sought to assist with documentation and template production. Programme co-ordinators are very good at facilitating appropriate communication forums with senior leadership and management to ensure that all organizational stakeholders are making the scheme a priority.

Formal mentoring schemes usually run for a specific period of time; few run for an indefinite period of time. Excellent project management skills are of huge benefit. A typical project manager will be skilled in creating structure using specific tools such as Gantt charts, decision matrices, risk assessments, project control sheets, budget control and finance variation documents, and so on. Clear and transparent structures and tools can help in managing complexity and navigating organizational nuances that may hinder scheme progress. Hand-in-hand with this are great time management skills, keeping abreast of project deliverables, crunch points and other people's time commitments. Delivering projects on time and on budget are two key outcomes from an organizational perspective.

The programme co-ordinator may be responsible for delivering training, preparing mentors and mentees for their roles successfully. If this is the case, knowledge of conceptual models will be important in order to articulate clearly the model applied within the organizational context. A colleague who is a mentoring programme co-ordinator and trainer described a recent experience to me:

> I was asked to deliver a training session to mentors and mentees in an Investment Bank. The client was keen that I emphasized the developmental nature of the mentoring relationships and the ownership needed to be taken by mentees to nurture and grow the relationship. For many of the participants it was their first experience of mentoring in a formal sense. A number of the participants were recent graduate entrants with little theoretical and practical understanding of what differentiates a developmental mentoring relationship from other types of mentoring relationship. This required me to distinguish developmental mentoring from the US-centric sponsorship mentoring approach, in order to illustrate the difference and help participants understand what was expected of them.

The programme co-ordinator will also need to be able to help participants understand their role and responsibilities and what this means from a pragmatic perspective. This might include mentors, mentees *and* mentoring relationship supervisors. Alongside this, mentor and mentee participants will need to understand and, ideally, practise the skills and techniques needed to develop their relationship. This might include skills such as: building rapport; active listening; questioning; giving and receiving feedback; dealing with road blocks and relationship droop; and closing the relationship. A colleague recently described to me the content of her training programme; the overview was as follows:

> All mentors and mentees attend a one-day training event together. At the event we help participants to understand and describe the purpose of the mentoring scheme; understand and articulate the role of the mentor and mentee; identify and develop the skills that are important for successful mentoring relationships; and recognize their behavior and their impact on others, adapting their situational approach.

If the programme co-ordinator does facilitate the training, thorough knowledge of the programme is required, alongside excellent knowledge and skills in training techniques. Training techniques will vary according to the content, approach and style. Being able to adopt a flexible approach to training based on the programme and participant needs is crucial.

Finally, programme co-ordinators may be responsible for the supervision of mentoring relationships. Supervision sometimes requires a high degree of skill in conflict management and counselling. This is very much dependent on each relationship and the degree to which the mentoring dyad is able to 'self-manage' their relationship. Scenario planning is helpful; preparing guidelines for a range of different situations and thinking through the options available is a useful tool in preparing.

Challenges and risks associated with the role of the programme co-ordinator

Programme co-ordinators are often the unsung heroes of mentoring programmes. They promote the programme to participants and corporate sponsors; protect it from the destructive forces of sudden economies and changes of management approach; and maintain the quality of the programme, often on limited budgets. During the implementation and maintenance phases of a mentoring programme, mistakes can be made and problems arise. Since formal mentoring takes place at two levels, the mistakes can be made on the programme level and the relationship level (Klasen and Clutterbuck, 2002). Being aware and alert to potential problems is essential in safeguarding the viability and long-term success of the mentoring programme. The potential challenges and risks at the programme and relationship level might include:

- Planning and preparation: this stage cannot be under-estimated; effective planning and preparation can certainly mitigate any unforeseen challenges and risks. It usually prevents issues such as unclear programme objectives and failure to gain public endorsement and senior management buy-in. Under-resourcing the programme is a common failing.
- Setting objectives and clear measurable outcomes, related to business priorities: in formal mentoring programmes, senior organizational sponsorship is unlikely to be forthcoming if the potential benefits are not clearly identified. The challenge is often in the *quantification* of benefits.
- Selecting and matching mentors and mentees: lack of clear selection criteria both for mentors and mentees can challenge the programme co-ordinator's ability to match effectively. Furthermore, not considering the mentee's preferences and failure to assess the fit between a mentee's needs and the mentor's knowledge and experience are common issues. Using an IT platform means that matching may be carried out between mentees and mentors without programme co-ordinator intuitive guidance, but this may have negative implications for quality of matches and ability of the programme co-ordinator to support relationships.
- Providing appropriate training: in a formal mentoring programme, mentees and mentors are required to fit into their new role quickly. Training supports this process by helping them

to understand their role and providing them with relevant skills and guidelines on managing their relationship. Training, which is relevant and sensitive to all participants, is vital in the preparation phase of a mentoring programme. However, the resources required to train mentees and mentors may be lacking, risking the quality of the relationships.

- Supporting mentees and mentors beyond the initial training to prepare participants for their roles. Regular 'check-ins' and briefing sessions might prove challenging in a resource-strained environment. However, the risk if this does occur is that mentees and mentors experience relationship droop as their focus and energies diminish.
- Encouraging mentors and mentee to establish the purpose of their association and to clarify their mutual expectations: only with a clear focus will discussions be meaningful, motivation maintained and results achieved.
- Ensuring relationships are neither over- nor under-managed: leaving most of the control with the mentee whilst providing gentle guidance. Within the framework of a formal mentoring programme, the individual mentoring pairs should be granted as much freedom as possible.
- Taking action to forestall breaches of confidentiality, as they damage the trust and confidence in all mentoring relationships within the programme, not just the immediate one.
- Poor clarity of the role of the line manager and the mentor: failing to distinguish between the role of the line manager and mentor may lead to confusion and sometimes conflict between mentor and line manager. The challenge is to engage the line manager in the process to gain their support and sponsorship and avoid conflict risks.
- Establishing a clear system for managing the relationships that come to an end. Formally closing a mentoring relationship is vitally important, particularly in relation to the identification of mutual learning. The challenge is encouraging participants to commit to the closing process and fully engage in the learning process. The risk if this stage is missed is that vital learning is overlooked and never fully recognized and articulated.
- Balancing formality and informality. 'The golden rule appears to be: a small dose of formality within the scheme and a large dose of informality in the individual relationship' (Klasen and Clutterbuck, 2002, p. 321).

CASE STUDY REFLECTIONS OF PROGRAMME CO-ORDINATORS

This section explores the experiences, challenges and reflections of two programme managers/co-ordinators responsible for a multi-organizational formal mentoring project.

Public sector developmental mentoring scheme – programme managers: Dr Julie Haddock-Millar and Chris Rigby

Programme outline

The aim of the project (also known as The Public Sector Diversity Mentoring Scheme) was to develop public sector mentors who would support the goal of increased employability for a diverse set of undergraduate student mentees who aspire to a career within the public sector. The unique project addressed the themes of employability and barriers faced by students from black and ethnic minorities (BME) and under-represented socio-economic groups. The key project partners were Middlesex University (MU), FDA (First Division Association) and Liverpool John Moores University (LJMU). The project commenced in 2012 and closed in 2014. The project objectives were as follows:

- Establish and develop a series of mentoring relationships; pairing 50 public sector graduate scheme entrants to mentor undergraduate students from MU (25) and LJMU (25) – 100 participants;
- support the recognition and development of transferable skills in the mentee and mentor group;
- enhance employment opportunities within the mentee group;
- identify and explore the barriers the mentee group face in successfully securing graduate scheme places;
- develop specific recommendations for the teaching and learning/student experience within Higher Education Institutes (HEIs) to support

students from BME and under-represented socio-economic groups relating to future employability;
- enhance learning and development opportunities for public sector mentors and offer the opportunity to utilize and refine existing skills;
- ensure applicants to public sector schemes in the future more closely resemble the community that the public sector serves.

Overall, the project aimed to have a long-term impact for the future employment of students in the public sector and to establish a nationwide relationship between Higher Education Institutions and public sector employers. The impact of the project was threefold. First, the project raised mentees' awareness of the range of career opportunities open to them in the public sector. Second, mentees and mentors had the opportunity to experience different forms of assessment and receive detailed, high-quality feedback on their performance. Third, with the support of their mentors, a significant number of mentees applied for a range of civil service graduate programmes and were successful.

Key learning points
Chris and I had previous experience of mentoring programme management, facilitating mentoring relationships, supporting our own mentees and working with our personal mentors. We were able to bring our varied experience to the programme. As with all projects, there were a number of key lessons along the way, which we summarize below:

1. The importance of establishing a Project Steering Group and regular communication between members of the group outside of planned meetings.
2. The importance of identifying and articulating concisely the strategic drivers for each partner.
3. The value of having a template protocol for processes, in this case *The International Standards for Mentoring Programmes in Employment* (ISMPE).
4. The value of having an external consultant to refer to/draw upon.
5. The critical importance of taking time to understand the culture and practice of partner organizations – this is particularly important in communications, where the same approach is not necessarily as effective for both mentees and mentors.
6. The value of capturing the process, especially the training days, on film, both as a record and as material for dissemination and promotion of future schemes.
7. The benefits of designing a survey tool to capture key data (a) electronically (in this case using Survey Monkey) rather than on paper, and (b) immediately after the training days, rather than playing catch-up later in the scheme.
8. The need to be vigilant and supportive in the early stages of the partnerships as communications are established, plus the need to respond to issues and concerns raised by participants.
9. The need to structure project timelines in sympathy with student and mentor availability and both the academic calendar and the 'policy cycle' for mentors, many of whom work to Ministerial teams and are impacted by the parliamentary timetable.
10. The critical importance of strong relationships within the University (a) at senior levels to act as champions and (b) central services such as Student Communications in order to publicize the schemes. We also found that a focused plan was required to identify appropriate channels and methods of communication to attract and engage students in the project.

In our experience, there are always challenges when several different organizations come together to develop a collaborative and cohesive formal mentoring programme. Perhaps the most powerful lesson learned was to be alert and responsive to the political and cultural sensitivities in a highly bureaucratic environment where protocol and process significantly influence the way in which people behave. This includes all members of the programme team, mentors and mentees. Despite our considerable experience in the fields of mentoring and professional development, there were occasions when we underestimated the influence of the organizational context on the programme processes and protocols. Going forward, we would spend more time understanding multi-stakeholder values, protocols, ways of working and explicit and implicit aims and objectives. This will heighten our ability to foresee potential political and cultural sensitivities and act accordingly.

Professional mentoring scheme (India, an e-mentoring programme) – programme manager: Chandana Sanyal

Programme outline

The aim of the e-mentoring scheme was to enhance students' learning experience and support their personal and career development. The scheme specifically sought to engage postgraduate students as mentees seeking to learn about human resource (HR) practices in an international context and thereby enhancing their global employment opportunities. The mentee participants were from postgraduate programmes such as a Masters in Human Resource Management (HRM), Masters in International HRM and Masters in Business Administration. The scheme recruited mentors who were HR practitioners in multinational organizations in India. Typical titles or roles included Vice President, Human Resources and Executive Vice President, Human Capital, drawn from across diverse sectors including aviation, automotive manufacturing, consulting, construction, manufacturing, IT consultancy services, engineering, telecommunications, social media and pharmaceuticals. These mentors committed to providing up to ten hours of mentoring to one student over a period of 3 to 4 months mainly by telephone, Skype or email and, if and where possible, by face-to-face communication.

Within the framework of the scheme, the mentor–mentee matching was based on personal preferences of industry, sector or previous educational background. To involve the mentors in the matching process, where possible, I offered two profiles of mentees for them to make their choice. I offered adequate opportunity to the mentors to discuss their options with me so that they could make an informed choice. I conducted one-to-one interviews with mentees as a part of the matching process. In supporting the start of the relationship, I provided both mentors and mentees brief pen portraits of each other to help them to develop their relationships. The mentors were supported by online material including a mentor toolkit and the mentees attended a development workshop which focused on the key drivers for the scheme and its structure and processes, including the code of conduct and the skills and behaviours that contribute to a successful mentor–mentee relationship. I ensured that the training material had been received and fully digested/understood by all participants.

Within this formal structure, the individual mentoring pairs were given the freedom to build and develop their relationships (Klasen and Clutterbuck, 2002). I provided monthly support sessions for mentees to help them to plan and structure their sessions to maximize their mentor–mentee conversations. Overall, the programme gave the mentees an opportunity to learn about organizational practices, particularly HR practices in an international context; *83% of the participants* agreed that e-mentoring provided a useful opportunity for learning. Some mentees received opportunities for networking and guidance on career development with options for work experience and placement both in India and the UK from their mentors. However, some mentor–mentee relationships did not progress and several required a high level of guidance and monitoring to move relationships through the 'mentoring phases'.

Key learning points

As the project manager of this programme, a key learning point was to acknowledge the unique character of this mentoring project and its participants. Firstly, this was not an in-house, intra-organizational programme; rather it involved participants from a range of disparate organizations, geographies, cultures and time zones. Secondly, the programme did not feature employee-to-employee relationships, meaning that the partnerships were not aligned and directed to a common organizational goal or performance criteria. Thirdly, unlike in-house programmes, this project was not about organizational knowledge sharing and organizational learning; it had individual mentee employability as its goal. This meant that the mentors needed support and guidance to ensure that the mentees' identified needs were clearly communicated to them so that the mentors could offer appropriate support. Similarly, the mentees needed support to build the confidence to be able to discuss their development issues openly with the mentors. The distance and remoteness between the mentors and mentees made this more challenging. Therefore, management of downtime/offline periods was critical in managing this programme. I had to carefully balance the degree and level of support needed to manage and support both mentors and mentees to develop and build rapport, ensure that the relationship was progressing and that both mentors and mentees were benefiting from the scheme.

CONCLUSION

The role, responsibilities, skills and competencies of the mentoring programme co-ordinator are largely derived from the reflective accounts of those engaged in mentoring programme management. In most situations, mentoring programmes operate in a highly complex, adaptive system, where the system's temporal equilibrium will be influenced both by internal organizational dynamics and the external environmental system (Clutterbuck, 2014). It is the interplay between the different aspects of mentoring programme management that are of particular interest. What is the 'ideal' mix of programme management knowledge and expertise that can help individuals, groups and organizations navigate their way through the intricacies of programme design, implementation and evaluation? To date, mentoring programme evaluation tends to focus on the experiences of the mentee and to a lesser extent the mentor. Going forward, capturing the programme co-ordinator's reflections and observations through a formal process would serve a community of specialists committed to the ongoing development and improvement of mentoring practice.

REFERENCES

Allen, T. D., Eby, L. T., O'Brien, K. E., and Lentz, E. (2008). The state of mentoring research: A qualitative review of current research methods and future research implications. *Journal of Vocational Behavior*, 73(3), 343–357.

Baker, Vicki L. (2015). People Strategy in Human Resources: Lessons for Mentoring in Higher *Education Mentoring and Tutoring: partnership in learning*, 23(1). Retrieved from http://dx.doi.org/10.1080/13611267.2015.1011034 (accessed 3 October, 2016).

Carroll, M. A. and Barnes, E. F. (2015). Strategies for enhancing diverse mentoring relationships in STEM fields. Retrieved from http://ijebcm.brookes.ac.uk/documents/vol13issue1-paper-04.pdf (accessed 3 October, 2016).

Clutterbuck, D. (2001). *Everyone Needs a Mentor – Fostering talent in your organisation*, 3rd edn., Chartered Institute of Personnel and Development (CIPD).

Clutterbuck, D. (2014). *Everyone Needs a Mentor*, 5th edn., Chartered Institute of Personnel and Development (CIPD).

Cranwell-Ward, J., Bossons, P. and Gover, S. (2004). *Mentoring – A Henley Review of Best Practice*. UK: Palgrave Macmillan.

Gibb, S. and Megginson, D. (1993). Inside corporate mentoring schemes: A new agenda of concerns. *Personnel Review*, 22(1), 40–54.

Haddock-Millar, J., Rigby, C., and Clutterbuck, D. (2012). Public sector mentoring scheme: exploring the development and delivery of mentoring programmes through a multi-stakeholder perspective.

Hatting, M., Coetze, M., and Schreuder, D. (2005). Implementing and sustaining mentoring programmes: A review of the application of best practices in the South African organisational context. *SA Journal of Human Resource Management*, *3*(3), 40–48.

ISMPE (2015). *International Standards for Mentoring Programmes in Employment.* Retrieved 14 December 14 2015, from: http://www.ismpe.com/standards.html

Jones, G. E. (1997). Advancement opportunity issues for persons with disabilities. *Human Resource Management Review*, *7*(1), 55–76.

Kim, S. (2007). Learning goal orientation, formal mentoring, and leadership competence in HRD: a conceptual model. *Journal of European Industrial Training*, *31*(3), 181–194.

Klasen, N. and Clutterbuck, D. (2002). *Implementing Mentoring Schemes – A practical guide to successful programs.* Oxford: Butterworth-Heinemann.

Kochan, F. (2013). Analyzing the relationships between culture and mentoring. *Mentoring and Tutoring: Partnership in Learning*, *21*(4), 412–430.

Lansing, J. S. (2003). Complex adaptive systems. *Annual Review of Anthropology*, 183–204.

Megginson, D., Clutterbuck, D., and Garvey, B. (2006). *Mentoring in action: A practical guide.* Great Britain: Kogan Page Publishers.

Mentoring Program Coordinator Guidelines, Consultative Group on International Agricultural Research (CGIAR), Gender and Diversity Mentoring Program (2009). Retrieved 14 December 2015, from: https://library.cgiar.org/bitstream/handle/10947/2746/42A_Mentoring%20Program%20Coordinator%20Guidelines%20_WP.pdf?sequence=1

Mitleton-Kelly, E. (1997). Organisation as co-evolving complex adaptive systems. British Academy of Management Conference, London 8–10 September.

Murray, M. (2001). *Beyond the Myths and Magic of Mentoring: How to Facilitate an Effective Mentoring Process* (New and Revised Edition). San Francisco: Jossey-Bass, John Wiley and Sons, Inc.

Ragins, B. R. and Kram, K. E. (2007). The landscape of mentoring in the 21st century. In B. R. Ragins and Kathy E. Kram (Eds). *The Handbook of Mentoring at Work: Theory, Research, and Practice.* Thousand Oaks, CA: Sage, 659–692.

Sanyal, C. and Rigby, C. (2013). Does e-mentoring work? The effectiveness and challenges of an international professional mentoring scheme. *Mentoring and Tutoring: Partnership in Learning*, 19(2), 139–156.

Waterman, S. and He, Y. (2011). Effects of mentoring programs on new teacher retention: A literature review. *Mentoring and Tutoring: Partnership in Learning*, *19*(2), 139–156.

Yedidia, M. J. and Bickel, J. (2001). Why aren't there more women leaders in academic medicine? The views of clinical department chairs. *Academic Medicine*, *76*(5), 453–465.

Supervision of Mentoring

Rodney K. Goodyear, Tony Rousmaniere and Jeff Zimmerman

SUPERVISION OF MENTORING

A growing international literature has documented the value of mentoring for the personal and professional development of mentees, for the organizations that employ them, and for the quality of the services these mentees provide (Allen et al., 2004; Clutterbuck, 2008; Eby and Lockwood, 2005; Megginson and Stokes, 2004; Tong and Kram, 2013). These effects have been important across many settings and disciplines. Yet mentors too often are left to develop competence for their role through 'example, trial and error, and peer observation' (Pfund et al., 2006, p. 3). This creates the substantial risk that the mentees they serve will receive ineffectual or even harmful mentoring (Burk and Eby, 2010; Eby et al., 2000).

The premise of this chapter is that training and supervision will foster and enhance mentor competence (Garvey and Westlander, 2013) and provide them with essential support. It assumes the transmission of effects depicted in Figure 17.1 (competent supervision of mentors) will have positive effects on those they mentor – and this, in the end, increases quality of service to the clients and organizations those mentees serve. The chapter draws from the small existing literature on mentor supervision as well as the larger psychotherapy supervision literature. To illustrate key points, we will conclude with a case illustration of a systemic mentoring scheme at a hypothetical metropolitan university teaching hospital (MUTH), and a list of recommendations for supervisors and administrators considering developing a similar scheme for their institution.

The supervision we discuss assumes an institutional structure that supports both mentoring and the supervision of mentors. This structure might be provided, for example, within corporations, universities (Keyser et al., 2008), national health systems (Viney and Harris, 2011), or trade associations (Iversen, 2011), as well as in healthcare

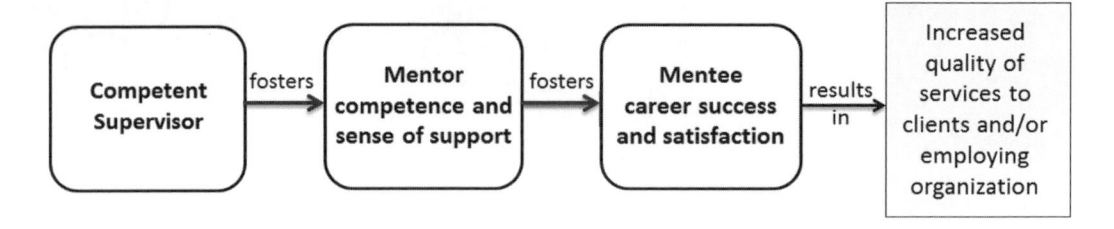

```
┌─────────────┐         ┌─────────────┐         ┌─────────────┐         ┌─────────────┐
│             │         │   Mentor    │         │   Mentee    │         │ Increased   │
│ Competent   │ fosters │ competence  │ fosters │career success│ results │ quality of  │
│ Supervisor  │────────▶│  and sense  │────────▶│and satisfaction│───in──▶│ services to │
│             │         │ of support  │         │             │         │clients and/or│
│             │         │             │         │             │         │ employing   │
└─────────────┘         └─────────────┘         └─────────────┘         │organization │
                                                                         └─────────────┘
```

Figure 17.1 Supervision's proximal and distal effects

practices outside of larger delivery systems. The advantages of working within these structures relates not only to the informational and other resources that this affords supervisors, mentors, and mentees, but also to a culture that helps shape expectations and makes mentoring a normative experience.

It is useful to establish at the outset that mentoring and supervisory relationships are similar to each other in a number of substantive ways. This isomorphism (White and Russell, 1997 [also called *parallel process*], Epstein, 1979) between the two functions is important in that what occurs in supervision of the mentor can often be modeled or otherwise reflected in the mentor's work with mentees. This sometimes can provide insights to the supervisor about what may be occurring between the mentor and mentee as, for example, when a particular relationship dynamic between mentor and mentee is being replicated between supervisor and mentor (Barrett, 2002). Also, it is because of isomorphism that much of what we discuss in this chapter about the purposes and processes of the supervision relationship extends as well to the mentor–mentee relationship.

Supervision to develop mentor competence

Supervision has been characterized both in the helping professions (Proctor, 1986) and in mentoring and coaching (Hawkins and Smith, 2013) as having formative, normative, and restorative purposes. These correspond, respectively, to the Kadushin and Harkness (2014) categories of educational, administrative (including protecting the public) and supportive supervision. In this first section of the chapter, we focus on the formative or educational functions, which foster competence in the person being supervised.

Mentors who have received training for their role have been shown to perform better than those who have not (Pfund et al., 2006). Training can help mentors enhance their skills, levels of professionalism, role identity and awareness, communication skills, and knowledge about the field (Garvey and Alred, 2000; Pfund et al., 2006). All of these are components of competence, which then benefits the mentees with whom the mentors are working. At the very least, mentor competence should help protect against mentoring's negative effects, which Tong and Kram (2013) have termed the 'dark side' of mentoring (p. 223).

These negative effects include mentee dissatisfaction (Allen, 2007), dysfunctional mentoring relationships (Scandura, 1998), mentor–mentee sexual tension (Ragins, 1989), unwarranted mentor credit-taking (Bickel and Rosenthal, 2011; Eby et al., 2004), and even mentor sabotage (Burk and Eby, 2010). Given the parallels that mentoring supervision has with psychotherapy supervision, it is unsurprising that these negative effects are similar to what has been documented to occur as inadequate or harmful supervision (Ellis et al., 2014).

But to help mentors develop and maintain competence requires that their supervisors be competent to supervise. To organize our discussion of the elements of that competence, we use the 'criteria for minimally adequate clinical supervision across disciplines' that Ellis et al. (2014, p. 439) proposed. They were speaking to the regulated work of supervisors of professional counsellors and psychotherapists, but their suggestions apply as well to the less regulated work of mentor supervisors. Specifically, they asserted that the minimally adequate supervisor:

1. Has the proper credentials as defined by the supervisor's discipline or profession;
2. Has the appropriate knowledge of and skills for clinical supervision and an awareness of his or her limitations;
3. Obtains a consent for supervision or uses a supervision contract;
4. Provides a minimum of one hour of face-to-face individual supervision per week;
5. Observes, reviews, or monitors supervisee's (i.e. mentor's) therapy/counseling sessions (or parts thereof);
6. Provides evaluative feedback to the supervisee (i.e. mentor) that is fair, respectful, honest, ongoing, and formal;
7. Promotes and is invested in the supervisee's (i.e. mentor's) welfare, professional growth, and development;
8. Is attentive to multicultural and diversity issues in supervision and in therapy/counseling (mentoring);
9. Maintains supervisee (i.e. mentor) confidentiality (as appropriate); and
10. Is aware of and attentive to the power differential (and boundaries) between the supervisee (i.e. mentor) and supervisor and its effects on the supervisory relationship. (p. 439)

In the sections that follow, we address these competence criteria as they pertain to those who supervise mentors.

Competence in the discipline and in the process of supervising

These first two competence criteria (Ellis et al., 2014) are the twin pillars on which supervisory competence rests, though the latter – competence in the process of supervising – typically bears the greater weight. A supervisor needs to know enough about the mentor's discipline to be credible and to anticipate issues that will come up in mentoring. But the greater emphasis is on competencies related to the supervisory process.

In light of our earlier observations about isomorphism, we would note that similar pillars of competence undergird the work of the mentors they supervise as well (i.e. competence in both their discipline and in mentoring). In this case, though, the pillars bear the weight more equally: mentors need competence in mentoring, but disciplinary competence is the content and focus of that mentoring.

Beginning with a supervision contract

A contract between supervisor and mentor provides an important mechanism for clarifying expectations that each party has for the other and the obligations of each. Although a written document is generally preferable because of the clarity it affords, supervision contracts can also be verbal. But whether it is oral or written, the contract negotiated at the outset of the supervision relationship provides the opportunity for a structured conversation about the tasks, methods, and goals of supervision.

Osborn and Davis (1996) recommended that a supervision contract speak to: (a) the purposes, goals, and objectives of supervision, (b) where, when, and how supervision will be done, (c) the methods of evaluation in supervision (which is more pertinent in some contexts than others), (d) the duties and responsibilities of the supervisor and person being supervised, (e) procedural considerations, including backup or emergency communication methods should that become necessary, and (f) a disclosure of the supervisor's scope of practice and areas of competency. In addition, Bernard and Goodyear (2014) suggest that the contract speak to the limits and scope of confidentiality, including what communication may be shared with superiors.

As an extension to the contracting process, supervisors might also engage in a role induction process (Bahrick et al., 1991), directly instructing the mentor about what will occur in supervision. As part of this process, it can be helpful for the supervisor to inquire about the mentor's previous experiences in supervision, as those may well prime the mentor to have positive or negative expectations regarding the new supervision.

In addition, role induction can be as important – and perhaps more so – for mentors to employ with mentees, who will vary in the expectations they bring to the mentoring process. When used to clarify those expectations, role induction can have a facilitative role in more quickly establishing an effective mentor–mentee relationship.

Specified times to meet

Ellis et al. (2014) suggest that supervision of mental health professionals should occur for at least one hour per week. However, specifying a particular schedule for the supervision of mentors may or may not make sense, depending on the nature of their work together and the context in which it occurs. For example, in many instances supervision occurs when the mentor experiences issues with which she or he would like help. And often mentoring supervision occurs in a group context, which would have a particular schedule. In any case, the frequency and length of supervision sessions should be discussed at the outset of the relationship and then honored by both parties.

Observes or otherwise monitors sessions

Psychotherapy supervisors rely primarily on trainee self-report (Noelle, 2002) and it is our impression that this is also the dominant source of 'data' in the supervision–mentoring context. We are not advocating that supervisors of mentors shift completely away from relying on mentor self-report, but we do want to address its limitations. In particular: regardless of how well-intentioned the person who is supervised or mentored, she or he can never capture in a self-report all the detail and contextual complexities of a situation for which they are seeking supervisory help, and will selectively remember details. Moreover, those who are being supervised inevitably make the deliberate choice not to report information (Ladany et al., 1996; Mehr et al., 2010). Therefore, to the extent that supervisors can get audio or even video recordings of mentor–mentee interactions, they will be able to provide more accurate and specific feedback to the mentors they are supervising.

Provides evaluative feedback

Feedback identifies discrepancies between a person's performance and that which is desired (Hattie and Timperley, 2007). This is meaningful in the supervision of mentors, though only to the extent that both supervisor and mentor are clear on what those desired mentoring behaviors are. There are a number of possible criteria that supervisor and mentor might choose to employ for this purpose. For example, Scandura and Viator (1994) found that mentoring has the three separate functions of career development, social support, and role modeling, and Johnson (2003) has suggested that the three types of abilities involved in mentoring to achieve these purposes are cognitive, emotional, and relational. These provide broad performance targets. Moreover, mentor supervision will likely be aided by the more recent measures, such as those of Fleming et al. (2013), that have been developed to better operationalize mentoring competence. Regardless of which framework or measure is used, though, feedback will be effective only insofar as the mentor is clear about it and the resulting performance goals.

Substantial literature now documents that continuous performance feedback is essential for skill acquisition (Ericsson, 1996, 2006). Thus, supervisors should use feedback (also known as formative evaluation) liberally, throughout the supervision process. Summative evaluation is, on the other hand, the assessment of a mentor's work or capabilities that is usually given at the completion of the supervisory process. Depending on the organizational context in which it occurs, it can have real occupational consequences for the person. Even in settings where that is not the case, evaluation can be threatening and so should be discussed openly, beginning with the development of the initial contract. To the extent that it is left unaddressed, the anxiety about the summative evaluation may increase supervisee non-disclosure or even cause supervisees harm.

Bernard and Goodyear (2014) described 'favorable conditions for evaluation' that may help inform models for evaluation in supervision of mentors. Among those was to remember that supervision is an unequal relationship and that it is natural for the person being supervised to feel exposed and therefore defensive during evaluations. They also remind us that evaluation should be mutual so that the mentor also has the opportunity to provide evaluative feedback to the supervisor.

Promotes the mentor's welfare, professional growth, and development

This criterion addresses both intent and capacity. In the case of mentor supervision, we assume appropriate intent. At issue is the capacity to promote mentors' welfare, professional growth, and development. That is, the mentor's competence is essential. This is a major focus of this chapter.

Attentiveness to multicultural and diversity issues

Members of every supervisor–mentor dyad will differ from one another on one or more demographic variables (e.g. race, ethnicity, class, sexual orientation, religion, gender, age). Similarly, each member of the dyad may also have stereotypic concepts about others that may be prejudicial and that affect the supervision. As a result, supervisors should consider themselves, as always, engaging in multicultural supervision.

These differences can have an even more pronounced effect on supervision if the mentor is from a marginalized or under-represented population. Sue et al. (1992) proposed a conceptual framework for cross-cultural counseling competencies that emphasize '(a) counselor awareness of own assumptions, values, and biases; and (b) understanding the worldview of the culturally different client' (p. 481). Because it can be difficult sometimes to discuss racial and other differences, sometimes termed 'difficult dialogues' (Toporek and Worthington, 2014), supervisors may be tempted to avoid those conversations. It is important, though, that supervisors signal their receptiveness to those discussions by initiating them at the very outset of the relationship and then being attentive to opportunities to do so throughout their work together with the mentor.

But in addition to their responsibility to work effectively with diversity within the supervisory relationship, supervisors are also responsible for helping the mentors they supervise to negotiate differences between themselves and their mentees. Many women and mentees of color believe that having a mentor of the same gender or race is important (Blake-Beard et al., 2011), but in instances where that it not possible, it is important that supervisors be able to help ensure that the mentors are offering the best and most appropriate services.

Attentiveness to power differences

In some mentoring relationships, the mentor can have greater power than the mentee, especially when the mentor has an evaluative or monitoring role (though not in the case of developmental mentoring or in reverse mentoring). These power differentials can also exist in the supervisor–mentor relationship. In fact, this power may have an even greater impact if the mentor's long-term employment (as opposed to a short-term training opportunity) may be affected by the supervisor's evaluations. These power differences speak to the importance of the empowered member of the dyad not only developing a collaborative relationship, but also openly discussing power differentials and having mechanisms for managing the interpersonal conflicts that occur between supervisor and mentor and between mentor and mentee.

Research from clinical supervision suggests that achieving collaboration in hierarchical relationships may be challenging, and especially so in relationships wherein the supervisor has formal (or even informal) evaluative responsibilities (Rousmaniere and Ellis, 2013). This challenge may be exacerbated by non-disclosure from the person being supervised, a phenomenon to which we allude earlier in the chapter. Non-disclosure has been found to be commonplace in data from multiple studies of clinical supervision (Mehr et al., 2010). In one study, 97% of psychology supervisees reported non-disclosure of important material in supervision, such as negative reactions to supervisors and clinical mistakes (Ladany et al., 1996). Therefore, supervisors are recommended to solicit feedback from mentors on a regular basis and maintain an open dialogue with the mentors they supervise about the goals and tasks of supervision, and the quality of the supervisory relationship.

Maintains confidentiality as appropriate

Mentoring can be successful only to the extent that the mentor is perceived as trustworthy. The same is true with respect to the supervision of those who mentor. Trustworthiness, in turn, depends on the extent to which the person being mentored or being supervised has confidence that the disclosure of information discussed will not be shared with others. Depending on the particular context, it is possible that there could be instances in which the supervisor (or the mentor) cannot assure complete confidentiality. If this is the case, then the circumstances under which there would be exceptions need to be made clear at the outset of the relationship, during the contracting period.

OTHER CONSIDERATIONS FOR THE SUPERVISOR

The previous section considered ways in which supervisors might demonstrate competence in their work with mentors. There are four additional considerations that are important to address. These are, in turn, the restorative function of supervision, the particular methods the supervisor might use, ethical considerations, and the importance of the supervisory alliance.

Supervision's restorative function

We have so far focused on supervision primarily as a means to foster mentor competence. But supervision also serves an important, 'restorative' function (Hawkins and Smith, 2013; Proctor, 1986, 2001) in that it can help mentors deal with stressors and maintain a sense of well-being. Lunsford et al. (2013) have documented, for example, that in addition to its rewarding aspects mentoring also has costs. These include psychosocial (burnout, anger, grief, loss) and career costs (reputational, especially in the case of mentees with poor performance records, and productivity). An effective supervisory relationship provides both a reflective space and a safe haven for the mentor to not only process these costs, but to obtain needed emotional support from the supervisors.

Methods of mentor supervision

Supervisors can use a variety of modalities and methods, including individual meetings with the mentors they supervise, group meetings, didactic lectures, workshops or 'intensives', assigning reading, and role plays (Garvey and Westlander, 2013; Mead et al., 1999). The duration of mentor supervision varies as widely as the methods. It can occur for a single session, a few sessions, or for a year or longer (e.g. Mead et al., 1999). Mentor supervisors and organizations should consider the goals for supervision, and structure the supervision timeline accordingly. If the goal of supervision is, for example, to help beginning mentors develop skills and professionalization and to monitor the quality of their work, then supervision should continue over a sufficiently long period in order to provide sufficient time for continuous performance observation and feedback (i.e. six to 12 months). If, on the other hand, the goal of supervision is to teach a relatively limited set of new concepts (i.e. how to help mentors with new laws or regulations), then a few hours of supervision may be sufficient.

One important factor to consider is that the supervisory working alliance takes time to build, and thus will not be strong for short-term supervision. This may be workable for limited knowledge acquisition, but will probably not be sufficient for skill acquisition or professionalization, as the process of continuous performance feedback is emotionally challenging for most who are supervised, and thus requires a strong supervisory working alliance that is built over time (Bernard and Goodyear, 2014).

The supervisory working alliance

Although there are varying perspectives in the literature regarding models of mentor development, there is widespread agreement that a high-quality supervisor–mentor relationship is essential for effective practice. For example, Barrett's (2002) model for mentor development assumes 'a relationship based on integrity, authenticity, and trust' (p. 282).

Megginson and Stokes (2004) report that the mentor literature often refers to supervisors with a familial tone, as a 'grandfather relationship' (p. 101). This finding closely mirrors the data from decades of research on psychotherapy supervision, showing that the supervisory relationship, termed the 'supervisory working alliance' (Bordin, 1983) is highly associated with effective clinical supervision (Bernard and Goodyear, 2014).

It is within the context of this supervisory alliance that the supervisor can also help the mentors develop and maintain effective learning alliances (Clutterbuck, 1998) with mentees. That is, the effectiveness of the work that the supervisor and mentor are able to accomplish together will affect the work that the mentor and mentee accomplish.

Bordin's (1979, 1983) conception of the working alliance involves three elements: agreement between the parties on what they are going to do (goals) and how they will do it (tasks), and then the relationship (bond) that develops between them as they engage in these tasks in pursuit of these goals. This speaks at least in part to the importance establishing that clarity of purpose that the supervision contract discussed above provides. It also, of course, speaks to the importance of the supervisor's trustworthiness that will enable the bond with the mentor to develop.

Ethics and professionalism

Supervisors are responsible both for demonstrating professionalism and for helping to foster it in the mentors they supervise. Key features of that professionalism include both comportment and an internalized sense of responsibility or accountability (Goodyear, 2015; Grus and Kaslow, 2014). That responsibility extends to behaving professionally.

Each of the many professions in which mentoring occurs will have its own ethical codes (often also varying somewhat by the country in which their professional organization is housed). There are, though, core moral principles that are foundational to virtually all of them (Beauchamp and Childress, 2001) and these have practical implications for supervisors of mentors. Although space prohibits a full discussion, we will note two of them. One is fidelity, which concerns dedication and trustworthiness to the person with whom we are working. In a mentoring context, this means, for example, not taking inappropriate personal credit for that person's work (Bickel and Rosenthal, 2011) and living up to agreements. The other, which is perhaps foremost among those core moral principles, is that of non-maleficence, refraining from doing harm, which is the principle being invoked in the Hippocratic Oath. Although this principle can be enacted in many ways, one is to avoid harmful dual relationships and perhaps the one that has received the most attention in the mentoring literature is sexual or romantic relationships (Barnett, 2008). Supervisors are responsible both for being vigilant for boundary crossings in their own relationships with the mentors they supervise *and* for helping mentors manage situations that have the risk for dual relationships with mentees.

The supervisor has two responsibilities with respect to professionalism and ethics. The first concerns his or her own behavior; the second concerns helping the mentor to behave ethically and with professionalism. This help can occur during discussions between the supervisor and mentor and also through the role modeling that the supervisor provides.

In the section that follows, we illustrate how some of the key points in this chapter might apply in practice. We then conclude the chapter with a summary and recommendations for mentor supervisors.

A CASE ILLUSTRATION

The case example we use is developed as a composite of a number of real-life examples. The setting is the large Metropolitan University Teaching Hospital (MUTH) serving a multi-culturally diverse community. MUTH has an equally diverse and multi-cultural staff of senior academicians and professionals (supervisors), more junior on-site and adjunct faculty (mentors), and residents and interns. Administratively the hospital is divided into separate departments often designated by medical specialty area (Emergency Medicine, Family Medicine, Surgery, Psychiatry, etc.). Each department has a Chief of Service and is essentially its own budgetary business center, managing delivery of care, personnel, and its own budget.

We will first look at MUTH from a systemic perspective, examining its need for cultural consistency across supervision and mentoring philosophy and practice. We will discuss the training MUTH provides so that the organization can build its core strengths in this area. We will then move to a more granular perspective, examining some of the key relationship challenges among various participants at different levels in the system.

Systemic challenges

One of the most consistent features in this organization is the diversity and variability of the individuals who compose the entire constellation of stakeholders, staff, trainees, and recipients of services. The diversity is not simply in terms of multi-cultural factors, but also permeates the agendas and *raison d'être* of the individuals involved. For example, each Chief of Service is focused on strengthening his/her department within the institution. They have prestige and power associated with their positions. Often their direct reports serve as supervisors to the mentors.

The supervisors all have major clinical responsibilities, often running programs within the Department. As such, they oversee the work of the more junior staff; people focused on securing their own place in the organization. These staff members mentor the interns and residents, who view themselves as affiliated but not permanent members of the staff. When we multiply these different vantage points and situational agendas by the natural competitiveness within the MUTH system, and then by the diversity across staff, residents, and interns, given their multi-cultural experiences as well as their very varied professional training programs outside of the MUTH system, we see an exponential rise in systemic dynamics and complexity.

However, the MUTH Board of Trustees and senior administrative team, professional organizations, and community of service recipients apply a set of expectations and values that need to permeate the system at large. These include, but are not limited to, the following: a) providing high-quality services to the community at large regardless of ability to pay, diagnosis, education, cultural background, language barriers, disability, etc., b) maintaining the highest standards around safe practice for providers and recipients of care, c) avoiding complex dual relationships, d) interacting in culturally competent ways with staff and service recipients, and e) providing appropriate and timely documentation for clinical service delivery and financial reimbursement.

Systemic infrastructure and training

MUTH has recognized the systemic challenges it faces. In response, it has implemented a training committee chaired by the Executive Vice President of its Medical Staff. The training committee (TC) has worked at identifying the core components of supervision and mentoring, as it believes that these are primary vehicles available for building any sense of organizational consistency to address the global expectations and values mentioned above. The TC has two primary initiatives. One is to train supervisors and the other is to train mentors. The intention here is to provide basic and ongoing training and skill development so there is this level of consistency and continuity across departments and throughout the organization.

One of the few inter-departmental activities that occur is the training of supervisors and mentors. In these meetings, department-specific initiatives are not on display and are not in competition with one another. Participants in the training are purposefully taken out of their cultural comfort zones and required to sit and work with members of other departments so as to build relationships and foster more organizational consistency.

Focus on relationships

Each of the training events for supervisors and mentors focuses on the values and expectations of MUTH. Supervisors are also taught to be keenly aware of the power they hold over the mentors. They are taught to respect this power, to provide a safe environment for the mentors, and to be sensitive to the trickle-down effects that can occur if they were to provide an unsafe environment. Compared to the more senior staff members who supervise, the mentors feel more insecure. They are newer to the field and generally do not have the seniority, power base, or tenure in the system.

Most mentees will be moving on to other settings after they complete their training; the mentors are trying to establish their own longevity with MUTH. The supervisors communicate with the Chief of Service and have an impact over mentors' job security and compensation. Yet, the mentors are also the conduits of information down the organizational chart to the mentees as well as up to the supervisors. If mentors convey or promote anxiety in the mentees this stress is likely to be passed on to the recipients of services. If the mentors do not feel safe, they will not openly discuss organizational issues and needs with the supervisors and will not look for input on mentoring particularly challenging mentees.

Mentors are trained in skills of listening, avoiding excessive autocratic mentoring, and how to foster growth and development of their mentees. They are taught to provide learning opportunities and an atmosphere of encouraged questioning to reduce ignorance and expand learning and skill development. Similar to the supervisors, they need the mentees to freely ask questions in order to promote professional skill development and continue to further the values and expectations of the organization.

Mentors and supervisors also need to be skilled in helping deal with transference/ relationship issues that develop between the mentors and mentees, as mentees may be dissatisfied with or feel uncomfortable with the direction and recommendations posed by mentors. Supervisors need to help mentors negotiate these potential minefields so that they can intervene with mentees in a supportive manner that is aligned with MUTH's values and mission.

For example, if a mentee is making comments that show a particular lack of multicultural sensitivity and awareness, the mentor needs to respond in a way that simultaneously is clear and also unlikely to elicit mentee anger or defensiveness. In so doing, the mentor needs to know that she or he has the support and backup of the supervisor in addressing this mentee need. This support can take the form of training in best practices for addressing this with the mentee (e.g. frank discussion, role plays, formal training, etc.).

In short, supervision and mentoring permeate the MUTH system. MUTH needs to have a sustained focus that broadly addresses this systemic element, supports the supervision and mentoring on the local (departmental and supervisory) level, and then channels it down to the specific mentor/mentee relationships.

We believe it essential that when constructing supervisory and mentoring practices each organization needs to do so taking into account its complex systemic forces and aligning them with the organization's culture and mission throughout the different levels of the institution.

CONCLUSION

This chapter focused on competent supervision of mentors. Figure 17.1 illustrates that supervisor competence is in the service of providing support for and increasing competence of the mentors (and decreasing the likelihood of negative or harmful mentoring). This, in turn, should increase (a) mentee career success and satisfaction, and (b) quality of service to clients or the employing organization.

We drew from the work of Ellis et al. (2014) to suggest some of the criteria that define adequate supervision of mentors. Among those were the importance of: (a) having the necessary skills to supervise; (b) using a supervision contract with the mentor, even if it is only in the form of a verbal agreement about respective roles and responsibilities; (c) providing the mentor with clear and ongoing evaluative feedback; (d) attending to issues of diversity in all its forms and helping the mentor do the same; (d) maintaining confidentiality as appropriate, and (d) maintaining an overall stance of promoting the mentor's development and welfare.

We noted that supervisors employ various methods (e.g. didactic lectures, workshops, role plays) and modalities (e.g. individual or group supervision) and that their interactions with mentors can vary significantly in frequency and duration. The supervisor's decisions about methods, modalities, duration, and frequency will all be affected by the goals of supervision. Whatever the form, though, successful supervision depends on an effective working alliance based on mutual trust as well as shared goals and expectations.

Finally, we discussed the supervisor's two responsibilities with respect to ethics and professionalism: the first concerns his or her own behavior and comportment; the latter concerns helping the mentor to behave ethically and professionally. We focused particularly on the moral principles of fidelity and non-maleficence (doing no harm). The former includes living up to agreements and not taking credit for another's work. The latter includes avoiding harmful dual relationships, especially those of a romantic or sexual nature.

REFERENCES

Allen, T. D. (2007). Mentoring relationships from the perspective of the mentor. In B.R. Ragins, and K.E. Kram (Eds.), *The Handbook of Mentoring at Work: Theory, research, and practice* (pp. 123–148). Thousand Oaks, CA: Sage.

Allen, T. D., Eby, L. T., Poteet, M. L., Lentz, E., and Lima, L. (2004). Career benefits associated with mentoring for protégés: A meta-analysis. *Journal of Applied Psychology*, *89*(1), 127–136.

Bahrick, A. S., Russell, R. K., and Salmi, S. W. (1991). The effects of role induction on trainees' perceptions of supervision. *Journal of Counseling and Development*, *69*(5), 434–438.

Barnett, J. E. (2008). Mentoring, boundaries, and multiple relationships: Opportunities and challenges. *Mentoring and Tutoring: Partnership in Learning*, *16*(1), 3–16.

Barrett, R. (2002). Mentor supervision and development-exploration of lived experience. *Career Development International*, *7*(5), 279–283.

Beauchamp, T. L., and Childress, J. F. (2001). *Principles of biomedical ethics*. New York, NY: Oxford University Press.

Bernard, J. M., and Goodyear, R. K. (2014). *Fundamentals of clinical supervision* (5th ed.). Needham Heights, MA: Allyn and Bacon.

Bickel, J., and Rosenthal, S. L. (2011). Difficult issues in mentoring: Recommendations on making the 'undiscussable' discussable. *Academic Medicine*, *86*(10), 1229–1234.

Blake-Beard, S., Bayne, M. L., Crosby, F. J., and Muller, C. B. (2011). Matching by race and gender in mentoring relationships: Keeping our eyes on the prize. *Journal of Social Issues*, *67*(3), 622–643.

Bordin, E. S. (1979). The generalizability of the psychoanalytic concept of the working alliance. *Psychotherapy: Theory, research & practice*, *16*(3), 252–260.

Bordin, E. S. (1983). A working alliance based model of supervision. *The Counseling Psychologist*, *11*, 35–42. doi:10.1177/0011000083111007.

Burk, H. G., and Eby, L. T. (2010). What keeps people in mentoring relationships when bad things happen? A field study from the protégé's perspective. *Journal of Vocational Behavior*, *77*(3), 437–446.

Clutterbuck, D. (1998). *Learning alliances: Tapping into talent*. London, England: CIPD Publishing.

Clutterbuck, D. (2008). What's happening in coaching and mentoring? And what is the difference between them? *Development and Learning in Organizations*, *22*(4), 8–10. doi: 10.1108/14777280810886364.

Eby, L. T., and Lockwood, A. (2005). Protégés' and mentors' reactions to participating in formal mentoring programs: A qualitative investigation. *Journal of Vocational Behavior*, *67*(3), 441–458.

Eby, L. T., Butts, M., Lockwood, A., and Simon, S. A. (2004). Protégés' negative mentoring experiences: Construct development and nomological validation. *Personnel Psychology*, *57*, 411–447.

Eby, L. T., McManus, S. E., Simon, S. A., and Russell, J. E. (2000). The protégé's perspective regarding negative mentoring experiences: The development of a taxonomy. *Journal of Vocational Behavior*, *57*(1), 1–21.

Ellis, M. V., Berger, L., Hanus, A. E., Ayala, E. E., Swords, B. A., and Siembor, M. (2014). Inadequate and harmful clinical supervision: Testing a revised framework and assessing occurrence. *The Counseling Psychologist*, 42, 434–472.

Epstein, L. (1979). Collusive selective inattention to the negative impact of the supervisory interaction. *Contemporary Psychoanalysis*, 22, 389–409.

Ericsson, K. A. (1996). The acquisition of expert performance: An introduction to some of the issues. In K. A. Ericsson (Ed.), *The road to excellence: The acquisition of expert performance in the arts and sciences, sports, and games* (pp. 1–50). Mahwah, NJ: Erlbaum.

Ericsson, K. A. (2006). The influence of experience and deliberate practice on the development of superior expert performance. In K. A. Ericsson, N. Charness, P. J. Feltovich, and R. R. Hoffman (Eds.), *The Cambridge handbook of expertise and expert performance* (pp. 683–703). Cambridge, UK: Cambridge University Press.

Fleming, M., House, M. S., Shewakramani, M. V., Yu, L., Garbutt, J., McGee, R., Kroenke, K., Abenin, Z., and Rubio, D. M. (2013). The mentoring competency assessment: Validation of a new instrument to evaluate skills of research mentors. *Academic Medicine: Journal of The Association Of American Medical Colleges*, 88(7), 1002–1008.

Garvey, B., and Alred, G. (2000). Educating mentors. *Mentoring and Tutoring*, 8(2), 113–126.

Garvey, R., and Westlander, G. (2013). Training Mentors – behaviors which bring positive outcomes in mentoring. In J. Passmore, D. Peterson, and T. Freire (Eds.), *The Wiley-Blackwell handbook of the psychology of coaching and mentoring* (pp. 243–265). New York, NY: John Wiley and Sons.

Goodyear, R. K. (2015). Using accountability mechanisms more intentionally: A framework and its implications for training professional psychologists. *American Psychologist*, 70, 736–743.

Grus, C. L., and Kaslow, N. J. (2014). Professionalism: Professional values and attitudes in psychology. In W. B. Johnson, and N. J. Kaslow (Eds.), *Oxford handbook of education and training in professional psychology* (pp. 491–509). New York, NY: Oxford University Press.

Hattie, J., and Timperley, H. (2007). The power of feedback. *Review of Educational Research*, 77(1), 81–112.

Hawkins, P., and Smith, N. (2013). *Coaching, mentoring, and organizational consultancy: Supervision and development* (2nd ed.). Maidenhead: Open University Press/McGraw Hill.

Iversen, E. (2011). Mentoring supervision with the Danish association of lawyers and economists. In T. Bachkirova, P. Jackson, and D. Clutterbuck (Eds.), *Coaching and mentoring supervision theory and practice* (pp. 258–264). Berkshire, England: Open University Press.

Johnson, W. B. (2003). A framework for conceptualizing competence to mentor. *Ethics and Behavior*, 13(2), 127–151.

Kadushin, A., and Harkness, D. (2014). *Supervision in social work*. NY: Columbia University Press.

Keyser, D. J., Lakoski, J. M., Lara-Cinisomo, S., Schultz, D. J., Williams, V. L., Zellers, D. F., and Pincus, H. A. (2008). Advancing institutional efforts to support research mentorship: A conceptual framework and self-assessment tool. *Academic Medicine*, 83(3), 217–225.

Kram, K. E. (1983). Phases of the mentor relationship. *Academy of Management Journal*, 26(4), 608–625.

Ladany, N., Hill, C., Corbett, M. M., and Nutt, E. A. (1996). Nature, extent, and importance of what psychotherapy trainees do not disclose to their supervisors. *Journal of Counseling Psychology*, 43, 10–24. doi:10.1037/0022-0167.43.1.10.

Lunsford, L. G., Baker, V., Griffin, K. A., and Johnson, W. B. (2013). Mentoring: A typology of costs for higher education faculty. *Mentoring and Tutoring: Partnership in Learning*, 21(2), 126–149.

Mead, G., Campbell, J., and Milan, M. (1999). Mentor and Athene: Supervising professional coaches and mentors. *Career Development International*, 4(5), 283–290. doi:10.1108/13620439910279770.

Megginson, D., and Stokes, P. (2004). Development and supervision for mentors. In *The Situational Mentor: An International Review of Competences and Capabilities in Mentoring*, pp. 94–107. Burlington, VT: Gower.

Mehr, K. E., Ladany, N., and Caskie, G. I. L. (2010). Trainee nondisclosure in supervision: What are they not telling you? *Counselling* and *Psychotherapy Research*, *10*, 103–113. doi:10.1080/14733141003712301.

Noelle, M. (2002). Self-report in supervision: Positive and negative slants. *The Clinical Supervisor*, *21*, 125–134.

Osborn, C. J., and Davis, T. E. (1996). The supervision contract: Making it perfectly clear. *The Clinical Supervisor*, *14*(2), 121–134.

Pfund, C., Pribbenow, C. M., Branchaw, J., Miller Lauffer, J., and Handelsman, J. (2006). The merits of training mentors. *Science*, *311*, 473–474.

Proctor, B. (1986). Supervision: A co-operative exercise in accountability. In A. Marken, and M. Payne (Eds.), *Enabling and ensuring: Supervision in practice*. Leicester National Youth Bureau/Council for Education and Training in Youth and Community Work.

Proctor, B. (2001). Training for the supervision alliance: Attitude, skills and intention. In T. Butterworth, J. R. Cutcliffe, and B. Proctor (Eds.), *Fundamental themes in clinical supervision*, pp. 25–46. New York, NY: Routledge.

Ragins, B. R. (1989). Barriers to mentoring: The female manager's dilemma. *Human Relations*, *42*(1), 1–22.

Rousmaniere, T. G., and Ellis, M. V. (2013). Developing the construct and measure of collaborative clinical supervision: The supervisee's perspective. *Training and Education in Professional Psychology*, *7*(4), 300–308.

Scandura, T. A. (1998). Dysfunctional mentoring relationships and outcomes. *Journal of Management*, *24*, 449–467.

Scandura, T. A., and Viator, R. E. (1994). Mentoring in public accounting firms: An analysis of mentor-protégé relationships, mentorship functions, and protégé turnover intentions. *Accounting, Organizations and Society*, *19*(8), 717–734.

Sue, D. W., Arredondo, P., and McDavis, R. J. (1992). Multicultural counseling competencies and standards: A call to the profession. *Journal of Counseling and Development*, *70*(4), 477–486.

Tong, C., and Kram, K. E. (2013). The efficacy of mentoring – the benefits for mentees, mentors, and organizations. In J. Passmore, D. B. Peterson, and T. Freire (Eds.), *The Wiley-Blackwell Handbook of the Psychology of Coaching and Mentoring*, pp. 217–242. Malden, MA: Wiley-Blackwell.

Toporek, R. L., and Worthington, R. L. (2014). Integrating service learning and difficult dialogues pedagogy to advance social justice training. *The Counseling Psychologist*, *42*, 919–945. doi:10.1177/0011000014545090.

Viney, R., and Harris, D. (2011). Mentoring supervision in the NHS. In T. Bachkirova, P. Jackson, and D. Clutterbuck (Eds.), *Coaching and mentoring supervision theory and practice*, pp. 251–257. Berkshire, England: Open University Press.

White, M. B., and Russell, C. S. (1997). Examining the multifaceted notion of isomorphism in marriage and family therapy supervision: A quest for conceptual clarity. *Journal of Marital and Family Therapy*, *23*(3), 315–333.

Keeping Emotions IN It: Emotionally Intelligent Mentoring

Rose Opengart and Laura Bierema

Most of us have heard the phrase 'Let's keep our emotions OUT of it' during potentially heated discussions, tense meetings, or disagreements. Yet, emotions are important barometers of the social exchange and context, and the ability to express, manage, and gauge emotions is an important interpersonal skill, particularly in mentoring relationships. What might happen if we were more accepting and attuned to our emotions in mentoring relationships?

Developmental relationships such as mentoring can enhance an individual's development. Traditionally, mentoring is a relationship between a more experienced individual (the mentor) and a less experienced individual (the protégé) (Kram, 1980). Mentoring involves close interpersonal interactions that focus on the protégé's career options and progress in the early, middle, or later career years, or it may be focused on the protégé's personal growth and development. An important aspect within this relationship is the emotional intelligence of both the parties involved.

An individual's abilities with interpersonal skills and sharing emotions is related to learning and success in mentoring (Kram, 1985; Liu et al., 2011). Interpersonal and social skills and the ability to express and manage emotions relate to the characteristics originally defined by Salovey and Mayer (1990) and Bar-On (1997) as emotional intelligence (EI). Emotional intelligence is defined as the ability to monitor and manage emotions successfully in interpersonal situations. Emotions shape social interactions (Fineman, 1993), and thus a process such as mentoring, which has interpersonal and social interaction as foundational activities, should be analyzed using the lens of emotion. Developmental relationships, including mentoring, significantly contribute towards upward career progression and can be further enhanced by understanding the connections between mentoring and emotional intelligence. A critical key to successful mentoring is missing without an understanding of the effect emotional intelligence has on these relationships.

The primary purpose of this chapter is to discuss the concept of emotional intelligence and its relationship to mentoring practice and research. The focus of this research is on mentoring partnerships within the workplace and, while our literature review was focused in the business realm, it may have relevance for mentoring in other fields.

The contents of this chapter are built upon an extensive systematic literature review, which is reported in detail in Opengart and Bierema (2015). Tranfield, Denyer, and Smart (2003) suggest that reviews of this type will 'improve the quality of the review process by synthesizing research in a systematic, transparent, and reproducible manner' (p. 209). Our goal was to provide conceptually rich descriptions of the phenomena of EI and mentoring and identify how they might interact to affect mentoring relationships.

Critical to systematic review is identifying the review research question (Step 1), because other aspects of the process flow from that (Tranfield et al., 2003). The main review question was 'What are the potential connections between emotional intelligence and mentoring?' We also examined whether there might be a relationship between the two and, lastly, sought to provide propositions and questions for future research.

Identifying relevant work (Step 2) involved a search of business-related online databases with keywords 'emotional intelligence' and 'mentoring', including only scholarly, peer-reviewed articles from journals generally regarded as at least a 'C' level in the Scimago journal rankings. The authors ensured representation from an interdisciplinary framework, as both mentoring and EI have been studied in many fields. This interdisciplinary search obtained a broad perspective and decreased potential bias in selecting articles written by familiar names.

After assessing studies for quality, those that were determined to be methodologically sound and informative were selected (Step 3). The next step (Step 4) included review and data synthesis, followed by a summary of the history and key concepts of emotional intelligence and mentoring. After reviewing theoretical and conceptual aspects of both areas, we drew connections between the literatures, specifically around aspects of mentoring involving emotional connections. Interpreting the findings (Step 5) was followed by examination of the implications associated with applying this perspective toward the development of successful mentoring relationships. We used our findings to develop a model of emotionally intelligent mentoring (EIM), which is detailed in this chapter.

This research examined mentoring relationships from an emotions lens and illustrated connections between emotional intelligence of both the mentor and the protégé with successful mentoring. While theoretical and exploratory, this research will initiate further empirical investigation into emotional intelligence as a moderator of the mentoring relationship – research that has barely been addressed in the mentoring literature. This research also breaks new ground by proposing a new concept: Emotionally Intelligent Mentoring.

EMOTIONAL INTELLIGENCE

This section defines emotional intelligence (EI), outlines key theoretical research on EI, and examines the implications of emotion in the workplace.

Defining emotional intelligence

The term 'emotional intelligence' was coined by Salovey and Mayer in 1990, although Bar-On developed the EQ (Emotional Quotient) Test in 1988. EI was later popularized by Goleman (1995). There are several definitions of EI, but the literature often associates the term with Goleman's (1995) trait-oriented definition: knowing and managing emotions, motivating oneself, recognizing emotions in others, and managing relationships. Goleman's definition also includes self-awareness, impulse control, delay of gratification, handling stress and anxiety, and empathy, with some arguing that his all-inclusive definition is not scientific and describes personality traits rather than intelligence and/or ability (Mayer et al., 2000).

Mayer, Salovey, and Caruso (2000) suggested that EI integrates psychological processes, including the appraisal and expression of emotions, assimilation of emotions in thoughts, and understanding, regulating, and managing emotions. The authors characterize their definition of emotional intelligence as an ability, as opposed to a set of personality traits (Mayer and Salovey, 1997; Mayer et al., 2000; Salovey and Mayer, 1990, 1994).

Bar-On (1997) described emotional intelligence as 'an array of noncognitive abilities, competencies, and skills that influence one's ability to succeed in coping with environmental demands and pressures' (p. 14). Salovey and Mayer (1990) defined emotional intelligence as 'the ability to monitor one's own and other's feelings and emotions, to discriminate among them, and to use this information to guide one's thinking and action' (p. 189).

There is still much debate around the definition of emotional intelligence as an ability or a collection of traits, and clarifying the definition is important. Table 18.1 illustrates the three streams of emotional intelligence within the framework of ability, trait, or mixed model definition, as defined by the authors who first presented it.

Mixed model perspective of EI

This research interprets emotional intelligence through the perspective of the mixed model. Some have argued that even the mixed model is too broad and has strayed from the core constructs of emotion and intelligence (Mayer et al., 2008), while others have suggested that the trait models are most 'guilty' of that. The mixed model perspective was deemed appropriate for this research because it incorporates previously identified elements important to mentoring success, including emotional and social skills, applied both inter-personally and intra-personally.

Each of the following, Salovey and Mayer (1990), Goleman and Cherniss (1998), and Bar-On (1997), have made important contributions to emotional intelligence. To better understand how EI might apply to mentoring, we have arranged key points of their definitions into a four-point perspective model appropriate for mentoring. These points comprise EI and the self, EI and others, integration of EI into thought, and assimilation of EI into action, and are summarized in Table 18.2.

Understanding EI and the self

Two critical aspects of emotional intelligence are awareness and self-management. Goleman and Cherniss' (1998) model emphasizes self-awareness, self-regulation,

Table 18.1 Three streams of definitions of Emotional Intelligence

Salovey & Mayer (1990)	Goleman & Cherniss (1998)	Bar-On (1997)
Ability Model	Trait Model	Mixed Model
Emotional Intelligence is: • The capacity to process information and reason with emotion • To perceive emotion • To integrate it into thought • To understand • To manage emotion	Emotional Intelligence is: • Self-awareness • Self-regulation • Self-motivation • Social awareness • Social skills	Emotional Intelligence is: • 'An array of non-cognitive abilities, competencies, and skills' (p. 14) • Intrapersonal EQ • Interpersonal EQ • Adaptability EQ • Stress management EQ • General mood EQ

Source: Opengart (2005), p. 51

Table 18.2 Four-point perspective of Emotional Intelligence (EI)

EI and the Self	EI and Others	EI and Thought	EI and Action
• Develops self-awareness, regulation, and motivation • Adapts during emotional moments • Learns from social interactions • Uses emotions to improve social and interpersonal effectiveness	• Possesses self-awareness and management of emotions • Exhibits intrapersonal and interpersonal EI • Gauges emotional states of others and adjusts behavior accordingly • Exhibits empathy toward others	• Able to reflect on emotions of self and others • Reasons with emotion • Perceives emotions • Understands emotions • Reflects on emotional states of self and others both during and after social interaction • Uses insights from reflection on emotions to shape future social interactions • Learns from emotional interactions	• Manages emotions • Adapts to others' emotional states • Manages stress • Controls mood • Evaluates emotional situations and identifies effective responses • Uses situational judgment • Selects best responses during conflict • Maintains calm • Offers support to others • Helps others identify emotions

and self-motivation. This insight into the self helps with emotional awareness, adapting (Bar-On, 1997) and managing the self effectively during emotional moments (Salovey and Mayer, 1990). Emotionally intelligent people are more likely to have and maintain successful relationships because of the ability to use emotions as a tool for improving social and interpersonal effectiveness (Kunnanatt, 2004). Two studies (Lopes et al., 2004; Lopes et al., 2005) found positive relationships between the ability to manage and regulate emotions and the quality of social interactions. (Both of the Lopes et al. studies controlled for personality traits.) This indicates that emotional intelligence facilitates social interactions.

Respecting EI and others

If self-management of emotions is lacking, it may make it more difficult to effectively engage with others. Social interaction requires emotional abilities because emotions serve to facilitate communication, convey information and intentions, and coordinate social encounters (Keltner and Haidt, 2001; Lopes et al., 2004).

Those wishing to serve as mentors or protégés need to master EI on a personal level before they are ready to develop a deeper understanding of another person's emotions.

Gaining social awareness (Goleman and Cherniss, 1998) and intrapersonal and interpersonal EQ (Bar-On, 1997), and possessing awareness of the emotional state of others helps people engage with each other. It helps mentors to gauge the emotional states of protégés and to be aware of emotions such as stress, anger, frustration, or excitement. The ability to tune into others' emotions helps with empathy and effectiveness of mentors, and helps protégés understand mentors' emotions and reactions.

Integrating EI into thought

Emotional intelligence involves complex processes that integrate emotion with cognition (Mayer and Salovey, 1997). Reflecting on emotion regarding both self and others is the process of integrating EI into thought. This transpires along with the capacity to process information and reason with emotion, and perceive and understand emotions (Goleman and Cherniss, 1998). The ability to reflect on one's emotional state, both during and after a personal interaction, is a key aspect of emotional intelligence. Mayer and Salovey (1997) proposed that emotions enter the cognitive system and, after being recognized and labeled, these emotions then alter thought. Thus, insights gained from reflections shape future interactions. This could take the form of a mentor reflecting on how interactions affected the protégé and vice versa, thus changing future approaches to the relationship.

Assimilating EI into action

The integration of EI into thought and self and other – awareness of others is next assimilated into action. This occurs through the management of emotions (Salovey and Mayer, 1990), social skills (Goleman and Cherniss, 1998), adaptation, mood control, and stress management (Bar-On, 1997). Emotions shape social transactions as well as contribute to organizational culture and structure (Fineman, 1993). Both emotional intelligence and affect have been shown to influence performance (Boyatzis et al., 2000; Cherniss, 2000; Cooper and Sawaf, 1997; Cherniss and Goleman, 2001; Reio and Callahan, 2004) and conflict management.

Lopes, Nezlek, Extremera, Hertel, Fernández-Berrocal, Schütz and Salovey (2011) examined conflict management and confirmed the importance of evaluating emotional situations and identifying effective responses. Results imply that situational judgment and effective responses may be helpful in managing conflicts, such as in mentoring relationships.

Research has revealed an inconsistency of assertions made by proponents of emotional intelligence (Zeidner et al., 2004), with some studies demonstrating negative results and little correlation between EI and performance (Janovics and Christiansen, 2001). One possible explanation for incongruences can be explained by Cote and Miners' (2006) finding that emotional intelligence predicted job performance well when cognitive intelligence was low. Thus, they indicated that high EI can make an impact only for employees with low cognitive intelligence.

More recent studies found positive relationships between emotional intelligence and job performance. Joseph and Newman (2010) examined the incremental validity of emotional intelligence within three groups: performance based, self-report ability measures, and self-report mixed models, and concluded that all three types of measures demonstrated incremental validity over and above personality traits and cognitive ability. Other research found all three main streams of EI research correlated with job performance (O'Boyle et al., 2011). One possibility for this connection relates to Salovey and Grewal's (2005) assertion that one must be aware of what is considered appropriate behavior within a particular context in order to use these skills. This points to the importance of linking mentoring with EI, as the mentor can provide contextual information that may have a significant impact on how the protégé interprets the social, political, or cultural environment of their work. Given the research demonstrating a positive relationship between EI and job performance, we add mentoring as a tool to further enhance job performance and proactively manage careers.

MENTORING

Managing one's career progress in today's increasingly complex, competitive global environment requires more competencies than ever before. One strategy for negotiating this rapidly changing world of work is mentoring, with a more seasoned professional guiding a more novice protégé through career decisions, development, and challenges.

Mentoring can facilitate career development and socialization into an organization or profession, contributing to career advancement, higher job satisfaction and self-esteem (Allen et al., 2004), promotions, higher salaries, better support networks, and greater satisfaction (Dreher and Cox, 1996; Eby and McManus, 2004; Murphy and Kram, 2014). Benefits may exist not only for the mentored employee, but also for the mentor and the organization (Allen et al., 2004; Eby et al., 2006). The next section defines mentoring, identifies phases of the mentoring relationship, and introduces potential problems in mentoring.

Defining mentoring

Definitions of mentoring vary somewhat (Haggard et al., 2011; Kram, 1985), ranging from developmental relationships, one-time career sponsorship, and coaching, to a committed, long-term, mutually beneficial formal relationship. Formal mentoring has been defined as an organizationally sanctioned learning relationship involving mentors sharing knowledge to advance a newer employee's career (Wanberg et al., 2003).

Mentoring has also been described as offering two types of support to protégés: career and psychosocial (Allen et al., 2008; Kram, 1983). Zey's (1984) definition of a mentor as someone 'who oversees the career and development of another person, usually a junior, through teaching, counseling, providing psychological support, protecting, and at times promoting or sponsoring' (p. 7) is less broad than Kram's (1980) definition, which describes both career and psychosocial support and mentoring phases. Kram described career support as offering protégés necessary career advancement skills, the opportunity for challenging and visible assignments, and psychosocial support including role modeling, confirmation, and counseling.

Phases of mentoring relationships

Kram's (1983, 1985) definition of mentoring included four phases: initiation, cultivation, separation, and redefinition. The *initiation* phase, or expectation-setting, lasts six to 12 months. The *cultivation* phase, two to five years, typically involves protégés receiving a wide range of career and psychosocial guidance. During the *separation* phase, the protégé becomes increasingly autonomous and in the *redefinition* phase the mentor and protégé begin to see each other as peers.

Haggard, Dougherty, Turban, and Wilbanks (2011) have suggested that the construct has changed since Kram's initial work in the early 1980s, particularly in terms of research. They reviewed evolving definitions, asserting that, while numerous definitions have been utilized, three common attributes distinguish mentoring relationships – reciprocity (mutuality of exchange), regular consistent interaction over some period of time, and developmental benefits (tied to the protégé's career).

This research focuses its application to practice on Kram's first two phases of mentoring – initiation and cultivation, and on how the concept and measurement of emotional intelligence may be an opportunity to improve the mentoring relationship as well as prevent and/or improve negative mentoring. These are the phases and areas where we propose that emotional and social skills, applied both inter-personally and intra-personally, are most likely to influence mentoring success.

Mentoring problems

More recently, researchers have adopted a critical lens toward mentoring. Most past research and writing on mentoring presupposed or indicated that it was a positive experience. However, these relationships can also be destructive and dysfunctional and result in negative effects on performance and attitudes (Eby and McManus, 2004; Kram, 1985; Scandura, 1998). Scandura (1998) suggested that these negative mentoring relationships may not occur frequently, yet the destructive consequences might be quite detrimental.

Negative emotions and behaviors from dysfunctional mentoring relationships may include aggressiveness, spoiling, envy, betrayal, abuse of power, psychological abuse, unresolved conflicts, over-dependence, deception, bullying, and jealousy (Eby and McManus, 2004; Ghosh et al., 2011; Scandura, 1998; Scandura and Pellegrini, 2007).

The causes of these negative mentoring experiences vary and are not well examined in the literature. Personality characteristics may affect mentoring success, including extraversion, self-esteem, need for achievement, and a positive affect (Scandura and Pellegrini, 2007). Eby and McManus (2004) concluded that individuals may have positive intentions, but still have ineffective relationships due to interpersonal difficulties. Wu, Turban, and Cheung (2012) concluded that social skills of both the mentor and protégé influence mentoring effectiveness. Additional authors have suggested that many aspects related to emotional intelligence, including mutual respect, trust, social awareness, self-awareness, social skills, confidentiality, common expectations, honesty, equality, and political astuteness (Clutterbuck, 2004; Hansman, 2002; Murphy and Kram, 2014), are critical to interpersonal functioning and a successful mentoring relationship. One factor may be emotional intelligence.

EMOTIONALLY INTELLIGENT MENTORING

Our review suggests that there may be a link between the quality of mentoring relationships and emotional intelligence (Brechtel, 2004; Grewal and Salovey, 2005) and that there should be much more research and discussion around this possibility. This systematic literature review has focused on emotional intelligence and mentoring in the business literature. We melded these streams into the concept of 'emotionally intelligent mentoring' (EIM). In this section we define EIM, illustrate how core mentoring functions can be further facilitated by emotional intelligence, and propose a model of EIM.

Defining emotionally intelligent mentoring (EIM)

Emotions permeate our experiences at work: joy over recognition or completing a difficult task, worry about a meeting or presentation, anger at a colleague for stealing an idea, stress about an organization downsizing, joy at the week's end… these are all emotional responses. How we manage each of these emotions in ourselves and perceive emotions in others is affected by emotional intelligence. While we are often told to keep our feelings to ourselves and not get emotional at work, dismissing our emotions is easier said than done. In addition, emotions may be an important dimension of work behavior of which mentors should be aware.

Mentoring has been described as an intense emotional relationship (Baum, 1992). The ability to handle this intensity is critical for the relationship to advance. As previously noted, mentoring can be exhilarating and rewarding when the process goes well, or can create anxiety and frustration when it does not. With all the potential emotions involved, one could conclude that effective mentors boast a high level of emotional intelligence in order to manage their own emotions, as well as model, monitor, and respond to the emotions of protégés.

Given the important role that highly developed emotional intelligence can play in mentoring relationships, we offer the following definition that melds the EI and mentoring literature into 'emotionally intelligent mentoring': 'Emotionally intelligent mentoring (EIM) is an intense, mutually beneficial developmental relationship between a mentor and protégé that depends upon and expands emotional and social skills in ways that inform thought and action, benefit the self and others, and result in career learning and advancement.'

The next sections provide breakdowns of the definition's key components and illustrate their meaning and connection to the literature.

Emotionally intelligent mentoring is an intense, mutually beneficial developmental relationship

Mentoring relationships must be able to sustain an intensely emotional level in order to develop into productive mentoring (Baum,

1992). Building trust, openness, and mutuality requires that both parties have well-developed emotional awareness, both towards the self and others, transparency of emotions, and the capacity to keep emotions in check. The more intimate the relationship and the more anxiety inherent in the relationship, the more critical the need for emotional intelligence (Allen et al., 2005; Fletcher and Ragins, 2007; Kram, 1996).

Powerful mentoring relationships are intense: they involve engagement in challenging conversations. The mutual and reciprocal nature of mentoring influences positive outcomes and the harmonizing of the mentor's and the protégé's personality characteristics (Ragins and Kram, 2007). Emotional engagement of both the mentor and the protégé is necessary for a successful relationship (Higgins and Kram, 2001; Sosik and Lee, 2002). The mentoring relationship 'is inherently reciprocal and interdependent' (Chun et al., 2010, p. 428). EIM assumes that benefits of the mentoring relationship are mutual and that both the mentor and protégé learn and grow from the affiliation.

Emotionally intelligent mentoring depends upon and expands the emotional and social skills of the mentor and protégé

Mentors need to be able to accurately appraise and understand protégé emotion. Having high emotional intelligence should enable them to better connect with their protégés (Lankau and Scandura, 2002) and successfully advance from phase one (initiation) to phase two (cultivation) (Kram, 1983, 1985).

Fineman (1993) contends that emotions shape interactions, and Kunnanatt (2004) suggests that they can be a tool for improving social and interpersonal effectiveness. Moore and Mamiseishvili (2012) stressed the importance of being aware of one's own emotions during an initial stage of mentoring and, similarly, Wolff, Pescosolido, and Druskat (2002) found that individuals with high awareness of emotions have less intense emotional reactions and communicate more effectively. Applying these findings to mentoring seems logical, as emotional awareness between mentor and protégé would be critical to a successful relationship, especially in the first two phases (Kram, 1983, 1985) when expectations are being set and guidance is crucial.

Just as Thelwell, Lane, Weston, and Greenlees (2008) argued that the key aspects of emotional intelligence are fundamental for a coach's effectiveness, so too would we argue about it being essential in a mentor. It has been suggested that mentors with emotional intelligence might be more effective at managing potential anxiety and intimacy than those without this ability (Cherniss, 2007). Emotional and social skills continue to be important throughout the mentoring relationship as the intensity increases and the focus is on the development, learning, and advancement of the protégé, but might be even more critical at the initial stages when the relationship is being initiated and trust is being built.

Emotionally intelligent mentoring informs thought and action

The experience of mentoring provides the opportunity for both the mentor and protégé to reflect on ideas and behaviors, learn from them, and modify future thought and action accordingly. Liu, Xu, and Weitz (2011) studied interns and found that those who were open with their emotions proactively shaped more positive internship experiences than those who were not. Those interns who hid emotional expression or who showed negative emotions indicated less learning and a less positive experience. This suggests a connection between emotions, quality of interpersonal interactions, learning and mentoring. We apply this to suggesting that willingness to display emotions opens the opportunity for critical thinking that informs future action and likely results in better outcomes.

A study on emotional intelligence and sports coaching revealed significant relationships between emotional intelligence and coaching efficacy (Thelwell et al., 2008). Barkham (2005) also offered several recommendations for how to be a successful protégé, including:

> Be open and honest...be prepared to listen and reflect...respect advice...continue to question your mentor and other colleagues...be prepared to ask for help...be sympathetic to others' problems in your workplace...be prepared to offer fresh ideas...be prepared to work hard...network...and enjoy the new life. (pp. 339–341)

These suggestions imply skills inherent in emotional intelligence. Mentors can help protégés reflect on their actions and align their emotions with their actions using dialogue and questioning about thought and action.

Emotionally intelligent mentoring benefits the self and others

Both the mentor and protégé can benefit from the developmental relationship. Barkham (2005) suggested that a new protégé may feel disoriented, disconcerted, bewildered, inadequate, and vulnerable; not wanting to burden anyone. Having emotional intelligence could help the protégé manage these feelings, explore, learn, and benefit from them. Similarly, a mentor with emotional intelligence will better be able to anticipate and address such emotions in the protégé, which in turn makes her or him a better mentor and person.

Emotionally intelligent mentoring results in career learning and advancement

The final part of our definition of emotionally intelligent mentoring states that mentoring is an opportunity for learning and growth to both the protégé and mentor. 'Relational mentoring theory' (Ragins et al., 2010) refers to the mutually interdependent, empathic, and empowering processes that create personal growth, development, and enrichment for mentors and protégés (Ragins and Verbos, 2007). Moberg (2008) argued that the mentor's role includes the moral and ethical education of the protégé. He makes several propositions for character development through mentoring, with emotion being one of the key aspects. In a similar vein, Woullard and Coats (2004) determined that undergraduate students' emotions toward the teaching profession changed significantly between exposure and becoming master teachers.

Emotional intelligence competencies exhibited by a person show his or her potential and support the learning of job-related skills (Cherniss and Goleman, 2001). Emotional intelligence predicts success in multiple domains, among them personal and work relationships (Salovey and Grewal, 2005). This should extend to a mentor and protégé's relationship as well.

HOW CORE MENTORING FUNCTIONS ARE STRENGTHENED BY EMOTIONAL INTELLIGENCE

This chapter makes the case for emotionally intelligent mentoring as a highly effective developmental relationship that provides a protégé and mentor mutual benefits. The matrix in Table 18.3 illustrates key points about how low and high levels of EIM might affect a mentor and protégé in the initiation and cultivation phases of mentoring. The critical learning point is that the abilities of both the mentor and the protégé in perceiving, understanding, and managing emotions in themselves and others should greatly impact their social interaction with each other and, thus, the effectiveness of the mentoring relationship. Many of the helpful aspects listed in the table will apply directly to the first two phases, initiation and cultivation, of the mentoring relationship. In addition, the emotional intelligence levels of both the protégé and mentor could increase as a result of their relationship, requiring practice, and reinforcement, of the very skills

Table 18.3 Low and high EIM and their impact on the mentoring relationship

High EIM Implications	**Mentors Better Able To:** • Use self-awareness • Connect with protégé • Handle intensity of relationship • Accurately assess feelings of protégé • Encourage protégé reflection on actions • Utilize personal emotions and draw on them to be effective mentor • Challenge protégé to deal with negative emotions • Help protégé with character development • Express empathy for protégé • Exhibit good role modeling • Urge protégé reflection on learning • Manage emotions	**Protégés Better Able To:** • Use self-awareness • Understand emotion of self and others • Facilitate expressiveness, responsiveness, and enthusiasm • Be open and honest • Listen and reflect; respect advice of mentor • Ask for help • Network • Manage emotions • Manage stress
Low EIM Implications	**Mentors Less Able To:** • Understand protégé needs • Gauge emotions • Appraise needs and feelings of protégé • Form a bond/have cohesion with protégé • Network both personally and on behalf of the protégé • Be transparent • Manage emotions	**Protégés Less Able To:** • Gauge emotions • Handle feelings such as vulnerability, feeling overwhelmed • Connect with mentor • Feel comfortable disclosing necessary information • Ask for help • Keep emotions in check

needed to be successful in the mentoring relationship.

A model of emotionally intelligent mentoring

Central to mentoring is *relationship* – the social interactions and the affiliation between a mentor and a protégé. The mentoring relationship must be mutual for it to be effective. Mentoring relationships thrive when both members have skill at perceiving, understanding, and managing emotions of self and others. Given the link between emotional intelligence and social interaction, and the fact that mentoring requires a relationship with social interaction, we have proposed Emotionally Intelligent Mentoring (EIM), where successful mentoring requires emotional intelligence and effective use of emotions and social skills.

The EIM perspective portrays how the emotional intelligence of both the mentor and the protégé are important in influencing mentoring effectiveness. This may result from many factors related to emotional intelligence, including openness to mentoring, increased learning capacity, ability to trust, self-awareness, ability to respond to feedback, and the increased practice and further development of these skills. Most clearly, the literature points to social skills inherent in emotional intelligence. In all cases, it is more important for the mentor than the protégé to come to the relationship with effective EI and mentoring relational skills since part of the role is to educate protégés in such behaviors. When they are absent or underdeveloped in the mentor, the mentoring outcomes will be lower. When they are present, the mentoring relationship is poised to be productive and effective. Table 18.4 illustrates four different mentoring relationships based on the levels of emotional intelligence and mentoring relational skills. Each quadrant will be discussed.

Nonproductive mentoring

When the mentor or protégé fall into the 'nonproductive' quadrant, there are likely

Table 18.4 Emotional Intelligence and mentoring relational skills matrix

Emotional Intelligence	**Emotive Mentoring** Accurate emotional gauging • Perception • Understanding Emotion management Emotional exaggeration Relational weakness • Poor Listening • Low Trust	**Productive Mentoring** Accurate emotional gauging • Perception • Understanding Emotion management Relational effectiveness Developed relational skills • Role modeling • Trust building • Protégé development Learning and development Career enhancement
	Nonproductive Mentoring Inaccurate or absent emotional gauging • Ignoring emotion • Misperception Emotional non-management or mismanagement • poor listening • low trust • emotional hijacking Relational weakness • Ineffective role modeling • Lack of trust • Inconsistent interaction • Absence of protégé development Mentoring and relational errors	**Relational Mentoring** Inaccurate or absent emotional gauging • Ignoring emotion • Misunderstanding Emotional non-management or mismanagement • poor listening • low trust • emotional hijacking Mentoring miscalculations Developed relational skills • Role modeling • Trust building • Protégé development Emotional errors
	Mentoring Relational Skills	

low emotional intelligence skills and the mentoring relationship may be at risk. Nonproductive mentoring is characterized by the inability to appropriately read emotional states or effectively manage the relationship. Emotions may be unmanaged or mismanaged. When emotions are not managed, individuals are susceptible to 'emotional hijacking' or allowing themselves to be carried away with emotion. This could result in ignoring, misperceiving, misunderstanding, or exaggerating emotions. A nonproductive mentor may fail to tune into cues and may overlook issues. It is likely that the mentor may mismanage emotions by not listening or failing to make adjustments to accommodate the emotional state of the protégé.

Nonproductive mentoring is also characterized by low relational skills, meaning that mentors may be ineffective at providing career and psychological support such as role modeling, confirmation, and counseling. Protégés may be unable or unwilling to express emotions or read those of the mentor, and/or have difficulty with reason and learning. When nonproductive behaviors are exhibited, initiating and cultivating a new mentoring relationship will be difficult, because these behaviors inhibit trust, reciprocity, interaction, and the developmental benefits that exist within effective mentoring relationships (Haggard et al., 2011).

Relational mentoring

Relational mentoring occurs when the protégé, mentor, or both, lack well-developed emotional intelligence skills, but have high relational abilities. This may signal that the individual(s) are not tuned into the emotional signals being sent by the other individual, but are good at cultivating relationships. Just as with nonproductive mentoring, the mentor may miss or ignore emotional cues and focus instead on the task of helping the protégé achieve stated goals. The mentoring will likely be consistent, fun, friendly, and productive, but may lack depth and the ability to address more challenging and enduring issues. In some ways, relational mentoring may be 'going through the motions' of mentoring without ever risking emotional exposure or vulnerability. The relational skills allow the mentoring relationship to be initiated and cultivated, but may fail to help the protégé make key career transitions and transformations.

Emotive mentoring

Emotive mentoring is characterized by highly developed emotional intelligence with correspondingly low relational skills. Participants may be highly aware of emotional states, but less capable of articulating them or building strong, productive working relationships. These mentoring relationships may also risk becoming over-focused on emotions and exaggerating them, rather than focusing on relational consequences or next steps. When energies are focused on emotion, the mentor may not push the protégé to learn from the experience or address the situation. The emotive focus might cause the protégé or mentor to take things too personally and be unable to separate themselves. Highly emotive mentors may not provide effective role modeling.

Productive mentoring

Productive mentoring melds highly developed emotional intelligence with effective relational skills, creating the conditions for emotionally intelligent mentoring. This type of mentoring results in a mutually beneficial relationship that results in learning and development for both the protégé and mentor. The mentor and protégé are attuned to the emotional states of themselves and others, integrate EI into thought, and assimilate EI into action. Productive mentoring conforms to our definition of emotionally intelligent mentoring (EIM) based on its intensity, mutuality, and developmental benefits. Both the protégé and mentor experience improved emotional and social skills as a result of the relationship, and the mentoring becomes a powerful influencer of thought and action. The mentoring benefits both the mentor and protégé, as well as others with whom they interact regularly.

IMPLICATIONS FOR ORGANIZATIONAL PRACTICE

The importance of EI and the implementation of EIM has important implications for the future of mentoring practice and research. Ideally, both the mentor and protégé would enter mentoring relationships with highly developed EI or develop it during the process. When this does not occur, it is more important for the mentor to have well-developed EI so that the protégé can receive mentoring that will result in improved professional behavior and a stronger mentoring process. When protégés have low EI, it is particularly important to pair them with a mentor who is strong in EI. Such deliberate pairings have the potential to deliver significant results (Singh et al., 2009). Because mentoring depends on the very social skills and interaction associated with emotional intelligence, the practice of these skills should also increase EI.

Evaluation of the mentoring program, therefore, should entail both a pre- and post-test, especially if developmental efforts were aimed toward increasing the protégé's EI. A measure of the mentoring effectiveness might be emotional intelligence levels and potential increases resulting from the mentoring experience. This marriage of emotional intelligence and mentoring may well result in heightened learning, more successful mentoring relationships, improved retention, and enhanced career development. Currently an instrument is under development to help measure levels of EI and mentoring relational skill (Bierema and Opengart, 2016).

Another strong potential implication of this research relates to mentor selection. With caution, organizations may want to consider administering established, validated emotional intelligence tests as part of the decision-making process when selecting mentors and protégés for formal mentoring programs. Caution is advised because this process should not result in elimination from a mentoring program (pre-program training could be considered) or in the replication of patriarchal and stereotypical behaviors.

Other implications for organizational practice include:

- Consider measuring the mentoring relational skills of the mentor
- Provide mentoring relational skills development (coaching, mentoring, training) to mentors who are low in this area
- Select those with high emotional intelligence who will most contribute and benefit from the relationship, or
- Deliberately pair a mentor of high emotional intelligence with a protégé who is low, if the goal is to increase the protégé's emotional intelligence
- Provide emotional intelligence training when needed, for mentors and/or mentees, focusing on those aspects that facilitate social interaction
- Administer both a pre-test and post-test of emotional intelligence if the mentoring is focused on developing EI

Implications for Future Research

This research provided a conceptual framework for Emotionally Intelligent Mentoring and its implication for practice based on an earlier systematic review of emotional intelligence and mentoring. Given the theoretical nature of this work, we recommend further empirical investigation. Questions for future empirical research might include the following:

- Does the level of emotional intelligence of both the mentor and the protégé influence the effectiveness of the mentoring relationship and, in particular, the initiation and cultivation phases of the mentoring relationship?
- Does the level of emotional intelligence of both the mentor and the protégé influence the positivity or negativity of the mentoring relationship?
- Which social and interaction-focused EI skills are most critical to mentoring success?
- Should emotional intelligence be measured as criteria in the selection of the mentor and protégé?
- How much might emotional intelligence further develop as a result of mentoring?
- Does the importance of emotional intelligence differ in different types of mentoring relationships?

These questions can be answered with further empirical testing of the theoretical propositions put forth in this research paper. It is important to determine the extent of the relationship between emotional intelligence and success of mentoring. The goal of emotionally intelligent mentoring has the potential to make mentoring relationships more powerful and productive. By keeping emotions IN it, mentors and protégés can have potentially richer, more rewarding relationships that yield positive career results.

REFERENCES

Allen, T. D., Day, R., and Lentz, E. (2005). The role of interpersonal comfort in mentoring relationships. *Journal of Career Development*, *31*, 155–169.

Allen, T. D., Eby, L. T., O'Brien, K. E., and Lentz, E. (2008). The state of mentoring research: A qualitative review of current research methods and future research implications. *Journal of Vocational Behavior*, *73*(3), 343–357.

Allen, T. D., Eby, M. L., Poteet, E., Lentz, L., and Lima, L. (2004). Outcomes associated with mentoring protégés: A meta-analysis. *Journal of Applied Psychology*, *89*, 127–136.

Barkham, J. (2005). Reflections and interpretations on life in academia: A mentee speaks. *Mentoring & Tutoring: Partnership in Learning*, *13*, 331–344.

Bar-On, R. (1997). *Bar-On Emotional Quotient Inventory (EQ-i): A test of emotional intelligence*. Toronto, Ontario, Canada: Multi-Health Systems.

Baum, H. S. (1992). Mentoring: Narcissistic fantasies and oedipal realities. *Human Relations, 45*, 223–245.

Bierema, L. L., and Opengart, R. (2016). Emotionally intelligent mentoring inventory. *Proceedings of the Academy of Human Resource Development Conference,* Jacksonville, FL.

Boyatzis, R., Goleman, D., and Rhee, K. (2000). Clustering competence in emotional intelligence: Insights from the Emotional Competence Inventory. In R. Bar-On and J. D. A. Parker (Eds.), *The handbook of emotional intelligence* (pp. 343–362). San Francisco, CA: Jossey-Bass.

Brechtel, M. E. (2004). The affective correlates of a good mentoring relationship. *Dissertation Abstracts International: Section B: The Sciences and Engineering, 64*(9-B), 4604.

Goleman, D., and Cherniss, C. (1998). Bringing emotional intelligence to the workplace: Technical report issued by the Consortium for Research on Emotional Intelligence in Organizations.

Cherniss, C. (Ed.). (2000). *Social and emotional competence in the workplace*. San Francisco, CA: Jossey-Bass.

Cherniss, C. (2007). The role of emotional intelligence in the mentoring process. In B. R. Ragins and K. E. Kram (Eds.), *The handbook of mentoring at work: Theory, research, and practice*. Thousand Oaks, CA: Sage.

Cherniss, C., and Goleman, D. (Eds.). (2001). *Training for emotional intelligence*. San Francisco, CA: Jossey-Bass.

Chun, J. U., Litzky, B. E., Sosik, J. J., Bechtold, D. C., and Godshalk, V. M. (2010). Emotional intelligence and trust in formal mentoring programs. *Group and Organization Management, 35*(4), 421–455.

Clutterbuck, D. (2004). *Everyone needs a mentor: Fostering talent in your organisation*. London, England: Charted Institute of Personnel Development.

Cooper, R. K., and Sawaf, A. (1997). *Executive EQ: Emotional intelligence in leaders and organizations*. New York, NY: Grosset/Putnam.

Cote, S., and Miners, C. T. (2006). Emotional intelligence, cognitive intelligence, and job performance. *Administrative Science Quarterly, 51*, 1–28.

Dreher, G. F., and Cox, T. H. (1996). Race, gender, and opportunity: A study of compensation attainment and the establishment of mentoring relationships. *Journal of Applied Psychology, 81*, 297–308.

Eby, L. T., Durley, J., Evans, S., and Ragins, B. R. (2006). The relationship between short-term mentoring benefits and long-term mentor outcomes. *Journal of Vocational Behavior, 69*, 424–444.

Eby, L. T., and McManus, S. E. (2004). The protégé's role in negative mentoring experiences. *Journal of Vocational Behavior, 65*, 255–275.

Fineman, S. E. (1993). *Emotion in organizations*. Thousand Oaks, CA: Sage.

Fletcher, J. K., and Ragins, B. R. (2007). Stone center relational cultural theory. In B. R. Ragins and K. E. Kram (Eds.), *The handbook of mentoring at work: Theory, research, and practice* (pp. 373–399). Thousand Oaks, CA: Sage.

Ghosh, R., Dierkes, S., and Falletta, S. (2011). Incivility spiral in mentoring relationships: Reconceptualizing negative mentoring as deviant workplace behavior. *Advances in Developing Human Resources, 13*, 22–39.

Goleman, D. (1995). *Emotional intelligence: Why it can matter more than IQ for character, health and lifelong achievement*. New York, NY: Bantam Books.

Goleman, D. (1998). *Working with emotional intelligence*. New York, NY: Bantam Books.

Grewal, D., and Salovey, P. (2005). Feeling smart: The science of emotional intelligence. *American Scientist, 93*, 330–339.

Haggard, D. L., Dougherty, T. W., Turban, D. B., and Wilbanks, J. E. (2011). Who is a mentor? A review of evolving definitions and implications for research. *Journal of Management, 37*, 280–304.

Hansman, C. A. (2002). Diversity and power in mentoring relationships. *Critical Perspectives on Mentoring: Trends and Issues, 39*–48.

Higgins, C., and Kram, K. (2001). Reconceptualizing mentoring at work: A developmental network. *The Academy of Management Review, 26*, 264–288.

Janovics, J., and Christiansen, N. D. (2001, April). *Emotional intelligence at the workplace*. Paper presented at the 16th Annual Conference of the Society of Industrial and Organizational Psychology, San Diego, CA.

Joseph, D. L., and Newman, D. A. (2010). Emotional intelligence: An integrative meta-analysis and cascading model. *Journal of Applied Psychology*, 95, 54–78.

Keltner, D., and Haidt, J. (2001). Social functions of emotions. In Mayne, Tracy J. (Ed); Bonanno, George A. (Ed). (2001). *Emotions: Currrent issues and future directions* (pp. 192–213). New York, NY, US: Guilford Press.

Kram, K. E. (1980). *Mentoring processes at work: Developmental relationships in managerial careers* (Doctoral dissertation). Yale University, New Haven, CT.

Kram, K. E. (1983). Phases of the mentor relationship. *Academy of Management Journal*, 26, 608–625.

Kram, K. E. (1985). Improving the mentoring process. *Training and Development Journal*, 39, 40–43.

Kram, K. E. (1996). A relational approach to career development. *The career is dead–Long live the career*, 132–157.

Kunnanatt, J. T. (2004). Emotional intelligence: The new science of interpersonal effectiveness. *Human Resource Development Quarterly*, 15, 489–495.

Lankau, M. J., and Scandura, T. A. (2002). An investigation of personal learning in mentoring relationships: Content, antecedents, and consequences. *Academy of Management Journal*, 45, 779–790.

Liu, Y., Xu, J., and Weitz, B. A. (2011). The role of emotional expression and mentoring in internship learning. *Academy of Management Learning and Education*, 10, 94–110.

Lopes, P. N., Brackett, M. A., Nezlek, J. B., Schütz, A., Sellin, I., and Salovey, P. (2004). Emotional intelligence and social interaction. *Personality and Social Psychology Bulletin*, 30, 1018–1034.

Lopes, P. N., Nezlek, J. B., Extremera, N., Hertel, J., Fernández-Berrocal, P., Schütz, A., and Salovey, P. (2011). Emotion regulation and the quality of social interaction: Does the ability to evaluate emotional situations and identify effective responses matter? *Journal of Personality*, 79, 429–467.

Lopes, P. N., Salovey, P., Côté, S., Beers, M., and Petty, R. E. (2005). Emotion regulation abilities and the quality of social interaction. *Emotion*, 5, 113–118.

Mayer, J. D., and Salovey, P. (1997). What is emotional intelligence? In P. Salovey and D. J. Sluyter (Eds.), *Emotional development and emotional intelligence: Educational implications* (pp. 3–31). New York, NY: Basic Books.

Mayer, J. D., Salovey, P., and Caruso, D. R. (2000). Emotional intelligence as zeitgeist, as personality, and as a mental ability. In R. Bar-On and J. Parker (Eds.), *The handbook of emotional intelligence* (pp. 92–117). San Francisco, CA: Jossey-Bass.

Mayer, J. D., Salovey, P., and Caruso, D. R. (2008). Emotional intelligence: New ability or eclectic traits? *American Psychologist*, 63, 503.

Moberg, D. J. (2008). Mentoring for protégé development. *Mentoring & Tutoring: Partnership in Learning*, 16, 91–103.

Moore, A., and Mamiseishvili, K. (2012). Examining the relationship between emotional intelligence and group cohesion. *Journal of Education for Business*, 87(5), 296–302.

Murphy, W., and Kram, K. (2014). *Strategic relationships at work: Creating your circle of mentors, sponsors, and peers for success in business and life*. New York, NY: McGraw-Hill.

O'Boyle, E. H., Humphrey, R. H., Pollack, J. M., Hawver, T. H., and Story, P. A. (2011). The relation between emotional intelligence and job performance: A meta-analysis. *Journal of Organizational Behavior*, 32, 788–818.

Opengart, R. (2005). Emotional intelligence and emotion work: Examining constructs from an interdisciplinary framework. *Human Resource Development Review*, 4, 49–62.

Opengart, R., and Bierema, L. (2015). Emotionally intelligent mentoring: Reconceptualizing effective mentoring relationships. *Human Resource Development Review*, 14(3), 234–258.

Ragins, B. R., and Kram, K. E. (2007). The roots and meaning of mentoring. In B. R. Ragins and K. E. Kram (Eds.), *The handbook of mentoring at work: Theory, research and practice* (pp. 3–15). Thousand Oaks, CA: Sage.

Ragins, B. R., and Kram, K. E. (2007). The landscape of mentoring in the 21st century. In B. R. Ragins and K. E. Kram (Eds.), *The handbook of mentoring at work: Theory, research, and practice* (pp. 659–687). Thousand Oaks, CA: Sage.

Ragins, B. R., Lyness, K. S., and Winkel, D. (2010, June). *Life spillovers: The impact of fear of home foreclosure on attitudes towards work, life and careers*. Paper presented at the 2010 Academy of Management Meeting, Montreal, Quebec, Canada.

Ragins, B. R., and Verbos, A. K. (2007). Positive relationships in action: Relational mentoring and mentoring schemas in the workplace. *Journal of Organizational Behavior, 13*, 169–174.

Reio, T., and Callahan, C. (2004). Affect, curiosity, and socialization related learning: A path analysis of antecedents to job performance. *Journal of Business and Psychology, 19*(1).

Salovey, P., and Grewal, D. (2005). The science of emotional intelligence. *Current Directions in Psychological Science, 14*(6), 281–285.

Salovey, P., and Mayer, J. D. (1990). Emotional intelligence. *Imagination, Cognition and Personality, 9*, 185–211.

Salovey, P., and Mayer, J. D. (1994). Some final thoughts about personality and intelligence. In R. J. Sternberg and P. Ruzgis (Eds.), *Personality and intelligence* (pp. 303–318). New York: Cambridge University Press.

Scandura, T. A. (1998). Dysfunctional mentoring relationships and outcomes. *Journal of Management, 24*(3), 449–467.

Scandura, T. A., and Pellegrini, E. K. (2007). Workplace mentoring: Theoretical approaches and methodological issues. In T. D. Allen and L. T. Eby (Eds.), *The Blackwell handbook of mentoring: A multiple perspectives approach* (pp. 71–91). Malden, MA: John Wiley and Sons.

Singh, R., Ragins, B. R., and Tharenou, P. (2009). Who gets a mentor? A longitudinal assessment of the rising star hypothesis. *Journal of Vocational Behavior, 74*(1), 11–17.

Sosik, J. J., and Lee, D. L. (2002). Mentoring in organizations: A social judgment perspective for developing tomorrow's leaders. *Journal of Leadership and Organizational Studies, 8*(4), 17–32.

Thelwell, R. C., Lane, A. M., Weston, N. J., and Greenlees, I. A. (2008). Examining relationships between emotional intelligence and coaching efficacy. *International Journal of Sport and Exercise Psychology, 6*(2), 224–235.

Tranfield, D., Denyer, D., and Smart, P. (2003). Towards a methodology for developing evidence-informed management knowledge by means of systematic review. *British journal of management, 14*(3), 207–222.

Wanberg, C. R, Welsh, E. T., and Hezlett, S. (2003). Mentoring research: A review and dynamic process model, research in personnel and human resources management. In *Research in Personnel and Human Resources Management, 22*, 39–124.

Wolff, S. B., Pescosolido, A. T., and Druskat, V. U. (2002). Emotional intelligence as the basis of leadership emergence in self-managing teams. *Leadership Quarterly, 13*, 505–522.

Woullard, R., and Coats, L. T. (2004). The community college role in preparing future teachers: The impact of a mentoring program for preservice teachers. *Community College Journal of Research and Practice, 28*(7).

Wu, S., Turban, D. B., and Cheung, Y. H. (2012). Social skill in workplace mentoring relationships. *Journal of Organizational Culture, Communications and Conflict, 16*(2), 61.

Zeidner, M., Matthews, G., and Roberts, R. D. (2004). Emotional intelligence in the workplace: A critical review. *Applied Psychology, 53*(3), 371–399.

Zey, M. G. (1984). *The mentor connection*. Homewood, IL: Dow Jones-Irwin.

PART III
The Contexts of Mentoring

Laura Gail Lunsford

We often focus on the individuals in the mentoring relationship when, in fact, the contexts shape greatly how mentoring relationships unfold. In this section, the authors write about the influence of contexts at an individual level (participant and relationship characteristics) and organizational level (expectations and outcomes). As a collective, this section examines features of individuals, relationships, and programs to understand mentoring effectiveness. Several themes run through these chapters that draw our attention to the importance of demographic characteristics, career stages, relationships, and diversity.

First, contexts influence who participates in mentoring and what mentoring activities and outcomes occur. The authors discuss how to recognize individual characteristics such as age, i.e. youth mentoring versus mentoring of adults, ethnicity, gender, citizenship, sexual orientation, and disabilities as potential proxies for different mentoring needs. For example, cadets in a military academy benefit from mentors who support development of leadership skills to excel in 'complex security environments', while corporate executives may need mentoring to 'accelerate their induction' period to the company. Youths from low-income backgrounds may need adult mentors to support school achievement, while female faculty members need mentors who can help them navigate a male-dominated work setting that may be alienating and isolating.

Second, the authors suggest that mentoring, even in seemingly similar organizational contexts, e.g. higher education or the same corporation, will vary by career stage. Undergraduate students may engage in peer-mentoring programs that orient them to college and increase their grades. In contrast, graduate students experience mentoring primarily through a relationship with a faculty advisor or supervisor who guides them in the discipline with the desired outcome of scholarly productivity. Receiving mentoring support at career-transition points is emphasized by several authors, especially for individuals in their early careers. Early-career professionals need orientation to their organization and norms, while mid-career or more experienced individuals benefit from mentors who enlarge their perspectives. Authors describe shifts from the industrial to the knowledge economy and to increasing multinational contexts that require mentors to support different skills, such as helping early-career school principals to handle 'task volume, diversity, and unpredictability'.

A third theme is the importance of the relationship as a context and a need to redirect mentoring relationships to promote reciprocity, reflection, collaboration, and learning. Transformative mentoring is more likely to occur when the protégé also takes an active role in creating and contributing to a relationship identity with their mentor as opposed to a situation in which mentors aspire to fix or inform their protégé. For example, supporting protégés to select their mentor, even when there is a required expectation to have one, is important in mentoring relationships in military academies. Some authors examine the quality of the mentoring relationship. In a military setting the ability to express positive and negative emotions was associated with better mentoring outcomes. Mentoring relationships cannot be assumed to be positive or reflective, as noted by an author studying teacher education who makes a case of the prevalence of judgementoring.

A need for greater appreciation of diversity in mentoring relationships is a fourth theme across contexts in organizational life and educational settings. Several authors decry a lack of diverse mentors for an increasingly diverse set of protégés across settings, e.g. business, youth mentoring, and education. Diversity is widely defined to include economic status, underrepresentation, ethnicity, gender, citizenship status, sexual orientation, etc. Mentors are needed who have an awareness of diversity and inclusion. People from underrepresented backgrounds may have different mentoring needs, and a failure to understand those needs may result in negative or non-existent mentoring experiences. For example, in corporate settings there is a greater need to mentor expatriates and handle cultural complexity. New principals, managers, and faculty members will encounter protégés who are demographically different from them. Another perspective on diversity is presented in a chapter on familial mentoring related to family businesses. Individuals from collectivist cultures, where one's identity is grounded in relationships with others, is more common than in individualist cultures, where one's identity is grounded in the self.

The authors provide suggestions for how program managers and mentors might be more inclusive and aware of diversity. Perhaps we need more open, and perhaps uncomfortable, discussions about social differences. Developing skills in Inter-Cultural Mentoring is another tactic. The authors highlight qualities of people and relationships that might enhance mentoring programs. For example, a change model of mentoring is proposed as well as an ONSIDE mentoring model. Better and more training for mentors and protégés is warranted. eMentoring is suggested as an avenue to increase access to mentoring for participants from diverse backgrounds. Mandating mentoring as one way to increase access is also proposed, along with the observation of the paradox it may create: the requirements may be resisted by potential protégés. Promoting choice in selecting mentors may be one way to overcome such a paradox.

The authors draw broadly on theory from the educational, organizational, and psychological literatures. Career-learning cycles highlight how mentoring is important at different career stages and transition points. A theory of Transformative Leadership suggests that mentoring may help future leaders transform their organizations. Leader–member exchange theory helps us to understand the exchanges made by mentors and mentees, while positionality theory acknowledges how an individual socially constructs their identity and related needs. It is suggested that mentoring scholars and practitioners draw more on the corporate strategies related to talent and diversity management. Ultimately, mentoring is about change and a Model of Change is proposed as a way to think about mentoring relationships and their outcomes.

More research is needed on how contexts influence mentoring. In particular, the authors note a need for conceptual clarity on terms like 'at risk', 'disadvantaged', 'cross-cultural', 'cross-racial', and 'inter-cultural'. We lack information about mentoring some diverse populations, e.g. LGBTQ, and more work is called for on non-Western populations. There is surprisingly little research on executive mentoring, perhaps because of the confidential nature of such relationships. Thus, new methods may be needed to understand these critical relationships. Future researchers might cross the scholarly divide and attempt to integrate talent development, succession planning and other human-resource functions more closely with mentoring initiatives and outcomes.

In sum, this section will raise the reader's awareness about contexts and their influence on mentoring relationships and outcomes. Even a cursory review of these chapters will provide ideas about how to think about relationships and contexts and promote transformation and learning in mentoring relationships.

Mentoring Disadvantaged Youth

Stella S. Kanchewa, Sarah E.O. Schwartz
and Jean E. Rhodes

INTRODUCTION

Young people who have adjusted well despite profound and persistent stress often attribute their success to the influence of a natural mentor, such as a special aunt, neighbor, or teacher. These assertions have been supported by a wealth of research highlighting the importance of supportive, intergenerational relationships with caring, non-parent adults, as a key resource for healthy development. In this chapter, we define youth mentoring, describe various approaches to it, and discuss a theoretical model for how it may work. Further, we present a systematic review of the research literature to examine the effectiveness of youth mentoring. Finally, we examine youth mentoring within the context of systemic economic disparities, specifically the role of mentors in supporting economically disadvantaged youth in the transition to adulthood.

YOUTH MENTORING

Youth mentoring is generally defined as a relationship, characterized by a strong connection, between an older or more experienced non-parental individual who provides guidance and support to a younger or less experienced mentee or protégé over time. This conceptualization of youth mentoring encompasses approaches varying in structure and context, ranging from formal relationships – in which mentees and mentors are matched through a program that outlines specific expectations about the parameters of the relationship (e.g. frequency and duration of contact) – to informal relationships that form organically between youth and older individuals within their existing social networks.

Informal mentoring

Informal or natural mentoring relationships between youth and older individuals are not a recent phenomenon. Throughout history, intergenerational relationships have served as a context within which communities can transmit knowledge, provide guidance, and offer support to younger generations within the community. Garvey (in Chapter 2 of this *Handbook*), provides a historical account of the origins of the term 'mentor'.

These relationships, which emerge from everyday connections with extended kin, teachers, neighbors, religious leaders, coaches, afterschool program staff, and other community members, play a significant role in the healthy development of young people. Informal mentors may be particularly important during adolescence, a time in development when individuals begin to navigate increasingly complex social-emotional, cognitive, and identity changes (Steinberg & Sheffield-Morris, 2001). As young people begin to navigate a balance between an increasing need for autonomy and shift towards peer culture, along with a desire to remain connected to important adults, mentors may be uniquely suited to support these efforts, as mentors inhabit a bridging role between adult and peer relationships (De Goede et al., 2009; Keller & Pryce, 2010). Informal mentors provide an alternate adult perspective and serve as a role model at a time when young people begin to grapple with questions about who they are and who they want to be in the world.

The vast majority (over 90%) of youth mentoring relationships in the United States consist of 'natural' or informal mentoring relationships (MENTOR, 2015). Studies show that natural mentoring relationships may be more enduring, with relationships lasting for multiple years (DuBois & Silverthorn, 2005; Hurd & Zimmerman, 2014). Despite these figures, a national survey indicates that a third of youth report not having any type of mentor in their lives (Bruce & Bridgeland, 2014). There may be a range of factors that explain why some youth do not have mentors, including the availability of adults who are willing to make a commitment to children who are not their own (Scales, 2003). The emergence of formal mentoring programs, in part, serves to increase young people's access to supportive, non-parental adults.

Formal mentoring

Formal youth mentoring programs provide youth with an opportunity to develop supportive relationships with mentors, typically volunteers, who may provide encouragement, guidance, and a role model. Under this model of youth mentoring, the program matches young people and mentors, and provides the infrastructure necessary to support the match. Programs may use a variety of matching criteria to bring together individuals; however, the distinguishing feature of formal youth mentoring relationships is that mentees and mentors do not know each other prior to the match.

Formal youth mentoring programs trace their roots to the progressive era of the early 1900s, a time when widening social class divides and concern over the perpetual vulnerability of children in economically disadvantaged circumstances led to the creation of a range of social service programs to address the needs of low-income youth (Freedman, 1993). The earliest program to emerge from this social movement was Big Brothers Big Sisters (BBBS), which remains the largest youth mentoring organization to date, with agencies in all 50 states in the United States and 14 countries.

The original model of formal mentoring was community-based mentoring (CBM). In the CBM model, programs have specific requirements that volunteer mentors must meet before they are matched with a young person, including a screening and training process (Rhodes, 2002). Youth in CBM are typically referred for mentoring by parental/ guardian figures who identify a need for mentoring, frequently due to individual and/or environmental challenges that the young person is encountering. Programs have expectations for the frequency of contact (typically four hours per month) and duration of the relationship (typically a minimum of one calendar year). In practice, relationship duration varies from premature terminations after a few meetings to lifelong relationships that endure beyond the requirements outlined by the formal program. Mentors and mentees engage in a variety of social activities in the community, including going out to eat, playing sports, attending museums and other cultural centers, and conversing more generally (Herrera et al., 2000). Increasingly, formal mentoring is being integrated into positive youth development programs in a variety of settings, such as athletic programs, after-school programs, work or apprenticeship programs, faith organizations, and other youth serving programs (DuBois & Karcher, 2014). While informal mentoring relationships may already exist within these contexts, formal mentoring serves as a more structured component of the organization's broader mission.

YOUTH INITIATED MENTORING

Traditionally, mentoring relationships have been categorized as natural mentoring, in which relationships develop organically without the presence of an outside agency, or as formal mentoring, in which an outside agency initiates and oversees the match. More recently, new models, such as Youth Initiated Mentoring (YIM), are emerging that integrate the two approaches. YIM is a model in which youth nominate mentors from their existing social network of non-parental adults. This formed match is then supported through the infrastructure of a formal program that provides screening, training, monitoring, and match support. Research indicated that YIM had positive effects on vocational, educational, and behavioral outcomes. Further, more enduring relationships were associated with greater benefits, particularly when youth chose their own mentor (as opposed to parents or program choice) and had a mentor from a similar background (Schwartz et al., 2013).

YIM may potentially provide the structure necessary to support a developing relationship for youth who may not have the skills to sustain a close mentoring relationship on their own. Indeed, other related approaches to YIM focus on strengthening youth's social capital networks, and empowering youth to identify, reach out to, and maintain relationships with mentors from these networks. Research on these approaches is relatively sparse, but emerging (e.g. Schwartz et al., 2016), and suggests the potential utility of YIM among youth from diverse backgrounds.

Taken together, these different approaches underscore the potential of mentoring, particularly the ways in which mentoring may be adapted into a variety of models to meet the needs of youth across a range of contexts.

WHAT IS THE EFFECTIVENESS OF YOUTH MENTORING?

The field of youth mentoring has experienced considerable research productivity within the last two decades. This research, drawn from impact evaluations, correlational and longitudinal studies, and meta-analyses, provides an opportunity to examine the benefits and limitations of youth mentoring as an intervention.

A comprehensive search of several databases – including PsycINFO, ERIC, PsychArticles, and ScienceDirect – was conducted to identify peer-reviewed journal articles and book chapters focusing on intergenerational relationships between youth and non-parental adults, specifically youth mentoring, as well as economic disparities and disadvantage. In addition, a review of technical reports from organizations that routinely evaluate mentoring initiatives (e.g. the former Public/Private Ventures, Office of Juvenile Justice and Delinquency) was included. The following search terminology was included within this search: 'mentor', or 'youth mentoring', or 'intergenerational relationships', or 'mentoring evaluation'; and 'economic disadvantage', or 'social class', or 'SES', or 'socioeconomic status', or 'disadvantaged', or 'at risk'.

Evidence of youth mentoring outcomes

What conclusions can be made about the effectiveness of youth mentoring from the extant literature? This section reviews research on the effects of natural and formal mentoring, and on variations in effectiveness within formal mentoring.

Research on natural mentoring, including cross-sectional and longitudinal studies, indicates that the presence of a natural mentoring relationship is associated with beneficial outcomes across several domains of wellbeing. Specifically, studies have shown that youth with natural mentoring relationships demonstrate more positive educational and vocational outcomes, such as: academic attitudes and attainment (DuBois & Silverthorn, 2005; Hurd et al., 2012; McDonald & Lambert, 2014); behavior, particularly risk-taking and substance use (Black et al., 2010; DuBois & Silverthorn, 2005; Whitney et al., 2011); and socioemotional and psychological wellbeing (Hurd et al., 2013; Hurd & Zimmerman, 2014; Whitney et al., 2011). In addition, research underscores the importance of having multiple natural mentors throughout critical points in development, such as in the transition from high school (Sánchez et al., 2011).

In contrast, evaluations of formal mentoring have shown relatively modest effects, with considerable variability across programs and populations (Rhodes, 2005). Grossman and Tierney (1998) conducted a landmark, random assignment, multi-site impact evaluation of BBBS community-based mentoring in the United States. They found positive effects for outcomes related to behavioral misconduct, drug and alcohol use, and social relationships. However, later findings from a multitude of program evaluations have ranged from positive effects across several domains, to no effects, and even negative effects (Bernstein et al., 2009; Karcher, 2008; McQuillin et al., 2011). Further, some studies have found positive effects that have eroded over time (Herrera et al., 2011).

Variations in program effectiveness may relate to differences in program models as more recent evaluations have focused on school-based mentoring (SBM) approaches, which are different in scope, structure, and focus from community-based models (e.g. Bernstein et al., 2009; Converse & Lignugaris-Kraft, 2009; Herrera et al., 2007; Karcher, 2008; Komosa-Hawkins, 2012; McQuillin et al., 2011). In addition, differences in mentoring effects may be influenced by differences in implementation of the intervention, research design and methodological considerations, as well as alignment of goals among key stakeholders (McQuillin et al., 2013; Wheeler et al., 2010).

Results from meta-analyses can, in part, reconcile differences in effects across evaluations of formal mentoring. Meta-analyses allow researchers to empirically summarize results across studies to estimate the overall effectiveness of a particular intervention. A strength of the meta-analytic approach is that it can overcome variability across studies (e.g. research design, methodology) and reveal trends within a field, and gaps that future researchers might address.

Meta-analyses have demonstrated the positive effects of formal mentoring. In a meta-analysis focused on outcomes related to juvenile delinquency, Tolan et al. (2014) found significant positive effects for delinquency and academic achievement, and some support for reduced aggression and drug use. In another meta-analysis focused on three major SBM evaluations, Wheeler et al. (2010) found positive effects on school-related outcomes (e.g. scholastic efficacy, misconduct, and absenteeism). These findings are consistent with those from the most comprehensive meta-analysis of formal mentoring programs to date by DuBois et al. (2011), which comprised 73 independent evaluations of formal mentoring programs that varied in model type and context, and examined a range of outcomes. They reported that mentoring is associated with positive development outcomes in behavioral, academic, and socio-emotional domains. The magnitude of the effect size in all these meta-analyses is modest, though comparable to those of other community and school-based youth programs, with effect sizes approximated in the .20 range (DuBois et al., 2011). Results from meta-analyses provide some evidence for the overall effectiveness of formal mentoring; however, these findings highlight gaps in the extant literature, particularly the need for a cross-cultural understanding of mentoring, and how mentoring addresses the needs of youth from diverse experiences. For instance, DuBois et al. (2011) included few international studies of youth mentoring.

Evidence of youth mentoring outcomes: international perspectives

To date, much of the youth mentoring literature has largely focused on programs in the United States. This section reviews a growing body of international research, including evaluations and studies of a variety of models from an array of countries. This research has ranged from large-scale, multi-site, longitudinal studies, to single-program, cross-sectional evaluations. Despite the range in models and methodology, the initiatives share similar objectives related to positive youth development, and findings from these studies suggest comparable benefits for a broad array of outcomes. Studies from programs in Canada, Israel, Australia, and Britain have found improvements in academic attitudes, motivation, and abilities (Big Brothers Big Sisters of Canada, 2013; Goldner & Mayseless, 2009; Lynch et al., 2015), and in vocational engagement (Newburn & Shiner, 2006), while programs in Ireland, Portugal, Israel, Rwanda, and New Zealand have found improvements in psychosocial outcomes, such as social competencies, self-concept, and perceived social support, and some mental health symptoms (Brown et al., 2009; DeWit et al., 2007; Dolan et al., 2011; Farruggia et al., 2011; Goldner & Mayseless, 2009; Simões & Alarcão, 2014). In addition, studies from Portugal have found positive effects of mentoring on youth's self-regulatory skills (Núñez et al., 2013). Finally, while some evaluations have found reductions in behavioral problems (e.g. aggression, bullying, and fighting) and increases in prosocial behavior (Big Brothers Big Sisters of Canada, 2013; Dolan et al., 2011), others have found no effects on substance use (Bodin & Leifman, 2011).

International perspectives on the effects of mentoring provide an opportunity to explore the potential of mentoring relationships in supporting the development of youth from diverse backgrounds. Current cross-cultural research suggests that mentoring may be a viable intervention; however, there is a need for ongoing research that further examines the role of mentoring in meeting specific cultural needs of youth across a range of societies. Further, researchers can explore culturally informed models of mentoring that adapt to the distinct norms of the culture within which they are embedded (Goldner & Scharf, 2014).

Evidence of youth mentoring outcomes: special populations

Formal mentoring programs serve youth with diverse needs and circumstances.

Increasingly, there are programs explicitly focused on more vulnerable youth, such as youth in the foster care system (Johnson & Pryce, 2013; Taussig & Culhane, 2010; Taussig et al., 2012), children with incarcerated parents (ICF International, 2011; Jarjoura et al., 2013), children in military families (Basualdo-Delmonico & Herrera, 2014), and youth who are involved with or at-risk for involvement with the juvenile justice system (Weiler et al., 2015). Results from evaluations of these programs suggest that mentoring can improve the wellbeing of youth within these circumstances, such as reductions in mental health problems; however, this existing research underscores a need for increased understanding of the ways in which formal mentoring can better support the needs of youth from special populations. Similarly, mentoring initiatives with a focus on supporting youth from specific identity groups, such as gender (Kuperminc et al., 2011; Henneberger et al., 2013), sexual orientation (Rummell, 2013), disability (Powers et al., 2015), ethnic (Hall, 2015; Johnson et al., 2014; Washington et al., 2007), and immigrant (Birman & Morland, 2014) identities have emerged, and need to be studied more extensively. Theory and research suggests there are benefits from mentoring relationships for youth from diverse backgrounds and circumstances. However, there is a need for more research to better understand the mechanisms through which mentoring promotes positive development among youth from diverse experiences, which can inform best practices.

VARIATIONS IN EFFECTIVENESS

Overall, research has demonstrated that formal mentoring relationships are associated with modest improvements in youth outcomes, which has encouraged researchers to examine factors that may account for these relatively modest effects. In this respect, studies point to possible moderators of program effectiveness. Research indicates three likely candidates: characteristics of the participants (youth and mentor); the relationship; and the program. In part, these moderators may also account for variations in effects across studies comprising different youth populations.

Youth and mentor characteristics

Youth and mentor demographic characteristics have been found to influence the outcomes and relationship processes of youth mentoring. For example, relationships with older mentees tend to be less close and less enduring than those with younger mentees (Grossman & Rhodes, 2002; Herrera et al., 2000; Rhodes et al., 2014; Thomson & Zand, 2010). Additionally, research shows that high school students may be less effective as mentors as compared to adult mentors, and that matches with high school and college student volunteers meet less frequently and are more likely to terminate prematurely (Grossman et al., 2012; Herrera et al., 2008; Rhodes et al., 2014). While age may matter, comprehensive training and support seem to mitigate its influence on relationship processes (Herrera et al., 2008). Similarly, some researchers suggest that work, vocational, and service-learning opportunities may be more effective contexts for the development of mentoring relationships with older youth (Hamilton & Hamilton, 2014).

Gender may influence mentoring relationships; research findings, however, have been mixed. Specifically, theory suggests that youth may enter mentoring relationships with different interpersonal needs and goals, while mentors may provide different types of support (Liang et al., 2014). Further, male and female youth are referred to mentoring for different reasons. Male referrals typically result when they are deemed to need an adult male role model and females due to difficulties in relationships with parental figures (Rhodes,

2002). Some research shows that programs serving a greater proportion of male youth may have stronger effects (DuBois et al., 2011), while matches with female mentees may be greater in relationship quality and duration (Rhodes et al., 2008; Zand et al., 2009). Likewise, most programs, particularly CBM relative to SBM, typically match youth with a mentor of the same gender, however, due to a limited pool of male mentors, male mentees may be matched with female mentors. While qualitative studies underscore the relative importance of same-gender matches (e.g. Spencer, 2007a), other studies examining the effects of gender matching indicate few differences in outcomes and relationship quality (Kanchewa et al., 2014).

Similarly, many programs attempt to match youth with mentors of similar racial, ethnic, or cultural backgrounds. In practice, however, matches often include individuals from different backgrounds, for example white mentors with mentees of color. Being matched with a mentor from a similar racial or ethnic background may be particularly valuable for some youth of color, especially in support of identity development (Sánchez et al., 2014). Some studies have found no statistically significant differences between youth in same- and different-race matches on outcomes and relationship processes (Rhodes et al., 2002), while other studies suggest variations in the relative importance that youth place on being matched with a mentor from a similar background (Syed et al., 2012). Future research can continue to examine nuanced models of the influence of racial, ethnic, and cultural identity in mentoring relationships, for example mediating pathways (e.g. Hurd et al., 2012). Importantly, meta-analysis data indicates that programs that match mentors and mentees based on common interests show greater effect sizes, suggesting the importance of considering mentor and mentee commonalities beyond demographic characteristics (DuBois et al., 2011).

Additional youth factors that may influence the processes and effects of mentoring relate to interpersonal histories, competencies, and expectations. For instance, some research suggests that certain personality characteristics – including agreeableness, openness, and conscientiousness – are associated with more positive mentoring experiences, and youth's social and academic adjustment (Goldner, 2015). Similarly, in consideration of the relationship-based focus of mentoring, findings suggest that mentees' and mentors' past attachments, or relationships formed with other significant individuals, may shape their experiences within the mentoring relationships (Goldner & Scharf, 2014; Leyton-Armakan et al., 2012). In fact, youth with more supportive parental relationships were more likely to report natural mentoring relationships (Zimmerman et al., 2002). Some research suggests that youth who have adequate, but not especially strong, connections with adults, benefit most from formal mentoring programs, when compared with youth who have relatively extensive and strong networks of positive relationships with adults or those with limited positive connections (Schwartz et al., 2011).

Mentor attributes, expectations, and interpersonal skills play a key role in the effectiveness of a given mentoring relationship, particularly when working with more vulnerable youth. For example, a study of high school student mentors showed that more vulnerable mentees who were matched with mentors who held more positive views of youth in general (prior to being matched with a mentee) showed improved outcomes, while those matched with mentors who held more negative views of youth showed no significant difference from youth without mentors (Karcher et al., 2010). Mentors' self-efficacy in their ability to mentor youth is also associated with higher-quality relationships (Karcher et al., 2005). Additionally, greater benefits from mentoring relationships are observed when mentors have prior experience in helping roles or occupations, or when there is a good fit between a mentor's educational or career experiences and the goals of the program (DuBois et al., 2002; DuBois et al., 2011). Mentors who take a youth-centered approach (i.e. allowing the relationship and activities to be guided primarily by the interests of the youth rather than the interests or expectations of the mentor) tend to be more effective (Chan et al., 2013; Jucovy, 2002). Relatedly, mentors who are more attuned to their mentee's preferences, concerns, and feelings are likely to have more successful relationships (Pryce, 2012). Furthermore, research demonstrates that when mentors take on more of an advocacy role in their relationships with mentees, youth show improved effects (DuBois et al., 2011). Other studies underscore the importance of realistic expectations about what a mentoring relationship will entail, to guard against a mentor's feelings of frustration or unfulfilled expectations, frequently identified as contributing to premature terminations (Spencer, 2007b). Finally, particularly since many mentors are working with mentees with different backgrounds and experiences from their own, an appreciation of, and openness to, understanding salient socioeconomic and cultural influences in their mentees' life is critical (Hirsch, 2005; Spencer, 2007b).

Overall, studies demonstrate ways in which youth and mentor characteristics moderate the effects and relationship processes of youth mentoring. In practice, it may be important to individually assess the relative salience of specific demographic factors, as well as interpersonal strengths and growth areas, to support the potential of each mentoring match.

Relationship characteristics

In addition to youth and mentor characteristics, three characteristics of the mentoring relationship itself have been shown to influence how effective the relationship is in improving benefits for youth. For example, research on both formal and informal mentoring relationships has highlighted the role of relationship quality, or youth and mentor reports of feelings of closeness, in predicting better outcomes for mentees (Bayer et al., 2015; DuBois & Silverthorn, 2005; Goldner & Mayseless, 2009; Hurd & Zimmerman, 2014; Thomson & Zand, 2010). Relationship duration also influences the effects of mentoring on youth, with those in longer relationships showing greater benefits from mentoring, and those in relationships that end prematurely, in some cases, showing negative effects when compared with non-mentored youth (Grossman & Rhodes, 2002; Grossman, et al., 2012; Herrera et al., 2007). Additionally, more frequent contact (often referred to as relationship intensity) is associated with improved youth outcomes (Herrera et al., 2000; Parra et al., 2002), and some research suggests that inconsistent attendance by mentors may have negative impacts on their mentees (Karcher, 2005). Taken together, these studies indicate that quality (of the mentoring relationship) and quantity (of time spent together) both matter in mentoring relationships. Moreover, expectations appear to play an important role, with failure to meet expectations around duration or frequency of meeting potentially having actual harmful effects.

Program characteristics

Program infrastructure and practices can play a key role in supporting mentoring relationships and the development of high-quality, enduring relationships. Significant progress has been made in the field of youth mentoring in identifying and implementing evidence-based practices supported by research. Specifically in the United States, The National Mentoring Organization (MENTOR) published the *Elements of Effective Practice for Mentoring*, a set of guidelines for youth mentoring programs (Mentor/ The National Mentoring Partnership, 2015). This document provides evidence-based standards for volunteer recruitment and screening, mentor and mentee training, expectations for frequency of contact and relationship duration, matching mentors with mentees, monitoring and supporting relationships, and ending relationships. In fact, meta-analysis results indicated that the effectiveness of a program increased based on the number of evidence-based practices it implemented (DuBois et al., 2011). In the future, researchers can expand these guidelines to include cross-cultural considerations inclusive of a variety of international programs.

Traditionally, mentoring programs have focused primarily on the relationship between the mentor and the mentee. Increasingly, researchers and practitioners are recognizing the importance of the role of parent and family involvement in supporting mentoring relationships (Keller, 2005). As a result, some programs are exploring strategies to reach out to and engage with families. Nevertheless, research suggests that program administrators could be more explicit in efforts to collaborate with families to enhance children's experiences with mentoring. For instance, more could be done to better facilitate consistent communication between mentors, parents/guardians, and program staff (Spencer & Basualdo-Delmonico, 2014; Spencer et al., 2011). Consideration of family involvement may be a more culturally consistent approach for some youth and families.

MODEL OF CHANGE

Based on empirical research and theory, Rhodes (2005) proposed a model for youth mentoring that identified key processes and conditions in mentoring relationships to facilitate positive youth outcomes (see Figure 19.1). As described in the model, mentoring relationships characterized by mutuality, trust, and empathy can influence youth through three interrelated development processes: socio-emotional, cognitive, and identity. These processes are expected to give rise to improved academic, behavioral, and psychological youth outcomes.

This model is informed by a number of psychological theories. Attachment theory, which proposes that children generalize representations and expectations of relationships based on previous relationship experiences (particularly with primary caregivers), suggests that children may approach mentoring relationships in ways that are consistent with these past representations and expectations. Alternatively, the development of a secure and trusting relationship with a mentor can positively influence how a child responds in other important relationships (Bowlby, 1988; Sroufe, 1995). Empirical research on mentoring has provided preliminary evidence for this latter point, indicating that high-quality mentoring relationships are associated with improvements in relationships with parents and teachers, changes which, in turn, are associated with improved outcomes such as grades, self-esteem, and substance use (Chan et al., 2013; Karcher et al., 2002; Rhodes et al., 2002; Rhodes et al., 2005).

Learning theories point to the role of relationships in cognitive development. Specifically, Lev Vygotsky described a 'zone of proximal development' that extends from what children can accomplish when problem solving independently, to the range of what they can do while working under adult guidance or with more capable peers (Vygotsky, 1978). The field of cognitive neuroscience lends support to this idea, demonstrating the ways in which relationships can alter the developing brain to influence mental processes and perceptions (Gopnik, 2009). Mentors can play a key role in supporting cognitive development by allowing children and adolescents to develop more general cognitive skills, such as problem-solving and abstract reasoning, and helping them to develop competence in specific areas (e.g. academic or extracurricular domains). Research has highlighted the role of mutual activities and youth-relevant conversation

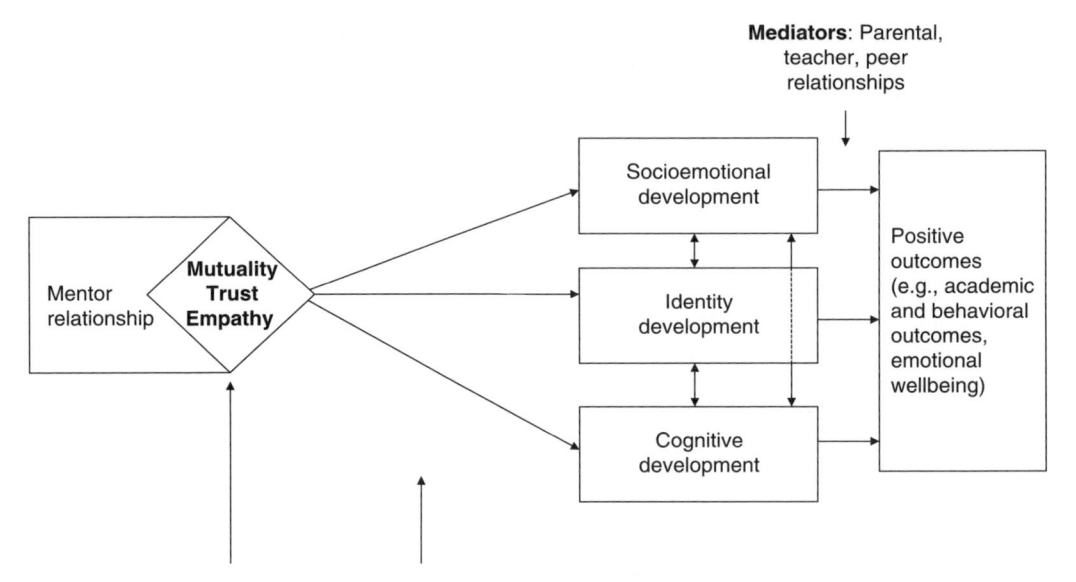

Figure 19.1 Model of Change

in facilitating youth's academic and social outcomes (Hamilton & Darling, 1996; Kanchewa et al., 2016; Larose et al., 2015; Parra et al., 2002).

Finally, researchers in identity development emphasize the role of relationships in identity formation. For example, Charles Cooley developed the idea of a 'looking glass self', which emphasized that one's sense of self is influenced by interpersonal interactions and others' perceptions of oneself. A related concept is that of 'possible selves', that is, ideas of what one could become in the future, including positive and negative possibilities (Markus & Nurius, 1986). Mentors are in an ideal position both to act as social mirrors to help youth develop self-perceptions, and to expose them to people and experiences, which may expand their ideas and beliefs about what they can become. Research on natural mentors provides some support for this idea, and indicates that non-parental adults can help youth reflect on the consequences (Sánchez et al., 2006). Other research shows an association between having a career mentor and having more aligned vocational aspirations and expectations (Hellenga et al., 2002). Nevertheless, although there is much theoretical, and some empirical, evidence to support these various pathways of development, there remains a need for research to support or challenge Rhodes' (2005) proposed model.

MENTORING AND YOUTH FROM ECONOMICALLY DISADVANTAGED BACKGROUNDS

While there is a need for continued research to reconcile variations in effects, factors that contribute to modest effects and address gaps and limitations, collectively, youth mentoring has the potential to support positive youth development, as indicated by research. One of the more pervasive challenges to positive youth development is economic disadvantage, including low socioeconomic status (SES) and poverty.

Within the United States, mentoring programs typically serve a large percentage of youth from economically disadvantaged backgrounds; in contrast, mentors tend to be from economically advantaged backgrounds (Deutsch et al., 2014; Freedman, 1993). Despite the potential role that economic disadvantage may play in youth's experiences of mentoring, there are a limited number of studies focusing on the effects of youth mentoring in the experiences of economically disadvantaged youth. In part, this limitation might relate to a lack of conceptual distinction and measurement challenges related to economic disadvantage. Specifically, several terms have frequently been used interchangeably within youth mentoring, including 'disadvantage' and 'at-risk', to describe mentees from a variety of circumstances, and the potential challenges that youth may encounter in relation to these circumstances (Deutsch et al., 2014; Thompson et al., 2013). While economic disadvantage may be encompassed within these terms, it is difficult to disentangle findings specific to economic disadvantage within this context.

Measurement of economic disadvantage has been equally variable across studies, as some researchers measure associated correlates (e.g. single-parent household), while others measure material resources, educational attainment, and demographic and community characteristics that relate to broader systemic inequalities (Deutsch et al., 2014; Huston & Bentley, 2010). Indeed, most youth mentoring studies have used correlates of economic disadvantage, including household composition and neighborhood characteristics, and proxies of economic status (e.g. caregiver occupation, free or reduced lunch), in addition to caregiver educational attainment (Deutsch et al., 2014). Some researchers have highlighted the limitations of extant measures within youth mentoring, including the lack of the social and psychological experience of social class (Deutsch et al., 2014), or within group variations (Thompson et al., 2013). Conceptualization and measurement of economic disadvantage has implications for the ways in which experiences of economic disadvantage can be better understood within youth mentoring, including relationship processes and outcomes (Yoshikawa et al., 2012). Further, there are international variations in economic disadvantage, which has implications for measurement and conceptualization across studies. Deutsch and colleagues (2014) present a model of mentoring and social class focusing on mediating and moderating processes that may influence the formation of effective mentoring relationships, and subsequent youth outcomes, which could serve as a conceptual framework for research on the youth mentoring experiences of youth from economically disadvantaged backgrounds.

Some researchers have found differential effects of mentoring for familial and environmental factors associated with economic disadvantage, such as household composition and housing stability. In a study of BBBS Ireland programs, Dolan and colleagues (2011) found that household composition moderated the effects of mentoring such that youth from single-parent households demonstrated increases in perceived parental support, whereas youth in two-parent households did not. Another study found that youth who had a greater number of stressful life events (e.g. frequent moves, caregiver unemployment) were less likely to be in enduring mentoring matches (Grossman et al., 2012). Other findings suggest that greater effects from mentoring are observed in programs serving youth with substantial environmental risk (e.g. neighborhood), that is, challenges related to economic circumstances (DuBois et al., 2011).

A few studies have further delineated the influence of economic disadvantage on youth mentoring outcomes. In a study of CBM with over 1,300 youth, Herrera and colleagues (2013) examined how variations in type and level of risk that youth experienced influenced the quality of the relationship formed with a mentor and the benefits derived from mentoring. These researchers defined risk as 'youth with one or more characteristics, behaviors, or features of their surrounding environments that research has associated with an increased likelihood of future problems' (p. 9). Risk was assessed with a baseline measure of circumstances in six areas of risk: economic adversity; family risk or stress; peer difficulties; academic challenges; problem behavior; and mental health concerns. From this information, the researchers developed four youth profiles that varied across two dimensions: risk type (individual or environmental); and risk level (low or high). There were youth with high environmental risk but comparatively low individual risk, youth with high individual risk but relatively low environmental risk, youth with high individual and environmental risk (the highest risk group), and youth low on both types of risk (the lowest risk group). Eighty-three percent of the youth lived in families experiencing economic adversity (e.g. potential eviction, difficulty paying bills). Moreover, 43% were in households with an income less than $20,000, and approximately 25% in households with an income less than $10,000. To put this in context, in 2013 the federal poverty threshold in the United States was $23,624 for a four-person, two-child, household (Jiang et al., 2015). Findings indicated that youth in all four profiles benefited equally from mentoring. Specifically, youth in the four profiles demonstrated better academic performance and peer relationships; however, the strongest effects were decreased depressive symptoms and a measure of overall positive change. These findings are encouraging, suggesting that mentoring can be an effective intervention for youth who bring with them challenges related to individual or environmental risk factors.

In another study, Thompson and colleagues (2013) examined within group variation of low SES among youth participating in a program with college mentors. The authors parsed out variation within a sample that would generally be categorized as 'impoverished'. Specifically, they used a caregiver report of SES that included weighted measures of caregiver occupation and educational attainment that accounts for household composition, with aggregated scores for individual or multiple caregivers. Whereas scores below 40 on the adapted measure of SES are typically indicative of extreme poverty, scores for the families participating in the study ranged from 11 to 49, suggesting diverse socioeconomic experiences among economically disadvantaged families. In addition, the authors examined associations between indicators of SES and youths' positive developmental assets (i.e. internal and external resources youth had that promoted healthy development), controlling for youths' age and number of siblings in household. Findings indicated that family SES, an aggregate of maternal and paternal education and occupation, was not associated with youth's overall assets at baseline; however, family SES was negatively associated with changes in youths' overall assets after mentoring, suggesting that youth from the lowest SES background derived the greatest benefits from mentoring, with increases in internal and external developmental assets.

In addition, researchers have examined the influence of matching based on SES characteristics on youth outcomes. In a study of social capital and relationship matching characteristics, Gaddis (2012) found no significant differences between mentees who were matched with a mentor from a higher social class relative to those matched with a mentor from a similar social class background, on alcohol and drug use, or on academic outcomes. This finding indicates few differences between matches with different social class configurations, which suggests that matching based on SES may not be a key predictor of youth outcomes. More research is needed, however, to replicate and further extend this research.

For example, it may be that other unmeasured factors (e.g. youth's perceptions of this match) may be more salient, and subsequently relate to effects.

Youth's experiences of economic disadvantage may influence the types of relationships that they form with mentors. A limited number of studies have explored relationship processes in the mentoring experiences of youth from economically disadvantaged backgrounds. Herrera and colleagues (2013) found that youth and mentors in four types of environmental and individual risk profiles reported relationships that were equally youth-centered, collaborative, close, and enduring, suggesting similar relationship quality across varying risk profiles. However, there were differences in the types of challenges that mentors encountered and reasons for match termination that related to the type of youth risk profile. Relative to those in matches with youth who had low environmental risk, mentors matched with youth with high environmental risk reported challenges in: establishing consistent meetings with their mentee; receiving support from the mentee's family; meeting the family's needs; and bridging across economic disparities. Notably, whereas 43% of youth were from households below the FPT, only about 12% of mentors had experienced similar circumstances, and about one-third had previous experience working with youth from impoverished backgrounds. Similarly, Spencer (2007b) found difficulties connecting across diverse experiences as a major theme among mentors whose relationships terminated early.

Taken together, these studies underscore the need for more research to gain a more nuanced understanding of the influence of economic disadvantage within youth's mentoring experiences. For instance, studies exploring mentee and family perspectives of mentoring within the context of economic disadvantage could greatly contribute to the field.

RECOMMENDATIONS FOR FUTURE RESEARCH

The reviewed literature presents an understanding of youth mentoring's effects, key factors and processes that influence benefits derived from mentoring for youth both in general and from economically disadvantaged backgrounds in particular. Youth mentoring programs typically target and serve a large percentage of youth from economically disadvantaged backgrounds. However, there remain gaps in the research on youth mentoring. Further, there are three limitations specific to the experiences of youth from economically disadvantaged backgrounds. Importantly, there is a need for continual conceptual clarity and operational definitions of frequently used terms, such as 'at-risk' and 'disadvantage', in relation to economic disadvantage, which has implications for the type of research methods employed, including measurement and design. Studies in which these constructs have been examined in-depth underscore the complexity, and demonstrate the importance, of more nuanced approaches (e.g. Herrera et al., 2013; Thompson et al., 2013). Further, conceptual delineation relates to the type of outcomes as specific constructs may relate to specific outcomes, which may inform the ways programs can intervene that align with the needs of youth from economically disadvantaged backgrounds (DuBois et al., 2006; Yoshikawa et al., 2012). Additional outcomes that may be more salient within the lives of youth from economically disadvantaged circumstances can be examined in future research. For instance, it may be that effective mentoring relationships positively impact youth through reductions in their stress levels. Alternatively, it may be that youth's mentoring involvement provides additional support for caregivers, which in turn helps to reduce their stress (Thompson et al., 2013). Studies of poverty suggest the potential mediating role of parental stress and behavior in the relationship between economic disadvantage and youth outcomes (Huston & Bentley, 2010; Yoshikawa et al., 2012). Given the increasing recognition of the importance of parents and families within the mentoring process (e.g. Spencer & Basualdo-Delmonico, 2014; Spencer et al., 2011), research that includes caregiver measures may provide a broader understanding of how youth's family systems may be influenced by mentoring. Finally, additional mediating mechanisms, related to economically disadvantaged youth's mentoring experiences and to moderating processes that may enhance these experiences, can be explored in future research.

More broadly, there are three directions for future research to address within the field of youth mentoring. First, there is a need for exploration of the mentoring experiences of youth from diverse backgrounds across all aspects of diversity, in addition to social class, as well as diverse international perspectives. Although some studies did address these issues, it will be important to develop an understanding of how mentoring works among different populations so that the potential benefits of mentoring may be maximized within the context of a variety of cultural backgrounds and experiences. This is particularly salient since mentoring relationships are often formed between individuals from different backgrounds. As such, it is crucial to attend not only to positive outcomes, but also the potential for harmful effects (Grossman & Rhodes, 2002; Grossman et al., 2012; Spencer, 2007). It would additionally be beneficial to investigate if certain models or approaches are more effective for youth from specific backgrounds, life experiences, and cultural contexts. Second, there is a need for systematic comparisons of the effects and relationship processes that occur in different approaches to youth mentoring. Recent exploration of new hybrid models of mentoring is promising, but there is little research on their effects, particularly in comparison to traditional models of mentoring. Research is also needed to establish the relative cost-effectiveness of various program practices, such as the type and amount of training and support offered to mentors. Finally, further studies are needed to investigate the proposed pathways in Rhodes' model of change, and whether such pathways generalize across contexts or if different pathways are more salient for different contexts or populations. Such research could further the field's understanding of mechanisms of change in youth mentoring intervention, which could, in turn, be used to inform program practice and promote improved outcomes.

PRACTICE AND POLICY IMPLICATIONS

Additionally, this review suggests five implications for practice. Generally, there is a need for programs to adopt evidence-based practices. *The Elements of Effective Practice* provides clear general guidelines for programs, but these guidelines are not consistently followed across programs. Second, more specific recommendations can be made for programs aiming to serve youth from economically disadvantaged backgrounds. The research identified in this review suggests the need for increased training and support for mentors about experiences of poverty and its effects on families and children. This support is particularly important since most volunteer mentors come from more economically advantaged backgrounds and may have little understanding of the experience of poverty. It is also essential for mentor training to provide opportunities for mentors to examine their assumptions and biases related to class status and poverty. Third, training may provide mentors with strategies around joining and relational skills, including taking a youth-centered approach. It is possible that matching around similar interests can provide additional feelings of connection. Moreover, providing support in strategies for partnering with parents and families may strengthen relationships and effects.

Fourth, research suggests the benefit of mentors taking on an advocacy role, for example, by connecting mentees with other resources and supports, in addition to focusing on the one-on-one relationship with their mentee. Moreover, approaches that empower youth to identify and reach out to supportive adults in their own networks may hold particular promise. Finally, mentors can advocate at the policy level to promote systems and policies that address economic inequities. Training and support can help mentors to understand their role as that of ally and avoid taking a paternalistic stance in their approach to advocacy or in the relationship itself.

CONCLUSION

Youth mentoring has the potential to promote positive outcomes among youth, including youth living in poverty. At the same time, there is a need for a greater understanding of the processes and effects of youth mentoring, specifically for youth from economically disadvantaged backgrounds. Such research may enable mentoring program administrators to better serve youth and harness the power of caring adult–youth relationships in supporting youth development.

REFERENCES

Basualdo-Delmonico, A., & Herrera, C. (2014). *Taking care of our own: Lessons learned about engaging military families in youth mentoring.* Philadelphia, PA: Amachi, Inc.

Bayer, A., Grossman, J. B., & DuBois, D. L. (2015). Using volunteer mentors to improve the academic outcomes of underserved students: The role of relationships. *Journal of Community Psychology, 43*(4), 408–29.

Bernstein, L., Rappaport, C., Olsho, L., Hunt, D., & Levin, M. (2009). *Impact evaluation of the U.S. Department of Education's Student Mentoring Program* (NCEE 2009–4047). Washington, DC: National Center for Education Evaluation and Regional Assistance, Institute of Education Sciences, U.S. Department of Education.

Big Brothers Big Sisters of Canada (2013). *Big Brothers Big Sisters launches 100 year celebration with largest mentoring study ever in Canada.* Retrieved August 3, 2015 from http://www.bigbrothersbigsisters.ca/en/home/newsevents/100yearcelebrationStudy.aspx

Birman, D., & Morland, L. (2014). Immigrant and refugee youth. In D. L. DuBois, & M. J. Karcher (Eds.), *Handbook of Youth Mentoring, 2nd Edition* (pp. 355–68). Thousand Oaks, CA: Sage Publications.

Black, D. S., Grenard, J. L., Sussman, S., & Rohrbach, L. A. (2010). The influence of school-based natural mentoring relationships on school attachment and subsequent adolescent risk behaviors. *Health Education Research, 25*(5), 892–902.

Bodin, M., & Leifman, H. (2011). A randomized effectiveness trial of an adult-to-youth mentoring program in Sweden. *Addiction Research and Theory, 19*(5), 438–47.

Bowlby, J. (1988). *A secure base: Parent–child attachment and healthy human development.* New York: Basic Books.

Brown, L., Thurman, T. R., Rice, J., Boris, N. W., Ntaganira, J., Nyirazinyoye, L., De Dieu, J. & Snider, L. (2009). Impact of a mentoring program on psychosocial wellbeing of youth in Rwanda: Results of a quasi-experimental study. *Vulnerable Children and Youth Studies, 4*(4), 288–99.

Bruce, M., & Bridgeland, J. (2014). *The mentoring effect: Young people's perspectives on the outcomes and availability of mentoring.* Washington, DC: Civic Enterprises with Hart Research Associates for MENTOR: The National Mentoring Partnership.

Chan, C. S., Rhodes, J. E., Howard, W. J., Lowe, S. R., Schwartz, S. E., & Herrera, C. (2013). Pathways of influence in school-based mentoring: The mediating role of parent and teacher relationships. *Journal of School Psychology, 51*(1), 129–42.

Converse, N., & Lingnugaris-Kraft, B. (2009). Evaluation of a SBM program for at-risk middle school youth. *Remedial and Special Education*, *30*(1), 33–46.

De Goede, I. H., Branje, S. J., & Meeus, W. H. (2009). Developmental changes in adolescents' perceptions of relationships with their parents. *Journal of Youth and Adolescence*, *38*(1), 75–88.

Deutsch, N. L., Lawrence, E. C., & Henneberger, A. K. (2014). Social class. In D. L. DuBois, & M. J. Karcher (Eds.), *Handbook of Youth Mentoring, 2nd Edition* (pp. 175–87). Thousand Oaks, CA: Sage.

DeWit, D. J., Lipman, E., Manzano-Munguia, M., Bisanz, J., Graham, K., Offord, D. R., O'Neill, E., Pepler, D., & Shaver, K. (2007). Feasibility of a randomized controlled trial for evaluating the effectiveness of the Big Brothers Big Sisters community match program at the national level. *Children and Youth Services Review*, *29*, 383–404.

Dolan, P., Brady, B., O'Regan, C., Russell, D., Canavan, J., & Forkan, C. (2011). *Big Brothers Big Sisters of Ireland: Evaluation study: Report one: Randomised controlled trial and implementation report*. Child and Family Research Centre, Galway.

DuBois, D. L., Doolittle, F., Yates, B. T., Silverthorn, N., & Tebes, J. K. (2006). Research methodology and youth mentoring. *Journal of Community Psychology*, *34*(6), 657–76.

DuBois, D. L., Holloway, B. E., Valentine, J. C., & Harris, C. (2002). Effectiveness of mentoring programs for youth: A meta-analytic review. *American Journal of Community Psychology*, *30*(2), 157–97.

Dubois, D. L., & Karcher, M. J. (2014). *Handbook of Youth Mentoring, 2nd Edition*. Thousand Oaks, CA: Sage.

DuBois, D. L., Portillo, N., Rhodes, J. E., Silverthorn, N., & Valentine, J. C. (2011). How effective are mentoring programs for youth? A systematic assessment of the evidence. *Psychological Science in the Public Interest*, *12*(2), 57–91. doi:10.1177/1529100611414806

DuBois, D. L., & Silverthorn, N. (2005). Characteristics of natural mentoring relationships and adolescent adjustment: Evidence from a national study. *Journal of Primary Prevention*, *26*, 69–92.

Farruggia, S. P., Bullen, P., Davidson, J., Dunphy, A., Solomon, F., & Collins, E. (2011). The effectiveness of youth mentoring programmes in New Zealand. *New Zealand Journal of Psychology*, *40*(3), 52–70.

Freedman, M. (1993). *The kindness of strangers: Adult mentors, urban youth, and the new volunteerism*. San Francisco: Jossey-Bass Inc.

Gaddis, S. M. (2012). What's in a relationship? An examination of social capital, race, and class in mentoring relationships. *Social Forces*, *90*(4), 1237–69.

Goldner, L. (2015). Protégés' personality traits, expectations, the quality of the mentoring relationship and adjustment: A big five analysis. *Child and Youth Care Forum*, 1–21. doi: 10.1007/s10566-015-9319-9

Goldner, L., & Mayseless, O. (2009). The quality of mentoring relationships and mentoring success. *Journal of Youth and Adolescence*, *38*(10), 1339–50.

Goldner, L., & Scharf, M. (2014). Attachment security, the quality of the mentoring relationship and protégés' adjustment. *Journal of Primary Prevention*, *35*(4), 267–79.

Gopnik, A. (2009). *The philosophical baby: What children's minds tell us about truth, love, and the meaning of life*. New York: Farrah, Strauss and Giroux.

Grossman, J. B., Chan, C., Schwartz, S., & Rhodes, J. E. (2012). The test of time in school-based mentoring: The role of relationship duration and re-matching on academic outcomes. *American Journal of Community Psychology*, *49*, 43–54.

Grossman, J. B., & Rhodes, J. E. (2002). The test of time: Predictors and effects of duration in youth mentoring relationships. *American Journal of Community Psychology*, *30*(2), 199–219.

Grossman, J. B., & Tierney, J. P. (1998). Does mentoring work? An impact study of the Big Brothers Big Sisters program. *Evaluation Review*, *22*, 403–26. doi: 10.1177/0193841X9802200304

Hall, H. R. (2015). Food for thought: Using critical pedagogy in mentoring African American adolescent males. *The Black Scholar: Journal of Black Studies and Research*, *45*(3), 39–53.

Hamilton, S. F., & Darling, N. (1996). Mentors in adolescents' lives. In K. Hurrelmann & S. F. Hamilton (Eds.), *Social problems and social contexts in adolescence: Perspectives across boundaries* (pp. 199–215). New York: Pergamon Press.

Hamilton, S. F., & Hamilton, M. A. (2014). Work and service-learning. In D. L. DuBois, & M. J. Karcher (Eds.), *Handbook of Youth Mentoring, 2nd Edition* (pp. 291–300). Thousand Oaks, CA: Sage.

Hellenga, K., Aber, M. S., & Rhodes, J. E. (2002). African American adolescent mothers' vocational aspiration-expectation gap: Individual, social and environmental influences. *Psychology of Women Quarterly*, *26*(3), 200–12.

Henneberger, A. K., Deutsch, N. L., Lawrence, E. C., & Sovik-Johnston, A. (2013). The young women leaders program: A mentoring program targeted toward adolescent girls. *School Mental Health*, *5*, 132–43.

Herrera, C., Kauh, T. J., Cooney, S. M., Grossman, J. B., & McMaken, J. (2008). *High school students as mentors: Findings from the Big Brothers Big Sisters school-based mentoring impact study*. Philadelphia, PA: Public/Private Ventures.

Herrera, C., DuBois, D. L., & Grossman, J. B. (2013). *The role of risk: Mentoring experiences and outcomes for youth with varying risk profiles*. New York: A Public/Private Ventures project distributed by MDRC.

Herrera, C., Grossman, J. B., Kauh, T. J., Feldman, A. F., & McMaken, J. (with Jucovy, L. Z.). (2007). *Making a difference in schools: The Big Brothers Big Sisters school-based mentoring impact study*. Philadelphia, PA: Public/Private Ventures.

Herrera, C., Grossman, J. B., Kauh, T. J., & McMaken, J. (2011). Mentoring in schools: An impact study of Big Brothers Big Sisters school-based mentoring. *Child Development*, *82*(1), 346–61.

Herrera, C., Sipe, C. L., McClanahan, W. S., Arbreton, A. J., & Pepper, S. K. (2000). *Mentoring school-age children: Relationship development in community-based and school-based programs*. Philadelphia, PA: Public/Private Ventures.

Hirsch, B. (2005). *A place to call home: After-school programs for urban youth*. Washington, DC: American Psychological Association and New York: Teachers College Press.

Hurd, N. M., Sánchez, B., Zimmerman, M. A., & Caldwell, C. H. (2012). Natural mentors, racial identity, and educational attainment among African American adolescents: Exploring pathways to success. *Child Development*, *83*(4), 1196–212.

Hurd, N. M., Varner, F. A., & Rowley, S. J. (2013). Involved-vigilant parenting and socio-emotional well-being among black youth: The moderating influence of natural mentoring relationships. *Journal of Youth and Adolescence*, *42*(10), 1583–95.

Hurd, N. M., & Zimmerman, M. A. (2014). An analysis of natural mentoring relationship profiles and associations with mentees' mental health: Considering links via support from important others. *American Journal of Community Psychology*, *53*(1–2), 25–36.

Huston, A. C., & Bentley, A. C. (2010). Human development in societal context. *The Annual Review of Psychology*, *61*, 411–37.

ICF International. (2011). *Mentoring children affected by incarceration: An evaluation of the Texas Amachi Program*. Fairfax, VA: Author.

Jarjoura, G. R., DuBois, D. L., Shlafer, R. J., & Haight, K. A. (2013). *Mentoring children of incarcerated parents: A synthesis of research and input from the listening session held by the Office of Juvenile Justice and Delinquency Prevention and the White House domestic policy council and office of public engagement*. Office of Juvenile Justice and Delinquency Prevention.

Jiang, Y., Ekono, M., & Skinner, C. (2015). *Basic facts about low-income children: Children under 18 years, 2013*. New York: National Center for Children in Poverty, Mailman School of Public Health, Columbia University.

Johnson, S. B., & Pryce, J. M. (2013). Therapeutic mentoring: Reducing the impact of trauma for foster youth. *Child Welfare*, *92*(3), 9–25.

Johnson, V. L., Simon, P., & Mun, E. (2014). A peer-led high school transition program increases graduation rates among Latino males. *Journal of Educational Research*, *107*(3), 186–96.

Jucovy, L. (2002). *Measuring the quality of mentor-youth relationships: A tool for mentoring programs*. Technical Assistance Packet. Philadelphia, PA: Public/Private Ventures.

Kanchewa, S. S., Rhodes, J. E., & Schwartz, S. E. O. (2016). *The influence of mentor-youth activity profiles on school-based youth mentoring relationship processes and outcomes*. Manuscript in preparation.

Kanchewa, S. S., Rhodes, J. E., Schwartz, S. E. O., & Olsho, L. E. W. (2014). An investigation of same- versus cross-gender matching for boys in formal school-based mentoring programs. *Applied Developmental Science*, *18*(1), 31–45.

Karcher, M. J. (2005). The effects of developmental mentoring and high school mentors' attendance on their younger mentees' self-esteem, social skills, and connectedness. *Psychology in the Schools*, *42*(1), 65–77.

Karcher, M. J. (2008). The study of mentoring in the learning environment (SMILE): A randomized evaluation of the effectiveness of school-based mentoring. *Prevention Science*, *9*, 99–113. doi: 10.1007/s11121-008-0083-z

Karcher, M. J., Davidson, A. J., Rhodes, J. E., & Herrera, C. (2010). Pygmalion in the program: The role of teenager peer mentors' attitudes in shaping their mentees' outcomes. *Applied Developmental Science*, *14*(4), 212–27.

Karcher, M. J., Davis III, C., & Powell, B. (2002). The effects of developmental mentoring on connectedness and academic achievement. *School Community Journal*, *12*(2), 35.

Karcher, M. J., Nakkula, M. J., & Harris, J. (2005). Developmental mentoring match characteristics: Correspondence between mentors' and mentees' assessments of relationship quality. *Journal of Primary Prevention*, *26*(2), 93–110.

Keller, T. E. (2005). A systemic model of the youth mentoring intervention. *Journal of Primary Prevention*, *26*(2), 169–88.

Keller, T. E., & Pryce, J. M. (2010). Mutual but unequal: Mentoring as a hybrid of familiar relationship roles. *New Directions for Youth Development*, *126*, 33–50.

Komosa-Hawkins, K. (2012). The impact of school-based mentoring on adolescents' social–emotional health. *Mentoring and Tutoring: Partnership in Learning*, *20*(3), 393–408.

Kuperminc, G. P., Thomason, J., DiMeo, M., & Broonfield-Massey, K. (2011). Cool Girls, Inc.: Promoting the positive development of urban preadolescent and early adolescent girls. *The Journal of Primary Prevention*, *32*(3–4), 171–83.

Larose, S., Savoie, J., DeWit, D. J., Lipman, E. L., & DuBois, D. L. (2015). The role of relational, recreational, and tutoring activities in the perceptions of received support and quality of mentoring relationship during a community-based mentoring relationship. *Journal of Community Psychology*, *43*(5), 527–44.

Leyton-Armakan, J., Lawrence, E., Deutsch, N., Williams, J. L., & Henneberger, A. (2012). Effective youth mentors: The relationship between initial characteristics of college women mentors and mentee satisfaction and outcome. *Journal of Community Psychology*, *40*(8), 906–20. doi: 10.1002/jcop.21491

Liang, B., Bogat, G. A., & Duffy, N. (2014). Gender in mentoring relationships. In D. L. DuBois, & M. J. Karcher (Eds.), *Handbook of Youth Mentoring, 2nd Edition* (pp. 159–73). Thousand Oaks, CA: Sage.

Lynch, J., Walker-Gibbs, B., & Herbert, S. (2015). Moving beyond a 'bums-on-seats' analysis of progress towards widening participation: reflections on the context, design and evaluation of an Australian government-funded mentoring programme. *Journal of Higher Education Policy and Management*, *37*(2), 144–58.

Markus, H., & Nurius, P. (1986). Possible selves. *American Psychologist*, *41*, 954–69.

McDonald, S., & Lambert, J. (2014). The long arm of mentoring: A counterfactual analysis of natural youth mentoring and employment outcomes in early careers. *American Journal of Community Psychology*, *54*(3–4), 262–73.

McQuillin, S., Smith, B., & Strait, G. (2011). Randomized evaluation of a single semester transitional mentoring program for first year middle school students: A cautionary result for brief, school-based mentoring programs. *Journal of Community Psychology*, *39*(7), 844–59.

McQuillin, S. D., Terry, J. D., Strait, G. G., & Smith, B. H. (2013). Innovation in school-based mentoring: matching the context, structure and goals of mentoring with evidence-based practices. *Advances in School Mental Health Promotion*, *6*(4), 280–94.

MENTOR/National Mentoring Partnership. (2015). *Elements of effective practice for mentoring* (4th ed.). Boston, MA: Author. Retrieved August 3, 2015 from http://www.

mentoring.org/images/uploads/Final_Elements_Publication_Fourth.pdf

Newburn, T., & Shiner, M. (2006). Young people, mentoring and social inclusion. *Youth Justice*, 6(1), 23–41.

Núñez, J. C., Rosário, P., Vallejo, G., & González-Pienda, J. A. (2013). A longitudinal assessment of the effectiveness of a school-based mentoring program in middle school. *Contemporary Educational Psychology*, 38(1), 11–21.

Parra, G. R., DuBois, D. L., Neville, H. A., Pugh-Lilly, A. O. & Pavinelli, N. (2002). Mentoring relationships for youth: Investigation of a process-oriented model. *Journal of Community Psychology*, 30(4), 367–88.

Powers, L. E., Schmidt, J., Sowers, J., & McCracken, K. (2015). Qualitative investigation of the influences of STEM mentors on youth with disabilities. *Career Development and Transition for Exceptional Individuals*, 38(1), 25–38.

Pryce, J. (2012). Mentor attunement: An approach to successful school-based mentoring relationships. *Child and Adolescent Social Work Journal*, 29, 285–305.

Rhodes, J. E. (2002). *Stand by me: The risks and rewards of mentoring today's youth*. Cambridge, MA: Harvard University Press.

Rhodes, J. E. (2005). A model of youth mentoring. In D. L. Dubois & M. K. Karcher (Eds.), *Handbook of Youth Mentoring* (pp. 30–43). Thousand Oaks, CA: Sage.

Rhodes, J. E., Grossman, J. B., & Resch, N. L. (2000). Agents of change: Pathways through which mentoring relationships influence adolescents' academic adjustment. *Child Development*, 71(6), 1662–71.

Rhodes, J. E., Lowe, S. R., Litchfield, L., & Walsh-Samp, K. (2008). The role of gender in youth mentoring relationship formation and duration. *Journal of Vocational Behavior*, 72, 183–92.

Rhodes, J. E., Reddy, R., & Grossman, J. (2005). The protective influence of mentoring on adolescents' substance abuse: Direct and indirect pathways. *Applied Developmental Science*, 9, 31–47.

Rhodes, J. E., Reddy, R., Grossman, J. B., & Lee, J. M. (2002). Volunteer mentoring relationships with minority youth: An analysis of same- versus cross-race matches. *Journal of Applied Social Psychology*, 32(10), 2114–33.

Rhodes, J. E., Schwartz, S. E. O., Willis, M. M., & Wu, M. B. (2014). Validating a mentoring relationship quality scale: Does match strength predict match length. *Youth and Society*. Advance online publication. doi: 10.1177/0044118X14531604

Rummell, C. L. (2013). A unique support for sexual-minority identity development: An interpretative phenomenological analysis of a long-term formal mentoring relationship between an adult and a youth from the gay community (unpublished doctoral dissertation). Portland, OR: Portland State University.

Sánchez, B., Colón-Torres, Y., Feuer, R., Roundfield, K. E., & Berardi, L. (2014). Race, ethnicity, and culture in mentoring relationship. In D. L. DuBois, & M. J. Karcher (Eds.), *Handbook of Youth Mentoring, 2nd Edition* (pp. 145–58). Thousand Oaks, CA: Sage.

Sánchez, B., Esparza, P., Berardi, L., & Pryce, J. (2011). Mentoring in the context of Latino youth's broader village during their transition from high school. *Youth and Society*, 43(1), 225–52.

Sánchez, B., Reyes, O., & Singh, J. (2006). Makin' it in college: The value of significant individuals in the lives of Mexican American adolescents. *Journal of Hispanic Higher Education*, 5(1), 48–67.

Scales, P. (2003). *Other people's kids: Social expectations and American adults' involvement with children and adolescents*. New York: Kluwer Academic/Plenum Publishers.

Schwartz, S. E. O., Kanchewa, S. S., Rhodes, J. E., Cutler, E., & Cunningham, J. (2016). 'I didn't know you could just ask': Empowering underrepresented college-bound students to recruit academic and career mentors. *Children and Youth Services Review*. Manuscript in press.

Schwartz, S. E. O., Rhodes, J. E., Chan, C. S., & Herrera, C. (2011). The impact of school-based mentoring on youth with different relational profiles. *Developmental Psychology*, 47(2), 450–62. doi: 10.1037/a0021379

Schwartz, S. E., Rhodes, J. E., Spencer, R., & Grossman, J. B. (2013). Youth initiated mentoring: Investigating a new approach to working with vulnerable adolescents. *American Journal of Community Psychology*, *52*(1–2), 155–69.

Simões, F., & Alarcão, M. (2014). Promoting well-being in school-based mentoring through basic psychological needs support: Does it really count? *Journal of Happiness Studies*, *15*(2), 407–24.

Spencer, R. (2007a). 'I just feel safe with him': Emotional closeness in male youth mentoring relationships. *Psychology of Men and Masculinity*, *8*(3), 185–98.

Spencer, R. (2007b). 'It's not what I expected': A qualitative study of youth mentoring relationship failures. *Journal of Adolescent Research*, *22*(4), 331–54. doi: 10.1177/0743558407301915

Spencer, R., & Basualdo-Delmonico, A. (2014). Family involvement in the youth mentoring process: A focus group study with program staff. *Children and Youth Services Review*, *41*, 75–82.

Spencer, R., Basualdo-Delmonico, A., & Lewis, T. O. (2011). Working to make it work: The role of parents in the youth mentoring process. *Journal of Community Psychology*, *39*(1), 51–9.

Sroufe, A. L. (1995). Contribution of attachment theory to developmental psychopathology. In E. A. Carlson, & A. L. Sroufe (Eds.), *Developmental Psychopathology*, vol. 1: *Theory and Methods* (pp. 581–617). New York: Plenum Press.

Steinberg, L., & Morris, A. S. (2001). Adolescent development. *Journal of Cognitive Education and Psychology*, *2*(1), 55–87.

Syed, M., Goza, B. K., Chemers, M. M., & Zurbriggen, E. L. (2012). Individual differences in preferences for matched-ethnic mentors among high-achieving ethnically diverse adolescents in STEM. *Child Development*, *83*(3), 896–910.

Taussig, H. N., & Culhane, S. E. (2010). Impact of a mentoring and skills group program on mental health outcomes for maltreated children in foster care. *Archives of Pediatrics and Adolescent Medicine*, *164*(8), 739–46.

Taussig, H. N., Culhane, S. E., Garrido, E., & Knudtson, M. D. (2012). RCT of mentoring and skills group program: Placement and permanency outcomes for foster youth. *Pediatrics*, e33–e39.

Thompson, R. B., Corsello, M., McReynolds, S., & Conklin-Powers, B. (2013). A longitudinal study of family socioeconomic status (SES) variables as predictors of socio-emotional resilience among mentored youth. *Mentoring & Tutoring Partnership in Learning*, *21*(4), 378–91.

Thomson, N. R., & Zand, D. H. (2010). Mentees' perceptions of their interpersonal relationships: The role of the mentor–youth bond. *Youth and Society*, *41*(3), 434–45.

Tolan, P. H., Henry, D. B., Schoeny, M. S., Lovegrove, P., & Nichols, E. (2014). Mentoring programs to affect delinquency and associated outcomes of youth at risk: A comprehensive meta-analytic review. *Journal of Experimental Criminology*, *10*(2), 179–206.

Vygotsky, L. S. (1978). *Mind in society: The development of higher psychological processes.* Cambridge, MA: Harvard University Press.

Washington, G., Johnson, T., Jones, J., & Langs, S. (2007). African American boys in relative care and a culturally centered group mentoring approach. *Social Work with Groups*, *30*(1), 45–69.

Weiler, L. M., Haddock, S. A., Zimmerman, T. S., Henry, K. L., Krafchick, J. L., & Youngblade, L. M. (2015). Time-limited, structured youth mentoring and adolescent problem behaviors. *Applied Developmental Science*, 1–10. doi: 10.1080/10888691.2015.1014484

Wheeler, M. E., Keller, T. E., & DuBois, D. L. (2010). Review of three recent randomized trials of school-based mentoring: Making sense of mixed findings. Social Policy Report. *Society for Research in Child Development*, *24*(3), 1–21.

Whitney, S. D., Hendricker, E. N., & Offutt, C. A. (2011). Moderating factors of natural mentoring relationships, problem behaviors, and emotional well-being. *Mentoring and Tutoring: Partnership in Learning*, *19*(1), 83–105.

Yoshikawa, H., Aber, J. L., & Beardslee, W. R. (2012). The effects of poverty on the mental, emotional, and behavioral health of children and youth. *American Psychologist*, *67*(4), 272–84.

Zand, D. H., Thomson, N., Cervantes, R., Espiritu, R., Klagholz, D., LaBlanc, L., & Taylor, A. (2009). The mentor-youth alliance: The role of mentoring relationships in promoting youth competence. *Journal of Adolescence*, *32*, 1–17.

Zimmerman, M. A., Bingenheimer, J. B., & Notaro, P. C. (2002). Natural mentors and adolescent resiliency: A study with urban youth. *American Journal of Community Psychology 30*, 221–43.

Mentoring in Higher Education

Laura Gail Lunsford, Gloria Crisp,
Erin L. Dolan and Brad Wuetherick

INTRODUCTION

Mentoring relationships are embedded in the educational process in higher education. This chapter reviews scholarly work on mentoring in higher education for undergraduates, graduate students, and faculty members. We consider the purposes, types, and outcomes of mentoring in each context. The informal focus on mentoring has given way to a proliferation of formal mentoring programs at universities around the world (González, 2001). Thus, we explore mentoring in educational contexts in the United States (USA), Australia, Canada, New Zealand, South Africa, and the United Kingdom (UK).

Our approach is to synthesize findings from the past ten years about mentoring that provide evidence as to what works for special populations/program types. The databases searched were: Academic Search Complete, Ebscohost, Psychology and Behavioral Sciences, SOCI Index, Education Full-Text (Wilson Web) full-text and peer-reviewed journals (excluding non-US and non-British work).

UNDERGRADUATE EDUCATION

Purpose of mentoring undergraduate students

The term mentoring describes a range of faculty–student, staff–student or student–student relationships (Crisp and Cruz, 2009; Gershenfeld, 2014; Jacobi, 1991). In descriptive reports and empirical studies of undergraduate mentoring these relationships are often defined at a programmatic or administrative level rather than from the perspective of the undergraduate, his or her mentor, or their relationship. Despite this focus, mentoring continues to be widely accepted as an effective mechanism for positively influencing undergraduate students (Eby and Dolan, 2015), including improving their academic performance (e.g. Fox et al., 2010), ensuring their persistence in university or in specific disciplines – such as science, technology, engineering, and mathematics (STEM) (e.g. Bettinger and Baker, 2011) – or easing their transition into new institutional or disciplinary cultures (e.g. Bordes and Arredondo, 2005). Some undergraduate mentoring programs aim to help students be successful in challenging experiences, such as a capstone projects (Pembridge, 2011), research experiences (e.g. Horowitz and Christopher, 2012), work-integrated learning (Ralph and Walker, 2010, 2013), or courses in which high levels of attrition are observed (e.g. Hryciw et al., 2013). Other programs aim to support underrepresented students, including: students from ethnic and racial backgrounds in STEM disciplines, women in physical sciences, mathematics, and engineering, and students who are first in their families to go to university (e.g. Wilson et al., 2012).

Types of undergraduate mentorship

Mentoring builds relationships with students, locates spaces where they get disconnected, and helps them reconnect when needed (Drake, 2011). Relationships may take a variety of forms and be distinguished by their duration, function, and source(s) of mentoring. Most research focuses on formal mentoring programs on university campuses (Erickson et al., 2009). However, mentoring may be informal and develop spontaneously and naturally (Eby and Allen, 2008). The amount of contact provided to students and the duration of informal and formal relationships also differs, with some relationships being limited to one meeting and others lasting over a decade (Crisp and Cruz, 2009).

Formal program components vary in terms of mentor training, activity type, and the mode of interaction between student and mentor (Larose et al., 2009). For instance, although traditionally mentoring has been provided in person, an increasing number of e-mentoring programs are being implemented across universities and include a combination of technology mediated (e.g. discussion boards), and face-to-face interactions with students (Shrestha et al., 2009).

While mentoring relationships are prevalent between faculty and undergraduate students, student relationships with university staff, peers, graduate students, family, friends, community members, and religious leaders have been shown to contribute to the educational success of students (Erickson et al., 2009). Further, mentoring may be experienced between a student and one individual or in small groups of two or more students and/or mentors (Crisp and Cruz, 2009). It is notable that the functions and roles of mentoring may differ by source and that students may benefit from having more than one mentor who provides different forms of support. For example, findings by D'Abate (2009) indicate that faculty regard their role to include teaching, sharing information, providing advice and feedback, and academic goal-setting tracking, whereas roles such as introducing, affirming and befriending may be better provided by peer-mentors.

Mentoring outcomes for undergraduates

Mentoring research and practice continues to develop through the work of a multidisciplinary and international group of scholars, each focusing on a specific educational context and/or target population (Eby and Allen, 2008). In recent years, researchers' attention has focused on mentoring outcomes for specific student groups, resulting in a growing knowledge base regarding how, and under what conditions, mentoring can be effective in supporting the development and success of undergraduate students. Overall, findings point to mentoring as a means of directly or indirectly improving academic outcomes, such as grade point average and persistence in higher education (Bordes-Edgar et al., 2011; Campbell and Campbell, 2007; Crisp, 2011).

Mentoring improves students' transition to university, by either helping them to attend university or once they are there, to be retained through to degree completion. A controlled evaluation of peer mentoring, designed to provide psychological support and academic advice to undergraduate students at universities in the UK, found that non-mentored students were four times as likely to consider leaving the university when compared to mentored students. Mentoring positively influences student outcomes such as:

- sense of belonging (O'Brien et al., 2012),
- capacity for socially responsible leadership (Campbell et al., 2012),
- deep and strategic learning approaches (Chester et al., 2013), and
- self-confidence in professional skills and abilities (Thiry et al., 2011).

There is further evidence that mentors may benefit from relationships with undergraduate students, including improved cognitive and socio-emotional growth, teaching, and communication skills (Dolan and Johnson, 2009).

There is a new line of work focused on students who are enrolled in community or technical colleges. For example, Khazanov (2011) used a quasi-experimental design to evaluate a peer-mentoring program for community college students enrolled in remedial or developmental classes. Findings revealed mentored students earned similar grades and were more likely to persist in college when compared to non-mentored students. Further, work by Barnett (2011) and Crisp (2010) suggested that mentoring may play an important role in helping community college students integrate, develop friends, and be satisfied with their academic experiences during college. Moreover, results from Barnett (2011) demonstrated the importance and value of community college students receiving validating interactions with faculty.

Although findings converge to suggest that mentoring is beneficial to undergraduate students, mentoring is not always effective, or may be less effective for certain groups or in certain contexts. The following subsections summarize recent findings that explain which mentoring outcomes may be influenced by mentor and student characteristics (e.g. at-risk, minority) and/or program type (e.g. STEM, undergraduate research).

Targeted undergraduate mentoring programs

Most undergraduate mentoring programs fit into three categories: undergraduate research mentoring, peer mentoring, or comprehensive mentoring. Each category is discussed separately below. There is a focus on science, technology, engineering, and mathematics (STEM) because STEM has been better funded (and thus more studied) relative to research on undergraduate mentoring in other disciplines.

Undergraduate research mentoring programs

Undergraduate research experiences (UREs) provide opportunities for students to gain authentic experience in their discipline of interest, develop as young professionals, strengthen their personal and professional (academic) identity development, and realize a variety of other cognitive, psychosocial, and behavioral outcomes (Laursen et al., 2010; Linn et al., 2015; Lopatto and Tobias, 2010; Palmer et al., 2015). Undergraduates who participate in research were typically apprenticed to more experienced individuals, such as faculty members, graduate or post-doctoral researchers, or upper-division undergraduates, who were considered to be their mentors (Burg et al., 2015; Feldman et al., 2013; Linn et al., 2015). Mentoring has been proposed as an important factor in maximizing student benefits of participating in research (Linn et al., 2015; Taraban and Logue, 2012; Thiry and Laursen, 2011). For the most part, however, UREs are loosely defined (Balster et al., 2010), and published descriptions of URE programs have not articulated how mentoring relationships are established, structured, or supported.

Undergraduate research offices and programs are increasingly prevalent on university campuses, and some match undergraduates with research mentors. For example, Burg and colleagues (2015) described a 'vertically integrated' mentoring structure for their STEM Incubator Course and two similar programs, the Freshman Research Initiative at The University of Texas at Austin and the Vertically-Integrated Projects Program at Georgia Tech. These programs engaged introductory-level undergraduates in research with guidance from graduate students and faculty. Undergraduates then had the option to continue research as peer mentors for the next cohort of students with coordination and guidance from a designated mentor coordinator.

Outside these structured programs, undergraduates find and establish informal relationships with research mentors, who normally receive little preparation or guidance on how to mentor undergraduate researchers. As a result, there has been a growth of local mechanisms (e.g. campus workshops and websites) and more formal curricula (e.g. Balster et al., 2010) for undergraduates to learn how to establish and navigate relationships with research mentors and to build the capacity of graduate students, postdoctoral researchers, and faculty to mentor undergraduates effectively (Pfund et al., 2006; Pfund et al., 2014). For example, *Entering Mentoring* (Handelsman, 2005) offers guidance to STEM research mentors on how to structure UREs, such as by defining goals and expectations for both protégés and mentors. *Entering Mentoring* and other mentor professional development curricula (see http://www.researchmentortraining.org/; http://mentor.unm.edu/online-resources [accessed September 22, 2015]) highlight common topics that arise when mentoring undergraduate researchers.

Few studies disaggregated the effects for undergraduates of participating in research from the effects of their relationships with research mentors. Russell, Hancock and McCullough (2007) surveyed 4,500 undergraduate students and 3,600 faculty members, graduate student and postdoctoral mentors and found that mentorship characteristics, such as involvement in decision-making and adequacy of mentor guidance, did not have a statistically significant impact on positive outcomes of undergraduate research. They argued, however, that:

> By far the most common suggestions that students made about how to improve undergraduate research programs concerned increased or more effective faculty guidance. We suspect that the absence of strong relationships on the structured questions reflects the complexity of the mentor's role rather than its unimportance. (Russell et al., 2007, 549)

Schultz and colleagues (2011) conducted one of the first empirical studies to delineate the outcomes of engaging in research versus being mentored. Their longitudinal study of STEM students, who were racial or ethnic minorities, examined the effects of participating in an undergraduate training program on students' persistence in their intentions to pursue science-related research careers, as compared to a propensity score matched control group. Undergraduates who reported participating in research were significantly more likely to continue in their intentions to pursue science-related research careers than matched control students, but there was not a similar effect for undergraduates who reported having a scientific mentor (i.e. faculty member, program staff member, graduate student, postdoctoral fellow, or scientific professional outside the university whom they considered to be a mentor). In contrast, in their longitudinal study of aspiring STEM majors with propensity score matched control students, Eagan and colleagues (2013) found that participating in research, mentoring by faculty, and interacting with graduate students/teaching assistants had distinct, significant, positive effects on undergraduates' intentions to pursue STEM graduate degrees. Contradictory results about the influence of mentoring in UREs are likely due to the limited methods used to measure mentoring, which generally do not take into account the quality or functions of mentoring relationships or mentors' levels of experience or preparation in mentoring (Johnson and Kaslow, 2014). The use of measures of mentoring competence (e.g. Fleming et al., 2013; Pfund et al., 2014) and mentoring functions (e.g. Schlosser and Gelso, 2001, 2005) may be useful for a more nuanced approach to studying the influence of mentoring in UREs.

Peer mentoring programs

Most peer mentoring programs aim to enhance students' sense of belonging at university and their academic persistence and success (Jacobi, 1991; Hill and Reddy, 2007; Nora and Crisp, 2007). Peer mentors function in ways that were reflective of other mentors, for example, by serving as role models and offering psychosocial and academic subject knowledge support (Colvin and Ashman, 2010; Terrion and Leonard, 2007; Terrion, 2012). Peer mentors connected their protégés to key resources by providing information about opportunities, helping protégés navigate their university, and acting as liaisons to faculty and other influential people. Peer mentoring programs achieved many of the same outcomes as other types of mentoring programs, including academic integration, retention, and success (e.g. Chester et al., 2013; Collings, Swanson, and Watkins, 2014; Hryciw et al., 2013).

Peer mentoring programs commonly target first-year undergraduates as protégés because the transition to university is an important time in students' decisions to continue in higher education and in particular disciplines (e.g. STEM; see Seymour and Hewitt, 1997). Further, upper-level undergraduates have recent, salient experience they can draw from in advising first-year students. Mentoring by peers can be particularly critical to early university students since students who do not connect to a peer group, or who have negative peer interactions, are more likely to be lost to attrition (Bean and Metzner, 1985; Tinto, 1975). Peer mentors afford advantages over faculty and staff mentors because they are more readily available and are perceived as more approachable, thus encouraging disclosure and trust formation. Peer mentors also face challenges unique to being a peer, including how to balance their own academic, personal, and professional priorities with those of their protégés, and how to establish and maintain contact with their protégés (Colvin and Ashman, 2010; Terrion and Leonard, 2007).

In contrast to programs that involve faculty or other professionals as mentors, peer mentoring programs often use a formal process for selecting mentors. Mentors may be selected according to criteria such as high level of academic achievement, interpersonal and communication skills, and conscientiousness, as well as a sincere interest in serving as a mentor, although the relative importance of these factors for the establishment of successful peer mentoring relationships has not been delineated (Terrion and Leonard, 2007). Some programs make efforts to match undergraduates and peer mentors based on socio-demographic characteristics, although research on the importance of matching based on race, ethnicity, or gender versus matching according to deep-level similarity or even dissimilarity (e.g. Sosik and Godshalk, 2005) is equivocal (Eby et al., 2013; Eby and Dolan, 2014; Terrion and Leonard, 2007).

Peer mentoring relationships are typically more structured than mentoring relationships observed in UREs. For example, many such programs start with formal opportunities for mentors and protégés to get acquainted, such as during a welcome event or a first-year seminar course (e.g. Holt and Berwise, 2012). There are often established expectations for mentor–protégé interactions at regular intervals, such as during a tutorial session or on an ad hoc basis, or at key time points (e.g. exam periods). Program administrators also expect more regular and systematic reporting about mentor–protégé interactions than in UREs. Peer mentors may meet with protégés one-on-one or in small groups (e.g. Collings et al., 2014), and can be volunteers or earn credit or pay. Some may even live in close proximity to their protégés to facilitate daily interactions (e.g. Kiyama and Luca, 2013). Most programs end formal relationships at natural points of closure, such as the end of a course, the end of the protégé's first year in college, or at graduation, although peer mentoring relationships may persist informally after the end of the formal program. Peer mentoring programs were more likely than other mentoring scenarios to provide formal mentor training in the form of workshops and regular meetings throughout the mentoring experience (e.g. Hryciw et al., 2012). These sessions aimed to build mentors' knowledge about how to engage with and support their protégés, and enhance mentors' awareness of issues that they and their protégés may face, and strategies for mitigating or resolving them.

Comprehensive mentoring programs

Keen interest in increasing diversity of university graduates and the STEM workforce has driven the establishment of multi-faceted mentoring programs that offer academic, social, and professional opportunities to students who are traditionally underserved, including underrepresented minority students, women in physics, mathematics, and engineering, and students who are first in their families to go to university. These efforts are grounded in research showing that underrepresented students leave university and STEM disciplines for reasons other than their capabilities (Ferrare and Lee, 2014; Seymour and Hewitt, 1997). We refer to these programs as *comprehensive mentoring programs*, which are responsive to theoretical (Pascarella, 1980; Tinto, 1975, 1993) and empirical work (e.g. Chemers et al., 2011; Gazley et al., 2014; Hurtado et al., 2009; Merolla and Serpe, 2013) on student socialization into academic and disciplinary cultures.

Comprehensive mentoring programs acknowledge that while cross-racial mentoring can be effective (Reddick and Pritchett, 2015) there are benefits to matching students with mentors of similar demographic characteristics. For instance, Campbell and Campbell (2007) found that ethnically matched pairs remained enrolled for more semesters and accumulated more units than did pairs who were not matched by ethnicity. Evidence suggests that students who were the first to attend college in their family, typically termed first generation, may approach and experience mentoring from more of a utilitarian perspective when compared to students with university-educated parents, who held a broader view of the relationship and were more likely to capitalize on social networking opportunities (Mekolichick and Gibbs, 2012). There is evidence from a well-designed experiment by Bettinger and Baker (2011) that mentoring may be more beneficial for male compared to female undergraduate students.

The Meyerhoff Scholars Program at University of Maryland, Baltimore County (Maton et al., 2000; Maton and Hrabowski, 2004) couples financial support in the form of scholarships and structured academic opportunities (e.g. summer bridge programming, undergraduate research opportunities, study groups, tutoring and being tutored) with mentoring by peers, academic advisors, faculty, and other professionals. Qualitative study of this program indicated that peer and faculty mentoring promoted a sense of belonging to the institution and the discipline and increased students' levels of self-efficacy and identity (Maton et al., 2000; Stolle-McAllister et al., 2011), all of which have been shown to improve students' academic engagement and achievement (Liang et al., 2002; Martin and Dowson, 2009). Peers and faculty serve as 'institutional agents' (Stanton-Salazar, 2011), which has been shown to be important for helping students find key information and opportunities and make connections within their institutions and disciplines (Crisp and Cruz, 2009; Eagan et al., 2013; Fuentes et al., 2014). Studies of the Meyerhoff Scholars Program and similar initiatives show that participating students have greater odds than non-participating students of persisting and succeeding in introductory science and math courses, earning higher GPAs, graduating with a STEM major, and pursuing STEM-related education or career paths after graduation, after controlling for gender, race/ethnicity, and high school achievement (Barlow and Villarejo, 2004; Slovacek et al., 2012; Villarejo and Barlow, 2007).

When considered holistically, these programs offer a full complement of mentoring functions, including the provision of psychosocial, role model, academic, and career-related support (Crisp, 2009; Nora and Crisp, 2007). Our review of scholarship on undergraduate mentoring identified an increasing number of mentoring programs and empirical work focused toward groups that have been traditionally underrepresented and underserved in higher education systems. Overall, evidence suggests that mentoring relationships may have benefits for underrepresented groups and may help reduce inequities in persistence and degree completion between Anglo/white and racial/ethnic minority groups (e.g. Bordes-Edgar et al., 2011). For instance, Hu and Ma (2010) found that having an assigned university mentor was positively related to the probability that minority students would persist at university. Further, Shotton, Oosahwe, and Cintron (2007) found peer mentors helped indigenous students overcome potential barriers by providing support and guidance, and by connecting them to the indigenous community on campus.

Mentoring similarities/differences across contexts

Research on mentoring outcomes in Canada, Australia, and the UK align with findings in US-focused studies. There is, however, a difference in the language used across these contexts. In the UK, Australia, and New Zealand, the research at both undergraduate and graduate student levels focuses on formal supervision, even though the characteristics of supervision they describe are what US scholars term mentorship (Grant and Manathunga, 2011; Lee, 2011; Manathunga and Goozée, 2007; Wisker, 2012[2005]). For example, Wisker's (2012[2005]) summary of the supervision literature in the UK articulated the characteristics of good research supervision as including supportive practices that nurtured the students' research skills development and development as an individual. These findings align with mentorship literature in the USA.

In Canada, the terms supervision and mentorship have been used interchangeably by scholars, however there is a recent move towards distinguishing between mentorship and supervision. The tension between supervision and mentorship is one of the fundamental differences in mentoring constructs. For example, Ralph (1998) first used the term supervision, through a model described as contextual supervision, to refer to how mentors adapt to student needs. Later, Ralph and Walker (2010, 2013) proferred the term 'adaptive mentorship' in their exploration of mentoring in the context of professional, work-integrated learning. These researchers argued that students in mentoring relationships may be located along two continua – confidence and competence. Further, mentorship provided to students must respond to student needs by adapting the mentor's stance between a task or support orientation for better outcomes from the mentorship experience (ibid.).

There is a dearth of research published in English beyond the primarily English-speaking contexts mentioned above on how the nature and outcomes of mentoring experiences vary across cultures (Buyukgoze-Kavas et al., 2010). Notably, Manathunga (2014) and Grant and Manathunga (2011) have explored how supervisory practices in doctoral education might need to change or evolve as a result of increasing student diversity within English-speaking institutions.

GRADUATE EDUCATION

Purposes of graduate student mentoring

As noted above, the terms mentoring and supervision are used interchangeably in non-US contexts and both terms are used here. The purposes of graduate student mentorship are to enhance the academic development (including development of research skills and a disciplinary identity), professional (career) development, and personal (psychosocial) development of graduate students. Mentors of graduate students may be formal advisors or supervisors, other faculty or research staff in the discipline or beyond, postdoctoral fellows, more senior graduate students, and peers. Mentoring by each of whom might manifest in different mentoring relationship dynamics. These mentoring relationships are important as 'graduate students experience lofty academic demands, high levels of stress and anxiety and conflicts between various responsibilities' (Hadjioannou et al., 2007: 160).

The quality of mentoring relationships may be important for particular groups of graduate students. For example, studies of international graduate students at US universities have reported different educational experiences than American students, in part because they have an added challenge of trying to adjust to a new environment and culture (Rose, 2005). Further, the reported graduate experiences of women, and of students from underrepresented, historically oppressed and diverse groups, suggest that mentoring relationships are critical in helping these students navigate an increasingly complex and difficult educational and career path through and beyond graduate school (Williams-Nickelson, 2009). Lechuga (2011) found that faculty–graduate student relationships, within the context of a STEM program with Latina/o faculty mentors, can be described by three broad descriptors that characterize faculty members' perceived roles and responsibilities as Allies, Ambassadors, and Master-Teachers.

Types of graduate mentorship

Researchers surveyed graduate students at 21 US universities and found that students experienced mentoring relationships in a variety of forms, including formal, informal, professional, and peer mentoring (Watson et al., 2009). There is a continuing tradition of a formal mentoring or master–apprentice model, where a supervisor works individually with a graduate student, which remains the archetype for graduate training. It is a model where the perceptions of both graduate students and leaders of graduate programs are positive (Rose, 2005).

Graduate supervision, in the inclusive sense in which supervision is used in the UK and Australian contexts, has been regarded primarily as an extension of research rather than as a form of teaching. Thus, it is considered a type of mentoring, where students gradually master appropriate disciplinary research knowledge over the course of their graduate education (Manathunga and Goozée, 2007). How individuals perceived their supervision and mentorship (Manathunga, 2005) influenced greatly their overall graduate experiences.

Unfortunately, faculty mentors and supervisors may assume that even new graduate students are 'always/already' autonomous scholars (Thomas, Lunsford, and Rodrigues, 2015). Further, university administrators similarly assume supervisors are 'always/already' effective at supervising and mentoring graduate students because they had completed (or 'endured') the process of conducting graduate research themselves (Manathunga and Goozée, 2007). It is possible that a faculty member might be an excellent supervisor (or mentor) but a poor mentor (or supervisor). Indeed,

> few supervisors are selected on, let alone trained in, advanced methods of supervision (and mentorship). Appointed supervisors therefore seldom have a conceptual map of what constitutes acceptable supervision (and mentorship). Supervisors themselves are often the products of poor supervision (and mentorship), and do not therefore hold experience of what constitutes competent supervision (and mentorship). (Dietz et al., 2006, 11)

Yob and Crawford (2012) have offered a conceptual model of the behaviors and skills needed to mentor doctoral students. The two domains of mentor behaviors and characteristics were academic and psychosocial. In the academic domain, four attributes were identified: competence, availability, induction, and challenge. In the psychosocial domain, three attributes were identified: the faculty member's personal qualities, communication, and emotional support.

Mentoring outcomes for graduate students

Overall, research demonstrates the importance of mentoring relationships in effective graduate education (Baker, Pifer and Flemion, 2013) and indicates that most graduate students perceive mentoring as important. In addition, findings demonstrate that the majority of graduate students receive mentoring support, typically from their faculty advisor but also from peers and other sources (e.g. Lunsford, 2012). Across disciplines and university contexts, mentoring relationships with faculty and peers are beneficial for graduate students. More specifically, mentoring has the potential to contribute to graduate students' socialization and academic support (Hadjioannou et al., 2007), and satisfaction with the program and/or advisor (McAllister et al., 2009). Further, there is a growing body of evidence demonstrating the relationship between mentoring and graduate students' research and writing productivity (e.g. Lunsford, 2012; Watson et al., 2009) including longitudinal research by Paglis, Green, and Bauer (2006) who studied doctoral students in the hard sciences over five and a half years and found mentoring to be related to students' research productivity and self-efficacy.

Despite the numerous positive outcomes, there is evidence that mentoring may not always benefit students and in some cases may serve to hinder graduate students' success. For instance, recent work found that female graduate students experienced feelings of self-doubt as a result of negative experiences with advising and mentoring, including difficulties engaging with a quality mentor (Welton, Mansfield and Lee, 2014). As such, it is important to recognize how mentoring may be experienced similarly or differently by different groups of students. Research by Rose (2005) identifies several notable differences in how mentoring may be influenced by both individual and sociocultural differences, including gender, age, and culture. In particular, findings revealed that female doctoral students at US universities considered a mentor's integrity to be more important to their definition of the ideal mentor when compared to male students. Findings also revealed an inverse relationship between the age of students and the perceived importance of the personal relationship aspect of mentoring. Similarly, international students considered a mentor's willingness to develop a personal relationship with them to be more important than domestic students.

Researchers have also been increasingly engaged in work to understand how mentoring is experienced among targeted groups of graduate students, in particular for those who have been traditionally underserved in higher education. For instance, Rudolph and colleagues (2015) sought to understand the mentoring experiences of Latina/o graduate students attending a US Hispanic serving institution, highlighting the importance of mentor openness, trust, commitment, availability, and grant assistance. Similarly, Pidgeon, Achibald and Hawkey (2014) studied Aboriginal graduate students in Canada who participated in a culturally relevant peer and mentoring program called SAGE. Findings showed that relationships between Aboriginal graduate students and faculty created networking opportunities and a sense of belonging. The program was also shown to foster self-accountability for students' academic studies. An evaluation of a mentoring program for lesbian, gay, bisexual, and transgender (LGBTQ) graduate students in social work education found students were looking for specific types of instrumental and psychosocial support from mentors as well as more mentor initiation of the relationship (McAllister et al., 2009).

A review of recent mentoring programs also revealed the importance of understanding the underlying conditions that promote success or impede successful graduate student mentoring relationships. For instance, findings by Rudolph and colleagues (2015) reveal that work obligations had a negative impact on mentoring for Latino males. Additionally, work by Hadjioannou and colleagues (2007) suggested that student-led mentoring groups may enhance the development of doctoral students' into scholars by providing mentors with the opportunity to support students in different ways and on different levels (e.g. peer review). Findings by Ortiz-Walters and Gilson (2005) indicated that African-American, Hispanic and indigenous graduate students may be more satisfied with, and receive more, psychosocial and instrumental support from mentors who are non-white. It appears that students' interpersonal comfort and commitment may mediate relationships between outcomes and superficial and deeper levels of similarity between mentors and graduate students. In cases where ethnic minority graduate students were mentored by white faculty or staff, qualitative findings by Chan, Yeh, and Krumboltz (2015) highlighted the importance of providing career support and guidance tailored for minorities, such as discussing career possibilities and building confidence. In addition, results of interviews with faculty mentors and doctoral students attending a research-intensive university in Australia suggested that students benefit from having a mentor who was adept at adapting to multiple cultural approaches (e.g. Australian and Chinese) to supervision (Manathunga, 2011).

ACADEMIC/FACULTY MENTORING

Purpose of academic mentoring

Academic mentoring refers to informal and formal efforts to mentor faculty members in higher education. Mentoring has been assumed to take place informally because of the tiered progression of academic careers (De Janasz and Sullivan, 2004). As such, formal mentoring is a recent phenomena that has been promoted in the USA through funding efforts such as the National Science Foundation Advance Program (http://www.nsf.gov/crssprgm/advance [accessed September 22, 2015]).

Research on informal mentoring efforts suggests that mentors support faculty in achieving a work/life balance as well as providing career guidance (Hagemeier et al., 2013; Metzger et al., 2013; Thomas et al., 2015). It has been viewed as the responsibility of senior faculty to mentor new faculty members.

Recent studies suggest that informal mentoring is available to about half of faculty members in academic medicine and that mentoring needs were more likely to be met for early and mid career individuals in tenure-track or tenured positions (Blood et al., 2012) than for individuals in instructor or full professor positions. Yet, 75 percent of faculty members without mentors desired one. Similarly, a study of faculty in pharmacy found that about 60 percent reported having an influential mentor and that 20 percent of these would not have pursued a faculty position without their mentor's encouragement (Hagemeier et al., 2013). A survey of law faculty in 44 institutions found that just over half reported having informal mentors (Haynes and Petrosko, 2009) and only three percent reported participation in a formal mentoring program.

Formal mentoring programs appear to be established because of requirements of professional bodies or because of priorities of university administrators. For example, the Association to Advance Collegiate Schools of Business requires mentoring of faculty as part of their accreditation process (Raymond and Kannon, 2014). University administrators support formal mentoring initiatives to mitigate problems related to job satisfaction and retention (Law et al., 2014), to address perceived shortages in the workforce – particularly in nursing (Sawatzky and Enns, 2009), and to help underrepresented academics attain experience in professional areas of grant writing and publishing (Mayer et al., 2009).

Types of academic mentoring

This section focuses on formal mentoring programs, most of which may be categorized by their focus on career stage (early career versus across ranks) and by their mentoring model (one-on-one versus networks).

Career stage

Formal mentoring programs for early career faculty focus on teaching and research responsibilities as well as achieving work–life balance and developing a career plan (Fleming et al., 2015; Law et al., 2014; Metzger et al., 2013; Thomas et al., 2015). These formal mentoring programs usually involve a series of workshops (e.g. Thomas et al., 2015) or a curriculum to achieve the program goals (e.g. Fleming et al., 2015).

There is an overwhelming focus on the needs of early career faculty. Over 90 percent of pharmacy departments offered a formal mentoring program targeted at early career faculty (Metzger et al., 2013). A task force convened by the American Association of Colleges in Pharmacy called for more attention to formal mentoring of mid career faculty. Their work suggested that early career faculty members need mentors from their institution while mid career faculty members need mentors from outside (Law et al., 2014). A study of faculty in liberal arts colleges also reported a lack of access to mentors at mid and late career (Baker et al., 2016).

Mentoring models

Over a decade ago mentoring scholars called for a broader understanding of mentoring relationships to extend beyond the traditional one-on-one relationships (Higgins and Kram, 2001). This work is beginning to make its way into academic mentoring programs as evidenced by a recent focus on supporting group and peer mentoring and professional learning communities (Pellegrino et al., 2014).

Group mentoring has been adopted by some faculties in medicine and appears to efficiently provide mentoring experiences. Most academic physicians in emergency medicine (98 per cent) listed lack of access to mentoring as an obstacle to their career progress (Yeung, Nuth, and Stiell, 2010). These researchers reported an increase in the career satisfaction and promotion rates of mentored faculty members who participated in a group telementoring program. A face-to-face group mentoring program for faculty in academic medicine also incorporated peer mentoring and increased the retention rate of mentored faculty members. Participants in this program reported higher knowledge, skills, and abilities as well as interconnectedness in the field than non-participants (Fleming et al., 2015). A pilot mentoring program for new faculty in science, agriculture, and the humanities in the United States purposely connected faculty with institutional mentors and advocated mentees to develop a mentoring network of four to five mentors within and external to their institution. Participants reported an increase in knowledge about their career and the institution (Thomas et al., 2015).

Interestingly, researchers suggest that race/ethnicity does not influence access to mentoring or mentoring outcomes (Eby et al., 2013; O'Brien et al., 2008), yet qualitative researchers rebut this claim (see Chapters 23 and 24 in this volume). This line of work suggests underrepresented faculty members may not be well served by what is perceived as a hierarchal, traditional model of mentoring.

Mentoring outcomes for faculty members

Scholars find that mentoring is associated with career and psychosocial benefits for faculty members. Early career faculty who are mentored are twice as likely to be promoted, more likely to report greater career satisfaction (Thomas et al., 2014; Yeung et al., 2010), and are more likely to stay in their jobs (Fleming et al., 2015). Further, junior faculty members with mentors report an increase in their skills and abilities (Jackevicius et al., 2014). It appears that mentees who focus on the skills needed for faculty work, such as writing and grant skills, gain confidence and productivity that lead to promotion and retention. Indeed, some faculty members report they would not have become faculty members without their mentors' encouragement and support (Hagemeier et al., 2013). There is less work on the benefits to faculty members in mid and late career, which is an avenue future researchers might explore.

CONCLUSION

The recent work on mentoring in higher education suggests that informal and formal mentoring is ubiquitous in the English-speaking countries examined here. Formal mentoring appears to be more frequent for undergraduate students than for graduate students or faculty members. Mentoring is presumed to be built into the advising/supervision function for graduate students. At the

Table 20.1 Purpose, types, and outcomes of mentoring for undergraduates, graduate students, and faculty members

	Purpose	Types of Mentoring	Outcomes
Undergraduates	Increase degree persistence Ease academic transitions Prepare for challenging experiences (graduate school, research, advanced courses) Support underrepresented students	Comprehensive E-mentoring Peer Research Natural/Informal	Grade point average Persistence in higher education Leadership skills Cognitive and socio-emotional growth (learning, sense of belonging)
Graduate students	Academic development Career development Personal development	Professional Peer Informal	Socialization Academic support Program/advisor satisfaction Scholarly productivity
Faculty	Increase job knowledge and satisfaction Increase retention	Early career Peer Networks	Career satisfaction Promotion and retention Job knowledge/skills

faculty level it is much less frequent, even when professional accrediting bodies require formal mentoring. This chapter highlighted the types of formal mentoring programs that have been well studied. For undergraduate students these programs focus on underrepresented groups or research mentoring, while professional and peer mentoring characterizes graduate student mentorship. In the faculty context mentoring usually focuses on the needs of early career faculty. Table 20.1 summarizes the purpose and type of mentoring and outcomes associated with each context.

Scholars report benefits of mentoring for those who participate in it. These outcomes relate to specific academic or job needs, depending on the population participating in mentoring. As researchers examine the nuances of mentoring, and what groups might benefit most from what types of mentoring, we may begin to find larger effect sizes. Future research might focus on understanding equivocal results related to different approachees to mentor-protege (or mentee) matching, on more clearly delineating what occurs during mentoring relationships and how this affects specific groups, and on studying the effects of mentoring at career stages currently under-represented in the literature (e.g., mid and late career faculty).

REFERENCES

Baker, V.L., Pifer, M.J., and Flemion, B. (2013). Process challenges and learning-based interaction in stage 2 of doctoral education: implications from two applied social science fields. *The Journal of Higher Education*, *84*(4), 449–76.

Baker, V.L., Pifer, M.J., and Lunsford, L.G. (2016). Faculty challenges across rank in liberal arts colleges: A human resources perspective. *The Journal of Faculty Development*, *30*(1), 23–30.

Balster, N., Pfund, C., Rediske, R., and Branchaw, J. (2010). Entering research: A course that creates community and structure for beginning undergraduate researchers in the STEM disciplines. *CBE – Life Sciences Education*, *9*, 108–18.

Barlow, A.E.L., and Villarejo, M. (2004). Making a difference for minorities: Evaluation of an educational enrichment program. *Journal of Research in Science Teaching*, *41*, 861–81.

Barnett, E.A. (2011). Validation experiences and persistence among community college students. *The Review of Higher Education*, *34*(2), 193–230.

Bean, J.P., and Metzner, B.S. (1985). A conceptual model of nontraditional undergraduate student attrition. *Review of Educational Research*, *55*, 485–540.

Bettinger, E., and Baker, R. (2011). The effects of student coaching in college: An evaluation of a randomized experiment in student mentoring. *National Bureau of Economic Research Working Paper 16881*. Retrieved from http://www.nber.org/papers/w16881 [accessed 15 September, 2015].

Blood, E.A., Ullrich, N.J., Hirshfeld-Becker, D.R., Seely, E.W., Connelly, M.T., Warfield, C.A., and Emans, S.J. (2012). Academic women faculty: are they finding the mentoring they need? *Journal of Women's Health*, *21*(11), 1201–08.

Bordes, V., and Arredondo, P. (2005). Mentoring and 1st-year Latina/o college students. *Journal of Hispanic Higher Education*, *4*(2), 114–33.

Bordes-Edgar, V., Arredondo, P., Kurpius, S.R., and Rund, J. (2011). A longitudinal analysis of Latina/o students' academic persistence. *Journal of Hispanic Higher Education*, *10*(4), 358–68. doi: 10.1177/1538192711423318

Burg, J., Pauca, V.P., Turkett, W., Fulp, E., Cho, S.S., Santago, P., Cañas, D., and Gage, H.D. (2015). Engaging non-traditional students in computer science through socially-inspired learning and sustained mentoring. In Proceedings of the 46th ACM Technical Symposium on Computer Science Education, New York: ACM, pp. 639–44.

Buyukgoze-Kavas, A., Taylor, J.M., Neimeyer, G.J., and Güneri, O.Y. (2010). The mentoring relationship: A comparison of counselling students in the United States of America and Turkey. *Counselling Psychology Quarterly*, *23*(4), 387–98.

Campbell, C.M., Smith, M., Dugan, J.P., and Komives, S.R. (2012). Mentors and college student leadership outcomes: The importance of position and process. *The Review of Higher Education*, *35*(4), 595–625.

Campbell, T.A., and Campbell, D.E. (2007). Outcomes of mentoring at-risk college students: Gender and ethnic matching effects. *Mentoring & Tutoring: Partnership in Learning*, 15(2), 135–48.

Chan, A.W., Yeh, C.J., and Krumboltz, J.D. (2015, June 8). Mentoring ethnic minority counseling and clinical psychology students: A multicultural, ecological, and relational model. *Journal of Counseling Psychology*. Advance online publication http://dx.doi.org/10.1037/cou0000079

Chemers, M.M., Zurbriggen, E.L., Syed, M., Goza, B.K., and Bearman, S. (2011). The role of efficacy and identity in science career commitment among underrepresented minority students. *Journal of Social Issues*, 67, 469–91.

Chester, A., Burton, L.J., Xenos, S., and Elgar, K. (2013). Peer mentoring: Supporting successful transition for first year undergraduate psychology students. *Australian Journal of Psychology*, 2013(65), 30–37. doi: 10.1111/ajpy.12006

Collings, R., Swanson, V., and Watkins, R. (2014). The impact of peer mentoring on levels of student wellbeing, integration and retention: a controlled comparative evaluation of residential students in UK. *Higher Education*, 68, 927–42.

Colvin, J.W., and Ashman, M. (2010). Roles, risks, and benefits of peer mentoring relationships in higher education. *Mentoring & Tutoring: Partnership in Learning*, 18, 121–34.

Crisp, G. (2009). Conceptualization and initial validation of the College Student Mentoring Scale (CSMS). *Journal of College Student Development*, 50, 177–94.

Crisp, G. (2010). The impact of mentoring on the success of community college students. *The Review of Higher Education*, 34(1), 39–60. doi: 10.1353/rhe.2010.0003

Crisp, G. (2011). The role of mentoring on the persistence decisions of undergraduate students attending a Hispanic serving institutions. *Enrollment Management Journal: Student Access, Finance and Success in Higher Education*, 5(1), 32–57.

Crisp, G., and Cruz, I. (2009). Mentoring college students: A critical review of the literature between 1990 and 2007. *Research in Higher Education*, 50(6), 525–45.

D'Abate, C.P. (2009). Defining mentoring in the first-year experience: One institution's approach to clarifying the meaning of mentoring first-year students. *Journal of The First-Year Experience and Students in Transition*, 21(1), 65–91.

De Janasz, S.C., & Sullivan, S.E. (2004). Multiple mentoring in academe: Developing the professorial network. *Journal of Vocational Behavior*, 64(2), 263–83.

Dietz, A.J., Jansen, J.D., and Wadee, A.A. (2006). *Effective PhD supervision and mentorship: A workbook based on experiences from South Africa and Netherlands*. South Africa-Netherlands research Programme on Alternatives in Development (SANPAD).

Dolan, E., and Johnson, D. (2009). Toward a holistic view of holistic undergraduate research experiences: An exploratory study of impact on graduate/postdoctoral mentors. *Journal of Science Education Technology*, 2009(18), 487–500.

Drake, J.K. (2011). The role of academic advising in student retention and persistence. *About Campus*, 16(3), 8–12.

Eagan, M.K., Hurtado, S., Chang, M.J., Garcia, G.A., Herrera, F.A., and Garibay, J.C. (2013). Making a difference in science education the impact of undergraduate research programs. *American Educational Research Journal*, 50, 683–713.

Eby, L.T., and Allen, T.D. (2008). Moving toward interdisciplinary dialogue in mentoring scholarship: An introduction to the special issue. *Journal of Vocational Behavior*, 72(2008), 159–67.

Eby, L.T., Allen, T.D., Hoffman, B.J., Baranik, L.E., Sauer, J.B., Baldwin, S., Morrison, M.A., Kinkade, K.M., Maher, C.P., Curtis, S., and Evans, S.C. (2013). An interdisciplinary meta-analysis of the potential antecedents, correlates, and consequences of protégé perceptions of mentoring. *Psychological Bulletin*, 139, 441–76.

Eby, L.T., and Dolan, E.L. (2015). Mentoring in postsecondary education and organizational settings. In *APA Handbook of Career Intervention, Volume 2: Applications*, P.J. Hartung, M.L. Savickas, and W.B. Walsh, eds., Washington, DC, USA: American Psychological Association, pp. 383–95.

Erickson, L.D., McDonald, S., and Elder, G.H. (2009). Informal mentors and education: Complementary or compensatory resources? *Sociology of Education*, *82*(4), 344–67.

Feldman, A., Divoll, K.A., and Rogan-Klyve, A. (2013). Becoming Researchers: The Participation of Undergraduate and Graduate Students in Scientific Research Groups. *Science Education*, *97*, 218–43.

Ferrare, J.J., and Lee, Y.G. (2014). *Should We Still be Talking About Leaving? A Comparative Examination of Social Inequality in Undergraduates' Major Switching Patterns* (WCER Working Paper No. 2014-5). Retrieved from University of Wisconsin–Madison, Wisconsin Center for Education Research website: http://www.wcer.wisc.edu/publications/workingPapers/papers.php (accessed on 9/22/2015)

Fleming, M., House, S., Hanson, V.S., Yu, L., Garbutt, J., McGee, R., Kroenke, K., Abedin, Z., and Rubio, D.M. (2013). The Mentoring Competency Assessment: Validation of a new instrument to evaluate skills of research mentors. *Academic Medicine*, *88*, 1002–8.

Fleming, G.M., Simmons, J.H., Xu, M., Gesell, S.B., Brown, R.F., Cutrer, W.B., … and Cooper, W. O. (2015). A facilitated peer mentoring program for junior faculty to promote professional development and peer networking. *Academic Medicine: Journal of the Association of American Medical Colleges*, *90*(6), 819–26.

Fox, A., Stevenson, L., Connelly, P., Duff, A., and Dunlop, A. (2010). Peer-mentoring undergraduate accounting students: The influence on approaches to learning and academic performance. *Active Learning in Higher Education*, *11*, 145–56.

Fuentes, M.V., Alvarado, A.R., Berdan, J., and DeAngelo, L. (2014). Mentorship Matters: Does Early Faculty Contact Lead to Quality Faculty Interaction? *Research in Higher Education*, *55*, 288–307.

Gazley, J.L., Remich, R., Naffziger-Hirsch, M.E., Keller, J., Campbell, P.B., and McGee, R. (2014). Beyond preparation: Identity, cultural capital, and readiness for graduate school in the biomedical sciences. *Journal of Research in Science Teaching*, *51*, 1021–48.

Gershenfeld, S. (2014). A review of undergraduate mentoring programs. *Review of Educational Research*, *84*, 365–91.

González, C. (2001). Undergraduate research, graduate mentoring, and the university's mission. *Science*, *293*(5535), 1624–26.

Grant, B., and Manathunga, C. (2011). Supervision and cultural difference: rethinking institutional pedagogies. *Innovations in Education and Teaching International*, *48*(4), 351–54.

Hadjioannou, X., Shelton, N.R., Fu, D., and Dhanarattigannon, J. (2007). The road to a doctoral degree: Co-travelers through a perilous passage. *College Student Journal*, *41*(1), 160–77.

Hagemeier, N.E., Murawski, M.M., and Popovich, N.G. (2013). The influence of faculty mentors on junior pharmacy faculty members' career decisions. *American Journal of Pharmaceutical Education*, *77*(3).

Handelsman, J. (2005). *Entering Mentoring : A seminar to train a new generation of scientists* (Madison, Wis.: Board of Regents of the University of Wisconsin System).

Haynes, R.K., and Petrosko, J.M. (2009). An investigation of mentoring and socialization among law faculty. *Mentoring and Tutoring: Partnership in Learning*, *17*(1), 41–52.

Higgins, M.C., and Kram, K.E. (2001). Reconceptualizing mentoring at work: A developmental network perspective. *Academy of Management Review*, *26*(2), 264–88.

Hill, R., and Reddy, P. (2007). Undergraduate peer mentoring: An investigation into processes, activities and outcomes. *Psychology Learning and Teaching*, *6*, 98–103.

Holt, L., and Berwise, C. (2012). Illuminating the process of peer mentoring: An examination and comparison of peer mentors' and first-year students' experiences. *Journal of The First-Year Experience and Students in Transition*, *24*, 19–43.

Horowitz, J., and Christopher, K.B. (2012). The research mentoring program: Serving the needs of graduate and undergraduate researchers. *Innovative Higher Education*, *38*, 105–16.

Hryciw, D.H., Tangalakis, K., Supple, B., and Best, G. (2013). Evaluation of a peer mentoring program for a mature cohort of first-year undergraduate paramedic students. *Advances in Physiology Education, 37*, 80–4.

Hu, S., and Ma, Y. (2010). Mentoring and student persistence in college: A study of the Washington State Achievers Program. *Innovative Higher Education*, *35*(5), 329–41.

Hurtado, S., Cabrera, N.L., Lin, M.H., Arellano, L., and Espinosa, L.L. (2009). Diversifying science: Underrepresented student experiences in structured research programs. *Research in Higher Education*, 50(2), 189–214.

Jackevicius, C.A., Le, J., Nazer, L., Hess, K., Wang, J., and Law, Anandi V. (2014). A formal mentorship program for faculty development. *American Journal of Pharmaceutical Education*, 78(5), Article 100.

Jacobi, M. (1991). Mentoring and undergraduate academic success: A literature review. *Review of Educational Research*, 61, 505–32.

Johnson, W.B., and Kaslow, N. (2014). *The Oxford handbook of education and training in professional psychology*. New York: Oxford University Press.

Khazanov, L. (2011). Mentoring at-risk students in a remedial mathematics course. *Mathematics and Computer Education*, 106–18.

Kiyama, J.M., and Luca, S.G. (2013). Structured opportunities: Exploring the social and academic benefits for peer mentors in retention programs. *Journal of College Student Retention: Research, Theory and Practice*, 15, 489–514.

Larose, S., Cyrenne, D., Garceau, O., Harvey, M., Guay, F., and Deschenes, C. (2009). Personal and social support factors involved in students' decision to participate in formal academic mentoring. *Journal of Vocational Behavior*, 74(2009), 108–16.

Laursen, S., Hunter, A.-B., Seymour, E., Thiry, H., and Melton, G. (2010). *Undergraduate Research in the Sciences: Engaging Students in Real Science*. San Francisco, CA: Wiley & Sons.

Law, A.V., Bottenberg, M.M., Brozick, A.H., Currie, J.D., DiVall, M.V., Haines, S.T., and Yablonski, E. (2014). A checklist for the development of faculty mentorship programs. *American Journal of Pharmaceutical Education*, 78(5), 98.

Lechuga, V.M. (2011). Faculty-graduate student mentoring relationships: Mentors' perceived roles and responsibilities. *Higher Education*, 62(6), 757–71.

Lee, A. (2011) *Successful research supervision: Advising students doing research*. New York, NY: Routledge.

Liang, B., Tracy, A.J., Taylor, C.A., and Williams, L.M. (2002). Mentoring college-age women: A relational approach. *American Journal of Community Psychology*, 30, 271–88.

Linn, M.C., Palmer, E., Baranger, A., Gerard, E., and Stone, E. (2015). Undergraduate research experiences: Impacts and opportunities. *Science*, 347, 1261757.

Lopatto, D., and Tobias, S. (2010). *Science in solution: The impact of undergraduate research on student learning*. Washington, DC: Council on Undergraduate Research.

Lunsford, L.G. (2012). Doctoral advising or mentoring? Effects on student outcomes. *Mentoring and Tutoring: Partnership in Learning*, 20(2), 251–70.

Manathunga, C. (2014). *Intercultural postgraduate supervision: Reimagining time, place and knowledge*. New York, NY: Routledge.

Manathunga, C. (2011). Moments of transculturation and assimilation: Post-colonial exploration of supervision and culture. *Innovations in Education and Teaching International*, 48(4), 367–76.

Manathunga, C. (2005). The development of research supervision: 'Turning the light on a private space'. *International Journal for Academic Development*, 10(1), 17–30.

Manathunga, C., and Goozée, J. (2007). Challenging the dual assumption of the 'always/already' autonomous student and effective supervisor. *Teaching in Higher Education*, 12(3), 309–22.

Martin, A.J., and Dowson, M. (2009). Interpersonal relationships, motivation, engagement, and achievement: Yields for theory, current issues, and educational practice. *Review of Educational Research*, 79, 327–65.

Maton, K.I., and Hrabowski III, F.A. (2004). Increasing the number of African American PhDs in the sciences and engineering: A strengths-based approach. *American Psychologist*, 59, 547–56.

Maton, K.I., Hrabowski, F.A.I., and Schmitt, C.L. (2000). African American college students excelling in the sciences: College and postcollege outcomes in the Meyerhoff Scholars Program. *Journal of Research in Science Teaching*, 37, 629–54.

Mayer, A.P., Files, J.A., Ko, M.G., and Blair, J.E. (2009). The academic quilting bee. *Journal*

of General Internal Medicine, 24(3), 427–9.
McAllister, C.A., Ahmedani, B.K., Harold, R.D., and Cramer, E.P. (2009). Targeted mentoring: Evaluation of a program. *Journal of Social Work Education*, 45(1), 89–104.
Mekolichick, J., and Gibbs, K. (2012). Understanding college generational status in the undergraduate research mentored relationship. *Council on Undergraduate Research Quarterly*, 33(2), 40–6.
Merolla, D.M., and Serpe, R.T. (2013). STEM enrichment programs and graduate school matriculation: the role of science identity salience. *Social Psychology of Education, 16*, 575–97.
Metzger, A.H., Hardy, Y.M., Jarvis, C., Stoner, S.C., Pitlick, M., Hilaire, M.L., and Lodise, N.M. (2013). Essential elements for a pharmacy practice mentoring program. *American Journal of Pharmaceutical Education*, 77(2), 23.
Nora, A., and Crisp, G. (2007). Mentoring students: Conceptualizing and validating the multi-dimensions of a support system. *Journal of College Student Retention: Research, Theory and Practice, 9*, 337–56.
O'Brien, K.E., Biga, A., Kessler, S.R., and Allen, T.D. (2008). A meta-analytic investigation of gender differences in mentoring. *Journal of Management*, 36(2), 537–54.
O'Brien, M., Llamas, M., and Stevens, E. (2012). Lessons learned from four years of peer mentoring in a tiered group program within education, *Journal of the Australia and New Zealand Student Services Association, 40*, 7–15.
Ortiz-Walters, R., and Gilson, L.L. (2005). Mentoring in academia: An examination of the experiences of protégés of color. *Journal of Vocational Behavior*, 67(2005), 459–75.
Paglis, L.L., Green, S.G., and Bauer, T.N. (2006). Does adviser mentoring add value? A longitudinal study of mentoring and doctoral student outcomes. *Research in Higher Education*, 47(4), 451–76.
Palmer, R., Hunt, A.N., Neal, M., and Wuetherick, B. (2015). Mentoring, undergraduate research, and identity development: A conceptual review and research agenda, *Mentoring and Tutoring: Partnership in Learning, 23*(5), 411–26.
Pascarella, E.T. (1980). Student-faculty informal contact and college outcomes. *Review of Educational Research, 50*, 545–95.
Pellegrino, K., Sweet, B., Kastner, J.D., Russell, H.A., and Reese, J. (2014). Becoming music teacher educators: Learning from and with each other in a professional development community. *International Journal of Music Education*, 32(4), 462–77.
Pembridge, J.J. (2011). *Mentoring in engineering capstone design courses: Beliefs and practices across disciplines* (Doctoral dissertation, Virginia Polytechnic Institute and State University).
Pfund, C., Pribbenow, C.M., Branchaw, J., Lauffer, S.M., and Handelsman, J. (2006). The merits of training mentors. *Science, 311*, 473–4.
Pfund, C., House, S.C., Asquith, P., Fleming, M.F., Buhr, K.A., Burnham, E.L., Gilmore, J.M.E., Huskins, W.C., McGee, R., Schurr, K., Shapiro, E.D., Spencer, K.C., and Sorkness, C.A. (2014). Training mentors of clinical and translational research scholars: A randomized controlled trial. *Academic Medicine, 89*, 774–82.
Pidgeon, M., Archibald, J., and Hawkey, C. (2014). Relationships matter: Supporting Aboriginal graduate students in British Columbia, Canada. *Canadian Journal of Higher Education*, 44(1), 1–21.
Ralph, E. (1998). *Developing practitioners: A handbook of contextual supervision*. Stillwater, Oklahoma: New Forums Press.
Ralph, E., and Walker, K. (2010). Rising with the tide: Applying Adaptive Mentorship© in the professional practicum. In A. Wright, M. Wilson, and D. MacIsaac (Eds.), *Collection of essays on learning and teaching: Between the tides*, Volume III (pp. 3–8). Hamilton, ON: McMaster University, Society for Teaching and Learning in Higher Education. Available from http://apps.medialab.uwindsor.ca/ ctl/ CELT/vol3/CELTVOL3.pdf [accessed 15 September 2015]
Ralph, E., and Walker, K. (2013). The promise of adaptive mentorship: What is the evidence?, *International Journal of Higher Education, 2*(2), p. 76–85.
Raymond, B.C., and Kannan, V.R. (2014). A survey of faculty mentoring programs in AACSB Schools of Business. *Journal of Management Education*, 38(6), 818–42.

Reddick, R.J., and Pritchett, K.O. (2015). 'I don't want to work in a world of Whiteness:' White faculty and their mentoring relationships with Black students. *The Journal of the Professoriate*, 54–84.

Rose, G.L. (2005). Group differences in graduate students' concepts of the ideal mentor. *Research in Higher Education*, 46(1), 53–80.

Rudolph, B.A., Castillo, C.P., Garcia, V.G., Martinez, A., and Navarro, F. (2015). Hispanic graduate students' mentoring themes: Gender roles in a bicultural context. *Journal of Hispanic Higher Education*, 14(3), 191–206.

Russell, S.H., Hancock, M.P., and McCullough, J. (2007). The benefits of undergraduate research experiences. *Science*, 316, 548–9.

Sawatzky, J.A.V., and Enns, C.L. (2009). A mentoring needs assessment: Validating mentorship in nursing education. *Journal of Professional Nursing*, 25(3), 145–50.

Schlosser, L.Z., and Gelso, C.J. (2001). Measuring the working alliance in advisor–advisee relationships in graduate school. *Journal of Counseling Psychology*, 48, 157–67.

Schlosser, L.Z., and Gelso, C.J. (2005). The Advisory Working Alliance Inventory – advisor version: Scale development and validation. *Journal of Counseling Psychology*, 52, 650–4.

Schultz, P.W., Hernandez, P.R., Woodcock, A., Estrada, M., Chance, R.C., Aguilar, M., and Serpe, R.T. (2011). Patching the pipeline reducing educational disparities in the sciences through minority training programs. *Educational Evaluation and Policy Analysis*, 33, 95–114.

Seymour, E., and Hewitt, N.M. (1997). *Talking about leaving: Why undergraduates leave the sciences*. Boulder, CO: Westview.

Shotton, H.J., Oosahwe, S.L., and Cintron, R. (2007). Stories of success: Experiences of American Indian students in a peer-mentoring retention program. *The Review of Higher Education*, 31(1), 81–107.

Shrestha, C.H., May, S., Edirisingha, P., Burke, L., and Linsey, T. (2009). From face-to-face to e-Mentoring: Does the 'e' add any value for mentors? *International Journal of Teaching and Learning in Higher Education*, 20(2), 116–24.

Slovacek, S., Whittinghill, J., Flenoury, L., and Wiseman, D. (2012). Promoting minority success in the sciences: The minority opportunities in research programs at CSULA. *Journal of Research in Science Teaching*, 49(2), 199–217.

Sosik, J.J., and Godshalk, V.M. (2005). Examining gender similarity and mentor's supervisory status in mentoring relationships. *Mentoring and Tutoring: Partnership in Learning*, 13, 39–52.

Stanton-Salazar, R.D. (2011). A social capital framework for the study of institutional agents and their role in the empowerment of low-status students and youth. *Youth Society*, 43, 1066–109.

Stolle-McAllister, K., Domingo, M.R.S., and Carrillo, A. (2011). The Meyerhoff Way: How the Meyerhoff Scholarship Program helps Black students succeed in the sciences, *Journal of Science Education and Technology*, 20, 5–16.

Taraban, R., and Logue, E. (2012). Academic factors that affect undergraduate research experiences. *Journal of Educational Psychology*, 104, 499–514.

Terrion, J.L. (2012). Student peer mentors as a navigational resource in higher education. In Fletcher, S., and Mullen, C.A., (Eds.), *The SAGE Handbook of Mentoring and Coaching in Education*, (pp. 383–96), Thousand Oaks, CA: Sage.

Terrion, J.L., and Leonard, D. (2007). A taxonomy of the characteristics of student peer mentors in higher education: findings from a literature review. *Mentoring and Tutoring: Partnership in Learning*, 15, 149–64.

Thiry, H., and Laursen, S.L. (2011). The role of student-advisor interactions in apprenticing undergraduate researchers into a scientific community of practice. *Journal of Science Education and Technology*, 20, 771–84.

Thiry, H., Laursen, S.L., and Hunter, A-B. (2011). What experiences help students become scientists?: A comparative study of research and other sources of personal and professional gains for STEM undergraduates? *The Journal of Higher Education*, 82(4), 357–88.

Thomas, D., Lunsford, L.G., and Rodrigues, H. (2015). Early career academic staff support: evaluating mentoring networks. *Journal of Higher Education Policy and Management*, 37(3), 320–9.

Tinto, V. (1975). Dropout from higher education: A theoretical synthesis of recent research. *Review of Educational Research, 45*, 89–125.

Tinto, V. (1993). Building Community. *Liberal Education, 79*, 16–21.

Villarejo, M., and Barlow, A.E. (2007). Evolution and evaluation of a biology enrichment program for minorities. *Journal of Women and Minorities in Science and Engineering, 13*(2), 119–44.

Watson II, J.C., Clement, D., Blom, L., and Grindley, E. (2009). Mentoring: Processes and perceptions of sport and exercise psychology graduate students. *Journal of Applied Sport Psychology, 21*, 231–46.

Welton, A.D., Mansfield, K.C., and Lee, P-L. (2014). Mentoring matters: An exploratory survey of educational leadership doctoral students' perspectives. *Mentoring and Tutoring: Partnership in Learning, 22*(5), 481–509.

Williams-Nickelson, C. (2009). Mentoring women graduate students: A model for professional psychology. *Professional Psychology: Research and Practice, 40*(3), 284–91.

Wilson, Z.S., Holmes, L., deGravelles, K., Sylvain, M.R., Batiste, L., Johnson, M., McGuire, S.Y., Pang, S.S., and Warner, I.M. (2012). Hierarchical mentoring: A transformative strategy for improving diversity and retention in undergraduate STEM disciplines. *Journal of Science Education and Technology, 21*, 148–56.

Wisker, G. (2005[2012]). The good supervisor. New York, NY: Palgrave Macmillan.

Yeung, M., Nuth, J., and Stiell, I. G. (2010). Mentoring in emergency medicine: the art and the evidence. *Canadian Journal of Emergency Medicine, 12*(2), 143–9.

Yob, I., and Crawford, L. (2012). Conceptual framework for mentoring doctoral students. *Higher Learning Research Communications, 2*(2), 34.

The Terrors of Judgementoring and the Case for ONSIDE Mentoring for Early Career Teachers

Andrew J. Hobson

INTRODUCTION

In this chapter I examine institution-based mentoring of early career school and college teachers. Research has shown that such mentoring can have a range of powerful, positive impacts on mentees, mentors, schools, colleges and education systems; yet, unless appropriate conditions for mentorship are created, mentoring can be ineffectual and even harmful. After defining the key concepts and outlining the research underpinning the chapter, I outline common ingredients of successful and effective mentoring for early career teachers in primary and secondary (K-12) schools and what in England we call 'further education' (FE).[1] Then, I argue that various failures at institutional and policy levels have contributed to inappropriate enactments of mentoring which have stunted professional learning and development (PLD) and had a deleterious effect on the well-being of many early career teachers. In doing so, I present new evidence from the UK and other international contexts on the nature, reach, causes and consequences of 'judgementoring' (Hobson and Malderez, 2013), a particular enactment of mentoring found to be detrimental to early career teachers' professional learning, development and well-being. Lastly, I offer a new research-informed mentoring framework, called *ONSIDE Mentoring*, that I consider would serve the needs of early career teachers – and the schools and colleges in which they are situated – far more effectively than existing approaches to mentoring deployed in the UK and elsewhere.

Developing earlier definitions by Malderez (2001), Hobson et al. (2009a) and Hobson and Malderez (2013), I define mentoring in this context as:

> a one-to-one relationship between a relatively inexperienced teacher (the mentee) and a relatively experienced teacher (the mentor), which aims to support the mentee's learning, development and well-being, and their integration into the cultures

of both the organisation in which they are employed and the wider profession.

This definition extends earlier ones by explicitly including support for mentees' well-being as an integral part of the mentor role. Support for the well-being of early career teachers is vital because:

1 the early years of teaching can be characterised by intense pressure and disillusionment (Bullough, 2005; Gold, 1996);
2 early career teachers often report feeling '*voiceless*', '*powerless*' and '*at the bottom of the pecking order*' in their schools and colleges (Hobson, 2009), and may generally be regarded as vulnerable learners, as Shanks (2014) argues:

> The vulnerability of new teachers can be understood as multiple layers of new experiences to deal with – a new profession, perhaps a new location, probably a brand new workplace with new colleagues, new students, continuing assessment and uncertainty as to whether they will obtain a new post for the subsequent school year. New teachers are in a vulnerable situation as a newcomer to their profession while they continue to learn about teaching and how to be a teacher. (Shanks, 2014, p.14; cf. Kelchtermans and Ballet, 2002; Johnson and Birkeland, 2003)

3 the provision of effective support for early career teachers can offset stress and fatigue, and support their retention in the profession (Kwakman, 2003; Johnson, 2004); and
4 higher levels of well-being are associated with increased teacher effectiveness (Day, 2008; Day and Kington, 2008).

Like most published literature on the subject, this chapter deals with the practice of mentoring as a one-to-one and formal arrangement, in which individuals are specifically designated to undertake the mentoring role, sometimes within the context of a wider scheme or programme. This is not to suggest that group mentoring and informal mentoring cannot and do not (also) have a positive impact on the professional learning, development and well-being of early career teachers. In this chapter, I use the terms early career teacher (ECT) and beginner teacher interchangeably to refer to those undertaking initial teacher preparation (ITP)[2] programmes or in their first three years as members of the profession.

THE UNDERPINNING RESEARCH

The chapter and its constituent arguments are informed by five empirical studies, two reviews of international research evidence on teacher mentoring, and several personal communications with some of my academic peers relating to the phenomenon of judgementoring. The empirical studies are

- Project 1: The mixed method *Becoming a Teacher* Project, which explored the nature and impact of teachers' experiences of initial teacher preparation, induction and early professional development in England (Hobson et al., 2009b);
- Project 2: The mixed method *Modes of Mentoring and Coaching* Project, which investigated the nature and impact of 'external' mentoring and coaching[3] associated with three national support programmes for teachers of science in England (Hobson et al., 2012);
- Project 3: A mixed method study of *Mentoring for Teachers and Lecturers in the Further Education and Skills Sector in England*, which examined the nature and impact of institution-based mentoring and the potential for external mentoring (Hobson et al., 2015);
- Project 4: A previously unpublished evaluation of an *External Mentoring Pilot* Project for trainee and qualified teachers of secondary English, developed and implemented at a university in the north of England, in partnership with local schools (2012–13);
- Project 5: *The Mentoring across Professions* study, which sought to explore what teacher mentoring can learn from the successful enactment of mentoring and coaching for employees in a range of sectors internationally (Hobson et al., 2016).

A summary overview of the methods of data generation and sample sizes associated with the five empirical studies is provided

Table 21.1 The five empirical research projects examined

Research project		Methods of data generation and achieved samples
Project 1	The Becoming a Teacher Project (2003–9)	Annual interviews with ECTs in primary and secondary schools across England at the end of their ITP (n=79), first (n=73), second (n=64) and third (n=56) years in post
		Regular email exchanges with ECTs in the above interview sample (46 ECTs during their first year in post, 45 during their second year and 36 during their third year)
		Annual surveys with ECTs in primary and secondary schools across England at the end of their ITP (n=3162), first year (n=2446), second year (n=1973) and third year (n=1638) in post
		Interviews with 15 school-based ITP mentors and 27 school-based induction mentors in primary and secondary schools across England
Project 2	The Modes of Mentoring and Coaching Project (2010–12)	Interviews with 28 (secondary science) ECTs across England who had experienced both institution-based and external mentoring
		Interviews with 13 external mentors
Project 3	Mentoring and Coaching for Teachers in the FE sector in England (2014–15)	Interviews with 40 participants (including 8 ECT mentees, 8 mentors and other stakeholders with a knowledge of mentoring and coaching) across 19 FE providers
		Online survey completed by 392 FE teachers and lecturers across England, 94 of whom were ECTs
Project 4	The External Mentoring Pilot Project (2012–13)	Open-ended survey with 8 ECTs located in 3 different schools in the North of England
		Two focus groups involving a total of 6 ECTs
Project 5	The Mentoring across Professions Study (2015–16)	32 interviews and documentary analysis relating to 10 exemplary mentoring and coaching programmes across six countries

Notes: This table does not list all data relating to each project; only data relevant to the current study.
All interviews conducted for Projects 1, 2, 3 and 5 may be described as 'part-structured' (Hobson and Townsend, 2010).

in Table 21.1. All five studies received institutional ethics approval. Data were generated and stored, and findings have been presented in accordance with the ethical guidelines of the British Education Research Association (BERA, 2004; BERA, 2011).

The discerning reader will have noticed that the primary focus of two of the five studies (Projects 2 and 4) was on the support provided to teachers by 'external mentors' (i.e. mentors not employed within the same institutions as the teachers they were supporting), while the main focus of this chapter is on school- and college-based mentoring. In fact, ECT participants in Projects 2 and 4 were in the relatively unique position of having recently experienced both institutional and external mentoring support. In comparing these experiences, they provided some of the most illuminating and powerful data generated to date on school- and college-based mentoring.

The initial review of literature informing this work comprised an analysis of the international evidence base on beginner teacher mentoring (Hobson et al., 2009a). This has been supplemented by a more selective review of literature published since that time, focusing on publications that discuss evaluative and judgemental approaches to mentoring, and judgementoring specifically.[4] Finally, I included in my dataset personal communications on the subject of judgementoring I had received from six researchers outside the UK. These communications took place via the media of e-mail and ResearchGate.[5]

ANALYTICAL FRAMEWORK

A thematic analysis (Braun and Clarke, 2006) was undertaken of: (a) previously published research findings from Projects 1–3;[6] (b) the published initial review of literature (Hobson et al., 2009a); (c) new data generated for Projects 4–5; (d) all publications retrieved for the subsequent literature review; and (e) personal communications with five international peers. The analyses were informed by the following research questions, which also provide an organising framework for the following three sections of this chapter:

1. What are the main ingredients of efficacious institution-based mentoring for ECTs?
2. How prevalent is judgementoring and what are the main causes and consequences of this phenomenon?
3. What are the key features of mentoring programmes and relationships that might forestall judgementoring and be embedded in a proposed new framework for mentoring ECTs?

Ingredients for efficacious teacher mentoring

International research evidence tells us that the potential gains of mentoring ECTs are substantial. For example, mentoring has been found to: help ECTs improve their skills of classroom and behaviour management, self-reflection and problem-solving; increase their confidence and self-esteem; and reduce feelings of isolation (Lindgren, 2005; McIntyre and Hagger, 1996). Research also shows that the provision of mentors for newly qualified teachers in particular, sometimes as part of a broader programme of induction support, can reduce their experiences of reality shock (Veenman, 1984), which is often associated with the transition from student to qualified teacher, and with coming to terms with the harsh realities of, for instance, a full or relatively full timetable and pupil indiscipline (Hagger et al., 2011).

Largely in consequence of these various benefits of mentoring, ECTs who are mentored are less likely to leave the profession than those who are not (Ingersoll and Kralik, 2004).[7] Conversely, some enactments of mentoring do not bring about these positive outcomes, and can even stunt beginner teachers' PLD (Feiman-Nemser et al., 1993; Ling, 2009), bring about anxiety and stress, and contribute to mentees' decisions to leave the profession (Beck and Kosnick, 2000; Maguire, 2001). Other problems can occur when newly qualified teachers who have benefited from mentoring support suffer an additional or delayed form of reality or transition shock, and feel unsupported, unprotected, exposed and vulnerable, as a result of formal mentoring (or wider induction support incorporating mentoring) coming to a sudden end, as is often the case at the end of their first year in post. Such a phenomenon has been termed 'reality aftershock' (Hobson and Ashby, 2012).

What, then, are the conditions in which mentorship is most likely to realise its potential benefits and least likely to have a damaging effect on ECTs? Research identifies several common ingredients for efficacious ECT mentoring, ranging from individual- and relationship-level factors, through organisational, to wider contextual and policy-level considerations. I summarise these below.

1. Mentees' openness to mentors and mentoring

Research shows that successful mentoring depends, to an extent, on characteristics and traits of individual mentees, including those of openness, willingness to change, and preparedness to operate outside of their comfort zones (Roehrig et al., 2008; cf. Searby, 2014; Valencic Zuljan and Vogrinc, 2007). Mentees need not necessarily possess all these characteristics at the start of a mentoring relationship, but they will need to develop them if they are to maximise the potential benefits of mentorship. The degree to which they are able to do so will be influenced by the skills of their individual mentors and the nature and extent of wider institutional and contextual support for mentoring, including various considerations addressed below.

2 Relational trust

One of the key ingredients for an effective mentoring relationship is the existence or development of trust between mentee and mentor (D'Souza, 2014; Ng, 2012), partly because this facilitates open and honest discussion. Whether or not trust can be established is itself dependent on a range of considerations, including the skills and dispositions of mentors, and whether the mentoring relationship is based on confidentiality (and mentees and mentors believe this to be the case). The latter may be facilitated by the existence of an appropriate mentoring contract and the way in which the mentoring programme is framed (Hobson et al., 2016), as well as further contextual considerations discussed below.

3 Mentors' use of appropriate mentoring strategies

Researchers have identified common strategies that are employed by mentors in successful mentoring programmes. Amongst these, effective mentors typically: provide ECTs with emotional and psychological support to help them feel welcome, accepted and included, and seek to build their confidence (Hascher et al., 2004; Rippon and Martin, 2006); encourage and support ECTs' critical interrogation of their own and others' practice (Harrison, Dymoke and Pell, 2006; Smith and Ingersoll, 2004); and provide them with an appropriate degree of both challenge (Daloz, 1986; Tang, 2003) and autonomy (Rajuan et al., 2007; Valencic Zuljan and Vogrinc, 2007). In addition, several studies (e.g. Bullough, 2005; Heilbronn et al., 2002; Young et al., 2005) report that ECTs often value mentor 'feedback' on their teaching, including being offered practical strategies for addressing any perceived limitations. The strategy of mentors observing and critically evaluating ECTs' teaching is not unproblematic, however, as will become clear in the ensuing discussion.

While mentoring strategies such as those outlined above have been shown to be effective across different international contexts, it is clear that, like teaching, mentoring is most successful where it is personalised and adapted to the specific support needs and current stages of development of individual mentees (Lindgren, 2005; Valencic Zuljan and Vogrinc, 2007). The extent to which mentors deploy appropriate, as opposed to inappropriate, mentoring strategies will be influenced by a range of other factors, including some if not all of those outlined below.

4 Mentor selection

Studies have shown that effective teachers do not always make effective mentors, and that mentoring tends to be more successful when mentors are carefully selected against relevant criteria (Yusko and Feiman-Nemser, 2008). Effective mentors exemplify models of good professional practice (Foster, 1999), possess excellent subject knowledge, and are trustworthy, approachable, supportive, empathetic, positive, non-judgemental and good listeners (Abell et al., 1995). They are also committed to mentoring, and to their own and their mentees' continuing PLD, and willing to 'make their work public' (Lindgren, 2005; Simpson et al., 2007).

5 Mentee-mentor matching

Mentoring tends to be more successful where care is taken to ensure an appropriate match of mentor and mentee (Wang, 2001). Pairing may thus be informed, for example, by a needs analysis of the mentee and consideration of the relevant expertise and experience of potential mentors, while some research has found that mentees who are able to select their mentor from a group of staff identified by their institution find the mentoring more beneficial than those whose mentors are chosen for them (Hobson et al., 2015). Research has also found that mentoring tends to be more successful where mentees are paired with mentors who teach (or taught) the same age-phase and/or subject or vocational specialism as themselves (Hobson et al., 2007; Smith and Ingersoll, 2004). This also helps to ensure that the mentor has credibility with the mentee, which is another factor in the establishment of a positive mentoring relationship (Kutsyuruba, 2012; Lejonberg et al., 2015).

Mechanisms should also exist which enable both mentees and mentors to opt out of the relationship and initiate the establishment of an alternative pairing – without risk of blame being apportioned to either party – should either feel that the relationship is not (or is no longer) productive (Association for Supervision and Curriculum Development, 1999).

6 Mentor (and mentee) preparation and development

Other things being equal, mentoring is more effective when mentors are able to take advantage of appropriate opportunities for both initial mentor preparation (Crasborn et al., 2008; Lejonberg et al., 2015), and ongoing development and networking with other mentors (Bullough, 2005; Graham, 1997). Studies suggest that, amongst other things, effective mentor preparation and development opportunities seek to help mentors develop their interpersonal skills (Rippon and Martin, 2006) and their ability to stimulate mentees' reflection on their actions (Crasborn et al., 2008), as well as help them to understand the importance and potential benefits of discussing pedagogical issues with mentees (Lindgren, 2005). While there is limited evidence for this in the literature on ECTs, evidence from other sectors shows that mentoring will also be enhanced by initial preparation or training for mentees, which may include a focus on developing reasonable and realistic expectations of mentors and mentoring, and how to take full advantage of mentoring support (Hobson et al., 2016).

7 Opportunities for regular and sustained contact between mentor and mentee

Studies show that mentoring is more effective where there is regular and sustained contact between mentor and mentee (Harrison et al., 2006; Hobson et al., 2015). This is facilitated in institutions that provide mentors with dedicated time in which to undertake the mentoring role, and where timetabling enables mentors and mentees to meet together during the school or college day (Bullough, 2005; Lee and Feng, 2007).

8 Reward and status

Some research has found that mentors tend to be more committed to mentoring, and thus more likely to be effective, where they receive financial recognition for undertaking the role and/or where being a mentor contributes to their status or prestige as teachers (Evans and Abbott, 1997; Simpson et al., 2007; Lee and Feng, 2007).

9 Mentoring coordinator role

Research has also found that, in organisations and programmes in which there are several mentor relationships, the success of mentoring schemes is enhanced through the provision of a mentoring coordinator role. The benefits accrue, in particular, through the role-holder's involvement in mentor selection, training and pairing, in acting as a central point of contact for mentees, and in monitoring interaction between mentors and mentees and intervening where appropriate (e.g. to ensure that mentees' entitlements are being met) (Malderez and Bodoczky, 1999; cf. Kochan et al., 2015).

10 Institutional and contextual support for mentoring

Several of the considerations outlined above relate to the broad issue of institutional support for and resourcing of mentoring, or the existence of an appropriate institutional 'architecture' (Cunningham, 2007). Mentoring tends to be more effective where it takes place in institutions which possess collegial learning environments (Edwards, 1998; Lee and Feng, 2007), and in contexts which are relatively free from excessive emphases on externally prescribed goals and agendas, such as those relating to teaching practices and teacher assessment (Edwards, 1998; Yusko and Feiman-Nemser, 2008). The potential for institutions to provide the kind of architecture outlined here may be enhanced or constrained by local, state or national government funding and directives.

One matter on which researchers have not reached a consensus relates to the issue of whether mentors should or should not be involved in formally assessing, evaluating or appraising the work of their mentees. Several studies (e.g. Bradbury and Koballa, 2008; Heilbronn et al., 2002; Ng, 2012) have indicated that mentoring has greater potential for success where this is not the case, but other researchers (e.g., Adey, 1997; Foster, 1999; Yusko and Feiman-Nemser, 2008) have argued that good mentors can effectively balance support, development and formal evaluation roles. I return to this moot point later in the chapter.

ENGLISH LESSONS TO AVOID – THE NATURE, REACH, CONSEQUENCES AND CAUSES OF JUDGEMENTORING

In a recent study which drew on a reanalysis of two major national datasets (Projects 1 and 2), Angi Malderez and I showed that, despite sporadic evidence of excellent practice, mentoring in teacher education in primary and secondary schools in England was failing to realise its potential. This failure could be explained by a systematic failure at the micro (mentoring relationship), meso (institutional) and macro (policy) levels to provide appropriate conditions for effective mentoring practice. We found, for example, that in many cases: mentors were not able to devote sufficient time to supporting mentees; schools did not employ rigorous methods of mentor selection; and mentors were not provided with appropriate mentor preparation and development opportunities. We also argued that schools and policymakers did not provide sufficient funding earmarked for school-based mentoring, or accord sufficient status to the mentoring role.

Moreover, Malderez and I highlighted a particular pathology of mentoring practice which we termed 'judgementoring' and defined as:

> a one to one relationship between a relatively inexperienced teacher (the mentee) and a relatively experienced one (the mentor) in which the latter, in revealing too readily and/or too often her/his own judgements on or evaluations of the mentee's planning and teaching (e.g. through 'comments', 'feedback', advice, praise or criticism), compromises the mentoring relationship and its potential benefits. (Hobson and Malderez, 2013, p. 90)

In short, we identified judgementoring as an inappropriate enactment of mentoring on the grounds that mentors – or judgementors – were explicitly evaluative and judgemental, and practiced an unnecessarily directive form of mentoring. In what follows, I provide new and consolidated evidence which extends our understanding of the nature, reach, causes and consequences of judgementoring in its enactment with ECTs.

Evidence of judgementoring: English disease or global judgementoring creep?

Qualitative data relating to Projects 1 and 2 show that in primary and secondary schools in England, judgementoring is perhaps most clearly exemplified in mentors' reliance upon and excessive use of the strategy of observing and 'providing feedback' on mentees' lessons. This is illustrated in the excerpt from a mentor interview below:

> [W]hen I talk to a trainee after [observing them teach] the thing I focus upon, first of all... is the good sound educational points... I make them feel that there are some good things coming out here. If there are points, which inevitably there will be, which need to be addressed, they must be addressed constructively... and [I] present the trainee with a set of strategies for dealing with [them]. (Mentor, Project 1)

The quotation above clearly shows that while this mentor had an apparent concern for the beginner teacher's well-being and professional development, they nonetheless focused on providing their own evaluation of the mentee's lesson and their own 'strategies for points that need to be addressed', based on their own judgements, experience and pedagogical insights, rather than facilitating and scaffolding *the mentee's own* critical reflection on their teaching attempt. Such judgemental, evaluative and directive mentoring practices were pervasive. Furthermore, there is evidence that not all mentors appeared to share the concern for their mentees' well-being expressed by the mentor quoted above. Indeed, some ECTs recounted experiences of mentors who they suggested dealt almost exclusively in *negative* judgements:

> [My mentor] would go 'this went very well but', and then he seemed to focus dreadfully on the things that hadn't gone so well. (Mentee, Project 1)

> [W]hatever you ask your mentor they would judge you on and [think] 'why doesn't she know that?' (Mentee, Project 2)

While in our 2013 paper Malderez and I noted that our data precluded us from estimating the prevalence of judgementoring within and beyond schools in England, others have since testified to its existence in English schools, and researchers suggest that the phenomenon is not uncommon to a range of other contexts. Firstly, for example, Lofthouse and Thomas (2014) presented clear evidence of judgementoring in their study of mentoring in initial teacher preparation in England, concluding that: *'The trend towards the practice of judgementoring [...] is illustrated through this case study, with students feeling judged against standards from very early in their school placements'* (p. 215).

Secondly, Duckworth and Maxwell (2015) concluded that their review of literature on mentoring in teacher training programmes in the FE sector in England *'demonstrates the prevalence of a "judgementoring" approach'* (p. 17). This conclusion is supported by the recent study of mentoring in the FE sector by myself and colleagues, which suggested that the following viewpoint expressed by an early career lecturer who had worked with a number of mentors was not uncommon: [The mentor's role is] *first of all to identify weaknesses of the [...] teacher, and then develop a plan of action addressing the weak points* (Mentee, Project 3).

In a case study of an FE college in-service teacher training programme on the south coast of England, Manning and Hobson (forthcoming) provide further triangulated evidence, drawn from observations of mentoring conversations and interviews with mentors and mentees, of judgemental and directive approaches to mentoring and of the less frequent use by some mentors of more developmental and non-directive (Clutterbuck, 1992; 2004) approaches. The study elaborates on the enactment of judgemental mentoring by detailing how mentors tended to set the agenda for meetings, lead discussion around their own evaluations of mentees' lessons, and provide strong advice in a relatively directive fashion.

Other researchers suggest that judgementoring exists to some degree in a range of other countries. Firstly, in the USA, D'Souza (2014) shows that ECTs reflected on how the development of trusting relationships with members of a research team compared favourably with school-based mentoring that one ECT described as *'contrived mentor relationships'* in which *'you meet, they watch you teach and give you feedback. They are looking for some kind of deficit*' (p. 179), while Lunsford (2016) noted that '*we found exactly this* [judgementoring] *in border schools in Arizona*'. Secondly, in Norway, Lejonberg et al. (2015) found that some mentors expressed '*beliefs consistent with judgementoring (evaluative or judgemental mentoring)*' (p. 142), notably about the importance of mentees hearing their (mentors') evaluations of mentees' teaching. Thirdly, in a national study of mentoring in early childhood education services and schools in New Zealand, Cameron et al. (2014, p. 65–6) '*saw examples of feedback that reflected what Hobson and Malderez (2013, p. 90) describe as "judgementoring"*'. Fourthly, Kourieos (2015) noted that the account of judgementoring provided in the original article (Hobson and Malderez, 2013) was '*so familiar to my own context*', namely pre-service language teacher education in Cyprus.

It is not entirely clear from the available evidence whether judgementoring has become more widespread in recent years and, if so, whether it continues to become so. Nonetheless, on the evidence presented above (and some additional evidence presented in the following two sub-sections of this chapter), we must entertain the possibility that we may be witnessing a period of *global judgementoring creep* which, as I elaborate below, may be connected to the spread of the 'terrors of performativity' (Ball, 2003) and the 'global educational reform movement' (GERM) (Sahlberg, 2010).[8] I now turn to a discussion of the consequences and causes of judgementoring in the current UK and global socio-historical context.

Consequences of judgementoring

It is clear from my own and others' research that the practice of judgementoring impedes the development of safe and trusting relationships between mentors and mentees, and that this is detrimental to mentees' PLD insofar as it results in ECTs:

1 being reluctant to seek the support of a mentor – because, for example *In the current climate, the wrong sort of head might use this as evidence that I wasn't performing* adequately. (ECT, Project 2).
2 refraining from being open and honest with mentors about their perceived PLD needs, which has been termed '*fabrication as strategic silence*' (Hobson and McIntyre, 2013).

> [Y]ou never want to mention any potential failings that you might have to your [school-based] mentor […] because you don't know what's going to go down in writing. (ECT, Project 2)
>
> Irrelevant of how wonderful and positive school based support and guidance is, there are always agendas and judgements attached – which restrict my willingness to share hopes, fears, concerns, ambitions. (ECT, Project 4)

3 avoiding forms of behaviour and interaction which they fear may draw attention to perceived weaknesses in their teaching capability or gaps in their knowledge, which has been termed '*fabrication as strategic avoidance*' (Hobson and McIntyre, 2013).

Fabrication as strategic avoidance may involve ECTs discouraging mentors and/or others from observing them teach classes they find difficult to manage, ignoring or failing to report problematic pupil behaviour, or as one beginner teacher put it, deliberately '*putting subject knowledge to the back*' (ECT, Project 2). 'Putting subject knowledge to the back' meant focusing, in their planning and teaching, on aspects of the curriculum about which ECTs felt confident, to avoid being asked awkward questions on aspects of the curriculum about which they did not feel confident: '*In terms of planning, the kids will ask you a question, something about physics and you're hoping no one will ask you*' (ECT, Project 2).

Judgementoring can impede beginner teachers' PLD in other ways, too. The relatively directive nature of judgementoring and the associated lack of autonomy that it affords to mentees can result in ECTs becoming over reliant on their mentors and developing a form of 'learned helplessness' (Maier and Seligman, 1976). In turn, this impedes the development of the important skills of critical reflection in and on practice (Schön, 1983), and of what Claxton (2004) terms 'learnacy' – defined in this context as ECTs' ability to manage their ongoing learning from their own and others' experiences of teaching (Malderez, 2015). Hence, Cameron et al. (2014) note that examples of judgementoring found in their New Zealand study led to mentees '*relying on mentor judgements*' at the expense of '*think*[ing] *critically about their own practice*' (p. 66).

Judgementoring also impedes ECTs' wellbeing. In our original study, Malderez and I noted that some beginner teachers who encountered judgementors described themselves as '*disheartened*', '*demoralised*', '*isolated*' or '*lonely*'. Similarly, Lofthouse and Thomas (2014) quote one student teacher who talked about '*getting disheartened about things you've done*' as a result of mentors '*judging you*' (p. 211), while an ECT participant in Project 4 stated that lesson '*observations* […] *have the power* […] *to make me feel like utter trash*'. It seems likely too that some ECTs' experience of reality aftershock (Hobson and Ashby, 2012) was caused or exacerbated by their prior experience of overly directive (judge)mentoring:

> [Y]ou go from always being looked at … to being by yourself and being very accountable very quickly. And that scared me at the time … that actually this is a class that if I screw up I have got to fix it… (Mentee, Project 1)

Related to the considerations discussed above, ECTs' experiences of judgementoring can also contribute to their decisions to discontinue initial teacher preparation, or leave the profession. An analysis of data from the Becoming a Teacher project (Project 1), for example, revealed that a common factor identified by student teachers who withdrew from initial teacher preparation programmes was poor relationships with mentors, and the receipt of mentor feedback that they regarded as unduly negative and critical (Chambers et al., 2010; Hobson et al., 2009c).

Causes of judgementoring

My analyses suggest that there are four broad and somewhat interconnected causes of judgementoring. First, the evidence presented above – and the wider evidence and datasets analysed for this study – suggest that a (and probably *the*) major cause is the fact that many and perhaps most schools and colleges who provide ECTs with mentors, assign those mentors to conflicting roles of formally evaluating and assessing the beginner teachers on the one hand, and supporting their PLD on the other. In some cases, the situation is compounded where ECTs' mentors are also their line managers or supervisors, a role which necessarily requires formal evaluation of their work. It is noteworthy that in the ten case studies of exemplary work-based mentoring and coaching schemes undertaken for Project 5, which found no evidence of judgementoring, mentoring and coaching were exclusively 'off-line' (i.e. separated from mentees' line-management/supervision) and mentors and coaches had no involvement in the formal evaluation of their mentees' performance. The *Mentoring Scheme Induction Brochure* of one of the case studies – the English Football Association Referee Mentoring Scheme – explicitly addresses the rationale for the mentoring being off-line in stating that this '*enables a more fully open relationship between mentor and referee and prevents the mentor from having a conflict of roles*' (cited in Hobson et al., 2016, p. 22).

Some of the ways in which 'on-line' mentoring can compromise the mentoring relationship are explained by a senior police officer interviewed for another Project 5 case study:

> There's no way I'd want to be mentored or coached by my line manager […] because you're so vulnerable […] for example, I might know

deep down that I've got a weakness that I'm hoping that I can sort out, but if I tell my line manager about that it's going to be in my next appraisal because they're suddenly aware of it [...] and if something's happened with a colleague or someone's really annoyed you and you're telling your line manager, you're putting them in a position where they've almost got to act. (Coachee, Project 5)

A second (and related) contributory factor to the enactment of judgementoring is particularly apparent in the findings of Project 3, which show that, apart from allocating mentors to trainee and newly qualified teachers, which is standard practice, many FE institutions selectively employ mentoring or coaching as a remedial strategy to address the perceived under-performance of a minority of staff. Interviewees from several institutions explained that teachers and lecturers are allocated a mentor or coach where their teaching is judged through lesson observations to be Grade 3 ('requires improvement') or 4 ('inadequate') in Ofsted terms.[9] In such a scenario, both early career and more experienced teachers will naturally associate mentoring with evaluations of and judgements on their teaching. Furthermore, such a scenario encourages a stigma to be attached to being mentored, which is likely to exacerbate the tendency towards fabrication as strategic silence and strategic avoidance, as the following excerpt from an interview with one FE college's head of professional development suggests:

I remember this woman recounting a story of going into the staffroom as a coach to work with someone and people there going 'Oh, have they come to pick on me?' [...] So it's actually [perceived to be] a bad thing. You know, it means you're doing something wrong if you're working with a mentor or working with a coach. (Project 3)

The third broad cause of judgementoring relates to the wider policy and cultural context within which mentoring in schools and colleges is situated. On the one hand, in some education systems, the practice at institutional level of involving mentors in the formal assessment and evaluation of their mentees' teaching actually reflects policy imperatives. With respect to initial teacher preparation for primary and secondary school teachers in England, Lofthouse and Thomas (2014) note that: '*The award of* [Qualified Teacher Status] *is judged by the subject mentor, professional tutor and university tutor as a collective. Thus, mentoring as a practice plays a pivotal role in the workplace learning experience **and assessment** of student teachers*' (Lofthouse and Thomas, 2014, pp. 201–2, emphasis added).

This association of formal assessment and evaluation with mentoring is also established in relation to newly qualified teachers (NQTs), as in the following wording from England's Department for Education's (2015) statutory guidance for schools:

The head teacher/principal must identify a person to act as the NQT's induction tutor, to provide day to day monitoring and support, **and co-ordination of assessment**. The induction tutor [...] should be able to provide effective coaching and mentoring [...] [and] review the NQT's progress at frequent intervals throughout the induction period [...] **NQTs should have formal assessments carried out by either the head teacher/principal or the induction tutor**. (Department for Education, 2015, pp. 16–17; emphasis added)

With regard to the English FE sector, Duckworth and Maxwell (2015) conclude that:

policy reforms [...] have imposed a model of mentoring that emphasises subject support and the assessment of teaching competence [...] and has led to judgemental rather than developmental approaches to mentoring [...] aligning with Hobson and Malderez's (2013) conceptualisation of 'judgementoring' in the schools sector. (Duckworth and Maxwell, 2015, p. 8)

On the other hand, and less directly, the involvement of mentors and others in routine formal evaluation of the work of ECTs (and teachers in general) in England has been encouraged by the government's role in embracing the '*Global Educational Reform*

Movement' (GERM) (Sahlberg, 2010) and what Ball (2003) refers to as *'the terrors of performativity'*, which are characterised by government control over the curriculum and workforce, and monitoring and 'inspection' of school, college and teacher effectiveness or 'performance'. Hence, vast amounts of time, energy and resources are committed to preparing for high-stakes Ofsted inspections, for example, and, given the very serious consequences of attracting an unfavourable Ofsted grade, school and college leadership teams invariably focus on seeking to bring about an immediate improvement in teachers' performance, as measured against external evaluation criteria, at the expense of a more developmental approach that might better support teachers' ongoing, medium- to longer-term professional learning, development and effectiveness.

While the specific examples cited above are from England, performativity and (by definition) GERM cross national borders and there are indications that an increased emphasis on monitoring and accountability in education is impacting on the mentoring of beginner teachers and others in a range of international contexts. For example, Ng (2012) notes that while mentoring and coaching in Singapore were *'premised on a developmental philosophy'*, tensions have arisen as mentors and coaches have become deployed *'in the critical area of appraisal linked to remuneration and career advancement'* (p. 31). Second, while mentors in Norway and other Scandinavian countries have generally been able to focus on supporting mentees' PLD without formally assessing them (Ulvik and Sunde, 2013), Lejonberg et al. (2015) note that *'mentors sometimes contribute to decisions regarding whether mentees should be hired or not'*, which *'might result in circumstances in which judgementoring is likely to occur'* (p. 145). Third, Lunsford (2016, personal communication) notes that *'the pressures for testing in the US I feel have really made judgementoring part of the pre-service teacher mentoring relationship'*.

Notwithstanding other likely contributory factors, such as the failure of many schools and colleges to employ sufficiently rigorous methods of mentor selection (based on appropriate selection criteria, such as potential to provide non-judgemental support), the fourth major cause of the widespread enactment of judgementoring is the frequent absence (well-established in the mentoring literature) of appropriate provision for mentor education and training. In the absence, in particular, of effective training in the use of non-judgemental and non-directive approaches to mentoring, mentors will inevitably draw on their own experiences of mentoring as mentees and/or on *'common sense'* pedagogical constructs such as *'teaching [or mentoring] is telling'* (Tomlinson, 1995). In a study of factors that support and hinder the development of leadership capacity in mentors working with beginner teachers in New Zealand, Thornton (2014) concluded that: *'Without in-depth professional learning opportunities, mentors are more likely to revert to telling the beginning teacher what to do or being overly critical, a practice described by Hobson and Malderez (2013) as judgementoring, rather than ensuring the learning is self-directed, tailored to the individual teacher'* (ibid., p. 27). Lejonberg et al.'s (2015) quantitative study in Norway found that, where appropriate, opportunities for mentor preparation and development *are* provided, *'mentor education contributes to lower reported levels of beliefs consistent with judgementoring'* (p. 149).

Combatting judgementoring

Earlier in this chapter, I identified a range of common ingredients associated with efficacious mentoring for ECTs. I then examined a particular pathology of mentoring that appears to have arisen, or become more widespread, as a result of some of those key ingredients being missing from the mentoring mix. The evidence suggests that the practice of judgementoring is occurring in a range of contexts internationally, to the detriment of ECTs' PLD, well-being and retention in the profession. If we value and have a sense of responsibility toward ECTs and their professional development and well-being, judgementoring must not be allowed to gain a stronger foothold. I thus highlight, in what follows, some ways in which policymakers, school and college leaders, and others who have a responsibility toward ECTs can avoid judgementoring and its harmful consequences, and instead seek to maximise the significant potential benefits of mentorship.

Firstly, evidence from Projects 2, 4 and 5 shows that judgementoring tends to be avoided and mentoring tends to be more effective where mentors are *external* to the organisation in which the mentee is employed. In particular, it was found that external mentors are more able than institution-based mentors to provide a safe or 'third space' (McIntyre and Hobson, 2016) within which mentees can openly share their hopes, fears and perceived limitations without fear of reprisals or repercussions. The following quotation illustrates the point:

> During our NQT year at [school] we work alongside [external mentor] who is employed by the school but is not a member of staff. He is a neutral party and a fantastic source of support and guidance. It is an important part of his role as a mentor that he is not a member of senior leadership. Because of his unbiased standpoint you really feel at the centre of the process – there are no hidden agendas; it's just about your progress […] By having direct access to a neutral forum I will be able to communicate professionally without consequence. (ECT, Project 4)

Whether it is practicable for schools and colleges to deploy external rather than institution-based mentors, however, is another matter, and this will depend on the specific context. Nonetheless, I suggest that schools and colleges take the external mentor option very seriously, at the very least, where there are no colleagues within the institution who meet the criteria for mentor selection and matching to a specific ECT – for example, where there is nobody who shares the same subject or vocational specialism.[10]

Turning to specific recommendations for policymakers, it should be noted that a common characteristic of the contexts of the ten case studies of exemplary work-based mentoring and coaching programmes examined in Project 5, in which judgementoring was notable by its absence, was that they were relatively free from external regulation and control. This highlights the fact that, in England, national policymakers exert a significant influence over education practice, including the content of school and college curricula and, in this case, teacher development and evaluation, with apparently little recourse to the findings of education research. It seems clear that this scenario has contributed to bringing about or (to the extent that it already existed) fuelling judgementoring. A second set of recommendations then, is to urge policymakers: (1) to reduce the emphasis on the formal monitoring, observation, assessment and evaluation of teachers' 'performance' (which is largely counter-productive if its main aim is to increase teacher effectiveness – Hargreaves and Fullan, 2012; Hobson and McIntyre, 2013); and (2) to reduce their micro-management of education more generally and seek to create a framework within which education policy and practice can become genuinely evidence-informed.

Despite the above critique of education policy, and notwithstanding the preponderance of research on teacher mentoring, it might be argued that one of the reasons why policymakers, school and college leaders and individual mentors have got it so wrong in encouraging and presiding over the terrors of judgementoring, is the lack of a specific research-informed framework for the mentoring of ECTs. I thus conclude this chapter by presenting such a framework, which I call *ONSIDE Mentoring*, which is born out of my analyses of data and previously published findings from the five empirical studies and two reviews of literature outlined earlier.

ONSIDE MENTORING

ONSIDE Mentoring shares key assumptions with, and advances, a number of other frameworks for and approaches to mentoring, coaching and professional learning and development – most notably:

1 developmental approaches to mentoring (Clutterbuck, 1992; 2004) and reflective practitioner approaches to PLD (Schön, 1983), which seek to empower mentees and promote their learnacy (Claxton, 2004);
2 growth and compassion-based approaches to mentoring and coaching (Boyatzis et al., 2013; Jack et al., 2013), which assume that mentees and coachees (in this case, ECTs) '*have the capacity for self-reflection and growth*' (Netolicky, 2016); and
3 scaffolding (Wood et al., 1976) – the sociocultural learning metaphor for the contingent (temporary and adjustable) support for an individual's learning and development provided by someone more experienced or adept at what they are seeking to learn or develop.

In addition, ONSIDE Mentoring draws on models of peer mentoring and is sympathetic to Hargreaves and Fullan's (2000) argument that, for various reasons, including

> developments in the science of teaching […] [and] the spread of information technologies […] [t]he old model of mentoring, where experts who are certain about their craft can pass on its principles to eager novices, no longer applies […] the new teacher may sometimes know more than the mentor about new teaching strategies. If the school assumes the mentor always knows best […] innovative new teachers might quickly experience the mentoring relationship as an oppressive one. (p. 52–3)

Hence, ONSIDE Mentoring does not assume that the mentor always knows best; rather, it promotes a non-hierarchical learning partnership (Zachary, 2009) that will benefit both mentor and mentee. Nonetheless, while ECTs doubtless benefit from participation in peer mentoring with one or more other ECTs (Cornu, 2005; Sorensen and Sears, 2005), ONSIDE Mentoring assumes that there is added value in ECTs being mentored by more experienced teachers. This is because more experienced teachers are likely to be more able than ECTs' immediate peers to effectively undertake some important mentor roles, including those identified by Malderez and Bodoczky (1999) as '*acculturator*' (helping mentees into full membership of the professional culture), '*sponsor*' (e.g. introducing the mentee to the 'right people') and '*model*' (e.g. demonstrating aspects of being a teacher in the specific context). It should also be noted that most of the literature identifying the various potential benefits and positive impacts of mentoring has been based on research into mentoring where the mentor is a more experienced teacher than the mentee.

Turning more explicitly now to what ONSIDE Mentoring involves, it comprises what I consider – based on the research outlined in this chapter – to be seven imperatives of mentoring relationships. These are set out (and the first six briefly elaborated) in Table 21.2, which also defines their polar opposites – what mentoring frameworks and relationships should avoid.

The seventh and overriding imperative of ONSIDE Mentoring is that, as the mnemonic implies, mentors' are first and foremost *on the side of – supporters, champions and advocates for – their mentees*. The status of ECTs as vulnerable learners (Shanks, 2014) at the bottom of the pecking order (Hobson, 2009) provides a moral and a practical imperative that someone *takes their side* (Becker, 1967; Gouldner, 1968) and that they are allocated a supporter in whom they can place their trust. ONSIDE Mentoring is thus part-predicated on the research-informed assumption that establishing relational trust is pivotal to the success of the mentoring relationship and, therefore, to enhancing mentees' learning, development and well-being.

Table 21.2 ONSIDE Mentoring

MENTORING IS/SHOULD BE...	MENTORING SHOULD NOT...
Off-line (i.e. separated from line-management) and non-hierarchical	Occur within hierarchical and power relationships that make it difficult to establish relational trust and for mentees to openly share their professional learning and development needs
Non-judgemental and non-evaluative	Be judgemental or involve mentors in formal evaluations or assessments of mentees' work, which can also impede the establishment or maintenance of a trusting relationship and (partly in consequence) of mentees' professional learning, development and well-being
Supportive of mentees' psycho-social needs and well-being	Focus solely on mentees' 'performance' or the development of their capability with no consideration for mentees' emotional or psychological state or their well-being (which are both important in their own right and impact on mentees' capacity to learn and develop)
Individualised – tailored to the specific and changing needs (emotional and developmental) of the mentee	Be one-size-fits-all, since any given mentoring strategy will be more or less relevant to and produce different (positive or negative) responses in different mentees
Developmental and growth-oriented – seeking to promote mentees' learnacy and provide them with appropriate degrees of challenge	Be solely or selectively deployed as a remedial strategy to 'correct' perceived deficiencies in professional practice, which can discourage mentees from taking advantage of the 'support' of mentors, and encourage them to fabricate their learning and development needs
Empowering – progressively non-directive to support mentees to become more autonomous and agentic	(Normally) be directive, in which mentors provide 'solutions' rather than supporting mentees to find their own, and which accords mentees little autonomy and agency, and encourages their dependency on the mentor

The off-line, non-judgemental, supportive and individualised (ONSI) elements of ONSIDE Mentoring are all designed to encourage the development of relational trust between mentor and mentee. Importantly, though, being on the mentee's side, winning their trust and supporting their well-being will sometimes require ONSIDE mentors to temporarily *not* promote other features of 'developmental' mentoring. This is because the experience of non-directive forms of mentoring can be potentially stressful for ECTs (especially in the early stages of their field or placement experiences as trainee teachers, or of their first teaching posts as newly qualified teachers), as can the provision of appropriate degrees of challenge that encourage mentees out of their comfort zones (Tang, 2003). To support ECTs' emotional and psychological needs and well-being, it will thus be necessary, on occasion, for mentors to adopt a relatively directive approach and offer them 'practical advice', notably where ECTs appear unable to find their own solutions and/or where the absence of a quick fix solution is considered potentially harmful to ECTs or the students in their care. ONSIDE Mentoring is thus *progressively* non-directive, *progressively* autonomy-promoting and *progressively* challenging, seeking to develop ECTs' learnacy to the extent that this is consistent with ensuring individual mentees are not exposed to too much stress or too many potential impediments to their well-being.

The ONSIDE Mentoring framework is consistent with, and extends, scholars' use of Wood et al.'s (1976) scaffolding metaphor in the context of mentoring and coaching ECTs (e.g. Collet, 2015; Edwards and Collison, 1996) and others. Brown and Palincsar (1986) explain that '*(a) the degree of aid, or scaffolding, is adapted to the learner's current state; (b) the amount of scaffolding decreases as the skill of the learner increases; (c) for a learner at any one skill level, greater assistance is given if task difficulty increases, and vice versa*' (p.38)

And Greenfield (1984) notes that scaffolding creates '*an environment which reduces [...] failure experiences at the early stages of learning a new skill*' (p. 119). In line with this, ONSIDE Mentors should: (a) provide sufficient scaffolded support to ensure ECTs do not perceive themselves to be failing, which would be detrimental to their well-being; whilst (b) progressively reduce the amount of scaffolding (i.e. make their mentoring increasingly non-directive) to accord ECTs greater autonomy, responsibility and challenge; yet (c) being ready to re-erect some temporary scaffold if necessary. In ONSIDE Mentoring, the erection or temporary reinstatement of scaffolding relates not only to mentees' skill level and to task difficulty, but also to their emotional and psychological preparedness for and response to specific experiences as teachers and as mentees.[11] By ensuring that mentees do not become dependent upon their mentors, but are empowered and become increasingly autonomous, ONSIDE Mentoring should help reduce the likelihood of reality aftershock (Hobson and Ashby, 2012) – difficulties experienced as a result of the sudden cessation of support when formal programmes of mentoring and induction come to an end.

Like all mentoring programmes, those based upon the ONSIDE Mentoring framework will be more likely to flourish where efforts are made to provide various other ingredients of efficacious teacher mentoring identified earlier, not least appropriate provision for mentor preparation and development. And such provision should include an explicit focus on the range of factors potentially affecting ECTs' PLD (Hobson and McIntyre, 2013) and well-being (Hobson and Maxwell, 2017), on means of developing trusting relationships (Bryk and Schneider, 2003), and on the various imperatives of ONSIDE Mentoring. Mentor preparation might also usefully include a 'contextual mentoring audit' (Malderez, 2015), which involves an examination of the extent to which the context is pro- or anti-mentoring in nature, and helps mentors to prepare strategies to shield their mentees from potential impediments to their PLD and well-being.

CONCLUSION

In this chapter, drawing on five empirical studies and two reviews of literature that I have led or undertaken, I make three main contributions to the literature on mentoring for early career teachers and mentoring more generally. First, I have outlined common ingredients for effective ECT mentoring that have been identified by previous research, and have extended this work by providing strong evidence for mentors' non-involvement in the formal assessment of mentees, which has been an area of contention amongst researchers in this area, and by showing that the widely used and acclaimed mentoring strategy of observing and providing feedback on ECTs' teaching can impede ECTs' PLD, learnacy and well-being. Secondly, I have extended what we know, and provided the most comprehensive account to date, of the nature, reach, consequences and causes of judgementoring (Hobson and Malderez, 2013). And thirdly, I have outlined and made the case for a new mentoring framework, which is sensitive to the specific needs and vulnerabilities of ECTs, and which I call ONSIDE Mentoring. I contend that, if implemented with and by appropriately prepared mentors, ONSIDE Mentoring will help to forestall and combat the terrors of judgementoring and its undesirable consequences, and help to maximise the potential benefits of mentorship.

In offering and commending ONSIDE Mentoring to policymakers, school and college leaders, mentor trainers and mentors, respectively, I anticipate the potential critique (or misunderstanding) that the framework is *one-sided*. That is, ONSIDE Mentoring may appear to place too much emphasis on the needs of the ECT at the expense of those of the school or college. However, I have explained earlier why, as vulnerable learners, ECTs need mentors to be on their side. I would also remind the reader that the aim of ECT mentoring, as I see it (and state in the definition of mentoring provided in the Introduction to this chapter), is to support the mentee's learning, development, well-being, *and integration into the cultures of the organisation in which they are employed* as well as the wider profession. As such, the ONSIDE Mentor will be consciously aware of the needs of the school or college in which the mentee is employed as well as those of the mentee, and will help the ECT develop an understanding of these to assist their integration into the culture of the organisation.[12] In addition, the school or college will undoubtedly benefit from having ECTs on their staff who – through the provision and support of ONSIDE Mentors – will be more able to take advantage of opportunities for professional learning and development, more likely to enjoy higher levels of well-being, and thus more likely to be committed to teaching and to the institution that is supporting them. In short, by being on the mentee's side, the ONSIDE Mentor is on the employing institution's side, and that of the wider profession.

While informed by my own and others' research on ECTs, the ONSIDE Mentoring framework is also informed by and wholly consistent with the findings from Project 5 – a study of ten exemplary mentoring and coaching programmes across various professions and sectors in six different countries. As such, the framework may be of interest and potentially applicable in other contexts, perhaps especially with respect to early career professionals who, like teachers, may generally be regarded as vulnerable learners.

I look forward to the response to the ONSIDE Mentoring framework from academics, practitioners and policymakers alike. I also look forward optimistically to the potential deployment of ONSIDE Mentoring, to research and evaluation studies of any such deployment and, perhaps most of all, to the potential contribution of ONSIDE Mentoring to the decline and fall of judgementoring.

Notes

1 The FE sector in England, also known as the Further Education and Skills, Post-Compulsory or Lifelong Learning sector, is large and diverse. It includes further education colleges, sixth form colleges, private and charitable training providers, adult and community learning providers, work-based learning providers, training departments of major employers, the armed services, the prison service, etc. (Lingfield, 2012).

2 The term *initial teacher preparation (ITP)* is used to refer to what is variously described as initial teacher education (ITE), initial teacher training (ITT) and pre-service teacher training. My preference for the use of ITP has been explained elsewhere (e.g. Hobson et al., 2008).

3 While I regard coaching as one of a number of aspects of a broader mentoring role, and one which relates to attempts to support an individual's development of one or more job-specific skills or capabilities (Hopkins-Thompson, 2000; Malderez and Bodoczky, 1999), others use coaching more broadly and in such a way that meets the definition of mentoring set out above. It is thus appropriate to include reference to some such literature and related programmes in this chapter, as it was in the projects underpinning it.

4 This included 35 sources listed in GoogleScholar as citing the original 'judgementoring' article (Hobson and Malderez, 2013) up to 31 May 2016; to which I added an article I co-authored that reports findings from a case study of mentoring provision in an FE college in-service teacher training programme in England (Manning and Hobson, forthcoming).

5 ResearchGate is a social networking site in which academics share research outputs, ask and answer questions, and find collaborators. For further information, see researchgate.net.

6 Thirteen publications (selected research reports and peer-reviewed journal articles) were reviewed, and are denoted with an asterisk in the Reference section of this chapter.

7 In this chapter I focus on the impacts of mentoring on ECTs. It is shown elsewhere that mentoring can also have a positive impact on mentors, and on mentees' and mentors' students and institutions (Hobson et al., 2009).

8 Performativity and GERM are characterised by government control over the school curriculum

and workforce, and monitoring and 'inspection' of school and teacher effectiveness or 'performance'.
9. The Office for Standards in Education, Children's Services and Skills (Ofsted) is the nonministerial department of the UK government that inspects and regulates services that care for children and young people, and services providing education and skills for learners of all ages in England, most notably schools.
10. For more information about external mentoring and its potential benefits for ECTs and teachers more generally, see Hobson et al. (2012); Hobson and McIntyre (2013); McIntyre and Hobson (2016).
11. A fuller discussion of the potential practical application of ONSIDE Mentoring is provided in Hobson (2016).
12. That said, we have seen that there are elements of some organisational cultures, and the culture of the wider teaching profession that militate against early career (and most likely other) teachers' PLD and well-being. ONSIDE mentors, supported by institutional mentoring coordinators and senior leadership teams, should thus seek to integrate critically reflective ECTs into the culture of their organisations and the wider profession, whilst empowering them to act as catalysts and change agents (Thornton, 2014) in bringing about improvements to those cultures, notably by supporting the development of supportive and collegial learning environments.

ACKNOWLEDGEMENTS

I am grateful to my mentoring mentors, Angi Malderez and Peter Tomlinson, to my trusted colleagues Lorraine Harrison and David Stephens, and to my *SAGE Handbook* Section Editor Laura Lunsford and *International Journal of Mentoring and Coaching in Education* (IJMCE) Co-Editor Linda Searby for their helpful comments. I also acknowledge the valuable contributions of all my co-researchers to the various 'underpinning research' projects, and to those who supported the projects financially and otherwise, including the Gatsby Charitable Foundation and the (then) Department for Children, Schools and Families (DCSF), General Teaching Council for England (GTCE) and Training and Development Agency for Schools (TDA).

REFERENCES

The 13 publications highlighted with an asterisk are those used for the thematic analysis of previously published research findings from Projects 1–3.

Abell, S.K., Dillon, D.R., Hopkins, C.J., McInerney, W.D. and O'Brien, D.G. (1995) 'Somebody to count on': Mentor/intern relationships in a beginning teacher internship program. *Teaching and Teacher Education*, *11*(2), 173–88.

Adey, K. (1997) First impressions do count: mentoring student teachers. *Teacher Development*, *1*(1), 123–33.

Association for Supervision and Curriculum Development (1999) *Mentoring to Improve Schools.* Alexandria, VA: ASDC.

Ball, S.J. (2003) The teacher's soul and the terrors of performativity, *Journal of Education Policy*, *18*(2), 215–28.

Beck, C. and Kosnick, C. (2000) Associate teachers in pre-service education: clarifying and enhancing their role, *Journal of Education for Teaching*, *26*(3), 207–24.

Becker, H.S. (1967) Whose side are we on? *Social Problems*, *14*, 239–47.

BERA (2004) *Revised Ethical Guidelines for Educational Research,* Nottingham: British Educational Research Association.

BERA (2011) *Ethical Guidelines for Educational Research,* London: British Educational Research Association.

Boyatzis, R.E., Smith, M.L., and Beveridge, A.J. (2013) Coaching with compassion: Inspiring health, well-being, and development in organizations, *The Journal of Applied Behavioral Science*, *49*(2), 153–78.

Bradbury, L.U. and Koballa, Jr., T.R. (2008) Borders to cross: Identifying sources of tension in mentor–intern relationships, *Teaching and Teacher Education*, *24*(8), 2132–45.

Braun,V. and Clarke, V. (2006) Using thematic analysis in psychology. *Qualitative Research in Psychology*, *3*(2), 77–101.

Brown, A.L. and Palincsar, A.S. (1986). *Guided, cooperative learning and individual knowledge acquisition. Technical Report No. 372.* Retrieved from http://eric.ed.gov/PDFS/ED270738.pdf (accessed 07 March 2016).

Bryk, A.S. and Schneider, B. (2003) Trust in schools: A core resource for school reform. *Creating Caring Schools*, 60(6), 40–5.

Bullough, R.V., Jr. (2005) Being and becoming a mentor: school-based teacher educators and teacher educator identity. *Teaching and Teacher Education*, 21(2), 143–55.

Cameron, M., Whatman, J., Hodgen, E., McLeod, L., Bright, N., Nuttall, J. and Nolan, A. (2014) Evaluation of the *Guidelines for induction and mentoring and mentor teachers*. Wellington: New Zealand Council for Educational Research.

*Chambers, G.N., Hobson, A.J., and Tracey, L. (2010) 'Teaching could be a fantastic job but…' Three stories of student teacher withdrawal from initial teacher preparation programmes in England. *Teachers and Teaching: Theory and Practice*, 16(1), 111–29.

Claxton, G. (2004) Learning is learnable (and we ought to teach it), in Cassell, J. (Ed.), *Ten Years On*. Bristol: The National Commission for Education Report, pp. 237–50.

Clutterbuck, D. (1992) *Mentoring*. Henley: Henley Distance Learning.

Clutterbuck, D.C. (2004) *Everyone Needs a Mentor: Fostering talent in your organisation*, London: Chartered Institute of Personnel and Development.

Collet, V.S. (2015) The Gradual Increase of Responsibility Model for coaching teachers: Scaffolds for change, *International Journal of Mentoring and Coaching in Education*, 4(4), 269–92.

Cornu, R.L. (2005) Peer mentoring: engaging pre-service teachers in mentoring one another, *Mentoring and Tutoring*, 13(3), 355–66.

Crasborn, F., Hennisson, P., Brouwer, N., Korthagen, F. and Bergen, T. (2008) Promoting versatility in mentor teachers' use of supervisory skills. *Teaching and Teacher Education*, 24(3), 499–514.

Cunningham, B. (2007) All the right features: towards an 'architecture' for mentoring trainee teachers in UK further education colleges, *Journal of Education for Teaching*, 33(1), 83–97.

Daloz, L.A. (1986) *Effective teaching and mentoring*. San Francisco: Jossey-Bass Publishers.

Day, C. (2008) Committed for life? Variations in teachers' work, lives and effectiveness, *Journal of Educational Change*, 9(3), 243–60.

Day, C. and Kington, A. (2008) Identity, well-being and effectiveness: the emotional contexts of teaching, *Pedagogy, Culture and Society*, 16(1), 7–23.

Department for Education (2015) *Induction for Newly Qualified Teachers (England): Statutory Guidance for Appropriate Bodies, Headteachers, School Staff and Governing Bodies*, retrieved from https://www.gov.uk/government/uploads/system/uploads/attachment_data/file/458233/Statutory_induction_guidance_for_newly_qualified_teachers.pdf (accessed 15 April 2016).

D'Souza, L.A. (2014) Bridging the gap for beginning teachers: researcher as mentor, *International Journal of Mentoring and Coaching in Education*, 3(2), 171–87.

Duckworth, V. and Maxwell, B. (2015) Extending the mentor role in initial teacher education: embracing social justice, *International Journal of Mentoring and Coaching in Education*, 4(1), 4–20.

Edwards, A. (1998) Mentoring student teachers in primary schools: assisting student teachers to become learners. *European Journal of Teacher Education*, 21(1), 47–62.

Edwards, A. and Collison, J. (1996) *Mentoring and developing practice in primary schools*. Buckingham: OUP.

Evans, L. and Abbott, I. (1997) Developing as mentors in school-based teacher training. *Teacher Development*, 1(1), 135–48.

Feiman-Nemser, S., Parker, M.B., and Zeichner, K. (1993) Are mentor teachers teacher educators?, in McIntyre, D., Hagger, H. and Wilkin, M. (Eds.), *Mentoring: Perspectives on School-Based Teacher Education*, London: Kogan Page, pp. 147–65.

Foster, R. (1999) School-based initial teacher training in England and France: trainee teachers' perspectives compared. *Mentoring and Tutoring: Partnership in Learning*, 7(2), 131–43.

Gold, Y. (1996) Beginner teacher support: attrition, mentoring and induction, in Sikula, J., Buttery, T.J. and Guyton, E. (Eds.), *Handbook of Research on Teacher Education*, New York: Macmillan, pp. 548–94.

Gouldner, A.W. (1968) The sociologist as partisan: Sociology and the Welfare State, *The American Sociologist*, 3(2), 103–16.

Graham, P. (1997) Tensions in the mentor teacher-student teacher relationship:

Creating productive sites for learning within a high school English teacher education program. *Teaching and Teacher Education*, *13*(5), 513–27.

Greenfield, P.M. (1984) A theory of the teacher in the learning activities of everyday life. In B. Rogoff and J. Lave (Eds.), *Everyday Cognition: Its Development in Social Context*, Cambridge, MA: Harvard University Press, pp. 117–38.

Hagger, H., Mutton, T., and Burn, K. (2011) Surprising but not shocking: The reality of the first year of teaching. *Cambridge Journal of Education*, *41*, 387–405.

Hargreaves, A. and Fullan, M. (2000) Mentoring in the new millennium, *Theory into Practice*, *29*(1), 50–6.

Hargreaves, A. and Fullan, M. (2012) *Professional capital: Transforming teaching in every school*. London and New York: Routledge.

Harrison, J., Dymoke, S. and Pell, T. (2006) Mentoring beginning teachers in secondary schools: An analysis of practice. *Teaching and Teacher Education*, *22*, 1055–67.

Hascher, T., Cocard, Y. and Moser, P. (2004) Forget about theory – practice is all? Student teachers' learning in practicum. *Teachers and Teaching: Theory and Practice*, *10*(6), 623–37.

Heilbronn, R., Jones, C., Bubb, S. and Totterdell, M. (2002) School-based induction tutors – a challenging role. *School Leadership and Management*, *22*(4), 371–88.

*Hobson, A.J. (2009) On being bottom of the pecking order: beginner teachers' perceptions and experiences of support. *Teacher Development*, *13*(4), 299–320.

Hobson, A.J. (2016) Judgementoring and how to avert it: Introducing ONSIDE Mentoring for beginning teachers. *International Journal of Mentoring and Coaching in Education*, *5*(2), 87–110.

*Hobson, A.J. and Ashby, P. (2012) Reality aftershock and how to avert it: second year teachers' experiences of support for their professional development. *Cambridge Journal of Education*, *42*(2), 177–96.

*Hobson, A.J. and Malderez, A. (2013) Judgementoring and other threats to realizing the potential of school-based mentoring in teacher education, *International Journal of Mentoring and Coaching in Education*, *2*(2), 89–108.

Hobson, A.J. and Maxwell, B. (2017), Supporting and inhibiting the well-being of early career secondary school teachers: extending self-determination theory, *British Educational Research Journal*.

*Hobson, A.J. and McIntyre, J. (2013) Teacher fabrication as an impediment to professional learning and development: the external mentor antidote, *Oxford Review of Education*, *39*(3), 345–65.

Hobson, A.J. and Townsend, A.J. (2010) Interviewing as educational research method(s). In: D. Hartas (Ed.), *Educational Research and Inquiry: Qualitative and Quantitative Approaches*. London: Continuum, pp. 223–38.

Hobson, A.J., Ashby, P., Malderez, A. and Tomlinson, P.D. (2009a) Mentoring beginning teachers: what we know and what we don't. *Teaching and Teacher Education*, *25*(1), 207–16.

Hobson, A.J., Castanheira, P., Doyle, K., Csigás, Z. and Clutterbuck, D. (2016) *The Mentoring across Professions (MaP) Project: What can teacher mentoring learn from international good practice in employee mentoring and coaching?* London: Gatsby Charitable Foundation. Retrieved from http://www.gatsby.org.uk/uploads/education/reports/pdf/mentoring-across-the-professions-final300816.pdf (accessed 23 September, 2016).

*Hobson, A.J., Giannakaki, M. and Chambers, G.N. (2009c) Who withdraws from initial teacher preparation programmes and why? *Educational Research*, *51*(3), 321–40.

*Hobson, A.J., Malderez, A., Tracey, L., Giannakaki, M.S., Pell, R.G. and Tomlinson, P.D. (2008) Student teachers' experiences of initial teacher preparation in England: core themes and variation, *Research Papers in Education*, *23*(4), 407–33.

*Hobson, A.J., Malderez, A., Tracey, L., Homer, M.S., Ashby, P., Mitchell, N., McIntyre, J., Cooper, D., Roper, T., Chambers, G.N. and Tomlinson, P.D. (2009b) *Becoming a teacher: teachers' experiences of initial teacher training, induction and early professional development*. London: Department for Children, Schools and Families.

*Hobson, A.J., Malderez, A., Tracey, L., Homer, M., Mitchell, N., Biddulph, M., Giannakaki, M.S., Rose, A., Pell, R.G., Chambers, G.N., Roper, T. and Tomlinson, P.D. (2007) *Newly qualified teachers' experiences of their first year of teaching: Findings from Phase III of the Becoming a Teacher project. Nottingham: Department for Children, Schools and Families.

*Hobson, A.J., Maxwell, B., Stevens, A., Doyle, K. and Malderez, A. (2015) *Mentoring and coaching for teachers in the Further Education and Skills Sector in England: full report*. London: Gatsby Charitable Foundation. Available at: http://www.gatsby.org.uk/uploads/education/reports/pdf/mentoring-full-report.pdf (accessed 7 March 2016).

*Hobson, A.J., McIntyre, J., Ashby, P., Hayward, V., Stevens, A. and Malderez, A. (2012) *The nature, impact and potential of external mentoring for teachers of physics and other subjects in England: full report*. London: Gatsby Charitable Foundation. Available at: http://www.gatsby.org.uk/~/media/Files/Education/Gatsby%20%20Impact%20of%20 Mentoring (accessed 7 March 2016).

Hopkins-Thompson, P.A. (2000) Colleagues helping colleagues: mentoring and coaching. *NASSP Bulletin*, 84(617), 29–36.

Ingersoll, R. and Kralik, J. (2004) *The impact of mentoring on teacher retention: What the research says*. Denver, CO: Education Commission of the States. Retrieved from http://citeseerx.ist.psu.edu/viewdoc/download?doi=10.1.1.486.3317andrep=rep1andtype=pdf (accessed 7 March, 2016).

Jack, A.I., Boyatzis, R.E., Khawaja, M.S., Passarelli, A.M. and Leckie, R.L. (2013) Visioning in the brain: An fMRI study of inspirational coaching and mentoring, *Social Neuroscience*, 8(4), 369–84.

Johnson, S. (2004) *Finders and keepers*. San Francisco: Wiley.

Johnson, S.M. and Birkeland, S.E. (2003) Pursuing a 'sense of success': New teachers explain their career decisions. *American Educational Research Journal*, 40(3), 581–617.

Kelchtermans, G. and Ballet, K. (2002) The micropolitics of teacher induction. A narrative-biographical study on teacher socialisation. *Teaching and Teacher Education*, 18(1), 105–20.

Kochan, F., Searby, L., George, M.P. and Mitchell Edge, J. (2015) Cultural influences in mentoring endeavors: applying the Cultural Framework Analysis Process, *IJMCE* 4(2), 86–106.

Kourieos, S. (2015) Personal communication, 25 December 2015.

Kutsyuruba, B. (2012) Teacher induction and mentorship policies: the pan-Canadian overview, *International Journal of Mentoring and Coaching in Education*, 1(3), 235–56.

Kwakman, K. (2003) Factors affecting teachers' participation in professional learning activities. *Teaching and Teacher Education* 19(2), 149–70.

Lee, J.C. and Feng, S. (2007) Mentoring support and the professional development of beginning teachers: a Chinese perspective. *Mentoring and Tutoring: Partnership in Learning*, 15(3), 243–63.

Lejonberg, E., Elstad, E. and Christophersen, K.A. (2015) Mentor education: challenging mentors' beliefs about mentoring, *International Journal of Mentoring and Coaching in Education*, 4(2), 142–58.

Lindgren, U. (2005) Experiences of beginning teachers in a school-based mentoring programme Sweden. *Educational Studies*, 31(3), 251–63.

Ling, L. (2009) Induction: making the leap, *Research in Comparative and International Education*, 4(1), 87–95.

Lingfield, R. (2012) *Professionalism in Further Education: Final report of the Independent Review Panel*. London: Department for Business, Innovations and Skills. Available at: www.gov.uk/government/uploads/system/uploads/attachment_data/file/34641/12-1198-professionalism-in-further-education-final.pdf (accessed 5 April, 2016).

Lofthouse, R. and Thomas, U. (2014) Mentoring student teachers; a vulnerable workplace learning practice, *International Journal of Mentoring and Coaching in Education*, 3(3), 201–18.

Lunsford, L.G. (2016) Personal communication, 2 February 2016 and 4 March 2016.

Maguire, M. (2001) Bullying and the postgraduate secondary school trainee: an English case study, *Journal of Education for Teaching*, 27(1), 95–109.

Maier, S.F. and Seligman, M.E.P. (1976) Learned helplessness: theory and evidence, *Journal of Experimental Psychology: General*, 105(1), 3–46.

Malderez, A. (2001) New ELT professionals, *English Teaching Professional*, 19(1), 57–8.

Malderez, A. (2015) On mentoring in supporting (English) teacher learning: where are we now?, in Hollo, D., and Karolyi, K. (Eds.), *Inspirations in foreign language teaching: Studies in language pedagogy and applied linguistics in honour of Peter Medgyes*, Harlow: Pearson, 21–32.

Malderez, A. and Bodoczky, C. (1999) *Mentor Courses: A resource book for trainer-trainers*. Cambridge: CUP.

Manning, C. and Hobson, A.J. (forthcoming) Judgemental and developmental mentoring in further education initial teacher education in England: mentor and mentee perspectives.

McIntyre, D. and Hagger, H. (1996) *Mentors in schools: developing the profession of teaching*. London: David Fulton.

*McIntyre, J. and Hobson, A.J. (2016) Supporting beginner teacher identity development: external mentors and the third space, *Research Papers in Education*, 31(2), 133–58.

Netolicky, D. (2016) Coaching for professional growth in one Australian school: 'oil in water', *International Journal of Mentoring and Coaching in Education*, 5(2), 66–86.

Ng, P.T. (2012) Mentoring and coaching educators in the Singapore education system, *International Journal of Mentoring and Coaching in Education*, 1(1), 24–35.

Rajuan, M., Douwe, B. and Verloop, N. (2007) The role of the cooperating teacher: bridging the gap between the expectations of cooperating teachers and student teachers. *Mentoring and Tutoring: Partnership in Learning*, 15(3), 223–42.

Rippon, J.H. and Martin, M. (2006) What makes a good induction supporter? *Teaching and Teacher Education*, 22(1), 84–99.

Roehrig, A.D., Bohn, C.M., Turner, J.E. and Pressley, M. (2008) Mentoring beginning primary teachers for exemplary teaching practices. *Teaching and Teacher Education*, 24(3), 684–702.

Sahlberg, P. (2010) Rethinking Accountability in a Knowledge Society, *Journal of Educational Change*, 11(1), 45–61.

Schön, D. (1983) *The reflective practitioner. How professionals think in action*, London: Temple Smith.

Searby, L. (2014) The protégé mentoring mindset: a framework for consideration, *International Journal of Mentoring and Coaching in Education*, 3(3), 255–276.

Shanks, R. (2014) A study of learners' situational vulnerability: new teachers in Scotland. *Education in the North*, 21(Special Issue), 2–20.

Simpson, T., Hastings, W. and Hill, B. (2007) 'I knew that she was watching me': the professional benefits of mentoring. *Teachers and Teaching: Theory and Practice*, 13(5), 481–98.

Smith, T. and Ingersoll, R. (2004) What are the effects of induction and mentoring on beginning teacher turnover? *American Educational Research Journal*, 41(3), 681–714.

Sorensen, P. and Sears, J. (2005) Collaborative practice in initial teacher education: the use of paired subject placements in the school practicum, *International Journal of Learning*, 14, 619–31.

Tang, S.Y.F. (2003) Challenge and support: the dynamics of student teachers' professional learning in the field experience. *Teaching and Teacher Education*, 19(5), 483–98.

Thornton, K. (2014) Mentors as educational leaders and change agents, *International Journal of Mentoring and Coaching in Education*, 3(1), 18–31.

Tomlinson, P.D. (1995), *Understanding mentoring: Reflective strategies for school-based teacher preparation*. Open University Press, Buckingham.

*Tracey L., Homer, M., Mitchell, N., Malderez, A., Hobson, A. J., Ashby, P. and Pell, G. (2008) *Teachers' experiences of their second year in post: Findings from Phase IV of the Becoming a Teacher project*. Nottingham: Department for Children, Schools and Families (DCSF).

Ulvik, M. and Sunde, E. (2013) The impact of mentor education: Does mentor education matter?, *Professional Development in Education*, 39(5), 754–70.

Valencic Zuljan, M. and Vogrinc, J. (2007) A mentor's aid in developing the competences of teacher trainees. *Educational Studies*, 33(4), 373–84.

Veenman, S.A.M. (1984) Perceived problems of beginning teachers. *Review of Educational Research*, 54, 143–78.

Wang, J. (2001) Contexts of mentoring and opportunities for learning to teach:

A comparative study of mentoring practice. *Teaching and Teacher Education*, *17*(1), 51–73.

Wood, D., Bruner, J. and Ross, G. (1976) The role of tutoring in problem solving. *Journal of Child Psychology and Child Psychiatry*, *17*(2), 89–100.

Young, J.R., Bullough, R.V., Draper, R.J., Smith, L.K. and Erickson, L.B. (2005) Novice teacher growth and personal models of mentoring: choosing compassion over inquiry, *Mentoring and Tutoring: Partnership in Learning*, *13*(2), 169–88.

Yusko, B. and Feiman-Nemser, S. (2008) Embracing Contraries: Combining Assistance and Assessment in New Teacher Induction. *Teachers College Record*, *110*(7), 1–12.

Zachary, L. (2009) *The mentor's guide*, San Francisco, CA: Jossey-Bass.

Mentoring Newcomer Immigrants: Tactics of and Recommendations for Successful Mentors

Roxanne B. Reeves

'If you light a lamp for someone, it will also brighten your own path.'

Buddhist Proverb

INTRODUCTION

What happens when mentors and mentees hold different cultural value systems and beliefs? What common understandings are needed to help these relationships flourish and to support knowledge transfer? What competencies are required to influence positively inter-cultural mentoring (ICM) relationships? These questions represent a delicate dance that juxtaposes social norms, societal pressures, and expectations with individual character attributes.

The need for mentor competence in navigating differences due to differing cultural and world-views should not be underestimated – for both members of the dyad seeking fruitful mentoring relationships. Recognizing the importance of local culture and context, this study draws on mentor feedback and reflection to examine the practices of mentors successful in mentoring immigrant entrepreneur newcomers and contributes to the understanding of IMC in several distinct ways.

The literature review describes Leader–Member Exchange theory (LMX) before reviewing inter-cultural mentoring literature with a focus on newcomer immigrant entrepreneurs; it concludes with a discussion of international mobility trends. Then the qualitative methods are described. Findings highlight mentor feedback and reflect on the seven themes which emerged that influence effective inter-cultural mentoring: mentees' culture; mentors' cultural self-awareness; building relationality and accessibility; sponsorship; deep learning; racism; and small-city truths. The chapter concludes with a discussion framed by LMX theory on the distinctive characteristics of mentoring in inter-cultural contexts.

LITERATURE REVIEW

This section presents LMX theory and an overview of inter-cultural mentoring literature. Suggestions for refining the term ICM and synthesizing the literature across contexts are proposed before reviewing the literature on inter-cultural mentoring of newcomer immigrant entrepreneurs. Finally, international mobility trends are discussed in relation to mentoring immigrant entrepreneurs, their settlement and associations, and their social and economic integration.

Leader–member exchange theory

LMX theory focuses on the quality of relationships, which posits that approaches taken by leaders are differentiated according to specific relationship qualities that exist among individuals (Scandura and Pellegrini, 2007). This theory suggests that some mentees may enjoy 'high-quality exchanges with their [mentor] characterized by a high degree of mutual trust, respect and obligation... whereas others experience low-quality exchanges' (ibid., p. 3). LMX theory points to the need to understand the quality of interactions within dyads, which has been associated with positive mentorship outcomes.

According to LMX theory, group members who report high satisfaction with their role in the group are less likely to leave the group and have greater chances of success. However, the main limitation of LMX research is that it is not effective at demarcating specific leader behaviors that promote high-quality relationships (Gerstner and Day, 1997; Keller and Dansereau, 1995; Liden et al., 1997; Scandura and Schriesheim, 1994). Nevertheless, LMX theory underlines the idea that robust relationships between mentor and mentee contribute to mentee success and remain a central goal.

Inter-cultural mentoring

A problem related to the reporting of research pertaining to ICM is ambiguity and conceptual confusion regarding the term ICM, in that the same construct varies from author to author. The present review recommends how mentoring literature might be synthesized across inter-cultural contexts and expands an earlier review of 123 manuscripts (Reeves, 2015) by further refining and simplifying categories assigned to ICM from four to three. These categories are defined below to clarify the terms; foreign-born newcomers is the category of interest for the present study.

Research on inter-cultural mentoring may be classified into three overarching categories: (a) foreign-born newcomers; (b) domestic-race based; and (c) global.

(a) Foreign-born newcomers are from countries with different ethnic backgrounds from their new country of residence (Petrovic, 2015; Reeves 2014a). They may, for example, be international students (Dimitrov, 2009; Kent et al., 2013; Lechuga, V.M., 2011; No-Gutiérrez P et al., 2014; Omar, 2015) or refugees (Askins, 2014; Merie, 2015), but they are primarily immigrants (Petrovic, 2015; Ramos and Yoshida, 2011; Reeves, in press).

(b) Domestic-race based mentoring is a term mostly used by US researchers. It refers to ethnic minority, American-born individuals who are visible minorities with non-dominant cultural backgrounds, but not recent immigrants to the US (Chan, 2008; Chandler et al., 2011; Hu et al., 2008; Kochan, 2002; Kochan and Pascarelli, 2003). However, when aboriginal populations are included in this category of domestic-race based mentoring, researchers from Canada, Australia, and New Zealand contribute to the field (Eskicioglu et al., 2014; Kervin et al., 2014; Mackinlay et al., 2014). Authors writing from this perspective highlight the relevancy of race and culture to dyads and the need for proficiencies in navigating cultural and/or worldview differences.

(c) Global refers to dyads that may cross boundaries of time, geography, and culture (Faustino, 2014; Philippart and Gluesing, 2012) and include: (a) virtual mentoring or e-mentoring; (b) mentoring in workplace settings both for traditional expatriate workers (AlMazrouei and Pech, 2014; Carraher et al., 2008; Purcell and Scheyvens, 2015; Rainoldi and Gölzner, 2014) and expatriates outside the boundaries of multinational corporations; and (c) pan-cultural mentoring, which refers to mentoring research from other countries supplementing or supplanting the preeminence of US/Anglo-Saxon research and illuminates cross-national variabilities in mentoring (Pekerti et al., 2015; also see, Case Studies of Mentoring around the Globe, Part IV this volume). Lunsford and Ochoa (2014) for example, discuss, in part, what mentoring means in the US-Mexico borderlands; Kervin et al. (2014) provide an Australian perspective, and Schultz-Nybacka and Sjödin (forthcoming) give a Swedish viewpoint.

ICM research includes divergent assumptions regarding the 'target', or the individual being mentored, and standard delineation. The confusion in criteria leads to faulty generalizations or incomplete models and theories. This study refines the overarching Reeves' framework (Reeves, 2015) to clarify terms related to ICM (see, Figure 22.1). Research specific to inter-cultural mentoring of newcomers is limited, particularly in terms of how inter-cultural differences may be negotiated and what skills and/or competencies are required of the mentor and mentee to influence cross-cultural mentoring relationships for immigrant newcomers.

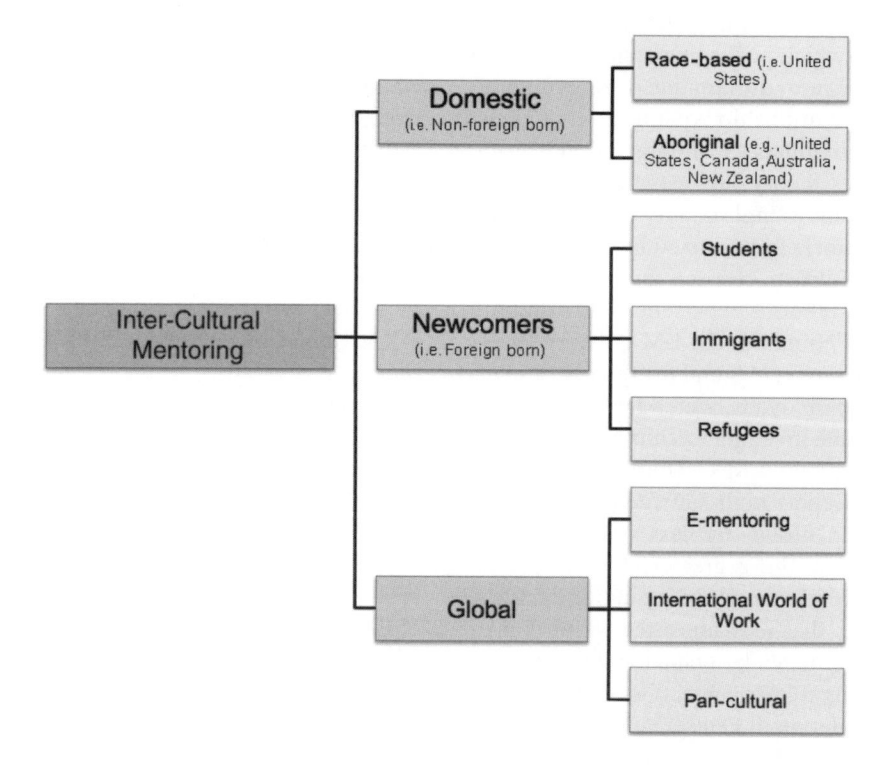

Figure 22.1 Proposed model for describing multiple meanings conferred on the term inter-cultural mentoring

Inter-cultural mentoring for immigrant entrepreneurs

Whereas mentoring and entrepreneurship have been researched extensively, fewer studies have focused on the intersection of these two topics, and how the needs of entrepreneurs are navigated *within* mentoring relationships (see, Reeves, 2014(b); Reeves, in press; St-Jean and Audet, 2013). According to Gravells (in St-Jean and Audet, 2013) relationships that focus on the mentee with [appropriately] high mentor involvement and *low* directivity (focus of concern is on mentor and mentor shows little involvement with the mentee) is ideal. In other words, 'mentoring is optimized when the mentor exhibits a maieutic approach, a directive style and significant involvement in the relationship... [i]t is of prime importance to get the mentee to talk, rather than provide them with examples of past experiences or advice based on these experiences' (St-Jean and Audet, 2013, p. 110).

There are well-documented financial challenges faced by entrepreneurs – including lack of financial capital (Brenner et al., 2010). However, additional challenges exist for immigrant entrepreneurs living in non-metropolitan immigrant gateways or non-traditional immigrant-receiving communities. Newcomers face obstacles and may lack contextual experience, connections, and resources when they live in small and medium cities SMCs that may not be large enough to support ethnic enclaves (Price and Chacko, 2009).

Due to a lack of existing networks and social integration newcomer immigrant entrepreneurs may struggle to develop positive reputations within the new business community (Brenner et al., 2010). These deficiencies may translate into insufficient knowledge of their new business milieu, which can further impede business-building efforts, and include a lack of understanding about: economic and social environments; legislation and regulations; and the local labour market (Brenner et al., 2010; Rath and Kloosterman, 2000). It is essential that they form social capital, shared memberships, and a web or network of social relationships that influence individual behaviour and thereby affect economic growth (Brenner et al., 2010; Reeves, in press). The question then becomes 'How may networks best be created for immigrant entrepreneurs' needs in new destination communities?'

Mobility trends

The twenty-first century has been called 'the age of migration' (Castles and Miller, 2009). There are about 232 million international migrants in the world today, more than ever before (United Nations, 2013). In light of the ongoing move toward economic globalization and current immigration trends the need for inter-cultural mentoring research and programming is likely to increase.

Three international mobility trends highlight the importance of examining how newcomer immigrants could be supported with inter-cultural mentoring. First, the potential for ICM continues to grow as workforce mobility increases, because of policies such as trade agreements between countries (Staff, 2013). *The Migration Observatory* (Coleman, 2013), notes that, '[n]et international migration is now the dominant element in population change in most Western European countries and in parts of the *Anglosphere* (USA, Canada, Australia, New Zealand)' (ibid., p. 2). Second, countries are increasingly relying upon immigrants to replenish shrinking populations. The intent is to reduce strain on publicly funded programmes and social security systems caused by rising dependency ratios (Brenner et al., 2010). Third, international migration is a global phenomenon growing in scope, complexity, and impact.

Researchers suggest that immigrant entrepreneurs are underprepared for the economic climate they encounter as business skills may not be transferable from one cultural or economic and regulatory setting to another (ibid.). For newcomer immigrants to SMCs, the absence of institutionally complete communities or strong ethnic economies in new gateway communities, means immigrants are unable to rely on their own community resources, an element considered instrumental for immigrant business development. Furthermore, immigrant newcomers living in SMCs who feel isolated and lack a sense of belonging are most at risk of leaving. Mentoring has the potential to combat this sense of isolation and may be critical to facilitate integration and encourage persistence. It is unclear if mentors of newcomer immigrant entrepreneurs are prepared to help their mentees adapt to a new cultural milieu. What is not known is: (a) how mentors perceive the diverse meanings of inter-cultural mentoring; (b) what skills/competencies are required of the mentor as they pertain to knowledge transfer and personal learning; (c) the significance of acculturation support; and (d) business and network gains.

THE PRESENT STUDY

Programme description

The Fredericton Business Immigrant Mentorship Program (BIMP) offered in New Brunswick (NB), Canada was selected as the setting from which to identify mentor-participants for this study (Populations: Fredericton 85,688; NB 753,914). The mentor pool comprised current/retired business owners from the Chamber of Commerce.

Purpose

The purpose of this study was to examine the practices of mentors who successfully mentored immigrant entrepreneur newcomers. The specific aims were to: (a) understand how mentors guide their mentees through manifold and varied demands to enhance the inter-cultural mentoring efforts and strategies of mentors and mentees; (b) inform practitioners (mentors/mentees) on the utility of the efforts of inter-cultural mentoring; and (c) further inform mentoring programme developers and managers who oversee ICM programmes.

Sample

A purposeful sampling strategy was adopted (Creswell, 2003) to uncover practices critical to inter-cultural mentoring. Five mentors from the BIMP programme, who were reported as 'high-caliber' by the BIMP administrator, were recruited to the study. Mentors were well established locally and provincially, either born in New Brunswick, Canada, or who had lived in the province for several decades; and been mentors in the programme for several years, some participants had returned after taking a short break.

Method

Qualitative data were collected through semi-structured interviews with open-ended questions. This study utilized self-reporting, employing a quantitative instrument, a retrospective survey questionnaire and qualitative, one-on-one interviews. Interviews provided data that explained and enhanced quantitative findings. All participants participated in face-to-face interviews at locations of their choice. Both paper survey and face-to-face interview were administered at the same session in June 2015, lasting between one and a half to two hours. This approach gave voice to what matters to mentors and why. Hearing the mentor testimonies permitted access to descriptions and personal viewpoints creating context and elaborating on or extending quantitative results. An in-depth understanding was sought in an effort to extract a 'thick description' (Denzin, 1989, p. 83), one that went below surface-level and captured nuances beyond readily observable phenomena.

Analysis

A qualitative analysis was appropriate and drew on testimonies of participants, providing insight into personal viewpoints and meanings attached to participants' experiences (Merriam, 1988). A process of inductive analysis identified themes important to participants, uncovered patterns that connected said themes, and created coded categories for the purpose of organization (Creswell, 2003). Analysis began at the point of data collection. The author wrote memos, recorded, and tracked analytical insights that emerged from interview data.

Design and instruments

Quantitative data were collected via a paper survey with Likert questions, as well as yes/no, radio and free text questions. There were seven sections in the survey relating to:

1 Demographics
2 Mentor perceptions
3 Meeting activities with mentee
4 Meeting logistics
5 Inter-cultural and learning matters
6 Concluding questions related to the programme
7 Summary Question: 'So, why do you bother? Is it worth the effort? What makes it worth the effort?'

Interviews were digitally recorded and explained. They expanded upon the survey data and questions and were embedded in a conversational interview approach (Patton, 2002). Thematic questions asked of mentors were:

1 What challenges do immigrant mentees and local mentors face concerning mentoring?
2 What extent does mentoring contribute to the success of newcomer immigrant entrepreneurs?
3 What challenges do mentors face with mentoring?
4 What gets in the way of/supports mentoring relationships?
5 What factors positively/negatively influence inter-cultural mentoring?

FINDINGS

Seven themes emerged from this study that directly influence the quality of ICM relationships: (a) mentees' culture; (b) mentors' cultural self-awareness; (c) significance of relationality and accessibility; (d) sponsorship (connection and protection); (e) listening and the art of asking questions; (f) racism; and (g) small town truths. Each theme is discussed below after the sample is described.

Sample description

The five mentors interviewed for this study were at the following stages in their careers: retired business owner ($n = 1$); current business owner and national trade association president ($n = 1$); retired business owner and executive director of a non-governmental organization ($n = 1$); and current business owner ($n = 2$). One mentor was from a first generation immigrant family of entrepreneurs who was an entrepreneur himself.

Mentee's culture

Mentors unanimously recounted episodes of bafflement and frustration, amusement and wonder brought on by their own flawed assumptions of sameness or ignorance of difference. Stereotypes were present in all relationships and were best discussed and exposed. Mentors were eager for material that captured the essence of differences. Mentors who had even basic cultural fluency reported the profound influence it had on their ability to adjust expectations, emotional reactions, and coping strategies.

> I used to get so frustrated with some of the Korean people, because I just didn't understand. I used to say 'Could you just tell me what you're trying to say? I mean what you're really really trying to say'. Then I was given the book *Korea Behind the Mask*. It was like the sun came out. WOW. Now I understand the importance of cultural context.

Mentors, on the whole, reported that even limited inter-cultural understanding helped provide more than a respectful nod to differences. Retrospectively, mentors related stories of how cultural understanding deepened their capacity to address the significance of cultural or worldview differences that they encountered; whereas prior to this mentors may have paid lip service to such pain points due to inexperience or may have even missed them all together.

> When I look back, I suppose, the more I knew about a culture the better the relationship… those relationships were deeper, more effective, and certainly more productive.

Cultivate cultural self-awareness

Mentors reported that when they began mentoring newcomer immigrants they did not overly value their own culture, nor did they recognize the importance of understanding their own culture. As one mentor reported:

> While at home [in Canada] we are often blind to ourselves and our own culture.

Because of these relationships, mentors began to examine their own personality, cultural traits, and worldviews. Over time mentors reported that the effort to know oneself offered the, often unexpected, capacity to understand others better.

> I'm a funny guy, but I've learned to put that aside – well at least until I know [my mentee] better and have a sense how they might take it. I do this to make them comfortable… and so that I'm not spending all my time explaining my jokes. These sessions need to be about them. You have to be self-aware regarding which of your *traits* will benefit them, when.

Building relationality and accessibility between mentor and mentee

Mentors unanimously reported that mentees routinely doubted the expressed and good intentions of mentors and that building a deep relationship had its obstacles. In the words of one mentor, 'trust is a major, major hurdle'.

> Some mentees would look at me and you can tell they are thinking 'Why are you so friendly? What do you want from me?' On occasion, I've actually came right out and said, 'Man, you have nothing I could possibly want, so don't worry about that… ask around'. I know it sounds rude, but sometime it's best to address the elephant in the room and to explain where we're coming from. We're excited to have these new people here and want them to stay, settle, grow our population, and become part of our city.

Each mentor was asked what was essential to building trust and relationality with newcomer mentees. Their answer was, unequivocally, *time*.

> First, you don't buy trust with a latte; it takes more than the occasional coffee. Only time can buy trust… That and I tell them to ask around; to ask a variety of people about me. Really, check around and find out what I'm about. Oh, and if you try to move too fast before you establish trust there's a real risk that you'll scare them away.

According to several mentors, 'just knowing the mentor is not enough'. Mentees need 'to get to know the individual behind the mentor in order to build trust'. Conversely, it's important that mentees know that mentors see them as more than just a 'business'. To that end, one mentor approached relationship building thus:

> I want them to 'meet me where I'm at', so I invited them over for a bonfire by the river. We're a musical family, so we get out our guitars and really enjoy the evening. Sometimes [mentees] think it's like a fairytale and well, it is in a way. And that's what they signed up for in small town Canada, but there'll be other things they're giving up and I like to have conversations about that as well. This transition must be really hard for them and I want them to know I'm trying to get that ... this is the stuff that these relationships are made of.

Mentors reported that they made real efforts to make mentees feel secure.

> Once trust is in 'play' and after [mentees] believe that you're not going to send them back then you're 'in'. That's when the relationship really changes. That's when we can 'get down to brass tacks'. That's when we can really start building their future here.

Seize opportunities for sponsorship: connection and protection

Some mentors depicted mentoring as a unique personal relationship, characterized by trust and the sharing of expertise and moral support. As one mentor put it:

> I feel like my mentees are, to a degree, in my care. I would deliberately take them to events and also attend business events that they were going to be at so that I could introduce them around. I acted as a bit of a filter; I wanted to protect them and make sure that the people they were meeting were reputable.

Another mentor summed up this point succinctly; after all, 'it's not what you know but who you know!'

> Knowing who not to call and who to avoid is as important as knowing who to call!

One mentor recounted how he counseled his mentees to approach locals:

> I advise my mentees to speak first. Just try your best and go for it! I tell them that if they do they'll find an awful lot of people eager to talk to them. I tell them that in my opinion, the locals aren't engaging you because they don't know if you speak English and they wouldn't want you to feel awkward, so just go ahead.

One mentor clearly stated a thought mentioned by other mentors, 'Creating a new network from scratch is tough; many [mentees] are unsure how to get out of the starting gate'.

> You're as much a resource person as you are a mentor; you're a bridge. You try to match up mentees with resources in the community. It's not always easy, but it's essential to be persistent.

Mentors suggested that modeling was important: 'It's important for them to see how other people relate to you... and how you do it... how you network and connect with people'. Most mentors reported that they knew they were being watched by their mentees – that they were modeling local practices and social norms for their mentee.

> I know that they watch you pretty closely and that they are trying to figure things out. What I do is to try to help them fit in. I monitor their confidence levels and bring them along in the conversation when it will help or jump in when it's called for. I want them to know I have their back.

Another mentor liked to arrive at events with his mentees to further support the mentees networking and acculturation efforts.

> It must be hard – hard and exhausting to be so new. Given that, I go with my mentees [to networking events] and I introduce them around then back off and watch. Then I shadow them a bit… that way I know if they need some help. The language can be tricky for some…. I also bring them along with me a bit as I'm networking so they can see how I interact with people and how people respond to me. Seeing how others respond to me seems to be important [to them]. It also helps with trust building.

When asked about how many connections he had helped his mentee to make, one participant responded:

> Subject matter experts and professionals I can count, beyond that the people I introduced my mentees to – well, that's countless. I also try to introduce them to communities like church organizations or sports teams. That can take some of the pressure off the mentor, and then they come to think 'wow I'm actually starting to fit in around here'. Or they say things like, 'it's crazy how approachable people are around here'. You know funerals and weddings are often the last local activities newcomers are invited to – so when appropriate I take [mentees] with me. Now around here those can be real cultural experiences!

Create deep learning: the importance of listening and the art of asking questions

Mentoring isn't about answering questions, a longtime BIMP mentor and wise entrepreneur reported, 'It's about asking questions – me asking mentees those questions they are on the cusp of asking themselves'.

> It's important to engage [my mentees] in conversations beyond business. They need to know that you see the full range of their identities: husband/wife, father/mother, past careers, hobbies, and so on. As a mentor, I try to get to their personal stories and share some of mine. It gives me insights into their strengths and weaknesses, and frames what they value and the skill sets they're bringing with them.

Mentors were, on the whole, pragmatic and spoke to the importance for both parties to know how the other works best – is it from doing, watching, listening, or from experimenting with new knowledge and subjects? One mentor reported that he felt the best approach was:

> To learn and then to guide [mentees] based on what you learned from them. It took me a while to figure this out… And then even longer to really know how to get them to open up. I've come to understand that you have to learn to *be slow to speak and quick to listen*… Becoming a good mentor takes time.

After what mentors referred to as 'good' mentoring sessions (one that incorporated more listening than speaking) mentors often acknowledged that they had a fuller understanding that, '[m]entees are burdened not only by the demands of creating a business, but also with the pressures of home, culture, and language intersecting in every mentees' life'.

> I haven't just become more culturally aware, I've become better at listening.
> 'You said this, but what are you really saying?'
> … You learn to listen not just to words but to everything.

When asked what the biggest ICM challenge was one mentor chimed in with, 'Did NOT listen!' Another mentor summed it up:

You make suggestions and the mentee nods and then they just go and do it their own way anyway. Almost every mentor will tell you that… There is a lot at stake, so we have to be careful of how we talk and what we say. In some cases it's their whole life savings that are on the line here!

According to another mentor,

[s]ome [mentees] think that they're smarter than we are – and I'm sure they are in some ways – but I know the terrain here… I'd like them to not necessarily do what I say, but when I offer advice I'd like them to at least take the time to check it's credibility. Sadly, over the years, we've seen some really poor business moves on the part of mentees – in spite of being forewarned! It's both heartbreaking and, as a mentor, discouraging… There's a bit of a challenge transitioning from being 'the nice guy' to 'the credible guy'.

> When [mentees] don't seriously explore the advice we give. When I say – think twice about buying that business, it may not be a good idea and then the next time we meet they've purchased it – an old haggard business that's turned over like 11 times. It's really discouraging! You try to help them avoid the minefields, the pitfalls.

Awareness of racism

Most mentors did not specifically use the word racism but did allude to 'unusual' challenges mentees sometimes came up against and to 'ignorant' people. Similarly, mentees were not overly explicit when they spoke with mentors about pernicious verbal and non-verbal encounters (Reeves, 2014a). Mentors were incensed by 'unwelcoming' behavior.

> Know if they're ignorant to you they're ignorant to everyone. They're just nasty. [If they act like that then] they're no friend of mine and you don't need them as one either!

Mentors wanted to 'get-in-on-this', in other words, ensure that their mentees weren't going to face this problem alone. Mentors weren't going to take any 'bullshit' from anyone and their mentees weren't either.

> Ask me the questions you're scared to ask? If odd things are going on you need to tell me. You live here now and we look out for each other here.

Appreciation of small-city realities

According to mentors many mentees struggled to both reconcile and internalize the implications of demographic and geo-social changes after moving to a SMC. According to one mentor:

> Many [mentees] come to a smaller city as much for a lifestyle change as anything, and while I know that, I try to remember that that doesn't necessarily make it any easier.

Mentors understood the importance of informing mentees about 'the good and the bad – the *ying* and the *yang*… [t]o a certain degree, small towns can be closed, and it can make it difficult. I try to help them navigate that'. Mentors, reported that '[t]hey're not always happy stories' with regard to retention and entrepreneurial successes. Interestingly, mentors reported that 'among their mentees who left many still stay in touch and in some ways [I think] still wish they could have made a go of it here'.

> I'm more aware of their difficulties integrating into a city that is known for being closed. It's made me more aware of the stumbling blocks. Overall, I have more of an understanding of what it takes for someone to pick up and come here, settle, and set up a business.

Mentors endeavoured to interpret small-city living for mentees: 'We're small so it's about who you know – you need a circle both to get things done and to build up a customer base'. Elaborating that 'the "locals" have roots, very deep roots through family, employment, or experience or whatever; they want to know about you and your connections to the community'. Under these conditions the support of a mentor can be critical.

> Around here when you do good business you make a living and you make friends. If you do it right you're looked on in a good light and develop a good reputation – here your reputation really means a lot.

DISCUSSION

There is a dearth of literature about what good mentors of immigrant newcomer mentee entrepreneurs in SMCs need to know. The themes identified above advance our understanding of the mentors' role in supporting newcomer immigrant entrepreneur mentees in SMCs. Overall, the findings offer insights into the behaviors involved in successful mentoring of newcomer immigrant entrepreneurs. Discussed below are the seven elements, as reported by mentors, that have direct implications for the quality of ICM relationships: (a) mentees' culture; (b) mentors' cultural self-awareness; (c) significance of relationality and accessibility; (d) sponsorship (connection and protection); (e) listening and the art of asking questions; (f) racism; and (g) small town truths. Each offering, from the mentor's perspective, more understanding of microprocesses that can be further distilled into: lifelong learning; social wealth; and small town survival skills.

Learning for life in our times

In relationships working from an initial position of difference, mentors emphasized the importance of dialogue regarding their unique backgrounds, interests, personalities, goals, and experiences. In other words, foundational to the creation of meaningful relationships is sensitivity to one's own and to others' culture/worldviews. Mentoring has taken education beyond formal training to embrace social learning arrangements. These arrangements assist information seekers to capitalize on the highly valuable, but often difficult or inaccessible, tacit knowledge that is accessible though conversation.

Further, high-level LMX relationships result in greater access to resources (Dansereau et al., 1975). Findings in this study corroborate claims that questions and conversations, geared toward understanding culture, worldviews, networks, and relationality, matter in that they are necessary for accessing both tacit and explicit knowledge that exist outside formal institutional learning. Still, mentors in this study expressed a high level of frustration over 'not being listened to'. Mentors recounted both their own stories of 'warnings' or advice gone unheeded by mentees and a plethora of stories they had heard from other mentors. Nevertheless, to newcomer mentees, mentors are often considered a natural resource. Mentors are veritable wells of information, resources, and experience for their mentees regarding the introduction to and familiarization with their new environment – an environment that consists of unwritten rules, conventions, norms, and practices that are not readily accessible to newcomers, who often lack invaluable connections and resources (Reeves, 2014b; Reeves, in press).

The results of this study captured challenges in effective, culturally sensitive mentoring. Mentors may possess inadequate knowledge about culture-specific challenges immigrant newcomers might encounter, including incidences of stereotyping, discrimination, and racism. Racism is subtle, hidden, and layered, and is perniciously perpetuated through discourse practices that include formal and informal policies; verbal, non-verbal, and written practices; and what is said and especially what is not said or practiced. Stanley (2012), defines racism as racializations that lead to exclusions with significant negative consequences for the excluded. When racism is combined with other barriers the result for immigrant newcomers can be double or triple jeopardy.

According to Este et al. (2012), experiences of racism can be

> compounded when those in power ignored problems of racism, or condoned unfair treatment... Through deliberate ignorance or condemnation of systemic and individual expressions of racism, those in leadership positions send the message that they supported, or did not care about, how people of colour and other marginalized groups were treated. (p.42).

There are many theories as to why groups perceive discrimination; however, when examined thoroughly, the evidence supports the case that discrimination is perceived because discrimination exists (Burke Wood and Wortley, 2010). In fact, empirical evidence indicates that discrimination may be an important force behind large and persistent disparities between migrant and non-migrant populations (OECD, 2008).

Who you know and how they help

Results showed the importance of building high-value relationships influenced by relationality and accessibility. Trust and relationship building are mentoring practices that have been found to be essential to dyad success (Hu et al., 2008; Frels and Onwegbuzie, 2012). The importance of building relationality and accessibility is echoed from a LMX perspective, when individuals receive quality support and care from, in this case, mentors, they reciprocate thus creating high-value, positive relationships founded on mutual trust between the mentor and mentee.

The perspectives and practices delineated here indicated that relationships were strengthened by sponsorship, exhibitions of public support, and that LMX relationships are advanced by meaningful communication (Graen et al., 1982). The interpersonal relationship generated by successful mentoring powerfully facilitates not just learning and moral support, but, equally important for entrepreneurs, access to networks. Mentors' Rolodexes or networks have the capacity to enhance the mentee's social capital and opportunities to network with people who may be able to help them meet their goals (Reeves, 2014b; Reeves, under review).

Moreover, mentor-driven networks may develop trust between members and redefine self-interest to consider the group as a whole, a key factor in high-yielding LMX relationships. Members may then choose to expand their identity to gain access to benefits. The development of trust within and among networks further encourages access to benefits through the promotion of resource exchanges (Besser and Miller, 2011). Existing scholarship that has examined immigrant retention rates illustrates the importance of connection; those least involved in structured groups and/or organizations are the most likely to move. *Movers*, those who leave within the first two years, participate in roughly half as many different types of groups or organizations (45%) as compared to stayers (81%) (Ramos and Yoshida, 2011). Newcomer immigrants who feel isolated and lack a sense of belonging are most at risk of leaving.

You're not from around here

The perks of living in a small town or SMC range from a stronger sense of community, to low property costs and taxes, to reduced crime rates. However, there are drawbacks to being in a SMC. Attributable not only to demographic differences but also geo-social changes, newcomer mentees may struggle to reconcile and adapt after moving to a SMC, thwarting retention and integration goals. Small and medium sized cities may be distinguished by their amenities – usually in the form of natural resources and space (mountains, lakes, rivers, beaches, wide open spaces) – and safety. The implications of the cultural dimensions can be neglected by mentors. Little is known about the social inclusion of immigrant newcomers nor the conditions under which immigrants thrive in SMCs (Ramos and Yoshida, 2011). Complexity is an inevitable feature of moving to a SMC and is, to varying degrees, different from what one might experience when moving to a metropolis (Reeves, 2014b; Reeves, in press).

CONCLUSION

Culturally competent mentoring may play a significant role in the acculturation and business success of immigrant newcomers. The question of how immigrant mentors perceived the diverse meanings of inter-cultural mentoring – or, more specifically, what skills and/or competencies were beneficial to the dyad – is an important one. The answers provide direction for future mentors, mentees, and organizations interested in enhancing inter-cultural mentoring efforts, and are relevant in a time of increasing migration, human resource transformation, flux, and globalization.

Mentoring is increasingly influenced by dissimilar worldviews. It is less and less a race-free or culture-free venture and warrants additional study. The participants in this study were positive and dedicated mentors, committed to creating an inter-cultural mentoring environment and who reported stories of programme impact and many successful mentoring relationships. The mentors' impressions and implications for practice suggest that powerful developmental, learning, and trusting relationships are frequent and attainable. The distinctive characteristics of mentoring in inter-cultural contexts included mentor participants' notions of mentoring and expanded the two functions traditionally used in mentoring studies (career versus psychosocial) to include being a role-model and the mentor as guide. Results also highlighted the importance of: cultural and worldviews; reflection; relationality and accessibility; the importance of listening and asking thoughtful and strategic questions; the dominance of psychosocial support for racialized newcomer immigrants to SMC; and the importance of local context. Moreover, this study highlights the central importance of facilitating personal learning/knowledge transfer, programme replication, retention, acculturation, and adaptation.

These results offer insights into inter-cultural mentoring for newcomer immigrants. Findings may spark interest for the future study of inter-cultural youth and faculty-student mentoring programmes, as well as expatriate mentoring efforts – all areas in need of targeted research. A contribution of this research is the expansion of mentoring research into the inter-cultural arena.

REFERENCES

AlMazrouei, H. and Pech, R.J. (2014). Expatriates in the UAE: Advance training eases cultural adjustments. *Journal of Business Strategy*, *35*(3), 47–54.

Askins, K. (2014). *Being together: Exploring the West End Refugee Service Befriending Scheme. Project Report*. Northumbria University, Newcastle-upon-Tyne. Retrieved on 21 September 2016 from http://eprints.gla.ac.uk/99205/1/99205.pdf

Besser, T.L. and Miller, N. (2011). The structural, social, and strategic factors associated with successful business networks. *Entrepreneurship & Regional Development*, *23*(3–4), 113–33.

Brenner, G.A., Menzies, T.V., Dionne, L., and Filion, L.J. (2010). How location and ethnicity affect ethnic entrepreneurs in three Canadian cities. *Thunderbird International Business Review*, *52*(2), 153–71.

Burke Wood, P. and Wortley, S. (2010). AlieNation: Racism, injustice and other obstacles to full citizenship. CERIS - Metropolis Centre, Working Paper No. 78. Retrieved on 21 September 2016 from http://search.library.utoronto.ca/details?9034857&uuid=cef94c98-0a85-440e-b1a7-d98da0cfbd35

Carraher, S.M., Sullivan, S.E., and Crocitto, M.M. (2008). Mentoring across global boundaries: An empirical examination of home- and host-country mentors on expatriate career outcomes. *Journal of International Business Studies*, *39*(8), 1310–26.

Castles, S. and Miller, M. (2009). *The age of migration*, (4th ed.). Basingstoke: Palgrave Macmillan.

Chan, D. (2008). So why ask me? Are self-reported data really that bad? In L.E. Charles and J.V. Robert (Eds.), *Statistical and methodological myths and urban legends: Received doctrine, verity, and fable in the organizational and social sciences* (pp. 309–35). New York: Routledge.

Chandler, D.E., Kram, K.E., and Yip, J. (2011). An ecological systems perspective on mentoring at work: A review and future prospects. *The Academy of Management Annals*, *5*(1), 519–70.

Coleman, D. (2013). Immigration, population and ethnicity: The UK in international perspective. *The Migration Observatory*. Retrieved from http://migrationobservatory.ox.ac.uk/briefings/immigration-population-and-ethnicity-uk-international-perspective

Creswell, J.W. (2003). *Research design: Qualitative, quantitative, and mixed methods approaches* (2nd ed.). Thousand Oaks, CA: Sage.

Dansereau, F., Graen, G.B., & Haga, W. (1975). A vertical dyad linkage approach to leadership in formal organizations. *Organizational Behavior and Human Performance*, *13*, 46–78.

Denzin, N.K. (1989). *Interpretive interactionism*. Newbury Park, CA: Sage.

Dimitrov, N. (2009). *Western guide to mentoring graduate students across cultures*. The University of Western Ontario, Teaching Support Centre. London, Ont.: University of Western Ontario. Retrieved on 21 September 2016 from https://www.uwo.ca/tsc/faculty_programs/pdf/PG_3_MentoringAcrossCultures.pdf

Eskicioglu, P., Halas, J., Sénéchal, M., Wood, L., McKay, E., Villeneuve, S., Shen, X., Dean, H., and McGavock, J.M. (2014). Peer mentoring for type 2 diabetes prevention in First Nations children. *Pediatrics*, *133*(6), 1624–31.

Este, D., Thomas Bernard, W., James, C.E., Benjamin, A., Lloyd B., and Turner, T. (2012). African Canadians: Employment and racism in the workplace. *Canadian Diversity/Diversité Canadienne*, (9)1, 40–3. Retrieved on 21 September 2016 from http://www.metropolis.net/pdfs/Diversite_Racism_2012_ACS.pdf

Faustino, G. (2014). *The role of the e-mentor in the social construction of knowledge in a cross-cultural learning environment*. (Doctoral dissertation). University of New Mexico. Division of Educational Leadership and Organizational Learning. Retrieved on 21 September 2016 from http://hdl.handle.net/1928/24246

Frels, R.K. and Onwegbuzie, A.J. (2012). The experiences of selected mentors: A cross-cultural examination of the dyadic relationship in school-based mentoring. *Mentoring and Tutoring: Partnership in Learning*, *20*(2), 181–206.

Gerstner, C.R. and Day, D.V. (1997). Metaanalytic review of leader-member exchange theory: Correlates and construct issues. *Journal of Applied Psychology*, *82*, 827–44.

Graen, G.B., Liden, R., & Hoel, W. (1982). Role of leadership in the employee withdrawal process. *Journal of Applied Psychology*, *67*(6), 868–872.

Hu, C., Thomas, K.M., and Lance, C.E. (2008). Intentions to initiate mentoring relationships: Understanding the impact of race, proactivity, feelings of deprivation, and relationship roles. *The Journal of Social Psychology*, *148*, 727–44.

Keller, T. and Dansereau, F. (1995). Leadership and empowerment: A social exchange perspective. *Human Relations*, *48*(21), 127–46.

Kent, A., Kochan, F., and Green, A.M. (2013). Cultural influences on mentoring programs and relationship. *International Journal of Mentoring and Coaching in Education*, *2*(3), 204–17.

Kervin, L., McMahon, S., O'Shea, S.E., and Harwood, V. (2014). *Digital storytelling: Capturing the stories of mentors in Australian Indigenous Mentoring Experience*. Retrieved from http://ro.uow.edu.au/sspapers/1264/

Kochan, F.K. (Ed.) (2002). *The organizational and human dimensions of successful* mentoring programs across diverse settings. Greenwich, CT: Information Age Publishing.

Kochan, F.K. and Pascarelli, J.T. (Eds.) (2003). *Global perspectives on mentoring: Transforming contexts, communities, and cultures*. Greenwich, CT: Information Age Publishing.

Lechuga, V.M. (2011). Faculty-graduate student mentoring relationships: Mentors' perceived roles and responsibilities. *Higher Education*, 62(6), 757–71.

Liden, R.C., Sparrowe, R.T., and Wayne, S.J. (1997). Leader-member exchange theory: The past and potential for the future. *Research in Personnel and Human Resources Management*, 15, 47–119.

Lunsford, L.G. and Ochoa, E. (2014). Culture and Mentoring: Teacher Preparation in the U. S. Mexico-Borderlands. In F. Kochan, A. Kent, and A. Green (Eds.), *Uncovering the Hidden Cultural Dynamics in Mentoring Programs and Relationships: Enhancing Practice and Research* (pp. 211–28) Greenwich, CT: Information Age Publishing.

Mackinlay, E., Barney, K., and Creagh, S. (2014). Becoming, belonging and being in the profession: Evaluating a mentoring program for Aboriginal and Torres Strait Islander initial teacher educators. In *Refereed Papers Collection, ATEA 2014: Australian Teacher Education Association Conference*, 186–99.

Merie, K. (2015). *Resettlement and self-sufficiency: Refugees' perceptions of social entrepreneurship in Arizona*. (Masters Thesis, Arizona State University). Retrieved from http://repository.asu.edu/attachments/150573/content/Merie_asu_0010N_14874.pdf

Merriam, S.B. (1988). *Case study research in educations: A qualitative approach*. San Francisco: Jossey-Bass Publishers.

No-Gutiérrez, P., Rodríguez-Conde, M.A., Zangrando, V., Seoane-Pardo, A.M., and Luatti, L. (2014). Peer tutoring at school with migrant students: Intercultural mentoring programme. In *Proceedings of the Second International Conference on Technological Ecosystems for Enhancing Multiculturality (TEEM '14)*. Retrieved on 21 September 2016 from http://doi.acm.org/10.1145/2669711.2669943

OECD (2008). Ending job discrimination. OECD Policy Brief, https://www.oecd.org/els/emp/Ending-job-discrimination-2008.pdf

Omar, F. (2015). Building rapport between international graduate students and their faculty advisors: Cross cultural mentoring relationships at the University of Guelph. *Dissertations and Thesis*. Masters Thesis, The University of Guelph. Retrieved on 15 August 2016 from https://atrium.lib.uoguelph.ca/xmlui/handle/10214/8734?show=full

Patton, M.Q. (2002). *Qualitative research and evaluation methods*. Thousand Oaks, CA: Sage.

Pekerti, A.A., Moeller, M., Thomas, D.C., and Napier, N.K. (2015). n-Culturals, the next cross-cultural challenge: Introducing a multicultural mentoring model program. *International Journal of Cross Cultural Management* 15, 5–25.

Petrovic, M. (2015). *Mentoring practices in Europe and North America: Strategies for improving immigrants' employment outcomes*. Brussels Migrant Policy Institute.

Philippart, N. and Gluesing, J. (2012). *Global e-mentoring: Overcoming virtual distances for an effective partnership*. Paper presented at the ICIC, Bengaluru, India.

Price, M. and Chacko, E. (2009). The mixed embeddedness of ethnic entrepreneurs in a new immigrant gateway. *Journal of Immigrant & Refugee Studies*, 7(3), 328–46.

Purcell, G. and Scheyvens, R. (2015). International business mentoring for development: The importance of local context and culture. *International Journal of Training and Development*, 19(3), 211–22.

Rainoldi, M. and Gölzner, H. (2014). Mentoring across cultures: Implications in managing expatriates' acculturation. *Kommunikation in Change und Risk*, 18, 147–64.

Ramos, H. and Yoshida, Y. (2011). Why do recent immigrants leave Atlantic Canada? Working Paper Series 32. Atlantic Metropolis Centre. Retrieved on 21 September 2016 from http://community.smu.ca/atlantic/documents/RamosYoshidaFINALWP32.pdf

Rath, J. and Kloosterman, R. (2000). Outsiders' business: A critical review of research on immigrant entrepreneurship. *International Migration Review*, 34(3), 657–81.

Reeves, R.B. (2014a). Corporate mentorship: An article-based examination of corporate and cross-cultural implications for organizations, mentors and mentees. Doctoral dissertation, University of New Brunswick, https://unbscholar.lib.unb.ca/islandora/object/unbscholar%3A8033.

Reeves, R. (2014b). Factors that foster successful cross-cultural mentoring relationships for immigrant entrepreneurs: An in-depth analysis. In F. Kochan, A. Kent, and A. Green (Eds.), *Uncovering the hidden cultural dynamics in mentoring programs and relationships: Enhancing practice and research* (pp. 79–101). Greenwich, CT: Information Age Publishing.

Reeves, R. (2015). What is cross-cultural mentoring? An integrative literature review and discussion of the term cross-cultural mentoring. *International Journal of Coaching and Mentoring. XIII*,(1), March.

Reeves, R. (in press) Inter-cultural mentoring for newcomer immigrants: Mentor perspectives and better practices. *International Journal of Evidence Based Coaching and Mentoring.*

Scandura, T.A. and Pellegrini, E.K. (2007). Workplace mentoring: Theoretical approaches and methodological issues. In T.D. Allen and L.T. Eby (Eds.), *Handbook of mentoring: A multiple perspective approach* (pp. 71–91). Malden, MA: Blackwell.

Scandura, T.A. and Schriesheim, C.A. (1994). Leader-member exchange and supervisor career mentoring as complementary constructs in leadership research. *Academy of Management Journal, 37*, 1588–602.

Schultz-Nybacka, P. and Sjödin, U. (forthcoming). Swedish mentors for immigrant entrepreneurs. In *Möjligheternas marknad: Om företagare med utländsk bakgrund, Tillväxtverket*. Retrieved on 21 September 2016 from http://www.snee.org/filer/papers/603.pdf

Staff (2013). Explainer: Why the Canada-EU trade deal will affect almost every industry. *The Globe and Mail*, October 18. http://www.theglobeandmail.com/news/politics/explainer-why-the-canada-eu-trade-deal-will-affect-almost-every-industry/article14937574/

Stanley, T. (2012). Analyzing racism in the Workplace. *Canadian Diversity/Diversité Canadienne* (9)1, 53–6.

St-Jean, E. and Audet, J. (2013). The effect of mentor intervention style in novice entrepreneur mentoring relationships. *Mentoring & Tutoring: Partnership in Learning, 21*(1), 96–119.

United Nations (2013). *Trends in international migrant stock: The 2013 revision – migrants by age and sex.* Department of Economic and Social Affairs, Population Division, United Nations database, POP/DB/MIG/Stock/Rev.2013/Age.

Race, Gender and Mentoring in Higher Education

Deirdre Cobb-Roberts, Talia Esnard,
Ann Unterreiner, Vonzell Agosto,
Zorka Karanxha, Makini Beck and Ke Wu

Women of color are increasingly represented, but often silenced, in academe. Institutions must therefore respond to the changing landscape by implementing programs and fostering climate that promote faculty success (Shollen et al., 2008). Mentoring that specifically caters to the needs of women faculty from different racial backgrounds can be an alternative to traditional mentoring practices that center on senior versus junior members of faculty, whether same race or across different racial groups. A focus on mentoring between women faculty across different races can support the development of intellectual, cross-cultural connectedness, as well as cultural and social capital within the group of participants (Agosto et al., 2016; Esnard et al., 2015; Johannessen and Unterreiner, 2010; Stanley, 2006; Turner et al., 2008). This line of mentoring research therefore seeks to unpack the complex web of relationships that are afforded to women faculty and the processes by which women of color benefit from mentoring across race, gender, institutions, cultures, time, and disciplines. While many scholars declare that there is risk associated with open discussions of social differences (i.e. race, culture, ethnicity), we support the position that such discussions are critical, not only for building cross-racial interactions (which can later transform into effective cross-cultural mentoring relationships), but also for providing relevant practices and ideas for traversing academia (Chan, 2008; Clutterbuck, 2007; Crutcher, 2007).

The increasing attention and advancing research related to cross-racial mentoring among women faculty provides deeper insights into the ways in which race and gender intersect to frame the networking and mentoring relationships that affect their professional experiences and journeys. What is required at this point, however, is a thorough examination of recent literature on mentoring among women faculty of color that moves such discussions beyond the identification of the problem; that is, the isolation and discrimination of women in higher education, to an exploration of emerging mentoring structures and processes that can support and advance not only their career in academe but also their successful negotiation of the complexities of such contexts. The purpose of this chapter therefore is to identify themes and gaps in the literature related to the question: How are women faculty of color mentoring and being mentored? This qualitative review presents a metasynthesis of the literature on mentoring among women faculty of color in higher education, with specific attention to the strengths, weaknesses, and controversies in the literature; an examination that points to avenues for future research.

THEORETICAL FRAMEWORK

The framework guiding this meta-synthesis is positionality theory. Positionality theory was conceptualized in the late 1980s and early 1990s and represents an addendum to standpoint theory (Harding, 1991) and, with more recent moorings of feminist standpoint theory (Harding, 2004) and Black feminist standpoint theory (Collins, 2000a). This particular theory was employed based on its focus on the individual, her position within the network (academy), and the collective effect on experiences and perceptions within the network (Cooks, 2003; Harley et al., 2002; West-Olatunji et al., 2010). From this framework, one's 'position' and his/her related experiences are tied to three major components: intersecting identities; power relations; and situational contexts (Kezar and Lester, 2010). The nature and dynamics of this position form the basis of a person's perceptions and experiences. A major premise of this theory is that the complexity of an individual's position impacts how they socially construct the world and adopt multiple identities as a response to these interpretations.

This framework allows one to examine the extent to which these perceptions and understandings of the shifting nature of one's positionality shape complex experiences for women faculty. Specifically, this framework centers on underrepresentation, marginality (based on the intersecting nature of gender, race, and ethnicity), relations of power, social interaction, multiple and complex identities, and the importance of networks as a critical source of empowerment in such contexts. Where women of color remain silenced in Predominantly White Institutions (PWIs) (Allen et al., 2004; Turner et al., 2008), such an examination can make apparent the ways in which they respond to continuous marginalization, construct their academic identities around these experiences and, more importantly, negotiate their positionality within such contexts.

MENTORING AND WOMEN FACULTY

Establishing a scholarly identity along with acclimating to a university culture are just a few of the challenges faced by early career faculty women in general and more specifically by women of color (Austin et al., 2007; Mullen and Forbes, 2000; Stanley and Lincoln, 2005). Where such institutional cultures within higher education can become highly politicized or exclusive (Allen et al., 2004; Stanley and Lincoln, 2005; Tillman, 2011), mentoring can provide the necessary support to advance and sustain the professional careers of women academics (Driscoll et al., 2009; Guise et al., 2012; Holmes and Terrell, 2004; Mullen, 2005). Variations within mentoring structures and their effects on the professional careers of women of color however remains a major contention in the literature. Below, therefore, we discuss research on two broad categories of literature on mentoring; traditional or dyadic mentoring; and mentoring of women of color.

Traditional mentoring

Traditional mentoring, in a US context, refers to a one-to-one hierarchical relationship in which there is a more experienced faculty member who functions as a guide, a model, a system of support, or a 'leader' to a less experienced person (Davis et al., 2011; Evans and Cokley, 2008; Jones and Osborne-Lampkin, 2013). Despite claims of the utility of the approach and its adaptation to various structures (formal, informal, face-to-face, online, short or long term) and functions over time (from career related to provision of social support), this form of traditional mentoring has been, and continues to be, critiqued in terms of its effectiveness or lack thereof, particularly for the career advancement of women of color. While there is a body of research that points to the importance of the relationship between mentor and protégé to the success of the marginalized scholar (Blake, 1999; Smith and Davidson, 1992), a growing number of researchers question the hierarchical and/or unidirectional nature of this process. Wherein a person of higher rank guides, instructs, leads, and facilitates the professional and personal development of White and, to a lesser extent, marginalized women faculty of color operating in Predominately White Institutions (Allen et al., 2008; Driscoll et al., 2009; Holmes et al., 2007). This type of mentoring often undermines the development of professional relationships and the provision of social support designed to secure the success of participating marginalized racial and gendered groups (Fries-Britt, 2000; Gaff et al., 2000). Where race and gender add to the dynamics of power relations inherent in traditional mentoring, many scholars have increasingly focused on emerging mentoring practices that center on the needs and experiences of women of color (Darwin and Palmer, 2009; Driscoll et al., 2009; Turner et al., 2008).

Mentoring among women of color

Over the past decades, non-traditional mentoring practices have materialized to address the mentoring needs and experiences of women faculty of color (Davis et al., 2012; Gregory, 2001; Johnson-Bailey and Cervero, 2004; Tillman, 2001, 2011). Mentoring among women of color in higher education, the structures they create and the processes that guide their activities remain underexplored. Scholars thus call for more holistic interrogations of experiences that capture the complexities and paradoxes of mentoring practices that specifically address their collective impact on the professional needs and situations of women of color in academia (Jean-Marie and Brooks, 2011; Johnson-Bailey and Cervero, 2008). These include, but are not limited to: (a) essential dimensions of mentoring among women of color (Barker, 2007; Gregory, 2001; Stanley, 2006); (b) explorations of contextual and relational processes that affect successful networking within this framework (Driscoll et al., 2009; Stanley and Lincoln, 2005), and; (c) the social relations tensions inherent in such mentoring networks which could affect productive outcomes (Esnard et al., 2015). Averting relational tensions within mentoring relationships involving women faculty from different racial and cultural backgrounds may require 'trust, honesty, a willingness to learn about self and others and the ability to share power and privilege' (Stanley and Lincoln, 2005, p. 46); other scholars make the case for ongoing discussions that also center on the structural, cultural, and discursive barriers to mentoring across racial groups (Meyer and Warren-Gordon, 2013; Shollen et al., 2008).

As a recently formed global cross-racial network of women faculty – specifically, Afro-Caribbean (2), Asian (Chinese), Caucasian, African American, Latina and Montenegrin from the United States and the Caribbean –

we see this review of existing research as critical to the advancement of research, the formation of viable and sustainable mentoring practices for women of color in academe and, by extension, the opening up of related professional possibilities. It is important to note that our use of the term women of color is part of a American framework that may not be recognized in other parts of the world (three group members were either born, raised and/or currently live outside of the United States). Women of color refers to any woman who is not White, acknowledging a common experience of racism in the United States. We limited our focus to mentoring among women faculty of color in higher education.

METHODS

This qualitative systematic review is a descriptive meta-synthesis of 22 academic journal publications from an eleven year period (2004–15) on the specific topic of mentoring among women of color in higher education. With the exception of one article, which problematized the experiences of women of color in Britain and Canada, all other scholarly papers accessed were based on research conducted in the United States. We used meta-synthesis to integrate results/findings from studies that focused on similar or connected topics or events (Thorne et al., 2004), in this case, mentoring between and among women faculty from different racial backgrounds. This remains a growing research field and this review points to the parameters that frame research in this field, and provides guidelines for future research on mentoring among women of color.

Process, exclusion/inclusion criteria

Our three-step process began in 2013 and concluded in 2015. In the first step, we listed key search terms that matched the research objectives of this meta-synthesis. We limited our search criteria to mentoring among women of color who were faculty members (regardless of discipline, institution, or geographic space).

During step one, our team searched ERIC, Google scholar and available institutional databases within our network (e.g. University of Montana, University of South Florida, University of Trinidad and Tobago, Villanova University) that provided access to prominent scholarly publications. All databases were utilized for their extensive repository of scholarly work in the area. From this process, we gathered a sample of 89 publications, which included journal articles, book chapters, books and dissertations. These publications were interdisciplinary, with articles that spanned areas such as education, social, legal and medical studies.

In step two, we evaluated the suitability of the 89 publications by applying exclusion/inclusion criteria at the level of title and abstract. Through a three-paired group system, we read and evaluated the publication abstracts to determine whether they were scholarly and met the search word criteria. From this paired process, team members engaged in a wider discussion with the group of six members to justify the choices for inclusion or exclusion. From this method, we subsequently reduced our initial sample of 89 works to 22 and removed all dissertations, books, book chapters, non-peer reviewed articles, and pamphlets.

In step three, we returned to the shortlisted articles and engaged in a more thorough, systematic and critical review of them. Within our paired group, we read each article, paying attention to patterns that emerged from the comparison of: (a) methods; (b) theoretical framework; (c) discipline; (d) findings; and (e) recommendations across the articles distributed to each group. During this paired process of critical analysis, we used memoing, diagramming and reflection on the data as a systematic approach to an examination of existing literature (Finfgeld-Connett, 2014). We employed Noblit and Hare's (1988) three stages to conducting a meta-synthesis: (a) reciprocal stage, recognizing themes and ideas; (b) refutational stage, recognizing themes that contradict the common themes and ideas; and (c) line of argument, constructing a summarizing argument of findings. This process allowed for the development of themes to be interpreted in relation to the framework on the positionality of women of color and the complexities that shape their responses.

FINDINGS

Our meta-synthesis aimed to understand the nature and extent of scholarship on the mentoring experiences of women of color in higher education. Four major themes emerged as part of this meta-synthesis: (a) the centrality of race and gender; (b) institutional contexts that affect the mentoring opportunities and practices of women of color; (c) the use of alternative types of mentoring (co-mentoring, peer mentoring, feminist mentoring, structured formal mentoring), and informal networks to advance their careers, and; (d) the importance of psycho-social support throughout the development of alternative mentoring structures and processes. All these themes were based on a qualitative review of the 22 articles.

Theme 1: Centrality of race and gender

Nineteen of the articles reviewed highlighted the centrality of race and gender to the marginalized experiences of women of color. Scholars commonly acknowledged: (a) the added complexities and tensions that race and gender bring to traditional mentoring; (b) the ineffectiveness of traditional mentoring as it relates to changing the marginalized positionalities of women of color; (c) the need for alternative structures and mentoring practices that address their cultural and institutional needs; and (d) the importance of assessing the implications of these emerging mentoring structures to the experiences and professional advancement of women of color. Of note however, were eight articles that advanced the need for continued interrogations of the ways in which the intersection of race and gender directly affects the mentoring process and/or experience of women of color, rather than just generalized experiences in academia (Blood et al., 2012; Davis et al., 2011; Holmes et al., 2007; Behar-Horenstein et al., 2012; Johnson-Bailey and Cervero, 2004, 2008; Jones and Osborne-Lampkin, 2013; Meyer and Warren-Gordon, 2013). In this regard, some researchers called on others to question monolithic notions of women of color while exploring related racial and sexualized experiences that complicate their professional networking and collaborative experiences.

Theme 2: Institutional mentoring context

Institutional contexts and dynamics also emerged as key areas in the literature on mentoring among women of color (Blood et al., 2012; Buzzanell et al., 2015; Davis et al., 2011 and 2012; Fries-Britt and Kelly, 2005; Johnson-Bailey and Cervero, 2004; Kent et al., 2013; Meyer and Warren-Gordon, 2013). One major starting point for researchers was the need for mentors to recognize the ways in which interracial dynamics embedded in organizational cultures silences the racial and ethnic peculiarities of mentees (Holmes et al., 2007). A few ($n = 3$) articles for instance, presented the notion of the diversity expert and/or Black Tax in the case of African American women, or the Cultural Tax in the case of women faculty from different ethnic backgrounds – as a demonstration of the negative ways in which closed cultures can affect the experiences of women faculty of color (Evans and Cokley, 2008; Meyer and Warren-Gordon, 2013; Shollen et al., 2008).

Where such practices become institutionalized and affect the power relations that define the formal mentoring experiences and identities of women of color, researchers contended that senior faculty must become culturally sensitive (Behar-Horenstein et al., 2012; Johnson-Bailey and Cervero, 2004; Shollen et al., 2008) to promote more authentic dialogue and collaboration between women faculty of different racial backgrounds (Stanley and Lincoln, 2005).

Theme 3: Alternative forms of mentoring

Ten of the articles reviewed celebrated the collaborative and collegial benefits of peer, co-mentoring and feminist mentoring as variations of informal networking (Chesney-Lind et al., 2006; Fries-Britt and Kelly, 2005; Jones and Osborne-Lampkin, 2013). These networks (or their structural variations) are collectively assessed as self-sustaining, trusting, motivating, validating, and seen as a safe haven (Davis et al., 2011 and 2012; Holmes et al., 2007; Jones and Osborne-Lampkin, 2013; Sorcinelli and Yun, 2007). A central focus for much of this literature therefore was the impact of alternative structures and processes in network formation and functionality on the shifting positionality of women in these networks and the related effect on their professional outcomes.

Peer mentoring relationships, for instance, were described as mentoring among faculty who share equal stature, similar interests, and/or occupy similar positions (Bottoms et al., 2013; Edmonson, 2012; Esnard et al., 2015; Fries-Britt and Kelly, 2005; Holmes et al., 2007; Jones and Osborne-Lampkin, 2013). In these cases, examinations offered needed insights into the utility and effectiveness of peer mentoring as a valid alternative to traditional or more hierarchical mentoring structures and approaches. As Bottoms and colleagues (2013) argued, peer mentoring can play an important role not only in the creative integration of social, personal and professional experience, but also in the development of supportive mechanisms that can address the diverse needs of faculty at various points of their academic trajectories.

The co-mentoring model is another structural alternative that rejects the inherent hierarchy of traditional mentoring. Described as an egalitarian model in which each participant has the opportunity to contribute to the growth of the other participant (Chesney-Lind et al., 2006; Holmes et al., 2007), this model is therefore a catalyst for ensuring mutual learning and empowerment based on accepted systems of social engagement within the group. For at least seven articles, this form of empowerment and more flexible relational processes sought to fill the void, particularly for women of color faculty in PWIs, when others within their academic community did not recognize their professional and/or institutional value (Davis et al., 2012; Fries-Britt and Kelly, 2005).

An extension of co-mentoring can be rooted in a feminist tradition that rests on an equal balance of power. This approach also acknowledges the emotional aspect of being an academic and the valuing of paid and unpaid work. The notion of unpaid work in this case is critical as the literature speaks to the nurturing roles that female faculty are often expected to play without professional reward (Diggs et al., 2009; Shollen et al., 2008). The characteristics of feminist mentoring explicate the importance of collaborative allies who: work at the margins with momentum; fight systems of oppression and relations of power; and recognize the significance of the personal and professional stance on the political impact of their roles and experiences in the academy (Chesney-Lind et al., 2006; Cowin et al., 2012). These scholarly pieces also center on the importance of reciprocity rather than deprivation, insofar as these related studies reject the assumption that the mentee/protégé is not in a position to do or provide anything for the senior person, as the mentee is too new and inexperienced (Holmes et al., 2007). The latter speaks to and calls into question a patriarchal and an Anglo-protestant ideology view of mentoring that is generally accepted within higher education and which initially banned women from educational participation at all levels. Where such questioning remains an ongoing part of the literature on mentoring among women faculty of different racial backgrounds, it brings into disrepute the discursive contexts that frame traditional mentoring in higher education. It also strengthens the inherent calls for the continued exploration of alternative frameworks that cater specifically to the professional needs of women of color who are continually marginalized in this process.

Theme 4: Psycho-social support

A fourth theme was the importance of shaping relevant and effective forms of psycho-social support for mentees in cross-racial relationships. Researchers who focused on this theme contended that both mentor and mentee can become victims of socially ingrained biases that operate at an unconscious level (Shollen et al., 2008). Two primary examples of which were: situations when the racialized and gendered nature of mentoring experiences framed the professional identities of women of color (Diggs et al., 2009); and when mentees were not being mentored, or being mentored inadequately, or where their work was devalued by being viewed as race work (Buzzanell et al., 2015; Evans and Cokley, 2008).

As part of rethinking the dynamics of psycho-social support and avoiding the negative effects of opposition rather than support (Behar-Horenstein et al., 2012; Cowin et al., 2012; Edmonson, 2012; Evans and Cokley, 2008; Shollen et al., 2008), scholars pointed to the need for:

1. open spaces of participation that increase, in more tangible ways, the prospects for tenure and promotion of women faculty of color (Behar-Horenstein et al., 2012; Cowin et al., 2012; Evans and Cokley, 2008; Shollen et al., 2008);
2. the need for greater collegiality and trust that can lead to the development of more positive professional identities (Edmonson, 2012; Fries-Britt and Kelly, 2005; Jones and Osborne-Lampkin, 2013; Simon et al., 2008);
3. relevant socialization processes (Jones and Osborne-Lampkin, 2013) that are capable of shifting the physical/cultural barriers to effective cross-race mentoring (Behar-Horenstein et al., 2012; Chesney-Lind et al., 2006; Diggs et al., 2009; Holmes et al., 2007; Shollen et al., 2008); and
4. reconfiguration of mentoring structures that allow for the development of formal or informal forms of networking and the professional career advancement of women of color (Davis et al., 2011 and 2012; Fries-Britt and Kelly, 2005; Holmes et al., 2007; Jones and Osborne-Lampkin, 2013). One such case was Sisters of the Academy (SOTA), designed to support and enhance the academic careers of Black women in higher education (Davis et al., 2011).

DISCUSSION

Much of the research centered on the need to recognize the ways gender and race intersect to shape the often silenced position of women of color in academe. As part of such related discussions, existing studies captured the role of gender and race in the creation and sustenance of structural, cultural, and social barriers to participation in formalized/institutionalized contexts. Many scholars highlighted the institutional and stratified contexts wherein women faculty of color strives to advance their professional careers and identities. Important aspects of such related discourses and examinations were: the culturally embedded, institutionalized, racialized, and gendered nature of power relations; the stifling and disempowering effects of such processes; and the collective weight of both on the professional trajectories of women of color. A central point within this related discourse was the need for and possibilities of cultural sensitivity moving beyond these structured and stratified limitations that exist even within multicultural institutional contexts. However, what remains clear is that more exploration is needed of the complexities that frame these contexts and how they intersect with gendered realities. For example, one shortfall in this literature on institutional contexts is the inability of existing studies to link these institutionalized experiences to the personal or familial challenges that women face. Advancing the field will require a deeper interrogation of demographics or personal factors related to family commitments (children), number of children, age of children, age of academic mothers and rank within the organization. Addressing these related contexts and lived experiences of women in academia may add to our understanding of the multifaceted realities that define their professional lives, practices, and trajectories.

Another theme identified was ineffective practices in traditional mentoring for women of color. A consensus that emerged from the literature was the ineffectiveness of traditional mentoring for dealing with issues of diversity within institutionalized workforces and the need for continuous reassessments of the mentoring structures and processes that women of color interact with, and the ways in which these interactions meet their professional and personal needs over time. This rethinking might include more pointed questioning of the ways in which race, ethnicity, positionality, power, institutional, or organizational cultures deny women access to existing mentoring programs and, by extension, impact the mentoring practices, beliefs and experiences of women in academia (Johnson-Bailey and Cervero, 2004, 2008; Meyer and Warren-Gordon, 2013).

At a practical level, our findings also revealed that examinations of cross-racial mentoring centered on the need for more flexible structures and functions that can advance the professional identities and needs of women of color. Specifically, scholars presented peer mentoring, co-mentoring, and feminist mentoring as emerging structures that can cater to the scholarly and professional needs of women of color. There is a need to revisit the role of the mentors and to embrace more open or flexible social support systems that can enhance the psycho-social and career related roles of mentors and, by extension, the success of women of color who are being mentored in the process. However, we observed that such examinations lacked any substantive description and analysis of the inherent dynamics that underlie supporting women of color and how these addressed the cultural peculiarities of the group. Where mentoring is an intricate dynamic dictated by institutional culture, personality, and competencies (Behar-Horenstein et al., 2012), we advocate the need for additional empirical research that also addresses the dynamics of negotiation, role of history, the relevance of contemporary racial and cultural protocols, collaborative practices among racially diverse colleagues, and the collective impact of these dynamics on academic performance, experience, and success.

Conceptually, cross-racial mentoring is presented as a desirable structural and epistemological alternative to traditional mentoring for women faculty of color. In the literature, cross-racial mentoring specifically refers to mentoring among women of color, regardless of discipline or institution and who are working with other women of color and/or White women or men. While mentoring cross-racially may occur within traditional mentoring structures and practices, the use of cross-racial mentoring in the literature suggests a deliberate focus on the nuances of mentoring cross-racially and the use of these racial and cultural differences in the practices and scholarly agenda within such groups. In so doing, our review showed that scholars frequently and synonymously used cross-racial and cross-cultural mentoring. Thus, what resulted was a blurring of these constructs as was the case in 22 of the reviewed journal articles (see Table 23.1) where there was little articulation of their distinctions and the independent effects of these factors on the professional outcomes of marginalized groups. This synonymous use of cross-racial and cross-cultural was problematic for conceptualizing, understanding and, by extension, measuring these two constructs. In exploring cross-cultural as opposed to cross-racial mentoring, Johnson-Bailey and Cervero (2004) offered a distinction through their story of the ways in which their cross-racial collaboration (between a Black and a White academic) specifically addressed the racial and cultural nuances that shaped their perception of each other and, inadvertently, their collaborative experiences. In this case, such recognition and interrogation of their racial and cultural differences paved the way for more productive collaborations that moved beyond their cultural and racial peculiarities. They thus define cross-cultural mentoring as a relationship that exists between people who are regarded as unequal 'on a hostile American stage' (p. 11), with a societal script that has been created to undermine the success of the cross-racial partnership. The dyad therefore is one of novice authority versus mentor credibility (Cowin et al., 2012), where trust and the ability to accept constructive critiques on issues related to race, gender, class, marginality, and discrimination remain critical. Despite this attempt to clarify these constructs, their blurring remains prevalent in the literature. This points to the need for clearer articulations of how these concepts differ and are related. Advancing this research field would therefore require some consideration of these aforementioned conceptual issues and the ways in which mentoring among cross-racial groups, or in this specific case women of color, can translate into cross-cultural practices where the emphasis is on the deliberate examination of cultural/racial histories and its implications for mentoring.

Methodologically, our findings show that this examination of cross-racial mentoring benefits from a rich diversity of research techniques, such as critical ethnography, surveys, counter storytelling, scholarly personal narrative, self-study, narrative analysis, focus group interviewing, literature review, autoethnography, thematic analysis, and mixed methods. The qualitative studies reviewed were cross-sectional. Thus, it is unknown how these mentoring approaches might change over time. Longitudinal studies, measuring the impact of emerging mentoring approaches for cross-race mentoring might help us know more about these changes. While we do not discount the value of such qualitative studies and we acknowledge the contribution of the qualitative literature on cross-racial mentoring for women faculty, it does not erase the need for the application of varying methodological and analytical approaches. The broadening of research methods may identify converging evidence of these practices in the examination of cross-racial mentoring at wider institutional and informal levels. We maintain that the work on cross-racial mentoring is not static but reflects a dynamic and ongoing process that evolves in response to the many unmet needs of women faculty of color. We therefore call for further deepening of such understandings through the continued application of these varied methodological approaches and extended timelines for actual observations of these practices.

CONCLUSION

Stanley and Lincoln (2005) posit that mentoring involves an invitation, a willingness to give and encourage and the perception of confidence and competence to create a mentoring relationship, and a mutual decision to participate. For women of color, traditional mentoring does not meet these mandates. Our meta-synthesis highlighted alternative forms of mentoring that were flexible enough to develop a spirit of collaboration and

Table 23.1 Articles reviewed for meta-synthesis

Themes*	Author(s) & Date	Journal	Methods	Findings
1, 2, 4	Beher-Horenstein, West-Olatunji, Moore, Houchen, & Roberts, 2012	Florida Journal of Educational Administration & Policy	Critical ethnography, case study	Mentors should be culturally competent and have an awareness of the systemic challenges faced by culturally diverse faculty. Informal mentoring beyond the borders of the academic unit is beneficial.
2	Blood, Ulrich, Hirschfeld-Becker, Seely, Connelly, Warfield, & Emans, 2012	Journal of Women's Health	Survey research	Mentoring gaps were addressed. Mentoring should be incorporated into the job expectation increasing the likelihood of successful relationships. Further, race was an important criterion in selecting a mentor.
3	Bottoms, Pegg, Adams, Wu, Smith-Risser, & Kern, 2013	Mentoring & Tutoring: Partnership in Learning	Narrative inquiry	Informal peer mentoring communities can play an important role in the mentoring of diverse faculty through multiple transitions.
1, 2, 4	Buzzanell, Long, Andeson, Kokini, & Batra, 2015	Management Communication Quarterly	Feminist postructural narrative	Feminist postructural accounts of women of color in engineering highlights the needs and frustrations that accompany the master narrative of mentoring. Further, more inclusion of women of color in STEM academic works space is important.
1, 3, 4	Chesney-Lind, Okomoto, & Irwin, 2006	Critical Criminology	Reflective inquiry on feminist mentoring	Feminist and multicultural mentoring involves: collaboration, relationships and political edge.
1, 3, 4	Cowin, Cohen, Ciechanowski, & Orozco, 2012	Journal of Education	Portraiture self-study of mentoring relationships	Mentees found the mentoring relationship beneficial in supporting their writing growth and in negotiating the emotional turbulence in their contexts.
1, 2, 3, 4	Davis, Chaney, Edwards, Thompson-Rogers, & Gines, 2012	The Negro Educational Review	Narrative inquiry	Findings revealed commonly derived benefits and program components through power and influence of mentoring affiliated with organized associations.
1, 4	Davis, Reynolds, & Jones, 2011	Florida Journal of Educational Administration & Policy	Narrative inquiry	Organized mentoring support for Black women tenure and tenure track faculty key strategies for productivity and expanding professional networks.
1, 2, 4	Diggs, Garrison-Wade, Estrada, & Galindo, 2009	Urban Review	Self-study	Formal and informal mentoring across racial lines was of value as a space for examining feelings and challenges for diversity contributions to institutional departments.
1, 3	Esnard, Cobb-Roberts, Agosto, Karanxha, Beck, Wu, & Unterreiner, 2015	Mentoring & Tutoring: Partnership in Learning	Narrative inquiry research	While productive orientations and shared experiences as women faculty of color promote supportive professional roles, the structural, relational and cultural dynamics subtly frame tensions.
1, 2, 3, 4	Evans & Cokley, 2008	Training and Education in Professional Psychology	Position article	Mentoring can enhance the career advancement of African American women faculty when being cognizant of the direct and indirect effects of sex and race on this group.
1, 4	Edmondson, 2012	Gender in Management: An International Journal	General review	Suggested tips for navigating challenging circumstances: seek feedback from white faculty; don't ignore feedback; observe how admin treats your peer coach; don't force friendships; adjust communication; take inventory of successes and failures.

(Continued)

Table 23.1 (Continued)

Themes*	Author(s) & Date	Journal	Methods	Findings
1, 2, 3, 4	Fries-Britt & Kelly, 2005	Urban Review	Narrative inquiry research	Peer mentoring of African American women and women of color fosters egalitarian dynamics, mutual empowerment and learning.
1, 3, 4	Holmes, Danley Land, and Hinton-Hudson, 2007	Negro Educational Review	Narrative research	Mentoring can increase black women's chances of success in academia and their tenure track transitions.
1, 2, 4	Johnson-Bailey & Cervero, 2004	Mentoring and Tutoring: Partnerships in Learning	Self-study	In a mentoring relationship of a Black woman and white male faculty, trust can overcome racism, invisibility and risk for minority women faculty. These components must be acknowledged if mentoring relationships are to be successful.
1, 3, 4	Jones & Osborne-Lampkin, 2013	Negro Educational Review	Qualitative interviewing	Mentoring community is valuable for Black women junior faculty advancement.
2	Kent, Kochan & Green, 2013	International Journal of Mentoring and Coaching in Education	Review of literature	Mentoring programs, although well meaning, may place mentees from traditionally excluded groups in a position that indicates to others they lack certain skills and knowledge. Cultural sensitivity and awareness is vital to successful mentoring.
1, 2, 4	Meyer & Warren-Gordon, 2013	The Qualitative Report	Autoethnography	Dysfunctional and negative mentoring experiences result in greater separation and seeking out of co-cultural challenges for minority faculty experiencing prejudice and discrimination in mentoring encounters.
1, 2, 4	Shollen, Bland, Taylor, Weber-Main, & Mulcahy, 2008	American Academic	Scholarly essay	Some criteria for mentoring women of color in faculty careers are: trust, open communication, encouragement, respect and egalitarian power relations. Further limited cultural taxation on minority faculty and pressures for being the representative diversity member of committees.
3	Sorcinelli & Yun, 2007	Change	Review of publications on mentoring	Mentoring is a vital contribution to academic careers for women and faculty of color. Further engaging in broader and more flexible mentoring networks are sources of great support.
1, 4	Simon, Roff, & Perry, 2008	Journal of Social Work Education	Survey research	Black female social work leaders provided more psychosocial and career mentoring support than they received as students and early faculty. Further least amount of support given to them was balancing family and career and they replicated this behavior.
1, 2	Stanley & Lincoln, 2005	Change	Scholarly essay	Cross-race mentoring is challenging for both mentor and protégé. The lessons learned from cross-race mentoring lead towards robust learning and higher education needs to pay closer attention to those on the margins.

*1 Centrality of race and gender; 2 institutional mentoring context; 3 alternate forms of mentoring; 4 psychosocial support synergy; which were continually negotiated and renegotiated across boundaries, peers, and institutions. Alternative mentoring, co-mentoring, feminist mentoring, structured formal mentoring, and informal networks are thus presented as important mentoring alternatives that may help retain women and minority faculty members, as they are greatly underrepresented in academia (Fries-Britt and Kelly, 2005; Holmes et al., 2007; Shollen et al., 2008). These are presented within a rich variation of qualitative approaches that are strong on the critique of traditional mentoring and the impact of alternative structures and practices that enhance their professional trajectories.

However, many gaps remain in the research. One major gap is the lack of clarity between what is cross-racial mentoring and what is cross-cultural mentoring. While a few scholars attempt to distinguish between the two constructs, much more application of this distinction is needed in the advancement of this research field (Crutcher, 2014; Johnson-Bailey and Cervero, 2004). Further discussions are needed around intersectionality that might extend our understanding beyond the traditional Black-White dyad and the ideology of privileging race over gender, or gender over race. Exploring multiple marginalities (i.e. class, sexual identity, religion) and other women of color across different disciplines would enhance the discussion of the relevance and importance of cross-racial mentoring within the academy.

Relatedly, there is a need for future scholars to develop and advance existing theoretical and methodological frameworks to analyze the nuanced mentoring experiences of women of color in cross-racial and cross-cultural relationships. The current literature delineates the importance of cross-racial mentoring but does not fully explicate how this type of mentoring will be accomplished, evaluated for effectiveness, or what spaces will be carved out for cross-racial and cross-cultural mentoring, and by whom? It is vital to acknowledge the tenets of power and positionality in any analysis that investigates cross-racial and cross-cultural mentoring. It is important to concede that the same constraints and systems of power, oppression, and imbalance can plague mentoring relationships. Thus, the quality, nature, and intent of the mentoring relationship should be investigated, as well as the institutional environment. Black feminist thought (Collins, 2000b), critical race feminism (Wing, 1997), LatCrit (Bernal, 2002), TribalCrit (Brayboy, 2005), and AsianCrit (Liu, 2009), as theoretical lenses may further ameliorate the issues and intersections associated with cross-cultural mentoring, along with its benefits and challenges.

We also insist that the emerging trends, foci, gaps, and directions for future research may be addressed when: (a) cross-racial mentoring is moved from the margins to the center of mentoring; (b) the intersections of race, gender, and culture are further interrogated; (c) there is some recognition that cross-racial mentoring has challenges that need to be fleshed out, and that; (d) some reenvisioning of the mentoring practices of diverse faculty within higher education can aid in the process. We call for future research agendas to explore the role of culture, dialogue, cultural sensitivity, and culturally based mentoring programs for the successful outcomes of cross-racial mentoring. Such explorations may have benefits for women of color who work in highly specialized fields (i.e. law, medicine, administration) and who continue to be underrepresented, in comparison to the general population.

REFERENCES

Agosto, V., Karanxha, Z., Unterreiner, A., Cobb-Roberts, D., Esnard, T., Wu, K., and Beck, M. (2016). Running bamboo: A mentoring network of women intending to thrive in academia. *NASPA Journal about Women in Higher Education,* 9(1), 74–89.

Allen, T. D., Eby, L. T., Poteet, M. L., Lentz, E., and Lima, L. (2004). Career benefits associated with mentoring for proteges: A meta analysis. *Journal of Applied Psychology*, 89(1), 127–36.

Austin, A. E., Sorcinelli, M. D., and McDaniels, M. (2007). Understanding new faculty background, aspirations, challenges, and growth. In R. P. Perry and J. C. Smart (Eds.), *The scholarship of teaching and learning in higher education: An evidence-based perspective* (pp. 39–89). Netherlands: Springer.

Barker, M. (2007). Cross-cultural mentoring in institutional contexts. *Negro Educational Review*, 58(1/2), 85–103.

Behar-Horenstein, L., West-Olatunji, C., Moore, T., Houchen, D., and Roberts, K. (2012). Resilience post tenure: The experience of an African American woman in a PWI. *Florida Journal of Educational Administration & Policy*, 5(2), 58–67.

Bernal, D. D. (2002). Critical race theory, Latino critical theory, and critical raced-gendered epistemologies: Recognizing students of color as holders and creators of knowledge. *Qualitative Inquiry*, 8(1), 105–26.

Blake, S. (1999). At the crossroads of race and gender: Lessons from the mentoring experiences of professional Black women. In Audrey J. Murrell, Faye J. Crosby, and Robin J. Ely (Eds.), *Mentoring dilemmas: Developmental relationships within multicultural organizations* (pp. 83–104). Mahwah, NJ: Lawrence Erlbaum Associates.

Blood, E. A., Ullrich, N. J., Hirshfeld-Becker, D. R., Seely, E. W., Connelly, M. T., Warfield, CA., and Emans, S. (2012). Academic women faculty: Are they finding the mentoring they need? *Journal of Women's Health*, 21(11), 1201–8. doi:10.1089/jwh.2012.3529

Bottoms, S., Pegg, J., Adams, A., Wu, K., Smith Risser, H., and Kern, A. L. (2013). Mentoring from the outside: The role of a peer mentoring community in the development of early career education faculty. *Mentoring & Tutoring: Partnership in Learning*, 21(2), 195–218.

Brayboy, B. M. J. (2005). Toward a tribal critical race theory in education. *The Urban Review*, 37(5), 425–46.

Buzzanell, P. M., Long, Z., Anderson, L. B., Kokini, K., and Batra, J. C. (2015). Mentoring in academe: A feminist poststructural lens on stories of women engineering faculty of color. *Management Communication Quarterly* 29(3), 440–57.

Chan, A. W. (2008). Mentoring ethnic minority, pre-doctoral students: an analysis of key mentor practices. *Mentoring & Tutoring: Partnership in Learning*, 16(3), 263–77.

Chesney-Lind, M., Okomoto, K. S., and Irwin, K. (2006). Thoughts on feminist mentoring: Experiences of faculty members from two generations in the academy. *Critical Criminology*, 14(1), 1–21.

Clutterbuck, D. (2007). An international perspective on mentoring. In B. R. Ragins and K. E. Kram, *The Handbook of Mentoring at Work: Theory, research, and practice*, (pp. 633–56). Thousand Oaks, CA: Sage.

Collins, P. H. (2000a). Gender, black feminism, and black political economy. *The Annals of the American Academy of Political and Social Science*, 568(1), 41–53.

Collins, P. H. (2000b). What's going on? Black feminist thought and the politics of postmodernism. *Working the ruins: Feminist poststructural theory and methods in education*, (pp. 41–73). New York, NY: Routledge.

Cooks, L. (2003). Pedagogy, performance, and positionality: Teaching about whiteness in interracial communication. *Communication Education*, 52(3–4), 245–57.

Cowin, K., Cohen, L., Ciechanowski, K., and Orozco, R. (2012). Portraits of mentor–junior faculty relationships: From power dynamics to collaboration. *Journal of Education*, 192(1), 37–47.

Crutcher, B. N. (2007). Mentoring across cultures. *Academe-Bulletin of the AAUP*, 93(4), 44.

Crutcher, B. N. (2014). Cross-cultural mentoring: A pathway to making excellence inclusive. *Liberal Education*, 100(2), 26.

Darwin, A., and Palmer, E. (2009). Mentoring circles in higher education. *Higher Education Research & Development*, 28(2), 125–36. doi:10.1080/07294360902725017

Davis, J., Chaney, C., Edwards, L., Thompson-Rogers, K., and Gines, K. (2011 & 2012). Academe as extreme sport: Black women, faculty development and networking. *The Negro Educational Review*, 62–3(1–4), 167–87.

Davis, D. J., Reynolds, R., and Jones, T. B. (2011). Promoting the inclusion of tenure earning Black women in academe: Lessons for leaders in education. *Florida Journal of Educational Administration & Policy*, *5*(1), 28–41.

Diggs, A. G., Garrison-Wade, F. D., Estrada, D., and Galindo, R. (2009). Smiling faces and colored spaces: The experiences of faculty of color pursuing tenure in the academy. *Urban Review*, *41*(4), 312–33.

Driscoll, L. G., Parkes, K. A. Tilley-Lubbs, G. A., Bril, J. M., and Bannister, V. R. P. (2009). Navigating the lonely sea: Peer mentoring and collaboration among aspiring women scholars. *Mentoring & Tutoring: Partnerships in Learning*, *17*(1), 5–21.

Edmonson, V. C. (2012). Reflections from a Black female in the promotion and tenure process. *Gender in Management: An Interdisciplinary Journal*, *27*(5), 331–45.

Esnard, T., Cobb-Roberts, D., Agosto, V., Karanxha, Z., Beck, M., Wu, K., and Unterreiner, A. (2015). Productive tensions in a cross-cultural peer mentoring women's network: A social capital perspective. *Mentoring & Tutoring: Partnership in Learning*, *23*(1), 19–36.

Evans, G. L., and Cokley, K. O. (2008). African American women and the academy: Using career mentoring to increase research productivity. *Training and Education in Professional Psychology*, *2*(1), 50–7.

Finfgeld-Connett, D. (2014). Use of content analysis to conduct knowledge-building and theory-generating qualitative systematic reviews. *Qualitative Research*, *14*(3), 341–52.

Fries-Britt, S. (2000). Developing support networks and seeking answers to questions. in M. Garcia (Ed.) *Succeeding in an academic career: A guide for faculty of color*, (pp. 39–56). Westport, CT: Greenwood Press.

Fries-Britt, S., and Kelly, B. T. (2005). Retaining each other: Narratives of two African American women in the academy. *The Urban Review*, *37*(3), 221–42.

Gaff, J. G., Pruitt-Logan, A. S., and Weibl, R. A. (2000). Building the faculty we need: Colleges and universities working together. Retrieved from http://www.preparing-faculty.org/ExecutiveSum.pdf (accessed 27 September, 2016).

Gregory, S. T. (2001). Black faculty women in the academy: History, status, and future. *The Journal of Negro Education*, *70*(3), 124–38.

Guise, J. M., Nagel, J. D., and Regensteiner, J. G. (2012). Best practices and pearls in interdisciplinary mentoring from building interdisciplinary research careers in Women's Health Directors. *Journal of Women's Health*, *21*(11), 1114–27.

Harding, S. 1991. *Whose Science? Whose Knowledge?* Ithaca, NY: Cornell University Press.

Harding, S. G. (2004). *The Feminist Standpoint Theory Reader: Intellectual and Political Controversies.* New York: Routledge.

Harley, D. A., Jolivette, K., McCormick, K., and Tice. (2002). Race, class, and gender: A constellation of positionalities with implications for counseling. *Journal of Multicultural Counseling and Development*, *30*(4), 216–23.

Holmes, S. L., Land, L.D., and Hinton-Hudson, V. (2007). Race still matters: Considerations for mentoring Black women in academe, *Negro Educational Review*, *58*(1–2), 105–29.

Holmes, S. L., and Terrell, M. C. (Eds.) (2004). Lifting as we climb: Mentoring the next generation of African American student affairs administrators [Special Issue]. *National Association of Student Affairs Professionals Journal* *7*(1), 1–134.

Jean-Marie, G., and Brooks, J. S. (2011). Mentoring and supportive networks for women of color in academe. In G. Jean-Marie and B. Lloyd-Jones (Eds.), *Women of color in higher education: Changing directions and new perspectives* (pp. 91–108). United Kingdom: Emerald Group.

Johannessen, B. G., and Unterreiner, A. (2010). Formal and informal mentoring for the 21st century. *Education and Society*, *28*(3), 31–49.

Johnson-Bailey, J., and Cervero, R. M. (2004). Mentoring in black and white: The intricacies of cross-cultural mentoring. *Mentoring and Tutoring: Partnerships in Learning*, *12*(1), 7–21.

Johnson-Bailey, J., and Cervero, R. M. (2008). Different worlds and divergent paths: Academic careers defined by race and gender. *Harvard Educational Review*, *78*(2), 311–32.

Jones, T., and Osborne-Lampkin, L. (2013). Black female faculty success and early career professional development. *Negro Educational Review*, *64*(1–4), 59–75.

Kent, A. M., Kochan, F., and Green, A. M. (2013). Cultural influences on mentoring programs and relationships: A critical review of research. *International Journal of Mentoring and Coaching in Education*, *2*(3), 204–17.

Kezar, A., and Lester, J. (2010). Breaking the barriers of essentialism in leadership research: Positionality as a promising approach. *Feminist Formations*, *22*(1), 163–85.

Liu, A. (2009). Critical race theory, Asian Americans, and higher education: A review of research. *InterActions: UCLA Journal of Education and Information Studies*, *5*(2).

Meyer, M., and Warren-Gordon, K. (2013). Marginal mentoring in the contact space: Diversified mentoring relationships at a mid-sized midwestern state university (MMSU). *The Qualitative Report*, *18*(38), 1–18.

Mullen, C. A. (2005). *The mentorship primer*. New York, NY: Peter Lang.

Mullen, C. A., and Forbes, S. A. (2000). Untenured faculty: Issues of transition, adjustment and mentorship. *Mentoring & Tutoring: Partnership in Learning*. *8*(1), 31–46.

Noblit, G. W., and Hare, R. D. (1988). *Meta Ethnography: synthesizing qualitative studies*. Sage: Newbury Park.

Shollen, S. L., Bland, C. J., Taylor, A. T., Weber-Main, A. M., and Mulcahy, P. A. (2008). Establishing effective mentoring relationships for faculty, especially across gender and ethnicity. *American Academic*, *4*(1), 131–58.

Simon, C. E., Roff, L., and Perry, A. (2008). Psychosocial and career mentoring: Female African American social work administrators' experiences. *Journal of Social Work Education*, *44*(1), 9–22.

Smith, E. P., and Davidson, II, W. S. (1992). Mentoring and the development of African American graduate students. *Journal of College Student Development 33*(6), 531–9.

Sorcinelli, M., and Yun, J. (2007). From mentor to mentoring networks: Mentoring in the new academy. *Change*, November/December, 58–61.

Stanley, C. (2006). Coloring the academic landscape: Faculty of color breaking silences in predominantly white colleges and universities. *American Educational Research Journal*, *43*(4), 701–36.

Stanley, C. A., and Lincoln, Y. S. (2005). Cross-race faculty mentoring. *Change: The Magazine of Higher Learning*, *37*, 44–50.

Thorne, S. E., Jensen, L., Kearney, M. H., Noblit, G. W., and Sandelowski, M. (2004). Qualitative metasynthesis: Reflections on methodological orientation and ideological agenda. *Qualitative Health Research*, *14*(10), 1342–65.

Tillman, L. C. (2001). Mentoring African faculty in predominantly white institutions. *Research in Higher Education*, *42*(3), 295–325.

Tillman, L. C. (2011). Sometimes I've felt like a motherless child. In S. Jackson and R. G. Johnson III (Eds.). *The Black professoriate: Negotiating a habitable space in the academy* (pp. 91–107). New York, NY: Peter Lang.

Turner, C. S. V., González, J. C., and Wood, J. L. (2008). Faculty of color in academe: What 20 years of literature tells us. *Journal of Diversity in Higher Education*, *1*(3), 139–68.

West-Olantunji, C., Shure, L., Pringle, R., Adams, T., Lewis, D., and Cholewa, B. (2010). Exploring how school counselors position low income African American girls in mathematics and science learners. *Professional School Counseling*, *13*(3), 184–95.

Wing, A. K. (Ed.). (1997). *Critical race feminism a reader*. New York: NYU Press.

Mentoring Diverse Populations

Nora Dominguez and Faith Sears

INTRODUCTION

Diversity is something we all encounter, be it at school, the workplace, or in our day-to-day activities. Diversity is not an old concept, however our ways of mentoring diverse populations might be. Older, well-known mentoring practices, are now out of their depth, having been developed constructively for homogenous populations that no longer characterize most of the workforce. New techniques addressing the evolving and dynamic nature of the socio-cultural environment are needed in place of methods that fail to account for or encourage diversity.

Over the past 40 years an active pursuit of diversification, both in educational settings and the workplace, has taken place through equal opportunity decrees and socially responsible initiatives around the world (e.g. Affirmative Action Laws – US; Employment Equity – Canada; Positive Discrimination – UK). In the United States, implementation of these initiatives and laws have shaped a more socially diverse workforce, in which over half of human resources are composed of minorities, immigrants, and women. These changes have led to increased productivity, innovation, and economic success (Swart et al., 2015). Unfortunately, this trend of increased diversity has not spread to greater diversity at the C-suite or executive levels. It remains difficult to develop and attract talent from diverse populations and then usher them into middle management and leadership positions (Thomas, 2001).

Mentoring programs have also been implemented to support a more equal environment and maximize the benefits of diversity in educational and workplace settings. However, while mentoring programs have been proven to positively increase graduation rates in higher education (Johnson, 2007), personnel retention, and satisfaction in organizations (Hegstad, 1999; Jossi, 1997; Murray, 2001), such programs seem to fail to promote the advancement of women and underrepresented minorities (URMs) into leadership and executive roles (Ragins, 1989; O'Neill, 2002). Scholars argue that these phenomena are the consequences of inadequate support and a lack of knowledge regarding diversified, cross-cultural mentoring relationships, in which mentors and mentees differ on the basis of race, ethnicity, gender, sexual orientation, disability, religion, socio-economic class, educational background, or other group memberships associated with power in organizations (O'Neill, 2002; Ragins, 1997, 2002a, 2002b, 2010).

New practices are needed to deal with the reality of an increasingly diverse workforce. Different groups of underrepresented mentees may have needs that are often unrecognized by teachers, managers, and leaders from majority populations. In this chapter we explore techniques in talent management and diversity training to satisfy the needs of mentors and mentees in diversified mentoring relationships. A particular focus remains on strategies that support the advancement of mentees who are traditionally underrepresented in executive and leadership positions. We begin with a targeted literature review that summarizes the challenges for the advancement of women, URM, and Lesbian, Gay, Transgender, Bisexual, and Queer (LGTBQ) populations. Next, we highlight diversity driven strategies that might improve our understanding of and effectiveness to deliver diversified mentoring relationships. We conclude with recommendations for future studies.

CHALLENGES FOR THE ADVANCEMENT OF WOMEN, URMS, AND LGTBQ POPULATIONS

Educational and income disparities

Diversity initiatives such as Affirmative Action in the United States, Employment Equity in Canada, and Positive Action in the United Kingdom, have existed for more than 45 years. In general, such initiatives were established to promote access to education, and equality in employment and pay for women and URMs. Despite these efforts educational and income disparities still prevail, because these initiatives are particularly 'ineffective at creating significant changes in gender balance at senior management and board levels in business and in government' (Swart et al., 2015, p. 203).

Despite having surpassed their male counterparts in the educational sphere, women find themselves on the wrong side of the gap that currently divides income based on gender. This is illustrated in part by the World Bank (2012), which found that 29% of post-secondary age youth were enrolled in tertiary education during 2010. Since 2000 average female enrollment in tertiary education has been higher than male enrollment (1.08 Gender Parity Index in 2010), with a female bias in all regions, except for South Asia and Sub-Saharan Africa. Despite increases in women's educational attainment, income disparities between males and females are prevalent in all regions, with a range from 8% in South Asian countries to 34% in Latin American countries. We could locate no global statistics for gender or racial/ethnicity disparities in attainment and/or income (IES, 2015; World Bank, 2012).

The United States, with higher levels of female participation in higher education than male, has mirrored global trends regarding the income gap between genders. During 2013 about one-third of the population completed tertiary education, but there were more women who did so (37% for females and 30% for males). Even though women make up the majority of the high-skilled workforce, there is a 26% gap in income between men and women. This gap affects females of all races/ethnicities, with a differential of 10% for Asian Americans and 46% for Hispanic/Latinas compared to the earnings of white men (IES, 2015; World Bank, 2012).

It is true that educational attainment has improved for minorities. Yet, there remain significant differentials in median annual earnings between people with less than high school completion and those with a high school diploma or who attained a bachelor's or higher degree were 25% and 109% respectively. When accounting for race, the income gap was even greater for African Americans (41%) and Hispanics (30%) (IES, 2015).

These statistics illustrate the inability of mentoring programs designed for academic success to translate that achievement into success in the workforce, especially for individuals who are commonly underrepresented. There is an assumption that mentoring programs have a positive impact on educational access, attainment, personnel retention and satisfaction in organizations for women, URMs, and LGTBQ populations (Hegstad, 1999; Johnson, 2007; Jossi, 1997; Murray, 2001), but that they fail to promote the advancement of women and underrepresented minorities to leadership and executive positions (Ragins, 1989; O'Neill, 2002) due to a lack of understanding of diversified mentoring relationships (O'Neill, 2002; Ragins, 1997, 2002, 2010). Therefore a better understanding of the dynamics of mentoring relationships must be forged through the exploration of specific needs and challenges documented in the literature for mentoring these particular populations.

Mentoring women

Despite progress in North American and European countries 'women still feel blocked, and a critical mass [in leadership positions] has not yet been achieved' (Swart et al., 2015). Many mentoring programs fail to meet the needs of female mentees when they do not adjust for gender-related needs, such as women's accounted difficulty in attaining positive mentors, career success, and other equality issues (Noe, 1988). Researchers report that women require support in: attaining sponsorship; identifying and overcoming barriers to their success; and advancing to leadership positions (Giscombe, 2007; Jonsen et al., 2010; McKeen and Bujaki, 2007). Furthermore, studies report underlying causes such as: low assertiveness, invisibility, lack of clarity, and other cultural obstructions (Janjuha-Jivraj, 2011); gender stereotypes (Jonsen et al., 2010); and hurdles like work/family conflict, lack of experience, and exclusion from networks (Giscombe, 2007). Barriers are often subtle rather than overt – for example a woman who is expecting a child may inadvertently be blocked from certain opportunities due to her anticipated maternity leave (Clutterbuck and Ragins, 2002b) – and are therefore difficult to identify.

According to McKeen and Bujaki (2007), seasoned mentors can help women to identify these problems early on in their careers. Mentors can facilitate the development and implementation of a plan of action by addressing key success factors and strategies to overcome barriers to success that are specific to their gender, contextualized as follows: 'A trusted guide, sponsor, and interpreter – a mentor – is critical to (a) assisting women in decoding the masculine culture in organizations, (b) promoting women's successful functioning and advancement in organizations, and (c) enhancing women's feelings of safety and belonging in such an environment' (p. 564).

Hewlett (2013) highlights the importance of having a champion in a senior position, an individual who effectively maneuvered the male dominated workforce and climbed the ladder of success is an example for women looking for career advancement. This technique, referred to as sponsorship, has gained importance for an individual's career growth and especially so for women who must also break through a 'glass ceiling', face stereotypes or overcome other gender-related barriers (Giscombe, 2007). Mentoring programs that provide sponsorship may help women gain recognition for their equal ability to contribute to their work environment and achieve success, as well as improve the confidence gap for women uncomfortable with self-promotion (Swart et al., 2015). Other women may find sponsorship helpful when experiencing the imposter syndrome (also called fraud syndrome), which refers to feelings and beliefs of being inadequate, incompetent, or inexperienced to hold a position, or undeserving of a promotion (Clance and Imes, 1978; Swart et al., 2015).

Support provided by trusted mentors can help manage these needs of women seeking career advancement by giving them access to internal networks, offering constructive feedback to increase their confidence, and promoting their visibility within the organization (Giscombe, 2007). There are, however, some behaviors that women should be aware of, including dysfunctional pairings, which result in harassment, exploitation, and sabotage, particularly when there is a large power differential between mentors and mentees. As a result, some female protégés may be apprehensive about becoming vulnerable by sharing their weaknesses with their male mentors, resulting in a less productive relationship with little psychosocial support (Clutterbuck and Richardson, 2014).

These problems can be addressed in different ways, one of which involves providing professional training for mentors and mentees that specifically addresses cross-gender strategies. Another approach is to expand the traditional dyadic relationship and embark on group mentorship, which reduces 'the likelihood of dysfunctionality, and in cross-gender pairings, meetings held in a group context could help avoid the nature of the relationship being misconstrued as somehow sexual in nature' (ibid., p. 2).

In summary, the literature suggests that women's advancement to leadership positions can be supported through the establishment of mentoring programs in which mentors and mentees develop a deep understanding of gender-specific needs and challenges. These needs may include networking and sponsorship activities, and the employment of a variety of strategies (like group mentorship) that reduce some of the pitfalls observed in cross-gender mentoring relationships.

Mentoring underrepresented minorities

The ethnic background of mentees may also influence their mentoring needs. Blake-Beard, Murrell, and Thomas (2007) asserted 'we cannot assume … that a single type of developmental constellation that produces social capital for majority individuals will have the same impact and operate by the same processes for people of color' (p. 237). Thus, there is an opportunity to examine mentoring practices specifically designed for URMs.

Four common needs of minorities reported in the literature are: forming strong ties; garnering psychosocial support; receiving feedback; and learning about organizational politics and tacit policies. These needs are certainly not unique to underrepresented minorities mentees, but failure to meet them is far more prevalent among URM groups (Blake-Beard et al., 2007; Bordes and Arredondo, 2005; Liang and Grossman, 2010; Zalaquett and Lopez, 2006).

In the last 15 years the need to establish strong and diversified developmental relationships and networks has been considered by mentoring scholars. Higgins and Kram (2001) acknowledge the benefits from a diversified developmental network with strong relationship ties, in the mentees' career development, personal learning, and organizational commitment. These strong ties also relate to the need of URMs to connect their jobs and community, and the need for emotional support (Bordes and Arredondo, 2005). Strong ties may alleviate the need for feedback. For example, after conducting a study on African American mentees, Liang and Grossman (2010) found that the closeness mentees felt with their mentor had a direct effect on the amount/quality of the feedback they received; furthermore:

> An important dilemma for the mentor is how to give useful feedback in a way that is encouraging rather than discouraging. While this dilemma may be relevant in most mentoring relationships, it may have particular significance for minorities who often face negative stereotypes about their group's lack of intelligence and ability to achieve. (p. 245)

Mentoring can acquaint URMs with organizational culture and practices. It can enlighten protégés to 'political realities' they may face by having a minority status within the organization (Ragins, 2002b). This realization and recognition of power structures that affect the mentee in an organization can be crucial to their success (Montoya, 2014). Zalaquett and Lopez (2006) discussed the effects of mentoring Latinas and Latinos in higher education and noted that mentors provide guidance in navigating a system in which mentees would otherwise receive minimal support. Crutcher (2014) advises mentors to see their mentees both as individuals and as a part of a larger social context.

Mentoring LGBTQ individuals

Research concerning the experiences of LGBTQ mentees is beginning to emerge, and suggests the prevalence of their specific needs for psychosocial support, inclusion, and awareness of the issues these individuals may experience in the workplace (Rummell and Chudnovsky, 2015). Church (2012) described how 'perceived workplace discrimination' (p. 118) prompted a lack of inclusion among LGBTQ mentees. Friskopp and Silerstein, (1996, as cited by Church, 2012, p. 118), and Wood (1994, as cited by Church, 2012, p. 118) note that 'gay employees are excluded from mentoring and networking relationships, which impair their opportunities for advancement in the organization'. The discrimination of LBGTQ members within mentoring relationships may derive from what Herek and Capitanio (1996, as cited in Church, 2012, p. 117) refer to as a 'courtesy stigma', a situation in which heterosexuals are assumed to be gay or lesbian because of their association or interaction with homosexuals. The exclusion of LBGTQ members from mentoring relationships may be fueled by a heterosexual's fear of this stigma, as well as a homosexual's fear of discrimination, as described by Church (2012):

> Fear of workplace discrimination inhibits relationship formation making informal mentor/mentee dyads for gay men and lesbians less likely to be formed. There may also be hesitation on the part of mentors to become involved with mentees of the same sex but different sexual orientations (i.e. heterosexual male mentor and gay male mentee) if the sexual orientations are known or suspected ... in the mentoring relationships that are with mentees of the same sex but different sexual orientations, not only may the mentor be subject to the possibility of sexual innuendo or rumor about the nature of the relationship (as with cross-gender relationships) but such innuendo or rumor would entail speculation about the sexual orientation of the mentor. (p. 117)

Developing an awareness of the barriers that exclude LBGTQ members from mentoring relationships, whether perceived workplace discrimination or courtesy stigmas, is necessary to formally integrate LBGTQ mentees into organizations and provide them with outlets for networking and other inclusionary activities. It is also necessary to provide these mentees with specific psychosocial support; Church (2012) notes that 'gay and lesbian mentees experiencing greater perceived workplace discrimination will need more psychosocial support to help them cope with the discrimination' (p. 118).

PROBLEMS WITH CURRENT MENTORING PRACTICES

There are two main problems with current mentoring practices in promoting the success and advancement to leadership positions of women, minorities, and LGTBQ populations. First, there is a lack of mentors from diverse backgrounds. Second, there is a lack of understanding of mentee's needs from underrepresented backgrounds due to unconscious bias.

Lack of diverse mentors

The insufficient numbers of mentors who are themselves diverse prevent a practical implementation of matching strategies based on demographic characteristics. An alternative is the recruitment of diverse mentors from outside the organization, perhaps through professional, industry, or community-based associations. Building a diverse pool of mentors will not happen immediately and will require sustained and intentional recruitment efforts and policies.

Unconscious bias

The second problem may be more complex. Since demographically similar mentors are rare, mentoring pairs are matched on other similarities. Problems within diversified mentoring relationships can easily occur. For example, male mentors may find themselves too protective of female mentees (Giscombe, 2007), or rumors of romantic relationships may arise (O'Neill, 2002; Ragins, 2002b). Strategies must be in place to mitigate these problems; diversity training may help sensitize members of diversified mentoring relationships to the potential problems – even if they feel they are unlikely to occur within their own relationship – and help prevent these problems before they begin.

A related problem is unintentional, but real, racist or sexist attitudes expressed as microaggression. Unfortunately, it has been shown that not being aware of one's own biases is a bias in and of itself (Kang 2009; Lee and Lebowitz, 2015). Unconscious biases may affect diverse mentoring relationships and an increasing literature suggests ways these biases evolve.

Unconscious bias refers to judgments people hold even when unaware of them. Scholars define biases as 'introspectively unidentified (or inaccurately identified) traces of past experience that mediate favorable or unfavorable thought, feeling, or action toward social objects' (Greenwald and Banji, 1995, as cited in Cameron, Payne, and Knobe, 2010, p. 274). Biases are inherent and systematic, but most importantly they are not active or conscious (Sandgren, 2014; Kang, 2009).

Biases, while being unintentional and unconscious, may have an effect on the success of a diverse mentoring relationship. In fact, Ragins (2002a) has stated that, 'It is clear that the development of mentoring relationships is guided not just by identification, but also by stereotypes, attitudes, attributions, and perceptions about what the other party brings to the relationship' (p. 33). Unconscious biases manifest themselves in 'little' things that can have major effects, such as the rate of callbacks or the interpretation of body language and facial expressions (Kang, 2009). The prevalence and importance of these biases have been studied thoroughly in the literature.

> When we deal with people, however, our lack of awareness of the assumptions, which we are drawing upon, often leads us into gross misunderstandings. We may see groups as much more different than they really are, or much more similar. Our assumptions create a framework of expectations, which can lead to self-fulfilling prophecies. (Clutterbuck and Ragins, 2002b, p. 115)

It is important that mentoring relationships do not support undesired status quos. The problem these biases present for mentoring relate to unfair expectations. For example, a male mentor may find himself unintentionally having lower expectations for his female mentee, despite believing that he does not judge her based on her gender. 'These stereotyping and attributional processes are pervasive and often unconscious, but may have a tremendous impact on the development and functioning of the mentoring relationship' (Ragins, 2002a, p. 34).

Research has shown that these mentors who hold such biases may detrimentally influence cross-gender relationships. Ragins (2002a), noted that:

> Mentors and mentees do not leave their group memberships behind when they enter a mentoring relationship ... These group memberships influence the mentoring relationship's development and effectiveness ... Specifically, gender may influence whether individuals are selected for a mentoring relationship, how they are viewed in the relationship by their partners or others in the organization, and even the overall effectiveness of the relationship. (p. 24)

It is important to educate mentoring participants about biases rather than having mentoring relationships be guided unconsciously by them (Page, 2006). Research reported that people who strive to overcome these biases can change them or their effects (Kang, 2009). The unconscious aspect of these biases makes it even more important for people to learn about them and reduce them.

ALTERNATIVE STRATEGIES

This section proposes solutions for creating effective diversified mentoring relationships. We draw from the field of *talent management* to propose strategies that alleviate challenges and barriers for women, URMs, and LGBTQ populations. *Diversity driven mentoring practices* are proposed to mitigate the challenges of diversified mentoring relationships, especially those that identify and act on unconscious or implicit biases.

Talent and diversity management

Talent and diversity management primarily focus on internal employee development (Harris and Foster, 2010), with a secondary focus on recruitment processes. Although, affirmative action practices have traditionally been used to satisfy quotas (especially at the recruitment stage), we propose a broader focus for talent and diversity management on the development and growth of mentor and mentee competencies for personal and professional development.

Talent management maintains a focus on merit rather than diversity. Such a focus empowers mentors from diverse backgrounds and provides underrepresented mentees with positive mentoring relationships. Talent management may be thought of as 'a comprehensive and integrated set of activities to ensure that the organization attracts, retains, motivates, and develops the talented people it needs now and in the future' (Baron and Armstrong, 2007, as cited in Harris and Foster, 2010, p. 423). This perspective operates on the notion of equality as meritocracy. 'The basic principle is that individuals are treated equally; individual talents and merits are the basis for extra support and preferential treatment given by the organization' (Bleijenberg et al., 2010, p. 5). Talent management allows companies to foster employees on the basis of the capacities that they bring to the organization (Heres and Benchop, 2010). Mentoring is often seen as the tool of talent management. We argue that the reverse should be true; talent management should be a tool for mentoring.

Diversity management, often a part of larger talent management initiatives (Bleijenberg et al., 2010), refers to a method that is 'more inclusive, proposing a broader understanding of individual differences that also include factors such as sexual orientation, skills, and experience' (Heres and Benchop, 2010, p. 438). Durska (2009) states that this perspective 'means taking advantage of all various experience, diverse knowledge, skills, predispositions and sensitivity in the entire organization or company'. Jonsen et al. (2010) write that it 'is about obtaining the best people in leadership positions and, in turn, supporting growth in the market and stronger relationships with our joint venture partners. It is about talent, growth, and competitiveness' (p. 558). Thus, it is clear that talent is important in diversity management. In fact, Heres and Benschop (2010) noted that:

> Part of the success of diversity management seems to lie in its meritocratic foundation; diversity management emphasizes, acknowledges, and values individual merits and qualities, and is therefore appealing to both individuals who seek recognition in their work environment and to organizations that seek high quality employees. (p. 437)

Another important distinction between the two management strategies, especially when looking at them separately instead of in conjunction, is that diversity management has a dual agenda (Heres and Benschop, 2010): while talent management can aim merely to foster an organization's goals and growth; diversity management also strives to increase diversity for the sake of diversity.

We advocate joining these perspectives to enable the best possible mentoring relationship for individuals from diverse backgrounds. The reason they are inadequate if used alone is twofold. First, talent management may not address the needs of diverse employees. Although talent management, in principle, should be demographically blind, women, URMs, and LGBTQ may not be perceived as 'talented' as other populations due to socio-cultural differences. Second, diversity management alone might be perceived as a system to meet quotas and compliance with affirmative action laws, rather than building diverse talent. Diversity and talent management are best utilized when there is a diversity of talent among an organization instead of merely demographic diversity (Page, 2007).

Diversity driven mentoring practices

The lack of mentors from underrepresented backgrounds in leadership positions and a failure to identify, comprehend, and relate to the specific needs of women, URMs, and LBGTQ mentees creates barriers to mobility and success, aggravating income and gender disparities for these populations. To confront these shortcomings, current practices must be modified, necessitating a change in how mentors think about the relationship compared to how they act, and in a way that is conducive to acknowledging the spectrum of needs of these populations. New practices in diversified mentoring relationships may benefit from actively providing mentees with access to underrepresented mentors, both inside and outside the organization, through the implementation of strategic recruitment practices. These practices should confront and identify instances of unconscious bias, the personal stereotypes we are unaware of in mentoring relationships, through actions that result in a collective modification of assumptions. Thomas (2001) describes a proactive approach to promote these changes in terms of a corporate culture tree, saying:

> Corporate culture is a kind of tree. Its roots are assumptions about the company and about the world. Its branches, leaves, and seeds are behavior. You can't change the leaves without changing the roots, and you can't grow peaches on an oak. Or rather, with the proper grafting, you *can* grow peaches on an oak—but they come out an awful lot like acorns—small and hard and not much fun to eat. So if you want to grow peaches, you have to make sure the tree's roots are peach friendly. (p. 17)

Therefore, it is important to address problematic assumptions or 'roots' to effectively change the outcomes and products of an organization.

An assumption that mentoring administrators need to challenge is described by Thomas (2001) as the notion 'that cream will rise to the top' (p. 17). He notes that although this conception is common, 'in most companies, what passes for cream rising to the top is actually cream being pulled or pushed to the top by an informal system of mentoring and sponsorship' (pp. 16–17). It is time to establish a system of mentoring and sponsorship that pushes or pulls mentees toward a more inclusive developmental success. To do so, mentoring programs across the board need to abandon outdated assumptions that ignore demographic differences in mentoring relationships.

As assumptions are challenged, it is important to employ new practices that seek to increase diversified mentoring relationships, and consequently meet the needs of participants, including mentors, mentees, and program administrators. Thomas describes the benefits of such practices as follows (2001): 'In the context of managing diversity, the question is not whether this system is maximally efficient, but whether it works for all employees. Executives who only sponsor people like themselves are not making much of a contribution to the cause of getting the best from every employee' (p. 19).

By understanding the present institutionalized misconception of diversity and talent management, we ultimately witness a need for foundational shifts in mentoring diverse populations. Our ability to embrace new practices that cater to a more diverse range of mentees is contingent on our modification of assumptions held within outdated mentoring practices. We challenge old institutionalized assumptions by proposing the application of four major strategies: inclusion; diversified matching; social networking; and diversity training.

Inclusion

Inclusion is an important principle in mentoring individuals from diverse backgrounds (Crutcher, 2014). Preeya (2014) observes that inclusion needs to be fostered as soon as such populations are integrated into an organization, as it may not occur on its own. Establishing mentoring programs with specific goals to promote the inclusion of underrepresented populations may increase a sense of belonging, a feeling of value and appreciation. Introducing inclusive mentoring programs in the workplace will also provide access to internal and external networks through connections and activities. Inclusive mentoring practices are especially important to increase the satisfaction and retention of mentees.

Clutterbuck and Ragins (2002a, b) propose dealing with diversity by recognizing differences and using this knowledge to pinpoint mentees' needs. Discussing diversity within the mentoring relationship is helpful in gaining a stronger mentoring relationship (Crutcher, 2014; Loue, 2011) and in creating a more inclusive environment for the mentee. This practice has been found to be more effective in meeting the mentee's needs than ignoring the differences in diversified mentoring relationships.

Diversified matching

Derived from socialization, social support, and social exchange theories, researchers have focused on investigating the nature, amount, and quality of social support provided by mentors (Young and Perrewe, 2000). The content of the information offered by the mentor and the mentor's own situation (career stage, position in the organization, power and influence, etc.) may influence the socialization process. This gives rise to the idea that a single mentor might not be able to satisfy all the developmental needs of a mentee and that mentees might choose to acquire information and model their behaviors on multiple sources (Chao, 2007; Blake-Beard et al., 2007). Therefore, Kram (1983) suggested the establishment of a constellation of mentoring relationships and more recently has introduced the idea of developmental mentoring networks (Higgins and Kram, 2001).

Pairing mentors and mentees who share similar backgrounds may show underrepresented populations that they are not alone and that there is a place within the organization for them. There are ways of looking at similar criteria to match mentors with mentees, but most commonly such criteria translate to demographic similarities involving ethnicity, gender, and sexual orientation (Loue, 2011). Matching exclusively on the basis of demographic similarities may not be in the best interest of mentees. However, we suggest that at least one mentor in a mentee's developmental network share either their gender, ethnicity, or sexual preference.

When demographic similarity matching is disregarded, assimilation may be forced and may result in what Thomas and Ely (2001) described as 'keeping people from identifying strongly and personally with their work' (p. 40). Assimilation of diverse and minority populations into the dominant culture is at odds with effective mentoring practices. Indeed, embracing and engaging one another's differences is crucial to success and creativity (Blake-Beard et al., 2007).

Mutual attraction, a psychological basis of mentorship, is influenced by demographic similarities, especially race (e.g. Byrne, 1971; Ensher and Murphy, 1997; Thomas, 1993). The strength of the desire for mentors of the same ethnicity is commonly linked to the mentee's age, researchers find, 'that young people tend to seek mentors from the same racial or ethnic background' (Liang and Grossman, 2010, p. 240). García and Henderson (2015) noted how Latinos felt about same-ethnicity mentors, as illustrated by one participant's comment: 'We don't have as many opportunities, and having a Latino/a mentor gives you that extra burst of hope, of yeah, we can' (p. 3). They also described a Latino/a mentor as someone who would understand the mentee to a greater degree as a cultural insider. According to two of the four participants, a cultural insider had helped with weighing career opportunities that involved relocating with cultural expectations/obligations (i.e. staying close to family). Some participants believed that being mentored by a Latino/a mentor would have a greater impact on them, academically and personally, including feeling increased self-confidence and motivation.

Thomas (1993) found that same-ethnicity mentoring relationships provided more psychosocial support because high levels of similarity can result in stronger identification with each other and a greater ability to trust (Blake-Beard et al., 2007). Understanding, 'how the mentee's culture affects him/her builds trust and rapport along with helping to identify the mentee's specific needs. In turn, mentees feel supported, affirmed, and empowered' (Chan, 2008, p. 263). Trust was important in allowing for needs to be met (Montoya, 2014), such as psychosocial support, and it was a crucial element to successful mentoring relationships (Crutcher, 2014). Racially diverse mentees may feel that same-race mentorships allow for a better understanding of their needs, as their mentor is likely to have encountered many of the same issues related to their minority status. Same-race mentors may provide proof that someone like the mentee can succeed.

Dynamics present in same-race mentoring also arise in cases of same-sex mentoring. A female mentor may show female mentees that it is possible to succeed, and may relate to facing the same barriers. Young people, regardless of ethnicity, have been shown to select same-sex mentors when possible (Liang and Grossman, 2010), and same gender mentors have been shown to have positive effects on adult, female professionals. McKeen and Bujaki (2007) report that 'female protégés with female mentors were more likely than those with male mentors to report that their mentors helped them integrate personal and professional aspects of their lives … and that women with female mentors were more involved in their jobs' (p. 208).

Despite the potential value, demographic matching may be difficult to accomplish.

Because of the various barriers minorities confront mentors of the same race, gender, and sexual orientation can be hard to find. Johnson-Bailey (2012) contextualizes this in regards to race, stating: 'While mentoring can be a crucial component that positively affects academic advancement, scholars and faculty of color continue to have difficulty in finding mentors, especially of the same racial background as themselves'. (Bierema, 2005; Hansman, 2002, 2005; Thomas, 1990 – as cited in Blake-Beard et al., 2007, p. 159).

However, researchers report that demographic differences may not be as important in mentoring relationships as perceived by underrepresented mentees. Thus, it may be more important for dyads to share some similarities in values or working styles rather than demographic characteristics (Sedlacek et al., 2010). In fact, studies report, 'mentees in cross-race matches might be just as satisfied as those in same-race matches if they perceive themselves to be similar to their mentors in other ways' (Liang and Grossman, 2010, p. 303). Ragins (2002b) found that in diverse mentoring relationships (cross-race/cross-gender) similarities such as shared values were even more important than in other types of mentoring relationships. It is only through these shared values that trust and understanding can be formed in cross-cultural or diverse mentoring relationships (Crutcher, 2014). Without this trust and understanding, these relationships are unlikely to succeed, and certainly will be unable to meet the needs of diverse populations.

These non-demographic similarities are often defined in terms of values and attitudes. For example, a mentor who believes strongly in being on time no matter what may be less successful with a mentor who prefers to take his time. Even if two people have different race, gender, sexual orientation, and cultural background (signifying an extremely diverse pair) the two may see each other as similar based on shared interests, beliefs, values, and so on. These similarities can lead not only to the same amount of success as demographically similar relationships, but also sometimes to even more success. One study found that, 'perceived attitudinal similarity was a better predictor of satisfaction with mentor and support received from the mentors than racial or gender similarity' (Ensher, Grant-Vallone, and Marelich, 2002, as cited in Ragins, 2010, p. 32). Similarity of some kind between mentor and mentee pairs is a proven good practice for mentoring diverse populations, especially when available mentors are not demographically similar and given that there is a lack of diversity among mentors, implementation of this practice is crucial (Loue, 2011).

Social networking

Social networking meets specific needs, such as: identification of institutional barriers for females; access to institutional guidance for ethnic minorities; and institutional inclusion for LGBTQ mentees. Most literature that explores the importance of social networking in mentoring relationships pertains to women and URMs, as these diverse populations are notoriously excluded from social networks. Reddick and Young (2012) acknowledge that, 'addressing networking for mentees of color is crucial' (p. 412), and Blake-Beard and colleagues (2007) expressed that mentees of color were excluded from, or lacked access to, existing social networks, especially in the workplace.

Even more obvious than the exclusion of URMs from social networks is the lack of access for women to male social networks – traditionally referred to as an old boys' network Giscombe (2007) – and it has been suggested that mentoring may be a remedy to this exclusion, providing women access to that network (Ragins and Sundstrom, 1989) and offering them the protection needed to deal with workplaces that may range from non-supportive to hostile.

Access to social networks is critical for women, especially professional women, as much upper-position recruiting is based on who you know and personal connections may provide access to, or at least notification of, available employment positions. Exclusion from these networks increases the likelihood for women to get the support offered by networks from their own direct supervisors (Cianni and Romberger, 1995; Ohlott et al., 1994; as cited in McKeen and Bujaki, 2007, p. 200); therefore, mentoring programs may reduce the gender gap in social networks (Jonsen et al., 2010).

Diversity training

Diversity training has been found to be organizationally relevant to mentoring programs for diverse populations (Clutterbuck and Ragins, 2002b; Colgan, 2011; Heres and Benschop, 2010; Jonsen et al., 2010). In a comprehensive study of over 13 gender-diverse mentoring programs, Giscombe (2007) found that most of the included programs showed indirect examples of gender bias. Giscombe (2007) subsequently concluded that this was because male mentors failed: 'To be alerted to the possibility that gender stereotyping may influence behavior in cross-gender relationships ... and that gender differences in organizational power might affect relationship dynamics' (Ragins and Sundstrom, 1989, as cited in Giscombe, 2007, p. 566).

Thus, diversity training may be an influential deterrent to unconscious bias. Simply by alerting mentors and mentees of the unconscious biases they hold may make a difference in the success of the mentoring relationships. 'Individuals in diversified mentoring relationships may reduce their reliance on stereotypes by employing a cognitive differentiation approach to dealing with others' (Ragins, 2002b, p. 34).

Diversity training often 'has two facets – an understanding of mentoring per se and an appreciation of the issues facing the target groups of mentees' (Clutterbuck and Ragins, 2002a, p. 117). In discussing the different ways diversity training can occur, these authors elaborate further on the idea of the two facets: 'The approaches may vary considerably, but the objectives are the same: To enhance the effectiveness of the relationship by increasing the sensitivity of one or both parties to the influence of stereotypes; to help people value and manage the differences between them' (p. 117).

Diversity training needs to focus on how sensitivity can increase the effectiveness of the mentoring relationship (Ragins, 2002a), and on valuing the differences between mentor and mentee. Training of this sort is not a new concept; however diversity training through the lens of unconscious biases is not prevalent in the mentoring field. 'Being aware of one's own stereotypes and helping the mentee recognize and explore their own are essential elements of diversity mentoring' (Clutterbuck, 2002, p. 117). Diversity training on unconscious bias would be useful when looking at the general goals of inclusion.

Awareness can help mentors and organizations become more inclusive of diverse populations, and training may allow mentors and mentees to find differences and similarities they may have not noticed otherwise due to unconscious biases. Mentors' awareness of unconscious bias may allow them to identify specific barriers faced by minorities, help mentees navigate the organization's political reality, and create inclusive environments for mentees. A focus on understanding the diverse collection of identities that exist within an institution is a valuable asset for improving the organizational climate and developing greater appreciation for the contributions of underrepresented populations.

The tools necessary to facilitate the process of diverse mentorship include: cultural humility; respect for others; active listening; honest introspection; openness to feedback on one's own values and priorities; openmindedness in considering other ways of thinking; and an appreciation for the synergy that cultural diversity brings to improving performance and bottom line success. Providing mentors and mentees with a roadmap of elements and effective behaviors and communication skills within this new model may allow mentees to develop a plan for professional development. Mentees will become aware of how the institution can support cultural diversity and how they can learn to navigate potential barriers to success.

An emphasis on cognitive diversity – for instance, the diverse perspectives that under-represented populations offer as a result of having different identities, cultural backgrounds, experiences, education, and training – have a proven effect on the development of better problem-solving skills (Page, 2007). Mentoring that is identity conscious and culturally relevant can be achieved through discussion and training of mentors and mentees alike, who learn to see differences as both assets and valuable contributions to mentoring relationships and the capacity and synergy with them. It is hoped that this synergistic process will, in turn, increase the institutional capacity for cross-cultural and intergenerational communication and collaboration, while cultivating the full potential and untapped human capital of women, URMs, and LGBTQ populations. Both career-related self-efficacy and institutional viability stand to gain from the implementation of such a process.

FUTURE RESEARCH

We propose four areas of mentoring for scholars to investigate. First, we agree with Clutterbuck and Ragins (2002b) who identified a need for research on how mentoring coordinators integrate the two facets of diversity mentoring. Such research might guide the establishment of effective practices to enhance diversified mentoring relationships.

Second, we add our voice to O'Neill (2002) and call for a better understanding of the psychosocial mentoring needs of diverse individuals. He noted that diverse mentoring relationships often only provide instrumental help. Yet, for progress to be made in organizations, there need to be friend-like bonds as well.

Third, more research is needed on the effects of same-demographic mentoring. Research shows that it is less important than previously perceived; it may be the case that the small samples are insufficient for such a conclusion. Further, the talent management perspective might be utilized in such studies. For research to be conclusive as to what types of similarities mandate effective practices for diverse mentoring relationship, access to both same-demographic mentors, and mentors with other similarities is needed.

Fourth, research is needed in areas not addressed in this chapter. For example, the mentoring needs of sexually or cross-culturally diverse populations still lacks academic depth. By developing a stronger research base related to the needs of these diverse populations, solutions for how mentoring can solve them can be hypothesized.

Finally, research is needed to examine whether talent management and diversity training can actually solve some of the challenges of current mentoring practices. These are new areas of scholarship and we have an opportunity to learn more about how talent and diversity management relate to effective mentoring.

CONCLUSION

A more socially diverse and educated workforce has led to increased productivity, innovation, and economic success around the globe; however, this trend has not been reflected in middle management and leadership positions. To maximize the benefits of diversity new mentoring programs that address specific barriers to the advancement of women, URMs, and LGBTQ populations are needed. Two major challenges that arise out of current mentoring practices are: a) the lack of diverse mentors; and b) a lack of understanding of the mentoring needs of mentees from underrepresented backgrounds due to prevailing unconscious biases. As shown in the literature, these populations might benefit from strategies drawn from talent and diversity management, and diversity driven mentoring practices promoting inclusion, diversified matching, social networking, and diversity training. Diversity training helps sensitize mentors to diversity issues and promote awareness of biases and, subsequently, prevent issues like sexism, racism, and discrimination. Further empirical research on this topic is needed to assess the impact of these strategies on the effectiveness of diversified mentoring relationships, as well as in career, personal learning, and organizational commitment outcomes.

REFERENCES

Baron, A., and Armstrong, M. (2007). *Human capital management: Achieving added value through people*. London: Kogage Ltd. http://www.123library.org/book_details/?id=98763

Blake-Beard, S., Murrell, A., and Thomas, D. (2007). Unfinished business: The impact of race on understanding mentoring relationships. In B. R. Ragins and K. Kram (Eds.), *The Handbook of Mentoring at Work* (pp. 223–47): Thousand Oaks, CA: Sage.

Bleijenbergh, I., Peters, P., and Poutsma, E. (2010). Diversity management beyond the business case. *Equality, Diversity and Inclusion: An International Journal*, 29(5), 413–21. doi:http://dx.doi.org/10.1108/02610151011052744

Bordes, V. A., and Arredondo, P. (2005). Mentoring and 1st year-latina/o college students. *Journal of Hispanic Higher Education*. 4(14).

Brdulak, H. (2009). Diversity management as a business model. *Kobieta i Biznes (1–4)*, 29–35. Retrieved from http://libproxy.unm.edu/login?url=http://search.proquest.com/docview/230452135?accountid=14613 (accessed 19 October, 2016).

Byrne, D. (1971). *The attraction paradigm*. NY: Academic Press.

Cameron, C., Payne, B., and Knobe, J. (2010). Do theories of implicit race bias change moral judgments? *Social Justice Research*, 23(4), 272–89. doi:10.1007/s11211-010-0118-z

Chan, A. W. (2008). Mentoring ethnic minority, pre-doctoral students: an analysis of key mentor practices. *Mentoring & Tutoring: Partnership In Learning*, 16(3).

Chao, G. (2007). Mentoring and organizational socialization: Networks for work adjustment. In B. Ragins and K. Kram (Eds.), *The handbook of mentoring at work* (pp. 179–96). Thousand Oaks, CA: Sage.

Church, R. (2012). National differences in effects of perceived workplace discrimination on the mentoring relationships of gay and lesbian mentees: *Journal of Organizational Culture, Communications and Conflict*, 16(2), 115–23.

Cianni, M., and Romberger, B. (1995). Perceived racial, ethnic, and gender differences in access to developmental experiences. *Group & Organization Management*, 20(4), 440.

Clance, P. R., and Imes, S. (1978). The imposter phenomenon in high achieving women: dynamics and therapeutic intervention. *Psychotherapy Theory, Research and Practice*, 15(3), 1–8.

Clutterbuck, D. R., and Ragins, B. R. (2002a). *Mentoring and diversity: An international perspective*. Oxford: Butterword-Heinemann.

Clutterbuck, D. R., and Ragins, B. R. (2002b). Some key issues for diversity mentoring. In Clutterbuck, D. R., and Ragins, B. R. (Eds.), *Mentoring and diversity: An international perspective*. Oxford: Butterword-Heinemann.

Clutterbuck, D. R., and Richardson, M. (2014). *Mentoring and sponsorship* [PDF], October 3. Retrieved from http://horizonsunlimited.com.au/pdf/Mentoring_and_Sponsorship.pdf (accessed 19 October, 2016).

Colgan, F. (2011). Equality, diversity and corporate responsibility. *Equality, Diversity and Inclusion: An International Journal*, 30(8), 719–34. http://dx.doi.org/10.1108/02610151111183225

Crutcher, B. N. (2014). Cross-cultural mentoring: A pathway to making excellence inclusive. *Liberal Education*, 100.

Durska, M. (2009). Diversity management: key concepts. *Kobieta i Biznes (1–4)*, 36–41. Retrieved from http://libproxy.unm.edu/login?url=http://search.proquest.com/docview/230452005?accountid=14613 (accessed 19 October, 2016).

Ensher, E. A. and Murphy, S. E. (1997). Effects of race, gender, perceived similarity, and contact on mentor relationships. *Journal of Vocational Behavior*, 50, 460–81.

García, I. O., and Henderson, S. J. (2015). Mentoring experiences of latina graduate students. *Multicultural Learning and Teaching*, 10(1), 91–109. doi:http://dx.doi.org/10.1515/mlt-2014-0003

Giscombe, K. (2007). Advancing women through the glass ceiling with formal mentoring. In K. K. Belle Rose Ragins (Ed.), *The handbook of mentoring in the workplace* (pp. 549–71). Thousand Oaks, CA: Sage.

Harris, L., and Foster, C. (2010). Aligning talent management with approaches to equality and diversity. *Equality, Diversity and Inclusion: An International Journal*, 29(5), 422–35. doi:http://dx.doi.org/10.1108/02610151011052753

Hegstad, C. (1999). Formal mentoring as a strategy for human resource development: A review of research. *Human Resource Development Quarterly*, 10(4), 383–90.

Heres, L., and Benschop, Y. (2010). Taming diversity: an exploratory study on the travel of a management fashion. *Equality, Diversity and Inclusion: An International Journal*, 29(5), 436–57. doi:http://dx.doi.org/10.1108/02610151011052762

Hewlett, S. A. (2013). *Forget a mentor, find a sponsor: The new way to fast-track your career*. Boston, MA: Harvard Business Review Press.

Higgins, M. C., and Kram, K. E. (2001). Reconceptualizing mentoring at work: A developmental network perspective. *The Academy of Management Review*, 26(2), 264–88.

IES National Center for Education Statistics (2015). *The condition of education 2015*. US Department of Education, NCES 2015–144. Retrieved from: http://nces.ed.gov/pubs2015/2015144.pdf (accessed 19 October, 2016).

Johnson-Bailey, J. (2012). Effects of race and racial dynamics on mentoring. In C. A. Mullen, Fletcher, S. J. (Eds.), *The SAGE handbook of mentoring and coaching in education* (pp. 155–69). Thousand Oaks, CA: Sage.

Johnson, W. (2007). Transformational supervision: When supervisors mentor. *Professional Psychology: Research and Practice*, 38(3), 259–67.

Jonsen, K., Maznevski, M. L., and Schneider, S. C. (2010). Gender differences in leadership – believing is seeing: implications for managing diversity. *Equality, Diversity and Inclusion: An International Journal*, 29(6), 549–72. doi:http://dx.doi.org/10.1108/02610151011067504

Jossi, F. (1997). Mentoring in changing times. *Training and Development*, 51(8), 50–4.

Kang, J. (2009). *Implicit Bias: A primer for courts*. National Campaign to Ensure the Racial and Ethnic Fairness of America's State Courts. Washington DC: National Center for State Courts.

Kram, K. (1983). Phases of the mentor relationship. *Academy of Management Journal*, 26(4), 608–25.

Lee, S. and Lebowitz, S. (2015). 20 Cognitive Biases that Screw Up Your Decisions. [Infographic], August 26. Retrieved from: http://www.businessinsider.com/

Liang, B., and Grossman, J. (2010). Diversity and Youth Mentoring Relationships. In T. D. Allen and Eby L. T. (Eds.), *The Blackwell handbook of mentoring* (pp. 239–58). Malden, MA: Blackwell Publishing.

Loue, S. (2011). *Mentoring HSP chart: Mentoring Health Science Professionals*. New York: Springer Publishing Company, LLC.

McKeen, C., and Bujaki, M. (2007). Gender and Mentoring. In K. K. Belle Rose Ragins (Ed.), *The handbook of mentoring at work* (pp. 197–222). Thousand Oaks, CA: Sage.

Murray, M. (2001). *Beyond the myths and magic of mentoring: How to facilitate an effective mentoring process, new and revised edition*. San Francisco, CA: Jossey-Bass.

Noe, R. A. (1988). Women and mentoring: A review and research agenda. *Academy of Management*, *13*(1), 65–78.

Ohlott, P. J., Ruderman, M. N. and McCauley, C. D. (1994). Gender differences in managers' developmental job experiences. *Academy of Management*, *37*(1), 46–67

O'Neill, R. (2002). Gender and race in mentoring relationships: A review of the literature. In D. R. Clutterbuck, Ragins, B. R. (Ed.), *Mentoring and diversity: an international perspective* (pp. 1–22). Oxford: Butterworth-Heinemann.

Page, S. (2007). *The difference: How the power of diversity creates better groups, firms, schools, and societies*. Princeton: Princeton University Press.

Preeya, D. (2014). Diversity and inclusion in an emerging market context. *Equality, Diversity and Inclusion: An International Journal*, *33*(3), 293–308. doi:http://dx.doi.org/10.1108/EDI-10-2012-0087

Ragins, B. R. (1989). Barriers to mentoring: The female manager's dilemma. *Human Relations*, *42*(1), 1–22. Retrieved from http://libproxy.unm.edu/login?url=http://search.ebscohost.com/login.aspx?direct=tru&db=eoah&AN=8488338&loginpage=Login.asp&site=ehost-live&scope=site (accessed 19 October, 2016).

Ragins, B. R. (1997). Antecedents of diversified mentoring relationships. *Journal of Vocational Behavior*, *51*(1), 90–109. doi:10.1006/jvbe.1997.1590

Ragins, B. R. (2002a). Understanding diversified mentoring relationships: Definitions, challenges, and strategies. In D. R. Clutterbuck, Ragins, B. R. (Eds.), *Mentoring and Diversity: An International Perspective*. Oxford: Butterworth-Heinemann.

Ragins, B. R. (2002b). Differences that make a difference: Common themes in the individual case studies of diversified mentoring relationships. In D. R. Clutterbuck, Ragins, B. R. (Eds.), *Mentoring and Diversity: An International Perspective*. Oxford: Butterworth-Heinemann.

Ragins, B. R. (2010). Diversity and workplace mentoring relationships. In T. D. Allen and Eby L. T. (Eds.), *The Blackwell handbook of mentoring* (pp. 281–300). Malden, MA: Blackwell Publishing.

Ragins, B. R., and Sundstrom, E. (1989). Gender and power in organizations: A longitudinal perspective. *Psychological Bulletin*, *105*, 51–8.

Reddick, R., and Young, M. (2012). Mentoring graduate students of color. In S. M. Fletcher, Carol (Ed.), *The SAGE handbook of mentoring and coaching in education* (pp. 412–29). Thousand Oaks, CA: Sage.

Rummell, C., and Chudnovsky, L. (Producers). (2015). Including and welcoming LGBTQ youth in mentoring programs. *Collaborative Mentoring Webinar Series*. Retrieved from: https://vimeo.com/128888831 (accessed June, 16 2016).

Sandgren, M. (2014). When glass ceilings meet glass walls. *Kennedy School Review*, *14*, 39–46. Retrieved from: http://libproxy.unm.edu/login?url=http://search.proquest.com/docview/1700330694?accountia=14613 (accessed 19 October, 2016).

Sedlacek, W. E., Benjamin, E., Schlosser, L. Z., and Sheu, H. B. (2010). Mentoring in academia: Considerations for diverse populations. In T. D. Allen and Eby L. T. (Eds.), *The Blackwell handbook of mentoring* (pp. 259–80). Malden, MA: Blackwell Publishing.

Swart, T., Chisholm, K., and Brown, P. (2015). *Neuroscience for leadership: Harnessing the brain gain advantage*. New York, NY: Palgrave Macmillan.

Thomas, D. A. (1993). Racial dynamics in cross-race developmental relationships. *Administrative Science Quarterly*, *38*, 169–94.

Thomas, T. A., and Ely, R. J. (2001). Making differences matter. *Managing diversity* (6th ed., p. 40). Boston, MA: Harvard Business School Press.

Thomas, R. R. (2001). From affirmative action to affirming diversity. *Managing diversity* (6th ed., pp. 1–32). Boston, MA: Harvard Business School Press.

World Bank (2012). *Access to education: Global report*. Retrieved from: http://datatopics.worldbank.org/education/wStateEdu/StateEducation.aspx (accessed 19 October, 2016).

Young, A. M., and Perrewe, P. L. (2000). What did you expect? An examination of career-related support and social support among mentors and protégés. *Journal of Management*, *26*(4), 611–32.

Zalaquett, C. P., and Lopez, A. D. (2006). Learning from the stories of successful undergraduate latina/latino students and the importance of mentoring. *Mentoring and Tutoring*, *14*(3), 337–53.

25

Mentoring Executives at the Workplace: A View of Practice and Research

Kirsten M. Poulsen

INTRODUCTION

The work of an executive can be tough and lonely, especially for the chief executive of an organization (the C-suite) (de Janasz and Peiperl, 2014, 2015). Moving up through the ranks and taking on more and more responsibility presents the executive with increasingly complex tasks and decisions (Charan et al., 2011). Additionally, the role of the executive has changed with the coming of the knowledge-driven society, where collaboration among knowledge workers is key, and with global markets, where cultural agility is required to collaborate and perform as an individual and as an organization.

There is a large body of research on mentoring within, and without, business indicating that mentoring is a proven approach for developing people in organizations. Mentoring fosters career success for mentees (Bozionelos et al., 2011; Høigaard and Mathisen, 2009; Singh et al., 2009) and provides benefits for mentors (Ghosh and Reijo Jr., 2013; Parise and Forret, 2007). In recent years, organizations have increased executive mentoring programs as a means of supporting talent development, enhancing retention, and planning for succession. However, executive mentoring has received little attention in the research literature. One reason for this may be that executives tend to keep their mentoring relationships very confidential. This chapter seeks to fill this void in the research knowledge base.

PURPOSE

The purpose of this chapter is to present an overview of the practice and research of executive mentoring. The chapter begins with an overview of the definition and evolution of executive mentoring and the shift in context from an industrial society to a knowledge society. This is followed by information about why organizations value executive mentoring, and the benefits to both executive and organization. The next section presents research on practice and provides examples from practice that look at strategic intent and at the matching, cultural complexity, and preparation of mentors and mentees. The chapter ends with a discussion of implications for research and the use of executive mentoring in organizations.

OVERVIEW OF EXECUTIVE MENTORING

Executive mentoring is framed by the context within which it functions and the manner in which the purposes and relationships are conceived. Thus, to understand executive mentoring it is necessary first to look at the different approaches to mentoring, mainly reflected in US and European approaches. While, there are differences in mentoring within different European countries, in general, the European approach tends to focus on 'the learning alliance tapping into talent' (Clutterbuck, 1998), 'mentoring as a learning partnership' (Poulsen, 2006), and 'enhancing the capacity and quality of thinking' (Clutterbuck, 2012). The US model is generally more focused on the mentor as a sponsor, protector, and advice-giver (Kram, 1988).

In the USA, Kram (1988) was the first to define mentoring functions – career and psychosocial functions – in an organizational context. This was in the context of voluntary, self-organized mentoring relationships taken up in large organizations, and would generally be the direct manager seeing talent in a younger employee. In most cases, both mentor and mentee were male.

Since then, we have seen a change from an industrial to a knowledge-driven society. These changes have resulted in an increase in knowledge workers, where knowledge is the main resource and the focus is on 'absorbing, creating and moving knowledge' (Correira de Sousa and van Dierendonck, 2010, p. 231). This context is characterized by the fact that experienced (older) leaders no longer have all the answers, and if they try to impose their knowledge and answers on the younger generation, they are ignoring what the younger generation can contribute to the success of the organization. At the same time, the organizational context has become more complex, more multicultural, more global, which also means that there is very seldom only one right answer to an issue.

This change in the societal and organizational context is changing the role of leaders and requires new leadership skills – such as the sharing of power in decision making, promoting a sense of community, and a more holistic approach to work (Correira de Sousa and van Dierendonck, 2010) – which connect with the motivational needs of knowledge workers: the need for autonomy, mastery, and working for the greater good (Pink, 2011). Additionally, these changes have brought about an evolution in the understanding of what mentoring is and what it can do which brings us back to the European approach to mentoring as a learning alliance (Clutterbuck, 1998) which can facilitate a double learning process (Poulsen and Wittrock, 2012).

Today, there is an abundance of definitions of mentoring, though there is little focus on defining executive mentoring. David Clutterbuck's working definition (in press) of executive mentoring describes it as a 'one-to-one learning relationship designed to support executives with the quality of their thinking and decision making in the context of the development of both their business and their own personal growth' (unpublished manuscript). Other authors simply talk about executive mentoring when the mentees (or mentors) are executives. Indirectly, they define the mentoring through the outcomes, such as: bringing in an outside perspective and a degree of objectivity (Larcker and Saslow, 2014); making better decisions; avoiding costly mistakes; becoming proficient in their roles faster (de Janasz and Peiperl, 2015); and accelerating the move upward in the organization (Pfleeger and Mertz, 1995). These outcomes are not that different from outcomes of mentoring in general. However, some authors focus on the potential role of mentors in alleviating the stress and loneliness at the top of an organization (Cooper and Quick, 2003; de Janasz and Peiperl, 2014, 2015), and the executive mentor is defined as 'a role model who has "made it" whose experience, wisdom and network are relevant to the mentee's job and career' (de Janasz and Peiperl, 2014, p. 5).

In this chapter, I define mentoring from two different perspectives and expand on these to define executive mentoring:

- **Mentoring from the perspective of the mentors and mentees**: Mentoring is a learning partnership between two people with different levels of experience, where both can achieve new learning, new insights and personal growth. Mentoring creates synergy between two people. (Poulsen, 2008, 2012)
- **Mentoring from the perspective of the organization**: Mentoring is a strategic development activity that supports the organization's vision, goals and values and the participant's own development needs and wishes. (Poulsen, 2008, 2012)
- **Executive mentoring**: Executive mentoring is a learning partnership between two executives at different levels in their career, where both can achieve new learning and insight, while enhancing their thinking and decision making in the context of developing their businesses and accelerating their personal growth.

When defining the term executive, most literature about leadership talks about the three levels of management:

- **Top/executive level** – board of directors and C-suite executives.
- **Mid-level management** – general managers, branch managers, department managers, and so on.
- **First-level management** – first-line managers, supervisors, section leaders, and so on.

However, I have chosen to define executive through the model of career transitions as presented in the *Leadership Pipeline* (Charan et al., 2011). I find this model is more valuable when looking to define mentoring for executives, as it not only presents the process of moving up through the hierarchy, but also presents the major points where leaders need to readjust their understanding of themselves, their tasks, and their organizations/businesses. These are significant points in a career where it can be especially valuable for the leader to have the support of a more experienced leader in managing change, stepping up to new challenges, and developing new self-understanding.

These transition points (see Figure 25.1) reflect the visible change in the formal role, responsibility, and tasks of the leader. Each point requires the development of new skills and competences and, as the complexity of the role increases, this becomes a more intense transformative learning process for the individual.

In smaller/medium-sized organizations, there may be a move from managing others to managing a function and then, as the

Figure 25.1 Career transition points (Charan, Drotter, and Noel, 2011)

ROLE	CAREER TRANSITION POINT
7 Managing an enterprise	From managing a group of businesses to managing an enterprise (multiple groups within the same organization)
6 Managing a group of businesses	From managing a business to managing a group of businesses
5 Managing a business	From managing a function to managing a business
4 Managing a function	From managing managers to managing a function
3 Managing managers	From managing others to managing managers
2 Managing others	From managing self to managing others
1 Managing self	

organization grows, to managing managers as subteams are established within the functional area. This is not necessarily a linear career progression, however, and the level of managing a business may be the highest level, depending on the size of the organization.

Charan, Drotter and Noel (2011) argue that it is when moving from managing a function to managing a business that the work of the leader becomes especially complex. The business leader not only needs to integrate and understand functions, but also needs to communicate clearly and effectively with diverse employee groups and balance short-term and long-term thinking. At this level, they argue, leaders 'need to stop *doing* every second of the day and reserve time for reflection and analysis' (Charan et al., 2011, p. 23). Others agree with this change in leadership functions and the abilities needed to be an effective leader. For example, in a global survey of leaders, 84% of respondents believed that 'the definition of effective leadership has changed in the past five years', and 60% said that 'leaders face challenges that go beyond their individual capacities' moving towards more collaborative leadership and leadership as a process (Martin, 2007). In another, international, study CEOs defined the top five leadership attributes as:

- retaining and developing talent
- managing complexity
- leading change
- leading with integrity
- having an entrepreneurial mind-set (Development Dimensions International [DDI], 2014, p. 9).

An obvious conclusion is that leadership is increasing in complexity, requiring more collaboration and an ability to communicate and engage, leading me to argue that leaders at all levels need to *stop doing* and *start thinking*. Therefore, in this chapter, executives are defined as managers managing managers.

Evolution of mentoring and the skills of mentors

The definition of mentoring is elusive and has changed over time. In essence, it is dependent upon the purposes of the mentoring program and the mentoring relationship, as well as on the organizational and individual readiness for the mentoring (Kochan, 2013; Poulsen and Wittrock, 2012). The manner in which mentoring is described and operationalized is presented in Figure 25.2.

In today's global marketplace, the focus will be on operationalizing mentoring at levels two and three. Traditional mentoring, which places the mentee as learner and the mentor as teacher, is not an appropriate approach. The reasons for this are described in more detail in the next section on the context of executive mentoring.

To form these types of mentoring relationships, a strong level of trust between mentor and mentee is essential. The mentor's proven track-record as a high level executive is what gives them credibility and becomes the foundation for trust (de Janasz and Peiperl, 2014, 2015). The relevant knowledge, experience and know-how of the executive scene means

Figure 25.2 Evolution/foci of mentoring definitions (Poulsen, 2008; Poulsen and Wittrock, 2012)

	Mentoring
Level 3 focus	A learning alliance enhancing the quality of thinking – where both can learn, gain new insights and together create new knowledge (similar to transformative mentoring [Kochan, 2013])
Level 2 focus	Mentor as a learning helper and guide – focusing on and supporting the mentee's learning – mentors do not have all answers, but can share knowledge and advice as relevant (similar to transitional mentoring [Kochan, 2013])
Level 1 focus	Mentors as sponsors, protectors and advice-givers – the mentor knows the answers and solutions – mentors focus on maintaining status quo (traditional mentoring [Kochan, 2013])

the mentor can pass on inside knowledge and help speed up the executive mentee's process of adaption (ibid.).

Additionally, executive mentors need to possess a number of attributes that permit them to foster and support the mentee's growth, while also being open to learning themselves. Included among these attributes are being motivated to serve as a mentor and having the welfare of the mentee as a central purpose of the relationship. The mentor must have a sense of intellectual curiosity, a continued desire for learning, and question relentlessly (Dumont, 2010). Also, mentors need to be very self-aware of their own emotions to be able to manage the mentoring relationship positively and with meaningful outcomes (Crumpton, 2015).

Context of executive mentoring

There are several arguments for focusing on the European approach – the third level approach – when engaging in executive mentoring. Among these are:

- **The shift from industrial to knowledge-driven economy.** In the knowledge society, knowledge is the only resource that grows when shared (van Weert, 2006). In the knowledge-driven economy, knowledge is not only transferred, but through sharing knowledge, new knowledge is created and transformed into learning, with new skills and new competences that allow people to take effective action. Too much focus on the sponsor, protector, and advice-giver approach to mentoring, risks the transfer of 'old' knowledge from the mentor to the mentee (or protégé) without taking the mentee's 'new' knowledge into account. This also means there is a risk of trying to solve tomorrow's challenges with yesterday's solutions! In the knowledge-driven economy learning alliance mentoring provides for knowledge to flow both ways and creates a mutual learning process (Poulsen and Wittrock, 2012).
- **The need for multinational leaders.** With the expanding global market for many corporations, global executives need special qualifications and skills to deal with unknown and often radically different cultures and environments. In a study of more than 12,000 leaders across 76 countries, it was found that 18% of all leaders and 37% of all executives had multinational responsibilities; the executives coordinated efforts across an average of 8.5 countries (Howard and Wellins, 2008). This global complexity has certainly increased since then. However, 62% of multinational executives described their preparation for their global roles as fair or poor (ibid.).
- **Mentoring is not a 'fix the mentee' tool.** Effective mentoring is not a one-dimensional focus on the mentee's learning. Rather, it is a multi-dimensional focus on learning for mentee, mentor and organization. A good example is when looking at mentoring for integrating minorities and other disenfranchised groups, such as women, who are traditionally excluded from executive leadership positions. Such issues cannot be solved by focusing on fixing the groups usually excluded. We also need to look at 'fixing the knowledge' and 'fixing the organization' (Schiebinger, 2008). When both mentors and mentees expect to learn and are willing to learn, there is a higher probability that things will change. As the mentors are often in powerful positions, when they change their perceptions and behaviors this can influence the whole organization. When mentors learn about the skills and talents of these excluded groups, they may come to appreciate them more, and they may become more open to recruiting and promoting them within the organization. Thus, mentoring can provide a double learning process (Clutterbuck et al., 2012).
- **The issue of power.** 'When people feel powerful or feel powerless, it influences their perception of others' (Yap as quoted in Resnick, 2013). Research on power shows that power is consistently related to dishonesty – and the psychological state of power increases the likelihood that individuals will focus on their own desires and ignore the consequences for others (Yap, 2013). Even the simple act of taking up a body posture of power (consciously or unconsciously because one is promoted to the corner office with the biggest chair and the biggest desk), will make a person feel more powerful and may lead the person to act accordingly. Another interesting part of Yap's (2013) research shows that a feeling of powerlessness can also lead to corrupt

behavior – and the more a person is focused on maintaining their safety and security, the more they will try to avoid the feeling of powerlessness, even using corrupt behavior. This confirms our own observations that the higher the leader moves up the leadership hierarchy, the more powerful the leader feels; and the more powerful an individual feels, the more tendency they have to believe in themselves and their skills. This feeling may lead mentors to believe that they have all the right answers, and if the mentees feel less powerful, they may either just cave in or they may resent and try to avoid the mentoring. Feeling powerful or powerless influences mentors' and mentees' perceptions of each other. Additionally, the more the mentoring approach is focused on the mentor having all the answers, the more power is given to the mentor (Bal et al., 2008).

- **The helping approach.** To quote Edgar H. Schein: 'Helping ... is to enable others to do something that they cannot do for themselves'.[1] The dilemma of helping is that in most cultures individuals do not want to be seen as needy and therefore are reluctant to ask for help. This is particularly true in cultures characterized by high power distance combined with a high score on uncertainty avoidance (Hofstede and Hofstede, 2005). With high power distance comes a high level of respect for superiors and less likelihood of challenging superiors and less openness to being challenged. With uncertainty avoidance comes an inclination to control and impose rules to provide emotional safety, which again feeds into less willingness to show vulnerability for both mentor and mentee. In executive mentoring, this is especially problematic when dealing with diversity issues with minorities. The moment a mentoring program is implemented for the traditionally excluded, it sends a signal that these individuals are not able to advance on their own (Clutterbuck et al., 2012). For example, some women in a program designed to foster their advancement in computer science careers, not only perceived their mentoring relationships as unsuccessful, but also viewed them as confirming their marginal status (Mertz and Pfleeger, 2002). This negative attitude impacts those who might mentor and those who are to be mentored, as they may not wish to be a part of such an initiative. Schein (2011) talks about the need to create 'cultural islands'. Ibarra, Ely and Kolb (2013) talk about 'creating safe "identity workspaces" to support transitions to bigger roles'. In both instances, the point is to create a space where the normal rules of the social order are temporarily suspended to create the psychological safety to explore and be able to talk about subjects that are usually not thought to be polite – or in this case, personal issues that are not normally on the business agenda.

Value and benefits of executive mentoring

Many organizations seem to forget that executives, despite their existing successes and long experience, might still benefit from being mentored. However, the moment executives at any level stop learning they endanger the potential of the whole organization and ultimately its continued existence.

Unfortunately, not much research has been done in the area of executive mentoring, and when executives are mentioned in the context of mentoring it is mainly in the role of mentors. However, in the research and writing that does exist, executives and their organizations find mentoring valuable and helpful for the following reasons:

- **Providing the CEO with a sounding board and preventing 'loneliness'.** As a CEO, the executive is at the top of the organization and therefore no longer has anyone at their own level internally to bounce ideas off without the risk of playing favorites, or compromising confidentiality (de Janasz and Peiperl, 2014). No internal colleague or mentor can be fully objective in a debate about issues within the organization. As a new CEO, it is even more important to learn the unwritten rules and how to play the C-suite game. Additionally, stress and loneliness at the top can cause a disconnectedness and a feeling of isolation, and lead to grandiose and risky projects initiated by feeling overly powerful (Cooper and Quick, 2003), as well as occasional loss of confidence and motivation. A top executive position requires a solid support network and a confidential outlet. In Janasz and Peiperl (2014), 71% of the C-suite executives gave mentoring credit for helping them improve company performance, 69% said they were making better decisions, and 76% said they were fulfilling stakeholder expectations better as a result of mentoring.

- **Accelerate induction.** Newly promoted or hired executives can benefit from having a mentor to support the transition from one role to the next, or from one organization to another. This will give the executive a relatively easier and faster introduction and integration into the role and the organization.
- **Retention.** There is still competition for top talent, and since there is no guarantee in an organization for when you can actually offer a promotion or a more demanding position to a top talent, a mentoring program can support their retention and give executives – the mentees – inspiration for untraditional career moves within the organization. At the same time, the mentors may learn to spot talent from other parts of the organization with different kinds of talents than they usually look for, and thus also open up more career opportunities.
- **Succession planning.** Mentoring programs for executives at all levels can help the succession process run more smoothly, while ensuring that tacit knowledge and leadership values are transferred, developed, and integrated. At the same time, mentors gain new learning for their own role as top level executives as they gain more insight into the talents and ambitions of their mentees (Larcker and Miles, 2010; Larcker and Saslow, 2014; Silvestri, 2013).
- **Providing learning opportunities for mentors.** Mentors also benefit from mentoring. 'Individuals who provided mentoring tended to be more satisfied and committed than those who had not been a mentor' (Ghosh and Reijo Jr., 2013). Mentors may achieve better job performance, job satisfaction, organizational commitment, and career success from mentoring (ibid.). Providing learning opportunities for mentors, as well as for mentees, facilitates a mutual, or double learning, process that increases the organizational effect of the mentoring program (Poulsen and Wittrock, 2012).

RESEARCH AND PRACTICE – CHALLENGES AND DILEMMAS

This part of the chapter looks at the following characteristics of executive mentoring, presenting research and sharing knowledge of practice – especially where no research exists:

- Mentoring programs – strategic intent
- Matching – finding a mentor for an executive
- Board members as mentors
- Mentoring expatriates
- Cultural complexity
- Preparation and training of mentors and mentees

Mentoring programs – strategic intent

To serve their strategic intent mentoring programs need clarity of purpose at both organizational and individual levels (ISMPE).[2] However, research shows that often succession plans are not connected with mentoring and internal talent development programs. Rather, they are treated as distinct activities. This means that these organizations miss the opportunity for a strategic link between assessing talent, developing talent, and ensuring both retention and succession pipelines (Larcker and Saslow, 2014). Mentoring may support and develop the individual, but there is no guarantee that it will provide strategic benefits for the organization, unless the mentoring programs are well designed and connected to company strategy. In the Global Leadership and Talent Index by Boston Consulting Group, those companies that rate themselves strongest on 20 leadership and talent management capabilities (one of them being 'Leaders devote significant time to leadership and talent' and another 'Make leaders accountable for talent development') increased their revenue 2.2 times faster and their profits 1.5 times faster than those companies that rated themselves the weakest (Bhalla et al., 2015).

While boards rate CEOs low in talent development and find one of the top weaknesses of CEOs to be mentoring skills (Larcker and Miles, 2013a), mentoring skills for developing internal talent is one of the highest rated skills that CEOs are working to develop

(Larcker and Miles, 2013b). Additionally, 69% of respondents to a 2010 survey on CEO succession planning think that a CEO successor needs to be 'ready now' to move into the CEO role while only 54% are grooming an executive for this position; and only 50% of the companies surveyed provide on-boarding or transition support for new CEOs (Larcker and Miles, 2010).

Matching – finding a mentor for an executive

One of the most important elements in the mentoring relationships is trust (de Janasz and Peiperl, 2015; Orser, 2013). When considering this issue, there is a difference between off-line mentoring, meaning the mentor is not the mentee's direct manager, and in-line mentoring, that is with a direct supervisor serving in this capacity. It may be very difficult for a mentee to share honestly with someone who evaluates them and, in fact, this is not considered to be best practice. Additionally, having input into the matching process is important to the perceived outcome of the mentoring program for both mentor and mentee (Allen et al., 2006).

However, a clear strategic intent is needed to define the right matching criteria that will support the strategic outcome of the program (Poulsen and Wittrock, 2012). Sometimes, an organization needs to go outside itself to find these mentors. For example, a public service organization in Denmark established an innovative mentoring program for executives to facilitate a change from a bureaucratic, rule-focused public organization culture to a more customer-focused, people-focused and business-oriented culture. The organization initiated a collaboration with a number of private corporations and the executives/mentees were matched with peer executives/mentors from those private corporations. These peer mentors provided the executives with: feedback; shared stories and new leadership approaches; and functioned as a sounding board for the reflection of the mentees. These activities helped the mentees gain new perspectives and facilitated a cultural change.

Some years ago, we were involved in a mentoring program for newly hired and newly promoted leaders at a large Danish IT provider. After the first year, when we were carrying out brush-up training for the mentors, one of the mentors came up to me with a question. He was a mid-level executive and explained that he had recently been assigned as a mentor to a new C-suite executive from a different business area. He was confused and nervous about how he could be a mentor for somebody higher up in the hierarchy and thought maybe this was a mistake. However, in this particular mentoring program we were looking at two outcomes, namely leadership development and cultural understanding and integration in the organization. Therefore, in this particular match where the mentee was an experienced high level executive newly hired into the organization, the mentor's role was not to 'teach leadership' to the new executive, but to share insights into the organizational culture, the unwritten rules, how to build networks and generally how to become part of the organization. In the same way, new executives can independently look for an internal mentor, or multiple mentors, to facilitate their integration into the job and the organization.

In a global mentoring program we are currently delivering, the mentors are C-suite executives who are mentoring executives at slightly lower levels – talents and successors – to prepare them for the final step into the C-suite, to support them in building networks across organizational boundaries, and to help them identify career opportunities in the organization. We have been very careful to match across business areas to ensure trust and confidentiality between mentors and mentees; and careful to select mentors who are not direct managers to any of the other mentees in the program to ensure both openness and confidentiality when working with the whole group.

Executives on their own can look for mentors internally or externally of the organization. For CEOs it is practically impossible to find mentors internally who can provide C-suite experience and organizational insight at the same time, while executives at slightly lower levels in larger organizations do have the opportunity for internal mentoring programs.

However, there are opportunities for CEOs and C-suite members to find mentors either from professional membership networks that provide matching between members or from professional providers of executive mentoring services. Many of these networks provide mentor training and matching services based on an assessment of the executive's/mentee's needs and wishes for a mentor.[3] Some, but not all, of these providers also provide training and accreditation for their mentors, focusing on selecting mentors who have not been negatively affected by their powerful positions (Resnick, 2013; Yap, 2013), and who have a servant-leader attitude and spirit of giving back.

Board members as mentors

Potential candidates for the role of executive mentor can be selected from the Board of Directors. When a board member assumes the role of mentor for the company CEO this may improve the company's competitive behavior and overall competitiveness (Offstein et al., 2011). These authors argue that mentoring CEOs is less about career progression, as the CEO is already at the top of his/her career, and more about influencing the company's competitive strategy. Board mentors can: support the CEO in developing and understanding the competitive environment; encourage the CEO to take bolder competitive moves; and support the CEO in making effective strategic decisions. All while providing sponsorship, protection, and coaching/counseling:

> Mentoring by the board of directors enables the CEO (and therefore the firm) to better understand the competitive environment and its implications in launching more informed and complex competitive actions. Similarly, sponsorship and protection through mentoring provides greater legitimacy to actions and encourages the CEO to undertake bold competitive actions of greater magnitude ... Thus, mentoring of the CEO by directors, in effect, is likely to increase the overall competitive advantage of the firm. (ibid.)

Board members mentoring CEOs can offer other benefits, such as providing the board with greater insight into the organization and the organizational performance (Larcker and Saslow, 2014), and the opportunity to build a closer relationship and collaboration between the CEO and the board.

One issue that does need to be addressed in such relationships is that the more the board mentors are seen as having a controlling and monitoring function, the less they will be able to provide the kind of mentoring in which trust builds openness. This mentoring relationship will be affected by board mentors' assumption of their role, the CEO and C-suite's assumption about the board mentor's function, and about how well the board mentor and CEO connect on a personal level.

Mentoring expatriates

Global and international organizations often provide their expatriates with cultural induction and training and sometimes follow up with an offer of coaching to enhance performance. Mentoring can be a good approach when the mentor has relevant expat experience and leadership experience to draw upon. Research on mentoring for expatriates across global boundaries, Carraher, Sullivan and Crocitto (2008) found that:

> having a host-country mentor had a significant positive effect on the expatriate's organizational knowledge, organizational knowledge-sharing,

job performance, promotability, and perceptions of teamwork. Having a home-country mentor had a significant positive effect only on organizational knowledge, job performance, and promotability ... having a home-country mentor had a significant but negative effect on the expatriate's organization identification and job satisfaction. (p. 1310)

This is interesting and the implications are that having a mentor in the host-country will help mentees to understand the cultural context of the job and the leadership style of the local organization and employees.

Cultural complexity

Mentoring programs for executives will often take place in a global context and have participants of many nationalities. This multicultural setting adds to the complexity of the program and its management, the matching, and the relationships (Kochan and Pascarelli, 2012). Thus, it is imperative that cultural perspectives in regards to the participants and the organization are taken into account when designing, implementing, and managing mentoring programs. As for matching across cultures or diversity dimensions, while some researchers conclude that the participants may be more satisfied with the match and the mentoring when they are matched on similarities, Kochan and Pascarelli (2012) conclude that 'having dissimilar backgrounds can sometimes result in both mentors and mentees gaining new insights and understanding of one another and broaden cultural understandings' (pp. 3–4). This makes very good sense when we are talking about executives in a global environment. Whether they are expats or simply need to collaborate across borders to lead and perform, they need to be able to perform successfully in a multicultural environment.

With the increase in global business and cross-cultural collaboration, there is a growing need for developing cross-cultural communication and collaboration skills – or cultural intelligence. Early and Mosakowski (2004) define cultural intelligence as 'an outsider's seemingly natural ability to interpret someone's unfamiliar and ambiguous gestures the way the person's compatriots would' (p. 140). However, this would indicate that cultural intelligence is an innate trait and based on observation rather than on action and interaction. A newer publication (Plum, 2007, p. 1) defines cultural intelligence as 'the ability to make oneself understood and the ability to create a fruitful collaboration in situations where cultural differences play a role'. Plum (2007, 2008) argues that cultural encounters have emotional, cognitive, and practical aspects, and that consequently cultural intelligence has three interdependent dimensions:

- **The emotional dimension** – intercultural engagement
- **The cognitive dimension** – cultural understanding
- **The action dimension** – intercultural communication

These three dimensions are equally important, influence each other, and help gain a deeper understanding of the mentor/mentee encounter to help improve its outcome. This is a dynamic model that seems to resonate with mentoring as a dynamic, collaborative learning process, where the relationship grows and changes throughout the mentoring process. Additionally, it supports the approach to mentoring as a double learning process. In a cultural encounter both mentor and mentee are learning about each other and about themselves. This model of cultural intelligence is based on the assumption that culture is not a fixed thing, but a collective phenomenon that changes over time, and the model can be used to deal with cultural and diversity dimensions in a broader sense.

An example of cultural influence

In a European mentoring program for executives we are providing kick-off seminars in which only the mentees participate. Normally both mentors and mentees would participate in such kick-off seminars to gain a common understanding of the program and its purpose, and to meet their match for the first time. The headquarters of this corporation is located in France and the majority of executives in both corporation and mentoring program come from France and Germany. The two barriers to having the mentors participate in the kick-off seminars are:

- Time – the mentors are the absolute top level executives across the divisions of the corporation and have difficulty prioritizing their time.
- Corporate culture – top level executives are expected to know what mentoring is, are expected to have the answers, and it is assumed that it would be embarrassing for them to realize they do not have all the answers.

Preparation and training of mentors and mentees

There seems to be a general consensus in practice and research that mentors and mentees need preparation and training for entering into a mentoring relationship (Brockbank and McGill, 2006; ISMPE), although it does not always happen. Training and its quality can have a positive impact on the relationship, the learning process, and the perceived outcomes (Allen et al., 2006). Additionally, there is an abundance of models and techniques for mentoring and many different ways of designing and implementing this training.

There is also an assumption in organizations that the higher up and the more experienced the leader is, the less the leader needs training for the mentor role. In our experience, this assumption is often based on an understanding of mentoring as a transfer of knowledge from mentor to mentee (the first level focus of mentoring). However, if we wish to promote the modern definition of mentoring as a mutual learning alliance and a double learning process that can also influence organizational learning, we need to communicate this to organizations and prepare mentors and mentees for this approach. This is also valid for internal executive mentoring programs.

Between 2009 and 2015 we have trained more than 6,000 mentors and mentees using the concept of situational mentoring and the mentor's many roles. Many of these were executives, including C-suite executives, but also many lower level leaders, newly appointed leaders, trainees and graduates, specialists, project and program managers; with healthcare professionals, university researchers and professors also among the participants. We have found that working with the ten situational mentor roles makes a lot of sense to mentors and mentees alike. It is a solid and collaborative tool that makes it easy for mentors and mentees to talk about mentoring in a very hands-on and concrete way. Additionally, it makes it very clear to mentors and mentees that mentoring is a shared responsibility and a learning process that can benefit not only the mentee, but also the mentor and the organization.

Situational mentoring is closely linked to the modern definition of mentoring (third level focus), while integrating the many different positions or roles of the mentor. It provides a platform for a more equal relationship between mentor and mentee by giving them the same tool for understanding what mentoring is and what mentoring can do. In this way, situational mentoring facilitates the double learning process. In the training, the mentors and mentees explore the ten situational mentor roles and gain an understanding of the different communication styles and learning opportunities they represent. These roles are presented in Figure 25.3.

Some research suggests that the tenth element in mentoring, sponsoring, is a distinct concept (Friday et al., 2004). Sponsoring can be defined as 'the process of a sponsor nominating or supporting a protégé's promotion' (ibid., p. 638). In our approach, sponsoring becomes one of the options the mentor can offer the mentee and which the mentee

Figure 25.3 Situational mentoring – the mentor's many roles (Poulsen, 2008, 2012; Poulsen and Wittrock, 2012)

1	Knowledge sharer	Shares professional knowledge about people, career, leadership, etc.
2	Storyteller	Tells stories from the mentor's own and other people's lives and careers to inspire mentees
3	Networker	Helps the mentee to form new ideas for developing relations and networks
4	Friend	Listens, encourages, and supports the mentee – without making demands
5	Coach	Asks questions that give the mentee new insights and new perspectives on a situation
6	Advisor	Gives expert advice based on the mentor's own professionalism and experience
7	Discussion partner	Challenges the mentee about assumptions, opportunities, and solutions
8	Door opener	Opens doors and invites the mentee to join networks
9	Critic	Provides the mentee with constructive criticism and feedback
10	Sponsor	Provides the mentee with career guidance and visibility

can ask for. Mentors assist aspiring executives through the sponsor role by helping to advance them within the organization, and the mentor can use the other roles to help the mentee enhance their competences and effectiveness in the job (Cao and Yang, 2013).

IMPLICATIONS FOR FUTURE RESEARCH AND PRACTICE

As the complexity of organizations and markets increase, continuous, lifelong learning is important to both executives and organizations to stay competitive and successful. Executive mentoring is one method to provide executives with a learning process that is both confidential and adapted to the individual's needs. However, there is still a need for more research in the field of executive mentoring. Some issues that require further examination include:

- Are multiple mentors better than one and how does that influence trust in the various mentoring relationships?
- What is the role of HR/program managers in executive mentoring programs?
- What are the most effective methods for evaluating the benefits of executive management without infringing confidentiality?
- What are the barriers to fostering the type of mentoring for executives that will foster personal and organizational growth and change?
- To what extent do individual, organizational, and societal cultural attributes influence mentoring foci, programs, and relationships?
- What are the real and potential impacts of technology on executive mentoring?

CONCLUSION

This chapter has sought to provide an overview of the issues in executive mentoring. If we are to have corporate environments in which creativity, quality, flexibility, and cross-functional as well as cross-cultural collaboration are to thrive, it is essential that the leaders of these organizations are open to learn and change, and will foster the development and growth of those who lead now and those who will lead in the future. Executive mentoring is a proven strategy to achieve these ends. However, its success is dependent upon ensuring that those who plan and execute such programs, and those who provide training for them, are aware of the manner in which these programs should be structured, the elements that foster and hinder their success, and the possibilities for strengthening such efforts in the future. It is hoped that this chapter provides some guidance in these areas and that it will stimulate further discussion, action, and research on this important topic.

Notes

1 Conference at Copenhagen Business School (CBS), March 16, 2010, on his new book, *Helping: How to offer, give, and receive help*.
2 International Standards of Mentoring Programmes in Employment (ISMPE). Originally developed by a group of researchers and consultants led by David Clutterbuck; recently this has become a part of the European Mentoring and Coaching Council's (EMCC) accreditation program. www.ismpe.org
3 Chairman Mentors International (CMi), www.cmi.eu.com; The Mentor Partnership LLC, www.thementorpartnership.com; Executive Business+Mentors, www.kmpplus.com

REFERENCES

Allen, T. D., Eby, L. T., and Lentz, E. (2006). The relationship between formal mentoring program characteristics and perceived program effectiveness. *Personnel Psychology*, 59, 125–53. doi:10.1016/j.jvb.2007.08.004

Bal, V., Campbell, M., Steed, J., and Meddings, K. (2008). *The role of power in effective leadership*. Center for Creative Leadership. Retrieved from http://insights.ccl.org/wpcontent/uploads/2015/04/roleOfPower.pdf (accessed 5 March, 2016).

Bhalla, V., Caye, J., Haen, P., Lovich, D., Ong, C. F., Rajagopalan, M., and Sharda, S. (2015). *The global leadership and talent index*. The Boston Consulting Group and World Federation of People Management Associations, March. Retrieved from https://www.bcgperspectives.com/content/articles/leadership_talent_human_resources_global_leadership_talent_index/ (accessed 25 March, 2016).

Bozionelos, N., Bozionelos, G., Kostopoulos, K., and Polychroniou, P. (2011). How providing mentoring relates to career success and organizational commitment. *Career Development International*, 16(5), 446–68. Retrieved from http://dx.doi.org/10.1108/13620431111167760 (accessed 8 July, 2015).

Brockbank, A., and McGill, I. (2006, reprinted 2009). *Facilitating reflective learning through mentoring and coaching*. London, UK: Kogan Page.

Cao, J., and Yang, Y. (2013). *What are mentoring and sponsoring and how do they impact organizations?* Retrieved from ILR School site: http://digitalcommons.ilr.cornell.edu/student/30/ (accessed 23 January, 2016).

Carraher, S. M., Sullivan, S. E., and Crocitto, M. M. (2008). Mentoring across global boundaries: An empirical examination of home- and host-country mentors on expatriate career outcomes. *Journal of International Business Studies*, 39, 1310–26. doi:10.1057/palgrave.jibs.8400407

Charan, R., Drotter, S., and Noel, J. (2011). *The leadership pipeline – How to build the leadership-powered company*. San Francisco: Jossey-Bass.

Clutterbuck, D. (1998). *Learning alliances tapping into talent*. London, UK: Institute of Personnel and Development.

Clutterbuck, D. (2012). Understanding diversity mentoring. In D. Clutterbuck, K. M. Poulsen, and F. Kochan (Eds.), *Developing successful diversity mentoring programmes*. London, UK: Open University Press.

Clutterbuck, D. (2016) (in press) *Mentoring Executives and Directors*, 2nd edition. New York: Routledge.

Clutterbuck, D., Poulsen, K. M., and Kochan, F. (2012). *Developing successful diversity mentoring programmes*. London, UK: Open University Press.

Cooper, C. L., and Quick, J. C. (2003). The stress and loneliness of success. *Counselling Psychology Quarterly*, 16(1), 1–7.

Correira de Sousa, M., and van Dierendonck, D. (2010). Knowledge workers, servant leadership and the search for meaning in knowledge-driven organizations. *On the Horizon*, 18(3), 230–9. http://dx.doi.org/10.1108/10748121011072681

Crumpton, M. A. (2015). The emotionally intelligent mentor. *Advances in Library Administration and Organization*, 34, 29–57. doi:10.1108/S0732-067120150000034002

de Janasz, S., and Peiperl, M. (2014). *Lonely at the top*. IMD and CMI. Retrieved from http://www.chairmanmentors.com/media/pdf/imd-report-jan14.pdf

de Janasz, S., and Peiperl, M. (2015). Managing yourself – CEOs need mentors too. *Harvard Business Review*, April, 100–3. Available https://hbr.org/2015/04/ceos-need-mentors-too

Development Dimensions International (DDI) (2014). Ready-Now Leaders: 25 Findings to meet tomorrow's business challenges. *Global Leadership Forecast 2014–2015.* Retrieved from http://www.ddiworld.com/glf2014

Dumont, S. C. (2010). *Mentoring at the top in large organizations.* The Mentor Partnership LLC, www.thementorpartnership.com

Early, P. C., and Mosakowski, E. (2004). Cultural intelligence. *Harvard Business Review, 2,* 139–46.

Friday, E., Friday, S. S., and Green, A. L. (2004). A reconceptualization of mentoring and sponsoring. *Management Decisions, 42*(5), 628–44. http://dx.doi.org/10.1108/00251740410538488

Ghosh, R., and Reijo Jr., T. G. (2013). Career benefits associated with mentoring for mentors: A meta-analysis. *Journal of Vocational Behavior, 83,* 106–16. Retrieved from http://dx.doi.org/10.1016/j.jvb.2013.03.011 (accessed 23 January, 2016).

Hofstede, G., and Hofstede, G. J. (2005). *Cultures and organizations software of the mind.* New York, NY: McGraw-Hill.

Høigaard, R., and Mathisen, P. (2009, August). Benefits of formal mentoring for female leaders. *International Journal of Evidence Based Coaching and Mentoring, 7*(2), 64–70. Retrieved from https://www.researchgate.net/publication/228482731_Benefits_of_ formal_mentoring_for_female_leaders (accessed 1 April, 2015).

Howard, A., and Wellins, R. S. (2008). *Global Leadership Forecast 2008–2009.* Development Dimensions International (DDI). Retrieved from http://www.ddiworld.com/DDI/media/trend-research/GLF2008-2009_Healthcare_Highlights_ddi.pdf?ext=.pdf (accessed 5 March, 2016).

Ibarra, H., Ely, R., and Kolb, D. (2013, September). Women rising: The unseen barriers. *Harvard Business Review, 91*(9), 60–6.

Kochan, F. (2013). Analyzing the relationships between culture and mentoring. *Mentoring and Tutoring: Partnership in Learning, 21*(4), 412–30.

Kochan, F., and Pascarelli, J. T. (2012). Perspectives on culture and mentoring in the global age. In S. Fletcher and C. A. Mullen, (Eds.), *Handbook of mentoring and coaching in education* (pp.184–98). Thousand Oaks, CA: Sage.

Kram, K. E. (1988). *Mentoring at work.* Lanham, MD: University Press of America.

Larcker, D. F., and Miles, S. (2010). 2010 *Survey on CEO succession planning.* Rock Center for Corporate Governance at Stanford University and Heidrick & Struggles. Retrieved from https://www.gsb.stanford.edu/sites/gsb/files/publication-pdf/cgri-survey-2010-ceo-succession.pdf (accessed 30 June, 2016).

Larcker, D. F., and Miles, S. (2013a). *Executive coaching survey.* Rock Center for Corporate Governance at Stanford University and The Miles Group. Retrieved from http://www.gsb.stanford.edu/sites/default/files/2013-ExecutiveCoachingSurvey.pdf (accessed 30 June, 2015).

Larcker, D. F., and Miles, S. (2013b). 2013 *CEO performance evaluation survey.* Rock Center for Corporate Governance at Stanford University and The Miles Group. Retrieved from http://www.gsb.stanford.edu/faculty-research/publications/2013-ceo-performance-evaluation-survey (accessed 30 June, 2015).

Larcker, D. F., and Saslow, S. (2014). *2014 Report on senior executive succession planning and talent development.* Rock Center for Corporate Governance at Stanford University and The Institute of Executive Development. Retrieved from http://www.gsb.stanford.edu/sites/default/files/2014%20Report%20on%20Senior%20Executive%20Succession%20Planning%20and%20Talent%20Development.pdf (accessed 1 April, 2015).

Martin, A. (2007). *The changing nature of leadership.* A Center for Creative Leadership (CCL) Research White Paper. Retrieved from http://insights.ccl.org/wp-content/uploads/2015/04/NatureLeadership.pdf (accessed 13 February, 2015).

Mertz, N., and Pfleeger, L. (2002). Using mentoring to advance females and minorities in a corporate environment. In F. K. Kochan (Ed.), *The organizational and human dimensions of successful mentoring programs and relationships.* (pp. 221–42). Greenwich, CT: Information Age Publishing Inc.

Offstein, E. H., Shah, A. J., and Gnyawali, D. R. (2011). Effects of CEO-BOD mentoring on firm competitive behavior. *Review of Business*, *32*(1), 75–88.

Orser, J. L. B. (2013). Fostering trust in mentoring relationships: An exploratory study. *Equality, Diversity and Inclusion: An International Journal*, *32*(4), 410–25.

Parise, M. R., and Forret, M. L. (2007). Formal mentoring programs. The relationship of program design and support to mentors' perception of benefits and costs. *Journal of Vocational Behavior*, *72*, 225–40. Doi: 10.1016/j.jvb.2007.10.011

Pfleeger, S. L., and Mertz, N. (1995, January). Executive mentoring – What makes it work? *Communications of the ACM*, *38*(1), 63–73.

Pink, D. H. (2011). *Drive: The surprising truth about what motivates us*. Edinburgh, UK: Canongate Books.

Plum, E. (2007). *Cultural intelligence*. London, UK: Libri Publishing. Retrieved from http://www.culturalintelligence.eu/ (accessed 3 March, 2016).

Plum, E. (2008). Cultural intelligence – The art of leading cultural complexity. London, UK: Libri Publishing.

Poulsen, K. M. (2006). Implementing successful mentoring programs: Career definition vs mentoring approach. *Industrial and Commercial Training*, *38*(5), 251–8. doi: 10.1108/00197850610677715

Poulsen, K. M. (2008). *Mentor+guiden*. Copenhagen, Denmark: KMP+ Publishing.

Poulsen, K. M. (2012), *The Mentor+Guide to Mentoring Programmes*. Copenhagen, Denmark: KMP+ Publishing

Poulsen, K. M., and Wittrock, C. (2012). *Mentorprogrammer i virksomheder og organisationer*. Copenhagen, Denmark: Dansk Jurist-og Økonomforbundets Forlag (DJØF Publishing).

Resnick, B. (2013). How power corrupts the mind. *The Atlantic*, July 9. Retrieved from http://www.theatlantic.com/health/archive/2013/07/how-power-corrupts-the-mind/277638/ (accessed 13 February, 2016).

Schein, E. H. (2011). *Helping: How to offer, give, and receive help*. San Francisco, CA: Berrett-Koehler Publishers, Inc.

Schiebinger, L. (2008). Getting more women into science: Knowledge issue. In L. Schiebinger (Ed.), *Gendered innovations in science and engineering*. Stanford, CA: Stanford University Press.

Silvestri, R. F. (2013). Building leaders through planned executive development. *Leader to Leader*, *Spring*, 19–25.

Singh, R., Ragins, B. R., and Tharenou, P. (2009). What matters most? The relative role of mentoring and career capital in career success. *Journal of Vocational Behavior*, *75*, 56–67. Retrieved from doi: 10.1016/j.jvb.2009.03.003 (accessed 30 June, 2015).

van Weert, T. J. (2006). Education of the twenty-first century: New professionalism in lifelong learning, knowledge development and knowledge sharing. *Education and Information Technology*, *11*, 217–37. doi: 10.1007/s10639-006-9018-0

Yap, A. J. (2013). How power and powerlessness corrupt. (Doctoral dissertation). Retrieved from http://academiccommons.columbia.edu/catalog/ac:188502 (accessed 30 June, 2015).

Early Career Faculty Mentoring: Career Cycles, Learning and Support

Vicki L. Baker and Aimee LaPointe Terosky

Workplace mentoring is one of the three most often examined types of mentoring in organizational studies and higher education (Allen and Eby, 2007). Eby et al. (2007) define it as mentoring that 'involves a relationship between a less experienced individual (protégé) and a more experienced person (mentor), where the purpose is the personal and professional growth of the protégé' (p. 16). Hall and Chandler (2007) have created a career framework for mentoring in the workplace comprised of four phases, which will be presented in more detail later in the chapter. This chapter examines mentoring at the early stage of career development and offers recommendations to support the development and advancement of individuals at the beginning of their career.

The chapter begins with an overview of the mentoring literature looking at the benefits of such relationships for protégé, mentor, and organization. This is followed by an overview of Hall's and Chandler's (2007) framework of career learning cycles as it relates to early career mentoring. We then illustrate how such concepts can support thinking and analysis of the early career stage cycle situating our focus in the context of the professoriate. Finally, we offer literature-based recommendations on how to enhance current approaches to mentoring during the early career stage.

BENEFITS OF MENTORING TO CAREER DEVELOPMENT

The newest generation of workers tends to seek new career challenges that appeal to and match their technological and business knowledge (McIlvaine, 2015). Changing demographics means that to remain competitive, business leaders must be concerned with and focused on doing what is necessary to attract, recruit, and maintain a strong workforce (Meinert, 2013). A proven strategy is to establish strong formal workplace mentoring programs that: show a high level of support (e.g. linked to reward structures, strong leadership involvement, involve collegial relationships); establish clear goals and objectives; and have well-defined selection and evaluative criteria (Kochan, 2002). Research indicates that such programs tend to result in positive outcomes for the mentee, mentor, and organization (De Janasz et al., 2003; Finkelstein and Poteet, 2007; Noe et al., 2002). Primary benefits for the mentee include: greater career satisfaction (Chao, 1997); higher promotion rates (Whitely et al., 1991); and an increased sense of belonging (Friday and Friday, 2002). Mentors experience: increased social capital and interpersonal skill development (Wright, and Werther Jr, 1991); revitalized interest in their career (Schulz, 1995); and more favorable job attitudes overall (Lentz and Allen, 2009). In the workplace, mentorships have also been found to serve as important career development tools that can result in positive organizational outcomes, including knowledge dissemination and sharing (Swap et al., 2001) and greater engagement as indicated by increases in organizational citizenship behaviors (Donaldson et al., 2000).

Positive workplace relationships are vital in helping an individual manage the rigors of their career trajectory and strong mentorships – created through formal programming, fostered by informal work connections, or as ingrained in the organizational culture – are an important strategy for creating those relationships. This is particularly important for individuals in their early career stage. Such relationships can help serve as: critical socializing agents (Thomas and Lankau, 2009); provide access to social capital and networking support (Blickle et al., 2009; Siebert et al., 2001); and help the early career entrant gain legitimacy (Chandler et al., 2011). Researchers have examined the influence of the 'right' mentor for the protégé in early career and found that protégés report greater career benefits when they have mentors who are perceived as being influential in their given organizational context (Arnold and Johnson, 1997). To provide a greater understanding of the connection between relationships and early career supports, we turn to Hall and Chandler's (2007) framework of career learning cycles and transitions.

CAREER LEARNING AND EARLY CAREER TRANSITIONS

Hall and Chandler (2007) sought to understand the role of and connection between a person's developmental network – defined as the group of individuals who take an active interest in supporting the protégé's advancement (Higgins and Kram, 2001) – and learning, as facilitated by career transitions. They described four stages (exploration, trial, establishment, mastery) that a protégé experiences in his or her early career. Relationships are not only vitally important during each of these four stages, but may serve as facilitators in enabling the focal individual to navigate each stage successfully. Relationships can also hinder development. Therefore, it becomes critically important to understand who provides support, what support is offered, and how and if the support enables an individual to transition through their intended career. In the following sections, we include a brief overview of Hall and Chandler's four distinct career stages of exploration, trial, establishment, and mastery.

Exploration

Exploration occurs when an individual contemplates potential careers or fields of work. The learner displays (and internalizes) a state of readiness for such change and illustrates that readiness by selecting a chosen career that is believed to reinforce his/her sense of self. One's mentors (or developers) provide critical insights as the 'outsiders' who offer guidance on the protégé's talents, skills, and strengths related to careers in which those talents can be realized and enhanced. Mentors also provide much needed support by way of helping the protégé develop realistic expectations and motivation toward pursuing the intended career path.

Trial

The trial stage begins once the individual decides on a career/field of interest and begins to engage in the activities and roles associated with the field as 'trials' or tests of fit (Ibarra, 1999). In other words, the new employee *tries on* the new role, or aspects of it, to determine the suitability, comfortability, and ease with which aspects of the new career align with personal values and interests. Three goals are pursued (and must be achieved) to successfully pass through this stage: (1) successful exit from the current role; (2) development of confidence in one's ability to cope in the new career; and (3) enjoying the sense-making process that accompanies said transition.

Establishment

Upon successful navigation of the trial stage, the individual enters the establishment stage where role learning begins. Role learning is defined as knowledge acquisition, including mastery of the social, organizational, and political norms (Morrison, 1995). At this stage, the protégé works to gain legitimacy by engaging in community practices that illustrate his/her competency (Lave and Wenger, 1991). Mentoring relationships become critically important at this stage as advice and counsel help guide the protégé toward assimilation and fit. The establishment and mastery stages, according to Hall and Chandler (2007), are where most mentoring studies are situated, particularly for early career entrants.

Mastery

The final stage, mastery, ensues when an individual moves from peripheral to full participation in the intended career. At this point, the protégé displays the ability to effectively engage with veterans in the professional and disciplinary domains and is able to perform the associated tasks (Lave and Wenger, 1991). 'Ideally, the mastery stage represents the time at which developers can bring learners smoothly toward the next role transition' (Hall and Chandler, 2007, p. 489).

HALL'S AND CHANDLER'S CAREER STAGE MODEL AND EARLY CAREER FACULTY

In the following section, we situate the notion of career learning and transitions in the professoriate, specifically early career faculty. Although some institutions, domestically and abroad, may offer similar or different experiences to the ones we describe, it is the following model that informs our thinking. In this model, the professoriate has three career stages (assistant, associate, full). Embedded in each career stage, are mini or condensed times of exploration, trial, establishment, and mastery. Typically, the early career faculty member is in the first career stage (assistant professor) for six years, unless more time is added (e.g. for parental leave). During this six-year timeframe, the faculty member may experience an interim review at the third year mark, or may be subject to yearly reviews, leading to the tenure decision from assistant to associate professor.

We now highlight the challenges facing early career faculty in moving from assistant professor to associate professor through each of the four stages of exploration, trial, establishment, and mastery. This is followed with literature-based recommendations on how to enhance current approaches to mentoring at each career phase. Although we structure this chapter on a stage model, we do note that, as with all stage theories, individual faculty members and their experiences within their careers are fluid and unique. Thus, faculty members may face challenges or require mentoring in different ways and at different points in their careers, so the Hall and Chandler stage model should be viewed as a helpful lens rather than a concrete process that all will follow in a linear manner.

EXPLORATION STAGE

Exploration stage challenges

Based on Hall's and Chandler's (2007) work, the exploration stage is defined as a time in which individuals consider potential avenues for their careers, and in turn, reflect on whether they fit within their career's roles and expectations. For the faculty career, much of the exploration stage occurs during graduate school when students not only decide if they will pursue an entry into a professorial career, but also at what type of institution they aspire to work. Thus, aspiring and early career academics need to look deeply into the profession's responsibilities for teaching, research, and service, its reward and advancement structures, and its challenges. This is particularly important at times like the present with reductions in full-time, tenure-track positions, tighter budgets, new pedagogical approaches, changing student demographics, and rising externally-mandated accountability and compliance measures (Altbach, 2015; Austin, 2002).

Alongside learning about the context and content of a faculty career, aspiring and early career faculty in the exploratory phase will need to determine if the academic career and/or different institutional contexts 'fit' with their own goals and dispositions. Recent surveys of aspiring academics found that their primary considerations for choosing a professorial position and/or institution included: conducting meaningful work; balancing teaching and research; achieving work-life balance; and maintaining quality living conditions (Finkelstein, 2015; see also Gibson, 2006; Trower, 2011a). Considered 'the signature of the millennial generation', (Finkelstein, 2015, p. 305), these primary indicators highlight that new faculty, in general, seek meaningful work that balances personal and the professional worlds more strongly than past generations of aspiring academics.

Exploration stage mentoring

As previously mentioned, much of the exploration stage occurs during doctoral studies under the guidance of academic advisors and therefore the significance of the advisor–student relationship during graduate school cannot be overlooked (Austin, 2002; Austin and McDaniels, 2006; Eddy and Hart, 2011; Gardner, 2010a; Lindholm, 2004; Noy and Ray, 2012; Sallee, 2011), particularly because positive relationships with advisors is one of the strongest predictors of doctoral retention (Golde, 2000; Mendoza, 2007). Scholars note that graduate school mentors are important for 'instrumental support', which includes mentoring on the 'survival skills for being academics in their disciplines' (Noy and Ray, 2012, p. 902); these survival skills include program completion, career advancement, social networks, research and publication collaborations, and job placement.

Yet, scholars and experts studying faculty work argue that graduate school preparation needs to rethink its current approach to advising the next generation of academics (ibid.), in large part because of the criticism that most doctoral graduates exit their programs with a limited understanding of the full career (Austin, 2002, 2011; Bieber and Worley, 2006; Jaeger et al., 2013). Critics also point out that programs primarily emphasize learning how to complete dissertation research and socialize their students toward the university model that emphasizes research productivity (Austin and McDaniels, 2006; Bieber and Worley, 2006; Gardner, 2010a; Golde and Dore, 2001; Weidman et al., 2001), despite the fact that most aspiring academics will acquire positions at institutions with teaching-focused missions 'with students who are much more diverse in backgrounds, social class, and abilities' (Altbach, 2015, p.13; see also Austin, 2011; Bieber and Worley, 2006; Golde and Dore, 2001).

With these concerns in mind, the mentoring that occurs during graduate school, typically between advisor and student, needs to provide a complete picture of the professorial career by emphasizing the following: (1) discussing all the career's responsibilities, not solely focusing on research; (2) highlighting the full range of experiences at different institutional types, beyond major research universities; (3) an overview of issues surrounding work–life balance; (4) encouraging reflection in terms of fit with the career and institutional types; and (5) providing organized, systematic professional development opportunities through teaching and research assistantships with guidance from mentors (Austin, 2002; Austin and McDaniels, 2006; Gardner, 2010b).

To better develop and support these mentoring skills in advisors, several scholars encourage the involvement of professional development personnel, human resources (HR) or organizational developers (OD) in providing professional growth opportunities that develop the mentoring skills of doctoral advisors (Austin, 2002; Gibson, 2006; Noy and Ray, 2012). Besides the need to enhance mentors' skills more generally, scholars also note that there needs to be intentional pairings of mentors–mentees around identity characteristics (e.g. gender, ethnicity, parent), when possible (Patton, 2009). Since women and faculty of color are likely to benefit from mentoring relationships with advisors with salient identity group characteristics, or with advisors who appreciate students (male or female) who are not aligned to masculine paradigms (e.g. competitiveness, hierarchy, sanctions) (Sallee, 2011), it is likewise important to ensure that they complete doctoral programs so that there is a strong pool of women and minorities from which to hire.

Lastly, scholars also highlight that the advisor–student relationship is not the only, and in some cases not even the primary, source of support; instead doctoral students' developmental networks with peers and external communities serve as significant influences during the exploration stage and therefore policies and actions that take into account this, oftentimes under-recognized form of support, are recommended (Austin, 2002; Baker, 2009; Bieber and Worley, 2006; Gardner, 2010a; Patton, 2009; Weidman and Stein, 2003).

TRIAL STAGE

Trial stage challenges

Following the exploratory stage, the trial stage, according to Hall and Chandler (2007), is a time in which an individual enters a career/field of interest and begins to perform the profession's responsibilities; it is also a time when an individual's sense of fit is tested. In terms of the early faculty career, the first three years of being an assistant professor is generally a time in which faculty members 'learn the ropes' of their specific positions and institutional contexts (Sorcinelli, 2000). This type of learning can range from an instrumental nature – such as how to operate a course management or communications system, how to complete required forms, or how to conduct office hours – to a scholarly nature – such as how to develop the content of a course, or how to establish connections to fellow scholars in one's area of expertise (Neumann, 2009). This instrumental and scholarly learning takes place within the contemporary American higher education context of financial and tenure-track employment concerns, changing student demographics and related pedagogical adjustments, and rising externally-mandated accountability and compliance measures (Altbach, 2015; Austin, 2002).

Although considered a time of great need in terms of learning and support, the extant literature characterizes the transition from doctoral studies to academic career as difficult for a number of reasons, including: lack of collegial relationships and related isolation; lack of strategies for integrating and balancing personal and professional lives; little or no feedback, recognition and/or reward from colleagues; lack of clear guidelines around the tenure and promotion process; and lack of networks supporting faculty members' scholarly learning (Austin, 2002). With these difficulties in mind, the trial stage can involve having to figure out roles, responsibilities, and fit within an academic career. This has often been a stage in which career faculty have had to 'historically…sink or swim on their own' (Finkelstein, 2015, p. 304).

Trial stage mentoring

In light of the view that the trial stage is one of sinking or swimming, it is important to consider how higher education institutions might support faculty members as they progress through this stage. Historically, the most common approach to supporting early career faculty has been traditional mentoring, where an experienced faculty member is formally assigned to an incoming faculty member within the same academic department, oftentimes with little or no guidelines or accountability. While the traditional mentoring structure has, for some, served as a source of great support, for others it has been ineffective or even detrimental (Feldman, 1999; Johnson, 2002). This happens, in part, because the power dynamics of traditional mentoring can result in: socializing one to believe there is only 'one right pathway' in the academy; a lack of salient identity characteristics between mentor and mentee; and lack of attention on the mentee from the mentor (Feldman, 1999; Johnson, 2002; Johnson and Huwe, 2002; Patton, 2009).

Based on shortcomings of traditional models of mentoring, experts recommend incorporating measures to address noted shortcomings in traditional mentoring structures, including: (1) intentionally selecting mentors based on a commitment to the mentoring process, shared interests between mentors–mentees, and/or common identity group characteristics; (2) providing time on a regular basis for the mentor–mentee relationship through course releases, service workload reductions, and/or established meeting times; (3) developing mentors' skill sets around how to mentor through systematic professional development and support; (5) sharing trends in new faculty needs with mentors so they can adapt accordingly; (6) developing policies/programs that integrate external communities/developmental networks; and (7) implementing an evaluation system that considers the work of mentoring in yearly evaluations or reward structures (Baker, 2009; Furco and Moely, 2012; Gibson, 2006; Lazerson et al., 2000; Patton, 2009; Ponjuan et al., 2011; Terosky et al., 2014).

ESTABLISHMENT STAGE

Establishment stage challenges

Situated at/after mid-tenure review for early career faculty, we characterize the establishment stage in Hall's and Chandler's (2007) model as a time in which faculty members have successfully navigated the trial stage and now begin to learn more deeply about, and shape, their roles and identities within their institutional contexts. In response to a mid-tenure review, faculty may find themselves grappling with their scholarly agenda and institutional identity for the purposes of shaping (or re-shaping) their academic careers around meaningful contributions and to meet expectations related to the tenure and promotion process (Hardré and Cox, 2009; Neumann and Terosky, 2007).

In regard to grappling with a scholarly agenda and identity, scholars of faculty work recognize that the professorial career is one that values highly the passion that originally drew people to the professorial career. Thus, the establishment stage is viewed as a time in which faculty are drawn to reconnect with their subject matter passions through their teaching, research, and service (Neumann, 2009; Neumann and Terosky, 2007).

At this stage, faculty need a better understanding of the tenure/promotion process, particularly in how it pertains to their own progress toward this goal. Yet, the extant literature notes that faculty members remain largely dissatisfied with their understanding of, and support related to, this process. 'One of the consistent complaints voiced by tenure-ladder faculty,' notes Finkelstein (2015), 'across all institutional types – was the lack of clear and explicit standards for satisfying tenure requirements' (p. 303). Without clearly communicated and enacted guidelines for tenure/promotion at institutions, faculty, especially women and faculty of color (Ponjuan et al., 2011), find navigating the system troublesome during the establishment phase.

Establishment stage mentoring

Based on recent studies, non-traditional forms of mentoring that include collaborative structures (e.g. peer mentoring, faculty learning communities, communities of practice, sense of community and collegiality, professional/disciplinary organizations' initiatives in learning communities, tenure/promotion support groups) benefit faculty as they reflect on and come to terms with their scholarly agenda, institutional identity, and progress toward tenure (Kezar, 2006; Terosky and Heasley, 2013). Whereas traditional, yet enhanced, forms of hierarchical mentoring might provide valuable networks for aspiring and current faculty in the exploration and trial stages, experts generally agree that pondering deep questions around future directions and one's scholarly place in an institution or field are well served in structures that promote collaboration among peers and communities (Creamer, 2004; Terosky and Heasley, 2013). In these collaborative structures, professors informally share expertise and passions around similar questions, concerns, and skills (Wenger and Snyder, 2000), while also upholding the perspective that all participants have talents and skills to contribute (Nunez et al., 2015).

The literature on academic careers emphasizes the significance of collaborative learning communities for faculty professional growth, motivation, teaching effectiveness, job satisfaction, and retention (Bozeman and Gaughan, 2011; Gappa et al., 2007; Hagedorn, 2000; Neumann, 2009; O'Meara et al., 2008; Rice et al., 2000; Rosser, 2004). This is especially important given recent findings about the preference of Generation X faculty for less of a top-down mentoring approach and more 'foster[ing] connections between naturally developing relationships, shared power, and collective action' (Gibson, 2006, p. 64). To researchers and faculty development practitioners, the strength of collaborative mentoring lies in its structure, namely informal, self-selected (Terosky et al., 2014), faculty-initiated groupings (Terosky and Gonzales, 2015) with colleagues who may reside in different departments or institutions (Baker, 2009; O'Meara and Niehaus, 2013; Patton, 2009; Terosky et al., 2014). These collaborations have the potential to serve as sites for professional relationships that foster intellectual growth, identity development, and assessments of tenure progress, especially for women and faculty of color who might not be served well in traditional mentoring structures (Patton, 2009).

Past research also indicates that initiatives, such as collaborative types of mentoring, are likely to fail if program developers/institutional leaders do not secure the involvement and buy-in of key constituents prior to launching the program (Furco and Moely, 2012; Kezar, 2006). To secure faculty buy-in, scholars recommend: clearly communicating the goals of the mentoring collaboration; providing opportunities for exploration of deeper level reflection while simultaneously remaining mindful of faculty time constraints; committing to on-going support of collaborative mentoring structures; rewarding participants through professional growth metrics and reward systems (Furco and Moely, 2012; Kezar, 2006; Lazerson et al., 2000); and addressing systemic organizational elements that hinder collaborative efforts (Kezar, 2006).

MASTERY STAGE

Mastery stage challenges

The final stage of Hall's and Chandler's model, the mastery stage, is characterized by individuals earning legitimacy in their field/career by demonstrating the ability to reach professional expectations and perform associated tasks. In terms of the early career faculty, the awarding of tenure and/or promotion occurs at this stage, and is oftentimes accompanied by a sense that faculty members no longer require support or mentoring. Yet, studies of early mid-career faculty note that this career phase is one of great transition as associate professors, no longer under the protection of pre-tenure status, are oftentimes called on to assume greater levels of service and administrative work (Baldwin et al., 2005; Gappa et al., 2007; Neumann and Terosky, 2007) with little to no mentoring or support in their new role.

It is not surprising, then, that recent surveys highlight that associate professors are the least satisfied rank in academia (Baldwin et al., 2005; Buch et al., 2011; DeAngelo et al., 2009; Jaschik, 2012; Trower, 2011a, 2011b; Wilson, 2012). Scholars explain these survey findings by suggesting that most faculty are caught off guard by their new workloads, and, as such, they need support in determining ways to manage their academic career, effectively. This need is particularly significant for populations historically burdened with excesses of service, such as women and faculty of color (Gappa et al., 2007; Glazer-Raymo, 2008; Terosky et al., 2014).

Mastery stage mentoring

Although the effectiveness of mentoring at all stages of Hall's and Chandler's model is criticized in the literature, the mastery stage is particularly noted for lacking support in addressing the needs of newly tenured faculty (Neumann and Terosky, 2007). At this stage, faculty needs include learning how to organize their time and focus on career advancement in the light of rising service/administrative loads. Thus, a combination of traditional mentoring, in which more experienced faculty provide expertise, and collaborative forms of mentoring, in which peers or learning communities share insights and reflections, would benefit faculty members during the mastery stage.

The content of mentoring during this period, should focus on facilitating newly tenured faculty members' skills in management (e.g. supervision of personnel, logistics and operations, budgeting), career design (e.g. how to craft the career in ways that promote one's scholarly and professional priorities), leadership (e.g. how to establish a mission/vision, how to reach goals and objectives, how to lead others), scholarly learning (e.g. how to contribute to one's scholarly field and knowledge base), and career advancement (e.g. how to meet expectations for promotion to full professor). These topics could be addressed: in induction processes guided by professional development support personnel; through one-on-one traditional mentoring with committed senior level faculty and administrators; and/or through collaborative mentoring structures with peers or a range of ranks (Austin, 2002; Gibson, 2006). Institutions can also promote the mentoring of faculty at the mastery stage by: creating, promoting, and rewarding participation in mentoring groups on management, leadership, and advancement; crediting the work of senior faculty who mentor others at this stage; and proactively publicizing and supporting faculty learning communities. Regardless of structure, whether traditional or collaborative forms of mentoring or a combination of both, experts highlight that recently tenured faculty members will continue to have professional growth needs throughout the remainder of their careers and intentional mentoring programs will better 'position faculty growth as ongoing and in a constant state of becoming' (O'Meara et al., 2008, p. 24).

DISCUSSION

Our aim in writing this chapter was to better understand how developmental relationships, such as mentorships, can support career learning and aid in career transitions. We conclude our chapter by offering our personal observations and future directions on these issues as evidenced in the mentoring literature.

The Hall and Chandler (2007) framework presented in this chapter helps illustrate the process through which career learning and transitions occur, allowing the protégé to be proactive about needs and supports to successfully navigate those transitions. Hence, we argue that a network of individuals is needed to support all early career individuals to be successful in their current career stage and as a means of preparing for the inevitable career transitions created by the current and ever-evolving career landscape. These networks can vary in type and purpose. For example, Hill and Lineback (2011) suggested creating three types of networks: *operational*, to support day-to-day work: *developmental*, to provide career and psychosocial health support; and *strategic,* which involves relationships aimed at supporting future career paths and goals. They argue that this third network, the strategic network, is often neglected since the other two networks usually develop organically. A strategic network requires: deliberate thinking about future professional and personal goals; a needs assessment to identify areas for support and further development; and a thoughtful inventory of those individuals who can provide the necessary support. Future research could explore the presence of strategic networks for early career professionals and the associated professional and personal outcomes.

We also suggest looking at new ways of supporting faculty, and other early career individuals, throughout their career trajectory journey. First, we believe that these efforts should not involve a top-down approach, but should be driven by the protégé. For faculty members, this means faculty leaders or developers should not be the drivers of such efforts, but they should work in collaboration with the early career individuals themselves to learn more about what support is needed. Such a collaboration should take lessons from those human resources/organizational developers who connect individual and organizational outcomes to each other. In other career contexts, this approach requires the protégé to be strategic (and reflective) about their intended career path, supports needed, and who is available to provide such support. At a minimum, a conversation with a direct supervisor and/or the human resource manager during performance appraisal time is recommended.

While formal networking and other mentoring experiences are essential, the importance of, and the need for, informal mentorships should not be forgotten. These informal mentorships should not be underestimated as important resources that round out the more deliberate, strategic efforts individuals (and organizations) engage in as they manage the ebbs and flows of their careers. Rather than long-term relationships that have a main goal(s) in mind, informal mentorships can serve as more short-term, or even one-off, opportunities for career learning or to fill the gap as an individual transition to the next phase of his/her career. In fact, some researchers have found that informal mentorships may be more beneficial than formal mentorships (Chao et al., 1992; Eby and Lockwood, 2005). Future research could explore the role and extent to which informal mentorships contribute to early career faculty members' transitions within and between stages of the professoriate.

Another important issue, supported in the mentoring literature and practice, is that formal mentoring programs need to be overhauled to acknowledge and correct the associated inherent challenges to their success. To that end, we suggest formal mentoring programs need to: (1) have input from the protégé; (2) be collaborative in nature to include peer to peer and other types of learning communities; (3) be individualized rather than a one-size-fits-all approach to mentoring; (4) account for the importance of content (and context) as a significant contributor to effectiveness; (5) be structured beyond initial matching and meeting opportunities; and (6) include extensive support, training, and accountability of mentors and protégés to support overall effectiveness of mentoring, and to achieve individual and organizational level outcomes (Campbell and Campbell, 2002).

Businesses and HR professionals are finding that a diverse workforce results in greater innovation and serves as a recruitment and retention tool, yet many institutions are still falling short in some critical areas (Egan, 2011). Yet, administrators tend not to fully understand how to attract and recruit promising new faculty from diverse backgrounds and, once hired, how to retain them (Finkelstein and Lacelle-Peterson, 1992; Sorcinelli and Austin, 1992). The sink or swim model common in the academy will no longer suffice. Rather, upper level administration and management need to have a commitment to new faculty and early career individuals and their success to attract and retain a talented, diverse workforce. They must also ensure that adequate resources are available to support these efforts.

Surveys have shown that work–life balance, quality of life, non-monetary incentives, and opportunities for advancement serve as key motivators for the current workforce and, as such, need to be accounted for in career support (Finkelstein, 2015; McCracken, 1999). Thus, it also seems apparent that more men and women who are dedicated to meaningful work and a work–life balance are placed in leadership positions so that these topics are discussed at the highest levels of the college/university or organization and are being addressed on a cultural level.

CONCLUSION

Our aim in this chapter was to focus on the importance of workplace mentoring relationships in the development of the early career professional and to provide an overview of the literature on this topic. We used Hall and Chandler's (2007) career cycles and learning framework to examine its usefulness in the context of the professoriate – specifically for the early career faculty member. We argue that the career stage approach, as outlined by Hall and Chandler (2007) is salient and useful, given the mini stages a faculty member experiences within and between the phases of his/her career, and the increasing challenges facing a professorial career with shifting demographics in future generations of doctoral students and early career faculty members – all of which call on the field of education to expand on the conversation on effective mentoring practices. Few studies attempt to explore the experiences of pre-tenure faculty at various career checkpoints, and the relationships that are present within that timeframe. A notable exception is the work of Ponjuan, Conley, and Trower (2011), in which they looked at professional and personal relationships with colleagues at different stages of pre-tenure. Therefore, our efforts in this chapter should be a meaningful contribution to this discussion as it offers a foundation framework for understanding the role of relationships in this understudied career stage.

While we situated this examination in the context of the professoriate and the experiences of early career faculty, recommendations offered could support mentoring efforts of early career individuals in other professional contexts. As Baker (2015) noted, business and higher education share fundamental similarities, such as seeking to attract and retain a talented workforce as a means of gaining and maintaining a competitive advantage. Furthermore, the 'face' of the employee is changing to include more women, underrepresented populations, and individuals motivated by personal growth and other unique career experiences. Such trends are present in both business and higher education, therefore, making an examination of the role of mentoring and career development at the early stages of one's career even more vital.

In summary, the traditional mentoring model – the dyadic relationship in which a more senior individual imparts knowledge to a novice – is antiquated given the changing career landscape. We offered recommendations in an effort to acknowledge the needs of a diverse population of employees, with a particular focus on the early career individual. There is a need to acknowledge: the role a variety of relationships play; the need for transparent and open dialogue in the workplace; and an understanding of workforce requirements and supports. We hope that the concepts presented here will foster meaningful dialogue, research, and action on this important topic.

REFERENCES

Allen, D., and Eby, L. T. (Eds.) (2007). *Blackwell handbook of mentoring: A multidisciplinary approach*. Oxford, UK: Blackwell.

Altbach, P. G. (2015). Building an academic career: A twenty-first century challenge. In M. Yudkevich, P. G. Altbach, and L. E. Rumbley (Eds.), *Young faculty in the twenty-first century: International perspectives*. Albany, NY: State University of New York Press.

Arnold, J., and Johnson, K. (1997). Mentoring in early career. *Human Resource Management Journal, 7*(4), 61–70.

Austin, A. E. (2002). Preparing the next generation of faculty: Graduate school as socialization to the academic career. *The Journal of Higher Education, 73*(1), 94–122.

Austin, A. E. (2011). The socialization of future faculty in a changing context: Traditions, challenges, and possibilities. In J. Hermanowicz (Ed.), *The American academic profession: Transformation in contemporary higher education*. Baltimore, MD: Johns Hopkins University Press.

Austin, A. E., and McDaniels, M. (2006). Preparing the professoriate of the future: Graduate student socialization for faculty roles. *Higher Education: Handbook of Theory and Research* (Vol. XXI, pp. 397–456). New York: Agathon Press.

Baker, V. (2009). Toward a theory of doctoral student professional identity development: A developmental networks approach. *Journal of Higher Education, 80*(1), 1–33.

Baker, V. L. (2015). People strategy in human resources: Lessons for mentoring in higher education. *Mentoring and Tutoring: Partnership in Learning, 23*(1), 6–18.

Baldwin, R. G., Lunceford, C. J., and Vanderlinden, K. E. (2005). Faculty in the middle years: Illuminating an overlooked phase of academic life. *The Review of Higher Education, 29*(1), 97–118.

Bieber, J. P., and Worley, L. K. (2006). Conceptualizing the academic life: Graduate students' perspectives. *The Journal of Higher Education, 77*(6), 1009–35.

Blickle, G., Witzki, A. H., and Schneider, P. B. (2009). Mentoring support and power: A three year predictive field study on protégé networking and career success.

Journal of Vocational Behavior, *74*(2), 181–9.

Bozeman, B., and Gaughan, M. (2011). Job satisfaction among university faculty: Individual, work, and institutional determinants. *The Journal of Higher Education*, *82*(2), 154–86.

Buch, K., Huet, Y., Rorrer, A., and Roberson, L. (2011). Removing the barriers to full professor: A mentoring program for associate professors. *Change: The Magazine of Higher Learning*, *43*(6), 38–45.

Campbell, T. A., and Campbell, D. E. (2002). Programmatic elements that enhance the mentoring relationship. In F. K. Kochan (Ed.), *The organizational and human dimension of successful mentoring across diverse settings* (pp. 69–82). Greenwich, CT: Information Age Publishing.

Chandler, D. E., Kram, K. E., and Yip, J. (2011). An ecological systems perspective on mentoring at work: A review and future prospects. *The Academy of Management Annals*, *5*(1), 519–70.

Chao, G. T. (1997). Mentoring phases and outcomes. *Journal of Vocational Behavior*, *51*(1), 15–28.

Chao, G. T., Walz, P. M., and Gardner, P. D. (1992). Formal and informal mentorships: A comparison on mentoring functions and contrast with nonmentored counterparts. *Personnel Psychology*, *45*(3), 619.

Creamer, E. G. (2004). Collaborators' attitudes about differences of opinion. *Journal of Higher Education*, *75*(5), 556–71.

DeAngelo, L., Hurtado, S., Pryor, J. H., Kelly, K. R., and Santos, J. L. (2009). *The American college teacher: National norms for the 2007–2008 HERI faculty survey*. Los Angeles, C.A.: Higher Education Research Institute, UCLA.

De Janasz, S. C., Sullivan, S. E., and Whiting, V. (2003). Mentor networks and career success: Lessons for turbulent times. *The Academy of Management Executive*, *17*(4), 78–91.

Donaldson, S. I., Ensher, E. A., and Grant-Vallone, E. J. (2000). Longitudinal examination of mentoring relationships on organizational commitment and citizenship behavior. *Journal of Career Development*, *26*(4), 233–49.

Eby, L. T., Rhodes, J., and Allen, T. D. (2007). Definition and evolution of mentoring. In T. D. Allen and L. T. Eby (Eds.), *Blackwell handbook of mentoring: A multidisciplinary approach* (pp. 7–20). Oxford, UK: Blackwell.

Eby, L. T., and Lockwood, A. (2005). Protégés' and mentors' reactions to participating in formal mentoring programs: A qualitative investigation. *Journal of Vocational Behavior*, *67*(3), 441–58.

Eddy, P. L., and Hart, J. (2011). Faculty in the hinterlands: Cultural anticipation and cultural reality. *Higher Education*, *63*, 751–69.

Egan, M. E. (2011). *Global diversity and inclusion: Fostering innovation through a diverse workforce*. New York: Forbes Insights. Retrieved online on May 20, 2015 from http://images.forbes.com/forbesinsights/StudyPDFs/Innovation_Through_Diversity.pdf

Feldman, D. C. (1999). Toxic mentors or toxic protégés? A critical re-examination of dysfunctional mentoring. *Human Resource Management Review*, *9*(3), 247–78.

Finkelstein, M. J. (2015). 'Do I still want to be a professor and, if so, can I?' Entering the American academic profession in the first decade of the twenty-first century. In M. Yudkevich, P. G. Altbach, and L. E. Rumbley (Eds.), *Young faculty in the twenty-first century: International perspectives*. Albany, NY: State University of New York Press.

Finkelstein, M. J., and Lacelle-Peterson, M. W. (1992). New and junior faculty: A review of the literature. *New Directions For Teaching And Learning*, *50*, 5–14.

Finkelstein, L. M., and Poteet, M. L. (2007). Best practices in formal mentoring programs in organizations. In T. Allen, and L. Eby (Eds.), *The Blackwell handbook of mentoring* (pp. 345–68). Oxford: Blackwell Publishing.

Friday, E., and Friday, S. S. (2002). Formal mentoring: is there a strategic fit? *Management Decision*, *40*(2), 152–7.

Furco, A., and Moely, B. E. (2012). Using learning communities to build faculty support for pedagogical innovation: A multi-campus study. *Journal of Higher Education*, *83*(1), 128–53.

Gappa, J., Austin, A., and Trice, A. (2007). *Rethinking faculty work: Higher education's strategic imperative*. San Francisco, CA: John Wiley and Sons.

Gardner, S. K. (2010a). Contrasting the socialization experiences of doctoral students in high- and low-completing departments: A qualitative analysis of disciplinary contexts at one institution. *Journal of Higher Education*, *81*(1), 61–81.

Gardner, S. K. (2010b). Keeping up with the Joneses: Socialization and culture in doctoral education at one striving institution. *The Journal of Higher Education*, *81*(6), 728–49.

Gibson, S. K. (2006). Mentoring of women faculty: The role of organizational politics and culture. *Innovative Higher Education*, *31*(1), 63–79.

Glazer-Raymo, J. (2008). The feminist agenda. In J. Glazer-Raymo (Ed.), *Unfinished agendas: New and continuing gender challenges in higher education*. Baltimore, MD: Johns Hopkins University Press.

Golde, C. M. (1998). Beginning graduate school: Explaining first-year. In M. S. Anderson (Ed.), *The experience of being in graduate school: An exploration* (pp. 55–64). San Francisco, CA: Jossey-Bass.

Golde, C. M. (2000). Should I stay or should I go? Student descriptions of the doctoral attrition process. *The Review of Higher Education*, *23*(2), 199–227.

Golde, C. M., and Dore, T. M. (2001). *At cross purposes: What the experiences of today's doctoral students reveal about doctoral education*. Philadelphia, PA: Pew Charitable Trusts.

Hagedorn, L. S. (2000). *What contributes to job satisfaction among faculty and staff. New directions for institutional research*, (p. 105). San Francisco, CA: Jossey-Bass.

Hall, D. T., and Chandler, D. E. (2007). Career cycles and mentoring. In B. R. Ragins and K. E. Kram (Eds.), *The handbook of mentoring at work: Theory, research, and practice* (pp. 471–97). Thousand Oaks, CA: Sage.

Hardré, P., and Cox, M. (2009). Evaluating faculty work: Expectations and standards of faculty performance in research universities. *Research Papers in Education*, *24*(4), 383–419.

Higgins, M. C., and Kram, K. E. (2001). Reconceptualizing mentoring at work: A developmental network perspective. *Academy of Management Review*, *26*(2), 264–88.

Hill, L., and Lineback, K. (2011). The three networks you need. *Harvard Business Review, March 3*. Retrieved on May 16, 2015. https://hbr.org/2011/03/the-three-networks-you-need.html

Ibarra, H. (1999). Provisional selves: Experimenting with image and identity in professional adaptation. *Administrative Science Quarterly*, *44*(4), 764–91.

Jaeger, A. J., Haley, K. J., Ampaw, F. D., and Levin, J. S. (2013). Understanding the career choice for underrepresented minority doctoral students in science and engineering. *Journal of Women and Minorities in Science and Engineering*, *19*(1), 1–16.

Jaschik, S. (2012). Unhappy associate professors. *Inside Higher Education, June 4*. Retrieved from http://www.insidehighered.com/news/2012/06/04/associate-professors-less-satisfied-those-other-ranks-survey-finds (accessed 12 April, 2014).

Johnson, W. B. (2002). The intentional mentor: Strategies and guidelines for the practice of mentoring. *Professional psychology: Research and practice*, *33*(1), 88.

Johnson, W. B., and Huwe, J. M. (2002). Toward a typology of mentorship dysfunction in graduate school. *Psychotherapy: Theory, Research, Practice, Training*, *39*(1), 44.

Kezar, A. J. (2006). Redesigning for collaboration in learning initiatives: An examination of four highly collaborative campuses. *Journal of Higher Education*, *77*(5), 804–38.

Kochan., F. K. (Ed.) (2002). *Examining the organizational and human dimensions of mentoring in diverse settings*. Greenwich, CT: Information Age Publishing Inc.

Lave, J., and Wenger, E. (1991). *Situated learning: Legitimate peripheral participation*. Cambridge, UK: Cambridge University Press.

Lazerson, M., Wagener, U., and Shumanis, N. (2000). What makes a revolution? *Change*, *32*(3), 12–20.

Lentz, E., and Allen, T. D. (2009). The role of mentoring others in the career plateauing phenomenon. *Group and Organization Management*, *34*(3), 358–84.

Lindholm, J. A. (2004). Pathways to the professoriate: The role of self, others, and environment in shaping academic career aspirations. *Journal of Higher Education*, *75*(6), 603–35.

McCracken, D. M. (1999). Winning the talent war for women. Sometimes it takes a revolution. *Harvard Business Review*, *78*(6), 159–60.

McIlvaine, A. R. (2015). Millennials in charge. *Human Resource Executive Online*. Retrieved July 15, 2015 from http://www.hreonline.com/HRE/view/story.jhtml?id=534358266

Meinert, D. (2013). Tailoring diversity practices produces different result. *HR Magazine*, *58*(7), 16.

Mendoza, P. (2007). Academic capitalism and doctoral student socialization: A case study. *Journal of Higher Education*, *78*(1), 71–96.

Morrison, E. W. (1995). Information usefulness and acquisition during organizational encounter. *Management Communication Quarterly*, *9*, 131–55.

Neumann, A. (2009). *Professing to learn: Creating tenured lives and careers in the American research university*. Baltimore, MD: The Johns Hopkins University Press.

Neumann, A., and Terosky, A. L. (2007). To give and to receive: Recently tenured professors' experiences of service in major research universities. *Journal of Higher Education*, *78*(3), 282–310.

Noe, R. A., Greenberger, D. B., and Wang, S. (2002). Mentoring: What we know and where we might go. *Research in Personnel and Human Resources Management*, *21*, 129–74.

Noy, S., and Ray, R. (2012). Graduate students' perceptions of their advisors: Is there systematic disadvantage in mentorship? *The Journal of Higher Education*, *83*(6), 876–914.

Nunez, A., Murakami, E. T., and Gonzales, L. D. (2015). Weaving authenticity and legitimacy: Latina faculty peer mentoring. *New Directions for Higher Education*, *50*(171), 87–96.

O'Meara, K., and Niehaus, E. (2013). *With a little help from my friends: The role of on and off campus relationships in faculty careers*. Paper presented at the annual meeting of the American Educational Research Association, April. San Francisco, CA.

O'Meara, K., Terosky, A. L., and Neumann, A. (2008). Faculty careers and work lives: A professional growth perspective. *ASHE Higher Education Report*, *34*(3), Jossey-Bass, San Francisco, CA.

Patton, L. D. (2009). My sister's keeper: A qualitative examination of mentoring experiences among African American women in graduate and professional schools. *Journal of Higher Education*, *80*(5), 510–37.

Ponjuan, L., Conley, V. M., and Trower, C. (2011). Career stage differences in pre-tenure track faculty perceptions of professional and personal relationships with colleagues. *The Journal of Higher Education*, *82*(3), 319–46.

Rice, R. E., Sorcinelli, M. D., and Austin, A. E. (2000). *Heeding new voices: Academic careers for a new generation*. New Pathways Working Paper Series, No. 7. Washington, DC: American Association for Higher Education.

Rosser, V. J. (2004). Faculty members' intentions to leave: A national study on their work-life and satisfaction. *Research in Higher Education*, *45*(3), 285–309.

Sallee, M. W. (2011). Performing masculinity: Considering gender in doctoral student socialization. *Journal of Higher Education*, *82*(2), 187–216.

Schulz, S. F. (1995). The benefits of mentoring. In M. W. Galbraith and N. H. Cohen (Eds.), *Mentoring: New strategies and challenges* (Vol. 66, p. 57–68). San Francisco: Jossey-Bass.

Seibert, S. E., Kraimer, M. L., and Liden, R. C. (2001). A social capital theory of career success. *Academy of Management Journal*, *44*(2), 219–37.

Sorcinelli, M. D. (2000). *Principles of good practice: Supporting early-career faculty. Guidance for deans, department chairs, and other academic leaders*. Washington, DC: AAHE Forum on Faculty Roles and Rewards.

Sorcinelli, M. D., and Austin, A. E. (1992). *Developing new and junior faculty* (Vol. 50). San Francisco: Jossey-Bass.

Swap, W., Leonard, D., Mimi Shields, M., and Abrams, L. (2001). Using mentoring and storytelling to transfer knowledge in the workplace. *Journal of Management Information Systems*, *18*(1), 95–114.

Terosky, A. L., and Gonzales, L. D. (2015). *Scholarly learning as vocation: A study of community and broad access liberal arts college faculty*. Paper presented at the annual meeting of the American Educational Research Association, Chicago, IL, April.

Terosky, A. L., and Heasley, C. (2013). *Sense of community for online faculty: A study of online course development and teaching*. Paper presented at the annual meeting of the American Educational Research Association, San Francisco, CA.

Terosky, A. L., O'Meara, K., and Campbell, C. M. (2014). Enabling possibility: Women associate professors' sense of agency in career advancement. *Journal of Diversity in Higher Education*, *7*(1), 58–76.

Thomas, C. H., and Lankau, M. J. (2009). Preventing burnout: The effects of LMX and mentoring on socialization, role stress, and burnout. *Human Resource Management*, *48*(3), 417–32.

Trower, C. A. (2011a). Senior faculty satisfaction: Perceptions of associate and full professors at seven public research universities. *TIAA-CREF Institute Research Dialogue*, *101*. Retrieved from http://www.tiaacref.org/ucm/groups/content/@ap_ucm_p_tcp_docs/documents/document/tiaa02030036.pdf (accessed 5 June, 2014).

Trower, C. A. (2011b). Senior Faculty Vitality. *Advancing Higher Education*. New York, NY: TIAA-CREF.

Weidman, J. C., Twale, D. J., and Stein, E. L. (2001). Socialization of graduate and professional students in higher education: A perilous passage? *ASHE-ERIC Higher Education Report*. San Francisco: Jossey-Bass.

Weidman, J. C. and Stein, E. L. (2003). Socialization of doctoral students to academic norms. *Research in higher education*, *44*(6), 641–656.

Wenger, E. C., and Snyder, W. M. (2000). Communities of practice: The organizational frontier. *Harvard Business Review*, *78*, 139–45.

Whitely, W., Dougherty, T. W., and Dreher, G. F. (1991). Relationship of career mentoring and socioeconomic origin to managers' and professionals' early career progress. *Academy of Management Journal*, *34*(2), 331–50.

Wilson, R. (2012). Why are associate professors so unhappy? *The Chronicle of Higher Education*, June 2.

Wright, R. G., and Werther Jr, W. B. (1991). Mentors at work. *Journal of Management Development*, *10*(3), 25–32.

Mentoring in Educational Leadership for Organizational Transformation

Gary M. Crow and Margaret Grogan

Mentoring has become a common, almost panacea-like, strategy for enhancing school leadership and promoting school reform. Frequently this strategy has been introduced in an a-theoretical manner that ignores the ultimate goal of mentoring, which we propose should be to enable transformative leadership practices and outcomes (Grogan and Crow, 2004). Additionally, the strategy is treated as a one-stop approach in which, during their preparation period, aspiring principals are assigned mentors with the assumption that this will enable them to be transformative leaders.

This approach ignores the leadership continuum that emphasizes the evolving development of leadership identities and skills (Sugrue, 2015). In recognition of this reality, several authors have acknowledged the importance of implementing mentoring across the leadership continuum (Duncan, 2012; Scott and Scott, 2013; Searby, 2010). Rhodes and Fletcher (2013) described mentoring and coaching as scaffolds for self-study and learning throughout a career.

The problem, on which this paper focuses, is how to make mentoring more transformative across the leadership continuum rather than viewing mentoring as a mechanism for maintaining a status quo version of the principal role.

We begin the chapter with a brief examination of how mentoring has been developed in educational leadership, including research on mentoring across the leadership continuum. Then, we draw on the theoretical framework of critical constructivism to propose the kind of mentoring that could result in transformative leadership. Next, using a case study, we consider some empirical evidence of mentoring relationships that developed well, but did not necessarily result in transformative leadership. We reexamine themes from the study through the critical constructivist lens to explore the transformative potential of mentoring relationships. Then, we discuss the implications of the study for mentoring transformative leaders. Finally, we offer suggestions about how certain mentoring relationships might allow mentors and protégés to be more deliberate in developing transformative practices.

LITERATURE ON MENTORING THROUGH THE LEADERSHIP CONTINUUM

Before discussing the specific literature on the role of mentoring at different stages of the leadership pipeline, it is helpful to understand the overall nature, participants, goals, and functions of mentoring. The typical way to understand the nature of mentoring is to point to the historical origin, based on Homer's *The Odyssey*, in which Odysseus left his son Telemachus to be taught and supported by his friend Mentor. The meaning portrayed in this epic was of the expert providing guidance, advice, and support to the novice. The typical meaning of mentoring in educational leadership has similarly been for an expert, veteran leader to provide mentoring to the newcomer, especially around the technical aspects of the role, such as using data for instructional decision-making. Although this is no doubt part of most mentoring arrangements, it does not exhaust the possibilities of the types of relationships or content that can be part of mentoring across the leadership continuum. Kram (1985) described a 'constellation of relationships' that can exist in mentoring, of which expert to novice is only one kind. Mullen and Lick (1999) expanded the nature of mentoring by reminding us of the value of peer mentoring, and other arrangements in which the direction of mentoring is more reciprocal. This notion of mentoring based on a constructivist understanding of learning (Crow, 2012) suggests that the nature and direction of mentoring can be bi-directional. It also suggests that mentoring can involve more than two participants, as in Mullen and Lick's (1999) 'circle of mentoring'.

This also leads to an expanded understanding of the functions of mentoring. Kram (1985) identified two functions: career, which focused on learning the technical aspects of the role and the movement to new roles; and psychosocial, which involves the needs of the individual novice in the work environment. Crow and Matthews (1998) proposed an expansion of Kram's two functions to three, which are more likely in mentoring educational leaders: (1) professional mentoring, focusing on the technical aspects of the role; (2) psychosocial mentoring, emphasizing the integration into a work culture and environment; and (3) career mentoring, centering on issues of career satisfaction, awareness, and advancement. These expanded functions reflect the recent acknowledgement by scholars of how, for example, the stress in new leaders requires mentoring. Lashway (2003; quoted by Gross, 2009) identified five causes of stress in new leaders: complexity; isolation; lonely job; assimilation; and role conflict. These functions of mentoring suggest two areas of content related to educational leaders' roles, technical and cultural (Greenfield, 1985). Greenfield distinguished these as learning 'how things are done', and 'how things are done around here'.

These descriptions of the nature, participants, functions, and content of mentoring in general beg the question regarding the goal of mentoring. The classic typology of roles (Schein, 1971) suggests three role orientations as approaches to the goal of socialization: custodianship; content innovation; and role innovation. Custodianship implies the acceptance of the 'knowledge base, strategic practices, and mission' (Crow and Matthews, 1998, p. 29) as determined by the occupation. Content innovation involves a rejection of, or dissatisfaction with, the customary ways of performing the role. Role innovation goes beyond this to reject the traditional mission of the role.

Several authors (Armstrong, 2010, 2012; Bengtson et al., 2013) have noted that the typical outcome of mentoring programs has been primarily custodial orientation. Van Maanen and Schein (1979) argued in their classic theory of professional socialization that one of the standard methods for perpetuating the status quo is to use veterans to train newcomers. Bengston and colleagues (2013) found this custodial response to be a typical feature of principal socialization. Several recent studies of the superintendency (Brunner and Grogan, 2007; Kowalski et al., 2010) found that it is likely that a more transformative response to the role may be affected not only by experience but by gender and race. This relates to the problem this paper attempts to remedy, how to make mentoring more transformative.

LITERATURE ON MENTORING ACROSS THE LEADERSHIP CONTINUUM

Understandably, the majority of literature on mentoring focuses on early career, that is, internship and induction of principals and assistant principals. This literature discusses needs, elements for successful mentoring, goals, and a growing literature on the role of gender and race. In terms of needs, Bristol and colleagues (2014) pointed to the complex practice landscape in which new principals and assistant principals find themselves and which influence the need for mentoring. This landscape means that mentors will need to respond to the 'reality shock' that new leaders face, given the high stakes, accountability policy environment (Spillane and Lee, 2014) and the process of crossing role boundaries that creates conflict and affective intensity in the principal role today (Cottrell and James, 2016).

Spillane and Lee (2014) pointed to the three core problems of practice embedded in this reality shock: task volume; diversity; and unpredictability. Oplatka (2012) provided more detail of what mentoring of novice principals has to address when he identified insufficient managerial competence, low practical experience in educational administration, and a greater propensity for making mistakes. Steyn (2013) added the issue of learning to respond to a predecessor's image and actions. Spillane and Anderson (2014) broadened the issues of learning to respond to the larger policy context, to handling the organizational context of the school or district. These authors acknowledge that learning to respond to these contextual factors involves sense-making processes that inform and constrain identity construction. Novices construct multiple, rather than unitary, identities that involve contradictions and inconsistencies. In addition to these technical aspects of the job, Oplatka (2012) mentioned two psychosocial issues to be addressed by mentors of novices, high levels of stress and a sense of loneliness.

Other literature on mentoring also points to several essential elements of successful mentoring for novice principals. These include helping new leaders navigate practice by integrating personal and professional knowledge (Crawford and Cowie, 2012), and adjusting foci and methods of mentoring over time to respond to the developmental needs of novice leaders (Brondyk and Searby, 2013; Lochmiller, 2013). Enomoto and Gardiner (2006) found that mentoring for prospective administrators included four types of relationships: mentor/protégé; administrator/intern; peer dyad; and mentoring team. This finding suggests that mentoring can and does take several forms.

Early career leader literature also identifies multiple goals/results of mentoring. As we mentioned previously, some literature focuses on the actual rather than espoused goal of mentoring. Armstrong (2010, 2012), Bengston and colleagues (2013), and Chen and Chen (2014) found that, typically, a more custodial orientation to the role results from mentoring. For example, Chen and Chen found that workplace training (such as mentoring) led to more obedient and docile administrators. However, Nash and Bangert (2014) found, in their quantitative study of over 212 public school principals, that principals' early leadership experiences and their relationships with mentors were the most likely factors to relate to transformational leadership behaviors.

A growing body of literature focuses on the role that gender and race play in mentoring. Informal, long-term relationships between mentors and their protégés were found to be mutually beneficial to women in all stages of their careers (Gardiner et al., 2000), unlike district-led 'grow-your-own' leadership programs that were found to be unsuccessful in attracting and retaining women in leadership positions (Sherman, 2005). Similarly, even for women in the early stages of their careers, the most effective mentoring approaches were non-hierarchical and focused on mutual learning (Peters, 2010). Both gender and ethnic background were found to affect the way mentoring for leadership was viewed; and same race mentoring supported the probability of success for future educational leaders of underrepresented minorities because these mentors were more aware of obstacles and issues the novice principals faced (Magdaleno, 2006; Shah, 2010).

Although mentoring at mid-career is probably very important in this high stakes accountability environment, where veteran principals are asked to take on new tasks and increase their focus on student learning, very little research on mentoring at this stage exists. Kissane-Long (2012) found that several mentoring issues were important for mid-career principals in developing instructional supervision skills, including developing skills in using probing questions, actionable feedback to teachers, establishing a focused line for lesson observation, and developing trusting relationships. It also appears that at this stage personalized or customized mentoring becomes more important (Kissane-Long, 2012).

As with mid-career mentoring, only a few studies were found that focused on mentoring for late career leaders. Cardno and Youngs (2013) described the need for a personalized and unique approach to mentoring for late career leaders. The program they examined used a school inquiry project to focus the mentoring on specific school leaders' needs. Oplatka (2010) identified later career leaders' tasks and issues, which are of concern for mentoring as demonstrating professional competence and personal success while dealing with diminished physical energy. The issues for mentoring included organizational commitment, personal energy, positive attitudes toward changes, a greater sense of professional competence, high self-confidence, and participative leadership style.

TRANSFORMATIVE VIEW OF MENTORING

Our conception of a transformative view of mentoring draws heavily on Crow's (2012) description of a critical-constructivist perspective on mentoring and is informed by Shields' (2010) theory of transformative leadership. Transformative suggests a fundamental change of perspective from maintaining the status quo to acting for social justice. 'Transformative concepts and social justice are closely connected through the shared goal of identifying and restructuring frameworks that generate inequity and disadvantage' (ibid., p. 566). This perspective proposes viewing mentoring as a learning tool, one that does not focus on the simple transmission of knowledge from an expert to a novice. Rather, this approach involves mentors and protégés in co-constructing the knowledge, skills, and identities of educational leadership. We define the 'fundamental quality of mentoring and coaching [a]s learning in which inquiry, sense making, and reflection are foundational' (Crow, 2012, p. 233). The transformative view of mentoring involves a reciprocal relationship between mentor and protégé (or multiple mentors and protégés). We argue that this is not a one-directional power relationship, but a relationship in which both mentor and protégé negotiate knowledge, skills, and dispositions.

In addition to the constructivist notion of learning on which this view of mentoring rests, its critical nature involves a goal that is transformative. The goal of mentoring in this view is not simply to maintain the status quo. Brockbank and McGill (2006) described it well when they said that mentors and protégés both 'have been able to see beyond, above, below and beside the taken-for-granted assumptions; the outcomes may be threatening to the status quo, and sometimes the consequence is that the individuals choose to leave or are excluded' (p. 17). Merriam and colleagues (2007) referred to this type of learning as transformational learning focused on 'fundamental change in the way we see ourselves and the world in which we live' (p. 130). Brown (2006) argued that new experiences designed to challenge thinking and question assumptions promote transformative learning. Within the transformative mentoring relationship, mentors and protégés engage in inquiry together.

This type of learning involves a new kind of role for mentors, one which Gehrke (1988) labeled 'gift giving', in which the mentor shares wisdom and awakening. 'There is a stirring, a recognition of the import of the gift, of the strength or talent, of the possibilities of one's life – a point where someone sees potential for genius in you' (ibid., p. 191). As Crow (2012) acknowledged, this mentoring role may appear to be a uni-directional activity from the mentor to the novice. However, the goal is transformational learning for both.

Although this approach to mentoring involves the development of knowledge and skills that are critical to do the job the transformative element of this view of mentoring emphasizes something else that has been largely ignored in current preparation and mentoring agendas, namely the development of identity. Several authors, including Lumby and English (2009), Scribner and Crow (2012), Moorosi (2012), and Crow, Day, and Moeller (in press) have noted a growing technocratic orientation to leadership development at all stages, which emphasizes skills and competencies but ignores beliefs, values, and identities. As Lumby and English (2009) argued, this orientation 'evades and miniaturizes the performance of leadership' (p. 95). The development of a leader's role identity is critical, since this is 'the internalized meanings of a role that individuals apply to themselves' (Burke and Stets, 2009, p. 114). 'The energy, motivation, drive that makes roles actually work require that individuals identify with, internalize, and become the role' (ibid., 2009, p. 38).

Our view of mentoring, then, involves a critical constructivist approach in which mentors and protégés together develop a sense of role identity which emphasizes transformation rather than maintenance of the status quo. Whether this occurs with aspiring principals, or in mid-career, or at movement to the superintendency (Brunner and Grogan, 2007; Kowalski et al., 2010), developing a transformative identity is critical. Mentoring then becomes a rich learning tool in which the mentor, while also learning, engenders an awakening to new ways of conceiving the leadership role and making sense of the need to transform leadership practices to address persistent educational inequities.

In summary, although scholars acknowledge the importance of viewing mentoring throughout the professional career, very little empirical investigation provides direction for practice in this way. In the next section, we describe an exception to this lack of research and highlight an empirical investigation of mentoring that includes various career stages. The study explores narratives of women educational leaders in long-term mentoring relationships. We do not assume that every mentoring instance described below resulted in transformative leadership practices or identity. However, we argue that this examination of the women's narratives provides examples that can be informative in understanding the type of career-long mentoring with a transformative leadership focus we are proposing.

NARRATIVES OF WOMEN IN MENTORING RELATIONSHIPS

Crow (2010) introduced the notion of a critical-constructivist perspective for mentoring and coaching to highlight both the learning aspect of the relationship between mentor and protégé and the impetus towards change that a critical lens generates. An excellent example of the learning aspect of the relationship is provided by Gardiner et al.'s (2000) case study of 36 pairs of mentors and protégés. The researchers investigated long-term mentoring relationships between a diverse selection of women and their mentors, men and women, who were primarily focused on the protégé's career development. What started out as uni-directional, mentoring relationships developed into multi-dimensional, mutually supportive relationships over time. In many cases, mentors and protégés changed roles and constructed new peer-to-peer relationships that engaged the meaning of educational leadership. Some of the relationships, but not all, provided support for leaders who wanted to transform their schools and districts to better serve marginalized students and families.

This section of the chapter re-analyzes the narratives in Gardiner et al.'s study (2000) using the critical-constructivist framework. In this process, we identified three themes: (1) professional identity development; (2) the meaning of a mentoring relationship; and (3) the moral dimension of mentoring.

Background of the study

The study of naturally-occurring mentoring relationships was conducted during the late 1990s in three different states, Maryland, Virginia, and Washington. In each state, one of three researchers identified women principals, superintendents, or other educational leaders who had been mentored into leadership positions by at least one or more mentors, who also agreed to participate in the study. There were 36 pairs and 62 participants. Fourteen participants were African American, four Latina/o and the rest Caucasian. Five of the mentors were male. A critical feminist theoretical framework was used to shape the interview protocol and to analyze the data (see Gardiner et al., 2000).

One of the most distinguishing features of this research study was that both sides of the mentoring story were heard. One researcher in each state interviewed, on separate occasions, both mentor and protégé, in each pair, for 60 to 90 minutes. The snowball technique was used to recruit participants from all corners of the three states. All interviews were recorded and transcribed. Each researcher analyzed her state data for themes particular to the state, and then, all three researchers conducted a cross-case analysis to understand the lived experiences of all the participants who were engaged in mentoring relationships.

Interview questions asked about the purpose of entering the relationship, specific tasks, skills, and/or information that was passed on, the roles mentors and protégés played, the meaning of mentoring, the benefits and costs of the relationship, ways to deal with conflicts and challenges within the relationship, and how mentorship can change educational leadership.

The study was an in-depth investigation into the extent to which women who aspire to educational leadership receive mentoring. The researchers were also interested in who initiated the relationships, because the traditional male model of mentoring, or grooming the next generation of leaders, usually begins with a 'tap' on the shoulder from a potential mentor.

At least six of the relationships in this study were initiated by protégés and, while all the relationships were considered to be informal ones, many of the relationships transitioned into mutually supportive ones where both members coached and advised each other. All the relationships were focused on career advancement, although some relationships developed before the protégé earned a teaching certificate. Some relationships grew out of community connections at church, or between women whose children were in the same school or class. The majority began as supervisory relationships when the mentor hired or began to work with the protégé as his or her subordinate. One of the most interesting and unexpected outcomes of this approach was that relationships were discovered between pairs and webs of women that had lasted many years. Some of the longest ones had developed over 20 years and the majority of the relationships had lasted over five years.

Professional identity development

If we think of mentoring as providing the opportunities for co-constructing professional identities, particularly in a dynamic, fluid way, we understand the potential of the mentoring relationship better. Gardiner et al. (2000) found quality mentoring developed in a variety of different settings, particularly when protégés expressed their leadership aspirations. The best connections occurred between women already holding leadership positions and aspirants when their career goals were made explicit. For example, as two different participants in the study explained:

> [Mentor gives guidance on] where to be with certain people and who was there. Did you meet so and so? Well you go meet so and so. Introduce yourself. And she would do the same for me if we were out. She would specifically bring people over, 'This is Doreen Ballard and she is one of the future leaders'. (p. 86)
>
> She made sure I knew who to network with ... She really had me get involved and know a lot of the state supervisors. And I did. So I know a lot of people at the state office by first name. And I can get a hold of anyone I need to if I have a question. (p. 86)

As the protégés interacted with their new colleagues, others began to see them as leadership aspirants, but more importantly, protégés began to think of themselves as legitimate leaders. Once they had been introduced as an aspiring superintendent, or principal, the identity formation began. In contrast, a superintendent in the study talked about not getting the mentoring she needed when she wanted to be a principal. It took her much longer because no one saw her in that role. She shared:

> I wanted to be principal, although people that I worked with here advised me, 'No you don't want to be a principal, you want to be a supervisor at the central office,' because that was for women and administration was for men. And because of that, even though the people that I worked with, my principal who loved me, thought I was a wonderful teacher, never had complaints about me, the people at central office loved me, I was well regarded in the school division, ... no one thought I should be principal. (p. 130)

As Crow (2012) argues 'an individual's identities do not come to the mentoring relationship totally developed' (p. 236). A mentor in the study talked about putting his protégés in challenging situations with the necessary guidance and opportunity for feedback.

> [I] put them in situations that won't damage them very much even if it screws them up a little bit; it won't hurt them terribly. It's important to have them move beyond the comfort zone where everything's just wonderful and sweetness and light and you sit around and talk, have a cup of coffee, and you don't get down to the serious work. (p. 64)

The study found that protégés value trying out new roles or taking professional risks in a safe mentoring relationship because they experience these as growth activities. As long as there are sensitive debriefing sessions that allow protégés to co-construct a leadership identity in tune with their own sense of self, the relationship has been helpful.

A participant recognized how leadership development is co-constructed in this way:

> And there was always this next step. ... [Mentor] was saying, 'You can do this.' I don't think there was anyone in our family [in leadership positions.] I look back at anyone I'm related to, people don't have management positions. We're the basic blue-collar worker, and so I never thought beyond that. So having someone push me was really good. I think that a lot of my success was that she had a vision that I could be there and I achieved it. (p. 121)

An African American principal talked of reaching out for the kind of support she needed to be viewed by others as legitimate in her new role. Learning from working with her mentor, she gained the courage to confront her supervisor and negotiate her role.

> My mentor [a retired high school principal, African American] had lots of problems because there was no support. I have a little more support, more than she, because I just went to my area director and said, 'Hey, I'm an African-American female. I have different needs. I need more support. I need you visible. I need the staff to know and I need the parents to know that you support me'. (p. 116)

Moreover, for some women of underrepresented communities who aspire to leadership, mentoring relationships have to provide the support for identity formation that is not only *not* available in the home, but sometimes actively discouraged at home. A Latina participant reflected on the advantage of her mentoring relationship.

> Sometimes in a relationship mentoring women of color, where the spouses are not receptive to this, you really are dancing on a fine line because they [protégés] want to do something different with their lives and they don't have the support at home. (p. 175)

Gardiner et al. (2000) found that:

> It is through the mentoring process that the protégé negotiates a new subject position. If the mentoring has truly served the needs of the protégé, the protégé has not only moved up the ranks in administration, but she has also found a way to lead from her new rank that reflects her own philosophies and convictions. She has not been forced to disguise herself or fit into a gendered or racially acceptable notion of leader. (p. 196)

This study certainly suggests that long-lasting mentoring relationships appear to provide fertile ground for the development of a strong leadership identity where the process is co-constructed. In the next section, a focus on the mentoring relationship itself reveals greater understanding of how this works.

The meaning of mentoring relationships

Crow (2012) asserts, 'Rather than identifying and transmitting a set of facts, skills, and practices, mentoring and coaching involve a creative process in which mentors and protégés together construct the knowledge of school leadership and make sense of the protégé's practice' (p. 233). To achieve this ideal learning, mentors and protégés need a multi-dimensional relationship, not one that sees learning as one-way, or uni-directional. Many relationships reported in Gardiner et al.'s study (2000) *evolved* into excellent examples of this, though few would have been characterized as such at the outset when most of the protégés reported a clear sense of learning from and emulating their mentor(s). This was most often the case with supervisory relationships for reasons inherent in the unequal status of the participants. For example, a mentor principal explained what she did for her protégé:

> The key thing you have to learn is dealing with other people. ... 'I want [protégé] to work with the math teachers during this [curriculum] adoption, and I want [math teachers] to change their thinking so that they're aligning with the [state] standards. ... to lead teachers, and to motivate

teachers into looking at it differently is the key part of educational leadership to me. (p. 80)

A new assistant principal noted that her mentor was very deliberate about what she wanted her protégés to learn:

> [Mentor] required that we watch her ... when she had a dilemma as an administrator, she walked it through with us as to what was going on in her head ... She required that we have daily logs ... it was very laborious and I hated doing it ... but we were new, we had to prove ourselves to those other people out there. (p. 57)

Some of the relationships that developed into more mutually beneficial ones were founded on a protégé's belief that the mentor was someone to emulate.

> When I saw [my mentor] run a meeting I thought, 'Now that's a good idea. I can do that and see how he got from point A to point B. ... I'm going to try that at my staff meetings'. ... or if he took me through a questioning time about why I wanted a certain program ... I thought 'Now when staff comes into me and they want new math cubes or whatever it might be, I can ask those kinds of questions and that would make sense'. (p. 88)

The overwhelming majority of participants in this study reported that their mentoring relationships changed over time. Mentors and protégés took new positions, left districts and what began as a largely hierarchical relationship matured into one of interdependence. Some participants used the term friendship to describe the mature relationship, but many did not, pointing out that:

> A friend is a person with whom you can casually go out with, eat lunch, and talk about all different kinds of things, other than professional duties. A mentor is a person who really ... shows interest and wants to help you succeed, and become more entrenched in your profession. (p. 131)

The best of the mature relationships appear to support Crow's (2012) idea of multidimensional co-constructivist relationships. For example, an associate superintendent talked of her protégés as:

> not always calling to ask for information or to ask for help. Sometimes they call just to bounce ideas off of you. You know, 'I was thinking about doing so-and-so, what do you think about that?' Or, 'If I did this, who should I involve in this activity ...' Or 'Do you think this is a good idea?' (p. 155)

The notion of peer mentoring also surfaced as an outgrowth of the once expert–novice relationship.

> I don't know if I would still be considered to be mentoring [protégé] as such now. I really think she has accomplished the levels, but I think I would still be an encourager to her. ... like with [other protégé] who still calls me once in a while, '... I've got this problem and I just don't know what to do with it.' That's a continuation of a mentoring relationship, but it has graduated. It has been elevated to a peer relationship. (p. 96)

The use of language in that quotation is telling. Mentoring relationships that developed into co-constructivist learning experiences for the participants, especially those that began informally for the purpose of supporting career advancement, appeared to 'graduate' or to become 'elevated' into multidimensional relationships. Perhaps some mentoring pairs never graduate because they do not develop relationships at all. It is quite possible that mentoring activity can be present between or among individuals who share professional interests, but, at least in this study, mentoring and being mentored was embedded in a long-term relationship. 'Most of the women in mentoring relationships in this study envisaged their mentorships lasting a lifetime, with many other mentors and protégés also part of the web of interconnections' (Gardiner et al., 2000, p. 97). The clearly expressed moral dimension of the relationships explained their long-term nature.

Mentoring guided by a moral compass

The ethic of care emerged as a key relationship element in this study. This ethic appeared to be necessary, if not sufficient, for quality mentoring offering co-constructivist identity development and the potential for transformative learning. Care for the needs of the protégé was identified in many mentor and protégé comments. One protégé remarked:

> I'm convinced that [mentors] have to care about the other person's success and well-being as an individual and as a professional. I say that because I know that's what motivated Pam. She didn't try to make me into a Pam Jr. That wasn't it at all. But she wanted me, Brenda, to succeed and to do well and she knew that I wanted that also. (p. 177)

In addition, in this study, mentoring relationships depended on shared professional values along with a feeling of goodwill towards a person. Mentors and protégés cared about the values and philosophies guiding their mentor's or protégé's educational leadership. Many participants suggested that they would not have remained in such long-lasting relationships had they not respected the other's child- and family-centered motivations for leading schools and districts. A mentor described whom she was willing to mentor:

> I look for people who are willing to take risks, who are anxious to try things, who believe fundamentally in the child and who I know will, bottom of the line, think of what will be best for the children regardless of the situation ... and who are very much trying to work with others. (p. 143)

A protégé doubted that she would have entered the mentoring relationship had she not respected her mentor's values:

> It reminds me of this saying, 'People don't care how much you know until they know how much you care.' ... I don't know that the experience [of being mentored] would be that valuable to me if there was no relationship between me and that person. And I don't mean that it has to be purely, purely affective in that they just lavish me with compliments and all this kind of thing. I guess for me, I have to recognize in that person leadership qualities that I want to emulate. (p. 159)

The experience of being in a mentoring relationship for many of these participants was predicated on knowing that they were in a relationship that furthered, in some way or other, their deeply held values about education. That, and the fact that they felt cared-for as individuals, resulted in transformative learning experiences. Using participants' words, Gardiner et al. (2000) summed it up this way: "'everyone can't be a mentor,' because not everyone is into relationship building ... and [prepared for] the high degree of nurturing in a mentoring relationship ... [or] the need to care enough about the person for them to be successful' (p. 93). Indeed, the mentoring process that emerged in the study was such an intense, powerful one that highly-valued principles and attitudes were transferred and mutually strengthened as the relationships deepened.

For example, although we are much more familiar with a distributed notion of leadership now, Gardiner et al. (2000) recognized the emergence of a new discourse on leadership that was clearly associated with openness and outreach, participation and collaboration. Stories about mentors and protégés illustrated such leadership priorities:

> [mentor] was very much a hands-on principal ... very much a teacher first, and that's what I believe in .... Her way of solving problems was to get people together, and have them talk about what happened. (p. 194)
>
> [protégé] believes in cooperative relationships, team kinds of decision-making ... I think she's comfortable with that versus the talk-down kind of leadership. So the fact that I was that way and wanting to share the decision-making and that type of thing, she felt comfortable with that. (p. 194)
>
> [I learned mentor]'s ... way of running a meeting ... being sure that people left feeling that they had gotten something done there, but yet giving people enough freedom so that they felt like they could breathe. (p. 194)

Without doubt, the other-focused, respectful basis upon which these relationships were developed inspired new learning. If we judge the success of the relationship to be the career advancement of the protégé, then, the majority of the relationships in Gardiner et al.'s (2000) study were exemplary. Although it is not known to what extent these relationships produced transformative leadership that challenged the status quo. Gardiner et al. noted some promising cases.

> He [mentor] really helped me in how to present a very controversial idea, something that would push the system. So when I'd go in to talk to him about something I'd want to do in this building, I knew what questions he was going to ask. And if I could answer those, I would probably get what I wanted for the building. And if I couldn't answer and support them with appropriate data then don't bother coming in. So his expectations were very high, and that taught me how to meet those challenges. (p. 84)

A principal mentor explained how she deliberately worked with her assistant principal protégé on exposing her to avenues for change as a participatory leader. She highlighted:

> Working with parents and hostile communities, understanding how to deal with parents, how you work with that. Giving [protégé] opportunities to take care of situations that are hostile or not particularly comfortable, but coaching [her] through the process and acting as a coach in difficult situations. (p. 83)

Some of the protégés in the study articulated their desire to move into leadership positions in order to effect change. Several were focused on addressing social injustices they had suffered themselves in their own lived experiences. However, the study was focused on the nature of mentoring for career development rather than on transformative practice. Mentors and protégés were drawn together because of shared values and beliefs, but not all wanted to challenge the status quo. Moreover, because mentors have knowledge of the skills and attitudes that are traditionally associated with leadership, and the goal is for the protégé to enter or climb the ladder of positions, mentors are unlikely to advocate for great change. Transformative leadership practice is more likely to emerge as leaders mature and learn how to dismantle unjust policies and practices while keeping their jobs. Examples of transformative learning in the study occurred as mentors and protégés grew professionally over time and acquired a second or third leadership opportunity.

Implications for mentoring to transform organizations

Although there is not evidence to suggest that all these mentoring relationships fostered transformative leadership, there are implications for mentoring to transform organizations arising from this study. First, the study highlighted the promise inherent in long-term mentoring relationships that develop multi-directionally. The major benefit of a co-constructivist mentoring relationship is that protégés learn how to lead on their own terms. Supportive yet challenging mentoring relationships like these develop protégés' leadership identities. In addition, if the relationship is multi-directional, the mentor's leadership identity also deepens. The value of being truly in a relationship with other educational leaders lies in the critical co-constructivist learning that can be facilitated by the trust and respect embedded in the relationship. It provides a safe space for the development of a critical consciousness of self and of others that precedes transformative practice (Brown, 2006). Thus, for transformative learning to occur, participants in the relationship must care about their mentoring partners and about the work in which they are engaged. Such mentoring is clearly a moral endeavor that requires individual commitment beyond attention to the instrumental goals of passing on information and skill development. This second implication suggests that unless there is a moral dimension to the mentoring relationship that prompts courageous action, the status quo will remain unchallenged. Because of the long-term nature of these relationships, many mentors in this study engaged in what could be seen as peer mentoring with their protégés over time. Thus, the third implication for mentoring for organizational transformation is that mentoring is valuable not only for novice leaders, but also across the leadership continuum.

Obviously, not all mentoring relationships are the same. Research is also needed to investigate whether formal mentoring programs have the same potential as informal ones. As Sherman (2005) found, some district-run programs offer only traditional approaches to leadership that did not attract women and other underrepresented individuals. Rather than rely on naturally-occurring mentoring opportunities, such as those Gardiner et al. (2000) studied, districts are encouraged to design mentoring webs that are deliberately focused on transformative leadership. They can identify potential mentors among principals who have had good success collaborating with their school communities to create equitable, diverse learning environments. The challenge will be to generate a deep, diverse pool of potential co-learners (teachers or assistant principals) who can benefit from the mentorship in a safe, nurturing way as participants in the study. We raise this issue because there are still few mentors for some women who aspire to educational leadership and for the many aspirants, women and men, whose communities are still greatly underrepresented in this field. The continued absence of diversity among principals and superintendents in the United States points to the fact that, desirable as it is, quality mentoring of any kind still eludes many women and underrepresented minorities. Further, individuals underrepresented in leadership positions are most often members of a community that has been under-served by traditional leadership practices and policies. To identify a mentor who can buffer such leaders or potential leaders as they engage in transformative leadership is crucial.

In addition to researching mentoring across the leadership continuum, universities and districts can play a valuable role in developing mentoring webs that acknowledge the need to ensure that effective, innovative, and transformative mentoring can occur at all stages. Research attests to the importance of universities and districts partnering at the preparation stages (Darling-Hammond et al., 2009), but we also encourage this type of partnering at successive career stages. The partnerships should not only acknowledge the knowledge and skills necessary for effective leadership, but should emphasize the identity construction necessary for transformative leadership. Leadership that challenges the status quo involves risk-taking that is unlikely to be supported in early career stages. Moreover, mentors that have been selected by districts not actively addressing educational inequities are unlikely to advocate the necessary risk-taking. To address this lack, McKenzie and Scheurich (2004) advocate for aspiring leaders in preparation programs to be assigned to mentor teacher classrooms in which they can observe, firsthand, transformative teaching practices. Indeed, several centers and programs focused on urban transformation across the country prepare and develop principals and other educational administrators who have been purposefully trained to challenge the status quo (such as the National Center for Urban School Transformation at San Diego State University, or the University of Illinois–Chicago, Ed.D. in Urban Education Leadership Program and the University of Texas–San Antonio, Urban School Leaders Collaborative, which have been recognized by the University Council on Educational Administration as exemplary programs). The university partners and their graduates are building teams of mentors going forward to tackle the necessary risks involved in organizational transformation and to successfully navigate the community and district politics.

CONCLUSION

Identity construction occurs at all career stages and provides the direction and motivation to lead in more innovative and critical ways. We acknowledge that identity construction toward more transformative leadership will probably be emphasized to a greater extent at mid and later career stages (Brunner and Grogan, 2007). However, we believe developing transformative leaders among principals and superintendents is critical for providing the kinds of mentors that novice principals need.

REFERENCES

Armstrong, D. (2010). Rites of passage: Coercion, compliance, and complicity in the socialization of new vice-principals. *The Teachers College Record*, *112*(3).

Armstrong, D. E. (2012). Connecting personal change and organizational passage in the transition from teacher to vice principal. *Journal of School Leadership*, *22*(3), 398–424.

Bengtson, E., Zepeda, S. J., and Parylo, O. (2013). School systems' practices of controlling socialization during principal succession looking through the lens of an organizational socialization theory. *Educational Management Administration & Leadership*, *41*(2), 143–64.

Bristol, L. S. M., Brown, L., and Esnard, T. (2014). Socialising principals: Early career primary school principals in Trinidad and Tobago. *Journal of Educational Administration and History*, *46*(1).

Brockbank, A., and McGill, I. (2006). *Facilitating reflective learning through mentoring and coaching*. London: Kogan Page.

Brondyk, S., and Searby, L. (2013). Best practices in mentoring: Complexities and possibilities. *International Journal of Mentoring and Coaching in Education*, *2*(3), 189–203.

Brown, K. M. (2006). Leadership for social justice and equity: Evaluating a transformative framework and andragogy. *Educational Administration Quarterly*, *42*(5), 700–45.

Brunner, C. C., and Grogan, M. (2007). *Women leading school systems: Uncommon roads to fulfillment*. Blue Ridge Summit, PA: Rowman & Littlefield Education.

Burke, P., and Stets, J. (2009). *Identity theory*. New York: Oxford University Press.

Cardno, C., and Youngs, H. (2013). Leadership development for experienced New Zealand principals: Perceptions of effectiveness. *Educational Management Administration and Leadership*, *41*(3), 256–71. Retrieved from http://doi.org/10.1177/1741143212474808

Chen, H. C., and Chen, M. J. (2014). How do local authorities prepare their headteachers in Taiwan? An exploration using Foucault's disciplinary power. *VODENJE*, *37*.

Cottrell, M., and James, C. (2016). Theorizing headteacher socialization from a role boundary perspective. *Educational Management Administration & Leadership*, *44*(1), 6–19.

Crawford, M., and Cowie, M. (2012). Bridging theory and practice in headship preparation: interpreting experience and challenging assumptions. *Educational Management Administration & Leadership*, *40*(2), 175–87.

Crow, G. M. (2012). A critical-constructivist perspective on mentoring and coaching for leadership. *The SAGE Handbook of Mentoring and Coaching in Education* (pp. 228–42). Thousand Oaks, CA: Sage.

Crow, G. M., and Matthews, L. J. (1998). *Finding one's way: How mentoring can lead to dynamic leadership*. Thousand Oaks, CA: Corwin Press.

Crow, G. M., Day, C., and Moeller, J. (In press). Framing research on school principals' identities. *International Journal of Leadership in Education*.

Darling-Hammond, L., Meyerson, D., LaPointe, M., and Orr, M. T. (2009). *Preparing principals for a changing world: Lessons from effective school leadership programs*. NY: John Wiley and Sons.

Duncan, H. E. (2012). Exploring gender differences in US school principals' professional development needs at different career stages. *Professional Development in Education*, *39*(3), 293–311. Retrieved from http://doi.org/10.1080/19415257.2012.722561

Enomoto, E. K., and Gardiner, M. E. (2006). Mentoring within internships: Socializing new school leaders. *Journal of School Leadership*, *16*(1), 34.

Gardiner, M. W., Enomoto, E. J., and Grogan, M. (2000). *Coloring outside the lines*. Albany, NY: State University of New York Press.

Gehrke, N. (1988). Toward a definition of mentoring. *Theory into Practice*, *27*(3), 190–4.

Greenfield, W. D. (1985). *Being and becoming a principal: Responses to work contexts and socialization processes*. Paper presented at the annual meeting of the American Educational Research Association, Chicago. ERIC Documentation Reproduction Service No. ED 254 932.

Grogan, M., and Crow, G. M. (2004). Mentoring in the context of educational leadership preparation and development – old wine in new bottles? Guest editor's introduction to special issue. *Educational Administration Quarterly*, 40(4), 463–7.

Gross, S. J. (2009). Establishing meaningful leadership mentoring in school settings. In M. D. Young, G. M. Crow, J. Murphy, and R. T. Ogawa (Eds.), *Handbook of research on the education of school leaders* (pp. 515–34). New York: Routledge.

Kissane-Long, A. L. (2012). Using mentor-coaching to refine instructional supervision skills of developing principals. PhD dissertation. Retrieved from http://escholarship.org/uc/item/1s67b773 (accessed 7 September, 2016).

Kowalski, T. J., Petersen, G. J., and Young, I. P. (2010). *The American school superintendent: 2010 decennial study*. Blue Ridge Summit, PA: Rowman & Littlefield Education.

Kram, K. E. (1985). *Mentoring at work: Developmental relationships in organizational life*. Glenview, IL: Scott, Foresman & Company.

Lashway, L. (2003). *Inducting school leaders*. Eugene, OR: CEPM Clearinghouse on Educational Management.

Lochmiller, C. R. (2013). Leadership coaching in an induction program for novice principals: A 3-year study. *Journal of Research on Leadership Education*, 9(1), 59–84.

Lumby, J., and English, F. (2009). From simplicism to complexity in leadership identity and preparation: Exploring the lineage and dark secrets. *International Journal of Leadership in Education*, 12(2), 95–114.

Magdaleno, K. R. (2006). Mentoring Latino school leaders. *Leadership*, 36(1), 12–14.

McKenzie, K. B., and Scheurich, J. J. (2004). Equity traps: A useful construct for preparing principals to lead schools that are successful with racially diverse students. *Educational Administration Quarterly*, 40(5), 601–32.

Merriam, S., Caffarella, R., and Baumgartner, L. (2007). *Learning in adulthood: A comprehensive guide* (3rd ed.). San Francisco, CA: John Wiley and Sons.

Moorosi, P. (2012). Mentoring for school leadership in South Africa: Diversity, dissimilarity and disadvantage. *Professional Development in Education*, 38(3), 487–503.

Mullen, C., and Lick, D. (Eds.). (1999). *New directions in mentoring: Creating a culture of synergy*. London: Falmer.

Nash, S., and Bangert, A. (2014). Exploring the relationships between principals' life experiences and transformational leadership behaviours. *International Journal of Leadership in Education*, 17(4), 462–80.

Oplatka, I. (2010). Principals in late career: Toward a conceptualization of principals' tasks and experiences in the pre-retirement period. *Educational Administration Quarterly*, 46(5), 776–815.

Oplatka, I. (2012). Towards a conceptualization of the early career stage of principalship: Current research, idiosyncrasies and future directions. *International Journal of Leadership in Education*, 15(2), 129–51.

Peters, A. (2010). Elements of successful mentoring of a female school leader. *Leadership and Policy in Schools*, 9(1), 108–29.

Rhodes, C., and Fletcher, S. (2013). Coaching and mentoring for self-efficacious leadership in schools. *International Journal of Mentoring and Coaching in Education*, 2(1), 47–63.

Schein, E. H. (1971). The individual, the organization, and the career: A conceptual scheme. *Journal of Applied Behavioral Science*, 7, 401–26.

Scott, S., and Scott, D. E. (2013). Principal preparation experiences. *Advances in Educational Administration*, 19, 45–70.

Scribner, S. P., and Crow, G. M. (2012). Employing professional identities: Case study of a high school principal in a reform setting. *Leadership and Policy in Schools*, 11(3), 243–74.

Searby, L. J. (2010). Preparing future principals: Facilitating the development of a mentoring mindset through graduate coursework. *Mentoring and Tutoring: Partnership in Learning*, 18(1), 5–22.

Shah, S. J. (2010). Re-thinking educational leadership: Exploring the impact of cultural and belief systems. *International Journal of Leadership in Education*, 13(1), 27–44.

Sherman, W. (2005). Preserving the status quo or renegotiating leadership: Women's experiences with a district-based aspiring leaders program. *Educational Administration Quarterly*, *41*(5), 707–40.

Shields, C. M. (2010). Transformative leadership: Working for equity in diverse contexts. *Educational Administration Quarterly*, *46*(4), 558–89.

Spillane, J. P., and Anderson, L. (2014). The architecture of anticipation and novices' emerging understandings of the principal position: Occupational sense making at the intersection of individual, organization, and institution. *Teachers College Record*, *116*(7).

Spillane, J. P., and Lee, L. C. (2014). Novice school principals' sense of ultimate responsibility problems of practice in transitioning to the principal's office. *Educational Administration Quarterly*, *50*(3), 431–65.

Steyn, G. M. (2013). Principal succession: The socialisation of a primary school principal in South Africa. *Koers–Bulletin for Christian Scholarship*, *78*(1), 9. Retrieved May 30, 2015, from http://www.scielo.org.za/scielo.php?script=sci_arttext&pid=S2304-85572013000100005&lng=en&tlng=pt

Sugrue, C. (2015). *Unmasking school leadership. A longitudinal life history of school leaders.* London: Springer.

Van Maanen, J., and Schein, E. H. (1979). Toward a theory of organizational socialization. In L. Cummings and B. Staw (Eds.), *Research in organizational behavior* (pp. 209–64). Greenwich, CT: JAI.

Mentoring in the Military[1]

Diane M. Ryan and Jeffrey D. Peterson

INTRODUCTION

The mission of the United States Military Academy is to educate, train, and inspire the Corps of Cadets so that each graduate is a commissioned leader of character committed to the values of Duty, Honor, Country and prepared for a career of professional excellence and service to the Nation as an officer in the United States Army. (USMA Strategic Plan, 2015: p.5)

Since 1802, West Point's primary contribution to the Nation has been and continues to be developing 'leaders of character' who serve America as commissioned officers in the United States Army. West Point's mission sets the audacious, aspirational goal that each graduate is a leader of character. In other words, the mission requires a 100% success rate. Any graduate who does not demonstrate the high character required of commissioned service in the Army is a mission failure for West Point. While this standard may seem unreasonable and unattainable, the requirement is understandable, given the complex security environment these graduates operate within, where a lapse in character by one graduate can have immediate and negative strategic consequences on others, and in some cases entire nations. Examples of such lapses are not difficult to find and each one negatively impacts the trust between the American public and the Army, in addition to making the mission more difficult. The strategic impact of one such error therefore requires West Point to continually ensure that it reaches this 100% success goal.

One way in which the institution attempts to achieve this goal is through the implementation of the West Point Leader Development System (WPLDS). The WPLDS is a systematic, integrated, and intensive process that synchronizes academic, physical, military, and character development programs to foster the character, competence, and commitment which are necessary for commissioned service (USMA, 2015). Each of the four programs provides experiences that comply with a research-based leader development model that includes five key components: readiness, developmental experience, reflection, new capacities and knowledge, and time (Kegan, 1982; Lewis et al., 2005; USMA, 2009). Within the context of this model, West Point emphasizes the critical role of mentors in the development process. Mentors guide cadets through reflection exercises that require cadets to think about what they learned from their developmental experiences within the context of preparing for commissioned service (USMA, 2009). The most important West Point strategic planning and program publications emphasize the crucial role of mentorship in achieving desired outcomes in all aspects of cadet development. A cursory reading of the *West Point Strategic Plan* (USMA, 2015), the *West Point Character Development Strategy* (USMA, 2014), the West Point *Character Program* (USMA, 2015), and the *West Point Leader Development System Handbook* (USMA, 2015) reveals a consistent emphasis on the crucial role of mentorship and a challenge to all staff and faculty to become mentors.

CHAPTER PURPOSE AND OVERVIEW

The purpose of this chapter is to present exploratory research on the mandatory mentorship requirement in a required academic course during a cadet's junior year. Although more details about the research design follow later in this chapter, this academic requirement presents an opportunity to examine the impact of a hybrid mentorship assignment that requires a cadet to find a mentor, but allows the cadet freedom to choose who will fulfill this role.

West Point's culture encourages mentorship throughout a cadet's experience and the faculty are encouraged to seek out protégés. In spite of this effort, a significant portion of cadets do not have a mentor by their third year at West Point. In an effort to encourage more cadet mentorship and to highlight the value of such endeavors to one's professional development, the core course in military leadership requires cadets to find a mentor for a series of graded exercises. As a result, those who do not already have a mentor must find one, and they have the freedom to choose whomever they want, with some constraints, which are described in detail later in this chapter. The structure of the assignment provides identification of two populations: those who already have a mentor and those who do not. This natural sorting allows us to examine any differences that exist between the groups for expectations of mentorship, the quality of the relationship, the attitude towards continuing the relationship, and the effect of this requirement on career aspirations. The research will help answer the question of how to increase the quantity and quality of mentorship relationships without undermining the desired policy outcome by mandating involuntary mentorship programs.

This chapter begins with an overview of mentorship in the Army in general and highlights how the mentoring culture in the larger institution relates to efforts at West Point. This is followed with a description of the aforementioned leadership course and the graded mentorship activity. The next sections convey the research design, methodology, and results. Finally, the discussion addresses implications for West Point and the Army, study limitations and recommendations for future research.

MENTORSHIP IN THE ARMY

West Point's emphasis on mentorship is closely connected to the Army's emphasis on the same. Because West Point graduates will immediately serve in the Army, they should understand the importance of mentorship and how to mentor others. Properly equipped and educated, West Point graduates can improve this endeavor throughout the Army. As a guide for West Point's mentorship activities,

Army leader development principles and doctrine emphasize the importance of effective mentorship. Numerous official Army publications clearly articulate the role of mentorship in effective leader development, and form the foundation of West Point's developmental model (ALDS, 2013; Department of the Army, 2012; Department of the Army, 2015).

Mentorship is not just a theoretical construct within the Army. Evidence shows that it is valued by all members of the officer corps, not only West Point graduates.[2] However, data also reveal that the Army could improve its mentoring culture. While most junior officers desire mentorship, many of them report they are not receiving the support and guidance they need (Martin, Reed, Collins and Dial, 2002; Riley, 2013; Wong, 2000). Senior officers also recognize the benefit of mentorship in their own professional development and most of them report having at least one mentor that helped them develop during their career (Martin et al., 2002).

US history provides many examples of Army officers who benefited greatly from effective mentorship. For instance, Generals Marshall, Eisenhower, and Patton were all beneficiaries of Major General Fox Conner's mentorship, without which they may not have risen to their prominent place in history (Cox, 2010). Finally, the military recognizes the body of scholarship that demonstrates mentorship benefits, such as job satisfaction, retention, and increased productivity (Johnson and Andersen, 2010). Clearly, the Army understands the importance and benefits of effective mentorship and expends considerable energy implementing leader development through this means.

However, the Army's emphasis on mentorship is no guarantee that it occurs effectively. In fact, the results are mixed. A survey of Senior Service College (SSC) officers found that 91% of students had at least one mentor (Johnson and Andersen, 2010). Although this finding seems promising, it is not necessarily an indicator of effective mentorship throughout the Army as SSC attendance is reserved for the top performers at, approximately, the 20-year career mark. Although this population is more likely to have experienced a mentoring relationship during their career, it is not clear if they were successful because they had a mentor or if they had a mentor because they were successful. Other surveys indicate a level of dissatisfaction among junior officers about the level of individual counseling and mentorship they receive from senior leaders (Riley et al., 2014). Hence, it is highly plausible that at least some segment of the Army officer population is unable to leverage quality mentorship to help them develop to their full potential.

Additionally, although officers indicate they would prefer to receive more mentorship, they do not support doing so via formal, mandatory mentorship programs (Martin et al., 2002). This is an important finding, because the Army often mandates activities it deems important. In this case, the Army's cultural norm would be to implement an involuntary mentorship program to ensure that every leader received mentorship whether they wanted it or not. Not only does research demonstrate this is not an optimal method, it also indicates that mandatory programs might actually undermine a protégé's intrinsic motivation and create resentment towards the mentorship program (Johnson and Andersen, 2010). This negative response to mandatory mentorship results in the Army confronting 'the paradox of program oversight' (ibid.). On one hand, the Army would like to increase the quantity of mentor relationships. On the other hand, mandatory mentorship programs might undermine the quality of mentor relationships. This paradox presents an opportunity to evaluate a different policy alternative for increasing mentorship in a military environment such as West Point, while at the same time ensuring everyone participates.

Another important aspect of the research context is the Army's misunderstanding and misuse of the words mentor and mentorship.

While most leaders would agree that mentorship is a critical component of an effective leader development program, there is less agreement about the concept of mentorship itself. Over time, the concept of mentorship expanded to encompass almost any personal or group development experience that involved the transfer of wisdom from one person to another, whether or not the supposed protégé wanted to receive the information. While this misinterpretation seems benign, the misconception of mentorship as an old boy network caused many to either resent or avoid mentorship experiences. The notion of favored treatment runs contrary to the military values of equality and meritocracy and could serve as a barrier to seeking mentorship out of concern for being perceived as a careerist, rather than a public servant.

This incoherent concept of mentorship creates confusion, disappointment, and resentment within the Army profession and might also provide an explanation for why more cadets have not established a mentoring relationship after two years in an environment that is fundamentally designed to facilitate and encourage mentorship. Prior to the most recent updates, Army leader development doctrine added to the confusion by sending mixed messages about counseling, coaching, and mentoring. Mentoring was described as something every leader would do for every subordinate in their charge on a daily basis. By conflating mentorship with routine leader behaviors the Army inadvertently set false expectations. To rectify this confusion and resulting junior officer disenchantment with mentorship, Martin et al. (2002) suggested publishing more clearly defined and distinct concepts of positive leader development with adequate performance counseling, senior leader role modeling, and senior leader development for high potential leaders.

The Army has taken steps to create a common understanding of mentorship within its leader development community of practice, which includes West Point. Recent Army doctrine defines mentoring as 'the voluntary developmental relationship that exists between a person of greater experience and a person of lesser experience that is characterized by mutual trust and respect' (Department of the Army, 2012). This clear definition of mentoring is useful for clarifying a mentorship relationship, but Army and West Point culture, as reflected in current use of the term mentor, has not caught up with doctrine.

As an integral part of the Army, West Point's culture provides several examples of incorrect usage of the terms mentor and mentorship. For example, if a cadet is found guilty of an Honor Code violation, the cadet may be enrolled in the Honor Mentorship Program under the tutelage of an officer approved by West Point leadership. This program is not voluntary and the cadet can be separated from the Academy if he or she does not complete the program. The cadet provides input into the mentor selection, but West Point approves the decision and sometimes overrides the cadet's first choice.

Another example of misusing the term mentor occurred in a required course taught to senior cadets on Officership. This course is a capstone professional development course designed to complete the identity transition from cadet to officer. The instructor for this course was called a mentor even though the cadets and the instructors had no choice over who was assigned to a specific seminar. Additionally, the graded requirements and evaluation changed the nature of the cadet–instructor relationship to something other than a relationship based on mutual respect and trust. Coaching is a better description of these mandatory developmental relationships.

Finally, overuse of the terms mentor and mentorship at West Point reveals a lack of understanding of the doctrinal definitions. Tactical officers have a senior–subordinate relationship with cadets, but are often described as cadet mentors for those cadets assigned to their company. Officers often refer to a correction they make on a cadet as providing mentorship instead of simply correcting behavior. Examples such as these regularly occur throughout the Army, continuing the confusion and conflicting messages about mentorship that existed in the late 1990s. Hence, it is essential to West Point and to the Army to promote a shared understanding of the concept of mentorship that includes the expectations and responsibilities of both mentors and protégés.

This shared understanding must also include the qualities desired in a mentor and the long-term impact of successful relationships. Mentors are often viewed in terms of their traits and behaviors: traits include both demographic characteristics and personal values, such as honor and integrity; behaviors are the actions mentors take on behalf of their protégés and fall into the general categories of career development and psychosocial support (Smith et al., 2005). Both West Point and the Army must consider these desired qualities in resourcing decisions. They need to retain the right types of people to serve as mentors, those who are also skilled in the necessary behaviors that facilitate successful relationship outcomes.

The organizational benefits of positive mentorship are well documented. Protégés in satisfying relationships report more positive work attitudes, and marginal relationships are actually more counterproductive than no mentorship at all (Ragins et al., 2000). A meta-analysis by Allen and colleagues (2004) revealed that mentored individuals report greater career satisfaction and commitment. Subsequently, a longitudinal study of 1,000 Army officers found that mentoring contributed to higher levels of both affective and continuance commitment (Payne and Huffman, 2005). Positive mentorship not only facilitates individual professional development, but ultimately strengthens the institution through more invested officers.

In summary, the Army's culture and doctrine recognizes that mentorship occupies a critical place in the leader development model. Both Army and West Point developmental frameworks emphasize the importance of mentorship and encourage all to seek mentoring and be mentors, as appropriate. There is a desire for more mentorship, yet the Army recognizes research that warns of negative outcomes for mandating mentorship programs requiring 100% participation. This context sets the stage for this chapter which examines the impact of one West Point academic course on leadership that requires all students to find a mentor as a graded requirement.

Given West Point's place in the Army, the institution has a unique opportunity to assess the influence of mentorship programs in a military context. West Point prepares officers to be mentors and research that explores West Point mentorship policies can inform Army policy decisions intended to increase mentorship. Although the Army as a whole appears to recognize the importance of mentoring in developing leaders of high character, and have built mentoring into the West Point curriculum, little research has been done to determine the effectiveness of these mentoring endeavors. This includes whether such programs achieve the desired outcomes and what impact they might have on one's commitment to a military career. This research will aid in addressing these issues.

Improving the mentorship culture at West Point

West Point's core curriculum includes a required leadership course that presents a hybrid approach to mandating a mentor relationship, while leaving room for individual choice in the mentor–mentee relationship. Every West Point cadet takes this required course, called Military Leadership, during the first or second semester of their junior year. The course has two main goals:

- Cadets will be better, more self-aware leaders who are capable of reflecting on and learning from their life and leadership experiences.
- Cadets will apply relevant frameworks, concepts and theory to their current leadership situations and demonstrate improvement as leaders.

Two of the major graded requirements for the class are a Leader Reflective Exercise and a Leadership Philosophy paper worth 10% and 20% of the course grade respectively. Both of these assignments require getting and reflecting on feedback from a formal mentor and capturing these thoughts on paper. However, improving the written product is only half of the purpose for the requirement. The other is to emphasize the utility of a mentor in one's personal and professional development.

Because there is no obligation in the USMA curriculum to have a designated mentor before this assignment, there is an assumption that not all cadets will have one, and that some will be unfamiliar with the process altogether. Therefore, the course syllabus briefly outlines the requirement and establishes some prerequisites. Among the constraints are that the mentor must be someone physically present at USMA, they must have significant leadership experience, and cannot be a family member or close friend. Additionally, cadets must provide documentation by the fifth class meeting that they have formally asked the mentor to participate. The mentor's role is not graded, but the mentor's input is part of the student's grade.

The hybrid nature of this requirement is a combination of formal and informal mentorship. The formal part is that each student is required to find a mentor. The informal part is that the student can find a mentor of their choosing within parameters set by the course director. Through this course requirement, West Point ensures that every cadet has at least one 'mentor' relationship opportunity prior to graduation and beginning their Army career. In other words, West Point increases the quantity of mentor relationships while attempting to preserve the quality of mentor relationships. Anecdotal evidence touts this specific requirement as a 'best practice' in cadet development, but it has never undergone any deliberate evaluation. The research design of this study allowed us to explore the program's impact on desired outcomes.

The West Point approach to mentorship is an important part of the context of this research. As previously discussed, cadets are immersed in a leader development environment with multiple opportunities to find a mentor. The military leadership course is one of many opportunities to find one. (USMA, 2009). For example, cadets are assigned to 'companies' of about 120 cadets under the direction of an active duty Army officer who sometimes becomes a mentor for a few cadets in the company. Cadets also develop relationships with members of the faculty who are charged by West Point leadership to mentor cadets outside the classroom. Many of these staff and faculty volunteer to lead cadet hobby clubs or athletic teams where they can develop mentoring relationships with cadet participants. There are also clubs under officer supervision that provide mentorship opportunities based on gender, ethnicity, and intellectual interests. Members of the staff and faculty also serve as cadet sponsors who provide a place to relax, do laundry, and enjoy home cooked food. Many of these sponsorship relationships develop into mentorship relationships over time.

By the time a cadet reaches their junior year, they have multiple opportunities to find a mentor in an environment that not only emphasizes mentorship, but has a large pool of potential mentors willing to fulfill that role. As a result, many of the cadets enrolled in the military leadership course already have a mentor for the assignment. However, some cadets have not yet found a mentor and this course requires them to identify someone for purposes of the graded assignment. This bifurcation of cadets completing the assignment enables us to compare outcomes between cadets who already have a mentor and those who are mandated to find one.

Research questions and design

As previously stated, the formal mentorship requirement in the military leadership course provides a unique opportunity to evaluate the impact of a semi-formal mentorship program on the aggregate as well as two distinct populations: cadets who complete the assignment with a mentor they have previously worked with and those who are working with a mentor for the first time. Previous work on peer effects makes the case that cadets are assigned to these groups randomly (Lyle and Smith, 2014). This random assignment alleviates concern that unobserved variable bias systematically affects developmental outcomes (Lyle, 2007). As a result, we can assert that all cadets have equal opportunities to find a mentor if they desire one. Therefore, by the time cadets enroll in the military leadership course, they have sorted into two groups based on unobserved criteria.

One group has already identified and worked with a mentor. Why they have done this is not known. Perhaps these cadets have a stronger desire for mentorship or believe they have more in common with staff and faculty than those who have not chosen a mentor. They may be actively involved with a club that provides more time with potential mentors who share common interests. These cadets might display a unique passion or talent that make a potential mentor willing to establish such a relationship.

Conversely, the other group has not engaged in a mentoring relationship. The reasons for this are also unknown. Perhaps the cadet does not desire a mentor because they don't understand how the relationship works or the potential benefits. They might not be receptive to input from a mentor for a variety of unknown reasons. It may also be true that potential mentors are reluctant to enter into a mentorship relationship because they perceive that the cadet lacks motivation or potential for future success.

Whatever the reason for cadets not having engaged a mentor prior to enrollment in the military leadership course, the requirement to find a mentor allows us to establish a quasi-experiment exploring some effects of mandatory mentorship on a group of cadets who do and do not have a mentorship relationship after spending two years in an environment purposefully designed to facilitate such affiliations. Furthermore, this study explored the effect of pre-existing mentoring relationships and the quality of these associations on career attitudes towards service as a commissioned officer.

As we considered important aspects of encouraging mentorship relationships between cadets and the West Point staff and faculty, several important questions emerged. First, we were concerned that confusion about the meaning and purpose of mentorship may be an obstacle to cadets seeking a mentor. We wondered if some cadets avoided mentorship simply because they lack understanding of what it means to be mentored and how they might benefit. If this is the case, then ensuring cadets understand mentorship may remove any hesitation that is preventing them from seeking a mentor.

Secondly, we considered the characteristics of the mentors chosen by the population of cadets who did not already have a mentor. We wanted to know whether they used the same criteria as those who already had a mentor and whether they picked the first available person just to fill the requirement. From a strategic standpoint we wanted to ascertain if the Academy provides a level playing field where everyone is able to find a mentor they are comfortable and eager to work with early on, or if there are segments of the cadet population who struggle to find someone that satisfies their developmental needs.

We also wanted to explore whether the cadets who already had a mentor received more benefit from the assignment than those who did not previously have a mentor. Another outcome we wanted to investigate was whether or not requiring a cadet to find a mentor results in increased long-term mentorship. If the mandatory relationships chosen by cadets evolve into a voluntary, long-term relationship then this program could be an effective way to increase mentorship throughout West Point and the Army.

Lastly, this research examined whether or not protégés' career aspirations and commitment are related to their satisfaction with their mentorship experience. It may be that cadets who are more committed to the Army seek out mentorship in preparation for service. If so, is the converse true?

The specific research questions asked were:

1. To what extent is there a common understanding of mentorship and expected outcomes between cadets with pre-existing mentors, and cadets without pre-existing mentors?
2. When mandated to find a mentor, to what extent do cadets with pre-existing mentors and those without them select mentors with the same qualities?
3. To what extent do mentorship outcomes differ between cadets in existing relationships and those with newly formed ones?
4. How likely are mandatory mentor relationships to develop into voluntary relationships?
5. To what extent do career intentions and organizational commitment attitudes differ between groups with pre-existing mentors and those without pre-existing mentors?

METHOD

Participants and procedures

This study utilized a convenience sample of cadets participating in the mandatory formal mentoring program for the Military Leadership academic course taken by all juniors at the United States Military Academy.[3] An online survey assessing various aspects of mentorship was developed and emailed to all enrolled students at the completion of the course, resulting in a response rate of 20%.

Measures

The survey commenced with two open-ended questions. First, respondents were asked 'In your own words, what is a mentor?' The second question prompted respondents to briefly describe their expectations of the mentoring process/relationship. The intent behind including these items up front was to promote thinking and reflection about the concept of mentorship prior to completing the remaining multiple choice responses.

To measure factors that influence mentor choice, protégés were asked to rank the three most important reasons for choosing a mentor in terms of practical considerations and desired mentor qualities from the following choices: existing relationship; good rapport; greatly admire; interest in mentor's career field/branch; mutual hobbies/interests; access to professional networks; or other specified reason. Protégés were also asked how long they knew their mentor prior to the course and in what capacity: current instructor; former instructor; extracurricular coach/club advisor; tactical officer; sponsor; acquaintance; or other specified individual. Finally, respondents were asked to indicate whether or not they had considered this person as their mentor prior to taking the course.

Relationship quality was defined by three components: tensility; emotional tone; and openness – based on the work of Dutton and Heaphy (2003) and a previous study by Lunsford (2015). Tensility was assessed with the item, 'I can count on my mentor/protégé even after difficult conversations'. Emotional tone was measured with the statement, 'I can express my feelings (good or bad) to my mentor/protégé'. The item, 'I think about new ideas as a result of conversations with my mentor/protégé' assessed openness. Respondents were asked to gauge their agreement with each statement using a six-point Likert scale, with a higher score indicating better relationship quality. Additionally, respondents were asked to estimate the likelihood, on a six-point Likert scale, that they would continue in a mentoring relationship with this particular mentor.

Career intentions and organizational attitudes were measured using items adapted from the Military Commitment Scale developed by Gade et al. (2003). Respondents were asked to indicate their agreement with statements that assessed their affective and continuance commitment to an Army career on a six-point Likert scale. Affective commitment is a measure of enthusiasm with regard to military service and was assessed with items such as 'I am happy with my decision to become an Army Officer' and 'I believe I will enjoy serving in the Army'. Items such as 'I intend to leave the Army after my initial service obligation' and 'I am committed to making the Army my career' measured continuance commitment. Responses were averaged to create a composite indicator of commitment, with a higher score representing more positive attitudes about the military as a career choice and stronger intentions to serve.

Demographics

The gender composition of the sample was of 80% men and 20% women. With regard to race, 63% of protégés reported identifying as White, followed by Asian (7.7%), Hispanic (6.2%), and African American (4.6%). The remainder of respondents indicated they were of mixed heritage (10.7%) or preferred not to answer (7.7%).[4]

RESULTS

The findings of this study are organized into four sub-sections. First, we compare the conceptualization of mentoring between those in an established relationship and those experiencing mentoring for the first time. Second, we look at the characteristics and qualities desired in mentors. Next, we look at the effects of mentor exposure on relationship outcomes. Finally, we examine the relationship between both mentor exposure and relationship outcomes to career intentions and commitment. The implications of each finding are addressed in the subsequent discussion section.

Defining mentoring and expectations

Protégés were asked to answer two open-ended questions regarding the definition of a mentor and their expectations for entering into a mentor relationship. With regard to defining a mentor, both protégés with a pre-existing mentorship relationship and those without appeared to have a fairly good shared understanding of what it means to be a mentor. Both groups generally considered a mentor to be a more experienced person who provides advice to someone less knowledgeable to help them develop and grow professionally. Examples of typical responses included:

A mentor is an experienced individual who exemplifies the qualities you want to have as a leader. They can be used for advice and ideas.

Somebody who you respect and look up to [sic] and can guide you to where you want to be. Generally somebody who is in the same position you would like to be in one day or the kind of person you aspire to be.

A mentor is someone who can provide an example and feedback on your personal qualities in an effort to develop you into a more capable individual.

In terms of expectations about the mentorship experience some subtle thematic differences emerged between experienced protégés and those working with mentors for the first time. Those in a pre-existing relationship more frequently recognized a mentor's investment in a protégé and their likely motivation. Some had clear ideas of the attributes desired in a mentor. For example:

I know a mentor is genuine in his or her concern with my development when he or she goes out of their way to mentor me. It is not required, they simply just want to help others.

I expect that in the mentoring process, the mentor listens to the issue or question the mentee has and offers advice based on their own experiences. Aside from the formal exchange of ideas, a mentor is someone whose everyday actions and behaviors inspire the mentee to be a certain way.

The mentoring relationship should be a combination of both personal and professional aspects. The mentor should possess a demeanor that encourages approachability and openness from the mentee while commanding a level of appropriate respect.

A small minority of experienced protégés recognized the benefits of mentorship to both parties in a relationship:

The mentor relationship is a two-way relationship. The mentee learns from the experiences and advice of the mentor while the mentor learns from the mentee's fresh perspective and deeper reflection on their experiences.

My expectations is [sic] a dynamic relationship that benefits all those involved. Mentors learn from the mentees and vice versa. They also share a deep and personal bond with one another.

In contrast, inexperienced protégés more frequently couched their expectations primarily in terms of what they expected to gain personally from the relationship:

My expectations were to get as much out of my mentor in regards to his experiences as a Platoon Leader, problems he may have faced, and how he overcame them to better himself and the others around him.

I expect my mentor to give me honest feedback that will help develop me and make me reconsider some decisions.

I expect my mentor to teach me what he/she has learned from first-hand experience. I expect him/her to be there when I need help or guidance on a personal or professional issue.

This group also appeared less optimistic about the prospect of working with a mentor:

Initially, I was not sure what to expect. However, as I learned more about the program, I expected my mentor to help me identify areas of improvement in my leadership style.

I expected the mentoring process to be like a story one of my instructors told the class. His battalion commander would always talk about his leadership philosophy every time the lieutenants were over for dinner. In other words, useful but dreadful.

I expected the mentoring process to be a waste of time. I expected it to be a 'check the box' thing that everyone did because they had to. I thought I may learn a few things but didn't expect to learn as much as I actually did.

Finally, a small minority of experienced protégés commented on the mutual responsibilities inherent in a mentoring relationship:

I would expect a mentor to be approachable and willing to listen. A mentee should have legitimate questions when they approach their mentor.

I believe most mentoring and communication between both parties is going to normally be started by the mentee and it's on the mentor to offer back constructive feedback.

Desired mentor qualities

Respondents were asked to rank their top three reasons for choosing a mentor. Over one quarter of respondents (26.1%) reported that admiration was the most important factor, followed by rapport (15.2%), and having a pre-existing relationship (11.1%). Only a small percentage of respondents considered other factors of mentor's career field/branch (6.1%), common interests (3%) and access to networks (1%) as most important. Furthermore, more than two-thirds of protégés considered choosing a person they admired, and half judged rapport to be among the top three reasons to choose a mentor.

A Mann-Whitney U test was conducted to determine if there were any significant differences between groups and their ranking of factors. Those who reported already having a mentor, predictably, were more likely to state a pre-existing relationship as the most important reason for choosing a mentor ($Z = -3.05$, $p > .05$). Additionally, cadets with pre-existing mentors were significantly more likely to consider branch choice ($Z = -1.97$, $p > .05$) and common interests ($Z = -2.40$, $p > .05$) as the most important factors in mentor selection.

There were no significant differences between the groups with regard to the demographic characteristics of their mentor choice. Nearly half (49.2%) of the protégés reported that they knew their mentor as a faculty member they had taken a class with since arriving at West Point. Extracurricular club advisor or athletic coach was the next most common response (18.5%), followed by an instructor they were presently taking a class with (12.3%). The length of time protégés reported knowing their mentor prior to beginning the formal mentoring relationship ranged from four months to four years with a mean of 18.3 months ($SD = 10.5$). Those already in a mentoring relationship reported knowing their mentor for 22 months on average ($SD = 11.4$), which significantly differed $t(63) = 2.93$, $p > .05$ from the inexperienced group who reported they knew their mentor (though not specifically engaged in a mentoring relationship with them) for an average of 14.79 months ($SD = 8.4$).

Furthermore, there were no significant differences between groups for the remaining factors that defined who military protégés chose as a mentor. All respondents overwhelmingly chose military officers as a program mentor (95.4%). No cadets indicated that they had been mentored by a non-commissioned officer and only 4.6% of respondents reported working with a civilian faculty member for this requirement. The majority of respondents (58.5%) chose officers in the rank of major/O-4 (i.e. those who have served at least nine years but not more than 15 in commissioned service), followed by lieutenant colonel/O-5 (18.5%), captain/O-3 (13.8%), and colonel/O-6 (4.6%).[5] Nearly half the protégés (48.4%) reported working with a member of a combat arms branch, followed by combat support (35.4%), and combat service support (13.8%). On a scale of zero to five, with zero being not at all likely and five being highly likely, the sample was almost evenly divided on the probability that they would choose the same career field in which their mentor was currently serving ($M = 2.62$, $SD = 1.86$).

Similarly, the majority of protégé respondents indicated that they had worked with a male (90.8%), and only 12% chose a mentor of the opposite sex. Further analysis to see if women and/or minorities were more likely to choose a female mentor was conducted. However, the results were only marginally significant, that is, cadets tended to choose male mentors more often than female ones, regardless of their own gender.

Mentor exposure and relationship outcomes

Overall, respondents strongly agreed that they had experienced a high-quality relationship with their mentor. Of the three factors that comprise relationship quality, emotional tone was assessed most highly ($M = 5.63$, $SD = .60$), followed by tensility ($M = 5.60$, $SD = .63$), then openness ($M = 5.58$, $SD = .71$). Subsequent t-tests were conducted to determine if a pre-existing relationship would predict better relationship outcomes. Emotional tone was the only factor that significantly differed between groups $t(63) = 2.38$, $p > .05$. Protégés in pre-existing relationships ($M = 5.81$, $SD = .40$) more strongly agreed that they were able to express their emotions with their mentor than those in new relationships ($M = 5.47$, $SD = .71$).

Almost 90% of the aggregate indicated that they were more likely than not to continue working with the same mentor even after the formal requirement of the course was complete, and more than three-quarters of this group strongly agreed that they intended to continue the relationship ($M = 4.19$, $SD = 1.1$). However, there was a significant difference in responses dependent on a pre-existing relationship $t(63) = 3.39$, $p > .001$. Cadets who already considered this person their mentor were more likely to continue the relationship post-course ($M = 4.6$, $SD = .67$) than those in a new relationship ($M = 3.8$, $SD = 1.2$).

Mentor exposure, relationship quality and career intentions

Finally, we explored the relationship between mentorship and career intentions to determine if cadets who engaged a mentor earlier in their career differed from those who had not in terms of their enthusiasm and intentions to pursue a military career. The aggregate commitment score mean was 4.52 ($SD = .71$) and less than 20% of respondents reported dissatisfaction with the prospect of a military career. There were no significant differences between groups with regard to commitment to the Army.

We also looked at the relationship between relationship quality and commitment. Of the three factors that comprise quality, only emotional tone was a significant predictor of commitment ($r = .213$, $p > .05$). Hence, protégés who reported feeling greater freedom to express their emotions with their mentor tended to have more positive attitudes and commitment to a career in military service.

DISCUSSION

In this chapter we set out to examine the semi-formal mentoring program at the United States Military Academy and determine if it achieves the desired outcomes. Initially we intended to gain a better understanding of the expectations emerging leaders have for mentorship, how well their needs are met, and how their experiences relate to their career intentions. Through the course of our research we discovered the emergence of two distinct groups, which provided additional context for our analysis: those who sought out a mentor before they were required to do so; and those who did not.

First, we wanted to assess how well protégés understood the concept of mentorship and what their expectations for a relationship were. While protégés across the board appeared to have a shared understanding of what a mentor is, the results were mixed in terms of their expectations. Both groups tended to be egocentric in describing what behaviors a mentor should engage in to provide the most benefit. Only experienced protégés commented on their own responsibilities for preparation and engagement. Thus, it appears that education about mentorship prior to engaging in a relationship can help with expectations and making the most of the experience. It also warrants further research to understand why some people are reluctant or unable to engage a mentor until mandated to do so.

The most important factors that protégés take into consideration when choosing a mentor are admiration and rapport, acknowledging the perceived value of both mentor traits and behaviors. This finding may explain previous research that questions the effectiveness of formal mentoring programs (Johnson and Andersen, 2010; Martin et al., 2002). If mentors are matched to protégés based on some superficial constellation of characteristics, it may not facilitate the level of intimacy needed for meaningful development to occur. While protégés in pre-existing relationships rated branch choice and common interests significantly higher than those who were not, the percentages were small and do not warrant further discussion.

In addition to observed trends in why protégés selected a specific mentor, there were also distinct patterns in who they chose. The most sought after mentors were White, male, mid-level combat-arms officers on the teaching faculty. This is also the most represented group at West Point and therefore the most available. However, considering the importance of admiration in the previous analysis, it is unclear if the demographic trends are more reflective of accessibility or result more from the referent power of the most privileged group in the Army (White, male, combat-arms). Given the Army's emphasis on diversity as a force multiplier in complex tasks and problem solving, and attrition concerns for women and minorities (Livingston, 2010; Smith, 2012), this is an area that warrants further research.

Next, we examined relationship quality to determine if the mandatory mentoring requirement could still produce desired outcomes. We found it to be the case that the majority of protégés reported a positive experience with their mentor at the conclusion of the course. Whether or not the relationship existed prior to beginning the assignment did not predict tensility or openness. However, those who had worked with their mentor previously reported a significantly higher emotional tone, that is the freedom to express their emotions, and were more confident that they would continue the mentoring relationship after the course was concluded. Emotional expressiveness may take longer to develop as it requires allowing oneself to be vulnerable and a certain amount of mutual trust, both of which may benefit from additional time (Chun et al., 2010). Furthermore, protégés who have invested this additional time in developing a mentoring relationship appear to be more committed to maintaining it in the future. Hence, the Academy might consider ways to more explicitly highlight the benefits of seeking mentorship early in one's development so that all cadets see this as the cultural norm.

Finally, although we expected that cadets who engaged in mentoring early on might be more committed to their career choice, we did not find this to be the case. All respondents, regardless of when or why they sought out a mentoring relationship, were positively committed to a career in military service. However, we did find emotional tone to predict commitment, suggesting that those who more freely express their emotions are more committed to a military career. Further research is warranted to determine if other variables can explain why some cadets are less able to express themselves emotionally and why this makes them less committed to military service.

Admittedly this study has several limitations. First, the sample size is relatively small, primarily due to technical difficulties with the Academy's email server during the time the survey was disseminated. Many cadets were well into final exams before they received an invitation, which significantly limited the response rate. We plan to replicate this study with modifications with the Class of 2017, which may allow us to overcome some of these limitations.

Also, the study may have been subject to selection bias. Because this was a voluntary survey it is possible that protégés who did not feel a positive connection with their mentor, or did not derive value from the experience were less motivated to respond. This would account for the relatively high assessment of relationship quality across both groups of participants.

Future studies should employ a more comprehensive research design. Only evaluating one half of a mentoring dyad paints an incomplete picture. A matched sample that compared mentor responses to their respective protégés would be informative and provide a more nuanced assessment of relationship quality. Additionally, collecting expectations pre-intervention and comparing those responses to post-intervention outcomes in a within-subjects design would more accurately measure the program's effectiveness.

In view of prior research which posits that formal mentoring programs can sometimes have less than optimal outcomes, this study highlights the potential of a semi-formal structure. For those emerging leaders who for some reason are reluctant to engage a mentor, even when presented with multiple opportunities to do so, this approach breaks the ice, so to speak. Protégés are mandated to participate in the program, but exercise an important choice in choosing a mentor. Considering the importance of admiration and rapport in mentorship, participants avoid the pitfalls of a forced match that may be unsuccessful. It is imperative that emerging leaders value and positively experience mentorship early in their leadership journey to help them develop to their full potential.

CONCLUSION

Effective mentorship is an essential component of an emerging leader's professional development. Future officers who attend West Point are provided with an environment rich in mentoring opportunities, yet this study reveals that some of them require more assistance than others to establish successful relationships. However, it also shows that West Point, with proper timing and emphasis, has great potential to model and set the conditions for positive mentorship that will not only provide professional benefits to individual leaders but also result in long-term improvements to the mentoring culture at the Academy and in the Army.

Notes

1 The views expressed in this chapter are those of the authors and do not purport to reflect the official policy or position of the Department of the Army, the Department of Defense, or the US Government.
2 West Point is just one of four possible sources of an officer commission. Officer Candidate School (OCS), Reserve Officer Training Corps (ROTC), and direct commission are the others. Approximately 20% of the active duty Officer Corps is produced by West Point annually, yet West Point graduates comprise more than 80% of the most senior leaders (four-star generals) currently serving in the Army (Lesinski, Pinter, Kucik & Lamm, 2011).
3 Invitations were only sent to those students enrolled in the Spring 2015 semester.
4 The demographic profile for the class of 2016 upon admission was as follows: men 84.1%, women 15.9%, White 76.2%, Asian 6.6%, Hispanic 8.6%, African American 8.6% (source: USMA Diversity Office).
5 This constitutes an over-representation of officers in the rank of Major/O4 who comprise approximately 34% of the staff and faculty, and an under-representation of other officer ranks of Captain/O3 (36%), Lieutenant Colonel/O5 (21%), and Colonel/O6 (8%).

REFERENCES

Allen, T. D., Eby, L. T., Poteet, M. L., Lentz, E., and Lima, L. (2004). Career benefits associated with mentoring for protégés: A meta-analysis. *Journal of Applied Psychology*, 89(1), 127–36.

Chun, J. U., Litzky, B. E., Sosik, J. J., Bechtold, D. C., and Godshalk, V. M. (2010). Emotional intelligence and trust in formal mentoring programs. *Group and Organization Management*, 35(4), 421–55.

Cox, E. (2010). Grey eminence: Fox Conner and the art of mentorship. *The Land Warfare Papers, No 78W*. Arlington, VA: Institute of Land Warfare, September 2010.

Dutton, J. E., and Heaphy, E. D. (2003). The power of high-quality connections. *Positive Organizational Scholarship: Foundations of a New Discipline*, 3, 263–78.

Gade, P. A., Tiggle, R. B., and Schumm, W. R. (2003). The measurement and consequences of military organizational commitment in soldiers and spouses. *Military Psychology*, 15, 191–207.

Johnson, W. B., and Andersen, G. R. (2010). Formal mentoring in the US military. *Naval War College Review*, 63(2), 113–26.

Kegan, R. (1982). *The evolving self*. Cambridge MA: Harvard University Press.

Lesinski, G., Pinter, J., Kucik, P., and Lamm, G. (2011). *Officer accessions flow model*. West Point, NY: Operations Research Center of Excellence, July 2011.

Lewis, P., Forsythe, G. B., Sweeney, P. J., Bartone, P., Bullis, C., and Snook, S. (2005). Identity development during the college years: Findings from the West Point longitudinal study. *Journal of College Student Development*, 46(4), 357–73.

Livingston, R. M. (2010). *Reality vs. myth: Mentoring reexamined* (Master's thesis). Retrieved from http://www.dtic.mil/dtic/tr/fulltext/u2/a526585.pdf [accessed 7 May, 2015].

Lunsford, L. G. (2015). *Protégés, mentors and job satisfaction: Faculty in liberal arts colleges.* Paper presented at the 2015 Annual Meeting of the American Educational Research Association, Chicago, IL.

Lyle, D. S. (2007). Estimating and interpreting peer and role model effects from randomly assigned social groups at West Point. *Review of Economics and Statistics*, *89*(2), 289–99.

Lyle, D. S., and Smith, J. Z. (2014). The effect of high performing mentors on junior officer promotion in the US Army. *Journal of Labor Economics*, *32*(2), 229–58.

Martin, G., Reed, G., Collins, R., and Dial, C. K. (2002). The road to mentoring: Paved with good intentions. *Parameters*, *32*(3), 115–27.

Payne, S.C., and Huffman, A. H. (2005). A longitudinal examination of the influence of mentoring on organizational commitment and turnover. *Academy of Management Journal*, *48*(1), 158–68.

Ragins, B. R., Cotton, J. R., and Miller, J. S. (2000). Marginal mentoring: The effects of type of mentor, quality of relationship, and program design on work and career attitudes. *Academy of Management*, *43*(8), 1177–94.

Riley, R., Hatfield, J., Freeman, T., Fallesen, J. J., and Gunther, K. M. (2014). *2013 Center for Army Leadership annual survey of army leadership (CASAL): Main findings (Technical Report 2014-01).* Retrieved from http://usacac.army.mil/sites/default/files/documents/cal/2013CASALMainFindingsTechnicalReport2014-01.pdf [accessed 10 June, 2015].

Smith, I. (2012). Why black officers still fail. Carlisle, PA: US Army War College *Parameters*, *40*(3), 1–16.

Smith, W. J., Howard, J. T., and Harrington, K. V. (2005). Essential formal mentor characteristics and functions in governmental and non-governmental organizations from the program administrator's and the mentor's perspective. Public Personnel Management, 34(1), 31–58.

US Army Center for Army Leadership (2013). *Advanced guide to MSAF coaching*, September. Ft. Leavenworth: Headquarters, Combined Arms Center.

USDA (US Department of the Army) (2012). ADRP 6–22: *Army leadership*, August 1. Washington, DC: Headquarters, Department of the Army.

USDA (2005). *Army mentorship handbook*, January 1. Rosslyn, VA: Headquarters, Department of the Army, DCS G-1.

USDA (2015). *Leader development*, June 30. Washington, DC: Headquarters, Department of the Army.

USMA (United States Military Academy) (2009). *Building capacity to lead.* West Point, NY: Office of the Superintendent.

USMA (2015, May). *West Point Leader Development System Handbook,* West Point, NY: Office of the Superintendent.

USMA (2015, March). *USMA strategic plan.* West Point, NY: Office of the Superintendent.

USMA (2014, December). *Character development strategy: Live honorably and build trust.* West Point, NY: Office of the Superintendent.

USMA (2015, May). *Character program.* West Point, NY: Office of the Superintendent.

Wong, L. (2000, October). *Generations apart: Xers and Boomers in the officer corps.* Carlisle, PA: Strategic Studies Institute.

An Historical Exploration of the Research and Practice of Familial Mentoring

Donnel Nunes and Leslie Dashew

INTRODUCTION

Mentoring between and among family members is part of an ancient form of social learning that predates the contemporary study of mentoring by thousands of years (Rogoff et al., 2003). In this chapter, we use the term *familial mentoring* to describe this relationship (Sanchez et al., 2008). It has been suggested that familial mentors represent the very origin of mentoring and the foundation for our future experiences as protégés and mentors (Johnson and Gastic, 2015). In fact, protégés as young as eight years old have been reported to have identified familial mentors.

Familial mentoring efforts are generally directed towards supporting the advancement of child-protégé participation in culturally congruent communities of practice (Johnson, 2002; Lave and Wenger, 1991; Nunes, 2013). The presence of mentors that include familial dyads has been connected to outcomes ranging across psychological and general health (Hurd and Zimmerman, 2010; Rhodes et al., 1992; Rhodes et al., 1994), social development, relationships, social capital, and academic success (Delgado-Gaitan and Ruiz, 1992; Hurd et al., 2013; Schwartz et al., 2013; Zimmerman et al., 2005).

Although the body of mentoring research that includes family members has been emerging over the last two decades (Delgado-Gaitan and Ruiz, 1992; DuBois and Silverthorn, 2005a, 2005b; Hurd et al., 2013; Rhodes et al., 1994; Sánchez et al., 2008; Zimmerman et al., 2005), investigation of these mentoring relationships remains an open frontier for study (Hamilton et al., in press; Sanchez et al., 2008). Some of the more common challenges associated with the study of familial mentoring include: concerns about the overlapping nature of family relationships and mentoring roles (Bearman et al., 2010; Darling et al., 2002); the complications associated with stress and conflict between parents and their children, which may impact the mentoring relationship

(Hurd & Zimmerman, 2010); a questionable belief that parenting equates to mentoring; and the potential for protégés to inadvertently limit the development of human and social capital typically associated with non-family mentoring relationships (DuBois and Silverthorn, 2005b). Additionally, findings from familial and non-family samples are commonly combined in general mentoring studies, making it difficult to examine the influence and impact of familial mentoring (Hamilton et al., in press). Such factors should not be equated with family members being somehow unacceptable candidates as mentors, nor does it suggest that their unique influence on mentoring outcomes should be overlooked. When identifying familial mentors, it should be evident that a family member possesses, at a minimum, either domain-specific expertise or is capable of the skillful provision of mentoring functions.

The purpose of this chapter is to bring clarity to the topic of familial mentoring, defined as a phenomenon in which mentors can be understood through the actions of immediate and extended family members, and through mentoring networks that include family and non-family mentors or important persons. Familial mentors are identified by their skill sets and the intention of their interactions (Nunes, 2013).

This chapter begins with two exemplars that include familial mentoring to provide the reader with a framework for understanding this phenomenon in practice. This is followed by a summary of the literature on this topic. The chapter concludes with a brief summary and suggestions for future research.

FAMILIAL MENTORING IN PRACTICE

This examination of familial mentoring begins with two case studies. The first case focuses on what many consider the origin of mentoring, the *Odyssey*, in which we are introduced to Mentor and his charge. The next example focuses on the familial mentoring experiences of the Forenzas (a pseudonym), a family of wine makers from Italy who immigrated to the United States during the mid twentieth century. Their story serves as a model for formalizing familial mentoring within the context of a family-owned business. Together, these cases demonstrate the dynamic and interwoven way that familial and non-family mentors come together in the lives of their protégés.

Family mentoring history: Homer's symbolic mentor

There is evidence to suggest that familial mentor-like practices were present 'in the earliest beginning of the human species' and that our drive to mentor may be 'part and parcel of our human DNA' (DuBois and Karcher, 2014, p. 3). Coupled with the existence of numerous cultural variations in terminology that can be equated with mentoring (Darling et al., 2002; Delgado-Gaitan, 1994), there is evidence that points to mentoring as, generally, a universal human experience. Thus, it appears that the scope of mentoring inquiry spans not merely decades, but millennia.

In what appears to be among the first literary references to the word mentor, the *Odyssey* highlights an ancient social learning practice that dates back to early human civilization. A critical analysis of the *Odyssey* points to an ancient history of mentor-like relationships that stemmed from and included family and non-family members working together in complex networks. Additionally, our interpretation of the *Odyssey* is one that makes explicit that the duties of the character, Mentor, were designated by and intended to replace those of an absent father. In essence, Mentor was a surrogate parent. The purpose of this position is to encourage readers to consider the historical position of familial mentoring relationships as viable dyads as we continue to advance our understanding of these relationships.

Symbolic mentor

Similar to present-day features of mentoring, relationships in Homeric society were guided by the concept of *cháris* (reciprocal favor) (Dova, 2012, para. 8). As a foundation, *cháris* conceptualizes the importance of honoring the actions of others through reciprocal favor. Frequent examples in the *Odyssey* demonstrate this principle with the exchange of gifts, acts of camaraderie, and through a graciousness and hospitality that was extended to all guests. This tradition continues in contemporary mentoring and is embodied in views that emphasize the shared and reciprocal nature of these learning relationships (Jacobi, 1991).

As was customary in this period, a child brought honor to their family by proving themselves capable of succeeding in the position of their parents (Dova, 2012). Common to practices associated with occupational inheritance, where it was assumed that younger generations would take over the work of their parents, older generations often played a directive role in the process of transition. In the *Odyssey*, it was the father, not the son, who selected Mentor (Dova, 2012; Homer, trans. 1998). In his first appearance, Mentor was introduced to readers as a trusted friend placed in the care of Odysseus' household. As the culture of the time would dictate, in this role he was responsible for the physical estate, the inhabitants, and expected to function in a paternal role to Telemachus, his mentee, and Odysseus' son.

It is important to note that Mentor was not Odysseus' equal. Furthermore, his position as surrogate was not intended to last for an extensive period. In an effort to elevate him as a capable surrogate relative to Odysseus, Homer merged Mentor with the goddess Athena in what we will refer to as *Symbolic Mentor*. We believe it is through this man/goddess fusion that Homer spoke to his own contemplations about what exactly comprises an exemplary mentor.

In book one, 'A Goddess Intervenes', Athena as Symbolic Mentor appeared before Telemachus in what could be understood as his time of need, delivering a renewed sense of hope and direction for the future. With the conviction of a goddess, Symbolic Mentor moved quickly to restore direction and clarity for the young prince. Reminding Telemachus of his lineage and noble heritage, and thus his cultural duty, Symbolic Mentor initiated a mentoring relationship that roused him from an apathetic state. Much like the story of any mentoring relationship, Symbolic Mentor inspired Telemachus to overcome his anguish and to take charge of his destiny. Through a well-crafted combination of emotional, psychosocial, and instrumental support (Jacobi, 1991), Telemachus was placed on the path to the 'realization of the dream' (Levinson, 1978, p. 98) that included self-discovery and reunification with the original mentor, his father.

The *Odyssey* also hints at another important fact, that the intended outcome of any mentoring story should be protégé focused. Ultimately, the greatness of a mentor is not intended to be central to the story. In fact, presenting the human form of Mentor as *lesser* than Odysseus may be yet another way to remind us of the peripheral nature of this role. It is important to note that in the climactic fight with the suitors, Symbolic Mentor fought alongside her human counterparts, not on behalf of them. The *Odyssey* ends, as should any good mentoring relationship, when the protégé blossoms through the supportive actions of a good mentor. For Odysseus this was a homecoming, for his son it was entry into manhood and reunification with his father.

Astute readers will find the *Odyssey* rich with examples of a Symbolic Mentor acting in roles that included patriarch, companion, guide, teacher, coach, guardian, and advisor. From instrumental backing that included the procurement of a boat and travel supplies, to psychosocial and emotional support in encouraging Telemachus to find his confidence when speaking to the king of a foreign land, Homer's epic outlines a relationship that includes functions consistent with numerous contemporary studies of mentoring.

The presence of these roles and functions suggests no major changes have occurred in the fundamental expectations of mentors, the needs of protégés, and the associated relational stages, since the advent of current research on non-family mentoring relationships. Any changes that might have occurred in mentoring relationships in families today are related primarily to variations in the perceived roles of the family. For example, at the time of the *Odyssey*, rural living and rigid social class structures limited accessibility to people and knowledge that naturally resulted in parents and family members often being the most skilled mentors for younger generations. During the later nineteenth century, industrialization introduced a shift from practices of occupational inheritance to occupational choice being more widely accepted (Savickas, 2007). With these shifts came a greater reliance on non-family persons to educate and contribute towards the development of younger generations. While we do not presume that all families from pre-industrial economies engaged in mentor-like parenting, we do speculate that the social and economic needs of a given family, culture, or time may be a factor worth examining in future research as relates to the prevalence of family member mentoring relationships in modern society. Our next case helps to illustrate the point.

FAMILY BUSINESS: THE CASE OF THE FORENZAS

From a practical standpoint, the field of family business consulting has much to offer in the way of practice-tested frameworks and strategies for familial mentoring relationships and their associated networks. Central to the development of these approaches has been the goal of family business advisors to cultivate relationships between family members that are both emotionally healthy and highly functional. The following case of the Forenzas, a third generation wine-making family, presents a familial mentoring scenario where parents who had been acting as the primary mentors to their children made the decision to hire a family business advisor to help formalize their efforts. Under the recommendation of the consultant, their efforts shifted to a network model. Led by the parents, under the guidance of the advisor, non-family mentors were selected to fill peripheral supportive roles that addressed gaps in the parents' knowledge and skill sets. Where the absence of the father required the assignment of a surrogate in the *Odyssey*, this case explores familial mentoring where the parents assume a central role and coordinate with non-family members as supports. Consistent with our definition of familial mentoring, the focus of this program was for the parents to help their children advance their participation within the family community and the practice of wine making.

The Forenza family

Originally from Italy, the Forenza family had been involved in wine making since the early 1900s. Deeply tied to their Italian roots, even after their move to the United States in the 1950s, the grandparents (Gen 1) continued to live and teach their children, Anthony and Franco (Gen 2), according to the culture and tradition of their previous home. Much like the practices of families in the time of Homer, Gen 2 was raised with the belief that participation in the family world of work was not only encouraged, but was also expected by both parents and children. As children, the majority of Gen 2's free time was occupied in peripheral tasks related to the family winery. The children were given duties across various aspects of the business that required progressive levels of competence as they grew. After high school, Gen 2 children attended college with the expectation that they would return to the family business after they had completed their programs. In this case, however, only Anthony returned to the vineyard.

Following those before them, Anthony's children (Gen 3), grew up in the vineyards where they were mentored in several areas, including wine making, business, and money management. Differing from the previous generation, Anthony and his wife, Margarita, were more deliberate and strategic about educating the next generation. They intentionally sought out ways to use resources from the winery to help their children develop skills they would find useful regardless of their future professional pathways. From the time they were young, their children were selling excess fruit from their own stand where they began learning about production, marketing, teamwork, and bookkeeping. At the end of each business day, they sat down with their parents who would ask questions and provide feedback about ways to improve business operations.

Partly as a response to the pressure they experienced from the previous generation and partly from a desire to make sure their children were not limited by the family business, the parents of Gen 3 encouraged their three children to pursue their own interests. Sarah, the youngest daughter, studied music; Simon, the middle child, studied agriculture; and the eldest, Stefan, was a business major. Their parents indicated that it would be an option to work in the family business, but only after demonstrating competence by working elsewhere.

In 2006, when the family was gathered for the holidays, they began discussing how the children might benefit from the family business legacy. Sarah was still pursuing her music education and thought she wanted to teach music. While she loved the family business, she was not ready to go in that direction. Both Stefan and Simon were interested in returning to the family business: Simon in the study of viticulture (cultivation of grapevines) and exploring how to optimize the growth of grapes; Stefan in how to position the company for growth, expanding distribution and exploring international sales.

Following this discussion, Anthony and Margarita began to think more about how to prepare the children to be their successors and to insure the continued success of the family business. While they both were well educated and had many years of experience with and in the family business, neither felt competent to set up a formal program for preparing their children for succession to the family business. It was at this point that they decided to seek a professional advisor to help with the transition.

During their first meeting with the consultant, Anthony and Margarita shared the family's intention of bringing the children into the business. Though they thought their children needed to understand the business in its entirety, they also believed strategies needed to be put in place to access the knowledge and experience the children had gained while in college and during their employment with other businesses. To support their goals, the parents, children, and the consultant developed a formal mentoring plan that included the addition of non-family mentors. Under the guidance of the advisor, the parents: (a) identified the core knowledge base needed by members of Gen 3; (b) created an advisory group of specialists who could serve as additional mentors (the field manager, wine maker, sales manager, and administrator); (c) developed systems of accountability to ensure that learning goals were being met; (d) provided formal opportunities for the children to reflect on what they learned, which included journals and scheduled discussions; (e) made assurances that the process could be modified when business or personal issues made the plan impractical (e.g. timing of grape picking and health issues); and (f) created ways to ensure that both familial and non-family mentors were comfortable with their roles and had the support they needed. Further, to clarify roles between family and business contexts, when parents acted as mentors they were referred to in their professional roles (rather than as mom or dad) to help manage the boundaries and reactions that might otherwise decrease the value of the learning experience.

During the course of the following year, Stefan and Simon began to attend staff meetings during which the management team evaluated various aspects of the business, including what was going well and the challenges that needed to be addressed. Over the course of this first year, they developed a greater understanding of how they could contribute to the business. As part of the formal mentoring structure, the meeting agenda included time where the children could ask questions about what was discussed and share their own thoughts and ideas.

At the end of the year, the mentoring team assembled to evaluate the process and to set goals for the coming year. With the support of the sales manager, Stefan proposed that it would be beneficial for him to spend some time at industry meetings and to begin building relationships with distributors who covered international markets. In response, the team identified and connected him to colleagues in their trade association who were willing to assume mentoring roles with Stefan with the intention of helping him learn more about global sales.

In recognition of the contribution Simon was making through his knowledge of viticulture, the team looked for community resources to encourage his ongoing learning. Drawing on the local university, the team helped Simon secure a research assistant position where he could continue to test his ideas and develop outside networks. Plans were also put in place to create opportunities for Simon to share what he was learning with the field managers and to implement ideas that could have a positive impact on the business.

At the completion of the second year, the consultant worked with the team to formally define the roles that Stefan and Simon would take in the business. Consistent with the model set by their parents, Stefan and Simon reported that they would like to work towards partnering and sharing leadership duties while specializing in their areas of interest. Stefan and Simon each took roles as junior members of their teams in the field and in sales. Since the company had an interest in growing international sales, Stefan was able to specialize in that area under the mentorship and supervision of the sales manager. Simon, who was more interested in the science of production, helped to develop new approaches to the cultivation of grapes and worked under the field manager to implement them. Sarah continued to maintain a peripheral role in the family business and began learning about ways for her to lead the family in evolving their family and ownership roles. She sought out professional training and began defining a role for herself as the head of family governance.

THE LITERATURE

We now turn from examples of the practice of familial mentoring to what the research says about this phenomenon. Our search focused on peer-reviewed literature where there was explicit reference to familial mentors in either the title or the abstract.

This section begins with an examination of the primary manner in which familial mentors appear in the literature, followed by information addressing the outcomes of these endeavors and some of the chief obstacles to conducting relevant research. In addition to these truncated searches, we conducted keyword searches that included the terms natural and informal mentors, along with family member identifiers (e.g. family member, mother, father, brother, sister, uncle, aunt, parent, extended family member, etc.).

Several electronic databases were used, including ERIC, Academic Search Complete, Business Source Complete, Psychology and Behavioral Sciences Collection, and PsycNET. Supplementary resources were identified from this primary search that included the identification of key studies and noteworthy authors. We also contacted several of these authors and made an effort to review materials they found to be significant. Because of the scarcity of dedicated familial mentoring studies, our findings include information gleaned from studies that merged familial with non-family mentors.

How familial mentors appear in the literature

Across the databases, various iterations of the word parent combined with truncated version of mentor, yielded the largest number of studies (N=179), but later review found the majority of these studies were specific to parents being mentored, not parents acting as mentors. While keyword searches that included natural mentoring, informal mentoring, or VIPs were useful in sorting literature, there were inconsistencies between and within these identifiers that diminished their functionality for the purpose of comparative research that included familial mentors.

Research on familial mentoring included studies which examined *specific* family members acting as mentors (parents, grandparents, siblings, etc.) and *group* studies where subjects could identify multiple mentors that included both family and non-family persons. In the case of group studies, we found the literature could be further divided into two sub-categories according to the parameters set by researchers. Specifically, group studies either: (a) allowed mentors to be identified without limitations based on their association to the protégé; or (b) included variations of the statement, 'other than your parent or whoever who raised you' (Rhodes et al., 1992, p. 449). To address the strengths

Table 29.1 Representation of categories in literature search

Category	Number of studies	% of Total
Family member specific		
Parents	6	
Grandparents	2	
Siblings	1	
Total family member specific	9	31%
Group studies		
Family and non-family mentors (parents included)	7	
Family and non-family mentors (parents excluded)	13	
Total group studies	20	68%
Total all studies	29	100%

and limitations associated with the inclusion/exclusion criteria of familial mentors in the various studies, we sorted the research into three categories: family member specific (parents, grandparents, siblings); family and non-family mentors with parents included; and family and non-family mentors with parents excluded. For a summary of research results see Table 29.1.

Specific family member

Studies in this category include explicit reference to the family role of the mentor relative to the protégé (e.g. mother, father, sister, brother, aunt, uncle, etc.). Findings from our search of role-specific studies were limited to parents, grandparents, and siblings. These studies typically focused on dyads where the familial mentor was often identified as, or later became, the primary mentor. Common among studies in this group was a practice of conflating everyday familial interactions to be the same as mentoring. Through vague definitions, family members were identified as mentors simply because they gave advice, advocated, or were identified as role models (Killoren and Roach, 2014; McGehee et al., 2007). Indicative of the emergent status of role-specific studies, they were few in number, reliant on small sample sizes, and geographically limited to studies from the United States.

Group studies

Problematic to many group studies was the practice of researchers merging findings in studies generated from familial and non-family mentors in their outcomes. Typically, the only distinctions made between these groups were those noted in descriptive statistics. At odds with this practice, researchers have identified differences in both outcomes and perceptions connected to the relational identity of mentors (Darling et al., 2002; Dubois and Silverthorn, 2005a; Hamilton et al., in press). Rather than suggest that this practice was born of poor design, we believe it is more accurate to interpret this as further evidence that the study of familial mentoring represents a gap in the broader mentoring literature. Given the clear limitations of the literature for drawing definitive conclusions about familial mentoring, portions of our findings reflect outcomes that have been associated with both familial and non-family mentors. Within the category of group studies, the literature could also be separated according to whether parents and primary caregivers were included or excluded.

Family and non-family mentors with parents included. Studies in this category included parents, immediate and extended family members, and non-related adults and peers. Samples in these studies bear the closest resemblance to how familial mentoring appears to exist in reality, composed of networks where the influence of familial and non-family mentors is dynamic in response to the needs of the protégé. Mirroring the relationships found in both the *Odyssey* and the Forenza family, these studies often included the identification of multiple mentors.

Family and non-family mentors with parents excluded. The greatest number of studies that included reference to familial mentors were those that used parameters from natural mentoring definitions for identifying mentors. Subjects in these studies were provided with variations of the statement, 'other than your parent or whoever raised you, is there an older person in your life who you go to for support and guidance' (DuBois and Silverthorn, 2005a, 2005b; Rhodes et al., 1992, p. 449) to consider when identifying mentors or very important people in their lives. Because of their connection to the well-established body of natural mentoring research, studies in this group more commonly included larger sample sizes, a focus on youth populations, and greater potential for producing generalizable findings (Hurd et al., 2013; Johnson and Gastic, 2015; Klaw and Rhodes, 1995; Klaw et al., 2003; Schwartz et al., 2013). While there are certainly numerous other natural mentoring studies that include family members, those that did not meet our inclusion criteria were not addressed.

OVERALL FINDINGS

The vast majority of familial mentoring research focuses on protégés from youth and young adult populations. Research included mentoring outcomes related to: teen pregnancy and parenting (Hurd and Zimmerman, 2010; Klaw et al., 2003); youth substance abuse (Strunin et al., 2015); education (Packard et al., 2004; Zalaquett et al., 2006); involved parenting (Hurd et al., 2013); the professional development of women (Abalkhail and Allan, 2015; Carter and Hart, 2010); and career development of deaf persons (Foster and MacLeod, 2004). Outcomes commonly used measures of: general health and well-being (Hurd and Zimmerman, 2010; Schwartz et al., 2013); psychological factors and duration of relationships (Schwartz et al., 2013); academic performance (Sanchez et al., 2008); perceived supports and benefits (Sanchez et al., 2006); and items specific to career development (Klaw and Rhodes, 1995).

When compared to the number of peer reviewed studies in general mentoring literature, those that highlighted familial mentors represented less than a fraction of one percent of this total body of knowledge. In contrast to what this may suggest about the prevalence of familial mentors, where the opportunity was given, participants identified family mentors at rates ranging from just under half (Hurd and Zimmerman, 2010) to nearly three quarters of all mentors in their lives (Klaw et al., 2003; Sanchez et al., 2008). The identities of familial mentors included parents (Abalkhail et al., 2015; Cook-Cottone, 2004), aunts, uncles, grandparents (Strunin et al., 2015; Klaw et al., 2003), siblings, and cousins (Sanchez et al., 2006; Sanchez et al., 2008).

In some reports (Klaw et al., 2003; Klaw and Rhodes, 1995) nearly three quarters of long-term mentoring relationships are between family members. An exception to this was noted among marginalized groups, including LGBT youth (Johnson and Gastic, 2015). As was the case with Telemachus, in the absence of a parent, youth rely more heavily on non-family mentors or other important persons. For youth in these situations, the negative effect of poor mentoring can be considerably more damaging, given the already existent social challenges faced by these populations (ibid.).

Culturally, the presence of familial mentors appears to be highest among groups that are collectivist in nature and where there is a high value placed on the connection between generations (Strunin et al., 2015). The Spanish word used to describe this value is *familismo* (ibid., p. 666). In both the *Odyssey* and the case of the Forenzas, the younger generations demonstrated this practice by drawing on elder family members as valuable sources of wisdom, knowledge, and instrumental support.

Though studies were overwhelmingly focused on samples from the United States (Hurd et al., 2013; Rhodes et al., 1992; Zimmerman et al., 2005), there is evidence that the broader experience of familial mentoring is somewhat generalizable (Darling et al., 2002). At the same time, there are aspects of mentoring that are influenced by culture, including power distance between mentor and protégé, expectations of familial involvement, protégé perceptions of family support, social and professional boundaries, and cultural expectations related to gender (Abalkhail and Allan, 2015; Cook-Cottone, 2004; Delgado-Gaitan and Ruiz, 1992).

Developmental trajectory of familial mentor relationships

As children progress through adolescence, their experience of mentoring also begins to shift. Where the mentoring experiences of children and young adolescents have been characterized primarily as dyadic experiences with familial mentors, later adolescents and young adults begin to seek out networks that commonly include non-family mentors and important others (Foster and MacLeod, 2004). Much like Telemachus daring to venture away from Ithaca, a similar trajectory appears to be characteristic of adolescents transitioning into adulthood. In some accounts, the frequency of non-family mentors has been reported to increase nearly three-fold during this time (Packard et al., 2004). Though familial mentoring relationships may continue during this period, protégés began to rely more heavily on mentoring that is offered by non-related peers and adults (Carter and Hart, 2010; Packard et al., 2004). A similar shift can be seen in the case of the Forenza family; after the children returned to the family business as young adults, efforts were made to connect them to mentors other than their parents, including non-family staff and community members.

Not without influence, the relationships between children and some of their immediate family members can have a significant effect on later mentoring relationships. Parenting styles and the perceptions of youth have been reported to have an influence on the likelihood that youth will connect to non-family mentors (Hurd et al., 2013; Rhodes et al., 1994). Specifically, adolescent mothers who reported higher levels of perceived acceptance by their mothers were more likely to have mentors and to report greater satisfaction with the support they were receiving from them (Rhodes et al., 1994). Additionally, children from homes that included involved-vigilant parents were more likely to later report non-family mentors (Hurd et al., 2013). In essence, children who experienced emotionally secure relationships (Bowlby, 1969) were more likely to report mentoring relationships with non-family mentors as they grew into adulthood.

Limiting effects of familial mentors

Though the presence of familial mentors was positively associated with several outcomes, including education, physical health, psychological well-being, reduced drug use, and greater physical activity, a review of evidence from a national study on youth and natural mentoring (DuBois and Silverthorn, 2005a) indicated the likelihood of positive outcomes was greater on nearly all of these factors when mentors were not family members. The only exception was related to psychological well-being, where familial mentors faired equally. Rather than consider this an argument against familial mentors, this can also be interpreted as further validation for pursuing coordinated networks, similar to the Forenza family and the model presented by Miller (1995), where mentors are drawn from the family and the respective community of practice of the protégé (i.e. school, business, trade groups, etc.).

Evidence suggests academic outcomes for young protégés might be particularly vulnerable to limitations associated with the educational level of familial mentors (Sanchez et al., 2008). Sanchez and associates (2008) attribute this to several factors: (a) the academic outcomes of protégés were influenced by the educational level of the primary mentor; (b) non-family mentors tended to have higher educational levels and, thus, higher levels of experience with educational institutions; and (c) mentoring relationships with family members extended over longer periods of time. Essentially, because mentoring relationships between family members are generally of longer duration than those between non-family members (Klaw et al., 2003; Sanchez et al., 2008), their prolonged influence can become a liability in cases where the mentor is limited by their own education and/or network.

Culturally driven roles

Variations in the roles and functions provided by familial mentors were noted between cultures. Examples in the literature included studies related to the mentoring experiences of ethnic minority families with school-age children in the United States (Cook-Cottone, 2004; Delgado-Gaitan and Ruiz, 1992) and professional women in the United Kingdom and Saudi Arabia (Abalkhail and Allan, 2015). In the case of school children, variations were motivated by the interactions of two culturally different groups. For professional women in the United Kingdom and Saudi Arabia, cultural differences were noted between these two groups, but were not addressed in terms of how they might influence any dealings between them.

Differences between the organizational culture of schools and the culture of a student's home led to familial mentors acting as cultural guides and advisors (Cook-Cottone, 2004; Delgado-Gaitan and Ruiz, 1992). These efforts were not unlike those of the Symbolic Mentor guiding the actions of Telemachus when he interacted with the chieftains from other lands. In such cases, parents acting as mentors to their children have been described as cultural brokers (Delgado-Gaitan and Ruiz,

1992, p. 51) and cultural mediators (Cook-Cottone, 2004; Delgado-Gaitan, 1994). When interacting with schools, parents were able to contextualize concerns and challenges through the cultural framework of the home in ways that promoted understanding and clarity for their children. Familial mentors provided encouragement, instruction, and advocacy for their children (Cook-Cottone, 2004) that was instrumental in helping students to adjust to the prevailing cultural orientation of the school. Further, when parents provided mentoring that included these supports, students and parents were perceived more favorably by teachers, students were less likely to drop out and more likely to access school resources that contribute to academic and social success (Cook-Cottone, 2004; Delgado-Gaitan and Ruiz, 1992). Parent mentors also reported feeling that they were valued as partners by school personnel and capable of providing meaningful help to their children (Cook-Cottone, 2004).

In Saudi Arabia, husbands and fathers assumed very directive positions in the lives of wives and daughters (Abalkhail and Allan, 2015). Providing a stark contrast between European and Middle Eastern familial mentoring experiences, professional women from the United Kingdom commonly associated mentoring with non-family persons, whereas females from Saudi Arabia relied heavily on family networks. Attributed to cultural and religious laws, women from Saudi Arabia reported mentoring relationships with male family members including fathers and husbands. These relationships were often expected to last the duration of a professional career. Driven by cultural and religious laws common in the Middle East, males were reported as acting in the role of 'guardian' (p. 160) to their female protégés. As guardian-mentor, a father or husband could intervene or advocate on behalf of a wife or daughter, even when they themselves had no professional affiliation with the given workplace or institution.

Program model for familial mentoring

The strategies and structures implemented by the Forenza family mirror a program model suggested by Miller (1995) that included the coordinated efforts of mentors from school, community, and home. Guided by standards for coordinated planning in mental health, the model included team planning and goals, ongoing training for members, considerations for sustainability, and regular meetings to insure fidelity in the delivery of mentoring and other supports. Mentors function as a collaborative network to provide encouragement, instrumental support, and the opportunity for youth to assume meaningful and contributory roles across and within each of the contexts.

Program features typically associated with best outcomes include: formal structure; support for matching based on shared interests; training for mentors; structured activities for dyads; encouraging regular contact; and fidelity of implementation (Schwartz et al., 2012; Strunin et al., 2015). There is also benefit for programs to support the teaching of cultural values (Strunin et al., 2015) and to strengthen connections between family members (Sanchez et al., 2006).

For families who may be in need of additional support from mental health professionals, targeted family therapies used in conjunction with formal mentoring programs can address negative patterns of behavior between family members (Strunin et al., 2015). In these cases, the use of extended family or non-family mentors can lessen the demands on parents and primary caregivers, providing possible respite that may contribute towards improved relationships (Hurd et al., 2013).

CHALLENGES TO FAMILIAL MENTORING RESEARCH

Almost universally, outcome reports were based on data generated from samples that included merged data from both familial and non-family mentors. When we consider studies that have identified findings with statistically significant differences relevant to these groups (DuBois and Silverthorn, 2005a; Hamilton et al., in press), the practice of merging familial and non-family data becomes highly questionable. In the majority of cases where studies reported differences between these groups, they were limited to the frequency at which protégés identified familial mentors.

With the exception of a small group of natural mentoring studies (Hurd et al., 2013; Johnson and Gastic, 2015; Klaw and Rhodes, 1995; Klaw et al., 2003; Schwartz et al., 2013), researchers generally relied on small sample sizes. Research was typically restricted to one-time measures and qualitative design. Suggesting the absence of consensus on parents and other primary caregivers acting as mentors (Bearman et al., 2010), it was common for researchers to exclude them as would-be mentors. While their exclusion may be useful in minimizing the influence of confounding variables that exist between the expected behaviors of certain family members and those typically associated with mentors (Darling et al., 2002); it comes at the risk of overlooking the contributions of parents and other caregivers that might otherwise be understood as mentoring.

Familiar to other areas of mentoring research, there were inconsistencies and conceptual problems among some of the definitions used by researchers to identify familial mentors. It was not unusual for researchers to cite singular or isolated mentoring functions provided by family members as evidence that mentoring was taking place (Killoren and Roach, 2014; McGehee et al., 2007). In certain cases, family members were identified as mentors simply because they provided advice or gave feedback.

Finally, there were clear issues related to current terminology. Searches were hindered by both the lack of agreed upon keywords and the presence of culturally equivocal terms to mentoring. Cultural terms were problematic because they raised the possibility of omitting relevant studies simply because they did not make specific reference to mentoring. Terms such as grandparenting (Neikrug, 2000; Waldrop et al., 1999), *Juku* and *senpai/kouhai* (Darling et al., 2002), and *consejos* (Delgado-Gaitan, 1994) have all been used to describe relationships and interactions very similar to mentoring.

CONCLUSION

At odds with the frequency at which family members are identified as mentors by protégés, research specific to this group was scarce and difficult to locate. Although findings suggest there may be aspects of mentoring relationships that transcend culture (Darling et al., 2002; Kent et al., 2012), existing literature was disproportionately limited to studies from the United States.

Research typically focused on protégés from youth and young adult populations. Literature could be broadly categorized according to the identity of mentors, where studies were either focused on relationships with *singular* family members (i.e. parents, grandparents, sisters, etc.) or *group* studies where mentors were identified from a broad range of family and non-family important persons that either included or excluded parents and primary caregivers.

Where familial mentoring relationships were often dominant in early years, over time they appear to give way to the increasing influence of non-family mentors and other important persons. In addition to this phenomenon being noted in the literature, examples could also be found in the *Odyssey* and in the case of the Forenza family. As part of his transition into adulthood, Telemachus left Ithaca in pursuit of the knowledge and support of a broader network from the surrounding lands. Similarly, Gen 3 of the Forenza family were encouraged to pursue their own interests and, upon their return, to develop relationships with mentors that not only included, but also extended beyond, their parents. Further, evidence suggests the nature of child attachment to parents could have an influence on the likelihood that they would later report having non-family mentors.

In concert with the model suggested by Miller (1995), the example of the Forenza family is worth considering as an exemplar for familial mentoring structures in Western cultures. Conversely, for families with limited resources, it reinforces the urgency for schools and community organizations to support efforts that facilitate connections with non-family mentors. Culture appears to have an influence between and within groups, as well as on the likelihood of mentors being familial and the roles expected of them. Cultural values, such as the Latino concept of *familismo*, influenced patterns of interactions that naturally supported familial mentoring relationships. When parents of Latino American youth acted as cultural mediators between school staff and students, benefits were experienced for all parties involved.

Addressing challenges through future research

Beyond the obvious need for more research, the field could benefit substantially from the adoption of precise language, agreed upon definitions, and research practices that recognize mentoring between and among family members as a unique area of study. We recommend the use of the term familial mentoring (Sanchez et al., 2008) for describing mentoring relationships that take place between family members and as a keyword that could be used to sort the relevant literature. To distinguish between family members who are merely being supportive and those who are mentoring, we propose the following guidelines as a starting point: (a) it should be evident that a family member is sharing domain expertise or is capable of the skillful provision of mentoring supports; and (b) the primary goal of the interaction is generating ways to support the advancement of child-protégé participation in a chosen community of practice (Johnson, 2002; Lave and Wenger, 1991; Nunes, 2013). These same standards can also be applied as alternatives to exclusion criteria based on the identity of family members. Given known differences between these two groups (DuBois and Silverthorn, 2005a; Hamilton et al., in press), where both are present, outcomes should include some level of between-group comparison to examine variance that may be attributable to the social role of mentors.

Moving forward, we endorse a research agenda similar to the one proposed by Chandler and Kram (2007). This outline calls for studies that examine non-Western populations and includes recommendations for examining mentoring practices and outcomes from individual, dyadic, and organization/network vantages. To this, we add the suggestion that studies should also include consideration of the influence of specific family roles and other family specific variables (i.e. ethnicity, culture, socio-economic status, education levels, parenting styles, etc.) on mentoring outcomes. The inclusion of these and other individual and group level variables will aid researchers in identifying the characteristics of exemplars, so that we can build an understanding of why some thrive where others struggle. Efforts could also be made to identify culturally equivocal terminology and explore the associated literature that addresses them. Qualitative ethnographic and grounded theory studies can be used as a starting point for mentoring researchers to identify the key issues associated with these relationships. Features identified from these studies could then be incorporated into longitudinal studies which may also include the use of growth models to examine reciprocal effects between mentors, protégés, and members of their networks.

Lastly, among the goals for future research should be the discovery and development of practical strategies that can be used to improve the outcomes of familial mentoring relationships. While researchers work to advance the theoretical understanding of familial mentoring relationships, equal priority should be placed on identifying teachable skill sets that enable familial mentors to transcend limitations associated with domain-specific knowledge, to include skills in the areas of communication, critical thinking, networking, and human development that could be seen as valuable to any mentor or protégé regardless of context. Further, the continued examination of case studies from family business contexts, similar to the Forenza family, could prove to be an excellent strategy for generating information that could immediately be put into practice.

REFERENCES

Abalkhail, J. M., and Allan, B. (2015). Women's career advancement: Mentoring and networking in Saudi Arabia and the UK. *Human Resource Development International*, 18(2), 153–68.

Bearman, S., Blake-Beard, S., Hunt, L., and Crosby, F. J. (2010). New directions in mentoring. In Allen, T. D., and Eby, L. T. (Eds). *The Blackwell handbook of mentoring: A multiple perspective approach* (pp. 375–95). Malden, MA: Wiley-Blackwell.

Bowlby, J. (1969). *Attachment and loss: Attachment (vol. 1)*. New York: Basic Books.

Carter, A. R., and Hart, A. (2010). Perspectives of mentoring: The Black female student-athlete. *Sport Management Review*, 13(4), 382–94.

Chandler, D. E., and Kram, E. K. (2007). Mentoring and developmental networks in the new career context. In Gunz, H., and Peiperl, M. (Eds). *Handbook of career studies* (pp. 241–67). Thousand Oaks, CA: Sage.

Cook-Cottone, C. (2004). Constructivism in family literacy practices: Parents as mentors. *Reading Improvement*, 41(4), 208.

Creswell, J. W., and Plano Clark, V. L. P. (2007). *Designing and conducting mixed method research*. Thousand Oaks, CA: Sage.

Darling, N., Hamilton, S., Toyokawa, T., and Matsuda, S. (2002). Naturally occurring mentoring in Japan and the United States: Social roles and correlates. *American Journal of Community Psychology*, 30(2), 245–70.

Delgado-Gaitan, C. (1994). Consejos: The power of cultural narratives. *Anthropology & Education Quarterly*, 25(3), 298–316.

Delgado-Gaitan, C., and Ruiz, N. T. (1992). Parent mentorship: Socializing children to school culture. *Educational Foundations*, 6(2), 45–69.

Dova, S. (2012). 'Kind like a father': On mentors and kings in the Odyssey. Center for Hellenic Studies. Retrieved from http://chs.harvard.edu/CHS/article/display/4351

DuBois, D. L., and Karcher, M. J. (2014). Youth mentoring in contemporary perspective. In D. L. DuBois and M. J. Karcher (Eds.), *Handbook of youth mentoring* (2nd ed., pp. 3–13). Thousand Oaks, CA: Sage.

DuBois, D. L., and Silverthorn, N. (2005a). Characteristics of natural mentoring relationships and adolescent adjustment: Evidence from a national study. *Journal of Primary Prevention*, 26(2), 69–92.

DuBois, D. L., and Silverthorn, N. (2005b). Natural mentoring relationships and adolescent health: Evidence from a national study. *American Journal of Public Health*, 95(3), 518–24.

Foster, S., and MacLeod, J. (2004). The role of mentoring relationships in the career development of successful deaf persons. *Journal of Deaf Studies and Deaf Education*, 9(4), 442–58.

Greeson, J. P., Thompson, A. E., Evans-Chase, M., and Ali, S. (2015). Child welfare professionals' attitudes and beliefs about child welfare-based natural mentoring for older youth in foster care. *Journal of Social Service Research*, 41(1), 93–112.

Hamilton, M. A., Hamilton, S. F., DuBois, D. L., and Sellers, D. E. (in press). *Functional roles of important non-family adults for youth*. New York: William T. Grant Foundation.

Higginbotham, B. J., MacArthur, S., and Dart, P. C. (2010). 4-H mentoring: Youth and families with promise – adult engagement and the development of strengths in youth. *Journal of Prevention & Intervention in the Community*, 38(3), 229–43.

Homer (1998). *The Odyssey* (trans. Fitzgerald, R.) New York: Farrar, Straus, and Giroux.

Hurd, N. M., Varner, F. A., and Rowley, S. J. (2013). Involved-vigilant parenting and socio-emotional well-being among black youth: The moderating influence of natural mentoring relationships. *Journal of Youth and Adolescence*, *42*(10), 1583–95.

Hurd, N., and Zimmerman, M. (2010). Natural mentors, mental health, and risk behaviors: A longitudinal analysis of African American adolescents transitioning into adulthood. *American Journal of Community Psychology*, *46*(1–2), 36–48.

Jacobi, M. (1991). Mentoring and undergraduate academic success: A literature review. *Review of Educational Research*, *61*(4), 505–32.

Johnson, W. B. (2002). The intentional mentor: Strategies and guidelines for the practice of mentoring. *Professional Psychology Research and Practice*, *33*(1), 88–96.

Johnson, D., and Gastic, B. (2015). Natural mentoring in the lives of sexual minority youth. *Journal of Community Psychology*, *43*(4), 395–407.

Kent, A., Kochan, F., and Green, A. (2012). Cultural influences on mentoring programs and relationships: a critical review of research. *International Journal of Mentoring and Coaching in Education*, *2*(3), 204–17.

Killoren, S. E., and Roach, A. L. (2014). Sibling conversations about dating and sexuality: Sisters as confidants, sources of support, and mentors. *Family Relations*, *63*(2), 232–43.

Klaw, E. L., and Rhodes, J. E. (1995). Mentor relationships and the career development of pregnant and parenting African-American teenagers. *Psychology of Women Quarterly*, *19*(4), 551.

Klaw, E. L., Rhodes, J. E., and Fitzgerald, L. F. (2003). Natural mentors in the lives of African American adolescent mothers: Tracking relationships over time. *Journal of Youth & Adolescence*, *32*(3), 223.

Lave, J., and Wenger, E. (1991). *Situated learning. Legitimate peripheral participation*. Cambridge, England: Cambridge University Press.

Levinson, D. J. (1978). *The seasons of a man's life*. New York: Random House LLC.

McGehee, D. V., Raby, M., Carney, C., Lee, J. D., and Reyes, M. L. (2007). Extending parental mentoring using an event-triggered video intervention in rural teen drivers. *Journal of Safety Research*, *38*(2), 215–27.

Miller, D. (1995). *Third-year evaluation report: Safe Policy*. Clarkston, WA: Asotin County Juvenile Services.

Neikrug, S. M. (2000). A new grandparenting: Dialogue and covenant through mentoring. *Journal of Gerontological Social Work*, *33*(3), 103–17.

Nunes, J. D. (2013). *Father/son mentor/mentee: The parent as the mentor*. Paper presented at the 2013 Mentoring Institute Conference. Albuquerque, NM.

Packard, B. W. L., Walsh, L., and Seidenberg, S. (2004). Will that be one mentor or two? A cross-sectional study of women's mentoring during college. *Mentoring and Tutoring: Partnership in Learning*, *12*(1), 71–85.

Rhodes, J. E., Contreras, J. M., and Mangelsdorf, S. C. (1994). Natural mentor relationships among Latina adolescent mothers: Psychological adjustment, moderating processes, and the role of early parental acceptance. *American Journal of Community Psychology*, *22*(2), 211–27.

Rhodes, J. E., Ebert, L., and Fischer, K. (1992). Natural mentors: An overlooked resource in the social networks of young, African American mothers. *American Journal of Community Psychology*, *20*(4), 445–61.

Rogoff, B., Paradise, R., Arauz, R. M., Correa-Chávez, M., and Angelillo, C. (2003). Firsthand learning through intent participation. *Annual Review of Psychology*, *54*(1), 175–203.

Sanchez, B., Esparza, P., and Colón, Y. (2008). Natural mentoring under the microscope: An investigation of mentoring relationships and Latino adolescents' academic performance. *Journal of Community Psychology*, *36*(4), 468–82.

Sanchez, B., Reyes, O., and Singh, J. (2006). A qualitative examination of the relationships that serve a mentoring function for Mexican American older adolescents. *Cultural Diversity and Ethnic Minority Psychology*, *12*(4), 615–31.

Savickas, M. L. (2007). Occupational choice. In H. Gunz, and M. Peiperl (Eds), *Handbook of career studies* (pp. 79–96). Thousand Oaks, CA: Sage.

Schwartz, S. O., Lowe, S. R., and Rhodes, J. E. (2012). Mentoring relationships and adolescent self-esteem. *Prevention Researcher*, *19*(2), 17–20.

Schwartz, S. O., Rhodes, J. E., Spencer, R., and Grossman, J. B. (2013). Youth initiated mentoring: Investigating a new approach to working with vulnerable adolescents. *American Journal of Community Psychology*, *52*(1–2), 155–69.

Strunin, L., Díaz-Martínez, A., Díaz-Martínez, L. R., Kuranz, S., Hernández-Ávila, C. A., Pantridge, C. E., and Fernández-Varela, H. (2015). Natural mentors and youth drinking: A qualitative study of Mexican youths. *Health Education Research*, *30*(4), 660–70.

Waldrop, D. P., Weber, J. A., Herald, S. L., Pruett, J., Cooper, K., and Juozapavicius, K. (1999). Wisdom and life experience: How grandfathers mentor their grandchildren. *Journal of Aging and Identity*, *4*(1), 33–46.

Zalaquett, C. P., Carlos, P., and Lopez, A. D. (2006). Learning from the stories of successful undergraduate Latina/Latino students: The importance of mentoring. *Mentoring & Tutoring*, *14*(3), 337–353.

Zimmerman, M. A., Bingenheimer, J. B., and Behrendt, D. E. (2005). Natural mentoring relationships. In D. DuBois and M. Karcher (Eds.), *Handbook of youth mentoring* (pp. 143–57). Thousand Oaks: Sage.

eMentoring: Computer Mediated Career Development for the Future

Laura Bierema

Several years ago I was sitting in my office when the telephone rang. A friendly voice – a woman doctoral student starting to learn about research – got right to the point: 'I am a fan of your work and have an idea you might be interested in pursuing.' She explained her idea and continued, 'I have two questions for you. Would you be interested in collaborating? And, would you be willing to mentor me?' I was immediately intrigued and was already studying electronic mentoring (eMentoring) at that time. My previous eMentoring relationship had been based on a very close face-to-face relationship that was interrupted by my relocation across the country, making virtual collaboration a necessity to complete my dissertation. In fact, I collaborated with that mentor on my first article on eMentoring (Bierema and Merriam, 2002).

My new protégé and I forged a plan and began working together. We worked from our respective US locations in Minnesota and Georgia to conduct a virtual research project using a social media platform as a data collection vehicle and submitted a proposal to an international conference. The first time we met face-to-face was at that conference in France, where we presented our research and even won a research prize (Rand and Bierema, 2009). Our colleagues at the conference were dumbfounded that we had never met face-to-face, yet were able to collaborate with such impressive results. Our virtual collaboration and mentoring relationship continues to this day and is an example of typical eMentoring that is not bound by geography, time, or prior relationship.

We are living in a global age of multinational corporations and individuals who are working, learning, and communicating from home across time and space. In this environment, learning and development activities in organizations are increasingly moving away from formal training programs toward facilitating informal, individual development plans that include coaching and mentoring (Simmonds and Zammit Lupi, 2009).

Likewise, mentoring endeavors between individuals are evolving to include individuals and groups communicating across time and space (Mullen, 2012). In this environment, eMentoring endeavors such as ours hold promise for minimizing geographical and cultural barriers that might have limited corporate mentoring programs and prevented individual and group mentoring dyads that are separated geographically from working together.

The purpose of this chapter is to present: an overview of eMentoring in practice; research over the past ten years (2005–2015); and to provide a guide to those interested in creating such programs. The literature informing the chapter was analyzed according to key themes that included definitions, key issues, benefits, challenges, technological infrastructure, research trends, and process models.

The chapter begins with a brief discussion of mentoring as a strategy for human and career development. This is followed by definitions and an overview of the context of eMentoring, including the roles of those involved, types of program benefits, and factors that facilitate and hinder its success. The next section of the paper provides an overview of themes gleaned from research on this topic. It also includes a summary chart which attempts to capture the essence of the findings. The chapter concludes with a section on the attributes of eMentoring and how to implement an eMentoring endeavor, and thoughts on the future of this important initiative.

AN OVERVIEW OF MENTORING AS A STRATEGY FOR GROWTH AND DEVELOPMENT

Before examining eMentoring, it is important to consider the structure, definition, and purposes of general mentoring. Buche (2008) states that mentoring 'consist[s] of a pair of individuals mutually committed to personal and professional growth within a specific context' (p. 36). Rix and Gold (2000) suggest that mentoring is synonymous with advising, supervising, coaching, assisting, guiding, leading, teaching, learning, readiness, compensation, support, and socialization. Several factors affect mentoring and the pursuit of new conceptualizations of it.

Mentoring has tangible and intangible career benefits (Burke et al., 2006; Eby et al., 2007), making it widely sought by aspiring professionals. Mentoring is well established as leading to higher levels of job and career satisfaction and success (Higgins, 2000; Higgins and Thomas, 2001; Van Emmerick, 2004). It is an important career development resource that helps acclimate protégés into an organization or profession, and position them for advancement. Mentoring has direct career benefits including more promotions, higher salaries, better support networks, and greater satisfaction for those who are involved in mentoring endeavors than for those who do not receive mentoring (Dreher and Cox, 1996; Eby and McManus, 2004).

Potential benefits of mentoring exist not only for the protégé, but also for the mentor and the organization (Allen et al., 2004; Eby et al., 2006). Mentoring relationships provide both psychological and career support (Kram, 1985). Mentors show protégés psychological support by providing acceptance, role modeling, affirmation, friendship, and coaching. Mentors provide career support by helping protégés navigate organizational culture, form developmental relationships, gain visibility, weigh career options, and process performance feedback. Organizations potentially benefit from eMentoring by promoting employee retention, reducing turnover, enhancing productivity, facilitating learning and knowledge transfer, developing employees, strengthening networks beyond the organization, providing more equitable access to mentoring, and developing a more diverse workforce.

EMENTORING IN A CONTEMPORARY CONTEXT

eMentoring is engagement in a developmental relationship between a mentor and a protégé that is mediated by a computer via email, chat, video conferencing, web, or message boards. eMentoring is also known as virtual mentoring, tele-mentoring, Internet mentoring, email mentoring, computer-mediated mentoring, or cyber-mentoring and is contrasted with tMentoring, or traditional mentoring, that is based on face-to-face developmental relationships. It is growing in use and importance as computer-mediated communication (CMC) becomes more prevalent within our work and personal lives.

> Given the growing number of CMC users and a business climate characterized by layoffs, worker mobility, boundaryless careers, and increased work demands, use of electronic means to expand one's network of developmental relationships is not only tenable, but also critical for career success. (de Janasz and Godshalk, 2013, p. 744)

Technology has enabled CMC via the Internet, email, instant messaging, social networking, and related technologies in ways that have changed when and how we communicate. World wide Internet use exceeds three billion, with approximately 40% of the world population accessing the Internet today, as compared to less than 1% in 1995, and over 96% of the US population having access to the Internet (Internet Live Stats). Facebook surpassed one billion registered accounts in 2015 and total social media accounts exceed two billion, with 3.6 billion unique mobile users and 1.6 billion active mobile social accounts (Kemp, 2015). People spend a lot of time on the Internet with the average user logging about four hours and 25 minutes per day (ibid.) and with 80% of smart phone users checking their phone within 15 minutes of waking up in the morning (Pinkham, 2013). Headlam-Wells, Gosland, and Craig (2006) noted that building online communities requires a combination of sociability (social interaction) and usability (human-computer interaction), although there has been more focus to date on supporting social interaction rather than designing usability.

eMentoring is described as a relationship (O'Neil et al., 2005; Risquez, 2008; Shrestha et al., 2009), a process (Hamilton and Scandura, 2003; Simmonds and Zammit Lupi 2009; Williams and Kim, 2011), and as distinct from face-to-face or tMentoring (Bierema and Hill, 2005; Bierema and Merriam, 2002; Perren, 2003; Risquez, 2008). Bierema and Merriam (2002) defined eMentoring as 'A computer mediated, mutually beneficial relationship between a mentor and a protégé that provides learning, advising, encouraging, promoting, and modeling, that is often boundaryless, egalitarian, and qualitatively different than traditional face-to-face mentoring' (p. 214). The virtual context of eMentoring requires different communication skills and interactions and allows more flexibility for creating and sustaining developmental relationships than face-to-face mentoring (Bierema and Hill, 2005; Bierema and Merriam, 2002).

eMentoring roles and types

eMentoring relies on technology and connectivity to link protégés and mentors. Mentoring traditionally serves at least three functions, to include vocational advising, psychological support, and role modeling (Ensher et al., 2003; Hamilton and Scandura, 2003). Mentor roles can focus on coaching, friendship, learning, or counseling. Vocational advising, psychological support, and role modeling are more difficult to provide in eMentoring contexts (Hamilton and Scandura, 2003) although improvements in virtual reality and visual applications are making this type of support more possible. Typically, mentors provide vocational mentoring that helps protégés with career planning and progress and may focus on things like making important career decisions about assignments, weighing opportunities or promotions, and learning new career skills such as negotiating interests, or supervising employees. Psychological support includes things like providing emotional support, serving as a sound board, and helping protégés navigate life balance challenges and receive constructive feedback. Role modeling is the opportunity for the protégé to directly observe how the mentor behaves, making this particularly challenging for virtual mentoring processes.

eMentoring nonprofit organizations have emerged over the past 20 years, such as iMentor, NetMentors.org, MentorNet, and the International Telementor Program. Long-term traditional mentoring programs, such as Big Brothers/Big Sisters and the National Mentoring Project, have started using online components. There have also been programs geared toward recruiting girls into science careers, such as GEM-Set (Girls Electronic Mentoring in Science, Engineering and Technology).

Benefits and attributes of eMentoring

The benefits of mentoring were presented earlier in the chapter. In addition to these positive outcomes, eMentoring provides additional benefits as compared to tMentoring due to its boundaryless nature, accessibility to a diverse range of participants, potential cost-effectiveness, dyad synergy, and capacity to promote reflection and learning.

eMentoring is boundaryless

tMentoring can be difficult due to organizational, individual, or interpersonal factors (Hamilton and Scandura, 2003). Organizational culture, policy, and hierarchy may make it difficult for all members to have equal access to mentoring. Organizational, social, and geographical contexts send social cues to their members, such as 'White men deserve developmental relationships with the best mentors'. These cues are diminished in eMentoring, affording women, people of color, and other marginalized populations opportunities to engage in mentoring with a lower propensity for implicit bias to contaminate the relationship.

eMentoring is not mediated by organization, social, or geographical context, unlike tMentoring. Thus, eMentoring diminishes traditional mentoring barriers by not posing limitations on geographical location or who can participate as mentors and protégés. This feature is important with workers increasingly dispersed across the globe and telecommuting becoming commonplace (Buche, 2008). Additionally, when mentoring is not confined to a certain organizational, social, or geographical context, the pool of available mentors and protégés expands exponentially.

Additionally, since eMentoring is not bound by time, place, or face-to-face communication, it is highly flexible for participants. Thus, eMentoring diminishes boundaries making mentoring more accessible, even in the current context of downsizing, increased mobility of the workforce, protean careers, and challenging work demands. This type of mentoring also makes it easier to work around family demands, work schedules, and time zones to engage in developmental relationships. It also widens potential mentoring relationships to the global community, increasing the pool of potential mentors and protégés. eMentoring also allows more frequent communication on a regular basis than traditional mentoring and can, in fact, be faster than some face-to-face relationships, which can suffer from the difficulty of arranging meetings (Clutterbuck, 2006).

eMentoring is accessible to a diverse range of participants

Although touted as a key career strategy, participation in traditional mentoring may be restricted in terms of who is able to partake, when, and by organization structure, interpersonal skills, cross-gender relationships, and ethnicity differences (Hamilton and Scandura, 2003). It is also well-documented that barriers to mentoring occur disproportionately across gender and ethnicity (ibid.). Research indicates that when it is available for women and people of color, eMentoring can boost their likelihood of initiating developmental relationships by increasing accessibility to mentors, equalizing salient differences between mentor and protégé, and deemphasizing demographic characteristics such as race, gender, age, or class (Ensher and Murphy, 2007). eMentoring has also been found to be more egalitarian, dialogical, and available across a more diverse spectrum of protégés than tMentoring (Bierema and Merriam, 2002; Headlam-Wells et al., 2006; Miller and Griffiths, 2005; Panapoulos and Sarri, 2013; Single and Single, 2005; Stewart, 2006).

eMentoring lessens barriers for women, people of color, and other marginalized populations who have more difficulty finding mentors and developing mentoring relationships due to implicit bias or mentor concerns about the relationship (e.g. sexual innuendo, different cultures) (Bierema and Hill, 2005; Fagenson-Eland and Lu, 2004). eMentoring has been found to be more egalitarian and accessible across diverse populations than tMentoring (Bierema and Hill, 2005; Fjermestad, 2004). The mentoring relationship can be documented and correspondence referred to at a future date. eMentoring is also flexible and accessible and may make it easier for individuals who face barriers in tMentoring based on gender, ethnicity, disability, geography, or who have family obligations that make engaging in mentoring during work hours difficult.

eMentoring can be a cost-effective approach to talent development

eMentoring can be highly cost effective (Tahmincioglu, 2004), particularly in informal mentoring relationships whereby the mentor and protégé strike up a relationship without participating in a formal, structured program. All it takes to get started is access to technology and a mutual agreement to engage in eMentoring. Although such organic eMentoring relationships are inexpensive propositions, formal mentoring programs that use a web-based mentoring management system may be costly to either create or purchase.

eMentoring can promote reflection, learning, and development

Mentoring relationships promote learning and eMentoring's often asynchronous nature allows time for reflection on the topics shared by the protégé and mentor. Mentoring has been shown to promote learning and development. Colky and Young (2006), for example, described mentoring as a process that 'brings together the inexperienced and the experienced in the hope that the former gains knowledge, skills, independence, and other benefits' (p. 437). Mullen (2005, 2009) likened mentoring to an educational process that engages dyads, groups, and cultures with teaching and learning. Mullen (2009) described it as 'a holistic form of teaching and learning that embraces the professional, personal, psychological, and career facets of a protégé's development, and such activities as advising, tutoring, coaching, and counseling' (p. 12). Taking a feminist approach to mentoring, Mullen (2009) advised that it should be a mutual learning process between the protégé and mentor that embraces critical reflection, risk taking, inquiry, and social justice.

Factors that facilitate eMentoring success

Research indicates that there are a number of factors, elements, and strategies that can foster eMentoring success. Technology advances with new devices, apps, and interfaces faster than we can keep up with readily. Thus it is vital that eMentoring participants have technological literacy (Bierema and Hill, 2005). Successful eMentoring is also reliant on having an adequate technology infrastructure that supports CMC (Buche, 2008).

Virtual mentoring can be facilitated through multiple multimedia platforms such as email, telephone, video conferencing, text messaging, social media, and virtual reality to allow the development of rich multimedia mentoring relationships. The ability to engage in easy access, real-time, free video exchange also makes it easier than previously to bond, read emotions, and provide role modeling.

Hamilton and Scandura (2003) suggested that the use of technology in the virtual mentoring process is mitigated by situational factors, social factors, and ease of use and usefulness. Situational factors include organizational culture and job characteristics. Organizations that are more advanced in their technology use and foster growth and learning will better position its workers for productive eMentoring relationships. Social factors include where co-workers and friends are comfortable with and appreciate technology and so tend to more readily adapt to and use new technologies. Thus, these individuals will be more likely to seek and use eMentoring. Ease of use and usefulness – how simple the technology is to use – influence the likelihood of its adoption.

In terms of success, gender, ethnicity, age and personality also impact technology use. Women tend to use it more for collaborative exchanges (Hamilton and Scandura, 2003).

Barriers to eMentoring

Although eMentoring has many benefits and can expand mentoring to a broader range of individuals across time and space, there are also some issues and factors that can hinder its success and value. Among the most prominent barriers are the cost and risk of mismatched dyads in formal programs, technological problems, individual differences that may impinge on the relationship, and challenges in providing effective role models. Research indicates that men are less aware of how they are being perceived in virtual space or how much they dominate virtual conversation as compared to women (Smith-Jentsch et al., 2008). Finally, there is a technology gap based on race, socioeconomic status, and age that may make it challenging for these groups to participate in eMentoring.

CMC-ed mentoring relationships are susceptible to weak ties, in which the social bonds are weaker due to the absence of nonverbal cues and body language characteristic of tMentoring. Lacking such cues increases the occurrence of miscommunication and misunderstanding (Rhodes et al., 2006). Challenges of eMentoring include miscommunication, decelerated pace of relationship development due to the nature and constraints of technology, higher reliance on a well-developed ability to write and use technology, technological breakdowns, lack of nonverbal cues, and privacy challenges (Clutterbuck, 2006; Ensher et al., 2003).

Another factor that can hinder the eMentoring process is the technology itself. eMentoring depends on the use of technology, particularly computing devices that require typing. The average person speaks much faster than they type, so this medium results in a lower exchange of information (Smith-Jentsch et al., 2008). This problem can be compounded by the lag time between messages and responses and can make the relationship feel disjointed and potentially lead to misunderstandings.

Individual differences in values, communication, interpersonal style, or contributions to the virtual nature of the relationship can also make forging and sustaining eMentoring relationships challenging. According to Cues Filtered Out Theory (Culnan and Markus, 1987), when visual and vocal cues are absent, as in the case of eMentoring, social inhibitions are diminished. This reality could have both positive and negative effects on the mentoring relationship. For example, the lack of visual cues makes it more difficult for the mentor to provide role modeling.

Although eMentoring has been found on a par with tMentoring in terms of career development and psychological support, it has proven less effective at providing role modeling from mentor to protégé (Hamilton and Scandura, 2003). Reasons for these differences, related to the factors discussed in this section are presented in Table 30.1, which compares tMentoring and eMentoring.

RESEARCH THEMES AND PRACTICE TRENDS IN EMENTORING

Although there is not an extensive body of literature on eMentoring, empirical studies on eMentoring are accumulating. These studies offer new understandings of formats and platforms for facilitating mentoring, the mentoring dyad (protégé and mentor), and the process of eMentoring. An overview of the salient issues identified in research on these topics is presented in this section.

Formats and platforms for eMentoring

The format of eMentoring – how the dyad uses technology to communicate – can take one or more forms, such as using CMC as: the primary mode of contact; the only mode of contact; the supplementary mode of contact; or only face-to-face contact. Platforms for mentoring – the types of technological

Table 30.1 Comparing tMentoring and eMentoring

Variable	tMentoring (traditional mentoring)	eMentoring (electronic mentoring)
Boundaries	Geographical/organizational similarity between mentor and protégé	Geographical dissimilarity between mentor and protégé, essentially boundaryless
Meeting mode	Generally face-to-face	Multiple modes that may include face-to-face, but also email and web-based applications
Meeting schedule	Synchronous, meetings planned in advance, dependent on mutually compatible schedules	Independent of time zone or schedule compatibility when asynchronous. Synchronous meetings require advance planning and compatible schedules
Nature of conversation	Spontaneous, unrehearsed discourse	Rehearsed, reflective dialogue that is often written; potential for spontaneous, unrehearsed discourse via video or telephone
Duration	Duration typically long term	Duration varies depending on mentoring goals
Accessibility based on demographics	Limited based on gender, race, and contextual constraints of the organization	Unlimited and more egalitarian across demographic and geographical lines
Formal cost considerations	High in terms of infrastructure, dyad pairing, and training	High in terms of electronic infrastructure, dyad pairing, training, monitoring, and troubleshooting
Informal cost considerations	Low, reliant on networks and proximity of dyad	Low, reliant on electronic infrastructure the dyad has ready access to
Hierarchical constraints	Rigid and limiting in terms of who has access to the mentor and process	Flexible and boundaryless
Privacy and confidentiality	Lower concerns as there is little or no documentation or monitoring of the mentoring	Higher privacy concerns due to the electronic trail of communication and monitoring characteristic of formal eMentoring
Benefits to protégé	Career support, psychological support, instrumental support, role modeling	Career support, psychological support, and instrumental support. Less role modeling is likely due to technological constraints
Benefits to mentor	Generative, professional, psychological, social	Technological skills, generative, professional development, psychological benefits, social benefits

interface used by the dyad – can take multiple forms, such as email, web streaming, virtual reality, or social networks.

Research on eMentoring formats

eMentoring can occur with a mixture of formats, ranging from entirely online to a blend such as mixing face-to-face meetings with electronic mentoring sessions. Examining differences between face-to-face mentoring and solely electronic eMentoring, Smith-Jentsch and colleagues (2008) found that mentoring solely in the electronic mode resulted in less psychosocial and career support, and a lower degree of protégé self-efficacy with male mentors. The researchers also discovered that male mentors tended to condense their statements more than females in the electronic realm. Overall, they found that dialogue interactivity was higher in an electronic context than with blended formats. The researchers concluded that women are more effective communicators when the risk of misinterpretation is high and that men were unaware of how ineffective they were in the eMentoring situation. They also found that higher degrees of interactivity resulted in higher self-efficacy and positive personal growth for protégés. Communication was more interactive via eMentoring than face-to-face dyads among the study participants and the researchers contended that theirs is the first study to provide empirical support for the Cues Filtered Out Theory (lower inhibitions in online context) in eMentoring.

Numerous studies have indicated that blended formats are more effective eMentoring arrangements then solely electronic relationships. Blended eMentoring combines a mixture of face-to-face mentoring with computer-mediated communication that may rely on text or email messages, telephone conversations, or web cameras. Headlam-Wells and colleagues (2006), for example, studied a university mentoring program for women that applied multiple formats for communication. They concluded that a blended approach (e.g. a mixture of face-to-face and online mentoring) is an effective way to build a mentoring relationship and that an initial face-to-face meeting helps jumpstart the relationship. Jacobs, Doyle, and Ryan (2015) conducted a retrospective, descriptive, qualitative study to understand the nature, perception, and impact on 29 graduates of an online post-professional doctoral program that used eMentoring. Their findings highlighted favorable features of eMentoring and how a multi-faceted approach, using a web camera or telephone to supplement email, worked effectively, with positive professional development results. Loureiro-Koechlin and Allan (2010) explored time, space, and structure in an e-learning and eMentoring project using structuration theory to understand theoretical explanations and how issues of time, space, and structure affect e-learning and eMentoring. They worked with women students and used collaborative software to create the mentoring format. They found the best formula for effective learning and mentoring was to blend the virtual interactions with face-to-face meetings, especially beneficial at the beginning of the program. When mentors or protégés were absent for long periods of time, it raised emotional responses to a poor working relationship. They found conflicting perceptions between mentors and protégés, in that mentors were located in 'fast time', where an exponential increase in information and communication technologies make it difficult to keep up and diminishes time for reflection, and protégés were located in 'slow time'. This discrepancy in time frames made it problematic to develop a mentoring routine.

Research on eMentoring platform

Smailes and Gannon-Leary (2011) conducted a literature review and case study that considered the advantages and disadvantages of three virtual mentoring models – virtual learning environments (VLEs), social networking sites, and virtual worlds – to facilitate peer mentoring among a diverse body of university students. VLEs are platforms to facilitate online learning and have the capacity to provide folders, email, quizzes and discussion boards. Social networking sites allow individuals to create personal profiles and engage in public social commentary, such as Facebook. Virtual worlds involve users becoming residents in a virtual community and creating avatars that engage in either fantasy- or reality-based environments, such as *Second Life*. Smailes and Gannon-Leary found that: VLEs are well-established yet lack excitement; social networking is popular but may not be embraced if appropriated by the institution; and virtual worlds are less familiar and require advanced skills to use effectively. Based on these findings, virtual platforms still have to make advances before eMentoring is fully embraced through VLEs, social networking, or virtual worlds.

The mentoring dyad (protégé and mentor)

eMentoring is enhanced by a well-paired, trained dyad. Building a productive mentoring dyad depends on a number of factors. The first is human interaction and the dynamics, the second is the environment, which in the case of eMentoring is a computer mediated one. deJanasz, Ensher and Heun (2008) conducted a study of eMentoring that paired business students with mentors. They found that a perceived similarity in terms of attitudes and values positively related to effective eMentoring relationships, while demographic similarity (gender, race) showed no relationship. Similar findings were corroborated by Eby and colleagues (2013). deJanasz, Ensher and Heun concluded:

> Perceived similarity is a strong predictor of e-mentoring effectiveness while actual similarity is not, suggest[ing] that the use of electronic means to establish mentoring relationships reduces the salience of observable differences in favor of value similarity even in early stage relationships such as the ones in this study. This finding is in contrast to an implication to the FtF mentoring literature: that demographic differences can initially impede mentors' and protégés' positive impressions, although this effect may dissipate over time. Therefore, e-mentoring may be especially helpful for minority and women protégés. (p. 405)

Mentoring dyad success was bolstered in a study of university eMentoring of women students by women mentors by offering online training in communication techniques and an opportunity to meet face-to-face at the start of the relationship, after dyads had been matched using a computer matching program (Headlam-Wells et al., 2006). The matching criteria was based on age, number of years of work experience, level of qualification, marital status, children, dependent care, life/career history, personal skills, professional skills, vocational sector, and personal values. The training curriculum also focused on the structure of the mentoring site, netiquette, and effective communication behaviors, such as politeness, civility, and confidentiality. E-moderators were provided in this study who served as a first point of contact for mentors serving as 'mentors to the mentors' (ibid., p. 373) and resource persons for the protégés. Organizers also took photographs to help the dyad develop an online identity. The participants received ongoing guidance and help during the mentoring process. The majority of the participants reported that they used a blended approach to the mentoring by using two or more different methods of communication. The mentors viewed the mentoring process as more effective than the protégés.

The mentoring dyad, the match of protégé and mentor, is crucial to mentoring success. How the match is made and the relationship cultivated impact whether the relationship will be effective. DiRenzo et al. (2010) attempted to explore the relationship between mentoring outcomes – such as program satisfaction, general, career, and fiscal self-efficacy – with the protégés attitudes and experience prior to the mentoring. They conducted a longitudinal study with a sample of

1,381 participants to develop and test a moderated mediation model of eMentoring. They found that frequency of interaction among the dyad moderates the protégés previous Internet experience and initial motivation to participate, and self- and task-efficacy.

Simmonds and Zammit Lupi (2009) studied the introduction of an eMentoring program into an international group of luxury hotels employing mixed methods to evaluate an eMentoring model they developed based on a review of the literature. They concluded that active involvement of the protégé in the matching process was crucial and led to more empowerment in the relationship and greater commitment. They proposed a new model for matching mentoring dyads to ensure the relationship was workable and expectations were met regarding meeting frequency.

deJanasz and Godshalk (2013) explored how dyad characteristics of interaction frequency, pre-existing relationship, perceived similarity, and relevant mentor knowledge affected the eMentoring process and impact on learning and satisfaction with a sample of undergraduate and graduate students engaged in eMentoring. They found interaction frequency positively related to career development and psychological support of the protégé, but not role modeling. If the protégé and mentor had a previous relationship, the eMentoring yielded higher satisfaction with mentor role modeling. Further, protégés' perception of the relevancy of eMentors' knowledge was positively associated with career development and role modeling.

eMentoring process

This section presents a compilation of research findings that compares empirically-based process models on the process of eMentoring, shown in Table 30.2. Empirical studies have tested various processes for structuring and facilitating eMentoring, building on our understanding of effective mentoring in tMentoring relationships.

Kram's (1983, 1985) definition of traditional mentoring included proposing four phases to a mentoring relationship: initiation, cultivation, separation, and redefinition. The *initiation* phase is the expectation-setting phase when the mentor and protégé become acquainted and set goals and objectives. This process should involve a gap analysis of where the protégé is and where she hopes to be (Colky and Young, 2006). It is generally characterized by ambiguity and uncertainty as the relationship is negotiated and a rapport is developed. Initiation is highly dependent on interactive communication if the relationship is to develop into a fruitful one (Buche, 2008). The *cultivation* phase typically involves protégés receiving a wide range of career and psychosocial guidance as the dyad develops rapport and trust. During the *separation* phase, the protégé becomes increasingly autonomous and independent and able to make choices without the mentor. The final *redefinition* phase is when the mentor and protégé begin to see each other as peers and the protégé develops an identity separate from the mentor. To develop the comparison in Table 30.2, I condensed Kram's four stages into three – initiation, cultivation, and termination – to best describe the process of eMentoring.

STRUCTURING AN EMENTORING PROGRAM

This section of the chapter moves from research to practice by providing a fuller discussion on how to develop an eMentoring process. It is hoped that, combined with the previously presented information, it will serve as a practical guide to establishing and implementing a successful eMentoring program.

eMentoring is on the rise, although it is still being developed and explored as a career and learning intervention and is underdeveloped academically (Headlam-Wells et al.,

Table 30.2 Virtual mentoring process models

Virtual mentoring phase	Hamilton & Scandura (2003)	Simmonds & Zammit Lupi (2009)	Williams & Kim (2011)	Akin & Hilbum (2007)	Headlam-Wells, Gosland, & Craig (2006)	Wong & Prekumar (2007)	De Janasz & Godshalk, 2013
Initiation	• Technology • Pairing • Expectations • Guidelines • Establishing relationship	• Weighted criteria (OD competency, professional skills, personal skills, values, interests and hobbies, and socio-economic background) to facilitate mentor and protégé matching, followed by interviews	• Structure (Time period, pairing, statement of purpose for relationship) • Learning objectives • Administrative support • Technical support • Communication tools	• Basic structure (pairing, duration, scheduled communication) • Learning objectives • Technical support	• Design structure (eMentoring site, communication media, resources, operational aspects) • Dyad pairing • Monitoring usage	• Purpose and long term plan • Incorporation of successful mentoring practices • Technology determination • Technology implementation • Recruitment plan for dyad • Eligibility screening for mentors and protégés • Strategy for matching mentors and protégés • Orientation for both mentors and protégés	• Dyad Antecedents • Interaction frequency • Pre-existing relationship • Perceived similarity • Relevant mentor knowledge • Comfort with CMC relationship
Cultivation	• Training • Netiquette • Technology support • Recognition • Celebrate success	• Web conferencing to facilitate mentoring relationship via voice over internet protocol (VOIP)	• eMentor training • eMentoring coaching support • In person eMentor gatherings	• Training • Coaching • Support		• Training for mentors and protégés • Monitoring • Support, recognition, and retention strategy	• eMentoring Received • Career development • Psychosocial support • Role Modeling
Termination	• Acknowledging accomplishments • Personal communication	• Evaluation by mentor • Evaluation by protégé	• eMentor evaluation	• Assessment		• Decision on steps for closure • Establish strategies for program evaluation	• Learning and Satisfaction • Enhanced skill self-efficacy • Increased course concept application • Learning via eMentoring • Satisfaction with relationship

2006; Perren, 2003; Risquez, 2008; Williams and Kim, 2011). eMentoring emerged in the 1990s without structure, process, or empirically tested models (Single and Single, 2005). Current research was summarized by Williams and Kim (2011) as consisting of eMentoring with students, broadly applied across settings and subjects, single case studies, specific discipline reviews, descriptions of specific eMentoring tools, assessment of benefits to the mentor and protégé, and evaluation reports of practitioner experiences. Williams and Kim also concluded that there is little evidence on which to base the creation of eMentoring structures and processes.

eMentoring programs are most effective when they are structured (Mihram, 2004; Williams and Kim, 2011). Emerging empirical studies provide evidence for a distinct process of formal eMentoring as summarized in Table 30.2. eMentoring structure provides a foundation for eMentoring relationships to flourish. It includes things like specifying the degree of structure, purpose of mentoring, learning objectives, time frame, and expected results. Even if eMentoring is informal, the dyad can elect to develop a structure that mirrors formal processes. Given Williams' and Kim's (2001) conclusion that the literature on designing eMentoring systems is scarce, this section of the chapter synthesizes existing models of eMentoring and proposes an eMentoring process with three phases: initiation, cultivation, and termination.

Initiation of eMentoring

The initiation phase involves activities such as pairing the eMentoring dyad (protégé and mentor), determining the eMentoring structure, ensuring the technology needs are met, and establishing ground rules and expectations. Initiation of eMentoring involves logistical, relational, and educational activities.

Logistical aspects of initiating eMentoring

Initiating an eMentoring process involves determining technical and practical issues. Headlam-Wells et al. (2006) conducted a case study of a university eMentoring program and illustrated the importance of blending social interaction with human–computer interaction to create and maintain an effective online mentoring community. The technical issues include what equipment will be used (computer hardware and software), and what media (Internet, social networks, telephone, etc.) will serve as the platform. Once the technical issues have been settled, practical issues related to timing and format should be decided. As discussed earlier in this article, there are a myriad combinations of CMC communication arrangements, ranging from solely online to blended. It is recommended that there be some face-to-face interaction if possible, as that has been shown to yield more effective, productive eMentoring relationships. Issues of timing also need to be decided in terms of the duration of the eMentoring engagement and the frequency of interaction.

Relational aspects of initiating eMentoring

Building a trusting, mutual relationship is key to a successful eMentoring process. We have already mentioned the importance of a functional mentoring dyad (protégé and mentor) that shares perceived similarity, interacts frequently, and builds trust. The relationship begins with pairing the dyad. Once the mentoring dyad is established, several factors affect the development and effectiveness of the relationship. Buche (2008) attempted to establish how trust developed in eMentoring relationships. Trust is imperative in mentoring relationships, especially when they are CMC. Building trust virtually in eMentoring is more challenging because it is more difficult to bridge geographical distance and build the relationship. Buche studied five women business leaders using focus group discussions to create a research model on the impact of CMC use on the development of trust. She found that miscommunication and misunderstandings are disruptive to the development of the relationship and are more likely to occur in eMentoring situations. The lack of visual cues, anonymity of CMC, and time lags can be particularly problematic in cultivating trust. She also found that maintaining the relationship was challenging given the reliance on CMC and the challenge of engaging in regular, continuous communication between both parties. Convenience is another factor, and here the benefits of eMentoring outweigh the other challenges. She also found that when media are imposed, neither party is satisfied. She concluded that trust is more difficult to cultivate in a CMC relationship.

Educational aspects of initiating eMentoring

The educational aspects of the mentoring relationship pertain to both technology and relationship. There may be a need to learn about the hardware, media, or format. Ideally, the dyad will have some support to ensure that the relationship is developmental. This involves focusing on how best to cultivate reflective practice, inquiry, and learning during the relationship. The dyad needs to be competent to give and receive feedback and engage in formative evaluation as the process unfolds. Both mentor and protégé need to be effective in this regard.

Cultivation

The next phase, cultivation, is the longest phase of eMentoring, where the relationship develops and flourishes. Undertakings in this phase include training, mentoring sessions via multiple media, reflecting on the mentoring and sharing feedback, and adjusting as necessary. Activities in this phase fall into four overlapping areas: preparation, engagement, support, and evaluation.

Preparation for eMentoring

Once the eMentoring relationship has been initiated, there are still learning needs to help develop and sustain the relationship, such as appropriate mentoring strategies for the mentor and protégé, netiquette, and technical skills. Participants in formal mentoring programs will be at an advantage since training programs are in place to help the dyad build the relationship. Informal eMentoring relationships can follow formal protocols to establish the expectations and ground rules for the mentoring.

Engagement in eMentoring

The bulk of the mentoring relationship occurs during cultivation, so the actual participation in mentoring activities occurs here. Interaction frequency has been shown to yield positive effects on learning and satisfaction with the mentoring process in both tMentoring and eMentoring (de Janasz and Godshalk, 2013). This includes meetings that may occur via multiple media, the writing of asynchronous responses, and the follow-up on recommendations outside the communication activities characterizing eMentoring. It is important for the dyad to determine frequency and structure at the beginning of the relationship and modify it as needed.

Learning through eMentoring

de Janasz and Godshalk (2013) summarized empirical studies showing a positive relationship between mentoring and protégé learning and satisfaction with the relationship. Protégés have reported that they were motivated to participate in formal mentoring based on their expectations of learning from the relationship (Allen and O'Brien, 2006; Eby and Lockwood, 2005). Yet, informal mentoring dyads result in higher protégé learning and goal attainment than formal pairings (Godshalk and Sosik, 2003; Ragins et al., 2000; Wanberg et al., 2003). Mentors have also reported a preference for protégés who are learning-focused and, in turn, provide learning opportunities. Learning-oriented protégés receive more mentoring (Godshalk and Sosik, 2003). The virtual, asynchronous context of eMentoring can allow the dyad more time to reflect on issues under discussion, often with a textual dialogue that makes it easy to follow and refer back to at the mentor's or protégé's own pace (Clutterbuck, 2006).

Support of eMentoring

The eMentoring relationship must be sustained through periodic process checks, feedback, and interventions, as needed. These activities occur organically and at the initiation of the mentor or protégé in informal relationships. Formal eMentoring programs have established procedures for coaching, monitoring, and intervening as necessary, to keep the mentoring on track and retain the relationship.

Evaluation of eMentoring

Evaluating the mentoring program occurs throughout the process and across the activities of the cultivation phase. Evaluation should include three types of data (Single and Muller, 1999): involvement data; formative data; and summative data. Involvement data includes the degree of participation of the mentors and protégés through amount of engagement, queries, and back-and forth exchanges between the dyad. Formative data deals with the mentoring process as it is in progress, such as how the participants perceive its effectiveness. Summative data focuses on the outcomes, such as career decisions or advancement of the protégé.

Termination

The final phase of eMentoring, termination, signifies the end of the mentoring relationship. Some programs have defined times, but when those are not present the dyad will have to determine what makes sense. Activities in this phase might include recognizing and celebrating accomplishments and evaluating the mentoring process. Activities differ in this phase according to whether the eMentoring is informal or formal.

CONCLUSION

Technology will continue to advance in ways that support eMentoring. The company Affectiva, for example, is pioneering ways to digitally interpret emotions from facial expressions using cameras inside computers and smartphones to 'read' expressions in real time, with the goal of providing more opportunities for emotional expression with these devices (Rebeck, 2015). This technology could give mentoring dyads real-time metrics on engagement, attention, and emotion that could help manage the relationship in new, more effective ways.

Our lives are increasingly computer mediated, whether we are making a banking transaction, scheduling a car service, shopping, making travel arrangements, or connecting with friends and family. Helping relationships, such as mentoring, are no longer confined to geographical or organizational boundaries. eMentoring has the potential to make mentoring more widely available to populations who have difficulty finding appropriate mentors, particularly women and people of color. This chapter has surveyed current research and best practices, and outlined a process for eMentoring for mentors, protégé's and organizations.

REFERENCES

Allen, L. T., Eby, M. L., Poteet, E., Lentz, L., and Lima, L. (2004). Outcomes associated with mentoring protégés: A meta-analysis. *Journal of Applied Psychology*, *89*(2004), 127–36.

Allen, T. D., and O'Brien, K. E. (2006). Formal mentoring programs and organizational attraction. *Human Resource Development Quarterly*, 17, 26–37.

Bierema, L. L., and Hill, J. (2005). Virtual mentoring and HRD. *Advances in Developing Human Resources*, 7(4), 556–68.

Bierema, L. L., and Merriam, S. B. (2002). E-mentoring: Using computer mediated communication to enhance the mentoring process. *Innovative Higher Education*, 26(3), 211–27.

Buche, M. W. (2008). Development of trust in electronic mentoring relationships. *International Journal of Networking and Virtual Organisations*, 5(1), 35–50.

Burke, R. J., Burgess, Z., and Fallon, B. (2006). Benefits of mentoring to Australian early career women managers and professionals. *Equal Opportunities International*, 25(1), 71–9.

Clutterbuck, D. (2006). *Everyone needs a mentor.* London: CIPD.

Colky, D. L., and Young, W. H. (2006). Mentoring in the virtual organization: Keys to building successful schools and businesses. *Mentoring & Tutoring*, 14(4), 433–47.

Culnan, M. J., and Markus, M. L. (1987). Information technologies. In F. M. Jablin, L. L. Putnam, K. H. Roberts, and L. W. Porter (Eds.), *Handbook of organizational communication: An interdisciplinary perspective* (pp. 420–43). Newbury Park, CA: Sage.

deJanasz, S. C., Ensher E. A., and Heun, C. (2008). Virtual relationships and real benefits: Using e-mentoring to connect business students with practicing managers. *Mentoring and Tutoring: Partnership in Learning*, 16(4), 394–411.

deJanasz, S. C., and Godshalk, V. M. (2013). The role of e-mentoring in protégés' learning and satisfaction. *Group & Organization Management*, 38(6), 743–74.

Dreher, G. F., and Cox, T. H. (1996). Race, gender, and opportunity: A study of compensation attainment and the establishment of mentoring relationships. *Journal of Applied Psychology*, 81, 297–308.

DiRenzo, M. S., Linnehan, F., Shao, P., and Rosenberg, W. L. (2010). A moderated mediation model of e-mentoring. *Journal of Vocational Behavior*, 76, 292–305.

Eby, L. T., Allen, T. D., Evans, S. C., Ng, T., and DuBois, D. L. (2007). Does mentoring matter? A multidisciplinary meta-analysis comparing mentored and non-mentored individuals. *Journal of Vocational Behavior*, 72(2), 254–67.

Eby, L. T., Allen, T. D., Hoffman, B. J., Baranik, L. E., Sauer, J. B., Baldwin, S., Morrison, M. A., Kinkade, K. M., Maher, C. P., Curtis, S., and Evans, S. C. (2013). An interdisciplinary meta-analysis of the potential antecedents, correlates, and consequences of protégé perceptions of mentoring. *Psychological Bulletin*, 139(2), 441.

Eby, L. T., Durley, J., Evans, S., and Ragins, B. R. (2006). The relationship between short-term mentoring benefits and long-term mentor outcomes, *Journal of Vocational Behavior*, 69, 424–44.

Eby, L. T., and Lockwood, A. (2005). Protégés' and mentors' reactions to participating in formal mentoring programs: A qualitative investigation. *Journal of Vocational Behavior*, 67, 441–59.

Eby, L. T., and McManus, S. E. (2004). The protégé's role in negative mentoring experiences. *Journal of Vocational Behavior*, 65(2), 255–75.

Ensher, E. A., Heun, C., and Blanchard, A. (2003). Online mentoring and computer-mediated communication: New directions in research. *Journal of Vocational Behavior*, 63, 264–88.

Ensher, E. A., and Murphy, S. E. (2007). Power mentoring. *Leadership Excellence*, 24(4), 14.

Fagenson-Eland, E. A., and Lu, R. Y. (2004). Virtual mentoring. In D. Clutterbuck, and G. Lane (Eds.), *The situational mentor: An international review of competences and capabilities in mentoring* (pp. 148–59). Aldershot: Gower Publishing.

Fjermestad, J. (2004). An analysis of communication mode in group support systems research. *Decision Support Systems* 37(2), 239–63.

Godshalk, V. M., and Sosik, J. J. (2003). Does mentor-protégé agreement on mentor leadership style influence the quality of mentoring relationships? *Group & Organization Management*, 25, 291–317.

Hamilton, B. A., and Scandura, T. A. (2003). E-mentoring: Implications for learning and development in a wired world. *Organizational Dynamics*, *31*(4), 388–402.

Headlam-Wells, J., Gosland, J., and Craig, J. (2006). Beyond the organization: The design and management of e-mentoring systems. *International Journal of Information Management*, *26*, 372–85.

Higgins, M. C. (2000). The more, the merrier. Multiple developmental relationships and work satisfaction. *Journal of Management Development*, *19*, 277–96.

Higgins, M. C., and Thomas, D. A. (2001). Constellations and careers: Toward understanding the effects of multiple developmental relationships. *Journal of Organizational Behavior*, *22*, 223–47.

Internet Live Stats. (n.d.). Retrieved on 12 October 2016 from http://www.internetlivestats.com/internet-users/

Jacobs, K., Doyle, N., and Ryan, C. (2015). The nature, perception, and impact of e-mentoring on post-professional occupational therapy doctoral students. *Occupational Therapy in Health Care*, *29*(2), 201–13.

Kemp, S. (2015, January). Digital, social and mobile worldwide in 2015. *We are Social*. Retrieved on 12 October 2016 from http://wearesocial.net/blog/2015/01/digital-social-mobile-worldwide-2015/

Kram, K. E. (1983). Phases of the mentor relationship. *Academy of Management Journal*, *26*, 608–25.

Kram, K. E. (1985). *Mentoring at work: Developmental relationships in organizational life*. Glenview, IL: Scott Foresman.

Loureiro-Koechlin, C., and Allan, B. (2010). Time, space and structure in an e-learning and e-mentoring project. *British Journal of Educational Technology*, *41*(5), 721–35.

Mihram, D. (2004). *E-Mentoring*. USC: Center for Excellence in Teaching.

Miller, H., and Griffeths, M. (2005). E-mentoring. In D. L. DuBois, and M. J. Karcher (Eds.), *Handbook of youth mentoring* (pp. 300–31). Thousand Oaks, CA: Sage.

Mullen, C. A. (2005). *Mentorship primer*. New York: Peter Lang.

Mullen, C. A. (2009). Re-imagining the human dimension of mentoring: A framework for research administration and the academy. *The Journal of Research Administration*, *40*(1), 10–31.

Mullen, C. A. (2012). Mentoring: An overview. In S. J. Fletcher and C. A. Mullen (Eds.), *The Sage handbook of mentoring and coaching in education* (pp. 7–23). London: Sage.

O'Neil, D. K., Weiler, M., and Sha, L. (2005). Software support for online mentoring programs: A research-inspired design. *Mentoring & Tutoring: Partnership in Learning*, *13*(1), 109–31.

Panopoulos, A. P., and Sarri, K. (2013). E-mentoring: The adoption process and innovation challenge. *International Journal of Information Management*, *33*, 217–26.

Perren, L. (2003). The role of e-mentoring in entrepreneurial education and support: A meta-review of academic literature. *Education & Training*, *45*(8–9), 517–26.

Pinkham, R. (2013). 80% of smartphone users check their phones before brushing their teeth … and other hot topics. *Constant Contact*, 5 April. Retrieved on 12 October 2016 from http://blogs.constantcontact.com/smartphone-usage-statistics/

Ragins, B. R., Cotton, J. L., and Miller, J. S. (2000). Marginal mentoring: The effects of type of mentoring, quality of relationship, and program design on work and career attitudes. *Academy of Management Journal*, *43*, 1177–94.

Rand, S., and Bierema, L. L. (2009). From 'old boy's networks' to women's leadership networks: Discovering the value of on-line social networks for HRD professionals. *Proceedings of the 10th International Conference on Human Resource Development Research and Practice across Europe*. Newcastle, England, June.

Rebeck, G. (2015). Five minutes with Rana el Kaliouby, co-founder and chief science and strategy officer, Affectiva. *Delta Sky Magazine*, *28*, 31.

Rhodes, J., Spencer, R., Saito, R., and Sipe, C. (2006). The promise and challenges of an emerging approach to youth development. *The Journal of Primary Prevention*, *27*, 497–513.

Risquez, A. (2008). E-mentoring: An extended practice, an emerging discipline. In F. J. Garcia-Penalvo (Ed.), *Advances in e-learning: Experiences and methodologies* (pp. 61–82). Hershey, PA: Information Science Publishing.

Rix, M., and Gold, J. (2000). 'With a little help from my academic friend': Mentoring change agents. *Mentoring and Tutoring: Partnership in Learning*, *8*(1), 47–62.

Shrestha, C. H., May, S. M., Edirisingha, P., Burke, L., and Linsey, T. (2009). From face-to-face to e-mentoring: Does the 'e' add any value for mentors? *International Journal of Teaching and Learning in Higher Education*, *20*(2), 116–24.

Simmonds, D., and Zammit Lupi, A. M. (2009). The matching process in e-mentoring: A case study in luxury hotels. *Journal of European Industrial Training*, *34*(4), 300–16.

Single, P. B., and Muller, C. (1999). *Electronic mentoring programs: A model to guide best practice and research*. Retrieved on 12 October 2016 from http://www.mentornet.net

Single, P. B., and Single, R. M. (2005). Mentoring and the technology revolution: How face-to-face mentoring sets the stage for e-mentoring. In F. K. Kochan and J. T. Pascarelli (Eds.), *Creating successful telementoring programs* (pp. 7–27). Greenwich, CT: Information Age Press.

Smailes, J., and Gannon-Leary, P. (2011). Peer mentoring – Is a virtual form of support a viable alternative? *Research in Learning Technology*, *19*(2), 129–42.

Smith-Jentsch, K. A., Scielzo, S. A., Yarbrough, C. S., and Rosopa, P. J. (2008). A comparison of face-to-face and electronic peer-mentoring: Interactions with mentor gender. *Journal of Vocational Behavior*, *72*, 193–206.

Stewart, S. (2006). A pilot study of email in an e-mentoring relationship. *Journal of Telemedicine and Telecare*, *12*, 83–5.

Tahmincioglu, E. (2004). Looking for a mentor? Technology can help make the right match. *Workforce Management*, *83*(13), 63–5.

Van Emmerick, H. I. J. (2004). The more you can get the better: Mentoring constellations and intrinsic career success. *Career Development International*, *9*, 578–94.

Wanberg, C. R., Welsh, E. T., and Hezlett, S. A. (2003). Mentoring research: A review and dynamic process model. *Research in Personnel and Human Resource Management*, *22*, 39–124.

Williams, S. L., and Kim, J. (2011). E-mentoring in online course projects: Description of an e-mentoring scheme. *International Journal of Evidence-Based Coaching and Mentoring*, *9*(2), 80–95.

PART IV

Case Studies of Mentoring Around the Globe

David A. Clutterbuck

INTRODUCTION

Our primary objective in selecting cases studies was to have as diverse as possible a distribution of cultures, geographical regions, types of mentoring and applications of mentoring, and to illustrate how core themes from the scholarly chapters reflect experience in the field. Many of the contributors of our case studies are not scholars, although some represent a growing phenomenon in the worlds of coaching and mentoring – the scholar-practitioner. These latter contributors tend to be people whose livelihoods are based on work as consultants or trainers in the mentoring field and who have chosen to enhance their practice and reputation through evidence-based research. One of the benefits of this small army is that the empirical study of mentoring is increasingly extending beyond academe and being enriched with credible observation and analysis from the field.

It is our belief as scholar-editors that, while large-scale, multi-organisational, multi-context, quantitative academic studies can be valuable in exploring the fundamentals of mentoring, it is through case studies that we gain deep insight into what works – especially in the context of the design and implementation of planned mentoring and mentoring programmes. Moreover, case studies at both individual and organisational level are a fruitful source of new themes for wider, multi-case studies.

Our geographical diversity covers all the major regions of the world, from Southern Africa to South America, Australasia to Afghanistan. We include examples from the worlds of commerce, the military and sport. And we report on both national and international programmes.

In the Introduction to this volume, we identified six lenses of mentoring: mentoring philosophy, mentoring context, mentoring application or practice, mentoring dynamics, the mentoring and the mentoring programme. In terms of *mentoring philosophy*, our case studies cover a spectrum from programmes, which emphasise transactional functions, such as knowledge sharing and hands-on support, to those which focus on learning and development and on self-discovery. Some programmes involve a level of hierarchical difference between mentor and mentee; others reflect more of a peer-mentoring model. Inevitably, most programmes draw to some extent on more than one philosophical base. The underlying assumptions of each programme affect its design, the nature of training and support for participants and the expected outcomes.

The *mentoring contexts* which we address in this section include leadership development, entrepreneurship, sport and career development – including one case exploring the role of mentoring in helping athletes establish new careers once their sporting prowess passes its peak. Even within contexts there are differences in approach. For example, there are significant differences in approach between entrepreneur mentoring programmes aimed at young people, female entrepreneurs and more general programmes. The international programmes, such as Mowgli and Youth Business International, can generally offer much more resource-rich support, because their scale is usually greater than comparable national programmes.

The range of *mentoring applications* extends from music to technical staff in the Afghan Air Force, being mentored by Italian peers; from project leaders in the Norwegian oil sector to members of disadvantaged communities, such as the Maori in New Zealand; and from doctors and dentists in the UK health service to the recruitment industry in Australia and New Zealand. The cases have a strong gender-diversity undercurrent, from female entrepreneurs in Finland to a Canadian programme to support women in the financial sector.

The ways in which the managers of each of the cases have chosen to design their *mentoring programmes* also vary considerably. Relatively few have taken advantage of the international standards to assess their programmes, although the Royal New Zealand Air Force has subjected its programme to rigorous review under the ISMPE (International Standards for Mentoring Programmes in Employment) and learned much from the discipline of reviewing every aspect of the programme. The factors that affect the design appear to be very varied, but some of the most commonly recurring ones are budget, the programme's intended beneficiaries and the logistics of meeting either face to face or virtually.

The *mentoring dynamics* and the mentoring conversation take us down a layer of analysis from the mentoring programmes. We have chosen, for reasons of space, not to include stand-alone cases of individual relationships. However, there are short, illustrative examples scattered throughout the cases.

In them you will find many examples of leading-edge good practice in areas such as mentor and mentee support, supervision, measurement, communication and sustainability. You will also find examples of setbacks, challenges and lessons learned.

Ubuntu and Transformational Mentoring in South Africa: 7 Principles of a Culturally Integrated Mentoring Response

Hilary Geber and Moyra Keane

INTRODUCTION

> Africans have a thing called Ubuntu. It is about the essence of being human. It is part of the gift that Africa is going to give to the world. ...We believe that a person is a person through other persons; that my humanity is caught up and bound up in yours. ...The solitary human being is a contradiction in terms, and therefore you seek to work for the common good because your humanity comes into its own in community, in belonging.
> (Archbishop Emeritus of Cape Town, Desmond Tutu, 1999)

Although many mentoring programmes are offered in South Africa every year, and some claim to be based on *Ubuntu,* the indigenous way of connecting with others (see, for example, 'Big Brother, Big Sister' and 'Novalis Ubuntu Institute' in Cape Town; 'Ubuntu Academy' in Cape Town; 'Ubuntu Youth' in KwaZulu-Natal), there is little explicit reference to how principles of *Ubuntu* are incorporated in these mentoring programmes. This culturally relevant approach is not explicitly explored nor is it addressed practically in management training (Geber and Keane, 2013) even though there are management books available on '*Ubuntu* in the workplace' (Boon, 1996; Mbigi, 2000; Mkhize, 2008; Msila, 2015). In instances where *Ubuntu* is specifically named in organisational mentor training, the content provides no indication of how a mentor centred in *Ubuntu* would engage from this perspective in the mentoring relationship. *Ubuntu* is typically invoked simply as a motivation for engagement.

There is also a scarcity of South African research into the field of *Ubuntu* coaching and mentoring. A special issue of the *International Journal of Evidence Based Coaching and Mentoring* 11: 2, August 2013) features eight articles on culture in coaching with only one article on South Africa. But, again, there is little guidance on ways to practically embed *Ubuntu* into mentoring programmes.

We advocate a mentoring model that is holistic – that is based on *Ubuntu* and community as a way of bridging the usual individual-focused Western worldview so that the mentoring aims and processes are more inclusive and culturally congruent in the South African context. This is important because both mentors and mentees, who may be from different cultures, typically view the interactions using unconscious assumptions or filters/lenses which may be limiting (if not alienating and confusing) for the mentees in South Africa. We use examples from numerous case studies to illustrate the need for an *Ubuntu* perspective and ways in which it may infuse the mentor–mentee relationship. In South Africa senior positions are still often held by white South Africans who then mentor younger black colleagues. In this context, it is imperative that there is awareness of not contributing to a patronising 'colonisation of the mind'. On the other hand, some mentoring programmes do have junior white staff being mentored by senior black managers. In such cases, there is an ideal opportunity to transform the status quo and to pioneer *Ubuntu* in mentoring. Finally, issues of race will hopefully become far less relevant as transformational mentoring contributes to harmonising relationships and communities.

Following on from this context we intend here to contrast some of the features of different worldview perspectives and contexts to open up a more transformational space that is inclusive and respectful of African ways of relating. The aim of mentoring should be the development of *Ubuntu,* which Archbishop Emeritus Desmond Tutu describes as the ultimate goal for any human being (Tutu, 1999). He goes further, extending beyond the individual to society, by claiming that 'Social harmony is for us the greatest good' (Tutu, 1999: 35).

UBUNTU

Ubuntu is defined in isiZulu as '*Umuntu ngumuntu ngabantu*' – a person is a person through other people. If these notions provide a focus for the workplace we would expect to see cohesive teamwork, interconnectedness, caring and being held by a collective vision (Msila, 2015). Compassion, kindness, and respect are the key values of *Ubuntu* espoused in the country's education policy (Department of Education, 2000). *Ubuntu* refers to an ontology and way of living that has significant differences from those of Western paradigms. This is not to say, of course, that humanism, empathy and relationship are not part of a Western paradigm but to emphasise that, on a continuum between individualism and interconnectedness, a traditional African worldview is located deeply in connection to community. Thus, beyond values of kindness and caring, *Ubuntu* is a way of experiencing being in the world. Rather than 'I think therefore I am', *Ubuntu* is defined as 'I am a human being because I belong'. As an organising principle in understanding the world, *Ubuntu* is more consistent with the Asian worldview (described, for example, by Nisbett, 2003). In an African worldview, community is not simply an aggregate sum of individuals, but a collectivity (Shutte, 2001). Another strong sense of the depth of *Ubuntu* beyond the common notions of moral integrity and having qualities of generosity is the belief that a person without *Ubuntu* is indeed not a person. Not all human beings are therefore persons. Personhood is acquired; and the notion of the community in which it is acquired could be a challenge for Western thinking. Ramose explains that the important process of initiation does not only incorporate one into personhood within the community of the living but also establishes a link between the initiated and the community of the living-dead or ancestors (Ramose, 1999).

It is important that we do not over-simplify or trivialise a worldview. We also caution against romanticising all aspects of any epistemology and ontology. As any Google search will quickly show, *Ubuntu* has become a buzzword, and multiculturalism is sometimes promoted zealously without problematising issues of complexity and dissonances. The self-awareness practices of mentoring and coaching as well as opportunities for seeing different perspectives are useful in keeping culture dynamic and constructive. Consider some of the shadow aspects of *Ubuntu* alluded to by Gorjestani (2010), the Chief Knowledge Officer for the African region of the World Bank: community loyalty sometimes leads to factions or xenophobia; respect for elders may inhibit change or lead to unwarranted loyalty; accepted hierarchical structures are often at odds with gender equity; fostering independence, a sense of agency and curiosity is not encouraged in young people who are not expected to question elders. Individual rights are not necessarily upheld in an *Ubuntu* perspective and even individual eccentricity may be unacceptable. These are areas that need to be discussed, acknowledged and negotiated while strengthening features relevant for mentoring programmes in contexts of multiple worldviews.

Imminent scholars, such as the Nobel Peace laureate, Maathai, have spoken against the loss of cultural identity:

> People without culture feel insecure and are obsessed with the acquisition of material things, which give them a temporary security...
>
> Without culture, a community loses self-awareness and guidance and grows weak and vulnerable. It disintegrates from within as it suffers a lack of identity, dignity, self-respect and a sense of destiny. (Maathai, 2004: 23)

The characteristics of identity, dignity, self-respect and destiny are directly related to mentoring goals and interactions – and are especially pertinent in a country where there is a legacy of exclusion and denigration of most of the population.

A deeper exploration of the features of an African worldview and its practical underpinning of personal growth is long overdue, where Black South Africans have been pushed to the margins of authentic participation.

In the following section we explore some of the features of an African worldview and *Ubuntu* and contrast this with a more Western worldview. We acknowledge that this very classification and the creation of binary oppositions is a feature of Western scientific thought! We suggest that, of course, there is a continuum across worldviews rather than a dichotomy and that people of one culture may, in fact, tend towards affiliating with the worldview of a different culture. However, we provide a table outlining features of an African worldview and a Western worldview which we have synthesised from three research sources (Table 31.1). Our aim is to note the less than universal assumptions we sometimes make about, for example, knowledge, relationships, self and personal success.

From this it is evident that one worldview may be inimical to another in obtuse and unconscious ways. There is likely to be accepted and assumed 'good practice' in our teaching, intended outcomes and processes that may be at odds with another culture's paradigms. These differences also provide an insight into values: the practical may be seen as more important than the abstract. Similarly, as an example, consider the value placed on 'competitiveness' in the West, as opposed to co-operation. Processes of assessment, league tables and competitiveness are privileged over co-operation; assertiveness over harmony; independence over interdependence. In Africa, sharing and reciprocity are norms throughout the continent (Nsamenang, 1992). On the one hand we can easily see how the spirit of mentoring fits well with this orientation; on the other we need to note that the drive for individual achievement, competitiveness and personal freedom with a sense of agency may cause dissonance.

Ubuntu *and transformational mentoring*

Mentoring with an awareness of different worldviews brings about change on a macro level in organisations and not only at an individual level (Ivey et al., 2013). This is an

Table 31.1 Contrasting worldview perspectives

African: Ubuntu worldview	Western worldview
The world is seen as holistic and anthropomorphic Substance is important	The world is categorised into dualities: living and non-living; mind and matter Form is important
Causes of events are complex; seek resonances; empathise with relevant players	Causes are linear and predictable; deterministic; scenario-writing and testing
Self Interdependence of all things is self-evident Linked to life stage and role; goals linked to community	Independence is prized Person has stable attributes, 'one true self', 'personality tests'; personal wishes and goals key
Relationships Basic; extensive; relating encouraged Taught to respect authority	Useful; often some isolation; 'networking' encouraged Encouraged to challenge authority
Argument / learning 'To argue with logical consistency … may not only be resented but also be regarded as immature' (Nisbett, 2003) Practical and/or allegory valued Knowledge gained through 'apprenticeship' ceremony, initiation	Logical argument considered an essential aspect of education Abstraction valued as a thinking tool Knowledge gained through formal courses
Structure Hierarchy valued as a norm	Aiming for equality assumed as universal value
Success Co-operation encouraged Success seen as a group goal Success relates to harmony / humility	Competitiveness encouraged Success seen as individual achievement Conflict and critique leads to achievement
Managing conflict Collective decision-making, practical	Trading, arguing from principles
Importance of place Place-based community valued	*Freedom of location* Expect to move often, as part of individual achievement
Freedom of action Collective, freedom available through community and support	Individual, unconstrained by relationships
Progress Up and down, circular; consultative	Linear, continuing; time efficient

This table is adapted and synthesised from Keane 2006; Nisbett 2003; Ogunniyi, 2004.

important factor where policies and practices in the workplace are changing (Geber, 2006).

The transformational model of mentoring (Geber, 2006) involves establishing learning alliances for professional development and a commitment to social and organisational change (Geber, 2003). An indigenous transformational mentoring programme integrates both Western and indigenous worldviews (Geber and Nyanjom, 2009). Mentors need to focus on reciprocal learning and be prepared to learn about African *Ubuntu* principles and their application from mentees. Being respectful, being aware of mentees' conditioning about respect for elders and experts and reflecting on how they interact with mentees is necessary in these cross-cultural relationships (Geber and Nyanjom, 2009). We now present a case-study example of a large-scale mentoring intervention.

Case-study example

In 2013 a jobs-fund partnership project by an environmental organisation aimed at creating sustainable job opportunities for 555 unemployed graduates and 245 school leavers with matric certificates. The support structure for this project was based on a transformational mentoring model giving the 800 participating young people workplace experience through a structured mentoring programme, together with skills development and training opportunities for a period of two and a half years. The participants, known as 'pioneers', were placed with one of the 43 partner organisations for the duration of the three-year project. There were approximately 350 mentors engaged in mentoring the participants and 50 regional coordinators working with them. The mentor engagements proved to be rewarding and worthwhile. Mentors indicated that they would be willing to share their newly acquired knowledge and skills with colleagues who were unable to attend the mentor workshops. A large community of mentoring practice has been established together with consistent and diligent mentoring of mentees using *Ubuntu* principles. Such a lengthy mentored internship has resulted in permanent jobs for 260 mentees to date. This is not insignificant in the context of an unemployment rate in South Africa of 26.4 per cent.[1]

Mentoring models, which focus on the traditional roles and functions of the mentee–mentor relationship, do not sufficiently address aspects of cross-cultural contexts. If mentors regard their mentees as 'apprentices' or 'protégés' they may reinforce the marginality of black mentees. In cross-cultural mentoring relationships, mentors play a crucial role in managing to overcome racial prejudice in the workplace. This is vitally important in South Africa, where black people are *not a minority population* but are under-represented in organisations for historical reasons. Mentors may have to make special and often creative efforts to integrate their mentees into work departments at the beginning of the mentoring relationship: being proactive in preventing the exploitation of mentees, offering mentees the opportunity of doing high-status work, even in a small way at first, and developing a sense of achievement through challenging work. Mentors need to become aware of and reflect on the reciprocal learning which ideally takes place in cross-cultural mentoring relationships. In so doing, mentors who fulfil all the functions which facilitate transformed relationships will have a long-term impact on the structure of organisations, particularly where the management or more senior staff is still predominantly white.

We have drawn out from case studies such as that above the key features for training mentors as well as practical steps for organisations.

The 7 principles of a culturally integrated mentoring response

- **Awareness:** Our ways of working are often habitual and culturally framed. Training needs to expose and explore assumptions, ways of talking and relating. Check how ways of interacting are working; suspend judgement; stretch one's range of Being-in-the-world.
- **Time and commitment:** From an **Ubuntu** perspective, time is valued less for getting things done quickly than for giving of one's time. Mentors and mentees may relax the pace to show respect for, and value in, the process.
- **Respect:** This is a core value that needs to be central to the training, mentoring relationship. Take specific care over language use and forms of address. 'Respect is not just about saying "please" or "thank you". It's about listening intently to others' ideas and not insisting that your ideas prevail ... It's about displaying characteristics of humility, generosity, and patience' (Louis, 2007, p. 133 in Khupe, 2014).
- **Explicit cultural references:** In the mentoring process mentor and mentee need to make explicit 'how things work' in my world/my context/my view.
- **Inclusion:** Finding ways to explicitly and warmly include the mentee – invite the mentee to functions, introduce them to colleagues, facilitate opportunities for them to join communities.
- **Care:** This is the underlying modality that underpins community and interconnection.
- **Story:** Telling stories is a powerful way to learn and relate, to share and to explore.

'When you see two people together you think: Ah, there is a story there!' (Achebe, 2003)

CONCLUSION

From an ontological perspective, the functions of a mentor include 'the development of trust, confidence and mutual respect between student and mentor' (Wadee et al., 2010: 33). The values that arise from this can easily be aligned to the *Ubuntu* worldview of communalism, cohesion, respect, generosity, mutual care, consensus and tradition (Metz, 2007). *Ubuntu*, as a relationship-centred paradigm, is a particularly well-suited framework for coaching and coaching training (Geber and Keane, 2013).

In mentoring processes where people understand that their cultural roots and worldviews are acknowledged rather than silenced and omitted they feel more secure in their self-development and in their mentors' efforts at developing their skills and experience. Transformational mentoring which explicitly includes *Ubuntu* is one way to go about being relevant in multicultural contexts and avoids unconscious projection of exclusive worldviews.

Note

1 Other case studies which have used a transformational mentoring model have been published and can be accessed in Geber (2014); Geber & Koyana (2012); Ivey et al. (2013).

REFERENCES

Achebe, C. (2003). Talk at University of the Witwatersrand, 16 September.
Boon, M. (1996). *The African way – The power of interactive leadership*. Sandton, South Africa: Zebra Press.
Department of Education (2000). *Values, education, democracy*. Pretoria: Department of Basic Education.
Geber, H. M. (2003). Fostering career development for Black academics in the new South Africa, in F. Kochan and J. Pascarelli, *Global perspectives of reconstructing context, learning communities, and cultures through mentoring*. Greenwich, CT: Information Age Publishing. pp 107–28.
Geber, H. M. (2006). Mentoring black junior academics at the University of the Witwatersrand, in D. Megginson, D. Clutterbuck, B. Garvey, P. Stokes and R. Garrett-Harris, *Mentoring in action: A practical guide*. 2nd edition. pp 94–101. London: Kogan Page.
Geber, H. (2014). An old tradition and the new beginning: Mentoring in Africa, in F. Kochan, A. Kent and A. M. Green, *Uncovering the cultural dynamics in mentoring programs and relationships: Enhancing practice and research*. Charlotte, NC: Information Age Publishing.
Geber, H. and Keane, M. (2013). Extending the worldview of coaching research and practice in Southern Africa: the concept of Ubuntu. *International Journal of Evidence Based Coaching and Mentoring*, 11(2), 8–17.
Geber, H. M. and Koyana, S. (2012). Mentoring of unemployed science graduates in South Africa. *Acta Academica*, 44(2), 88–109.
Geber, H. and Nyanjom, J. A. (2009). Mentor development in higher education in Botswana: How important is reflective practice. *South African Journal of Higher Education*, 23(5), 894–911.
Gorjestani, N. (2010). Indigenous knowledge for development: Opportunities and challenges. A paper based on presentation to UNCAD Conference on Traditional Knowledge in Geneva, 1 November, 2000. Retrieved from http://www.worldbank.org/afr/ik/ikpaper_0102.pdf (accessed on 14 June, 2016).
Ivey, P., Geber, H. and Nänni, I. (2013). Uncovering the cultural dynamics in mentoring programs and relationships: Enhancing practice and research. *International Journal of Evidence Based Coaching and Mentoring*, 11(1), 85–111.
Keane, M. (2006). Understanding science curriculum and research in rural Kwa-Zulu Natal. Unpublished PhD thesis. University of the Witwatersrand. Johannesburg.
Khupe, C. 2014. Indigenous knowledge and school: Possibilities for integration. Unpublished PhD thesis. University of the Witwatersrand. Johannesburg.

Louis, R. P. (2007). Can you hear us now? Voices from the margin: Using indigenous methodologies in geographic research. *Geographical Research,* 45(2), 130–39.

Maathai, W. (2004). *Nobel Lecture,* Oslo, December.

Mbigi, L. (2000). *In search of the African business renaissance: An African cultural perspective.* Randburg, South Africa: Knowledge Resources.

Metz, T. (2007). Toward an African moral theory. *Journal of Political Philosophy,* 15(3), 321–41.

Mkhize, N. (2008). Ubuntu and harmony: An African approach to morality and ethics. In R. Nicholson, (ed.) *Persons in community: African ethics in a global culture.* Scottsville: University of KwaZulu-Natal Press. 35–44.

Msila, V. (2015). UBUNTU: Shaping the current workplace with (African) wisdom. Johannesburg: Knowres Publishing.

Nisbett, R. E. (2003). The geography of thought: How Asians and Westerners think differently and why. New York: Free Press.

Nsamenang, A. B. (1992). *Human development in cultural context: A third world perspective.* Newbury Park, CA: Sage.

Ogunniyi, M. B. (2004). The challenge of preparing and equipping science teachers in higher education to integrate scientific knowledge and IKS for their learners. *South African Journal of Higher Education,* 18, 289–304.

Ramose, M. B. (1999). African philosophy through Ubuntu. Mond Books. Retrieved from http://repository.uvt.nl/id/ir-uvt-nl:oai:wo.uvt.nl:80540 (accessed 14 September, 2016).

Shutte, A. (2001). *Ubuntu: An ethic for a new South Africa.* Cape Town: Cluster Publications.

Tutu, D. (1999). *No future without forgiveness.* New York: Random House.

Wadee, A. A., Keane, M., Dietz, T. and Hay, D. (2010). *Effective PhD supervision: Mentorship and coaching.* Amsterdam: Rozenberg Publishers.

E-Mentoring Women in Resources: Lessons Learned from an Australian Programme

Melissa Richardson

BACKGROUND

The resources industry is enormously important to the Australian economy, representing more than $195 billion in annual exports and employing over 229,000 people. Whilst women make up over 46 per cent of the Australian workforce, their participation rate in the resources sector is 16 per cent of the industry workforce. This female participation rate has hardly increased in recent years, and very few of the women employed are in operational and/or leadership roles.

The Australian Women in Resources Alliance (AWRA) is an initiative led by national resource-industry employer group the Australian Mines and Metals Association (AMMA), dedicated to helping employers attract, retain and reap the rewards of women in resources workplaces. In 2012 AWRA identified that a formal mentoring program for women in resources could be a key way to support attraction and retention of women and help grow female workforce participation to 25 per cent by 2020. However, there were two key barriers to delivering an effective mentoring program:

1. Mine sites and oil and gas operations are often in remote locations which would make face-to-face mentoring inaccessible to many women.
2. The resources sector utilises complex roster arrangements for many job roles, making connection between mentoring partners potentially difficult, if they are required to 'meet' in a traditional way.

An e-mentoring solution was deemed to be the answer. With the help of mentoring consultancy Art of Mentoring and the Australian Government, AWRA rolled out the first cohort of its programme in early 2013. Since then, over 200 females working in the industry have been matched with female and male mentors from outside their own companies, in a mentoring programme administered entirely virtually. In May 2015, the AWRA e-Mentoring Programme was showcased at the Global Summit for Women as Australia's example of an effective programme for women in the workforce.

PROGRAMME DESIGN AND STRUCTURE

With accessibility such a key issue, it was clear that the programme had to be virtual (i.e. it would be unlikely that mentoring pairs, programme managers and trainers could physically meet). Further, with the large number of participants that AWRA wanted to attract, it was also clear that an online mentoring platform would be needed for efficient programme administration. This would enable easy online access to mentoring resource materials for participants and provide the AWRA programme managers with a central platform for applications, matching and communications with participants.

Virtual: The pros and cons

A virtual programme has some clear advantages – for example, the ability to provide mentoring access to anyone at any time would open mentoring to women working in remote locations. In a review of e-mentoring literature, Thompson et al. (2010) note that electronic communication forms have been found to have some advantages over traditional face-to-face mentoring. Electronic media such as email can mitigate against social cues such as status getting in the way of mentoring relationships, and, being an asynchronous medium, email allows more considered messages between partners.

Some of the disadvantages are also obvious. Whilst there is a rapidly growing industry in 'cyber coaching', which demonstrates that coaching relationships can be built without the richness of face-to-face interaction, some people nevertheless find it difficult to build rapport using telephone, teleconferencing, email or text. Zey (2011) notes that in virtual relationships some mentoring activities, like shadowing (where the mentee physically follows and observes the mentor in action), role modelling and attending events together, cannot be used. Thompson et al. also suggest that engagement and persistence can be problematic in virtual relationships.

Houck (2011) draws on research from the fields of generational differences and virtual teams to suggest that in virtual mentoring there is a need for frequent communication, and that younger generations, whilst more comfortable with virtual technologies, may need more structure than their older counterparts. Millennials, it is claimed, also like group activities.

Design principles

With all this in mind, some key design principles emerged:

1. Rather than offer a 'self-serve' mentoring option – where a single mentee searches for a mentor online – we would roll the programme out in 'cohorts' so that the mentees in particular would feel connected as a group and possibly build connections with other mentees in their cohort.
2. Whilst face-to-face events could not be offered, each cohort would have at least three webinar-event opportunities to prepare them for their mentoring relationships, allow them to connect with others in the programme and to provide closure once the programme and/or mentoring relationship was completed.
3. Relatively 'high-touch' programme management would be needed to help keep mentoring relationships on track. This could be made easier by using automated emails for regular communications as well as phone calls to participants and webinar check-ins.
4. Training is always a critical success factor in formal mentoring programmes. In this programme, the training would need to address the usual topics plus how to use the mentoring platform and how to make the most of virtual relationships, including suggested frequency of contact (every 2–4 weeks).

Programme structure

Phase 1

In Phase 1, seven cohorts and over 100 mentoring pairs were matched and supported in a nine-month programme, between February 2013 and May 2014. The steps were:

1. Application by mentees and mentors;
2. Matching by programme administrators, using the mentoring platform matching tool as a guide but overriding with qualitative information about each applicant;
3. Programme introduction and training by webinar for mentors and mentees in separate groups;
4. A progress-review webinar after three months, for mentors and mentees in separate groups;
5. Programme evaluations sent out after initial matching, after three months and on programme completion.

Phase 2

At the end of Phase 1 a major review was made of the programme and the steps were changed to:

1. Intensive pre-marketing through industry bodies and employers;
2. Preliminary application by mentees and mentors to check their suitability for the programme;
3. Upon being accepted into the programme, compulsory viewing of a 20-minute video outlining programme expectations before final admission for matching;
4. Matching by programme administrators, using the mentoring platform matching tool as a guide but overriding with qualitative information about each applicant – the matching algorithm was changed and is now providing better matches;
5. Multimedia online training for mentors and mentees;
6. Programme introduction webinars for mentors and mentees in separate groups;
7. A progress-review webinar after three months, for mentors and mentees in separate groups;
8. A programme-close webinar;
9. Programme evaluations sent out after initial matching, after three months and on programme completion as well as a year on from commencing the programme;
10. Implementation of a 'Certificate of Appreciation' which is also used as an indirect marketing tool to attract new mentors and mentees into the programme.

Reasons for the changes

Pre-marketing

Due to a wide-scale transition in the Australian resource industry from major project construction to a less labour-intensive production phase, coupled with commercial pressures from commodity-price fluctuations, AWRA has placed greater emphasis on organisational engagement to recruit both mentors and mentees into the AWRA e-Mentoring programme.

Pre-matching video

A requirement to watch the video meant that mentees in particular were clearer about what to expect from the mentoring programme and what it could or couldn't deliver. This was in response to a drop-out rate of over 30 per cent amongst mentees in Phase 1. The drop-out rate is now 15 per cent, which is considered acceptable.

Multimedia online training

Training by webinar, limited to short sessions of up to an hour, has considerable limitations compared with face-to-face training, in which a trainer can demonstrate mentoring techniques and facilitate participant interaction. The programme has now incorporated an online multimedia format, containing mentor and mentee video interviews, video demonstrations of key mentoring skills and downloadable mentoring tools in addition to its existing training (webinars).

The online training has increased access for people who cannot attend webinars due to work rosters. Greater access to better training may have contributed to lowering the drop-out rate.

Programme-close webinar

This was part of the original programme design but omitted due to budget constraints.

Participants in Phase 1 noted and regretted the lack of programme closure and this step has now been added.

Another change that was made was in the frequency and size of cohort launches. Initially the cohorts were rolled out too close together (every fortnight to monthly), and the aim was for 25 pairs per cohort. In Phase 2 the cohorts are spaced further apart (on average 30–40 days apart) and each cohort contains 10–15 pairs. This has improved the quality of matches and allows the programme managers to more easily keep track of pairs and stay in touch with them, which seems to be needed. Also in Phase 1, there was not enough follow-up with applicants who could not be matched. They were invited into later cohorts but by then had lost interest. Now, mentees are told they may have to wait a few months for an appropriate mentor, and programme administrators stay in touch until then.

RESULTS

After completion, eighty-seven per cent of mentees said they had achieved the goals they set for themselves in the programme; almost a third rated the mentoring experience as 'one of the best things I have done', with almost all of the remaining two thirds rating it as 'quite good'. Eighty per cent were satisfied with the programme structure and resource materials and Eighty-seven per cent said they would stay in contact with their mentor after the programme. Eighty-five per cent of participants said they had contact every 2–4 weeks (which was the recommended frequency). Most participants used telephone and email with their mentoring partner, with some using Skype or FaceTime.

A great deal of qualitative information has been collected about programme benefits to participants. The feedback from both mentors and mentees is in line with feedback expected from any mentoring programme. AWRA has a number of case studies of mentoring pairs on their website: http://awra.org.au/programs/awra-e-mentoring-program (accessed 5 September, 2016).

A small number of Phase 1 participants responded to an additional survey one year after the programme. Eighty-three per cent of mentees were still in contact with their mentors. All said that contact via electronic media was very effective.

Mentees and mentors were asked to say how much impact the mentoring programme had had on a number of aspects, ranging from skill acquisition to job promotion. The highest level of impact for mentees was reported to be on self-awareness, self-confidence, personal growth and development and the likelihood of continuing to work in the industry. For mentors, positive impact from their participation was reported to include self-awareness, personal learning and growth, sense of well-being and development of leadership capacity.

LESSON LEARNED

This case study demonstrates that virtual mentoring can be very effective but needs careful planning. The evaluation results are in line with results expected from face-to-face mentoring. The AWRA programme appears to be delivering a high-quality mentoring experience to both mentees and mentors in spite of being virtual. Whilst it is too early to say with certainty whether the programme is meeting the objective of helping to attract and retain women in the resources sector, it is encouraging that in the one-year-post-programme survey a considerable number of mentees noted that mentoring had a highly positive impact on the likelihood of them continuing to work in the industry.

Our key recommendations for implementation of a virtual mentoring programme, based on our learning from this case study, are:

1 Do not under-estimate the programme administration and programme structure required to run

a virtual programme. Because of the nature of virtual relationships, we believe there is a need to track and stay in touch with mentoring pairs, to an even greater extent than when the programme is run face-to-face. In this programme, emails were sent every 2–3 weeks in the first four months, with a reminder of actions to take and with tips on how to capitalise on the programme and the relationship. Thereafter, the frequency can be reduced because the mentoring relationship has its own momentum.
2. As with any programme, good matching is critical. If using an online mentoring programme-administration platform, the programme administrators need to understand and be able to influence the matching algorithm used by the software and fine tune this until quality matches result. The platform match suggestions are a guide only and sometimes need to be overridden when other criteria are important.
3. High-quality online training appears to be more effective than webinar training and, based on anecdotal feedback, is more enjoyable and can be done when it suits the participant.
4. Don't leave mentees and mentors 'on the bench' too long without frequently communicating with them, otherwise they lose interest.
5. The programme-close event is important. If budget does not allow an 'event' then a clear programme-close communication is still needed.
6. A number of changes to the programme structure including a pre-matching step of having participants watch an on-boarding video appears to have reduced drop-out rates in this programme and is recommended. This is the equivalent of an information session that participants may attend before face-to-face programmes, in order to decide if the programme is appropriate for them.

WHERE TO FROM HERE?

This programme will continue into 2018 with government funding. We will continue to gather data and make adjustments. Hopefully there will be sufficient data by then to show that the programme is meeting its strategic goal of supporting attraction and retention of women in the sector.

REFERENCES

Houck, Christiana (2011). Multigenerational and virtual: how do we build a mentoring program for today's workforce? *Performance Improvement*, Vol. 50, No. 2, 25–30.

Thompson, L., Jeffries, M. and Topping, K. (2010). E-mentoring for e-learning development. *Innovations in Education and Teaching International*, Vol. 47, No. 3, 305–15.

Zey, M. (2011). Virtual mentoring: the challenges and opportunities of electronically mediated formal mentor programs. *Review of Business Research*, Vol. 11, No. 4, 141–52.

Mentoring Novice Teachers: An Online Experience in Brazil

Aline Maria de Medeiros Rodrigues Reali, Maria da Graça Nicoletti Mizukami and Regina Maria Simões Puccinelli Tancredi

Mentorship programs are increasingly common in state policy in the USA and Europe but vary greatly in their design (Feiman-Nemser, 2001). One important current strategy to address new teachers' isolation, frustration, and failure is formal mentorship programs, which pairs new teachers with their veteran colleagues. It is considered a promising avenue for the professional development of inexperienced professionals and of those who work as mentors themselves (Sundli, 2007). It is also a challenging activity because of a number of factors associated with the interactive processes between mentors and mentees: conflicting ideas and attitudes, lack of confidence, partial information, incompatible schedules, and communication difficulties.

Mentors are educators and, as such, teachers. Their practice, therefore, occurs in conflicting, complex situations subjected to multiple, contradictory forces (Kennedy, 2006). Such practices are usually rooted in knowledge constructed along their personal and professional trajectories and act as 'lenses' or 'filters' (Fairbanks et al., 2010) through which they conceive learning as well as guide their practices. The kind of teaching and learning required nowadays demands that these professionals learn from their own practices and professional contexts instead of just acquiring new strategies and activities.

Among teaching characteristics, learning to teach and learning to be a teacher are unending lifelong processes, thus professional teaching competence cannot be only acquired through formal education. Because of this and the ever changing nature of today's world, it is necessary to provide practicing teachers with support to enable them to grow professionally throughout their careers (Marcelo García, 2011).

Considering the Brazilian context, our goal in this chapter is to focus on the Online Mentorship Program (OMP) – its conception, implementation/phases, and results – developed by researchers from a public university and teachers from public elementary schools.

AN OVERVIEW CONSIDERING INITIATIVES OF FORMATIVE PROCESSES FOR NOVICE TEACHERS IN BRAZIL

Although the Brazilian literature on the initial phases of a teaching career is quite considerable, the literature related to mentorship programs for novice teachers is rather limited. It seems that public policies do not take into account the formative needs of professionals in the first years of immersion in schools. In this context, studies on expert teachers mentoring novice teachers in how to teach are scarce.

Brazilian professional teaching contexts seldom allocate resources to mitigate the difficulties inherent to this or subsequent career phases because, traditionally, schools in Brazil have not systematized novice teachers' induction and professional development.

THE ONLINE MENTORSHIP PROGRAM (OMP) – CHARACTERISTICS

The OMP aims at educating mentors to work via the *Portal dos Professores* (Teachers' Web Portal, www.portaldosprofessores. ufscar.br) with novice primary/elementary schoolteachers and at investigating the processes involved and also the contributions of a professional-development program for mentors and their mentees.

The mentorship model adopts a methodological approach that assumes novice teachers will reflect on their own practices in view of adults' learning characteristics and the professional contexts of elementary schools. Focusing on the novices' formative needs and difficulties, the OMP is characterized as adopting an open curriculum, to be developed in process. Every novice teacher enrolled in the program is assisted by a mentor (an experienced teacher), who guides her or him throughout the program, which consists of two modules (a 120-hour module lasting approximately one year, followed by a 60-hour module lasing six months).

The group of mentors consisted of ten teachers, who were selected for their extended and diverse professional experience, with more than 15 years of teaching practices. Each one attended to three mentees simultaneously (Figure 33.1). They were generally perceived by their school communities as successful teachers, and just four of them had had any previous experience in teacher education. None of them had ever worked in distance education.

Forty-one novice teachers attended the OMP. The OMP had no institutional affiliation with any educational system of basic education. Three researchers were responsible for the initiative.

By means of the OMP we sought to promote, understand, and investigate:

- the professional development processes of mentors and novice teachers interacting by email;
- the use of a virtual learning environment and narrative accounts as investigative and formative tools, as the Teaching and Learning Experiences (TLE);[1]
- how experienced teachers' (mentors) knowledge base is constructed and developed during the mentorship process, and how it may be developed and shaped in light of the mentors' online communication with novices during a given period of time.

The investigation adopted theoretical perspectives that seek to understand – by means of methods involving learning and reflection – the complexity of processes which are natural to school life and the participants' unique specificities. These research and intervention models imply getting to know the reality of teachers' work, what they think, what they do, and why they do it to reflect on collaboratively lived situations and, whenever necessary, to build strategies to deal with them considering their schools' and communities' particularities. In order to achieve this goal, it is necessary to establish a two-way work process with the schools and their teachers,

Common problems faced by novice teachers.

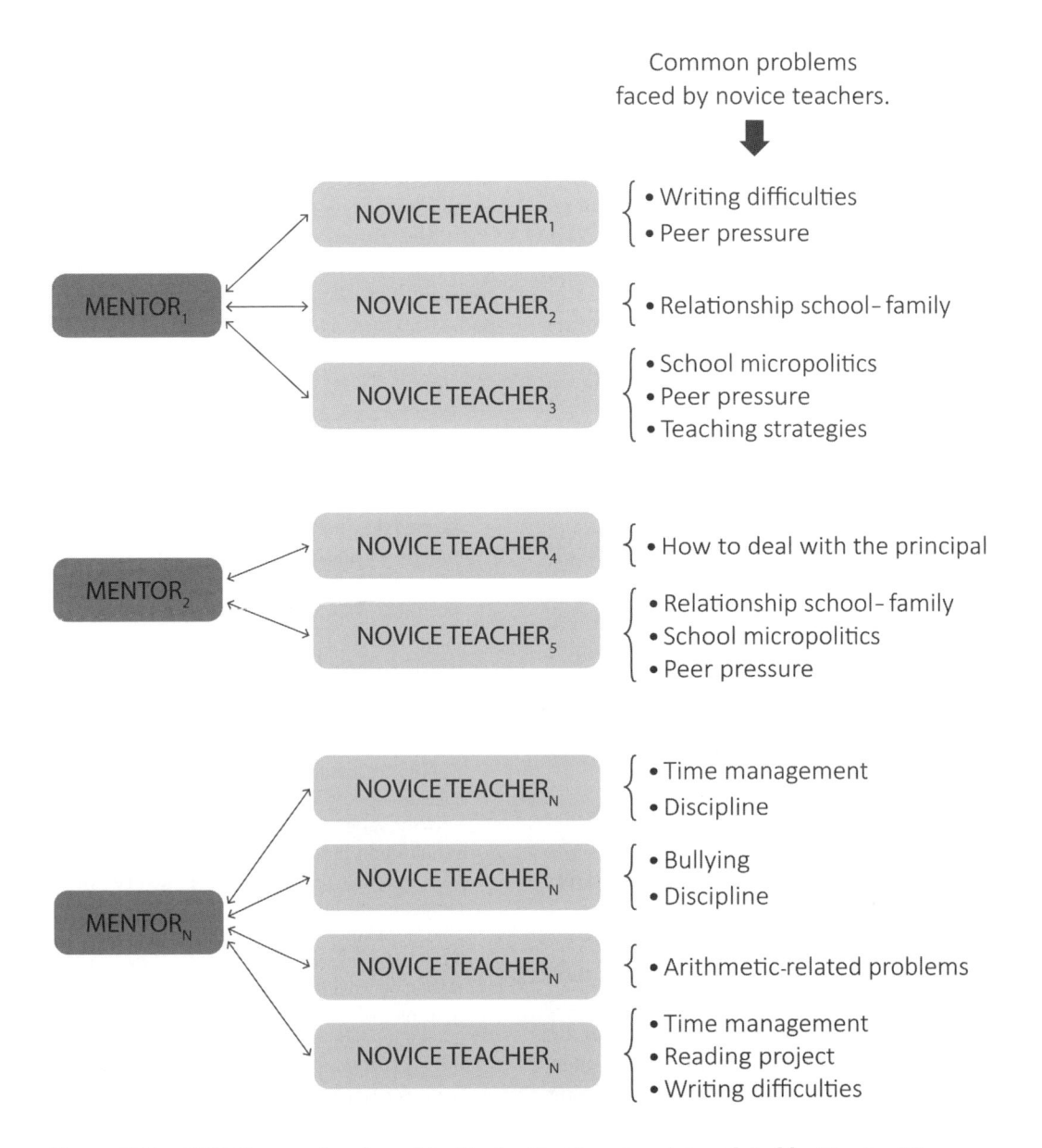

- MENTOR₁ → NOVICE TEACHER₁
  - Writing difficulties
  - Peer pressure
- MENTOR₁ ↔ NOVICE TEACHER₂
  - Relationship school–family
- MENTOR₁ → NOVICE TEACHER₃
  - School micropolitics
  - Peer pressure
  - Teaching strategies

- MENTOR₂ → NOVICE TEACHER₄
  - How to deal with the principal
- MENTOR₂ ↔ NOVICE TEACHER₅
  - Relationship school–family
  - School micropolitics
  - Peer pressure

- MENTORₙ → NOVICE TEACHERₙ
  - Time management
  - Discipline
- MENTORₙ → NOVICE TEACHERₙ
  - Bullying
  - Discipline
- MENTORₙ ↔ NOVICE TEACHERₙ
  - Arithmetic-related problems
- MENTORₙ → NOVICE TEACHERₙ
  - Time management
  - Reading project
  - Writing difficulties

Figure 33.1 CTLE themes developed by Novice Teachers I and A assisted by Mentor MI

avoiding seeing them as mere suppliers of research data.

Moreover, it is assumed that communication-technology advances, especially the internet, may greatly amplify social interactions and become a promising mentorship tool. Programs developed through this medium are often called 'virtual mentorship' or 'telementorship' (Knapczyk et al., 2005), and emails and teleconferences can provide assistance when face-to-face contact between mentors and mentees is unfeasible or unnecessary.

It was assumed that by investigating these aspects it would be possible to contribute to the planning of teachers' development and educational programs based on collaboration at their workplace.

In order to fully explore the research objectives, the data have been mainly collected through the mentors' and novice teachers' written narratives (daily email exchanges, reflective journals, teaching cases) and the mentors' oral narratives, collected at weekly meetings with the researchers. The information about the novice teachers and their interactions with their mentors was then compiled weekly, which raised the issues to be discussed at the weekly meeting between the mentors and researchers. These meetings helped to define the characteristics of the OMP and its deployments as well as to promote the mentors' professional development. The data related to the meetings were also compiled along a timeline and assisted the researchers in following them up. Therefore, both sets of data were used to define the intervention pace and steps as well as to construct answers to the research questions. Due to these options the study was also of a descriptive–analytical nature.

THE OMP RESEARCH-INTERVENTION DEVELOPMENT

The OMP was developed through three stages. In the first stage, which lasted eight months, the researchers and future mentors devised the program from the future mentors' conceptions of teaching, learning, knowledge, students, teachers, school, and curriculum, as well as from what they thought they needed to learn to act as mentors. The basic features, presuppositions, curriculum, activities, and duration of the OMP were delineated in the same fashion. The second stage, which lasted about three months, involved the mentors undergoing a learning process to use the virtual learning environment adopted by the OMP. The third stage, which lasted 25 months, every mentor assisted two or three novice teachers by means of emails exchanged between them and their novice-teacher partner. The weekly meetings with the researchers were maintained during this period to discuss how the OMP was evolving and to assist with professional development.

In the three and a half years, almost 5,750 messages were exchanged between mentors and their novice teacher partners, and 4,480 messages were exchanged between mentors and researchers.

Some results and developments

1 Although all of the mentor-novice dyads constructed their unique paths throughout the development of the OMP, at their own pace and following their own pattern, the investigation illustrated that these paths were observed to follow a *vital cycle* consisting of distinct phases: familiarization, development/intensification, and disengagement, which, in turn, displayed specific characteristics, goals, and procedures.
2 Each of these phases involved the mentors and novices discussing different themes, demanded specific support from the mentors (in view of the novices' varied formative needs, related to their socialization process in a school culture and to their teaching practices), and presented critical moments and periods, which promoted observable learning.
3 As a way to cope with some difficulties in managing novices' requests and evaluating the outcomes of their suggestions, mentors designed a working plan (the TLEs) with the novices, with the possibility of intervention, to mitigate/solve the reported problems by the novices.

The TLE themes developed by Novice Teachers I and A assisted by Mentor MI are presented in Table 33.1.

The results suggest the significance of developing *formative strategies*, such as TLEs, that take into account daily situations encountered by teachers, the teacher learning processes and characteristics, and that promote reflective processes and bonding among teachers in order to build strong communities of practice. It was also useful to question the

Table 33.1 TLE themes developed by Novice Teachers I and A assisted by Mentor MI

Novice teacher	Teaching and Learning Experience (TLE)
Novice Teacher I	Diagnostic evaluation
	Register book – ongoing analysis and reflection
	ESL activities for children
	Audio-visual materials/resources
	Methodology and activity – conceptualization
	Adult literacy education – Paulo Freire's method
	Organization of pedagogical work – planning weekly schedule
	Teaching Portuguese at public schools – reading/writing, grouping of contents, student unruliness
	Halloween festivity – reflective register of activities
	Computer classes – educational links
	Meaningful learning
	Yearly schedule of English lessons – preschool and first grades of elementary school
	Class planning – 3rd grade (English)
	Didactics and supervised training
	Interdisciplinarity/Project World Cup
	Teaching cases – CEAD
	Didactic projects
Novice Teacher A	Diagnostic evaluation (exploration) – analysis of student performance
	Classroom management – student unruliness
	Planning PTA meeting for effective participation
	Insertion of students with special needs
	Heterogeneity of students – how to deal with it
	Reallocation of students – a good solution to problems?
	Reflective register as a tool for teacher development
	Diversifying activities for literacy classes
	Planning productive groupings
	Didactic materials

pedagogical work and to identify the dilemmas and difficulties faced by teachers. It favored the observation and improvement of novice teachers' pedagogical practices. In theoretical terms, carrying out the TLEs showed the importance of pedagogical practices in teachers' process of knowledge construction informed by theory as well as the inquiring or reflexive processes.

What a teacher should know can be understood as the knowledge set – of different natures – that teachers require to teach, and different categories can be adopted to describe it – for example, pedagogical content, subject-matter content, technological content, and context content (Borges and Tardif, 2001; Shulman, 1987).

The data showed that the mentors – in the role of teacher educators – have, in addition to the development of online teaching-related knowledge, a multidisciplinary knowledge base at least on two levels: one related to the novice teachers they mentored and the other associated with the students of the novice teachers (Achinstein and Athanases, 2005). In fact, they developed a multifocal vision about what they need to know to teach novice teachers how to teach, since they simultaneously and permanently articulated and took into consideration both their novice teachers' formative needs and those of their novice teachers' students, including the teaching learning processes they (mentors and novices) were subject to, as well as intervening factors and teaching-practice contexts.

It was noticed that mentors usually conducted the online mentorship process by considering the difficulties faced by the novices, as well as the themes and contents of which they have more mastery and/or experience. This pattern was associated with the help and

Table 33.2 Phases/Steps of the Teaching and Learning Experiences (TLE) conducted by the novice with the mentors' supervision

TLE	Components	Description
Step 1	Definition of intervention theme	Identification of theme to be developed in TLE (teaching of content of any curricular component, case of a particular student, theme related to school life, students' lives, school–families interactions, specific teaching/learning difficulties, pedagogical coordination, and transversal themes).
Step 2	Planning of TLE	Negotiation of TLE theme between mentors and novice teachers: – Elicitation of clear TLE goals; – Initial selection of activities to be developed; – Preliminary selection of sources/materials to be used; – Eliciting how to develop this experience; – Elicitation of experience steps (from beginning to end).
Step 3 (concomitant with Step 2)	Definition of TLE registering procedures	Selection of procedures to follow up and register TLE: – Descriptive journal of activities planned and carried out; – Reflective journal; – Register of student discourse; – Report of meetings; – Account of critical events; – Register of observations of classrooms, parents, students, lunch breaks, and so forth.
Step 4	Writing TLE plan	Writing final plan of TLE to be developed, containing information related to previous steps.
Step 5	Developing and registering TLE	Implementation of procedures and detailed description of occurrences (for example, observations, points of view, impressions, justifications, expectations, difficulties, and accomplishments).
Step 6	Evaluating and writing descriptive report on TLE	Systematization and evaluation of TLE including analysis of and reflection on processes.
Step 7	Conception of teaching case about professional development (Module 1) and lived process (Module 2)	Final reflection on TLE via teaching case.

assistance of others mentors and illustrates the importance of the collaborative work.

Table 33.2 presents a systematization of these results. It should be remarked that the following organization does not intend to set up domain taxonomy or even embrace all that a mentor should know in order to help their mentees.

These results point to complexity of the knowledge base requested by the OMP and, consequently, of educating professionals to perform this function. Its description enabled a more detailed conception of what constitutes the knowledge of a mentor or teacher educator in internet-mediated mentorship processes. These data are relevant in view of the paucity of studies on teacher educators in Brazil and may serve as foundation for the analysis of formative processes for mentors and other educators as well as for their design.

CONCLUSION

The investigation and development of the OMP were challenging processes: it has been a much more complex enterprise than an equivalent face-to-face program, because it demands entirely new logistics. It was observed that peer communication, in an environment where questioning is welcome, is an essential factor in the mentors' individual professional development as well as in their contact with the novice teachers. For the mentees, the difficulties related to their professional teaching practice of the first years were worked out with the mentors who helped them during their participation in the OMP. It was evidenced that the professional knowledge constructed by them during this initiative enabled them not only to 'learn from the experience ... but [from] thinking about it' (Mizukami, 2004, p. 7).

Note

1 Teaching and Learning Experiences (TLEs) are structured on teaching and learning situations, planned by the researchers and implemented by the teachers from themes deemed by the latter, collectively, to be of individual and collective interest. These experiences are circumscribed processes, which may involve actions with small groups of teachers or in classrooms, involving the teacher and students, and usually deriving from practical difficulties related to the understanding of curricular components, challenges posed by public policies, or the school's daily activities (Mizukami et al., 2010, p. 116).

REFERENCES

Achinstein, B., and Athanases, S. Z. (2005). Focusing new teachers on diversity and equity: Toward a knowledge base for mentors. *Teaching and Teacher Education*, *21*, 843–62.

Borges, C., and Tardif, M. (2001). Os saberes dos docentes e a sua formação. *Educação e Sociedade*, *74*, 11–26.

Fairbanks, C. M., Duffy, G. D., Faircloth, B. S., He, Y., Levin, B., Rohr, J., and Stein, C. (2010). Beyond knowledge: Exploring why some teachers are more thoughtfully adaptive than others. *Journal of Teacher Education*, *61*(1–2), 61–171.

Feiman-Nemser, S. (2001). From preparation to practice: Designing a continuum to strengthen and sustain teaching. *Teachers College Record*, *103*(6), 1013–55.

Kennedy, M. (2006). Knowledge and vision in teaching. *Journal of Teacher Education*, *57*, 205–11.

Knapczyk, D. R., Hew, K. F., Frey, T. J., and Wall-Marencik, W. (2005). Evaluation of online mentoring of practicum for limited licensed teachers. *Teacher Education and Special Education*, *28*(3–4), 207–20.

Marcelo García, C. (2011). Políticas de inserción en la docencia: De eslabón perdido a puente para El desarrollo profesional docente. *Serie Documentos*, *52*. Retrieved from http//www.preal.org/PublicacionN.asp (accessed 5 September, 2016).

Mizukami, M. G. N. (2004). Aprendizagem da docência: Algumas contribuições de L. S. Shulman. *Educação*, *29*(2), 76–92.

Shulman, L. S. (1987). Knowledge and teaching: Foundations of the new reform. *Harvard Educational Review*, *57*(1), 1–22.

Sundli, L. (2007). Mentoring: a new mantra for education? *Teaching and Teacher Education*, *23*, 201–14.

Mowgli Foundation – Mentoring to Empower Entrepreneurial and Economic Development

Kathleen Bury and Amanda Edwards

Established in 2008 by successful serial entrepreneur, Tony Bury, the Mowgli Foundation (Mowgli) is an international mentoring organisation, which has been pioneering and specialising in entrepreneurial mentoring and embedding leadership development through the philosophy of mentoring, in the Middle East and North Africa (MENA) and the UK, for the sole purpose of empowering entrepreneurial and economic development.

Mowgli provides mentoring that inspires, connects and guides entrepreneurs and leaders to overcome life's personal and business challenges through interactive, experiential and transformational programmes. Each programme begins with a Kickstart workshop, which sees the preparation and training of mentors and, depending upon the programme's target beneficiaries, the matching of entrepreneurs with the trained mentors, within a unique environment for accelerated relationship building and the facilitation of a structured period of ongoing support. This period of ongoing support and supervision seeks to embed the mentor's learning, develop the peer-to-peer support network within the group and further enhance engagement and relationship building, to provide for the highest levels of quality and sustainability of the mentoring relationships.

Mowgli has delivered over 95 programmes in 14 countries – Algeria, Bahrain, Egypt, Jordan, Lebanon, Libya, Morocco, Palestine, Qatar, Saudi Arabia, Syria, Tunisia, Yemen and the UK – and has engaged over 1,770 alumni members within a learning and mentoring focused global alumni network. In December 2012, Mowgli was recognised with the Mohammed bin Rashid Award for Young Business Leaders Award for the 'Best Mentor Network in the Arab Region' and in 2016 won the Employment Generation award at the Ta'atheer Social Impact Awards, received the European Quality Award accreditation from the European Mentoring and Coaching Council for its Mowgli Mentoring Experience (MME) programme syllabus and was nominated as the Start Up Program of the Year at the Arabian Business Awards.

MENTORING IN ENTREPRENEURSHIP

The incubation, development and support of sustainable entrepreneurship and small- and medium-sized enterprises (SME) can play a vital role in increasing employment and economic generation. In the MENA region, the youth-unemployment rate currently stands at 27 per cent (18–35 year olds) and is the highest globally. Between 50 and 80 million jobs are required over the next 10 years to maintain the current levels of unemployment, signifying the requirement for a 40 per cent expansion in available jobs (Arabia Monitor, World Bank 2012). This is a highly daunting goal.

A key way to address this huge unemployment challenge is the incubation, development and support of sustainable entrepreneurship and SMEs. To foster an environment conducive to private-enterprise development, a number of factors are required:

- Strengthening of regulatory frameworks
- Access to infrastructure
- Access to capital
- Strengthening of human capital through the access to appropriate business skills training and mentoring

Human capital is defined as the knowledge and skills acquired through formal and informal learning that resides within individuals (Becker, 1964) and relates to intergenerational transmission of knowledge and learning behaviours (Roberts, 2001). The development of human capital is a key challenge for the entrepreneurship ecosystem; and the support and empowerment of the entrepreneur's core spirit (resilience, motivation and confidence), as well as the development of their skills, behaviours and mindset, is critical to their long-term success (Mowgli Foundation, 2016). Mowgli's mission is focused on developing human and entrepreneurial capital through holistic mentorship, which focuses on their personal and professional development.

WHY MENTORING?

Mowgli defines mentoring as 'having someone who tells you what you need to know, not necessarily what you want to hear' and a mentor as 'someone who stands beside you in a shoulder-to-shoulder relationship and works with you to empower you to develop your own leadership, thought process, decision-making capabilities and provides you with the necessary confidence to take the risks inherent in both your business and personal development'.

On every entrepreneurial journey, the business the entrepreneur is nurturing will have a lifetime of development, overseen, guided and indeed lived by the entrepreneur him or herself. As a result, the entrepreneurial learning often goes through several distinct phases of growth and development, along with the business. Within these phases, three of the most challenging times when Mowgli believes an entrepreneur can benefit from a highly skilled mentor are:

- Start up
- Growth
- Success

During each of these key transitional stages a mentor can provide vital guidance and support to entrepreneurs to support them in finding the courage and resources to move their business forward. In the UK, when an SME leader is mentored, the business is twice as likely to surpass its fifth anniversary of being in business, therefore enhancing the business's profitability, sustainability and ability to expand its workforce.

Business mentoring is still a relatively new concept in the MENA region. A recent study showed that approximately 40 per cent of entrepreneurs do not have a mentor (Wamda, 2014). While informal mentoring relationships between friends and family members are reasonably commonplace, true and focused entrepreneurial mentoring is still in its infancy. Mowgli invests heavily in the raising of awareness of the importance and

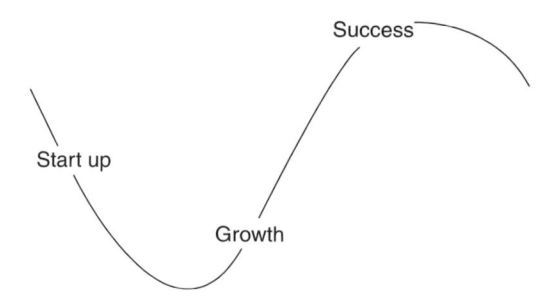

Figure 34.1 The three critical stages of an entrepreneur's journey when they need a mentor

benefits of mentoring in order to make it a cornerstone of entrepreneurial and human-capacity development.

Furthermore, Mowgli advocates a 'serve to lead' philosophy of mentoring, whereby the mentor volunteers his/her time with no expectation of return, including financial, and seeks to ensure that mentoring is paid forward through the mentoring of others. This serves to embed a culture of mentoring and leadership development within the community.

THE MOWGLI MENTORING EXPERIENCE (MME)

Mowgli has developed a highly innovative and experiential Mowgli Mentoring Experience (MME) syllabus that can be tailored to meet the needs of various target audiences: start up, growth and exiting entrepreneurs, microfinance institutions/micro-entrepreneurs and youth/corporate leaders. The Kickstart workshop, with which each programme begins, focuses primarily on the training of mentors. Following this, a mix of entrepreneur–mentor matching, learning and speed-mentoring sessions and the facilitation of a structured and supervised period of ongoing support, usually for one year, is undertaken.

The mentor-training programme seeks to develop the leadership skills of professionals through Mowgli's 'serve to lead' mentoring philosophy and practices, developing the qualities and competencies associated with strong leadership and providing them with the foundation tools, techniques and mindset to be able to effectively support those they wish to mentor.

The entrepreneur–mentor matching seeks to ensure effective and successful pairings for mutual growth and development. The 12 month period of ongoing relationship facilitation seeks to provide supervision and support to ensure the mentoring relationships stay on course and deliver against the entrepreneur's set goals, further enhance the peer-to-peer support network and provide additional learning and networking opportunities. Feedback is sourced from both the entrepreneurs and mentors at regular intervals throughout the programmes.

Mowgli-trained Lead and Co-facilitators deliver the Kickstart workshop to groups of 12 entrepreneurs and 12 mentors – the optimum number of participants for Mowgli's programme design. All of Mowgli's facilitators are required to participate in a Mowgli programme as a mentor and are hand-selected by Mowgli's Coach Facilitators. Following the selection, they are trained in a 2–3-day Train of Facilitator (ToF) workshop, during which they develop a deeper understanding of mentoring, the Mowgli programme and its objectives. Following this, they undertake a supervised 2–3-year period of development with Mowgli, where they graduate from Trainee to Co-Facilitator and then on to Lead Facilitator. Graduation from one development stage to another is based on demonstration of their capabilities against a set of core competencies and feedback from entrepreneurs, mentors, fellow facilitators and Mowgli's Coach Facilitators.

To be selected for the Mowgli mentoring programme, entrepreneurs and mentors are required to complete a registration form and be interviewed, to ensure quality, commitment and fit. Applications are assessed against pre-defined and set selection criteria, which is tailored against the project need, which Mowgli regards as a necessary foundation for effective mentoring to take place.

Mowgli's entrepreneur-selection criteria typically centres around:

- A developed business with a structure, secured funding and vision, trading for at least a year (this differs for micro-entrepreneurs)
- Personal qualities of leadership
- Commitment to owning and driving the mentoring relationship for one year (minimum of 2 hours per month plus the initial Kickstart workshop)
- Understanding of the MME programme
- Willingness to take part in regular monitoring and pass on the philosophy and benefits of mentoring

Mowgli's mentor-selection criteria typically centres around:

- A successful track record as an entrepreneur, senior executive or professional with 5+ years of cash flow/ P&L management experience
- Wide and diverse network and cross-border professional experience
- Understanding of the unique MME programme, Mowgli's mentoring philosophy, principles and practice
- Commitment to the mentoring relationship for one year (minimum of 2 hours per month plus the initial 3-day Kickstart workshop)
- Willingness to pass on the philosophy and benefits of mentoring

While it is important for a business mentor to have achieved a certain level of business experience, of equal importance are a mentor's personal attributes. Mowgli defines a good mentor as someone the entrepreneur can trust, who shows humility, approaches the mentoring relationship holistically and is motivated by a desire to serve the entrepreneurs' needs. These personal qualities are further developed during the Kickstart workshop and the 1-year mentoring programme.

Mentoring for mutual growth and development

The beneficiaries of mentoring are far reaching; however, Mowgli predominantly focuses on two key parties:

1 The entrepreneurs, who are mentored, benefit from being supported on a holistic basis, eradicating their feeling of loneliness on the journey and furthering their personal and business growth and development. As a ripple effect, their employees are also able to benefit from the mentoring through the creation of new jobs, the safeguarding of existing jobs and working within a mentoring-centred organisation, as well as with leaders, who 'serve to lead'.
2 The individuals, who are trained as mentors, not only further develop themselves holistically through the mentoring experience, they become better leaders within their workplaces, families and wider communities and pass on the mentoring philosophy where they can.

The evolution of Mowgli Foundation

In the 8 years since Mowgli launched its first programme, Mowgli's core team has grown from 2 to 8. Mowgli has a Board of Trustees of 6 and has developed a pool of 23 trained Facilitators including trainees. Mowgli's headquarters are based in the UK and is locally embedded in the MENA ecosystem, with teams based in Jordan, Morocco and the UAE, as well as Kenya.

The first Mowgli mentoring programme was delivered in 2009 in Jordan, where Mowgli contracted two trained facilitators, including the Programme Designer/Coach

Facilitator, to deliver the mentoring programmes. In 2012, Mowgli trained a further 5 Facilitators to expand the facilitator pool and began its recruitment of local facilitators to be able to offer the mentoring programmes in English, Arabic and French. Since its inception in 2008, Mowgli has evolved and adapted to meet the needs of the ecosystem and beneficiaries across all stages of the entrepreneurial life cycle.

The far-reaching impact of entrepreneurial mentoring

As a result of Mowgli's mentoring programmes, over 790 entrepreneurs have been sourced and matched with trained volunteer mentors, and over 980 volunteer professionals have been trained as mentors. Mowgli's three desired areas of impact are:

- Economic growth, job creation and safeguarding
- Business growth, sustainability and success
- Personal growth and strengthening of leadership

An independent study found Mowgli's projects produced an average Return on Mentoring Investment (ROMI) of 890% (Mowgli Foundation, 2015). Beneficiaries readily acknowledge the transformational nature of Mowgli's approach, and many have gone onto become mentors themselves.

In addition to determining the ROMI, feedback is collected from the entrepreneurs and mentors at the beginning of the programme and at quarterly intervals over the year. Analysis of the feedback indicates that over 3,470 jobs have been created and safeguarded by Mowgli Entrepreneurs, that on average each entrepreneur creates 3.3 jobs and safeguards 90+% of the their existing employees/jobs during their mentoring year (Mowgli Foundation, 2015).

At the end of their mentoring year, 89 per cent of Mowgli Entrepreneurs' businesses remained operational, 71 per cent said they feel more confident to move their business onto the next growth stage, 51 per cent increased their client list/secured more contracts and 43 per cent of entrepreneurs increased their turnover.

In addition to the impact of mentoring on their business, the majority or entrepreneurs said that mentoring had supported their personal development. 81 per cent of Mowgli Entrepreneurs felt more confident in general, 76 per cent developed confidence in their business decision-making skills, 82 per cent of Mowgli Mentors said they would recommend the programme to others, 85 per cent said they had developed their capacity for empathy, 79 per cent developed their leadership, coaching and active skills and 77 per cent said they had developed a deeper sense of self-awareness.

Mowgli fundamentally believes that the mentors should also benefit from the mentoring experience: 83 per cent of Mowgli Mentors said they had benefited from the programme, 85 per cent said they had developed their capacity for empathy, 79 per cent developed their coaching and active listening skills and 77 per cent said they had developed a deeper sense of self-awareness.

The benefits of the mentoring programme extend much further, to the wider community. 76 per cent of mentors said they would like to mentor again and 71 per cent of entrepreneurs said they would like to mentor another entrepreneur. Seventy per cent of Mowgli Mentors said they use the mentoring skills they developed in a professional setting with junior colleagues or with others and 56 per cent made direct changes in their working lives following the program. Further impact data can be found at http://mowgli.org.uk/our-impact.

Challenges and ways forward

Delivering an effective mentoring programme is not without its challenges. The top four challenges faced by Mowgli in delivering the mentoring programmes are:

1 The recruitment of quality entrepreneurs and mentors who are open to and are committed to

the mentoring programme. Both the entrepreneur and the mentor need to be able to dedicate adequate time to the relationship and stringent human-centric recruitment processes need to be adopted.
2. Understanding of the difference between mentoring and business advice and what the role of the mentor is; a mentor is not a consultant, financial provider or business-plan writer, for example. Regular Mentoring Awareness Sessions and Expectation Setting Sessions need to be built into any mentoring programme within an emerging and immature market.
3. Understanding of the programme and the openness to engage with holistic mentoring. Entrepreneurs need to be empowered to open up to their mentor and to drive the mentoring relationship. Mentors need to be empowered to be open with their mentee and serve the entrepreneur's needs rather than their own. The Kickstart workshop and ongoing support facilitates consistent messaging to ensure that each party manages their own expectations and a productive mentoring relationship can flourish.
4. Securing funding to deliver mentoring programmes that focus heavily on the training of mentors, matching and/or ongoing support with the objective of empowering entrepreneurial and economic development when operating within an environment that focuses more on financial than human-capital development. Continuous engagement with key stakeholders and communication of the return on mentoring investment (ROMI) is critical to proving the value that holistic mentoring offers.

Mowgli's learning nuggets

After six years operating in the MENA region, Mowgli has learnt a number of important lessons.

Think local

Building a network of local partnerships and fostering community-level engagement increases the reach and impact of the mentoring programme. In addition, training local facilitators and mentors, and hiring employees from within the region, builds credibility and ensures that the programmes remain culturally relevant.

Provide training

While some other mentoring programmes do not train volunteer mentors, Mowgli has found that this is a critical component in increasing the potential of the mentoring relationships, both from a quality and a longevity perspective. The mentors feel more confident and are committed to the mentoring relationship and are better equipped to serve their mentee.

Listening, learning and adapting

Listening to the needs and feedback of the beneficiaries, partners and stakeholders and then embedding this is key to ensuring continuous improvement. In fact, adapting your service offering is critical for the success of any business operation.

Capture the impact

Monitoring the mentoring relationships through regular feedback from the participants has enabled Mowgli to measure the programme's impact and provide support to relationships that may be struggling. The monitoring support also serves to formalise the mentoring relationship and ensures the entrepreneurs' and mentors' commitment remains consistent throughout the year.

Face-to-face

Working with entrepreneurs, especially across the MENA region, highlights the importance of face-to-face interaction. While other forms of communication are useful for entrepreneurs and mentors to stay in touch, accelerated relationship building during a Kickstart workshop is essential, and face-to-face meetings throughout the ongoing support period are highly beneficial for building a strong mentoring relationship based on trust and open communication.

Duration of mentoring programme

While mentoring relationships do not have to continue for a set amount of time, Mowgli has found that committing to a

1-year relationship means entrepreneurs and mentors have time to foster a strong relationship based on mutual growth and development. It gives the entrepreneur and mentor a milestone to work towards and sets the foundations for the mentoring relationships to continue beyond the year.

Chemistry

Instead of focusing on matching entrepreneurs to mentors based upon industry sector, Mowgli has found that a more holistic approach, where Mowgli Facilitators match the pairs based on their personal chemistry during the workshop, works well in enabling the foundation of a successful mentoring relationship.

Long-term sustainability of mentoring

Mowgli has already achieved the goals it set out in 2008, when it commenced operations. Now that the first phase has been successfully accomplished, it is launching its second phase, as there is always more to accomplish.

In addition to expanding into Sub Saharan Africa and going global, Mowgli's long-term vision is to empower local ecosystem partners, who fundamentally believe in the power of mentoring and wish to secure mentoring as a cornerstone of entrepreneurial and leadership development to establish local mentoring organisations (LMO) within their respective country. The establishment of these LMOs will be managed and driven to satisfy the specific mentoring needs of their beneficiaries, with Mowgli providing the infrastructure, systems, process and programme IP under a franchise model.

In addition, Mowgli seeks to ensure the quality of mentoring provision in each of the countries it operates in, both today and in the future, and is in the process of developing a Mentor Accreditation Programme.

With a critical alumni base of over 1,770, Mowgli seeks to provide alumni members with opportunities and support for lifelong learning and development through an online and offline alumni platform.

REFERENCES

Arabia Monitor, World Bank (2012) Retrieved from http://www.mowgli.org.uk/sites/default/files/121109_FINAL_Arabia%20Monitor%20Article%20Regional%20Views%20-%20Entrepreneurship_Press%20Release.pdf (accessed 30 September, 2016).

Becker, G.S. (1964) *Human Capital: A Theoretical and Empirical Analysis, with Special Reference to Education*. Chicago and London: University of Chicago Press.

Mowgli Foundation (2015) Empowering Entrepreneurs for Economic Growth Impact Report 2015. Retrieved from http://www.mowgli.org.uk/sites/default/files/Mowgli_2015_ImpactReport.pdf (accessed 3 January, 2017).

Mowgli Foundation (2016) Nurturing Human Capital: The Missing Piece of MENA's Entrepreneurship Puzzle. Retrieved from http://mowgli.org.uk/sites/default/files/Nurturing%20Human%20Capital.pdf (accessed 3 January, 2017).

Roberts, J. (2001) *Class in Modern Britain*. Oxford: Open University Press.

Wamda (2014) Retrieved from http://www.wamda.com/research/the-mentor-effect (accessed 30 September, 2016).

Rhea Challenge Mentoring Learning Alliance Program for Female Entrepreneurs in Finland

Mikaela Nyström and Eeva-Liisa Heinaro

What an energy boost!

You can feel the energy and inspiration in the room – 36 ladies are ready to start their mentoring learning alliances for the following year. You can feel the excitement of the 18 ambitious and dynamic female entrepreneurial mentees, each the founder of their own start-up company, each at different phases of the organizational life cycle. They are ready to kick off the mentoring learning alliances with their mentors, professional and powerful leaders in Finland from the GAIA Network. GAIA members are female leaders with long experience and a solid knowledge of business leadership and management. The Rhea Challenge has begun!

The idea of Rhea Challenge was born in spring 2014, with the goal of supporting female entrepreneurs in setting up and developing their businesses through mentoring provided by members of GAIA.

Female entrepreneurs in Finland currently make up 31 percent of the total number of entrepreneurs. Young female entrepreneurs are a minority: approximately 80 percent of entrepreneurs starting their own companies in Finland are male and only 20 percent are female (European Commission Statistical Rate on Women Entrepreneurs 2014). The aim of Rhea Challenge is to help the businesses of young female entrepreneurs grow past the first stages, increase their turnover, and enable the employment of more people, thus supporting the development of the Finnish economy.

The project team, which consists of representatives from GAIA and EY (formerly known as Ernst and Young), recognized the need for a program that supported female entrepreneurship. They decided to ensure a program of sufficient size, targeting a minimum of 20 mentor–mentee pairs. During the fall of 2014, a three-month period of planning, marketing, and content development, as well as the application process, was launched. Members of GAIA volunteered and were selected to be mentors for the Rhea Challenge. They were categorized by current company segment/position and previous experience. The mentors represent a wide selection of business and industry backgrounds, such as consumer goods, IT, HR, and general management. Mentors have an average of more than 20 years of working experience, advancing to senior positions in their respective companies relatively quickly. Some have also started their own companies.

The Rhea Challenge was promoted at several events in universities and institutes, through business-angels networks and contacts, as well as at SLUSH (www.slush.org) in November 2014. During the same month, an article in the Finnish business magazine Talouselämä was published, presenting the first matched mentor and mentee pair, in order to market the opportunity. These actions led to the Rhea Challenge receiving over 50 applications. Mentees' application forms developed into a map consisting of business idea, background, and specific mentoring needs, such as finance, leadership, management, or strategy.

The average age of the mentees is 30. Most have an academic degree or higher-level education. Approximately half of them have only worked for themselves, either setting up their current company or being otherwise self-employed.

In order to create suitable pairs, the mapping process focused on the fit between the mentor's background and knowledge and the mentee's business idea and unique mentoring needs. This created what at surface level seemed to be unusual combinations of mentors and mentees, with, for example, a manufacturing-industry professional becoming the mentor of a beauty entrepreneur. In most cases, despite the seemingly different interests of some of the pairs, this approach gave good results. Finally, 18 pairs were matched and the kick-off, 'What is a mentoring learning alliance?', was held in March 2015.

In their first mentoring meeting, mentors were expected to focus on mentees' business needs, business-development strategies, and business financing as part of direction setting and building the relationship. The project team developed a set of development criteria for the businesses, to be followed up on after one year.

In the mentoring program, four joint sessions for all mentors and mentees were planned, to give room for networking and sharing participants' own best practice and pitfalls. The project team also wanted to share theories and input around mentoring, time management, self-managed leadership, business models, and so on. A workbook was developed, which included a learning log for documentation and reflection of the one-year learning alliance.

Six months later, in August 2015, 17 pairs had continued with the program. One pair ended their learning alliance due to time management and scheduling challenges.

Mentoring program flow

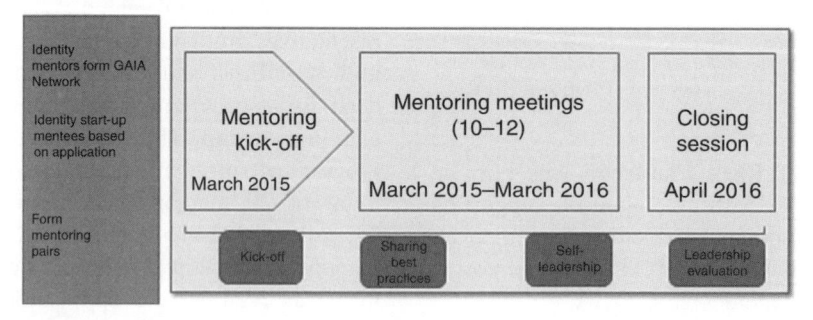

Figure 35.1 A kick-off with all mentors and mentees was held in March and a mid-review in October. A workshop related to time and stress management was held in December; and a closing evaluation and feedback session was held in April 2016, when the one-year program came to an end

KEY LEARNING FROM THE MENTORING LEARNING ALLIANCES SO FAR

Prior to the program, expectations included focusing on business targets as well as personal development and leadership. However, the main focus has been on start-up business targets, such as to implement strategy and clarify vision. Gender (female entrepreneur) has not been a business-related topic for the pairs, implying that this is not an issue in this entrepreneurial context.

Added value has been gained by both mentors and mentees through taking the time to slow down and reflect on relevant issues. An open and honest dialogue has allowed the development of a more holistic and objective view of their businesses and their own roles as leaders.

The sessions have provided structure and analyses related to business planning and strategy as well as company culture and values. Discussions have given new insights and increased understanding of partnering, investments, financial agreements, contracts, and client networks. In the beginning of the process the mentor's role was that of a listener, coach, and sounding board, but it evolved to the role of critical friend and challenger, as well as a bridge and networker (see Figure 35.2, David Clutterbuck's mentor role grid).

LESSONS LEARNED SO FAR FOR THE MENTEES AND MENTORS

Shrinking the elephant

The feedback from the interviewed mentees indicated that time spent voicing their thoughts and concerns with their mentors was well spent, as it allowed them to reflect on and demystify their business challenges. Mentees feel that they have gained more confidence as leaders and received motivational support for their business ideas and vision. The support of the mentor has given the mentee courage to take risks and inspired them to believe in themselves and their business idea. They have also developed a better understanding of their role as a leader of their team and their start up.

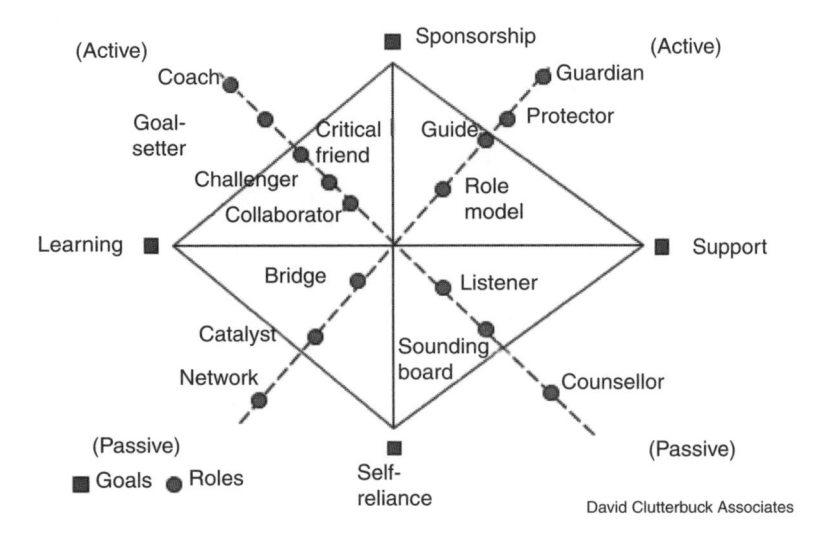

Figure 35.2 Different roles of the mentor

Seeing the invisible gorilla

Questions from mentors have helped mentees to see alternatives and ways to move forward. By distancing themselves from daily tasks, the mentees have been able to develop a more holistic perspective on their business as well as the ability to look at their business strategies more critically. The mentors have taught the mentees to appreciate their own achievements.

End to end – from idea to implementation and following up with reflective learning

Discussions with mentors have helped mentees to work in a more structured manner instead of an ad hoc flow. Also, following up actions and results has helped mentees to improve their working practices in areas such as recruitment, leadership role, contracts, and financial management.

Boosted energy

For the mentors, access to young business leaders and dynamic start-up entrepreneurial females has been both inspirational and a great learning opportunity. Mutual learning, fun, inspiration, the opportunity to step into another world with a different culture and clock speed – these have all been much appreciated. Access to young, inspirational, and dynamic entrepreneurs has given the mentors a lot of energy for their own work challenges. Some even experienced reverse mentoring and true mutual learning as part of their mentoring learning alliance. Both mentors and mentees felt that in having a female pair the focus was not just to 'cut the bullshit' and focus on the hard facts. It also evolved learning to deal with emotional and intuitive issues. In this context of rapport building, the gender aspect had a big, positive impact.

LESSONS LEARNED FROM THE PROGRAM SO FAR

Both mentors and mentees look forward to face-to-face sessions, where they meet, share best practices and pitfalls, learn from each other, get benchmarks ... and support each other.

The program ended with a closing session in April 2016, where the following metrics were collected:

- Selected financial metrics such as turnover and number of personnel
- A pulse survey conducted after each joint session with identical sets of questions to provide material on the development of aspects of personal strength. The pulse survey was completed by both mentors and mentees. Joint sessions and pulse surveys were held in March 2015, October 2015, December 2015, and April 2016. The pulse survey provided metrics on:
  - personal development of the mentee
  - on the development of the start-up company
  - feedback and value added of the structured mentoring learning alliance program for female entrepreneurs

Interim results

The first pulse survey and the feedback from individual mentees, contacted by the project team members, indicates that the start-up companies and the mentees themselves are in such different life-cycle phases that common metrics are difficult to find. In addition, the needs of each mentee are individual and so varied that common denominators are few. However, the success rate of the project can so far be considered high, as 17 pairs out of 18 are continuing their work.

A mentoring program such as this is valuable, because the ability to think like an entrepreneur and to have a start-up mind-set with innovation, risk-taking, courage and great learning agility, is also important for the success of larger organizations and businesses in today's disruptive business environment.

Intercultural Relationships and Mentoring: The Italian Air Force on an Afghanistan NATO Training Mission, Shindand

Matteo Perchiazzi

INTRODUCTION

The Italian School of Mentoring (SIM) of Florence is unique in Italy. It was founded in 2010, as the result of more than fifteen years of research, consulting, training and exchange of good practices on the topic of mentoring by its founder and creator, Matteo Perchiazzi. The activity of the school is based on four main areas: consulting, research, training and certification, with the aim of creating communities of practice and professional bodies in mentoring. The core business of the school is the structuring of formal paths of mentoring and training in key project management for formal SIM mentoring certificat.(SIM n.d.).

SIM supported the Italian Air Force, using mentoring as part of NATO's Training Mission in Afghanistan, which began in July 2010 and ended in 2014. The aim of the mission was to facilitate the process of transition to full Afghan military independence. SIM and CEFODIMA–ISMA (Institute of Military Sciences and Aviation) trained about 400 mentors/ advisors to mentor staff belonging to the Afghan military airport at Shindand, the future centre of excellence and training for the entire Afghan Air Force (Aeronautica Militare, n.d.). Italian mentors were chosen from outstanding experts in all the professionals of a military airport: from the organization of the food to firefighting; from professionals involved in refuelling to MI17 helicopter pilots; and from transportation to the commander-in-chief of the entire mission.

It was a gigantic programme, in which, for four and half years, a group of mentors were sent to Shindand every six months, where SIM facilitated:

- Designing (initial and ongoing adaptation) of the mentoring scheme
- Training mentors
- Assisting mentors weekly, through the Italian Air Force reserved and classified channel e-platform

- Ongoing evaluation through monthly mentor diaries to create lessons learnt within a knowledge-management system
- Capturing additional learning through focus groups and individual interviews, with every group coming back after the mission
- Six-monthly evaluation of the impact of the mission.

Much of the information about this mission is classified, including the financial investment, so we decided to focus this case study on the development of the relationship in such a difficult and different intercultural environment and the impact of mentoring in developing autonomy through exchanging values.

Mentoring is a developmental and learning-support methodology, aimed at promoting individual potential, which takes place in an exchange relationship (formal or informal) between a mentor – an agent of socialization, natural facilitator, 'older friend', *passepartout* for the adult world, continual source of reference – and a mentee – a less experienced person, student or learner.

Mentoring was born as a natural and spontaneous relationship, in which the experience and wisdom of the mentor are able to stimulate both the processes of self-learning and learning in a mentee, and also the development of values, along with a shared sense of belonging and motivation within the relationship. Mentoring is therefore based on a significant relationship, during which both mentor and mentee have an experience of personal growth, with mutual learning. One of the characteristics of mentoring, compared to other forms of help with personal development, lies in the exchange, giving and receiving the gifts of wisdom and knowledge. The mentor is a positive role model, a guide at certain times of transition for the mentee, who inspires a change that leads to new forms of participation in significant activities within a community.

In Italy, we started to study, theorize and experience structured mentoring in 2000 (CAMEO, 2004; Progetto MAITRE n.d.), in a wide range of applications, ranging from school to work, from vocational guidance to entrepreneurship, from sports to prisons and from military schools to the army (Perchiazzi, 2009).

The content of the mentoring conversations, from which the relationship develops, is never the same, is closely linked to the needs of the mentee and relates strongly to the context in which the relationship takes place. The Afghanistan context was very different from anything experienced in Italy or elsewhere in Western Europe. For example, typically, mentoring relationships expect the mentee to take control. However, in the context of this programme, mentors were expected to drive the process, because mentees, while not necessarily reluctant to take part, had little concept of what was involved and what would be required of them.

SPECIFIC ELEMENTS OF THE IMPLEMENTATION PROCESS: TRAINING, EVALUATION, COMMUNICATION IN THE PROGRAMME

Project EMPIRE – Empowerment through Mentoring (2007–9) (Progetto EMPIRE n.d.) outlined good practice for public-sector mentoring programmes at European level and established guidelines for the design of formal mentoring. These include mentors having appropriate tools and being supported in their continuous learning in order to be effective in their roles.

A key part of this educational process – this knowledge-management system – was the 'diary' of each mentor. This ongoing monitoring tool was the main instrument for collecting empirical data about the performance of each relationship, the results it produced, the identification of any problems and the remedial strategies adopted. The diary has been crucial in identifying those strategies/elements/teaching techniques/devices which have been successful and those which have failed, from the point of view of the relationship. Important information included the purpose and focus of the relationship (on, for instance, career scope, professional development, or cultural development), any difficulties encountered and how they were dealt with, and how each pair built and strengthened rapport. We paid particular attention to how each mentor built the relationship and how mentor and mentee communicated and worked with their values. We also used the diary to assess the mentee's growth in terms of degree of autonomy and greater awareness of their professional military roles. The diaries were sent to the research team on a monthly basis and were analysed through a content-analysis methodology that transformed it from a pure reading activity to a process for qualitative identification of the key recurring themes.

Lessons learnt

Empirical evidence emerging from qualitative and quantitative analysis of approximately 470 diaries during the period November 2010–November 2012 allowed us to see how mentoring supported the mentees in their daily life and work. It helped to improve communication, provided a sense of belonging and transferred tools for professional and organizational enrichment. It also resulted in extensive cultural exchange and appreciation of cultural diversity. We were able to see the role of mentoring in conveying cultural values, by creating relationships that are built on a foundation of trust, empathy and equal interchange, and by using this foundation to define, pursue and achieve professional goals. The results in this extreme setting so far support the view that mentoring can be successfully applied in any context (social, business, school, etc.) in which we can meet different cultures.

The sample of diaries shows that mentoring engaged with Afghans belonging to several different ethnic groups, but particularly Pashtun (45 per cent), Tajik (21 per cent), other (17 per cent) and Hazara (4 per cent). This suggests that our experience can also be extrapolated to other tribes and ethnic groups in other contexts (Figure 36.1).

The typical aims of mentoring as a learning method relate to the transmitting of the specific job-role experience: helping the learner (mentee) to take better control of their organizational role and career path.

Our analysis explored the most important constraints on the mentoring relationship. We classified them into four types: learning constraints, relational constraints, cultural constraints and operating–logistic constraints (Figure 36.2).

Learning constraints relate to the professional starting point and basic level of commitment – does the mentee want to be

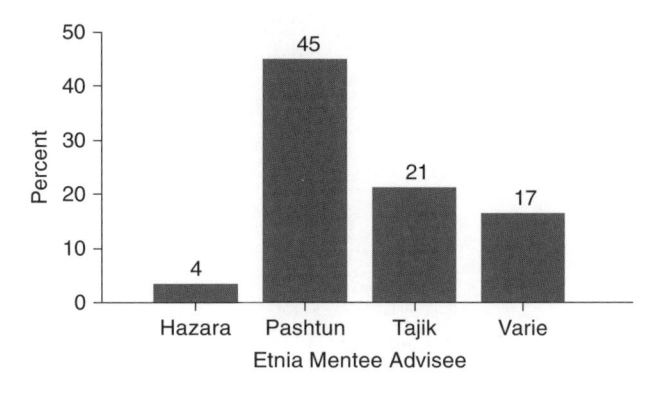

Figure 36.1 Afghan Army mentee by ethnicity

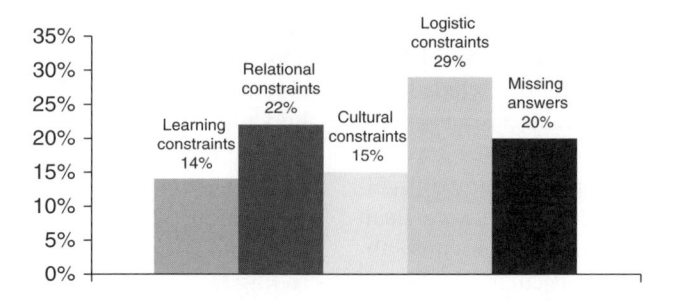

Figure 36.2 Constraints of mentoring relationship

involved or not? Other constraints derived from relational communication, from cultural differences and from operational issues, such as the organization of mentoring within the daily military-base activities. As can be seen from Figure 36.2, cultural constraints are only 15 per cent of the constraints limiting the success of mentoring, and, together with relational constraints, which arise in part from difficulties relating to language and culture, make up only 37 per cent of the overall problems of the relationship. The relationship is mediated by an interpreter, who translates from Italian to English and English to Farsi Dhari, the main language in Afghanistan – so it is hardly surprising that some problems occurred!

To overcome these constraints, mentors on the mission were asked to describe how they went about establishing an effective learning relationship. We were looking in particular for what went well – the strengths of the relationships. The surprising data were that, for a mentoring relationship in this difficult environment, the most critical strengths related to sharing values (59 per cent of the examples) and military ethics (30 per cent) (Figure 36.3). From the diaries we classified four types of strength: 'the culture', 'the values' transmitted and identified in the relationship, 'the military ethic' (i.e. all the values that can be traced back to the mentality of a military organization) and the relationship itself.

Further analysis of the category of military ethics demonstrated the importance of being a role model (understanding of the role), with 18 per cent, and 'respect for the roles' (22 per cent) (Figure 36.4 (left)). Figure 36.4 (right) details the values that helped to establish an effective mentoring relationship: 'trust and cooperation' (34 per cent), 'respect' (26 per cent), 'friendship' (11 per cent) and 'hospitality'.

Further analysis (Figure 36.5) indicates that for a really effective mentoring relationship in a military context the key shared values are 'duty and discipline', 'respect and

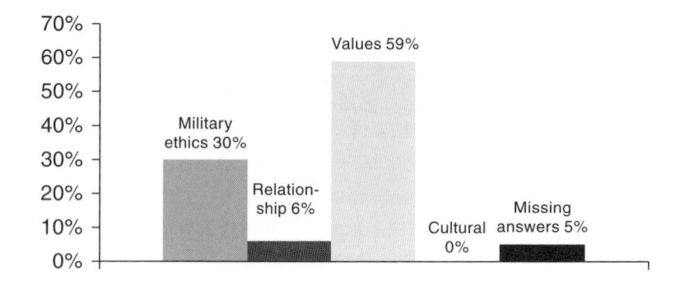

Figure 36.3 Strengths of mentoring relationship

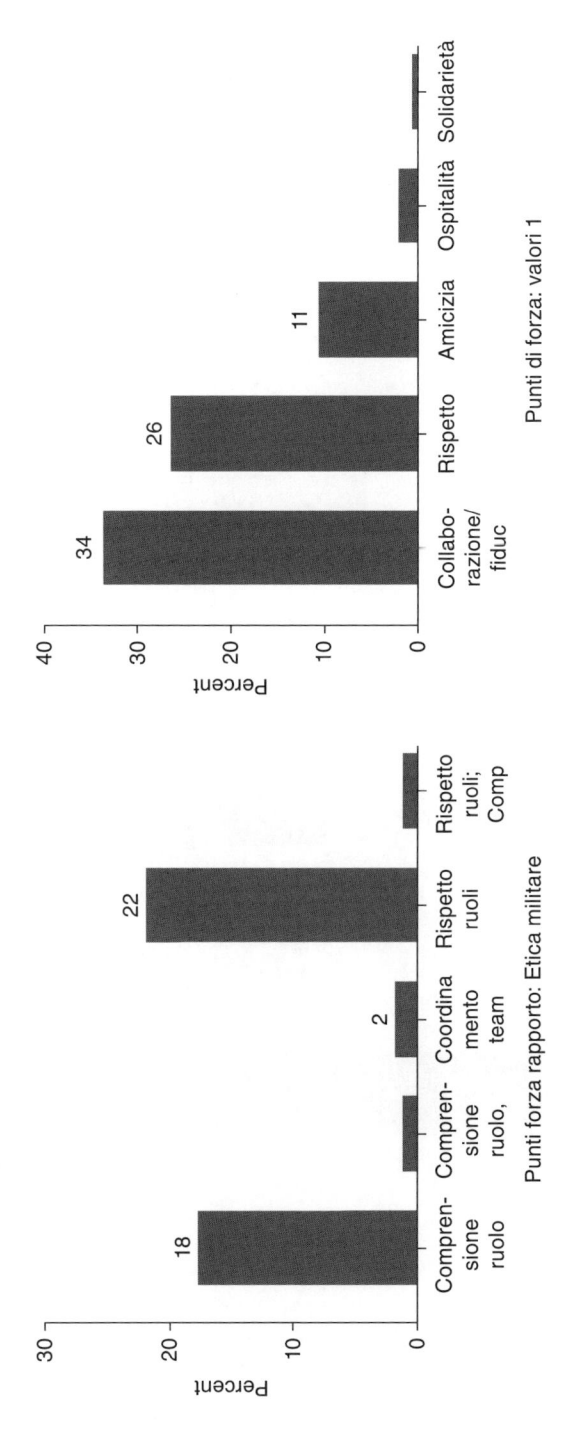

INTERCULTURAL RELATIONSHIPS AND MENTORING 535

Figure 36.4 Details of military ethics and values in mentoring relationships

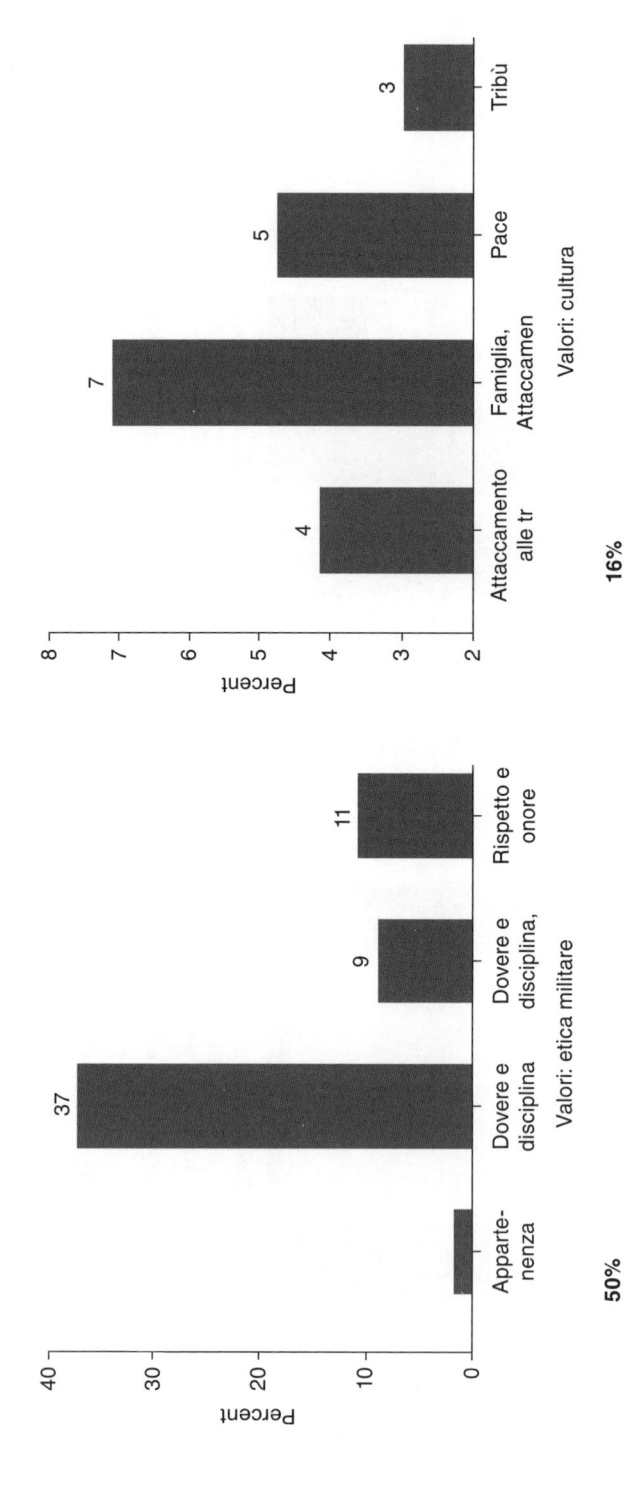

Figure 36.5 Details of values shown in mentoring relationships in the categories 'military ethics' and 'culture'

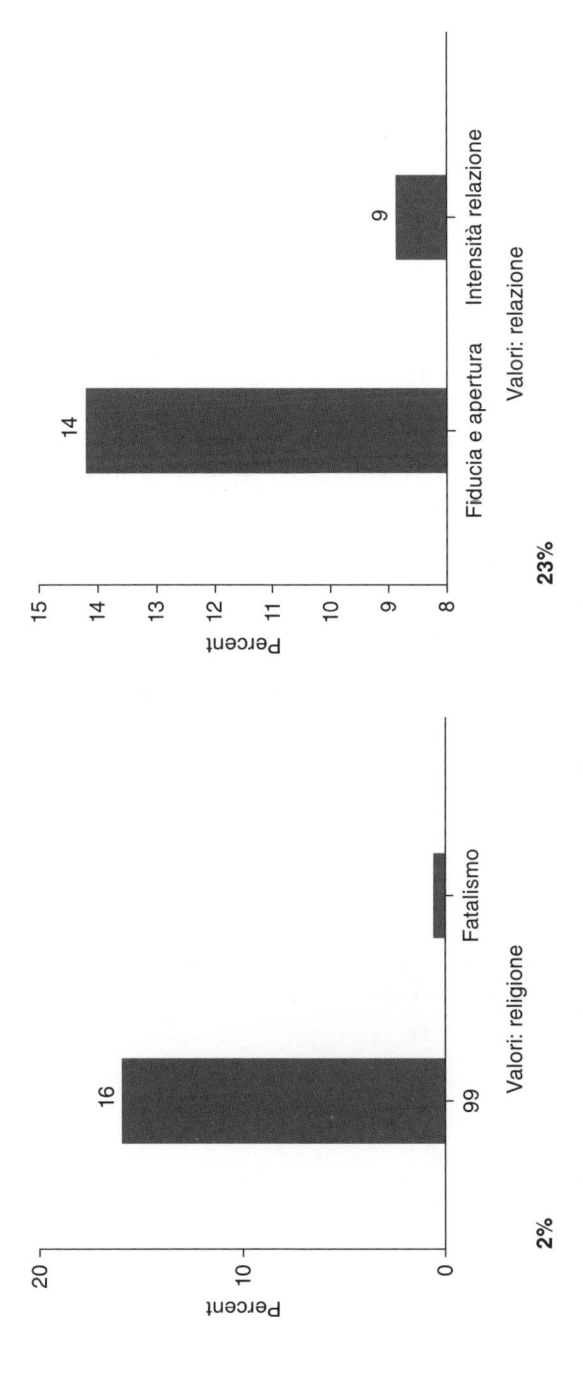

Figure 36.6 Details of values shown in mentoring relationships in the categories 'religion' and 'relationship'

honour' and 'sense of belonging'. Key factors within the category 'culture' are 'attachment to traditions', 'family' and 'peace' – and a small emphasis on tribal loyalty.

Another extremely interesting issue is that resulting from the 'religion' and 'relationship' categories that emerged in attitudes towards the value mentor (Figure 36.6).

It might be expected that religion would play a major role in values applied to mentoring. However, apart from 'fatalism' ('If God wills'), religious values do not appear to be relevant within the mentoring relationship. Another important value category is 'the relationship' itself (23 per cent), which is related to the values of 'trust and openness' (14 per cent) and 'intensity of the relationship' (9 per cent).

The simple data and their classifications indicate clearly that it is possible to have positive and beneficial communication and learning mentoring relationships between very different cultures and religions by focusing on building relationships that have universal value-concepts, or meta values, such as:

- Collaboration and trust
- Respect
- Friendship
- Devotion to family
- Attachment to the traditions
- Peace.

A sub level of communication in our analysis is 'universal and military ethics'. In terms of mentoring rapport, this is related to sharing your professional identity and belonging to the same 'professional community'. In particular, we identified dimensions including:

- Mutual understanding of the roles
- Respect for the role
- Duty and discipline
- Respect and honour.

In this extreme setting and environment, the results support three closely related conclusions:

- It is possible to establish intercultural communication using universal values and meta values
- Mentoring promotes the transfer of professional experience by building a relationship based on trust, listening and shared values
- Mentoring promotes intercultural communication and can be successfully applied in any context (social, business, school, etc.), in which you can meet different cultures and different ethnic groups.

REFERENCES

Aeronautica Militare. http://www.aeronautica.difesa.it
Cameo, ISFOL, 2004.
Perchiazzi, M., Learning Mentoring, Transeuropa Edizioni, Massa, 2009.
Progetto EMPIRE, http://www.filprato.it/10/ita/index.html
Progetto MAITRE, http://www.amitie.it/maitre/it
SIM, www.scuolaitalianadimentoring.com

The Virtual Māori Mentoring Programme, Massey Business School, New Zealand

Vasudha B and Farah Palmer

INTRODUCTION

The ever expanding reach of technology has led, over the past few years, to virtual mentoring finding a place not only in organizations but also in areas such as educational institutions and youth programmes. This has given rise to newer models of virtual mentoring, each with its own set of distinctive features. The Māori Mentoring Programme (MMP), which was first rolled out in 2014, is a virtual mentoring programme for Māori students enrolled as distance students in the first year of the Bachelor of Business Studies course in the Business School of Massey University, New Zealand.

Peer mentoring has been recognized as an effective mentoring strategy for students (Grant-Vallone and Ensher, 2000), and the MMP utilizes some aspects of this approach while bringing in some new and unique features that have made it an extremely successful initiative in Massey University. The MMP benefits both the student mentors and student protégés while simultaneously contributing to the broader objective of Māori development in New Zealand.

THE EDUCATIONAL PIPELINE FOR MĀORI

According to the 2013 New Zealand Census (Statistics New Zealand, n.d.), one in seven people, or 14.9 per cent, of those living in New Zealand belong to the Māori ethnic group, and 12.3 per cent of Māori women and 7.4 per cent of Māori men reported having a bachelor's degree or higher as their highest qualification. These figures were highest for a bachelor's degree (75 per cent) and lowest for a doctorate (1.8 per cent), indicating that Māori students trickled down the educational pipeline as they moved up from a bachelor's to a doctoral degree, even though the total number of Māori with no formal degree had decreased to 33 per cent in 2013 from 39 per cent in 2006.

MENTORING FOR MĀORI STUDENTS IN TERTIARY EDUCATION

Education has been identified to be essential for improving the health, standard of living and employment figures of Māori in New Zealand. However, work and *whanau* (extended-family) commitments often lead to stress among Māori students and significantly influence their decision to study full time or part time and discontinue or underperform in tertiary studies (Koia, 2015).

Mentoring has been recognized as a valuable intervention for increasing the retention and participation of Māori students in tertiary education, where it is understood as the process of supporting the self-development of students in order to motivate and inspire them intellectually (Darwin and Palmer, 2009; *Kaiako pono: Mentoring for Māori learners in the tertiary sector*, 2010). This is evident in the proliferation of mentoring programmes in the tertiary-education sector, such as the University of Auckland's Vision 20:20 programme and Massey University's Te Rau Puawai Programme (Ratima et al., 2007) in the past few years in New Zealand.

Te Puni Kōkiri and Aotearoa National Centre for Tertiary Teaching Excellence's study in 2010 suggested that Māori mentoring programmes for tertiary students provided an environment that aligned with Māori culture and values, in turn influencing student success. This led to increased completion rates and enabled the students to overcome barriers that they faced when they entered tertiary education, such as shyness, isolation and communication issues (Koia, 2015).

MASSEY UNIVERSITY'S COMMITMENT TOWARDS MĀORI STUDENTS

Among New Zealand universities, Massey University has the highest number of Māori students enrolled (22 per cent) and has identified Māori student recruitment, retention and completion as critical factors in achieving the university's investment-plan targets. The successful elements of existing programmes, such as the Te Rau Puawai Bursary Programme in the College of Humanities and Social Science (a well-established programme with proven benefits that has been running since 1999 in collaboration with the Health Workforce New Zealand), as well as other factors influencing Māori student success, including various theoretical models of student engagement, were considered (Greenwood and Aika, 2009; Russell and Slater, 2011; Leach and Zepke, 2011; Nash and Oprescu, 2013) by Massey University in order to develop a plan for the increased recruitment and retention of Māori students (Office of the AVC Māori and Pasifika, 2014).

Providing student support and advisory services is one of the components of this plan, and several approaches are currently being undertaken for achieving this objective. The Te Rau Whakaara Māori Student Advisors approach, which has now been discontinued due to structural changes, was one of the programmes rolled out to enhance Māori student recruitment and retention.

THE VIRTUAL MĀORI MENTORING PROGRAMME, MASSEY BUSINESS SCHOOL

The MMP is one of the more specific strategies employed in the Massey Business School for enabling engagement with Māori students and ensuring their success. This was developed with the intention of contributing to individual student outcomes and also to Māori development in general.

The Office of AVC Māori and Pasifika, Massey University, observed that some of the factors that influence the failure and non-retention rates of university students are their ethnicity (i.e. Māori or Pasifika), being a first-time student and distance study. A 2013 review showed that 33 per cent of all Māori students enrolled in the first year of undergraduate study were in the Business School, the second highest enrolment in Massey University, and 70 per cent of them studied via distance. However, only 47 per cent of distance Māori students passed the papers taken, in contrast to 70 per cent of internal students. Therefore, the distance students were identified as the group likely to have the greatest benefit from the programme.

Massey University came up with the idea of mentoring these students virtually in a joint initiative of the Massey Business School, the National Centre of Teaching and Learning, the National Call Centre and the Office of the AVC Māori and Pasifika. This programme was piloted in September, 2014 for two core papers in the Bachelor of Business Studies (BBS) course, with inputs from Te Rangiwhenua and Te Ohu Whai Pakihi. Te Rangiwhenua is a group established in 2003 with the goal of improving the voice of Māori staff in the Business School at Massey University. Te Ohu Whai Pakihi (Te Ohu) is the Māori Development Working Group that was established in 2013 to deliberate on the objectives of Massey University and the Business School that relate to Māori strategic goals. The MMP was underpinned by Kia Marama 2020 (Massey University's Māori strategy), Massey University's investment plan and New Zealand's Treaty of Waitangi. The Treaty of Waitangi, or Te Tiriti o Waitangi, was the covenant prepared in 1840 and signed by representatives of Māori and the British Crown for the Māori and the British settlers to live together in New Zealand under the governance of some common laws (Archives New Zealand, n.d.). In the present context, the Waitangi Tribunal (since 1975) and the courts have considered the overall ideas, intentions and goals of the treaty and identified its principles on an individual case basis (Te Ara, n.d.). The principles of the Treaty were described as participation, partnership and protection by The Royal Commission on Social Policy in 1988 (Te Ara, n.d.). Some principles of the Treaty have become well established, some have developed over time, while some remain controversial. In light of the principles of the Treaty and Massey's strategic direction, the MMP focused on developing the leadership skills of the student mentors who were seniors (*tuakana*) and at the same time aimed to increase Māori achievement among the distance-mode junior students (*teina*) enrolled in first year of the BBS course.

MMP 2014

A mentoring team was developed that included student mentors, administrative support staff, a mentor Supervisor, Policy and Cultural Advisor from the Office of the AVC Māori and Pasifika and the Chair of Te Ohu Whai Pakihi. The student mentors were supervised by the mentor Supervisor, who reviewed the guidance and advice that they were providing to the student protégés.

The student mentors were internal students based in Palmerston North, New Zealand and selected on the basis of their academic performance and leadership potential. They all identified as Māori and wanted to work towards developing their cultural identity, and they were keen to help other Māori students achieve their academic potential. They were also felt to have the necessary life experience that would enable them to develop a rapport with the distance students and advise them suitably. A total of seven Māori students were selected for this position in 2014. They were all in year two or three and enrolled in business-related papers.

The student mentors were trained to provide mentoring advice on the course and any other academic assistance over the phone and/or by email. A mentoring manual was developed for reference, and weekly telephone sessions (5pm to 8pm) were conducted along with mentoring training sessions. Māori cultural practices like reciting *whakapapa* (genealogy), *pepeha* (introductions) and *mihi* (greetings) to the group, which often included *karakia* (prayer), were introduced into the weekly mentoring sessions. *Pepeha* includes details of where an individual comes from and sometimes their *whakapapa* or genealogy (Mead, 2003). *Mihi* are formal greetings to welcome somebody and *karakia* are Māori prayers believed to increase the chances of positive outcomes in important events (Mead, 2003). The results of this mentoring programme were very positive, with over 50 per cent of students doing very well or with minor issues, and only 16 per cent dropping out during the course. The students appreciated having mentors to guide and support them during the course. As a result of the positive results, the MMP was extended for the year 2015.

MMP 2015

In 2015, the objective of MMP was to begin two weeks ahead of the semester to provide enrolment and workload advice and then continue to offer weekly advice and support on course-related issues during the semester for eight weeks. The students who were targeted for this programme in 2015 were Māori students studying BBS core papers at 100-level by distance and who were in Massey University for the first time.

There were 10 student mentors in 2015 and a Supervisor who organized and supervised the phone-out mentoring sessions on a weekly basis. The mentors spent 3 hours every week on a shift basis to provide enrolment advice (prior to start of the course) and course advice. Their interactions and advice were managed by the Supervisor, who provided another level of advice and was in charge of follow-ups and planning future sessions. Results at the end of semester one indicated an overall pass rate of 75 per cent for the students who participated in the MMP programme. The most recent figures, for 2015, show an 11 per cent improvement in completion rates across all core BBS papers for the semester. Another important outcome was assisting Maori students who would have otherwise failed due to other commitments or issues to withdraw from the course without financial penalty (Koia, 2015). As a result of its success in 2014 and 2015, the Massey Business School expressed its commitment to continue this programme in 2016. Efforts are also in progress to expand this programme into other colleges in Massey University.

BENEFITS

Besides the immediate retention and completion outcomes for Māori students, by supporting them in achieving educational qualifications and enhancing their educational outcomes, the MMP contributes to Māori development by creating leadership-development opportunities for the Māori student mentors. Anecdotal evidence suggests the mentors themselves experience a sense of *kotahitanga* (unity) and *whanaungatanga* (kinship) with each other, forming friendships that extend beyond the mentoring role and communicating regularly through a Māori Mentoring Facebook page. According to Massey Business School, this contribution of the programme towards Māori in Aotearoa is its most valuable aspect.

A preliminary survey suggests that the perceived benefits of the mentoring programme included being able to interact more freely with Māori student mentors than with lecturers when they were struggling, and the reassurance of knowing that if they had trouble with understanding the expectations of academic reading or writing there was someone to help who had recently experienced these papers themselves. Student protégés felt that the first few weeks of the course were overwhelming for most students and it helped greatly to have support during that time, in particular for those with family responsibilities like young children, elderly care, etc., who felt that it was great to know there was support available to them, even via distance. Having Māori student mentors contributed significantly towards forming a rapport with the Māori student protégés and towards the overwhelming success of the programme.

REPLICATING THE VIRTUAL MMP MODEL

The MMP is an example of virtual mentoring in an educational setting that was initially developed for a niche group of people enrolled in specific papers in the Business School at Massey University. However, the success of the programme and the positive outcomes make this a model that can be replicated across other settings and outside of a specific cohort, region or even country. Universities are increasingly leveraging technology to enrol larger numbers of students and expand their reach both nationally and internationally, and virtual mentoring is a natural extension of that strategy. The MMP serves as an excellent example of a virtual mentoring programme that can enable institutions to meet their own diversity goals as well as the larger diversity goals of society.

REFERENCES

Archives New Zealand (n.d.). Treaty of Waitangi – Te Tiriti o Waitangi. Retrieved from http://archives.govt.nz/exhibitions/treaty (accessed 30 September, 2016).

Darwin, A. and Palmer, E. (2009). Mentoring circles in higher education. *Higher Education Research and Development*, 28 (2): 125–36.

Grant-Vallone, E. J. and Ensher, E. A. (2000). Effects of peer mentoring on types of mentor support, program satisfaction and graduate student stress: A dyadic perspective. *Journal of College Student Development*, 41: 637–42.

Greenwood, J. and Aika, L-H. (2009). *Hei Tauira: Teaching and Learning for Success for Māori in Tertiary Settings*. Retrieved from https://akoaotearoa.ac.nz/download/ng/file/group-3846/n3866-hei-tauira—full-report.pdf (accessed 28 December, 2016).

Kaiako pono: Mentoring for Māori learners in the tertiary sector (2010). Wellington, New Zealand: Ako Aotearoa National Centre for Tertiary Education Excellence and Te Puni Korkiri.

Koia, M. (2015). *Māori mentoring report*. Palmerston North, New Zealand: Massey University.

Leach, L. and Zepke, N. (2011). Engaging students in learning: A review of a conceptual organiser. *Higher Education Research and Development*, *30*(2), 193–204. doi:10.1080/07294360.2010.509761

Mead, H. M. (2003). *Tikanga Māori: Living by Māori values*. Wellington, New Zealand: Huia.

Nash, G. and Oprescu, F. I. (2013). From drowning to bouncing: the SKIM model for informing academic processes that are energy-builders rather than energy-suckers. Proceedings of the 16th International First Year in Higher Education Conference: 1–10. Retrieved from http://research.usc.edu.au/vital/access/manager/Repository?exact=sm_creator%3A%22Nash%2C+G%22&f0=sm_creator%3A%22Oprescu%2C+F+I%22 (accessed 30 September, 2016).

Office of the Assistant Vice-Chancellor, Mäori and Pasifika (2013). *Kia Marama* 2010. Retrieved from https://www.massey.ac.nz/massey/fms/About%20Massey/Documents/kia-marama-maori@massey-2013.pdf (accessed 30 September, 2016).

Office of the AVC Māori and Pasifika (2014). *Achieving significant increases in Māori student retention and completion* [discussion paper]. Palmerston North, New Zealand: Massey University.

Ratima, M. M., Brown, R. M., Garrett, N. K. G., Waikere, E., Ngawati, R. M., Aspin, C. and Potaka, U. (2007). Strengthening Māori participation in the New Zealand health and disability workforce. *The Medical Journal of Australia*, 186 (10): 541–3.

Russell, B. and Slater, G. L. (2011). Factors that encourage student engagement: insights from a case study of 'first time' students in a New Zealand university. *Journal of University Teaching and Learning Practice*, 8 (1). Retreived from http://ro.uow.edu.au/cgi/viewcontent.cgi?article=1083&context=jutlp (accessed 28 December 2016).

Statistics New Zealand (n.d.). NZ.Stat. Retrieved from http://nzdotstat.stats.govt.nz/wbos/Index.aspx

Te Ara: The Encyclopaedia of New Zealand (n.d.). Principles of the Treaty of Waitangi. Retrieved from http://www.teara.govt.nz/en/principles-of-the-treaty-of-waitangi-nga-matapono-o-te-triti/page-1 (accessed 30 September, 2016).

Statoil Mentoring Program for Leaders in Projects

Jennybeth Ekeland and Åse Velure

ABOUT STATOIL

Statoil is an international energy company present in more than 30 countries around the world and has high ambitions for international growth. Statoil's largest activities are located in Norway. The company is the largest operator on the Norwegian continental shelf and a license holder in numerous oil and gas fields. The onshore facilities in Norway are active within areas such as gas treatment, crude oil reception, refinement, and methanol production.

THE PLE AND THE PLE MENTORING PROGRAM

The PLE Mentoring program (PLE MP) was carried out from 2005 to 2011, a continuation of the Project Leadership Experience (PLE), a leadership development program initiated by Statoil's Project Academy (PA). The vision of the PA is to develop and sustain a community of project executives, professionals, and leaders that consistently delivers extraordinary short- and long-term project results in dynamic national and international operating environments. The target group of PLE was current and future project leaders, and one of the main targets of the program was to inject more leadership into Statoil's project. Nineteen classes with 21 participants each took part in the PLE, i.e. close to 400 participants (mentees) joined the PLE MP. We estimate that about 150 mentors were engaged, having from one to a record of five mentees.

THE PLE MENTORING PROGRAM

The PLE MP was designed according to the success criteria in the International Standards for Mentoring Programmes in Employment

(ISMPE) and developed and executed according to the North European tradition of mentoring. This tradition puts mentoring in a development context where the main intention is to focus on personal and professional growth and increased awareness as a continuous learning process.

Mentors and mentor training

The Statoil PA nominated the mentors, mainly highly experienced project directors and some line managers/directors. The matching process that followed was run by the program director and AFF lead consultant. Like the mentees, all mentors, including repeat participants, were asked upfront to fill in a form with answers to questions relevant for drawing a picture of their qualities and making the best possible match.

The purpose of the training was to qualify a number of experienced leaders as mentors, and, because of the volume needed, a solid mentor pool was established. The mentor training made it possible to create common ground for the mentors on issues important to Statoil. They were introduced to PLE content, e.g. strategic project leadership, management challenges and dilemmas, the leadership pipeline, and transition thinking.

Objectives and structure

The PLE MP objectives were to extend and strengthen the learning process initiated by the PLE program, with special focus on leadership dimensions to enhance business and project performance. A mentee personal-development plan from the PLE was an important tool in the transition from PLE to PLE MP.

The MP had the objective of strengthening and enforcing learning by:

- Reinforcing concepts
- Adapting to different learning styles
- Providing real-life application to concepts
- Extending skill development
- Strengthening the participants' network
- Sharing best practices.

The MP consisted of three one-day workshops for each of the mentor and mentee classes (max of 42 participants) and one half-day workshop with mentees only. The sessions' specific intent was as follows:

- First, the best start to the relationship (Getting Started)
- Second, calibrating the quality of the relationship and exchanging experience in the early phase (Feeling the Pulse)
- Third, keeping focus on mentee ambitions and proactivity (Energizing the Relation)
- Finally, summing up and formally closing the relationship (Touch Ground).

Two facilitators (one each from Statoil and AFF at NHH Norwegian School of Economics (AFF)) were present at all sessions.

Resources needed and applied

The PLE and PLE MP had strong and conclusive support from the top management. In the early stage of the PLE MP, each mentor received a letter from Statoil CEO Helge Lund about the importance of the mentor role in developing excellent project leaders, thus giving the mentors an important status in the organization.

The PLE initiative was firmly anchored within the Statoil's Project Academy. In addition to a highly qualified administrative staff, a dedicated in-house program director had operational responsibility for the program, alongside their facilitating work in the program. AFF was the external partner in the design and facilitation of both the PLE and the PLE MP.

Reviews and changes

There was a close and exploratory dialogue between AFF and Statoil throughout the program. Midway, a student study gave valuable input. As for the MP, we consistently collected feedback based on participant experiences through a café dialogue at the close of the fourth session. Based on the study, evaluation, and feedback, a few key changes were made:

- The mentoring masterclass was reduced from two days to one through a more intensive learning process, combined with increased time spent on sharing experiences and coaching the mentor group at class sessions.
- In 2009, an online follow-up system was developed and introduced. It had two aims: firstly, to serve as a mentee tool for planning and keeping count of the meetings; and, secondly, to serve as a program-management tool to monitor progress and indicate support and the need for interventions. Not being mandatory, it was only used by about one in two mentees and so did not represent sufficient value-added.

In addition, we looked at content and choice of processes to increase program efficiency, and smaller revisions were introduced.

Changes as a result of mentoring

There was a close link between the PLE and PLE MP, and it is difficult to single out effects from the PLE MP itself. The volume of participants, with more than 550 mentees and mentors altogether, a program period of more than 6 years, from 2005 to 2011, indicates that, in addition to individual and project-team effects, there can be effects on an organizational level. Based on participants' feedback, we believe the program contributed to:

- Organizational development through common language (PLE), extended network (PLE and PLE MP), and development of a culture for learning (PLE and PLE MP)
- More attention to the leadership mindset and the behavioral part of deliveries. Key words from the evaluations and the student study are:
  o Increased self-awareness
  o Distinguishing leadership and management in practical work
  o More precise and courageous communication
  o Importance of motivation
  o Reputation awareness etc.

THE STATOIL HYDRO MERGER

In December 2006, the merger between Statoil and Hydro was announced, with effect from October 1, 2007. From the second half of 2007 the PLE and consequently the PLE MP welcomed participants from the Hydro organization. This was a unique opportunity, intense and thrilling, to explore similarities and differences in project planning and execution, including leadership and management role diversity across the merging companies. From a PLE MP perspective, we observed that:

- There was a positive effect on the integration process (for example, the meetings between mentor and mentee helped the mentee make sense of job opportunities and choices in a new and demanding situation)
- It helped them identify and explore leadership differences between Statoil and Hydro
- It supported the exchange of ideas and experience between organizational units.

The PLE MP seemed to have played an important role, being highly appreciated as an alignment arena by both mentors and mentees.

The student study of the PLE MP

Statoil initiated a study where students at the University of Oslo, from a spread of relevant fields (work and organizational psychology, culture and communication, social studies and social economics), took a closer look at possible effects of the PLE and PLE MP. Data was collected from the pilot class and through to class 6 (a maximum of 150 respondents). The main findings related to the MP part were:

- The MP served a bridging function from the PLE insights into everyday project challenges and dilemmas
- The MP made it easier to focus on and give priority to the PLE development goals and ambitions
- The MP had the function of a grounding arena after a personally challenging PLE.

Based on the survey, 50 percent of the respondents had entered new positions, and there was a payroll increase among the participant group. We cannot document any linear 'cause and effect', but it indicates that the PLE and PLE MP had a career effect, which was one of the intentions of the program. The overall response was that most mentees were very satisfied with the MP and their mentor. The students found a correlation between satisfaction and frequency of meetings.

Challenges

Evaluation, feedback, and the student study outlined some challenges:

- Organizational and top-management commitment seemed to fade after some years.
- Mentor presence at class sessions declined. A hypothesis could be that an attitude of 'Been there, seen that' evolved for mentors over time. It also seems as if ambition levels changed in later stages of the program.
- The geographical distance between mentor and mentee, as a result of changes in job role or location, including international assignments, made it difficult to keep continuity in the meetings.
- Demanding work situations made it difficult for about a third (29 percent) of the mentees to give priority to the meetings with their mentor.

Lessons learned that might be useful to other organizations

- In a two-phase program, the first part with a leadership programme and a second part with a mentoring programme, the second part (PLE MP) would benefit from a more explicit stop and start – e.g. with a new selection process and application renewal for the next step (PLE MP). A new and second selection process could have crystallized commitment to further learning, development areas, and career ambitions.
- An e-mentoring solution would be useful both to compensate for the geographical distance between mentor and mentee but also as an efficient digital tool in itself.
- It is essential that the commitment and involvement of top-management is maintained throughout the entire program. The motivation of both mentors and mentees would likely have declined without this support.
- Mentoring for project leaders can be a very efficient strategy in an organizational learning perspective. Few positions have as many connections and relations as project leaders.
- As the Statoil case shows, mentoring can be a very potent approach when it comes to major organizational changes, such as mergers, in large organizations.
- There should have been more research and measurements on the organizational effects and contributions of such an important, high-profile programme as Statoil PLE and PLE MP.

A Case Study of Mentoring in a Military Context

Wendy Baker and Warrant Officer Viti Flanagan

He aha tee mea nui o te ao? He tangata! He tangata! He tangata!

What is the most important thing in the world? It is people! It is people! It is people! (New Zealand Maori proverb)

The Royal New Zealand Air Force (RNZAF) sits within a bi-cultural European and Maori society, with significant diasporas from the South Pacific, Asia and beyond. New Zealand is considered a modern nation, which in 1893 was the first country where women gained the right to vote. In 2014 the RNZAF became the first armed service worldwide to be awarded gold accreditation by the International Standards for Mentoring Programmes in Employment (ISMPE).

The origins of the RNZAF began in 1909 with the gift of a Bleriot aircraft to New Zealand by the Imperial Air Committee in London. This led the way to New Zealanders flying over the battlefields of Europe in World War One and the subsequent formation of the RNZAF in 1937. Since its inception, and from the bottom of the Pacific, the RNZAF have sent aircraft and personnel worldwide to serve in a multitude of conflicts, peacekeeping operations and humanitarian missions.

Over time, the RNZAF has faced the challenge of remaining nimble during peacetime cutbacks and aircraft acquisitions and upgrades. With fewer than 3,000 personnel, there has been a move from the muscles to the minds of those who serve. It is within this constantly changing military environment that the RNZAF mentoring programme was established in 2008. The initial vision was to embed mentoring capability and processes into the RNZAF culture by providing personnel with the opportunity to further develop their service values of professionalism, integrity and teamwork, while developing leadership attributes and building networks.

When the mentoring programme was conceived the RNZAF was looking for ways to achieve two strategic goals – namely, Resource Optimisation and Enabling Processes – as part of their vision and competency framework. They wanted to foster the potential of their bright, innovative, ambitious and energetic young people. Furthermore, they wanted to tap into the talent of their experienced people. This included utilising the experience, motivation and networks of Senior Non Commissioned Officers (SNCOs) who did not currently have subordinates. It was envisioned there would be natural synergistic benefits if these people were brought together in mentoring partnerships outside the usual strict military hierarchical environment.

With this notion in mind, the RNZAF engaged the services and expertise of the New Zealand Coaching and Mentoring Centre (NZCMC) to assist in the design and implementation phases of a mentoring programme. This collaboration was to ensure the principles of good mentoring practice were blended with the strategic direction of the RNZAF. At the same time a group of volunteers were formed to become the RNZAF Base Auckland Mentoring Advisory Team (MAT). Four months was invested in planning, designing and influencing in the lead up to the launch of the 12-month pilot programme. The 12-month timeframe aligned with the expected life of a mentoring partnership. The pilot programme was intended as a precursor to implementing mentoring across the RNZAF.

The MAT picked up the challenge of holding true to mentoring best practice while operating within a strict military hierarchal environment. For the pilot programme only, mentees were invited by MAT members to participate. This enhanced the probability of early success stories. Subsequent participants were always to be volunteers, in that mentees and mentors self-selected into the programme, which contrasts with the military environment, where compulsion is the norm. It was also important to compare mentoring with coaching in a military environment. In the military coaching often occurs when a less experienced person learns how to achieve particular tasks.

The programme also cut across rank and service areas, resulting in relationships between a mentor and mentee being outside the chain of command and outside trade groups where possible. To reinforce this point, participants attended mentoring training in civilian attire – a break with tradition. Furthermore, it was accepted that sometimes a mentee's goals and aspirations might not always be obviously linked to organisational strategic objectives. Most importantly, the programme was not aimed at personnel requiring remedial training. The programme was in no way meant to detract from the normal trade and general coaching provided in the workplace and there was no connection with performance-management systems. The privacy of the mentoring relationship was considered sacrosanct and could only be transgressed if both parties agreed or if there was a breach of ethics or RNZAF orders.

A great deal of work behind the scenes occurred with developing mentoring programme guidelines – such as clear criteria for selection of mentees and mentors. The potential mentees were junior personnel who displayed self-motivation, commitment to their own goals, capacity to invest time into the programme, including their own time, and commitment to the RNZAF. Mentors were predominantly from SNCOs and above. It was seen as ideal for (but not limited to) those without staff who would benefit from engaging with junior personnel. The pilot recruitment process resulted in 15 mentoring pairs being established who then attended a combined mentee/mentor training workshop run by the NZCMC. On ANZAC Day, 25 April 2008 (a significant day for New Zealanders), the mentoring programme was launched.

During the pilot the MAT was there to:

- Support and encourage the success of mentoring relationships
- Monitor the policy and guidelines
- Promote the programme
- Ensure all participants were trained
- Provide clear communication around expectations

- Review the mentoring process periodically
- Uphold the principles of good mentoring
- Troubleshoot and be willing to problem solve if things went wrong

Fortunately, the existing strengths of the RNZAF provided fertile ground for the pilot programme and increased the likelihood of success. The strengths included: robust equity policies, a strong theme of cultural awareness overlaying day-to-day operations, and an ethical culture. Furthermore, the RNZAF tends to recruit people who align with these values both in uniform and as civilian employees. Additionally, the welfare-support structure is strong and goes back to the beginnings of the RNZAF.

There was a strong correlation between the success of the pilot programme and the support from significant senior ranked personnel. Chief of Air Force, Air Vice Marshall Graham Lintott, championed the programme. He went so far as to attend mentoring training as a participant – a huge leadership statement to the rest of the RNZAF personnel. This combined with the enthusiastic support, encouragement and leadership shown by the Warrant Officer of Air Force, Warrant Officer Keith Gell, who helped drive the programme towards success.

At the end of the pilot, there were glowing evaluations, and mentoring was seen to have the potential to support the intended objectives. Some of the mentoring relationships continued on a less formal basis and this continues to be a theme today. The programme was then rolled out across the RNZAF and the MAT replicated on each Base. While this occurred the NZCMC and RNZAF personnel collaborated to build the internal capacity of the RNZAF to administer, manage and provide the training themselves.

The mentoring programme continued to grow as news of its success spread and participation increased. It grew from a focus on developing junior ranks to being available Air Force-wide for all ranks and civilian staff, plus group mentoring was developed. Due to mentoring programmes not yet existing in the Army and Navy, the Air Force embraced interested personnel from those services. This helped grow the programme from the small pilot in 2008 to close to 700 personnel having participated to date. This has required an Air Force-wide database to manage interest and partnerships and to allow a grand picture of participation.

Throughout this time, there has been continued leadership and budgetary support from subsequent Chiefs of Air Force. The programme maintained its link to the RNZAF's strategic objectives and the day-to-day management and training continued to be run by volunteers. This included a volunteer Air Force coordinator.

As the programme grew in size the challenge for the volunteers was their available time to coordinate the programme, keep policy up-to-date with changes and keep Bases unified in their approach, outside of maintaining the programme's basic principles. Volunteer has been one of the most significant challenges with competing demands of workloads and often deployments.

In 2013 the former Chief of Air Force, Air Vice Marshall Peter Stockwell, asked how the programme currently benchmarked itself. This gave rise to exploring an early programme aspiration of gaining international accreditation. On the advice of NZCMC, the ISMPE accreditation process was used as a benchmarking and review opportunity. As this coincided with the levelling off of MAT volunteer capacity, a part-time RNZAF Mentoring Coordinator position was established in 2014. This position advanced accreditation and took some of the administration tasks such as surveying and reporting from Base MATs. They were also able to focus on mentoring governance RNZAF wide, with a report line directly to the Warrant Officer of Air Force.

During the accreditation journey every area of the mentoring programme was examined, and it became a motivational process taking the programme to another level.

It was a challenge overlaying a non-military compliance framework on the programme. Thinking required reframing and civilian concepts translating into a military context. 'The accreditation allows us to benchmark our own programme against other international organisations. It demonstrates to New Zealanders that the RNZAF is a forward-thinking employer that values individuals for their diversity of thought and action as well as their aspirations' stated Air Vice Marshall Yardley, Chief of Air Force (New Zealand Defence Force, 2014).

The accreditation process underscored that the RNZAF could take pride in the programme which had been created as well as satisfaction from mentoring that was already being done well. The programme was reinvigorated as the RNZAF measured itself against the ISMPEs six core strands (International Standards for Mentoring Programmes in Employment, 2014):

- Clarity of purpose
- Stakeholder training and briefing
- Processes for selection and matching
- Processes for measurement and review
- Maintaining high standards of ethics and pastoral care
- Administration and support

The accreditation core standards prompted investigation into areas that were ripe for development. Checking that participants are aware of the need to regularly review the quality of their mentoring relationship is an example of this. The process resulted in the amendment of every supporting document from policy to marketing flyers and the creation of new material. The intranet website was sharpened to make it a one-stop information centre, and the RNZAF mentoring steering group was created. An annual audit against internal processes and a mid-accreditation-cycle audit against ISMPEs standards was scheduled. An important development was the scheduling of a RNZAF mentoring conference every 18 months.

Internal programme measures were created to allow measurement against standards and to drive performance through improvements. Survey format and questions were improved to align with measures. It improved the critical analysis of survey data, turning it into meaningful knowledge which better informed a participant's thoughts and experiences. In collaboration with the NZCMC mentoring support posts are now delivered throughout a mentoring life cycle.

Feedback from Professor David Clutterbuck, the ISMPE auditor, included the following:

> I was impressed with the high quality mentoring programme in place at the RNZAF and the gold standard is well deserved. In assessing the RNZAF, I found they have strong processes, a high level of ethics and pastoral care, the mentors and mentees are not only committed at the highest level, but also well supported and the programme is delivering measurable benefits. (Clutterbuck, 2015)

The mentoring profile was raised along with expectations of delivery and performance. Managing and meeting these expectations has been made considerably easier with a dedicated RNZAF Coordinator in place.

The RNZAF purposely designed a mentee-centric programme, with the relationship driven by the mentees. However, it was found that mentees are at times hesitant about making contact and procrastinate when they should just 'get on with it'. The training was amended to account for this and mentors are encouraged to foster the mentee being more active to keep the relationship thriving. Mentors know to approach this with a light touch to maintain mentoring principles.

When establishing the programme there was a fair amount of scepticism. There were concerns that the confidential nature of mentoring might undermine the chain of command and that it could be used for remedying sub-standard work performance. The most common misunderstanding is that 'we do it anyway, so why do we need this formalised programme'. The programme continues to dispel these myths through actions, education and sound leadership from the top.

The nature of the military is that personnel are quite mobile, with courses, deployments and postings taking them away from their home Base. This results in regular meetings between mentors and mentees being difficult for some, which continues to challenge the programme. This mobility also affects the capability of Base MATs to fully operate at times. Naturally, there are also security considerations when using other communication channels to conduct mentoring meetings from afar.

The new survey framework has a much higher response rate (over 50 per cent) and extreme responses continue to be good learning points for the programme. The RNZAF are currently raising MAT skills through advanced training and increasing the number of trainers to spread the delivery load, plus group mentoring has been reinvigorated. The Coordinator continues to be the only employee focused solely on mentoring.

Looking to the future there is a focus on increasing the engagement of senior leaders in mentoring. Due to the initial foci on junior personnel, mentoring is not often seen as a personal development tool for senior officers and managers. Exploration of various communication channels for use when partnerships are temporarily apart is also occurring.

The continued support from the top by successive Chiefs of Air Force and Warrant Officers of Air Force is one of the most important factors in the sustainability of the programme. They have been resolute in their support. Mentoring is seen as helpful in building co-learning relationships across the boundaries of rank and job roles, thereby enhancing the qualities that a modern military organisation requires of its service men and women.

When initiating a mentoring programme in a military context, the experience of the RNZAF recommends the following:

- Secure the support of the organisation's top leader
- Make the programme mentee-centric
- Start small and adapt for your culture and any micro-cultures you may have
- Connect with an external organisation to provide advice
- Use benchmarking as a useful tool – it can be a driver of positive change
- Keep the programme design simple and limit bureaucracy
- Have a person dedicated to running the programme as the manager/coordinator
- Select people who are the right fit for MATs, trainers and as the manager/coordinator
- Do not compromise on matches – they are critical to mentoring success
- Create a budget and gain sufficient funds for the programme from initial inception
- Use short simple surveys as feedback tools

REFERENCES

Clutterbuck, D. (2015). NZ Air Force mentors attain ISMPE gold standard. *Coaching at work*, 10(1), p. 7.

International Standards for Mentoring Programmes in Employment (2014). *Accredited assessor's guide April 2014.* UK.

New Zealand Defence Force (2014). *Air Force first international military to be awarded gold standard for mentoring.* Retrieved June 27, 2015 from http://www.nzdf.mil.nz/news/media-releases/2014/20141118-afnwliem.htm.

Sanofi Aventis Case Study, Poland

Mariola Czechowska-Fraczak, Anna Jarzębska and Malgorzata Jastrzebska

Sanofi is a global pharmaceutical company, which has been present in Poland for more than 20 years. Its operations are well established and the company is well respected by clients and customers. Over the past 5 years, Sanofi went through a phase of changing the strategy and enlarging its portfolio. As a result, Sanofi acquired different companies and brands worldwide (for example, Genzyme) as well as in Poland (for example, Nepentes). This created a bigger company, with a very large portfolio and diversified culture, including ways of working, levels of knowledge and competencies of employees. In turn, this created a need for a new generation of leaders.

The company's human capital is no less diversified, with strong female participation and a relatively (in comparison to other European affiliates of Sanofi) young population. There is a wide mixture of generations, including baby boomers and Generations X, Y and Z. The labour-turnover rate is at the general market level; however, it is higher than in other Sanofi affiliates in Europe.

Mind Partners with David Clutterbuck Partnership were contacted by Sanofi Poland in 2013 to discuss possible ways of developing the company's high- and early-potential employees. It was clear to both sides that classic ways of growing leaders were not applicable to this group, which included a high proportion of Generation Y employees. Building a mentoring culture suited the needs of both employees and the company. It was felt that mentoring could flourish in Sanofi, because it met key criteria defined by Clutterbuck:

- support and quality management from the center
- flexibility in delivery in divisions
- shared definition of mentoring, along with localised cultural adaptation.

Both parties agreed that the main goals to be achieved would be:

- Sharing knowledge and experience to make sure that it rests within organisation
- Keeping talent within the organisation
- Increasing motivation and engagement of high/early potentials
- Helping talented employees grow within the organisation
- Initiating cross-company communication and cooperation/breaking down silos.

From the company point of view, Sanofi Poland wanted to develop mentoring as a powerful personal-development and empowerment tool that could help develop a mature and transverse vision of the business. The company believed that mentoring could give huge benefits to mentees – the future leaders – but also to mentors – the current leaders and experts. Mentors would have the opportunity to share their knowledge and experience with younger colleagues, motivating them, reassuring them in their role and increasing their engagement and loyalty.

From the HR point of view, Sanofi Poland wanted mentoring to align with and support other HR initiatives. The organisation wants to see mentoring as:

- flexible
- across all functions
- driven by principles of mutual benefits to both sides: mentees and mentors
- adapted to mentees' and mentors' needs
- relatively informal but with appropriate support and competence.

The organisation wanted to create an environment where asking and giving advice is encouraged.

Additionally, as an objective for the mentees, Sanofi Poland wanted them to:

- benefit from the experience of mentors
- be provided with opportunities to develop:
    - leadership and management skills
    - business and strategic 'helicopter view'
    - strategic thinking and transverse view of the business
- increase their visibility and broaden their networks.

THE INITIAL PLAN/STRATEGY

Mind Partners together with Sanofi Poland HR Department prepared an initial plan/strategy to introduce the mentoring culture within the organisation.

The initial plan defined:

- ways of engaging top management in the process by connecting them to learning and mentoring
- the use of the Human Resources Department not only to coordinate the mentoring process but, more importantly, to be internal experts and support
- suitable time and financial resources.

The strategic planning process covered:

- defining vision, strategy and tactics that would support the implementation of the mentoring culture – in line with *International Standards for Mentoring Programs in Employment*
- knowledge resources (Mind Partners together with David Clutterbuck Partnership were designated to train and supervise future mentors)
- communication strategy directed to specific target audiences in/out of organisation
- advanced matching
- implementation steps (including kick-off meeting, education of mentees)
- mentor supervision.

MENTORING PROGRAMME PLAN

The strategy was presented by the Sanofi Poland HR Director and Mind Partners to the management team in a mentoring style, i.e. via dialogue – mindful listening, asking powerful questions, showing respect for other people's opinions and being patient. Top management quickly became deeply engaged in mentoring, with the first mentors being recruited from that group. Six management-team members decided to play an active role as mentors (at that time this was more than 70 per cent of them). The strategy dialogue ensured that all parties had the same goal in mind: make sure that the Sanofi Poland's top

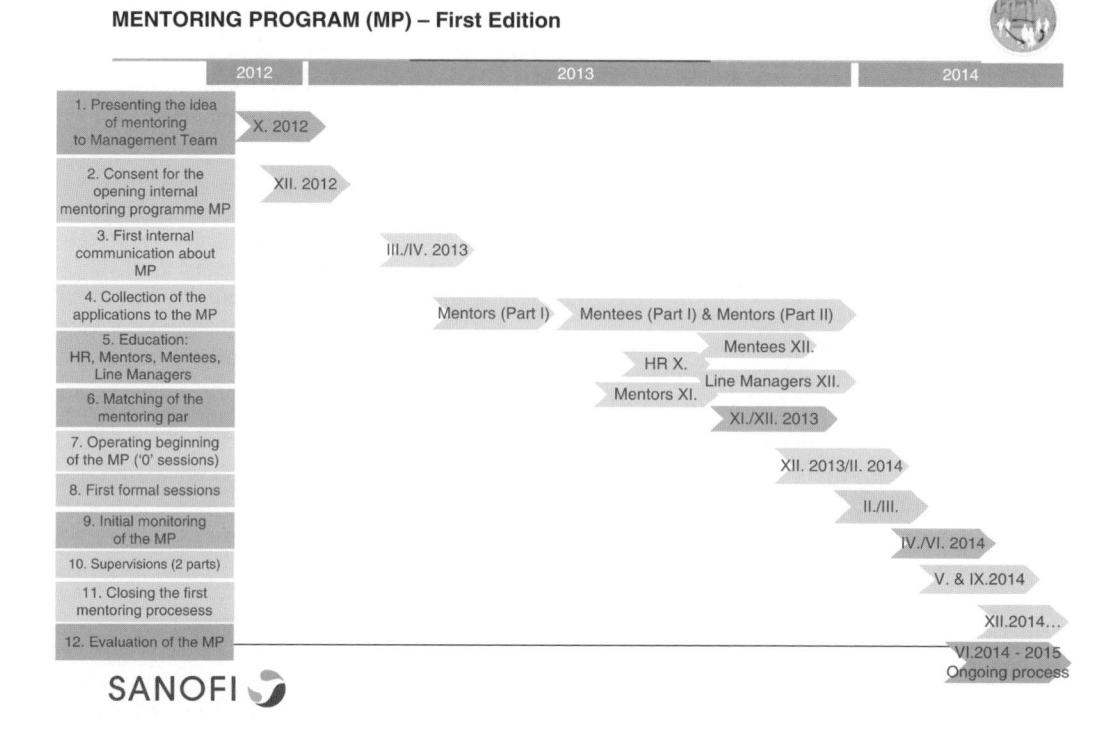

Figure 40.1 First edition of the Mentoring Program – the project flow

talents had the best possible environment in which to grow and help the organisation grow as well.

A Programme Coordinator was tasked with:

- educating all stakeholders
- making sure that all mentoring standards are met
- creating action plans
- matching mentoring pairs
- putting in place ongoing support to all the participants
- keeping in contact with all stakeholders involved
- liaising with external experts
- monitoring and evaluating the whole process.

Key Success Factors to the process included setting goals and measuring them but also implementing well targeted communication and a carefully planned and executed training programme. This covered:

- externally resourced training for the HR team – as a provider of the whole process
- externally resourced training for all mentors
- internal training for mentees – created and led by the Mentoring Programme Coordinator and HR Development Manager
- educational meeting with managers of mentees – delivered by HR
- externally resourced supervision for mentors – two times per cadre.

Communication:

- 360 communication directed to:
    - all participants (mentors and mentees)
    - line managers.

This involved direct communications and personal meetings with Coordinator of the Mentoring Programme (face-to-face meetings), email communication to all the programme participations (mentees, mentors, line managers) and, sometimes, phone conversations with the sales-force mentors.

Effectiveness measures:

- questionnaires to be completed by mentors and mentees separately
- at the same time, individual meetings with all the participants summarising the benefits and challenges coming from participation in the mentoring programme.

Table 40.1 below illustrates the data gathered at the end of the programme.

Lessons learned

- The HR Department didn't suggest any deadlines or time limits for the relationships, allowing mentoring pairs to work together for as long as they needed. It was suggested that they aim to have approximately 10 sessions. We observed that this creates some disorganisation, as some mentees are ready very quickly, while some need a timeframe to follow. In the next edition well defined and communicated timelines will be presented.
- The organisation trained more mentors than it actually needed for the pilot to ensure there would be a mentor for each mentee. However, for the one mentor who was left without a mentee it was not a developmental experience. After several discussions between the mentor and the Mentoring Programme Coordinator they found the reason why the former was not chosen by the mentee – it was because of a lack of managerial experience, which was really important for the mentee – and it was decided that the mentor will be invited to the supervisions to get more contact with real mentoring situations. (It is also interesting that the same mentor take part in the second edition of the programme as a mentee.)
- In the pilot mentoring programme, 15 mentoring pairs were initiated. This proved to be too many for the HR Department to manage effectively with one coordinator, though it now has the experience to do so.
- The programme had an impact on the understanding of both mentors and mentees about the whole diversified business of Sanofi Poland – for example, a mentor from the legal department is now more familiar with vaccine business due to the mentoring relation with a mentee from that division.
- An 'individual approach' during the whole process is needed and expected.
- 'You have the choice' attitude is needed and expected.
- The programme is ideal for introducing and understanding new businesses within the group.
- There is satisfaction on both sides (mentor and mentee): feeling of being 'chosen'.
- Mentoring can be a tool for mentors against burnout (especially for mentors with more than 10 years within a company).
- Mentoring can be used as a framework for a group of mentors who want/are open to advice from another mentor (e.g. business issue, financial issue).

Challenges

- engagement – by the mentee side, if here was no energy and engagement;
- time management – if the mentee did not plan all the meetings with his/her mentor in the early stage of the process; and sometimes the break between sessions was too long (2 months);
- acceptance issue – by the presentation of Mentor, Mentee inform, the Coordinator of the Programme, that it will be better to get another person as a Mentor – of course there was no possibility to choose the Mentor but on the beginning there was such a case;

Table 40.1 Data gathered at the end of the mentoring programme

Mentors	Mentees
The rate at which the goal was realised (0–100%).	The rate at which the goal was realised (0–100%).
What has most influenced achievement of the mentoring goal?	What has most influenced achievement of the mentoring goal?
How has your participation in the mentoring programme in the role of mentor had an impact on your personal development?	Would you recommend participation in the mentoring programme?
Do you want to be a mentor in this program again?	Additional comments/recommendations for improvement.

- concerns on the 'boss side' – there was a situation when the line manager of one of the mentees wanted to know more about the mentoring process of his mentee and the information about the goal was not enough for him.

What the company still has to accomplish

Sanofi Poland HR Department's next task is to complete its analysis of the pilot and communicate what it learns to the organisation as a crucial part of laying the ground for further development of the programme. There is still work to do to consolidate trust and confidence among the management team and the general manager in mentoring as a tool for talent development. Thereafter, further strategies will be put in place to continue the journey towards creating a mentoring culture.

Among ideas being examined are:

- extending the cross-mentoring concept to include pairings with mentors and mentees in other companies
- group mentoring
- continuing the development of mentors through 'mind groups' – peer-to-peer learning groups – as a kind of supervision, where each mentor supports the others by finding the best way to solve mentoring issues and problems (groups of 4–6 mentors with mentoring experience of at least 2 sessions).

The company is also analysing the possibility of setting up more systemic measures of mentoring effectiveness, which would involve collecting data from multiple perspectives, e.g. mentees' superiors. It would lend credibility to the measures and to the programme itself.

TESTIMONIALS

Testimonials - Mentees

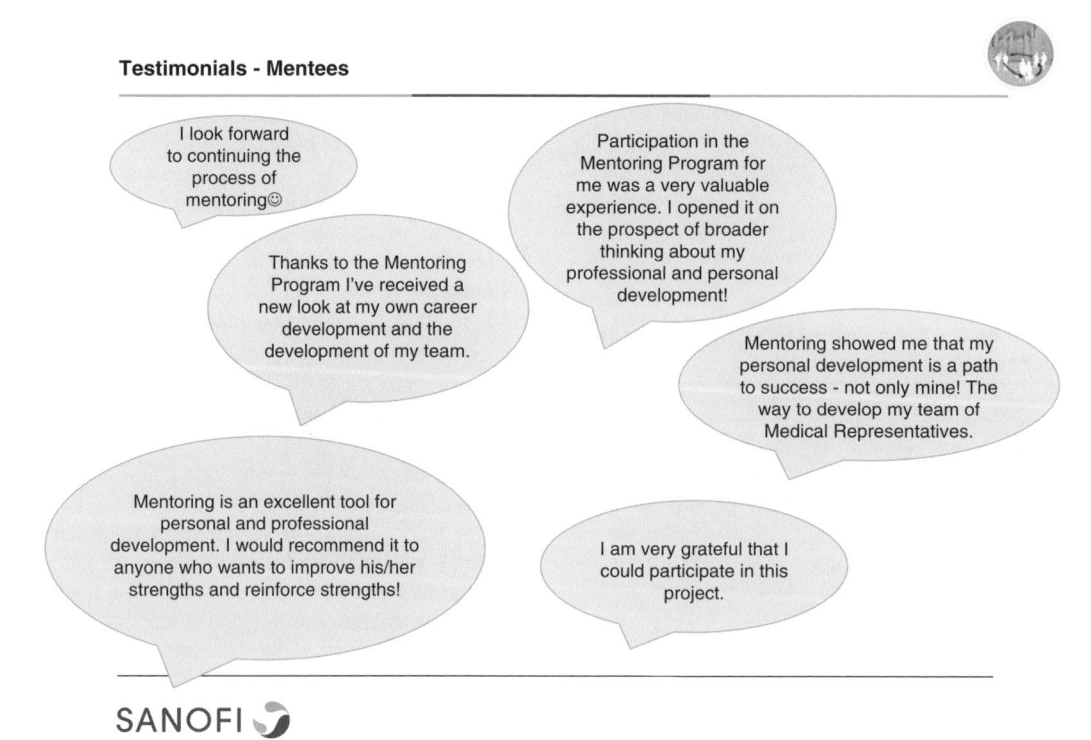

- I look forward to continuing the process of mentoring☺
- Thanks to the Mentoring Program I've received a new look at my own career development and the development of my team.
- Participation in the Mentoring Program for me was a very valuable experience. I opened it on the prospect of broader thinking about my professional and personal development!
- Mentoring showed me that my personal development is a path to success - not only mine! The way to develop my team of Medical Representatives.
- Mentoring is an excellent tool for personal and professional development. I would recommend it to anyone who wants to improve his/her strengths and reinforce strengths!
- I am very grateful that I could participate in this project.

SANOFI

Figure 40.2 Testimonials of the mentee – after closing the first edition of the Mentoring Program

Testimonials - Mentors

- I am delighted with the program :-)

- It's interesting, developing experience integrating people from different areas of the company by such a Program.
I think it's perceived by the mentee as a reward and a unique formula for individual development.

- Each mentoring session with Mentee was very inspiring and stimulating for me.

- I consider this program as a valuable and growing one for people in our organization. It's professional preparation before the start of the program and support during the process (workshops supervisory) provide comfortable conditions for the participation in this program for both Mentee and the Mentor.

- Due to the process itself had during his lifetime greater insight into themselves and their work.
I was able to look at myself from a distance, my behaviors and motivations.
This experience also helped me in a new way to approach the work with my direct team.

SANOFI

Figure 40.3 Testimonials of the mentors – after closing the first edition of the Mentoring Program

The WomenWinWin Mentoring Programme (WWWMP), Portugal

Ana Oliveira Pinto

INTRODUCTION

WWWMP is a one-year programme for women in Portugal who are entrepreneurs and business owners. It exposes mentees to the community of successful entrepreneurs and business owners/developers. It promotes the transfer between them of tacit entrepreneurial knowledge and expertise on how to start a business and develop it in a sustainable way.

The programme was developed within WWW – WomenWinWin – Connecting Business and Women (http://www.womenwinwin.com/), a non-profit organisation based in Lisbon, Portugal. WWWMP's mission is to foster, develop and strengthen women's entrepreneurship through a proprietary technological platform.

The program was launched in July 2014, with 13 pairs. It is now on its second cohort (October 2015–September 2016), with 16 pairs. It is a volunteer programme, so all the support team, as well as the mentors, work *pro bono*. There is sponsorship from a couple of Portuguese companies, as well as partnerships with a few other international organisations and individuals.

THE PROGRAMME'S MISSION, PURPOSE AND GOALS

The mission of WWWMP is to deliver quality business mentoring to enhance women-owned businesses in Portugal. The professional/business accomplishments resulting from the mentoring relationship are the main purpose of the programme, but the impact of the program has already proved to be broader – it fosters participants' self-confidence and self-esteem, which in turn propels initiative, courage and an entrepreneurial mindset (attitude and vision).

Besides this, WWWMP aims to influence at a systemic level, by:

- recognising the distinctive nature of female entrepreneurship (motivational factors, problems and challenges) and, thus, suggesting practical recommendations to enhance female entrepreneurship in Portugal
- sharing mentoring best practice and serving as a sounding board on mentoring-programme design and execution for women entrepreneurs/businesswomen.

PROGRAMME CHARACTERISTICS

One-to-one relationship

The programme entails a one-on-one mentoring relationship within a year. WWWMP suggests that mentor and mentee meet at least once a month.

Synergy mechanisms

Besides the core one-to-one mentoring relationship, the programme includes other mechanisms that make use of the possibilities of being in a group and in a structured programme. The aim is to promote a community of learning, resources and support, where synergies and diversity of thought are possible, as well as to contribute to developing within the mentees a mindset where time to reflect and learn is valued and where they are able to make more strategic and meaningful decisions. These mechanisms are:

- Thematic group mentoring sessions (three)

These sessions are 4 hours in length, entail the invitation of an entrepreneur/business expert and are based on the philosophy of action learning.

- Buddy system

We suggest that mentees regularly meet with one or a few other mentees during the one-year mentoring programme to make an alliance of support and encouragement, with the clear purpose of being mutual sounding boards, particularly with regard to the mentoring process and the issues that they are being mentored on.

- Alumni

The alumni scheme is a mechanism to provide sustainability and momentum for former mentees continuing their development work and to broaden their net of relations by connecting with new mentees (and mentors) of the following cohorts, potentially expanding the program's impact going forward and contributing to creating an expanded learning community.

Entrepreneurial mindset profile (partnership with Eckert College, Leadership Development Institute)

The EMP – Entrepreneurial Mindset Profile (http://edpmindset.com/) – is a self-assessment questionnaire developed by Eckerd College Leadership Development Institute, based on extensive research into the traits, motivations and skills of entrepreneurs. The EMP tracks both the personality and the cognitive style, or mindset, of the women entrepreneur, using 14 items. Mentees have the opportunity of getting a debriefing of their results from a qualified coach in a 4-hour group feedback session. They also receive a Development Guide with suggestions for development, recommended resources and guidelines for successful action planning.

Mentees have the opportunity to do this self-assessment at the beginning of their mentoring journey and also at the end, providing them with a perspective on how they have changed. Mentors also give the mentees their perceptions at the end, enriching the analysis and contributing to mentees being more aware of their characteristics and attitudes towards entrepreneurship. The EMP is also a powerful wake-up call to mentees, as it enables a broader sense of what is needed to be an effective entrepreneur and the style of life required. Mentors also have the opportunity to do the same self-assessment.

Support and follow-up

Another factor relevant to the success of WWWMP is the periodic follow-up (by telephone or in person, at least four times during the programme) with both mentors and mentees. This is done by part of the WWWWMP team (the 'Angel') and its aim is to reinforce the sustainability of the mentoring process by providing time to analyse progress and the mentoring relationship, put things in perspective, assure alignment with the philosophy and positioning of the programme and contribute to the accomplishment of the mentee's goals and the mentor's and mentee's expectations.

In this second cohort, there is the additional aim of providing support for mentors in a group setting each quarter. We facilitate a peer-group session, where mentors can share with each other their mentoring experience and approach, giving them the opportunity to be more conscious of their mentoring style and proficiency in mentoring skills. Another objective is to tap into mentors' tacit knowledge and incorporate their tools, approaches and strategies into the Mentoring Manual written for cohort one and revised for cohort two.

Matching process

We believe that the mentoring relationship is more likely to be successful if the match is successful. Therefore, there is always a rationale for the matching, and significant investment is made in making this process effective, transparent and open.

The WWWMP team takes responsibility for proposing the matches between mentees and mentors, beginning with a rigorous application process. Based on this, the team matches each mentee's development needs and expectations with mentors' experience and skills, paying attention to the perception of good chemistry and fit in order to foster a learning environment where trust and sharing are fundamental. There is also a values-and-style analysis in the matching, intuitively used, which has proved to be relevant.

The matches are validated by the mentee and mentor, but the WWWMP team considers it important to propose pairings, because it knows the mentor pool and can add value in supporting the mentee's understanding of their needs, personal characteristics and developmental priorities.

The application process starts with accessing information about the programme (its philosophy and goals, code of conduct and expected responsibilities) and the pre-selection requirements for participating, which are as follows:

For mentees to:

- have a desire to substantially grow their business
- display internal and external integrity as a business owner
- be willing to invest the time – meet with a mentor at least once per month and attend 75 per cent of the programme's initiatives.

For mentors to:

- be a veteran business owner or a top-level executive with experience in starting or restructuring a business
- be willing to openly share business know-how (both successes and failures)
- be willing to commit to meeting with a mentee regularly for one year, at least once per month
- act on a voluntary basis – that is to say, without remuneration – and commit to refrain from direct involvement in the company led by their mentee for two years following the end of the mentoring programme.

The second element is to complete the application. The application form (available online) aims to enable participants to provide not only general personal information but also to reflect on and record other relevant items about their business and expectations relating to WWWMP. It asks mentors and mentees to describe their preferences, personal interests, areas of expertise, availability, experience as a mentor/mentee and reasons for participating in the programme.

The mentees are also asked to provide as far as possible a clear outline of their goals and learning objectives and corresponding criteria for measuring success measurement criteria. They are asked to provide their professional biographies, too.

Afterwards, mentees are interviewed at two different points by two different WWWMP team members. This enables the team to 'get a sense' of each mentee candidate.

Finally, a selection committee analyses the completed applications to make decisions on matching mentors and mentees.

So far this matching method has worked very well. Participants have said that the fit is successful and, in fact, one of the critical factors in the effectiveness of the programme.

Quality assurance, evaluation and continuous improvement mindset

WWWMP aims to add value to women entrepreneurs. That is why we set high standards – and we are aware that a lot is at stake by making this explicit. The design of the WWWMP is based on the ISMPE – International Standards for Mentoring Programmes in Employment (http://www.ismpe.com/) and benefits from cooperation with David Clutterbuck (http://www.davidclutterbuckpartnership.com/) as well as Gaby Marcon Clarke (http://www.shinepeopleandplaces.co.uk/). The WWWMP also entails a structured evaluation of each cohort, with a mid- and end-programme surveys.

LESSONS LEARNED AND FUTURE CHALLENGES

The first cohort of WWWMP was a pilot and enabled us to test some solutions and gain a clearer notion of what is required to make the programme as impactful and effective as possible. The second cohort will be a further test to consolidate some of our views and assumptions.

A key lesson is that the determination to make the programme a valuable experience for participants has been critical. This mindset stresses the importance of choosing the right people (both in the management team and as participants). We observe that there is an attitude and competence profile that is particularly suitable for implementing and participating in a volunteer mentoring programme. The characteristics that we have perceived as being relevant include a sense of ownership and commitment, a solutions-focused mindset, the ability to see opportunities in difficult situations, a bias for action, resilience and a willingness to make the difference.

To go full circle, it also seems that to guarantee involvement of the right people you need to operate at a high standard of service and really add value for participants (team members included). To make this happen requires following up closely on what is happening on the ground, and this clearly requires investment of time, energy and discipline. Mentoring is a resource-intensive investment, and the sustainability of a volunteer mentoring program is in itself an issue.

There are other lessons related to the mentoring itself and aligned with the mentoring literature, including the following:

- It is important to clarify what mentoring is and is not, and to be clear and transparent with participants about what they can expect from mentoring and what it entails in terms of roles, responsibilities, expectations and principles of operation. This is fundamental to guarantee effectiveness in the mentoring relationship.
- There are, definitely, special issues within entrepreneurial and business mentoring for women – addressing the psychological and belief system is as important as addressing the business issues and challenges. Also, the rhythm and length of sessions in business mentoring should be

tailor-made, especially compared with corporate mentoring/career-development mentoring. The first cohort showed that mentees' needs varied greatly according to their specific developmental requirements, the personal styles of both mentee and mentor and the contextual constraints and specificities of mentee and mentor.
- Mentoring can be of great value for both parties involved – it prompts self-reflection and, therefore, self-awareness, and it challenges thinking, enabling fresh insights, different perspectives and possibilities. This is true for both mentees and mentors.
- The results of the first cohort show that mentees valued highly the mentoring component of the programme, and that, as a result of their participation in the programme, they are willing to become mentors themselves, as a way to give back.

Mentoring others is an instinctive behaviour for many people. This can be a challenge, especially within a hierarchical and patriarchal culture, such as that which persists in Portugal, where every successful businessman/woman is automatically perceived to be a good mentor and a role model for leadership. It takes additional effort and investment to support and educate mentors in developing their ethical practice and in their continuous personal development as mentors and leaders. Similarly, it takes additional effort to educate women mentees in how to benefit most from the mentoring relationship and programme. This is especially so in the context of mentoring women on their entrepreneurial and business development journey. Having a busy and stressful day job running their businesses makes it difficult to find the time and energy to build the skills of mentoring and being mentored and to engage in the reflection needed for the critical tasks of sharing knowledge, exchanging experiences and tracking what really delivers results and adds value.

Youth Business International

Hoang Anh Thi Le and Laura Rana

Youth Business International (YBI) is a global network of 47 independent non-profit organisations ('members') spanning 43 countries, enabling aspiring young entrepreneurs (aged 18–35) to start and grow sustainable businesses with the potential to employ local people, build local supply chains and strengthen local communities. The YBI network is facilitated by a London-based Network Team, which co-ordinates and leads global activity and has responsibility for driving network growth and quality, including through the delivery of capacity development services to members. As such, our network combines global expertise with local experience.

YBI operates across high-, medium- and low-income countries – we are mandated to work anywhere with a youth-unemployment challenge, which means our work covers a wide range of contexts, from Argentina to Australia, Bangladesh to Belgium. Our members provide integrated support to underserved[1] young entrepreneurs, which typically include training, mentoring and other business-development services, combined in many cases with provision and/or facilitation of finance (generally loans). YBI members adapt this support to the needs and opportunities in their local context, working in partnership with governments, businesses and multilateral and civil-society organisations.

In 2014, YBI supported the start-up, strengthening and growth of 20,696 youth-led businesses.[2] Mentoring is often a key part of the support package that our members provide to young entrepreneurs. It is also a vital ingredient in the success of that support package, helping to ensure any finance is used effectively and complements the non-financial elements. Moreover, it is central to what makes the YBI model unique, distinguishing our approach from other microcredit-centred initiatives. Our network currently encompasses over 15,000 volunteer business mentors. These mentors are largely drawn from the local business community, most commonly from the SME (small- and medium-sized enterprise) community, occasionally also complemented with employees of large corporations, both national and international.

A successful mentoring relationship can significantly enhance young entrepreneurs' success. Mentors inspire and empower the young entrepreneurs they support to reach their personal and professional potential. Mentees can turn to their mentors for a wide range of support, from gaining particular skills they need to run their businesses to simply providing a source of encouragement. Mentoring relationships build self-confidence and self-reliance. Experience from across the YBI network suggests that when mentoring is delivered in a structured and professional way, it can make a real difference to entrepreneurs, reducing their risk profile and enhancing their personal and commercial credentials.

By unlocking the collective power of the business community, volunteer mentoring has the potential to have a transformative effect. YBI's global research has shown that 84 per cent of the entrepreneurs supported felt more confident running their business as a result of the non-financial support they have received, highlighting mentoring in particular.[3]

Research by our Canadian member, Futurpreneur Canada (previously the Canadian Youth Business Foundation), found that their annual loan-write-off rate decreased steadily from 11.4 per cent in 2004, when mentoring became mandatory for entrepreneurs, to 5.7 per cent in 2010.[4]

How we work

YBI provides a number of capacity development services to our members in the area of mentoring.[5] These include but are not limited to:

- Supporting members to build formal, structured mentoring programmes through YBI's flagship mentoring capacity development support
- Helping members to strengthen their existing mentoring programmes through targeted support
- Providing remote Skype coaching to members' Mentoring Managers
- Hosting global mentoring master-classes, in which members are invited to share innovations and challenges and learn from world-leading experts
- Providing access to an online mentoring community, through which members can share good practice and news and access YBI's resources. The aim of the online group is to foster a stronger sense of being part of a global community.

YBI's flagship mentoring capacity development support

YBI provides members with intensive capacity development support for the full design or redesign of a member's mentoring programme. This currently encompasses two in-country workshops: (1) YBI's Methodology Build Workshop and (2) a Bespoke Workshop, which is supplemented by additional remote support for 12 months.

The **Methodology Build Workshop** is an interactive workshop (typically lasting three days) that takes members through the step-by-step processes involved in building a mentoring programme. It is also an opportunity for staff and relevant stakeholders to participate as 'mentors' in YBI's mentor-induction training. This enables the implementing team to learn what mentoring is and gives them exposure to the knowledge, skills and attitudes needed for a successful relationship. For external stakeholders, it is an opportunity to engage with the mentoring programme before its launch. YBI also takes members through the mentee-induction workshop so they understand its importance. By the end of the workshop, members have a clearer understanding of the steps they need to take to build a formal, structured mentoring programme.

When the member is ready, YBI will run a **Bespoke Workshop** based on the needs of the member. Typically, this will take the form of a 'train the trainer' workshop but may also encompass other support interventions such as supporting the member with matching or performing a mid-term evaluation of the pilot. In the case of a 'train the trainer' workshop, which is an active, skills-building workshop (again, typically three days), members are given the opportunity to learn the content and practise the facilitation skills they will need to deliver their own mentor- and mentee-induction workshops. The workshop includes a variety of learning opportunities, such as understanding mentoring models, skills development and skills practice. It is structured around a highly participative and experiential learning process, with many opportunities to practise skills, share experience and receive developmental feedback.

Throughout a YBI mentoring capacity development intervention, YBI's mentoring team is available to support and coach members through phone calls and web conferences. This remote support follows a structured process and colleagues are encouraged to complete a development plan and reflection notes. In addition to this one-on-one support, colleagues also receive full access to YBI's mentoring knowledge library and the online community.

As a result of YBI interventions in this area, mentoring managers, mentors and entrepreneurs have seen the immediate benefits of the implementation of a structured and formal mentoring programme:

> PerMicroLab's mentoring programme is professional and well-structured in comparison with other volunteering initiatives. Our mentors like the fact that they're involved in a serious organisation who cares about them, as shown by the fact that we offer a structured recruitment and training process... we don't just take anyone in, I care about quality! (Federica Paviolo, Mentoring Coordinator, Youth Business Italy)

KEY LEARNING

- Experience from the network suggests that if a member is building and launching a brand new mentoring programme, or if they are going to make a large-scale change to their existing mentoring programme, starting with a pilot is a sensible option. A pilot is important to test new systems and processes and then make the necessary changes before launch or 'going live'. The pilot is an excellent opportunity to solicit both positive and constructive feedback.
- We have found that for members launching a pilot mentoring programme, 25 mentoring relationships is a realistic and manageable target, as it can help the organisation to obtain a clear picture of what is and isn't working but doesn't create unrealistic expectations of major change in the organisation. For organisations that may have national operations with a number of regional centres/offices, we recommend that no more than two centres launch a pilot.
- It is important to understand that the mentors are first and foremost volunteers and, as such, it is not only a mentoring programme they are implementing but a *volunteering programme*. Volunteers can offer a number of services to an organisation besides mentoring – for example, training support, coordination of mentors, etc., and therefore our members need to ensure that their volunteers experience a professional and structured end-to-end process.
- Implementing a volunteer mentoring programme will mean gradual but significant change to the organisation and its offering to entrepreneurs. If an organisation's field officers or loan officers have previously provided mentoring or coaching-type services to entrepreneurs, it's important to have their buy-in, as a mentoring programme may lead to a significant change to their roles.
- For YBI, the mentoring team needs to understand that a mentoring programme involves significant change for a member. This means it has been crucial for those leading on mentoring capacity development in YBI to understand organisational-change methodology to ensure the success of projects we are supporting.
- A mentoring manager or coordinator is fundamental to the success of an organisation's mentoring programme. The organisation may choose to involve a number of staff in the mentoring programme, but it is essential to establish a main point of contact and authority who has the capacity and authority to manage the programme overall. They will manage every aspect of the mentoring programme and be its main

ambassador and contact point for the mentors and mentees.
- It may seem premature to think about succession planning, but it is an essential part of the planning process and therefore needs sufficient attention. In the YBI network, mentoring programmes have failed because the mentoring manager has left with key institutional knowledge and no safeguards to protect the systems, processes and relationships they have created.
- As the YBI approach to mentoring is often such a new concept for organisations to implement, it is really important to get buy-in from senior management from the outset. In Spain, for example, having senior staff attend the initial training workshop on mentoring meant they were able to see what it was all about and understand its value, which made them very committed to and supportive of the mentoring programme going forwards. Indeed, the mentoring manager highlighted that the head of her organisation has himself become a mentor with the organisation.
- It is important to train multiple members of staff so that expertise is not lost if the key staff member who receives the support leaves the organisation.
- Where possible, securing local pro bono support from e.g. a local consultancy firm can add valuable project management skills to the team. Several YBI members have benefitted from local consultancy support to develop their mentoring strategy and implementation plans to provide valuable support to implementation plans.
- Rolling out our online mentoring community, known as the 'Mentoring All Stars', has shown us that for communities of practice to be most impactful, the person leading the community (in this case YBI's Head of Mentoring) needs to engage in active facilitation (posting relevant content from within and beyond YBI's knowledge library, tagging group members, etc.) and promotion (for example, raising awareness of the benefits of joining the community during in-country visits to members).
- Stakeholders generally understand the positive effects mentoring can have on an entrepreneur's personal and professional development. However where possible, monetising the financial contribution of mentoring may help stakeholders to understand the monetary value of mentoring. One of our members found that the volunteering mentoring services provided by their mentors over 12 months was the equivalent of £1.2m – their stakeholders definitely took notice!

Challenges

Volunteer business mentoring is a new concept in many of the countries we work with. However, we have found that volunteering exists in every culture whether it is through religious organisations, local charities, schools, etc. Our members have started to engage more widely with these organisations in order to attract individuals who are interested in giving their time and sharing their business knowledge. Local business associations, such as the local chapters of Rotary or Lions Clubs, Chambers of Commerce, or other local equivalents, are great sources of business mentors.

There are a number of languages spoken across our network, one of the predominant ones being Spanish. To support our Spanish-speaking members, YBI has trained mentoring managers from Spain and Argentina to deliver YBI's methodology with our Latin American members. YBI's future strategy is to engage a number of network advisors to work regionally using the YBI global methodology tailored to the local context.

Success stories

YBI's capacity development methodology is unique in the entrepreneur-mentoring space, and YBI is seen as a trailblazer in the sector. We have advanced our position as a thought leader through the development of resources such as a Guide to Group Mentoring and a series of advanced-mentoring workshops, as well as a highly successful online community of practice, enabling global-level knowledge and experience-sharing.

In Spain, the youth-unemployment rate between the ages of 16 and 24 has soared to 57 per cent. Tomillo (an organisation based in Madrid) and Autoocupació (based in Barcelona) independently provide start-up support to entrepreneurs of all ages and jointly have over 30 years' experience in training, technical support and access to finance. However, they both lacked the provision of post-start-up support for the entrepreneurs they supported. Drawing on the technical experience of YBI, Youth Business Spain embarked on the building of a high-quality volunteer business-mentoring programme to extend and improve support for entrepreneurs to improve their chances of creating successful and sustainable businesses.

In 2013, YBI provided 12 months of support to Youth Business Spain to build and launch Spain's first volunteer business-mentoring programme. Currently, Youth Business Spain has nine delivery partners (Ronsel, Gaztenpresa, Maimona, Creas, Aprofem, Aire, Mentor Day, Tomillo and Autoocupació) that have supported over 700 entrepreneurs with one-to-one business mentoring. By 2018, together with their regional partners, it aims to reach its ambitious target of 2,500 mentoring relationships.

In Uganda, an estimated 380,000 youths per annum are released into the job market to compete for a mere 90,000 jobs. As such, about 25 per cent of them are absorbed and the remaining 75 per cent remain either unemployed or underemployed. Enterprise Uganda's mission is to develop a new generation of dynamic Ugandan entrepreneurs by actively providing support to micro-, small- and medium-scale enterprises and corporate organisations to enhance their productivity, growth and competitiveness. In 2013, YBI embarked on a project to help Enterprise Uganda to design and implement a volunteer business-mentoring programme. By April 2015, 362 entrepreneurs had access to mentoring services, and recent evaluations have found that one hour of mentoring per month contributes US$50 to a business's operation.

Notes

1 For YBI, under-served means unable to access the financial, knowledge or human capital needed to start and grow a business.
2 YBI (2015) Network Review 2015, http://www.youthbusiness.org/wp-content/uploads/2015/07/YBI_networkreview_inside-2015-Art.pdf
3 http://www.youthbusiness.org/wp-content/uploads/2012/08/YouthEntrepreneurshipSurvey2011.pdf
4 http://www.youthbusiness.org/wp-content/uploads/2012/08/BeyondCollateral.pdf
5 In addition, we have capacity development programmes in the areas of entrepreneurship training, monitoring, evaluation and learning, and technology, and we are in the process of developing a programme focused on social entrepreneurship.

Mentoring in Music and the City: A Comparison of Schemes for City Businesswomen and High-Performing Early-Career Professional Musicians

Esther Cavett

BACKGROUND AND CONTEXT

This case study compares two mentoring schemes in operation as at August 2015, both designed by the author. Each involves business people as mentors, but they have very different mentee populations and the schemes are very different sizes. The contrasts and similarities between the way the schemes were set up and run may assist others considering the best formulation for their own mentoring scheme.

The first scheme, the Citymothers Scheme (CMS), which the author oversees on an ongoing basis, was started in June 2014. Following the reporting date of this chapter, the CMS was opened to men as well as women mentees. It is a programme for the networking organisation Cityparents (http://www.cityparents.co.uk), which is a membership organization of over 10,000 working parents in the City of London, and was started in response to member demand. The scheme has paired around 400 mentors and mentees and 'offers a supportive and confidential environment in which to discuss and think through issues regarding a mentee's work and parenting role from the perspective of managing her career and work-life balance'. Mentees are mothers with ages ranging from mid 20s to late 40s, working in junior to senior positions within largely City-based jobs; mentors can be male or female and are more senior in their profession than their mentee. The mentoring relationship is assumed to run for a year within the scheme (though it might continue longer than that informally), with pairs meeting approximately every six weeks. Mentees pay a nominal fee, which goes towards the cost of administration.

As a consequence of her experience with the CMS, the author was commissioned to advise the staff of the City Music Foundation (the 'CMF', see http://www.citymusicfoundation.org) on structuring and delivering their mentoring scheme (the 'CMFS') for early-career musicians selected by competitive audition (the 'mentee' can be an instrumental combination, such as a duet partnership or ensemble, rather than an individual). This is a relatively new organization, providing support by means of professional-development seminars and workshops, and artistic and now business mentoring. The mentors are 'senior business people who offer their own perspective on how CMF Artists can strategically build a business – the business of being a successful performing musician in the 21st Century'. The scheme has approximately 15 mentoring pairs each year, who are asked to meet at least once a quarter over the course of a year. A special feature of the scheme is the transfer of skill in one area (business) to people who are highly skilled in another (musical performance).

The impetus for setting up the scheme came from discussions between the CMF and the Bank of New York Mellon (BNYM), a large international investment bank, which has a record of supporting the arts and a strong tradition of providing internal mentoring for its staff; BNYM provided the majority of mentors. The CMF does not charge artists or mentors for their involvement in the scheme.

APPLICATION PROCESS

The very different sizes of the schemes led to different application processes. The CMS invites applications twice a year, in contrast to some other large schemes where people can apply throughout the year. This frequency was chosen because matching is done on the basis of mentees requesting mentors to have certain characteristics and mentors offering skills in particular areas, so the larger the pool, the greater the chance of good matches. All members of Citymothers are notified that an 'application window' is open for a period of approximately two weeks, and some detailed FAQs are available on the website explaining the application process and ethos of the scheme. Citymothers staff do not have capacity to answer individual queries routinely, so all information about the scheme needs to be available on its webpage.

Applicants for the CMS fill out a Survey Monkey (www.surveymonkey.com) electronic application form, which has evolved during the life of the scheme. Mentors and mentees provide information to assist matching, including their age, type of job, years of experience in that area of work, ages of children and preferred location for meeting. The mentee form lists a number of skills, such as work/life balance, inter-office relationships, developing business acumen, parenting and so on, and asks applicants to prioritize the areas they wish to focus on with their mentor; there are also free-text questions such as 'what would you wish to gain from a mentoring relationship?' and 'what experience in your mentor might be most useful to you?'. The mentor forms have a parallel sequence of questions. Mentors rank the skills they feel most able to assist mentees with and answer free-text questions including 'what might you bring to a mentoring relationship and what might you gain from one?'. Mentors also provide an anonymised biography, and the second stage of the matching is to send all mentee applicants a copy of these biographies so they can indicate their 'top picks', thus involving them in the selection process. Due to the size of the scheme Women Ahead (www.women-ahead.org) have assisted with the matching.

For the CMFS, the application process is more bespoke. The mentors were mostly recruited from the CMF's existing contacts, and the mentoring programme has since proven particularly attractive to new contacts of the CMF, providing a way to engage them in the CMF's work. Hard-copy application questionnaires were sent to mentors and mentees, covering similar ground, and the open-text questions were designed to start both mentors and mentees thinking about business mentoring and what they want to gain from it. The matching was made by CMF staff on the basis of the questionnaires and through prior knowledge of most of the mentors and mentees.

INDUCTION

Despite their obvious contrasts, the schemes share certain features, designed to ensure the efficacy of the mentoring and the safety of the mentee. Thus each starts with an induction for both mentors and mentees, in the form of either an online training e-book written by the author, in the case of the CMS, or a seminar supported by written take-away materials, in the case of the CMFS. In each case the induction sets out the aims of the scheme, defines what is expected of mentors and mentees in terms of behaviour and then offers practical exercises and materials, often based on standard coaching models, such as the GROW model (Whitmore, 2009). Mentees are asked to 'drive the relationship' and take responsibility for arranging meetings and for their self-development. Mentors are encouraged to be mindful of their triple role: someone who has 'been there and got the t-shirt', who is as a source of practical or industry-specific insights and who acts as coach, encouraging reflection rather than providing active guidance. Mentors and mentees are asked to create a clear 'contract' regarding practical matters such as the place and time of the meeting, as well as initial goals, which can be refined during the course of the relationship. This contract is a point of reference during the course of the year. The induction also goes over the most important aspects of the code of conduct, which applicants to both schemes have been asked to read and agree to before joining the scheme.

CODE OF CONDUCT

The code of conduct for each scheme (called 'guidelines' in the case of the CMFS) incorporates key features of the ethical code of the Association of Coaching and the European Mentoring and Coaching Council. Thus the importance of boundary management and confidentiality are emphasized, as is the importance of a coach not coaching beyond his or her areas of competence or when incapacitated. Mentoring pairs are asked to reflect on the mentoring process regularly and to acknowledge the aims of the scheme, as referred to in the induction process, and provide timely feedback to the scheme organizers so as to evaluate the efficacy of the scheme. In addition, there is a section explaining how the scheme complies with the UK Data Protection Act. The code names the author (a trained executive coach, who carries indemnity cover for coaching and mentoring) as point of contact for any substantive queries or concerns; however, the codes make clear that it is the responsibility of the individual pairs, as adults with full capacity, to manage their relationship appropriately within the scheme guidelines.

ONGOING MANAGEMENT AND FEEDBACK

The schemes are managed on an ongoing basis to ensure quality, troubleshoot problems and establish value for participants (Allen et al., 2008). Ideally, mentoring schemes should be evaluated through a combination of an initial baseline test of participant attitudes and expectations prior to the scheme starting; a review of how confident participants feel about the process of mentoring and their own functions within it after induction and any subsequent training; and regular reviews by participants of the quality of their relationship to check if goals are being achieved or need adjustment. In addition, individual feedback should be considered in conjunction with pooled data, and outcomes compared to initial baseline evaluation.

Feedback on the performance of the mentee during the course of the mentoring year could be gathered from mentees, mentors and from third parties. The problems with using attainment of goals as a measure of success are well documented, including the fact that goals may change or that any positive change cannot be definitively attributed to the mentoring rather than some external circumstance.

In reality, it is unlikely that schemes without significant resources will always achieve the above.

In the case of the CMS, the following features are in place:

- Initial benchmarking in the application forms
- Mentoring e-booklet (i.e. the handouts for the training session) containing guidance and further reading
- Assistance of the scheme director if called upon by members of the scheme
- A drop in conference calls offered immediately following the close of the scheme, for any queries to be answered
- A survey/telephone call from the scheme director shortly after the close of each application window, regarding feedback on the application process
- Mentoring surgeries, on a first-come-first-served basis, on 'good mentoring conversations', delivered by the scheme director
- Occasional reminders from the scheme director saying she would appreciate informal feedback on the mentoring process
- Each cohort emailed for informal feedback towards the end of the mentoring year.

In the case of the CMF, following an in-person induction seminar, the internal scheme administrator emailed all mentoring pairs to introduce them officially and send them the code of conduct. Since then she has contacted mentors and mentees individually (personal meetings, emails, phone calls, through colleagues) to follow up on progress and ensure that the guidelines have been signed and returned. The feedback from mentors and mentees has generally been very positive, but not very specific.

Examples of feedback include:

- 'I'm feeling so positive and inspired' (musician mentee); 'it was the first time that she was thinking about goals and career planning in this way' (business mentor)
- 'We are extremely positive about our mentoring relationship and have regular meetings and contact and also we have met to discuss progress over lunch' (pianist, member of chamber ensemble)
- 'Mentoring was for me and about me. I'd never given myself permission to take myself and my progression seriously before. I was so busy taking my obligations to others seriously I didn't realise that the one project I was not focussing on was my own self development. I think on a whole different level now' (mentee for the CMS).

EVALUATION

Ongoing management and feedback does not provide statistically valid evaluation. With a small scheme such as the CMFS this is difficult to achieve, but CMS has a large enough cohort to obtain some statistically meaningful analysis, so research has been commissioned which follows British Psychological Society Code of Human Research Ethics. Questions used and validated by psychologists in many other contexts were inserted into initial application forms and will be followed up at the end of the scheme year. It is anticipated that responses will be interpreted in light of previous analyses of general personality traits in the population at large. The data collected in this survey will be analysed on a 'group basis'; at no point will individual responses be analysed. The data is kept confidential and will be destroyed at the end of the evaluation process. It is hoped that results will assist understanding of how to develop the scheme in the future – for example, determining if certain types of participant are more likely to benefit from a particular approach. Whether this research can be effectively undertaken will depend on the level of responses to the closing questionnaires, and we know that long-term engagement of mentors and mentees is one of the greatest challenges of large schemes (Clutterbuck, 2015).

LIABILITY

Both schemes involve adults working with adults and do not therefore need to consider matters relevant to schemes mentoring children, teenagers or vulnerable adults. Nevertheless, we wanted positive confirmation from CMS applicants in their application forms and from CMFS applicants in their signed 'guidelines' that they understand and agree that mentees take personal responsibility for their own development and choices and that it is their responsibility to obtain relevant professional or personal advice, if needed, before taking or refraining to take any specific actions in relation to career and personal life. Advice or information provided by a mentor, Citymothers or the CMF (as applicable) or any scheme director or administrator is not a substitute for such professional or personal advice.

CONCLUSION

Both programmes are relatively new and are evolving. They were structured following a review of the extensive literature available on starting and running mentoring schemes and of other mentoring schemes offered both online and face-to-face (Connor and Pokora, 2012; Garvey et al., 2009; Kay and Hinds, 2012; Megginson et al., 2006). The framework of each scheme has worked well; what is more challenging is ensuring the continuing engagement of mentor and mentee over the lifecycle of the mentoring relationship. Detailed formal evaluation is complex and expensive. We urge those developing schemes to consider their design so that evaluation is possible and a body of knowledge is developed and can be shared.

REFERENCES

Allen, T.D., Eby, L., O'Brien, K.E. and Lentz, E. (2008). 'The state of mentoring research: A qualitative review of current research methods and future research implications', *Journal of Vocational Behavior*, 73: 343–57. doi:10.1016/j.jvb.2007.08.004

British Psychological Society (2014). 'Code of Human Research Ethics'. Leicester: The British Psychological Society.

Clutterbuck, D. (2015). 'Measuring and evaluating mentoring', unpublished seminar paper.

Connor, M. and Pokora, J. (2012). *Coaching and Mentoring at Work: developing effective practice* (2nd ed.). Maidenhead: McGraw Hill.

Garvey, R., Stokes, P. and Megginson, D. (2009). *Coaching and Mentoring: theory and practice*. London: Sage.

Kay, D. and Hinds, R. (2012). *A Practical Guide to Mentoring: using coaching and mentoring skills to help others achieve their goals* (5th ed.). Oxford: How To Books.

Megginson, D., Clutterbuck, D., Garvey, B., Stoke, P. and Garrett-Harris, R. (2006). *Mentoring in Action: a practical guide* (2nd ed.). London: Kogan Page.

Whitmore, John (2009 [1992]). *Coaching for performance: GROWing human potential and purpose: the principles and practice of coaching and leadership*. People skills for professionals (4th ed.). Boston: Nicholas Brealey.

Mentoring Irish Rugby Players for Life After Rugby

Paula King

On the 5 November 2013, IRUPA, the Irish Rugby Union Players' Association, announced the launch of its Business Mentoring Programme in partnership with the Institute of Directors in Ireland (IoD).

IRUPA was founded in 2001 to help to promote and protect its members both during and after their careers. It first began offering services in the area of player development with the appointment of a Player Services Advisor in 2008. Today the association runs a nationwide Player Development Programme and has five Player Development Managers (PDMs) around the country, facilitating player development at all levels. IRUPA is the collective voice of players on all issues and through its Executive Board it advocates for player welfare within the Irish Rugby Football Union (IRFU). Its members are supported across a range of issues, from contract disputes to career development. The mentoring system launched with the IoD is one example of IRUPA aiming to help further in the development of all young men and women playing professional rugby in Ireland.

The IoD is the representative body for over 2,300 directors and senior executives within the private and public sectors in Ireland. From chief executives, managing directors and senior executives to board members and chairpersons, the IoD membership covers the breadth of industry, ranging from start-up companies, SMEs and not-for-profit organisations to large companies, multinational corporations and public-sector bodies.

Creating this unique link through the mentoring programme enabled talented rugby players to be partnered with talented business people.

Prior to the announcement of the launch, the foundations were put in place for the programme, commencing with an invitation to IoD members to respond to a request to partake in this mentoring initiative. An overwhelming response was received from the members and, throughout the summer of 2013, the IoD worked in conjunction with

IRUPA to develop panels of mentors who could offer a wide range of skills and experience which players could access. The role of the IoD mentors was to assist players in post-playing career planning, the setting of non-rugby-related goals, including educational and personal development, and facilitate industry-specific experience. The role of the mentor was also seen as one of advice, support, encouragement and networking opportunities and introductions. For players at these levels, the focus is always about preparation, and this initiative was an opportunity for them to apply the same approach in developing their off-field careers. Mentors and players were matched based on a range of factors, including common interests, educational background, professional interests, skills and geographical proximity, with players in each province taking a 'hands-on' approach to selecting a suitable mentor.

Nearly 100 mentors were assigned to the initiative from the IoD, with the aspiration that 60 players would be involved in the programme.

REASON FOR EMBARKING ON THE MENTORING PROGRAMME

Drawing together research which has been carried out into the transition for a top athlete from his or her sport to a career which will provide them with both the financial security and a fulfilled life, many studies have described the vulnerability attached to athletes during this process and how this vulnerability adds to the transitional stress.

Research recognises the dedication it takes to achieve and maintain professionalism or elite standards, but this may come at a cost (Pearson and Petitpas, 1990). The narrowing of focus may alter the developmental perspective and inhibit certain life skills and life experiences, which would be of assistance in career planning and personal planning (Blann, 1985; Pearson and Petitpas, 1990; Sowa and Gressard, 1983).

Other studies have shown that there is a reduced level of career maturity in top athletes. A potential explanation for this reduced level may be found by examining developmental theory. As individuals reach late adolescence, they are faced with the task of establishing their personal identity (Chickering, 1969; Erikson, 1959). As explained by Marcia et al. (1993), identity development necessitates an active exploration of possible roles and behaviours, followed by a commitment to the occupational and ideological options that are most consistent with an individual's values, needs, interests and skills. It has been proposed that the commitment and exclusive dedication necessary to excel in sport may restrict athletes' opportunities to engage in exploratory behaviour (Chartrand and Lent, 1987; Pearson and Petitpas, 1990), which is critical for subsequent personal and career-identity development (Super, 1957). Individuals who make commitments to roles without engaging in exploratory behaviour are said to be in a state of identity foreclosure (Marcia et al., 1993).

Foreclosure may be brought on by the demands and expectations of the environment or may be a result of individual choice (Danish et al., 2004). In college undergraduates, identity foreclosure has also been associated with a dependent decision-making style, in which responsibility for important decisions (e.g. career choices) is deferred to others (Blustein and Phillips, 1990). Several authors have suggested that the physical and psychological demands of intercollegiate athletics, coupled with the restrictiveness of the athletic system, may isolate athletes from mainstream college activities, restrict their opportunities for exploratory behaviour and promote identity foreclosure (Chartrand and Lent, 1987; Nelson, 1983; Petitpas and Champagne, 1988). Consistent with these findings and the theoretical propositions of Jordaan (1963) and Super (1957), research has shown that many athletes have restricted career and educational plans (Blann, 1985; Kennedy and Dimick, 1987; Sowa and Gressard, 1983). In addition to identity foreclosure, another aspect of self-identity, athletic identity, may be relevant to the career-decision-making process in athletes. Part of multidimensional self-concept, athletic identity consists of the cognitive, affective, behavioural and social concomitants of identifying with the athlete role (Brewer et al., 1993). It has been suggested that many athletes either lack the time or interest to do career planning or view it as a threat to their athletic identity and their dream of being a professional athlete (Kennedy and Dimick, 1987).

Taking the above research into account, it has been hypothesized that individuals with a strong and exclusive commitment to the athlete role are less prepared for post-sport careers than individuals less invested in the athlete role (Baillie and Danish, 1992; Pearson and Petitpas, 1990). In support of this argument, athletic identity has been inversely related to post-sport career planning before retirement from elite amateur sport (Lavallee et al., 1997) and ease of adjustment following sport-career termination (Hinitz, 1989; Lavallee et al., 1997).

However, we cannot ignore the many positive aspects of athletic identity and the many skills that players learn while they are playing that could be transferred to business.

High athletic identity, while associated with restricted personal development, can lead to positive experiences for athletes (Sparkes, 1998). It is highly correlated with athletic performance, higher commitment in training and a focus on sporting goals (Callero, 1985; Horton and Mack, 2000). It has also been linked to high levels of self-confidence, positive self-image and healthy lifestyle habits (Callero, 1985; Horton and Mack, 2000). A strong athletic identity does not necessarily mean that an athlete will not be able to develop successfully in other areas outside of sport, but solely emphasizing the athlete role, with little exploration of alternative identities, can be associated with negative outcomes (Brewer et al., 1993; Coakley, 1993; Miller and Kerr, 2003).

The sport-business-mentoring relationship can be beneficial to both parties, as players have usually developed sports-based life skills that can be transferred to the business world. Gould and Carson (2008) defined sport-based life skills as 'those internal personal assets, characteristics and skills such as goal setting, emotional control, self-esteem, and hard work ethic that can be facilitated or developed in sport and are transferred for use in non-sport settings' (p. 60). These life skills can be behavioural (communicating effectively with peers and adults) or cognitive (making effective decisions); interpersonal (being assertive) or intrapersonal (setting goals) (Danish et al., 2004).

The inspiration behind this initiative was, therefore, that while these skills are transferable, players may not always be confident in their ability to transfer them. Having a mentor to help them identify the skills that they have and how these are applied in the business world would therefore be beneficial. Having access to a mentor whom the athlete respects provides a fresh perspective and encourages future career planning.

APPROACH AND METHODOLOGY

Following the appointment of the 100 mentors to the mentoring programme, the IoD and IRUPA issued guidelines outlining the vision for the programme, including:

1 Core principles of the mentoring programme
2 Mentoring guidelines
3 What players should expect
4 Key contacts for the programme
5 FAQs.

Core principles

Confidentiality – all issues discussed between mentor and player are confidential.

Guidance – mentors will offer advice and guidance and assist with self-development.

Post-rugby planning – the relationship should concern itself with non-rugby-related issues and focus on helping a player ready themselves for their post-rugby career. This should include advice and assistance with work placement opportunities, possible educational opportunities, advice on obtaining a work–life balance and development of skills such as leadership or public speaking.

Goal setting – mentors will help players set non-rugby-related goals, including educational and personal development, lifestyle and family. Goals will be shared with the mentor and reviewed on an ongoing basis.

Mutual challenge and learning – there should be mutual benefit for both parties in the mentoring relationship, in terms of exchanging ideas, creating and establishing goals and developing self-awareness.

Person focused – academy players often need to juggle their rugby lives with college responsibilities. This programme will take this into consideration and the programme timings will be tailored individually.

Mentoring guidelines

The following guidelines were issued to all mentors and players:

- Once matched with a player, mentors should take the initiative at the start and make initial contact with their player.
- If at any stage throughout the course of the mentoring relationship, a player fails to get back in contact with their mentor after two attempts, the mentor should advise their regional IoD mentoring representative, who will contact IRUPA. Having been contacted by IRUPA, if the player still fails to make contact, they may be removed from the mentoring programme.
- Mentors and players should aim to meet 3–4 times a year.
- Ideally, the initial meeting and at least one meeting a year should be face-to-face.
- An agenda should be set for each meeting, with follow-up at every subsequent meeting.
- Each mentoring relationship is unique and a flexible approach must be taken in each case. However, mentors should be willing to share their own insights and experiences, to encourage and support players to build connections and, if possible, to facilitate opportunities to gain industry experience during or after their playing career.

A mentor should:

- *Ask questions and challenge*
- *Suggest networking opportunities*
- *Boost confidence and encourage*
- *Offer advice, but the decision to act on it will be for the player*
- *Nudge, not nag.*

> While the initial meeting should be about getting to know each other, it should also set out how the relationship will operate, and the mentor and player should agree on all aspects together.
> Mentors and players should tell each other their initial expectations – expectations may be realistic or may need to be re-focused.
> Mentors and players should agree on procedures and goals for the relationship in general going forward.
> Mentors and players should agree on the role and responsibilities of the mentor.
> Mentors and players should agree on the role and responsibilities of the player.
> Mentors and players should agree on how many meetings they will have – and when, where and how long?
> Mentors and players should exchange contact details and determine an appropriate level of contact outside of face-to-face meetings.
> Mentors and players should agree on any preparation needed by both the player and mentor in advance of meetings.
> As early as possible, the mentor and player should set out goals and a plan of action for the player.
> Subsequent meetings should assess progress towards goals, re-assess goals and add new goals, as required.

There was a recognition that, in some instances, mentors might feel they personally were not able to assist a player in a particular area. In this case they were encouraged to continue to act as a mentor while introducing the player to other people who could offer assistance. However, such introductions should only be made having consulted with the player.

What players were advised to expect

- Mentoring can assist players to set and clarify goals, keep them focused while working to achieve those goals and provide advice, support and encouragement.
- Players should discuss aims and goals, find out their strengths and weaknesses and get advice on areas they need to improve upon. Players should not expect their mentor to help with all problems.
- The success of a mentoring relationship will depend, to a large degree, upon the player's attitude and commitment. Players are expected to be proactive and work with their mentor in order to achieve success.
- The mentor should assist the player to assess career options post-rugby and to formulate plans.
- The player should make the decisions and take the responsibility.
- Players are encouraged to focus on what they want to achieve and on how to do so. Mentoring is not the same as counselling; players shouldn't expect a shoulder to cry on.
- Mentoring relationships cannot answer or solve all questions or issues for a player. It is important that the player is realistic about what can be achieved; this is why setting goals at the outset is so important.

Key learning outcomes

Supply versus demand. One of the key challenges since the mentoring programme was established has been managing supply versus demand. When the IoD sought expressions of interest from its members to join the mentoring programme, it was heavily oversubscribed in all provinces. A broad mix of skills, expertise and backgrounds was created on provincial panels in order to meet the needs of a diverse player base. Once three panels were established – approximately 90 IoD members in total – supply-versus-demand issues continued, as the mentors involved outnumbered players.

Managing expectations. One of the key challenges in the process has been managing expectations on both sides. From a mentor perspective, all have been enthusiastic and keen to get involved; however, as outlined below, not all players are ready for a formal/structured mentoring relationship. Facilitating networking and connections between players and mentors has been far more beneficial and has enabled relationships to form organically. Expectations were perhaps overly ambitious at the outset, and through trial and error the programme is finding the right balance to create fruitful and worthwhile interactions between players and mentors.

Real need. Unless there is a real need from a player for a mentor, the player will disengage. Networking events, where players and prospective mentors mingle, tend to result in a better introduction to the concept of mentoring; pairings cannot necessarily be forced.

Scheduling. As the players train practically daily, and mentors generally work full-time in business, making time to meet can be challenging, especially for national-level players and extremely busy or self-employed/entrepreneurial mentors.

Time. It takes time to build a relationship. Players may not immediately appreciate the time and attention that the mentor has given to the process.

Lack of understanding/clarity. Some players have suggested that they are unsure of what is expected of them in a mentoring relationship. They have a sense that it is good for their off-field development but don't really know why. Often the players meet a mentor once or twice but then the process stalls as both player and mentor waited for the other to get in touch.

Future career. Some players have an idea of what they want to do, but most don't have a very clear path in their minds, so they are reluctant to engage with a mentor as they feel they might be wasting the mentor's time.

Possible over management. There may have been a perception that there was a greater need from players – and a less formalized approach, where a player comes with a specific need or question, or perhaps is looking for some work experience or internship, has fostered better engagement between players and mentors. There needs to be understanding by mentors, too, i.e. although they have signed up and are ready to devote their time to becoming mentors, they may not be called upon (as there is only a limited number of players) and that this is no reflection on their experience, qualification or skill set.

CASE STUDIES

Player 1 experience

I suppose some of the challenges for athletes is obviously the serious injuries that you as a player can receive in the game. Also I think knowing and trying to figure out what you are going to do after rugby is also a challenge for most athletes.

My hopes and dreams from a rugby point of view are to play for Ireland and to fulfil my full potential as a player before I retire. Outside rugby it would be to set up and run a successful business of my own, be happy and enjoy life.

The fact that I know I will succeed and get to where I want to go in rugby and in life if I always work hard enough for it. And also I believe the set-backs you receive make you stronger for it.

I believe it's very important not just to meet new business people who might be handy to know in the future but also it gives you the confidence of how to act in a real job later in life. Also gets rugby players out of their comfort zone and into a realisation of the real world a little, prepares them for after rugby more.

This mentoring really made me appreciate what I do for a living as I saw what it was like to be sat inside an office all day! Helped hugely to keep me very busy during a tough time of injury and also makes you have another type of discipline in your life which is good.

Player 2 experience

Challenges for top athletes:

Elite or professional sport will rarely be a lifelong career. The nature of high performance is that it requires a complete commitment and dedication to train and compete at the highest level. In such a drive to fulfil one's potential, other aspects of life such as career development, social commitments and non-sporting interests can often be put 'on the back burner'. The challenge for athletes is to manage performance influencing factors while maintaining and developing themselves in aspects of their lives other than sport, as well as planning for the future.

My own hopes and dreams are to live a happy and meaningful life! To enjoy time with people who are important to me and to pursue different challenges in order to get the best out of life!

I believe on some level that I can overcome difficulty, and I tend to have quite good perspective – failure or disappointment in the sporting arena is small stuff compared to so many people who have genuine difficulties to deal with in their lives. It's sort of a challenge within myself to see how much I can extend myself I guess. Having a great support network is key, and also looking for inspiration everywhere to keep your own will fueled.

Sports people tend to be so invested in their career that their identity is completely built around them as a sportsperson. A mentor can help to develop the athlete as a whole person and help and guide them to fulfil their potential in other areas of life, and in doing so prepare them for life after sport. A mentoring relationship can give the mentee invaluable insight, knowledge and perspective that they otherwise would not get. It can also provide them with opportunities to try new things or develop new skills.

The value my mentoring relationship has had is that I have had a space to discover, to be me, to have a thinking partner who knows what the business I would like to get in to is like, and also who has come to understand my strengths and how I could plug them in to the world. I have been able to appreciate the value of my sporting experience and how I can use that now, and in the future. I have had the opportunity to learn from you and with you, and you have given me the chance to trial and give things a go, with support and feedback. Mostly you have been there to serve me out of your own good will.

This has been the cornerstone of what I feel is a very good relationship. I feel I have developed as a whole person, in knowledge, skill, understanding, I am awake to possibilities, I am far more than just a sportsperson.

REFERENCES

Baillie, P. and Danish, S. (1992). Understanding the career transition of athletes. *The Sport Psychologist*, 6, 77–88.

Blann, F. (1985). Intercollegiate athlete competition and students' educational and career plans. Journal of College Student Personnel, 26, 115–18.

Blustein, D. L. and Phillips, Susan D. (1990) Relations between Ego Identity Statutes andDecision-Making Styles. *Journal of Counseling Psychology,* 37(2), 160–68.

Brewer, B. W., Van Raalte, J. L., and Linder, D. E. (1993). Athletic identity: Hercules' muscle or Achilles heel? *International Journal of Sport Psychology*, 6, 279–88.

Callero, P. L. (1985). Role-identity salience. *Social Psychology Quarterly,* 48(3), 203–15.

Coakley, J. (1993). *Sport in Society: Issues and Controversies*, Irwin/McGraw-Hill.

Chartrand, J. M. and Lent, R. W (1987). Handbook of Counselling Psychology (3rd edition). New York: Wiley.

Chickering, A. W. (1969). *Education and Identity*, San Francisco, Jossey – Bass, series in higher education.

Danish, S. J., Forneris, T., Hodge, K., and Heke, I. (2004). Enhancing youth development through sport. *World Leisure*, 3, 38–49.

Erikson, E. H. (1959). *Identity and the Life Cycle: selected papers 1959.* New York: International Universities Press, Psychological Issues (Series).

Gould, D. and Carson, S. (2008). Life skills development through sport: current status and future directions. *International Review of Sport and Exercise Psychology*, 1(1), 58–78. Available at: http://www.tandfonline.com/doi/abs/10.1080/17509840701834573 [accessed 25 September, 2014].

Hinitz, B. F. (1989). *A Mini-History of Early Childhood Education*. In Bauch. (Ed.) Early Childhood in the Schools. NEA Aspects of Learning Series. Washington D.C: National Education Association.

Horton, R. S. and Mack, D. E. (2000). Athletic identity in marathon runners: functional focus or dysfunctional commitment? *Journal of Sport Behavior,* 23, 101–16.

Kennedy, S. R. and Dimick, K. M. (1987) Career-Maturity and Professional Sports Expectations of College Football and Basketball Players. *Journal of College Student Personnel*, 28(4), 293–97.

Lavallee, D., Grove, J. R. and Gordon, S. (1997). The causes of career termination from sport and their relationship to post-retirement adjustment among EliteAmateur athletes in Australia. *Australian Psychologist*, 32(2), 131–5. Available at: http://doi.wiley.com/10.1080/00050069708257366 [Accessed 29 September, 2014].

Marcia, J. E., Waterman, A. S., Matteson, D. R., Archer, S. L., and Orlofsky, J. L. (1993). *Ego identity: a Handbook for Psychosocial Research*. New York: Springer-Verlag.

Miller, P. S. and Kerr, G. A. (2003). The role experimentation of intercollegiate student athletes. *The Sport Psychologist,* 17, 196–219.

Nelson, W. E. et al. (1983), *Textbook of Pediatrics* Philadelphia (etc): W.B Saunders, 1983

Pearson, R. and Petitpas, A. J. (1990). Transitions of athletes: development and preventive perspective. *Journal of Counselling and Development*, 69, 7–10.

Petitpas, A. and Champagne, D. E. (1988). Developmental programming for intercollegiate athletes. *Journal of College Student Development,* 29 (5), 454–460.

Singer, R. N., Murphy, M. and Tennant, L. K. (eds), *Handbook of Research on Sport Psychology* (pp. 571–86). New York: Macmillan Publishing Company.

Sowa, C. and Gressard, C. (1983). Athletic participation – its relationship to student-development. *Journal of College Student Personnel*, 24, 236–9.

Sparkes, A. (1998). Athletic identity: an Achilles' heel to the survival of self. *Qualitative Health Research*, 8(5), 644–64.

Super, D. E. (1957). *The Psychology of Careers.* New York: Harper & Row.

Welchman, K. (2000). Erik Erikson: *His Life, Work, and Significance*. Buckingham: Open University Press.

Peer Mentoring: A Powerful Tool to Accelerate the Learning Experience

Mariano Ulanovsky and Patricia Pérez

This chapter's objective is to share Skeylls' experience with peer mentoring, in partnership with Perez Companc Foundation, and the different approach that we decided to adopt regarding this specific type of developmental relationship.

Perez Companc Foundation provides scholarships to students of all educational levels. Considering the difficulties that some of these students have in joining the labor market, Perez Companc Foundation hired Skeylls, a human-resources organization based in Buenos Aires, to design and run a training program to help them get a good job and excel at it.

As is well known, employment is a huge issue for young people all over the world: according to the ILO (International Labour Organization), unemployment affects young people much more than adults: two out of three unemployed individuals are youngsters. The ILO has pointed out the risk of a generation of young people that combines unemployment, inactivity and precarious work in developing or emerging countries. Argentina is one of these countries.

According to the latest data collected by the INDEC (the Argentine National Institute for Statistics and Census), in 2007 24 percent of young people were unemployed, more than twice the general unemployment rate (10 percent by that time) and more than three times the adult unemployment rate (7 percent).

In addition, many parents in Argentina think that it is better for their children to finish their studies before entering the job market. Therefore, when students obtain their college degree, they have no working experience at all, decreasing their chances of getting a good job in Argentina, where working while receiving college education used to be common and expected 10 years ago.

Since 2012, Skeylls has been implementing a three-stage program that combines training, coaching, simulation, and peer mentoring in order to achieve an effective learning experience in both academic and working environments. To date, 151 students have taken part in this program.

The program includes two different levels: *employment skills*, for those students that are not working at the time they join the program, and *skills to succeed at work*, for those who are already working.

For both levels, the three-step program run by Skeylls includes:

1 Introduction
2 Simulation
3 Real World Training.

The *Introduction* is an eight-hour training session focused on providing relevant information about the job market, getting to know each participant and developing interpersonal and communication skills.

During the eight-hour *Simulation*, the students go through a simulation lab, where they train their ability to get through a job interview or a challenging job situation. The simulation parts are played by actors and all of them are recorded, so the students have the opportunity to watch themselves, make a self-assessment and improve their performances. This stage is also very helpful in strengthening the bonds among the students.

During the *Real World Training* phase, the students have to practice in the real world the skills they have been training, in order to get their first job or to improve their performances at work.

The peer-mentoring model takes place in this third stage.

During the first year of the program, in 2012, Skeylls decided to run a peer-mentoring program with the traditional hierarchical mentoring approach, i.e. advanced students assisting junior students. One widespread definition of peer mentoring states that 'it is a process through which a more experienced individual encourages and assists a less experienced individual develop his or her potential within a shared area of interest' (Debra Gillman, *The Power of Peer Mentoring*, 2006, p. 5).

In our 2012 program, students at the second level assisted those who were still searching for a job (first level). In this first attempt, we faced some difficulties:

- While most mentors were very enthusiastic with their new role and the idea of assisting others, many protégés did not appear to be so motivated with the process
- The number of mentors was insufficient to match the potential protégés
- Despite the extremely short gap between mentor and protégé in terms of program level (one year from junior to advanced level), some dyads showed important difficulties in terms of understanding each other's needs and expectations.

Regarding the latter point, the asymmetric component of mentoring (Eby and Allen, 2002; Kram, 1985; McManus and Russell, 1997; Ragins 1997) did not appear to be effective for this particular group of students.

Taking into account the outcomes of that first experience, we decided to implement a different, more symmetric, peer-mentoring model in 2013. In doing so, we used the 'pilot/co-pilot' analogy. This time, during the third stage of the program, each student became 'pilot' for his or her own development and 'co-pilot' for a second student's progress. In most cases, members of each 'pilot/co-pilot' team belonged to the same program level. Pilots and co-pilots had the goal of assisting each other in the development of the skills each of them needed to get a job (first level) or to improve their performance in it (second level).

Through this pilot experience, we strived to answer Barry Bozeman and Mary Feeney's question: 'Is it appropriate to think of mentoring as multidimensional, such that one member of a dyad can be the mentor in one or more realms and (for the same dyad) the protégé in other realms?' (Bozeman and Feeney, 2007).

It had become clear to us that students of the same level of the program had very diverse stages of development for specific soft skills, personal experience, or even the technical or hard skills required to successfully look for and get a job. Therefore, symmetry in terms of age or academic stage did not prevent students from having different levels of knowledge, experience, or skill in specific domains. Those specific or partial inequalities varied from one student to another in such a way that each participant could benefit from the other's knowledge, experience, or skill in a particular domain.

We designed the matching process in such a way that the students were in charge of choosing their own mentors/co-pilots. Through a series of pre-designed and guided activities, students offered their strengths as potential 'co-pilots' to other students. At the same time, they searched for the abilities they needed from their future 'co-pilots' to help them in their own development plan. Even though a facilitator coordinated the whole process, the students themselves performed the matching process. The methodology here was focused on creating the right activities to help students succeed in choosing their peer mentors.

Here are two examples of these successful partnerships that would have probably never been reached through traditional matching.

Example A: Agustín, a passionate literature student, highly creative but with a low sense of reality, who was having a hard time searching for a job, and Florencia, a marketing student, very practical and result-oriented, who was facing some troubles with 'extremely' creative colleagues. They assisted each other in a way no facilitator would have thought of, exceeding their own and other people's expectations: Agustín started a systematic process to get a job and Florencia improved her relationships with her creative fellow colleagues. They did not become close friends, but they really assisted each other!

Friendship is a possible but not a necessary outcome of a mentoring process (Bozeman and Feeney, 2007). But the 'process of informal transmission of knowledge, social capital and psychosocial support perceived by the recipient as relevant to (…) professional development', required by Bozeman and Feeney (2007, p. 731) to define mentoring was present both ways: from Agustín to Florencia, and from Florencia to Agustín.

Example B: Sofía, an orthodontist student, who spent most of her time studying had highly developed communication skills but lacked social life and time to work; and Thiago, a very sociable young man with poor vocabulary, who was facing difficulties getting a job. Sofía assisted Thiago in improving his vocabulary and communication skills, and Thiago assisted Sofía in socializing. As a result, Thiago got a job and Sofía realized that she did not want to become an orthodontist, improved her social life, decided to become a psychologist and is currently looking for a job in that field. They continue to be very good friends.

Given the positive outcomes of the 2013 pilot experience, we have continued implementing the program with this mutual peer-mentoring model. We have faced many challenges, for which we have designed different courses of action.

The most important of these challenges is that the whole peer-mentoring process relies on what happens between dyads out of the training sessions, far from the facilitators' control and supervision. While some dyads were very enthusiastic, pro-active, and, therefore, successful in setting the mentoring relationship and reaching the expected goals, others simply vanished due to lack of initiative, distraction, or other inherent causes. In 2014, Skeylls implemented a follow-up process based on a progress report e-mailed by each participant to the program coordinator. For 2015, we added a series of personal and virtual interviews, where the program coordinator actively follows and offers assistance to each dyad.

Another challenge is, of course, the matching itself. A good match is critical for the success of the program. Students have the ability to choose the partner who best fulfills their needs. This enhances responsibility, commitment, and eagerness to learn. Our self-driven matching process has proved to be much more effective than the previous facilitator-driven one. However, it is far from being flawless. Many students ended up realizing that their co-pilot choice was not an effective one. In order to reduce risk of failure in the matching process, we added a series of self-awareness activities to the first and second stages of our program, along with a deeper assessment of choice criteria as one of the first activities in our third stage.

Up to this point, this particular peer-mentoring approach has proved to be a high-impact, low-cost knowledge- and skill-transmission strategy. There is no way that we could have reached similar outcomes through a formal training process without facing the high costs that multiple, customized, and, in some cases, even individual training sessions would have carried.

We consider that this strategy enhances the students' learning capacity. It opens possibilities for people to develop the eagerness to learn and increases responsibility and accountability. Trust is fundamental: the whole process has low control levels and a high level of trust. During the last three years of the program, symmetry has proved to be a key factor in building trustful relationships. Furthermore, in the words of Bozeman and Feeney, 'peers inevitably impart knowledge by example and usually more directly' than people in a higher academic or professional position (Bozeman and Feeney, 2007, p. 729).

We believe it is necessary to build more symmetric relationships in educational and working environments in order to change the way we learn. Due to the expansion of the internet and social networks, relationships have become flatter, and the educational system has not yet caught up with current needs. In terms of developmental skills, young students learn much faster from other young students than from 'teachers' who no longer share their interests and standards.

Nowadays, what we are able to learn is much more important than what we know. This is the key challenge that education is facing: the need to change focus from teaching to learning. We believe that this particular peer-mentoring model can be an effective resource for this purpose.

As Heraclitus stated, the only thing that remains constant in life is change itself. Change has been a constant also in terms of the theory, conceptualization, and practical applications of mentoring. As the concept of mentoring has evolved from its earlier strongly hierarchical definitions (Kram, 1980, 1983, 1985; Levinson et al., 1978; Noe, 1988; Scandura and Schriesheim, 1994) towards a broader concept that includes peer-mentoring (Bozionelos, 2004; Eby, 1997), we challenge our colleagues and ourselves to explore a possible next step in mentoring evolution, that of mutual peer mentoring, where two individuals can be one another's mentor, as long as it is in different domains, where they have unequal knowledge, experience, or skill (Bozeman and Feeney, 2007).

REFERENCES

Bozeman, B. and Feeney, Mary K. 2007. Toward a Useful Theory of Mentoring. *Administration & Society*, 39(6), 719–739.

Bozionelos, N. 2004. Mentoring provided: Relation to mentor's career success, personality, and mentoring received. *Journal of Vocational Behavior*, 64, 24–46.

Eby, L.T. 1997. Alternative forms of mentoring in changing organizational environments: A conceptual extension of the mentoring literature. *Journal of Vocational Behavior*, 51, 125–144.

Eby, L. T. and Allen, T. D. 2002. Further investigation of protégés' negative mentoring experiences: Patterns and outcomes. *Group & Organization Management*, 27(4), 456–479.

Kram, K.E. 1980. Mentoring processes at work: Developing relationships in managerial careers. Unpublished doctoral dissertation. Yale University, New Haven.

Kram, K.E. 1983. Phases of the mentor relationship. *Academy of Management Journal*, 26: 608–625.

Kram, K.E. 1985. *Mentoring at work: Developmental relationships in organizational life*. Glenview, Ill: Scott, Foresman.

Levinson, D.J., Darrow, C.N., Klein, E.B., Levinson, M.A. and Mc Kee, B. 1978. *Seasons of a Man's Life*. New York: Knof.

McManus, S. E. and Russell, J. E. A. 1997. New directions for mentoring research: An examination of related constructs. *Journal of Vocational Behavior, 51*(1), 145–161.

Noe, R.A. 1988. An investigation of the determinants of successful assigned mentoring relationships. *Personnel Psychology*, 41, 457–479.

Ragins, B. R. 1997. Antecedents of diversified mentoring relationships. *Journal of Vocational Behavior, 51*(1), 90–109.

Scandura, T.A. and Schriesheim, C.A. 1994. Leader-member exchange and supervisor career mentoring as complementary constructs in leadership research. *Academy of Management Journal*, 37, 1588–1602.

International Labor Organization (ILO). 2015. *Social Perspective and Employment in the world*. Published on ILO Website.

Social Security, Employment and Work Ministry of Argentina. *Diagnosis of Youth Unemployment* (Ministerio de Trabajo, Empleo y Seguridad Social, *Diagnóstico del Desempleo Juvenil*). 2007. Based on the National Institute of Statistics and Census (INDEC Argentina, *Encuesta Permanente de Hogares*). Published on the official web site of the Social Security, Employment and Work Ministry of Argentina.

Gillman, D. 2006. Waisman Center University of Wisconsin–Madison University Center for Excellence in Developmental Disabilities, *The Power of Peer Mentoring*.

46

A Multi-Country Mentoring Programme across Eurasia with Anadolu Efes

Tim Bright and David Megginson

INTRODUCTION

This chapter is about a multi-country mentoring programme run within the Anadolu Efes beer group, which operates a total of 15 breweries in Turkey, Russia, Kazakhstan, Moldova, Ukraine and Georgia, and is the market leader in Turkey, Kazakhstan, Georgia and Moldova. Anadolu Efes is part of the Anadolu Group, a major business group headquartered in Istanbul, Turkey, made up of 75 companies with 29,000 employees and strong corporate governance and social-responsibility practices.

The programme was designed and delivered by Professor David Megginson and Tim Bright, based on materials developed over many years by Professor Megginson. The programme structure and methodology was developed in close cooperation with Anadolu Efes's Group Human Resources (HR) team. At least one member of that team was present in every workshop and supervision session.

The aims of the mentoring programme included building connections across different parts of the organisation and building a sense of belonging to a multinational organisation for employees, who may be based in locations many hours' travel away from each other. Developing the mentors' coaching and mentoring skills to use in their daily business life was also an explicit goal of the programme.

The mentors and mentees were selected by group HR: the mentors were the most senior executives in the organization, the mentees high-potential mid-level managers. Participants came from all the countries mentioned above. The programme lasted for one year, with a guideline of one two-hour mentoring meeting per month. All participants were volunteers and could withdraw from the programme at any time if they wanted.

STRUCTURE

The initial workshops were held in Moscow in March 2010 over three days. On Day 1, the mentees had a full-day workshop, which introduced them to the programme and key concepts and gave them a chance to practise mentoring on real issues. On Day 2, the mentors had a full-day workshop similar to that of the mentees', while the mentees worked with HR on their development plans. In the evening of Day 2 there was a cocktail reception for all participants, hosted by the CEO, and the mentees got a chance to talk to all the mentors they didn't already know and then submit three names of mentors they would like to work with. This could not include anyone in their own reporting line. After the reception, the programme consultants and group HR completed the matching of mentor and mentee pairs. On the morning of Day 3, the pairs were announced, and the mentors had a morning workshop, continuing from Day 2 and focusing on mentoring skills, while the mentees worked to prepare for their first mentoring meeting. The formal programme ended with a lunch together, and each pair then had time in the afternoon to have their first mentoring meeting, face to face over several hours.

In the workshops, there was a clear emphasis on the importance of building a strong relationship at the start of the programme, and not immediately jumping into issues in the first meeting. The first meeting was positioned as a chance for each participant to get to know their partner well.

The first mentoring meeting happened face to face, and we encouraged the mentees to have their next one or two meetings face to face if possible, and there was some budgetary support for this. Mentors were deliberately matched 'for difference' with mentees from other locations, national cultures and business functions. This meant many subsequent meetings had to happen by videoconference. We organised two follow-up supervision sessions during the year, in different locations, with the mentees attending in the morning and the mentors in the afternoon. Participants were encouraged to schedule face-to-face sessions on those days as well.

The programme was designed to be transparent: the same 'Mentoring Guide' was presented to all participants, and the programme was presented as a learning experience for all. In subsequent years, we have combined mentors and mentees for supervision and some workshop sessions, and this has also been effective.

This mentoring programme was clearly positioned as 'mentee-led'. Only the mentees had a say in who they would be paired with, and the mentees received considerable training and support so that they could shape the mentoring relationship and manage the mentoring agenda according to their needs and wants.

OUTCOMES

Overall, the programme was seen as a success and it has been repeated in subsequent years, with kick-off workshops held in different cities where the Group is present. The programme has been seen as supporting talent-management initiatives across the company and improving retention and development. The three-day format for the initial workshops worked well, and we have repeated this with other clients where participants are coming from different locations. It is a considerable investment of resources and time, but it can often be combined with other events that bring people together in one location. The three-day structure builds a sense of excitement and importance around the programme, and creates the opportunity for a range of useful conversations. Having the first meeting on Day 3 adds immediacy to the workshops, with mentors and mentees knowing that they will very soon apply what they are using. The open-ended structure on Day 3 allows mentors and mentees to have a long first meeting and to effectively lay the foundation for their relationship. We observed that many pairs met for long periods, and if one of them was in their home location it gave them an opportunity to take their partner to their workplace. In other programmes we've noticed that some pairs don't have their first mentoring meeting for several weeks, and this structure avoids that risk and adds real momentum to the programme.

LOCATION ISSUES

The location issue is not straightforward. In this case a clear goal was to build connections across a widely spread group. It was difficult for some pairs to meet face to face because of the time and costs involved. Many used videoconferencing effectively, but some reported that they did not like using this methodology. Some pairs chose to do all meetings face to face; others were happy to mix face-to-face meetings with video calls. A number of mentees chose to fly considerable distances to meet their mentors and commented that the journey to and from the mentoring session gave them valuable time to prepare for and reflect on the meeting. The business has seen a number of benefits from these interactions between people from different functions and locations, including information sharing and coming up with new solutions to business challenges. Many mentors and mentees have stayed in close touch after the end of the formal programme, and this provides benefits to them and the business.

OBSERVATIONS

Having a clearly designated programme manager (from group HR) was essential, and the fact that this person was in every workshop and supervision session gave great continuity to the programme. The programme manager is able to access people that the consultants can't, and they are easily reachable by all the participants when they have questions to ask.

Participants had strong, divergent opinions on whether mentoring can be done effectively by videoconference or by phone. Some expressed a strong preference for face-to-face mentoring; others did not. This did not seem to be related to age, but may vary according to national culture.

Clarity in purpose and design is essential. Participants come to the programme with many different ideas about 'mentoring'. Rather than spending time on confusing debates about terminology in different cultures, it is essential to agree what the terms mean for us in this context. An explicit focus on the 'skilled mentee' driving the process is also important to the success of this programme. The most active and motivated mentees appear to get the most benefit from the programme. We have also observed significant change in mentors' behaviours; the mentoring relationship gives them a safe area in which to practise coaching skills such as listening and asking good questions, which they can then apply in their daily business role. Overall, based on the feedback received from the participants and other stakeholders, the design and implementation of the programme has effectively met the needs of the organisation and the individual participants.

Mentoring Women in Canada's Financial Sector

Joanne Leck and Catherine Mossop

CONTEXT

According to ESDC (Employment and Social Development Canada, 2015), organizations seeking to hire employees in the financial sector are expected to experience a labour shortage over the next decade. The majority of job openings are projected to arise from retirements. Workers in these occupations are generally older and tend to retire somewhat earlier than other workers. Consequently, there is a pressing need to train and develop younger workers to occupy these senior roles.

Over 52.9 per cent of the financial industry's labour force is comprised of women (Employment Equity Act Annual Report, 2013). Catalyst (2015), a non-profit organization whose mission is to work with organizations to expand opportunities for women, reported that among organizations in the S&P 500 (finance and insurance), women are underrepresented as CEOs (1.4 per cent), board members (19.8 per cent) and executive/senior-level officials (27.8 per cent). As a response to these inequities, on 15 October, 2014, the Canadian securities regulators announced amendments to Canada's corporate-governance disclosure practices to include the mandatory disclosure of the number of women on boards and in executive-officer positions (Ontario Securities Commission, 2015). In addition, organizations must disclose their policies and future targets regarding the representation of women on the board. Canadian companies are recognizing both that this underutilized source of talent is a resource that can be developed to occupy senior roles and ensure future growth, and that this new regulatory transparency may impact investors making investment and voting decisions. As a consequence of these two realities, the need to develop young female workers has become paramount.

CASE STUDY – CI FINANCIAL

CI Financial (CI), employing over 1300 employees, is Canada's third-largest investment-fund company and second-largest publicly traded fund company. Initiated by senior executives in 2012, with an interest in addressing some of the unique and different issues women face in managing their careers, mentorship was seen as a way to help the women of CI to build their leadership capabilities. In the summer of 2012, CI announced the inception of a pilot programme to focus on 'Women Mentoring Women in Leadership'. The mission for the programme was twofold. First, to grow and prepare junior women to manage and lead in a more complex environment. Second, to build capabilities in managing complex relationships on the job and to understand the scope and broad impact of the business in a global market place.

Participants

Eight women executives were invited to participate as the first mentors. Due to an overwhelming response in mentee applications, the programme was designed to launch eight one-on-one mentor–mentee pairs in September 2012 and a second mentee match six months later. Each formal mentoring relationship is expected to continue for twelve months, after which participants may continue informally if they so choose. Matching has continued at six-month intervals for a current total of twenty-eight mentee participants and nine mentors (two women executives are no longer formal mentors due to travel schedules, and two male executives were added to the roster). For the mentors, the staggered approach provides six months for development of trust and a natural flow to one relationship prior to commencing a new relationship. At the time of the programme evaluation, six mentors had had the experience of three mentoring relationships.

Programme design

The programme was designed for each cohort to run for twelve months. Following a women-only networking event focused on the role of mentoring in careers, prospective mentees applied to the programme. To establish the credibility and culture for the programme, prospective mentees were asked to complete an application that included a paragraph stating what they hoped to learn; then the applicant's management lead provided a letter indicating why they supported the participation of their staff in the programme. This management-sign-off step was critical to assure leadership support at the strategic and operational levels and reduce risk. The programme committee subsequently matched the mentee to the mentor based on the following criteria: cross-functional/divisional areas of the business; learning goals matched to strengths/offering of the mentor; and location (in the first cohort, two mentoring pairs were remote matches). All mentors and mentees attended a mandatory programme launch and orientation which served to explain the process and the tools and resources that would be provided (for example, quarterly women-only networking events, Birkman™ leadership assessment, Cascade to Wisdom field guides for mentors and protégés). Mentor Exchanges and Mentee Exchanges were organized to provide ongoing learning for mentors and as a check-in for mentees to support them in achieving the depth in their relationship required to engage in strategic conversations – the point at which transformational learning begins to take place.

The programme design was reviewed in the second year and was deemed to be effective, needing only minor adjustments and enhancements. Two main recommendations were made. As there is a shortage of women executives, the first was to introduce male mentors in order to sustain the programme and prepare for growth. Research has demonstrated that, while women often favour psychosocial support (for example, receiving support from others, mentor commitment, discussion of personal problems), it is the career-related support (for example, sponsorship, exposure and visibility, coaching, protection and challenging assignments) that advances their careers. Since many studies have demonstrated that female mentors provide more psychosocial support and less career-related support than their male counterparts (O'Brien et al., 2010), introducing more male mentors could increase the mentees' exposure to career-related support. Note, however, that the results of the CI mentoring programme suggested that the type of mentoring support did not differ between male and female mentors. This may be due to the training that was provided prior to the mentoring initiative that outlined the types and forms of mentoring that were expected.

As video conferencing is now readily available in other CI locations, the second recommendation was to introduce and support more 'remote pairings' (i.e. matches where the mentee and mentor are geographically apart). The types of support that were discussed included making arrangements for the pair to meet in person, encouraging the use of communication technology (for example, video conferencing, Google Hangout) and creating a remote mentor group (Mentor Exchange). While e-Mentoring may not be as effective as face-to-face mentoring, it does have some advantages. E-mentoring provides unlimited access to a greater number of mentors, offers greater flexibility in establishing and sustaining relationships, removes geographical barriers and blurs demographic and personal differences that can lead to negative biases and stereotyping (Leck et al., 2013).

Evaluation

At the end of the twelve months, the programme was evaluated using a five-point Likert scale (1–strongly disagree, 3–neither agree nor disagree, 5–strongly agree) on several criteria, including mentor satisfaction, mentee satisfaction, leadership development and competency development. Open-ended questions also queried the benefits of participating in the programme, recommended changes for the future and whether participants would recommend the programme to others and why. The results of the survey of all three twelve-month groups follow.

Mentor satisfaction

Of the nine items assessing mentor satisfaction, only one was unanimously rated as satisfactory by all mentors ('The program team (HR and Consultants) provided the right amount of support throughout'). Dissatisfaction with three items ('I felt my mentee valued my input and time', 'I made progress on my own development goals' and 'Where and how we met worked well for our relationship') was reported by one mentor – this mentoring relationship was remote, with a time-zone differential, and further investigation by the programme consultant discovered that the mentee did not have private space for telephone meetings, did not attend the orientation and expectations were related to career advancement rather than the programme goals for leadership development. All other items were rated as either highly satisfied, satisfied or 'neither satisfied nor dissatisfied' ('My mentee was a good match for me', 'My mentee made significant progress on the goals and objectives we set on the outset', 'There was an appropriate time interval between meetings', 'The time commitment required for the program was appropriate').

Mentee satisfaction

The scale used to measure mentor satisfaction was modified to measure mentee satisfaction. Only one item was unanimously rated as satisfactory by all mentees ('I felt my mentor valued my input and time'). All but one mentee felt that their mentor was a good match. Overall, most programme elements were perceived to be satisfactory; however, three mentees were dissatisfied with keeping to scheduled meeting times. Those mentees who reported that they booked their meetings for the twelve months at the launch of their relationship, reported higher success in maintaining their meeting schedule.

Leadership development

Nine items measured the perceived development of leadership skills. Overall, most mentees agreed that participating in the programme allowed them to: 1) set realistic short- and long-term personal goals; 2) be more self-aware; 3) increase self-control; 4) expand knowledge and effectiveness in their current role; 5) expand into a more complex role; 6) develop new perspectives and practices; 7) build a strategic network; 8) balance work and personal life; and 9) develop a broader perspective of CI. The programme was most successful in increasing self-awareness and least successful in helping mentees attain work–life balance. Only one mentee expressed dissatisfaction, specifically in the last three items described above.

Competency development

Nine items measured the perceived development of mentee competencies and capabilities. Mentees expressed strong agreement in their belief that the programme allowed them to: 1) engage in reflective thinking; 2) influence change in others; 3) increase understanding of the needs of others; 4) develop alternate strategies; and 5) improve decision making. To a lesser extent, mentees also believed that the programme allowed them to: 1) use resources effectively; 2) deal with poor performers; 3) identify and capitalize on others' strengths; and 4) influence and hold others accountable. One mentee was dissatisfied with the programme with respect to the last three items above.

Overall benefits and recommendations

Mentees were interviewed to gather richer data on their perceptions of the programme. First, mentees were asked to provide an example of what they are doing differently as a result of the programme. Several themes emerged: mentees gave examples that demonstrated that they had greater confidence, more information, greater perspective, improved approaches to handling problems and improved strategic decision-making skills. Second, mentees were asked to describe the benefits of participating in the programme. Their responses included benefits such as strong networking, improved relationships, greater confidence, access to advice and broader perspective and insights. Third, mentees were asked to recommend changes to the programme. Their recommendations included more assistance during the start of the programme, more networking with fellow mentees and greater diversity among the mentors (diversity here means to expand to and include other divisions and sister organizations). Finally, mentees were asked how they would respond if one of their colleagues asked about the programme. All respondents indicated that they would recommend the programme to others; one mentee highlighted the need for a good match, however.

CONCLUSION

The programme's objective was to build leadership skills and improve competencies and capabilities among women in management and prepare them for more complex roles. The survey results strongly suggest that the mentees perceived that the programme was succeeding in achieving its objectives. However, a true measure of a programme's success is best measured with quantifiable and objective criteria, such as pay increases, promotions, transfers, assignment of strategic projects, investment in additional training and even resignations (by those accepting better jobs elsewhere). Since the inception of the programme, there have been twenty-eight mentee participants, 15 per cent have received a promotion, several have become mentors, and the salary base has increased by 13 per cent over two years. Mentees and mentors self-report increased confidence, improved decision-making and improved managerial and leadership effectiveness. The impact of the success has resulted in other valuable yet non-measurable elements that have contributed to the business, namely: the retention of talented women in an environment of high demand for such talent; enhanced corporate reputation and attraction of high-calibre talent to the organization; positive and credible visibility at board and shareholder level. While the participants are achieving excellent outcomes, it is worth noting the programme elements that contribute to the success of mentoring within CI, most notably:

- A clear business case for the programme
- Credible leadership of the programme committee and its administration
- Ongoing women-only networking and speaker events
- Executive and management leads supporting the participation of their staff
- Continuous involvement of participants as ambassadors for the programme, facilitators at networking events, speakers at external events and mentees becoming mentors

- Ongoing mentor development and reflective practice
- Thoughtful integration of male mentors while retaining the culture of the programme

With this success, CI plans to continue and add other mentoring initiatives in the workplace.

REFERENCES

Catalyst (2015). http://www.catalyst.org/knowledge/women-sp-500-finance-and-insurance-0 (accessed 1 April, 2015).

Employment and Social Development Canada (2015). http://www23.hrsdc.gc.ca/occupationsummarydetail.jsp?&tid=18 (accessed 1 April, 2015).

Employment Equity Annual Report (2013). http://www.labour.gc.ca/eng/standards_equity/eq/pubs_eq/annual_reports/2013/index.shtml accessed 1 April, 2015.

Leck, J.D., Elliott, C., Bourgeois, E. and Kemp, K. (2013). Mentoring a diverse workforce: SSHRC knowledge synthesis final report. http://www.sshrc-crsh.gc.ca/society-societe/knowledge_mobilization-mobilisation_des_connaissances/index-eng.aspx (accessed 3 October, 2016).

O'Brien, K.E., Biga, A., Kessler, S.R. and Allen, T.D. (2010). A meta-analytic investigation of gender differences in mentoring. *Journal of Management*, 36(2), 537–54.

Ontario Securities Commission (2015). https://www.osc.gov.on.ca/en/NewsEvents_nr_20141015_csa-regarding-disclosure-of-women.htm (accessed 1 April, 2015).

Coaching and Mentoring Doctors and Dentists – A Case Study

Rebecca Viney and Denise Harris

INTRODUCTION

This case study describes the coaching and mentoring scheme set up by the London Deanery.[1] It will identify the factors that contributed to the success of this award-winning service and the impact of the mentors' behaviour and attitude in influencing a coaching culture across the National Health Service (NHS) in London and beyond.

In 2008 each deanery in England was given funding to support doctors and dentists who were in transition following a substantive NHS training reorganisation. London chose to invest some of the funds in a six-month project to develop a mentoring scheme.

BACKGROUND

Coaching and mentoring are still relatively new in the NHS but there is increasing acknowledgement of the value of such support for healthcare professionals (Viney and Paice, 2010; Viney and Harris, 2011; Steven et al., 2008; Abbasi, 2008; Bachkirova et al., 2015). This is important, particularly as the demands on doctors, dentists and all staff in the NHS are well publicised (Gerada, 2014).

PLANNING THE SERVICE

At the time the London service was set up, there were few mentoring schemes for doctors and most had not flourished or lasted long. These schemes were usually speciality-specific and designed for 'doctors in difficulty'.

The service in London was different in that it was set up for doctors and dentists in transition and was designed to provide developmental rather than remedial support. The vision was to establish a service that would be positive and sustainable. It was therefore important that the person who would lead the development of the service had the vision and skills to deliver this.

Dr Rebecca Viney was appointed to this role. As a GP Educationalist, she brought considerable experience of supporting doctors in transition as well as an approach to leadership that was inclusive.

Her first priority was to gather as much information as possible about existing mentoring schemes for doctors and other healthcare professionals. This included the mentors' experience of mentoring doctors, details of the training, management and quality-assurance processes, how they measured value for money and cost effectiveness, the challenges they encountered and their ideas of the factors that impacted on the potential for a scheme to thrive. In addition, she extensively researched the topic of mentoring.

The lead created twelve essential tenets, from the information gathered. These were:

1 Voluntary participation
2 Confidentiality
3 Externality (accessing a mentor from another organisation)
4 Choice
5 Mentee preparation
6 Trained mentors
7 Supervision and continuing professional development for the mentor
8 Agreements
9 Ethics
10 Limited number of sessions
11 No blame
12 Monitoring, evaluation and review

One of the reasons given for the failure of other schemes was the reluctance of doctors to ask for something that might indicate they were in difficulty. The London service adopted the model of situational leadership (Driver, 2011) in order to reinforce the focus on development.

SETTING UP THE SERVICE

It was decided that medical educationalists should be recruited as mentors. This was for two main reasons. They already had substantial transferable skills, knowledge and experience and they were in a position of influence with networking links across organisations. This meant they were ideally placed to introduce the new approach.

The assumption was that they would develop the new skills, incorporate them into their existing portfolio and deliver them within their organisations and specialities. However, this was not as straightforward as expected.

One challenge was convincing the potential mentors that they would need three days' training and then ongoing development to hone their skills. Some of those invited to apply to be a mentor felt that they did not need training and were keen to give the young plenty of advice using their own experience. Even some of the most open-minded of the senior doctors felt that three days of training was excessive and that it would be difficult for them to get the time away from their departments.

Those who expressed interest were invited to 'gateway days'. They were observed delivering a mentoring session and allocated to one of three categories: assessed as having the skills to begin mentoring immediately; accepted onto the mentor register with a requirement that they attend top-up training in the next three months; and invited to undertake the three-day training. The majority undertook the three-day training and were then reassessed.

The second challenge was that doctors and dentists spend ten to fifteen years training so that they can diagnose, problem solve and give patients their very best advice. They are used to being the expert, so those that did attend the training found that not giving advice was unbelievably difficult.

A third challenge was establishing the idea that it was possible to mentor across specialties. The suggestion that a surgeon could mentor a general practitioner (GP) or pathologist seemed very wrong to most people. However, it was soon apparent to the newly trained mentors that if they did overcome their anxiety of mentoring someone from a different area, it helped to address the previous challenge. It was in fact much easier if they were not seen as an 'expert'. They could move to the mindset of seeing the other person as resourceful, with potential to find their own solutions.

DEVELOPMENT OF THE SERVICE

The service grew and developed to include representatives from the wide range of specialties in medicine and dentistry across the NHS in London. At first, the funding was agreed annually; however, after approximately three years it became permanent, recognising the value and impact that the service had on challenging and changing culture.

The service remained primarily for doctors, although after two years it was made available to other NHS staff. It was also renamed 'coaching and mentoring' in recognition of the fact that the practitioners were using coaching skills.

In developing the service, the lead continued to model a collaborative approach. She invited the mentors and mentees to contribute ideas and suggestions for development, which she then encouraged them to become involved in or lead on. This included giving taster sessions, becoming involved in training delivery, setting up local schemes, and using the internet to mentor medics in the developing world.

Another important factor that supported the growth and success of the service was the focus on regular supervision and professional development. This served several purposes: it strengthened the community of practice enabling networking opportunities across organisational and specialist boundaries; it created a strong culture of teamwork; and it provided an opportunity to quality assure the mentoring being offered.

The mentors were encouraged and supported to further develop their skills by taking higher qualifications in coaching and mentoring. They also found that their careers flourished.

By 2010 over 500 doctors and dentists had applied to be mentored and the story of the success of the service began to spread. Mentees and mentors moved area and shared stories of their experience. The lead also had opportunities to deliver taster sessions and formal presentations at medical-education conferences across the UK and further afield.

The developing national recognition of the success of the service resulted in enquiries from medical educationalists in other areas. They asked for advice and access to the materials that London had produced so they could launch coaching and mentoring in their own areas. The lead decided to produce a report of the development of the service and commissioned a new mentor who was passionate about the subject to write it with her (Viney and Paice, 2010).

In late 2010 Dr Viney attended the Harvard Leadership and Healthcare Coaching Conference in Boston, Massachusetts and came across 'coaching for health'. This approach enabled patients to take ownership of their health, motivated them to make lifestyle changes and generally improved both their mental and physical health. She returned to England and discovered a 'coaching for health' pilot for practice nurses being run in Suffolk by Andrew McDowell and Dr Penny Newman.

The concept was introduced to the London Deanery mentors and in late 2011 funding was found for a 'coaching for health' pilot in London. The training was delivered by expert coaching trainers alongside Deanery mentors and over the next three months over 300 healthcare workers, mainly young doctors, were trained in the approach. This has had a significant impact on patient enablement (Rogers and Maini, 2016).

EVALUATION

Over a period of six years in excess of 2,000 doctors and dentists applied to be mentored by the service and over 650 medical educationalists were substantively trained in the skills of coaching and mentoring. These trained mentors recognised the power of mentoring and coaching in developing people and their skills. Their enthusiasm was significant in contributing to the success of the service and in advancing the goal of embedding '…a culture of coaching and mentoring across London's NHS' (Viney and Paice, 2010, p. 36).

The service has been formally evaluated twice. The first evaluation was undertaken by Sheffield Hallam University after the first year and showed there were clear benefits of mentoring (Chadwick-Coule and Garvey, 2009).

In 2012 Oxford Brookes University was commissioned to evaluate the quality assurance and efficacy of coaching and mentoring. The measures used were self-efficacy, engagement and self-compassion. This revealed that between two and four mentoring sessions resulted in significantly enhanced scores in these areas. In addition, the mentors themselves found that being a mentor had a strong positive impact on their career development (Bachkirova et al., 2015).

THE FUTURE

In 2013 the General Medical Council reviewed their Good Medical Practice guidelines, the core text for doctors to remain registered. It was relaunched and included 'mentoring' for the first time.

> You should be willing to find and take part in structured support opportunities … (for example, mentoring). You should do this when you join an organisation and whenever your role changes significantly throughout your career.

> You should be willing to take on a mentoring role for more junior doctors and other healthcare professionals. (General Medical Council, 2013)

In 2014 the delivery of medical education was reorganised. The mentoring service continues to serve the doctors in speciality training in London; however, the coaching and mentoring of trained GPs and consultants is now devolved to trusts and GP employers.

The legacy of the original vision is that coaching and mentoring are now both available and seen as something that is part of good practice for doctors. The mentors that were trained continue to practise their skills, and coaching and mentoring are increasingly being used by NHS Trusts to support and develop their staff.

Note

1 Deaneries were the regional organisations responsible for postgraduate medical and dental training in the UK until 2014, when this transferred to Health Education England (HEE).

REFERENCES

Abbasi, K. (2008). Mentoring and the meaning of soul. *Journal of the Royal Society of Medicine*, 101(11): 523.

Bachkirova, T., Arthur, L. and Reading, E. (2015). Evaluating a coaching and mentoring programme: Challenges and solutions, *International Coaching Psychology Review*. 10(2), pp.175–189.

Chadwick-Coule, T. and Garvey, R. (2009). *London Deanery Mentoring Service: A Formative and Developmental Evaluation of Working Practices and Outcomes*. Unpublished report. Sheffield: Sheffield Business School, Sheffield Hallam University.

Driver, M. (2011). *Coaching Positively: Lessons for Coaches from Positive Psychology*. Maidenhead: Open University Press/McGraw Hill.

General Medical Council (2013). *Good Medical Practice*. London: General Medical Council, retrieved from www.gmc-uk.org/guidance (accessed 3 August, 2015).

Gerada, C. (2014). Something is profoundly wrong with the NHS today. *British Medical Journal,* Retrieved from http://careers.bmj.com/careers/advice/view-article.html?id=20018022 (accessed 25 June, 2014).

Rogers, J. and Maini, A. (2016). *Coaching for Health: Why It Works and How to Do It.* Maidenhead: Open University Press.

Steven, A., Oxley, J. and Fleming, W.G. (2008). Mentoring for NHS doctors: Perceived benefits across the personal-professional interface. *Journal of the Royal Society of Medicine* 101(11): 552–7.

Viney, R. and Harris, D. (2011). Mentoring supervision for doctors and dentists in a National Health Service (NHS) Deanery. In T. Bachkirova, P. Jackson and D. Clutterbuck (eds), *Coaching and Mentoring Supervision Theory and Practice.* Maidenhead: Open University Press, pp. 251–7.

Viney, R. and Paice, E. (2010). *The First Five Hundred: A Report on London Deanery's Coaching and Mentoring Service 2008–2010.* London: London Deanery.

Swarovski Case Study

Emily Cosgrove and Petra Lockhart

Founded in 1895 in Austria, Swarovski designs, manufactures, and markets high-quality crystals, genuine gemstones, and created stones as well as finished products such as jewelry, accessories, and lighting. Now run by the fifth generation of family members, the Swarovski Crystal Business has a global reach, with approximately 2,560 stores in around 170 countries, more than 25,000 employees, and revenue of about €2.33 billion in 2014.

Together with its sister companies, Swarovski Optik (optical devices) and Tyrolit (abrasives), Swarovski Crystal Business forms the Swarovski Group. In 2014, the Group generated revenue of about €3.05 billion and employed more than 30,000 people. The Swarovski Foundation was set up in 2012 to honor the philanthropic spirit of founder Daniel Swarovski. Its mission is to support creativity and culture, promote well-being, and conserve natural resources.

The pilot internal mentoring program was initiated and launched by Petra Lockhart, Global VP for Learning and Development and sponsored by Anna Cocca, Global Finance and Administration HR Business Partner. Pockets of mentoring and examples of informal mentoring were already in place at Swarovski, but they had not yet established a shared approach to mentoring across the businesses. Both Lockhart and Cocca were clear from the start that the approach to mentoring at Swarovski was to be at the developmental end of the spectrum rather than sponsorship. This decision was informed partly through a desire to support the development of senior leaders within the organization in the role of mentor, to enhance their leadership skills, and support their own self-reflection journeys.

According to Lockhart, 'Mentoring helps us develop our trust and confidence in leaders, support our women in leadership agenda, our leadership culture and philosophy, and our skills enablement'.

The team encountered very little pushback from colleagues globally regarding launching the program. The US launch was slightly delayed because the region was going through a major reorganization. While on a visit to Hong Kong, Petra Lockhart shared an update on the mentoring pilot in Europe with Francis Belin, Senior Vice President Greater China, Consumer Goods Business, and he was keen to support a program he believed in and to trail blaze in his region. He has subsequently spoken very highly of the program and is an active ambassador for mentoring. In 2016, the European Senior Vice President of the Consumer Goods Business will also join the program representing his region. This sponsorship of the mentoring program by senior individuals across the business has greatly influenced the success of the program.

The team was clear that it needed external support to establish a robust program with a strong learning element and chose to work with The Conversation Space, who helped them to design the program and to run and support all the key learning elements.

PILOT 2014

The pilot in June 2014, which involved eleven mentoring pairs across Europe, included line-manager briefings, design and delivery of both mentee and mentor workshops, supporting materials, and action-learning telephone follow-up.

Mentees were selected from an identified high-potential talent pool, giving specific focus to encouraging and supporting women in leadership, while not excluding men from taking part. The main criterion for choosing mentors for the pilot was high commitment to the project. It was a key aim of the program design that mentors would become the ambassadors for mentoring and this, along with their high level of seniority, has been one important element in getting additional people on-board.

Following four months of planning and design, the program launched and offered the following key areas of support:

- Initial support for both mentors and mentees through highly interactive and challenging workshops.
- Ongoing action-learning sets as an approach to offer mentors facilitated and peer supervision.
- Mid-point reviews for all mentees.
- An informal evening event for all new mentees and mentors to meet before mentees find out who their mentors are. This provided an opportunity for participants to network with others from across the different functions and hierarchies within the organization.
- Creative thinking around how to inform participants of their match, including handwritten cards and careful timing.
- Providing all mentees and mentors with their own reflection journal from the start of the process. Program sponsors modelled these themselves and attended all training.
- Providing full briefings for all line managers of mentees, including a live Q&A session.
- Sharing the story at every opportunity, across both business and support functions.
- Sharing example evaluation questions for Swarovski to run this aspect of the program internally.

ROLL OUT 2015 AND BEYOND

The global roll-out began in Asia Pacific in February 2015 with another twelve mentoring pairs, and this followed the same format as the pilot, with the program sponsored by Francis Belin, Senior VP Asia Pacific.

The second Europe cohort rolled out in April 2015, with more than double the number of mentoring pairs than in the pilot, and the second Asia Pacific cohort launched in summer 2015. Continued roll out is planned with the launch of the first Mentoring@ Swarovski program in South America in spring 2016 and a further two cohorts in Europe, in Switzerland and Austria.

As part of building sustainability for the program, and shifting it to be supported internally, a Train the Trainer (TTT) event was held in April 2015. Ten internal human-resource and learning-and-development practitioners were supported over two days to take on the role of internally supporting the mentoring programs at a regional level. This group continues to meet to share good practice and maintain the community of mentoring practitioners.

Evaluation

The internal team at Swarovski managed the overall evaluation of the scheme using the Kirkpatrick model (Kirpatrick and Kirkpatrick, 2006) as a baseline and ensuring measurement took place at both levels 1 and 2, as follows:

- Happy Sheets after the initial training – to support Kirkpatrick level 1.
- Action-learning sessions with mentors and mid-point calls/meetings with mentees, which have also started to include some aspects of action learning – to support Kirkpatrick level 2.

The feedback has led to some small changes to the launch-workshop content, including the use of more experiential exercises and more transparency on the matching process.

The evaluation approach for 2016 will be to:

- Send out an online survey to both mentors and mentees.
- Use the Employee Engagement Survey and cluster mentors and mentees into separate groups in order to analyze their level of engagement, enablement, and confidence in leaders.
- Analyze mentees' career progression – for example, in taking on new roles or lateral moves.

Challenges and lessons

Some eighteen months on from the pilot, there are almost 100 participants actively involved in the mentoring program. So far, there has been a 100 percent roll over of mentors, all of whom have taken on a new mentee, and around two thirds of mentees have been promoted or have taken on extra responsibility in their role. There is a substantial waiting list to become both a mentee and a mentor, with 30 percent of mentees' line managers expressing an interest to be actively involved in the program.

The great success of the pilot provided a strong business case to ensure enthusiasm and buy in for a speedy global roll-out.

The greatest challenge for the program was geography. The program is global, and, with one of its core ambitions being to grow the one-to-one mentoring relationships, the ability to connect in person and get face-to-face time was important. Swarovski met this by supporting mentoring pairs to meet face to face at the end of each of the launch training workshops for initial conversations and by encouraging pairs to find opportunities to meet when traveling for business. The majority of pairs who were separated by distance have been able to meet face to face at least twice, and they ensure they stay in regular contact through video conferencing, phone calls, and apps such as WhatsApp.

It was also interesting to note that, as the program has grown, with numbers soon to exceed 100, Swarovski chose to support the mentoring through regional HR hubs and has continued to match 'by hand', using local knowledge. They consider this to have a huge advantage over the use of mentor-matching software, which they decided would offer lower success rates for initiating strong and lasting mentoring relationships.

The team at Swarovski and The Conversation Space felt that the following worked particularly well for this scheme and contributed to its successful outcomes:

1. *Choice of program owner is critical* – having the global head of L&D and global head of HR had huge impact on launching, getting buy-in for and supporting the mentoring.
2. *Select your mentors carefully* – ensure they are eager to be involved and have influence to spread the word. If you can, include senior sponsors as mentors.

3 *Support your mentees and your mentors along the journey* – the more energy you invest in continuing the conversation after kick-off, the more dividends you will reap.
4 *Support global programs both centrally and locally* – both for more successful matching and for ongoing troubleshooting.
5 *Make it enjoyable!* – The energy and enjoyment that Lockhart and her team have built into the program and openly shared about the mentoring is contagious and has created a culture of desirability.

The future for mentoring at Swarovski is to build on the success encountered so far. This will involve rolling out the program in other regions, expanding it into other sectors in the business, and continuing to develop people internally to support and manage the programs. Key initiatives are:

- Hold TTT events, focused on how to facilitate and deliver action learning effectively.
- Hold further TTT events on delivering-learning workshops.
- Launch the mentoring program in North America.
- Run at least six new waves of trained mentors and mentees (three in Europe, one in Asia Pacific, one in Latin America and one in the US).
- Look into reverse mentoring.
- Expand the program to the retail population (through the new Swarovski Retail Academy).

REFERENCE

Kirpatrick, D.L. and Kirkpatrick, J.D. (2006) *Evaluating Training Programs: The Four Levels*. San Francisco, CA: Berrett-Koehler Publishers Inc.

Mentoring across an Industry – the Recruitment Industry in Australia and New Zealand

Vanessa Fudge and Akram Sabbagh

The recruitment industry in Australia and New Zealand has historically suffered from a tarnished reputation predominantly due to the highly transactional behaviours of some recruiters, especially evidenced during difficult economic climates when vacant roles are scarce and competition is high.

The industry body for the recruitment-services sector in Australia and New Zealand, the Recruitment Consultant Services Association (RCSA), representing 3,300 company and individual members, was seeking a way to overcome this obstacle and raise the overall perception of its membership to attract and retain new talent to the industry in line with its stated vision of 'shaping our profession through standards, knowledge and influence'.

Despite this reputational hurdle, recruitment professionals tend to be people-oriented, highly social individuals who demonstrate within their industry a significant degree of collaboration and networking between professionals. This is not surprising given that their work is all about understanding people to accurately match them to the right job roles.

In 2011 the RCSA launched an initiative called the PEARL (Professional Emerging and Aspiring Recruitment Leaders) programme to develop the leadership skills in the next generation of recruitment professionals. The PEARL committee comprises established and aspiring leaders from across the industry.

With the support of external facilitation through a team coaching process, an industry-wide mentoring programme was conceived in the first PEARL committee meeting, with the stated objective to 'create an industry reputation that professionals could be proud of'.

Halfway through the committee meeting, it became apparent that established leaders were dominating the conversation and the emerging leaders were barely able to make comments. When the facilitating coach brought this observation to the room's awareness, members were able to consider how this was reflecting the dynamics across the industry and their inability to listen to their own emerging leaders.

Mentoring was agreed to be the vehicle to reverse this trend and to impact upon the negative reputation of the industry. From here on in it would be their job and that of the RCSA via its marketing engine to sell the programme to the members.

For the RCSA there was a strong business case to support the PEARL mentoring programme. Since the global financial crisis the industry had experienced a significant loss of talent and the industry body was seeking ways to proactively reverse this alarming trend and rebuild their membership base. By involving the committee of member representatives there was strong buy-in from the programme's inception.

> 'The objectives of the PEARL Programme are to foster relationships that are mutually beneficial for mentors and mentees and to contribute to the profession and the industry.'
> Steve Granland, CEO RCSA

The initial plan was to conduct a pilot programme in 2012 that would span the geographical membership base of the RCSA. This included four state territories in Australia (New South Wales, Western Australia, Queensland and Victoria) as well as Auckland and Wellington in New Zealand. This pilot programme included a total of twenty-four mentor/mentee pairs.

The strategy was to provide upfront mentor and mentee training as well as quarterly facilitated peer meets for mentors and mentees separately. The challenge was to provide these in a face-to-face format across the six geographies. This was made possible by leveraging the AltusQ team of coaches across Australia and New Zealand, who were willing to volunteer their time with the objective of spreading goodwill for their mentoring-programme methodology and coaching skills.

The roll-out included a total of five coaches, who, wherever possible, ran their training and follow-up meets in parallel (except where different time zones applied, in the case of Western Australia and New Zealand).

> 'When I actually joined the programme... I was starting my own company and I really needed that support going into a whole new business, not really sure of how things were really going to go. So having a support of a mentor during the early stages of my business has been a real benefit...'
> Kate Taylor APRCSA, Managing Director, Taylor Care Recruitment

Other contributors required to run the pilot successfully beyond the coaching team were supplied by the RCSA both from the governing committee and via an appointed programme co-ordinator. The committee took on the responsibility of matching mentors and mentees, which they managed based on a thorough application process and their knowledge of the industry in general and the mentors in particular. The programme co-ordinator administered the application and registration process as well as conducting follow-up phone calls with the mentors and mentees to monitor progress throughout the pilot. This person was also instrumental in ensuring busy mentors and mentees made it not only to the training but also to quarterly meets by initiating follow-up phone calls with anyone who had not proactively registered for these events.

Resources in the form of programme tools were provided by the AltusQ coaching team, who had trialled their methodology on several enterprise clients already, although not yet at an industry level. These included a code of ethics for participants, application forms and process for participants, programme launch communications, a sponsor's guide, a mentoring guidebook, a mentee learning journal, training materials and articles of interest to maintain programme engagement as well as evaluation surveys.

The final role for serious consideration in any successful mentoring programme was, of course, a programme sponsor. This was given to the CEO of the RCSA to promote the programme publicly at the annual industry conference as well as regular industry forums and educational events.

Given that the programme trainers and facilitators were first and foremost experienced practitioners of team and executive coaching, there was a strong emphasis in both the upfront skills training as well as the quarterly meets on self awareness, active listening, addressing the mentees' agenda and navigating conversations using a coaching framework.

These skills were imparted via an interactive, experiential approach in initial half-day training workshops and then reinforced via the quarterly facilitated meets held separately for mentors and mentees in each location, where the coaches deliberately modelled 'open agenda' coaching in order to demonstrate the impact of the process that had been endorsed from the start. The challenge was drawing participants along to an open-agenda coaching approach and getting them to put to one side their wish to know what would be covered. To fill the rooms, high-level agendas were crafted, mainly as marketing collateral, only to be placed visibly to one side during the coaching sessions in order to demonstrate that there is no better agenda than the one you unearth in your next session in the moment with your participant. Once participants had experienced the value of this approach, they were able to take it into their individual sessions.

The coaching team also acknowledged the real risk to the programme, i.e. that of mentees being approached by their mentors for roles and thereby 'poached' from their current organisation. If this were to occur, the sourcing of mentees would become increasingly difficult due to the fears of their employers, and the programme would only serve to further erode the reputation of the industry. This risk was raised at the governing-committee level, and it was promptly decided that a zero-tolerance policy would apply. With several industry mentors quick to warn mentors across the programme, and with the coaching team drawing making comments in all introductory sessions, no such examples have emerged in the now four-year duration of the programme.

At the end of the first-year pilot, both mentors and the mentees were surveyed to determine the value of the pilot programme. Fourteen mentors and sixteen mentees responded to the survey, giving a total representation of 63 per cent of total pilot participants.

Mentees were asked to rate the following statement on a five-point scale from 'strongly agree' to 'disagree': *The mentoring programme has increased my perception of the professionalism of our industry*. Seventy-five per cent of mentees responded that they agreed or strongly agreed with this statement, with the remaining responses falling in the neutral category.

Mentors were asked to rate their overall satisfaction with the mentoring programme on a five-point scale, from 'highly satisfied' to 'highly dissatisfied'. Ninety-three per cent of respondents rated themselves as highly satisfied or satisfied, with the remaining single respondent providing a neutral rating. Mentors were also asked if they would be willing to continue in the programme beyond the pilot in a mentoring role. Seventy-nine per cent of mentor respondents indicated they would like to continue mentoring into year two, with the remaining indicating that they were 'undecided'.

Mentors and mentees were also asked in several questions to evaluate the survey qualitatively. For example, they were asked: *Has the mentoring programme developed your leadership skills in any identifiable way? If so, in what way?*

Comments ranged from 'better listening skills' and 'more focus in development techniques' through to 'not really, I have always done coaching and mentoring'.

Mentors were asked: *What have you learned from being a mentor?*

Responses ranged from 'sticking to a few simple issues and holding people to account is powerful', 'comparing their problems with our problems' and 'better planning around all personal development conversations' through to 'to adapt and attend a meeting not knowing what will be covered until you get there!'.

Mentees were asked: *What benefits have you received from the mentoring programme?*

Responses ranged from 'massive benefits, I have grown professionally and personally' and 'a lot of professional growth and maturity to deal with constant change within my organisation' through to 'I now have someone outside the business that I can talk to completely confidentially'.

Mentees were also asked: *What have you learned from being a mentee?*

Responses included 'that the answers I seek all come from me but need to be coached out of me', 'growth comes from asking for help and guidance to make the right decision and rectify mistakes' and 'the importance of continuing to develop and grow' through to 'the importance of empowering staff – I have now rolled out a similar programme for my junior and senior staff'.

The survey also homed in on changes recommended by the first-year programme participants for the future programme roll-out.

Mentors were asked: *To enhance the mentoring programme in the future there should be...*

Answers included:

- 'Better matching, opting out or grace period for mentees to change mentors'
- 'An accountability aspect assigned to mentees to drive the programme'
- 'The industry body to do more telephone follow-up to monitor programme progress'
- 'Keep it simple so that it can reach more people'.

Mentees were asked: What would you like to see changed for the programme moving into the future?

Responses ranged from 'nothing' through to:

- 'Better organisation of quarterly meets'
- 'To be able to continue a relationship with the mentor'
- 'More interactions between mentees to share experiences'
- 'A closer fit when matching mentors to mentees'

To incorporate this feedback, the matching process was adjusted in year two to take into consideration the seniority of the mentors and to more closely align them with mentees in terms of relevance of experience. The programme co-ordinator also committed to phone-call follow-up each quarter immediately prior to the quarterly meets, with the dual purpose of monitoring feedback as well as lifting attendance at the quarterly meets.

In addition to this it was agreed to act more quickly on any apparent mismatches at the start of the programme, particularly where participants were not making themselves available for the commitments of the programme. To encourage more interaction between mentees, other leadership-programme elements were introduced to complement the mentoring programme and enhance the overall PEARL development programme, including leadership master-classes and annual consultants' forums.

Following the pilot, the programme has now run for three more years, with an intake now underway for year five. Table 50.1 breaks down the participants per year:

The drop off in 2015 has been attributed to the introduction of an application fee for

Table 50.1 PEARL mentoring-programme participants

Year	Total participants
2012	48
2013	122
2014	100
2015	66

mentees when (there was no charge previously). This coincided with the introduction of an automated programme platform that was designed to decrease the administration tasks placed on the programme co-ordinator and provide an access point for all programme information and tools. Unfortunately, neither mentors nor mentees demonstrated a high utilisation of the platform, and it has been decided to discontinue this cost in light of insufficient returns.

Keeping mentor numbers up has been a perennial concern. In 2014 a useful discovery was made at the annual industry conference. Industry leaders were very happy to be tapped on the shoulder and asked to participate as mentors, even though they had not volunteered previously. This discovery resulted in several high-profile industry speakers participating as mentors, which in turn drove up the mentor applications by adding credibility and kudos to the programme.

> 'I think we are in a time where our credibility is challenged and we need to establish a relevance for our industry and the RCSA...The PEARL programme is so essential in bringing out the young people, encouraging ethical behaviour, encouraging professionalism and establishing a value or a worth of what they are doing in the committee. I think if we don't do that, then our industry is under a lot more threat than it may currently be in this very challenging environment.'
>
> John Hartland FRCSA, Director
> *ERG Workforce* Mentor

For the 2015 programme roll-out, seventeen mentors and thirteen mentees responded to the feedback survey – a 45 per cent response rate. There are positive signs for the ongoing success of the programme: 46 per cent of mentee respondents stated that they were interested in playing the mentor role next time, and 100 per cent of mentee and mentor respondents stated that they would be highly likely or likely to recommend the programme to others.

In addition, 100 per cent of mentee respondents stated that the programme had changed their leadership style significantly or moderately, and 53 per cent of mentors reported a significant or moderate impact on their leadership style.

Programme elements were rated in terms of their impact on overall programme satisfaction on a scale of 1 to 5, where 5 was highly beneficial and 1 not beneficial. The results, listing various programme features in order of relevance, are shown for mentees in Table 50.2 and mentors in Table 50.3.

Many valuable lessons have been gained through the four years of this industry programme, including, but not limited to, the importance of a strong galvanising vision and a motivated programme steering committee and programme administrator; the power of a

Table 50.2 PEARL Programme 2015 – mentee feedback on programme impact

Programme feature	Perceived positive impact on mentee programme satisfaction
Time spent with mentor	4.46
Care and attention of the committee given to the matching process	4.31
Emotional support from mentoring relationship	4.31
New leadership and communication skills	4.23
Increased awareness applicable to work and personal life	4.15
Industry knowledge applicable to business role	4.08
Decision making and/or problem-solving skills	4
Increased engagement in the industry	3.75
Training and quarterly meets to reinforce skills	3.33
Contact and follow-up with industry association	3.31
Ability to connect with industry peers via training and quarterly programme meets	3.15
Training and quarterly meets for networking purposes	2.69

Table 50.3 PEARL Programme 2015 – Mentor feedback on programme impact

Programme feature	Perceived positive impact on mentor programme satisfaction
Satisfaction from helping someone	4.65
Ability to connect with industry peers via quarterly peer-mentoring meetings	4.12
Contact and follow-up with industry association	4.12
Care and attention of the committee given to the matching process	4.06
Increased self awareness and personal reflection	4.06
Enhanced listening and communication skills	4.06
Time spent with mentee	4
Training and quarterly meets to reinforce skills	3.94
A fresh industry perspective from your mentee	3.76
Improved leadership skills	3.63
Commercial ideas to implement in your own business	2.88

> 'I think this is a very important program and is something I am very passionate about as I am an emerging leader in this industry… for us to move forward into the future as the recruitment industry it's important that we learn the pearls of wisdoms we can from the leaders before us, but also be coming in with new innovative ways that we can input into the next generation and the future of the industry.
>
> 'This programme really is the making of you if you allow it to be.'
>
> Kate Taylor APRCSA, Managing Director, Taylor Care Recruitment

team of coaches in supporting a team of mentors and mentees; and the need for sufficient structure to support a consistent commitment and quality of mentoring.

For mentees, the highest value was placed on the time with their mentor, the care demonstrated in the matching process and the emotional support from the mentoring relationship.

For mentors it was the satisfaction of helping someone, the ability to connect with industry peers via quarterly peer-mentoring meetings and the contact and follow-up by the industry association.

> 'I thoroughly enjoyed my time with the many experienced, intelligent mentors, as well as working with the mentees. It's a quality programme and I am very proud to be a part of it.'
>
> Karen Palmer MRCSA, Mentor

A future step for this programme is to use peer mentoring to link internal recruiters within organisations with external recruiters providing services. This has the potential to drive further industry relevance and forge closer links between those providing the services and those seeking to build their internal talent base.

Following the results of the PEARL programme and the referrals generated, there are now several other industry-mentoring programmes underway, including in the technology, defence, education, creative arts and not-for-profit sectors.

Commonwealth of Australia Statutory Authority

Anna Blackman

THE ORGANISATION

Australia is a marine nation. With 85 per cent of the population living on the coastal fringe, and a maritime industry worth $47 billion per annum, the Australian community and economy depend on effective management of coastal waters. Good management of these resources requires timely, accurate and relevant information for managers, policy-makers, industry and the community.

For over 40 years, a Commonwealth of Australia Statutory Authority (SA) has played a pivotal role in providing this information for Australia's tropical northern waters. Fisheries, offshore oil and gas, mining, reef tourism and aquaculture have all benefited from the research geared towards the protection and sustainable development of marine resources. This data and environmental intelligence allow the SA to understand the marine context and system changes that underwrite the protection of Australia's marine biodiversity and marine economy.

Unique features of the operating environment

The SA maintains specialised, world-class marine research facilities in support of its objectives and has a staff of 199 of whom 69 (35 per cent) are women.

Business case

In June 2010, the Federal Sex Discrimination Commissioner had announced a Gender Equality Blueprint setting out approaches to implementing the recommendations of the 2008 report *Gender equality: what matters to Australian women and men* (Cerise, S. & Black & White Media Australia, 2008). The recommendations are:

- Balancing paid work and family and caring responsibilities
- Ensuring women's lifetime economic security
- Promoting women in leadership

- Preventing violence against women and sexual harassment
- Strengthening national gender-equality laws, agencies and monitoring.

The SA identified that women were under-represented in leadership positions and needed specific consideration when planning their careers. These aspects are important to support and retain women and become an employer of choice for women.

There were no women in the Executive Team and they were under-represented at the executive and higher management levels of the organisation. The roles primarily filled by women were:

- Research scientists (18)
- Research support staff (20)
- Technical and corporate (31).

In order to make changes a group of female employees approached the Human Resources Manager to develop a mentoring programme within the SA.

The initial plan/strategy

The initial plan was to offer the female staff a seminar addressing the Gender Equality Blueprint, with an opportunity for those who wished to receive individual coaching from an external coach. Staff were to be offered this opportunity during paid work time.

Selling the strategy

SA leadership sought an opportunity for female staff to define their aspirations, explore their workplace options, identify their goals and define the actions required to meet those goals.

A proposal was put forward to the CEO, which outlined the Gender Equality Blueprint. A local organisation that offers leadership programmes was approached by staff to develop and empower women within the organisation. Subsequently, a seminar for female staff was given. The seminar was complemented by a series of one-on-one coaching sessions for all seminar participants, with the opportunity for the participants to engage with a mentor.

Resources and roles

The SA offered those interested in the programme time allocations to complete the programme, funding to pay for the consultants to conduct the mentoring/coaching and an opportunity to review the programme at the end with a view to extend. The programme was developed by the local organisation that provided external coaches for the participants.

Implementation

The implementation process was designed as follows see Table 51.1 below:

In practice

Seventeen women (25 per cent of the female workforce) participated. Fifteen women completed a pre-coaching survey and seventeen completed the post-coaching survey.

After the seminar, sixteen women completed two sessions of individual coaching. Of those, twelve went on to complete three sessions, while seven completed four sessions and two completed five or more sessions. All but two completed the programme.

Reviews and changes in the programme

A two-hour recap session with participants and the external consulting business was held midway through the programme so that the

Table 51.1 Implementation process

One-day seminar	Up to three sessions of coaching	Two-hour recap/ progression	Up to two sessions	Half-day report-back workshop
Inform participants: • SA intent (possible brief by CEO) • SA facts (from SA 2011–12 Annual Report) • Experiences of other women in the APSC (choices, mentoring and networking) • Participants decide on a direction, i.e. *Yes, No* or *Don't Know* • Facilitate discussion on next steps: • *Yes* and *Don't Know* = continue • *No* = end • Define goals for next stage for discussion with coaches	• Tactical structured coaching to identify: • 'Interferences' to: • Meeting goals such as skills and capability gaps • Identifying actions to address • Implementing action • Networking opportunities • Criteria for ideal mentor • Finding the mentor	• Sharing experience and progress • Networking • Options for improvement • Next steps	• Tactical situational coaching to support goal attainment • Continuation (if necessary of structured coaching)	• Sharing experience and progress • Networking • Feedback to CEO/programme sponsor • Next steps
Outputs: • Improved Self-awareness • Decision to proceed (*yes, no, don't know/may be*) • SA women's aspirational profile	Outputs: • Improved Self-awareness • Decision to proceed (*yes, no*) • Solutions to gaps 70/20/10 • Mentor criteria • Potential mentor	Outputs: • Strengthened network • Establish mentor relationship • Personal/professional growth	Outputs: • Improved Self-awareness • Solutions to gaps 70/20/10 • Mentor criteria • Grow mentoring relationship	

sessions could be modified to the participants' needs.

The overall programme was reviewed by pre and post surveys. A summary of findings from the pre-programme survey was provided to the participants during the two-hour recap sessions. Findings and a comparison with the pre-survey results were provided to participants and the learning organisation during the half-day report-back workshop.

Changes in the participants

Pre and post surveys reported that female staff members felt that personal development was the most important achievement of the sessions: self-awareness, perspective on how to move toward the future, work/life balance and increased confidence.

Participants initially identified professional development as an expectation from the coaching sessions. Practical tasks such as setting short-term goals, training needs, time management, staff conflict, delegation and coping strategies were identified as important. Surprisingly, post-coaching participants only identified improved networks/networking skills and workforce planning as areas of achievement. This may indicate that other areas of achievement such as personal development, achievement tools and work/life balance were more important than professional development.

Around one third of the female staff wanted to learn more about career direction

Table 51.2   Coachee expectations

Prompted focus on what I want out of life.

I found it inspiring to do the sessions while on leave and really appreciated that the sessions could be held at my house when the baby was asleep. The sessions included more about my personal life than I expected and helped me get a clearer view of the relationship between my work life and my private life.

I expected the programme to only focus on professional/work issues, but we addressed many personal matters that seemed to underpin my effectiveness in the work environment. I was pleasantly surprised at how effective the approach was.

It was as much about personal issues as professional.

A platform to identify resources and networks across general themes instead of only within my limited professional focus.

---

and about how to advance their career. After the sessions, survey participants identified that coaching helped them to gain clarity between work and personal goals and with analysing and setting career goals.

When asked to articulate the ways the coaching programme differed from their initial expectations, some participants were surprised, and grateful, that the programme and the coaching addressed both professional and personal issues (see Table 51.2 above).

Challenges

Because of the support from the SA, challenges were identified within the group rather than from external factors. Prior to the programme, 46 per cent of participants thought lack of time would be a barrier. Preoccupation with work matters worried 43 per cent, and 14 per cent were preoccupied with personal matters. Subsequently, these percentages fell slightly to 43 per cent, 42 per cent and 12 per cent respectively.

What still needs to be accomplished

It is difficult to see how empowering change in one sector of an organisation can last if not everyone has been part of the change process. As one participant said, 'available to all is a good suggestion – I feel everyone at SA (men, women, older, younger) would benefit from this programme'. Similarly, another participant urged the organisation to develop a planned response: 'If SA is going to integrate, it would be nice to see a bit of a model about what they envision future needs to be'.

Other participants focused more on developing their own needs, including more practical advice, access to coaching support, professional library resources and further follow-up.

What lessons learned might be useful to other organisations?

For organisations looking at implementing programmes to help develop staff it is important to have a good understanding of what the client organisation wants to achieve but also the participants – sometimes these goals are aligned and sometimes they are not. Be very clear in what it is that each party wants to achieve.

REFERENCE

Cerise, S., and Black and White Media Australia. (2008). Gender equality: What matters to Australian women and men. In C. Goldie & K. O'Connell (Eds.), *The Listening Tour Community Report* (pp. 1–24). Sydney: Human Rights and Equal Opportunity Commission.

UCLan, Centre for Volunteering and Community Leadership: Mentoring Practice

Ridwanah Gurjee

The Centre for Volunteering and Community Leadership (CVCL) is noted for its work in developing community cohesion and active citizenship projects at the University of Central Lancashire (UCLan). CVCL is a social enterprise that has delivered significant regional, national and international high-impact outcomes in the areas of youth development and community mentoring programmes alongside academic, vocational and bespoke Continuing Professional Development (CPD) courses at UCLan. Its key functions are to encourage mentoring and community engagement, raise the aspirations of our students and increase access to opportunities for education and employment. The mission of CVCL is to 'Empower, Engage and Enable' students in the direct delivery of community projects. A particular project – the focus of this chapter – is the case study of UCLan Student Mentoring in the Community.

The UCLan Student Mentoring in the Community is a validated 20-credit, year-long module that is available to all Year 2 undergraduate students across the university, with the additional external recognition of a Level 3 Certificate in Mentoring from the Institute of Leadership and Management. This is a work-based-learning qualification that recognises achievements and personal development in a mentoring setting. Students are offered the opportunity to enhance their understanding of mentoring pedagogy and then apply their learning in the role of a mentor in the community. This could either be with young people in educational settings, community centres, or care homes or vulnerable adults experiencing homelessness, loneliness or suffering from mental health issues. All students participating in this opportunity must complete an enhanced criminal-record check from the Disclosure and Barring Service (DBS). This executive agency of the Home Office has been set up to ensure safer recruitment decisions and identify those people who may be unsuitable to work with children or vulnerable adults (Home Office,

2015). Thus, only those students receiving satisfactory DBS clearance are able to participate.

Furthermore, mentoring in the community at UCLan is underpinned by the philosophy of Paulo Freire (1993: 96). He highlighted the concept of 'banking education', where the teacher deposits information and students are repositories. Freire (1993: 88) identifies the need to develop dialogue around what you are learning and why you are learning. For him, education is a culture action, not an everyday experience; it should have direct relevance to people's lives, and so it is important for CVCL to embark on mentoring programmes that initiate such encounters. Freire (1993: 88) also talks about problem-posing in the educational process and how exchange must be dialogical, working in small groups to encourage contribution. Here mentors use dialogue to engage mentees in action/reflection praxis to develop consciousness or self realisation – an integral part of this community-based methodology.

Many research evaluations, such as Grossman and Gary (1997: 9), report mentoring to be a promising approach which provides people, particularly the younger generation, with guidance, support and positive adult role models. Similarly, empirical research by Melling and Gurjee (2013) on the UCLan mentoring scheme concludes that mentoring programmes result in a wide range of tangible benefits, including the personal and professional development of students as well as providing them with the ability to gain key transferable skills for life and future employment.

The review process of the UCLan Student Mentoring in the Community included both a qualitative and quantitative approach. A high level of importance was placed on gaining a detailed insight into the mentors' and mentees' feelings, attitudes, levels of self-esteem and confidence, so as to measure impact. A qualitative approach was deemed particularly useful in order to draw out this information and make trustworthy conclusions.

Subsequently, it was also important to incorporate a quantitative approach in order to obtain 'hard' information from the mentees about their opinions and attitudes relating to the mentoring experience so enabling patterns could be observed and comparisons made (Cohen et al., 2011: 381). In addition to basing the fieldwork around the mentor and mentees, mentor co-ordinators from the community projects were also interviewed, providing a collaborative notion and a deeper insight into the mentees' achievements and progression, as advocated by DuBois et al. (2006: 658).

Finally, the research analysed student portfolios that reflected on the mentor role, completed as part of the module assessment. This additional method provided detailed information on both the mentors' and mentees' experiences, but, coming from the mentors' perspective, focused on the impact of mentoring with regard to personal and skills development and the influence/impact they feel they had on their mentee. These reflections provide supporting evidence and examples of situations that the mentor and mentee faced as a team as well as the social context of mentoring and the influences it has.

The results have generally identified mentoring as a positive experience for the student mentors, with some key areas of personal development that they will take with them in all aspects of their future life. The portfolios have been an extremely useful tool to allow students to reflect on their personal development and the process of mentoring, as proposed by Putnam (2000). The students have highlighted a number of key skills, including communication, team building, problem solving and leadership.

Furthermore, Knowles and Parsons' (2009: 205) research findings highlighted that mentoring is generally perceived in a positive way (as 'good'); however, there was no evidence of the impact of mentoring on behaviour and attendance. This is a different story in the UCLan research, as the results have identified many positive attributes to mentoring, such as 'good', 'enjoyable' and 'massively beneficial', as well as outlining some 'hard' and 'soft' outcomes on positive behaviour, attitudes and, particularly, personal and professional development.

The semi-structured interviews with mentor co-ordinators also highlighted 'hard' and 'soft' outcomes, as proposed by Clayden and Stein (2005: 34). Mentees, according to their mentors, enhanced their self-esteem and personal qualities, and they demonstrated changes in their behaviour and attitude by engaging in extra-curricular activities.

Another key aspect from the study by Clayden and Stein (2005: 34) shared by the UCLan students is that the mentor training was extremely valuable to them and supported them in their mentoring relationship. However, it could be important to incorporate 'instrumental' and 'expressive' mentoring styles into the training sessions in order for them to acknowledge and characterise some of the approaches that they are adopting (Gurjee, 2014).

This applied-learning environment, followed by reflective reviews and portfolio development, are central to CVCL and provide students with the opportunity to acknowledge the benefits – more often than not they are 'invisible' benefits – that they take away from the practical experience of mentoring (Kamvounias et al., 2008).

One of the aspects that was particularly difficult in this research was the analysis and decoding of the word 'challenge'. This was mainly because some students were communicating this as a positive aspect of their experience, whereas there were some mentors who were describing the challenge of the mentoring experience negatively. Thus, during the data-analysis process it has been really important to be very conscious of ensuring that researcher bias and subjectivity do not creep into the findings.

Other challenges identified by the co-ordinators include funding and the need for more research to be carried out on the impact of mentoring initiatives. This will not only help to secure funding streams but also highlight the significance and impact of such projects.

This project may also offer further opportunities for CVCL to support student mentoring in other contexts and internationally – for example, in orphanages within deprived countries, such as India or Pakistan. There is also the concept of e-mentoring, which is coming to fore, and how it can play an integral part within mentoring in comparison to traditional, face-to-face relationships.

Future research could also involve looking at the characteristics and processes of mentoring adopted by students, as these could possibly influence the quality and effectiveness of mentoring relationships, as explored by Rhodes and DuBois (2006: 3). It is important to look how interaction impacts on mentoring relationships, such as short-term mentoring in comparison to long-term mentoring and emotional connection versus a prescriptive approach. These are variables that influence the effectiveness of a mentoring relationship. By making an effort to explore these aspects in more detail, we will not only enhance the understanding of mentoring but also provide our students with quality first-hand empirical research on the characteristics and process of an effective mentoring relationship.

REFERENCES

Clayden, J. and Stein, M. (2005). *Mentoring Young People Leaving Care – 'Someone for me'*. Joseph Rowntree Foundation: York.

Cohen, L., Manion, L. and Morrison, K. (2011). *Research Methods in Education*. Seventh Edition. Routledge: London.

DuBois, D. L., Doolittle, F., Yates, B. T., Silverthorn, N. and Kraemer-Tebes, J. (2006). Research Methodology and Youth Mentoring. *Journal of Community Psychology*. Volume 34, Issue 6, Pages 657–76.

Freire, P. (1993). *Pedagogy of the Oppressed*. Continuum International Publishing Group Ltd: London and New York.

Grossman, J. B. and Gary, E. M. (1997). *Mentoring – A Proven Delinquency*

Prevention Strategy. Office of Juvenile Justice and Delinquency Prevention, US Department of Justice: Washington DC.

Gurjee, R. (2014). *An Exploration of Instrumental versus Expressive Mentoring: A Research Abstract.* Connect – International Mentoring Association, at http://mentoringassociation.org/connect/instrumental-vs-expressive-mentoring/ (accessed on 2 December 2015).

Home Office (2015). *About the Criminal Records Bureau.* Accessed online on 30 November, 2015 at https://www.gov.uk/government/organisations/disclosure-and-barring-service

Kamvounias, P., McGrath-Champ, S. and Yip, J. (2008). 'Gifts' in Mentoring: Mentees' Reflections on an Academic Development Program. *International Journal for Academic Development.* Volume 13, Issue 1, Pages 17–25.

Knowles, C. and Parsons, C. (2009). Evaluating a Formalized Peer Mentoring Program: A Student Voice and Impact Audit. *Pastoral Care in Education.* Volume 27, Issue 3, Pages 205–18.

Melling, A. and Gurjee, R. (2013). Researching the Impact of Student Mentoring in the Community. *International Journal of Social Work and Human Services Practice.* Horizon Research Publishing, Volume 1, Issue 1, Pages 1–8, at http://www.hrpub.org/download/201309/ijrh.2013.010101.pdf (accessed 2 December, 2015).

Putman, R. (2000). *Bowling Alone.* New York: Touchstone.

Rhodes, J. E. and DuBois, D. L. (2006). Understanding and Facilitating the Youth Mentoring Movement. *Social Policy Report.* Volume 20, Issue 3, Pages 3–19.

The Bacchus Mentoring Scheme: Enhancing the Alumni and Student Experience

Judie Gannon

A persistent challenge within even successful University undergraduate programmes is ensuring students are adequately prepared for their graduate careers. The Bacchus Mentoring Scheme aimed to improve transitions from university, within the specialist vocational area of international hospitality and tourism management from the Oxford School of Hospitality Management, into the industry. The programmes and School achieve high employability records for their graduates, but there is evidence that mentoring may remedy the number of graduates that tend to leave the sector after a few years of early-management experience and improve their networks of industry contacts. There is evidence, too, that mentoring is a feature of successful careers in the international hospitality and tourism industry, so prior exposure to mentoring can further enhance young managers' abilities to seek out suitable mentors and benefit from this intervention (Garavan et al., 2006). The Bacchus Mentoring scheme also presented an opportunity to position the programmes in an increasingly competitive higher-education environment, with increased focus on graduate employability, career development and a distinctive and meaningful student experience (Hazelkorn, 2015). Within the UK higher-education context there is a growing interest in developing alumni engagement and relations to facilitate these new foci. This scheme created new ways for the School to work with its alumni, industry friends and contacts who were keen to contribute to the student experience and the School's success.

PULLING THE PLAN TOGETHER

The mentoring scheme takes its name from the Bacchus Society, which is made up of students, alumni and staff from the School, part of the Business Faculty at Oxford Brookes University. A proposal was initiated and developed between key faculty members and the alumni arm of the society for a mentoring scheme in which, initially, only final-year undergraduates would be mentored by alumni and other industry supporters of the School. For several years the School had examined ways of offering more widespread engagement opportunities for alumni, and the chance to mentor students to support their successful transition (and long-term retention) into the industry was strongly advocated by active alumni. A committee was formed in 2007 to develop the mentoring scheme, comprising two members of the teaching team (including the author), three representatives of the alumni and two members of staff from the central University alumni office. The support of the University central alumni office was critical to help build the argument for the mentoring scheme and added weight to the case within the institution. A plan was developed to implement mentoring within the academic year 2008–9, with two teams within the committee tasked with separate activities. The first team focused on identifying good practice, drawing on expertise across the University and the wider mentoring and coaching community, and then preparing training and resources for students (mentees) and mentors. The second team concentrated on recruiting mentors through networks of alumni cohorts and School staff. The scheme was sold to potential mentors as a way of 'giving back' to the School and University and enhancing opportunities for recruiting and retaining graduates and Generation Y employees. Potential mentors were asked to compile a profile, detailing their career experiences to date, to help students identify mentoring preferences and support faculty members in the matching process. The 2008–9 launch plan also included a mentor briefing session and a separate matching and mentor–mentee-meeting event. The two teams were coordinated by the author as the initiator of the scheme and an academic within the School.

An early challenge faced by the committee was to sell the strategy to senior managers within the Faculty and wider University. Initial support for resources, such as catering, rooms and mentoring documentation, were secured by persuading this group of managers of the added value for the student experience and the wider impact of alumni engagement. The central alumni office and School senior-management team were particularly pivotal in securing a small amount of funding, including the time for the academics involved to achieve the launch of the scheme. The profile of the participating alumni also helped raise awareness of the initiative and further convince senior managers at the Faculty and University levels of the viability and benefits of the scheme.

THE FIRST YEAR OF THE SCHEME

The first run of the scheme comprised 44 mentors and 92 students, so most mentors worked with two students and a handful worked with three. In accordance with the academic year, the scheme ran from October through to the following May, across the final year of the undergraduate programme. Following concerns about widening participation and student engagement, the committee agreed to tie the scheme to a module on career planning and development. However, it was agreed that as the first year was essentially a trial, no aspect of participation in the scheme would be formally assessed. Likewise, the committee had concerns over mentors' engagement and their ability to spend time away from their businesses but agreed that a day-long mentor-briefing event would be appropriate. This was scheduled before the beginning of the academic year to ensure there were no limitations placed on accessing rooms and facilities. The sessions centred on the philosophy and content of the undergraduate programmes within the School, the student-support mechanisms on offer from the University and the student profile, alongside mentoring skills and good practice (including contracting and boundary setting, active listening and developing questioning techniques). A local consultant and trainer experienced in graduate development and recruitment facilitated the sessions alongside the author. The planning stages and initial consultation with alumni had identified that mentors would value the opportunity to network and practise their skills and knowledge. Accordingly, the briefing day factored in these aspects, and feedback was extremely positive about the mentor-briefing event. The students were briefed one week later, with their sessions focusing upon the value of mentoring and how to make the most of mentoring experiences. Students were asked to review the mentors' profiles, identify their top five preferences and justify these choices in relation to their career aspirations and personal goals. The initial matching of mentors and mentees provided a substantial challenge for the academic team. Student preferences were submitted only ten days before the matching and networking event, but working with colleagues who knew the students well from their previous studies helped, along with the students' own stated preferences, to identify the best matches.

Based upon the good-practice evidence collected by the academic team, and wider expertise, both mentors and mentees were provided with mentoring guides, which included further details on ideas for maintaining a positive relationship, topics to discuss during mentoring meetings and support services. As part of these guides, participants were recommended to record their mentoring interactions and experiences, setting goals for meetings and following up on actions agreed within sessions. The mentors were spread across the UK and Europe, so flexibility in communicating within the mentoring dyads was another point emphasised at both briefing events.

The launch matching event, where all mentees and mentors were introduced to each other, provided the team with specific challenges, due to a campus redevelopment and limited availability of resources (rooms and car-parking spaces). The event began by welcoming only the mentors and then allocating them to rooms across the University, where the mentees were then introduced. Initial tasks involved ice-breaker activities before matches were announced and mentors and mentees were given time to exchange contact details and begin to develop their mentoring contracts. The School deployed as many of its academic staff as it could to coordinate the different groups of mentors and mentees, which, while it created timetabling problems, hugely increased wider staff buy-in for the scheme and introduced mentors to more of the School's academic team. The committee undertook a preliminary evaluation of the matching and launch event and received very positive reactions. Only the logistical problems were experienced by mentors presenting the main issues and the team enacted plans to tackle these in future versions of the scheme.

One shortcoming of the initial plan developed by the committee for the Bacchus Mentoring scheme was the limited acknowledgement of the important role communication would play. While the mentees, as students, were easy to contact, due to ongoing teaching connections the team did not anticipate the extent of communication which would emerge on the mentors' side. This ranged from mentors seeking ongoing mentoring advice and support, media contacts initiated by mentors and wider interest from mentors to recruit new mentors from their own alumni and organisational networks – and, more generally, to know more about the progress of the scheme. The academic team sought to tackle these issues by introducing all mentors to the School e-magazine, the Bacchus Bulletin, and developing their own quarterly e-newsletter, focused solely on the mentoring scheme. The team also became versed in managing contacts from the press due to the unanticipated interest in the initiative. Recognising the personal nature of the mentoring relationships and the importance of retaining mentors for subsequent years of the scheme, the author also telephoned all mentors to establish their experiences of the mentoring. This was extremely informative and helped identify several issues for subsequent briefings and resources, including managing expectations and tactics for engaging less motivated students. It was also decided that a 'finale' event would be used to bring the first year of the scheme to an end and provide a final opportunity for mentors and mentees to meet and to celebrate the scheme. An online survey was then used to garner further feedback, which was fed back to participants in the newsletter.

Building upon the scheme's success

By the end of the first year the scheme was recognised as a significant success, not only by the mentors and mentees but the organising committee and the wider University. It had also been a challenging learning journey, as the time needed to administer the scheme, liaise with mentors and mentees and deal with enquiries had been unforeseen. Issues of data protection had prevented mentors from accessing the University virtual learning environment as a way to administer and manage communication for all scheme members. This led to one mentor offering her company's IT system to the scheme so that mentors and mentees could share a common platform for resources, and mentor profiles could be permanently accessible. In later years the scheme has been able to purchase an online mentoring tool, which has substantially professionalised the mentoring experiences of all concerned.

The importance of providing ongoing support for mentoring relationships was acknowledged after the first year. A small percentage of students struggle with their final-year studies, and this means their engagement with the mentoring opportunity needs to be managed carefully. Likewise, some mentors have had to withdraw due to changes in their personal or professional lives. Managing mentors' and mentees' expectations is crucial where such disturbances and fractures in relationships may occur. Following on from the feedback from the first year of the scheme, a more structured approach was adopted for the mentoring interactions and a greater emphasis was placed on managing expectations and having difficult conversations to move mentoring relationships forward in the briefing sessions and resources. In subsequent years students have also been asked to develop profiles so that mentors can engage with the students' experiences and expectations. This has helped establish diversity in the mentoring community, and mentors and mentees alike are much more confident in communicating their mentoring preferences with the academic team. After five years the remit of the mentoring scheme expanded to include postgraduate students within the School. The higher proportion of international students in this cohort has presented the challenge of managing a different set of student expectations and engagement. However, mentors and mentees have responded equally well to the prospect of enhancing their international networks.

The number of mentors has substantially increased since the first year of the scheme – 180 mentors are now registered – primarily due to word of mouth and wider recommendations from alumni and existing mentors. In more recent years the first group of mentors who experienced the scheme as mentees have become involved as mentors too. In recognition of mentors' many commitments, the mentor briefings are now held on the morning of the matching events. Mentors have also supported the scheme by offering their hospitality businesses in central London as venues for the mentoring-scheme events. The team has also worked with members of the International Centre for Coaching and Mentoring Studies to provide online mentoring support and resources, adding flexibility to mentors' development. Resourcing the scheme remains a challenge within the dynamic higher-education setting of fee implementation and a more competitive environment for students. Support from the mentors themselves, as well as the contribution of their time, has been invaluable; however, it is philanthropic donations which sustain the scheme on a year-to-year basis. The original remit of the mentoring scheme has paid dividends for the School and the wider institution. Specifically, the scheme has helped the School's programmes create and sustain a strong graduate-recruitment reputation, which means employers seek out graduates from their programmes due to their employability, networking skills and ability to transition into industry roles effectively.

REFERENCES

Garavan, T.N., O'Brien, F. and O'Hanlon, D. (2006). Career advancement of hotel managers since graduation: a comparative study, *Personnel Review*, 35(3), pp. 252–80.

Hazelkorn, E. (2015). *Rankings and the reshaping of higher education: The battle for world-class excellence*. Basingstoke: Palgrave Macmillan.

How Might Mentoring Work? Starting to Lift the Lid on the Black Box

Sally Lawson

This short study describes peer-to-peer mentoring in specialist workforce development and explores the challenge of knowing more about how mentoring works. It looks beyond how mentoring is done. It draws on research into a mentoring programme for a group of non-medical practitioners working in neuro services, where mentoring was interpreted as a developmental relationship, outside the person's usual organisational hierarchy or accountability, which supports significant and meaningful changes in thinking, feeling or actions, for work or self (after Megginson et al., 2006).

The mentoring framework proposed by Megginson et al. (2006: 4) informs this study. Their multi-level perspective encompasses the *mentoring culture* and *scheme design,* encircling *relationships, episodes* and *techniques* and, centrally, the *moment* or *moments* of change. It is used here to consider how mentoring worked in a dyad, linking the relationship qualities that were embedded in each episode or conversation and the way these were expressed in techniques, especially the use of questions that enabled the mentee to recount, reflect, reappraise and respond differently from the way they might have done without mentoring – their moment.

It begins with the background to the mentoring programme, followed by an appreciation of mentoring from participants' feedback. This leads to the study, an exemplar that draws on mentoring stories emerging from a dyad, focusing on one way in which mentoring worked. This informs the start of a theory (Lawson, 2017). The narratives come from the author's PhD research into this mentoring programme, a longitudinal study using realist evaluation methodology to understand how it worked, 'for whom, in what circumstance and in what respects' (Pawson and Tilley, 2004: 2).

BACKGROUND TO THE MENTORING PROGRAMME, 2009–11

The programme was the workforce component of an innovative partnership-improvement infrastructure set up by a commissioning-led network across the north east of England. The aim was to use strategic funding to accelerate local implementation of the National Service Framework for Long-term Conditions (Department of Health, 2005). It created complementary opportunities for people who use neuro services, practitioners, managers, commissioners and researchers to learn and work together to increase capacity and capability and improve services and outcomes (summarised by Lawson, 2012).

Describing this project within the mentoring framework, the mentoring programme (*mentoring scheme design*) was a part-time, broadly based learning, development and change programme for eighteen participants, delivered in six modules from November 2009 to March 2011. Participants included both experienced and less experienced practitioners as mentors and mentees, seconded from all sectors, thirteen different organisations and seven different practitioner groups. Teaching and facilitation drew on substantial local expertise in policy, practice and research to challenge perspectives on current and future services and inform participants' work in moving change forward. Twenty change projects were carried out, anchored in participants' own organisations, and from one of these, Mentoring in the Workplace, two additional mentees were involved. Action research enabled participants to evaluate their work as well as the programme (Akhurst, 2011; Akhurst and Lawson, 2013).

A dedicated mentoring module gave ten experienced practitioners the opportunity to gain competence and confidence as mentors, with an option to undertake portfolio and assignment-based accreditation up to master's level through a local university. The module was developed and delivered by an independent provider with recognised expertise and experience in this approach, with learning resources underpinned by evidence of good practice. It included taught elements, e.g. introduction to mentoring, emotional intelligence; support elements for the mentors, i.e. a personal development review and plan, action learning sets; and the mentoring experience with mentees. Additional themes were added to the module as it progressed, responding to feedback from those involved.

Developmental mentoring (*the relationship, episodes, techniques* and *moments*) was central to the programme, supporting the achievement of mentees' personal and practice-career outcomes and similarly benefiting the mentors. Mentoring was not only the key Programme intervention but became part of its collaborative approach, its *culture*. Mentors and mentees were matched outside their own organisation and practitioner group. Mentees set the goals and direction of mentoring conversations whilst taking responsibility for their own learning and development. The format and timing of contact between mentors and mentees was determined by each pairing in their contract. The content of the mentoring conversations was confidential.

PARTICIPANTS' APPRECIATION OF MENTORING

In both the mentoring programme and mentoring relationships, the focus was on a developmental, partnership approach to understanding and valuing individual and group differences and commonalities to create a vibrant community of learning, practice and discovery (*mentoring culture*). This infiltrated one-to-one relationships and conversations as well as wider group discussions, strengthening participants' knowledge, attitudes, beliefs and behaviours and contributing to defining the values and norms of the group.

In the programme's summative evaluations (Akhurst, 2011; Carson, 2011; Lawson,

2011), participants reported meaningful changes:

- Developing confidence and competence as mentors: *both Myers Briggs Type Indicators and Emotional Intelligence have been life changing – not just work and mentoring, but my whole life approach*;
- Finding new ways of learning together: *to explore ideas, how to change what you are already doing; look at things from a different angle… and provides a non-judgemental environment – feel comfortable to develop skills and knowledge and fill in gaps in the learning process*;
- Working differently and making a difference, in partnership with people accessing services: *with a different set of questions, taking it from the other person's perspective… I have taken the pressure off myself to be the expert. The person using the service is having their priorities heard and we can work to achieve those. It's more meaningful for the individual and more satisfying for me*;
- Making operational changes: *a mentee is now using a mentoring approach to the learning and development of practitioners in her team, opening doors, breaking down barriers of specialist roles and encouraging staff to take responsibility for their own learning and development. This has freed up waiting times and re-distributed the caseload*; and
- Networking and influencing strategically: *neurological experience in tandem with an understanding of the mentoring process brings the mentor to a new place which allows you as a mentor to effect change: for example, working with budget holders, other practitioners and service users/carers to make the necessary changes required.*

So, how might developmental mentoring work to enable changes and impacts such as these?

MENTORING STORIES

The following stories were shared with the researcher in separate, semi-structured interviews with a matched mentee and mentor. They were encouraged to reflect on their experience of mentoring and particularly what had changed for the mentee and how. What impact did it have for her? For that to happen, what was it in mentoring or about mentoring that she responded to and what was her response? Finally, what was going on for her at that time that made her respond to that particular opportunity in that way? Analysis revealed causal patterns in the way mentoring had worked for her.

Unknowingly, both the mentee and the mentor talked about the same mentee experience. It was about an impasse overcome, highlighting the significance of support and challenge in their mentoring relationship, in their contacts (in person, by phone and email) and in the mentor's technique of using questions to elicit reflective stories and discussion that enabled the mentee to move forward. This changed the quality of the mentee's thinking and as a result, the quality of what she was then able to achieve through a greater sense of agency.

The mentee's story: ideas, plus support, lead to action…

The mentee worked as a practitioner in *a good service that could be better.* It was dominated by NHS hierarchies and the medical model. She was an activist, comfortable with change and risk, but perhaps also a covert theorist, enjoying structure and purpose and not overwhelmed by complexity or challenge in her day-to-day practice.

With her mentor, she was quick to raise the issue of a service improvement opportunity at work – keen to make progress but not knowing how to change things.

In her interview with the researcher, the mentee gave an account of the significant contextual imbalances which had left her stuck. On the positive side, she saw herself as *a clinical expert with plenty of improvement ideas* and *a passion for changing neuro services.* Conversely, she said she was *frustrated and disheartened* by gaps in her strategic knowledge, with *no idea how to take things forward,* made worse by *a lack of time at work.* Additionally, she felt she had no support, because her *manager's thought processes aligned with the organisation. Good ideas were 'taken on board' but led to no movement.* Organisationally, she felt that *neuro was not a priority or on people's agenda; there were not the right people with enough knowledge to help move things forward; they had limited perceptions of my profession, grade and role... or the need for a neuro champion in the organisation.*

Asked about the resources she connected with in mentoring, she spoke about what she valued in the mentoring relationship, reinforced in the programme itself, making it different to management or supervision at work: *there was time... a place – all in same room... and people – diversity but with a shared passion, vision and language.* She valued this opportunity and became confident in the relationship, accessing the mentor's wider experience and expertise: *knowing someone was there to bat things out with... that there was support and challenge,* including *setting objectives and a structure to make progress.* In addition, she appreciated the mentor's questions which caused her to slow down and created the space for her to think about things differently: *'Is that the only way? Could you do something different?' – all in a conversational style... talking things through was a reflective process.* This was new territory for this activist and it was here that she addressed the contexts she believed restricted her, reconnected with the strengths she had lost sight of and explored options on ways forward she had not envisaged. This enabled her to formulate a plan and act on it: *I'm not sure I would have got to that point myself.*

Her moment was the decision to do fairly simple things. She chose to meet the key medical consultant... *having the confidence to do that... with the belief in what you're doing, the benefit of that and what the implication of that action will be... understanding my own risk-taking powers and just managing the risk... breaking down all the invisible stereotypes and traditions and this changed beliefs of myself and others.* As a result of this meeting and further conversations, service changes were made.

Since her experience of the partnership approach with the mentor and of using it to good effect with the consultant, her sense of self-efficacy and agency has stayed with her. They have influenced her practice and particularly the purpose and content of what she does and how she does it: *and that's made me a much better clinician – and what makes me a little bit different to other clinicians – quite different.* She has recently moved to a significant leadership position.

The mentor's story: you wouldn't say that, but you'd find a way of saying that... and find a way to use the power of the powerful...

The mentor had years of experience and expertise as a practitioner, leading services with the social model at their core and working extremely effectively with a partnership and improvement approach. This brought reflector and theorist styles to mentoring, with a strong dose of pragmatism and practicality.

In the research interview, the mentor interpreted the same story as *a light bulb moment for her.* The mentoring relationship and their conversations supported and challenged the mentee to create more positive conditions for change, resonant with her approach. The mentor's technique, and particularly the corresponding style and content of questions, enabled the mentee to reconnect with her strengths: *trying to find out what and where she was coming from.* The mentor challenged her perception of the inhibiting, disempowering contexts that prevented her doing anything: *I was probably a bit more proactive.* The same circumstances still existed but their perceived relevance and influence diminished. She could then focus on where change might come from: *she was no different to lots of people who are in awe of these consultants... and that stopped her trying to move their service forward – the consultant was the block.* Drawing on years of finding ways forward with similar situations at work, the mentor offered examples of practical, small steps that the mentee could choose to action, including, pivotally: *simply go and sit down and talk to him, explaining what the situation is.* The mentee made progress: *she went away and did that and came back saying, 'it worked, I've done it, it was fine' – and that was a big boost for her.*

FROM CASUAL PATTERNS TO THE START OF A THEORY

These mentee and mentor stories bring the levels of the mentoring framework into relief: the relationship, episodes, techniques and moments within a specific culture and design. Further, these accounts of how mentoring worked for them, point to a provisional hypothesis about the importance of *change conversations and shared reflection* as one of many significant aspects of developmental mentoring in practice. This might be expressed as follows: 'By taking regular time out of work in a developmentally focused dyad to which both the mentee and mentor are committed, the questioning and listening in change conversations evoke shared reflection on the mentee's story, enhanced by the mentor's expertise, experience and broader view. Over time, this enables the mentee to generate new ways of thinking about an issue, consider options, decide what to do and action that change. Further conversations and reflection about that experience consolidate the mentee's development, including their sense of agency'.

However, to achieve a credible theory that might explain how developmental mentoring works requires the generation of additional hypotheses and the evaluation of more narrative data, with greater depth and from wider sources. As well as primary evaluations, this might involve the synthesis of studies from mentoring as well as developmental or helping relationships in other fields, their conversations and techniques, further informed by theories of behavioural change, for example. A reference for this approach is Pawson's realist review of youth mentoring (2006: chapter 6).

As a result, emergent theories about what is happening and how it works, at and between levels in the mentoring framework might better inform the knowledge and evolving practice of developmental mentoring as a complex intervention.

REFERENCES

Akhurst, J. 2011. *Neurosciences Workforce Innovations Programme (North East): Mentorship Programme*. Action Research Report. Middlesbrough: North East Neurosciences Network.

Akhurst, J. and Lawson, S. 2013. Workforce innovation through mentoring; an action research approach to programme evaluation. *International Journal of Therapy and Rehabilitation,* 20(8): 410–16.

Carson, S. 2011. *Evaluation and Outcomes Report – North East Workforce Innovations Programme 2009–2011*. Mentorship Development Module. Middlesbrough: North East Neurosciences Network.

Department of Health. 2005. *National Service Framework for Long-term Conditions.* London: Department of Health.

Lawson, S. 2011. *Workforce Innovations Programme: Change and Benefit Realisation Report*. Middlesbrough: North East Neurosciences Network.

Lawson, S. 2012. Improving outcomes through workforce innovations. *Occupational Therapy News,* February 2012: 22–3.

Lawson, S. 2017. Mentoring in specialist workforce development: a realist evaluation. Unpublished PhD thesis. Leeds University.

Megginson, D., Clutterbuck, D., Garvey, B., Stokes, P. and Garrett-Harris, R. 2006. *Mentoring in Action*. London: Kogan Page.

Pawson, R. and Tilley, N. 2004. *Realist Evaluation*. Available at: http://www.communitymatters.com.au/RE_chapter.pdf (downloaded 21 January, 2013).

Pawson, R. 2006. *Evidence-based Policy. A Realist Perspective*. London: Sage.

Crossing Thresholds Career-Mentoring Programme for Women in the UK Civil Service

Fiona McInnes-Craig

INTRODUCTION

Thresholds have gained a solid reputation in the UK public sector for delivering highly effective career support at affordable prices.

Crossing Thresholds is a year-long mentoring programme for women in the UK Civil Service who want to develop their career in a structured and supportive environment. The mentoring partnerships are underpinned with five themed facilitated modules, peer support groups, shadowing assignments and 'hot topic' learning events facilitated by the participants themselves.

To date 105 cohorts have completed or are underway, with more than 2,000 mentoring partnerships.

On average, 76 per cent of participants get promoted or move to a more suitable job within a year of completing the programme.

ORIGIN AND AIMS

The Crossing Thresholds programme was originally developed for the Department for International Development (DFID) in response to a study into diversity barriers to career progression. Women who took part in the study had identified particular difficulties for those who wanted to progress, and highlighted the need for mentoring and coaching.

DFID's Diversity Adviser had come across Thresholds at an Opportunity Now showcase event, and she felt that our innovative approach was just what was needed. There was pressure within the organisation to use a more 'tried and tested' organisation; however, she was able to get the green light for one pilot programme.

Senior DFID staff responded in large numbers to a request for mentors, and the mentor-training workshops were well attended.

The aim of the programme was to stimulate participants' thinking about what they wanted in their careers and support them to take strategic action to achieve it.

The pilot programme began in January 2006 with 18 partnerships. It had quite a loose structure: a two-day career goal-setting and action-planning workshop, followed by broadly themed modules at two-monthly intervals, with internal speakers and lively discussions. Participants were paired with one of their short-listed mentors. Mentoring sessions were generally one hour per month, with partnerships having the flexibility to adjust this around their needs and availability. Although the majority of the sessions were face to face, because of the international nature of the organisation some people were paired with a mentor overseas, and these sessions were by videoconference.

REFINING THE PROGRAMME

Thresholds has always strived to be a 'learning organisation'. We begin any event or programme with a clear vision of the results we want (and agreed with our clients), which acts as a reference point throughout the design, delivery and evaluation. Regular feedback is central to our ability to make strategic adjustments and course corrections in order to achieve the vision we have set out.

With Crossing Thresholds the vision was clear – to support each mentee to identify and achieve their career goal within their chosen time frame. In addition we wanted each person to gain transferrable skills they could apply to any personal or work goal in the future.

Throughout each programme the key questions we asked ourselves were 'Is this achieving our vision?' and 'How could this be even more effective?'. The regular wealth of input and feedback from mentees and mentors was combined with our own experience and learning to produce one of the most successful programmes DFID has ever run (so we are told!).

EVALUATION OF THE PILOT

The evaluation of the pilot was done in two parts: seven months into the programme mentees completed an interim survey. The findings were immediately used to make improvements to the programme and also helped shape the second programme, which was just starting. A more thorough evaluation was undertaken during the pilot programme's final group event. We also got detailed feedback from the mentors.

Most participants had made tangible progress towards their goals, including substantive promotion to the next grade, temporary promotion, lateral moves to more desirable jobs and strategic secondments. From all the feedback it became clear that the programme was having a powerful impact on participants' careers, specifically:

- Space and time to think 'outside the box'
- Increased clarity of direction and career focus
- A better understanding of the organisational culture and what it takes to progress
- Learning from those who have already attained more senior grades
- Increased visibility inside and outside the department
- Confidence to approach senior colleagues for advice
- Greater self-belief and sense of readiness for promotion
- Support – both emotional and practical – from being part of a network of female peers
- Sharing useful practical tips from mentors – both one's own and others'

LESSONS LEARNED AND IMPLEMENTED

1 We needed to make our expectations of the time commitment much clearer to the mentors taking part

We saw from mentee feedback a clear link between the time given by mentors and the benefit mentees received from the relationship. Some mentors only gave a short time to them, e.g. 15–30 minutes. Some mentors fulfilled their commitment to the 10 sessions they had signed up for, while others only managed four or five. In the few instances where there was a combination of these two things, i.e. only a few brief discussions, their mentees clearly got less benefit from the programme.

2   Mentors and mentees need to share mutual expectations at the start

Some mentees felt let down by their mentors, whether because they cancelled sessions without suggesting alternative dates, didn't contact them for long periods, didn't seem to have prepared for sessions or only made brief times available. We saw the need in future to encourage the partnerships to start off by sharing their expectations of each other and setting out an informal contract, which would form a reference point for any future deviations from the agreement. We would also encourage mentees to be proactive about booking several sessions with their mentor in advance, in case a session has to be postponed.

3   Mentees want their thinking to be challenged and stretched

Although many mentees commented on the value of the support and encouragement they received, many also appreciated having their assumptions challenged and being pushed to think things through for themselves.

4   Mentors need to see how their role fits with the wider programme

We saw that the few mentors who didn't fully understand the wider context for their role tended to focus on the more immediate issues which their mentees were facing (e.g. a job application) rather than more strategic career-progression issues.

5   Geography needn't be a barrier to effective partnerships

We found, to our delight, that geographic distance needn't be a barrier to contact. As was recommended, the partnerships made use of a variety of communications media for mentoring sessions: people often benefited as much from a telephone session and email feedback as face-to-face contact.

6   Mentees need to be encouraged to give feedback to their mentors

There was clearly some variance in mentoring quality and ability. Some mentees were keen to give feedback to their mentors but were unsure or lacking confidence about doing this. We would therefore encourage mentees to develop the habit of giving feedback to their mentors in relation to what they wanted more (or less) of, and, where necessary, holding their mentors to account for what they had agreed to.

IN SUMMARY

In total, five Crossing Thresholds programmes were run at DFID, which resulted in a measurable increase in the proportion of women progressing to the Senior Civil Service.

The Crossing Thresholds programme was the central pillar of DFID's Opportunity Now award in 2006.

Expansion across the Civil Service

The Civil Service has always taken the issue of representation very seriously, and the launch of the Diversity 10 Point Plan highlighted the need for all Government Departments to consider what support they needed to offer women in order to 'level the playing field'.

In 2009, Crossing Thresholds was opened up to women civil servants from all Departments and Executive Agencies. At first it was run as an external programme, requiring applicants to provide a business case.

In 2014 it was incorporated into the Civil Service Learning (CSL) Curriculum, which has resulted in it being much more widely available across the Civil Service.

Using end-of-module and end-of-programme feedback, the programme has been continuously refined. The initial programmes were held in London; however, in the last two years it has expanded across the UK, including Wales and Scotland, and there have also been a number of courses run in Africa and Asia.

Long-term results

One year after the end of each programme we ask everyone in that cohort to complete an online survey to find out the lasting impact from being on the programme. As mentioned above, on average 76 per cent of participants get promoted or move to a more suitable job within a year of completing the programme.

Beyond that, we have created a global support network of 'Thresholders', who have all been on a similar development journey and have ongoing access to resources and alumni networking events.

Keys to a successful mentoring partnership

The following are some things we recommend to mentees:

- Agree at the outset the frequency, length, structure and logistics for the sessions. Take responsibility for suggesting dates and making sure they get in both your diaries. Block-booking a number of sessions or setting up a recurring Outlook event can work well. Decide between you what you will do if a session gets cancelled. Don't be put off if a session gets cancelled – take the initiative and get a new date arranged asap.
- Set out your goals for the mentoring partnership and take responsibility for what you want from each of the sessions. It helps to approach mentoring sessions in the 'learning mode', rather than 'performing mode'.
- Prepare in advance for each session and send a reminder/agenda/update to your mentor a couple of days beforehand. It's really useful to take time to reflect on previous discussions before you go into a session, which allows discussions to build on each other. Take notes of each session and send your mentor a typed-up record of your discussion afterwards, with action points highlighted. Take action between sessions. Inform your mentor about your successes along the way.
- Decide how you will evaluate the relationship along the way. Build in time for giving and receiving feedback at the end of each session, so you know that the sessions are serving their purpose or what else you need to do. For example, this might include encouraging your mentor to challenge and stretch your thinking.
- Use your career action plan as a focus of your work together. You may also want to make a list of relevant topics to look at – for example, as you work through the modules, make their themes the topic of your discussions. This approach will help to keep your sessions both fresh and inspiring, and preparation for each module with subsequent evaluation will help you get the best from your programme as well as your mentoring. Be prepared to ask for specific help if appropriate – for example, looking over an application form.
- Be honest and open. Show your appreciation for your mentor's support.

A Self-Managed Mentee-Led Mentoring Programme for Vodafone Turkey

Tim Bright

INTRODUCTION

This chapter is about an ongoing mentoring programme within Vodafone Turkey. Vodafone is a leading mobile-communications operator in Turkey, with over 21 million customers and more than 3,000 employees. The programme was designed and delivered together with Vodafone Turkey's human-resources (HR) team.

THE NEED

The leadership of Vodafone Turkey is committed to mentoring as a development methodology. However, there were concerns that a 'typical' mentoring programme might not meet the organisation's needs. Vodafone Turkey is an extremely fast-paced environment, with all staff working to meet multiple goals under significant pressure in an atmosphere of constant change. It is extremely difficult for senior leaders to commit time to programmes such as mentoring, or even to gather all at the same time and place for a workshop. Also, the employee population is self-confident and savvy and can have a limited attention span for corporate initiatives. People development can often lose out to other items on the pressing business agenda.

In mentoring programmes in other contexts we have seen concerns about matching, challenges to select and maintain a pool of mentors, some mentees not being fully committed to the programme and a drop-off in engagement during the process for some pairs. We were particularly concerned about these risks within this organisation.

Within Vodafone Turkey there was an expressed need for more mentoring and developmental conversations to happen across the organisation, for a programme to quickly scale rather than just being provided for a number of designated 'high talents', and for it to be sustainable over the medium term across the organisation.

THE DESIGN

The mentoring programme is designed as completely voluntary and totally driven by the mentee. The scheme design is as follows:

- Any employee can be a mentee.
- Anyone who wants to be a mentee needs to select their own mentor within the company and approach them. The mentor can't be in their own reporting line.
- People who are approached to be mentors can accept or reject the invite as they wish. Each mentor can work with a maximum of three mentees at any one time.
- Once a pair is established the mentee should inform their HR contact.
- Information on the programme and e-learning tools for mentoring (videos, presentations, methodology) are provided to everyone in the company.
- Half day training workshops for mentees and mentors are offered for all participants.
- Mentoring pairs are recommended to meet once per month over 12 months.
- HR will support mentors or mentees who approach them for input or guidance. Participants can also approach the external consultant for support.
- Two-hour follow-up/supervision sessions are run periodically (two to three times each year) and separately for mentees and mentors. Attendance is voluntary.
- Short 'pulse check' email surveys are sent to mentors and mentees, with a maximum of five questions to get feedback on their participation in the programme.
- The formal programme in terms of HR support and follow-up ends after a year. After that mentees are encouraged to choose a different mentor to work with if they want to continue in a mentoring relationship.

PRINCIPLES

The programme is designed to be as 'light touch' as possible and to put the responsibility for managing the programme fully on the mentee. It is also completely voluntary, so there is no requirement for HR to select mentees or mentors or to follow up on whether they are meeting or not. This avoids many of the challenges of selecting suitable mentors and mentees and how to manage the pool.

The scheme design is very transparent: all participants have access to the same tools and materials. Participants are encouraged to be open about their mentoring relationships. A number of participants are simultaneously mentors and mentees, and they are free to attend either the mentee or mentor workshop or both. The content of each workshop is largely the same but focuses on the concerns of either mentees or mentors.

OUTCOMES

Together with HR we had concerns about how employees would react to this programme and whether it would be difficult to manage. At the time of writing we are coming to the end of the first year of the programme and the reactions so far have been very positive.

Participation in the programme has been much higher than expected. Because of the demand from people who want to be mentees we have started three 'waves' of participation over time, offering the workshops to new participants. Over 200 mentoring pairs have now started working together. If we had worked with a typical approach of selecting a pool of mentors we would not have had more than 20 or 30 pairs active at this stage.

There has been a great deal of enthusiasm around the programme, and many participants are both mentors and mentees. The mentees have a great sense of ownership as they have selected themselves for the programme and chosen their own mentor. We believe this will make the relationships more sustainable as well.

CHALLENGES

There have been a number of issues to manage. A number of senior leaders have been approached by many potential mentees and have found it difficult to choose who to work with and how to reject others. The rule that they can work with a maximum of three people at once gives them some help in this. Also, the guideline that relationships should last for a year has given them the opportunity to offer to work with a mentee at the end of the current year's programme.

There have also been significant demands on the time of the HR team, with mentees and mentors asking for support over issues such as choosing a mentor and how to manage the process effectively. These conversations have also given the HR team an opportunity to work effectively with their internal clients and contribute to their development.

Some participants (mentees and volunteer mentors) didn't immediately find a partner, and the HR team has helped them find a match.

A number of mentees chose mentors from departments where they think they might want to work in the future. At first we were concerned about this and potential conflicts of interest, but we have come to see it as a good thing, as it can support employee rotation within the organisation, which is a leadership aim (and it probably increases retention as well).

LEARNING

We have learned that we need to be very clear about the role of sponsorship. Lots of mentees are looking for sponsorship, and some mentors are prepared to offer it. We were careful to define sponsorship and developmental mentoring as different things. We have said in the workshops and on other occasions that sponsors are useful and that employees should find a number of sponsors, both internal and external, but that for this programme we are focused on developmental mentoring, and we shouldn't confuse the two.

The self-service nature of this programme has generally been effective. Although we wanted to run full-day workshops to present and discuss a range of material, we found that half-day workshops have much higher attendance rates, and we have provided other materials via Vodafone's e-learning portal.

The role of the internal programme manager has been critical to success. Also important is the role of front line HR Business Partners, who all need to be comfortable talking about the programme and dealing with questions.

Based on our experience so far, this programme design appears to be a good fit for the particular context we are working in and has avoided some of the challenges of programmes with selected pools of mentors and mentees who are matched by the organisation. This self-managed, mentee-led programme has led to a huge number of development-focused conversations that probably wouldn't have happened otherwise, has unleashed a great deal of energy and focus on people's own development and has increased effective cross-functional communication within Vodafone Turkey.

INDEX

Aarhus University, 170, 228
Abdelrahman, Nahed, xiv; *co–author of Chapter 8*
Abedin, Z., 144
Aboriginal graduate students, 325
academic careers, 56–7
academic monitoring
    purpose of, 325–6
    types of, 326–7
Achebe, C., 505
adult development, 25, 30, 106
adult learning theory, 71
advocacy role, 110, 302, 309
Affectiva (company), 495
affirmative action, 395–6
Afghanistan, 531
Agosto, Vonzell, xiv; *co-author of Chapter 23*
Alberta Mentoring Partnership, 126
alignment of mentoring with object-ives, 218–21, 224, 251
Allan, B., 489
Allen, T.D., 26, 52, 54, 60–1, 67, 78, 81, 146, 215, 455
Alred, G., 16, 178
Amabile, T., 28
American Association of Colleges of Pharmacy, 326
American College of Physicians (ACP), 214
Anadolu Efes (company), 587
analogical reasoning, 198–9
Anderson, E.M., 16, 149
Anderson, L., 438
Apple, M.W., 34
apprenticeship model, 20–1, 36, 69
Aragon, Louis, 23, 25
Archibald, J., 325
Arksey, H., 120
Armstrong, M., 395
Aryee, S., 5
aspirations, *extrinsic* and *intrinsic*, 173
assimilation, 398
Association to Advance Collegiate Schools of Business, 326

Athena, 2–3, 68
'atmosphere' for mentoring, 7
attachment theory, 97–8, 303
Audet, J., 361
Australia, 508–12, 604–13
authoritarianism, 37
autonomy, 115

Bacchus Mentoring Scheme, 618–22
Bach, B.W., 161, 165
Baker, R., 321
Baker, Vicki L., xiv, 212, 251, 431; *author of Chapter 14 and co-author of Chapter 26*
Baker, Wendy, xiv; *co-author of Chapter 39*
Ball, S.J., 345–6
Bangert, A., 439
Barkham, J., 282
Barnett, E.A., 318
Bar-On, R., 276
Baron, A., 395
Barrett, R., 193, 267
barrier transcendence, 36–7
baseball professionals, 94–5
Bauer, T.N., 324
Beck, Makini, xiv; *co-author of Chapter 23*
beginner teachers, 336; *see also* early career teachers
behaviorist theories, 72
behavioural awareness, 145
behavioural outcomes of mentoring, 235–8
Behnke, S., 110
Belin, Francis, 601
benchmarks, use of, 238–43
beneficence, principle of, 114
Bengtson, E., 438
Bennetts, C., 24–5
Bennis, Warren, 231
Benschop, Y., 395–6
Bernard, J.M., 263–5
best practice
    in mentoring, 54, 69, 79
    in mentoring research, 58

Bettinger, E., 321
Bhide, Sadhana, xiv; *author of Chapter 13*
bias, unconscious, 384, 400–2
Bierema, Laura, xv, 484; *author of Chapter 30 and co-author of Chapter 18*
Big Brothers and Big Sisters movements, 185, 296, 298
Birmingham, 228
Black, L.L., 178
Blackman, Anna, xv; *author of Chapter 51*
Blake-Beard, S., 191, 392, 399
Bleijenberg, I., 395
Blevins-Knabe, B., 112
Blewden, M., 232
'blockers' amongst mentors, 146
board members as mentors, 414
Bodoczky, C., 348
Bordin, E.S., 267
Boswell, Jennifer, xv; *co-author of Chapter 8*
Bottoms, S., 379
Bouquillon, E.A., 160–1, 165
Bourdieu, Pierre, 126
Boyzatis, Richard, 177
Bozeman, Barry, 53, 59–60, 157, 583, 585
Brazil, 513–19
Bright, J.E.H., 173–4
Bright, Tim, xv, 587; *author of Chapter 56 and co-author of Chapter 46*
Brim, J.B., 172
Bristol, L.S.M., 438
Brockbank, A., 144–5, 163–4, 440
Brodeur, P., 59
Brondyk, S., 54, 58, 79
Bronfenbrenner, U., 99
Brounstein, M., 16
Brown, A.L., 349
Brown, K.M., 440
Browne-Ferrigno, T., 37–8, 40
Buche, M.W., 483, 493–4
Buddha, 119
Bujaki, M., 391, 398
Bullis, C., 161, 165
Burg, J., 319
Burke, P., 440
Bury, Kathleen, xv; *co-author of Chapter 34*
business mentoring, 149, 213–14
Byron, Lord, 24

Calafell, B.M., 25
Cameron, David, 28
Cameron, M., 343–4
Campbell, C., 69, 81
Campbell, T.A. and D.E., 321
Canada, 322, 590–4
Caraccioli, L.A., 23–4
Cardno, C., 439
career development mentoring, 76–8, 89, 105–6, 149, 421–2, 437, 445–6, 483–5, 629–32
'career stage' models, 73, 422–31
career transition points, 292, 408–9
Carolina Covenant, 215
Carraher, S.M., 202, 414–15
Carroll, S.J., 144
Carson, S., 577
Caruso, J.A., 186
Caruso, P., 276
cascade mentoring, 36
Castles, S., 361
cause-and-effect relationships, 56–7, 78
Cavett, Esther, xvi, 570; *author of Chapter 43*
centralized and *decentralized* mentoring programmes, 248
Centre for Volunteering and Community Leadership (CVCL), 614–16
Cervero, R.M., 382
'champions' for mentoring, 190, 196
Chan, A.W., 325
Chandler, D.E., 55, 58–60, 165, 421–30, 478
change discourse, 28
Chao, G.T., 160–1, 164, 216
Charan, R., 409
cháris concept, 468
charting of data, 121
Chen, H.C. and M.J., 438–9
Cherniss, C., 276–7
Chesterfield, Lord, 24
Cheung, Y.H., 280
chief executive officers (CEOs), 411–14
chivalry, 19–20
Church, R., 393
Cintron, R., 322
City Music Foundation (CMF), 570–4
Citymothers Scheme (CMS), 570–4
clarification of issues, 7
clarity of purpose, 148
Clarke, P.P., 21

Claxton, G., 344
Clayden, J., 616
'climates' for mentoring, 4
Clutterbuck, David A., xiii, 4–7, 25, 39, 54, 69, 71, 76–7, 145–7, 150, 152, 159–63, 178, 180, 185–8, 195–9, 202, 231, 233, 248–9, 253, 394, 397, 400–1, 407, 552, 554, 563; *author of Introduction to Part IV, co-author of Chapters 1 and 11 and co-editor*
coaching
    definitions of, 174
    as distinct from mentoring, 39–40
    literature on, 174–7
    supervision of, 151
    types of, 39
Coats, L.T., 282
Cobb Roberts, Deirdre, xvi; *co–author of Chapter 23*
Cocca, Anna, 600
co-constructivism, 446
codes of ethics, 106, 109, 114–15
cognitivist theories, 72
Colky, D.L., 486
collaborative mentoring, 41–2, 47
collectivist cultures, 151
collegiality, 38
Colley, H., 17–18, 26
Collins, A., 57
Collins, P.H., 25
Columbus, Christopher, 236
co-mentoring, 379, 381
communication skills, 145, 150
community-based mentoring (CBM), 296–8
comparative studies, 57–8
competencies, 76–9, 148–50
    definition of, 109
    need for research on, 153
competency frameworks, 143
competitive advantage, 224
complex adaptive systems, 150–1, 153, 247, 259
'comprehensive mentoring programs', 321–2
computer-mediated communication (CMC), 484, 493–5
conceptual modelling, 145
confidentiality, 110, 266
Conley, V.M., 431
constructive development theory, 73
constructivism, 72, 443–5

context of mentoring, 2–4, 54–6, 149, 165, 247, 291–3, 410–11, 438, 500
    importance of, 228
contextual intelligence, 198–9
control within mentoring, 12
conversation within mentoring, 2, 6–7
Cooley, Charles, 304
Cooper, A.M., 143–4, 146
corporate culture, 396
Cosgrove, Emily, xvi; *co-author of Chapter 49*
Cote, S., 278
Cotton, J.L., 216
Cotton, R.D., 94–5
Coulter, Ernest, 185
Coutu, D., 175–6
Cox, E., 175
Craig, J., 484
Cranwell-Ward, J., 190, 195–6
Crawford, L., 324
Crisp, Gloria, xvi, 318; *co-author of Chapter 20*
critical reflection, 72
Crocitto, M.M., 202, 414–15
cross-cultural contacts, 265, 401
cross-cultural mentoring, 58, 382, 385
Crossing Thresholds programme, 629–32
cross-race and cross-gender mentoring, 381–2, 385, 398
Crow, Gary M., xvi, 36–7, 437–44; *co–author of Chapter 27*
Crutcher, B.N., 393
'cues filtered out' theory, 487
cultural complexity, 415–16
cultural differences, 202
cultural intelligence, 415
cultural mentoring, 45–6, 126
cultural self-awareness, 364
culturally-competent mentoring, 370
culturally-sensitive mentoring, 379
Czechowska-Fraczak, Mariola, xvii; *author of Chapter 40*

D'Abate, C.P. 317
Darwin, A., 28, 42, 77
Dashew, Leslie, xvii; *co-author of Chapter 29*
David, S., 170, 176–7
Davis, T.E., 263
Deci, E.L., 171, 173
De Four-Babb, J., 56

de Janasz, S.C., 484, 491, 494
democracy, 34
democratic mentoring, 37–8, 41–3
Denmark, V.M., 144
density of a network, 93–4
Denyer, D., 275
Denzin, N.K., 362
Departmentt for International Development (DFID), 629–30
dependence on the mentor, 41
Derrick, K.S., 126
'destroyers' amongst mentors, 146
Deutsch, N.L., 305
developer data matrix, 91–2
developmental coaching, 39
developmental mentoring, 149–50, 186–7, 197, 397
developmental networks, 75, 88–100, 422, 425
    analysis of, 92
    assessment of, 90–5
    characteristics of, 89
    definition of, 89
    diversity in, 93
    ecological view of, 98–100
    in practice, 95–7
    research on, 88–90, 97–100
    size of, 92
    structure of, 90–1
    typology of, 89
developmental relationships, 70–1, 107, 274, 282
developmental theories, 73–4
Dewey, John, 43
dialogue, 181
digital technology, 40, 47, 202
DiRenzo, M.S., 490–1
discrimination, 369
distributed mentoring, 97
diversified cultures, 124–5
diversified mentoring, 97, 292, 389–402
diversity, concept of, 389
diversity management, 395–7, 401
diversity mentoring, 213
diversity training, 400–2
Dobrow, S.R., 94
doctoral students, mentoring of, 324
doctors, mentoring of, 595–8
Dolan, Erin L., xvii; *co-author of Chapter 20*
Dolan, P., 305

Dominguez, Nora, xiii, 71; *author of Chapter 5, co-author of Chapters 1 and 24 and co-editor*
Dondero, G.M., 26
Dougherty, T.W., 279
Dreher, G., 73–4
Drotter, S., 409
Druskat, V.U., 291
DuBois, D.L., 236, 299, 467, 616
Dubrin, A.J., 178
Duckworth, V., 342, 345
'dumpers' amongst mentors, 146
Durska, M., 395
Dutton, J.E., 458
Dvorak, R., 144
Dweck, Carol, 173
dynamics of mentoring, 2, 4–5, 199, 500

Eagan, M.K., 320
Early, P.C., 415
early career teachers (ECTs), 336–51
    efficacious mentoring for, 338–41
Eby, L.T., 16, 26, 71, 78, 146, 215, 230–1, 235–6, 280, 421
ecological systems theory, 99–100
economic disadvantage, 304–9
ecosystems, *inner* and *outer*, 140
education, mentoring in, 44–6, 95, 122–3, 149, 214, 236, 416, 423–31, 436–9, 443–4, 513–19; *see also* early career teachers; higher education
educational disparities, 390–1
Edwards, Amanda, xvii; *co-author of Chapter 34*
Edwards, R., 16
effectiveness of mentoring, 6–8
    benchmarking of, 238–43
    measurement of, 227–43
Egan, T.M., 215
Eisenhower, Dwight D., 453
Ekeland, Jennybeth, xvii; *co-author of Chapter 38*
Ellis, M.V., 264, 270
Elman, N.S., 212
Ely, R., 398, 411
Emelo, R., 126
e-mentoring, 40, 47, 126, 150, 152–3, 164, 192, 317, 482–95
    barriers to, 487–8
    benefits and attributes of, 485–6

compared with traditional type of
mentoring, 488
cultivation phase of, 494
definition of, 484
evaluation of, 495
formats and platforms for, 488–90
initiation of, 493–4
learning by means of, 494–5
the mentor–protégé dyad in, 490–4
preparation for, 494
processes for structuring and facil-itation
of, 491–3
to promote reflection, learning and
development, 486
research on, 489–90
roles in and types of, 484–5
support for, 495
termination of, 495
emotional intelligence, 109, 140, 146, 274–86
assimilated into action, 278
definition of, 274
implications for organizational
practice, 285–6
mixed-model approach to, 276–8
emotional intimacy, 111
emotionally-intelligent mentoring (EIM), 274–6, 280–5
emotive mentoring, 285
English, F., 440
Enomoto, E.K., 438
Ensher, E.A., 399, 490
entrepreneurship, 521–2, 527
Esnard, Talia, xvii–xviii, 56; *co–author of Chapter 23*
Espstein, R.M. 109
'establishment' stage in a career, 423, 426–8
Este, D., 369
ethical considerations, 105–15, 128, 268, 271
ethnicity, 38–9, 42–3, 439
European approach to coaching, 176
European approach to mentoring, 71, 163–4, 187, 407, 410
European Mentoring and Coaching Council
(EMCC), 114, 197, 241–2
evaluation, *formative* and *summative*, 195, 265
evaluation of mentoring, 55–6, 140, 152–3,
195–6, 228–35, 243, 252–3, 259, 285, 495
evaluation plans, 227–8, 238, 243

evaluation template, 238
evidence-based practices, 302–3, 308
executive coaching, 96
executive mentoring, 291, 293, 406–12, 415, 417
context of, 410–11
definitions of, 407–8
individual countries' approaches to, 189
value and benefits of, 411–12
executives
definition of, 408
induction of, 412
responsibilities of, 406, 410
retention of, 412
expatriates, mentoring for 414–15
expectations, *unrealistic* or *not clearly defined* 236
experiential learning, 196–7
exploitation of mentees, 112, 114
'exploration' stage in a career, 422–5

face-to-face mentoring, 40, 150, 164
facilitators of learning, 152
faculty mentoring, 326–8; *see also* women
in academia
fair treatment, 112–13, 115
familial mentoring, 465–79
challenges in, 466–7, 474–9
history of, 467
in practice, 467–9
family businesses, 469–73
literature on, 471–3
family relationships, 303
feedback, 77, 264–5
Feeney, Mary K., 53, 59–60, 157, 583, 585
Feldon, D.F., 48
feminism and feminist scholarship, 37, 41, 379–81, 385
Fénelon, F.S. de la M., 16, 21–9, 69
Feren, D.B., 144
Ferro, A., 60
fidelity, 115, 268, 271
fiduciary relationships, 114
financial sector, 590–4
Fineman, S.E., 281
Finkelstein, L., 81, 216–17
Finkelstein, M.J., 427
Finland, 527–30
Fischler, L., 41, 71–2, 178

Flanagan, Viti, xviii; *co-author of Chapter 39*
Fleming, M., 264
Fletcher, S., 436
'focal person' role, 88
Football Association (English), 344
formal mentoring, 37–41, 108, 156–7, 230, 246–7, 296–300, 317, 336
    definitions of, 213
    see also mentoring programmes
Fredericton Business Immigrant Mentoring Program, 362
Freedman, M., 26
Freire, Paulo, 615
Friday, E. and S.S,. 218
Fudge, Vanessa, xviii; *co-author of Chapter 50*
Fullan, M., 348
functions of mentoring, 5–6, 75–6, 160, 437, 484; *see also* psycho-social functions of mentoring

Gaddis, S.M., 306
Gade, P.A., 458–9
Galinsky, A.D., 171
Gallimore, R.G., 43
Gannon, Judie, xviii; *author of Chapter 53*
Gannon-Leary, P., 489–90
Gant, G., 215
Garcia, I.O., 398
Gardiner, M.E., 438
Gardiner, M.W., 441–7
Gardner, P.D., 216
Garvey, Bob, xix, 16, 144, 178, 185, 190–1, 296; *author of Chapter 2*
Gary, E.M., 615
Gay, B., 20
Geber, Hilary, xix; *co-author of Chapter 31*
Gehrke, N., 440
Gell, Keith, 551
gender issues, 38–9, 97, 124, 374, 378–81, 439
General Electric, 172
General Medical Council, 598
GenXers, mentoring of, 127
Gershenfeld, S., 54, 61
'get in get on' (GIGO) schemes, 161–2
Ghosh, R., 412
Giannantonio, C.M., 144
Gibb, S., 18–19, 190, 247
Gibson, S.K., 427
Gill, J., 26

Gillman, Debra, 583
Gilson, L.L., 325
Giscombe, K., 399–400
Glenaffric Ltd, 232
global financial crisis (2008), 29
global mentoring, 126, 196
globalisation, 28
'goal', definitions of, 169–71, 174
'goal-blindness', 171
goal-focused coaching (GFC), 175
goal-free mentoring, 181
goal orientation, 176, 181
goal research, 174
goal-setting, 41, 169–72, 175–9
goal theory, 171
goals, 169–82
    clarification of, 145
    difficulty related to task performance, 171
    introjected, 173
    of mentor and mentee, 179–80
    multiple, 172
Godshalk, V.M., 75, 181, 484, 491, 494
Gold, J., 483
Goleman, D., 275–7
good practice in mentoring, 79–82, 141
Goodyear, Rodney K., xix, 263–5; *co–author of Chapter 17*
Gorjestani, N., 503
Gosland, J., 484
Gould, D., 577
graduate students, mentoring of, 323–8
Grandland, Steve, 605
Grant, A.M., 170, 175
Grant, B., 323
Grassinger, R., 69
Greek mythology, 2; *see also* 'The Odyssey'
Green, M.T., 178
Green, S.G., 324
Greenfield, P.M., 349–50
Greenfield, W.D., 437
Greenlees, I.A., 281
Grewal, D., 278–80
Grogan, Margaret, xix; *co-author of Chapter 27*
Grossman, J.B., 26, 298, 392–3, 398–9, 615
grounded theory, 68
group mentoring, 38, 47, 58, 95, 97, 126–7, 326, 336
Groves, K.S., 127

GROW model, 174–5
Gurjee, Ridwanah, xix–xx, 615; *author of Chapter 52*

Haddock, Millar, Julie, xiii, 161, 256–8; *author of Chapters 4 and 10, author of Introduction to Part II, co–author of Chapter 1 and co–editor*
Hadjioannou, X., 323, 325
Hager, M., 71
Haggard, D.L., 279
Hale, R., 5
Hall, D.T., 421–30
Hamilton, B.A., 150, 487
Hancock, M.P., 319
Hare, R.D., 378
Hargreaves, A., 348
Harkness, D., 262
Harris, Denise, xx; *co-author of Chapter 48*
Hartland, John, 608
Hawkey, C., 325
Hawkins, P., 175–6, 179
He, Y., 55–6, 58
Headlam-Wells, J., 484, 489, 493
healthcare, mentoring in, 214–15; *see also* doctors
Heaphy, E.D., 458
Heinaro, Eeva-Liisa, xx; *co-author of Chapter 35*
Henderson, S.J., 398
Heraclitus, 585
Herdman, J., 236
Heres, L., 395–6
Herrera, C., 305–7
Heun, C., 490
Hewlett, S.A., 391
Higgins, M.C., 16, 75, 89, 94, 392
'high flyers', 147
higher education, mentoring in 316–28; *see also* women in academia
high-stakes assessments, 110
Hill, L., 429
Hoang Anh Thi Le, xxiii; *co-author of Chapter 42*
Hobson, Andrew J., xx–xxi, 341–6; *author of Chapter 21*
Hollister, L.R., 214
Homer, 17, 468; *see also* 'The Odyssey'
Honoria, 24
Houck, Christiana, 509

Houston-Philpot, K.R., 215
Hu, S., 322
Huizing, R.L., 38, 40, 42, 47, 58
'human becoming', 27, 29–30
human capital, definition of, 74, 521
humour, sense of, 145
Hundert, E.M., 109

Ibarra, H., 171, 411
identity development, 42, 45, 47, 440–3, 446–7
immigrants
    as entrepreneurs, 361–2, 368
    mentoring of and by, 370
implementation proposals for mentoring programmes, 250–1
'imposter syndrome' affecting women, 392
'inattentional blindness', 171
inclusion, principle of, 397
income disparities, 390–1
induction as distinct from mentoring, 40
informal mentoring, 37–9, 108, 156–7, 230, 246, 296, 317, 336, 429–30, 447
informed consent process, 108
instrumental behaviors of mentors, 76–7
inter-cultural mentoring (ICM), 58, 358–63, 366
International Institute for Coaching and Mentoring (IIC&M), 240–1
International Journal of Coaching and Mentoring (IJCM), 119–21
International Journal of Mentoring and Coaching in Education (IJMCE), 119–21
International Mentoring Association (IMA), 79–80
international scope for mentoring, 46
International Standards for Coaching and Mentoring (SMCP), 197
International Standards for Mentoring Programmes in Employment (ISMPE), 8, 80, 151, 240
Internet use, 484
interpersonal skills
    for mentees, 146
    for mentors, 144
Investors in People (IiP), 242–3
Irby, Beverly J., xxi, 126; *co-author of Chapter 8*
Ireland, 575–81
Islington Housing Services, 228
Italian School of Mentoring, 531

'itches', 180
Ives, Y., 175

Janssen, S., 53, 55, 57, 89, 165
Jewel Tea Company, 69–70
JIVE Mentoring Programmes, 192
Johns, R., 59, 61
Johnson, P., 26
Johnson, W. Brad, xxi, 107, 144, 264; *author of Chapter 7*
Johnson-Bailey, J., 382, 398–9
Jones, J., 148
Jones, R., 57
Jones, T., 20
Jong, M.D., 165
Jonsen, K., 395–6
Joseph, D.L., 278
journals, 58, 119
Judge, T.A., 59
'judgementoring', 336, 341–50
  causes of, 344–6
  combatting of, 346–8
  consequences of, 343–4
  definition of, 341
  evidence of, 341–2

Kadushin, A., 262
Kamehameha Early Education Project (KEEP), 43
Kammeyer-Mueller, J.D., 59
Kanchewa, Stella S., xxii; *co-author of Chapter 19*
Kant, Immanuel, 25
Karanxha, Zorka, xxii; *co-author of Chapter 23*
Karcher, M.A., 230, 236
Kass, J.D., 29
Kaufmann, C., 175–6
Kayes, D.C., 171
Keane, Moyra, xxii; *co-author of Chapter 31*
Kegan, Robert, 17
Kennedy, John F., 172
Khazanov, L., 318
Kilburg, R.R., 174
Kim, J., 493
Kim, S., 127
King, Paula, xxii; *author of Chapter 44*
Kirkpatrick, Donald, 234–5
Kissane-Long, A.L., 439

Klasen, N., 190, 195–6, 248–9
knowing–doing gap, 197
knowledge-driven economy, 410
knowledge workers, 407
Knowles, C., 615
Kochan, Frances K. xiii, 1–2, 45, 55, 58, 80, 415; *author of Introduction to Part I, co-author of Chapter 1 and co-editor*
Koczka, Terezia, xxii; *author of Chapter 16*
Kolb, D., 411
Kourieos, S., 343
Kram, Kathy E., xxii–xxiii, 4–5, 16, 21, 37, 41–2, 48, 70, 73, 75–8, 89, 105, 157–8, 160–1, 163, 165, 185–6, 236, 392, 397, 478; *co-author of Chapter 6*
Krumboltz, J.D., 325
Kunnanatt, J.T., 281
Kwoh, Leslie, 213–14

Lane, A.M., 281
Lane, G., 69
Lankau, M., 70–1
Lansing, J.S., 150
Lara-Alecio, Rafael, xxiii; *co-author of Chapter 8*
Larrick, R.P., 171
Lasch, C., 28
Lashway, L., 437
Laske, Otto, 177
Latham, Gary, 171
Laukhuf, R.L., 57
Lawrence-Lightfoot, S., 25
Lawson, Sally, xxiii; *author of Chapter 54*
leader–member exchange (LMX) theory, 74–5, 292–3, 358–9, 368–9
leadership
  custodial orientation to, 437–8
  technocratic orientation to, 440
leadership concept, 58
leadership continuum, 436–7, 446–7
leadership development, 95, 213, 443
leadership identity, 443, 446
leadership mentoring, 38
Leadership Pipeline, 408
leadership qualities and skills, 407, 409
Lean, E., 16
'learnacy', 344, 349–50
'learned helplessness', 343–4

learning
  intensity of, 148
  self-managed, 145
learning experiences, 445
learning goals, 172, 181
learning opportunities, 412, 494–5
learning theories, 71–3, 303
Lechuga, V.M., 323
Leck, Joanne, xxiii–xxiv; *co-author of Chapter 47*
Lee, A.W., 21
Lee, D., 160–1, 165
Lee, F.K., 5
Lee, L.C., 438
Lejonberg, E., 343, 346
Leonard, D., 57
levels of evidence-based intervention effectiveness (LEBIE), 61
Levinson, Daniel J., 24–5, 70, 73, 106–7
Lewes, Jane, xxiv; *co-author of Chapter 15*
LGBT[Q] (lesbian, gay, bisexual, trans-gender [and queer]) communities, 325
  mentoring for, 391, 393
Liang, B., 392–3, 398–9
Lick, D., 437
Liebnau, D., 172
Lincoln, Y.S., 376, 385
Lineback, K., 429
Linley, A., 175
Lintott, Graham, 551
literature reviews, 35, 52–61, 67–8
Liu, Y., 281
Locke, Edwin, 171
Lockhart, Petra, xxiv, 600–1; *co-author of Chapter 49*
Lofthouse, R., 342, 344–5
London Deanery, 595–8
longitudinal research, 60–1, 78, 163, 165, 237, 243
'looking glass self', 304
Lopes, P.N., 277–8
Lopez, A.D., 393
Los Angeles Children's Hospital, 215
Louis XIV, 23
Loureiro-Koechlin, C., 489
love
  in a mentoring relationship, 24–5, 30
  triangulation theory of, 111

Lucasse Shannon, A., 16
Lumby, J., 440
Lunsford, Laura Gail, 181, 266–7, 343, 346, 360; *author of Introduction to Part III, co-author of Chapters 1 and 20 and co-editor*

Ma, Y., 322
Maathai, W., 503
McCarthy, G., 178
McCullough, J., 319
McDonald, S., 93
McDonalds fast food chain, 26
McDowell, Andrew, 597
McGill, I., 144–5, 163–4, 440
McInnes-Craig, Fiona, *author of Chapter 55*
McIntyre, J., 343
McKee, Anne, 173
McKeen, C., 391, 398
McKenzie, K.B., 447
Mackey, H., 42
MacLennan, N., 195
McManus, S.E., 280
macro influences on mentoring programmes, 228
Mael, F.A., 215
Malderez, Angi, 341–50
Malone, T.A., 57
Mamiseishvili, K., 281
managerialism, 25–9
Manathunga, C., 323
Manning, C., 342
Mao, J., 99
Māori Mentoring Programme (MMP), 539–43
Marshall, George Catlett, 453
Martin, G., 454
Maryland University, 321–2
Massey University (New Zealand), 540–3
'mastery' stage in a career, 423, 428–9
matching of mentors to mentees, 81, 191, 255, 296–301, 306–8, 321, 339–40, 397–8, 413–15
Matthews, L.J., 437
Maxwell, B., 342, 345
Mayer, J.D., 274–7
Megginson, David, xxiv, 18–19, 144, 160, 178, 186, 188, 202, 247, 267, 587, 623; *co-author of Chapters 11 and 46*
Melling, A., 615
mental maps, 113

mentee-led mentoring, 633–5
mentees
    development of, 195
    effectiveness in, 146–7
Mentor (Fénelon's character), 21–4
Mentor (Homer's character), 15–19, 29, 68, 437, 467–8
MENTOR (US national mentoring organization), 302
'mentor', definition and use of the word, 69–70, 186, 279
'mentor capital' (Irby), 126
Mentor Self-Efficacy Scale, 60
mentoring
    application and practice of, 2, 5–6, 75–8, 500
    benefits of, 77–8, 164, 190, 422, 523
    definitions of, 11, 35–6, 53–4, 70–1, 107, 144, 149, 186, 202, 279, 335, 407–9, 416, 454, 483, 491, 521
    as a discipline in its own right, 128
    as distinct from supervision, 322
    elements of success in, 438, 486–7
    and emotional intelligence, 279–85
    goals and objectives of, 41, 54, 140, 152, 255, 436–7, 440
    good practice in, 69, 79–80
    history of, 1, 11, 15–16, 68–70
    philosophy of, 1–3, 16–18, 21–30, 500
    problems with, 36–7, 46–7, 279–80, 283–4, 324, 393–5
    as a relational system, 100
    theoretical frameworks of, 71–5
    traditional form of, 376, 381, 385
    typologies of, 125–6, 145
    see also evaluation of mentoring; functions of mentoring
mentoring circles, 12, 42–4, 96–7
mentoring cycle, 156–66
mentoring discourses, 186–8
mentoring measurements, 231, 237–8, 253
mentoring moments, 188
mentoring organisations, 197–8
mentoring programme co-ordinators, 152, 246–59, 340
    challenges and risks for, 255–6
    competencies needed by, 253–5
    reflections of, 256–9
    role and responsibilities of, 248–53
mentoring programmes, 2, 7–8, 67, 96, 98, 123–4, 157, 187–200, 212–17, 430, 447
    benefits of, 197–8, 215–16
    clarification of purpose for, 7, 190
    design and development of, 140, 151–2, 188–91, 200
    drawbacks of, 216
    effective practices in, 216–17
    management infuences on, 247–56
    operational components of, 54
    phases of, 249
    purposes of, 213
    setting-up of, 191–2
    strategic intent in, 412–13
    support and supervision in, 151, 192–5
mentoring relationship continuum (MRC), 107, 109–10
mentoring relationships, 124–5
    changing nature of, 140
    common problems with, 107
    definitions of, 149
    dysfunctional, 12, 78, 278–80
    effectiveness in, 147–8
    initiation of, 179–80, 441–2
    intensity of, 302
    interactional nature of, 139, 165
    management of, 82
    meaning of, 443–4
    'natural', 296, 298
    nature of, 105–7
    phases in, 140–1, 156, 162–3, 279
    quality of, 76
    strength of, 109–10
    see also multi-country mentoring programmes
Mentoring and Tutoring: Partnership in Learning (journal) (M&T) 119–21
mentors
    benefits gained by, 126, 186–7, 483
    characteristics and behaviors of, 76–7
    competencies needed by, 108–10, 113, 115, 144–6, 149, 262–3, 410
    development of, 193–5
    ethical issues for, 107–15
    ineffectiveness in, 146
    lack of a diverse pool of, 384
    practical approaches for, 178–81
    workloads of, 48

meritocracy, 29
Merriam, S., 78, 146, 440, 484
Merrick, Lis, xxiv–xxv, 187, 190, 196–7, 199; *author of Chapter 12*
meta-analyses, 298–9
meta-synthesis, 378, 385
Meyerhoff Scholars Program, 321–2
Mezirow, J., 72
mid-career mentoring, 439
migrants in the world, number of, 361
military mentoring, 291–2, 451–64, 531–8, 549–53
Millennials, mentoring for, 127
Miller, D., 475, 478
Miller, M., 361
Mind Partners, 554–5
mindsets, 77, 173
MIners, C.T., 278
minority groups, 197, 411
Missirian, A.K., 158–61, 163
Mitchell, M.E., 60
Mitchell, T.R., 172
Mitleton-Kelly, E. 150
Mizukami, Maria da Graça Nicoletti, xxv, 519; *co-author of Chapter 33*
Moberg, D.J., 282
Model of Change, 303–4
modeling of practices and norms, 365
Montesquieu, Baron de, 23
Moore, A., 281
moral principles, 268, 271
moral stance, *moral context* and *moral pedagogy*, 113
mosaic theory of mentoring, 42–3
Mosakowski, E., 415
Mossop, Catherine, xxv; *co-author of Chapter 47*
motivation, *extrinsic* and *intrinsic*, 172–3
motives for mentoring, 26
Mowgli Foundation, 520–6
Mullen, Carol A., xxv–xxvi, 39, 43, 46–8, 69, 80, 437, 486; *author of Chapter 3*
multi-country mentoring programmes, 202–11
    elements fostering success in, 205–6
    recruitment and retention of mentors for, 207
    return on investment, 208
    support from the human resources community for, 206-7
multicultural environments, 415

multinational companies, 196
multiple-level comentoring, 44–5
multiple relationships, 112, 115
multiplexity in relationships, 94–5
Murakami, E.T., 37
Murphy, Eileen, xxvi, 232; *co-author of Chapter 15*
Murray, M., 248
Murrell, A., 392
Muth, R., 37–8, 40

narrative analysis, 16
Nash, S., 439
National (US) Mentoring Organization (MENTOR), 302
National Occupational Standards (NOS) for Coaching and Mentoring, 238–40
'nested' systems, 98–9
Netolicky, D., 348
network, types of, 429
networks for mentoring, 56, 75, 126, 164–5, 199
New Zealand, 604–9
Newman, D.A., 278
Newman, Penny, 597
Ng, P.T., 346
Nietzsche, Friedrich, 19
Noblit, G.W., 378
Noe, R.A., 178
Noel, J., 409
non-maleficence, principle of, 114–15, 268, 271
novice mentors, 193–5
Nunes, Donnel, xxvi; *co-author of Chapter 29*
Núñez, A.M., 37
Nyström, Mikaela, xxvi; *co-author of Chapter 35*

O'Boyle, E.H., 278
Ochoa, E., 360
'The Odyssey', 15–21, 68, 185, 437, 467–9, 473, 477
Office for Standards in Education (Ofsted), 346
old boys' network, 399
Olian, J.D., 144
O'Malley, L., 120
O'Meara, K., 429
O'Neill, R., 401
'on-line' and 'off-line' mentoring, 344
ONSIDE Mentoring, 347–51
Oosahwe, S.L., 322
Opengart, Rose *co-author of Chapter 18*

Oplatka, I., 438–9
Ordonez, Lisa, 171–2
organic approach to design of mentoring schemes, 191
organisational benefits of mentoring, 140, 197–8, 212, 215–16, 224, 483
organisational climate, 4, 172
organisational culture, 98, 151, 188, 475
Ortiz-Walters, R., 325
Osborn, C.J., 263
O'Shea, P.G., 215
outcomes of mentoring
    evidence on, 106, 317–18, 327–8, 407–8, 438
    focus on, 181
    individual- and *organisational-* level, 140
    positive or *negative*, 164
Owen, H.D., 126

Page, S., 164
Paglis, L.L., 324
Palincsar, A.S., 349
Palmer, A., 143–4, 146
Palmer, E., 42
Palmer, Farah, xxvi; *co-author of Chapter 37*
Palmer, Karen, 609
pan-cultural mentoring, 360
parental roles, 303
Parse, R.R., 27
Parsloe, E., 186–7
Parsons, C., 615
Pascarelli, J.T., 415
Passmore, J., 174
Patton, George Smith, 453
Patton, M.Q., 229
Pawson, R., 623, 627
PEARL (Professional Emerging and Aspiring Recruitment Leaders) programme, 604–9
peer coaching, 39
peer mentoring, 47, 123, 198, 318–21, 326–7, 379, 381, 539, 582–5, 623
Pellegrini, E. 76, 78
Pemberton, C. 175
Perchiazzi, Matteo, xxvi–xxvii, 531; *author of Chapter 36*
Pérez, Patricia, xxvii; *co-author of Chapter 45*
Perez Companc Foundation, 582–3
performance goals, 80
person centeredness, 29–30, 144

personal information, disclosure of, 112
Pescosolido, A.T., 291
Peterson, Doug, 219–23
Peterson, Jeffrey D., xxvii; *co–author of Chapter 28*
Pfeffer, J., 197
Pfund, C., 261
Phillips, J., 234–5
Pidgeon, M., 325
Pinto, Ana Oliveira, xxvii; *author of Chapter 41*
Plaut, S.M., 114
Plum, E., 415
Podsen, I.J., 144
Pollock, R., 156, 160
Ponjuan, L., 431
Porter, T.M., 27–8
Portugal, 560–4
positionality theory, 293
positioning theory, 375
'possible selves', 304
Poteet, M.L., 81, 216–17
Poulsen, Kirsten M., xxviii, 407; *author of Chapter 25*
power relations, 266, 410–11
Preeya, D., 397
privacy, protection of, 110, 115
process mentoring (Gibb), 190–1
productive and nonproductive mentoring, 283–5
professional mentoring, 437
professionalism, 108, 267–8, 271, 442–5
Profetis, G., 125
prospect theory, 171
proximal development, theory of, 73
Pryor, R.G.L., 173–4
psychological support, 380–1, 398, 485
psychosocial functions of mentoring, 76–8, 89, 105, 141, 437
Puetzer, M., 178
Purkiss, J., 19
Putnam, R., 615
'Pygmalion' syndrome, 158–9

qualitative research, 59–60
quantitative studies, 125
questions, asking of, 366, 368

race-related issues, 374, 378–81
racism, 367–9, 394
    definition of, 369

radical humanism, 27–30
Ragins, Belle R., 89, 97, 105, 109, 113, 146, 216, 282, 394–401
Ralph, E., 322
Ramaswami, A., 73–4
Rana, Laura *co-author of Chapter 42*
rapport and rapport-building, 140, 148, 150, 159, 162
reachability, concept of, 93
Recruitment Consultant Services Association (RCSA), 604–6
recruitment industry, 604–9
Reddick, R., 38, 399
Reeves, Roxanne B., xxviii, 58, 360; *author of Chapter 22*
referrals to mentoring, 300
reflective mentors and reflexive mentors, 194–5
reflective practice, 231
reframing, *objective* and *subjective*, 72
Refworks tool, 120
Reijo, T.G. Jr, 412
relational behaviors, 76
relational mentoring, 89, 284–5
relational skills training, 96
relationship 'droop', 140
relationship management, 145, 150
religious beliefs, 196
research on mentoring, 52–62, 74, 195, 489–90
    best practice in, 58
    critical issues in, 53
    on developmental networks, 88–90, 97–100
    on families, 471–9
    future prospects for, 12–13, 46–8, 56–7, 62, 82, 97–8, 119, 125–8, 139–40, 153, 164–5, 205, 209, 286, 307–8, 385–6, 401, 417, 478–9
    lack of rigour in, 60–1
    mixed-methods type, 59
    scope of, 34–5
    types of study, 58
return on investment (ROI), 208, 234
reverse mentoring, 39–40, 198, 213–14
Rhea Challenge, 527–30
Rhodes, C., 436
Rhodes, Jean E., xxix, 303, 308, 616; *co-author of Chapter 19*
Richardson, J. 44
Richardson, Melissa, xxviii; *author of Chapter 32*

Rigby, Chris, 162, 256–8
Riggio, R.E., 128
Riley, P., 21
risk-taking, 171, 306
Ritchie, J., 121
Rix, M., 483
Roberts, A., 17–18, 22
Rodenhauser, P., 144
Rodrigues Reali, Aline Maria de Medeiros, xxviii–xxix; *co–author of Chapter 33*
Rogers, Carl, 29
role modelling, 5, 76, 198, 485
Rose, G.L., 324
Rosser, M.H., 215
Rousmaniere, Tony, xxix; *co–author of Chapter 17*
Rousseau, Jean Jacques, 23
Royal New Zealand Air Force (RNZAF), 549–53
Rudisill, J.R., 144
Rudolph, B.A., 325
rugby, 575–81
Rushdie, Salman, 16
Russell, S.H., 319
Ryan, Diane M. xxix; *co-author of Chapter 28*
Ryan, R., 171, 173

Sabbagh, Akram, xxix; *co-author of Chapter 50*
St-Jean, E., 361
Salovey, P., 274–80
same-race and same-gender mentoring, 398
Sanchez, B., 475
Sanofi (company), 554–9
Sanyal, Chandana, xxx, 162, 258–9; *author of Chapter 9*
Saudi Arabia, 476
'scaffolding' of learning, 348–50
Scandura, T.A., 76, 78, 150, 264, 279, 487
Schein, Edgar H., 411, 437–8
schemas for mentoring, 113
Scheurich, J.J., 447
scholar-practitioners. 499
school-based mentoring (SBM), 298–9
Schultz, P.W., 319
Schunk, D.H., 39, 47–8
Schwartz, Sarah E.O., xxx; *co–author of Chapter 19*
scoping analysis, 119–21
Scoular, A., 175

Scriven, M., 231
Searby, L., 54, 58, 77, 79
Sears, Faith *co-author of Chapter 24*
second-wave mentoring, 196–7
selection of mentors and mentees, 81, 286, 292, 297, 339
self-awareness, 145
self-confidence, 147
self-determination theory, 171, 173
self-directed learning, 72
self-disclosure, 111–12
self-efficacy, 301
self-regulated mentoring, 41
senior management role, 190, 249
sexism, 394
sexual feelings, 111
'shadowing', 69
Shannon, A.L., 149
Shannon, K., 42
Shape Corporation, 219–24
Shapiro, S.M., 181
Shea, G., 145
Shearing, C., 28
Shen, Y., 99
Sherman, W., 447
Shields, C.M., 439
Shotton, H.J., 322
Silva, D., 113
Silver, W.S., 172
Simmonds, D., 491
Singh, R., 146
Single, Peg Boyle, 39–40, 47
Single, R.M., 47
situational mentoring, 126, 417
Skeylls organization, 582–3
Smailes, J., 489–90
small-city living, 367–8
small- and medium-sized enterprises (SMEs), 521
Smart, P., 275
SMART goals, 170, 172–4
Smith, M.A., 215
Smith, N., 175, 179
Smith, R., 16
Smith-Jentsch, K.A., 489
'so what' question, 61
social capital, 74, 369
social control, 26–7, 30
social equality, 41

social learning, 73, 148, 368
social network theory, 75
social networking, 399–400, 489–90
social theories, 73–5
socialization, 74, 437–8
socio-economic status (SES), 306
Sontag, L., 80
Sosik, J.J., 75, 160–1, 165, 181
South Africa, 501–2, 505
Sparta, 17
Spencer, L., 121
Spencer, R., 307
Spillane, J.P., 438
sponsoring role, definition of, 416–17
sponsorship mentoring, 147, 149, 186–8
sports and sports people, 4
Srivastava, S.B., 98
stakeholders, 190–1, 196, 228–31, 254
    groups of, 229–30
standards for mentoring, 238–40
standard-setting, 80
standpoint theory, 375
Stanley, C.A., 376, 385
Stanley, T., 369
Starr, J., 16, 174
Statoil (company), 545–8
Statutory Authority (SA) of the Commonwealth of Australia, 610–13
Stein, M., 616
'STEM' subjects (science, technology, engineering and mathematics), 317–23
Stephenson, J., 20
stepped approaches to design of mentoring programmes, 189
Sternberg, R., 106, 111, 198
Stets, J., 440
Steyn, G.M., 438
Stockwell, Peter, 551
Stokes, P., 178, 190, 193, 267
Stone, F., 69
strategic networks, 429
Straus, S.E., 230
stress, causes of, 437
stretch goals, 172
striving for mentoring, 249–50
success, definition of, 169–70
succession planning, 127–8, 412–13
succession potential, 147

Sue, D.W., 265
Sullivan, S.E., 202, 414–15
summarisation, 7
Sundstrom, E., 400
supervision of mentoring, 151, 192–4, 261–71
    adequacy of, 262–3, 270
    contracts for, 263
    methods used in, 267, 270–1
    restorative function of, 266–7
    similarity to other forms of supervision, 262
supervision of research, 322
Sutton, R., 197
Swarovski (company), 600–3
Swart, T., 390–1
synchronicity of events, 199
systematic review, 275

tacit knowledge, 198–9, 368
talent development and management programs, 126, 140, 395–6, 401, 486
talent mentoring wheel, 187–8
Tancredi, Regina Maria Simões Puccinelli, xxx; *co-author of Chapter 33*
Taylor, Kate, 605, 609
teachers
    mentoring of, 513–19
    professional development of, 44–5
team coaching, 39
Terosky, Aimee LaPointe, xxx; *co-author of Chapter 26*
Terrion, J.L., 57
Tharenou, P., 146
Tharp, R.G., 43
Thelwell, R.C., 281
theory applied to practice, 75
Theory of Change, 234
Thomas, D., 392
Thomas, R.R., 396–7
Thomas, T.A., 398
Thomas, U., 342–5
Thompson, L., 509
Thompson, R.B., 306
Thornton, K., 346
Tickle, L., 16
Tierney, J.P., 26, 298
ties, strength, of, 92–5
Tilley, N., 623
'time chunking', 199

'time warping', 199
Tolan, P.H., 298
Tom, A.R., 113
Tomlinson, P.D., 346
Tong, C., 262
Tong, Fuhui, xxx–xxxi; *co-author of Chapter 8*
topical mentoring, 125–7
Torrance, E.P., 25
traditional mentoring, 488
Training Evaluation Model (Kirkpatrick), 234
training of mentors and mentees, 127, 152, 191–2, 221–2, 254–6, 262, 392, 401, 416, 586
Tranfield, D., 275
transformative leadership, 446–8
transformative learning, 72, 445–6
transformative mentoring, 292, 439–41, 503–4
transparency, 115
'trial' stage in a career, 423, 425–6
Trower, C., 431
trust, 339, 369, 409, 413–14, 493–4
Turban, D.B., 5, 279–80
Turkey, 633–5
Tutu, Desmond, 501–2

Ubuntu, 501–6
    definition of, 502
UCINET program, 92
Ulanovsky, Mariano, xxxi; *co-author of Chapter 45*
undergraduate research experiences (UREs), 318–20
undergraduate students, mentoring of, 316–22, 327
underrepresented minorities (URMs), 389–93
    mentoring of, 392–3
United States approach to coaching, 176
United States approach to mentoring, 71, 149, 151, 163–4, 196, 214, 407
United States Military Academy (USMA), 458, 462; *see also* West Point
University of Central Lancashire (UCLan), 614–16
Unterreiner, Ann, xxxi; *co-author of Chapter 23*
Usher, R., 16

Vasudha B, xiv–xv; *co-author of Chapter 37*
values, 175, 177, 445–6
Van Maanen, J., 438
Velure, Åse, xxxi; *co-author of Chapter 38*

Viator, R.E., 264
Viney, Rebecca, 596–7; *co-author of Chapter 48*
virtual learning environments (VLEs), 489–90
virtual mentoring, 126–7
    pros and *cons* of, 509
virtual worlds, 489–90
Vodafone Turkey, 633–5
'VUCA' environment, 198–9
vulnerability of mentees, 114
Vuuren, M., 165
Vygotsky, L.S., 73, 303

Walker, K., 322
Walz, P., 216
Waterman, S., 55–6, 58
Weitz, B.A., 281
Welch, Jack, 214
well-being of mentees, support for, 336
West Point, 451–7, 461–4
    mentorship culture at, 455–6
Westland, P.R., 162–3
Weston, N.J., 281
Wheeler, M.E., 299
Whitmore, John, 174
Wilbanks, J.E., 279
Williams, S.L., 493
Wilson, J.A., 212
Winter, D.A., 179
Wisconsin University Logic Model, 232–3, 236
Wisker, G., 322
Wolff, S.B., 291
women
    in academia, 374–86
    in the financial sector, 590–4
    as mentors and mentees, 77, 97, 124, 391–2, 439–48
    role and status of, 17
WomenWinWin Mentoring Programme (WWWMP), 560–4
Wong, H.K., 40
Wood, D., 349

'working alliance' concept, 148, 267, 271
workplace mentoring, 213, 236, 421–2
worldviews, 503–4
Wosket, V., 164
Woullard, R., 282
Wray, M., 187
Writers in Training (WIT), 43–4
Wu, S., 280
Wuetherick, Brad, xxxii; *co-author of Chapter 20*

Xi, J., 281

Yan, S., 95–6
Yap, A.J., 410–11
Yeh, C.J., 325
Yip, Jeffrey, xxxii, 165; *co-author of Chapter 6*
Yob, I., 324
York, P.J., 231–2
Young, M., 399
Young, M.D., 38
Young, W.H., 486
Youngs, H., 439
Youth Business International (YBI), 565–9
youth-centered approaches, 302
youth-initiated mentoring (YIM), 297
youth mentoring, 26–7, 236, 295–309
    effectiveness of, 297–300
    international perspectives on, 299
    outcomes of, 298–9
    for special populations, 299–300
    for those from disadvantaged backgrounds, 304–7

Zachary, L., 41, 71–2, 80, 82, 178
Zalaquett, C.P., 393
Zambrana, R.E. 59
Zammit Lupi, A.M., 491
Zey, M.G., 147, 185–6, 279, 509
Zimmerman, Jeff, xxii; *co-author of Chapter 17*
zone of proximal development, 303